Explorations in
CORE MATH

for Common Core
Algebra 2

HOUGHTON MIFFLIN HARCOURT

Contents

COMMON CORE

Chapter 3 Polynomial Functions

Chapter 4 Exponential and Logarithmic Functions

Chapter 8   Data Analysis and Statistics

Chapter 9   Sequences and Series

Chapter 10   Trigonometric Functions

Chapter 11 Trigonometric Graphs and Identities

Chapter 12 Conic Sections

Learning the Standards for Mathematical Practice

The Common Core State Standards include eight Standards for Mathematical Practice. Here's how *Explorations in Core Math Algebra 2* helps students learn those standards as they master the Standards for Mathematical Content.

1 Make sense of problems and persevere in solving them.

In *Explorations in Core Math Algebra 2*, students will work through Explores and Examples that present a solution pathway for them to follow. They will be asked questions along the way so that they gain an understanding of the solution process, and then they will apply what they've learned in the Practice for the lesson.

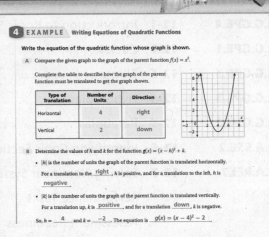

2 Reason abstractly and quantitatively.

When students solve a real-world problem in *Explorations in Core Math Algebra 2*, they will learn to represent the situation symbolically by translating the problem into a mathematical expression or equation. Students will use these mathematical models to solve the problem and then state their answers in terms of the problem context. They will reflect on the solution process in order to check their answers for reasonableness and to draw conclusions.

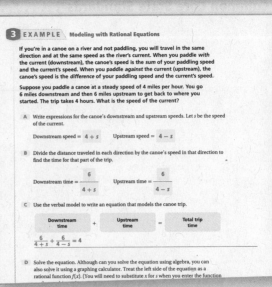

③ Construct viable arguments and critique the reasoning of others.

Throughout *Explorations in Core Math Algebra 2*, students will be asked to make conjectures, construct a mathematical argument, explain their reasoning, and justify their conclusions. Reflect questions offer opportunities for cooperative learning and class discussion. Students will have additional opportunities to critique reasoning in Error Analysis problems.

③ EXAMPLE Proving That the Sum of a Rational Number and an Irrational Number Is Irrational

Given that the set of rational numbers is closed under addition, prove that the sum of a rational number and an irrational number is an irrational number.

Let a be a rational number, let b be an irrational number, and let $a + b = c$. Assume that c is rational.

Rewrite $a + b = c$ as $b = -a + c$ by adding $-a$ to both sides. Because $-a$ and c are both ___rational___ and the set of rational numbers is closed under addition, $-a + c$ must be ___rational___, which means that b is ___rational___.

This contradicts the condition that b be irrational. So, the assumption that c is rational must be false, which means that c, the sum of a rational number and an irrational number, is ___irrational___.

REFLECT

3a. Indirect proof is also called *proof by contradiction*. What is the contradiction in the preceding proof?

The number b cannot be both rational and irrational.

3b. Compare an indirect proof to a counterexample.

A counterexample shows that a statement is false by finding an example that

22. **Error Analysis** A student simplified the expression $\sqrt[3]{x^2} \cdot \sqrt{x}$ by writing
$\sqrt[3]{x^2} \cdot \sqrt{x} = x^{\frac{2}{3}} \cdot x^{\frac{1}{3}} = x^{\frac{2}{3} + \frac{1}{3}} = x^{\frac{3}{3}} = x^2$. Describe and correct the student's error.

$\sqrt[3]{x^2} = x^{\frac{2}{3}}$, not $x^{\frac{1}{3}}$; $\sqrt[3]{x^2} \cdot \sqrt{x} = x^{\frac{2}{3}} \cdot x^{\frac{1}{2}} = x^{\frac{2}{3} + \frac{1}{2}} = x^{\frac{7}{6}} = x^{1 + \frac{1}{6}} = x^1 \cdot x^{\frac{1}{6}} = x \cdot \sqrt[6]{x}$

④ Model with mathematics.

Explorations in Core Math Algebra 2 presents problems in a variety of contexts such as science, business, and everyday life. Students will use mathematical models such as expressions, equations, tables, and graphs to represent the information in the problem and to solve the problem. Then they will interpret their results in context.

④ EXAMPLE Modeling Quadratic Functions in Vertex Form

The shape of a bridge support can be modeled by $f(x) = -\frac{1}{600}(x - 300)^2 + 150$, where x is the horizontal distance in feet from the left end of the bridge and $f(x)$ is the height in feet above the bridge deck. Sketch a graph of the support. Then determine the maximum height of the support above the bridge deck and the width of the support at the level of the bridge deck.

A Graph the function.

• The vertex of the graph is ___(300, 150)___

• Find the point at the left end of the support ($x = 0$).

Since $f(0) = $___0___, the point ___(0, 0)___ represents the left end.

• Use symmetry to find the point at the right end of the support.

Since the left end is 300 feet to the left of the vertex, the right end will be 300 feet to the right of the vertex.

The point ___(600, 0)___ represents the right end.

• Find two other points on the support.

$(120, 96)$ and $(480, 96)$

• Sketch the graph.

B Determine the maximum height of the support.

The maximum of the function is ___150___

So, the maximum height of the bridge support is ___150___ feet.

C Determine the width of the bridge support at the level of the bridge deck.

The distance from the left end to the right end is ___600___ feet.

So, the width is ___600___ feet at the level of the bridge deck.

REFLECT

4a. Explain how you know that the y-coordinate of the right end of the support is 0.

The support has the shape of a parabola, so it is symmetric. The left end has a y-coordinate of 0, so the right end must also have a y-coordinate of 0.

4b. What does the vertex represent in this situation?

the point on the support above the midpoint of the bridge deck and at the greatest height above the bridge deck

5 Use appropriate tools strategically.

Students will use a variety of tools in *Explorations in Core Math Algebra 2,* including manipulatives, paper and pencil, and technology. They might use manipulatives to develop concepts, paper and pencil to practice skills, and technology (such as graphing calculators, spreadsheets, or geometry software) to investigate more complicated mathematical ideas.

The Natural Base, e
Going Deeper

Essential question: *How does the graph of $f(x) = e^x$ compare to graphs of exponential functions with other bases?*

CC.9-12.F.IF.2

1 EXPLORE Investigating $\left(1 + \frac{1}{x}\right)^x$

A Enter the expression $\left(1 + \frac{1}{x}\right)^x$ as Y_1 in your calculator's equation editor.

B Evaluate the function at the values of x shown in the table below. To do so, press **VARS**, select **Y-VARS**, and then select **1:Function**. In the function menu, select **1:Y_1**. Then use parentheses to evaluate the function at a value of x, as shown at right.

```
Y₁(10)
          2.59374246
```

C Complete the table by writing all of the digits displayed on your calculator.

x	$\left(1 + \frac{1}{x}\right)^x$	x	$\left(1 + \frac{1}{x}\right)^x$
1	2	10,000	2.718145927
10	2.59374246	100,000	2.718268237
100	2.704813829	1,000,000	2.718280469
1000	2.716923932	10,000,000	2.718281693

D Find the value of e^1 on your calculator. To do so, press **2nd** **LN** e^x and enter 1 as the exponent. Write all of the digits displayed on your calculator.

2.718281828

REFLECT

1a. What happens to the value of $1 + \frac{1}{x}$ as x increases without bound?

The value decreases, approaching 1, but not reaching 1.

1 EXPLORE Investigating a Geometric Series

CC.9-12.A.SSE.1*,
CC.9-12.A.SSE.1a*,
CC.9-12.A.SSE.1b*,
CC.9-12.A.SSE.4

A Start with a rectangular sheet of paper and assume the sheet has an area of 1 square unit. Cut the sheet in half and lay down one of the half-pieces. Then cut the remaining piece in half, and lay down one of the quarter-pieces. Continue the process: At each stage, cut the remaining piece in half, and lay down one of the halves. As you lay pieces down, arrange them to rebuild the original sheet of paper.

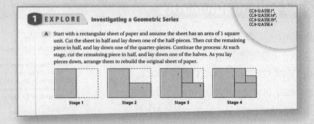

Stage 1   Stage 2   Stage 3   Stage 4

6 Attend to precision.

Precision refers not only to the correctness of arithmetic calculations, algebraic manipulations, and geometric reasoning but also to the proper use of mathematical language, symbols, and units to communicate mathematical ideas. Throughout *Explorations in Core Math Algebra 2* students will demonstrate their skills in these areas when they are asked to calculate, describe, show, explain, prove, and predict.

REFLECT

2a. How do you know that $ps + qr$ and qs are integers?

The set of integers is closed under addition and multiplication, so both expressions represent integers.

2b. Why does $a + b = \frac{ps + qr}{qs}$ prove that the set of rational numbers is closed under addition?

Because a and b are any two rational numbers and $a + b$ is also a rational number, the sum of any two rational numbers must be a rational number.

2c. Given that the set of rational numbers is closed under addition, how can you prove that the set of rational numbers is closed under subtraction?

Write $a - b$ as $a + (-b)$. If b is a rational number, then $-b$ is also rational. The rational numbers are closed under addition, so $a + (-b)$ is rational.

19. If $z_1 = a + bi$ and $z_2 = c + di$, show that $|z_1 \cdot z_2| = |z_1| \cdot |z_2|$.

$|z_1 \cdot z_2| = |(a + bi)(c + di)| = |(ac - bd) + (ad + bc)i| = \sqrt{(ac - bd)^2 + (ad + bc)^2} =$
$\sqrt{a^2c^2 - 2abcd + b^2d^2 + a^2d^2 + 2abcd + b^2c^2} = \sqrt{a^2c^2 + a^2d^2 + b^2c^2 + b^2d^2} =$
$\sqrt{a^2(c^2 + d^2) + b^2(c^2 + d^2)} = \sqrt{(a^2 + b^2)(c^2 + d^2)} = \sqrt{a^2 + b^2} \cdot \sqrt{c^2 + d^2} =$
$|z_1| \cdot |z_2|.$

20. Let $z_3 = z_1 \cdot z_2$. When you divide z_3 by z_1 and get z_2 as the quotient, how can you use the absolute values of z_3 and z_1 as a check on z_2? (*Hint:* See Exercise 19.)

Divide $|z_3|$ by $|z_1|$; the result should equal $|z_2|$ because $\frac{|z_3|}{|z_1|} = \frac{|z_1 \cdot z_2|}{|z_1|} = \frac{|z_1| \cdot |z_2|}{|z_1|} = |z_2|.$

7 Look for and make use of structure.

In *Explorations in Core Math Algebra 2*, students will look for patterns or regularity in mathematical structures such as expressions, equations, geometric figures, and graphs. Becoming familiar with underlying structures will help students build their understanding of more complicated mathematical ideas.

Value of Discriminant	Number of Real Solutions
$b^2 - 4ac > 0$	Two real solutions: $x = \dfrac{-b + \sqrt{b^2 - 4ac}}{2a}$ and $x = \dfrac{-b - \sqrt{b^2 - 4ac}}{2a}$
$b^2 - 4ac = 0$	One real solution: $x = -\dfrac{b}{2a}$
$b^2 - 4ac < 0$	No real solutions

Value of Discriminant	Number of Complex Solutions
$b^2 - 4ac > 0$	Two real solutions
$b^2 - 4ac = 0$	One real solution
$b^2 - 4ac < 0$	Two imaginary solutions

8 Look for and express regularity in repeated reasoning.

In *Explorations in Core Math Algebra 2,* students will have the opportunity to explore and reflect on mathematical processes in order to come up with general methods for performing calculations and solving problems.

1 EXAMPLE Graphing $f(x) = ax^2$ when $|a| > 1$

Graph each quadratic function using the same coordinate plane. (The graph of the parent function is shown.)

A $g(x) = 2x^2$

x	−3	−2	−1	0	1	2	3
$g(x) = 2x^2$	18	8	2	0	2	8	18

B $g(x) = -2x^2$

x	−3	−2	−1	0	1	2	3
$g(x) = -2x^2$	−18	−8	−2	0	−2	−8	−18

REFLECT

1a. In general, how does the y-coordinate of a point on the graph of $g(x) = 2x^2$ compare with the y-coordinate of a point on the graph of $f(x) = x^2$ when the points have the same x-coordinate?

The y-coordinate of a point on the graph of $g(x)$ is 2 times the y-coordinate of a point on the graph of $f(x)$.

1b. Describe the graph of $g(x) = 2x^2$ as a transformation of the graph of $f(x) = x^2$. Use the word *stretch* in your description.

The graph of $g(x)$ is a vertical stretch of the graph of $f(x)$ by a factor of 2.

1c. What transformation occurs when the value of a in $g(x) = ax^2$ is negative?

Reflection across the x-axis

CHAPTER 1

Foundations for Functions

Foundations for Functions

Chapter Focus

In this chapter you will examine the characteristics of functions and their graphs. You will learn to understand functions as transformations of parent functions. You will also learn to model paired data using linear functions.

Chapter at a Glance

COMMON CORE

Lesson		Standards for Mathematical Content
1-1	Exploring Transformations	CC.9-12.F.IF.5, CC.9-12.F.BF.3
1-2	Introduction to Parent Functions	CC.9-12.F.BF.3
1-3	Transforming Linear Functions	CC.9-12.F.BF.3
1-4	Curve Fitting with Linear Models	CC.9-12.S.ID.6a, CC.9-12.S.ID.6b, CC.9-12.S.ID.6c
	Performance Tasks	
	Assessment Readiness	

COMMON CORE **PROFESSIONAL DEVELOPMENT** **CC.9-12.F.BF.3**

In this chapter, students examine the effects of changing parameters of various functions on their graphs with respect to a given parent function. They describe these effects using transformations. In particular, they observe how some parameter changes result in a translation, while others result in reflections, and still others result in stretches or compressions.

Unpacking the Standards

Understanding the standards and the vocabulary terms in the standards will help you know exactly what you are expected to learn in this chapter.

COMMON CORE **CC.9-12.F.BF.3**

Identify the effect on the graph of replacing $f(x)$ by $f(x) + k$, $k\,f(x)$ ... for specific values of k (both positive and negative); ...

Key Vocabulary
compression *(compresión)* A transformation that pushes the points of a graph horizontally toward the y-axis or vertically toward the x-axis.
reflection *(reflexión)* A transformation that reflects, or "flips," a graph or figure across a line, called the line of reflection, such that each reflected point is the same distance from the line of reflection but is on the opposite side of the line.
stretch *(estiramiento)* A transformation that pulls the points of a graph horizontally away from the y-axis or vertically away from the x-axis.
transformation *(transformación)* A change in the position, size, or shape of a figure or graph.
translation *(traslación)* A transformation that shifts or slides every point of a figure or graph the same distance in the same direction.

What It Means For You   Lessons 1-1, 1-2, 1-3

You can change a function by adding or multiplying by a constant. The result will be a new function that is a transformation of the original function.

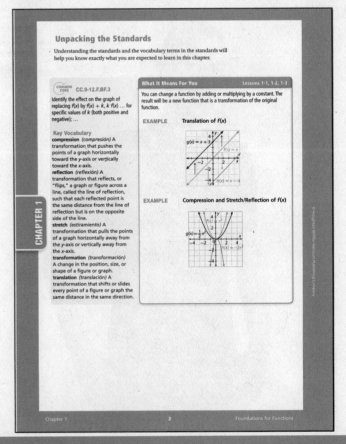

EXAMPLE   **Translation of $f(x)$**

EXAMPLE   **Compression and Stretch/Reflection of $f(x)$**

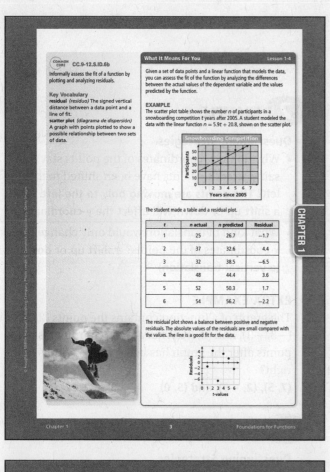

CC.9-12.S.ID.6b

Informally assess the fit of a function by plotting and analyzing residuals.

Key Vocabulary
residual *(residuo)* The signed vertical distance between a data point and a line of fit.
scatter plot *(diagrama de dispersión)* A graph with points plotted to show a possible relationship between two sets of data.

What It Means For You
Lesson 1-4

Given a set of data points and a linear function that models the data, you can assess the fit of the function by analyzing the differences between the actual values of the dependent variable and the values predicted by the function.

EXAMPLE
The scatter plot table shows the number n of participants in a snowboarding competition t years after 2005. A student modeled the data with the linear function $n = 5.9t + 20.8$, shown on the scatter plot.

Snowboarding Competition

Participants / Years since 2005

The student made a table and a residual plot.

t	n actual	n predicted	Residual
1	25	26.7	−1.7
2	37	32.6	4.4
3	32	38.5	−6.5
4	48	44.4	3.6
5	52	50.3	1.7
6	54	56.2	−2.2

The residual plot shows a balance between positive and negative residuals. The absolute values of the residuals are small compared with the values. The line is a good fit for the data.

Residuals / t-values

Key Vocabulary

compression *(compresión)* A transformation that pushes the points of a graph horizontally toward the y-axis or vertically toward the x-axis.

linear function *(función lineal)* A function that can be written in the form $f(x) = mx + b$, where x is the independent variable and m and b are real numbers. Its graph is a line.

parent function *(función madre)* The simplest function with the defining characteristics of the family. Functions in the same family are transformations of their parent function.

reflection *(reflexión)* A transformation that reflects, or "flips," a graph or figure across a line, called the line of reflection, such that each reflected point is the same distance from the line of reflection but is on the opposite side of the line.

residual *(residuo)* The signed vertical distance between a data point and a line of fit.

scatter plot *(diagrama de dispersión)* A graph with points plotted to show a possible relationship between two sets of data.

slope *(pendiente)* A measure of the steepness of a line. If (x_1, y_1) and (x_2, y_2) are any two points on the line, the slope of the line, known as m, is represented by the equation $m = \frac{y_2 - y_1}{x_2 - x_1}$.

stretch *(estiramiento)* A transformation that pulls the points of a graph horizontally away from the y-axis or vertically away from the x-axis.

transformation *(transformación)* A change in the position, size, or shape of a figure or graph.

translation *(translación)* A transformation that shifts or slides every point of a figure or graph the same distance in the same direction.

x-intercept *(intersección con el eje x)* The x-coordinate(s) of the point(s) where a graph intersects the x-axis.

y-intercept *(intersección con el eje y)* The y-coordinate(s) of the point(s) where a graph intersects the y-axis.

MATHEMATICAL PRACTICE

The Common Core Standards for Mathematical Practice describe varieties of expertise that mathematics educators at all levels should seek to develop in their students. Opportunities to develop these practices are integrated throughout this program.

1. Make sense of problems and persevere in solving them.
2. Reason abstractly and quantitatively.
3. Construct viable arguments and critique the reasoning of others.
4. Model with mathematics.
5. Use appropriate tools strategically.
6. Attend to precision.
7. Look for and make use of structure.
8. Look for and express regularity in repeated reasoning.

COMMON CORE PROFESSIONAL DEVELOPMENT
CC.9-12.S.ID.6b*

In this chapter, students will fit linear equations to data in scatter plots. They will also learn to find and plot residuals. Then they will use residual plots to assess how well a model fits a data set.

1-1 Exploring Transformations
Going Deeper

Essential question: *What patterns govern transformations of functions?*

COMMON Standards for
CORE Mathematical Content

CC.9-12.F.BF.3 Identify the effect on the graph of replacing $f(x)$ by $f(x) + k$, $k\,f(x)$, $f(kx)$, and $f(x + k)$ for specific values of k (both positive and negative); …

CC.9-12.F.IF.5 Relate the domain of a function to its graph and, where applicable, to the quantitative relationship it describes.*

Prerequisites

Previous courses

Math Background

Transformations change the graph of a function. When students understand the basic transformations (translation, reflection, stretch and compression), they are better able to understand how to write the equation of a graph, and how to identify the graph of a function that has been transformed. Example 4, for instance, will help students prepare for a functional interpretation of horizontal stretches and compressions.

INTRODUCE

Show students how the value of a number changes as its position on the number line changes. Show students the coordinate plane, reminding them that the x-axis of the coordinate plane is a representation of the one-dimensional number line. Show students how the y-coordinates of points change as the points move up and down.

TEACH

1 EXPLORE

Questioning Strategies

• What happens to the value of the x-coordinate of a point as it moves to the right along the x-axis? as it moves to the left? **It increases; it decreases.**

• What happens to the value of the y-coordinate of a point as it moves up along the y-axis? as it moves down? **It increases; it decreases.**

2 EXAMPLE

Questioning Strategies

• Why do the y-coordinates of the points stay the same after the points have been shifted to the left? **The points are moving only to the left. Only a shift up or down will affect the y-coordinates.**

• What kind of translation would only change the y-coordinates of the points? **a shift up or down (a vertical translation)**

EXTRA EXAMPLE

The graph of a function contains the points $(2, 5)$, $(-3, -3)$, and $(0, 0)$. What are the coordinates of the points after the graph has been shifted 5 units to the right?
(7, 5), (2, −3), and (5, 0)

3 EXAMPLE

Questioning Strategies

• What are the coordinates of the origin after it has been reflected across the x-axis? **(0, 0)**

• Which points do not change after a reflection across the x-axis? **points on the x-axis**

EXTRA EXAMPLE

The graph of a function contains the points $(5, 6)$, $(0, -8)$, $(-3, 1)$, and $(-4, -2)$. What are the coordinates of the points after the graph has been reflected across the x-axis?
(5, −6), (0, 8), (−3, −1), and (−4, 2)

1-1

Video Tutor

Exploring Transformations
Going Deeper

Essential question: *What patterns govern transformations of functions?*

CC.9-12.F.BF.3
1 EXPLORE Translating Points

Translate the point (−2, 5) three units to the left and two units down.

To translate three units to the left, **subtract** 3 from the ___x___ -coordinate.

To translate two units down, **subtract** 2 from the ___y___ -coordinate.

Translating (−2, 5) three units to the left and two units down results in the

point __(−5, 3)__ .

> **REFLECT**
>
> **1a.** When you translate a point left or right, how do you change the coordinates of the point?
>
> Add (if translating right) or subtract (if translating left) to the x-coordinate.
>
> **1b.** When you translate up or down, how do you change the coordinates of the point?
>
> Add (if translating up) or subtract (if translating down) to the y-coordinate.

CC.9-12.F.BF.3
2 EXAMPLE Translating a Function

Translate the graph of f(x) three units to the left.

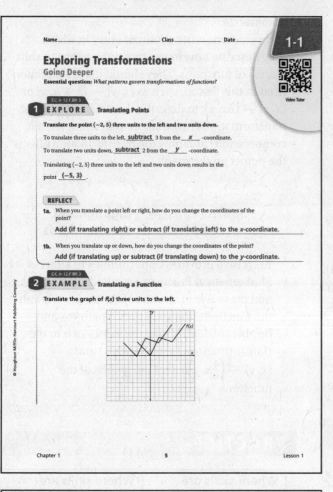

> **REFLECT**
>
> **2a.** How do the x-coordinates of the points on the graph change after being shifted to the left?
>
> The x-coordinates of the points on the graph decrease by 3.
>
> **2b.** How do the y-coordinates change after being shifted to the left?
>
> The y-coordinates of the points on the graph stay the same.

CC.9-12.F.IF.5
3 EXAMPLE Reflecting a Function

Reflect the graph of f(x) across the x-axis.

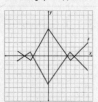

> **REFLECT**
>
> **3a.** Fill in the table to show how points on the graph of change after the graph is reflected over the x-axis.
>
> | Original Function | Transformation |
> | --- | --- |
> | (−7, 1) | (−7, −1) |
> | (−4, −1) | (−4, 1) |
> | (0, 6) | (0, −6) |
> | (5, −1) | (5, 1) |
>
> **3b.** How do the y-coordinates of the points change after being reflected over the x-axis?
>
> The y-coordinates are multiplied by −1.
>
> **3c.** How do the x-coordinates of the points change after being reflected over the x-axis?
>
> The x-coordinates of the points do not change.

© Houghton Mifflin Harcourt Publishing Company

Notes

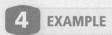

4 EXAMPLE

Questioning Strategies

- If you multiply the *x*-coordinate of a point by a whole number, does the point move closer to or further from the *y*-axis? further

- If you multiply the *x*-coordinate of a point by a number between 0 and 1, does the point move closer to or further from the *y*-axis? closer

- If you multiply the *y*-coordinate of a point by a whole number, do you think the point would move closer to or further from the *x*-axis? further

EXTRA EXAMPLE

The graph of a function contains the points $(-4, 2)$, $(0, -3)$, $(5, 1)$, and $(8, -2)$. What are the coordinates of the points under a horizontal compression by a factor of $\frac{1}{2}$?
$(-2, 2)$, $(0, -3)$, $(2.5, 1)$, and $(4, -2)$

Teaching Strategy

After students complete Example 4 (but before they answer the Reflect questions), have them repeat Example 4 using the transformations $(x, y) \rightarrow (3x, y)$ and $(x, y) \rightarrow \left(\frac{1}{3}x, y\right)$. Ask students if they notice any patterns. Some students may need to use the transformations $(x, y) \rightarrow (4x, y)$ and $(x, y) \rightarrow \left(\frac{1}{4}x, y\right)$ as well before they identify the pattern.

CLOSE

Essential Question

What patterns govern transformations of functions?
Graphs of functions can be transformed by translation, reflection, stretch, or compression. If a constant is added to or subtracted from the *x*-coordinates of the points on a graph, the graph shifts left or right. If a constant is added to or subtracted from the *y*-coordinates, the graph is shifted up or down. If the *y*-coordinates of the points on a graph are multiplied by −1, the graph is reflected across the *x*-axis. If the *x*-coordinates are multiplied by −1, the graph is reflected across the *y*-axis. If the *x*-coordinates of the points on a graph are multiplied by a positive number, the graph is stretched or compressed horizontally. Although it is not shown in this lesson, if the *y*-coordinates of the points on a graph are multiplied by a positive number, the graph is stretched or compressed vertically.

Summarize

Have students write a journal entry in which they describe how to use transformations to shift graphs of functions. They should use the notation used in this lesson, such as $(x, y) \rightarrow (x + a, y)$ or $(x, y) \rightarrow (ax, y)$, to describe the different types of transformations (translation, reflection, stretch, compression) and how the transformation affects the points on the graph.

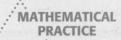 **Highlighting the Standards**

Exercise 6 provides opportunities to address Mathematical Practices Standard 7 (Look for and make use of structure). As students graph the functions, they will notice patterns and be able to identify how the values of *a* in the transformations $(x, y) \rightarrow (ax, y)$ and $(x, y) \rightarrow \left(\frac{1}{a}x, y\right)$ affect the graphs of the functions.

PRACTICE

Where skills are taught	Where skills are practiced
1 EXPLORE	EXS. 1–3
2 EXAMPLE	EX. 4
3 EXAMPLE	EX. 5
4 EXAMPLE	EX. 6

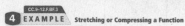

4 **EXAMPLE** CC.9-12.F.BF.3   Stretching or Compressing a Function

Consider the transformations $(x, y) \rightarrow (2x, y)$ and $(x, y) \rightarrow \left(\frac{1}{2}x, y\right)$. You will use the tables below to see the effects of these transformations on the graph of $f(x) = x^2$. Complete the table with values of $2x$ and $\frac{1}{2}x$ that correspond to the given values of x.

2x	x	y = x²
−4	−2	4
−2	−1	1
0	0	0
1	1	1
2	2	4

½x	x	y = x²
−1	−2	4
−½	−1	1
0	0	0
½	1	1
1	2	4

The graph of $f(x) = x^2$ is shown on the grids. Plot the points $(2x, y)$ from your table on the coordinate grid on the left. Connect them with a smooth curve. Do the same for the points $\left(\frac{1}{2}x, y\right)$ on the coordinate grid on the right.

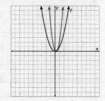

REFLECT

4a. A transformation of the form $(x, y) \rightarrow (ax, y)$ is a horizontal stretch or compression. Based on the graphs above, for what kinds of numbers a do you think that the transformation $(x, y) \rightarrow (ax, y)$ is a horizontal compression?

numbers between 0 and 1

4b. For what kinds of numbers a do you think that the transformation $(x, y) \rightarrow (ax, y)$ is a horizontal stretch?

numbers greater than 1

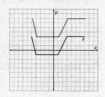

© Houghton Mifflin Harcourt Publishing Company

PRACTICE

Perform the given translation on the point $(5, -3)$ and give the coordinates of the translated point.

1. 6 units right

(11, −3)

2. 2 units up

(5, −1)

3. 1 unit right, 7 units down

(6, −10)

Use a table to perform each transformation of $y = f(x)$.

4. translation 4 units up

Original Function	Transformation
(−5, 2)	(−5, 6)
(−4, −1)	(−4, 3)
(1, −1)	(1, 3)
(3, 3)	(3, 7)
(7, 3)	(7, 7)

5. reflection across the y-axis

Original Function	Transformation
(−5, 0)	(5, 0)
(−3, 3)	(3, 3)
(0, 0)	(0, 0)
(2, −2)	(−2, −2)
(6, 2)	(−6, 2)

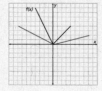

6. horizontal stretch by a factor of 4

Original Function	Transformation
(−4, 8)	(−16, 8)
(−1, 2)	(−4, 2)
(0, 0)	(0, 0)
(2, 2)	(8, 2)
(4, 4)	(16, 4)

© Houghton Mifflin Harcourt Publishing Company

Assign these pages to help your students practice and apply important lesson concepts. For additional exercises, see the Student Edition.

Answers

Additional Practice

1. $(-1, 5)$ **2.** $(2, -1)$

3. $(6, 7)$

4.

$x - 1$	x	y	$y - 5$
-4	-3	3	-2
-2	-1	1	-4
0	1	2	-3
1	2	1	-4
2	3	2	-3

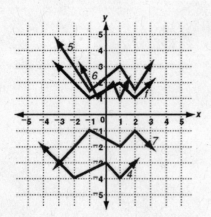

5.

x	y	$\frac{3}{2}y$
-3	3	$\frac{9}{2}$
-1	1	$\frac{3}{2}$
1	2	3
2	1	$\frac{3}{2}$
3	2	3

6.

$\frac{1}{2}x$	x	y
$-\frac{3}{2}$	-3	3
$-\frac{1}{2}$	-1	1
$\frac{1}{2}$	1	2
1	2	1
$\frac{3}{2}$	3	2

7.

x	y	$-y$
-3	3	-3
-1	1	-1
1	2	-2
2	1	-1
3	2	-2

8. Profits are reduced by 10%; vertical compression; $(x, 0.9y)$.

Problem Solving

1. $120; $160; $220; $240

2. $40 per hour   **3.** $20 per hour

4. Translated down 15 units

5. Possible answers: A line would go from $(0, 160)$ to $(3, 160)$ with no open circle; the range would not include any numbers less than 160.

6. He would have to pay more to rent the Art Center.

7. A   **8.** J

Name_____ Class_____ Date_____ **1-1**

Additional Practice

Perform the given translation on the point (2, 5) and give the coordinates of the translated point.

1. left 3 units

2. down 6 units

3. right 4 units, up 2 units

_____   _____   _____

Use the table to perform each transformation of $y = f(x)$. Use the same coordinate plane as the original function.

4. translation left 1 unit, down 5 units

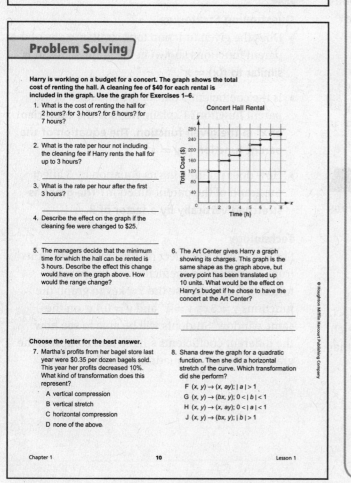

x	y
–3	3
–1	1
1	2
2	1
3	2

5. vertical stretch factor of $\frac{3}{2}$

x	y	
–3	3	
–1	1	
1	2	
2	1	
3	2	

6. horizontal compression factor of $\frac{1}{2}$

x	y
–3	3
–1	1
1	2
2	1
3	2

7. reflection across x-axis

x	y
–3	3
–1	1
1	2
2	1
3	2

Solve.

8. George has a goal for the number of computers he wants to sell each month for the next 6 months at his computer store. He draws a graph to show his projected profits for that period. Then he decides to discount the prices by 10%. How will this affect his profits? Identify the transformation to his graph and describe how to find the ordered pairs for the transformation.

_____

_____

Problem Solving

Harry is working on a budget for a concert. The graph shows the total cost of renting the hall. A cleaning fee of $40 for each rental is included in the graph. Use the graph for Exercises 1–6.

1. What is the cost of renting the hall for 2 hours? for 3 hours? for 6 hours? for 7 hours?

_____

2. What is the rate per hour not including the cleaning fee if Harry rents the hall for up to 3 hours?

_____

3. What is the rate per hour after the first 3 hours?

_____

4. Describe the effect on the graph if the cleaning fee were changed to $25.

_____

Concert Hall Rental

5. The managers decide that the minimum time for which the hall can be rented is 3 hours. Describe the effect this change would have on the graph above. How would the range change?

_____

_____

_____

6. The Art Center gives Harry a graph showing its charges. This graph is the same shape as the graph above, but every point has been translated up 10 units. What would be the effect on Harry's budget if he chose to have the concert at the Art Center?

_____

_____

_____

Choose the letter for the best answer.

7. Martha's profits from her bagel store last year were $0.35 per dozen bagels sold. This year her profits decreased 10%. What kind of transformation does this represent?

A vertical compression

B vertical stretch

C horizontal compression

D none of the above

8. Shana drew the graph for a quadratic function. Then she did a horizontal stretch of the curve. Which transformation did she perform?

F $(x, y) \rightarrow (x, ay)$; $|a| > 1$

G $(x, y) \rightarrow (bx, y)$; $0 < |b| < 1$

H $(x, y) \rightarrow (x, ay)$; $0 < |a| < 1$

J $(x, y) \rightarrow (bx, y)$; $|b| > 1$

1-2

Introduction to Parent Functions
Going Deeper

Essential question: *How do parent functions help you visualize the graph of a function?*

COMMON CORE Standards for Mathematical Content

CC.9-12.F.BF.3 Identify the effect on the graph of replacing $f(x)$ by $f(x) + k$, $k\,f(x)$, $f(kx)$, and $f(x + k)$ for specific values of k (both positive and negative); find the value of k given the graphs. Experiment with cases and illustrate an explanation of the effects on the graph using technology...

Prerequisites
Exploring Transformations

Vocabulary
parent function

Math Background
Students encounter many functions in their study of mathematics. The simplest are the parent functions, including the parent linear function $f(x) = x$, the parent quadratic function $f(x) = x^2$, the parent cubic function $f(x) = x^3$, and the parent square root function $f(x) = \sqrt{x}$. Each parent function is the building block for the functions in its family. Understanding the parent functions is a first step in understanding equations and graphs of functions in general.

INTRODUCE

Students should already be familiar with the graphs of some parent functions. Sketch the parabola $y = x^2$ and point out some of the points on the graph. Ask what would happen to those points if you moved the parabola up one unit on the coordinate plane. Students should recognize that, for instance, $(0, 0)$ would move to $(0, 1)$ and, in fact, that any point (x, y) would move to $(x, y + 1)$. Sketch the new parabola. Students may also recognize that the equation of the new parabola is $y = x^2 + 1$.

TEACH

1 EXPLORE

Questioning Strategies

- Does the given function look similar to any of the parent functions shown in the graphs? **Yes, it is similar to $f(x) = x^3$.**

- What expression does the given function contain instead of x? **$x + 4$**

- How do you think subtracting 4 from the x-value in the equation of a function would affect the graph of the function? **The graph would be shifted 4 units to the right.**

2 EXPLORE

Questioning Strategies

- Does the given function look similar to any of the parent functions shown in the graphs? **Yes, it is similar to $f(x) = x^2$.**

- Is the coefficient 3 part of the equation of the parent function? Explain. **No, 3 is the coefficient of x^2 in the given function. The equation of the parent function is $y = x^2$.**

- How does multiplying its equation by 3 affect the graph of the parent function? **The graph is stretched vertically by a factor of 3.**

Technology
Show students the effect on the graph that results from changing the coefficients of the parent function $f(x) = x^2$. Use the Y= key to graph the functions $y = 3x^2$, $y = x^2$ and $y = 0.1x^2$ on the same window. Students will be able to see how the different coefficients stretch and compress the graph of the parent quadratic function.

Name_____ Class_____ Date_____

1-2

Introduction to Parent Functions
Going Deeper

Essential question: *How do parent functions help you visualize the graph of a function?*

The *parent function* of a family of functions is the simplest function with the defining characteristics of the family. Parent functions help you understand the shape of a graph. You can graph many of the functions you will study by applying one or more transformations to one of the parent graphs.

Commonly used parent functions and their graphs are shown below:

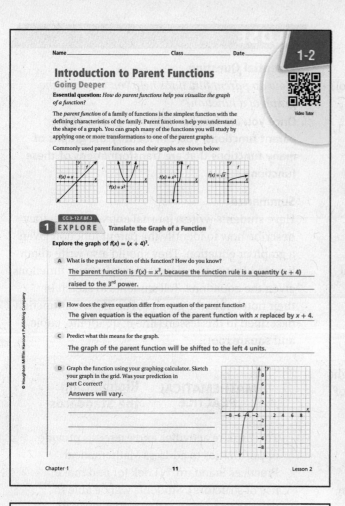

CC.9–12.F.BF.3

1 EXPLORE Translate the Graph of a Function

Explore the graph of $f(x) = (x + 4)^3$.

A What is the parent function of this function? How do you know?

The parent function is $f(x) = x^3$, because the function rule is a quantity $(x + 4)$ raised to the 3rd power.

B How does the given equation differ from equation of the parent function?

The given equation is the equation of the parent function with x replaced by $x + 4$.

C Predict what this means for the graph.

The graph of the parent function will be shifted to the left 4 units.

D Graph the function using your graphing calculator. Sketch your graph in the grid. Was your prediction in part C correct?

Answers will vary.

REFLECT

1a. How can you change the equation of a parent function if you want to shift it to the left or right?

Add (if translating left) or subtract (if translating right) to the input value.

1b. By replacing x with $x + 4$ in the parent function, you shift it 4 units to the left. Why does adding 4 to x shift the graph in the negative direction? Explain.

Answers will vary. Sample answer: If 4 is being added to x, the value of x will need to be 4 less to obtain the same output value for the function.

When the word 'stretch' is used alone, it refers to a vertical stretch by default.

CC.9–12.F.BF.3

2 EXPLORE Graph the Stretch of a Function

Explore the graph of $f(x) = 3x^2$.

A What is the parent function of this function? How do you know?

The parent function is $f(x) = x^2$. The given equation involves a constant times x^2.

B How does the given equation differ from the equation of the parent function?

In the given equation, x^2 is multiplied by 3.

C Predict what this means for the graph.

The graph of the parent function will be stretched vertically by a factor of 3.

D Graph the function using your graphing calculator. Sketch your graph in the grid below. Was your prediction in part C correct?

Answers will vary.

© Houghton Mifflin Harcourt Publishing Company

Questioning Strategies

- Which parent function involves a radical symbol?
  the square root function

- If the y-coordinate of a point is multiplied by -1, how is the point reflected? It is reflected across the x-axis.

- If a negative sign appears before $f(x)$, which coordinate is negated, the x-coordinate or the y-coordinate? the y-coordinate

Avoid Common Errors

Students often confuse the direction of horizontal translations of parent functions. Remind them that adding a positive constant to the x in the equation of a parent function shifts the function to the left, while subtracting a positive constant from the x shifts the function to the right. This is counterintuitive because to shift a point to the right, one adds a positive constant to the x-coordinate of the point.

Differentiated Instruction

Show students examples of the transformations discussed in the Avoid Common Errors section above. Then ask them to choose a parent function, add a positive constant to x, and graph the new function. Have students repeat the exercise, but ask them to *subtract* a positive constant from x. Students should compare their results and discuss what they see.

CLOSE

Essential Question

How do parent functions help you visualize the graph of a function?

Once you are familiar with the graphs of the parent functions, you can identify the graphs of many functions that are transformations of these functions.

Summarize

Have students write a journal entry in which they describe how to identify the parent function given a graph or equation. They should also write about how to identify transformations of parent functions given the equations. Tell students to sketch in their notebooks the graphs of each parent function described in this lesson (linear, quadratic, cubic, and square root).

> **MATHEMATICAL PRACTICE**   **Highlighting the Standards**
>
> The Explore activities and exercises provide opportunities to address Mathematical Practices Standard 7 (Look for and make use of structure). Students will be able to write the equation of a function given its graph, because they will be able to recognize the graph as a transformation of a parent function. Students will know the graphs of the parent functions as well as how changes in the equations of those functions transform their graphs. They will be able to look at a function and immediately have an idea of what its graph looks like.

PRACTICE

Where skills are taught	Where skills are practiced
1 EXPLORE	EXS. 1, 2, 6, 9
2 EXPLORE	EXS. 4, 7, 8, 11, 12
3 EXPLORE	EXS. 3, 5, 10

REFLECT

2a. How does multiplying $f(x)$ in the parent function by a constant change the graph?

The parent function stretches vertically.

2b. How would the graph change if the constant were a number between 0 and 1?

The graph of the parent function would be compressed vertically.

3 EXPLORE Graph the Reflection of a Function
CC.9-12.F.BF.3

Explore the graph of $f(x) = -\sqrt{x}$.

A What is the parent function of this function? How do you know?

The parent function is $f(x) = \sqrt{x}$. The given equation involves a constant times $\sqrt{x}$.

B How does the given equation differ from the equation of the parent function?

In the given equation, $\sqrt{x}$ is multiplied by -1.

C Predict what this means for the graph.

The graph of the parent function will be reflected across the x-axis.

D Graph the function using your graphing calculator. Sketch your graph in the grid below. Was your prediction in part C correct?

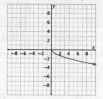

Answers may vary.

REFLECT

3a. How does multiplying $f(x)$ by -1 affect the graph?

The graph of the parent function is reflected across the x-axis.

3b. What would happen to the function if x were multiplied by -1 instead of $f(x)$? Why?

The parent function would be reflected across the y-axis; the x-values would be negated.

PRACTICE

1. The graph shows a translation of the function $f(x) = x$.

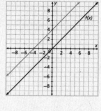

a. Describe the translation in two different ways.

A vertical shift of 4 units up, and a horizontal shift of 4 units left.

b. Explain why the translations are the same.

The equation of the shifted graph is $y = x + 4$, which is both $f(x + 4)$ and $f(x) + 4$. The transformation can be thought of as acting on the x-coordinates or on the y-coordinates.

c. Other parent functions do not have this same feature. Use the parent function $y = x^2$ to explain why.

The equation $y = x^2 + 4$ and $y = (x + 4)^2$ are not equivalent.

Identify the parent function from the function rule. Describe the transformation of the parent function that each function represents. Use your graphing calculator to check your answers.

2. $f(x) = (x + 2)^2$
$f(x) = x^2$; shifted 2 units to the left

3. $g(x) = -x^3$
$f(x) = x^3$; reflected in x-axis

4. $f(x) = 5x^2$
$f(x) = x^2$; vertical stretch by factor of 5

5. $g(x) = \sqrt{-x}$
$f(x) = \sqrt{x}$; reflected in y-axis

6. $f(x) = (x - 3)^3$
$f(x) = x^3$; shifted 3 units right

7. $g(x) = 0.5x^2$
$f(x) = x^2$; vert. compression by factor of 0.5

8. $f(x) = 4\sqrt{x}$
$f(x) = \sqrt{x}$; vert. stretch by factor of 4

9. $g(x) = x + 5$
$f(x) = x$; shift 5 units up (or 5 units left)

10. $f(x) = -x$
$f(x) = x$; reflect in x- or y- axis

11. $g(x) = 3x$
$f(x) = x$; vert. stretch by factor of 3 or horiz. comp. by factor of $\frac{1}{3}$

12. Why are the graphs of $f(x) = x^2$ and $f(-x) = (-x)^2$ the same graph? Explain algebraically and using the graph.

Algebraically: $(-x)^2 = (-x)(-x) = x^2$, which is the same as $f(x)$.

Using the graph: the graph of the function is symmetric about the y-axis and when it is reflected over the y-axis, the function maps onto itself.

Assign these pages to help your students practice and apply important lesson concepts. For additional exercises, see the Student Edition.

Answers

Additional Practice

1. Square root; translation 4 units left

2. Cubic; translation 4 units right

3. Quadratic; horizontal compression

4. Cubic; translation 1 unit down

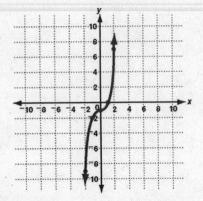

5. Square root; vertical compression

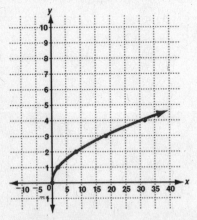

6. The domain is the same for both functions, all real numbers. The range for the linear function is all real numbers, but the range for the quadratic function is all real numbers greater than or equal to 0.

7. The domain and the range for the cubic function are all real numbers. The domain and the range for the square-root function are all real numbers greater than or equal to 0.

Problem Solving

1. The graph of $f(x) = 7x + 2$ is translated up 2 units and the line is steeper by a factor of 7.

2. 44; yes; Possible answer: I tried points (3, 23), (4, 30), (5, 37), (7, 51), (8, 58); when x has a value greater than 6, the points do not match well.

3. The graph of $f(x) = x^2 + 5$ is translated up 5 units.

4. 41; not exactly; Possible answer: I tried points (2, 9), (4, 21), (5, 30), (8, 69), (10, 105), and (12, 149), and they match reasonably well.

5. Possible answer: The quadratic parent function translated up 5 units best models these data.

Additional Practice

Identify the parent function for *h* from its function rule. Then graph *h* on your calculator and describe what transformation of the parent function it represents.

1. $h(x) = \sqrt{x+4}$

2. $h(x) = (x-4)^3$

3. $h(x) = 4x^2$

_____   _____   _____

_____   _____   _____

Graph the data from the table. Describe the parent function and the transformation that best approximates the data set.

4.
x	−2	−1	0	1	2
y	−9	−2	−1	0	7

5.
x	0	2	8	18	32
y	0	1	2	3	4

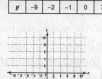
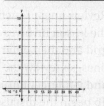

6. Compare the domain and the range for the parent quadratic function to the domain and the range for the parent linear function.

_____

_____

_____

7. Compare the domain and the range for the parent square-root function to the domain and the range for the parent cubic function.

_____

_____

_____

_____

Problem Solving

Katy and Peter are writing a paper about the history and use of cell phones. They make a graph of the data in the table. They want to determine the parent function for the graph.

Cell Phone Subscribers in the United States (estimated in millions)			
1991	7.6	1997	55.3
1992	11.0	1998	69.2
1993	16.0	1999	86.0
1994	24.1	2000	109.5
1995	33.8	2001	128.4
1996	44.0	2002	140.8

U.S. Cell Phone Subscribers

1. Peter wants to compare the graph to the function $f(x) = 7x + 2$. How would the graph of $f(x) = 7x + 2$ compare to its parent function $f(x) = x$?

_____

2. What is the value $f(x) = 7x + 2$ for 1996, when $x = 6$? Does that point fit the graph? Try some other values of x for the function $f(x) = 7x + 2$. How well do the results fit the range of the graph?

_____

3. Katy wants to compare the graph to the function $f(x) = x^2 + 5$. How would the graph of $f(x) = x^2 + 5$ compare to its parent function $f(x) = x^2$?

_____

4. Find the value of $f(x) = x^2 + 5$ for 1996, when $x = 6$? Does that point fit the graph? Try some other values of x for the function $f(x) = x^2 + 5$. How well do the results fit the range of the graph?

_____

5. Which parent function and transformation best models these data?

_____

Notes

Transforming Linear Functions
Going Deeper

Essential question: *How can a linear function be understood as the transformation of another linear function?*

Standards for Mathematical Content

CC.9-12.F.BF.3 Identify the effect on the graph of replacing $f(x)$ by $f(x) + k$, $k f(x)$, $f(kx)$, and $f(x + k)$ for specific values of k (both positive and negative); find the value of k given the graphs. Experiment with cases and illustrate an explanation of the effects on the graph using technology. ...

Prerequisites

Exploring Transformations

Introduction to Parent Functions

Math Background

A transformation changes a graph's size, shape, position, or orientation. Although this lesson deals exclusively with transformations of linear functions, most of the results can be extended to polynomial functions in general and to certain other functions, such as absolute value functions. For example, $y = -f(x)$ reflects the graph of f across the x-axis, while $y = f(-x)$ reflects it across the y-axis. The function $y = f(x - k)$ translates the graph of f horizontally k units while $y = f(x) + k$ translates the graph vertically k units. The function $y = af(x)$ stretches the graph of f vertically if $|a| > 1$, and compresses it vertically if $0 < |a| < 1$. However, linear functions have some unique properties. For instance, a vertical stretch of a linear function is also a horizontal compression, and a vertical compression is also a horizontal stretch.

INTRODUCE

Review linear functions with the students. Part of the lesson involves drawing lines on a coordinate grid and then determining the equations of those lines, so review the process of determining slope and y-intercept from the graph of a linear function. To begin the discussion of transformations of linear functions, ask students to determine the coordinates of the point (3, 4) after it has been translated 5 units left and 7 units down. (−2, −3) Then ask them to write the coordinates of the point (x, y) after a horizontal translation of h units and a vertical translation of k units. $(x + h, y + k)$

TEACH

1 EXPLORE

Questioning Strategies

- Why do the two lines in the diagram have the same slope? **Because points on the graph of f are translated the same distance vertically to produce the graph of g, the new line is parallel to (and therefore has the same slope as) the first.**

- The graphs of linear functions f and g are parallel. Compare the equations of the functions. **With the equations written in $y = mx + b$ form, the slopes m are equal. The y-intercepts, b, are not the same because the lines are parallel. The point (0, b) cannot be on both lines.**

2 EXPLORE

Questioning Strategies

- The graph of $y = x$ is translated n units up and then n units right. What is the equation of the resulting line? $y = x$

- The graph of $y = f(x)$ is translated p units horizontally and then q units vertically. What is the equation of the resulting line? $y = f(x - p) + q$

continued

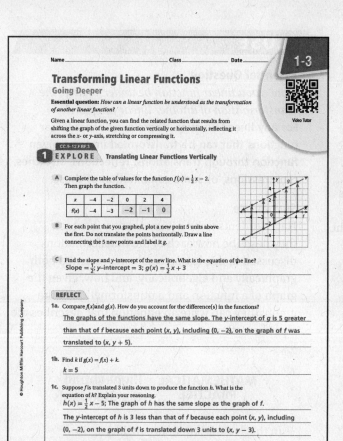

Transforming Linear Functions
Going Deeper

Essential question: *How can a linear function be understood as the transformation of another linear function?*

Given a linear function, you can find the related function that results from shifting the graph of the given function vertically or horizontally, reflecting it across the x- or y-axis, stretching or compressing it.

CC.9-12.F.BF.3

1 EXPLORE   Translating Linear Functions Vertically

A Complete the table of values for the function $f(x) = \frac{1}{2}x - 2$. Then graph the function.

x	−4	−2	0	2	4
f(x)	−4	−3	−2	−1	0

B For each point that you graphed, plot a new point 5 units above the first. Do not translate the points horizontally. Draw a line connecting the 5 new points and label it g.

C Find the slope and y-intercept of the new line. What is the equation of the line?
Slope = $\frac{1}{2}$; y-intercept = 3; $g(x) = \frac{1}{2}x + 3$

REFLECT

1a. Compare f(x) and g(x). How do you account for the difference(s) in the functions?

The graphs of the functions have the same slope. The y-intercept of g is 5 greater than that of f because each point (x, y), including (0, −2), on the graph of f was translated to (x, y + 5).

1b. Find k if $g(x) = f(x) + k$.

$k = 5$

1c. Suppose f is translated 3 units down to produce the function h. What is the equation of h? Explain your reasoning.

$h(x) = \frac{1}{2}x - 5$; The graph of h has the same slope as the graph of f.

The y-intercept of h is 3 less than that of f because each point (x, y), including (0, −2), on the graph of f is translated down 3 units to (x, y − 3).

Chapter 1   17   Lesson 3

© Houghton Mifflin Harcourt Publishing Company

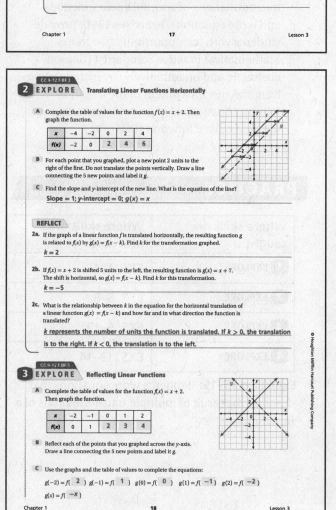

CC.9-12.F.BF.3

2 EXPLORE   Translating Linear Functions Horizontally

A Complete the table of values for the function $f(x) = x + 2$. Then graph the function.

x	−4	−2	0	2	4
f(x)	−2	0	2	4	6

B For each point that you graphed, plot a new point 2 units to the right of the first. Do not translate the points vertically. Draw a line connecting the 5 new points and label it g.

C Find the slope and y-intercept of the new line. What is the equation of the line?
Slope = 1; y-intercept = 0; $g(x) = x$

REFLECT

2a. If the graph of a linear function f is translated horizontally, the resulting function g is related to f(x) by $g(x) = f(x - k)$. Find k for the transformation graphed.

$k = 2$

2b. If $f(x) = x + 2$ is shifted 5 units to the left, the resulting function is $g(x) = x + 7$. The shift is horizontal, so $g(x) = f(x - k)$. Find k for this transformation.

$k = -5$

2c. What is the relationship between k in the equation for the horizontal translation of a linear function $g(x) = f(x - k)$ and how far and in what direction the function is translated?

k represents the number of units the function is translated. If $k > 0$, the translation is to the right. If $k < 0$, the translation is to the left.

CC.9-12.F.BF.1

3 EXPLORE   Reflecting Linear Functions

A Complete the table of values for the function $f(x) = x + 2$. Then graph the function.

x	−2	−1	0	1	2
f(x)	0	1	2	3	4

B Reflect each of the points that you graphed across the y-axis. Draw a line connecting the 5 new points and label it g.

C Use the graphs and the table of values to complete the equations:

$g(-2) = f(\ 2\ )$ $g(-1) = f(\ 1\ )$ $g(0) = f(\ 0\ )$ $g(1) = f(\ -1\ )$ $g(2) = f(\ -2\ )$

$g(x) = f(\ -x\ )$

Chapter 1   18   Lesson 3

© Houghton Mifflin Harcourt Publishing Company

Avoid Common Errors

The general equation for vertical translations, $g(x) = f(x) + k$, makes intuitive sense, because $k > 0$ indicates an upward translation of the graph and $k < 0$ indicates a downward translation. The same is not true of the general equation for horizontal translations, $g(x) = f(x - k)$. For example, it appears that $g(x) = f(x - 3)$ represents a translation of 3 units to the left, i.e., in a negative direction, when in fact the translation is to the right. Bring this fact to students' attention.

 EXPLORE

Questioning Strategies

• What is the equation of the graph of $y = mx + b$ after it is reflected across the x-axis? after it is reflected across the y-axis? $y = -mx - b$; $y = -mx + b$

• What is $g(x)$, the equation of the graph of linear function $f(x)$ after its reflection across the y-axis, followed by a vertical translation of k units? $g(x) = f(-x) + k$

 EXPLORE

Questioning Strategies

• Is there a value of n for which the transformation $j(x) = nf(x)$ transforms the function $f(x) = x$ so that its graph is the y-axis? Explain. No; n represents the slope of the line $y = nx$, and the slope of the y-axis is undefined.

• How can you tell whether the transformation $g(x) = nf(x)$ vertically stretches or compresses the graph of $f(x) = x$? For $0 < n < 1$, the transformation vertically compresses $f(x)$. For $n > 1$, it vertically stretches $f(x)$.

CLOSE

Essential Question

How can a linear function be understood as the transformation of another linear function?
For any linear function, there exist other linear functions that can be transformed into the given function through translations, reflections, stretches, compressions, or some combination of these.

Summarize

Have students write a journal entry in which they describe how each of the transformations discussed in this lesson can be represented both graphically and algebraically, and how, given the graph of a function and a transformation of the graph, they can write an equation that describes the transformation.

MATHEMATICAL PRACTICE	Highlighting the Standards

In this lesson, students consider transformations of specific linear functions and write equations. Exercises 15–19 provide students with the opportunity to address Mathematical Practice Standard 4 (Reason abstractly and quantitatively) by extrapolating from the specific content of the lesson to writing equations of given transformations of the generalized function $f(x)$.

PRACTICE

Where skills are taught	Where skills are practiced
1 EXPLORE	EXS. 1–4
2 EXPLORE	EXS. 5–8
3 EXPLORE	EXS. 9–12
4 EXPLORE	EXS. 13–14

Exercises 15–19: Students write equations that describe the result of multiple transformations of a function.

REFLECT

3a. The graph of $f(x) = x + 2$ is reflected across the x-axis. The image, h, is shown in the graph. Use the graph to write the order pairs $(x, f(x))$ and $(x, h(x))$ for $x = -3, -2, -1, 0, 1, 2,$ and 3.

f: $(-3, -1), (-2, 0), (-1, 1), (0, 2), (1, 3), (2, 4), (3, 5)$

h: $(-3, 1), (-2, 0), (-1, -1), (0, -2), (1, -3), (2, -4),$ $(3, -5)$

3b. Write $h(x)$ in terms of $f(x)$: $h(x) = \underline{-f(x)}$

CC.9-12.F.BF.3

4 EXPLORE   Compressing or Stretching Functions Vertically

A The graph of $f(x) = x$ is shown. For each of the values $x = 0, 2, 4,$ 6, and 8, plot the point that is halfway between the x-axis and the point (x, x). That is, compress the graph of f vertically. Then draw a line through the points and label the graph h.

B Explain how the y-coordinate of each point $(x, h(x))$ is related to the y-coordinate of the point $(x, f(x))$. Then write a rule for h in terms of $f(x)$.

$h(x)$ is one-half $f(x)$; $h(x) = \frac{1}{2} f(x).$

REFLECT

4a. Compare the segments of the graphs of f and h for which the endpoints have x-coordinates 2 and 8. How do the two segments show that h is a vertical compression of f?

The segment of the graph of h is shorter than the segment of the graph of f.

4b. The graph of h appears to be a counterclockwise rotation of the graph of f. Tell how you know that this is not true.

If it were a rotation, the segments in part a would be the same length.

4c. Explain why the vertical compression $h(x) = \frac{1}{2} f(x) = \frac{1}{2} x$ is also a horizontal stretch.

The rule for h can also be thought of as $h = \left(\frac{1}{2} x\right)$, which is a horizontal stretch.

4d. Give a value of k for which $h(x) = k f(x)$ is a vertical stretch of f. Explain your reasoning.

Any number greater than 1. Sample answer: Each point on h is k times as far from the x-axis as the corresponding point on f is.

PRACTICE

Linear function f is transformed to produce g. Write $g(x)$ in terms of $f(x)$.

1. $f(x) = 3x$ is translated 6 units up.
$g(x) = 3x + 6$

2. $f(x) = x - 6$ is translated 3 units down.
$g(x) = x - 9$

3. $f(x) = -x$ is translated 2 units up.
$g(x) = -x + 2$

4. $f(x) = -4x + 5$ is translated 6 units down.
$g(x) = -4x - 1$

5. $f(x) = 4x + 3$ is translated 2 units left.
$g(x) = 4x + 11$

6. $f(x) = -3x$ is translated 5 units right.
$g(x) = -3x + 15$

7. $f(x) = 13x$ is translated 3 units to the left.
$g(x) = 13x + 39$

8. $f(x) = 2x + 9$ is translated 7 units right.
$g(x) = 2x - 5$

9. $f(x) = 2x$ is reflected across the y-axis.
$g(x) = -2x$

10. $f(x) = x - 7$ is reflected across the x-axis.
$g(x) = -x + 7$

11. $f(x) = -x + 5$ is reflected across the y-axis.
$g(x) = x + 5$

12. $f(x) = -2x + 11$ is reflected across the x-axis.
$g(x) = 2x - 11$

Choose from the following phrases the appropriate description(s) of g as a transformation of f: *vertical compression, vertical stretch, horizontal compression, horizontal stretch*.

13. $g(x) = \frac{3}{4} f(x)$ vertical compression, horizontal stretch

14. $g(x) = 3f(x)$ vertical stretch, horizontal compression

Linear function f is transformed twice to produce g. Write $g(x)$ in terms of $f(x)$. You can use a graphing calculator to check your answers.

15. f is translated 5 units down, then 4 units right. $g(x) = f(x - 4) - 5$

16. f is translated 5 units right, then 4 units down. $g(x) = f(x - 5) - 4$

17. f is reflected across the x-axis, then across the y-axis. $g(x) = -f(-x)$

18. f is translated 6 units up, then reflected across the x-axis. $g(x) = -f(x) - 6$

19. f is translated 4 units right, then reflected across the y-axis. $g(x) = f(-x + 4)$

Assign these pages to help your students practice
and apply important lesson concepts. For
additional exercises, see the Student Edition.

Answers

Additional Practice

1. $g(x) = 2x + 3$

2. $g(x) = -\frac{1}{10}x + \frac{1}{5}$

3. $g(x) = -x - 3$ **4.** $g(x) = 4.6x + 7$

5. $g(x) = 1.19x - 2.1$ **6.** $g(x) = \frac{5}{2}x - 2$

7. $g(x) = 3.2x - 9.6$

8. a. $g(x) = 1.5[1 + 0.75\,(5x - 1)] = 5.625x + 0.375$

   b. Vertical stretch by a factor of 1.5

Problem Solving

1. $C(p) = 0.55p + 2.25$

2. $J(p) = 0.55p + 3.5$

3. Possible answer: The slopes are the same so the lines are parallel.

4. y-intercept of $C(p)$ is 2.25; y-intercept of $J(p)$ is 3.5; the cost of the cover.

5. The line is shifted up.

6. $1000

7. B   **8.** D

Name_____ Class_____ Date_____

Additional Practice

Let g(x) be the indicated transformation of f(x). Write the rule for g(x).

1.

horizontal translation
left 3 units

_____

2.

vertical compression by
a factor of $\frac{1}{5}$

_____

3.

reflection across the
y-axis

_____

4. linear function defined by the table; horizontal stretch by
a factor of 2.3

x	−5	0	7
y	−3	7	21

5. $f(x) = 1.7x - 3$; vertical compression by a factor of 0.7

_____

Let g(x) be the indicated combined transformation of f(x) = x. Write the rule for g(x).

6. vertical translation down 2 units followed by a
horizontal compression by a factor of $\frac{2}{5}$ _____

7. horizontal stretch by a factor of 3.2 followed by
a horizontal translation right 3 units   _____

Solve.

8. The Red Cab Taxi Service used to charge $1.00 for the first $\frac{1}{5}$ mile and $0.75 for each

additional $\frac{1}{5}$ mile. The company just raised its rates by a factor of 1.5.

a. Write a new price function g(x) for a taxi ride.

_____

b. Describe the transformation(s) that have been applied.

_____

© Houghton Mifflin Harcourt Publishing Company

Problem Solving

**The students in Ms. Hari's English class are planning to print a
booklet of their creative writings. Use the table of publishing prices.**

1. The students decide to print a booklet containing
black and white text only. Write a function, C(p), to
show the cost of printing a booklet of p pages with
a cover that also has text only.

Publishing Prices		
	Text Only	Color Graphic
Per page	$0.55	$1.25
Cover	$2.25	$3.50

2. Julie wants the booklet cover to have a color
graphic. Write a new function, J(p), to show this
cost for a booklet of p pages.

_____

3. What is the slope of each function? What does the slope tell you
about the relationship of the lines?

_____

4. What is the y-intercept of each function? What is represented by
the y-intercept?

_____

5. Describe the transformation that has been applied to the graph by
the decision to change the cover.

_____

6. Oscar suggests that the booklet have 30 pages, one for each person in
the class. What is the cost of printing 50 booklets, using the function J(p)?

_____

Choose the letter for the best answer.

7. Lee writes a function for the cost of p
pages, all in color, with a plain text
cover. What transformation does this
apply to the graph of C(p)?

A Horizontal stretch

B Horizontal compression

C Vertical stretch

D Vertical compression

8. Tina finds a printer who will print text
pages at $0.25 a page, with a color
cover for $2.00. Using this printer, what
is the cost of 50 booklets of 30 pages
each?

A $950

B $725

C $600

D $475

© Houghton Mifflin Harcourt Publishing Company

Curve Fitting with Linear Models
Going Deeper

Essential question: *How do you find a linear model for a set of paired numerical data, and how do you evaluate the goodness of fit?*

COMMON CORE **Standards for Mathematical Content**

CC.9-12.F.BF.1 Write a function that describes a relationship between two quantities.*

CC.9-12.F.BF.1a Determine an explicit expression ... from a context.*

CC.9-12.F.LE.5 Interpret the parameters in a linear ... function in terms of a context.*

CC.9-12.S.ID.6 Represent data on two quantitative variables on a scatter plot, and describe how the variables are related.*

CC.9-12.S.ID.6a Fit a function to the data; use functions fitted to data to solve problems in the context of the data.*

CC.9-12.S.ID.6b Informally assess the fit of a function by plotting and analyzing residuals.*

CC.9-12.S.ID.6c Fit a linear function for a scatter plot that suggests a linear association.*

CC.9-12.S.ID.7 Interpret the slope (rate of change) and the intercept (constant term) of a linear model in the context of the data.*

Vocabulary
residual
residual plot
interpolation
extrapolation

Prerequisites
Graphing linear functions
Writing linear functions

Math Background

In this lesson, students will make a scatter plot for a set of paired numerical data, draw a line of fit on the scatter plot, and then find the equation of the line of fit. To find a line of fit in the form $y = mx + b$, use two given data points close to the line and then find the line's slope, $m = \dfrac{y_2 - y_1}{y_2 - x_1}$. Then use m and one of the points to find the y-intercept, b, where

$$b = y_1 - \frac{y_2 - y_1}{y_2 - x_1}(x_1).$$

Residuals can be used to assess how well a model fits a data set. Residuals that are small and random indicate a good fit. If there are many large residuals or if there is a pattern to the residuals, then a new model may be needed. For a data point (x, y_d) and the corresponding point (x, y_m) on the model, the residual is $y_d - y_m$.

INTRODUCE

Remind students that in a linear relationship, as the input values increase by one unit, the differences in the consecutive output values are constant, as shown in the table below.

College Tuition	
Year	Amount ($)
0	10,000
1	11,000
2	12,000
3	13,000

Remind students how to find the slope of a line containing the points $(-4, 1)$ and $(3, 6)$. $\dfrac{5}{7}$

Name_____ Class_____ Date_____

1-4

Curve Fitting with Linear Models
Going Deeper

Essential question: *How do you find a linear model for a set of paired numerical data, and how do you evaluate the goodness of fit?*

When paired numerical data have a strong positive or negative correlation, you can find a linear model for the data. The process is called *fitting a line to the data* or *finding a line of fit for the data*.

Video Tutor

CC.9-12.S.ID.6c

1 EXAMPLE Finding a Line of Fit for Data

The table lists the median age of females living in the United States based on the results of the U.S. Census over the past few decades. Determine whether a linear model is reasonable for the data. If so, find a linear model for the data.

Year	Median Age of Females
1970	29.2
1980	31.3
1990	34.0
2000	36.5
2010	38.2

A Identify the independent and dependent variables, and specify how you will represent them.

The independent variable is time, so use the variable t. Rather than let t take on the values 1970, 1980, and so on, define t as the number of years since 1970.

The dependent variable is the median age of females. Although you could simply use the variable a, you can use F as a subscript to remind yourself that only median *female* ages are being considered. So, the dependent variable is a_F.

B Make a table of paired values of t and a_F. Then draw a scatter plot.

t	a_F
0	29.2
10	31.3
20	34.0
30	36.5
40	38.2

Time (years since 1970)

C Draw a line of fit on the scatter plot.

Using a ruler, draw a line that passes as close as possible to the plotted points. Your line does not necessarily have to pass through any of the points, but you should try to balance points above and below the line.

D Find the equation of the line of fit.

Suppose that a student drew a line of fit that happens to pass through the data points (20, 34.0) and (30, 36.5). Complete the steps below to find the equation of the student's line. (Note that x and y are used as the independent and dependent variables for the purposes of finding the line's slope and y-intercept.)

1. Find the slope.

$m = \dfrac{y_2 - y_1}{x_2 - x_1}$

$m = \dfrac{36.5 - 34.0}{30 - 20}$

$m = \underline{0.25}$

2. Find the y-intercept using (20, 34.0).

$y = mx + b$

$34.0 = 0.25 (20) + b$

$34.0 = 5 + b$

$29.0 = b$

So, in terms of the variables t and a_F, the equation of the line of fit is

$a_F = 0.25t + 29$

Perform similar calculations to find the equation of your line of fit.

Equation of your line of fit: _Answers will vary._

REFLECT

1a. What type of correlation does the scatter plot show?

A strong positive correlation

1b. Before you placed a ruler on the scatter plot to draw a line of fit, you may have thought that the plotted points were perfectly linear. How does the table tell you that they are not?

If the points were perfectly linear, the difference in consecutive values of the

dependent variable would be constant because the values of the independent

variable are equally spaced. But the median age increased by 2.1 from 1970 to

1980 and by 2.7 from 1980 to 1990.

1c. For your line of fit, interpret the slope and a_F-intercept in the context of the data.

The slope is the rate of change in median female age per year; the a_F-intercept

is the median female age in the initial year (1970).

© Houghton Mifflin Harcourt Publishing Company

1 EXAMPLE

Questioning Strategies

- Why is a linear model reasonable for the data? The points of the scatter plot roughly follow a line.

- When can there be more than one reasonable equation of the line of fit for a data set? when the data points are not perfectly linear

- Why does the scatter plot show points with a strong positive correlation? The correlation is strong because the points are very tight along the line of fit; the correlation is positive because the dependent values are increasing as the independent values are increasing.

Avoid Common Errors

Students may have difficulty drawing a line of fit on a scatter plot if they are trying to include actual data points on the line. While it is desirable to include points on the line, they should try to balance the number of points above the line with the number of points below the line. Tell students it is more important to locate the line so that the points are evenly distributed above and below the line.

EXTRA EXAMPLE

The table lists the estimated number of wireless industry (primarily cellular telephone) subscribers in the United States over a five-year period, measured in June of each year. Determine whether a linear model is reasonable for the data. If so, find a linear model for the data.

Year (as of June)	Number of Subscribers (millions)
2005	194.5
2006	219.7
2007	243.4
2008	262.7
2009	276.6

A scatter plot shows that a linear model is reasonable for the data. Sample answer for line of fit: $s = 20.7t + 197.9$ where t is the number of years since 2005 (answers will vary but the value of the coefficients should be similar to this answer).

2 EXAMPLE

Questioning Strategies

- Why do two points in part A have residuals of 0? They are data points used to find the model.

- How would you describe the suitability of the model if a pattern in the residuals showed that they are decreasing as the values of x are increasing? The model may not be suitable.

Differentiated Instruction

Help visual learners understand how to interpret the scatter plot of the residuals for the model and how their scatter plot compares with a scatter plot of residuals that shows a random tight distribution of points about the x-axis.

EXTRA EXAMPLE

A student fit the line $s = 19.3t + 204.8$ to the data in the previous example. Make a residual plot and evaluate the goodness of fit.

Residuals are -10.3, -4.4, 0, 0, and -5.4. There are two residuals with a value of zero, but there are no positive residuals, so there is not a balance between the positive and negative residuals. So, the distribution is not random. The absolute values of the residuals are small compared with the values, and the only pattern is the lack of positive residuals. The line fits the data somewhat but is a relatively poor model. A model with a mix of positive and negative residuals would be better.

continued

Residuals You can evaluate a linear model's goodness of fit using *residuals*. A **residual** is the difference between an actual value of the dependent variable and the value predicted by the linear model. After calculating residuals, you can draw a **residual plot**, which is a scatter plot of points whose x-coordinates are the values of the independent variable and whose y-coordinates are the corresponding residuals.

Whether the fit of a line to data is suitable and good depends on the distribution of the residuals, as illustrated below.

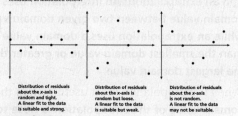

Distribution of residuals about the x-axis is random and tight. A linear fit to the data is suitable and strong.

Distribution of residuals about the x-axis is random but loose. A linear fit to the data is suitable but weak.

Distribution of residuals about the x-axis is not random. A linear fit to the data may not be suitable.

CC.9-12.S.ID.6b

2 EXAMPLE Creating a Residual Plot and Evaluating Fit

A student fit the line $a_F = 0.25t + 29$ to the data in the previous example. Make a residual plot and evaluate the goodness of fit.

A Calculate the residuals. Substitute each value of t into the equation to find the value predicted for a_F by the linear model. Then subtract predicted from actual to find the residual.

t	a_F actual	a_F predicted	Residual
0	29.2	29.0	0.2
10	31.3	31.5	−0.2
20	34.0	34.0	0
30	36.5	36.5	0
40	38.2	39.0	−0.8

B Plot the residuals.

C Evaluate the suitability of a linear fit and the goodness of the fit.

- Is there a balance between positive and negative residuals?
  There is one positive and two negatives, but the negatives have a greater
  absolute value than the positive if you add them.

- Is there a pattern to the residuals? If so, describe it.
  The residuals have no apparent pattern.

- Is the absolute value of each residual small relative to a_F (actual)? For instance, when $t = 0$, the residual is 0.2 and the value of a_F is 29.2, so the relative size of the residual is $\frac{0.2}{29.2} \approx 0.7\%$, which is quite small.
  The absolute values of the residuals are all small.

- What is your overall evaluation of the suitability and goodness of the linear fit?
  The line is an appropriate model for the data and fits the data fairly well.

REFLECT

2a. Use the table and graph below to find the residuals for your line of fit from the first Example and then make a residual plot. Answers will vary.

t	a_F actual	a_F predicted	Residual
0	29.2		
10	31.3		
20	34.0		
30	36.5		
40	38.2		

2b. Evaluate the suitability and goodness of the fit for your line of fit.
  Answers will vary.

2c. Suppose the line of fit with equation $a_F = 0.25t + 29$ is changed to $a_F = 0.25t + 28.8$. What effect does this change have on the residuals? On the residual plot? Is the new line a better fit to the data? Explain.
  Residuals increase by 0.2; points in plot are translated 0.2 unit up; now there are
  3 positive residuals and 1 negative one, but the sum of the residuals is now closer
  to 0, so the fit may be slightly better.

Notes

Avoid Common Errors

Some students may expect that since the lesson is about linear models, a graph of the residuals should form a straight line. Make sure students understand that the residuals indicate a good fit only if they cluster randomly around the *x*-axis, preferably with a tight distribution that resembles a horizontal line. However, if the residuals have a tight linear distribution that veers away from the *x*-axis, this indicates a poor fit.

Differentiated Instruction

Advanced students may be interested in knowing that they can find more than one equation of the line of fit, and that they can compare their models with other students to determine which one may be the best fitting model.

MATHEMATICAL PRACTICE   **Highlighting the Standards**

2 EXAMPLE   addresses Standard 2 (Reason abstractly and quantitatively). Draw students' attention to the use of multiple representations for the residuals, both as a table and as a scatter plot. Specifically, ask students why a scatter plot of residuals is helpful in determining whether a model for data is suitable and good.

---

3 EXAMPLE

Questioning Strategies

• What is the difference between an interpolation and an extrapolation? **An interpolation uses a domain value between two given domain values, while an extrapolation uses a domain value less than the smallest domain value or greater than the largest domain value.**

• When is extrapolation most useful? **when the domain value of the extrapolation is close to the given domain values**

• If the independent variable is time, is a prediction about a future value interpolation or extrapolation? **extrapolation**

• If the independent variable is time, is a prediction about a past value interpolation or extrapolation? **It could be either, depending on whether the date in question is before or after the earliest date in the given data set.**

Technology

Students may benefit from using a spreadsheet to find the interpolated values of the model for the years 1970 to 2010. Ask them to enter 1970 as year 0 in cell A1; then, have students enter $= A1 + 1$ in cell A2 and the model for 1970 as $0.25*A1 + 29$ in cell B1. Then, they should use the FILL DOWN feature of the spreadsheet to find the values for all years between 1970 and 2010.

EXTRA EXAMPLE

Using the model $s = 20.7t + 197.9$, predict the total number of wireless subscribers in December 2006 (midway between the 2006 and 2007 data in Extra Example 1) and in June 2015. Identify each prediction as an interpolation or an extrapolation. **Dec. 2006: 229 million, interpolation; June 2015: 405 million, extrapolation**

Making Predictions A linear model establishes the dependent variable as a linear function of the independent variable, and you can use the function to make predictions. The accuracy of a prediction depends not only on the model's goodness of fit but also on the value of the independent variable for which you're making the prediction.

A model's domain is determined by the least and greatest values of the independent variable found in the data set. For instance, the least and greatest t-values for the median age data are 0 (for 1970) and 40 (for 2010), so the domain of any model for the data is $\{t \mid 0 \le t \le 40\}$. Making a prediction using a value of the independent variable from *within* the model's domain is called **interpolation**. Making a prediction using a value from *outside* the domain is called **extrapolation**. As you might expect, you can have greater confidence in an interpolation than in an extrapolation.

CC.9–12.S.ID.6a

3 E X A M P L E   Making Predictions Using a Linear Model

Using the model $a_F = 0.25t + 29$, predict the median age of females in 1995 and in 2015. Identify each prediction as an interpolation or as an extrapolation.

A To make a prediction about 1995, let $t =$ __25__. Then to the nearest

tenth, the predicted value of a_F is $a_F = 0.25\left(\underline{25} \right) + 29 \approx$ __35.3__.

Because the t-value falls __within__ the model's domain,

the prediction is an __interpolation__.

B To make a prediction about 2015, let $t =$ __45__. Then to the nearest

tenth, the predicted value of a_F is $a_F = 0.25\left(\underline{45} \right) + 29 \approx$ __40.3__.

Because the t-value falls __outside__ the model's domain, the

prediction is an __extrapolation__.

REFLECT

3a. Use your linear model to predict the median age of females in 1995 and 2015.

__Answers will vary.__

3b. The Census Bureau gives 35.5 as the median age of females for 1995 and an estimate of 38.4 for 2015. Which of your predictions using your linear model was more accurate? Explain.

__Answers will vary but should be based on comparing differences between__

__actual and predicted values.__

PRACTICE

Answers to parts c–e are based on the sample answer in part b.

1. The table lists the median age of males living in the United States based on the results of the U.S. Census over the past few decades.

Year	1970	1980	1990	2000	2010
Median Age of Males	26.8	28.8	31.6	34.0	35.5

a. Let t represent time (in years since 1970), and let a_M represent the median age of males. Make a table of paired values of t and a_M. Then draw a scatter plot.

t	a_M
0	26.8
10	28.8
20	31.6
30	34.0
40	35.5

b. Draw a line of fit on the scatter plot and find an equation of the line.

Sample answer: $a_M = 0.24t + 26.6$

c. Calculate the residuals, and make a residual plot.

t	a_M actual	a_M predicted	Residual
0	26.8	26.6	0.2
10	28.8	29.0	−0.2
20	31.6	31.4	0.2
30	34.0	33.8	0.2
40	35.5	36.2	−0.7

d. Evaluate the suitability of a linear fit and the goodness of the fit.

__The line is an appropriate model for the data and fits the data fairly well.__

Essential Question

How do you find a linear model for a set of paired numerical data, and how do you evaluate the goodness of fit?

Identify the independent and dependent variables, make a scatter plot of the data, draw a line of fit on the scatter plot, and find the equation of the line of fit. To determine the goodness of fit, find the residuals and see whether the distribution of residuals about the *x*-axis is random and tight.

Summarize

Have students complete the graphic organizer below.

Distribution of residuals about the *x*-axis is...	Goodness of fit is ...
random and tight.	suitable and strong.
random and loose.	suitable and weak.
not random.	not suitable.

Where skills are taught	Where skills are practiced
1 EXAMPLE	EXS. 1a, 1b, 4a, 4b, 4c
2 EXAMPLE	EXS. 1c, 1d, 4d, 4e
3 EXAMPLE	EX. 1e

Exercise 2: Students compare data from two different models. Students should focus on the characteristics of the models, in particular slope and intercepts.

Exercise 3: Students will have to consider reasons why a model that works over a known data range may not hold up in the future. This should help reinforce the statement in the lesson that extrapolations tend to be less reliable than interpolations.

e. Predict the median age of males in 1995 and 2015. Identify each prediction as an interpolation or an extrapolation, and then compare the predictions with these median ages of males from the Census Bureau: 33.2 in 1995 and an estimated 35.9 in 2015.

1995 age is 32.6 and is an interpolation; 2015 age is 37.4 and is an extrapolation.

The 1995 interpolation is a better approximation to the Census Bureau data

than the 2015 extrapolation.

2. Compare the equations of your lines of fit for the median age of females and the median age of males. When referring to any constants in those equations, be sure to interpret them in the context of the data.

Answers will vary, but students should find that the slopes (rates of change in

median age) are roughly equal while the a-intercepts (median ages in 1970)

differ by about 2.

3. Explain why it isn't reasonable to use linear models to predict the median age of females or males far into the future.

The predictions made from a linear model will grow at a constant rate from year

to year but median ages will not. The growth in median ages is likely to slow

down and might even reverse (start decreasing).

4. The table lists, for various lengths (in centimeters), the median weight (in kilograms) of male infants and female infants (ages 0−36 months) in the United States.

Length (cm)	50	60	70	80	90	100
Median Weight (kg) of Male Infants	3.4	5.9	8.4	10.8	13.0	15.5
Median Weight (kg) of Female Infants	3.4	5.8	8.3	10.6	12.8	15.2

a. Let l represent an infant's length in excess of 50 centimeters. (For instance, for an infant whose length is 60 cm, $l = 10$.) Let w_M represent the median weight of male infants, and let w_F represent the median weight of female infants. Make a table of paired values of l and either w_M or w_F (whichever you prefer).

l	0	10	20	30	40	50
w						

Answers will vary.

b. Draw a scatter plot of the paired data. Answers will vary.

c. Draw a line of fit on the scatter plot and find the equation of the line. According to your model, at what rate does weight change with respect to length?

Answers will vary. Sample answers: $w_M = 0.244l + 3.4$; $w_F = 0.238l + 3.4$.

Weight increases 0.244 kg (boys) or 0.238 kg (girls) per 1 cm increase in length.

d. Calculate the residuals, and make a residual plot. Answers will vary.

l	w actual	w predicted	Residual
0			
10			
20			
30			
40			
50			

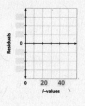

e. Evaluate the suitability of a linear fit and the goodness of the fit.

Answers will vary.

© Houghton Mifflin Harcourt Publishing Company

Assign these pages to help your students practice and apply important lesson concepts. For additional exercises, see the Student Edition.

Answers

Additional Practice

1.

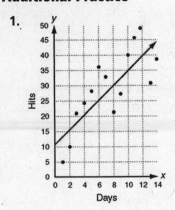

$y = 2.5x + 11$

2. b. $r = 0.848$

c. $y = 0.33x - 11.33$

d. Possible answer: about 50 photos

3. Possible answer: If the slope is negative, the correlation coefficient is negative. If the slope is positive, the correlation coefficient is positive.

Problem Solving

1. Negative correlation

2.

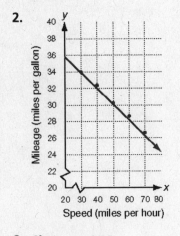

3. Slope ≈ -0.15

4. Possible answer: $y \approx -0.15x + 38$

5. $r \approx -0.98$

6. Possible answer: There is a strong negative correlation.

7. $y \approx -0.175x + 39.85$

8. A   **9.** C

Name_____ Class_____ Date_____ **1-4**

Additional Practice

Solve.

1. Vern created a website about his school's sports teams. He has a hit counter on his site that lets him know how many people have visited the site. The table shows the number of hits the site received each day for the first two weeks. Make a scatter plot for the data using the day as the independent variable. Sketch a line of best fit and find its equation.

Lincoln High Website														
Day	1	2	3	4	5	6	7	8	9	10	11	12	13	14
Hits	5	10	21	24	28	36	33	21	27	40	46	50	31	38

2. A photographer hiked through the Grand Canyon. Each day she filled a photo memory card with images. When she returned from the trip, she deleted some photos, saving only the best. The table shows the number of photos she kept from all those taken for each memory card.

   a. Use a graphing calculator to make a scatter plot of the data. Use the number of photos taken as the independent variable.

   b. Find the correlation coefficient.

   _____

   c. Write the equation of the line of best fit.

   _____

   d. Predict the number of photos this photographer will keep if she takes 200 photos.

   _____

Grand Canyon Photos	
Photos Taken	Photos Kept
117	25
128	31
140	39
157	52
110	21
188	45
170	42

3. What is the relationship between the slope of a line and its correlation coefficient?

_____

_____

© Houghton Mifflin Harcourt Publishing Company

Problem Solving

As a science project, Shelley is studying the relationship of car mileage (miles per gallon) and speed (miles per hour). The table shows the data Shelley gathered using her family's hybrid vehicle.

Speed (miles per hour)	30	40	50	60	70
Mileage (miles per gallon)	34.0	33.5	31.5	29.0	27.5

1. Make a scatter plot of the data. Identify the correlation.

   _____

2. Sketch a line of best fit on the graph.

3. Use two points on the line to find the slope.

   _____

4. Use the point-slope form to write an equation that models the data.

   _____

5. Use a graphing calculator to plot the data. Find the value of the correlation coefficient r.

6. What does the value of r tell you about the data?

   _____

7. What equation do you find with the calculator for the line of best fit?

   _____

Use the equation you wrote in Exercise 4. Choose the letter for the best answer.

8. Predict the mileage for a speed of 55 miles per hour.

   A 30
   B 34
   C 39
   D 46

9. Predict the speed if the mileage is 28 miles per gallon.

   A 32
   B 35
   C 67
   D 75

© Houghton Mifflin Harcourt Publishing Company

This page provides students with the opportunity to apply concepts from the Common Core in real-world problem situations. There are three different levels of performance tasks:

⭐ **Novice:** These are short word problems that require students to apply the math they have learned in straightforward, real-world situations.

⭐⭐ **Apprentice:** These are more involved problems that guide students step-by-step through more complex tasks. These exercises include more complicated reasoning, writing, and open-ended elements.

⭐⭐⭐ **Expert:** These are open-ended, non-routine problems that, instead of stepping the students through, ask them to choose their own methods for solving and justify their answers and reasoning.

Sample answers

1a. $y(x) = 20 + 8x$; slope 8 and y-intercept 20.

 b. $y(x) = 8x$; the graph is shifted down 20 units.

2a. $0.25; the slope of $A(n)$ is 0.75, and the slope of $B(n)$ is 0.5.

 b. $k = \frac{3}{2}$ or 1.5.

3. Scoring Guide:

Task	Possible points
a	1 point for the correct answer that 300 is the number of calories burned per hour of exercise Monday through Friday
b	1 point for the correct answer that the graph will be shifted down 375 units
c	2 points for the correct equation, $c(h) = 750 + 400h$, and 2 points for correctly explaining that the graph will become steeper but the y-intercept will stay at 750

Total possible points: 6

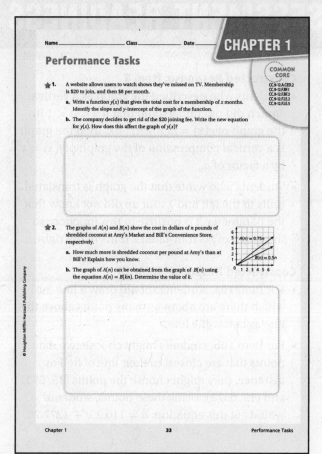

Name _____ Class _____ Date _____

Performance Tasks

CHAPTER 1

COMMON
CORE
CC 9-12.A.CED.2
CC 9-12.F.BF.1
CC 9-12.F.BF.3
CC 9-12.F.LE.2
CC 9-12.F.LE.5

★ 1. A website allows users to watch shows they've missed on TV. Membership is $20 to join, and then $8 per month.

    a. Write a function $y(x)$ that gives the total cost for a membership of x months. Identify the slope and y-intercept of the graph of the function.

    b. The company decides to get rid of the $20 joining fee. Write the new equation for $y(x)$. How does this affect the graph of $y(x)$?

★ 2. The graphs of $A(n)$ and $B(n)$ show the cost in dollars of n pounds of shredded coconut at Amy's Market and Bill's Convenience Store, respectively.

    a. How much more is shredded coconut per pound at Amy's than at Bill's? Explain how you know.

    b. The graph of $A(n)$ can be obtained from the graph of $B(n)$ using the equation $A(n) = B(kn)$. Determine the value of k.

© Houghton Mifflin Harcourt Publishing Company

Chapter 1   33   Performance Tasks

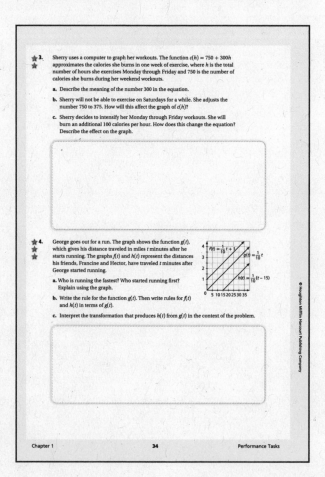

★ 3. Sherry uses a computer to graph her workouts. The function $c(h) = 750 + 300h$ approximates the calories she burns in one week of exercise, where h is the total number of hours she exercises Monday through Friday and 750 is the number of calories she burns during her weekend workouts.

    a. Describe the meaning of the number 300 in the equation.

    b. Sherry will not be able to exercise on Saturdays for a while. She adjusts the number 750 to 375. How will this affect the graph of $c(h)$?

    c. Sherry decides to intensify her Monday through Friday workouts. She will burn an additional 100 calories per hour. How does this change the equation? Describe the effect on the graph.

★ 4. George goes out for a run. The graph shows the function $g(t)$, which gives his distance traveled in miles t minutes after he starts running. The graphs $f(t)$ and $h(t)$ represent the distances his friends, Francine and Hector, have traveled t minutes after George started running.

    a. Who is running the fastest? Who started running first? Explain using the graph.

    b. Write the rule for the function $g(t)$. Then write rules for $f(t)$ and $h(t)$ in terms of $g(t)$.

    c. Interpret the transformation that produces $h(t)$ from $g(t)$ in the context of the problem.

© Houghton Mifflin Harcourt Publishing Company

Chapter 1   34   Performance Tasks

---

4. Scoring Guide:

Task	Possible points
a	1 point for the correct answer that they are all running at the same speed, because the lines are all parallel or have the same slope, and 1 point for the correct answer that Francine started running first, because her distance was 1 mile at the time George started running
b	1 point for $g(t) = \frac{1}{10}t$, 1 point for $f(t) = g(t) + 1$ or equivalent, and 1 point for $h(t) = g(t - 15)$ or equivalent
c	1 point for the correct answer that the 15-unit horizontal translation to the right means that Hector started running 15 minutes after George did

Total possible points: 6

CHAPTER 1 COMMON CORE ASSESSMENT READINESS

...

COMMON CORE CORRELATION

Standard	Items
CC.9-12.F.IF.4*	4
CC.9-12.F.IF.7a*	9
CC.9-12.F.IF.7b*	10
CC.9-12.F.BF.3	1, 2, 3, 4, 5, 8, 9, 10
CC.9-12.F.LE.5*	11
CC.9-12.S.ID.6a*	7, 11
CC.9-12.S.ID.6b*	5, 11
CC.9-12.S.ID.6c*	11
CC.9-12.S.ID.7*	11
CC.9-12.S.ID.8*	11

TEST PREP DOCTOR ⊕

Multiple Choice: Item 1
- Students who chose **A** translated the point 2 units right and 3 units down.
- Students who chose **C** translated the point 3 units left and 2 units down.
- Students who chose **D** translated the point 3 units right and 2 units up.

Multiple Choice: Item 6
- Students who chose **F** or **G** did not recognize that the parameter a in $g(x) = ax^2$ results in a vertical stretch or compression (and possibly a reflection across the x-axis) of the graph of $f(x) = x^2$, but not a vertical translation of the graph of f.
- Students who chose **J** recognized that the parameter a in $g(x) = ax^2$ results in a vertical stretch and shrink of the graph of $f(x) = x^2$, but thought that the stretch/compression factor is the reciprocal of a rather than a itself.

Constructed Response: Item 8
- Students who described the graph as a vertical stretch did not understand that if $0 < a < 1$ in the graph of $g(x) = a(x - h)^3 + k$, then the graph is a vertical compression of the graph of $f(x) = x^3$ by a factor of a.
- Students who wrote that the graph is translated 2 units to the left and 1 unit up did not know that the parameter h is positive in this function, so the graph of f is translated 2 units to the right.

Constructed Response: Item 10
- For Item **10a**, students should draw a line for which there are about as many points above the line as below the line.
- For Item **10b**, students might choose two data points that are closest to their line of fit. For instance, they might choose the points (15, 5931) and (19, 6372). Using these points, students would get this equation: $a = 110.25t + 4277.25$.

Name _____ Class _____ Date _____

MULTIPLE CHOICE

1. The point $(-2, 7)$ is translated 3 units right and 2 units down. What are the coordinates of the translated point?

A. $(0, 4)$

B. $(1, 5)$

C. $(-5, 5)$

D. $(1, 9)$

2. The graph of which function is stretched vertically and reflected in the x-axis as compared to the parent function $f(x) = x^3$?

F. $g(x) = 3x^3$ H. $g(x) = \frac{1}{3}x^3$

G. $g(x) = -3x^3$ J. $g(x) = -\frac{1}{3}x^3$

3. The graph of $g(x) = (x + 4)^2 - 1$ can be obtained from the graph of $f(x) = x^2$ using which transformations?

A. Translate 4 units up and 1 unit left.

B. Translate 4 units up and 1 unit right.

C. Translate 4 units left and 1 unit down.

D. Translate 4 units right and 1 unit down.

4. How would the graphs of $f(x) = 4x - 1$ and $g(x) = 4x - 2$ compare if graphed on the same coordinate plane?

F. The graph of f would be 1 unit above the graph of g.

G. The graph of f would be twice as steep as the graph of g.

H. The graph of g would be twice as steep as the graph of f.

J. The graphs would intersect at $(0, 4)$.

5. A student fit a line to data, then made the residual plot shown. Based on analyzing the residual plot, what can you conclude about the data?

A. A linear fit to the data may not be suitable.

B. A linear fit to the data is suitable, and the fit is strong.

C. A linear fit to the data is suitable, but the fit is weak.

D. No conclusion can be drawn.

6. Which of the following describes a way to use the parent quadratic function $f(x) = x^2$ to graph the function $g(x) = 2x^2$?

F. Translate the graph of f 2 units right.

G. Translate the graph of f 2 units down.

H. Stretch the graph of f vertically by a factor of 2.

J. Compress the graph of f vertically by a factor of $\frac{1}{2}$.

7. A student used the model $n = 0.49t + 15.2$, where t is the number of seasons since 2005, and n is the number of wins, to describe the high school basketball team's winning record over an 8-year period. Use the model to predict the number of wins in the 2015 season to the nearest whole number.

A. 18 wins   **C.** 20 wins

B. 23 wins   D. 26 wins

© Houghton Mifflin Harcourt Publishing Company

CONSTRUCTED RESPONSE

8. a. Graph the function $g(x) = \frac{1}{4}(x - 2)^3 + 1$.

b. Describe how to transform the graph of $f(x) = x^3$ to obtain the graph of $g(x) = \frac{1}{4}(x - 2)^3 + 1$.

Compress the graph of $f(x) = x^3$

vertically by a factor of $\frac{1}{4}$.

Then translate 2 units right and

1 unit up.

9. a. Graph $g(x) = -2x + 1$.

b. Describe transformations that you could perform on the graph of $f(x) = x$ to obtain the graph of g.

Sample answer: Vertical stretch

by a factor of 2; reflection in the

x-axis; translation 1 unit up.

c. If the graph of g is translated 3 units to the right to obtain the graph of h, what is the equation for h?

$h(x) = -2(x - 3) + 1$

10. The amount that households in the United States spent on food was studied over a number of years. The table shows the amount a in millions of dollars in given years, where $t = 0$ represents the year the study began.

t	a	t	a
0	4296	16	6111
5	4505	17	6133
10	5158	18	6443
15	5931	19	6372

a. Draw a line of fit on the scatter plot.

b. Find an equation of your line of fit.

Answer will vary.

c. Perform linear regression to find the equation of the line of best fit and the correlation coefficient.

$a = 122.1t + 4092.6$; 0.9865

d. Create a residual plot on a graphing calculator. Evaluate the suitability and goodness of fit of the regression equation.

The points are randomly distributed about the t-axis, so a linear fit is suitable. The correlation is strong and the points are close to the t-axis, so the fit is good.

© Houghton Mifflin Harcourt Publishing Company

CHAPTER 2

Quadratic Functions

Quadratic Functions

Chapter Focus

In this chapter, you will learn how to recognize, graph, and write quadratic functions in standard form, vertex form, and intercept form. You will identify the vertex and the intercepts of the graphs of quadratic functions. You will also use quadratic functions to model and solve real-world problems.

Just as rational and irrational numbers together form the set of real numbers, imaginary numbers and real numbers together form a set called the complex numbers. You will learn to perform operations with complex numbers, and you will see how complex numbers allow you to solve quadratic equations that you weren't able to solve in Algebra 1.

Chapter at a Glance

COMMON CORE

Lesson		Standards for Mathematical Content
2-1	Using Transformations to Graph Quadratic Functions	CC.9-12.F.IF.7a, CC.9-12.F.BF.3
2-2	Properties of Quadratic Functions in Standard Form	CC.9-12.F.IF.7, CC.9-12.F.IF.7a
2-3	Solving Quadratic Equations by Graphing and Factoring	CC.9-12.F.IF.8, CC.9-12.F.IF.8a
2-4	Completing the Square	CC.9-12.F.IF.8, CC.9-12.F.IF.8a
2-5	Complex Numbers and Roots	CC.9-12.N.CN.1
2-6	The Quadratic Formula	CC.9-12.N.CN.7, CC.9-12.A.REI.4b
2-7	Solving Quadratic Inequalities	CC.9-12.A.CED.1
2-8	Curve Fitting with Quadratic Models	CC.9-12.N.Q.1, CC.9-12.A.SSE.1, CC.9-12. A.CED.2, CC.9-12.A.CED.3, CC.9-12.F.IF.4, CC.9-12.F.IF.7a
2-9	Operations with Complex Numbers	CC.9-12.N.CN.2, CC.9-12.N.CN.3(+)
	Performance Tasks	
	Assessment Readiness	

COMMON CORE PROFESSIONAL DEVELOPMENT

CC.9-12.F.IF.7a*
CC.9-12.A.REI.4b

In this chapter, students will continue to develop their understanding of quadratic functions and their graphs. They will apply this knowledge in real-world situations involving projectile motion.

Unpacking the Standards

Understanding the standards and the vocabulary terms in the standards will help you know exactly what you are expected to learn in this chapter.

COMMON CORE CC.9-12.F.IF.7a

Graph ... quadratic functions and show intercepts, maxima, and minima.

Key Vocabulary
quadratic function *(función cuadrática)* A function that can be written in the form $f(x) = ax^2 + bx + c$, where a, b, and c are real numbers and $a \neq 0$, or in the form $f(x) = a(x - h)^2 + k$, where a, h, and k are real numbers and $a \neq 0$.
x-intercept *(intersección con el eje x)* The x-coordinate(s) of the point(s) where a graph intersects the x-axis.
y-intercept *(intersección con el eje y)* The y-coordinate(s) of the point(s) where a graph intersects the y-axis.
maximum/minimum value of a function *(máximo/mínimo de una función)* The y-value of the highest/lowest point on the graph of the function.

What It Means For You   Lessons 2-1, 2-2, 2-3, 2-4, 2-5

The graph of a quadratic function has key features that are helpful when interpreting a real-world quadratic model: the intercepts and the maximum or minimum value.

EXAMPLE   Graph of $y = x^2 + 2x - 3$

The x-intercepts are −3 and 1.

The minimum value is −4.

The y-intercept is −3.

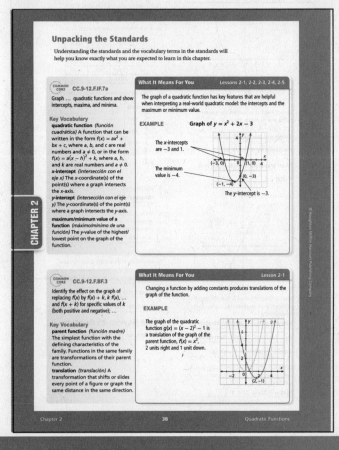

COMMON CORE CC.9-12.F.BF.3

Identify the effect on the graph of replacing $f(x)$ by $f(x) + k$, $k\,f(x)$, ... and $f(x + k)$ for specific values of k (both positive and negative); ...

Key Vocabulary
parent function *(función madre)* The simplest function with the defining characteristics of the family. Functions in the same family are transformations of their parent function.
translation *(translación)* A transformation that shifts or slides every point of a figure or graph the same distance in the same direction.

What It Means For You   Lesson 2-1

Changing a function by adding constants produces translations of the graph of the function.

EXAMPLE

The graph of the quadratic function $g(x) = (x - 2)^2 - 1$ is a translation of the graph of the parent function, $f(x) = x^2$, 2 units right and 1 unit down.

CC.9-12.N.CN.2

Use the relation $i^2 = -1$ and the commutative, associative, and distributive properties to add, subtract, and multiply complex numbers.

Key Vocabulary

complex number *(número complejo)* Any number that can be written as $a + bi$, where a and b are real numbers and $i = \sqrt{-1}$.

What It Means For You Lesson 2-9

Whole numbers, integers, real numbers, and so on, are all members of a larger set called the complex numbers. You can use the same properties of operations with all of them.

EXAMPLE

$(4 + i)(3 - 2i)$
$= 4(3 - 2i) + i(3 + 2i)$ *Distributive Property*
$= 12 - 8i + 3i - 2i^2$ *Distributive Property*
$= 12 - 8i + 3i + 2$ $i^2 = -1$
$= (12 + 2) + (-8i + 3i)$ *Associative/Commutative Properties*
$= 14 - 5i$ *Add real parts and imaginary parts.*

 CC.9-12.A.REI.4b

Solve quadratic equations by inspection (e.g., for $x^2 = 49$), taking square roots, completing the square, the quadratic formula and factoring, as appropriate to the initial form of the equation. Recognize when the quadratic formula gives complex solutions and write them as $a \pm bi$ for real numbers a and b.

Key Vocabulary

quadratic equation *(ecuación cuadrática)* An equation that can be written in the form $ax^2 + bx + c = 0$, where a, b, and c are real numbers and $a \neq 0$.

completing the square *(completar el cuadrado)* A process used to form a perfect-square trinomial. To complete the square of $x^2 + bx$, add $\left(\frac{b}{2}\right)^2$.

Quadratic Formula *(fórmula cuadrática)* The formula
$$x = \frac{-b \pm \sqrt{b^2 - 4ac}}{2a}$$
which gives solutions, or roots, of equations in the form $ax^2 + bx + c = 0$, where a, b, and c are real numbers and $a \neq 0$.

What It Means For You Lessons 2-3, 2-4, 2-5, 2-6

Knowing how to solve quadratic equations gives you tools to understand many situations, including the laws of motion. Recognizing the best solution method for a situation allows you to work efficiently.

EXAMPLE

The height h in feet of a baseball leaving a certain batter's bat is $h(t) = -16t^2 + 63t + 4$, where t is in seconds. When does the ball hit the ground?

$-16t^2 + 63t + 4 = 0$ *The ball hits the ground when $h = 0$.*
$-1(16t + 1)(t - 4) = 0$ *You can factor the equation.*
$t = -\frac{1}{16}$ or $t = 4$ *The factors give these solutions.*

The ball hits the ground in 4 seconds. (The negative value is not reasonable in the real-world context.)

Key Vocabulary

absolute value of a complex number *(valor absoluto de un número complejo)* The absolute value of $a + bi$ is the distance from the origin to the point (a, b) in the complex plane and is denoted $|a + bi| = \sqrt{a^2 + b^2}$.

axis of symmetry *(eje de simetría)* A line that divides a plane figure or a graph into two congruent reflected halves.

completing the square *(completar el cuadrado)* A process used to form a perfect-square trinomial. To complete the square of $x^2 + bx$, add $\left(\frac{b}{2}\right)^2$.

complex conjugate *(conjugado complejo)* The complex conjugate of any complex number $a + bi$, denoted $\overline{a + bi}$, is $a - bi$.

complex number *(número complejo)* Any number that can be written as $a + bi$, where a and b are real numbers and $i = \sqrt{-1}$.

complex plane *(plano complejo)* A set of coordinate axes in which the horizontal axis is the real axis and the vertical axis is the imaginary axis; used to graph complex numbers.

imaginary unit *(unidad imaginaria)* The unit in the imaginary number system, $\sqrt{-1}$.

imaginary number *(número imaginario)* The square root of a negative number, written in the form bi, where b is a real number and i is the imaginary unit, $\sqrt{-1}$. Also called a *pure imaginary number*.

maximum/minimum value of a function *(máximo/mínimo de una función)* The y-value of the highest/lowest point on the graph of the function.

parabola *(parábola)* The shape of the graph of a quadratic function.

quadratic equation *(ecuación cuadrática)* An equation that can be written in the form $ax^2 + bx + c = 0$, where a, b, and c are real numbers and $a \neq 0$.

Quadratic Formula *(fórmula cuadrática)* The formula $x = \frac{-b \pm \sqrt{b^2 - 4ac}}{2a}$ which gives solutions, or roots, of equations in the form $ax^2 + bx + c = 0$, where $a \neq 0$.

quadratic function *(función cuadrática)* A function that can be written in the form $f(x) = ax^2 + bx + c = 0$, where a, b, and c are real numbers and $a \neq 0$, or in the form $f(x) = a(x - h)^2 + k$, where a, h, and k are real numbers and $a \neq 0$.

vertex of a parabola *(vértice de una parábola)* The point on the parabola that lies on the axis of symmetry.

x-intercept *(intersección con el eje x)* The x-coordinate(s) of the point(s) where a graph intersects the x-axis.

y-intercept *(intersección con el eje y)* The y-coordinate(s) of the point(s) where a graph intersects the y-axis.

zero of a function *(cero de una función)* For the function f, any number x such that $f(x) = 0$.

Using Transformations to Graph Quadratic Functions

Extension: Graphing Quadratic Functions in Vertex Form

Essential question: *How can you graph the function* $f(x) = a(x - h)^2 + k$?

CC.9-12.A.CED.2 ... graph equations on coordinate axes with labels and scales.*

CC.9-12.F.IF.2 Use function notation, evaluate functions for inputs in their domains, and interpret statements that use function notation in terms of a context.

CC.9-12.F.IF.7 Graph functions expressed symbolically and show key features of the graph ...*

CC.9-12.F.IF.7a Graph ... quadratic functions and show intercepts, maxima, and minima.*

CC.9-12.F.BF.3 Identify the effect on the graph of replacing $f(x)$ by $f(x) + k$, $kf(x)$, ... and $f(x + k)$ for specific values of k (both positive and negative); find the value of k given the graphs.
Also: CC.9-12.F.IF.9

Vocabulary
vertex form
zero of a function

Prerequisites
Graphing functions of the form $f(x) = (x - h)^2 + k$ and of the form $f(x) = ax^2$

Math Background
Quadratic functions are used in a variety of real-world applications. In this lesson, students will use them to model the shape of a curved bridge support.

INTRODUCE

Ask students to recall what effect h and k have on the graph of the function $f(x) = (x - h)^2 + k$. **horizontal and vertical translation** Ask students to recall what effect a has on the graph of $f(x) = ax^2$. **It stretches or shrinks the graph vertically, and it reflects the graph across the x-axis if negative.**

TEACH

 ENGAGE

Questioning Strategies

- Describe the zero of a linear function of the form $f(x) = mx + b$ where $m \neq 0$ in terms of its graph. **The zero is the x-value of the point where the line crosses the x-axis.**

- A linear function $f(x) = mx + b$ where $m = 0$ is called a *constant function*. If $b \neq 0$, how many zeros does the constant function $f(x) = b$ have? How is this evident from the graph of $f(x)$? **$f(x)$ has no zeros; the graph of $f(x)$ is a horizontal line that does not cross the x-axis.**

- The zeros of a function are x-values. What is the y-value that corresponds to these x-values? **0**

Name _____ Class _____ Date _____

2-1

Video Tutor

Using Transformations to Graph Quadratic Functions

Extension: Graphing Quadratic Functions in Vertex Form

Essential question: How can you graph the function $f(x) = a(x - h)^2 + k$?

CC.9-12.F.BF.3

1 ENGAGE   Understanding Vertex Form

The **vertex form** of a quadratic function is $f(x) = a(x - h)^2 + k$. The vertex of the graph of a quadratic function in vertex form is (h, k).

$$f(x) = a(x - h)^2 + k$$

a indicates a vertical stretch or shrink and/or a reflection across the x-axis.	h indicates a horizontal translation.	k indicates a vertical translation.

A **zero of a function** is an input value x that makes the output value $f(x)$ equal 0. You can estimate the zeros of a quadratic function by observing where the graph crosses the x-axis.

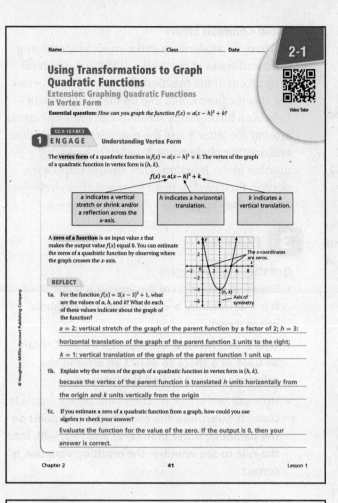

The x-coordinates are zeros.

(h, k)

Axis of symmetry

REFLECT

1a. For the function $f(x) = 2(x - 3)^2 + 1$, what are the values of a, h, and k? What do each of these values indicate about the graph of the function?

$a = 2$: vertical stretch of the graph of the parent function by a factor of 2; $h = 3$:

horizontal translation of the graph of the parent function 3 units to the right;

$k = 1$: vertical translation of the graph of the parent function 1 unit up.

1b. Explain why the vertex of the graph of a quadratic function in vertex form is (h, k).

because the vertex of the parent function is translated h units horizontally from

the origin and k units vertically from the origin

1c. If you estimate a zero of a quadratic function from a graph, how could you use algebra to check your answer?

Evaluate the function for the value of the zero. If the output is 0, then your

answer is correct.

Chapter 2   41   Lesson 1

CC.9-12.F.IF.7a

2 EXAMPLE   Graphing $f(x) = a(x - h)^2 + k$

Graph the function $f(x) = 2(x + 1)^2 - 2$. Identify the vertex, minimum or maximum, axis of symmetry, and zeros of the function.

A   Identify and graph the vertex.

$h = $ ___−1___

$k = $ ___−2___

The vertex of the graph is ___$(−1, −2)$___.

B   Identify the coordinates of points to the left and right of the vertex.

x	−3	−2	0	1
f(x)	6	0	0	6

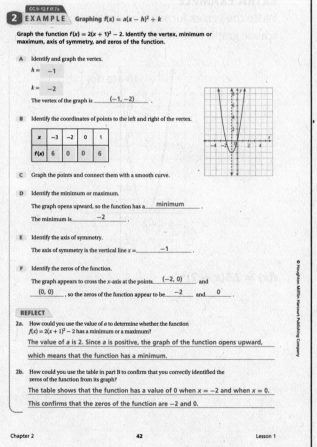

C   Graph the points and connect them with a smooth curve.

D   Identify the minimum or maximum.

The graph opens upward, so the function has a ___minimum___.

The minimum is ___−2___.

E   Identify the axis of symmetry.

The axis of symmetry is the vertical line $x = $ ___−1___.

F   Identify the zeros of the function.

The graph appears to cross the x-axis at the points ___$(−2, 0)$___ and

___$(0, 0)$___, so the zeros of the function appear to be ___−2___ and ___0___.

REFLECT

2a. How could you use the value of a to determine whether the function $f(x) = 2(x + 1)^2 - 2$ has a minimum or a maximum?

The value of a is 2. Since a is positive, the graph of the function opens upward,

which means that the function has a minimum.

2b. How could you use the table in part B to confirm that you correctly identified the zeros of the function from its graph?

The table shows that the function has a value of 0 when $x = −2$ and when $x = 0$.

This confirms that the zeros of the function are −2 and 0.

Chapter 2   42   Lesson 1

© Houghton Mifflin Harcourt Publishing Company

2 EXAMPLE

Questioning Strategies

- How would the graph be different if $a = -2$ rather than $a = 2$? Describe the vertex and the direction in which the parabola opens. **The vertex is unchanged. The graph opens down.**

- Make a table of values for $g(x) = -2(x + 1)^2 - 2$ for $x = -3, -2, -1, 0,$ and 1. $g(x) = -10, -4, -2, -4, -10$

- Explain why the vertex of the graph of $g(x) = -2(x + 1)^2 - 2$ stays the same as the vertex of the graph of $f(x)$. **The value of h is still -1, and the value of k is still -2, so the vertex remains at $(-1, -2)$.**

- What are the zeros of $g(x) = -2(x + 1)^2 - 2$? **There are no zeros.**

EXTRA EXAMPLE

Graph the function $f(x) = -3(x - 4)^2 - 1$. Identify the vertex, minimum or maximum, axis of symmetry, and zeros of the function.

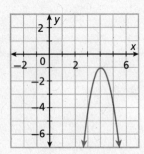

The vertex is $(4, -1)$; the maximum is -1; the axis of symmetry is $x = 4$; there are no zeros.

Technology

Students can graph the quadratic function in the Example using a calculator and compare this graph to the one they drew by hand. However, reinforce to students that prior to graphing a quadratic function in vertex form on a graphing calculator, they should identify the vertex and know which way the parabola opens.

Avoid Common Errors

It is easy for students to make errors in identifying the coordinates of the vertex. Writing the general vertex form of the function directly above or below the specific function to line up the variables will help. As a further step, students can draw one circle around the letter h and the number in the function, and another circle around the letter k and the number in the function. They should include the signs in their circles. If, for instance, they circle $-h$ and $+4$, they know that $-h = +4$, or $h = -4$.

3 EXAMPLE

Questioning Strategies

- Based on the graph of the function, is $a < 0$, or is $a > 0$? Explain. **$a < 0$ because the parabola opens down.**

- Why is determining the sign of a helpful? **It can be used as a check to detect an error in the calculations used to find the value of a.**

- How can you check whether your function rule is correct? **Substitute the coordinates of a point on the parabola, other than $(2, 2)$ and $(-2, -6)$, into the rule to see whether the resulting equation is correct.**

EXTRA EXAMPLE

Write the vertex form of the quadratic function whose graph is shown.

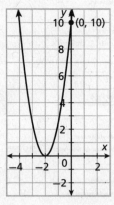

$f(x) = 2.5(x + 2)^2$

3 EXAMPLE CC.9-12.F.BF.3 Writing Equations in Vertex Form

Write the vertex form of the quadratic function whose graph is shown.

A Use the vertex of the graph to identify the values of h and k.

The vertex of the graph is (2, 2)

$h = $ 2

$k = $ 2

Substitute the values of h and k into the vertex form:

$f(x) = a(x - 2)^2 + 2$

B Use the point $(-2, -6)$ to identify the value of a.

$f(x) = a(x - 2)^2 + 2$	Vertex form
$-6 = a(-2 - 2)^2 + 2$	Substitute -6 for $f(x)$ and -2 for x.
$-6 = a(16) + 2$	Simplify.
$-8 = a(16)$	Subtract 2 from both sides.
$-\frac{1}{2} = a$	Divide both sides by 16.

Substitute the value of a into the vertex form:

$f(x) = -\frac{1}{2}(x - 2)^2 + 2$

So, the vertex form of the function shown in the graph is

$f(x) = -\frac{1}{2}(x - 2)^2 + 2$.

REFLECT

3a. How can you tell by looking at the graph that the value of a is negative?

The graph opens downward, which indicates a reflection of the graph of the

parent function across the x-axis. A reflection across the x-axis results in a

negative value of a.

3b. Describe the graph of the given function as a transformation of the parent
quadratic function.

Reflection across the x-axis, vertical shrink by a factor of $\frac{1}{2}$, and translation

2 units to the right and 2 units up

---

4 EXAMPLE CC.9-12.F.IF.7a Modeling Quadratic Functions in Vertex Form

The shape of a bridge support can be modeled by $f(x) = -\frac{1}{600}(x - 300)^2 + 150$,
where x is the horizontal distance in feet from the left end of the bridge and
$f(x)$ is the height in feet above the bridge deck. Sketch a graph of the support.
Then determine the maximum height of the support above the bridge deck and
the width of the support at the level of the bridge deck.

A Graph the function.

• The vertex of the graph is (300, 150) .

• Find the point at the left end of the support ($x = 0$).

Since $f(0) = $ 0 , the point (0, 0) represents the left end.

• Use symmetry to find the point at the right end of the support.

Since the left end is 300 feet to the left of the vertex, the right end will be 300 feet to
the right of the vertex.

The point (600, 0) represents the right end.

• Find two other points on the support.

$\left(120, 96\right)$ and $\left(480, 96\right)$

• Sketch the graph.

B Determine the maximum height of the support.

The maximum of the function is 150 .

So, the maximum height of the bridge support is 150 feet.

C Determine the width of the bridge support at the level of the bridge deck.

The distance from the left end to the right end is 600 feet.

So, the width is 600 feet at the level of the bridge deck.

REFLECT

4a. Explain how you know that the y-coordinate of the right end of the support is 0.

The support has the shape of a parabola, so it is symmetric. The left end has a

y-coordinate of 0, so the right end must also have a y-coordinate of 0.

4b. What does the vertex represent in this situation?

the point on the support above the midpoint of the bridge deck and at the

greatest height above the bridge deck

Questioning Strategies

- What shape does the bridge support have? How do you know? **Parabola; it is represented by a quadratic function.**

- Why is the graph only in the first quadrant? **In this situation, the values of x and $f(x)$ represent distance and height. Distance and height cannot be negative.**

⟋⟍ **MATHEMATICAL** **Highlighting**
∴∴∴ **PRACTICE** **the Standards**

4 EXAMPLE is an opportunity to address Mathematical Practice Standard 4 (Model with mathematics). Students will describe the quadratic relationship between the height of a bridge support and the horizontal distance from the base of the support. They will sketch a graph of the quadratic function (which is the shape of the bridge support) and identify and use the zeros and the vertex of the function to determine physical quantities.

EXTRA EXAMPLE

The shape of a highway tunnel through a mountain can be modeled by $f(x) = -\frac{1}{15}(x - 20)^2 + 27$, where x is the horizontal distance in feet from the left edge of the tunnel and $f(x)$ is the height in feet above the highway. Sketch a graph of the function. Determine the maximum height of the tunnel and the width of the tunnel.

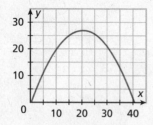

height = 27 ft; width = 40 ft

CLOSE

Essential Question

How can you graph the function $f(x) = a(x - h)^2 + k$?
To graph the function $f(x) = a(x - h)^2 + k$, first identify the vertex as (h, k). Determine whether the parabola will open up or down by examining whether $a > 0$ or $a < 0$. Then, choose two x-values on one side of the vertex and calculate their y-values. Using symmetry, find two points on the other side of the vertex. Finally, graph the function.

Summarize

Students should write a journal entry to describe how to graph the vertex form of a quadratic function by hand. They should mention the value of a, the vertex, and how they will use symmetry to help them graph the function. Next, they should address how they would check the graph of a quadratic function obtained from a calculator.

PRACTICE

Where skills are taught	Where skills are practiced
2 EXAMPLE	EXS. 1–4
3 EXAMPLE	EXS. 5, 6
4 EXAMPLE	EXS. 7, 8

Exercises 9 and 10: Students extend what they learned in **2** EXAMPLE and **3** EXAMPLE to compare the maximum or minimum of two quadratic functions—one given as an equation and the other as a graph.

PRACTICE

Graph each quadratic function. Identify the vertex, minimum or maximum, axis of symmetry, and zeros of the function.

1. $f(x) = -2x^2 + 8$

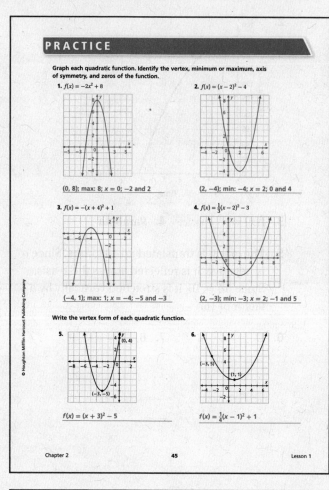

(0, 8); max: 8; $x = 0$; −2 and 2

2. $f(x) = (x - 2)^2 - 4$

(2, −4); min: −4; $x = 2$; 0 and 4

3. $f(x) = -(x + 4)^2 + 1$

(−4, 1); max: 1; $x = -4$; −5 and −3

4. $f(x) = \frac{1}{3}(x - 2)^2 - 3$

(2, −3); min: −3; $x = 2$; −1 and 5

Write the vertex form of each quadratic function.

5.

$f(x) = (x + 3)^2 - 5$

6.

$f(x) = \frac{1}{4}(x - 1)^2 + 1$

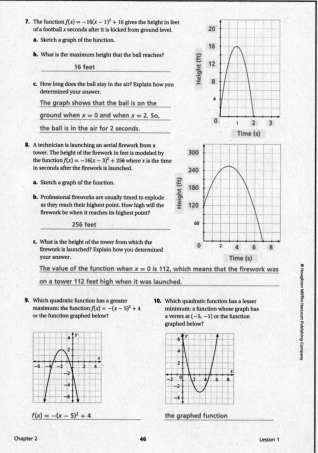

7. The function $f(x) = -16(x - 1)^2 + 16$ gives the height in feet of a football x seconds after it is kicked from ground level.

a. Sketch a graph of the function.

b. What is the maximum height that the ball reaches?

16 feet

c. How long does the ball stay in the air? Explain how you determined your answer.

The graph shows that the ball is on the ground when $x = 0$ and when $x = 2$. So, the ball is in the air for 2 seconds.

8. A technician is launching an aerial firework from a tower. The height of the firework in feet is modeled by the function $f(x) = -16(x - 3)^2 + 256$ where x is the time in seconds after the firework is launched.

a. Sketch a graph of the function.

b. Professional fireworks are usually timed to explode as they reach their highest point. How high will the firework be when it reaches its highest point?

256 feet

c. What is the height of the tower from which the firework is launched? Explain how you determined your answer.

The value of the function when $x = 0$ is 112, which means that the firework was on a tower 112 feet high when it was launched.

9. Which quadratic function has a greater maximum: the function $f(x) = -(x - 5)^2 + 4$ or the function graphed below?

$f(x) = -(x - 5)^2 + 4$

10. Which quadratic function has a lesser minimum: a function whose graph has a vertex at (−5, −1) or the function graphed below?

the graphed function

ADDITIONAL PRACTICE AND PROBLEM SOLVING

Assign these pages to help your students practice and apply important lesson concepts. For additional exercises, see the Student Edition.

Answers

Additional Practice

1.

x	$f(x) = x^2 + 2x - 1$	$(x, f(x))$
-2	-1	$(-2, -1)$
-1	-2	$(-1, -2)$
0	-1	$(0, -1)$
1	2	$(1, 2)$
2	7	$(2, 7)$

2. Translated 2 units right, 2 units up

3. Reflected across the x-axis and horizontal compression by a factor of 3

4. Horizontal stretch by a factor of 2

5. $g(x) = -\left(\frac{1}{3}x\right)^2 - 2$

6. Vertical translation; possible answer: at a given time a ball dropped from tower A will be 200 feet higher than a ball dropped from tower B at the same time. Tower A is 200 feet taller than tower B.

Problem Solving

1.

Time (t)	$f(t) = -16t^2 + 185$	$(t, f(t))$
0	$f(0) = -16(0)^2 + 185$	$(0, 185)$
1	$f(1) = -16(1)^2 + 185$	$(1, 169)$
2	$f(2) = -16(2)^2 + 185$	$(2, 121)$
3	$f(3) = -16(3)^2 + 185$	$(3, 41)$
4	$f(4) = -16(4)^2 + 185$	$(4, -71)$

2.

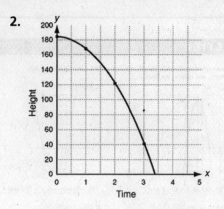

3. $f(x) = x^2$

4. Parabola

5. The graph is translated up 185 units. Since a is negative, it is reflected across the x-axis. Since $|a| = 16$, it is stretched vertically by a factor of 16.

6. D

7. B

2-1

Name_____ Class_____ Date_____

Additional Practice

Graph the function by using a table.

1. $f(x) = x^2 + 2x - 1$

x	$f(x) = x^2 + 2x - 1$	$(x, f(x))$
-2		
-1		
0		
1		
2		

Using the graph of $f(x) = x^2$ as a guide, describe the transformations, and then graph each function. Label each function on the graph.

2. $h(x) = (x - 2)^2 + 2$

3. $h(x) = -(3x)^2$

4. $h(x) = \left(\frac{1}{2}x\right)^2$

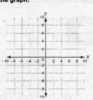

Use the description to write a quadratic function in vertex form.

5. The parent function $f(x) = x^2$ is reflected across the x-axis, horizontally stretched by a factor of 3 and translated 2 units down to create function g.

_____

6. A ball dropped from the top of tower A can be modeled by the function $h(t) = -9.8t^2 + 400$, where t is the time after it is dropped and $h(t)$ is its height at that time. A ball dropped from the top of tower B can be modeled by the function $h(t) = -9.8t^2 + 200$. What transformation describes this change? What does this transformation mean?

_____

_____

Problem Solving

Christa and Jelani are standing at the top of the Leaning Tower of Pisa in Italy, 185 feet above the ground. Jelani wonders what the path of a dropped object would be as it falls to the ground from the top of the tower. The height of an object after t seconds is given by the function, $f(t) = -16t^2 + 185$.

1. Complete the table to show the height, $f(t)$, of the object for different values of t.

2. Plot the ordered pairs from the table and draw the graph to show the path of the object.

Time (t)	$f(t) = -16t^2 + 185$	$(t, f(t))$
0	$f(0) = -16(0)^2 + 185$	
1	$f(1) = -16(1)^2 + 185$	
2		
3		
4		

3. What is the parent function for the graph? _____

4. What is the name for this U-shaped curve? _____

5. Describe the transformations of the parent function into $f(t) = -16t^2 + 185$, which describes the path of an object falling from 185 feet.

_____

Choose the letter for the best answer.

6. Mario dropped a wrench from the top of a sailboat mast 58 feet high. Which function describes the path of the falling wrench?

   A $f(t) = 16(t - 58)^2 - 185$

   B $f(t) = -16(t - 58)^2 + 185$

   C $f(t) = 16t^2 - 58$

   D $f(t) = -16t^2 + 58$

7. Delle wants to transform the parent function $f(t) = t^2$ into $f(t) = -4(t - 0.6)^2 + 6$. Which is NOT a step in that transformation?

   A Translation 6 units up

   B Translation 0.6 unit left

   C Reflection across the x-axis

   D Vertical stretch by a factor of 4

Properties of Quadratic Functions in Standard Form
Going Deeper

Essential question: *How is the structure of a quadratic equation related to the structure of the parabola it describes?*

COMMON CORE **Standards for Mathematical Content**

CC.9-12.F.IF.7 Graph functions expressed symbolically and show key features of the graph, by hand in simple cases...*

CC.9-12.F.IF.7a Graph linear and quadratic functions and show intercepts, maxima, and minima.*

Prerequisites

Using Transformations to Graph Quadratic Functions

Math Background

The graph of a quadratic function is a parabola. Quadratic functions are the first non-linear functions that students study. Stress to students that, when they graph parabolas, they should not attempt to draw straight lines between the points. Also note the symmetrical properties of the parabola. The axis of symmetry is the line that reflects the parabola onto itself. The vertex is the point at which the axis of symmetry intersects the parabola.

INTRODUCE

Start the lesson with a discussion about symmetry. Have students give examples of common objects or shapes that show symmetry, such as the capital letters A and B. Next, lead into a discussion of parabolas. Explain how symmetry can be used to find points on a parabola, including the vertex. Explain how students can use the symmetry of a parabola to find its axis of symmetry (by taking the average of the *x*-values of two points on the parabola with the same *y*-values).

TEACH

1 EXPLORE

Questioning Strategies

- How can you use the graph to find the axis of symmetry? **The parabola can be reflected onto itself across the axis of symmetry.**

- How can you find points on the graph of a function? **Substitute *x*-values into the equation of the function and calculate the corresponding *y*-values.**

- For a quadratic equation in standard form, how can you use the value of *a* to tell whether the associated parabola opens upward or downward? **If $a > 0$, it opens upward; if $a < 0$, it opens downward.**

2 EXAMPLE

Questioning Strategies

- What is the relationship between the vertex and the axis of symmetry of a parabola? **The vertex is the point where the axis of symmetry and the parabola intersect.**

EXTRA EXAMPLE

What is the axis of symmetry of the parabola $y = x^2 + 4x + 10$? What are the coordinates of the vertex? **axis of symmetry: $x = -2$; vertex: $(-2, 6)$**

Name_____ Class_____ Date_____

2-2

Properties of Quadratic Functions in Standard Form
Going Deeper

Essential question: *How is the structure of a quadratic equation related to the structure of the parabola it describes?*

The standard form of a quadratic function is $f(x) = ax^2 + bx + c$, where a, b and c are constants and $a \neq 0$. The graph of a quadratic function is a parabola.

Video Tutor

1 EXPLORE CC.9-12.F.IF.7a **Find the Axis of Symmetry and Vertex from a Graph**

Find the axis of symmetry and vertex by graphing.

A Complete the table of values below. Sketch the graph of $y = x^2 - 4x + 5$.

x	y = x² − 4x + 5
0	5
1	2
2	1
3	2
4	5

What is the axis of symmetry of the parabola? $x = 2$
What is the vertex of the parabola? (2, 1)
What is the y-intercept of the parabola? (0, 5)
In which direction does the parabola open? upward

B Complete the table of values below. Sketch the graph of $y = 2x^2 + 4x + 1$.

x	y = 2x² + 4x + 1
−3	7
−2	1
−1	−1
0	1
1	7

What is the axis of symmetry of the parabola? $x = -1$
What is the vertex of the parabola? (−1, −1)
What is the y-intercept of the parabola? (0, 1)
In which direction does the parabola open? upward

© Houghton Mifflin Harcourt Publishing Company

REFLECT

1. How is the equation of the axis of symmetry related to coefficients a and b in Part A? How is the equation of the axis of symmetry related to coefficients a and b in Part C? Write a rule for the equation of the axis of symmetry based on the values of a and b.

The sign of the axis of symmetry is the opposite of the sign of b, and the numeric part is half the quotient of $\frac{b}{a}$. $x = \frac{-b}{2a}$.

2 EXAMPLE CC.9-12.F.IF.7 **Find the Axis of Symmetry and Vertex from a Table**

A Complete the table of values below.

x	y = x² + x + 2
−2	4
−1	2
0	2
1	4
2	8

B Between which two x-values is the axis of symmetry located? −1 and 0
What is the axis of symmetry of the parabola? $x = -0.5$
How did you find the axis of symmetry?

The axis of symmetry is halfway between each pair of points that share a y-value.

How can you find the vertex of the parabola once you know the axis of symmetry?

If the axis of symmetry is $x = a$, then a is the x-coordinate of the vertex. Substitute a for x in the equation of the parabola to calculate the y-coordinate.

What is the vertex of the parabola? (−0.5, 1.75)

© Houghton Mifflin Harcourt Publishing Company

CLOSE

Essential Question

How is the structure of a quadratic equation related to the structure of the parabola it describes?

The standard form of a quadratic equation is $ax^2 + bx + c = 0$. When a is positive, the parabola opens upward. When a is negative, the parabola opens downward. The value of c is the y-intercept of the parabola. The axis of symmetry of the parabola is given by the equation $x = \frac{-b}{2a}$.

Summarize

Have students write a journal entry in which they describe how to graph a parabola given a quadratic equation. They should explain how to determine the axis of symmetry and vertex of a parabola given a quadratic equation in standard form. Tell students to sketch the graph of a parabola in their notebooks, labeling the axis of symmetry, vertex, x-intercepts (if applicable), and y-intercept.

MATHEMATICAL PRACTICE — Highlighting the Standards

The Explore activity, Example, and exercises provide opportunities to address Mathematical Practices Standard 7 (Look for and make use of structure). Students study the structure of parabolas. They also use Standard 3 (Construct viable arguments and critique the reasoning of others) when finding the axis of symmetry in Example 2.

PRACTICE

Where skills are taught	Where skills are practiced
1 EXPLORE	EXS. 1–2
2 EXAMPLE	EXS. 3–5

REFLECT

2a. How might you find the axis of symmetry of a parabola if you are given a table of values?

If there are two points that have the same y-value, the axis of symmetry is

halfway between those points.

2b. Why is the axis of symmetry halfway between two points on the parabola that have the same y-value?

The parabola is symmetric about the axis of symmetry.

PRACTICE

Complete the table of values and sketch the graph. Identify the axis of symmetry, vertex, and y-intercept of each parabola.

1. $y = x^2 + 6x - 1$

x	$y = x^2 + 6x - 1$
−5	−6
−4	−9
−3	−10
−2	−9
−1	−6

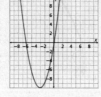

Axis of symmetry: $x = -3$

Vertex: (−3, −10)

y-intercept: (0, 1)

2. $y = 4x^2 + 8x - 5$

x	$y = 4x^2 + 8x - 5$
−3	7
−2	−5
−1	−9
0	−5
1	7

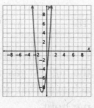

Axis of symmetry: $x = -1$

Vertex: (−1, −9)

y-intercept: (0, −5)

Complete the table of values. Identify the axis of symmetry, vertex, and y-intercept of each parabola.

3. $y = -2x^2 + 2x + 1$

x	$y = -2x^2 + 2x + 1$
−2	−11
−1	−3
0	1
1	1
2	−3

Axis of symmetry: $x = 0.5$

Vertex: (0.5, 1.5)

y-intercept: (0, 1)

4. $y = x^2 + 3x - 2$

x	$y = x^2 + 3x - 2$
−4	2
−3	−2
−2	−4
−1	−4
0	−2

Axis of symmetry: $x = -1.5$

Vertex: (−1.5, −4.25)

y-intercept: (0, 1)

5. $y = -x^2 - x - 4$

x	$y = -x^2 - x - 4$
−3	−10
−2	−6
−1	−4
0	−4
1	−6

Axis of symmetry: $x = -0.5$

Vertex: (−0.5, −3.75)

y-intercept: (0, −4)

Assign these pages to help your students practice and apply important lesson concepts. For additional exercises, see the Student Edition.

Answers

Additional Practice

1. $x = 2$

2. $x = \frac{3}{4}$

3. $x = -3$

4. a. Downward

   b. $x = 1.5$

   c. $(1.5, 3.25)$

   d. 1

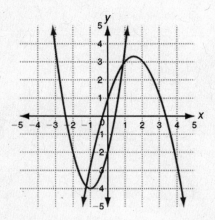

5. a. Upward

   b. $x = -1$

   c. $(-1, -4)$

   d. -2

6. Minimum: 0; domain: all real numbers; range: $\{y \mid y \geq 0\}$

7. Maximum: 8.25; domain: all real numbers; range: $\{y \mid y \leq 8.25\}$

8. Day 45; 182,250 records

Problem Solving

1. $a < 0$, so the graph opens downward.

2. $x = 40$ **3.** -30

4. $(40, 18)$

5.

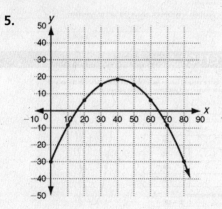

6. a. Maximum

   b. 18

   c. Possible answer: 18 miles per gallon is the highest gas mileage that this car will achieve. That occurs at a speed of 40 miles per hour.

7. D   **8.** C

2-2

Name_____ Class_____ Date_____

Additional Practice

Identify the axis of symmetry for the graph of each function.

1. $g(x) = x^2 - 4x + 2$

2. $h(x) = -8x^2 + 12x - 11$

3. $k(x) = -4(x + 3)^2 + 9$

_____   _____   _____

For each function, (a) determine whether the graph opens upward or downward, (b) find the axis of symmetry, (c) find the vertex, and (d) find the y-intercept. Then graph the function.

4. $f(x) = -x^2 + 3x + 1$

   a. Upward or downward _____

   b. Axis of symmetry _____

   c. Vertex _____

   d. y-intercept _____

5. $g(x) = 2x^2 + 4x - 2$

   a. Upward or downward _____

   b. Axis of symmetry _____

   c. Vertex _____

   d. y-intercept _____

Find the minimum or maximum value of each function. Then state the domain and range of the function.

6. $g(x) = x^2 - 2x + 1$

7. $h(x) = -5x^2 + 15x - 3$

Solve.

8. A record label uses the following function to model the sales of a new release.

$$a(t) = -90t^2 + 8100t$$

The number of albums sold is a function of time, t, in days. On which day were the most albums sold? What is the maximum number of albums sold on that day?

_____

Problem Solving

Kim wants to buy a used car with good gas mileage. He knows that the miles per gallon, or mileage, varies according to various factors, including the speed. He finds that highway mileage for the make and model he wants can be approximated by the function $f(s) = -0.03s^2 + 2.4s - 30$, where s is the speed in miles per hour. He wants to graph this function to estimate possible gas mileages at various speeds.

1. Determine whether the graph opens upward or downward. _____

2. Identify the axis of symmetry for the graph of the function. _____

3. Find the y-intercept. _____

4. Find the vertex. _____

5. Graph the function.

6. a. Does the curve have a maximum or a minimum value? _____

   b. What is the value of the y-coordinate at the maximum or minimum? _____

   c. Explain what this point means in terms of gas mileage.

_____

A ball is hit into the air from a height of 4 feet. The function $g(t) = -16t^2 + 120t + 4$ can be used to model the height of the ball where t is the time in seconds after the ball is hit. Choose the letter for the best answer.

7. About how long is the ball in the air?

   A 3.5 seconds

   B 3.75 seconds

   C 7 seconds

   D 7.5 seconds

8. What is the maximum height the ball reaches?

   A 108 feet

   B 124 feet

   C 229 feet

   D 394 feet

Solving Quadratic Equations by Graphing and Factoring
Extension: Intercept Form

Essential question: How do you determine where the graph of a quadratic function crosses the x-axis?

COMMON CORE **Standards for Mathematical Content**

CC.9-12.A.SSE.3 Choose and produce an equivalent form of an expression to reveal and explain properties of the quantity represented by the expression.*

CC.9-12.A.SSE.3a Factor a quadratic expression to reveal the zeros of the function it defines.*

CC.9-12.A.CED.2 ... graph equations on coordinate axes with labels and scales.*

CC.9-12.F.IF.2 Use function notation, evaluate functions for inputs in their domains and interpret statements that use function notation in terms of a context.

CC.9-12.F.IF.7 Graph functions expressed symbolically and show key features of the graph ...*

CC.9-12.F.IF.7a Graph ... quadratic functions and show intercepts, maxima, and minima.*

CC.9-12.F.IF.8 Write a function defined by an expression in different but equivalent forms to reveal and explain different properties of the function.

CC.9-12.F.IF.8a Use the process of factoring ... in a quadratic function to show zeros, extreme values, and symmetry of the graph, and interpret these in terms of a context.

Vocabulary
intercept form

Prerequisites
Factoring $ax^2 + bx + c$

Math Background
Zeros can be found for many different types of functions, such as linear, quadratic, polynomial, logarithmic, exponential, and trigonometric. These functions are used to describe many different physical phenomena. Finding zeros of functions is a useful tool for determining information about the real-world situations modeled by these functions.

INTRODUCE

Have students state the general vertex form of a quadratic function. Ask them how they can find the coordinates of the vertex from this form. Ask them what other key characteristics they have found for quadratic functions (the zeros or *x*-intercepts). Explain that they will learn how to write a quadratic function in intercept form from which they can easily read the *x*-intercepts of the function's graph. Remind students that all three forms (standard, vertex, and intercept) of a given quadratic function are equivalent.

TEACH

1 EXPLORE

Questioning Strategies

- In part A, is there another method you can use to rewrite the expression? Explain. **Yes; you can use the FOIL method to multiply the binomials.**

- Describe a method you can use in parts A and B to check your work. **Substitute a value for x into both the original expression and the rewritten expression to ensure that the values of both expressions are the same.**

- In part B, if you were given the function $f(x) = x^2 - 3x - 4$ instead of the expression, explain how you would find the zeros of the function. **Set the function equal to zero and use the zero-product property.**

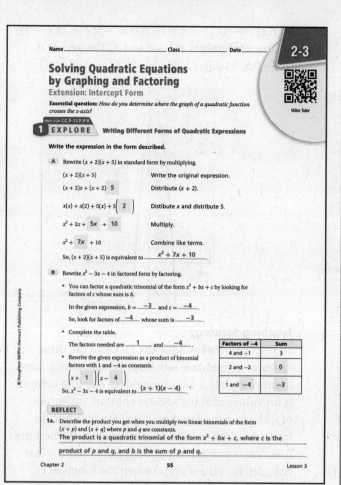

Name _____ Class _____ Date _____

Solving Quadratic Equations by Graphing and Factoring

Extension: Intercept Form

Essential question: *How do you determine where the graph of a quadratic function crosses the x-axis?*

PREP FOR CC.9-12.F.IF.8

1 EXPLORE Writing Different Forms of Quadratic Expressions

Write the expression in the form described.

A Rewrite $(x + 2)(x + 5)$ in standard form by multiplying.

$(x + 2)(x + 5)$	Write the original expression.
$(x + 2)x + (x + 2)\ 5$	Distribute $(x + 2)$.
$x(x) + x(2) + 5(x) + 5\left(\ 2\ \right)$	Distibute x and distribute 5.
$x^2 + 2x + \ 5x\ + \ 10$	Multiply.
$x^2 + \ 7x\ + 10$	Combine like terms.

So, $(x + 2)(x + 5)$ is equivalent to $\ x^2 + 7x + 10$

B Rewrite $x^2 - 3x - 4$ in factored form by factoring.

* You can factor a quadratic trinomial of the form $x^2 + bx + c$ by looking for factors of c whose sum is b.

In the given expression, $b = \ -3$ and $c = \ -4$.

So, look for factors of $\ -4$ whose sum is $\ -3$.

* Complete the table.

The factors needed are $\ 1$ and $\ -4$.

Factors of −4	Sum
4 and −1	3
2 and −2	0
1 and −4	−3

* Rewrite the given expression as a product of binomial factors with 1 and −4 as constants.

$$\left(x + \ 1\ \right)\left(x - \ 4\ \right)$$

So, $x^2 - 3x - 4$ is equivalent to $\ (x + 1)(x - 4)$

REFLECT

1a. Describe the product you get when you multiply two linear binomials of the form $(x + p)$ and $(x + q)$ where p and q are constants.

The product is a quadratic trinomial of the form $x^2 + bx + c$, where c is the

product of p and q, and b is the sum of p and q.

© Houghton Mifflin Harcourt Publishing Company

REFLECT

1b. In part B, how could you check that you factored the given expression correctly?

Multiply the binomials to check whether the product is the same as the

given expression.

The **intercept form** of a quadratic function is $f(x) = a(x - p)(x - q)$. The values of p and q are the x-intercepts of the function's graph, or the zeros of the function.

You can multiply to change a quadratic function in intercept form to standard form, and you can factor to change a quadratic function in standard form to intercept form.

CC.9-12.F.IF.8a

2 EXAMPLE Graphing $f(x) = a(x - p)(x - q)$

Write each function in intercept form. Identify the x-intercepts and vertex of the function's graph. Then graph the function.

A $f(x) = x^2 - 8x + 12$

* Write the function in intercept form by factoring the trinomial.

$$f(x) = \left(x - \ 2\ \right)\left(x - \ 6\ \right)$$ Factor the trinomial.

* Identify the x-intercepts.

The x-intercepts are $\ 2$ and $\ 6$.

So, the graph includes the points (2, 0) and $\left(\ 6\ , 0\right)$.

* Identify the vertex.

Based on the symmetry of the parabola, the x-coordinate of the vertex must be halfway between the x-coordinates of the points (2, 0) and (6, 0).

The x-coordinate of the vertex is $\frac{2 + 6}{2} = \ 4$.

Substitute this value of x into the function rule to find the y-coordinate of the vertex.

$f(4) = \left(\ 4\ - 2\right)\left(\ 4\ - 6\right)$ Substitute 4 for x.

$f(4) = \left(\ 2\ \right)\left(\ -2\ \right)$ Simplify the factors.

$f(4) = \ -4$ Multiply.

So, the vertex is $\left(\ 4\ , \ -4\ \right)$.

* Graph the function using the x-intercepts and the vertex.

© Houghton Mifflin Harcourt Publishing Company

Questioning Strategies

- In part A, state the two conditions that must be satisfied by the factors of the constant term. **Their product must be 12, and their sum must be −8.**

- In part A, how do you know that both binomial factors are of the form $(x - \underline{\quad})$? **The constant term is positive, so its factors must both be negative or must both be positive. Because the coefficient of x is negative, the factors of the constant term must both be negative.**

- In part A, what is the value of a? **1** Which way should the parabola open? **up**

- In part B, why was $-\frac{1}{3}$ factored out instead of just $\frac{1}{3}$? **To make the factoring easier, you want the coefficient of x^2 to be positive.**

- In part B, does the parabola open up or down? How do you know? **Down; a is negative.**

EXTRA EXAMPLE

Write each function in intercept form. Identify the x-intercepts and vertex of the function's graph. Then graph the function.

A. $f(x) = x^2 - 6x + 5$ $f(x) = (x - 5)(x - 1)$; the x-intercepts are 5 and 1. The vertex is $(3, -4)$.

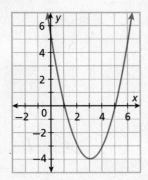

B. $f(x) = -5x^2 - 5x + 10$ $f(x) = -5(x + 2)(x - 1)$; the x-intercepts are −2 and 1. The vertex is $(-0.5, 11.25)$.

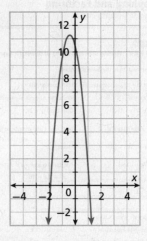

Teaching Strategy

To help students solidify the fact that the three forms of a quadratic function are equivalent, have them complete a 4-column table. The first column is for values of x; the second column, for values of $f(x)$ when the function is written in intercept form; the third column, for values of $f(x)$ when the function is written in standard form; and the last column, for values of $f(x)$ when the function is written in vertex form. Include at least five rows for five different values of x.

Give students a quadratic function in standard form and have them factor it. Once students have factored the function and found the vertex, they write three x-values—the two intercepts and the x-coordinate of the vertex. Then, they can choose two other x-values. Students will find $f(x)$ for each value of x three different times, once for each form of the equation. All three equations should yield the same value for $f(x)$, thus demonstrating that the forms are equivalent.

B $f(x) = -\frac{1}{3}x^2 + \frac{4}{3}x + \frac{5}{3}$

- Write the function in intercept form by factoring the trinomial.

$f(x) = -\frac{1}{3}\left(x^2 - \boxed{4}\, x - \boxed{5}\right)$ Factor out $-\frac{1}{3}$ so that the coefficient of x^2 is 1.

$f(x) = -\frac{1}{3}\left(x - \boxed{5}\right)\left(x + \boxed{1}\right)$ Factor the trinomial.

- Identify the x-intercepts.

The x-intercepts are $\underline{5}$ and $\underline{-1}$

So, the graph includes the points $\left(\boxed{5}, 0\right)$ and $\left(\boxed{-1}, 0\right)$.

- Identify the vertex.

The x-coordinate of the vertex must be halfway between the x-coordinates of the

points (5, 0) and $\left(\boxed{-1}, 0\right)$.

The x-coordinate of the vertex is $\dfrac{\boxed{5} + \boxed{-1}}{2} = \boxed{2}$.

Substitute this value of x into the function rule to find the y-coordinate of the vertex.

$f(2) = -\frac{1}{3}\left(\boxed{2} - 5\right)\left(\boxed{2} + 1\right)$ Substitute 2 for x.

$f(2) = -\frac{1}{3}\left(\boxed{-3}\right)\left(\boxed{3}\right)$ Simplify the factors.

$f(2) = \boxed{3}$ Multiply.

So, the vertex is $\left(\boxed{2}, \boxed{3}\right)$.

- Graph the function using the x-intercepts and the vertex.

REFLECT

2a. Describe another way that you could have found the vertex of the graph of the function in part A.

Sample answer: Write the function in vertex form. Then use the values of

h and k in the vertex form to write the coordinates of the vertex.

2b. In part B, how could you tell that the parabola opens downward by looking at the standard form of the quadratic function?

The value of a is negative, which means that the graph of the function is a

reflection of the graph of the parent function across the x-axis.

2c. A student claims that you can find the x-coordinate of the vertex of the graph of a quadratic function by averaging the values of p and q from the intercept form of the function. Is the student's claim correct? Explain.

Correct; The values of p and q are the x-intercepts of the function. Averaging p

and q gives an x-value that is halfway between them. Based on symmetry, the

x-coordinate of the vertex is halfway between the x-intercepts.

3 EXAMPLE   CC.9-12.F.IF.8a   Writing a Quadratic Model in Intercept Form

The cross-sectional shape of the archway of a bridge is modeled by the function $f(x) = -0.5x^2 + 2x$, where $f(x)$ is the height in meters of a point on the arch and x is the distance in meters from the left end of the arch's base. How wide is the arch at its base? Will a wagon that is 2 meters wide and 1.75 meters tall fit under the arch?

A Write the function in intercept form.

$f(x) = -0.5\left(x^2 - \boxed{4}\, x\right)$ Factor out -0.5 so that the coefficient of x^2 is 1.

$f(x) = -0.5(x)\left(x - \boxed{4}\right)$ Factor the binomial.

$f(x) = -0.5(x - 0)\left(x - \boxed{4}\right)$ Write the intercept form.

B Identify the x-intercepts and the vertex.

The x-intercepts are $\underline{0}$ and $\underline{4}$

The x-coordinate of the vertex is $\dfrac{\boxed{0} + \boxed{4}}{2} = \boxed{2}$.

Find the y-coordinate of the vertex.

$f(2) = -0.5\left(\boxed{2} - 0\right)\left(\boxed{2} - 4\right)$ Substitute 2 for x.

$f(2) = -0.5\left(\boxed{2}\right)\left(\boxed{-2}\right) = \boxed{2}$ Simplify.

The vertex is $\left(\boxed{2}, \boxed{2}\right)$.

C Graph the function using the x-intercepts and the vertex.

D Use the graph to solve the problem.

The width of the arch at its base is $\underline{4}$ meters.
Sketch the wagon on your graph. Will the wagon fit under the arch? Explain.

No; when the wagon is centered on the arch,

the top corners are slightly higher than the arch.

Distance from left end (m)

© Houghton Mifflin Harcourt Publishing Company

Questioning Strategies

- What does the shape of the parabola represent in terms of the situation? **the actual shape of the archway**

- Which way do you expect the parabola to open? How do you know both mathematically and in terms of the situation? **Down; $a < 0$; also, the arch under a bridge must open down.**

EXTRA EXAMPLE

The shape of a tunnel is modeled by the function $f(x) = -0.2x^2 + 2x$ where $f(x)$ is the height from the ground in meters of a point on the tunnel and x is the distance in meters from the left edge of the tunnel. How wide is the tunnel at its base? Will 2 trucks that are each 4 meters tall and 2.6 meters wide be able to pass through the tunnel? **10 meters wide; no**

⋰ MATHEMATICAL PRACTICE **Highlighting the Standards**

3 EXAMPLE is an opportunity to address Mathematical Practice Standard 4 (Model with mathematics). Students must not only model the archway of the bridge described in the problem by drawing its graph but also determine whether a wagon will fit under the arch. This is done by modeling the wagon using a rectangle on the same grid as that of the model of the archway. Students must then look at the two models together and correctly determine that the wagon will not fit.

CLOSE

Essential Question

How do you determine where the graph of a quadratic function crosses the x-axis?
You can find the x-intercepts of the graph of a quadratic function in standard form by factoring the function to get its intercept form. If the function is not factorable, the x-intercepts can be found by using the quadratic formula to find the zeros of the function.

Summarize

Have students construct a graphic organizer showing the graph of a quadratic function and its equation in vertex form, intercept form, and standard form. The organizer should show how to "translate" among the forms. Students should choose an initial function in intercept form to be sure its graph has two real x-intercepts. A sample is shown.

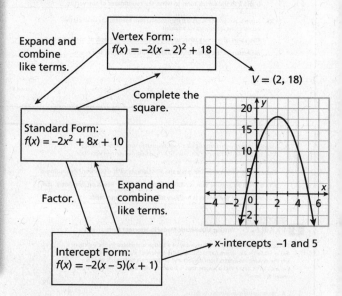

Expand and combine like terms.

Vertex Form:
$f(x) = -2(x - 2)^2 + 18$

$V = (2, 18)$

Complete the square.

Standard Form:
$f(x) = -2x^2 + 8x + 10$

Factor.

Expand and combine like terms.

Intercept Form:
$f(x) = -2(x - 5)(x + 1)$

x-intercepts −1 and 5

PRACTICE

Where skills are taught	Where skills are practiced
2 EXAMPLE	EXS. 1–4
3 EXAMPLE	EXS. 5, 6

REFLECT

3a. What do the x-intercepts represent in this situation?

The x-coordinates of the points where the arch touches the ground, where an

x-coordinate is the horizontal distance in meters from the left end of the arch.

3b. Explain how you used the graph to find the width of the arch at its base.

I found the distance between the points where the graph crosses the x-axis.

This distance is 4 units, so the arch is 4 meters wide.

3c. Explain how you modeled the shape of the wagon on the graph.

I drew a rectangle 2 units wide and 1.75 units high. I placed the bottom side of

the rectangle on the x-axis and centered the rectangle horizontally on the axis of

symmetry of the parabola.

3d. What are the x-coordinates of the left and right sides of the model of the wagon?
Evaluate the function modeling the arch for these x-values. Do the results verify
your conclusion about whether the wagon will fit under the arch? Explain.

1 and 3; $f(1) = f(3) = 1.5$; yes; The arch is 1.5 meters high at these x-values,

and the height of the wagon is 1.75 meters, so the wagon is too tall to fit.

PRACTICE

Write each function in intercept form. Identify the x-intercepts and vertex of the
function's graph. Then graph the function.

1. $f(x) = x^2 + 6x + 5$

$f(x) = (x + 5)(x + 1);$
-5 and -1; $(-3, -4)$

2. $f(x) = x^2 - 2x - 8$

$f(x) = (x + 2)(x - 4);$
-2 and 4; $(1, -9)$

© Houghton Mifflin Harcourt Publishing Company

Write each function in intercept form. Identify the x-intercepts and vertex of the
function's graph. Then graph the function.

3. $f(x) = 2x^2 - 8x + 6$

$f(x) = 2(x - 1)(x - 3)$; 1 and 3; $(2, -2)$

4. $f(x) = -3x^2 + 24x - 45$

$f(x) = -3(x - 3)(x - 5)$; 3 and 5; $(4, 3)$

5. In a football game, Tony attempts to kick a field goal at a distance of 40 yards
from the goal post. The path of the kicked football is given by the equation
$y = -0.02x^2 + 0.9x$ where x is the horizontal distance in yards and y is the
vertical distance in yards.

a. Write the equation in intercept form.

$y = -0.02x(x - 45)$

b. Identify the x-intercepts and the vertex.

$0, 45$; $(22.5, 10.125)$

c. Graph the equation in the first quadrant.

d. The horizontal bar of the goal post is 10 feet above the ground.
Does the ball go over the bar? Explain.

Yes, because the height of the ball at $x = 40$ yards

is $y = 4$ yards $= 12$ feet, so the ball clears the bar

by 2 feet.

6. Consider the function $f(x) = 2x^2 + 12x + 18$.

a. Write the function in intercept form. What is the relationship between p and q?

$f(x) = 2(x + 3)(x + 3)$; $p = q$

b. What is the relationship between the graph's x-intercepts and its vertex?
Explain.

There is a single x-intercept that occurs at the vertex because the graph is

tangent to the x-axis at the vertex.

c. What is the vertex form of a quadratic function if $p = q$ in the intercept form of
the function?

$f(x) = a(x - p)^2$

© Houghton Mifflin Harcourt Publishing Company

Assign these pages to help your students practice and apply important lesson concepts. For additional exercises, see the Student Edition.

Answers

Additional Practice

1.

x	−4	−3	−2	−1	0
f(x)	2	0	0	2	5

−2 and −3

2.

x	−2	0	2	4	6
f(x)	−7	5	9	5	−7

−1 and 5

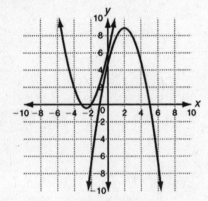

3. −3
4. −0.5, −4

5. −5, 4
6. $\dfrac{2}{3}$

7. −0.75, 0.75
8. $f(x) = x^2 - 5x - 14$

9. $f(x) = x^2 + 7x - 8$
10. About 7.5 s

Problem Solving

1. **a.** $a = -16$, $b = 80$, $c = 0$

   b. $t = \dfrac{-80}{2(-16)} = 2.5$ seconds

   c. 100 feet

   d. 5 seconds

2. **a.** $h(t) = -16t^2 + 80t + 21$

   b. $(4t + 1)(-4t + 21) = 0$

   c. Possible answer: Erin has the roots correct. Set each factor equal to 0 and solve for t. But the rocket will stay in the air 5.25 seconds. (The negative root represents the time before launch since the rocket is starting at 21 feet, not at ground level.)

3. A
4. C

Name_____ Class_____ Date_____

Additional Practice

Find the zeros of each function by using a graph and a table.

1. $f(x) = x^2 + 5x + 6$

x	−4	−3	−2	−1	0
f(x)					

_____

2. $g(x) = -x^2 + 4x + 5$

x	−2	0	2	4	6
f(x)					

_____

Find the zeros of each function by factoring.

3. $h(x) = -x^2 - 6x - 9$ 4. $f(x) = 2x^2 + 9x + 4$ 5. $g(x) = x^2 + x - 20$

_____   _____   _____

Find the roots of each equation by factoring.

6. $12x = 9x^2 + 4$ 7. $16x^2 = 9$

_____   _____

Write a quadratic function in standard form for each given set of zeros.

8. −2 and 7   9. 1 and −8

_____   _____

Solve.

10. The quadratic function that approximates the height of a javelin throw is $h(t) = -0.08t^2 + 4.48$, where t is the time in seconds after it is thrown and h is the javelin's height in feet. How long will it take for the javelin to hit the ground?   _____

Problem Solving

Erin and her friends launch a rocket from ground level vertically into the air with an initial velocity of 80 feet per second. The height of the rocket, $h(t)$, after t seconds is given by $h(t) = -16t^2 + 80t$.

1. They want to find out how high they can expect the rocket to go and how long it will be in the air.

   a. Use the standard form $f(x) = ax^2 + bx + c$ to find values for a, b, and c.

   b. Use the coordinates for the vertex of the path of the rocket to find t, the number of seconds the rocket will be in the air before it starts its downward path.   _____

   c. Substitute the value for t in the given function to find the maximum height of the rocket. How high can they expect their rocket to go?   _____

   d. Megan points out that the rocket will have a height of zero again when it returns to the ground. How long will the rocket stay in the air?   _____

2. Megan gets ready to launch the same rocket from a platform 21 feet above the ground with the same initial velocity. How long will the rocket stay in the air this time?

   a. Write a function that represents the rocket's path for this launch.   _____

   b. Factor the corresponding equation to find the values for t when h is zero.   _____

   c. Erin says that the roots of the equation are $t = 5.25$ and $t = -20.25$ and that the rocket will stay in the air 5.5 seconds. Megan says she is wrong. Who is correct? How do you know?

   _____

   _____

Choose the letter for the best answer.

3. Which function models the path of a rocket that lands 3 seconds after launch?

   A $h(t) = -16t^2 + 32t + 48$

   B $h(t) = -16t^2 + 32t + 10.5$

   C $h(t) = -16t^2 + 40t + 48$

   D $h(t) = -16t^2 + 40t + 10.5$

4. Megan reads about a rocket whose path can be modeled by the function $h(t) = -16t^2 + 100t + 15$. Which could be the initial velocity and launch height?

   A 15 ft/s; 100 ft off the ground

   B 16 ft/s; 100 ft off the ground

   C 100 ft/s; 15 ft off the ground

   D 171 ft/s; 15 ft off the ground

Completing the Square
Connection: Vertex Form of Quadratic Equations

Essential question: *How do you convert quadratic functions to vertex form,* $f(x) = a(x - h)^2 + k?$

COMMON CORE Standards for Mathematical Content

CC.9-12.A.SSE.3 Choose and produce an equivalent form of an expression to reveal and explain properties of the quantity represented by the expression.*

CC.9-12.A.SSE.3b Complete the square in a quadratic expression to reveal the maximum or minimum value of the function it defines.*

CC.9-12.A.CED.2 ... graph equations on coordinate axes with labels and scales.*

CC.9-12.F.IF.2 Use function notation, evaluate functions for inputs in their domains ...

CC.9-12.A.F.IF.7 Graph functions expressed symbolically and show key features of the graph ...*

CC.9-12.F.IF.7a Graph ... quadratic functions and show intercepts, maxima, and minima.*

CC.9-12.F.IF.8 Write a function defined by an expression in different but equivalent forms to reveal and explain different properties of the function.

CC.9-12.F.IF.8a Use the process of factoring and completing the square in a quadratic function to show zeros, extreme values, and symmetry of the graph, and interpret these in terms of a context.

Vocabulary
standard form

Prerequisites
Completing the square
Graphing quadratic functions in vertex form

Math Background
Quadratic functions can be written in a variety of forms: standard form, $f(x) = ax^2 + bx + c$; vertex form, $f(x) = a(x - h)^2 + k$; and intercept form, $f(x) = a(x - p)(x - q)$. Since they are all equivalent, it is possible to convert from one form to another.

INTRODUCE

Remind students how to determine the value of c that makes $x^2 + bx + c$ a perfect square trinomial: Take half the coefficient of x and square it, so $c = \left(\frac{b}{2}\right)^2$ and $x^2 + bx + \left(\frac{b}{2}\right)^2 = \left(x + \frac{b}{2}\right)^2$. Point out that if students are completing the square on the rule for a function, such as $f(x) = x^2 + bx$, they must add a form of 0 to produce an equivalent rule. In other words, they must both add $\left(\frac{b}{2}\right)^2$ and subtract it, which results in the function $f(x) = x^2 + bx + \left(\frac{b}{2}\right)^2 - \left(\frac{b}{2}\right)^2$, or $f(x) = \left(x + \frac{b}{2}\right)^2 - \left(\frac{b}{2}\right)^2$.

TEACH

1 EXPLORE

Questioning Strategies

• In part A, how do you expand $(x - 4)^2$? **You can use the square of a binomial pattern or FOIL.**

• In part A, how are the graphs of $f(x) = 2(x - 4)^2 + 3$ and $f(x) = 2x^2 - 16x + 35$ related to each other? **They are the same.**

• In part B, how do you determine that the value to add is 9? **To complete the square on $x^2 + 6x$, you have to add $\left(\frac{6}{2}\right)^2$, or 9.**

• In part B, why do you have to subtract 9 as well? **To keep the function rule the same; by adding 9 and then subtracting 9, you have essentially added 0 to the rule; thus, it has not changed.**

continued

Name_____ Class_____ Date_____

2-4

Completing the Square
Connection: Vertex Form of Quadratic Equations

Essential question: *How do you convert quadratic functions to vertex form,*
$f(x) = a(x - h)^2 + k$?

Video Tutor

CC.9-12.F.IF.8

1 EXPLORE   Writing Quadratic Functions in Different Forms

Write the quadratic function in the form described.

A Write the function $f(x) = 2(x - 4)^2 + 3$ in the form $f(x) = ax^2 + bx + c$.

$f(x) = 2(x - 4)^2 + 3$

$f(x) = 2\left(x^2 - \boxed{8}x + \boxed{16}\right) + 3$ Multiply to expand $(x - 4)^2$.

$f(x) = 2(x^2) - \boxed{2}(8x) + \boxed{2}(16) + 3$ Distribute 2.

$f(x) = 2x^2 - \boxed{16}x + \boxed{32} + 3$ Multiply.

$f(x) = 2x^2 - 16x + \boxed{35}$ Combine like terms.

So, $f(x) = 2(x - 4)^2 + 3$ is equivalent to $\underline{f(x) = 2x^2 - 16x + 35}$

B Write the function $f(x) = x^2 + 6x + 4$ in vertex form.

Recall that the vertex form of a quadratic function is $f(x) = a(x - h)^2 + k$.
Write the given function in vertex form by completing the square.

$f(x) = x^2 + 6x + 4$

$f(x) = \left(x^2 + 6x + \boxed{}\right) + 4 - \boxed{}$ Set up for completing the square.

$f(x) = (x^2 + 6x + 9) + 4 - 9$ Add a constant so the expression inside the parentheses is a perfect square trinomial. Subtract the constant to keep the equation balanced.

$f(x) = \left(x + \boxed{3}\right)^2 + 4 - 9$ Write $(x^2 + 6x + 9)$ as a binomial squared.

$f(x) = (x + 3)^2 - \boxed{5}$ Combine like terms.

So, $f(x) = x^2 + 6x + 4$ is equivalent to $\underline{f(x) = (x + 3)^2 - 5}$

REFLECT

1a. In part A, how does the value of a of the function in vertex form compare with the value of a when the function is in the form $f(x) = ax^2 + bx + c$?

The value of a in both forms is the same, 2.

Chapter 2   63   Lesson 4

1b. In part B, how could you check that you found the vertex form of the quadratic equation correctly?

Use the vertex form to write the equation in the form $f(x) = ax^2 + bx + c$. Then
check that the values of a, b, and c match those given in the original equation.

1c. Describe how to complete the square for the quadratic expression

$x^2 + 8x + \boxed{}$

Divide the coefficient of x by 2, and square the quotient: $\left(\frac{8}{2}\right)^2 = 16$.

Add the result to the quadratic expression: $x^2 + 8x + 16$.

The **standard form** of a quadratic equation is $f(x) = ax^2 + bx + c$. Any quadratic function in standard form can be written in vertex form, and any quadratic function in vertex form can be written in standard form.

CC.9-12.F.IF.8a

2 EXAMPLE   Graphing by Completing the Square

Graph the function by first writing it in vertex form. Then give the maximum or minimum of the function and identify its zeros.

A $f(x) = x^2 - 8x + 12$

• Write the function in vertex form.

$f(x) = \left(x^2 - 8x + \boxed{}\right) + 12 - \boxed{}$ Set up for completing the square.

$f(x) = \left(x^2 - 8x + \boxed{16}\right) + 12 - \boxed{16}$ Add a constant to complete the square. Subtract the constant to keep the equation balanced.

$f(x) = \left(x - \boxed{4}\right)^2 + 12 - 16$ Write the expression in parentheses as a binomial squared.

$f(x) = (x - 4)^2 - \boxed{4}$ Combine like terms.

• Sketch a graph of the function.

The vertex is $\underline{(4, -4)}$

Two points to the left of the vertex are

$\left(2, \boxed{0}\right)$ and $\left(3, \boxed{-3}\right)$.

Two points to the right of the vertex are

$\left(5, \boxed{-3}\right)$ and $\left(6, \boxed{0}\right)$.

• Describe the function's properties.

The minimum is $\underline{-4}$

The zeros are $\underline{2}$ and $\underline{6}$

Chapter 2   64   Lesson 4

Differentiated Instruction

Students who are having difficulty completing the square in part B can work with algebra tiles. They should model $x^2 + 6x + 4$ using tiles, with 3 x-tiles to the right of the x^2-tile and 3 x-tiles below the x^2-tile. Once they have the tiles laid out, they should move the 1-tiles, as a group, off to the side. Students should then add enough positive 1-tiles to the x^2-tile and six x-tiles to complete the square (9 tiles). They add an equal number of negative 1-tiles to their separated group of four 1-tiles so that the net amount added is 0. Combining the 1-tiles off to the side gives 5 negative 1-tiles, or –5. Students then write the expression as a square of a binomial, $(x + 3)^2$, plus the number of 1-tiles off to the side. The final expression, $(x + 3)^2 - 5$, is equal to the original one, since students have simply added a form of 0 to the original.

2 EXAMPLE

- In part A, how do you determine what number to add (and subtract) to complete the square? Take half of the coefficient of x and square it; $\left(\frac{b}{2}\right)^2 = \left(\frac{8}{2}\right)^2 = 16$

- In part B, why do you multiply 9 by −2 before you subtract it? The 9 being added to complete the square on $x^2 + 6x$ is being multiplied by −2, the number that was originally factored out of the variable terms of the function rule. Essentially, you are adding −18 to the function rule, so you have to subtract −18 to keep the equation balanced.

EXTRA EXAMPLE

Graph the function by first writing it in vertex form. Then give the maximum or minimum of the function and identify its zeros.

A. $f(x) = x^2 + x - 6$

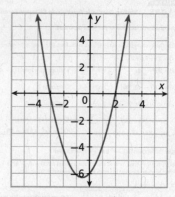

$f(x) = (x + 0.5)^2 - 6.25$; minimum $= -6.25$; The zeros are −3 and 2.

B. $f(x) = 3x^2 - 6x + 8$

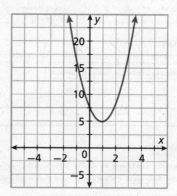

$f(x) = 3(x - 1)^2 + 5$;

minimum $= 5$; no zeros

MATHEMATICAL PRACTICE   **Highlighting the Standards**

2 EXAMPLE is an opportunity to address Mathematical Practice Standard 8 (Look for and express regularity in repeated reasoning). When transitioning from standard to vertex form, students will need to perform the same series of steps outlined in the Example no matter what the coefficients are. Students can check the reasonableness of their results by checking that the vertex (from the vertex form) satisfies the standard form and by ensuring that the parabola opens in the direction they expect based on the value of a.

B $f(x) = -2x^2 - 12x - 16$

* Write the function in vertex form.

$f(x) = -2\,(x^2 + 6x) - 16$ — Factor the variable terms so that the coefficient of x^2 is 1.

$f(x) = -2\left(x^2 + 6x + \boxed{}\right) - 16 - \boxed{}$ — Set up for completing the square.

$f(x) = -2\left(x^2 + 6x + \boxed{9}\right) - 16 - (-2)\ \boxed{9}$ — Complete the square. Since the constant is multiplied by -2, subtract the product of -2 and the constant to keep the equation balanced.

$f(x) = -2\left(x + \boxed{3}\right)^2 - 16 - (-2)9$ — Write the expression in parentheses as a binomial squared.

$f(x) = -2(x + 3)^2 - 16 - \boxed{-18}$ — Simplify $(-2)9$.

$f(x) = -2(x + 3)^2 + \boxed{2}$ — Combine like terms.

* Sketch a graph of the function.

The vertex is $\underline{(-3, 2)}$

Two points to the left of the vertex are

$\left(-5,\ \boxed{-6}\right)$ and $\left(-4,\ \boxed{0}\right)$

Two points to the right of the vertex are

$\left(-2,\ \boxed{0}\right)$ and $\left(-1,\ \boxed{-6}\right)$

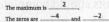

* Describe the function's properties.

The maximum is $\underline{\hspace{0.3cm}2\hspace{0.3cm}}$

The zeros are $\underline{\hspace{0.3cm}-4\hspace{0.3cm}}$ and $\underline{\hspace{0.3cm}-2\hspace{0.3cm}}$

REFLECT

2a. How do you keep the equation of a quadratic function balanced when completing the square?

Subtract the constant that you add to complete the square. If the constant is multiplied by a number, subtract the product of the constant and the number.

2b. In part B, why do you factor out -2 from the variable terms before completing the square?

-2 is the coefficient of x^2, and it is easier to complete the square when the coefficient of x^2 is 1.

Chapter 2   65   Lesson 4

2c. Why might the vertex form of a quadratic equation be more useful in some situations than the standard form?

In vertex form, you can use the values of a, h, and k to easily identify the vertex, the axis of symmetry, and the maximum or minimum of the function and its graph.

CC.9-12.F.IF.8a

3 EXAMPLE   Modeling Quadratic Functions in Standard Form

The function $h(t) = -16t^2 + 64t$ gives the height h in feet of a golf ball t seconds after it is hit. The ball has a height of 48 feet after 1 second. Use the symmetry of the function's graph to determine the other time at which the ball will have a height of 48 feet.

A Write the function in vertex form.

$h(t) = \boxed{-16}\ (t^2 - 4t)$ — Factor so that the coefficient of t^2 is 1.

$h(t) = -16\left(t^2 - 4t + \boxed{4}\right) - (-16)\ \boxed{4}$ — Complete the square and keep the equation balanced.

$h(t) = -16\left(t - \boxed{2}\right)^2 - (-16)4$ — Write the expression in parentheses as a binomial squared.

$h(t) = -16(t - 2)^2 + \boxed{64}$ — Simplify.

B Use symmetry to sketch a graph of the function and solve the problem.

The vertex is $\underline{(2, 64)}$

The point $\left(0,\ \boxed{0}\right)$ is on the graph.

This point is 2 units to the left of the vertex. Based on symmetry, there is a point 2 units to the right of the vertex with the same y-coordinate at $\left(\boxed{4},\, 0\right)$.

The point $(1, 48)$ is on the graph. Based on symmetry, the point $\left(\boxed{3},\, 48\right)$ is also on the graph.

So, the ball will have a height of 48 feet after 1 second and again after $\underline{\ 3\ }$ seconds.

REFLECT

3a. How can you check your answer to the problem?

Evaluate the original function for $t = 3$ and check that the value of the function is 48.

Chapter 2   66   Lesson 4

Notes

© Houghton Mifflin Harcourt Publishing Company

Questioning Strategies

- In this problem, which variable describes the horizontal distance that the golf ball travels? There isn't a variable that describes horizontal distance. t describes the time, and $h(t)$ describes the vertical distance above the ground.

- What is the axis of symmetry for this parabola? $x = 2$

- For how long is the ball in the air? How can you tell? **4 sec; the ball is on the ground when $h(t) = 0$. This occurs at $t = 0$ and at $t = 4$.**

EXTRA EXAMPLE

The function $h(t) = -16t^2 + 48t$ gives the height h in feet of a football t seconds after it is kicked off a tee. The ball has a height of 32 feet after 1 second. Write the function in vertex form and then graph the function. Use the symmetry of the function's graph to determine the other time at which the ball will have a height of 32 feet.
$h(t) = -16(t - 1.5)^2 + 36$

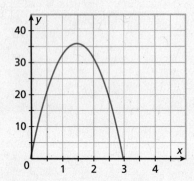

At 2 seconds, the ball will have a height of 32 feet.

CLOSE

Essential Question

How do you convert quadratic functions to vertex form, $f(x) = a(x - h)^2 + k$?

You can convert quadratic functions from standard form $f(x) = ax^2 + bx + c$ to vertex form by completing the square on $ax^2 + bx$. You have to add and subtract the same constant to keep the equation balanced.

Summarize

Students should write a journal entry that summarizes what they know about the graphs of quadratic functions. They should write a quadratic function in vertex form, sketch its graph, and then write the function in standard form. To complete their summary, students should complete the square on the standard form to move back to the (original) vertex form of the function.

PRACTICE

Where skills are taught	Where skills are practiced
2 EXAMPLE	EXS. 1–4
3 EXAMPLE	EXS. 5, 6

3b. What is the maximum height that the ball reaches? How do you know?

The vertex form of the function indicates that the vertex is (2, 64). This means

that the ball reaches a maximum height of 64 feet 2 seconds after it is hit.

3c. If you know the coordinates of a point to the left of the vertex of the graph of a quadratic function, how can you use symmetry to find the coordinates of another point on the graph?

The second point will be the same distance to the right of the vertex as the

first point is to the left of the vertex. The second point will have the same

y-coordinate as the first point.

PRACTICE

Graph each function by first writing it in vertex form. Then give the maximum or minimum of the function and identify its zeros.

1. $f(x) = x^2 - 6x + 9$

$f(x) = (x - 3)^2$; min: 0; 3

2. $f(x) = x^2 - 2x - 3$

$f(x) = (x - 1)^2 - 4$; min: −4; −1 and 3

3. $f(x) = -7x^2 - 14x$

$f(x) = -7(x + 1)^2 + 7$; max: 7; −2 and 0

4. $f(x) = 3x^2 - 12x + 9$

$f(x) = 3(x - 2)^2 - 3$; min: −3; 1 and 3

---

5. A company is marketing a new toy. The function $s(p) = -50p^2 + 3000p$ models how the total sales s of the toy, in dollars, depend on the price p of the toy, in dollars.

a. Complete the square to write the function in vertex form and then graph the function.

$s(p) = -50(p - 30)^2 + 45,000$

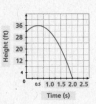

b. What is the vertex of the graph of the function? What does the vertex represent in this situation?

(30, 45,000); the toy price ($30) that is

predicted to result in the greatest total

sales ($45,000)

c. The model predicts that total sales will be $40,000 when the toy price is $20. At what other price does the model predict that total sales will be $40,000? Use the symmetry of the graph to support your answer.

$40; The point (20, 40,000) is 10 units to the left of the vertex. Based on

the symmetry of the graph, there will also be a point 10 units to the right

of the vertex with a y-coordinate of 40,000. This point is (40, 40,000).

6. A circus performer throws a ball from a height of 32 feet. The model $h(t) = -16t^2 + 16t + 32$ gives the height of the ball in feet t seconds after it is thrown.

a. Complete the square to write the function in vertex form and then graph the function.

$h(t) = -16(t - 0.5)^2 + 36$

b. What is the maximum height that the ball reaches?

36 feet

c. What is a reasonable domain of the function? Explain.

$\{t \mid 0 \le t \le 2\}$; Only nonnegative values of

t and h make sense, so t cannot be less than 0.

h is negative for values of t greater than 2, so t

must be less than equal to 2.

d. What is the y-intercept of the function's graph? What does it represent in this situation? What do you notice about the y-intercept and the value of c when the function is written in standard form?

32; The height in feet from which the ball is thrown.

The y-intercept and the value of c are the same.

ADDITIONAL PRACTICE AND PROBLEM SOLVING

Assign these pages to help your students practice and apply important lesson concepts. For additional exercises, see the Student Edition.

Answers

Additional Practice

1. $x = \pm 2\sqrt{6}$ **2.** $x = 7 \pm 3\sqrt{2}$

3. $4; (x - 2)^2$ **4.** $36; (x + 6)^2$

5. $d = \dfrac{5}{2} \pm \dfrac{\sqrt{41}}{2}$ **6.** $x = -3, 1$

7. $x = 3 \pm \sqrt{19}$ **8.** $x = -\dfrac{3}{2} \pm \dfrac{\sqrt{13}}{2}$

9. $f(x) = (x - 3)^2 - 11; (3, -11)$

10. $g(x) = (x - 2)^2 - 3; (2, -3)$

11. $h(x) = 3(x - 1)^2 - 18; (1, -18)$

12. $f(x) = -2(x + 4)^2 + 36; (-4, 36)$

13. a. Base = 8 ft, height = 20 ft

b. Base = 10 ft, height = 16 ft

Problem Solving

1. a. $15 = -5t^2 + 30t$

b. $t^2 - 6t = -3$

c. $t = 0.6, 5.4$

d. Possible answer: He is partially correct. The flare will first reach 15 meters at 0.6 second after firing and then again at 5.4 seconds. (The function has two solutions.)

e. Possible answer: He is correct. The flare will first reach 15 meters at 0.6 second after firing. Also, the difference between 5.4 and 0.6 seconds (the two solutions) is 4.8 seconds, which is about 5 seconds.

Name_____ Class_____ Date_____

Additional Practice

Solve each equation.

1. $2x^2 - 6 = 42$

2. $x^2 - 14x + 49 = 18$

_____ _____

Complete the square for each expression. Write the resulting expression as a binomial squared.

3. $x^2 - 4x +$ _____

4. $x^2 + 12x +$ _____

_____ _____

Solve each equation by completing the square.

5. $2d^2 = 8 + 10d$

6. $x^2 + 2x = 3$

_____ _____

7. $-3x^2 + 18x = -30$

8. $4x^2 = -12x + 4$

_____ _____

Write each function in vertex form, and identify its vertex.

9. $f(x) = x^2 - 6x - 2$

10. $f(x) = x^2 - 4x + 1$

_____ _____

11. $h(x) = 3x^2 - 6x - 15$

12. $f(x) = -2x^2 - 16x + 4$

_____ _____

Solve.

13. Nathan made a triangular pennant for the band booster club. The area of the pennant is 80 square feet. The base of the pennant is 12 feet shorter than the height.

a. What are the lengths of the base and height of the pennant?

_____

b. What are the dimensions of the pennant if the base is only 6 feet shorter than the height?

_____

Problem Solving

Sean and Mason run out of gas while fishing from their boat in the bay. They set off an emergency flare with an initial vertical velocity of 30 meters per second. The height of the flare in meters can be modeled by $h(t) = -5t^2 + 30t$, where t represents the number of seconds after launch.

1. Sean thinks the flare should reach at least 15 meters to be seen from the shore. They want to know how long the flare will take to reach this height.

a. Write an equation to determine how long it will take the flare to reach 15 meters. _____

b. Simplify the function so you can complete the square. _____

c. Solve the equation by completing the square. _____

d. Mason thinks that the flare will reach 15 meters in 5.4 seconds. Is he correct? Explain.

_____

e. Sean thinks the flare will reach 15 meters sooner, but then the flare will stay above 15 meters for about 5 seconds. Is he correct? Explain.

_____

2. Sean wants to know how high the flare will reach above the surface of the water.

a. Write the function in vertex form, factoring so the coefficient of t^2 is 1. _____

b. Complete the square using the vertex form of the function. _____

c. How high will the flare reach? _____

Choose the letter for the best answer.

3. Use the vertex form of the function to determine how long after firing the flare it will reach its maximum height.

A 3 s

B 5 s

C 9 s

D 15 s

4. The boys fire a similar flare from the deck 5 meters above the water level. Which statement is correct?

A The flare will reach 45 m in 3 s.

B The flare will reach 50 m in 3 s.

C The flare will reach 45 m in 3.5 s.

D The flare will reach 50 m in 3.5 s.

Notes

2-5

Complex Numbers and Roots
Going Deeper

Essential question: *What is a complex number?*

COMMON CORE Standards for Mathematical Content

CC.9-12.N.CN.1 Know there is a complex number i such that $i^2 = -1$, and every complex number has the form $a + bi$ with a and b real.

Vocabulary

complex number

complex plane

imaginary unit

pure imaginary number

Prerequisites

Completing the Square

Math Background

By combining real and imaginary numbers, the class of complex numbers $a + bi$ is created, where a and b are real numbers and i is the imaginary unit. The imaginary unit i is defined as $\sqrt{-1}$. The real numbers are a subset of the complex number system. They are the case of $a + bi$ where b equals zero. The pure imaginary numbers are another subset of the complex number system. They are the case of $a + bi$ where a equals zero.

INTRODUCE

Ask students to imagine that they lived at a long-ago time when only the natural number system 1, 2, 3,... was known. Ask how they would have solved the equation $x + 5 = 5$. Elicit that the equation could not have been solved without the concept of zero. Present in succession each of the following equations, illustrating that none could be solved without the use of a new system of numbers: $3x = 2$ (rational numbers/fractions); $x + 5 = 4$ (negative numbers); $x^2 = 5$ (irrational numbers). Conclude by stating that this lesson introduces complex numbers which are used to solve equations like $x^2 = -1$.

TEACH

1 EXPLORE

Questioning Strategies

- Why can't you find a real number n with the property $n^2 = -4$? *n must be a positive or negative real number. Whether n is positive or negative, n^2 is positive. n^2 cannot equal a negative number.*

- How can you show that the real number system is a subset of the complex numbers? *Any real number a can be written as a complex number $a + bi$, where $b = 0$.*

- Under what conditions is the complex number $a + bi$ equal to the complex number $c + di$? *$a = c$ and $b = d$*

- Classify each of the following as a real number or as a pure imaginary number: i; i^2; i^3; i^4. Explain your reasoning. *i is the imaginary unit, a pure imaginary number; $i^2 = -1$, a real number; $i^3 = i^2 \cdot i = (-1)i = -i$, a pure imaginary number; $i^4 = i^2 \cdot i^2 = -1(-1) = 1$, a real number*

Name _____ Class _____ Date _____

Complex Numbers and Roots
Going Deeper

2-5

Essential question: *What is a complex number?*

CC.9-12.N.CN.1

1 EXPLORE   Understanding Complex Numbers

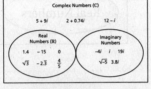

Consider the quadratic equations $x^2 - 1 = 0$ and $x^2 + 1 = 0$. You can solve the equations using square roots.

$$x^2 - 1 = 0 \qquad\qquad x^2 + 1 = 0$$
$$x^2 = 1 \qquad\qquad x^2 = -1$$
$$x = \pm\sqrt{1} = \pm 1 \qquad x = \pm\sqrt{-1}$$

A The first equation has two solutions, 1 and -1. The second equation also has two solutions, $\sqrt{-1}$ and $-\sqrt{-1}$. Which of these four solutions are real numbers?   **1 and -1**

B The graphs of $y = x^2 - 1$ and $y = x^2 + 1$ are shown. How do the graphs confirm your answer to part **A**?
The first graph has x-intercepts of 1 and -1, its two
real solutions. The second graph has no x-intercepts,
so it has no real solutions.

When the graph of a quadratic function $f(x)$ does not cross the x-axis, the solutions of $f(x) = 0$ involve the *imaginary unit i*.

C Previously you have used the Product Property $\sqrt{ab} = \sqrt{a} \cdot \sqrt{b}$ to simplify square roots of nonnegative numbers. Now extend the property to situations where $a = -1$ or $b = -1$. Simplify the following square roots by writing them in terms of the so-called **imaginary unit** i, which equals $\sqrt{-1}$.

$$\sqrt{-2} = \sqrt{-1 \cdot 2} = \sqrt{-1} \cdot \sqrt{2} = i\sqrt{2} \qquad \sqrt{-4} = \sqrt{-1 \cdot 4} = \sqrt{4} \cdot \sqrt{-1} = 2i$$

A **complex number** is a number that can be written in the form $a + bi$, where a and b are real numbers and $i = \sqrt{-1}$. The set of real numbers is a subset of the complex numbers C. Every complex number has a real part a and an imaginary part b.

Complex Numbers (C)
$5 + 9i$ $2 + 0.74i$ $12 - i$

Real Numbers (R)	Imaginary Numbers
1.4 -15 0	$-4i$ i $19i$
$\sqrt{3}$ $-2.\overline{3}$ $\frac{4}{5}$	$\sqrt{-5}$ $3.8i$

Real part   Imaginary part
↓   ↓
a + $b\,i$

Real numbers are complex numbers where $b = 0$. Imaginary numbers are complex numbers where $a = 0$ and $b \neq 0$. These are sometimes called **pure imaginary numbers**.

The complex numbers that are neither real nor imaginary, such as $5 + 9i$, are called *nonreal numbers*. In general, the nonreal numbers $a + bi$ are those in which both $a \neq 0$ and $b \neq 0$.

REFLECT

1a. How many real solutions does $x^2 + 4 = 0$ have? How many nonreal solutions? Explain.
The solutions to the equation are $2i$ and $-2i$, so there are two nonreal solutions.

1b. What is the value of i^2? Explain.
-1; The square of the square root of a quantity is the quantity itself.

1c. Using just the three set names shown in the Venn diagram on the previous page, name all sets to which each of the following numbers belong.

$1 - 2i$ **complex**

$-2i$ **imaginary (or pure imaginary); complex**

-2 **real; complex**

CC.9-12.N.CN.1

2 ENGAGE   The Complex Plane

Every real number corresponds to a point on the real number line. Similarly, every complex number corresponds to a point in the **complex plane**.

In the complex plane, real numbers are represented on a horizontal axis called the *real axis*. Pure imaginary numbers are represented on a vertical axis called the *pure imaginary* axis. Complex numbers that are neither real numbers nor pure imaginary numbers are represented in the plane formed by these axes.

It is important to recognize that the complex plane is not the same as the x-y coordinate plane that you are familiar with. In the x-y plane, real numbers are represented on both the x-axis and the y-axis.

REFLECT

2a. Describe how you would plot the following points in the complex plane.

7 **Mark a point at 7 on the real axis.**

$-4i$ **Mark a point at -4 on the pure imaginary axis.**

$-6 + 2i$ **Start at the origin. Move left 6 units and up 2 units and mark a point.**

2b. What complex number is represented by the origin of the complex plane?
$0 + 0i$ or 0

© Houghton Mifflin Harcourt Publishing Company

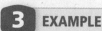
Questioning Strategies

- Describe how you could locate the complex number $m + ni$ on the complex plane. **Sample: Draw a vertical line through m on the real axis and a horizontal line through n on the pure imaginary axis. $m + ni$ will be located at the intersection of the lines.**

- Can you graph the line $y = 3x + 4$ on the complex plane? Explain. **No; The y-coordinate of any point on the line $y = 3x + 4$ is a real number. Numbers on the vertical axis of the complex plane are imaginary.**

3 EXAMPLE

Questioning Strategies

- What numbers are their own complex conjugates? **the real numbers**

EXTRA EXAMPLE
Find each complex conjugate.

A. $-5 + 2i$ **$-5 - 2i$**

B. $3 - 7i$ **$3 + 7i$**

C. 2 **2**

D. $-3i$ **$3i$**

4 EXPLORE

Questioning Strategies

- How could you check to see if your solutions to the quadratic equation in part A were correct? **You could substitute them in the original equation and see if a true statement results.**

Avoid Common Errors
Students may write the complex conjugate of $a + bi$ as $-a - bi$. Caution them to change the sign of only bi when they write the complex conjugate, and not the sign of a.

CLOSE

Essential Question
What is a complex number?
A complex number is a number that can be written in the form $a + bi$, where a and b are real numbers and $i = \sqrt{-1}$. A complex number $a + bi$ has a real part a and an imaginary part b. Real numbers are complex numbers where $b = 0$. Imaginary numbers, sometimes called pure imaginary numbers, are complex numbers where $a = 0$ and $b \neq 0$.

Summarize
Have students copy the graphic organizer and enter complex numbers that you name into the proper locations.

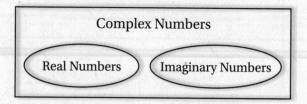

MATHEMATICAL PRACTICE   **Highlighting the Standards**

Exercises 13–18 provide opportunities to address Mathematical Practices Standard 7 (Look for and make use of structure). Quadratic equations are equations of degree 2, and therefore have a maximum of two real solutions. Sometimes the two real solutions are a double root, such as $x = -1$ for the equation $x^2 - 2x + 1 = 0$. However, many quadratic equations like $x^2 + 2x + 1 = 0$ have zero real solutions. With the introduction of complex numbers, we can now find two solutions for all quadratic equations, which was not possible before.

PRACTICE

Where skills are taught	Where skills are practiced
1 EXPLORE	EXS. 1–16
3 EXAMPLE	EXS. 17–22
4 EXPLORE	EXS. 23–24

The **complex conjugate** of any real number $a + bi$ is the complex number $a - bi$.

3 EXAMPLE Finding Complex Conjugates

Find each complex conjugate.

A	$3 + 5i$	B	$-6 - i$	C	12	D	$-2i$
	$3 - 5i$		$-6 + i$		12		$2i$

REFLECT

3a. What is the conjugate of the conjugate of a complex number $a + bi$? Explain.

$a + bi$; the conjugate of $a + bi$ is $a - bi$, and the conjugate of $a - bi$, or $a + (-bi)$,

is $a - (-bi)$, or $a + bi$.

4 EXPLORE Graphing Complex Conjugates

A Use the quadratic formula to solve $x^2 - 4x + 5 = 0$.

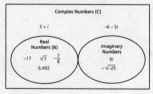

$$x_1 = \frac{-4 + \sqrt{-4^2 - 4 \cdot 1 \cdot 5}}{2 \cdot 1} \qquad x_2 = \frac{-4 - \sqrt{-4^2 - 4 \cdot 1 \cdot 5}}{2 \cdot 1}$$

$$= \frac{4 + \sqrt{-4}}{2} \qquad\qquad = \frac{4 - \sqrt{-4}}{2}$$

$$= 2 + i \qquad\qquad\qquad = 2 - i$$

B Graph the solutions on the complex plane.

REFLECT

4a. Why are nonreal roots of a quadratic equation complex conjugates?

The imaginary part of each nonreal root arises from the discriminant in the quadratic

equation, which both adds and subtracts the imaginary part to the real part. So, if we

call the real part a and the imaginary part b, the roots are $a + bi$ and $a - bi$.

4b. Describe the locations of the graphs of a complex number and its conjugate relative
to the real axis. Explain why the relationship exists.

The points are symmetric (mirror images) about the real axis. The point $a + bi$ is

located b units above a on the real axis. The point $a - bi$ is located b units below a.

PRACTICE

Write each number in its proper location in the Venn diagram.

1. $3 + i$
2. -17
3. $\sqrt{7}$
4. $9i$
5. $-6 - 5i$
6. $-\frac{7}{8}$
7. 6.492
8. $-\sqrt{-25}$

Complex Numbers (C)

$3 + i$ $-6 - 5i$

Real Numbers (R)

-17 $\sqrt{7}$ $-\frac{7}{8}$

6.492

Imaginary Numbers

$9i$

$-\sqrt{-25}$

Write the square roots of each number in terms of i.

9. -9 $3i$ and $-3i$
10. -7 $i\sqrt{7}$ and $-i\sqrt{7}$
11. -1 i and $-i$
12. -100 $10i$ and $-10i$

Solve.

13. $x^2 - 16 = 0$ 4 and -4
14. $x^2 + 16 = 0$ $4i$ and $-4i$
15. $x^2 - 5 = 0$ $\sqrt{5}$ and $-\sqrt{5}$
16. $x^2 + 5 = 0$ $i\sqrt{5}$ and $-i\sqrt{5}$

Find each complex conjugate.

17. $7 - 2i$ $7 + 2i$
18. 9 9
19. $6i$ $-6i$
20. $-8i$ $8i$
21. $-1 - 9i$ $-1 + 9i$
22. $12 + 5i$ $12 - 5i$

Solve. Then graph the solutions on the complex plane.

23. $x^2 + 2x + 5 = 0$
$x = -1 + 4i$
$x = -1 - 4i$

24. $x^2 - 6x + 13 = 0$
$x = -3 + 2i$
$x = -3 - 2i$

Notes

Assign these pages to help your students practice and apply important lesson concepts. For additional exercises, see the Student Edition.

Answers

Additional Practice

1. $4i\sqrt{2}$

2. $6i\sqrt{2}$

3. $\frac{1}{3}i$

4. $x = \pm 3i\sqrt{3}$

5. $x = \pm i\sqrt{7}$

6. $x = \pm 4i\sqrt{3}$

7. $x = \pm i\sqrt{21}$

8. $x = 4, y = 5$

9. $x = -\frac{1}{3}, y = \frac{1}{2}$

10. $x = 1 \pm i\sqrt{3}$

11. $x = -3 \pm i\sqrt{5}$

12. $-3 - i$

13. $-4 - 3i$

14. $-11i$

15. $3 \pm i\sqrt{11}$

Problem Solving

1. a. $t = 1 \pm \dfrac{i}{2}$

   b. No; possible answer: the roots are imaginary numbers.

2. a.

b	Function	Roots
24	$d(t) = 16t^2 - 24t + 20$	$\frac{1}{4}\left(3 \pm i\sqrt{11}\right)$
32	$d(t) = 16t^2 - \underline{}t + 20$	$1 \pm \frac{i}{2}$
40	$d(t) = 16t^2 - \underline{}t + 20$	$\frac{1}{4}\left(5 \pm \sqrt{5}\right)$
48	$d(t) = 16t^2 - \underline{}t + 20$	$\frac{3}{2} \pm \sqrt{1}$

   b. $b = 40$ and 48

   c. Possible answer: Real roots mean that ringing the bell is possible.

3. About 36 feet per second

4. C

5. D

Additional Practice

Express each number in terms of _i_.

1. $\sqrt{-32}$

2. $2\sqrt{-18}$

3. $\sqrt{\dfrac{1}{9}}$

_____   _____   _____

Solve each equation.

4. $3x^2 + 81 = 0$

5. $4x^2 = -28$

6. $\dfrac{1}{4}x^2 + 12 = 0$

7. $6x^2 = -126$

Find the values of _x_ and _y_ that make each equation true.

8. $2x - 20i = 8 - (4y)i$

9. $5i - 6x = (10y)i + 2$

_____   _____

Find the zeros of each function.

10. $f(x) = x^2 - 2x + 4$

11. $g(x) = x^2 + 6x + 14$

_____   _____

Find each complex conjugate.

12. $i - 3$

13. $3i - 4$

14. $11i$

_____   _____   _____

Solve.

15. The impedance of an electrical circuit is a way of measuring how much the circuit impedes the flow of electricity. The impedance can be a complex number. A circuit is being designed that must have an impedance that satisfies the function $f(x) = 2x^2 - 12x + 40$, where _x_ is a measure of the impedance. Find the zeros of the function.

_____

Problem Solving

At a carnival, a new attraction allows contestants to jump off a springboard onto a platform to be launched vertically into the air. The object is to ring a bell located 20 feet overhead. The distance from the bell in feet is modeled by the function $dt = 16t^2 - bt + 20$, where _t_ is the time in seconds after leaving the platform, and _b_ is the takeoff velocity from the platform.

1. Kate watches some of the contestants. She theorizes that if the platform launches a contestant with a takeoff velocity of at least 32 feet per second, the contestant can ring the bell.

   a. Find the zeros for the function using 32 feet per second as the takeoff velocity.   _____

   b. Is Kate's theory valid? Explain.

   _____

2. Mirko suggests they vary the value of _b_ and determine for which values of _b_ the roots are real.

   a. Complete the table to show the roots for different values of _b_.

   b. For which values of _b_ in the table are the roots real?

   c. What difference does it make if the roots are real?

_b_	Function	Roots
24	$d(t) = 16t^2 - 24t + 20$	
32	$d(t) = 16t^2 - \_\_t + 20$	
40	$d(t) = 16t^2 - \_\_t + 20$	
48	$d(t) = 16t^2 - \_\_t + 20$	

3. Using the results from the table, and the function, estimate the minimum takeoff velocity needed for a contestant to be able to ring the bell.   _____

Choose the letter for the best answer.

4. Mirko suggests using four bells at heights of 15, 20, 25, and 30 feet from the platform. How many of the bells can a contestant reach if the takeoff velocity is 32 feet per second?

   A 3   C 1
   B 2   D 0

5. At what height must a bell be placed for a contestant to reach it with a takeoff velocity of 48 feet per second?

   A 20 feet or less
   B 25 feet or less
   C 30 feet or less
   D 36 feet or less

The Quadratic Formula
Going Deeper

Essential question: *When does a quadratic equation have nonreal solutions, and how do you find them?*

○○○ **COMMON** Standards for
○ **CORE** **Mathematical Content**

CC.9-12.N.CN.7 Solve quadratic equations with real coefficients that have complex solutions.

CC.9-12.A.REI.4 Solve quadratic equations in one variable.

CC.9-12.A.REI.4b Solve quadratic equations by ... the quadratic formula ... Recognize when the quadratic formula gives complex solutions and write them as $a \pm bi$ for real numbers a and b.

Also: CC.9-12.N.CN.1, CC.9-12.N.CN.2, CC.9-12.N.CN.8(+)

Prerequisites
Quadratic formula

Multiplying binomials

Multiplying complex numbers

Math Background
In Algebra 1, students used the quadratic formula to find the solutions to a quadratic equation. If the expression $b^2 - 4ac$ (the discriminant) in the quadratic formula was negative, students learned there were no real solutions. In this lesson, students will find the nonreal solutions to quadratic equations. When the discriminant is negative, then $\sqrt{b^2 - 4ac}$ is rewritten as $\sqrt{(-1) \cdot (4ac - b^2)}$, or $\sqrt{-1} \cdot \sqrt{4ac - b^2}$. This simplifies to $\left(\sqrt{4ac - b^2}\right)i$. The solutions are then expressed as nonreal numbers. By examining the discriminant, the number and type of solutions to a quadratic equation can be summarized as follows:

Value of Discriminant	Number and type of solutions
$b^2 - 4ac > 0$	two real solutions
$b^2 - 4ac = 0$	one real solution
$b^2 - 4ac < 0$	two nonreal solutions

INTRODUCE
Draw the following parabolas on the board.

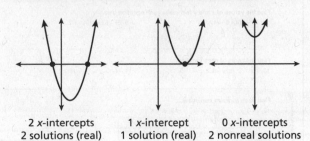

2 x-intercepts	1 x-intercept	0 x-intercepts
2 solutions (real)	1 solution (real)	2 nonreal solutions

Remind students that if $f(x)$ is a quadratic function, then the solutions of the equation $f(x) = 0$ give the x-intercepts of the function's graph. If the graph of $f(x)$ does not cross the x-axis, then there are no x-intercepts and the equation $f(x) = 0$ has no real solutions. Tell students they will now learn how to find all of the complex solutions of quadratic equations.

TEACH

1 **ENGAGE**

Questioning Strategies
- Why are there two solutions if $b^2 - 4ac > 0$ in the quadratic formula $x = \dfrac{-b \pm \sqrt{b^2 - 4ac}}{2a}$?
  The radical expression is preceded by $\pm$. In one case the radical is added to $-b$, and in the other the radical is subtracted from $-b$, resulting in two solutions.

- Why are there always two solutions to a quadratic equation that has nonreal solutions? How are they related? **Since $\sqrt{b^2 - 4ac}$ is not zero, its value will be both added to and subtracted from $-b$ in the numerator, resulting in two solutions; they are complex conjugates.**

- What is the general solution of a quadratic equation with only one solution? $-\dfrac{b}{2a}$

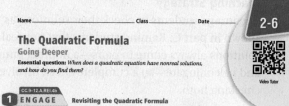

Name_____ Class_____ Date_____

2-6

The Quadratic Formula
Going Deeper

Essential question: *When does a quadratic equation have nonreal solutions, and how do you find them?*

Video Tutor

1 ENGAGE Revisiting the Quadratic Formula

CC.9-12.A.REI.4b

You have solved quadratic equations of the form $ax^2 + bx + c = 0$, where the coefficients a, b, and c are real numbers and $a \neq 0$, in several ways. One way was by using the *quadratic formula*:

$$x = \frac{-b \pm \sqrt{b^2 - 4ac}}{2a}$$

The radical $\sqrt{b^2 - 4ac}$ has meaning in the real number system only if the radicand $b^2 - 4ac$ is nonnegative. The radicand determines the number of real solutions and for this reason is called the *discriminant* for the quadratic equation. The table below summarizes the possible numbers of real solutions of a quadratic equation.

Value of Discriminant	Number of Real Solutions
$b^2 - 4ac > 0$	Two real solutions: $x = \frac{-b + \sqrt{b^2 - 4ac}}{2a}$ and $x = \frac{-b - \sqrt{b^2 - 4ac}}{2a}$
$b^2 - 4ac = 0$	One real solution: $x = -\frac{b}{2a}$
$b^2 - 4ac < 0$	No real solutions

When you solve a quadratic equation in the complex number system, where the radical $\sqrt{b^2 - 4ac}$ has meaning no matter what the value of the radicand is, the equation always has solutions. The table below summarizes the possible numbers of complex solutions of a quadratic equation.

Value of Discriminant	Number of Complex Solutions
$b^2 - 4ac > 0$	Two real solutions
$b^2 - 4ac = 0$	One real solution
$b^2 - 4ac < 0$	Two nonreal solutions

The table below gives three simple quadratic equations having different numbers and types of complex solutions.

Equation	Value of Discriminant	Solutions
$x^2 - 1 = 0$	$0^2 - 4(1)(-1) = 4$	$x = \pm 1$ (two real solutions)
$x^2 = 0$	$0^2 - 4(1)(0) = 0$	$x = 0$ (one real solution)
$x^2 + 1 = 0$	$0^2 - 4(1)(1) = -4$	$x = \pm i$ (two nonreal solutions)

REFLECT

1a. Use the discriminant to explain why the equation $x^2 + 2x - 3 = 0$ has two real solutions while the equation $x^2 + 2x + 3 = 0$ has no real solutions.

For the first equation, $b^2 - 4ac = 2^2 - 4(1)(-3) = 4 + 12 = 16 > 0$; for the second

equation, $b^2 - 4ac = 2^2 - 4(1)(3) = 4 - 12 = -8 < 0$

1b. For what value of c does the equation $x^2 + 2x + c = 0$ have exactly one real solution? Explain.

$c = 1$ because then $b^2 - 4ac = 2^2 - 4(1)(1) = 4 - 4 = 0$

2 EXAMPLE Finding the Complex Solutions of a Quadratic Equation

CC.9-12.N.CN.7

Tell whether the solutions of $x^2 + 4 = 0$ are real or nonreal. Then find the solutions.

A Use the discriminant to determine the number and type of solutions.

$b^2 - 4ac = \;0\;^2 - 4(\;1\;)(\;4\;) = \;-16$

Because $b^2 - 4ac \; < \; 0$, there are two ___nonreal___ solutions.

B Use the quadratic formula to solve the equation.

$x = \frac{-b \pm \sqrt{b^2 - 4ac}}{2a}$ Write the quadratic formula.

$= \frac{-\;0\;\pm \sqrt{-16}}{2(\;1\;)}$ Substitute values. For the radicand $b^2 - 4ac$, use the value from part A.

$= \frac{\pm 4i}{2}$ Simplify the numerator, and simplify the denominator.

$= \pm 2i$ Simplify the fraction.

REFLECT

2a. Describe how you can check the solutions of a quadratic equation. Use the method to check the solutions of $x^2 + 4 = 0$.

Substitute the solutions into the equation to see if they produce a true statement;

$(\pm 2i)^2 + 4 = -4 + 4 = 0$, so the solutions check.

2b. Why is it important to write a quadratic equation in the form $ax^2 + bx + c = 0$ before identifying the values of a, b, and c? For instance, why should you write $x^2 = -4$ as $x^2 + 4 = 0$ before using the quadratic formula to solve the equation?

You need to know the correct signs of a, b, and c; for instance, if you use

$c = -4$ when solving $x^2 = -4$, you will get two real solutions rather than

two nonreal solutions.

© Houghton Mifflin Harcourt Publishing Company

2 EXAMPLE

Questioning Strategies

- In part A, is the discriminant the solution to the quadratic equation? No; it gives only the type and number of solutions.

- In part B, why does a discriminant of -16 give you two nonreal solutions? There are two solutions because the quadratic formula uses a $\pm$ symbol. The solutions are nonreal because evaluating the formula requires finding the square root of a negative number.

EXTRA EXAMPLE

Tell whether the solutions of $x^2 + 25 = 0$ are real or nonreal. Then find the solutions.
nonreal solutions; $\pm 5i$

<table>
<tr><td colspan="7">MATHEMATICAL PRACTICE   Highlighting the Standards</td></tr>
<tr><td colspan="7">If students have difficulty evaluating $b^2 - 4ac$, you can provide a connection to Mathematical Practice Standard 6 (Attend to precision). Have them organize the variables as shown in the table below. Have them fill in the table for $3x^2 + 2x + 5 = 0$ and then predict the number and type of solutions.</td></tr>
</table>

a	b	c	b^2	$4ac$	$b^2 - 4ac$	number/type of solutions
3	2	5	4	60	-56	2 nonreal

Avoid Common Errors

Make sure that students do not leave the i under the radical sign when solving quadratic equations: $\sqrt{-5} \neq \sqrt{5i}$; $\sqrt{-5} = i\sqrt{5}$. If students have trouble with this, have them rewrite the radical first: $\sqrt{-5} = \sqrt{-1} \cdot \sqrt{5} = i\sqrt{5}$

3 EXAMPLE

Questioning Strategies

- Why can $(x - (2 + 3i))(x - (2 - 3i))$ be called a factorization of $x^2 - 4x + 13$? The product equals $x^2 - 4x + 13$.

- You are given that $(1 + 3i)$ is a solution to a quadratic equation. What is another solution? Why? $(1 - 3i)$; nonreal solutions to quadratic equations come in pairs and are conjugates of one another.

Teaching Strategy

Encourage students to check their solutions as shown in part C. Remind students that nonreal solutions always come in pairs—a nonreal number and its conjugate—so a complete check involves checking both.

EXTRA EXAMPLE

Tell whether the solutions of $x^2 + 4x + 5 = 0$ are real or nonreal. Then find the solutions.
nonreal solutions; $-2 \pm i$

CLOSE

Essential Question

When does a quadratic equation have nonreal solutions, and how do you find them?
When the value of the discriminant is negative, the quadratic equation will have two nonreal solutions. You find the solutions by using the quadratic formula to solve the equation, writing the solutions as a pair of complex conjugates of the form $a \pm bi$.

Summarize

Have students summarize how to use the discriminant to help solve any quadratic equation. Have them include examples of quadratic equations with one or two real solutions and with two nonreal solutions.

PRACTICE

Where skills are taught	Where skills are practiced
1 ENGAGE	EXS. 1–9
2 EXAMPLE	EXS. 10–12
3 EXAMPLE	EXS. 13–18

Exercise 19: Students extend what they learned in 3 EXAMPLE to finding a quick way to check the solutions of a quadratic equation.

3 EXAMPLE CC.9-12.N.CN.7 Finding the Complex Solutions of a Quadratic Equation

Tell whether the solutions of $x^2 - 4x + 13 = 0$ are real or nonreal. Then find the solutions.

A Use the discriminant to determine the number and type of solutions.

$b^2 - 4ac = (-4)^2 - 4(\underline{1})(\underline{13}) = -36$

Because $b^2 - 4ac < 0$, there are two __nonreal__ solutions.

B Use the quadratic formula to solve the equation.

$x = \dfrac{-b \pm \sqrt{b^2 - 4ac}}{2a}$ Write the quadratic formula.

$= \dfrac{-(-4) \pm \sqrt{-36}}{2(1)}$ Substitute values. For the radicand $b^2 - 4ac$, use the value from part A.

$= \dfrac{4 \pm 6i}{2}$ Simplify the numerator, and simplify the denominator.

$= 2 \pm 3i$ Simplify the fraction.

C One of the solutions is $x_1 = 2 + 3i$. Check this solution by substituting it into the equation to see if it produces a true statement.

$x^2 - 4x + 13 = (2 + 3i)^2 - 4(2 + 3i) + 13$ Substitute.

$= (-5 + 12i) - 4(2 + 3i) + 13$ Square.

$= (-5 + 12i) + (-8 - 12i) + 13$ Multiply.

$= 0$.   Simplify.

REFLECT

3a. Describe what will change in each step of the check in part C when you substitute the other solution, x_2.

First step: each $3i$ becomes $-3i$; second step: $12i$ becomes $-12i$ and $3i$ becomes $-3i$;

third step: $12i$ becomes $-12i$ and $-12i$ becomes $12i$; fourth step: no change

3b. Does the equation $x^2 + 4x + 13 = 0$ have the *same number and type of solutions* as $x^2 - 4x + 13 = 0$? Does it have the *same solutions*? Explain.

Yes, because $4^2 - 4(1)(13) = (-4)^2 - 4(1)(13) = -36$; no, because the real parts of

the solutions of the first and second equations are -2 and 2, respectively.

3c. Use the solutions x_1 and x_2 to write the expression $(x - x_1)(x - x_2)$. Multiply the binomials. What do you notice?

$(x - (2 + 3i))(x - (2 - 3i)) = x^2 - 4x + 13$; this is the quadratic expression that

appears in the equation.

© Houghton Mifflin Harcourt Publishing Company

PRACTICE

Find the number and type of solutions of each equation.

1. $x^2 - 9 = 0$

2 real solutions

2. $x^2 + 16 = 0$

2 nonreal solutions

3. $x^2 = 0$

1 real solution

4. $x^2 - 2x + 4 = 0$

2 nonreal solutions

5. $x^2 - 10x + 25 = 0$

1 real solution

6. $x^2 - 3x - 10 = 0$

2 real solutions

7. $x^2 + 12x = -36$

1 real solution

8. $2x^2 + 5 = -3x$

2 nonreal solutions

9. $3x^2 = 7 - 4x$

2 real solutions

Find the complex solutions of each equation.

10. $x^2 + 49 = 0$

$\pm 7i$

11. $x^2 + 5 = 0$

$\pm i\sqrt{5}$

12. $4x^2 + 9 = 0$

$\pm \dfrac{3}{2}i$

13. $x^2 - 2x + 2 = 0$

$1 \pm i$

14. $x^2 - 6x + 13 = 0$

$3 \pm 2i$

15. $x^2 + 10x + 29 = 0$

$-5 \pm 2i$

16. $5x^2 - 2x + 1 = 0$

$\dfrac{1}{5} \pm \dfrac{2}{5}i$

17. $9x^2 + 12x + 5 = 0$

$-\dfrac{2}{3} \pm \dfrac{1}{3}i$

18. $2x^2 - 6x + 7 = 0$

$\dfrac{3}{2} \pm \dfrac{\sqrt{5}}{2}i$

19. Multiplying the binomials in $(x - x_1)(x - x_2)$ gives $x^2 - (x_1 + x_2)x + x_1 x_2$.

a. Explain why x_1 and x_2 are solutions of the equation $(x - x_1)(x - x_2) = 0$ as well as the equation $x^2 - (x_1 + x_2)x + x_1 x_2 = 0$.

Substituting x_1 or x_2 into either equation produces a true statement.

b. For the equation $x^2 - (x_1 + x_2)x + x_1 x_2 = 0$, how is the coefficient of the x-term related to the equation's solutions? How is the constant term related to the solutions?

The opposite of the sum of the solutions; the product of the solutions

c. Describe a quick way to check the solutions x_1 and x_2 of an equation in the form $x^2 + bx + c = 0$. Then check to see if $x_1 = 2 + i$ and $x_2 = 2 - i$ are solutions of the equation $x^2 - 4x + 5 = 0$.

Check to see if $-(x_1 + x_2) = b$ and $x_1 x_2 = c$; $-[(2 + i) + (2 - i)] = -4$ and

$(2 + i)(2 - i) = 5$.

© Houghton Mifflin Harcourt Publishing Company

Assign these pages to help your students practice
and apply important lesson concepts. For
additional exercises, see the Student Edition.

Answers

Additional Practice

1. $x = -9, -1$ **2.** $x = -1 \pm \sqrt{7}$

3. $x = 0.5$ **4.** $x = -3, 1$

5. $x = -1, -0.5$ **6.** $x = \dfrac{-5 \pm \sqrt{37}}{2}$

7. Two nonreal solutions

8. Two real solutions

9. One real solution

10. a. 0.5 s

   b. 15 ft

   c. 1 s

Problem Solving

1. a. $t = -0.25, 1.5$ **b.** 30 ft

2. a. $t = -0.23, 1.61$; 35.4 ft

   b. $t = -0.21, 1.77$; 44.3 ft

   c. $t = -0.19, 1.94$; 54.3 ft

3. C   **4.** C

2-6

Additional Practice

Find the zeros of each function by using the Quadratic Formula.

1. $f(x) = x^2 + 10x + 9$

_____

2. $g(x) = 2x^2 + 4x - 12$

_____

3. $h(x) = 3x^2 - 3x + \dfrac{3}{4}$

_____

4. $f(x) = x^2 + 2x - 3$

_____

5. $g(x) = 2x^2 + 3x + 1$

_____

6. $g(x) = x^2 + 5x - 3$

_____

Find the type and number of solutions for each equation.

7. $x^2 - 3x = -8$

_____

8. $x^2 + 4x = -3$

_____

9. $2x^2 - 12x = -18$

_____

Solve.

10. A newspaper delivery person in a car is tossing folded newspapers from the car window to driveways. The speed of the car is 30 feet per second, and the driver does not slow down. The newspapers are tossed horizontally from a height of 4 feet above the ground. The height of the papers as they are thrown can be modeled by $y = -16t^2 + 4$, and the distance they travel to the driveway is $d = 30t$.

a. How long does it take for a newspaper to land?

_____

b. From how many feet before the driveway must the papers be thrown?

_____

c. The delivery person starts to throw the newspapers at an angle and the height of the papers as they travel can now be modeled by $y = -16t^2 + 12t + 4$. How long does it take the papers to reach the ground now?

_____

Problem Solving

In a shot-put event, Jenna tosses her last shot from a position of about 6 feet above the ground with an initial vertical and horizontal velocity of 20 feet per second. The height of the shot is modeled by the function $h(t) = -16t^2 + 20t + 6$, where t is the time in seconds after the toss. The horizontal distance traveled after t seconds is modeled by $d(t) = 20t$.

1. Jenna wants to know the exact distance the shot travels at a velocity of 20 feet per second.

a. Use the Quadratic Formula $t = \dfrac{-b \pm \sqrt{b^2 - 4ac}}{2a}$ to solve the height function for t.

_____

b. Use the value for t and the distance function to find the distance her shot travels.

_____

2. Jenna is working to improve her performance. She makes a table to show how the horizontal distance varies with velocity. Complete the table.

	Velocity (ft/s)	Formula	Time (s)	Distance (ft)
a.	22	$t = \dfrac{-22 \pm \sqrt{(22)^2 - 4(-16)(6)}}{2(-16)}$		
b.	25			
c.	28			

Jenna has not reached her full potential yet. Her goal is to toss the shot from a height of 6 feet 6 inches with a vertical and horizontal velocity of 30 feet per second. Choose the letter for the best answer.

3. If she achieves her goal, how long will her shot stay in the air?

A 1.65 s

B 1.87 s

C 2.07 s

D 2.27 s

4. If she achieves her goal, what horizontal distance will the shot travel?

A 41.4 ft

B 56.1 ft

C 62.1 ft

D 68.1 ft

Notes

Solving Quadratic Inequalities
Going Deeper

Essential question: How can you visualize the solution of a quadratic inequality?

COMMON Standards for
CORE Mathematical Content

CC.9-12.A.CED.1 Create equations and inequalities in one variable and use them to solve problems. Include equations arising from linear and quadratic functions....*

CC.9-12.A.CED.3 Represent constraints by equations or inequalities, and by systems of equations and/or inequalities, and interpret solutions as viable or non-viable options in a modeling context.*

CC.9-12.A.REI.11 Explain why the x-coordinates of the points where the graphs of the equations $y = f(x)$ and $y = g(x)$ intersect are the solutions of the equation $f(x) = g(x)$; find the solutions approximately, e.g. using technology to graph the functions, make tables of values, or find successive approximations...*

Math Background

Quadratic inequalities can be used to solve many real-world problems. Functions related to area are typically quadratic and inequalities involving these functions can be solved using the methods described in this lesson. Other applications include profit functions and functions that model the motion of a particle thrown into the air.

INTRODUCE

Review linear inequalities with students. Then remind students how to solve quadratic equations in one variable. Point out that solving quadratic inequalities is similar to solving linear inequalities. Tell students that in this lesson, they will learn graphing methods for solving quadratic inequalities.

TEACH

EXAMPLE

Questioning Strategies

• When solving the inequality, why do you look at points on the parabola that are graphed at or below the line $y = 7$? **The inequality includes the symbol for less than or equal to.**

• How is subtracting 7 from both sides of the inequality similar to transforming the graph of the parabola? **It is like translating the graph down 7 units.**

EXTRA EXAMPLE

Solve $x^2 + 4x - 18 < 3$ by graphing each side of the inequality as a function. **$-7 < x < 3$**

CLOSE

Essential Question

How can you visualize the solution of a quadratic inequality?
The solution of a quadratic inequality in the form $ax^2 + bx + c > 0$ is the set of x-coordinates from the points on the part of the parabola $y = ax^2 + bx + c$ that is graphed above the x-axis. The solution of a quadratic inequality in the form $ax^2 + bx + c < 0$ is the set of x-coordinates from the points on the part of the parabola $y = ax^2 + bx + c$ that is graphed below the x-axis.

Summarize

Have students write a journal entry describing how to solve a quadratic inequality by graphing. They should explain two different methods for solving the inequality $x^2 - 2x - 8 < 7$. The journal entry should also compare and contrast quadratic inequalities with linear inequalities.

The exercises provide students with opportunities to address Mathematical Practices Standard 5 (Use appropriate tools strategically). Students use technology to graph equations and to find the intersection of two curves. By graphing, they are able to solve quadratic inequalities in two ways.

PRACTICE

Where skills are taught	Where skills are practiced
1 EXAMPLE	EXS. 1–18

2-7

Solving Quadratic Inequalities
Going Deeper

Essential question: *How can you visualize the solution of a quadratic inequality?*

Video Tutor

CC.9-12.A.CED.1

1 EXAMPLE Solve a Quadratic Inequality in More Than One Way

Solve $x^2 - 2x - 8 \leq 7$ by graphing each side of the inequality as a function.

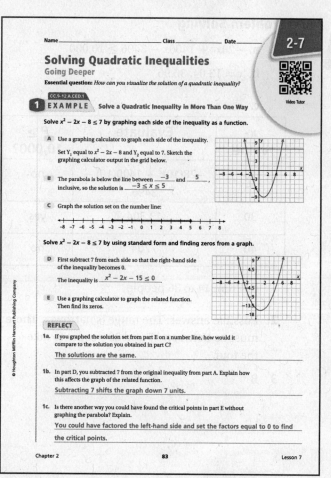

A Use a graphing calculator to graph each side of the inequality.

Set Y_1 equal to $x^2 - 2x - 8$ and Y_2 equal to 7. Sketch the graphing calculator output in the grid below.

B The parabola is below the line between ___−3___ and ___5___, inclusive, so the solution is ___$-3 \leq x \leq 5$___.

C Graph the solution set on the number line:

Solve $x^2 - 2x - 8 \leq 7$ by using standard form and finding zeros from a graph.

D First subtract 7 from each side so that the right-hand side of the inequality becomes 0.

The inequality is ___$x^2 - 2x - 15 \leq 0$___.

E Use a graphing calculator to graph the related function. Then find its zeros.

REFLECT

1a. If you graphed the solution set from part E on a number line, how would it compare to the solution you obtained in part C?

The solutions are the same.

1b. In part D, you subtracted 7 from the original inequality from part A. Explain how this affects the graph of the related function.

Subtracting 7 shifts the graph down 7 units.

1c. Is there another way you could have found the critical points in part E without graphing the parabola? Explain.

You could have factored the left-hand side and set the factors equal to 0 to find the critical points.

PRACTICE

Solve each inequality by graphing.

1. $x^2 - 7 < 2$

    ___$-3 < x < 3$___

2. $x^2 + 8x - 15 \leq 5$

    ___$-10 \leq x \leq 2$___

3. $x^2 + 4x + 5 \geq 1$

    ___$x \geq -2$___

4. $x^2 + 5x + 1 > -3$

    ___$x > -1$ or $x < -4$___

5. $x^2 - 10x + 18 < 2$

    ___$2 < x < 8$___

6. $x^2 - x - 50 \leq 6$

    ___$-7 \leq x \leq 8$___

7. $x^2 + 8x + 10 \geq 3$

    ___$x \leq -7$ or $x \geq -1$___

8. $x^2 + x - 14 \geq 6$

    ___$x \leq -5$ or $x \geq 4$___

Solve each inequality using any method. Explain your choice.

9. $x^2 + 4x - 1 < 4$

    ___$-5 < x < 1$___

10. $x^2 + 3x + 4 \leq 2$

    ___$-2 \leq x \leq -1$___

11. $x^2 + 7x - 10 \geq 8$

    ___$x \leq -9$ or $x \geq 2$___

12. $x^2 + 2x - 60 > 3$

    ___$-9 < x < 7$___

13. $2x^2 - 9x - 1 < 4$

    ___$-\frac{1}{2} < x < 5$___

14. $3x^2 - 7x + 1 \leq -1$

    ___$\frac{1}{3} \leq x \leq 2$___

15. $2x^2 + 13x + 10 \geq 4$

    ___$x \leq -6$ or $x \geq -\frac{1}{2}$___

16. $5x^2 - 36x - 30 < 2$

    ___$-\frac{4}{5} < x < 8$___

17. Which types of quadratic inequalities do you prefer to solve by graphing rather than algebraically? Explain.

Answers will vary. Sample: It is easier to solve quadratic inequalities in which the

leading coefficient is not equal to 1 by graphing because it is difficult to factor

quadratic expressions when the leading coefficient is not equal to 1.

18. Explain why solving the inequality $x^2 - 2x - 30 < 5$ is the same as solving the inequality $x^2 - 2x - 35 < 0$. Give both an algebraic and a graphical explanation.

Algebraic: The inequalities are the same because the second inequality is obtained

by subtracting 5 from each side in the first inequality.

Geometric: The second graph is the first graph translated down 5 units, so the

x-values identified in the solution remain the same.

Notes

Assign these pages to help your students practice and apply important lesson concepts. For additional exercises, see the Student Edition.

Answers

Additional Practice

1.

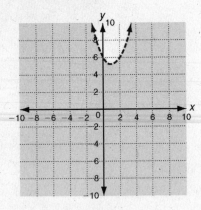

2.

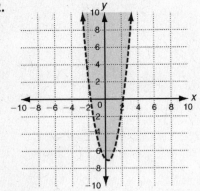

3. $-7 \leq x \leq 4$ **4.** $x < 3$ or $x > 6$

5. $x < -1$ or $x > 3$ **6.** $-5 < x < -1$

7. $x \leq 2$ or $x \geq 6$ **8.** $-\frac{4}{3} \leq x \leq 1$

9. More than 30 but fewer than 60

Problem Solving

1. a. $-28x^2 + 1400x - 3496 \geq 10,000$

b. $x = 13.04, 36.96$

c.

x-value	Evaluate	$P \geq$ 10,000?
10	$-28(10)^2 + 1400(10) - 3496$	no
30	13,304	yes
40	7704	no

d. From 14 to 36 people

2. Possible answer: The range is narrower. There must be between 17 and 33 people to take the tour.

3. B   **4.** B

Name_____ Class_____ Date_____

Additional Practice

Graph each inequality.

1. $y < x^2 - 2x + 6$

2. $y > 2x^2 - x - 7$

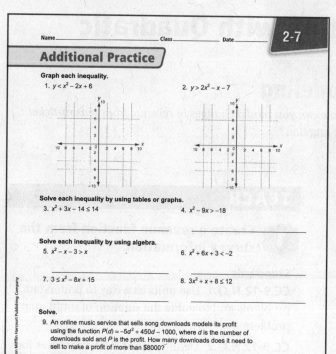

Solve each inequality by using tables or graphs.

3. $x^2 + 3x - 14 \le 14$

4. $x^2 - 9x > -18$

Solve each inequality by using algebra.

5. $x^2 - x - 3 > x$

6. $x^2 + 6x + 3 < -2$

7. $3 \le x^2 - 8x + 15$

8. $3x^2 + x + 8 \le 12$

Solve.

9. An online music service that sells song downloads models its profit using the function $P(d) = -5d^2 + 450d - 1000$, where d is the number of downloads sold and P is the profit. How many downloads does it need to sell to make a profit of more than $8000?

Problem Solving

The manager at Travel Tours is proposing a fall tour to Australia and New Zealand. He works out the details and finds that the profit P for x persons is $P(x) = -28x^2 + 1400x - 3496$. The owner of Travel Tours has decided that the tour will be canceled if the profit is less than $10,000.

1. a. Write an inequality that you could use to find the number of people needed to make the tour possible.　_____

   b. Solve the related equation to find the critical values.　_____

   c. Test an x-value in each interval.

x-value	Evaluate	$P \ge 10,000$?
10	$-28(10)^2 + 1400(10) - 3496$	
30		
40		

   d. How many people will Travel Tours need to make the tour possible?　_____

2. A year later, the owner of Travel Tours decides that the Australia/New Zealand tour will have to make a profit of at least $12,000 for the tour to be possible. What effect will this have on the range of people able to take this tour?

The manager plans a tour to the Fiji Islands and determines that the profit P for x persons is $P(x) = -40x^2 + 1920x - 3200$. Choose the letter for the best answer.

3. In order to make $10,000 profit, how many people will it take for this tour to happen?

   A Between 9 and 39 people

   B Between 14 and 36 people

   C At least 22 people

   D At least 30 people

4. The owner thinks the company should make at least $15,000 profit on the Fiji Islands tour. How many people will it take for the tour to happen?

   A Between 9 and 39 people

   B Between 13 and 35 people

   C At least 22 people

   D At least 35 people

Curve Fitting with Quadratic Models
Focus on Modeling

Essential question: *How can you model changes in revenue from season-ticket sales using a quadratic function?*

COMMON CORE Standards for Mathematical Content

The following standards are addressed in this lesson. (An asterisk indicates that a standard is also a Modeling standard.) For more detailed information, see each section of the lesson.

Number and Quantity: CC.9-12.N.Q.1*, CC.9-12.N.Q.2*

Algebra: CC.9-12.A.SSE.1*, CC.9-12.A.APR.1, CC.9-12.A.CED.1*, CC.9-12.A.CED.2*, CC.9-12.A.CED.3*, CC.9-12.A.REI.3, CC.9-12.A.REI.4

Functions: CC.9-12.F.IF.2, CC.9-12.F.IF.4*, CC.9-12.F.IF.5*, CC.9-12.F.IF.6*, CC.9-12.F.IF.7*, CC.9-12.F.IF.7a*, CC.9-12.F.IF.8, CC.9-12.F.IF.8a, CC.9-12.F.BF.1* CC.9-12.F.BF.1a*

Prerequisites
- Quadratic functions in intercept form
- Quadratic functions in vertex form
- Real solutions of quadratic equations

Math Background
In this lesson, students write a quadratic function that models revenue from season-ticket sales. When they study calculus, students will learn how to use differentiation to solve maximization problems like this one. In the meantime, this modeling lesson will show students that the tools and concepts they already have at their disposal can be used to solve the problem.

INTRODUCE

Ask students to discuss the repercussions that may occur when a business raises the price of an item. Help students understand that, on the one hand, revenue (which is the price of the item times the number of items sold) is likely to increase. On the other hand, these gains could be offset by fewer items being sold. Explain to students that they will use a quadratic function to model a business situation involving a price increase.

TEACH

1 **Create a revenue function from the survey information.**

Standards
CC.9-12.N.Q.1 Use units as a way to understand problems and to guide the solution of multi-step problems; ...*

CC.9-12.N.Q.2 Define appropriate quantities for the purpose of descriptive modeling.*

CC.9-12.A.SSE.1 Interpret expressions that represent a quantity in terms of its context.*

CC.9-12.A.CED.2 Create equations in two ... variables to represent relationships between quantities; ...*

CC.9-12.F.IF.2 Use function notation, evaluate functions for inputs in their domains, and interpret statements that use function notation in terms of a context.

CC.9-12.F.BF.1 Write a function that describes a relationship between two quantities.*

CC.9-12.F.BF.1a Determine an explicit expression ... from a context.*

Questioning Strategies
- What is the current revenue from season-ticket sales? How do you know? **200 • $50 = $10,000; this is the value that you obtain from** $R(n)$ **when** $n = 0$.

- How can you use your revenue function to find the revenue after three $5 price increases? What is the price in this case? How many season-ticket holders are there? **Evaluate** $R(n)$ **when** $n = 3$; **price is $50 + $5 • 3 = $65; number of season-ticket holders is** $200 - 10 • 3 = 170$.

Teaching Strategy
If students have difficulty writing an expression for the number of season-ticket holders after n price increases, suggest that they make a table showing values of n and the corresponding numbers of season-ticket holders. Then, encourage students to look for and describe any patterns in the table.

Curve Fitting with Quadratic Models
Focus on Modeling

Essential question: *How can you model changes in revenue from season-ticket sales using a quadratic function?*

Video Tutor

A community theater currently sells 200 season tickets at $50 each. In order to increase its season-ticket revenue without increasing the number of season tickets that it sells, the theater surveys its season-ticket holders to see if they would be willing to pay more. The survey finds that for every $5 increase in the price of a season ticket, the theater would lose 10 season-ticket holders. What action, if any, should the theater take to increase revenue?

1 Create a revenue function from the survey information.

A Let *n* be the number of $5 price increases in the cost of a season ticket. Write an expression for the cost of a season ticket after *n* price increases.

$50 + 5n$
_____

B Write an expression for the number of season-ticket holders after *n* price increases.

$200 - 10n$
_____

C The revenue generated from season-ticket sales is given below in words. Use this verbal model and your expressions from steps 1A and 1B to write an algebraic rule for the revenue function $R(n)$.

Revenue from season tickets	=	Number of season-ticket holders	·	Price of a season ticket

$$R(n) = (200 - 10n)(50 + 5n)$$

D As a check on your function rule, find the value of $R(0)$. Tell what this number represents and whether it agrees with the problem statement.

$R(0) = 10{,}000$; this is the current revenue and agrees with the problem.

REFLECT

1a. What units are associated with the expressions that you wrote in steps 1A and 1B?

For $50 + 5n$, the units are dollars per ticket; for $200 - 10n$, the units are tickets.

1b. When you multiply the units for the expressions, what units do you get for the revenue? Are they the units you expect?

Dollars; yes, because (dollars per ticket) · (tickets) = dollars

2 Determine the domain of the revenue function.

A Because *n* is the number of $5 price increases in the cost of a season ticket, you might think that the domain of the revenue function $R(n)$ is the set of whole numbers. However, given that increases in price result in losses of customers, what eventually happens to the number of season-ticket holders as *n* increases?

The number of season-ticket holders eventually becomes negative.

B Determine a constraint on the values of *n*. That is, write and solve an inequality that represents an upper bound on the values of *n*.

$200 - 10n \geq 0$; $n \leq 20$

C State a reasonable domain for the revenue function.

$\{0, 1, 2, \ldots, 20\}$

REFLECT

2. When the value of *n* reaches its upper bound, what will happen to the value of $R(n)$? Why?

$R(20) = 0$ because the number of season-ticket holders becomes 0.

3 Graph the revenue function.

A Complete the tables of values for the revenue function.

n	R(n)
0	10,000
1	10,450
2	10,800
3	11,050
4	11,200
5	11,250
6	11,200
7	11,050
8	10,800
9	10,450
10	10,000

n	R(n)
11	9,450
12	8,800
13	8,050
14	7,200
15	6,250
16	5,200
17	4,050
18	2,800
19	1,450
20	0

Notes

2 Determine the domain of the revenue function.

Standards
CC.9-12.A.CED.3 Represent constraints by ... inequalities, ... and interpret solutions as viable or nonviable options in a modeling context.*

CC.9-12.A.REI.3 Solve linear ... inequalities in one variable ...

CC.9-12.F.IF.2 Use function notation, evaluate functions for inputs in their domains, and interpret statements that use function notation in terms of a context.

CC.9-12.F.IF.5 Relate the domain of a function to its graph and, where applicable, to the quantitative relationship it describes.*

Questioning Strategies
- What happens if you evaluate the revenue function for $n = 21$? Why does this happen? $R(21)$ **is negative because the number of season-ticket holders becomes negative when $n = 21$.**
- What is the domain of a function? **The domain of a function is the values of the independent variable for which the function is defined.**
- What is meant by a *reasonable domain*? **A reasonable domain consists of the values of the independent variable that make sense in the context of the real-world situation.**

Teaching Strategy
If students are unable to determine the domain of the revenue function based on its equation, encourage them to move on and make the tables and/or graph in step 3 of the problem. Once students have had this additional hands-on experience working with the function, they may find it easier to describe the domain.

3 Graph the revenue function.

Standards
CC.9-12.N.Q.1 ... choose and interpret the scale and the origin in graphs and data displays.*

CC.9-12.A.CED.2 Create equations in two or more variables to represent relationships between quantities; graph equations on coordinate axes with labels and scales.*

CC.9-12.F.IF.7a Graph ... quadratic functions and show intercepts, maxima, and minima.*

Questioning Strategies
- In general, how do the values of $R(n)$ change in your tables? **They increase and then decrease.**
- What range of values should you show on the horizontal axis of your graph? on the vertical axis? $0 \leq n \leq 20;\ 0 \leq R(n) \leq 12{,}000$

Avoid Common Errors
When students draw the graph of $R(n)$, they may draw a smooth curve through the points they plotted. Remind them that a reasonable domain of $R(n)$ consists of whole-number values of n from 0 to 20, inclusive. Therefore, the graph of the function is actually a set of discrete points rather than a smooth curve.

4 Analyze the revenue function.

Standards
CC.9-12.F.IF.4 For a function that models a relationship between two quantities, interpret key features of graphs and tables in terms of the quantities ...*

Questioning Strategies
- Which values of n result in an increase in revenue? Which values of n result in a decrease in revenue? How do you know? $0 \leq n \leq 5$; **the plotted plots rise on the interval** $0 \leq n \leq 5$; $5 \leq n \leq 20$; **the plotted plots fall on the interval** $5 \leq n \leq 20$
- How can you find the maximum value of $R(n)$ from your tables? How can you find the maximum value from your graph? **Look for the greatest value in the $R(n)$ column; look for the highest point on the graph and read its y-coordinate.**

continued

B Graph the revenue function. Be sure to label the axes with the quantities they represent and indicate the axis scales by showing numbers for some grid lines.

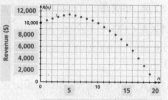

Number of price increases

REFLECT

3. Enter the revenue function on a graphing calculator. Set the viewing window to match that of the grid above, then graph the function. Is your graph identical to the one on the graphing calculator? If not, describe and explain any differences. Which graph is correct, and why?

Not identical; the graph is an unbroken curve rather than

discrete points. The manual graph is correct, because you can't sell a fraction

of a ticket.

4 Analyze the revenue function.

A For what values of n does $R(n)$ increase? For what values of n does $R(n)$ decrease?

$0 \le n \le 5;\ 5 \le n \le 20$

B At what value of n does $R(n)$ take on its maximum value? What is the maximum value?

$n = 5;\ R(5) = 11{,}250$

C Write a brief paragraph describing what action the theater should take to maximize revenue. Include what happens to the number of season-ticket holders as well as the season-ticket price.

Maximize revenue by increasing the price of a season ticket to $75.

The number of ticket holders drops to 150, but revenue increases to

$11,250.

REFLECT

4. Identify the intercepts of the graph, and explain what they represent in the context of generating revenue from season-ticket sales.

Vertical intercept: 10,000, the current revenue;

horizontal intercept: 20, the greatest number of price increases

EXTEND

1. Show that the revenue function from step 1C is a quadratic function by multiplying the two factors and collecting like terms to obtain a function of the form $R(n) = an^2 + bn + c$ where a, b, and c are constants.

$R(n) = (200 - 10n)(50 + 5n) = 10{,}000 + 1{,}000n - 500n - 50n^2 =$

$-50n^2 + 500n + 10{,}000$

2. A quadratic function $f(x) = ax^2 + bx + c$ has a maximum value at $x = -\frac{b}{2a}$ if $a < 0$ or a minimum value at $x = -\frac{b}{2a}$ if $a > 0$. Confirm that this property is true for the rewritten revenue function from Exercise 1.

For $R(n) = -50n^2 + 500n + 10{,}000$, $a = -50$ and $b = 500$, so

$-\frac{b}{2a} = 5$, which agrees with the fact that the function has a

maximum at $n = 5$.

3. Complete the square on the rewritten revenue function from Exercise 1 to obtain a function of the form $R(n) = a(n - h)^2 + k$ where a, h, and k are constants. Using this vertex form, identify the vertex of the graph of $R(n)$ and check to see whether it agrees with your answers for step 4B.

$R(n) = -50n^2 + 500n + 10{,}000 = -50(n^2 - 10n) + 10{,}000 =$

$-50(n^2 - 10n + 25) + 10{,}000 + 50(25) = -50(n - 5)^2 + 11{,}250,$

so a maximum of 11,250 occurs at $n = 5$.

continued

Teaching Strategy

You may wish to have students use their calculators to find the maximum. To do so, have students display the graph on the calculator. Then, have them press **2nd** **TRACE** and select **4:maximum**. The calculator will ask for a left bound, a right bound, and a guess. Students should use the arrow keys to move along the graph to enter these values. Once the guess has been entered, the calculator will give the coordinates of the vertex, whose y-coordinate is the function's maximum.

CLOSE

Essential Question

How can you model changes in revenue from season-ticket sales using a quadratic function? Write expressions for the cost of a ticket after n price increases and for the number of season-ticket holders after n price increases. Use these expressions to write a quadratic revenue function $R(n)$. Then, use a table or graph to find the maximum value of $R(n)$.

Summarize

Have students write a journal entry in which they provide a one-page summary of their findings for the manager of the community theater.

> ⋰ MATHEMATICAL **Highlighting**
> PRACTICE **the Standards**
>
> If you have students summarize their findings as suggested in the preceding Summarize note, you can use the summaries to address Mathematical Practice Standard 3 (Construct viable arguments and critique the reasoning of others). Have pairs of students exchange their summaries and comment on the clarity and completeness of the argument made by their partner to the manager of the community theater.

EXTEND

CC.9-12.A.APR.1 ... multiply polynomials. **(Ex. 1)**

CC.9-12.A.CED.1 Create equations ... in one variable and use them to solve problems.* **(Ex. 6)**

CC.9-12.A.REI.4 Solve quadratic equations in one variable. **(Ex. 6)**

CC.9-12.F.IF.4 For a function that models a relationship between two quantities, interpret key features of graphs and tables in terms of the quantities, ... * **(Exs. 2, 7)**

CC.9-12.F.IF.6 Calculate and interpret the average rate of change of a function (presented ... as a table) over a specified interval ... * **(Ex. 5)**

CC.9-12.F.IF.8a Use the process of factoring and completing the square in a quadratic function to show ... extreme values, and symmetry of the graph, and interpret these in terms of a context. **(Exs. 3, 4)**

4. When graphing the revenue function in step 3B, you may have noticed that $R(0) = R(10)$, $R(1) = R(9)$, $R(2) = R(8)$, $R(3) = R(7)$, and $R(4) = R(6)$. Use the rewritten revenue function from Exercise 3 to explain those observations.

Each pair of n-values (0 and 10, 1 and 9, etc.) is the same

distance from 5, so $(n - 5)^2$, and therefore $R(n)$, has the same

value for each pair.

5. Using your tables of values from step 3A, calculate the rate of change in $R(n)$ for consecutive values of n. (The rate of change in $R(n)$ is given by the fraction $\frac{\text{change in } R(n)}{\text{change in } n}$, but because the values of n are consecutive whole numbers, the change in n is always 1 and the rate of change in $R(n)$ is just the change in $R(n)$.) Describe what happens to the rates of change in $R(n)$, and relate them to your answers to the questions in step 4A.

n	$R(n)$	Change in $R(n)$		n	$R(n)$	Change in $R(n)$
0	10,000	—		11	9,450	−550
1	10,450	450		12	8,800	−650
2	10,800	350		13	8,050	−750
3	11,050	250		14	7,200	−850
4	11,200	150		15	6,250	−950
5	11,250	50		16	5,200	−1050
6	11,200	−50		17	4,050	−1150
7	11,050	−150		18	2,800	−1250
8	10,800	−250		19	1,450	−1350
9	10,450	−350		20	0	−1450
10	10,000	−450				

The changes are positive and then negative, which means

that $R(n)$ increases and then decreases.

6. Rather than maximize season-ticket revenue, suppose the theater wants to increase the current revenue by just 8%. Using the revenue function from step 1C, write and solve a quadratic equation, and interpret the solution(s).

_$(200 - 10n)(50 + 5n) = 1.08(10,000)$; $-50n^2 + 500n + 10,000 =$_

$10,800$; $n^2 - 10n + 16 = 0$; $(n - 2)(n - 8) = 0$; $n = 2$ or 8; set

ticket price at \$60 or \$90

7. Predict what would happen to revenue if the theater lost fewer than 10 season-ticket holders for every \$5 increase in the price of a ticket. Then check your prediction by creating and analyzing a model for the situation.

Prediction: The maximum revenue would increase. For instance, if only

5 season-ticket holders are lost per \$5 increase, the revenue function is

$R(n) = (200 - 5n)(50 + 5n)$ and the maximum revenue is \$15,625.

Notes

Assign these pages to help your students practice
and apply important lesson concepts. For
additional exercises, see the Student Edition.

Answers

Additional Practice

1. Yes, because all the second differences are 2

2. No, because the second differences are not
   constant

3. $f(x) = x^2 + 2x - 8$

4. $f(x) = -x^2 + 8x - 7$

5. $f(x) = x^2 - 4x - 6$ 6. $f(x) = 2x^2 - x + 3$

7. a. $E = 2v^2$

   b. 50 joules

   c. 8 m/s

Problem Solving

1. a. Yes; possible answer: the first differences of
      the y-values in the table are not constant.
      The second differences are constant (3).
      So this data represents a quadratic function.

   b. $\begin{cases} 25a + 5b + c = 7 \\ 100a + 10b + c = 17 \\ 400a + 20b + c = 46 \end{cases}$

   c. $a = 0.06$, $b = 1.1$, $c = 0$

   d. $f(x) = 0.06x^2 + 1.1x$

   e. 282 ft

2. B   3. C

Notes

Additional Practice

Determine whether each data set could represent a quadratic function. Explain.

1.

x	−1	0	1	2	3
y	35	22	11	2	−5

_____

2.

x	−2	0	2	4	6
y	18	10	6	2	1

_____

Write a quadratic equation that fits each set of points.

3. (0, −8), (2, 0), and (−3, −5)

4. (−1, −16), (2, 5), and (5, 8)

5. (−2, 6), (0, −6), and (3, −9)

6. (1, 4), (−2, 13), and (0, 3)

Solve.

7. The data table shows the energy, E, of a certain object in joules at a given velocity, v, in meters per second.

Energy (joules)	4.5	12.5	24.5	40.5
Velocity (m/s)	1.5	2.5	3.5	4.5

a. Find the quadratic relationship between the energy and velocity of the object. _____

b. What is the energy of an object with a speed of 5 m/s? _____

c. What is the velocity of the object if the energy is 128 joules? _____

Problem Solving

Ellen and Kelly test Ellen's new car in an empty parking lot. They mark a braking line where Ellen applies the brakes. Kelly then measures the distance from that line to the place where Ellen stops, for speeds from 5 miles per hour to 25 miles per hour.

Brake Test					
Speed (mi/h)	5	10	15	20	25
Stopping Distance (ft)	7	17	30	46	65

1. Ellen wants to know the stopping distance at 60 miles per hour. She cannot drive the car at this speed in the parking lot, so they decide to try curve fitting, using the data they have collected.

a. Can you use a quadratic function to represent the data in the table? Explain how you know.

_____

_____

b. Use three points to write a system of equations to find a, b, and c in $f(x) = ax^2 + bx + c$. _____

c. Use any method to solve 3 equations with 3 variables. Find the values for a, b, and c. _____

d. Write the quadratic function that models the stopping distance of Ellen's car. _____

e. What is the stopping distance of Ellen's car at 60 miles per hour? _____

The table shows the sizes and prices of decorative square patio tiles. Choose the letter for the best answer.

Patio Tiles Sale					
Side Length (in.)	6	9	12	15	18
Price Each ($)	1.44	3.24	5.76	9.00	12.96

2. What quadratic function models the price of the patio tiles?

A $P(x) = 0.4x^2$

B $P(x) = 0.04x^2$

C $P(x) = 0.04x^2 + 0.4x$

D $P(x) = 0.04x^2 + x + 0.4$

3. What is the second difference constant for the data in the table?

A 1.44

B 1.08

C 0.72

D 0.36

Operations with Complex Numbers
Going Deeper

Essential question: *How do you add, subtract, multiply, and divide complex numbers?*

COMMON CORE **Standards for Mathematical Content**

CC.9-12.N.CN.1 Know there is a complex number i such that $i^2 = -1$, and every complex number has the form $a + bi$ with a and b real.

CC.9-12.N.CN.2 Use the relation $i^2 = -1$ and the commutative, associative, and distributive properties to add, subtract, and multiply complex numbers.

CC.9-12.N.CN.3(+) Find the conjugate of a complex number; use conjugates to find moduli and quotients of complex numbers.

Vocabulary

imaginary unit   complex number

imaginary number   pure imaginary number

conjugate   absolute value

Prerequisites

Solving quadratic equations

Adding and multiplying binomials

Pythagorean Theorem

Math Background

Solving some quadratic equations requires taking square roots of negative numbers. Such equations have no real solutions. However, the solutions can be expressed using complex numbers. A complex number is of the form $a + bi$, where a and b are real numbers and $i = \sqrt{-1}$. If $b = 0$, the complex number is a real number. If $a = 0$, it is an imaginary number.

This lesson presents three mathematical concepts: (1) what the conjugate of a complex number is, (2) what the absolute value (modulus) of a complex number is and how conjugates are related to absolute value, and (3) what it means to divide complex numbers and the role that conjugates play in the division process.

Although the definition of a conjugate (i.e., that the conjugate of a complex number $z = a + bi$ is $\bar{z} = a - bi$) is simple, students need to understand that it is essentially three definitions rolled into one: (1) for a real number a, the conjugate is just a;

(2) for an imaginary number bi, the conjugate is $-bi$; and (3) for all other complex numbers $a + bi$, the conjugate is $a - bi$.

The definition of the absolute value of a complex number is most easily understood from a geometric point of view by plotting the complex number in the complex plane. The absolute value of $z = a + bi$ can then be interpreted as the distance of the point (a, bi) from the origin.

The idea of distance is an extension of the geometric interpretation of the absolute value of a real number: If a is a real number plotted on the real number line, then $|a|$ is the distance of a from 0. Students should understand the connection between these two notions of absolute value: Given that $|z|$ is defined to be $\sqrt{a^2 + b^2}$, you can write the real number a in the complex form $a + 0i$ so that $|a| = \sqrt{a^2 + 0^2} = \sqrt{a^2}$. Taking the square root of the square of the real number a always results in either a if $a \geq 0$ or $-a$ if $a < 0$. Returning to the geometric interpretation of absolute value, you know that on the real number line, every nonzero real number and its opposite have the same absolute value. The analogue to this fact in the complex plane is that all complex numbers that lie on the circle centered at the origin with radius $\sqrt{a^2 + b^2}$ have the same absolute value. Among these points are $z = a + bi$, $\bar{z} = a - bi$, $-z = -a - bi$, and $-\bar{z} = -a + bi$.

INTRODUCE

Review the discriminant $b^2 - 4ac$ from the quadratic formula. Remind students that if the discriminant is negative, a quadratic equation has no real solutions. This is because solving the quadratic formula when the discriminant is negative requires taking the square root of a negative number. In this lesson, students will learn how to express such solutions using complex numbers.

Remind students that the product of two complex numbers can be found using the FOIL method. Make sure students understand that i^2 is -1 so that they can simplify the results of the FOIL method.

Name_____ Class_____ Date_____

Operations with Complex Numbers
Going Deeper

2-9

Video Tutor

Essential question: *How do you add, subtract, and multiply complex numbers?*

To add or subtract complex numbers, add or subtract their real parts and add or subtract their nonreal parts. You can use the distributive property to add or subtract the nonreal parts. For instance, $3i + 2i = (3 + 2)i = 5i$.

CC.9-12.N.CN.2

1 EXAMPLE   Adding and Subtracting Complex Numbers

A $(8 + 3i) + (7 + 5i) = \left(\boxed{8} + \boxed{7} \right) + \left(\boxed{3}i + \boxed{5}i \right)$ Collect real parts, and collect nonreal parts.

$= \boxed{15} + \boxed{8}i$ Add real parts, and add nonreal parts.

B $(8 + 3i) - (7 + 5i) = \left(\boxed{8} - \boxed{7} \right) + \left(\boxed{3}i - \boxed{5}i \right)$ Collect real parts, and collect nonreal parts.

$= \boxed{1} + \left(\boxed{-2i} \right)$ Subtract real parts, and subtract nonreal parts.

$= \boxed{1} - 2i$ Write the number without parentheses.

REFLECT

1a. Give an example of two complex numbers whose sum is a real number. Find the sum of the numbers.

Sample answer: $2 + 3i$ and $2 - 3i$; $(2 + 3i) + (2 - 3i) = 4$

1b. Give an example of two complex numbers whose sum is an imaginary number. Find the sum of the numbers.

Sample answer: $-5 + 2i$ and $5 + 6i$; $(-5 + 2i) + (5 + 6i) = 8i$

1c. What properties (extended to nonreal numbers) allow you to collect the real parts and nonreal parts of two complex numbers being added?

Commutative and associative properties of addition

To multiply two complex numbers, use the distributive property to multiply each part of one of the numbers with each part of the other. Then simplify by using the fact that $i^2 = -1$ and combining like terms. The general multiplication pattern is shown below.

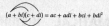
$(a + bi)(c + di) = ac + adi + bci + bdi^2$

CC.9-12.N.CN.2

2 EXAMPLE   Multiplying Complex Numbers

A $(5 + 3i)(9 + 8i) = 45 + \boxed{40}i + \boxed{27}i + 24i^2$ Multiply.

$= 45 + \boxed{40}i + \boxed{27}i + 24(-1)$ $i^2 = -1$

$= 21 + 67i$ Combine like terms.

B $(8 + 12i)(4 - 2i) = 32 - 16i + 48i + \left(\boxed{-24i^2} \right)$ Multiply.

$= 32 + 32i + \boxed{24}$ $i^2 = -1$

$= 56 + 32i$ Combine like terms.

REFLECT

2a. How is multiplying $(5 + 3i)(9 + 8i)$ like multiplying $(5 + 3x)(9 + 8x)$? How is it different?

The distributive property is used to multiply both expressions. For the first expression, you need to replace i^2 with -1 and combine the like terms. For the second expression, you only combine the like terms.

2b. What is the product of $a + bi$ and $a - bi$ where a and b are real numbers, $a \neq 0$, and $b \neq 0$? Classify the product as a real number or a nonreal number. Explain.

$(a + bi)(a - bi) = a^2 - abi + abi - (bi)^2 = a^2 + b^2$; because a and b are real numbers, the product is a real number.

2c. What is the square of $a + bi$ where a and b are real numbers, $a \neq 0$, and $b \neq 0$? Classify the square as a real number, an imaginary number, or neither.

$(a + bi)^2 = a^2 + 2abi + (bi)^2 = (a^2 - b^2) + 2abi$; because $a \neq 0$ and $b \neq 0$, $2ab \neq 0$, so the square is neither.

2d. If you multiply a nonzero real number and a nonreal number, is the product real or nonreal? Explain.

Nonreal; $a(b + ci) = ab + aci$, which is nonreal since ab and ac are real and $ac \neq 0$.

Notes

1 EXAMPLE

Questioning Strategies

- Can the sum of two complex numbers be 0? **Yes, if both the real parts and the nonreal parts are opposites of each other**

- When is the sum of two complex numbers an imaginary number? **when the real parts are opposites**

EXTRA EXAMPLE
Add or subtract.

A. $(6 + 3i) + (-2 + 5i)$ $4 + 8i$

B. $(-2 + 7i) - (3 + i)$ $-5 + 6i$

2 EXAMPLE

Questioning Strategies

- How is multiplying two complex numbers similar to the FOIL method? **The same steps are used when multiplying two complex numbers as when multiplying two binomials.**

- If you use the FOIL method to multiply two complex numbers, which of the F, O, I, or L products are real? Which are nonreal? **F and L; O and I**

- Why isn't the product of two complex numbers a trinomial? **The product of two complex numbers has an i^2-term. Since $i^2 = -1$, the i^2-term is real and can be added to the other real term.**

Avoid Common Errors
Remind students that after they use FOIL to multiply two imaginary numbers, they are not finished simplifying the result until the answer is in the form $a + bi$. That means that the i^2-term must be simplified and added to the other real term.

Teaching Strategy
Reinforce how FOIL is used to multiply two binomials, such as the product of $2 + 3x$ and $1 - 4x$, before asking students to use FOIL to multiply two imaginary numbers, such as the product of $2 + 3i$ and $1 - 4i$. Show the work for the binomials and for the imaginary numbers side-by-side and ask students to point out the similarities and differences in the steps.

EXTRA EXAMPLE
Multiply.

A. $(4 + 2i)(3 + 5i)$ $2 + 26i$

B. $(-2 + 5i)(3 - 4i)$ $14 + 23i$

3 EXPLORE

Questioning Strategies

- Why is the product of a complex number and its conjugate always a real number? **If you use FOIL, the middle terms containing i add to zero. Since the coefficient of the i-term is zero, the number is real.**

4 ENGAGE

Questioning Strategies

- Why is the absolute value of a complex number always a real number? $|a + bi| = \sqrt{a^2 + b^2}$; **since a^2 and b^2 are both positive, $\sqrt{a^2 + b^2}$ is a real number.**

MATHEMATICAL PRACTICE   Highlighting the Standards

In **4 ENGAGE** and its Reflect questions, students address Mathematical Practice Standard 7 (Look for and make use of structure). By analyzing the graph and applying the Pythagorean Theorem, students find the relationship between the absolute value of a complex number and the coordinates of the complex number when graphed in the complex plane.

5 EXAMPLE

Questioning Strategies

- How is the absolute value of a complex number similar to the absolute value of a real number? **Both are real numbers indicating the distance of the number from the origin.**

EXTRA EXAMPLE
Compare the absolute values of $2 - i$ and $4 + 3i$.
$|2 - i| < |4 + 3i|$ because $\sqrt{5} < 5$.

Let $z = a + bi$ be a complex number. The **conjugate** of z is $\bar{z} = a - bi$. For example, the conjugate of $4 + 7i$ is $4 - 7i$.

Finding Products of Complex Numbers and Their Conjugates

A Complete the table.

z	$\bar{z}$	$z \cdot \bar{z}$
$4 + 7i$	$4 - 7i$	65
$5 - 2i$	$5 + 2i$	29
$3i$	$-3i$	9
-6	-6	36

B Generalize the results: If $z = a + bi$, then in terms of a and b,
$z \cdot \bar{z} = (a + bi)(a - bi) = a^2 - (bi)^2 = a^2 - b^2 i^2 = a^2 - b^2(-1) = \underline{\;a^2 + b^2\;}$.

REFLECT

3a. Is the product $z \cdot \bar{z}$ a real number or an nonreal number? Explain.

Real; a and b are real, and the sum of their squares is real.

Understanding the Absolute Value of a Complex Number

A complex number can be represented by a point in the *complex plane* having real numbers on its horizontal axis and pure imaginary numbers on its vertical axis. If $z = a + bi$, then the coordinates of the point representing z are (a, bi).

For any complex number not on one of the axes, you can draw a right triangle as shown. The lengths of the legs are the real numbers $|a|$ and $|b|$. The **absolute value** of the complex number z, written as $|z|$, is the length of the hypotenuse. The absolute value of z is also called the *modulus* of z.

For the special case of $z = a + 0i$, the graph of z is a point on the real axis, and $|z| = |a|$. Similarly, for the special case of $z = 0 + bi$, the graph of z is a point on the pure imaginary axis, and $|z| = |b|$.

REFLECT

4a. If $z = a + bi$, use the Pythagorean Theorem to express $|z|$ in terms of a and b. (Note that $|a|^2$ can simply be written as a^2 and $|b|^2$ as b^2.)

$|z| = \sqrt{|a|^2 + |b|^2} = \sqrt{a^2 + b^2}$

4b. Show that the formula you wrote for Question 2a also applies to the special cases $z = a + 0i$ and $z = 0 + bi$. Use the fact that if x is a real number, then $\sqrt{x^2} = |x|$.

If $z = a + 0i$, then $|z| = \sqrt{a^2 + 0^2} = \sqrt{a^2} = |a|$; if $z = 0 + bi$, then

$|z| = \sqrt{0^2 + b^2} = \sqrt{b^2} = |b|$.

4c. How is $|z|$ related to $z \cdot \bar{z}$?

$|z|^2 = z \cdot \bar{z}$ or $|z| = \sqrt{z \cdot \bar{z}}$

Comparing Absolute Values The set of real numbers is an *ordered set* because for any two real numbers a and b, you can determine whether $a < b$, $a = b$, or $a > b$. The set of complex numbers, however, is not an ordered set. For instance, you cannot compare the numbers $3 + 4i$ and $1 - 5i$ other than to say that they are not equal.

Because the absolute value of a complex number is a real number, you *can* compare the absolute values of two complex numbers. Just as you can interpret the absolute value of a real number geometrically as the number's distance from 0 on the real number line, you can interpret the absolute value of a complex number geometrically as the number's distance from the origin of the complex plane.

Comparing Absolute Values of Complex Numbers

Compare the absolute values of $3 + 4i$ and $1 - 5i$.

A Find each absolute value.

$|3 + 4i| = \sqrt{3^2 + 4^2} = \sqrt{25} = 5$

$|1 - 5i| = \sqrt{1^2 + (-5)^2} = \sqrt{26}$

B Compare the absolute values.

$|3 + 4i| < |1 - 5i|$ because $5 < \sqrt{26}$.

REFLECT

5a. What does the comparison of $|3 + 4i|$ and $|1 - 5i|$ tell you about the points in the complex plane representing $3 + 4i$ and $1 - 5i$?

The point representing $3 + 4i$ is closer to the origin of the complex plane than the point representing $1 - 5i$.

5b. In part A you found that $|3 + 4i| = 5$. Give three other complex numbers that have an absolute value of 5.

$-3 + 4i$, $-3 - 4i$, and $3 - 4i$ (although any $z = a + bi$ where $a^2 + b^2 = 25$ also works)

Notes

6 EXAMPLE

Questioning Strategies

- How is the conjugate of the denominator used to divide two complex numbers? **The numerator and denominator are both multiplied by the conjugate of the denominator to give an expression with a real number in the denominator.**

EXTRA EXAMPLE

Divide.

A. $\dfrac{9 + 3i}{3i}$ $1 - 3i$

B. $\dfrac{10 - 10i}{2 + i}$ $2 - 6i$

C. $\dfrac{4 + 2i}{3 + 3i}$ $1 - \dfrac{1}{3}i$

CLOSE

Essential Question

How do you add, subtract, multiply, and divide complex numbers?

Adding and subtracting complex numbers is similar to adding and subtracting binomial expressions with variables. You can use FOIL to multiply complex numbers; then, simplify so the answer is expressed as $a + bi$. If $z = a + bi$, then the conjugate of z is $a - bi$, and $|z| = \sqrt{a^2 + b^2}$. To divide complex numbers, you must first express them in fraction form and then multiply the numerator and the denominator by the conjugate of the denominator.

Summarize

Have students add examples to the graphic organizers shown below. Students can pair off, exchange their entries, and comment on the accuracy of the operations their partner did on complex numbers. Sample answers are given.

Nonreal Number: $a + bi, b \neq 0$
Sum: $(4 + 2i) + (-2 + i) = 2 + 3i$
Product: $(3 - 4i)(2 + 5i) = 26 + 7i$
Pure Imaginary Number: $bi, b \neq 0$
Sum: $-8i + 3i = -5i$
Product: $6i\,(4i) = -24$
Real Number: a
Sum: $6 + 3 = 9$
Product: $4(-2) = -8$

Have students add examples to the graphic organizer below to demonstrate what they have learned about dividing complex numbers.

$$\frac{z_1}{z_2} = \frac{3 + 2i}{1 + 2i} = \frac{3 + 2i}{1 + 2i} \cdot \frac{1 - 2i}{1 - 2i}$$

$$= \frac{(3 + 2i)(1 - 2i)}{(1 + 2i)(1 - 2i)}$$

$$= \frac{3 + 2i - 6i - 4i^2}{5}$$

$$= \frac{7}{5} - \frac{4}{5}i$$

PRACTICE

Where skills are taught	Where skills are practiced
1 EXAMPLE	EXS. 1–4
2 EXAMPLE	EXS. 5–10
4 ENGAGE	EXS. 12–14
5 EXAMPLE	EXS. 15–16
6 EXAMPLE	EXS. 17–19

Exercise 11: Students simply $i^{18} \cdot i^{23}$ in two ways.

Exercises 20–23: Students explore properties of the absolute value of complex numbers.

Dividing Complex Numbers To divide two complex numbers $a + bi$ and $c + di$, express the quotient as $\frac{a+bi}{c+di}$. You can write this fraction as a single complex number by multiplying the numerator and denominator by the conjugate of the denominator and then simplifying.

CC.9-12.N.CN.3(+)

6 EXAMPLE Dividing Complex Numbers

Divide.

A $\frac{6-4i}{2i} = \frac{6-4i}{2i} \cdot \frac{-2i}{-2i}$ Multiply the numerator and denominator by the conjugate of the denominator.

$= \frac{-8-12i}{4}$ Multiply the numerators, and multiply the denominators. Simplify each product.

$= -2 - 3i$ Write in the form $a + bi$.

B $\frac{10-15i}{2+i} = \frac{10-15i}{2+i} \cdot \frac{2-i}{2-i}$ Multiply the numerator and denominator by the conjugate of the denominator.

$= \frac{5-40i}{5}$ Multiply the numerators, and multiply the denominators. Simplify each product.

$= 1 - 8i$ Write in the form $a + bi$.

C $\frac{1}{2+2i} = \frac{1}{2+2i} \cdot \frac{2-2i}{2-2i}$ Multiply the numerator and denominator by the conjugate of the denominator.

$= \frac{2-2i}{8}$ Multiply the numerators, and multiply the denominators. Simplify each product.

$= \frac{1}{4} - \frac{1}{4}i$ Write in the form $a + bi$.

REFLECT

6a. How can you use multiplication to check the quotient that you obtain when you divide one complex number by another? Illustrate this procedure using the quotient from part A.

Multiply the quotient by the divisor to see if you get the dividend;

$(-2 - 3i)(2i) = -4i - 6i^2 = -4i - 6(-1) = 6 - 4i$.

6b. Find the absolute values of the dividend, the divisor, and the quotient in part A. How are these absolute values related?

$|6 - 4i| = \sqrt{52} = 2\sqrt{13}$, $|2i| = \sqrt{4} = 2$, and $|-2 - 3i| = \sqrt{13}$; the absolute value

of the dividend divided by the absolute value of the divisor gives the absolute

value of the quotient.

PRACTICE

Add or subtract.

1. $10i - 2i$ ___8i___

2. $9i - (13 + 7i)$ ___$-13 + 2i$___

3. $(9 - 8i) - (6 - 4i)$ ___$3 - 4i$___

4. $(3 + 15i) - (-5 + i)$ ___$8 + 14i$___

Multiply.

5. $-2(1 - 3i)$ ___$-2 + 6i$___

6. $5i(-5 + 2i)$ ___$-10 - 25i$___

7. $(4 - 8i)(5 - 6i)$ ___$-28 - 64i$___

8. $(5 + 4i)(3 + 9i)$ ___$-21 + 57i$___

9. $(1 + 2i)^2$ ___$-3 + 4i$___

10. $(2 - i)^2$ ___$3 - 4i$___

11. Find the values i^1, i^2, i^3, and i^4. Use these to find the product $i^{18} \cdot i^{23}$ two ways: (1) by simplifying each power before multiplying, and (2) by using the product of powers property and then simplifying.

$i^1 = i$, $i^2 = -1$, $i^3 = -i$, $i^4 = 1$

$i^{18} = -1$ and $i^{23} = -i$, so $i^{18} \cdot i^{23} = (-1)(-i) = i$; $i^{18} \cdot i^{23} = i^{41} = i$

Find the absolute value of each complex number.

12. $4 + 3i$ ___5___

13. $5i$ ___5___

14. $-3 - 2i$ ___$\sqrt{13}$___

Compare the absolute values of each pair of complex numbers.

15. $1 + 2i, 2 - i$ ___$|1 + 2i| = |2 - i|$___

16. $7 - 2i, 6 + 4i$ ___$|7 - 2i| > |6 + 4i|$___

Divide.

17. $\frac{-3-2i}{i}$ ___$-2 + 3i$___

18. $\frac{8-12i}{5+3i}$ ___$\frac{2}{17} - \frac{42}{17}i$___

19. $\frac{5+2i}{3+6i}$ ___$\frac{3}{5} - \frac{8}{15}i$___

20. For a complex number z, compare $|z|$ and $|\bar{z}|$. Explain the relationship two ways: using algebra and using a geometric interpretation.

$|z| = |\bar{z}|$; if $z = a + bi$, then $\bar{z} = a - bi$, $|z| = \sqrt{a^2 + b^2}$, and $|\bar{z}| = \sqrt{a^2 + (-b)^2} =$

$\sqrt{a^2 + b^2}$; $\bar{z}$ can be represented by the point $(a, -bi)$, which is the reflection in

the x-axis of the point (a, bi) representing z, so $\bar{z}$ is the same distance as z from

the origin.

21. For a real number a, $|a| = |-a|$. Show that this property also applies to a complex number and its opposite.

If $z = a + bi$, then $-z = -a - bi$ and $|-z| = |-a - bi| = \sqrt{(-a)^2 + (-b)^2} =$

$\sqrt{a^2 + b^2} = |z|$.

Notes

ADDITIONAL PRACTICE AND PROBLEM SOLVING

Assign these pages to help your students practice and apply important lesson concepts. For additional exercises, see the Student Edition.

Answers

Additional Practice

1–5.

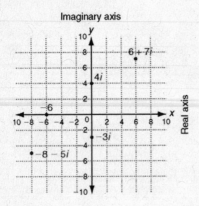

6. $2\sqrt{5}$ **7.** $\sqrt{26}$

8. 3   **9.** $5 - 7i$

10. $-1 - 10i$ **11.** $-7 + 10i$

12. $9 + 6i$ **13.** $3 + 14i$

14. $9 + 20i$ **15.** $\dfrac{4}{3} - \dfrac{2}{3}i$

16. $\dfrac{14}{17} + \dfrac{5}{17}i$ **17.** $-2i$

18. $8 + 2i$

Problem Solving

1.

n	$Z_{n+1} = (Z_n)^2 + c$	Z_{n+1}
0	$Z_1 = 1 + 2i$	$Z_1 = 1 + 2i$
1	$Z_2 = (1 + 2i)^2 + 1$	$Z_2 = -2 + 4i$
2	$Z_3 = (-2 + 4i)^2 + 1$	$Z_3 = -11 - 16i$
3	$Z_4 = (-11 - 16i)^2 + 1$	$Z_4 = -134 + 352i$

2. $(-13, -35i)$; possible answer: this point cannot be generated using the given formula.

3. D   **4.** B

5. A   **6.** C

Name_____ Class_____ Date_____

Additional Practice

Graph each complex number.

1. -6
2. $4i$
3. $6 + 7i$
4. $-8 - 5i$
5. $-3i$

Find each absolute value.

6. $|4 + 2i|$

7. $|5 - i|$

8. $|-3i|$

_____ _____ _____

Add or subtract. Write the result in the form $a + bi$.

9. $(-1 + 2i) + (6 - 9i)$

10. $(3 - 3i) - (4 + 7i)$

11. $(-5 + 2i) + (-2 + 8i)$

_____ _____ _____

Multiply. Write the result in the form $a + bi$.

12. $3i(2 - 3i)$

13. $(4 + 5i)(2 + i)$

14. $(-1 + 6i)(3 - 2i)$

_____ _____ _____

Simplify.

15. $\dfrac{2 + 4i}{3i}$

16. $\dfrac{3 + 2i}{4 + i}$

17. $2i^{11}$

_____ _____ _____

Solve.

18. In electronics, the total resistance to the flow of electricity in a circuit is called the impedance, Z. Impedance is represented by a complex number. The total impedance in a series circuit is the sum of individual impedances. The impedance in one part of a circuit is $Z_1 = 3 + 4i$. In another part of a circuit, the impedance is $Z_1 = 5 - 2i$. What is the total impedance of the circuit?

_____

Problem Solving

Hannah and Aoki are designing fractals. Aoki recalls that many fractals are based on the Julia Set, whose formula is $Z_{n+1} = (Z_n)^2 + c$, where c is a constant. Hannah suggests they make their own fractal pattern using this formula, where $c = 1$ and $Z_1 = 1 + 2i$.

1. Complete the table to show values of n and Z_n.

n	$Z_{n+1} = (Z_n)^2 + c$	Z_n
0	$Z_1 = 1 + 2i$	$Z_1 = 1 + 2i$
1	$Z_2 = (1 + 2i)^2 + 1$	$Z_2 =$
2	$Z_3 = (_____)^2 + 1$	$Z_3 =$
3	$Z_4 = (_____)^2 + 1$	$Z_4 =$

2. Four points are shown on the complex plane. Which point is not part of the fractal pattern they have created? Explain.

_____

Choose the letter for the best answer.

3. Aoki creates a second pattern by changing the value of c to 3. What happens to Z_n as n increases?

   A The imaginary part is always twice the real part.

   B The real and imaginary parts become equal.

   C The real part becomes zero.

   D The imaginary part becomes zero.

5. Aoki takes Hannah's new formula, leaves $c = 1$, and sets $Z_1 = \dfrac{1}{1 + 2i}$. What is the value of Z_3?

   A $Z_3 = -11 - 16i$

   B $Z_3 = 2 + 2i$

   C $Z_3 = 0.48 - 0.16i$

   D $Z_3 = 147.4 + i$

4. Hannah changes the formula to $Z_{n+1} = \dfrac{1}{(Z_n)^2} + c$. Leaving $c = 1$ and $Z_1 = 1 + 2i$, what is the value of Z_2?

   A $0.48 - 0.16i$

   B $0.88 - 0.16i$

   C $1.2 - 0.4i$

   D $2.2 - 0.4i$

6. Hannah reverts to $Z_{n+1} = (Z_n)^2 + c$. She sets $Z_1 = i$ and $c = i$. Which statement is NOT true?

   A Z_n flip-flops between $(-1 + i)$ and $(-i)$.

   B The coefficient of i never reaches 2.

   C The imaginary part becomes zero.

   D On a graph $Z_1 - Z_3$ create a triangle.

Notes

This page provides students with the opportunity to apply concepts from the Common Core in real-world problem situations. There are three different levels of performance tasks:

⭐ **Novice:** These are short word problems that require students to apply the math they have learned in straightforward, real-world situations.

⭐⭐ **Apprentice:** These are more involved problems that guide students step-by-step through more complex tasks. These exercises include more complicated reasoning, writing, and open-ended elements.

⭐⭐⭐ **Expert:** These are open-ended, non-routine problems that, instead of stepping the students through, ask them to choose their own methods for solving and justify their answers and reasoning.

Sample answers

1. No; possible explanation: There is no solution to the system $\begin{cases} h = 15t - 4.9t^2 + 2 \\ h = 20 \end{cases}$, so the ball cannot hit the camera because it never reaches a height of 20 m.

2. Possible argument:

$$(a + bi)(a - bi) = a^2 + abi - abi - b^2(i^2)$$
$$= a^2 - (-1)\,b^2$$
$$= a^2 + b^2$$

So the product of a complex number and its conjugate has no imaginary part, and it is always a real number.

3. Scoring Guide:

Task	Possible points
a	1 point for correctly inserting the values into the formula and factoring, and 1 point for correctly finding the solutions: $75 = \frac{1}{2}(6)t^2$ $0 = 3t^2 - 75$ $0 = t^2 - 25$ $0 = (t + 5)(t - 5)$ $t = -5, 5$
b	1 point for identifying that the solutions represent times of 5 and -5 seconds, and 1 point for stating that the negative solution is irrelevant
c	1 point for correctly finding the reaction distance (before the brakes are engaged) to be (2 s)(28 m/s) = 56 m, and 1 point for finding the total distance, 75 m + 56 m = 131 m, and converting it to about 430 ft

Total possible points: 6

CHAPTER 2

COMMON
CORE
CC-9-12.N.CN.1, 2, 3
CC-9-12.A.REI.7
CC-9-12.F.IF.8a
CC-9-12.S.ID.6a

Performance Tasks

★ **1.** A football quarterback throws a long pass whose height h in meters can be modeled by $h = 15t - 4.9t^2 + 2$ where t is the time in seconds. A camera hangs from a wire 20 meters off the ground. Could the ball hit the camera? Explain your reasoning.

★ **2.** Give an argument that a complex number, $a + bi$, multiplied by its conjugate, always results in a real number.

★ **3.** Vehicle braking performance data uses 60 mph (or 28 m/s) to 0 mph. However, the published data is often unrealistic for the average driver and road conditions. To calculate how long it takes a vehicle to stop, assuming a constant deceleration, you can use the formula $d = \frac{1}{2}at^2$, where d is the distance traveled while stopping, a is the acceleration (deceleration), and t is the time. For a new hybrid car the published stopping distance is 75 meters and its constant deceleration is 6 m/s².

   a. Substitute the given values into $d = \frac{1}{2}at^2$ and simplify the equation. Group all the terms on one side of the equation and use factoring to solve.

   b. What do the solutions represent? Are all solutions meaningful? Explain.

   c. The stopping time provided does not include the driver recognition and reaction time, which can add about 2 seconds to the stopping time. Find the reaction distance by multiplying the speed (before stopping begins) times the reaction time. What is the total distance the vehicle travels, including the reaction distance? Convert this distance to feet using 1 m = 3.3 ft.

continued

★★★ **4.** Examine the data for plasma HDTVs of the same brand and model.

   a. What would you expect the maximum power consumption of a 54 inch HDTV of the same brand and model to be? Explain how you found your answer, and include any models you use and explain why you chose them.

   b. If the 54 inch plasma HDTV is on for 5 hours each day, what is the maximum number of kilowatt-hours it uses in a year? What is the maximum annual cost of operating a 54 inch plasma HDTV if electricity costs $0.12 per kilowatt-hour? (*Hint:* Kilowatt-hours can be found by multiplying the wattage of an item by the number of hours it is in use, then dividing by 1000.)

Plasma HDTVs	
Diagonal Screen Size (inch)	Maximum Power Consumption (watts)
42	485
46	526
50	584
60	800

4. Scoring Guide:

Task	Possible points
a	3 points for giving an appropriate model and explaining why they chose it, and 1 point for using that model to find the energy consumption for a 54-inch TV, for example: When graphed, the data follows part of a U-shaped curve, so I used a quadratic model, $W(x) = 0.514x^2 - 34.9x + 1044$, where x is the length of the diagonal in inches and W is the maximum power consumption in watts, and $W(54) \approx 658$ watts.
b	1 point for correctly finding the number of kilowatt-hours per year and 1 point for finding the maximum cost. Using the number of Watts given in part **a** gives an answer of about 1201 kilowatt-hours at a total cost of $144

Total possible points: 6

Standard	Items
CC.9-12.N.Q.1*	12
CC.9-12.N.CN.1	3
CC.9-12.N.CN.2	6, 14
CC.9-12.N.CN.3(+)	7, 8, 9
CC.9-12.N.CN.7	14
CC.9-12.A.SSE.3a*	5
CC.9-12.A.SSE.3b*	13
CC.9-12.A.CED.2*	11
CC.9-12.A.CED.3*	12
CC.9-12.A.REI.4b	14
CC.9-12.F.IF.4*	12
CC.9-12.F.IF.5*	12
CC.9-12.F.IF.7a*	10, 13
CC.9-12.F.IF.8a	2
CC.9-12.F.BF.1*	1, 12
CC.9-12.F.BF.3	4

TEST PREP DOCTOR ✚

Multiple Choice: Item 1
- Students who chose **A** or **B** did not include the reflection of the parent function.
- Students who chose **B** or **D** did not recognize the effect of $|a| < 1$, which is a vertical compression.

Multiple Choice: Item 2
- Students who chose **G** or **J** found the intercepts, not the axis of symmetry.
- Students who chose **H** either did not correctly evaluate the midpoint between the intercepts or thought that the y-axis is always the axis of symmetry.

Multiple Choice: Item 4
- Students who chose **G** mistakenly thought the graph is reflected across the y-axis. It is symmetric about the y-axis but reflected across the x-axis.
- Students who chose **H** or **J** confused the effect of h or k on the graph of the parent function with the effect of a on the parent graph.

Multiple Choice: Item 6
- Students who chose **F** did not find the middle term correctly with FOIL. They should have added $36i$ to $6i$ to get $42i$.
- Students who chose **G** may have incorrectly thought the product of $2i$ and $-9i$ is -18 instead of 18.
- Students who chose **J** added -12 and 18 incorrectly to get -6 instead of 6.

Multiple Choice: Item 10
- Students who chose **F** did not recognize the equivalence of this form of the function with the forms in **G** and **H**.
- Students who chose **G** did not recognize that the vertex is $(-1, 32)$.
- Students who chose **H** did not recognize the intercepts are -5 and 3.

Constructed Response: Item 11
- Likely errors in writing the function include writing a function for the area of the entire quilt with the border, or failing to account for needing a border on all four sides of the quilt, which increases both the length and the width by $2x$.
- Students who did not interpret the meaning of $f(0.5)$ correctly may not understand the functional dependence of area on the width of the border.

Constructed Response: Item 13
- Students may not have completed the square correctly. If they did complete the square correctly, they could have made an error with the signs of h and k in identifying the coordinates of the vertex.

CHAPTER 2 COMMON CORE ASSESSMENT READINESS

Name _____ Class _____ Date _____

MULTIPLE CHOICE

1. The graph of which function is a reflection and vertical stretch of the parent quadratic function?

A. $f(x) = 3x^2$ C. $f(x) = -3x^2$ (circled)

B. $f(x) = 0.3x^2$ D. $f(x) = -0.3x^2$

2. What is the axis of symmetry of the graph of $f(x) = (x + 1)(x + 5)$?

F. $x = -3$ (circled)   H. $x = 0$

G. $x = -1$ J. $x = 5$

3. What is the definition of a complex number?

A. A number of the form $a + bi$ where a and b are real (circled)

B. A number of the form $a + bi$ where $a = 0$ and b is real

C. A number of the form $a + bi$ where a is real and $b = 0$

D. A number of the form $a + bi$ where $a = 0$, b is real, and $b \neq 0$

4. Which of the following describes the graph of $f(x) = -2x^2$ as a transformation of the graph of the parent quadratic function?

F. reflection across the x-axis and vertical stretch by a factor of 2 (circled)

G. reflection across the y-axis and vertical shrink by a factor of 2

H. translation 2 units left

J. translation 2 units down

5. What is the minimum value of $f(x) = 5x^2 + 10x + 10$?

A. -5 C. 1

B. -1 D. 5 (circled)

6. What is the simplified form of the product $(-4 + 2i)(3 - 9i)$?

F. $6 - 42i$ H. $6 + 42i$ (circled)

G. $-30 - 42i$ J. $-6 + 42i$

7. What is the conjugate of $2 - 3i$?

A. $-2 - 3i$ C. $3 + 2i$

B. $2 + 3i$ (circled)   D. $3 - 2i$

8. What is the simplified form of the quotient $\frac{1 - 4i}{-2 + i}$?

F. $-2 + \frac{7}{5}i$ H. $\frac{2}{5} + 3i$

G. $-\frac{6}{5} + \frac{7}{5}i$ (circled)   J. $\frac{2}{5} + \frac{9}{5}i$

9. What is $|-1 - i|$?

A. $1 + i$ C. $\sqrt{2}$ (circled)

B. 1 D. 0

10. Which of the following functions does *not* have the graph shown below?

F. $f(x) = -2x^2 - 4x + 30$

G. $f(x) = -2(x + 1)^2 + 32$

H. $f(x) = -2(x + 5)(x - 3)$

J. $f(x) = -2(x - 5)(x + 3)$ (circled)

© Houghton Mifflin Harcourt Publishing Company

CONSTRUCTED RESPONSE

11. Amanda is adding a border to a rectangular quilt with a length of 4 feet and a width of 3 feet. The border has a width of x feet. Write a quadratic function $f(x)$ in standard form for the area of the border in square feet. What is $f(0.5)$ and what does it represent?

$f(x) = 4x^2 + 14x$; $f(0.5) = 8$; the area

in square feet of the border when the

width of the border is 0.5 foot

12. The function $f(x) = -16x^2 + 40x$ models the height in feet of a football x seconds after it is kicked from the ground.

a. Graph the function.

(graph: Height (ft) vs Time (s))

b. What does the origin of the graph represent?

The height of the ball when it is

kicked; the ball has a height of

0 feet after 0 seconds.

c. What is a reasonable domain of the function? Explain.

Domain: $\{x \mid 0 \le x \le 2.5\}$;

The height of the ball must be

nonnegative; this occurs only

between 0 seconds and 2.5 seconds.

d. What is the maximum of the function, and what does it represent in this situation?

25; The greatest height that the

ball reaches is 25 feet.

13. Write the function $f(x) = 3x^2 - 6x + 5$ in vertex form. Identify the vertex of the function's graph. Then graph the function.

$f(x) = 3(x - 1)^2 + 2$

vertex: (1 , 2)

(graph)

14. Consider the equation $x^2 - 4x + 5 = 0$.

a. Without solving the equation, tell whether it has real or nonreal solutions. Explain how you know.

Nonreal; the discriminant

$b^2 - 4ac = (-4)^2 - 4(1)(5) =$

$16 - 20 = -4 < 0$

b. What are the solutions of the equation?

$2 \pm i$

c. Evaluate $x^2 - 4x + 5$ for each solution. Show your results each time you perform an operation (squaring, multiplying, subtracting, and adding). What can you conclude?

$(2 + i)^2 - 4(2 + i) + 5 = (3 + 4i) -$

$4(2 + i) + 5 = (3 + 4i) - (8 + 4i) +$

$5 = -5 + 5 = 0$; $(2 - i)^2 - 4(2 - i)$

$+ 5 = (3 - 4i) - 4(2 - i) + 5 =$

$(3 - 4i) - (8 - 4i) + 5 = -5 + 5 =$

0; because the value is 0 in each

case, both solutions check.

© Houghton Mifflin Harcourt Publishing Company

CHAPTER 3

Polynomial Functions

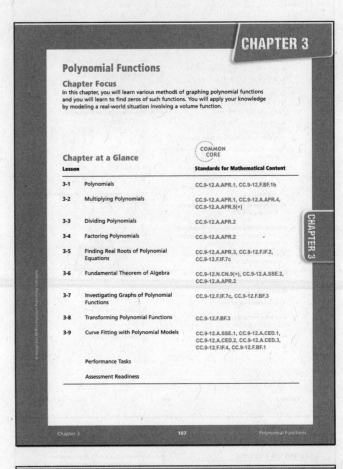

Polynomial Functions

Chapter Focus
In this chapter, you will learn various methods of graphing polynomial functions and you will learn to find zeros of such functions. You will apply your knowledge by modeling a real-world situation involving a volume function.

Chapter at a Glance

COMMON CORE

Lesson		Standards for Mathematical Content
3-1	Polynomials	CC.9-12.A.APR.1, CC.9-12.F.BF.1b
3-2	Multiplying Polynomials	CC.9-12.A.APR.1, CC.9-12.A.APR.4, CC.9-12.A.APR.5(+)
3-3	Dividing Polynomials	CC.9-12.A.APR.2
3-4	Factoring Polynomials	CC.9-12.A.APR.2
3-5	Finding Real Roots of Polynomial Equations	CC.9-12.A.APR.3, CC.9-12.F.IF.2, CC.9-12.F.IF.7c
3-6	Fundamental Theorem of Algebra	CC.9-12.N.CN.9(+), CC.9-12.A.SSE.2, CC.9-12.A.APR.2
3-7	Investigating Graphs of Polynomial Functions	CC.9-12.F.IF.7c, CC.9-12.F.BF.3
3-8	Transforming Polynomial Functions	CC.9-12.F.BF.3
3-9	Curve Fitting with Polynomial Models	CC.9-12.A.SSE.1, CC.9-12.A.CED.1, CC.9-12.A.CED.2, CC.9-12.A.CED.3, CC.9-12.F.IF.4, CC.9-12.F.BF.1
	Performance Tasks	
	Assessment Readiness	

COMMON CORE PROFESSIONAL DEVELOPMENT
CC.9-12.F.IF.7c*

In previous courses, students learned to graph linear and quadratic functions and identify the intercepts, maxima, and minima. Building on this knowledge, students in Advanced Algebra will graph polynomial functions. They will identify zeros by factoring. Students learn to apply the skill of factoring polynomials to examining the characteristics of functions.

Unpacking the Standards
Understanding the standards and the vocabulary terms in the standards will help you know exactly what you are expected to learn in this chapter.

COMMON CORE CC.9-12.F.IF.7c
Graph polynomial functions, identifying zeros when suitable factorizations are available, and showing end behavior.

Key Vocabulary
polynomial function (función polynomial) A function whose rule is a polynomial.
zero of a function (cero de una función) For the function f, any number x such that $f(x) = 0$.

What It Means For You   Lessons 3-1, 3-5, 3-7, 3-8
You can find zeros of a polynomial function by locating where the graph of the function crosses the x-axis.

EXAMPLE
The volume of a box is modeled by the function
$V(x) = 4x^3 - 20x^2 + 24x$, or
$V(x) = 4x(x - 2)(x - 3)$.
The zeros of $V(x)$ are also the x-intercepts of the graph:
$x = 0$, $x = 2$, and $x = 3$.

COMMON CORE CC.9-12.A.APR.5(+)
Know and apply the Binomial Theorem for the expansion of $(x + y)^n$ in powers of x and y for a positive integer n, where x and y are any numbers, with coefficients determined for example by Pascal's Triangle.

Key Vocabulary
Binomial Theorem (Teorema de los binomios) For any positive integer n,
$(x + y)^n = {}_nC_0 x^n y^0 + {}_nC_1 x^{n-1} y^1 + {}_nC_2 x^{n-2} y^2 + \dots + {}_nC_{n-1} x^1 y^{n-1} + {}_nC_n x^0 y^n$
Pascal's triangle (triángulo de Pascal) A triangular arrangement of numbers in which every row starts and ends with 1 and each other number is the sum of the two numbers above it.

What It Means For You   Lesson 3-2
You can use the number patterns in Pascal's Triangle to find the coefficients when you raise a binomial like $(x + y)$ to a power.

EXAMPLE   Pascal's triangle and binomial expansion

$$1$$
$$1 \quad 1$$
$$1 \quad 2 \quad 1$$
$$1 \quad 3 \quad 3 \quad 1$$
Row 4: $$1 \quad 4 \quad 6 \quad 4 \quad 1$$

4th power: $(x + y)^4 = 1x^4 + 4x^3y + 6x^2y^2 + 4xy^3 + 1y^4$

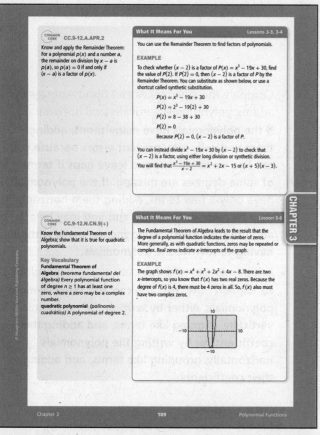

CC.9-12.A.APR.2

Know and apply the Remainder Theorem: For a polynomial $p(x)$ and a number a, the remainder on division by $x - a$ is $p(a)$, so $p(a) = 0$ if and only if $(x - a)$ is a factor of $p(x)$.

What It Means For You — Lessons 3-3, 3-4

You can use the Remainder Theorem to find factors of polynomials.

EXAMPLE

To check whether $(x - 2)$ is a factor of $P(x) = x^3 - 19x + 30$, find the value of $P(2)$. If $P(2) = 0$, then $(x - 2)$ is a factor of P by the Remainder Theorem. You can substitute as shown below, or use a shortcut called synthetic substitution.

$$P(x) = x^3 - 19x + 30$$
$$P(2) = 2^3 - 19(2) + 30$$
$$P(2) = 8 - 38 + 30$$
$$P(2) = 0$$

Because $P(2) = 0$, $(x - 2)$ is a factor of P.

You can instead divide $x^3 - 19x + 30$ by $(x - 2)$ to check that $(x - 2)$ is a factor, using either long division or synthetic division. You will find that $\frac{x^3 - 19x + 30}{x - 2} = x^2 + 2x - 15$ or $(x + 5)(x - 3)$.

CC.9-12.N.CN.9(+)

Know the Fundamental Theorem of Algebra; show that it is true for quadratic polynomials.

Key Vocabulary

Fundamental Theorem of Algebra (*teorema fundamental del álgebra*) Every polynomial function of degree $n \geq 1$ has at least one zero, where a zero may be a complex number.

quadratic polynomial (*polinomio cuadrático*) A polynomial of degree 2.

What It Means For You — Lesson 3-6

The Fundamental Theorem of Algebra leads to the result that the degree of a polynomial function indicates the number of zeros. More generally, as with quadratic functions, zeros may be repeated or complex. Real zeros indicate x-intercepts of the graph.

EXAMPLE

The graph shows $f(x) = x^4 + x^3 + 2x^2 + 4x - 8$. There are two x-intercepts, so you know that $f(x)$ has two real zeros. Because the degree of $f(x)$ is 4, there must be 4 zeros in all. So, $f(x)$ also must have two complex zeros.

Key Vocabulary

Binomial Theorem (*Teorema de los binomios*) For any positive integer n, $(x + y)^n = {}_nC_0 x^n y^0 + {}_nC_1 x^{n-1} y^1 + {}_nC_2 x^{n-2} y^2 + \ldots + {}_nC_{n-1} x^1 y^{n-1} + {}_nC_n x^0 y^n$.

degree of a monomial (*grado de un monomio*) The sum of the exponents of the variables in the monomial.

degree of a polynomial (*grado de un polonomio*) The degree of the term of the polynomial with the greatest degree.

end behavior (*comportamiento extremo*) The trends in the y-values of a function as the x-values approach positive and negative infinity.

Factor Theorem (*Teorema del factor*) For any polynomial $P(x)$, $(x - a)$ is a factor of $P(x)$ if and only if $P(a) = 0$.

Fundamental Theorem of Algebra (*Teorema fundamental del álgebra*) Every polynomial function of degree $n \geq 1$ has at least one zero, where a zero may be a complex number.

Pascal's triangle (*triángulo de Pascal*) A triangular arrangement of numbers in which every row starts and ends with 1 and each other number is the sum of the two numbers above it.

polynomial (*polinomio*) A monomial or a sum or difference of monomials.

polynomial function (*función polinomial*) A function whose rule is a polynomial.

quadratic polynomial (*polinomio cuadrático*) A polynomial of degree 2.

synthetic division (*división sintética*) A shorthand method of dividing by a linear binomial of the form $(x - a)$ by writing only the coefficients of the polynomials.

synthetic substitution (*sustitución sintética*) A method used to evaluate a polynomial function.

transformation (*transformación*) A change in the position, size, or shape of a figure or graph.

turning point (*punto de inflexión*) A point on the graph of a function that corresponds to a local maximum (or minimum) where the graph changes from increasing to decreasing (or vice versa).

zero of a function (*cero de una función*) For the function f, any number x such that $f(x) = 0$.

CHAPTER 3

COMMON CORE PROFESSIONAL DEVELOPMENT — **CC.9-12.N.CN.9(+)**

Students will extend their knowledge of complex numbers and the fact that every quadratic equation with real coefficients is solvable over the complex numbers to the Fundamental Theorem of Algebra. A solid understanding of complex numbers and the Fundamental Theorem of Algebra creates a foundation for students to advance their studies into solving various types of equations, investigating functions, and sketching their graphs.

Polynomials
Going Deeper

Essential question: *How do you add and subtract polynomials?*

COMMON CORE **Standards for Mathematical Content**

CC.9-12.A.APR.1 Understand that polynomials form a system analogous to the integers, namely, they are closed under the operations of addition, subtraction, ...; add, subtract ... polynomials.

CC.9-12.F.BF.1 Write a function that describes a relationship between two quantities.*

CC.9-12.F.BF.1b Combine standard function types using arithmetic operations.*

Also: CC.9-12.A.SSE.1*

Prerequisites

Closure of the set of integers

Defining polynomials

Math Background

Students are familiar with integer operations and understand that the integer system is closed under the operations of addition, subtraction, and multiplication. Students are also familiar with polynomials, have learned to identify the degree of a polynomial, and can write a polynomial in standard form.

INTRODUCE

Review integer operations, emphasizing that the integer system is closed under the operations of addition, subtraction, and multiplication.

TEACH

1 EXAMPLE

Questioning Strategies

- Are the commutative and associative properties of addition true for the addition of polynomials? Yes, the sum will be the same regardless of the order in which polynomials are added. If there are three or more polynomials being added, the sum will be the same regardless of how the polynomials are grouped.

- Compare the advantages and disadvantages of adding polynomials vertically and horizontally. If the polynomials have many terms, adding them vertically may prevent errors because you can line up like terms and leave gaps if terms of some degrees are missing. If the polynomials have only a few terms, adding them horizontally may be more convenient, and you may be able to add the coefficients using mental math without having to rewrite the polynomials.

- Is it possible to add three or more polynomials? If so, explain how. Yes, you can add three or more polynomials, either by writing the polynomials vertically, aligning like terms, and adding their coefficients or by writing the polynomials horizontally, grouping like terms, and adding their coefficients.

EXTRA EXAMPLE

Add $(4x^3 + 11x^2 + 8x + 5) + (7x^2 - 5x + 9)$.

$4x^3 + 18x^2 + 3x + 14$

2 EXAMPLE

Questioning Strategies

- Is it necessary to write polynomials in standard form before subtracting them? No, as long as you group like terms before subtracting and keep track of signs correctly, the results will be the same. However, it is good practice to write the difference as a polynomial in standard form.

- Is it necessary to use the method of rewriting the subtraction of polynomials as the addition of the opposite as in the given examples? No, although this may reduce the chance of error. If you can accurately subtract the coefficients of like terms rather than adding opposites, the results will be the same.

continued

Name_____ Class_____ Date_____

3-1

Polynomials
Going Deeper

Essential question: *How do you add and subtract polynomials?*

A **monomial** is a number or a product of numbers and variables with whole-number exponents. For example, 6, $3x^3$, and $-2xy^2$ are all monomials. A **polynomial** is a monomial or a sum of monomials. For example, $-4x^9 + 5x^2 + 1$ is a polynomial.

The **degree of a monomial** is the sum of the exponents of the variables. The **degree of a polynomial** is the degree of the term with the greatest degree. For example, the polynomial $-4x^9 + 5x^2 + 1$ has degree 9.

To add or subtract polynomials, you combine like terms. You can add or subtract horizontally or vertically.

CC.9-12.A.APR.1
1 EXAMPLE Adding Polynomials

Add.

A $(3x^3 + 12x^2 + 9x + 6) + (5x^2 - 6x + 7)$

Use a vertical arrangement.

$$\begin{array}{r} 3x^3 + 12x^2 + 9x + 6 \\ 5x^2 - 6x + 7 \\ \hline \underline{3}\,x^3 + \underline{17}\,x^2 + \underline{3}\,x + \underline{13} \end{array}$$

Write the polynomials, aligning like terms.

Add the coefficients of like terms.

B $(2x - 7x^2) + (x^2 - 2x + 1)$

Use a horizontal arrangement.

$(-7x^2 + 2x) + (x^2 - 2x + 1)$ Write the polynomials in standard form.

$= (-7x^2 + \underline{x^2}) + (2x - \underline{2x}) + \underline{1}$ Group like terms.

$= \underline{-6x^2} + 0x + \underline{1}$ Add the coefficients of like terms.

$= \underline{-6x^2} + \underline{1}$ Simplify.

REFLECT

1a. Do you get the same results whether you add polynomials vertically or horizontally? Why or why not?

Yes; in either case you find the sum by combining like terms, so the results of the two methods are the same.

1b. Is the sum of two polynomials always another polynomial? Explain.

Yes; the two addends consist of a sum of monomials. After adding, the result also consists of a sum of monomials, so it is a polynomial.

1c. Is the sum of two polynomials of degree 5 always a polynomial of degree 5? Give an example to explain your answer.

No; for example, $(x^5 + 3x) + (-x^5 + 6x) = 9x$.

To subtract polynomials, you add the opposite of the subtracted polynomial. The following example shows how to use this method with the vertical and horizontal formats.

CC.9-12.A.APR.1
2 EXAMPLE Subtracting Polynomials

Subtract.

A $(2 + 9x^2) - (-6x^2 - 2x + 1)$

Use a vertical arrangement.

$$\begin{array}{r} 9x^2 \qquad + 2 \\ 6x^2 + 2x - 1 \\ \hline \underline{15}\,x^2 + \underline{2}\,x + \underline{1} \end{array}$$

Write the first polynomial in standard form.

Add the opposite of the second polynomial.

Add the coefficients of like terms.

B $(6x^3 + 3x^2 + 2x + 9) - (4x^3 + 8x^2 - 2x + 5)$

Use a horizontal arrangement.

$(6x^3 + 3x^2 + 2x + 9) - (4x^3 + 8x^2 - 2x + 5)$ Write the polynomials.

$= (6x^3 + 3x^2 + 2x + 9) + (-4x^3 - 8x^2 + 2x - 5)$ Add the opposite.

$= (6x^3 - \underline{4x^3}) + (3x^2 - \underline{8x^2}) + (\underline{2x} + 2x) + (\underline{9} - 5)$ Group like terms.

$= \underline{2}\,x^3 - \underline{5}\,x^2 + \underline{4}\,x + \underline{4}$ Add the coefficients of like terms.

REFLECT

2a. How is subtracting polynomials similar to subtracting integers?

You subtract integers by adding the opposite of the subtracted integer; you subtract polynomials by adding the opposite of the subtracted polynomial.

2b. In part A, you leave a gap in the polynomial $9x^2 + 2$ when you write the subtraction problem vertically. Why?

The polynomial does not have an x term, so you must leave a gap for like terms to align properly.

2c. Is the difference of two polynomials always another polynomial? Explain.

Yes; finding a difference of two polynomials is equivalent to finding the sum of the first polynomial and the opposite of the second polynomial, and the sum of two polynomials is always another polynomial.

© Houghton Mifflin Harcourt Publishing Company

2 EXAMPLE continued

Avoid Common Errors

Regardless of the method students use to subtract polynomials, a common error is that instead of distributing the subtraction operation to all terms in the second polynomial, only the first term is subtracted while the others are added. Remind students to always be aware of this potential mistake. Also, encourage students to check their answers. Just as a numerical difference can be checked by addition, students can check a polynomial difference by addition.

EXTRA EXAMPLE

Subtract $(4 + 7x^2) - (-5x^2 - 3x + 2)$.
$12x^2 + 3x + 2$

3 EXAMPLE

Questioning Strategies

• Would adding or subtracting polynomials help you find the difference between the estimated number of female students in 2000 and 2005? Explain. No; you would have to evaluate $F(x)$ for $x = 0$ and $x = 5$ and find the difference between the results.

• How could you use the model to find the total enrollment in 2003? Since x represents the number of years since 2000, evaluate $T(x)$ for $x = 3$.

MATHEMATICAL PRACTICE | Highlighting the Standards

3 EXAMPLE and its Reflect questions offer an opportunity to address Mathematical Practice Standard 4 (Model with mathematics). Many real-world situations in fields ranging from education and business to engineering and physics can be modeled by polynomial functions. In this example, students are given polynomials that model male and female high school enrollment in the United States. By adding and subtracting polynomials, students extend the model to determine the total high school enrollment and the difference between male and female enrollment.

EXTRA EXAMPLE

For the presidential elections from 1980 to 2008, the votes cast for the Democratic candidate can be modeled by $D(x) = 0.00230x^3 - 0.0625x^2 + 1.17x + 34.9$ where x is the number of years since 1980 and $D(x)$ is the number of Democratic votes cast in millions. The votes cast for the Republican candidate in these elections can be modeled by $R(x) = -0.00140x^4 + 0.0809x^3 - 1.41x^2 + 7.29x + 43.5$ where x is the number of years since 1980 and $R(x)$ is the number of Republican votes cast in millions. Write a model for the total Democratic and Republican votes cast in the presidential elections from 1980 to 2008, and use it to estimate the total Democratic and Republican votes cast in the 2000 election. $T(x) = -0.00140x^4 + 0.0832x^3 - 1.4725x^2 + 8.46x + 78.4$; $T(20) = 100.2$, so about 100.2 million votes were cast for the Democratic and Republican candidates in the 2000 election.

CLOSE

Essential Question

How do you add and subtract polynomials?
You can add polynomials by writing the polynomials vertically, aligning like terms, and adding their coefficients. You can also add the polynomials by writing them horizontally, grouping like terms, and adding their coefficients. To subtract polynomials, you can add the opposite of the polynomial being subtracted by using either the vertical or the horizontal addition method.

Summarize

Have students make a table describing the methods for adding and subtracting polynomials horizontally and vertically. For each method, students should provide an example.

PRACTICE

Where skills are taught	Where skills are practiced
1 EXAMPLE	EXS. 1–4
2 EXAMPLE	EXS. 5–10
3 EXAMPLE	EX. 11

Exercise 12: Students identify an error made by another student when subtracting polynomials.

3 EXAMPLE CC.9-12.F.BF.1b Modeling High School Populations

According to data from the U.S. Census Bureau for the period 2000–2007, the number of male students enrolled in high school in the United States can be approximated by the function $M(x) = -0.004x^3 + 0.037x^2 + 0.049x + 8.11$ where x is the number of years since 2000 and $M(x)$ is the number of male students in millions. The number of female students enrolled in high school in the United States can be approximated by the function $F(x) = -0.006x^3 + 0.029x^2 + 0.165x + 7.67$ where x is the number of years since 2000 and $F(x)$ is the number of female students in millions. Estimate the total number of students enrolled in high school in the United States in 2007.

A Make a plan. The problem asks for the total number of students in 2007. First find $T(x) = M(x) + F(x)$ to find a model for the total enrollment. Then evaluate $T(x)$ at an appropriate value of x to find the total enrollment in 2007.

B Add the polynomials.

$-0.004x^3 +$ $0.037x^2 +$ $0.049x + 8.11$ Write the polynomials, aligning like terms.

$\underline{-0.006x^3 +}$ $\underline{0.029x^2 +}$ $\underline{0.165x + 7.67}$

$\underline{-0.01}x^3 + \underline{0.066}x^2 + \underline{0.214}x + \underline{15.78}$ Add the coefficients of like terms.

$T(x) = \underline{-0.01x^3 + 0.066x^2 + 0.214x + 15.78}$

C Evaluate $T(x)$.

For 2007, $x = 7$. Use a calculator to evaluate $T(7)$. Round to one decimal place.

$T(7) \approx$ ____17.1____

So, there were approximately ____17,100,000____ high school students in 2007.

REFLECT

3a. Is it possible to solve this problem without adding the polynomials? Explain.

Yes; you can evaluate $M(x)$ and $F(x)$ separately for $x = 7$ and then add the results.

3b. Explain how you can use the given information to estimate how many more male high school students than female high school students there were in the United States in 2007.

First find $D(x) = M(x) - F(x)$; then evaluate $D(x)$ for $x = 7$.

$D(x) = M(x) - F(x) = 0.002x^3 + 0.008x^2 - 0.116x + 0.44;$

$D(7) \approx 0.7$, so there were about 700,000 more male students than female students in 2007.

PRACTICE

Add or subtract.

1. $(2x^4 - 6x^2 + 8) + (-x^4 + 2x^2 - 12)$

$x^4 - 4x^2 - 4$

2. $(7x^2 - 2x + 1) + (8x^3 + 2x^2 + 5x - 4)$

$8x^3 + 9x^2 + 3x - 3$

3. $(5x^2 - 6x^3 + 16) + (9x^4 + 3x + 7x^4)$

$7x^4 + 3x^3 + 5x^2 + 3x + 16$

4. $(-3x^3 - 7x^5 - 3) + (5x^2 + 3x^3 + 7x^5)$

$5x^2 - 3$

5. $(2x^4 - 6x^2 + 8) - (-x^4 + 2x^2 - 12)$

$3x^4 - 8x^2 + 20$

6. $(x^3 + 25) - (-x^2 - 18x - 8)$

$x^3 + x^2 + 18x + 33$

7. $(2x^2 + 3x + 1) - (7x^2 - 2x + 7x^3)$

$-7x^3 - 5x^2 + 5x + 1$

8. $(12x^2 + 3) - (15x^2 - 4x + 9x^4 + 7)$

$-9x^4 - 3x^2 + 4x - 4$

9. $(14x^4 - x^3 + 2x^2 + 5x + 15) - (10x^4 + 3x^3 - 5x^2 - 6x + 4)$

$4x^4 - 4x^3 + 7x^2 + 11x + 11$

10. $(-6x^3 + 10x + 26) + (5x^2 - 6x^5 + 7x) + (3 - 22x^4)$

$-6x^5 - 22x^4 - 6x^3 + 5x^2 + 17x + 29$

11. According to data from the U.S. Census Bureau, the total number of people in the United States labor force can be approximated by the function $T(x) = -0.011x^2 + 2x + 107$, where x is the number of years since 1980 and $T(x)$ is the number of workers in millions. The number of women in the United States labor force can be approximated by the function $W(x) = -0.012x^2 + 1.26x + 45.5$.

a. Write a polynomial function $M(x)$ that models the number of men in the labor force.

$M(x) = 0.001x^2 + 0.74x + 61.5$

b. Estimate the number of men in the labor force in 2008. Explain how you made your estimate.

Approximately 83,000,000; evaluate $M(x)$ for $x = 28$.

12. Error Analysis A student was asked to find the difference $(4x^5 - 3x^4 + 6x^2) - (7x^5 - 6x^4 + x^3)$. The student's work is shown at right. Identify the student's error and give the correct difference.

The student did not distribute the negative sign in the second polynomial. The correct difference is

$-3x^5 + 3x^4 - x^3 + 6x^2.$

$\begin{aligned} 4x^5 - 3x^4 \quad\quad + 6x^2 \\ -7x^5 - 6x^4 + x^3 \quad\quad \\ \hline -3x^5 - 9x^4 + x^3 + 6x^2 \end{aligned}$

3. $SA = \pi\left(\dfrac{d}{2}\right)(d - 0.6) + \pi d(d + 4) + \pi\left(\dfrac{d}{2}\right)^2$

4. B   **5.** C

6. C   **7.** B

ADDITIONAL PRACTICE AND PROBLEM SOLVING

Assign these pages to help your students practice and apply important lesson concepts. For additional exercises, see the Student Edition.

Answers

Additional Practice

1. 2   **2.** 7

3. 11

4. $-4x^3 + x^2 + 7x + 6$; -4; 3; 4; cubic polynomial with 4 terms

5. $2x^5 + 7x^4 + x^2 - 12x - 3$; 2; 5; 5; quintic polynomial with 5 terms

6. $11x^3 + x^2 + 3x + 4$

7. $-3x^3 - 8x^2 - 6x - 4$

8. $3x^4 + x^3 + 10x^2 + 7$

9. $-x^7 + 21x^2 + 9x - 6$

10. Tom forgot that to subtract a polynomial, he should have added the opposite of each of the terms of the second polynomial.
The correct answer is $-x^4 - 8x^2 + 8x - 1$.

11. a. 161 ft and 105 ft

    b. The height of the baseball 3 s after being hit by the bat and the height of the baseball 5 s after being hit by the bat

Problem Solving

1. a. $SA = \pi\left(\dfrac{d}{2}\right)^2 + \pi\left(\dfrac{d}{2}\right)s$

    b. Possible answer: πrs because it gives the surface area of the curved part of the cone, not the circular base; the base is against the cylinder so it isn't part of the surface area of the castle.

2. a. $SA = \dfrac{\pi d^2}{2} + dh\pi$

    b. Possible answer: just the curved part and one base; the top of the cylinder is hidden because the cone sits on it.

Additional Practice

Identify the degree of each monomial.

1. $6x^2$ 2. $3p^3m^4$ 3. $2x^8y^3$

_____ _____ _____

Rewrite each polynomial in standard form. Then identify the leading coefficient, degree, and number of terms. Name the polynomial.

4. $6 + 7x - 4x^3 + x^2$

_____

5. $x^2 - 3 + 2x^5 + 7x^4 - 12x$

_____

Add or subtract. Write your answer in standard form.

6. $\left(2x^2 - 2x + 6\right) + \left(11x^3 - x^2 - 2 + 5x\right)$ 7. $\left(x^2 - 8\right) - \left(3x^3 - 6x - 4 + 9x^2\right)$

_____ _____

8. $\left(5x^4 + x^2\right) + \left(7 + 9x^2 - 2x^4 + x^3\right)$ 9. $\left(12x^2 + x\right) - \left(6 - 9x^2 + x^7 - 8x\right)$

_____ _____

10. Find and correct the error in Tom's calculation below.

$$(2x^4 - 3x^2 + 5x + 1) - (3x^4 + 5x^2 - 3x + 2) = ?$$

$\quad\quad (2x^4 - 3x^2 + 5x + 1)$
$\underline{-(3x^4 + 5x^2 - 3x + 2)}$
$\quad\quad -x^2 - 2x^2 + 2x - 1$

Solve.

11. The height, h, in feet, of a baseball after being struck by a bat can be approximated by $h(t) = -16t^2 + 100t + 5$, where t is measured in seconds.

   a. Evaluate $h(t)$ for $t = 3$ and $t = 5$. _____

   b. Describe what the values of the function from part a represent.

_____

_____

Problem Solving

As part of a project to build a model castle, Julian wants to find the surface area of solid towers of various sizes, shaped like the one shown in the figure below. The diameter of the circular base is d inches, the height of the cylinder is $d + 4$ inches, and the slant height of the right circular cone is $d - 0.6$ inch.

1. The general formula for the lateral surface area of a cone is $SA = \pi r^2 - \pi rs$, where r is the radius of the base, and s is the slant height of the cone.

   a. Write the formula in terms of d.

     _____

   b. What part of the formula will you use to find the surface area of the cone part of the model? Why?

     _____

     _____

2. The general formula for the surface area of a cylinder (with radius r and height h) is $SA = 2\pi r^2 + 2\pi rh$.

   a. Write the formula in terms of d. _____

   b. What part of the formula will you use to find the surface area of the cylinder part of the model? Why?

3. Write a general polynomial expression for the surface area of the model tower.

_____

Choose the letter for the best answer.

4. What is the approximate surface area in square inches of a tower with a diameter of 5 inches?

   A 278   C 44
   B 196   D 38

5. What is the approximate surface area in square inches of a tower with a diameter of 10 inches?

   A 176   C 666
   B 278   D 1174

6. What is the approximate surface area in square inches of a tower where the height of the cylinder is 12 inches?

   A 931   C 445
   B 716   D 395

7. What is the approximate surface area in square inches of a tower where the slant height of the cone is 3.4 inches?

   A 103   C 158
   B 134   D 268

3-2 Multiplying Polynomials
Going Deeper

Essential question: *How do you multiply polynomials?*

COMMON CORE **Standards for Mathematical Content**

CC.9-12.A.APR.1 Understand that polynomials form a system analogous to the integers, namely, they are closed under the operations of ... multiplication; ... multiply polynomials.

CC.9-12.A.APR.4 Prove polynomial identities and use them to describe numerical relationships.

CC.9-12.A.APR.5(+) Know and apply the Binomial Theorem for the expansion of $(x + y)^n$ in powers of x and y for a positive integer n, where x and y are any numbers, with coefficients determined for example by Pascal's Triangle.

Prerequisites

Closure of the set of integers

Adding polynomials

Multiplying polynomials

Math Background

Students are familiar with integer operations and understand that the integers are closed under the operations of addition, subtraction, and multiplication. In the previous lesson, students learned to add and subtract polynomials, and discovered that like the integers, polynomials are closed under addition and subtraction.

INTRODUCE

Review polynomial addition and subtraction, emphasizing that like the integers, polynomials are closed under addition and subtraction. Ask students if they think that polynomials are also closed under multiplication, and have them explain their reasoning.

TEACH

1 EXAMPLE

Questioning Strategies

• Is the Commutative Property of Multiplication true for the multiplication of polynomials? Yes, the product will be the same regardless of the order in which polynomials are multiplied.

• After you have multiplied two polynomials, how can you check to make sure you have not missed any terms in the process? Before simplifying, the product of a polynomial with m terms and a polynomial with n terms has mn terms, so count the number of terms in the product.

Teaching Strategy

Students may benefit from reviewing the FOIL method for finding the product of two binomials. FOIL is an acronym that stands for "First," "Outer," "Inner," and "Last," and it refers to pairings of the terms when the binomials are multiplied horizontally. Students should understand that the FOIL method works only for multiplying binomials, but the general principle behind FOIL still applies when multiplying two polynomials: Each term of one polynomial must be multiplied with each term of the other.

EXTRA EXAMPLE

Find the product $(2x - 3)(3x^3 - x^2 + 6)$.
$6x^4 - 11x^3 + 3x^2 + 12x - 18$

Name_____ Class_____ Date_____

3-2

Multiplying Polynomials
Going Deeper

Essential question: *How do you multiply polynomials?*

To multiply two polynomials, you use the distributive property so that every term in the first factor is multiplied by every term in the second factor. You also use the product of powers property ($a^m \cdot a^n = a^{m+n}$) each time you multiply two terms.

Video Tutor

CC.9-12.A.APR.1

1 EXAMPLE Multiplying Polynomials

Find the product.

A $(4x^2)(2x^3 - x^2 + 5)$

$= (4x^2)(2x^3) + (4x^2)(-x^2) + (4x^2)(5)$ ⟶ Distributive property

$= 8x^5 - \underline{4x^4} + \underline{20x^2}$ ⟶ Multiply monomials.

B $(x - 3)(-x^2 + 2x + 1)$

Method 1: Use a horizontal arrangement.

$(x - 3)(-x^2 + 2x + 1)$

$= x(-x^2) + x(2x) + x(1) - 3(-x^2) - 3(2x) - 3(1)$ ⟶ Distribute x and then -3.

$= -x^3 + \underline{2x^2} + x + \underline{3x^2} - \underline{6x} - 3$ ⟶ Multiply monomials.

$= -x^3 + \underline{5x^2} - \underline{5x} - \underline{3}$ ⟶ Combine like terms.

Method 2: Use a vertical arrangement.

$$
\begin{array}{r}
-x^2 + 2x + 1 \\
x - 3 \\
\hline
3x^2 - 6x - 3 \\
-x^3 + 2x^2 + x \\
\hline
-x^3 + 5x^2 - 5x - 3
\end{array}
$$

Write the polynomials vertically.

Multiply $(-x^2 + 2x + 1)$ by -3.

Multiply $(-x^2 + 2x + 1)$ by x.

Add.

REFLECT

1a. Is the product of two polynomials always another polynomial? Explain.

Yes; after using the distributive property and multiplying monomials, the product

consists of a sum of monomials, so it is a polynomial.

1b. If one polynomial has m terms and the other has n terms, how many terms does the product of the polynomials have before it is simplified?

The product has mn terms.

© Houghton Mifflin Harcourt Publishing Company

There are several special products that occur so frequently that it is helpful to recognize their patterns and develop rules for the products. These rules are summarized in the table.

Special Product Rules	
Sum and Difference	$(a + b)(a - b) = a^2 - b^2$
Square of a Binomial	$(a + b)^2 = a^2 + 2ab + b^2$
	$(a - b)^2 = a^2 - 2ab + b^2$
Cube of a Binomial	$(a + b)^3 = a^3 + 3a^2b + 3ab^2 + b^3$
	$(a - b)^3 = a^3 - 3a^2b + 3ab^2 - b^3$

CC.9-12.A.APR.4

2 EXAMPLE Justifying and Applying a Special Product Rule

Justify the sum and difference rule. Then use it to find the product $(4x^2 + 15)(4x^2 - 15)$.

A Justify the rule.

$(a + b)(a - b) = a \cdot a + a(-b) + \underline{ba} + \underline{b(-b)}$ ⟶ Distribute a and then b.

$= a^2 - ab + \underline{ba} + \underline{-b^2}$ ⟶ Multiply monomials.

$= \underline{a^2} - \underline{b^2}$ ⟶ Combine like terms.

B Find the product $(4x^2 + 15)(4x^2 - 15)$.

$(4x^2 + 15)(4x^2 - 15) = (\underline{4x^2})^2 - (\underline{15})^2$ ⟶ Sum and difference rule

$= \underline{16x^4 - 225}$ ⟶ Simplify.

REFLECT

2a. **Error Analysis** A student was asked to find the square of $7x + 3$. The student quickly wrote $(7x + 3)^2 = 49x^2 + 9$. Identify the student's error and provide the correct answer.

The student forgot the middle term, $2ab$, in the rule for the square of a binomial.

The correct answer is $49x^2 + 42x + 9$.

2b. Show how to justify the rule for the cube of a binomial, $(a + b)^3$.

$(a + b)^3 = (a + b)(a + b)(a + b)$

$= (a + b)(a^2 + 2ab + b^2)$

$= a^3 + 2a^2b + ab^2 + ba^2 + 2ab^2 + b^3$

$= a^3 + 3a^2b + 3ab^2 + b^3$

© Houghton Mifflin Harcourt Publishing Company

Questioning Strategies

- In part A, how could the FOIL method help you? **It would help you find the four terms in the product (before like terms are combined).**

- In part B, what would the product be if the binomials being multiplied were $4x + 15$ and $4x - 15$? **$16x^2 - 225$**

Avoid Common Errors

When using the rules for special products, students often forget to apply exponents to the coefficients of terms in the binomial. Suggest that students first write the coefficient and variable within parentheses, with the exponent applied to both, and then simplify.

EXTRA EXAMPLE

Find the product $(2x^2 + 7)(2x^2 - 7)$. **$4x^4 - 49$**

3 EXAMPLE

Questioning Strategies

- When applying the special product rule for the square of a binomial to $(x^2 - y^2)^2$, which terms are substituted for a and b in the rule $(a - b)^2 = a^2 - 2ab + b^2$? **The term x^2 is substituted for a, and the term y^2 is substituted for b.**

- What is another way to find the product $(x^2 + y^2)^2$ if the special product rule for the square of a binomial is not applied? **Write the product as $(x^2 + y^2)(x^2 + y^2)$ and use the Distributive Property to multiply every term in the first factor by every term in the second factor, resulting in a total of four terms. Then, simplify the product by combining the two x^2y^2-terms.**

MATHEMATICAL PRACTICE   Highlighting the Standards

2 EXAMPLE , **3 EXAMPLE** , and their Reflect questions offer an opportunity to address Mathematical Practice Standard 3 (Construct viable arguments and critique the reasoning of others). Students use what they have learned about multiplying polynomials to justify the special product rule for the sum and difference. Then, students identify an error made by another student when applying the special product rule for the square of a binomial. Finally, students extend their understanding of multiplying polynomials and applying special product rules when they verify Euclid's formula.

Differentiated Instruction

Visual learners may benefit from drawing a right triangle with side lengths generated by Euclid's formula. For example, if students generate a Pythagorean triple by using $x = 4$ and $y = 2$, they can draw a right triangle with legs 12 cm and 16 cm in length, and a hypotenuse 20 cm in length. Students can then use their triangle to relate Euclid's formula to the Pythagorean theorem $a^2 + b^2 = c^2$.

EXTRA EXAMPLE

Use Euclid's formula to generate a Pythagorean triple with $x = 7$ and $y = 2$. **45, 28, 53**

CC.9-12.A.APR.4

3 EXAMPLE Applying Special Products

Recall that a *Pythagorean triple* is a set of positive integers, a, b, and c, such that $a^2 + b^2 = c^2$. Euclid's formula states that if x and y are positive integers with $x > y$, then $x^2 - y^2$, $2xy$, and $x^2 + y^2$ form a Pythagorean triple.

$$(x^2 - y^2)^2 + (2xy)^2 = (x^2 + y^2)^2$$

Verify Euclid's formula. Then use the formula to generate a Pythagorean triple with $x = 5$ and $y = 3$.

A Show that $(x^2 - y^2)^2 + (2xy)^2 = (x^2 + y^2)^2$.

Step 1: Simplify the left side of the equation.

$(x^2 - y^2)^2 = (\underline{x^2})^2 - 2 \cdot \underline{x^2} \cdot \underline{y^2} + (\underline{y^2})^2$ Square of a binomial

$\qquad = \underline{x^4 - 2x^2y^2 + y^4}$. Simplify.

$(2xy)^2 = \underline{4x^2y^2}$ Simplify.

So, $(x^2 - y^2)^2 + (2xy)^2 = \underline{x^4 + 2x^2y^2 + y^4}$ Add.

Step 2: Simplify the right side of the equation.

$(x^2 + y^2)^2 = (\underline{x^2})^2 + 2 \cdot \underline{x^2} \cdot \underline{y^2} + (\underline{y^2})^2$ Square of a binomial

$\qquad = \underline{x^4 + 2x^2y^2 + y^4}$ Simplify.

Step 3: Compare the expressions on both sides of the equation.

The expressions on both sides of the equation equal $\underline{x^4 + 2x^2y^2 + y^4}$.

So, Euclid's formula is valid.

B Use the formula to generate a Pythagorean triple with $x = 5$ and $y = 3$.

$a = x^2 - y^2 = (\underline{5})^2 - (\underline{3})^2 = \underline{25} - \underline{9} = \underline{16}$

$b = 2xy = 2 \cdot \underline{5} \cdot \underline{3} = \underline{30}$

$c = x^2 + y^2 = (\underline{5})^2 + (\underline{3})^2 = \underline{25} + \underline{9} = \underline{34}$

So, the Pythagorean triple is $a = \underline{16}$, $b = \underline{30}$, and $c = \underline{34}$.

REFLECT

3a. Describe how you can check the Pythagorean triple. Then perform the check.

Check that $a^2 + b^2 = c^2$; $16^2 + 30^2 = 256 + 900 = 1156$ and $34^2 = 1156$.

Pascal's Triangle is a famous number pattern named after the French mathematician Blaise Pascal (1623–1662). You can use Pascal's Triangle to help you expand a power of a binomial of the form $(a + b)^n$.

PREP FOR CC.9-12.A.APR.5(+)

4 EXPLORE Generating Pascal's Triangle

You can generate Pascal's Triangle by making a tree diagram as shown below. Starting at the top of the diagram, there are two paths from each node to the nodes beneath it, the left path (L) and the right path (R). You can describe a path from the top down to any node using lefts and rights.

There is only one possible path to each node in row 1. In row 2, there is only one possible path (LL) to the first node and only one possible path (RR) to the last node, but there are two possible paths (LR and RL) to the center node.

A Complete rows 3 and 4 of Pascal's Triangle. In each node, write the number of possible paths from the top down to that node.

B Look for patterns in the tree diagram.

What is the value in the first and last node in each row? $\underline{1}$

For the other nodes, what is the relationship of the value in the node to the two values above it?

Each value is the sum of the two values above it.

C Use the patterns to complete rows 5 and 6 of Pascal's Triangle.

Row 0:   1

Row 1:   1   1

Row 2:   1   2   1

Row 3:   1   3   3   1

Row 4: 1   4   6   4   1

Row 5: 1   5 10 10   5   1

Row 6: 1 6 15 20 15 6 1

Questioning Strategies

- Which row of Pascal's Triangle has 12 values? **row 11**

- What do you notice if you read any row of Pascal's Triangle from left to right or from right to left? **The values are the same when read in either direction. Each row is symmetric about a vertical line through the number at the top of the triangle.**

- Is there a limit to the number of rows in Pascal's Triangle? **No, Pascal's Triangle can have infinitely many rows.**

Teaching Strategy

If time permits, students may be interested to learn more about Blaise Pascal and Pascal's Triangle. Born in 1623, Pascal was a child prodigy who was building calculating machines by the time he was a teenager. The computer programming language Pascal is named for him. Encourage students to look for other patterns in Pascal's Triangle, such as horizontal sums (the rows add to powers of 2) and patterns that form the Fibonacci sequence.

Differentiated Instruction

Kinesthetic learners may benefit from moving a physical object, such as coin or other marker, along the paths in Pascal's Triangle. For instance, you can give each of 16 students a unique pathway to follow using a four-letter sequence of Ls and Rs, such as RRLR. Those 16 students can then move their markers along the paths to determine at what node in row 4 of the triangle they land. By surveying the 16 students, you can find how many students landed at each of the five nodes in row 4, thereby generating the numbers in that row of Pascal's Triangle.

5 EXPLORE

Questioning Strategies

- In part A, what is another way of obtaining the expansion of $(a + b)^3$? **Use the special product rule for the cube of a binomial.**

- What position in Pascal's Triangle is represented as $_5C_2$? Explain. **Position 2 of row 5; $_nC_r$ represents position r of row n.**

- How is the number of paths to any given node in row n of Pascal's Triangle related to the corresponding term of the expanded form of $(a + b)^n$? **The number of paths is the coefficient of the corresponding term.**

Teaching Strategy

By the time students expand $(a + b)^4$ by multiplying $(a + b)(a + b)^3$ in step A, they will recognize that there is an advantage to learning an easier way to expand powers of binomials. Point out how the simple pattern of Pascal's Triangle gives the coefficients of terms in a binomial expansion that were previously so difficult to calculate. Explain to students that as they become mathematically fluent, they will learn many more ways that mathematics can make a seemingly complex task easy.

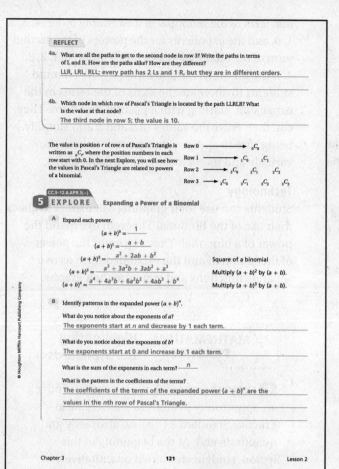

REFLECT

4a. What are all the paths to get to the second node in row 3? Write the paths in terms of L and R. How are the paths alike? How are they different?

LLR, LRL, RLL; every path has 2 Ls and 1 R, but they are in different orders.

4b. Which node in which row of Pascal's Triangle is located by the path LLRLR? What is the value at that node?

The third node in row 5; the value is 10.

The value in position r of row n of Pascal's Triangle is written as $_nC_r$, where the position numbers in each row start with 0. In the next Explore, you will see how the values in Pascal's Triangle are related to powers of a binomial.

Row 0 → $_0C_0$

Row 1 → $_1C_0$ $_1C_1$

Row 2 → $_2C_0$ $_2C_1$ $_2C_2$

Row 3 → $_3C_0$ $_3C_1$ $_3C_2$ $_3C_3$

CC.9-12.A.APR.5(+)

5 EXPLORE Expanding a Power of a Binomial

A Expand each power.

$$(a + b)^0 = 1$$
$$(a + b)^1 = a + b$$
$$(a + b)^2 = a^2 + 2ab + b^2$$ Square of a binomial
$$(a + b)^3 = a^3 + 3a^2b + 3ab^2 + a^3$$ Multiply $(a + b)^2$ by $(a + b)$.
$$(a + b)^4 = a^4 + 4a^3b + 6a^2b^2 + 4ab^3 + b^4$$ Multiply $(a + b)^3$ by $(a + b)$.

B Identify patterns in the expanded power $(a + b)^n$.

What do you notice about the exponents of a?
The exponents start at n and decrease by 1 each term.

What do you notice about the exponents of b?
The exponents start at 0 and increase by 1 each term.

What is the sum of the exponents in each term? _n_

What is the pattern in the coefficients of the terms?
The coefficients of the terms of the expanded power $(a + b)^n$ are the
values in the nth row of Pascal's Triangle.

© Houghton Mifflin Harcourt Publishing Company

REFLECT

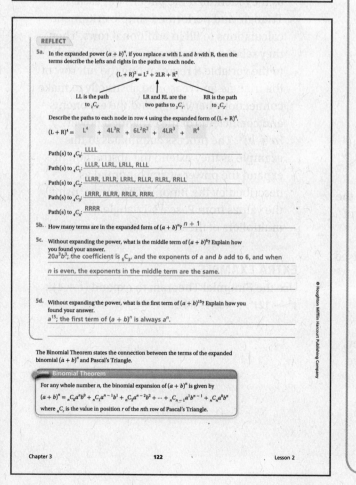

5a. In the expanded power $(a + b)^n$, if you replace a with L and b with R, then the terms describe the lefts and rights in the paths to each node.

$$(L + R)^2 = L^2 + 2LR + R^2$$

LL is the path to $_2C_0$.

LR and RL are the two paths to $_2C_1$.

RR is the path to $_2C_r$.

Describe the paths to each node in row 4 using the expanded form of $(L + R)^4$.

$$(L + R)^4 = L^4 + 4L^3R + 6L^2R^2 + 4LR^3 + R^4$$

Path(s) to $_4C_0$: LLLL

Path(s) to $_4C_1$: LLLR, LLRL, LRLL, RLLL

Path(s) to $_4C_2$: LLRR, LRLR, LRRL, RLLR, RLRL, RRLL

Path(s) to $_4C_3$: LRRR, RLRR, RRLR, RRRL

Path(s) to $_4C_4$: RRRR

5b. How many terms are in the expanded form of $(a + b)^n$? _$n + 1$_

5c. Without expanding the power, what is the middle term of $(a + b)^6$? Explain how you found your answer.

$20a^3b^3$; the coefficient is $_6C_3$, and the exponents of a and b add to 6, and when
n is even, the exponents in the middle term are the same.

5d. Without expanding the power, what is the first term of $(a + b)^{15}$? Explain how you found your answer.

a^{15}; the first term of $(a + b)^n$ is always a^n.

The Binomial Theorem states the connection between the terms of the expanded binomial $(a + b)^n$ and Pascal's Triangle.

Binomial Theorem

For any whole number n, the binomial expansion of $(a + b)^n$ is given by

$$(a + b)^n = {}_nC_0 a^n b^0 + {}_nC_1 a^{n-1} b^1 + {}_nC_2 a^{n-2} b^2 + \cdots + {}_nC_{n-1} a^1 b^{n-1} + {}_nC_n a^0 b^n$$

where $_nC_r$ is the value in position r of the nth row of Pascal's Triangle.

© Houghton Mifflin Harcourt Publishing Company

Questioning Strategies

- If a term in a binomial being raised to a power has a coefficient other than 1, what happens to that coefficient when the power is expanded using the Binomial Theorem? Give an example. **The coefficient is raised to the same power as the variable for each term and then multiplied by the corresponding value from Pascal's triangle. For example, the expansion rule for $(2x + y)^3$ is $a^3 + 3a^2b + 3ab^2 + b^3$. Substituting $2x$ for a and y for b, the expansion becomes $((2x)^3 + 3(2x)^2y + 3(2x)y^2 + y^3) = 8x^3 + 12x^2y + 6xy^2 + y^3$.**

- Describe the steps to expand $(3c + 2d)^4$ using the Binomial Theorem. **Expand $(a + b)^4$ to get $a^4 + 4a^3b + 6a^2b^2 + 4ab^3 + b^4$. Substitute $3c$ for a and $2d$ for b; then, simplify: $(3c)^4 + 4(3c)^3(2d) + 6(3c)^2(2d)^2 + 4(3c)(2d)^3 + (2d)^4 = 81c^4 + 216c^3d + 216c^2d^2 + 96cd^3 + 16d^4$.**

Teaching Strategy

Many students find it helpful to write out a copy of Pascal's Triangle before expanding $(a + b)^n$, especially as values of n increase. Help students remember how to create Pascal's Triangle by writing one 1 in row 0 and two 1s in row 1, and then using the pattern that they discovered in **4 EXPLORE** to generate additional rows.

Avoid Common Errors

When expanding a power of a binomial like $(2x + 3)^4$, students may raise the x in $2x$ to appropriate powers but not the coefficient 2. For instance, they may think that the first term in the expansion of $(2x + 3)^4$ is $2x^4$ instead of $(2x)^4 = 16x^4$. Similarly, students may forget to use the numbers from Pascal's Triangle in an expansion. For instance, they may think that the second term in the expansion of $(2x + 3)^4$ is $(2x)^3(3)^1 = 24x^3$ instead of $4(2x)^3(3)^1 = 96x^3$.

Before beginning the expansion of a binomial raised to a power, some students may find it helpful to write out a "fill-in-the-blank" product, such as $(\_ + \_)^4 = (\_)^4 + 4(\_)^3(\_) + 6(\_)^2(\_)^2 + 4(\_)(\_)^3 + (\_)^4$. First, have them find the appropriate numbers from Pascal's Triangle. Then, they can fill in the exponents for the powers of the

first term of the binomial in descending order: 4, 3, 2, 1, 0, and the exponents for the powers of the second term of the binomial in ascending order: 0, 1, 2, 3, 4. If the binomial has the form $(a - b)^n$, remind students to alternate the signs of the terms in the expansion, starting with a positive first term. They can then enter the values of a and b and simplify, being sure to apply each exponent to both the variable and its coefficient for variable terms.

Technology

Students can use their graphing calculators to check their use of the Binomial Theorem to expand the power of a binomial. They can enter the power of the binomial and the expanded form as two separate functions and compare their graphs.

MATHEMATICAL PRACTICE — Highlighting the Standards

6 EXAMPLE and its Reflect questions offer an opportunity to address Mathematical Practice Standard 2 (Reason abstractly and quantitatively). At the beginning of this lesson, students reasoned quantitatively as they identified the pattern of Pascal's Triangle and performed simple arithmetic calculations to fill in additional rows. Then, they related the values in Pascal's Triangle to the variable n representing the nth row of the triangle and reasoned abstractly to make connections between n and the exponents and coefficients of the expanded power $(a + b)^n$. The process culminates in this example as they extend the abstraction to expand the power of any binomial as described by the Binomial Theorem, using the values from Pascal's Triangle as multipliers of the terms in the expansion.

EXTRA EXAMPLE

Use the Binomial Theorem to expand $(t - 4)^3$.
$t^3 - 12t^2 + 48t - 64$

6 EXAMPLE CC.9-12.A.APR.5(+) Using the Binomial Theorem to Expand a Power

Use the Binomial Theorem to expand each power of a binomial.

A $(s-2)^3$

Step 1: Identify the values in row 3 of Pascal's Triangle. 1   3   3   1

Step 2: Expand the power as described in the Binomial Theorem, using the values from Pascal's Triangle as coefficients.

$$1 \ s^3 \ (-2)^0 + 3 \ s^2 \ (-2)^1 + 3 \ s^1 \ (-2)^2 + 1 \ s^0 \ (-2)^3$$

Step 3: Simplify.

So, $(s-2)^3 = s^3 - 6s^2 + 12s - 8$

B $(x+y)^5$

Step 1: Identify the values in row 5 of Pascal's Triangle. 1   5   10   10   5   1

Step 2: Expand the power as described by the Binomial Theorem, using the values from Pascal's Triangle as coefficients.

$$1 \ x^5 \ y^0 + 5 \ x^4 \ y^1 + 10 \ x^3 \ y^2 + 10 \ x^2 \ y^3 + 5 \ x^1 \ y^4 + 1 \ x^0 \ y^5$$

Step 3: Simplify.

So, $(x+y)^5 = x^5 + 5x^4y + 10x^3y^2 + 10x^2y^3 + 5xy^4 + y^5$

REFLECT

6a. What do you notice about the signs of the terms in the expanded form of $(s-2)^3$? Why does this happen?

The signs alternate between positive and negative. This happens because −2 to an
even power is positive and −2 to an odd power is negative.

6b. If the number 11 is written as the binomial $(10+1)$, how can you use the Binomial Theorem to find 11^2, 11^3, and 11^4? What is the pattern in the digits?

$11^2 = 10^2 + 2(10)(1) + 1^2 = 121$; $11^3 = 10^3 + 3(10^2)(1) + 3(10)(1^2) + 1^3 = 1331$;
$11^4 = 10^4 + 4(10^3)(1) + 6(10^2)(1^2) + 4(10)(1^3) + 1^4 = 14641$; the digits are the
values in the rows of Pascal's Triangle.

PRACTICE

Find each product.

1. $(2x^3)(2x^2 - 9x + 3)$

$4x^5 - 18x^4 + 6x^3$

2. $(x+5)(3x^2 - x + 1)$

$3x^3 + 14x^2 - 4x + 5$

3. $(x-4)(x-6)$

$x^2 - 10x + 24$

4. $(3+x^3)(-x+x^2+7)$

$x^5 - x^4 + 7x^3 + 3x^2 - 3x + 21$

5. $(4x^2 + 2x + 2)(2x^2 - x + 3)$

$8x^4 + 14x^2 + 4x + 6$

6. $(2x^4 - 5x^2)(6x + 4x^2)$

$8x^6 + 12x^5 - 20x^4 - 30x^3$

7. $(x+y)(2x-y)$

$2x^2 + xy - y^2$

8. $(x+2y)(x^2 + xy + y^2)$

$x^3 + 3x^2y + 3xy^2 + 2y^3$

9. $(3x^2 - x + 2x^3 - 2)(2x+3)$

$4x^4 + 12x^3 + 7x^2 - 7x - 6$

10. $(x^3)(x^2 - 3)(3x + 1)$

$3x^6 + x^5 - 9x^4 - 3x^3$

Use the Binomial Theorem to expand each power of a binomial.

11. $(x-1)^4$

$x^4 - 4x^3 + 6x^2 - 4x + 1$

12. $(2m+5)^3$

$8m^3 + 60m^2 + 150m + 125$

13. $(c+2d)^3$

$c^3 + 6c^2d + 12cd^2 + 8d^3$

14. $(2x-2)^4$

$16x^4 - 64x^3 + 96x^2 - 64x + 16$

15. $(8-m)^3$

$512 - 192m + 24m^2 - m^3$

16. $(3s+2t)^4$

$81s^4 + 216s^3t + 216s^2t^2 + 96st^3 + 16t^4$

17. $(3+t)^5$

$243 + 405t + 270t^2 + 90t^3 + 15t^4 + t^5$

18. $(x-y)^5$

$x^5 - 5x^4y + 10x^3y^2 - 10x^2y^3 + 5xy^4 - y^5$

19. $(2n+1)^6$

$64n^6 + 192n^5 + 240n^4 + 160n^3 + 60n^2 + 12n + 1$

20. $(p-2q)^6$

$p^6 - 12p^5q + 60p^4q^2 - 160p^3q^3 + 240p^2q^4 - 192pq^5 + 64q^6$

Essential Question

How do you multiply polynomials?

You can use the Distributive Property to multiply every term in the first factor by every term in the second factor. For two polynomials with m and n terms, the resulting product will have mn terms before simplifying. Some polynomials can also be multiplied using special product rules, including the sum and difference, square of a binomial, and cube of a binomial rules. To expand a binomial raised to the nth power, identify the values in row n of Pascal's Triangle. Expand the power as described in the Binomial Theorem, using the values from Pascal's Triangle as multipliers of the terms. Then, simplify.

Summarize

Have students make a table describing the methods for multiplying polynomials. Give examples for multiplying monomials, binomials, and trinomials, as well as for using special product rules.

Where skills are taught	Where skills are practiced
1 EXAMPLE	EXS. 1–10
2 EXAMPLE	EX. 21
3 EXAMPLE	EX. 23
5 EXPLORE	EX. 26
6 EXAMPLE	EXS. 11–20

Exercise 22: Students apply the sum and difference rule to multiply integers by mental math.

Exercises 24 and 25: Students apply the Binomial Theorem to functions of the form $f(x) = a(x - h)^n + k$, demonstrating that they are polynomial functions.

Exercise 27: Students use a calculator to expand the power of a binomial using the Binomial Theorem.

21. Justify the rule for the square of a binomial, $(a + b)^2 = a^2 + 2ab + b^2$. Then use it to expand $(2x^3 + 6y)^2$.

$(a + b)^2 = (a + b)(a + b) = a \cdot a + a \cdot b + b \cdot a + b \cdot b = a^2 + ab + ba + b^2 = a^2 + 2ab + b^2$;

$(2x^3 + 6y)^2 = (2x^3)^2 + 2(2x^3)(6y) + (6y)^2 = 4x^6 + 24x^3y + 36y^2$

22. The sum and difference rule is useful for mental-math calculations. Explain how you can use the rule and mental math to calculate $32 \cdot 28$. (*Hint:* $32 \cdot 28 = (30 + 2)(30 - 2)$.)

$32 \cdot 28 = (30 + 2)(30 - 2)$; by the sum and difference rule, this is equal to

$30^2 - 2^2$, which is easy to calculate by mental math: $30^2 - 2^2 = 900 - 4 = 896$.

23. You can generate a Pythagorean triple by choosing a positive integer m and letting $a = 2m$, $b = m^2 - 1$, and $c = m^2 + 1$. Show that this formula generates a Pythagorean triple. Then use the formula to generate a Pythagorean triple with $m = 5$.

$a^2 + b^2 = (2m)^2 + (m^2 - 1)^2 = 4m^2 + m^4 - 2m^2 + 1 = m^4 + 2m^2 + 1$;

$c^2 = (m^2 + 1)^2 = m^4 + 2m^2 + 1$; so $a^2 + b^2 = c^2$.

When $m = 5$, the Pythagorean triple is $a = 10$, $b = 24$, and $c = 26$.

24. Previously, you graphed functions of the form $f(x) = a(x - h)^n + k$.

a. What is the expanded form of $a(x - h)^3 + k$?

$ax^3 - 3ax^2h + 3axh^2 - ah^3 + k$

b. Is this function a polynomial? Why or why not?

Yes; the function consists of a sum of monomials.

c. What is the constant term in the expanded form of $a(x - h)^3 + k$? What does this represent in the graph of the function?

$-ah^3 + k$; it is the y-intercept of the graph.

© Houghton Mifflin Harcourt Publishing Company

25. What is the leading term of the expanded form of $f(x) = a(x - h)^n + k$? What is the constant term? Explain how you know.

ax^n; $a(-h)^n + k$; when $(x - h)^n$ is expanded using the Binomial Theorem, the first term is x^n and the last term is $(-h)^n$. Each term of the expanded form is multiplied by a, and k is added to the constant term.

26. If n is even, the expanded form of $(a + b)^n$ has an odd number of terms. For example, the expansion of $(a + b)^2$ is $a^2 + 2ab + b^2$ and the expansion of $(a + b)^4$ is $a^4 + 4a^3b + 6a^2b^2 + 4ab^3 + b^4$. Write an expression for the middle term of the expanded form of $(a + b)^n$ when n is an even number. Explain your reasoning.

$_nC_{\frac{n}{2}}(a^{\frac{n}{2}}b^{\frac{n}{2}})$; When there are an odd number of terms, the value of r in $_nC_r$ for the middle term is always half the value of n. Also when there are an odd number of terms, the exponents of a and b in the middle term are always equal and both are half the value of n.

27. You can use a graphing calculator to evaluate $_nC_r$. First enter the value of n, then press MATH, select **PRB**, then select **3:nCr**. Now enter the value of r, and then press ENTER. Use a calculator to help you expand $(x + 1)^9$.

$x^9 + 9x^8 + 36x^7 + 84x^6 + 126x^5 + 126x^4 + 84x^3 + 36x^2 + 9x + 1$

© Houghton Mifflin Harcourt Publishing Company

Assign these pages to help your students practice and apply important lesson concepts. For additional exercises, see the Student Edition.

Answers

Additional Practice

1. $12x^4 + 4x^2$

2. $-9x^3 - 18x^2 - 36x$

3. $-6x^5 - 42x^4 + 24x^3 - 18x^2$

4. $-4x^6 + 10x^5 - 7x^4 + 2x^3$

5. $-35m^3n^4 + 10m^4n^3 - 30m^3$

6. $xy^2 + 2xy - 12x + 2y^2 + 4y - 24$

7. $4p^3 - p^2 + 4p^2q - 2pq - 8pq^2 - q^2 - 8q^3$

8. $2x^2y^2 + 6x^3 + xy^3 + 3x^2y - y^3 - 3xy$

9. $27x^3 - 27x^2 + 9x - 1$

10. $x^4 - 16x^3 + 96x^2 - 256x + 256$

11. $3a^2 - 24ab + 48b^2$

12. $5x^6 - 30x^4y + 60x^2y^2 - 40y^3$

13. $8y^5 + 14y^4 + 7y^3 + y^2$

Problem Solving

1.

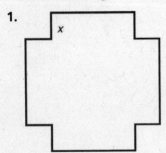

2. $24 - 2x$

3. $V = (x)(24 - 2x)(24 - 2x)$

4. $V = 4x^3 - 96x^2 + 576x$

5. Possible answer: The side length of the finished box is $24 - 2x$, and $24 - 2(12) = 0$.

6. 800; 972; 1024; 980; 864

7. **a.** 4

   b. Possible answer: The volume increases up to $x = 4$ and then decreases after that.

   c. 4 by 16 by 16 inches

Additional Practice

Find each product.

1. $4x^2(3x^2 + 1)$

2. $-9x(x^2 + 2x + 4)$

3. $-6x^2(x^3 + 7x^2 - 4x + 3)$

4. $x^3(-4x^3 + 10x^2 - 7x + 2)$

5. $-5m^3(7n^4 - 2mn^3 + 6)$

6. $(x + 2)(y^2 + 2y - 12)$

7. $(p + q)(4p^2 - p - 8q^2 - q)$

8. $(2x^2 + xy - y)(y^2 + 3x)$

Expand each expression.

9. $(3x - 1)^3$

10. $(x - 4)^4$

11. $3(a - 4b)^2$

12. $5\left(x^2 - 2y^3\right)^3$

Solve.

13. A biologist has found that the number of branches on a certain rare tree in its first few years of life can be modeled by the polynomial $b(y) = 4y^2 + y$. The number of leaves on each branch can be modeled by the polynomial $l(y) = 2y^3 + 3y^2 + y$, where y is the number of years after the tree reaches a height of 6 feet. Write a polynomial describing the total number of leaves on the tree.

Problem Solving

Latesha is making an open wooden toy box to hold the building blocks at her day care center. She has a square panel of cedar with side length of 24 inches. The first step is to cut out congruent squares from each corner. She needs to know what the side length of the cutout square should be in order for the finished toy box to have the greatest volume possible.

1. Draw a sketch to help solve the problem.

2. The toy box will be square and x inches deep. Write an expression for the side length of the finished box.
_____

3. Write an equation to represent the volume.
_____

4. Express the volume as the sum of monomials.
_____

5. Latesha decides to try some possible values for x. She knows that x must be less than 12. Explain why.
_____

6. Complete the table for each value of x. Round each volume to the nearest square inch.

x (in.)	2	3	4	5	6
Volume (sq in.)					

7. Latesha decides that she will use an integer value for x, so that she does not have to cut fractions of an inch.
   a. What value for x should she choose?
   _____
   b. Explain why this is the best choice.
   _____

   c. What are the dimensions of her finished toy box?
   _____

Notes

Dividing Polynomials
Going Deeper

Essential question: *What is the relationship between polynomial division and the Remainder Theorem?*

Standards for Mathematical Content

CC.9-12.A.APR.1 Understand that polynomials form a system analogous to the integers, namely, they are closed under the operations of addition, subtraction, and multiplication ...

CC.9-12.A.APR.2 Know and apply the Remainder Theorem: For a polynomial $p(x)$ and a number a, the remainder on division by $x - a$ is $p(a)$, so $p(a) = 0$ if and only if $(x - a)$ is a factor of $p(x)$.

Vocabulary

synthetic division

synthetic substitution

Prerequisites

Closure of the set of integers

Multiplying polynomials

Math Background

Students have learned to add, subtract, and multiply polynomials. Students also explored the property of closure and concluded that the set of polynomials is closed under addition, subtraction, and multiplication in a way that is analogous to the set of integers. In this lesson, they will explore division of polynomials, discovering that the set of polynomials, like the set of integers, is *not* closed under the operation of division.

INTRODUCE

Point out the parallels between addition, subtraction, and multiplication of integers and the same operations for the set of polynomials. Ask: Is the set of integers closed under division? No. Do you think the set of polynomials is closed under division? No. Review numerical long division and explain that polynomial long division is similar.

TEACH

1 EXAMPLE

Questioning Strategies

- When using long division to find $4517 \div 58$, you may think that the first digit of the quotient is 9, because $45 \div 5 = 9$. However, $9 \times 58 = 522$, which is greater than 451, so 9 is too large for the first digit. Do similar situations arise when using long division to divide polynomials? **No, because at each step of the division process, you are dividing monomials to obtain the next term in the quotient. As long as the degree of the monomial from the dividend is greater than or equal to the monomial from the divisor, the quotient of the monomials is another monomial.**

- Why is the quotient of the polynomials in the Example *not* a polynomial? **A polynomial does not have variables in the denominators in any of its terms.**

- How could you check that division of polynomials using long division has been performed correctly? **Multiply the quotient by the divisor and then add the remainder. The resulting polynomial should be equal to the polynomial that is the dividend.**

Teaching Strategies

Students who normally divide with a calculator may benefit from a review of numerical long division. As a review, work a numerical long division and a polynomial long division side-by-side, showing the steps of each simultaneously. Remind students to take special care with the signs when subtracting polynomials to avoid careless mistakes. Encourage students to write neatly and keep terms aligned.

EXTRA EXAMPLE

Divide $3x^3 + x^2 - 4x$ by $x - 1$ using long division.
$3x^2 + 4x$

Name_____ Class_____ Date_____

Dividing Polynomials
Going Deeper

Essential question: *What is the relationship between polynomial division and the Remainder Theorem?*

You can use long division to divide a polynomial by another polynomial of a lower degree. The process is similar to dividing numbers.

Video Tutor

PREP FOR CC.9-12.A.APR.2

1 EXAMPLE   Using Long Division to Divide Polynomials

Divide $2x^3 + 4x^2 + 5$ by $x - 3$ using long division.

A Write the quotient in long division format with the polynomials written in standard form. Remember to include terms with a coefficient of 0.

$$
\begin{array}{r}
2x^2 + 10x + 30 \\
x - 3 \overline{)\,2x^3 + 4x^2 + 0x + 5} \\
-(2x^3 - 6x^2) \\
\hline
10x^2 + 0x \\
-(10x^2 - 30x) \\
\hline
30x + 5 \\
-(30x - 90) \\
\hline
95
\end{array}
$$

Divide $2x^3$ by x. Write $2x^2$ above $2x^3$.
Multiply $2x^2$ by $x - 3$ and subtract.
Bring down the next term. Divide $10x^2$ by x.
Multiply $10x$ by $x - 3$ and subtract.
Bring down the next term. Divide $30x$ by x.
Multiply 30 by $x - 3$ and subtract.
Write the remainder.

B Write the quotient. The last term of the quotient is the remainder in fraction form.

$$\frac{2x^3 + 4x^2 + 5}{x - 3} = 2x^2 + 10x + 30 + \frac{95}{x - 3}$$

REFLECT

1a. When you perform long division of polynomials, why must the degree of the remainder be less than the degree of the divisor?

If this were not the case, it would be possible to continue the long division

process.

1b. Is the set of polynomials closed under division? Why or why not?

No; the quotient of the polynomials in the example is not a polynomial.

CC.9-12.A.APR.2

2 ENGAGE   Understanding the Remainder Theorem

When you divide $2x^3 + 4x^2 + 5$ by $x - 3$, you get a remainder of 95. If you evaluate the polynomial $2x^3 + 4x^2 + 5$ for $x = 3$, you get $2(3)^3 + 4(3)^2 + 5 = 2(27) + 4(9) + 5 = 95$. This is an illustration of the Remainder Theorem.

> **Remainder Theorem**
>
> If a polynomial $p(x)$ is divided by $x - a$, then the remainder r is $p(a)$.

You can use the Remainder Theorem to evaluate polynomials. To find $p(a)$, you divide the polynomial $p(x)$ by $x - a$ and find the remainder.

A shorthand method for dividing a polynomial by $x - a$ is called **synthetic division**. The process is similar to long division, but you work only with the coefficients. Here are the steps for using synthetic division to find the quotient $(2x^3 + 4x^2 + 5) \div (x - 3)$. In this case, $p(x) = 2x^3 + 4x^2 + 5$ and $a = 3$.

Step 1: Write the coefficients of $p(x)$ in the top row.

Step 2: Write the value of a to the left.

Step 3: Bring down the first coefficient.

Step 4: Multiply by a and place the result below the next coefficient, then add. Continue to the last column.

$$
\begin{array}{c|ccccc}
3 & 2 & 4 & 0 & 5 \\
  &   & 6 & 30 & 90 \\
\hline
  & 2 & 10 & 30 & 95
\end{array}
$$

The coefficients of the quotient, $2x^2 + 10x + 30$, are shown in the bottom row, and the last value, 95, is the remainder. By the Remainder Theorem, this is also the value of $p(3)$. Because synthetic division may be used to evaluate polynomials, the process is also known as **synthetic substitution**.

REFLECT

2a. If a polynomial $p(x)$ is divided by $x - a$, then $\frac{p(x)}{x-a} = q(x) + \frac{r}{x-a}$, where $q(x)$ is the quotient and r is the remainder. This is the first step in the proof of the Remainder Theorem. Complete the proof.

$\frac{p(x)}{x-a} = q(x) + \frac{r}{x-a}$	Given
$(x - a)\frac{p(x)}{x-a} = (x - a)\left(q(x) + \frac{r}{x-a}\right)$	Multiply both sides by $x - a$.
$p(x) = (x - a)q(x) + \boxed{r}$	Distributive property and simplification
$p(a) = (a - a)q(a) + \boxed{r}$	Substitute a for x.
$p(a) = \boxed{0} \cdot q(a) + \boxed{r}$	Simplify $a - a$.
$p(a) = \boxed{r}$	Simplify.

Questioning Strategies

- If a polynomial $p(x)$ is divided by $x - a$ and $p(a) \neq 0$, is the quotient a polynomial? Explain. **No; if $p(a) \neq 0$, then the quotient contains a term with the remainder $p(a) = r$ in the numerator and $x - a$ in the denominator.**

- In the synthetic division shown, if you replaced the 3 in the box at the upper left with a 4, what division problem would be represented by the synthetic division? **$(2x^3 + 4x^2 + 5) \div (x - 4)$**

- If you replaced the 3 in the box at the upper left in the synthetic division with a -3, what division problem would be represented by the synthetic division? **$(2x^3 + 4x^2 + 5) \div (x + 3)$**

Avoid Common Errors

Students may think that the entire bottom row of numbers in a synthetic division represents the quotient. For instance, in the problem shown, students may think that the quotient is $2x^3 + 10x^2 + 30x + 95$. Point out to students that if they were to multiply this "quotient" by the divisor, $x - 3$, they would get a polynomial of degree 4, which is obviously not the degree of the dividend. Students should understand that using a divisor of degree 1 results in a quotient whose degree is 1 less than the degree of the dividend. So, the quotient has 1 less term than the dividend does. In the bottom row of a synthetic division, then, all the numbers *except for the last one* are coefficients of the quotient, and the last number (which can be "boxed off" from the others) is the remainder.

3 EXAMPLE

Questioning Strategies

- A student filled in the bottom row of the synthetic division as 3, 29, -146, and -710. What error did the student make? **The student subtracted the second line of numbers from the top line of numbers instead of adding.**

- What number would you place in the box at the upper left to find $(3x^3 + 14x^2 - x + 20) \div (x - 7)$ using synthetic division? **7**

- What numbers would be placed along the top row to find $(2x^3 - 13x^2 + x - 25) \div (x + 5)$ using synthetic division? **2, -13, 1, and -25**

Differentiated Instruction

Interpersonal learners may benefit from taking turns with a partner filling in the missing numbers

in a synthetic division problem. Students could be given the option to make a mistake on purpose to keep the other partner attentive to possible errors that can occur in the process.

Avoid Common Errors

Synthetic division involves copying and manipulating numbers in a format that is removed from the context of the polynomials, which increases the chance for error. Remind students to be careful to avoid errors like incorrectly copying coefficients, using the wrong sign for the number in the box, and subtracting the numbers in the second row instead of adding.

EXTRA EXAMPLE

Divide $6x^3 + 23x^2 - x + 12$ by $x + 4$ using synthetic division. **$6x^2 - x + 3$**

CLOSE

Essential Question

What is the relationship between polynomial division and the Remainder Theorem?
The Remainder Theorem says that if a polynomial $p(x)$ is divided by a linear binomial of the form $x - a$, the remainder r of that division is equal to the result of evaluating $p(x)$ for $x = a$.

Summarize

Have students write a journal entry describing how polynomial division is related to the Remainder Theorem. Ask them to provide at least two examples that illustrate the relationship.

PRACTICE

Where skills are taught	Where skills are practiced
1 EXAMPLE	EXS. 1–6
3 EXAMPLE	EXS. 7–12

Exercise 13: Students identify an error made by another student when performing synthetic division.

Exercise 14: Students analyze closure of the set of polynomials.

Exercise 15: Students write a polynomial given its quotient and divisor.

Exercise 16: Students write a polynomial division problem and its quotient represented by a given synthetic division.

CC.9-12.A.APR.2

3 EXAMPLE   Using Synthetic Division

Divide $3x^3 + 14x^2 - x + 20$ by $x + 5$ using synthetic division.

A Write the coefficients of $p(x)$ in the top row.

B Write the divisor in the form $x - a$.

$x + 5 = x - (-5)$, so $a = \underline{-5}$

C Write the value of a in the upper left corner.

D Bring down the first coefficient. Multiply by a and place the result below the next coefficient, then add. Continue to the last column.

E Write the quotient: $\underline{3x^2 - x + 4}$

-5	3	14	-1	20
		-15	5	-20
	3	-1	4	0

REFLECT

3a. What is the remainder in this example? How do you know?

The value in the lower right corner of the synthetic division is the remainder, so the remainder is 0.

3b. Can you use synthetic division to divide $3x^3 + 14x^2 - x + 20$ by $x^2 + 5$? Why or why not?

No; to use synthetic division, the divisor must be a linear binomial of the form $x - a$.

PRACTICE

Divide using long division.

1. $(5x^3 - 8x^2 - x - 4) \div (x - 2)$

$5x^2 + 2x + 3 + \dfrac{2}{x - 2}$

2. $(6x^2 + 16x^2 + 3x - 2) \div (x + 1)$

$6x^2 + 10x - 7 + \dfrac{5}{x + 1}$

3. $(x^3 + 7x^2 + 5x + 35) \div (x + 7)$

$x^2 + 5$

4. $(7x^3 + 9x^2 + 13) \div (x - 3)$

$7x^2 + 30x + 90 + \dfrac{283}{x - 3}$

5. $(4x^2 - 6x + 6) \div (2x + 1)$

$2x - 4 + \dfrac{10}{2x + 1}$

6. $(15x^3 + 16x^2 + x - 2) \div (3x + 2)$

$5x^2 + 2x - 1$

Divide using synthetic division.

7. $(4x^3 + 5x^2 + 2x + 16) \div (x + 2)$

$4x^2 - 3x + 8$

8. $(2x^3 - 22x^2 + 3x - 33) \div (x - 11)$

$2x^2 + 3$

9. $(4x^4 + 2x^2 - 3x - 9) \div (x + 1)$

$4x^3 - 4x^2 + 6x - 9$

10. $(6x^3 - 5x^2 - 3x + 2) \div \left(x - \frac{1}{2}\right)$

$6x^2 - 2x - 4$

11. $(3x^3 - x + 7) \div (x + 3)$

$3x^2 - 9x + 26 - \dfrac{71}{x + 3}$

12. $(6x^3 - 4x^2 + 2x + 17) \div (x - 4)$

$6x^2 + 20x + 82 + \dfrac{345}{x - 4}$

13. Error Analysis A student was asked to find the quotient $(4x^3 + x^2 + 2x + 1) \div (x + 2)$. The student's work is shown at right. Identify the student's error and provide the correct quotient.

The student should have used -2 in the upper left corner of the synthetic division. The correct quotient is $4x^2 - 7x + 16 - \dfrac{31}{x + 2}$.

2	4	1	2	1
		8	18	40
	4	9	20	41

So, $(4x^3 + x^2 + 2x + 1) \div (x + 2) = 4x^2 + 9x + 20 + \dfrac{41}{x + 2}$.

14. The set of polynomials is analogous to a set of numbers you have studied. To determine which, consider the following questions about closure.

a. Under which operations is the set of polynomials closed?

addition, subtraction, and multiplication

b. Which set of the numbers discussed in Lesson 1-1 is closed under the same set of operations?

integers

15. When the polynomial $p(x)$ is divided by $x - 1$, the quotient is $-2x^2 + 3x + 5 + \dfrac{12}{x - 1}$. What is $p(x)$? How did you find $p(x)$?

$p(x) = -2x^3 + 5x^2 + 2x + 7$; multiply the quotient by $x - 1$.

16. Determine the values of a, b, and c in the synthetic division shown at right. Then tell what polynomial division problem and quotient are represented by the synthetic division.

$a = 1$, $b = -5$, $c = 4$; $(x^3 - 2x^2 + 4x + 1) \div (x + 3)$

$= x^2 - 5x + 19 - \dfrac{6}{x + 3}$.

-3	a	-2	c	1
		-3	15	-57
	1	b	19	-56

© Houghton Mifflin Harcourt Publishing Company

Assign these pages to help your students practice and apply important lesson concepts. For additional exercises, see the Student Edition.

Answers

Additional Practice

1. $x + 2$

2. $2x^2 + 1$

3. $-3x + 2$

4. $3x^2 - \dfrac{14}{x + 3}$

5. $3x - 2$

6. $5x - 19 + \dfrac{69}{x + 3}$

7. $9x + 2 + \dfrac{5}{x - 1}$

8. $-6x + 47 - \dfrac{339}{x + 7}$

9. $P(3) = 11$

10. $P(-2) = -36$

11. $2t + 10$

Problem Solving

1. $\dfrac{\sqrt{3}}{4}x^2$

2. B

3. C

4. A

5. D

Additional Practice

Divide by using long division.

1. $(x^2 - x - 6) \div (x - 3)$

2. $(2x^3 - 10x^2 + x - 5) \div (x - 5)$

3. $(-3x^2 + 20x - 12) \div (x - 6)$

4. $(3x^3 + 9x^2 - 14) \div (x + 3)$

Divide by using synthetic division.

5. $(3x^2 - 8x + 4) \div (x - 2)$

6. $(5x^2 - 4x + 12) \div (x + 3)$

7. $(9x^2 - 7x + 3) \div (x - 1)$

8. $(-6x^2 + 5x - 10) \div (x + 7)$

Use synthetic substitution to evaluate the polynomial for the given value.

9. $P(x) = 4x^2 - 9x + 2$ for $x = 3$

10. $P(x) = -3x^2 + 10x - 4$ for $x = -2$

Solve.

11. The total number of dollars donated each year to a small charitable organization has followed the trend $d(t) = 2t^3 + 10t^2 + 2000t + 10,000$, where d is dollars and t is the number of years since 1990. The total number of donors each year has followed the trend $p(t) = t^2 + 1000$. Write an expression describing the average number of dollars per donor.

Problem Solving

An art class is making pedestals in the shape of regular prisms to display sculptures in an art show. Blake is in charge of the mirrors for the tops of the pedestals. He needs to estimate the total area of the mirrored surfaces. He will use that total to help determine the amount of mirrored product to purchase.

The figures below show the shape of the bases for each of the three kinds of prisms that will be used for pedestals. Each regular polygon has a side length of x. Recall that, for a prism, $V = Bh$.

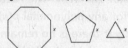

1. The triangular prism has a height of $2x + 1$ and its volume can be modeled by $V(x) = \dfrac{\sqrt{3}}{2}x^3 + \dfrac{\sqrt{3}}{4}x^2$. What is the area of the top of the pedestal?

Choose the letter for the best answer.

2. The volume of the pentagonal prism can be modeled by $V = 6.88x^3 - 1.72x^2$. Which expression represents the area of the top of the prism if the height is $4x - 1$?

   A $0.57x^2$

   B $1.72x^2$

   C $2.28x^2$

   D $6.88x^2$

3. The volume of the octagonal prism can be modeled by $V = 4.83x^3 - 24.15x^2$. Which expression represents the area of the top of the prism if the height is $x - 5$?

   A $48.3x^2$

   B $38.64x^2$

   C $4.83x^2$

   D $3.86x^2$

4. Which expression represents the total area that will be mirrored?

   A $A = x^2\left(\dfrac{\sqrt{3}}{4} + 6.55\right)$

   B $A = 6.98x$

   C $A = 12.58x^3 + 22.86x^2$

   D $A = \sqrt{6.98x}$

5. If $x = 5$, what is the total mirrored area in square units?

   A 6.98

   B 34.9

   C 69.8

   D 174.5

Notes

3-4

Factoring Polynomials
Connection: The Remainder Theorem

Essential question: *What is the relationship between polynomial division and the Factor Theorem?*

COMMON CORE **Standards for Mathematical Content**

CC.9-12.A.APR.2 Know and apply the Remainder Theorem: For a polynomial $p(x)$ and a number a, the remainder on division by $x - a$ is $p(a)$, so $p(a) = 0$ if and only if $(x - a)$ is a factor of $p(x)$.

Prerequisites
Multiplying polynomials
Synthetic division, synthetic substitution

Math Background
In the previous lesson, students used long division and synthetic division to find the quotient when a polynomial is divided by a binomial. Students are also familiar with using the distributive property to find the product of two polynomials.

INTRODUCE

Review the process of synthetic division, using $(2x^3 - 3x^2 + 4x - 7) \div (x - 1)$ which has a remainder and $(x^3 - 2x^2 - 7x + 2) \div (x + 2)$ which does not. Emphasize the difference between the final entries, the first being –4 and the second being 0. Write the two quotients as polynomials and point out the rational expression representing the remainder in the first division. Remind students that the dividend in a division problem (either of the polynomials in the problems here) can be written as the product of the divisor and the quotient.

1 ENGAGE

Questioning Strategies
- If a number is divided by one of its factors, what is the remainder? Give an example. **0; 5 is a factor of 35, and $35 \div 5 = 7$ with no remainder.**
- According to the Factor Theorem, what is the remainder when a polynomial is divided by any of its factors? **0**
- The Factor Theorem is stated using "if and only if." Rewrite the statement of the theorem using two if-then statements. **If $x - a$ is a factor of $p(x)$, then $p(a) = 0$. If $p(a) = 0$, then $x - a$ is a factor of $p(x)$.**

2 EXAMPLE

Questioning Strategies
- Could you show that $x^2 + 6x + 3$ is a factor of $p(x) = x^3 + 2x^2 - 21x - 12$ by using synthetic division to divide $p(x)$ by $x^2 + 6x + 3$? **No, synthetic division can be used only when the divisor is a linear binomial of the form $x - a$.**
- What does the Factor Theorem tell you if you use synthetic division to evaluate $p(-4)$? **Since the remainder is not zero, $x + 4$ is not a factor of $p(x)$.**

Technology
Students can use their graphing calculators and the Remainder Theorem to check their answer when performing synthetic division. Enter $Y_1 = p(x)$, and use the TABLE feature to find $p(a)$, which should match the remainder.

EXTRA EXAMPLE
Write $p(x) = x^3 + 2x^2 - 13x - 6$ as the product of $x - 3$ and another factor. **$(x - 3)(x^2 + 5x + 2)$**

CLOSE

Essential Question
What is the relationship between polynomial division and the Factor Theorem? **The Factor Theorem says that for any polynomial $p(x)$, $x - a$ is a factor if and only if there is no remainder r (that is, $p(a) = 0$) when $p(x)$ is divided by $x - a$.**

Summarize
Have students write a journal entry describing how polynomial division is related to the Factor Theorem. Ask them to provide at least two examples that illustrate the relationship.

PRACTICE

Where skills are taught	Where skills are practiced
2 EXAMPLE	EX. 1

Exercise 2: Students use their graphing calculators to factor a polynomial completely by applying the Factor Theorem.

Name_____ Class_____ Date_____

3-4

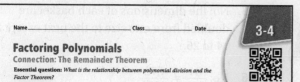

Video Tutor

Factoring Polynomials

Connection: The Remainder Theorem

Essential question: *What is the relationship between polynomial division and the Factor Theorem?*

CC.9-12.A.APR.2

1 ENGAGE   Understanding the Factor Theorem

When you use synthetic division to divide $3x^3 + 14x^2 - x + 20$ by $x + 5$, the remainder is 0. Therefore the divisor is a factor of the polynomial, as shown below.

$(x + 5)(3x^2 - x + 4) = x(3x^2) + x(-x) + x(4) + 5(3x^2) + 5(-x) + 5(4)$ Distribute each term.

$\qquad\qquad\qquad\quad = 3x^3 - x^2 + 4x + 15x^2 - 5x + 20$ Multiply.

$\qquad\qquad\qquad\quad = 3x^3 + 14x^2 - x + 20$ Combine like terms.

This shows that the product of $x + 5$ and $3x^2 - x + 4$ is the original polynomial, $3x^3 + 14x^2 - x + 20$. So, the divisor is a factor of the original polynomial.

The above observation is generalized in the Factor Theorem.

> **Factor Theorem**
>
> For any polynomial $p(x)$, $x - a$ is a factor if and only if $p(a) = 0$.

REFLECT

1a. Complete the proof of the Factor Theorem for a polynomial $p(x)$ divided by a linear binomial $x - a$ with quotient $q(x)$ and remainder r.

The proof has two parts: if $p(a) = 0$, then $x - a$ is a factor of $p(x)$, and if $x - a$ is a factor of $p(x)$, then $p(a) = 0$.

Part 1: Assume that $p(a) = 0$.

$p(a) = 0$	Given
$r = \underline{\quad p(a) \quad}$	Remainder Theorem
$p(x) = (x - a)q(x) + \underline{\quad p(a) \quad}$	Dividend = Divisor $\cdot$ Quotient + Remainder
$p(x) = (x - a)q(x) + \underline{\quad 0 \quad}$	Substitute 0 for $p(a)$.
$p(x) = \underline{\quad (x - a)q(x) \quad}$	Simplify.
$x - a$ is a factor of $p(x)$.	Definition of factor

Part 2: Assume that $x - a$ is a factor of $p(x)$.

$x - a$ is a factor of $p(x)$.	Given
$p(x) = (x - a)q(x)$	Definition of factor
$p(a) = \underline{\quad (a - a)q(a) \quad}$	Substitute a for x.
$p(a) = \underline{\quad 0 \quad}$	Simplify.

CC.9-12.A.APR.2

2 EXAMPLE   Using the Factor Theorem

Show that $x - 4$ is a factor of $p(x) = x^3 + 2x^2 - 21x - 12$. Then write $p(x)$ as the product of $x - 4$ and another factor.

A Evaluate $p(4)$ by using synthetic substitution. Complete the process at the right.

B The synthetic substitution shows that $p(4) = \underline{\quad 0 \quad}$.

So, by the Factor Theorem, $x - 4$ is a factor of $p(x)$.

4	1	2	−21	−12
		4	24	12
	1	6	3	0

C Write the polynomial as the product of $x - 4$ and the quotient.

From the synthetic substitution, $(x^3 + 2x^2 - 21x - 12) \div (x - 4) = \underline{\quad x^2 + 6x + 3 \quad}$.

So, $p(x) = x^3 + 2x^2 - 21x - 12 = (\underline{\quad x - 4 \quad})(\underline{\quad x^2 + 6x + 3 \quad})$.

REFLECT

2a. Show how to check the factorization you wrote in the last step.

$(x - 4)(x^2 + 6x + 3) = x(x^2) + x(6x) + x(3) - 4(x^2) - 4(6x) - 4(3) =$

$x^3 + 6x^2 + 3x - 4x^2 - 24x - 12 = x^3 + 2x^2 - 21x - 12$

PRACTICE

1. a. Show that $x + 6$ is a factor of $p(x) = x^3 + 6x^2 - 16x - 96$. Then write $p(x)$ as the product of $x + 6$ and another factor.

Using synthetic substitution, $p(-6) = 0$, so by the Factor Theorem, $x + 6$ is a

factor of $p(x)$; $p(x) = (x + 6)(x^2 - 16)$.

b. Factor $p(x) = x^3 + 6x^2 - 16x - 96$ completely. That is, write $p(x)$ as a product of linear factors. Describe the strategy you used.

$x^2 - 16$ is a difference of squares, so $x^2 - 16 = (x + 4)(x - 4)$ and

$p(x) = (x + 6)(x + 4)(x - 4)$.

2. Use the Table feature of your graphing calculator to complete the table of values for $p(x) = x^4 - 2x^3 - 9x^2 + 2x + 8$. Use your results to factor $p(x)$ completely. Justify your answer.

$p(x) = (x + 2)(x + 1)(x - 1)(x - 4)$; the

zeros of $p(x)$ are $-2, -1, 1,$ and 4, so by

the Factor Theorem, $x + 2$, $x + 1$,

$x - 1$, and $x - 4$ are factors of $p(x)$.

x	$p(x)$	x	$p(x)$
−4	240	1	0
−3	56	2	−24
−2	0	3	−40
−1	0	4	0
0	8	5	168

© Houghton Mifflin Harcourt Publishing Company

Assign these pages to help your students practice and apply important lesson concepts. For additional exercises, see the Student Edition.

Answers

Additional Practice

1. Yes
2. No

3. Yes
4. No

5. $x(2x - 1)(x + 1)$ **6.** $(4x + 1)(x^2 - 2)$

7. $(5x^3 + 1)(x^2 - 1)$

8. $2x(x + 3)(x^2 - 3x + 9)$

9. $(4x - 1)(16x^2 + 4x + 1)$

10. $3x(x + 2)(x^2 - 2x + 4)$

11. $2016; -(x - 10)(x^2 - 6x + 14)$

Problem Solving

1. a. $-2, 4, 6$
   b. $(x + 2)(x - 4)(x - 6)$

2. a. $-4, -1, 0$
   b. $(2x + 2)(x + 4)(x)$

3. a. $5, 8, 9$
   b. $(x - 5)(x - 8)(x - 9)$

4.

Basket	Dimensions (in terms of x)	Actual Dimensions	Volume
A	$(x - 5), (x - 8), (x - 9)$	7 by 4 by 3	84 cubic units
B	$(x + 2), (x - 4), (x - 6)$	14 by 8 by 6	672 cubic units
C	$(2x + 2), (x + 4), (x)$	26 by 16 by 12	4992 cubic units

5. No; the dimensions of each basket are doubled from one size to the next except for 14 to 26.

6. No; $\dfrac{84}{672} \neq \dfrac{672}{4992}$

Additional Practice

Name_____ Class_____ Date_____

Determine whether the given binomial is a factor of the polynomial $P(x)$.

1. $(x - 4)$; $P(x) = x^2 + 8x - 48$

2. $(x + 5)$; $P(x) = 2x^2 - 6x - 1$

3. $(x - 6)$; $P(x) = -2x^2 + 15x - 18$

4. $(x + 3)$; $P(x) = 2x^2 - x + 7$

Factor each expression.

5. $2x^4 + 2x^3 - x^2 - x$

6. $4x^3 + x^2 - 8x - 2$

7. $5x^6 - 5x^4 + x^3 - x$

8. $2x^4 + 54x$

9. $64x^3 - 1$

10. $3x^4 + 24x$

Solve.

11. Since 2006, the water level in a certain pond has been modeled by the polynomial $d(x) = -x^3 + 16x^2 - 74x + 140$, where the depth d, is measured in feet over x years. Identify the year that the pond will dry up. Use the graph to factor $d(x)$.

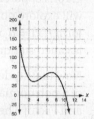

Problem Solving

Paulo is drawing plans for a set of three proportional nesting baskets, in the shape of open rectangular prisms.

1. The volume for the middle-sized basket (B) can be modeled by the function $V_B(x) = x^3 - 8x^2 + 4x + 48$. Use the graph to factor V_B.

   a. What are the values of x where $V_B = 0$?

   b. Use these zeros to write the factors.

2. The volume for the largest basket (C) can be modeled by the function $V_C(x) = 2x^3 + 10x^2 + 8x$. Use the graph to factor V_C.

   a. What are the values of x where $V_C = 0$?

   b. Use these zeros to write the factors.

3. The volume for the smallest basket (A) can be modeled by the function $V_A(x) = x^3 - 22x^2 + 157x - 360$. Use the graph to factor V_A.

   a. What are the values of x where $V_A = 0$?

   b. Use these zeros to write the factors.

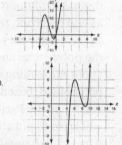

4. Complete the table. Use $x = 12$ units to find the actual dimensions and volume.

Basket	Dimensions (in terms of x)	Actual Dimensions	Volume
A			
B			
C			

5. Are the actual dimensions of the three baskets proportional? Explain.

6. Are the volumes of the three baskets proportional? Explain.

Finding Real Roots of Polynomial Equations

Extension: Graphing Factorable Polynomial Functions

Essential question: *How do you use zeros to graph polynomial functions?*

COMMON **Standards for**
CORE **Mathematical Content**

CC.9-12.A.SSE.2 Use the structure of an expression to identify ways to rewrite it.

CC.9-12.A.APR.3 Identify zeros of polynomials when suitable factorizations are available, and use the zeros to construct a rough graph of the function defined by the polynomial.

CC.9-12.A.CED.2 Create equations in two … variables to represent relationships between quantities; graph equations on coordinate axes with labels and scales.*

CC.9-12.F.IF.2 Use function notation, evaluate functions for inputs in their domains, and interpret statements that use function notation in terms of a context.

CC.9-12.F.IF.7 Graph functions expressed symbolically and show key features of the graph, by hand in simple cases and using technology for more complicated cases.*

CC.9-12.F.IF.7c Graph polynomial functions, identifying zeros when suitable factorizations are available, and showing end behavior.*

Also: CC.9-12.F.IF.9

Vocabulary

monomial, polynomial, degree of a monomial, degree of a polynomial, polynomial function

Prerequisites

Understanding end behavior

Determining end behavior

Dividing polynomials

Math Background

Previously, students investigated polynomials functions written in the form $f(x) = a(x - h)^n + k$. This form enables students to graph polynomial functions by transforming the graphs of parent functions. In this lesson, students will explore polynomial functions written in the form $f(x) = a_n x^n + a_{n-1} x^{n-1} + \cdots + a_1 x + a_0$, which is called standard form.

Now that students know how to find the factors of a polynomial using the Remainder Theorem and Factor Theorem, they will graph factorable polynomial functions in factored form.

INTRODUCE

Explain to students that they have already been graphing polynomial functions that are written in the form $f(x) = a(x - h)^n + k$. They will now be graphing polynomial functions written in standard form, and this form requires different graphing techniques.

This lesson brings together many of the topics covered previously. Start by drawing the graph of a general polynomial function on the board, and discuss the important features of the function, such as end behavior, zeros, maxima and minima. Ask students how they would determine the degree of the polynomial and what they could determine about the leading coefficient and the factors of the polynomial, based on the end behavior and zeros and using the Factor Theorem. Tell students they will learn to put all of these pieces together in order to graph polynomials that can be factored.

Name_____ Class_____ Date_____

3-5

Finding Real Roots of Polynomial Equations

Extension: Graphing Factorable Polynomial Functions

Essential question: *How do you use zeros to graph polynomial functions?*

Video Tutor

PREP FOR CC.9-12.F.IF.7c

1 ENGAGE   Understanding Polynomial Functions

A **polynomial function** can be written as $f(x) = a_n x^n + a_{n-1}x^{n-1} + \cdots + a_1 x + a_0$ where the coefficients $a_n, \ldots, a_1, a_0$ are real numbers. This is known as *standard form*. Note that linear functions are polynomial functions of degree 1 and quadratic functions are polynomial functions of degree 2. The functions you have graphed in the form $f(x) = a(x-h)^n + k$ are also polynomial functions, as you will see in later lessons.

The end behavior of a polynomial function $f(x) = a_n x^n + a_{n-1}x^{n-1} + \cdots + a_1 x + a_0$ is determined by the term with the greatest degree, $a_n x^n$.

Polynomial End Behavior

n	a_n	As $x \to +\infty$	As $x \to -\infty$	Graph
Even	Positive	$f(x) \to +\infty$	$f(x) \to +\infty$	
Even	Negative	$f(x) \to -\infty$	$f(x) \to -\infty$	
Odd	Positive	$f(x) \to +\infty$	$f(x) \to -\infty$	
Odd	Negative	$f(x) \to -\infty$	$f(x) \to +\infty$	

You know how to use transformations to help you graph functions of the form $f(x) = a(x-h)^n + k$. If a polynomial function is not written in this form, then other graphing methods must be used. You will learn several methods throughout this unit, but the most basic is to plot points and connect them with a smooth curve, taking into account the end behavior of the function.

Chapter 3   139   Lesson 5

In general, the higher the degree of a polynomial, the more complex the graph. Here are some typical graphs for polynomials of degree n.

Degree 1
Linear

Degree 2
Quadratic

Degree 3
Cubic

Degree 4
Quartic

REFLECT

1a. Evaluate each term of the polynomial $f(x) = x^4 + 2x^3 - 5x^2 + 2x - 3$ for $x = 10$ and $x = -10$. Explain why the end behavior is determined by the term with the greatest degree.

For $x = 10$: 10,000; 2000; −500; 20; −3. For $x = -10$: 10,000; −2000; −500; −20; −3.

The term with the greatest degree has a much greater absolute value than any other term when $|x|$ is large.

1b. Describe the end behavior of $f(x) = -2x^3 + 3x^2 - x - 3$. Explain your reasoning.

The end behavior of $f(x)$ is the same as the end behavior of $y = -2x^3$; so

$f(x) \to -\infty$ as $x \to +\infty$ and $f(x) \to +\infty$ as $x \to -\infty$.

The *nested form* of a polynomial has the form $f(x) = (((ax + b)x + c)x + d)x \ldots)$. It is often simpler to evaluate polynomials in nested form.

CC.9-12.F.IF.2

2 EXAMPLE   Writing Polynomials in Nested Form

Write $f(x) = x^3 + 2x^2 - 5x - 6$ in nested form.

$f(x) = x^3 + 2x^2 - 5x - 6$ Write the function.

$f(x) = (\boxed{x^2 + 2x - 5})x - 6$ Factor an x out of the first three terms.

$f(x) = ((\boxed{x + 2})x - 5)x - 6$ Factor an x out of the first two terms in parentheses.

REFLECT

2a. Use the standard form and the nested form to evaluate the polynomial for $x = 3$. Then compare both methods. Which is easier? Why?

Standard form: $f(3) = (3)^3 + 2(3)^2 - 5(3) - 6 = 24$

Nested form: $f(3) = ((3 + 2)3 - 5)3 - 6 = 24$

Nested form is easier, because there are no exponents to evaluate.

Chapter 3   140   Lesson 5

TEACH

1 ENGAGE

Questioning Strategies

- What is the degree of the polynomial $3x^2 + 2x^4$? Explain. **The degree is 4, which is the degree of $2x^4$, the term with the greatest degree. The degree of the polynomial is easier to determine if the polynomial is written in standard form: $2x^4 + 3x^2$.**

- The end behavior of a polynomial function $f(x)$ is $f(x) \to -\infty$ as $x \to +\infty$ and $f(x) \to +\infty$ as $x \to -\infty$. What can you tell about the degree of the polynomial and the coefficient a_n? **The degree is odd, and the coefficient a_n is negative.**

Differentiated Instruction

Understanding the concept of the degree of a polynomial is important in determining the end behavior of polynomial functions and, therefore, in graphing polynomial functions. English language learners may benefit from a rigorous review of finding degrees of polynomials, some in standard form and others with terms in varying orders of degree. Focus on polynomials that contain only single-variable monomials.

2 EXAMPLE

Questioning Strategies

- When a polynomial is in nested form, how is the number of pairs of parentheses related to the degree of the polynomial? **The number of pairs of parentheses is one less than the degree of the polynomial.**

- If a polynomial is in nested form, how can you write it in standard form? **Start with the leftmost expression in parentheses and multiply it by the x that was factored out. Repeat until all parentheses are removed.**

Avoid Common Errors

When writing any expression that contains many parentheses, a common error is that the number of left parentheses and the number of right parentheses do not match. Remind students that parentheses come in pairs and encourage them to count the number of left parentheses and the number of right parentheses to make sure they are the same.

EXTRA EXAMPLE

Write $f(x) = x^3 + 3x^2 - 6x - 8$ in nested form.
$f(x) = ((x + 3)x - 6)x - 8$

3 EXAMPLE

Questioning Strategies

- What do you notice about the degree of $f(x)$ and the number of zeros $f(x)$ has? **The degree is 3 and there are 3 zeros.**

- When does a polynomial function of degree 8 have a minimum? a maximum? **If a_n is positive, the function has a minimum; if a_n is negative, the function has a maximum. The graph can also have local minimums and maximums.**

MATHEMATICAL PRACTICE — Highlighting the Standards

3 EXAMPLE and its Reflect questions offer an opportunity to address Mathematical Practice Standard 3 (Construct viable arguments and critique the reasoning of others). Based on the degree of a polynomial and the characteristics of its coefficients, students can give a viable description of the graph of the polynomial. Students can also use what they know about polynomials to critique a description of the graph given by another student.

Technology

Students can check their graphs by using their graphing calculators. Remind students that if the graph is not visible, they may have to change the settings for the viewing window. Once the graph is displayed, students can also check the zeros by pressing `2nd` `TRACE` (CALC) and choosing **2:zero.**

The graph will be displayed, and students will be prompted to enter a left bound, a right bound, and a guess for the value of the zero. This can be done by entering the numerical values or by moving the cursor to locations left of, right of, or near an x-intercept and pressing `ENTER`. The x-intercept, which is a zero of the function, is then displayed. The process can be repeated for finding other zeros of the function.

EXTRA EXAMPLE

Graph $f(x) = x^3 + 3x^2 - 6x - 8$. The graph has the same end behavior as $f(x) = x^3$ and zeros at -4, -1, and 2.

3 EXAMPLE CC.9-12.F.IF.7c **Graphing Polynomials**

Graph $f(x) = x^3 + 2x^2 - 5x - 6$.

A Determine the end behavior of the graph. The end behavior is determined by the leading term, x^3.

So, as $x \to +\infty$, $f(x) \to$ ___$+\infty$___ , and as $x \to -\infty$, $f(x) \to$ ___$-\infty$___ .

B Complete the table of values. Use the nested form from the previous example to evaluate the polynomial.

x	−3	−2	−1	0	1	2	3
$f(x)$	0	4	0	−6	−8	0	24

C Plot the points from the table on the graph, omitting any points whose y-values are much greater than or much less than the other y-values on the graph.

D Draw a smooth curve through the plotted points, keeping in mind the end behavior of the graph.

REFLECT

3a. What are the zeros of the function? How can you identify them from the graph?

−3, −1, and 2; the zeros occur where the graph intersects the x-axis.

3b. What are the approximate values of x for which the function is increasing? decreasing?

The function is increasing for approximately $x < -2$ and $x > 1$; the function is

decreasing for approximately $-2 < x < 1$.

3c. A student wrote that $f(x)$ has a minimum value of approximately −8. Do you agree or disagree? Why?

Disagree; there is a *local* minimum of approximately −8, but the function has

no minimum value.

3d. Without graphing, what do you think the graph of $g(x) = -x^3 - 2x^2 + 5x + 6$ looks like? Why?

The graph of $g(x)$ is a reflection of the graph of $f(x)$ in the x-axis because

$g(x) = -f(x)$.

© Houghton Mifflin Harcourt Publishing Company

Now you will sketch a variety of polynomial functions. You do not need to put values on the y-axis. The emphasis is on showing the overall shape of the graph and its x-intercepts.

4 EXPLORE CC.9-12.F.IF.7c **Investigating the Behavior of Graphs Near Zeros**

Use a graphing calculator to graph each function. Sketch the graphs on the axes provided below. Then complete the table.

A $f(x) = (x - 1)(x - 2)(x - 3)(x - 4)$

B $g(x) = (x - 1)^2(x - 2)(x - 3)$

C $h(x) = (x - 1)^3(x - 2)$

D $j(x) = (x - 1)^4$

E

Examining Zeros	$f(x)$	$g(x)$	$h(x)$	$j(x)$
What are the zeros of the function?	1, 2, 3, 4	1, 2, 3	1, 2	1
How many times does each zero occur in the factorization?	1, 2, 3, 4: 1 time	1: 2 times 2, 3: 1 time	1: 3 times 2: 1 time	1: 4 times
At which zero(s) does the graph cross the x-axis?	1, 2, 3, 4	2, 3	1, 2	none
At which zero(s) is the graph tangent to the x-axis?	none	1	none	1

REFLECT

4a. Based on your results, make a generalization about the number of times a zero occurs in the factorization of a function and whether the graph of the function crosses or is tangent to the x-axis at that zero.

The graph crosses the x-axis at the zero if the zero occurs an odd number of times.

The graph is tangent to the x-axis at the zero if the zero occurs an even number

of times.

© Houghton Mifflin Harcourt Publishing Company

4 EXPLORE

Questioning Strategies

- If you write all four polynomial functions in standard form, what do you notice about the degree of each polynomial? **Each polynomial has a degree of 4.**

- Looking at the table, how are the zeros of the functions related to the degrees of the functions? **Each polynomial has a degree of 4 and the total number of times zeros occur for each function is 4.**

Teaching Strategy

To review previous lessons, as well as reinforce new concepts learned in this example, draw the graph for part B on the board. Have students take turns identifying the parts of the graph that show what the function's end behavior is, where the function increases or decreases, where minimum or maximum values occur, and where zeros occur. Also have students keep count of the zeros, with separate totals for zeros at which the graph crosses the x-axis and zeros at which the graph is tangent to the x-axis.

Technology

Have students zoom in very closely around each zero and compare the shape of the graph with the graph of a function of the form $f(x) = x^n$. Students should notice that when they zoom in around a zero that occurs once in the factorization, the graph will look like the graph of $f(x) = x$ (a line). If the zero occurs twice, the graph will look like the graph of $f(x) = x^2$ (a parabola). If the zero occurs three times, the graph will look like the graph of $f(x) = x^3$. And if the zero occurs four times, the graph will look like the graph of $f(x) = x^4$.

5 EXAMPLE

Questioning Strategies

- What is $f(0)$? What does this tell you about the graph? **12; it is the graph's y-intercept.**

- How do you know that the graph is tangent to the x-axis at $x = -2$? **The zero -2 occurs twice in the factorization, and the graph of a polynomial function is tangent to the x-axis at the zero if the zero occurs an even number of times.**

Avoid Common Errors

To determine end behavior, students can multiply all factors, but they may make errors in the complex calculation. Point out to students that the end behavior is determined by the term with the greatest degree. If a function is written in factored form, then the highest-degree term is the product of all the first terms of the factors, as long as any repeated factors are considered individually. So, if $f(x) = (3x + 1)^2(x - 1) = (3x + 1)(3x + 1)(x - 1)$, then the leading term is $(3x)(3x)(x) = 9x^3$, and the polynomial has the same end behavior as $f(x) = x^3$.

The y-intercept can also be found by multiplying the constant terms in the factors, $(1)(1)(-1) = -1$.

EXTRA EXAMPLE

Sketch the graph of
$f(x) = (x - 2)^2(x + 1)(x + 2)(x + 3)$. The graph shows that $f(x) \longrightarrow -\infty$ as $x \longrightarrow -\infty$ and $f(x) \longrightarrow +\infty$ as $x \longrightarrow +\infty$, and has x-intercepts -3, -2, -1, and 2, crossing the x-axis at each negative x-intercept and tangent to the x-axis at the positive x-intercept.

6 ENGAGE

Questioning Strategies

- For any polynomial function written in standard form, will all numbers of the form $\frac{c}{b}$, where c is a factor of the constant term a_0 and b is a factor of the leading coefficient a_n, be zeros of the function? **No, the Rational Zero Theorem just says that every rational zero is a number of this form, not that every number of this form is a rational zero.**

- Is every zero of a polynomial function represented in the set of numbers given by the Rational Zero Theorem? **No, the Rational Zero Theorem gives only those zeros that are rational numbers. A polynomial function can also have zeros that are irrational numbers (or even imaginary numbers if you allow zeros from the set of complex numbers).**

continued

The factored form of a polynomial is useful for graphing because the zeros can easily be determined. The degree of a polynomial in factored form is the sum of the degrees of the factors.

CC.9-12.F.IF.7c

5 EXAMPLE   Sketching the Graph of a Factored Polynomial Function

Sketch the graph of $f(x) = (x + 2)^2(x + 1)(x - 2)(x - 3)$.

A Determine the end behavior.

The degree of the polynomial is the sum of the degrees of the factors.

So, the degree of $f(x)$ is ___5___.

If you multiply the factors to write $f(x)$ standard form, $a_nx^n + a_{n-1}x^{n-1} + \cdots + a_1x + a_0$, the leading coefficient a_n is ___1___.

Because the degree is odd and the leading coefficient is positive,

$f(x) \rightarrow$ ___$+\infty$___ as $x \rightarrow +\infty$ and $f(x) \rightarrow$ ___$-\infty$___ as $x \rightarrow -\infty$.

B Describe the behavior at the zeros.

The zeros of the function are _____$-2, -1, 2,$ and 3_____.

Identify how many times each zero occurs in the factorization.

___-2 occurs 2 times; -1, 2, and 3 each occur 1 time.___

Determine the zero(s) at which the graph crosses the x-axis.

___$-1, 2,$ and 3___

Determine the zero(s) at which the graph is tangent to the x-axis.

___-2___

C Sketch the graph at right. Use the end behavior to determine where to start and end. You may find it helpful to plot a few points between the zeros to help get the general shape of the graph.

REFLECT

5a. Can you determine how many times a zero occurs in the factorization of a polynomial function just by looking at the graph of the function? Explain.

___No; you can tell only whether a zero occurs an even or odd number___

___of times in the factorization.___

PREP FOR CC.9-12.A.APR.3

6 ENGAGE   The Rational Zero Theorem

If you multiply the factors of the function $f(x) = (x - 1)(x - 2)(x - 3)(x - 4)$, you can write $f(x)$ in standard form as follows.

$$f(x) = x^4 - 10x^3 + 35x^2 - 50x + 24$$

So, $f(x)$ is a polynomial with integer coefficients that begins with the term x^4 and ends with the term 24. The zeros of $f(x)$ are 1, 2, 3, and 4. Notice that each zero is a factor of the constant term, 24.

Now consider the function $g(x) = (2x - 1)(3x - 2)(4x - 3)(5x - 4)$. If you multiply the factors, you can write $g(x)$ in standard form as follows.

$$g(x) = 120x^4 - 326x^3 + 329x^2 - 146x + 24$$

So, $g(x)$ is a polynomial with integer coefficients that begins with the term $120x^4$ and ends with the term 24. The zeros of $g(x)$ are $\frac{1}{2}, \frac{2}{3}, \frac{3}{4},$ and $\frac{4}{5}$. In this case, the numerator of each zero is a factor of the constant term, 24, and the denominator of each zero is a factor of the leading coefficient, 120.

These examples illustrate the Rational Zero Theorem.

Rational Zero Theorem

If $p(x) = a_nx^n + a_{n-1}x^{n-1} + \cdots + a_2x^2 + a_1x + a_0$ has integer coefficients, then every rational zero of $p(x)$ is a number of the following form:

$$\frac{c}{b} = \frac{\text{factor of constant term } a_0}{\text{factor of leading coefficient } a_n}$$

REFLECT

6a. If $\frac{c}{b}$ is a rational zero of a polynomial function $p(x)$, explain why $bx - c$ must be a factor of the polynomial.

Since $p\left(\frac{c}{b}\right) = 0$, $x - \frac{c}{b}$ is a factor of $p(x)$ by the Factor Theorem.

So, $p(x) = \left(x - \frac{c}{b}\right)q(x)$ and $p(x) = \frac{b}{b}\left(x - \frac{c}{b}\right)q(x) = \frac{1}{b}(bx - c)q(x)$,

which shows that $bx - c$ is a factor of $p(x)$.

CC.9-12.A.APR.3

7 EXAMPLE   Using the Rational Zero Theorem

Sketch the graph of $f(x) = x^3 - x^2 - 8x + 12$.

A Use the Rational Zero Theorem to identify the possible rational zeros of $f(x)$.

The constant term is 12.

Integer factors of the constant term are $\pm1, \pm2, \pm3, \pm4, \pm6,$ and ±12.

The leading coefficient is ___1___.

Integer factors of the leading coefficient are ___±1___.

Notes

- If the leading coefficient of a polynomial function with integer coefficients is 1, what can you conclude about the function's rational zeros? Explain. They must be integers because when you apply the Rational Zero Theorem in this case, b can equal only 1 or -1 in $\frac{c}{b}$.

Differentiated Instruction

Analytical learners may benefit from answering the Reflect question and then testing their algebraic reasoning by working through the zeros given for the functions $f(x)$ and $g(x)$ in the Engage. Point out that in the algebraic conclusion of the Reflect question, the function $q(x)$ represents the quotient when $p(x)$ is divided by $x - \frac{c}{b}$.

7 EXAMPLE

Questioning Strategies

- Since the Rational Zero Theorem can generate many possible rational zeros, what rule of thumb could you follow to determine which possible zero(s) to test first? You can first test possible zeros that are integers because the function will be easier to evaluate for those numbers.

- Describe the steps to find the other zeros of $f(x) = x^3 - x^2 - 8x + 12$ if the possible rational zero -3 is tested first. The results of the synthetic substitution can be used to write the product $(x + 3)(x^2 - 4x + 4)$, which can then be factored as $(x + 3)(x - 2)(x - 2)$. The result is the same: the zeros are -3 and 2, with 2 occurring twice.

MATHEMATICAL PRACTICE   Highlighting the Standards

7 EXAMPLE and its Reflect questions offer an opportunity to address Mathematical Practice Standard 8 (Look for and express regularity in repeated reasoning). Students use the Rational Zero Theorem to identify a list of possible rational zeros for a polynomial function of degree three and then test possible zeros until one actual zero is found. Students identify one linear factor and then use the results of the synthetic substitution to rewrite the polynomial as the product of a linear factor and a quadratic factor. They then factor the quadratic factor, identify the zeros and end behavior, and graph the function. For functions of greater degree, the process can be repeated by testing for other actual zeros from the list of possible rational zeros generated by the Rational Zero Theorem. Another approach is to use the Rational Zero Theorem to identify one actual zero and its related linear factor, rewrite the polynomial as a product of that linear factor and another polynomial factor, and repeat the process for the other polynomial factor. (The second approach greatly reduces the number of possible rational zeros at each stage.)

EXTRA EXAMPLE

For the polynomial $p(x) = 2x^3 - 7x^2 + 2x + 3$, use the Rational Zero Theorem to identify the possible rational zeros; then, factor the polynomial completely, and sketch the function's graph. Possible zeros: ± 1, ± 3, $\pm\frac{1}{2}$, $\pm\frac{3}{2}$; $p(x) = (x - 1)(x - 3)(2x + 1)$; the graph shows that $f(x) \to -\infty$ as $x \to -\infty$ and $f(x) \to +\infty$ as $x \to +\infty$, and has x-intercepts 1, 3, and $-\frac{1}{2}$, crossing the x-axis at each x-intercept.

By the Rational Zero Theorem, the possible rational zeros of $f(x)$ are all rational numbers of the form $\frac{c}{b}$ where c is a factor of the constant term and b is a factor of the leading coefficient.

List all the possible rational zeros.

Possible rational zeros: $\underline{\pm 1,\ \pm 2,\ \pm 3,\ \pm 4,\ \pm 6,\ \pm 12}$

B Test the possible rational zeros until you find one that is an actual zero.

Use synthetic substitution to test 1 and 2.

1	1	−1	−8	12
		1	0	−8
	1	0	−8	4

2	1	−1	−8	12
		2	2	−12
	1	1	−6	0

So, $\underline{\ 2\ }$ is a zero, and therefore $\underline{\ x-2\ }$ is a factor of $f(x)$.

C Factor $f(x) = x^3 - x^2 - 8x + 12$ completely.

Use the results of the synthetic substitution to write $f(x)$ as the product of a linear factor and a quadratic factor.

$f(x) = (\ \underline{x-2}\ )(\ \underline{x^2 + x - 6}\ )$

Factor the quadratic factor to write $f(x)$ as a product of linear factors.

$f(x) = (\ \underline{x-2}\ )(\ \underline{x-2}\ )(\ \underline{x+3}\ )$

Use the factorization to identify the other zeros of $f(x)$.

$\underline{2 \text{ and } -3}$

How many times does each zero occur in the factorization?

$\underline{2 \text{ occurs two times};\ -3 \text{ occurs one time.}}$

D Determine the end behavior.

$f(x) \to \underline{\ +\infty\ }$ as $x \to +\infty$ and $f(x) \to \underline{\ -\infty\ }$ as $x \to -\infty$.

E Sketch the graph of the function on the coordinate plane at right.

REFLECT

7a. How did you determine where the graph crosses the x-axis and where it is tangent to the x-axis?

The graph crosses at any zero that occurs an odd number of times in the factorization (i.e., at $x = -3$) and is tangent at any zero that occurs an even number of times (i.e., at $x = 2$).

7b. How did factoring the polynomial help you graph the function?

By setting each factor equal to zero and solving, you can identify all the zeros of the function, which are the x-intercepts of the function's graph.

7c. How did using the Rational Zero Theorem to find one zero help you find the other zeros?

Using synthetic substitution to find one zero gives the coefficients of the quadratic factor, which can easily be factored into two linear factors.

PRACTICE

Write each polynomial function in nested form. Then sketch the graph by plotting points and using end behavior.

1. $f(x) = x^4 - 4x^2$

$f(x) = \underline{(((x)x - 4)x)x}$

2. $f(x) = -x^3 + 4x^2 - x - 6$

$f(x) = \underline{((-x + 4)x - 1)x - 6}$

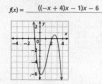

3. $f(x) = x^3 - x^2 - 4x + 4$

$f(x) = \underline{((x - 1)x - 4)x + 4}$

4. $f(x) = -x^4 + 4x^3 - 2x^2 - 4x + 3$

$f(x) = \underline{(((-x + 4)x - 2)x - 4)x + 3}$

© Houghton Mifflin Harcourt Publishing Company

Essential Question

How do you use zeros to graph polynomial functions?

A polynomial function can be graphed by determining end behavior, using zeros to plot points along the *x*-axis, and drawing a smooth curve through those points, keeping end behavior in mind.

Summarize

Have students extend the table in **1 ENGAGE**. For each end behavior, students can write a polynomial with the given end behavior. They can then graph the polynomial and identify its zeros, intervals where the function is increasing or decreasing, minimums or maximums, and local minimums or maximums.

Have students make a flow chart illustrating the process of graphing a factorable polynomial function. Choose one polynomial function from Practice Exercises 10–13 and describe how each step would be applied.

Where skills are taught	Where skills are practiced
2 EXAMPLE	EXS. 1–4
3 EXAMPLE	EXS. 1–4
5 EXAMPLE	EXS. 6–9
7 EXAMPLE	EXS. 11–13

Exercise 5: Students identify the characteristic of the graph of a polynomial function that indicates the function has a double root.

Exercise 14: Given the zeros of a polynomial function, students write the function.

5. Given the graph of a polynomial function, how can you tell if a given zero occurs an even or an odd number of times?

If the graph is tangent to the x-axis at that zero, the zero occurs an even number of times. If the graph crosses the x-axis, the zero occurs an odd number of times.

Sketch the graph of each factored polynomial function.

6. $f(x) = (x - 3)(x + 2)^2$

7. $g(x) = (x + 1)^6$

8. $h(x) = (x + 3)(x + 1)^2(x - 1)$

9. $j(x) = (x + 2)^3(x - 3)^2$

10. From 2000 to 2010, the profit (in thousands of dollars) for a small business is modeled by $P(x) = -x^3 + 9x^2 - 6x - 16$, where x is the number of years since 2000.

  a. Sketch a graph of the function at right.

  b. What are the zeros of the function in the domain $0 \le x \le 10$?

  2 and 8

  c. What do the zeros represent?

  The business broke even in 2002 and 2008.

Use the Rational Zero Theorem to identify the possible zeros of each function. Then factor the polynomial completely. Finally, identify the actual zeros and sketch the graph of the function.

10. $f(x) = x^3 - 2x^2 - x + 2$

Possible zeros:
±1, ±2

Factored form of function:
$f(x) = (x + 1)(x - 1)(x - 2)$

Actual zeros:
−1, 1, 2

11. $g(x) = x^3 - 2x^2 - 11x + 12$

Possible zeros:
±1, ±2, ±3, ±4, ±6, ±12

Factored form of function:
$g(x) = (x + 3)(x - 1)(x - 4)$

Actual zeros:
−3, 1, 4

12. $h(x) = 2x^4 - 5x^3 - 11x^2 + 20x + 12$

Possible zeros:
$\pm\frac{1}{2}$, ±1, $\pm\frac{3}{2}$, ±2, ±3, ±4, ±6, ±8, ±12

Factored form of function:
$h(x) = (x + 2)(2x + 1)(x - 2)(x - 3)$

Actual zeros:
−2, $-\frac{1}{2}$, 2, 3

13. The polynomial function $p(x)$ has degree 3, and its zeros are −3, 4, and 6. What do you think is the equation of $p(x)$? Do you think there could be more than one possibility? Explain.

$p(x) = (x + 3)(x - 4)(x - 6)$; any constant multiple of $p(x)$ will also have degree 3 and the same zeros, so the equation could be any function of the form

$p(x) = a(x + 3)(x - 4)(x - 6)$ where $a \neq 0$.

Assign these pages to help your students practice and apply important lesson concepts. For additional exercises, see the Student Edition.

Answers

Additional Practice

1. $\dfrac{1}{3}, \dfrac{\sqrt{3}}{3}, -\dfrac{\sqrt{3}}{3}$

2. $-4, 0, 6$

3. $-7, 0, 1$

4. $-2, 0, 4$

5. $x = -1$ with multiplicity 3

6. $x = 3$ with multiplicity 1; $x = -4$ with multiplicity 2

7. $-4, 1, -7$

8. $-5, -\dfrac{1}{3}, 2$

9. a. $x^3 + x^2 - 2x - 8 = 0$

   b. $\pm 1, \pm 2, \pm 4, \pm 8$

   c. $2, \dfrac{-3 \pm i\sqrt{7}}{2}$; no, 2 of the roots are irrational numbers.

   d. 2 m wide, 4 m long, and 1 m deep

Problem Solving

1. $V = w(w + 10)(w - 14)$

2. $w^3 - 4w^2 - 140w - 76{,}725 = 0$

3. No; yes; no
   The constant term is 76,725, which is not a multiple or 4 or 10, but is a multiple of 5.

4. Students should test possible roots that are multiples of 5 but not multiples of 10, such as 35, 45, and 55.

5. C

6. A

Additional Practice

Solve each polynomial equation by factoring.

1. $9x^3 - 3x^2 - 3x + 1 = 0$

   _____

2. $x^5 - 2x^4 - 24x^3 = 0$

   _____

3. $3x^5 + 18x^4 - 21x^3 = 0$

   _____

4. $-x^4 + 2x^3 + 8x^2 = 0$

   _____

Identify the roots of each equation. State the multiplicity of each root.

5. $x^3 + 3x^2 + 3x + 1 = 0$

   _____

6. $x^3 + 5x^2 - 8x - 48 = 0$

   _____

Identify all the real roots of each equation.

7. $x^3 + 10x^2 + 17x = 28$

   _____

8. $3x^3 + 10x^2 - 27x = 10$

   _____

Solve.

9. An engineer is designing a storage compartment in a spacecraft. The compartment must be 2 meters longer than it is wide and its depth must be 1 meter less than its width. The volume of the compartment must be 8 cubic meters.

   a. Write an equation to model the volume of the compartment.

   _____

   b. List all possible rational roots.

   _____

   c. Use synthetic division to find the roots of the polynomial equation. Are the roots all rational numbers?

   _____

   d. What are the dimensions of the storage compartment? _____

Problem Solving

Most airlines have rules concerning the size of checked baggage. The rules for Budget Airline are such that the dimensions of the largest bag cannot exceed 45 in. by 55 in. by 62 in. A designer is drawing plans for a piece of luggage that athletes can use to carry their equipment. It will have a volume of 76,725 cubic inches. The length is 10 in. greater than the width and the depth is 14 in. less than the width. What are the dimensions of this piece of luggage?

1. Write an equation in factored form to model the volume of the piece of luggage.

   _____

2. Multiply and set the equation equal to zero.

   _____

3. Think about possible roots of the equation. Could a root be a multiple

   of 4? _____ a multiple of 5? _____

   a multiple of 10? _____. How do you know?

   _____

4. Use synthetic substitution to test possible roots. Choose positive integers that are factors of the constant term and reasonable in the context of the problem.

Possible Root	1	-4	-140	-76,725

   _____

Choose the letter for the best answer.

5. Which equation represents the factored polynomial?

   A $(w + 55)(w^2 + 25w + 1550) = 0$

   B $(w - 35)(w^2 + 60w + 1405) = 0$

   C $(w - 45)(w^2 + 41w + 1705) = 0$

   D $(w - 4)(w^2 - 140w + 76,725) = 0$

6. Which could be the dimensions of this piece of luggage?

   A 31 in. by 45 in. by 55 in.

   B 45 in. by 55 in. by 55 in.

   C 45 in. by 45 in. by 55 in.

   D 45 in. by 55 in. by 62 in.

Fundamental Theorem of Algebra
Going Deeper

Essential question: *How can you find zeros of polynomial functions?*

COMMON Standards for
CORE   Mathematical Content

CC.9-12.N.CN.9(+) Know the Fundamental Theorem of Algebra; show that it is true for quadratic polynomials.

CC.9-12.A.SSE.2 Use the structure of an expression to identify ways to rewrite it.

CC.9-12.A.APR.2 Know and apply the Remainder Theorem; For a polynomial $p(x)$ and a number a, the remainder on division by $x - a$ is $p(a)$, so $p(a) = 0$ if and only if $(x - a)$ is a factor of $p(x)$.

Also: CC.9-12.N.CN.8(+)

Prerequisites
Recognizing special products

Expanding powers of binomials

Finding rational zeros

Math Background
Previously students used the Rational Zero Theorem to identify possible rational zeros for polynomial functions written in standard form and then used synthetic substitution to test for actual zeros. An alternative method of finding zeros is to factor a polynomial and then set each factor equal to 0. Factoring a polynomial is the reverse of multiplying its factors, so the skills that students learned earlier, such as finding special products and expanding powers of binomials using the Binomial Theorem, are useful in this lesson.

INTRODUCE

Review the special product rules and the Binomial Theorem. Explain that rules for special products and the Binomial Theorem can be applied in reverse to factor polynomials. Write some polynomials on the board and ask students to identify them as sum-and-difference, square of a binomial, cube of a binomial, or other expanded power of a binomial. Then, have them work

backward to try to figure out what factors were multiplied to get each special product.

TEACH

1 EXAMPLE

Questioning Strategies
- Will the coefficients in the expansion of $f(x) = (2x + 5)^3$ exactly match the numbers 1, 3, 3, and 1 in row 3 of Pascal's Triangle? Explain. **No; the numbers from Pascal's Triangle get multiplied by powers of 2 and 5: the expansion of $f(x) = (2x + 5)^3$ is $f(x) = 8x^3 + 60x^2 + 150x + 125$.**

- Can you use the Binomial Theorem to find the zeros of $f(x) = 8x^3 + 60x^2 + 150x + 125$? If so, explain how. **Yes; examining the relationship between the numbers 1, 3, 3, and 1 from row 3 of Pascal's triangle and the coefficients 8, 60, 150, and 125 shows that $8 = 2^3$, $60 = 3 \cdot 2^2 \cdot 5$, $150 = 3 \cdot 2 \cdot 5^2$, and $125 = 5^3$. So, $f(x) = (2x + 5)^3$ and the only zero of $f(x)$ is $-\frac{5}{2}$, which occurs 3 times.**

Teaching Strategy
To gain facility in recognizing polynomials that are special products, students might benefit from some sort of game or matching exercise between a set of polynomials in standard form and another equivalent set in factored form.

Avoid Common Errors
When finding the zeros of $f(x) = (x + 1)^3$, students may say the zero is 1 because they are accustomed to thinking that a is a zero when $x - a$ is a factor without realizing that $x + 1$ needs to be in the form of a difference: $x - (-1)$. Remind students to check whether $f(x) = 0$: in this case, $f(-1) = 0$ but $f(1) = 8$.

EXTRA EXAMPLE
Find the zeros of
$g(x) = x^6 + 6x^5 + 15x^4 + 20x^3 + 15x^2 + 6x + 1$ and write the function in factored form. **−1, which occurs six times; $g(x) = (x + 1)^6$**

Name _____ Class _____ Date _____

3-6

Video Tutor

Fundamental Theorem of Algebra
Going Deeper

Essential question: *How can you find zeros of polynomial functions?*

So far, you have found only rational zeros of polynomial functions.
In this lesson you will review the various techniques for finding
rational zeros and employ those techniques on polynomial functions
whose zeros may not all be rational numbers.

CC.9-12.A.SSE.2

1 EXAMPLE Using the Binomial Theorem to Find Zeros

Find the zeros of $f(x) = x^3 + 3x^2 + 3x + 1$ and write the function in
factored form.

A Write the coefficients of the terms of the polynomial.

1, 3, 3, 1

How are these coefficients related to Pascal's Triangle?

They are the values from row 3 of Pascal's Triangle.

Identify the corresponding binomial expansion.

$(a + b)^3 = a^3 + 3a^2b + 3ab^2 + b^3$

B Use the binomial expansion to rewrite the function in the form $(a + b)^n$.

$f(x) = \left(x + 1 \right)^3$

C Identify the zero(s) of the function.

The only zero of $f(x)$ is −1.

How many times does each zero occur? Explain.

The only zero, −1, occurs 3 times because the factor $x + 1$ occurs 3 times.

So, the zero of $f(x)$ is   −1

The factored form of $f(x)$ is $f(x) = (x + 1)^3$

REFLECT

1a. Can you always use the Binomial Theorem in this way to find the zeros of a polynomial
function? Explain.

No, but the Binomial Theorem is useful if the coefficients of the terms of

the polynomial correspond to a row of Pascal's Triangle.

1b. Without actually graphing, describe the graph of $f(x)$.

The graph has the same shape as the graph of $y = x^3$ but is translated 1 unit left.

CC.9-12.A.APR.2

2 EXAMPLE Using the Rational Zero Theorem to Find Zeros

Find the zeros of $g(x) = x^3 - x^2 - 2x + 2$ and write the function in factored form.

A Use the Rational Zero Theorem to identify possible rational zeros.

Integer factors of the constant term are   ±1, ±2

Integer factors of the leading coefficient are   ±1

By the Rational Zero Theorem, the possible rational zeros of $g(x)$ are all rational
numbers $\frac{c}{b}$ where c is a factor of the constant term and b is a factor
of the leading coefficient.

Possible rational zeros are   ±1, ±2

B Use synthetic substitution to test each possible rational zero to identify any actual
rational zeros.

The function $g(x)$ has one rational zero, which is   1

So, $x -$ 1   is a factor of $g(x)$.

C Use synthetic division to identify the other factors of the polynomial.

Divide $g(x)$ by $x -$ 1   . Complete the synthetic
division at right.

The quotient is   1 $x^2 +$ 0 $x -$ 2

1	1	−1	−2	2
		1	0	−2
	1	0	−2	0

Write $g(x)$ as a product of two factors.

$g(x) = (x -$ 1 $)(x^2 -$ 2 $)$

The zeros of the quadratic factor are $\pm\sqrt{2}$

Write the quadratic factor as a product of two linear factors.

$(x - \sqrt{2})(x + \sqrt{2})$

D Identify the zeros of the function.

The zeros of $g(x)$ are $1, \sqrt{2}, -\sqrt{2}$

E Write the function in factored form.

The factored form is $g(x) = (x -$ 1 $)(x -$ $\sqrt{2}$ $)(x +$ $\sqrt{2}$ $)$.

REFLECT

2a. When you used the Rational Zero Theorem, did your list of possible zeros include
all of the actual zeros of $g(x)$? Why or why not?

No; only the rational zero, 1, is in the list. The other zeros, $\pm\sqrt{2}$, are irrational,

so they are not included.

2b. How can you check that you wrote the factored form of $g(x)$ correctly?

Multiply the factors; the product should be the original function $g(x)$.

Questioning Strategies

- Explain how the Rational Zero Theorem can help you find zeros that are not rational. **The Rational Zero Theorem can be used to identify rational zeros and the corresponding factors. Then, other methods, such as the quadratic formula, may be used to find other zeros that are irrational or imaginary.**

- Can you use the Rational Zero Theorem to help you write a polynomial function in factored form if the function has no rational zeros? **No, the Rational Zero Theorem can only be used to find rational zeros.**

Teaching Strategy

To reinforce how to find both rational and irrational zeros, have students create their own polynomial functions that have both rational and irrational zeros. To do this, have students write one factor of the form $x - a$, where a is rational, and another factor of the form $x^2 + b$ where $b > 0$. Have them multiply these factors to obtain a polynomial in standard form. Students can exchange their polynomial functions and use the Rational Zero Theorem to find all the zeros.

EXTRA EXAMPLE

Find the zeros of $g(x) = x^3 - x^2 - 7x + 7$ and write the function in factored form. **1, $\sqrt{7}$, $-\sqrt{7}$; $g(x) = (x - 1)(x - \sqrt{7})(x + \sqrt{7})$**

3 EXAMPLE

Questioning Strategies

- Could you use a special product to find the zeros of $h(x) = 25x^4 + 20x^2 + 4$? If so, explain how. **Yes; the function can be rewritten as the square of a binomial: $h(x) = (5x^2 + 2)^2$. Then find the zeros of $5x^2 + 2$.**

- If you do not recognize the form of a function as a special product, is it still possible to find the zeros of the function? **Yes, you can still use other factoring techniques and the Rational Zero Theorem to write the function in factored form.**

Avoid Common Errors

When using special products to factor polynomial functions, remind students to write the exponents correctly. For example, since the difference of two squares is given by $a^2 - b^2 = (a + b)(a - b)$, students may factor $x^4 - 16$ as $(x + 4)(x - 4)$ rather than as $(x^2 + 4)(x^2 - 4)$.

.·······:
: MATHEMATICAL   **Highlighting**
:   PRACTICE   **the Standards**
:·······:

3 EXAMPLE   and its Reflect questions offer an opportunity to address Mathematical Practice Standard 7 (Look for and make use of structure). In previous lessons, students learned to multiply polynomials in a more efficient way by using rules for special products. Specific patterns were identified in the structure of some polynomial products: the difference of two squares, the square of a binomial, and the cube of a binomial. In this example, students recognize that the structure of the polynomial $x^4 - 16$ is the difference of two squares.

EXTRA EXAMPLE

Find the zeros of $h(x) = x^4 - 256$ and write the function in factored form. **$-4i$, $4i$, -4, 4; $h(x) = (x + 4i)(x - 4i)(x + 4)(x - 4)$**

3 EXAMPLE Using Special Products to Find Zeros

CC.9-12.A.SSE.2

Find the zeros of $h(x) = x^4 - 16$ and write the function in factored form.

A Rewrite the function as a special product.

What type of special polynomial is $x^4 - 16$?

The expression is a difference of squares ($a^2 - b^2$).

Factor the polynomial.

$$f(x) = (x^2 + 4)(\underline{\quad x^2 \quad} - \underline{\quad 4 \quad})$$

B Find the zeros for each factor of the special product.

$$x^2 + 4 = 0 \qquad\qquad x^2 - \underline{4} = 0$$
$$x^2 = -4 \qquad\qquad x^2 = \underline{4}$$
$$x = \pm\sqrt{-4} \qquad\qquad x = \pm\sqrt{\underline{4}}$$
$$x = \pm 2i \qquad\qquad x = \pm \underline{2}$$

C Identify the zeros of the function.

The zeros of $h(x)$ are $\underline{-2i, 2i, -2, 2}$.

D Write the function in factored form.

The factored form is $h(x) = (x + \underline{2i})(x - \underline{2i})(x + \underline{2})(x - \underline{2})$.

REFLECT

3a. How many x-intercepts does the graph of $h(x)$ have? What are they? Explain how you know.

There are two x-intercepts: −2 and 2. The real zeros correspond to points where

the graph of $h(x)$ intersects the x-axis.

3b. Show how you can check the imaginary zeros of $h(x)$.

Check that $h(2i) = 0$ and $h(-2i) = 0$; $h(2i) = (2i)^4 - 16 = 2^4 i^4 - 16 = 16(1) - 16 = 0$;

$h(-2i) = (-2i)^4 - 16 = (-2)^4 i^4 - 16 = 16(1) - 16 = 0$.

3c. In general, how many zeros does the function $f(x) = x^4 - a$ have when a is a positive integer? What are the zeros?

There are 4 zeros: $\sqrt[4]{a}, -\sqrt[4]{a}, i\sqrt[4]{a}$, and $-i\sqrt[4]{a}$.

3d. Could you use the method of the example to find the zeros of $k(x) = x^4 + 16$? Explain.

No; $x^4 + 16$ is not a difference of two squares.

4 ENGAGE Understanding the Fundamental Theorem of Algebra

CC.9-12.N.CN.9(+)

The table summarizes the functions from the three examples. Notice that the number of zeros equals the degree of the polynomial as long as repeated zeros are counted multiple times. Irrational and imaginary zeros must also be taken into account.

Function	Degree	Zeros	Number of Zeros
$f(x) = x^3 + 3x^2 + 3x + 1$	3	−1 (occurs 3 times)	3
$g(x) = x^3 - x^2 - 2x + 2$	3	$1, \sqrt{2}, -\sqrt{2}$	3
$h(x) = x^4 - 16$	4	$-2i, 2i, -2, 2$	4

The table can help you understand the Fundamental Theorem of Algebra.

> **Fundamental Theorem of Algebra**
>
> If $f(x)$ is a polynomial of degree n, then $f(x)$ has at least one zero in the set of complex numbers.
>
> **Corollary:** If $f(x)$ is a polynomial of degree n, then $f(x)$ has exactly n zeros, provided that repeated zeros are counted multiple times.

REFLECT

4a. How does the quadratic formula prove the Fundamental Theorem of Algebra for the case $n = 2$?

The formula gives two real zeros if $b^2 - 4ac > 0$, one real zero if $b^2 - 4ac = 0$,

and two complex zeros if $b^2 - 4ac < 0$. In every case, there is at least one zero

in the set of complex numbers.

4b. If you apply the Fundamental Theorem of Algebra to any polynomial function $f(x)$, you can conclude that $f(x)$ has one complex zero z_1. So, by the Factor Theorem, $x - z_1$ is a factor of $f(x)$. This means $f(x) = (x - z_1)q_1(x)$ where $q_1(x)$ is a polynomial whose degree is one less than the degree of $f(x)$. Explain how you can use this idea and repeatedly apply the Fundamental Theorem of Algebra to prove the corollary of the theorem.

The quotient $q_1(x)$ is a polynomial function, so by the Fundamental Theorem of

Algebra, $q_1(x)$ has one complex zero z_2. So, $f(x) = (x - z_1)(x - z_2)q_2(x)$ where $q_2(x)$

is a polynomial whose degree is two less than the degree of $f(x)$. You can continue

this process until $q_n(x)$ is a factor of degree 1 and n complex zeros of $f(x)$ have

been identified.

4c. Can you conclude that $f(x) = x^5 - 4x^2 + \frac{1}{x}$ has 5 zeros? Why or why not?

No; the Fundamental Theorem of Algebra applies only to polynomials.

Questioning Strategies

- Suppose that a polynomial function has two zeros, $\frac{1}{2}$ and $-\frac{1}{2}$. Do these zeros satisfy the requirement of the Fundamental Theorem of Algebra which states that a polynomial $f(x)$ of degree n has at least one zero in the set of complex numbers? **Yes, $\frac{1}{2}$ and $-\frac{1}{2}$ are real numbers. Complex numbers are numbers of the form $a + bi$, where a and b are real numbers, and real numbers are complex numbers for which the value of b is 0. So, all real numbers are complex numbers, and $\frac{1}{2}$ and $-\frac{1}{2}$ satisfy the requirement.**

- A polynomial function of degree 4 has only the zeros -2, 3, and 4. How can this be true given the requirement of the Corollary of the Fundamental Theorem of Algebra which states that a polynomial of degree n has exactly n zeros? **One of the zeros must occur twice. The corollary requires that repeated zeros be counted multiple times.**

Technology

Encourage students to use their graphing calculators to check their factorizations of polynomials. Have students enter the polynomial functions into their graphing calculators and display the graphs so they can see the points where the graph crosses or is tangent to the x-axis. (Remind students that they may have to adjust window settings.)

By examining graphs, students should see that if a polynomial function of degree n has n different real zeros, then its graph crosses the x-axis at n different points, and that if the graph crosses or is tangent to the x-axis at fewer than n points, then some zeros are repeated.

CLOSE

Essential Question

How can you find zeros of polynomial functions?
You can factor the polynomial to find zeros. For some polynomials, you can use the Binomial Theorem or rules for special products to help you identify factors. You can also use the Rational Zero Theorem to identify possible rational zeros and then you can test them to see whether they are actual zeros. If one factor has degree 2, you can use the quadratic formula to find irrational or imaginary zeros.

Summarize

Have students make a table with each row describing a strategy for finding zeros of polynomial functions, including using the Binomial Theorem, rules for special products, and the Rational Zero Theorem. Include an example for each strategy.

PRACTICE

Where skills are taught	Where skills are practiced
1 EXAMPLE	EXS. 1–3
2 EXAMPLE	EXS. 4, 5, 9
3 EXAMPLE	EXS. 6–8, 10

Exercise 11: Given the zeros of a polynomial function, students write the function.

Exercise 12: Students use the corollary of the Fundamental Theorem of Algebra to determine the number of zeros for a function $p(x)$ that is the product of two polynomials whose degrees are given.

Exercises 13–14: Given one numeral zero and one radical zero of a polynomial function, students first use the Fundamental Theorem of Algebra to determine the number of other zeros for the function, and then identify two of those zeros using the fact that nonreal zeros and radical zeros occur in conjugate pairs.

PRACTICE

Find the zeros of the function and write the function in factored form.

1. $f(x) = x^4 + 4x^3 + 6x^2 + 4x + 1$

The zeros of $f(x)$ are

___−1 (occurs 4 times)___

The factored form is

$f(x) =$ ___$(x + 1)^4$___

2. $g(x) = x^3 - 3x^2 + 3x - 1$

The zeros of $g(x)$ are

___1 (occurs 3 times)___

The factored form is

$g(x) =$ ___$(x - 1)^3$___

3. $f(x) = x^5 + 5x^4 + 10x^3 + 10x^2 + 5x + 1$

The zeros of $f(x)$ are

___−1 (occurs 5 times)___

The factored form is

$f(x) =$ ___$(x + 1)^5$___

4. $g(x) = x^3 - x^2 - 3x + 3$

The zeros of $g(x)$ are

___$1, \sqrt{3}, -\sqrt{3}$___

The factored form is

$g(x) =$ ___$(x - 1)(x + \sqrt{3})(x - \sqrt{3})$___

5. $f(x) = x^3 + 2x^2 - 5x - 10$

The zeros of $f(x)$ are

___$-2, \sqrt{5}, -\sqrt{5}$___

The factored form is

$f(x) =$ ___$(x + 2)(x + \sqrt{5})(x - \sqrt{5})$___

6. $g(x) = x^4 - 81$

The zeros of $g(x)$ are

___$-3i, 3i, -3, 3$___

The factored form is

$g(x) =$ ___$(x + 3i)(x - 3i)(x + 3)(x - 3)$___

7. $f(x) = x^4 - 8x^2 + 16$

The zeros of $f(x)$ are

___$2, -2$ (each occurs 2 times)___

The factored form is

$f(x) =$ ___$(x + 2)^2(x - 2)^2$___

8. $g(x) = 16x^4 - 1$

The zeros of $g(x)$ are

___$\frac{1}{2}i, -\frac{1}{2}i, \frac{1}{2}, -\frac{1}{2}$___

The factored form is

$g(x) =$ ___$(2x + i)(2x - i)(2x + 1)(2x - 1)$___

9. $f(x) = x^4 - 4x^3 - 6x^2 + 40x - 40$

The zeros of $f(x)$ are

___2 (occurs twice), $\sqrt{10}, -\sqrt{10}$___

The factored form is

$f(x) =$ ___$(x - 2)^2(x + \sqrt{10})(x - \sqrt{10})$___

10. $g(x) = x^5 + 2x^3 + x$

The zeros of $g(x)$ are

___$0, i$ (occurs twice), $-i$ (occurs twice)___

The factored form is

$g(x) =$ ___$x(x + i)^2(x - i)^2$___

© Houghton Mifflin Harcourt Publishing Company

---

11. A polynomial function has exactly four zeros: $2, -2, \sqrt{3},$ and $-\sqrt{3}$. Use standard form to write the simplest function with these zeros. Describe your method.

$f(x) = x^4 - 7x^2 + 12$; use the zeros to write the factors, then multiply the factors:

$f(x) = (x - 2)(x + 2)(x - \sqrt{3})(x + \sqrt{3}) = (x^2 - 4)(x^2 - 3) = x^4 - 7x^2 + 12.$

12. Suppose $p(x)$ is the product of a polynomial of degree 5 and a cubic polynomial. How many zeros does $p(x)$ have? Explain.

8; $p(x)$ has degree $5 + 3 = 8$, so it has 8 zeros by the corollary to the

Fundamental Theorem of Algebra.

Suppose $q(x)$ is a polynomial function of degree 5 and you know that two of the zeros are $2i$ and $\sqrt{6}$.

13. How many other zeros does the function $q(x)$ have? Justify your answer.

3 other zeros. Sample answer: By the corollary to the Fundamental Theorem

of Algebra, the polynomial function has 5 zeros because its degree is 5. Since 2

zeros are known, there are $5 - 2 = 3$ other zeros.

14. Can you identify any of the other zeros of the function? If so, give them and explain how you know they are zeros.

Yes; $-2i$ and $-\sqrt{6}$. Sample answer: Both nonreal zeros and radical zeros always

occur in pairs. In general, if ai is a zero of a polynomial function, then $-ai$ is also;

similarly, if $\sqrt{a}$ is a zero of the function, then $-\sqrt{a}$ is as well.

© Houghton Mifflin Harcourt Publishing Company

Assign these pages to help your students practice and apply important lesson concepts. For additional exercises, see the Student Edition.

Answers

Additional Practice

1. $P(x) = x^3 - 2x^2 - 11x + 12$

2. $P(x) = x^3 - \frac{7}{2}x^2 - \frac{17}{2}x + 5$

3. $P(x) = x^5 - 4x^4 + x^3 - 4x^2 - 12x + 48$

4. $P(x) = x^5 + 5x^4 + 7x^3 + 35x^2 - 18x - 90$

5. $x = i, -i, -3$, and 5

6. $x = 2, -2, 2i$, and $-2i$

7. $x = -4i, 4i, 2$, and 6

8. $x = -3i, 3i$, and -3

9. $V(t) = t^3 - 10t^2 + 23t - 14$

Problem Solving

1. a. $V = 4\pi r^2$

   b. $V = \frac{1}{2}\left(\frac{4}{3}\pi r^3\right)$

2. $\frac{13}{12}\pi = 4\pi r^2 + \frac{2}{3}\pi r^3$

3. $8r^3 + 48r^2 - 13 = 0$

4.

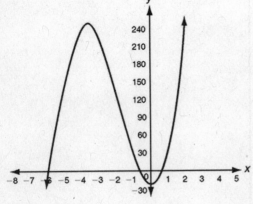

5. $\frac{1}{2}$

6. $x = \frac{-26 \pm 21.6}{8}$; both these roots are negative, so they cannot be the radius.

7. 0.5 inch

3-6

Additional Practice

Write the simplest polynomial function with the given roots.

1. 1, 4, and –3

2. $\frac{1}{2}$, 5, and –2

_____

_____

3. $2i$, $\sqrt{3}$, and 4

4. $\sqrt{2}$, –5, and –3i

_____

_____

Solve each equation by finding all roots.

5. $x^4 - 2x^3 - 14x^2 - 2x - 15 = 0$

6. $x^4 - 16 = 0$

_____

_____

7. $x^4 + 4x^3 + 4x^2 + 64x - 192 = 0$

8. $x^3 + 3x^2 + 9x + 27 = 0$

_____

_____

Solve.

9. An electrical circuit is designed such that its output voltage, V, measured in volts, can be either positive or negative. The voltage of the circuit passes through zero at $t = 1$, 2, and 7 seconds. Write the simplest polynomial describing the voltage $V(t)$.

_____

Problem Solving

A company that makes accessories for cars needs a container like that shown at the right to hold touch-up paint. The hemispherical top will be fitted with a brush applicator. The cylindrical part of the container should be 4 inches tall. The volume of the entire container is $\frac{13}{12}\pi$ cubic inches. Find the value of x, the radius of the hemisphere.

1. a. Write a formula for the volume of the cylindrical part of the container.

_____

b. Write a formula for the volume of the hemispherical part of the container.

_____

2. Write an equation to represent the total volume of the container.

_____

3. Write the equation in standard form.

_____

4. Graph the equation with a graphing calculator. Hint: Use a window with x-values from –8 to 5 with a scale of 1, and y-values from –20 to 250 with a scale of 30 to see the general shape of the graph. Sketch the graph.
Then focus on the area of the positive root by using a window of –8 to 3 on the x-axis and –20 to 20 on the y-axis. Use Trace to help you find a possible positive root.

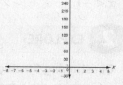

5. Verify the root using synthetic substitution. What is the positive root?

_____

6. Use the Quadratic Formula to find approximate values for the other two roots. Explain why these two roots cannot also be solutions to the problem.

_____

7. What is the value of x, the radius of the hemisphere, for this paint container?

_____

Investigating Graphs of Polynomial Functions
Going Deeper

Essential question: *How does the value of n affect the behavior of the function* $f(x) = x^n$?

COMMON **Standards for**
CORE **Mathematical Content**

CC.9-12.F.IF.7 Graph functions expressed symbolically and show key features of the graph, by hand in simple cases and using technology for more complicated cases.*

CC.9-12.F.IF.7c Graph polynomial functions, identifying zeros when suitable factorizations are available, and showing end behavior.*

CC.9-12.F.BF.3 Identify the effect on the graph of replacing $f(x)$ by ... $f(kx)$ ... for specific values of k ...

Vocabulary
end behavior
even function
odd function

Prerequisites
Graphing $f(x) = x^2$

Math Background
Students are familiar with the graphs of $f(x) = x$ and $f(x) = x^2$ and their characteristics, such as symmetry and end behavior. In this lesson, students will extend their understanding to graphs of functions of the form $f(x) = x^n$ where n is a whole number as they investigate how the value of n affects the behavior of the graph.

INTRODUCE

Compare and contrast the graphs of the parent linear function, $f(x) = x$, and the parent quadratic function, $f(x) = x^2$. Note that both graphs pass through the origin, but the graph of $f(x) = x$ crosses the x-axis while the graph of $f(x) = x^2$ is *tangent* to the x-axis. Also note that both functions increase without bound as x increases without bound, so both graphs rise without bound in Quadrant I. But as x decreases without bound, $f(x) = x$ *decreases* without bound while $f(x) = x^2$ *increases* without bound. So, the graph of $f(x) = x$ falls without bound in Quadrant III while the graph of $f(x) = x^2$ rises without bound in Quadrant II.

TEACH

1 EXPLORE

Materials
graphing calculator

Questioning Strategies
• If you graph $f(x) = x^8$, what will the function have in common with the functions $f(x) = x^2$, $f(x) = x^4$, and $f(x) = x^6$? **All of the functions have a zero at x = 0, a minimum value of 0, the y-axis as a line of symmetry for their graphs, and the same end behavior.**

• For the function $f(x) = x^{10}$, what happens to the values of $f(x)$ as x increases without bound, and how is this observed in its graph? **The values of f(x) also increase without bound, and the graph rises without bound as you move along the positive y-axis.**

Technology
Students may benefit from using different viewing windows to observe how the graphs of $f(x) = x^n$ are related for different values of n. For example, have students set the viewing window to Xmin = 0, Xmax = 1, Ymin = 0, and Ymax = 1 and graph all three functions. Then, set the window to Xmin = −10, Xmax = 10, Ymin = 0, and Ymax = 100. Note that the order of the graphs of $f(x) = x^2, f(x) = x^4$, and $f(x) = x^6$, from top to bottom, is reversed for the intervals $0 < x < 1$ and $x > 1$ as well as for the intervals $−1 < x < 0$ and $x < −1$.

2 EXPLORE

Questioning Strategies
• Compare the symmetry of the graphs of $f(x) = x^{11}$ and $f(x) = x^{12}$. **The graph of f(x) = x^{11} has 180° rotational symmetry about the origin. The graph of f(x) = x^{12} has reflection symmetry in the y-axis.**

continued

Name_____ Class_____ Date_____

3-7

Investigating Graphs of Polynomial Functions
Going Deeper

Essential question: *How does the value of n affect the behavior of the function $f(x) = x^n$?*

CC.9-12.F.IF.7c

1 EXPLORE   Graphing $f(x) = x^n$ When n is Even

Follow these steps to investigate the graphs of $f(x) = x^2$, $f(x) = x^4$, and $f(x) = x^6$.

A   Set the viewing window of your graphing calculator as shown.

B   Enter the functions $f(x) = x^2$, $f(x) = x^4$, and $f(x) = x^6$ in the equation editor as shown.

C   Graph the functions on the coordinate plane at right by sketching what you see on your calculator.

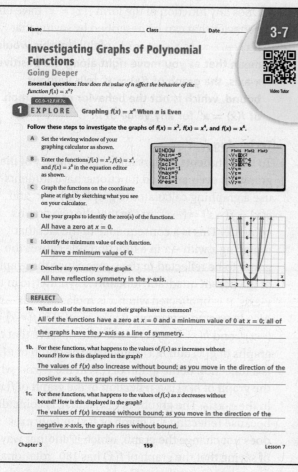

```
WINDOW
Xmin=-5
Xmax=5
Xscl=1
Ymin=-1
Ymax=9
Yscl=1
Xres=1
```

```
Plot1 Plot2 Plot3
\Y1■X^2
\Y2■X^4
\Y3■X^6
\Y4=
\Y5=
\Y6=
\Y7=
```

D   Use your graphs to identify the zero(s) of the functions.

All have a zero at $x = 0$.

E   Identify the minimum value of each function.

All have a minimum value of 0.

F   Describe any symmetry of the graphs.

All have reflection symmetry in the y-axis.

REFLECT

1a. What do all of the functions and their graphs have in common?

All of the functions have a zero at $x = 0$ and a minimum value of 0 at $x = 0$; all of the graphs have the y-axis as a line of symmetry.

1b. For these functions, what happens to the values of $f(x)$ as x increases without bound? How is this displayed in the graph?

The values of $f(x)$ also increase without bound; as you move in the direction of the positive x-axis, the graph rises without bound.

1c. For these functions, what happens to the values of $f(x)$ as x decreases without bound? How is this displayed in the graph?

The values of $f(x)$ increase without bound; as you move in the direction of the negative x-axis, the graph rises without bound.

CC.9-12.F.IF.7c

2 EXPLORE   Graphing $f(x) = x^n$ When n is Odd

Follow these steps to investigate the graphs of $f(x) = x$, $f(x) = x^3$, and $f(x) = x^5$.

A   Set the viewing window of your graphing calculator as shown.

B   Enter the functions $f(x) = x$, $f(x) = x^3$, and $f(x) = x^5$ in the equation editor as shown.

C   Graph the functions on the coordinate plane at right by sketching what you see on your calculator.

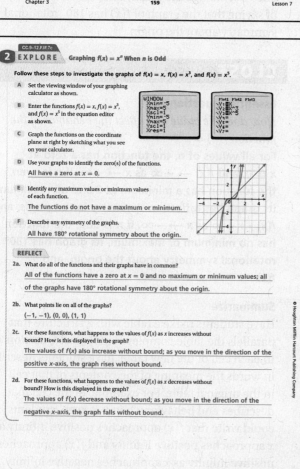

```
WINDOW
Xmin=-5
Xmax=5
Xscl=1
Ymin=-5
Ymax=5
Yscl=1
Xres=1
```

```
Plot1 Plot2 Plot3
\Y1■X
\Y2■X^3
\Y3■X^5
\Y4=
\Y5=
\Y6=
\Y7=
```

D   Use your graphs to identify the zero(s) of the functions.

All have a zero at $x = 0$.

E   Identify any maximum values or minimum values of each function.

The functions do not have a maximum or minimum.

F   Describe any symmetry of the graphs.

All have 180° rotational symmetry about the origin.

REFLECT

2a. What do all of the functions and their graphs have in common?

All of the functions have a zero at $x = 0$ and no maximum or minimum values; all of the graphs have 180° rotational symmetry about the origin.

2b. What points lie on all of the graphs?

$(-1, -1)$, $(0, 0)$, $(1, 1)$

2c. For these functions, what happens to the values of $f(x)$ as x increases without bound? How is this displayed in the graph?

The values of $f(x)$ also increase without bound; as you move in the direction of the positive x-axis, the graph rises without bound.

2d. For these functions, what happens to the values of $f(x)$ as x decreases without bound? How is this displayed in the graph?

The values of $f(x)$ decrease without bound; as you move in the direction of the negative x-axis, the graph falls without bound.

© Houghton Mifflin Harcourt Publishing Company

- Compare what happens to the graphs of $f(x) = x^{11}$ and $f(x) = x^{12}$ as x decreases without bound. **The graph of $f(x) = x^{11}$ falls without bound. The graph of $f(x) = x^{12}$ rises without bound.**

Teaching Strategy

Have students graph all the following functions on the same axes: $f(x) = x$, $f(x) = x^2$, $f(x) = x^3$, $f(x) = x^4$, $f(x) = x^5$, and $f(x) = x^6$ Have students compare the graphs for $0 < x < 1$, $x > 1$, $-1 < x < 0$, and $x < -1$. Ask students how the graphs of $f(x) = x^n$ are related for different values of n. Have students predict how the graphs would change if they used the absolute value of each odd function: $f(x) = |x|$, $f(x) = |x^3|$, and $f(x) = |x^5|$. Then, have them graph to confirm their conjectures.

MATHEMATICAL PRACTICE — Highlighting the Standards

2 EXPLORE and its Reflect questions offer an opportunity to address Mathematical Practice Standard 7 (Look for and make use of structure). In this Explore and the previous Explore, students investigate the graph of $f(x) = x^n$ for different values of n. Students discover that the characteristics of the graphs, including minimum values, symmetry, and end behavior, are determined by whether the value of n is even or odd.

3 ENGAGE

Questioning Strategies

- Suppose $f(x) \to +\infty$ as $x \to -\infty$. What does this statement tell you about the graph of $f(x) = x^n$ and the direction in which you are moving on the x-axis? What can you say about the value of n? **The statement says that as you move to the left along the negative x-axis so that x decreases without bound, the graph of $f(x) = x^n$ rises without bound. This is a characteristic of the graph of $f(x) = x^n$ when n is even.**

- Does any function of the form $f(x) = x^n$ have end behavior that can be described by saying that $f(x) \to -\infty$ as $x \to +\infty$? Explain. **No; this would mean that as you move right along the positive x-axis, the graph of $f(x) = x^n$ falls without bound, which is not the behavior of the graph of $f(x) = x^n$ for any value of n.**

Technology

To help students understand the symmetry of the graphs of even and odd functions, have students use a graphing calculator to graph $f(x) = x^2$ and $g(x) = f(-x) = (-x)^2$ to see that the two graphs coincide. This is a consequence of the fact that replacing x with $-x$ in a function rule causes the graph to be reflected in the y-axis. Since the graph of the parent quadratic function is symmetric in the y-axis, it is unaffected when x is replaced with $-x$. Also have students graph $f(x) = x^3$, $g(x) = f(-x) = (-x)^3$, and $h(x) = -f(x) = -x^3$ and observe that the graphs of $g(x)$ and $h(x)$ coincide. The graph of $g(x)$ is a reflection of the graph of $f(x)$ in the y-axis, while the graph of $h(x)$ is a reflection of the graph of $f(x)$ in the x-axis. The graphs of $g(x)$ and $h(x)$ coincide because reflecting the graph of $f(x)$ in *both* axes does not change the graph, which is another way of saying that the graph of $f(x)$ has 180° rotational symmetry about the origin.

CLOSE

Essential Question

How does the value of n affect the behavior of the function $f(x) = x^n$?

For all values of n, the function has a zero at $x = 0$, and $f(x) \to +\infty$ as $x \to +\infty$. If n is even, the function has a minimum at 0 and no maximum, its graph has reflection symmetry in the y-axis, and $f(x) \to +\infty$ as $x \to -\infty$. If n is odd, the function has no minimum or maximum, its graph has 180° rotational symmetry about the origin, and $f(x) \to -\infty$ as $x \to -\infty$.

Summarize

Have students make a table with a structure that parallels the table completed in Reflect Question 3f. In each cell of the new table, have students describe in words the meaning of the contents of that cell in the original table. For example, in the cell that describes end behavior when n is even, students could write that $f(x)$ approaches positive infinity as x approaches positive infinity and $f(x)$ approaches positive infinity as x approaches negative infinity.

3 ENGAGE   Describing Characteristics of Functions

CC.9-12.F.BF.3

The **end behavior** of a function is a description of the values of the function as x increases without bound or decreases without bound.

For example, for $f(x) = x^3$, the values of $f(x)$ increase without bound as x increases without bound. You can say that $f(x)$ approaches positive infinity as x approaches positive infinity. This may be abbreviated as "$f(x) \to +\infty$ as $x \to +\infty$."

Also, the values of $f(x)$ decrease without bound as x decreases without bound. You can say that $f(x)$ approaches negative infinity as x approaches negative infinity. This may be abbreviated as "$f(x) \to -\infty$ as $x \to -\infty$."

A function is an **even function** if $f(-x) = f(x)$ for all values of x. This means that if the point (x, y) is on the graph, then the point $(-x, y)$ is also on the graph, so the graph is symmetric with respect to the y-axis.

A function is an **odd function** if $f(-x) = -f(x)$ for all values of x. This means that if the point (x, y) is on the graph, then the point $(-x, -y)$ is also on the graph, so the graph has 180° rotational symmetry about the origin.

The Graph of an Even Function	The Graph of an Odd Function

REFLECT

3a. For the function $g(x)$, you are told that $g(1000) = 5{,}000{,}000$. Is it possible to make any conclusions about the end behavior of $g(x)$? Explain.

No, end behavior depends only on how the function behaves as x increases or decreases without bound, not on particular values.

3b. What can you say about the end behavior of $f(x) = x^n$ when n is even?

$f(x) \to +\infty$ as $x \to +\infty$ and $f(x) \to +\infty$ as $x \to -\infty$.

3c. What can you say about the end behavior of $f(x) = x^n$ when n is odd?

$f(x) \to +\infty$ as $x \to +\infty$ and $f(x) \to -\infty$ as $x \to -\infty$.

3d. Explain why any function of the form $f(x) = x^n$ is an even function if n is even.

If n is even, then $(-x)^n = x^n$ for all values of x. So, $f(-x) = f(x)$ for all values of x and $f(x)$ is even.

3e. Explain why any function of the form $f(x) = x^n$ is an odd function if n is odd.

If n is odd, then $(-x)^n = -x^n$ for all values of x. So, $f(-x) = -f(x)$ for all values of x and $f(x)$ is odd.

3f. Complete the table.

	Characteristics of $f(x) = x^n$	
	n is even	**n is odd**
Sketch of graph of $f(x) = x^n$		
End behavior	As $x \to +\infty$, $f(x) \to$ $+\infty$, As $x \to -\infty$, $f(x) \to$ $+\infty$.	As $x \to +\infty$, $f(x) \to$ $+\infty$, As $x \to -\infty$, $f(x) \to$ $-\infty$.
Zeros	$x =$ 0	$x =$ 0
Maximum or minimum values	Maximum: none Minimum: 0	Maximum: none Minimum: none
Symmetry	reflection symmetry in y-axis	180° rotational symmetry about origin
Even or odd function	even	odd

Assign these pages to help your students practice and apply important lesson concepts. For additional exercises, see the Student Edition.

Answers

Additional Practice

1. 2; 5; as $x \to +\infty$, $P(x) \to +\infty$; and as $x \to -\infty$, $P(x) \to -\infty$

2. -4; 2; as $x \to -\infty$, $Q(x) \to -\infty$; and as $x \to +\infty$, $Q(x) \to -\infty$

3. Even; negative   **4.** Even; positive

5. Odd; positive

6. ± 1, ± 2, ± 3, ± 4, ± 6, ± 12

7. -4, -3, and 1

8. As $x \to +\infty$, $P(x) \to +\infty$, and as $x \to -\infty$, $P(x) \to -\infty$

9.

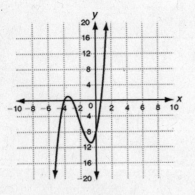

10. About 5400 in year 20

Problem Solving

1. $V(x) = x(11 - 2x)(17 - 2x)$

2. a. $4x^3 - 56x^2 + 187x = 0$

   b. Positive

   c. Odd

   d. As $x \to +\infty$, $V \to +\infty$, and as $x \to -\infty$, $V \to -\infty$.

3. a. 2

   b. About 183 and -64

4. Values of x greater than 5.5 or less than 0

5. About 2.3 and 183

6. 183 cubic inches

7. 2.3 in. by 6.4 in. by 12.4 in.

8. A   **9.** D

Name_____ Class_____ Date_____

Additional Practice

Identify the leading coefficient, degree, and end behavior.

1. $P(x) = 2x^5 - 6x^3 + x^2 - 2$

2. $Q(x) = -4x^2 + x - 1$

Identify whether the function graphed has an odd or even degree and a positive or negative leading coefficient.

3.

4.

5.

Graph the function $P(x) = x^3 + 6x^2 + 5x - 12$.

6. Identify the possible rational roots.
   _____

7. Identify the zeros.
   _____

8. Describe the end behavior of the function.
   _____

9. Sketch the graph of the function.

Solve.

10. The number, $N(y)$, of subscribers to a local magazine can be modeled by the function $N(y) = 0.1y^4 - 3y^3 + 10y^2 - 30y + 10,000$, where y is the number of years since the magazine was founded. Graph the polynomial on a graphing calculator and find the minimum number of subscribers and the year in which this occurs.
   _____

Problem Solving

The Spanish Club members are baking and selling fruit bars to raise money for a trip. They are going to make open boxes to display the bars from sheets of cardboard that are 11 inches by 17 inches. They will cut a square from each corner and fold up the sides and tape them. Find the maximum value for the volume of the box and find its dimensions.

1. Write a formula to represent the volume of the box. _____

2. a. Write the equation in standard form. _____

   b. Is the leading coefficient positive or negative? _____

   c. Is the degree of the polynomial even or odd? _____

   d. Describe the end behavior of the graph.
      _____

3. Use a graphing calculator to graph the equation. Hint: Try a window from –10 to 10 on the x-axis, with a scale of 1, and from –500 to 500 on the y-axis, with a scale of 100.

   a. How many turning points does the graph have? _____

   b. Estimate the local maxima and minima from the graph. _____

4. What values of x are excluded as solutions because they do not make sense for this problem? _____

5. Use the CALC menu on your graphing calculator to find the approximate values of x and y at the local maximum for the graph. _____

6. What is the maximum volume of the box? _____

7. What are the dimensions of the box to the nearest tenth of an inch?
   _____

Choose the letter for the best answer.

8. Arturo is going to build a dog run using one side of his house and 100 feet of fencing. His design has an area that can be modeled by $A(x) = 100x - 7x^2$. What is the maximum area he can enclose?

   A 357 ft²   C 100 ft²

   B 204 ft²   D 70 ft²

9. In order to eliminate some choices on a standardized test, Ruth identifies which of these functions could NOT have a local maximum.

   A $F(x) = -7x^2 + 5x + 2$

   B $F(x) = -7x^3 + 5x - 11$

   C $F(x) = 7x^3 - 5x^2 - 2$

   D $F(x) = 7x^2 - 3x - 18$

Transforming Polynomial Functions
Going Deeper

Essential question: *What are the effects of the constants a, h, and k on the graph of* $f(x) = a(x - h)^n + k$*?*

Standards for Mathematical Content

CC.9-12.F.IF.7 Graph functions expressed symbolically and show key features of the graph, by hand in simple cases ...*

CC.9-12.F.IF.7c Graph polynomial functions, identifying zeros when suitable factorizations are available, and showing end behavior.*

CC.9-12.F.BF.3 Identify the effect on the graph of replacing $f(x)$ by $f(x) + k$, $k f(x)$, ... and $f(x + k)$ for specific values of k (both positive and negative); find the value of k given the graphs. Experiment with cases and illustrate an explanation of the effects on the graph ...

Also: CC.9-12.A.CED.2*, CC.9-12.F.IF.2, CC.9-12.F.IF.9

Prerequisites

Graphing $f(x) = x^n$

Translating the graph of $f(x) = x^n$

Math Background

Previously, students became familiar with the graph of the parent quadratic function $f(x) = x^2$ and how values of the constants h and k affect the graph of $f(x) = (x - h)^2 + k$. In previous lessons, students investigated graphs of functions of the form $f(x) = x^n$ and found that whether n is even or odd has a great effect on the graph of $f(x) = x^n$. In this lesson, students will extend that knowledge to translating the graph of $f(x) = x^n$ and understanding how values of the constants h and k affect the graph of $f(x) = (x - h)^n + k$.

INTRODUCE

Review the function $f(x) = x^2$ and how values of the constants h and k in $f(x) = (x - h)^2 + k$ affect the graph of the function. Also, review how the value of n affects the graph of $f(x) = x^n$.

TEACH

1 EXAMPLE

Questioning Strategies
- When n is even, how can you determine whether the turning point of the graph of $f(x) = x^n + k$ will be located above or below the x-axis? If $k > 0$, the turning point will be located above the x-axis. If $k < 0$, the turning point will be located below the x-axis.
- When $k > 0$, what can you determine about the zero of $f(x) = x^3 + k$ by looking at the graph of the function? Explain. When $k > 0$, the zero of the function $f(x) = x^3 + k$ will have a value that is less than zero because when the graph is translated $|k|$ units up, it intersects the x-axis at a point where $x < 0$.

Teaching Strategy
Students should be reminded that when a graph of a function is translated, the location of the graph on the coordinate plane changes, but the graph otherwise stays the same. As a way to help students understand this, have them trace the graph of $f(x) = x^n$. Students can then either relocate the tracing on the same coordinate plane or use it on a different coordinate plane of the same size and scale.

EXTRA EXAMPLE
Graph $g(x) = x^4 - 5$. It is the graph of the parent function $f(x) = x^4$ translated 5 units down.

Name_____ Class_____ Date_____

3-8

Transforming Polynomial Functions
Going Deeper

Essential question: *What are the effects of the constants a, h, and k on the graph of*
$f(x) = a(x - h)^n + k?$

In this lesson, you will explore transformations of the graph of $f(x) = x^n$.
First, you will focus on translations.

Video Tutor

CC.9-12.F.BF.3
1 EXAMPLE   Graphing $f(x) = x^n + k$

Graph each function.

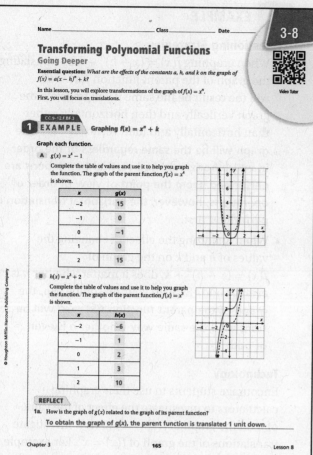

A $g(x) = x^4 - 1$

Complete the table of values and use it to help you graph
the function. The graph of the parent function $f(x) = x^4$
is shown.

x	g(x)
−2	15
−1	0
0	−1
1	0
2	15

B $h(x) = x^3 + 2$

Complete the table of values and use it to help you graph
the function. The graph of the parent function $f(x) = x^3$
is shown.

x	h(x)
−2	−6
−1	1
0	2
1	3
2	10

REFLECT

1a. How is the graph of $g(x)$ related to the graph of its parent function?

To obtain the graph of $g(x)$, the parent function is translated 1 unit down.

Chapter 3   165   Lesson 8

1b. How is the graph of $h(x)$ related to the graph of its parent function?

To obtain the graph of $h(x)$, the parent function is translated 2 units up.

1c. In general, how do you think the graph of $j(x) = x^n + k$ is related to the graph of its
parent function?

To obtain the graph of $j(x)$, the parent function is translated $|k|$ units up if
$k > 0$ and $|k|$ units down if $k < 0$.

CC.9-12.F.BF.3
2 EXAMPLE   Graphing $f(x) = (x - h)^n$

Graph each function.

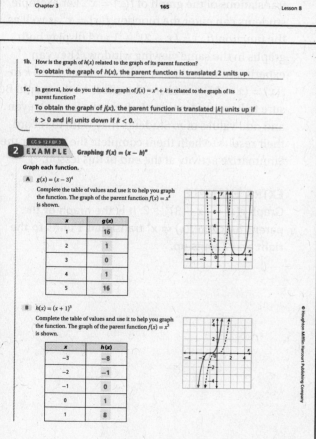

A $g(x) = (x - 3)^4$

Complete the table of values and use it to help you graph
the function. The graph of the parent function $f(x) = x^4$
is shown.

x	g(x)
1	16
2	1
3	0
4	1
5	16

B $h(x) = (x + 1)^3$

Complete the table of values and use it to help you graph
the function. The graph of the parent function $f(x) = x^3$
is shown.

x	h(x)
−3	−8
−2	−1
−1	0
0	1
1	8

© Houghton Mifflin Harcourt Publishing Company

Chapter 3   166   Lesson 8

Questioning Strategies

- If n is even, how does the value of h affect the minimum of the function $f(x) = (x - h)^n$? Explain. **When n is even, the minimum of the function $f(x) = (x - h)^n$ is zero for any value of h; changing the value of h results only in a horizontal translation of the graph, so the minimum is not affected.**

- How does the value of h affect the zero of the function $f(x) = (x - h)^n$? Explain. **The zero is h, because the graph of $f(x) = (x - h)^n$ intersects the x-axis at $(h, 0)$.**

Avoid Common Errors

When translating the graph of $f(x) = (x - h)^n$, students commonly interpret the sign of h incorrectly and translate the parent graph in the wrong direction. A major cause of this error is the presence of the subtraction sign in the expression $x - h$. Remind students that this subtraction sign is not the sign of h. In the expression $x - 2$, for instance, $h = 2$ (a positive number), so the translation is to the right. To identify the value of h in the expression $x + 2$, students should rewrite it as $x - (-2)$, which means that $h = -2$, so the translation is to the left.

EXTRA EXAMPLE

Graph $h(x) = (x + 2)^3$. **It is the graph of the parent function $f(x) = x^3$ translated 2 units left.**

Questioning Strategies

- When graphing $f(x) = (x - h)^n + k$ by translating the graph of the parent function $f(x) = x^n$, will the result be the same if you translate the graph vertically and then horizontally rather than horizontally and then vertically? **Yes, the graph will be the same regardless of the order in which horizontal and vertical translations are performed. From the point of view of order of operations, however, the horizontal translation is performed first.**

- When analyzing the effect of changing the values of h and k on the graph of $f(x) = (x - h)^n + k$, does it matter whether n is even or odd? Explain your reasoning. **No, the graph of the parent function $f(x) = x^n$ will be translated the same way whether n is even or odd.**

Technology

Encourage students to use their graphing calculators to investigate the effect of the value of n on the graph of $f(x) = x^n$, to now investigate translations of the graph of $f(x) = x^n$. For example, students can enter the function $f(x) = x^3$ as well as the function $f(x) = (x - 2)^3 + 1$ and display both graphs in the same viewing window. They can experiment with changing the values of h and k in $f(x) = (x - h)^n + k$ to see the effect on the graph. Be sure to have students explore graphs for both even and odd values of n. Students may want to record their results to help them complete the table for the Summarize activity at the end of this lesson.

EXTRA EXAMPLE

Graph $g(x) = (x - 3)^4 + 2$. **It is the graph of the parent function $f(x) = x^4$ translated 3 units to the right and 2 units up.**

REFLECT

2a. How is the graph of $g(x)$ related to the graph of its parent function?

To obtain the graph of $g(x)$, the parent function is translated 3 units right.

2b. How is the graph of $h(x)$ related to the graph of its parent function?

To obtain the graph of $h(x)$, the parent function is translated 1 unit left.

2c. In general, how do you think the graph of $j(x) = (x - h)^n$ is related to the graph of its parent function?

To obtain the graph of $j(x)$, the parent function is translated $|h|$ units right if $h > 0$ and $|h|$ units left if $h < 0$.

CC.9-12.F.BF.3
3 EXAMPLE Graphing $f(x) = (x - h)^n + k$

Graph $g(x) = (x - 2)^3 + 1$.

A The graph of the parent function, $f(x) = x^3$, is shown. Determine how the graph of $g(x)$ is related to the graph of $f(x)$.

Since $g(x) = (x - 2)^3 + 1$, $h = \underline{2}$ and $k = \underline{1}$.

Complete the table to describe how the graph of the parent function must be translated to obtain the graph of $g(x)$.

Type of Translation	Number of Units	Direction
Horizontal	2	right
Vertical	1	up

B Use the translations you identified to help you draw the graph of $g(x)$.

REFLECT

3a. Compare the domain and range of $g(x) = (x - 2)^3 + 1$ to the domain and range of the parent function $f(x) = x^3$.

The domain and range of both functions are all real numbers.

3b. How is the graph of $h(x) = (x + 17)^8 - 6$ related to the graph of $f(x) = x^8$?

To obtain the graph of $h(x)$, the graph of $f(x)$ is translated 17 units left and 6 units down.

CC.9-12.F.BF.3
4 EXAMPLE Writing the Equation of a Function

The graph of $g(x)$ is the graph of $f(x) = x^4$ after a horizontal and vertical translation. Write the equation of $g(x)$.

A Complete the table to describe how the graph of the parent function must be translated to obtain the graph of $g(x)$. (*Hint:* Consider how the "turning point" (0, 0) on the graph of $f(x)$ must be translated to obtain the turning point on the graph of $g(x)$.)

Type of Translation	Number of Units	Direction
Horizontal	1	left
Vertical	6	down

B Determine the values of h and k in the equation $g(x) = (x - h)^4 + k$.

Based on the translations, $h = \underline{-1}$ and $k = \underline{-6}$.

So, $g(x) = \underline{(x + 1)^4 - 6}$.

REFLECT

4a. Compare the domain and range of $g(x)$ to the domain and range of the parent function $f(x) = x^4$.

The domain of both functions is all real numbers. The range of $f(x)$ is all real numbers greater than or equal to 0; the range of $g(x)$ is all real numbers greater than or equal to -6.

4b. Suppose the graph of $g(x)$ is translated 3 units right and 2 units up to give the graph of $h(x)$. Explain how you can write the equation of $h(x)$.

These translations move the turning point of the graph to $(2, -4)$, so the equation is $h(x) = (x - 2)^4 - 4$.

4c. In general, do translations change the end behavior of a function of the form $f(x) = x^n$? Give a specific example.

No, translations do not change end behavior. For example, the end behavior of $f(x) = x^4$ is $f(x) \to +\infty$ as $x \to +\infty$ and $f(x) \to +\infty$ as $x \to -\infty$. The function $g(x) = (x - 1)^4 - 6$ has the same end behavior.

Questioning Strategies

- What is the value of $g(x) = (x - h)^4 + k$ for $x = h$? How is the corresponding point on the graph of $g(x)$ related to the turning point on the graph of $f(x)$? $g(h) = k$; the corresponding point (h, k) on the graph of $g(x)$ is the translation of the turning point $(0, 0)$ on the graph of $f(x)$, so it is the turning point on the graph of $g(x)$.

- What is the equation of the axis of symmetry for the graph of $g(x)$? Which translation (horizontal or vertical) determines the location of the axis of symmetry? Why? $x = -1$; horizontal; vertical lines are affected by horizontal translations but not vertical translations.

MATHEMATICAL PRACTICE   **Highlighting the Standards**

4 EXAMPLE and its Reflect questions offer an opportunity to address Mathematical Practice Standard 2 (Reason abstractly and quantitatively). Students look at a graph of a function of the form $f(x) = x^n$ and determine the distance and direction that the graph has been translated horizontally and vertically. They then use this quantitative information algebraically as they determine the values of h and k and write an equation of the form $f(x) = (x - h)^n + k$ for the translated graph.

EXTRA EXAMPLE

The graph of $g(x)$ is the graph of $f(x) = x^5$ after a horizontal translation 3 units to the left and a vertical translation 2 units down. Write the equation of $g(x)$. $g(x) = (x + 3)^5 - 2$

Questioning Strategies

- How is the graph of $j(x) = \frac{1}{2} x^4$ related to the graphs of $f(x)$ and $g(x)$ in part A? The graph of $f(x)$ is shrunk vertically by a factor of 0.5 to obtain the graph of $j(x)$. The graph of $g(x)$ is stretched vertically by a factor of 2 to obtain the graph of $j(x)$. All three functions have the same minimum and end behavior.

- If (x, y) is a point on the graph of $g(x) = ax^n$ where n is even, is $(-x, -y)$ a point of the graph of $h(x) = -ax^n$? Explain. Yes; the graph of the function $h(x) = -ax^n$ is a reflection across the x-axis of the graph of $g(x) = ax^n$, so if (x, y) is on the graph of $g(x)$, then $(x, -y)$ is on the reflected graph. The point $(-x, -y)$ is a reflection of the point $(x, -y)$ across the y-axis. If n is even, then the graph has reflection symmetry in the y-axis, so the point $(-x, -y)$ is on the graph of $h(x)$.

EXTRA EXAMPLE

Graph $g(x) = \frac{1}{2}x^2$ and $h(x) = -\frac{1}{2}x^2$. The graph of $g(x)$ is a vertical shrink of the graph of $f(x) = x^2$ that passes through $(-2, 2)$, $(0, 0)$, and $(2, 2)$. The graph of $h(x)$ is a reflection of the graph of $g(x)$ across the x-axis.

Questioning Strategies

- If n is even and $a < 0$, how is the turning point of the graph of $g(x) = a(x - h)^n + k$ related to the turning point of the graph of $f(x) = x^n$? What about the maximum or minimum value that occurs at the turning point? The turning point of the graph of $g(x)$ is (h, k) and k is a maximum. The turning point of the graph of $f(x)$ is $(0, 0)$ and 0 is a minimum.

continued

As you have learned, the values of h and k in the function $f(x) = a(x - h)^n + k$ correspond to a horizontal and vertical translation of the graph of the parent function. Now you will investigate the effects of the constant a.

CC.9-12.F.BF.3

5 EXAMPLE Graphing $f(x) = ax^n$

Graph each pair of functions.

A $g(x) = \frac{1}{4}x^4$ and $h(x) = -\frac{1}{4}x^4$

Complete the table of values and use it to help you graph the functions.
The graph of the parent function $f(x) = x^4$ is shown.

x	g(x)	h(x)
−2	4	−4
−1	$\frac{1}{4}$	$-\frac{1}{4}$
0	0	0
1	$\frac{1}{4}$	$-\frac{1}{4}$
2	4	−4

B $g(x) = 2x^3$ and $h(x) = -2x^3$

Complete the table of values and use it to help you graph the functions.
The graph of the parent function $f(x) = x^3$ is shown.

x	g(x)	h(x)
−2	−16	16
−1	−2	2
0	0	0
1	2	−2
2	16	−16

REFLECT

5a. How is the graph of $f(x) = ax^n$ related to the graph of the parent function $f(x) = x^n$ when $a > 1$? when $0 < a < 1$?

For $a > 1$, the graph of the parent function is stretched vertically.

For $0 < a < 1$, the graph is shrunk vertically.

5b. How is the graph of $f(x) = ax^n$ related to the graph of the parent function $f(x) = x^n$ when $a < -1$? when $-1 < a < 0$?

For $a < -1$, the graph of the parent function is stretched vertically and reflected across the x-axis. For $-1 < a < 0$, the graph is shrunk vertically and reflected across the x-axis.

5c. How is the end behavior of the graph of $f(x) = ax^n$ related to the end behavior of the graph of the parent function $f(x) = x^n$?

If $a > 0$, the end behavior of both graphs is the same.

If $a < 0$, the end behavior is the opposite.

CC.9-12.F.BF.3

6 EXAMPLE Graphing $f(x) = a(x - h)^n + k$

Graph $g(x) = 3(x - 2)^4 - 4$.

A The graph of the parent function $f(x) = x^4$ is shown. Determine how the graph of $g(x)$ is related to the graph of $f(x)$.

First perform any vertical stretches, shrinks, and reflections.

For $g(x)$, $a = \underline{3}$. The graph of $f(x)$ is stretched vertically and there is no reflection.

B For $g(x)$, $h = \underline{2}$ and $k = \underline{-4}$.

Complete the table to describe how the graph of the parent function must be translated to obtain the graph of $g(x)$.

Type of Translation	Number of Units	Direction
Horizontal	2	right
Vertical	4	down

C Use the transformations you identified to help you draw the graph of $g(x)$.

REFLECT

6a. Describe how you think the graph of $g(x) = -0.5(x + 1)^5 - 1$ is related to the graph of the parent function $f(x) = x^5$. Check your prediction by graphing the functions on your calculator.

The graph of f(x) is reflected in the x-axis, shrunk vertically by a factor of

0.5, and translated 1 unit left and 1 unit down.

- If n is odd and $a < 0$, how is the end behavior of $g(x) = a(x - h)^n + k$ related to the end behavior of $f(x) = x^n$? The end behaviors are opposites: As $x \to +\infty$, $f(x) \to +\infty$ and $g(x) \to -\infty$. As $x \to -\infty$, $f(x) \to -\infty$ and $g(x) \to +\infty$.

EXTRA EXAMPLE
Graph $g(x) = 2(x - 1)^4 - 3$. The graph of $f(x) = x^4$ is stretched vertically by a factor of 2 and then translated 1 unit to the right and 3 units down.

> **MATHEMATICAL PRACTICE**   **Highlighting the Standards**
>
> 6 EXAMPLE   and its Reflect questions offer an opportunity to address Mathematical Practice Standard 8 (Look for and express regularity in repeated reasoning). In this unit, students build upon patterns they have observed regarding the effects of parameters on the graph of the function $f(x) = a(x - h)^n + k$.

7 EXAMPLE

Questioning Strategies

- What is the image of the point $(0, 0)$? How can you tell? How does this relate to the values of h and k? $(-2, 3)$; the "symmetry point" of the graph of the parent function is translated to the symmetry point of $g(x)$. The x-coordinate of the image of $(0, 0)$ is h, and the y-coordinate is k.

- If n were even, how would you determine the values of h and k? The point $(0, 0)$ is the turning point of the graph of the parent function. The image of this point is the turning point of the translated graph and has coordinates (h, k).

- How can you use the images of $(0, 0)$ and $(1, 1)$ to find the value of a? Find the difference in the y-coordinates in the image points. The image of $(0, 0)$ is (h, k), and the image of $(1, 1)$ is $(h + 1, k + a)$.

Technology
Students can check the equations they write by graphing the functions on their graphing calculators. Use the TRACE or TABLE feature to identify coordinates of points in the resulting graph.

EXTRA EXAMPLE
The graph of $g(x)$ is the graph of $f(x) = x^3$ after it has been stretched vertically by a factor of 3, reflected across the x-axis, and translated left 4 units and up 1 unit. Write the equation of $g(x)$.
$g(x) = -3(x + 4)^3 + 1$

7 EXAMPLE Writing the Equation of a Function

The graph of $g(x)$ is the graph of $f(x) = x^3$ after a series of transformations. Write the equation of $g(x)$.

A Complete the table to describe how the graph of the parent function must be translated to obtain the graph of $g(x)$. (*Hint:* Consider how the "symmetry point" $(0, 0)$ on the graph of $f(x)$ must be translated to obtain the symmetry point on the graph of $g(x)$.)

Type of Translation	Number of Units	Direction
Horizontal	2	left
Vertical	3	up

So, $h = \underline{-2}$ and $k = \underline{3}$.

B Determine the value of a in the equation $g(x) = a(x - h)^3 + k$.

The image of the point $(0, 0)$ is $\underline{(-2, 3)}$.

The image of the point $(1, 1)$ is $\underline{(-1, 1)}$.

The vertical distance between $(0, 0)$ and $(1, 1)$ is 1 unit.

The vertical distance between the images of $(0, 0)$ and $(1, 1)$ is $\underline{2}$ units.

This means that $|a| = \underline{2}$.

The graph of the parent function is reflected across the x-axis, so $a \underline{<} 0$.

So, the value of a is $\underline{-2}$.

C Use the values of h, k, and a to write the equation: $g(x) = \underline{-2(x + 2)^3 + 3}$.

REFLECT

7a. The graph of $g(x)$ contains $(-3, 5)$. Check that your equation from part C is correct by showing that $(-3, 5)$ satisfies the equation.

$g(-3) = -2(-3 + 2)^3 + 3 = -2(-1)^3 + 3 = -2(-1) + 3 = 2 + 3 = 5$

7b. Suppose the graph of $g(x)$ is translated 4 units right and 5 units down to give the graph of $h(x)$. What is the equation of $h(x)$?

$h(x) = -2(x - 2)^3 - 2$

7c. The transformation of $f(x)$ into $g(x)$ above involved all of translation, reflection, and stretching. Would it change the final equation to perform these transformations in a different order? Why or why not?

No. The transformations are independent of each other.

Chapter 3   171   Lesson 8

PRACTICE

Graph each function.

1. $f(x) = x^3 - 2$

2. $f(x) = x^6 + 1$

3. $f(x) = (x + 2)^4$

4. $f(x) = (x - 3)^5$

5. $f(x) = (x - 1)^4 + 2$

6. $f(x) = (x + 2)^3 - 2$

7. Without graphing, explain how the graph of $g(x) = (x - 5)^7 - 1.3$ is related to the graph of $f(x) = x^7$.

To obtain the graph of $g(x)$, the graph of $f(x)$ is translated 5 units right and 1.3 units down.

Chapter 3   172   Lesson 8

Essential Question

What are the effects of the constants a, h, and k on the graph of $f(x) = a(x - h)^n + k$?

The graph of $f(x) = (x - h)^n + k$ is a translation of the graph of the parent function $f(x) = x^n$. The graph of the parent function is translated h units to the right if $h > 0$, $|h|$ units to the left if $h < 0$, k units up if $k > 0$, and $|k|$ units down if $k < 0$.

If $a > 1$, the graph of the parent function is stretched vertically by a factor of a. If $0 < a < 1$, the graph is shrunk vertically by a factor of a. If $a < -1$, the graph of the parent function is stretched vertically by a factor of $|a|$ and reflected across the x-axis. If $-1 < a < 0$, the graph of the parent function is shrunk vertically by a factor of $|a|$ and reflected across the x-axis.

Summarize

Have students make a table showing the effects of the constants *a, h,* and *k* on the graph of $f(x) = a(x - h)^n + k$ if $a > 1$, $a < -1$, $0 < a < 1$, and $-1 < a < 0$. In the table, have students include a sketch of the graph, as well as information about how changing the values of *a, h,* and *k* affects function characteristics like zeros, minimum and maximum values, symmetry, and end behavior.

Where skills are taught	Where skills are practiced
❶ EXAMPLE	EXS. 1, 2
❷ EXAMPLE	EXS. 3, 4
❸ EXAMPLE	EXS. 5–7
❹ EXAMPLE	EXS. 12–14
❺ EXAMPLE	EXS. 8–9
❻ EXAMPLE	EXS. 10–11
❼ EXAMPLE	EXS. 17–18

Exercise 15: Students investigate turning points of the graphs of $f(x) = (x - h)^n + k$ and how turning points are related to whether n is even or odd.

Exercise 16: Students identify an error when a graph is translated.

Exercise 19: Students apply their knowledge of stretching, shrinking, and reflecting the graph of $f(x) = x^3$ to a problem involving the volumes of spheres and cubes.

Graph each function.

8. $f(x) = 2x^4$

9. $f(x) = -\frac{1}{2}x^3$

10. $f(x) = -(x-3)^4 + 1$

11. $f(x) = 2(x+1)^3 - 2$

The graph of $g(x)$ is the graph of $f(x) = x^3$ after a horizontal and vertical translation. Write the equation of $g(x)$.

12.

$y = (x-3)^3 + 2$

13.

$y = (x+2)^3 - 3$

14. Suppose you translate the graph of $y = (x-2)^5 - 7$ left 4 units and up 3 units. What is the equation of the resulting graph?

$y = (x+2)^5 - 4$

---

15. A turning point on the graph of a function is a point where the graph changes from increasing to decreasing, or from decreasing to increasing. A turning point corresponds to a local maximum or local minimum.

a. Does the graph of $y = x^4$ have a turning point? If so, what is it?

Yes; (0, 0)

b. Does the graph of $y = (x+5)^4 + 4$ have a turning point? If so, what is it?

Yes; (−5, 4)

c. For even values of n, what is the turning point of $y = (x-h)^n + k$? Why is this true only when n is even?

(h, k); there is no turning point when n is odd.

16. **Error Analysis** A student was asked to graph the function $g(x) = (x+3)^4 - 2$. The student's work is shown at right. Identify the error and explain how the student should have graphed the function. Graph the function correctly.

The student translated the graph of $f(x) = x^4$ right 3 units and down 2 units, but the student should have translated the graph of $f(x)$ left 3 units and down 2 units.

The graph of $g(x)$ is the graph of $f(x) = x^4$ after a series of transformations. Write the equation of $g(x)$.

17.

$g(x) = -(x+3)^4 + 4$

18.

$g(x) = \frac{1}{4}x^4 - 4$

19. $S(x) = \frac{4}{3}\pi\left(\frac{x}{2}\right)^3$ gives the volume of a sphere with diameter x, and $C(x) = x^3$ gives the volume of a cube with edge length x. Explain why the volume of a sphere with diameter x is less than the volume of a cube with edge length x.

$S(x) = \frac{4}{3}\pi\left(\frac{x}{2}\right)^3 = \frac{4}{3}\pi\left(\frac{x^3}{8}\right) = \frac{\pi}{6}x^3$ and $C(x) = x^3$, so $S(x) < C(x)$ because $\frac{\pi}{6} < 1$.

Assign these pages to help your students practice and apply important lesson concepts. For additional exercises, see the Student Edition.

Answers

Additional Practice

1. $g(x) = (x + 4)^3 + 1$

2. $g(x) = 3x^3 + 3$

3. $g(x) = \left(\frac{1}{2}x\right)^3 + 1$

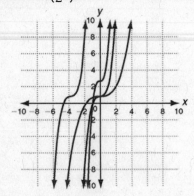

4. $g(x) = x^3 + 4x^2 + 5x + 12$

5. $g(x) = x^3 - 4x^2 + 5x - 12$

6. Vertically compressed by a factor of 4

7. Translated 3 units down

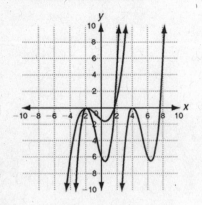

8. $-x^3 + 4x^2 + x + 11$

9. $\frac{1}{4}(x - 3)^3 + (x - 3)^2 - \frac{1}{4}(x - 3) + \frac{5}{4}$

10. $N(t) = 8t^2 - 2t + 4000$

Problem Solving

1. $N(x) = 0.02x^3 + 0.4x^2 + 0.2x + 235$

2. Vertical translation of 200 units up

3.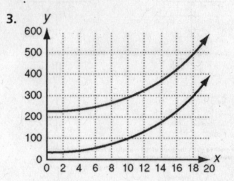

4. Because only positive values have meaning in the context of the problem.

5. An additional 200 cars are passing through the intersection every week.

6. Possible answer: $R(x) = C(x) - 30$; vertical shift of 30 units down

7. $2C(x) = 0.04x^3 + 0.8x^2 + 0.4x + 70$; possible answer: a new mall opened at the intersection.

3-8

Additional Practice

For $f(x) = x^3 + 1$, write the rule for each function and sketch its graph.

1. $g(x) = f(x + 4)$

_____

2. $g(x) = 3f(x)$

_____

3. $g(x) = f\left(\frac{1}{2}x\right)$

_____

Let $f(x) = -x^3 + 4x^2 - 5x + 12$. Write a function $g(x)$ that performs each transformation.

4. Reflect $f(x)$ across the y-axis

5. Reflect $f(x)$ across the x-axis

Let $f(x) = x^3 + 2x^2 - 3x - 6$. Describe $g(x)$ as a transformation of $f(x)$ and graph.

6. $g(x) = \frac{1}{4}f(x)$

_____

7. $g(x) = f(x - 6)$

_____

Write a function that transforms $f(x) = x^3 + 4x^2 - x + 5$ in each of the following ways. Support your solution by using a graphing calculator.

8. Move 6 units up and reflect across the y-axis.

_____

9. Compress vertically by a factor of 0.25 and move 3 units right.

_____

Solve.

10. The number of participants, N, in a new Internet political forum during each month of the first year can be modeled by $N(t) = 4t^2 - t + 2000$, where t is the number of months since January. In the second year, the number of forum participants doubled compared to the same month in the previous year. Write a function that describes the number of forum participants in the second year.

_____

Problem Solving

A traffic engineer determines that the number of cars passing through a certain intersection each week can be modeled by $C(x) = 0.02x^3 + 0.4x^2 + 0.2x + 35$, where x is the number of weeks since the survey began. A new road has just opened that affects the traffic at that intersection. Let $N(x) = C(x) + 200$.

1. Find the rule for $N(x)$.

_____

2. What transformation of $C(x)$ is represented by $N(x)$?

_____

3. On the graph of $C(x)$, sketch the graph for $N(x)$.

4. Use a graphing calculator to graph $N(x)$. Use a window from 0 to 20 with a scale of 1 on the x-axis and from 0 to 500 with a scale of 1 on the y-axis. Compare it to your sketch. Explain why only the values in Quadrant 1 are considered for this problem.

_____

5. Explain the meaning of the transformation of $C(x)$ into $N(x)$ in terms of the weekly number of cars passing through the intersection.

_____

6. Emergency roadwork temporarily closes off most of the traffic to this intersection. Write a function $R(x)$ that could model the effect on $C(x)$ Explain how the graph of $C(x)$ might be transformed into $R(x)$.

_____

7. Describe the transformation $2C(x)$ by writing the new rule and explaining the change in the context of the problem.

_____

3-9

Curve Fitting with Polynomial Models
Focus on Modeling

Essential question: *How can you use polynomial functions to model and solve real-world problems?*

The following standards are addressed in this lesson. (An asterisk indicates that a standard is also a Modeling standard.) For more detailed information, see each section of the lesson.

Algebra: CC.9-12.A.SSE.1*, CC.9-12.A.SSE.1a*, CC.9-12.A.APR.1, CC.9-12.A.CED.1*, CC.9-12.A.CED.2*, CC.9-12.A.CED.3*, CC.9-12.A.REI.11*

Functions: CC.9-12.F.IF.4*, CC.9-12.F.IF.5*, CC.9-12.F.IF.7*, CC.9-12.F.IF.7c*, CC.9-12.F.BF.1*, CC.9-12.F.BF.1a*

Prerequisites
Graphing polynomial functions

Adding, subtracting, and multiplying polynomial expressions

Solving polynomial equations

Math Background
Students write a polynomial function for the volume of a box. They use the Rational Zero Theorem to find the dimensions of the box and analyze the graph of the function to find the maximum volume of the box.

INTRODUCE

Point out that volume models can be used for a wide range of real-world situations, from engineering and manufacturing to everyday applications like mailing a package.

TEACH

1 **Write a volume function.**

Standards
CC.9-12.A.SSE.1 Interpret expressions that represent a quantity in terms of its context.*

CC.9-12.A.SSE.1a Interpret parts of an expression, such as … factors …*

CC.9-12.A.CED.2 Create equations in two … variables to represent relationships between quantities …*

CC.9-12.F.BF.1 Write a function that describes a relationship between two quantities.*

CC.9-12.F.BF.1a Determine an explicit expression … from a context.*

Questioning Strategies
- How is the expression for the height of the box related to expressions for the length and the width of the box? **The expression for the height is *x*, which is the amount cut from each end of the 10-inch length, represented as 10 − 2*x*, and from each end of the 8-inch width, represented as 8 − 2*x*.**

- What would the rule for $V(x)$ be if the piece of cardboard were a square with side length 8 inches? $V(x) = x(8 - 2x)^2$

2 **Determine the domain of the volume function.**

Standards
CC.9-12.A.CED.3 Represent constraints by … inequalities …*

CC.9-12.F.IF.5 Relate the domain of a function … to the quantitative relationship it describes.*

Questioning Strategies
- Why do the constraints on *x* for the length and width not simply require that *x* be nonnegative? **The constraints on *x* describe those values of *x* that make the expressions for the length and width result in nonnegative values.**

- How can you generalize from this situation to finding the domain for any volume function? **Since length, height, and width will always be nonnegative, the domain of a volume function will always require that the independent variable takes on only values that make each dimension nonnegative.**

3-9

Curve Fitting with Polynomial Models
Focus on Modeling

Essential question: *How can you use polynomial functions to model and solve real-world problems?*

Video Tutor

> Y̶ou are making an open rectangular box for an art project. To make the box, you cut out a square from each corner of a rectangular piece of cardboard and fold up the flaps to create an open box as shown below.
>
>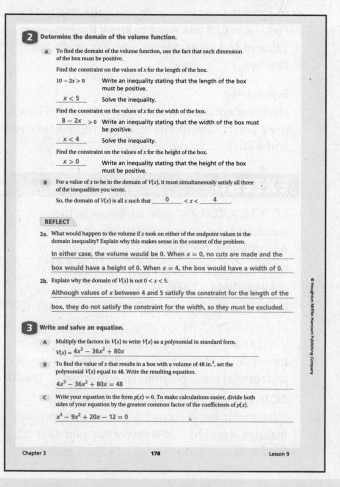
>
> The original rectangular piece of cardboard is 10 inches long and 8 inches wide. If x is the side length in inches of each square that is cut from the corners, what value or values of x will result in a box with a volume of 48 in.³? Is this the greatest possible volume? Explain.

1 Write a volume function.

A Use the figure to help you write expressions for the length, width, and height of the box.

Length of box: $10 - 2x$

Width of box: _____ $8 - 2x$ _____

Height of box: _____ x _____

B The volume of the box is the product of the length, width, and height. Use the expressions you wrote above to write a function $V(x)$ that models the volume of the box.

$V(x) = (10 - 2x)(8 - 2x)x$

REFLECT

1a. What units are associated with the expressions for the length, width, and height? What are the units for the volume of the box?

inches; cubic inches

1b. How can you use your function $V(x)$ to find the volume of the box when squares with sides of length 3 inches are cut from the corners of the cardboard? What are the dimensions of the box in this case?

$V(3) = (4)(2)(3) = 24$ in.³; the dimensions are 4 in. × 2 in. × 3 in.

---

2 Determine the domain of the volume function.

A To find the domain of the volume function, use the fact that each dimension of the box must be positive.

Find the constraint on the values of x for the length of the box.

$10 - 2x > 0$ — Write an inequality stating that the length of the box must be positive.

$x < 5$ — Solve the inequality.

Find the constraint on the values of x for the width of the box.

$8 - 2x > 0$ — Write an inequality stating that the width of the box must be positive.

$x < 4$ — Solve the inequality.

Find the constraint on the values of x for the height of the box.

$x > 0$ — Write an inequality stating that the height of the box must be positive.

B For a value of x to be in the domain of $V(x)$, it must simultaneously satisfy all three of the inequalities you wrote.

So, the domain of $V(x)$ is all x such that _____ 0 _____ $< x <$ _____ 4 _____.

REFLECT

2a. What would happen to the volume if x took on either of the endpoint values in the domain inequality? Explain why this makes sense in the context of the problem.

In either case, the volume would be 0. When $x = 0$, no cuts are made and the box would have a height of 0. When $x = 4$, the box would have a width of 0.

2b. Explain why the domain of $V(x)$ is not $0 < x < 5$.

Although values of x between 4 and 5 satisfy the constraint for the length of the box, they do not satisfy the constraint for the width, so they must be excluded.

3 Write and solve an equation.

A Multiply the factors in $V(x)$ to write $V(x)$ as a polynomial in standard form.

$V(x) = 4x^3 - 36x^2 + 80x$

B To find the value of x that results in a box with a volume of 48 in.³, set the polynomial $V(x)$ equal to 48. Write the resulting equation.

$4x^3 - 36x^2 + 80x = 48$

C Write your equation in the form $p(x) = 0$. To make calculations easier, divide both sides of your equation by the greatest common factor of the coefficients of $p(x)$.

$x^3 - 9x^2 + 20x - 12 = 0$

Notes

3 Write and solve an equation.

Standards

CC.9-12.A.APR.1 ... multiply polynomials.

CC.9-12.A.CED.1 Create equations ... in one variable and use them to solve problems.*

Questioning Strategies

- How does writing the polynomial in standard form help you solve the equation? **You can then use the Rational Zero Theorem to identify possible rational zeros.**

- According to the Fundamental Theorem of Algebra, how many zeros will any volume function have? Explain. **3; a volume function is always of degree 3.**

4 Graph the volume function and determine the local maximum.

Standards

CC.9-12.F.IF.4 For a function that models a relationship between two quantities, interpret key features of graphs ... in terms of the quantities ...*

CC.9-12.F.IF.7 Graph functions expressed symbolically and show key features of the graph, ... using technology for more complicated cases.*

CC.9-12.F.IF.7c Graph polynomial functions ...*

Questioning Strategies

- How can you use your graphing calculator to find the values of x that result in a volume of 48 in.^{3}? **Enter and graph a second function as $Y_2 = 48$ and then use the Intersect feature to find the x-values where the two graphs intersect.**

- For any volume less than the maximum, how many different boxes are possible? Explain. **2, because there are two x-values for any $V(x)$-value less than the maximum, and each x-value results in a unique box.**

CLOSE

Essential Question

How can you use polynomial functions to model and solve real-world problems?
Write a polynomial function $f(x)$ to model the situation. Restrict the domain of $f(x)$ to account for any real-world constraints. If you want to know the value(s) of x for which $f(x) = c$, you can use the Rational Zero Theorem and other techniques to solve the equation once you write it in the form $f(x) - c = 0$. If you want to know the maximum value of $f(x)$ on its domain, you can graph the function.

Summarize

Have students write a one-page summary of how to use a polynomial model to write a volume function and solve volume problems.

EXTEND

CC.9-12.A.CED.2 Create equations in two ... variables to represent relationships between quantities ...* (Ex. 1)

CC.9-12.A.CED.3 Represent constraints by ... inequalities ...* (Ex. 2)

CC.9-12.A.REI.11 Explain why the x-coordinates of the points where the graphs of the equations $y = f(x)$ and $y = g(x)$ intersect are the solutions of the equation $f(x) = g(x)$ ... Include cases where $f(x)$ and/or $g(x)$ are ... polynomial ... functions.* (Ex. 3)

CC.9-12.F.IF.4 For a function that models a relationship between two quantities, interpret key features of graphs ... in terms of the quantities ...* (Exs. 4, 5)

D Solve the equation. First determine the possible rational zeros of $p(x)$.

$\pm1, \pm2, \pm3, \pm4, \pm6, \pm12$

Use synthetic substitution to find a zero of $p(x)$. Then factor $p(x)$ completely to find the remaining zeros.

The zeros of $p(x)$ are 1, 2, and 6

E Interpret the results. Which of the zeros are in the domain of $V(x)$?

1 and 2

For each of these zeros, what are the corresponding dimensions of the box?

When $x = 1$, the box is 8 in. $\times$ 6 in. $\times$ 1 in.

When $x = 2$, the box is 6 in. $\times$ 4 in. $\times$ 2 in.

REFLECT

3a. Check that the values of x that you found above result in a box with a volume of 48 in.^{3}

When $x = 1$, the volume is $8 \times 6 \times 1 = 48$ in.^{3}

When $x = 2$, the volume is $6 \times 4 \times 2 = 48$ in.^{3}

3b. Given that it's possible to create a box with a volume of 48 in.^{3}, do you think it's possible to create a box with a volume of 24 in.^{3}? Explain.

Yes; if $V(x)$ takes on a value of 0 when $x = 0$ and $V(x)$ takes on a value of 48 when $x = 1$, then $V(x)$ must take on all values between 0 and 48 for $0 < x < 1$.

---

4 Graph the volume function and determine the local maximum.

A Use a graphing calculator to graph the volume function $V(x)$.

Step 1: Enter $V(x)$ in the equation editor.

Step 2: Use the domain of $V(x)$ and the fact that the volume can be at least 48 in.^{3} to help you choose an appropriate viewing window.

Step 3: Graph the function. Sketch the graph on the coordinate plane at right.

B Find the maximum value of the function within the domain.

Step 1: Press [2nd] [TRACE], then select **4:maximum.**

Step 2: Use the arrow keys to move along the graph to select a left bound, a right bound, and a guess. Press [ENTER] after each of these.

At what point does the maximum value occur? Round the coordinates to the nearest tenth.

(1.5, 52.5)

REFLECT

4a. Interpret the result. What do the coordinates of the point where the maximum value occurs represent in the context of the problem?

The box has a maximum volume of about 52.5 in.^{3} when the squares cut from each corner have side lengths of about 1.5 in.

4b. How does your graph of $V(x)$ support the domain you found earlier?

The graph shows that the volume is positive for values of x between 0 and 4.

4c. You know that $V(x)$ has a maximum value on the domain $0 < x < 4$, but does $V(x)$ have a maximum value when the domain is not restricted (that is, when x can be any real number)? Explain.

No; the graph of $V(x)$ eventually rises without bound as x increases without bound, so $V(x)$ has no greatest value when x can be any real number.

EXTEND

1. Suppose you have a second piece of cardboard that is 16 inches long and 6 inches wide. What is the volume function for this box when squares of side length x are cut from the corners of the cardboard?

$V(x) = (16 - 2x)(6 - 2x)x$

2. What is the domain of this volume function?

$0 < x < 3$

3. Graph this volume function in the same viewing window as the volume function for the box made from the 10-by-8 piece of cardboard. Then use the calculator's Intersect feature to find the coordinates of the point or points where the graphs intersect.

The graphs intersect at (2, 48).

4. What do the coordinates of the points of intersection represent in the context of the problem?

When $x = 2$ in., both boxes have a volume of 48 in.^{3}

5. Suppose you can make a box from only one of the pieces of cardboard and you want to make a box with the greatest possible volume. Which piece of cardboard should you use? How is your answer supported by the graphs of the volume functions?

The graphs show that the box with the greatest possible volume made from the 16-by-6 piece of cardboard has a greater volume (approximately 59.3 in.^{3}) than the box with the greatest possible volume made from the 10-by-8 piece of cardboard.

Assign these pages to help your students practice
and apply important lesson concepts. For
additional exercises, see the Student Edition.

Answers

Additional Practice

1. Box A: $V(x) = (12 - 2x)(7 - 2x)x$; domain:
   $0 < x < 3.5$

   Box B: $V(x) = (12 - 2x)(9 - 2x)x$; domain:
   $0 < x < 4.5$

2. Box A: 50 cm^3

   Box B: 70 cm^3

3. Box A: $V(x) = 4x^3 - 38x^2 + 84x$;

   Box B: $V(x) = 4x^3 - 42x^2 + 108x$

4. Check students' graphs. Box B; The graph for
   Box A shows that for $0 < x < 3.5$, $V(x)$ is always
   less than 80. The graph for Box A shows that
   for $0 < x < 4.5$, $V(x)$ has a maximum value of
   about 81.9. The volume of Box B is 80 cm^3
   when x is 2.

Problem Solving

1. Side lengths greater than 0 and less than
   3 inches

2. 2 inches; 8 in.^{3}

3. Check students' graphs. 16 in.^{3}; Possible
   explanation: I graphed the equation
   $y = (6 - 2x)(6 - 2x)x$ for the values $0 < x < 3$.
   For these values, the graph reaches a
   maximum at (1, 16).

4. B

5. G

6. B

7. C

8. D

Additional Practice

The diagrams show patterns for making two boxes. For each box, a square of side length x centimeters is cut from each corner of a rectangular piece of cardboard. The flaps are folded up to form the box. Use the diagrams for Exercises 1–4.

Box A

7 cm

12 cm

$x$cm

Box B

9 cm

12 cm

$x$cm

1. Write a function $V(x)$ that models the volume of each box. Find the domain of each function.

   Box A _____

   Box B _____

2. Find the volume of each box if a square of side length 1 centimeter is cut from each corner.

   Box A _____   Box B _____

3. For each function, multiply the factors in $V(x)$ to write it as a polynomial in standard form.

   Box A _____

   Box B _____

4. Graph each function on a graphing calculator. Which box could have a volume of 80 cubic centimeters? How do you know? Then find the value of x that produces a volume of 80 cubic centimeters.

   _____

   _____

   _____

   _____

Problem Solving

Sue cuts identical squares out of the corners of the cardboard square shown, then folds up the flaps to make a box. Use this information for Exercises 1–3.

6in.

6in.

1. Describe the possible side lengths Sue can use for the squares she cuts from the corners of the box.

   _____

2. Sue wants the box to be cube-shaped. What side length should she use for each of the squares she cuts from the corners? What will be the volume of the box?

   _____

3. Use a graphing calculator to find the maximum possible volume for Sue's box. Explain your procedure.

   _____

   _____

Choose the best answer.

A rectangular prism has sides of length x, $0.5x$, and $x - 1$ inches. Its volume is 9 cubic inches. Use this information for Exercises 4–6.

4. Which equation models the situation?

   A $0.5x^3 - 0.5x = 9$

   B $0.5x^3 - 0.5x^2 = 9$

   C $0.5x^2 - 0.5x^2 = 9$

   D $(0.5x)(x - 1) = 9$

5. What are the possible rational solutions of the equation in Exercise 1?

   F $\pm\frac{1}{1}, \pm\frac{1}{2}, \pm\frac{1}{3}, \pm\frac{1}{6}, \pm\frac{1}{9}, \pm\frac{1}{18}$

   G $\pm\frac{1}{1}, \pm\frac{2}{1}, \pm\frac{3}{1}, \pm\frac{6}{1}, \pm\frac{9}{1}, \pm\frac{18}{1}$

   H $\pm\frac{1}{1}, \pm\frac{3}{1}, \pm\frac{9}{1}$

   J $\pm\frac{1}{1}, \pm\frac{1}{3}, \pm\frac{1}{9}$

6. What is the length of the shortest side of the prism?

   A 1 in.   C 2 in.

   B 1.5 in.   D 3 in.

7. The volume of a rectangular prism is 225 cubic centimeters. The base of the prism is a square, and the height of the prism is 4 centimeters greater than a side length of the base. What is the height of the prism?

   A 4 cm   C 9 cm

   B 5 cm   D 25 cm

8. A pyramid-shaped sculpture has a volume of 18 cubic inches. The length of a side of the square base of the pyramid is 3 inches less than the height of the pyramid. What equation could model this situation?

   A $x^3 - 3x^2 = 18$

   B $x^3 - 3x^2 = 54$

   C $x^3 - 6x^2 + 9x = 18$

   D $x^3 - 6x^2 + 9x = 54$

Notes

This page provides students with the opportunity to apply concepts from the Common Core in real-world problem situations. There are three different levels of performance tasks:

⭐ **Novice:** These are short word problems that require students to apply the math they have learned in straightforward, real-world situations.

⭐⭐ **Apprentice:** These are more involved problems that guide students step-by-step through more complex tasks. These exercises include more complicated reasoning, writing, and open-ended elements.

⭐⭐⭐ **Expert:** These are open-ended, non-routine problems that, instead of stepping the students through, ask them to choose their own methods for solving and justify their answers and reasoning.

Sample answers

1. $9x - 18$. Possible explanation: The area of the paper was originally x^2 square inches. After Jeremy finished cutting, the area was $(x - 6)(x - 3) = x^2 - 3x - 6x + 18 = (x^2 - 9x + 18)$ square inches. Therefore, to find the total area in square inches of the scrap that he discarded, subtract the second area from the first area: $x^2 - (x^2 - 9x + 18) = x^2 - x^2 + 9x - 18 = 9x - 18$

2. $x^3 - 4x^2 - 11x + 30 = (x - 2)(x - 5)(x + 3)$. Possible explanation: the customer's polynomial is incorrect because he reversed the signs of the measurement changes.

3. Scoring Guide:

Task	Possible points
a	1 point for finding that the fourth differences are constant, so a fourth degree polynomial would be best.
b	1 point for correctly choosing a quartic regression and 1 point for correctly determining the function to be $P(x) = -x^4 + x^3 - 2x^2 - x + 100,000$
c	1 point for correctly determining the expected average price, $97,837, for properties sold in 2015
d	1 point for correctly answering that the function $P(x)$ will not be valid indefinitely and 1 point for a correct explanation, for example: eventually the function predicts a price lower than zero, which does not make sense in this context.

Total possible points: 6

CHAPTER 3

Performance Tasks

COMMON
CORE
CC-9-12.A.SSE.2
CC-9-12.A.APR.3
CC-9-12.A.CED.2

★ 1. Jeremy had a square piece of gift wrapping paper with a side length of x inches that he used to wrap a present. First he cut 6 inches off the right side of the paper and discarded the rectangular scrap. Next he cut 3 inches off the top of the paper and again discarded the rectangular scrap. What expression represents the total area in square inches of the scraps that he discarded? Justify your answer.

★ 2. A customer at a self-storage facility was offered a choice between a storage unit shaped like a cube and another unit that is 2 feet longer, 5 feet wider, and 3 feet shorter than the first unit. The customer thinks that if the volume of the cube is x^3, the volume of the other unit would be $x^3 - 4x^2 - 11x + 30$. Is the customer correct? Factor the polynomial to check.

★ 3. The table shows the average price of the properties sold by a real estate agency for each of the years from 2009 to 2014.

Year	Price	Year	Price
2009	$99,997	2012	$99,772
2010	$99,982	2013	$99,445
2011	$99,925	2014	$98,842

    a. Use finite differences to find the degree of polynomial that would best model this data.

    b. Use a graphing calculator to perform a regression and determine the function $P(x)$ that models the data. Let your x-values be the number of years since 2008. (Round the parameters of the regression to whole numbers.)

    c. What can the real estate agency expect the average price to be for the properties sold in 2015?

continued

    d. Will the function $P(x)$ that you found in part b continue to model the average price of the properties sold indefinitely? Explain.

★ 4. A band's concert revenue can be modeled by $R(t) = t^6 - 64$, and its average price per ticket sold can be modeled by $P(t) = t^2 - 4$, where t is the hours of advertising purchased. The band wants to find the function $Q(t)$, which represents the number of tickets sold.

    a. Why can $t^6 - 64$ be thought of as the difference of two squares? Write it as the product of two binomials.

    b. Write the function $Q(t) = \frac{R(t)}{P(t)}$ and simplify it so that $Q(t)$ is written as a quartic polynomial.

4. Scoring Guide:

Task	Possible points
a	2 points for correctly explaining that $t^6 - 64$ can be thought of as the difference of two squares because $(t^3)^2 = t^6$ and $8^2 = 64$, and 1 point for correctly finding $t^6 - 64 = (t^3 - 8)(t^3 + 8)$
b	1 point for writing $Q(t) = \frac{(t^3 + 8)(t^3 - 8)}{t^2 - 4}$ (with or without factoring) and 2 points for correctly simplifying the quotient to $Q(t) = t^4 + 4t^2 + 16$

Total possible points: 6

COMMON CORE CORRELATION

Standard	Items
CC.9-12.N.CN.9(+)	1
CC.9-12.A.SSE.2	2
CC.9-12.A.APR.1	4, 10
CC.9-12.A.APR.2	6, 11
CC.9-12.A.APR.3	7, 8
CC.9-12.A.APR.5(+)	5
CC.9-12.A.CED.1*	14
CC.9-12.A.CED.2*	12
CC.9-12.A.CED.3*	13
CC.9-12.F.IF.2	11
CC.9-12.F.IF.4*	3
CC.9-12.F.IF.7c*	3
CC.9-12.F.BF.1*	12, 15
CC.9-12.F.BF.3	9

TEST PREP DOCTOR ⊕

Multiple Choice: Item 3
- Students who chose **A** did not take into account the negative sign in the leading term $-x^5$.

- Students who chose **B** or **C** identified the end behavior for a polynomial of even degree.

Multiple Choice: Item 5
- Students who chose **B** used a 4 instead of a 1 for the constant term.

- Students who chose **C** used a 4 instead of a 1 as the leading coefficient.

- Students who chose **D** used a 4 instead of a 1 for both the leading coefficient and the constant term.

Multiple Choice: Item 7
- Students who chose **A** factored $f(x) = x^2 - 9$.

- Students who chose **C** incorrectly identified $f(x) = x^2 + 9$ as the square of a binomial.

- Students who chose **D** used the wrong sign in one of the factors.

Constructed Response: Item 9
- Students who incorrectly graphed and described the end behavior of $g(x)$ may not understand the effect of the value of n on the graph of $g(x) = a(x - h)^n + k$.

- Students who incorrectly graphed and described the stretching of the graph of $f(x)$ may not understand the effect of the value of a on the graph of $g(x) = a(x - h)^n + k$.

- Students who incorrectly graphed and described the reflection of the graph of $f(x)$ may not understand the effect of the sign of a on the graph of $g(x) = a(x - h)^n + k$.

- Students who incorrectly graphed and described the horizontal and/or vertical translations of the graph of $f(x)$ may not understand the effects of the values of h and k on the graph of $g(x) = a(x - h)^n + k$.

Constructed Response: Item 11
- Students who performed the synthetic substitution correctly and determined that -6 is a zero of $f(x)$ do not understand how to interpret the results of synthetic substitution. They may not understand that -6 would be a zero only if $f(-6)$, the last number in the bottom row, were zero.

- Students who determined that -6 is a zero of $f(x)$ may have mistakenly tested to see whether 6 is a zero of $f(x)$. Evaluating $f(x)$ for $x = 6$ results in 0.

- Students who performed the synthetic substitution incorrectly may not have understood the process of synthetic substitution, such as subtracting numbers in the second row from numbers in the top row instead of adding.

CHAPTER 3 COMMON CORE ASSESSMENT READINESS

Name _____ Class _____ Date _____

MULTIPLE CHOICE

1. Which theorem states that if $f(x)$ is a polynomial of degree n, then $f(x)$ has at least one zero in the set of complex numbers?

A. Rational Zero Theorem

B. Factor Theorem

C. Remainder Theorem

D. Fundamental Theorem of Algebra

2. Which is a factored form of $x^4 - 16$?

F. $(x^2 - 2)(x^2 + 2)$

G. $(x^2 + 4)(x^2 - 2)(x^2 + 2)$

H. $(x^2 + 4)(x - 2)(x + 2)$

J. $(x^2 + 4)(x - 4)(x + 4)$

3. Christopher is drawing the graph of $f(x) = -x^5 + 2x^4 + x^3 + 3x^2 - 8x + 1$. How should he show the end behavior of the function?

A. $f(x) \to +\infty$ as $x \to +\infty$ and $f(x) \to -\infty$ as $x \to -\infty$

B. $f(x) \to -\infty$ as $x \to +\infty$ and $f(x) \to -\infty$ as $x \to -\infty$

C. $f(x) \to +\infty$ as $x \to +\infty$ and $f(x) \to +\infty$ as $x \to -\infty$

D. $f(x) \to -\infty$ as $x \to +\infty$ and $f(x) \to +\infty$ as $x \to -\infty$

4. Under which operation(s) is the set of polynomials closed?

F. addition only

G. addition and multiplication only

H. addition, subtraction, and multiplication only

J. addition, subtraction, multiplication, and division

5. Which expression is the expansion of $(x + 1)^4$?

A. $x^4 + 4x^3 + 6x^2 + 4x + 1$

B. $x^4 + 4x^3 + 6x^2 + 4x + 4$

C. $4x^4 + 4x^3 + 6x^2 + 4x + 1$

D. $4x^4 + 4x^3 + 6x^2 + 4x + 4$

6. If $x - a$ is a factor of a polynomial $p(x)$, which statement *must* be true?

F. $x + a$ is a factor of $p(x)$.

G. $p(a) = 1$

H. If $p(x)$ is divided by $x - a$, the remainder is 0.

J. If $p(x)$ is divided by $x - a$, the remainder is a.

7. Which factorization can you use to find the zeros of $f(x) = x^2 + 9$?

A. $(x + 3)(x - 3)$ C. $(x + 3)(x + 3)$

B. $(x + 3i)(x - 3i)$ D. $(x + 3i)(x + 3i)$

8. Which could be the rule for the function $f(x)$ whose graph is below?

F. $f(x) = 2x^3 - 2x^2 - 16x + 24$

G. $f(x) = 2x^3 + 2x^2 - 16x - 24$

H. $f(x) = 2x^3 + 16x^2 + 42x + 36$

J. $f(x) = 2x^3 - 16x^2 + 42x - 36$

CONSTRUCTED RESPONSE

9. Graph $g(x) = -2(x - 1)^3 - 4$. Describe the transformations of the graph of the parent function $f(x) = x^3$ that produce this graph.

The graph of $f(x)$ is stretched vertically

by a factor of 2, reflected across the

x-axis, and translated 1 unit right

and 4 units down.

10. Given the functions $p(x) = 3x^3 - 4x^2 + 7$ and $q(x) = 4x + 10 + 4x^2$, find $p(x) + q(x)$ and $p(x) - q(x)$.

$p(x) + q(x) = 3x^3 + 4x + 17$;

$p(x) - q(x) = 3x^3 - 8x^2 - 4x - 3$

11. Is -6 a zero of $f(x) = x^3 - 5x^2 - 8x + 12$? Show how you can use synthetic substitution to determine the answer.

No; use synthetic substitution to

evaluate $f(x)$ for $x = -6$:

The remainder is not 0, so -6 is not

a zero.

For Items 12–15, use the figure and the information below.

You make a box by cutting out a square from each corner of a rectangular sheet of cardboard and folding up the flaps as shown below.

12. Write a function $V(x)$ to represent the volume of the box. Explain how you wrote $V(x)$.

$V(x) = 4x^3 - 30x^2 + 56x$; multiply

expressions that represent length

$(8 - 2x)$, width $(7 - 2x)$, and

height (x).

13. What is the domain of $V(x)$? Justify your answer.

$0 < x < 3.5$; each dimension must be

positive, so find the intersection of

$8 - 2x > 0$, $7 - 2x > 0$, and $x > 0$.

14. Write and solve an equation to find the two values of x that result in a box with a volume of 15 in.³ Use your calculator to help you solve the equation.

$4x^3 - 30x^2 + 56x - 15 = 0$;

$x \approx 0.32$ in. and $x \approx 2.5$ in.

15. What maximum volume can a box made from a 7-by-8 sheet of cardboard have? What size square must you cut from each corner?

About 30.9 in.³; a square with a side

length of about 1.24 in.

Exponential and Logarithmic Functions

Exponential and Logarithmic Functions

Chapter Focus

A logarithmic function is the inverse of an exponential function. In an exponential function, the exponent is the input, so in a logarithmic function, the exponent is the output. You will learn how to graph logarithmic functions by hand and by using a graphing calculator. You will explore and verify properties of logarithms and use those properties to solve logarithmic equations. Along the way, you will learn about the irrational number e and see applications of exponential functions, including compound interest and population growth. You will also revisit exponential equations and learn a new way to solve them. Throughout this chapter, you will see applications of logarithms, which include the decibel scale, compound interest, and half-lives of radioactive substances.

Chapter at a Glance

COMMON CORE

Lesson		Standards for Mathematical Content
4-1	Exponential Functions, Growth and Decay	CC.9-12.F.IF.7e, CC.9-12.F.LE.3
4-2	Inverses of Relations and Functions	CC.9-12.F.IF.7a, CC.9-12.F.BF.4, CC.9-12.F.BF.4a
4-3	Logarithmic Functions	CC.9-12.F.IF.7e, CC.9-12.F.BF.5(+)
4-4	Properties of Logarithms	CC.9-12.F.IF.2, CC.9-12.F.BF.5(+)
4-5	Exponential and Logarithmic Equations and Inequalities	CC.9-12.A.SSE.3c, CC.9-12.A.REI.11, CC.9-12.F.BF.5(+), CC.9-12.F.LE.4
4-6	The Natural Base, e	CC.9-12.F.IF.2, CC.9-12.F.IF.7e, CC.9-12.F.BF.3
4-7	Transforming Exponential and Logarithmic Functions	CC.9-12.F.BF.3
4-8	Curve Fitting with Exponential and Logarithmic Models	CC.9-12.A.CED.2, CC.9-12.A.CED.4, CC.9-12.F.IF.2, CC.9-12.F.IF.4, CC.9-12.F.BF.1, CC.9-12.F.BF.1a
	Performance Tasks	
	Assessment Readiness	

COMMON CORE PROFESSIONAL DEVELOPMENT CC.9-12.F.BF.5(+)

In Advanced Algebra, students will expand their knowledge of linear and quadratic functions to include exponential and logarithmic cases. Students will understand the relationship between exponential and logarithmic functions based on their prior knowledge of inverse functions.

Unpacking the Standards

Understanding the standards and the vocabulary terms in the standards will help you know exactly what you are expected to learn in this chapter.

COMMON CORE CC.9-12.F.BF.5(+)
Understand the inverse relationship between exponents and logarithms and use this relationship to solve problems involving logarithms and exponents.

Key Vocabulary
inverse function (*función inversa*) The function that results from exchanging the input and output values of a one-to-one function. The inverse of $f(x)$ is denoted $f^{-1}(x)$.
logarithm (*logaritmo*) The exponent that a specified base must be raised to in order to get a certain value.

What It Means For You *Lessons 4-2, 4-3, 4-4*

Logarithmic functions and exponential functions are inverse functions. The input of an exponential function is an exponent and the output is a power. The input of a logarithmic function is a power, and the output is an exponent.

EXAMPLE
When working with logarithms, remember that *a logarithm is an exponent*. In both equations below, b is the base, and the logarithm x is the exponent.

Exponential Equation   Logarithmic Equation

$$b^x = a \qquad \log_b a = x$$

$$b > 0, b \neq 1$$

Read: b to the x equals a.
Think: When I raise b to the xth power, I get a.

Read: log base b of a equals x.
Think: x is the exponent on the base b that gives me a.

COMMON CORE CC.9-12.F.IF.7e
Graph exponential and logarithmic functions, showing intercepts and end behavior, ...

Key Vocabulary
exponential function (*función exponencial*) A function of the form $f(x) = ab^x$, where a and b are real numbers with $a \neq 0$, $b > 0$, and $b \neq 1$.
logarithmic function (*función logarítmica*) A function of the form $f(x) = \log_b x$, where $b \neq 1$ and $b > 0$, which is the inverse of the exponential function $f(x) = b^x$.

What It Means For You *Lessons 4-1, 4-3, 4-6*

Exponential functions represent growth or decay. Because exponential and logarithmic functions are inverse functions, the graph of an exponential function and its inverse logarithmic function are reflections in the line $y = x$.

EXAMPLE
For the function $f(x) = 3^x$, the input 2 gives the output 9. So, for the inverse function $f^{-1}(x) = \log_3 x$, the input 9 gives the output 2.
The y-intercept, 1, of $f(x) = 3^x$ is the x-intercept of $f^{-1}(x) = \log_3 x$.

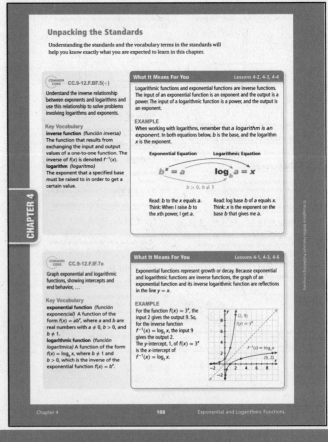

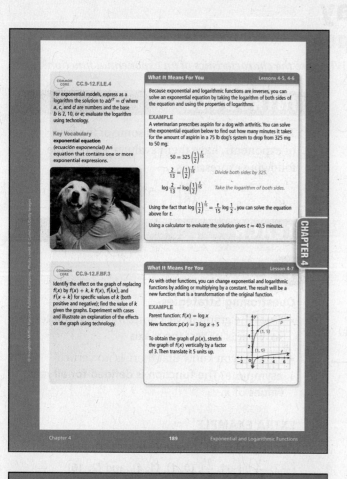

CC.9-12.F.LE.4

For exponential models, express as a logarithm the solution to $ab^{ct} = d$ where a, c, and d are numbers and the base b is 2, 10, or e; evaluate the logarithm using technology.

Key Vocabulary

exponential equation *(ecuación exponencial)* An equation that contains one or more exponential expressions.

What It Means For You
Lessons 4-5, 4-6

Because exponential and logarithmic functions are inverses, you can solve an exponential equation by taking the logarithm of both sides of the equation and using the properties of logarithms.

EXAMPLE

A veterinarian prescribes aspirin for a dog with arthritis. You can solve the exponential equation below to find out how many minutes it takes for the amount of aspirin in a 75 lb dog's system to drop from 325 mg to 50 mg.

$$50 = 325 \left(\frac{1}{2}\right)^{\frac{t}{15}}$$

$$\frac{2}{13} = \left(\frac{1}{2}\right)^{\frac{t}{15}} \qquad \text{Divide both sides by 325.}$$

$$\log \frac{2}{13} = \log \left(\frac{1}{2}\right)^{\frac{t}{15}} \qquad \text{Take the logarithm of both sides.}$$

Using the fact that $\log \left(\frac{1}{2}\right)^{\frac{t}{15}} = \frac{t}{15} \log \frac{1}{2}$, you can solve the equation above for t.

Using a calculator to evaluate the solution gives $t \approx 40.5$ minutes.

CC.9-12.F.BF.3

Identify the effect on the graph of replacing $f(x)$ by $f(x) + k$, $k\, f(x)$, $f(kx)$, and $f(x + k)$ for specific values of k (both positive and negative); find the value of k given the graphs. Experiment with cases and illustrate an explanation of the effects on the graph using technology.

What It Means For You
Lesson 4-7

As with other functions, you can change exponential and logarithmic functions by adding or multiplying by a constant. The result will be a new function that is a transformation of the original function.

EXAMPLE

Parent function: $f(x) = \log x$

New function: $p(x) = 3 \log x + 5$

To obtain the graph of $p(x)$, stretch the graph of $f(x)$ vertically by a factor of 3. Then translate it 5 units up.

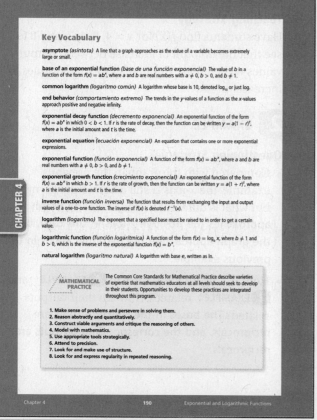

Key Vocabulary

asymptote *(asíntota)* A line that a graph approaches as the value of a variable becomes extremely large or small.

base of an exponential function *(base de una función exponencial)* The value of b in a function of the form $f(x) = ab^x$, where a and b are real numbers with $a \neq 0$, $b > 0$, and $b \neq 1$.

common logarithm *(logaritmo común)* A logarithm whose base is 10, denoted $\log_{10}$ or just log.

end behavior *(comportamiento extremo)* The trends in the y-values of a function as the x-values approach positive and negative infinity.

exponential decay function *(decremento exponencial)* An exponential function of the form $f(x) = ab^x$ in which $0 < b < 1$. If r is the rate of decay, then the function can be written $y = a(1 - r)^t$, where a is the initial amount and t is the time.

exponential equation *(ecuación exponencial)* An equation that contains one or more exponential expressions.

exponential function *(función exponencial)* A function of the form $f(x) = ab^x$, where a and b are real numbers with $a \neq 0$, $b > 0$, and $b \neq 1$.

exponential growth function *(crecimiento exponencial)* An exponential function of the form $f(x) = ab^x$ in which $b > 1$. If r is the rate of growth, then the function can be written $y = a(1 + r)^t$, where a is the initial amount and t is the time.

inverse function *(función inversa)* The function that results from exchanging the input and output values of a one-to-one function. The inverse of $f(x)$ is denoted $f^{-1}(x)$.

logarithm *(logaritmo)* The exponent that a specified base must be raised to in order to get a certain value.

logarithmic function *(función logarítmica)* A function of the form $f(x) = \log_b x$, where $b \neq 1$ and $b > 0$, which is the inverse of the exponential function $f(x) = b^x$.

natural logarithm *(logaritmo natural)* A logarithm with base e, written as ln.

MATHEMATICAL PRACTICE

The Common Core Standards for Mathematical Practice describe varieties of expertise that mathematics educators at all levels should seek to develop in their students. Opportunities to develop these practices are integrated throughout this program.

1. Make sense of problems and persevere in solving them.
2. Reason abstractly and quantitatively.
3. Construct viable arguments and critique the reasoning of others.
4. Model with mathematics.
5. Use appropriate tools strategically.
6. Attend to precision.
7. Look for and make use of structure.
8. Look for and express regularity in repeated reasoning.

COMMON CORE PROFESSIONAL DEVELOPMENT   CC.9-12.F.LE.4*

In previous courses, students have used inverse operations to solve linear equations. In previous Advanced Algebra lessons, students have learned the inverse relationship between exponents and logarithms. Using these concepts, students will solve an exponential equation by taking the logarithm of both sides of the equation.

Exponential Functions, Growth and Decay
Going Deeper

Essential question: What are the characteristics of an exponential function?

COMMON CORE Standards for Mathematical Content

CC.9-12.F.IF.2 Use function notation, evaluate functions for inputs in their domains, ...

CC.9-12.F.IF.7 Graph functions expressed symbolically and show key features of the graph, by hand in simple cases ...*

CC.9-12.F.IF.7e Graph exponential ... functions, showing intercepts and end behavior, ...*

CC.9-12.F.LE.3 Observe using graphs and tables that a quantity increasing exponentially eventually exceeds a quantity increasing linearly, quadratically, or (more generally) as a polynomial function.*

Vocabulary

exponential function

exponential growth function

exponential decay function

Prerequisites

Evaluating integer exponents

Properties of exponents

Math Background

An exponential function is not just a function with an exponent but a function whose independent variable is in the exponent. Therefore, $f(x) = 2^x$ is an exponential function, but $g(x) = x^2$ is not. Students should enter this lesson comfortable with evaluating powers with zero and negative exponents.

Students will graph most of the exponential functions in this lesson by hand. They will see that the graphs of exponential growth functions approach the negative x-axis as x decreases without bound while the graphs of exponential decay functions approach the positive x-axis as x increases without bound, so the x-axis is an asymptote for the graph of any function of the form $f(x) = b^x$ where $b > 0$ and $b \neq 1$. In subsequent lessons, students will transform the graphs of exponential functions and discover how the transformations affect the asymptote, y-intercept, and rate of increase or decrease.

INTRODUCE

To help remind students of some of the laws of exponents, have them evaluate each of the following expressions.

$$4^0 \quad 1 \quad \left(\frac{1}{8}\right)^{-3} \quad 512 \quad 10^{-2} \quad \frac{1}{100}$$

TEACH

1 EXAMPLE

Questioning Strategies

- Does the graph have a horizontal asymptote? If so, what is it? **Yes; the x-axis**

- How do you know that there is no vertical asymptote? **The function is defined for all real values of x.**

EXTRA EXAMPLE

Graph $f(x) = 4^x$. The curve passes through $\left(-2, \frac{1}{16}\right)$, $\left(-1, \frac{1}{4}\right)$, (0, 1), (1, 4), and (2, 16).

Teaching Strategy

Have students find $f(x)$ for $x = 4, 5, 6, 7,$ and 8 to see that the *amount* of increase between output values will increase dramatically as x continues to increase.

2 EXAMPLE

Questioning Strategies

- Compared with the graph in the previous example, the x-axis is still a horizontal asymptote, but what is different in this case? **The graph approaches the positive x-axis in this case, but the graph approached the negative x-axis in the previous example.**

- How are the function rules in **1 EXAMPLE** and **2 EXAMPLE** related? How are their outputs related? **The bases in the function rules are reciprocals, and the corresponding outputs are reciprocals.**

continued

Name_____ Class_____ Date_____

Exponential Functions, Growth and Decay
Going Deeper

4-1

Video Tutor

Essential question: *What are the characteristics of an exponential function?*

In an **exponential function**, the variable is an exponent. The parent function is $f(x) = b^x$, where b is any real number greater than 0, except 1.

CC.9-12.F.IF.7e

1 EXAMPLE Graphing $f(x) = b^x$ for $b > 1$

Graph $f(x) = 2^x$.

A Complete the table of values below.

B Plot the points on the graph and connect the points with a smooth curve.

x	$f(x) = 2^x$
−3	$2^{-3} = \frac{1}{2^3} = \frac{1}{8}$
−2	$\frac{1}{4}$
−1	$\frac{1}{2}$
0	1
1	2
2	4
3	8

REFLECT

1a. What happens to $f(x)$ as x increases without bound? What happens to $f(x)$ as x decreases without bound?

As x increases without bound, $f(x)$ increases without bound; as x decreases without bound, $f(x)$ approaches 0.

1b. Does the graph intersect the x-axis? Explain how you know.

No; $f(x)$ gets increasingly close to 0 as x decreases without bound, but it never equals 0. Since $f(x)$ is always positive, the x-axis is an asymptote.

1c. What are the domain and range of $f(x)$?

Domain: all real numbers; range: all positive real numbers.

© Houghton Mifflin Harcourt Publishing Company

Chapter 4   191   Lesson 1

CC.9-12.F.IF.7e

2 EXAMPLE Graphing $f(x) = b^x$ for $0 < b < 1$

Graph $f(x) = \left(\frac{1}{2}\right)^x$.

A Complete the table of values below.

B Plot the points on the graph and connect the points with a smooth curve.

x	$f(x) = \left(\frac{1}{2}\right)^x$
−3	$\left(\frac{1}{2}\right)^{-3} = (2)^3 = 8$
−2	4
−1	2
0	1
1	$\frac{1}{2}$
2	$\frac{1}{4}$
3	$\frac{1}{8}$

REFLECT

2a. What happens to $f(x)$ as x increases without bound? What happens to $f(x)$ as x decreases without bound?

As x increases without bound, $f(x)$ approaches 0; as x decreases without bound, $f(x)$ increases without bound.

2b. How do the domain and range of $f(x) = \left(\frac{1}{2}\right)^x$ compare to the domain and range of $f(x) = 2^x$?

Both functions have a domain of all real numbers and a range of all positive real numbers.

2c. What do you notice about the y-intercepts of the graphs of $f(x) = \left(\frac{1}{2}\right)^x$ and $f(x) = 2^x$? Why does this make sense?

The y-intercept of both graphs is 1. This makes sense since $b^0 = 1$ for any nonzero value of b.

2d. What transformation can you use to obtain the graph of $f(x) = \left(\frac{1}{2}\right)^x$ from the graph of $f(x) = 2^x$?

Reflection across the y-axis

© Houghton Mifflin Harcourt Publishing Company

Chapter 4   192   Lesson 1

EXTRA EXAMPLE

Graph $f(x) = \left(\frac{1}{4}\right)^x$. The curve passes through

$(-2, 16)$, $(-1, 4)$, $(0, 1)$, $\left(1, \frac{1}{4}\right)$, and $\left(2, \frac{1}{16}\right)$.

Differentiated Instruction

Have students copy the graph of $f(x) = \left(\frac{1}{2}\right)^x$ on the same grid used for the graph of $f(x) = 2^x$ so they can confirm that the y-axis acts as a line of reflection for transforming one graph to the other.

MATHEMATICAL PRACTICE   **Highlighting the Standards**

1 EXAMPLE   and **2** EXAMPLE   include opportunities to address Mathematical Practice Standard 8 (Look for and express regularity in repeated reasoning). Show students how they can continue the patterns in the output columns. As x increases in **2** EXAMPLE , the numbers in the denominators of the unit fractions double. So, without even evaluating the function, you can determine that $f(x)$ equals $\frac{1}{16}$, $\frac{1}{32}$, and $\frac{1}{64}$ when x equals 4, 5, and 6, respectively.

---

3   **ENGAGE**

Questioning Strategies

- How can you determine whether an exponential function models growth or decay just by looking at its graph? Exponential growth functions increase from left to right, and exponential decay functions decrease from left to right.

- Can you automatically conclude that an exponential function models decay if the base of the power is a fraction or decimal? Explain. No, some fractions and decimals have a value greater than one, such as 2.5 and $\frac{7}{2}$, and these bases produce exponential growth functions.

- For any acceptable value of b in an exponential function $f(x) = b^x$, what is the value of $f(x)$ if $x = -1$? $\frac{1}{b}$

Differentiated Instruction

For kinesthetic learners, draw a coordinate plane on the board so that the origin is about shoulder height of a given student. Have the student stand in front of the plane so his or her body aligns with the y-axis and then arrange his or her arms to roughly model the graph of an exponential function for different values of b. Choose values for both growth and decay, such as 0.5, 3, and 8.

4   **EXPLORE**

Questioning Strategies

- Do all three functions have the same end behavior as x decreases without bound? No, as x decreases without bound, $f(x)$ and $g(x)$ decrease without bound, but $h(x)$ approaches 0.

- Do all three functions have the same end behavior as x increases without bound? Yes, all three functions increase without bound as x increases without bound.

- As x increases without bound, how do you think the output values for a polynomial function with a greater exponent, such as $f(x) = x^5$, would compare to those of an exponential function whose base matches the exponent? For the same x-values, the output values for the exponential function would eventually exceed those of the polynomial function.

Technology

The table in part A may lead students to think that $h(x) \geq g(x)$ for all x. You might have students enter the two functions on their graphing calculators and examine a table of values starting at $x = 2.4$ with an increment of 0.1. They will see that $h(x) < g(x)$ for $x = 2.5, 2.6, 2.7, 2.8,$ and 2.9. (From the table in part A, students already know that $h(x) = g(x)$ when $x = 3$. The function values are also equal when $x \approx 2.48$. So, for x from about 2.48 to 3, $h(x) < g(x)$.)

3 ENGAGE CC.9-12.F.IF.7e   Recognizing Types of Exponential Functions

A function of the form $f(x) = b^x$ is an **exponential growth function** if $b > 1$ and an **exponential decay function** if $0 < b < 1$.

Exponential Growth $f(x) = b^x$ for $b > 1$	Exponential Decay $f(x) = b^x$ for $0 < b < 1$

REFLECT

3a. Describe the end behavior of an exponential growth function.

$f(x)$ approaches 0 as x decreases without bound and $f(x)$ increases without bound as x increases without bound.

3b. Describe the end behavior of an exponential decay function.

$f(x)$ increases without bound as x decreases without bound and $f(x)$ approaches 0 as x increases without bound.

3c. Explain why the point $(1, b)$ is always on the graph of $f(x) = b^x$.

Any number raised to the first power equals that number.

3d. Explain why the point $(0, 1)$ is always on the graph of $f(x) = b^x$.

Any number (except 0) raised to the 0 power equals 1.

3e. Are $f(x) = 3^x$ and $g(x) = 5^x$ both exponential growth functions or both exponential decay functions? Although they have the same end behavior, how you do think their graphs differ? Explain your reasoning.

Both are exponential growth functions. The graph of $g(x)$ rises more quickly than the graph of $f(x)$ as x increases without bound, and the graph of $g(x)$ falls more quickly than the graph of $f(x)$ as x decreases without bound.

3f. Are $f(x) = \left(\frac{1}{3}\right)^x$ and $g(x) = \left(\frac{1}{5}\right)^x$ both exponential growth functions or both exponential decay functions? Although they have the same end behavior, how do you think their graphs differ? Explain your reasoning.

Both are exponential decay functions. The graph of $g(x)$ falls more quickly than the graph of $f(x)$ as x increases without bound, and the graph of $g(x)$ rises more quickly than the graph of $f(x)$ as x decreases without bound.

Chapter 4   193   Lesson 1

---

4 EXPLORE CC.9-12.F.LE.3   Comparing Linear, Cubic, and Exponential Functions

Compare each of the functions $f(x) = x + 3$ and $g(x) = x^3$ to the exponential function $h(x) = 3^x$ for $x \geq 0$.

A   Complete the table of values for the three functions.

x	$f(x) = x + 3$	$g(x) = x^3$	$h(x) = 3^x$
0	3	0	1
1	4	1	3
2	5	8	9
3	6	27	27
4	7	64	81
5	8	125	243

B   The graph of $h(x) = 3^x$ is shown on the coordinate grid below. Graph $f(x) = x + 3$ on the same grid.

C   The graph of $h(x) = 3^x$ is shown on the coordinate grid below. Graph $g(x) = x^3$ on the same grid.

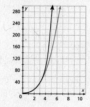

REFLECT

4a. How do the values of $h(x)$ compare to those of $f(x)$ and $g(x)$ as x increases without bound?

For the same x-value, the value of $h(x)$ may start out less than the values of $f(x)$ and $g(x)$, but the value of $h(x)$ eventually becomes greater than the values of $f(x)$ and $g(x)$ as x increases without bound.

Chapter 4   194   Lesson 1

Essential Question

What are the characteristics of an exponential function?

The graph is a curve that rises from left to right at an increasing rate when the base is greater than 1. The curve falls from left to right when the base is between 0 and 1. The domain is all real numbers, but the range is restricted to positive numbers because a power with a positive base cannot yield a negative number. This gives the graph a horizontal asymptote at the *x*-axis.

Summarize

Have students make a graphic organizer to compare and contrast exponential growth functions and exponential decay functions. One possibility is shown below.

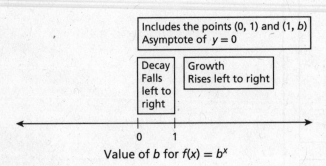

Value of *b* for $f(x) = b^x$

Where skills are taught	Where skills are practiced
1 EXAMPLE	EX. 6
2 EXAMPLE	EX. 7
3 ENGAGE	EXS. 1–4, 13
4 EXPLORE	EX. 8

Exercise 5: Students consider the restriction that *b* cannot be 1 in the definition of an exponential function.

Exercise 9: Students use their graphing calculators to compare another pair of exponential growth and decay functions whose bases are reciprocals.

Exercise 10: Students use the fact that every graph in the form $f(x) = b^x$ passes through $(1, b)$ to determine the rule for a given graph.

Exercises 11 and 12: Students use the properties of exponents to explain, generally, how *y* will change under certain circumstances.

Exercise 14: Students compare linear growth with exponential growth.

PRACTICE

Tell whether the function describes an exponential growth function or an exponential decay function. Explain how you know without graphing.

1. $f(x) = 0.9^x$

Exponential decay; $b = 0.9$ and 0.9 is between 0 and 1.

2. $g(x) = 4.5^x$

Exponential growth; $b = 4.5$ and 4.5 is greater than 1.

3. $h(x) = \left(\frac{5}{2}\right)^x$

Exponential growth; $b = 2.5$ and 2.5 is greater than 1.

4. $k(x) = \left(\frac{3}{4}\right)^x$

Exponential decay; $b = 0.75$ and 0.75 is between 0 and 1.

5. In an exponential function, $f(x) = b^x$, b is not allowed to be 1. Explain why this restriction exists.

If $b = 1$, the function is not exponential; in this case, it is the constant function $f(x) = 1$ because 1 raised to any power equals 1.

6. Complete the table for $f(x) = 4^x$. Then sketch the graph of the function.

x	f(x)
−1	0.25
0	1
1	4
2	16
3	64

7. Complete the table for $f(x) = \left(\frac{1}{3}\right)^x$. Then sketch the graph of the function.

x	f(x)
−3	27
−2	9
−1	3
0	1
1	$\frac{1}{3}$

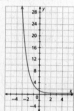

8. Compare the graph of $f(x) = 2^x$ to the graph of $g(x) = x^2$.

The graph of $g(x)$ has a line of symmetry, while the graph of $f(x)$ does not. As x increases without bound, the graph of $f(x)$ rises more quickly than the graph of $g(x)$. As x decreases without bound, the graph of $f(x)$ approaches 0 while the graph of $g(x)$ increases without bound.

9. Enter the functions $f(x) = 10^x$ and $g(x) = \left(\frac{1}{10}\right)^x$ into your graphing calculator.

a. Look at a table of values for the two functions. For a given x-value, how do the corresponding function values compare?

They are reciprocals of each other.

b. Look at graphs of the two functions. How are the two graphs related to each other?

The graphs are reflections of each other across the y-axis.

10. The graph of an exponential function $f(x) = b^x$ is shown.

a. Which of the labeled points, (0, 1) or (1, 5), allows you to determine the value of b? Why doesn't the other point help?

(1, 5); (0, 1) doesn't help because the graphs of all functions of the form $f(x) = b^x$ pass through (0, 1)

b. What is the value of b? Explain how you know.

$b = 5$ because $f(1) = b^1 = b = 5$

11. Given an exponential function $y = b^x$, when you double the value of x, how does the value of y change? Explain.

The value of y is squared because $b^{2x} = (b^x)^2 = y^2$.

12. Given an exponential function $y = b^x$, when you add 2 to the value of x, how does the value of y change? Explain.

The value of y is multiplied by b^2 because $b^{x+2} = b^x \cdot b^2 = b^2 \cdot y$.

13. Error Analysis A student says that the function $f(x) = \left(\frac{1}{0.5}\right)^x$ is an exponential decay function. Explain the student's error.

$f(x) = b^x$ is an exponential decay function when $0 < b < 1$, but in this case $b = 2$.

14. One method of cutting a long piece of string into smaller pieces is to make individual cuts, so that 1 cut results in 2 pieces, 2 cuts result in 3 pieces, and so on. Another method of cutting the string is to fold it onto itself and cut the folded end, then fold the pieces onto themselves and cut their folded ends at the same time, and continue to fold and cut, so that 1 cut results in 2 pieces, 2 cuts result in 4 pieces, and so on. For each method, write a function that gives the number p of pieces in terms of the number c of cuts. Which function grows faster? Why?

Method 1: $p = c + 1$; method 2: $p = 2^c$; $p = 2^c$ because exponential growth beats linear growth

Assign these pages to help your students practice
and apply important lesson concepts. For
additional exercises, see the Student Edition.

Answers

Additional Practice

1. Growth

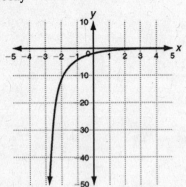

2. Decay

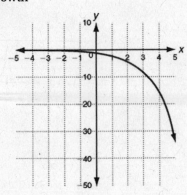

3. Decay

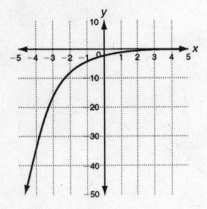

4. Growth

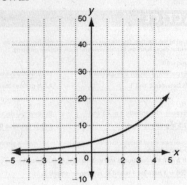

5. a.

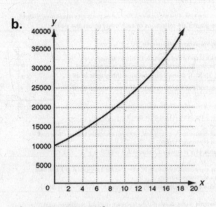

b. 2010

Problem Solving

1. $m(t) = 10{,}200(1 + 0.029)^t$

2. 8; 12; 16; 20
11,436; 12,821; 14,374; 16,116; 18,068

3. He drove more miles; about 5,900 miles more.

4. a. $n(t) = 10{,}200(1 + 0.078)^t$

b.

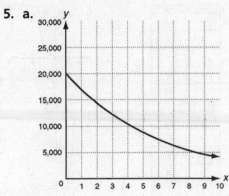

About 34,000 miles

c. He drove fewer miles than the average light
truck driver by about 12,000 miles.

5. D   **6.** G

Additional Practice

Tell whether the function shows growth or decay. Then graph.

1. $g(x) = -(2)^x$

2. $h(x) = -0.5(0.2)^x$

3. $j(x) = -2(0.5)^x$

4. $p(x) = 4(1.4)^x$

Solve.

5. A certain car's value depreciates about 15% each year. This is modeled by the function

$V(t) = 20,000(0.85)^t$

where $20,000 is the value of a brand-new model.

a. Graph the function.

b. Suppose the car was worth $20,000 in 2005. What is the first year that the value of this car will be worth less than half of that value?

Problem Solving

Justin drove his pickup truck about 22,000 miles in 2004. He read that in 1988 the average residential vehicle traveled about 10,200 miles, which increased by about 2.9% per year through 2004.

1. Write a function for the average mileage, $m(t)$, as a function of t, the time in years since 1988.

2. Assume that the 2.9% increase is valid through 2008 and use your function to complete the table to show the average annual miles driven.

Year	1988	1992	1996	2000	2004	2008
t	0	4				
m (t)	10,200					

3. Did Justin drive more or fewer miles than the average residential vehicle driver in 2004? by how much (to the nearest 100 miles)?

4. Later Justin read that the annual mileage for light trucks increased by 7.8% per year from 1988 to 2004.

a. Write a function for the average miles driven for a light truck, $n(t)$, as a function of t, the time in years since 1988. He assumes that the average number of miles driven in 1988 was 10,200.

b. Graph the function. Then use your graph to estimate the average number of miles driven (to the nearest 1000) for a light truck in 2004.

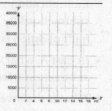

c. Did Justin drive more or fewer miles than the average light truck driver in 2004? by how much?

Justin bought his truck new for $32,000. Its value decreases 9.0% each year. Choose the letter for the best answer.

5. Which function represents the yearly value of Justin's truck?

A $f(t) = 32,000(1 + 0.9)^t$

B $f(t) = 32,000(1 - 0.9)^t$

C $f(t) = 32,000(1 + 0.09)^t$

D $f(t) = 32,000(1 - 0.09)^t$

6. When will the value of Justin's truck fall below half of what he paid for it?

F In 6 years

G In 8 years

H In 10 years

J In 12 years

Inverses of Relations and Functions
Going Deeper

Essential question: *How do you find the inverse of a function, and how is the original function related to its inverse?*

COMMON CORE Standards for Mathematical Content

CC.9-12.A.CED.2 Create equations in two ... variables to represent relationships between quantities; graph equations on coordinate axes with labels and scales.*

CC.9-12.F.IF.2 Use function notation, evaluate functions for inputs in their domains, and interpret statements that use function notation in terms of a context.

CC.9-12.F.IF.7 Graph functions expressed symbolically and show key features of the graph ...*

CC.9-12.F.IF.7a Graph linear ... functions ...*

CC.9-12.F.BF.4 Find inverse functions.

CC.9-12.F.BF.4a Solve an equation of the form $f(x) = c$ for a simple function f that has an inverse and write an expression for the inverse.

Also: CC.9-12.A.CED.4*, CC.9-12.F.IF.7d(+)

Vocabulary
inverse functions

Prerequisites
Functions
Graphing linear functions
Graphing rational functions

Math Background
A relation is a mapping of the elements of one set of numbers to the elements of another set, which produces a set of ordered pairs. A relation is a function if, for every input, there is exactly one output. The graph of a relation is a function if it passes the *vertical line test*, that is, if every possible vertical line drawn through the graph intersects it in at most one point.

A function takes an input, applies a rule, and gives an output. The inverse of that function will use that output as its input and apply a rule to give the input of the original function as its output.

INTRODUCE

Tell students you have a secret number. If you multiply by 2, add 3, and divide by 7, in that order, the number becomes 5. Have students find your secret number and explain how they found it. **The number is 16. Perform inverse operations on 5 in the reverse order.**

TEACH

1 ENGAGE

Questioning Strategies
- What are some points on the graph of $f(x) = 2$? **Sample answers: (−3, 2), (0, 2), (4, 2)**
- Is $f(x) = 2$ a function? Is its inverse a function? Explain. **Yes, each input has only one output. No, the input of 2 has infinitely many outputs.**
- What must be true about a function if its inverse is not a function? **The function must pair at least two inputs with the same output.**

Avoid Common Errors
Students often read $f^{-1}(x)$ as raising a function to the −1 power. Stress that −1 is not an exponent even though it is written as a superscript.

2 EXPLORE

Questioning Strategies
- In part A, how do you know that the multiplication is performed before the subtraction? **By the order of operations, multiplication is performed before subtraction.**
- In part A, what would be the rule if the subtraction were performed first? $f(x) = 3(x − 2)$
- What is the inverse function of $f(x) = 3(x − 2)$? $f^{-1}(x) = \frac{x}{3} + 2$

Name_____ Class_____ Date_____

4-2

Inverses of Relations and Functions
Going Deeper

Essential question: *How do you find the inverse of a function, and how is the original function related to its inverse?*

CC.9-12.F.BF.4

1 ENGAGE   Understanding the Inverse of a Function

The mapping diagram on the left shows a function. If you reverse the arrows in the mapping diagram as shown on the right, the original outputs become the inputs, and the original inputs become the outputs.

Inputs   Outputs   Outputs   Inputs

1 → 2   1 → 2
3 → 4   3 → 4
5 → 6   5 → 6

If you reverse the arrows in a mapping diagram of a function and the new mapping diagram also represents a function, this new function is said to be the *inverse* of the original function. Functions that undo each other are called **inverse functions**.

The notation $f^{-1}(x)$ indicates the inverse of a function $f(x)$. The domain of $f^{-1}(x)$ is the range of $f(x)$, and the range of $f^{-1}(x)$ is the domain of $f(x)$.

REFLECT

1a. How do you know that each mapping diagram shows a function?

Each input has exactly one output.

1b. The domain of a function $f(x)$ is the set {10, 20, 30}. What does this information tell you about $f^{-1}(x)$?

The range of $f^{-1}(x)$ is {10, 20, 30}.

1c. If the graph of a function $f(x)$ includes the point (3, 0), what point must the graph of $f^{-1}(x)$ include? Explain.

(0, 3); If $f(3) = 0$, then $f^{-1}(0) = 3$, and the graph of $f^{-1}(x)$ must include (0, 3).

CC.9-12.F.BF.4

2 EXPLORE   Finding $f^{-1}(x)$ by Using Inverse Operations

Find the inverse function $f^{-1}(x)$ for the function $f(x) = 3x - 2$.

A Describe the sequence of operations performed on an input value x by the function $f(x)$.

• First, multiply by ___3___.
• Second, _subtract 2_.

B Describe the inverse of each operation listed in step A, but in reverse order.

• First, add ___2___.
• Second, _divide_ by 3.

C Write a function rule for $f^{-1}(x)$ that matches the steps you described in step B.

$x + 2$ First, add 2 to the variable.

$\dfrac{x + 2}{3}$ Second, _divide_ the sum by 3.

$f^{-1}(x) = \dfrac{x + 2}{3}$ Write the rule for the inverse function.

D Complete the tables to verify that you found the rule for the inverse function correctly. Use the outputs from the first table as the inputs for the second table.

| Function $f(x) = 3x - 2$ | | Inverse Function | |
Input x	Output $f(x)$	Input x	Output $f^{-1}(x)$
0	−2	−2	0
2	4	4	2
4	10	10	4
6	16	16	6

REFLECT

2a. Explain how the tables show that you found the inverse of the function correctly.

The inputs in one table are the same as the outputs in the other table, and vice versa.

2b. Why do you reverse the order of the steps when writing the inverse operations in part B?

To undo the operations in the original function, you need to work backward. Start by undoing the last operation in the original function. Then undo the first operation.

2c. Could the rule for $f^{-1}(x)$ be written as $\frac{x}{3} + 2$? Explain why or why not.

No; to undo the operations in the original function, first add 2 and then divide by 3. This expression shows dividing by 3 first and then adding 2.

© Houghton Mifflin Harcourt Publishing Company

3 EXAMPLE

Questioning Strategies

- What are the two operations in $f(x)$ in the order they are performed?
  multiplication and subtraction
- What are the two operations in $f^{-1}(x)$ in the order they are performed?
  addition and division
- What is $f(0)$? **−2**
- What is $f^{-1}(-2)$? **0**

EXTRA EXAMPLE

Find the inverse function $f^{-1}(x)$ for the function $f(x) = \frac{x-4}{3}$. $f^{-1}(x) = 3x + 4$

Teaching Strategy

Show students that they can reverse the steps in finding the inverse function. They could first switch x and y and then solve for y.

Teaching Strategy

Encourage students to always test an inverse function using the fact that if $f(a) = b$, then $f^{-1}(b) = a$.

4 EXAMPLE

Questioning Strategies

- How do you know from their function rules that both $f(x)$ and $f^{-1}(x)$ are linear?
  Each has the form $y = mx + b$.
- What is the y-intercept of the graph of $f(x)$? **−2**
- What is the x-intercept of the graph of $f^{-1}(x)$? **−2**
- Why does the y-intercept of the graph of $f(x)$ equal the x-intercept of the graph of $f^{-1}(x)$?
  When you switch the coordinates of $(0, -2)$, you get $(-2, 0)$.

EXTRA EXAMPLE

Graph the function $f(x) = \frac{1}{2}x + 5$ and its inverse. **The graph of $f(x)$ passes through $(0, 5)$ and $(2, 6)$. The graph of $f^{-1}(x) = 2(x - 5) = 2x - 10$ passes through $(5, 0)$ and $(6, 2)$.**

Differentiated Instruction

Visual learners will benefit from folding their papers over the line $y = x$. They will easily be able to see that $f(x)$ and $f^{-1}(x)$ are reflections of each other over that line.

Teaching Strategy

Have students draw segments connecting $(-2, 0)$ to $(0, -2)$ and $(2, 4)$ to $(4, 2)$ to see that the line $y = x$ is the perpendicular bisector of those segments.

5 EXAMPLE

Questioning Strategies

- Given that the distance function is $d(t) = 100 - 50t$, what is $d(0)$? What does this value represent? **100; it represents the distance (in miles) left to travel when Mr. Williams has driven for 0 hours.**
- Given that the inverse function is $t(d) = 2 - \frac{d}{50}$, what is $t(0)$? What does this value represent?
  2; it represents the time (in hours) left to travel when Mr. Williams has driven 0 miles.

EXTRA EXAMPLE

The function $a(t) = 25 + 40t$ gives the amount a (in dollars) that a cleaning company charges as a function of the time t (in hours) spent cleaning. Write the inverse of this function and tell what the inverse represents. $t(a) = \frac{a - 25}{40}$; **it gives the time t (in hours) that the company will clean as a function of the amount a (in dollars) that a customer is willing to spend on cleaning.**

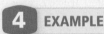

MATHEMATICAL PRACTICE — **Highlighting the Standards**

5 EXAMPLE includes opportunities to address Mathematical Practice Standard 4 (Model with mathematics). After finding an inverse function, students must be able to interpret it in the context of the situation. Discuss how the units are switched in the domain and range because the input and the output of the function are reversed. Draw a simple mapping diagram for the situation. Label the left side *hours* and the right side *miles*. Include a few values in each set, such as 0 in the *hours* set and 100 in the *miles* set. Ask students to draw arrows in the proper direction for the function $d(t)$. Then, on a copy of the mapping diagram, have them draw arrows in the proper direction for the function $t(d)$.

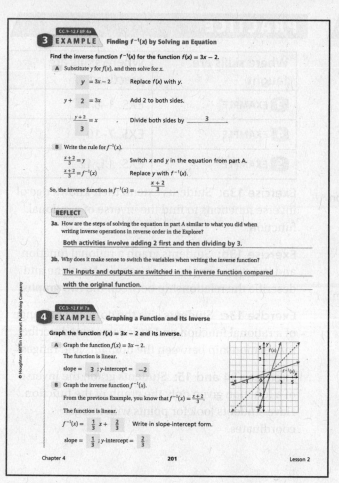

3 EXAMPLE Finding $f^{-1}(x)$ by Solving an Equation

CC.9-12.F.BF.4a

Find the inverse function $f^{-1}(x)$ for the function $f(x) = 3x - 2$.

A Substitute y for $f(x)$, and then solve for x.

$y = 3x - 2$ Replace $f(x)$ with y.

$y + \boxed{2} = 3x$ Add 2 to both sides.

$\dfrac{y+2}{3} = x$ Divide both sides by $\underline{\quad 3 \quad}$

B Write the rule for $f^{-1}(x)$.

$\dfrac{x+2}{3} = y$ Switch x and y in the equation from part A.

$\dfrac{x+2}{3} = f^{-1}(x)$ Replace y with $f^{-1}(x)$.

So, the inverse function is $f^{-1}(x) = \underline{\dfrac{x+2}{3}}$

REFLECT

3a. How are the steps of solving the equation in part A similar to what you did when writing inverse operations in reverse order in the Explore?

Both activities involve adding 2 first and then dividing by 3.

3b. Why does it make sense to switch the variables when writing the inverse function?

The inputs and outputs are switched in the inverse function compared with the original function.

4 EXAMPLE Graphing a Function and Its Inverse

CC.9-12.F.IF.7a

Graph the function $f(x) = 3x - 2$ and its inverse.

A Graph the function $f(x) = 3x - 2$.

The function is linear.

slope = $\boxed{3}$; y-intercept = $\boxed{-2}$

B Graph the inverse function $f^{-1}(x)$.

From the previous Example, you know that $f^{-1}(x) = \dfrac{x+2}{3}$.

The function is linear.

$f^{-1}(x) = \boxed{\dfrac{1}{3}} x + \boxed{\dfrac{2}{3}}$ Write in slope-intercept form.

slope = $\boxed{\dfrac{1}{3}}$; y-intercept = $\boxed{\dfrac{2}{3}}$

© Houghton Mifflin Harcourt Publishing Company

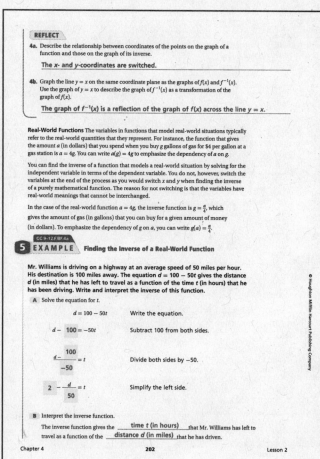

REFLECT

4a. Describe the relationship between coordinates of the points on the graph of a function and those on the graph of its inverse.

The x- and y-coordinates are switched.

4b. Graph the line $y = x$ on the same coordinate plane as the graphs of $f(x)$ and $f^{-1}(x)$. Use the graph of $y = x$ to describe the graph of $f^{-1}(x)$ as a transformation of the graph of $f(x)$.

The graph of $f^{-1}(x)$ is a reflection of the graph of $f(x)$ across the line $y = x$.

Real-World Functions The variables in functions that model real-world situations typically refer to the real-world quantities that they represent. For instance, the function that gives the amount a (in dollars) that you spend when you buy g gallons of gas for $4 per gallon at a gas station is $a = 4g$. You can write $a(g) = 4g$ to emphasize the dependency of a on g.

You can find the inverse of a function that models a real-world situation by solving for the independent variable in terms of the dependent variable. You do not, however, switch the variables at the end of the process as you would switch x and y when finding the inverse of a purely mathematical function. The reason for not switching is that the variables have real-world meanings that cannot be interchanged.

In the case of the real-world function $a = 4g$, the inverse function is $g = \dfrac{a}{4}$, which gives the amount of gas (in gallons) that you can buy for a given amount of money (in dollars). To emphasize the dependency of g on a, you can write $g(a) = \dfrac{a}{4}$.

5 EXAMPLE Finding the Inverse of a Real-World Function

CC.9-12.F.BF.4a

Mr. Williams is driving on a highway at an average speed of 50 miles per hour. His destination is 100 miles away. The equation $d = 100 - 50t$ gives the distance d (in miles) that he has left to travel as a function of the time t (in hours) that he has been driving. Write and interpret the inverse of this function.

A Solve the equation for t.

$d = 100 - 50t$ Write the equation.

$d - \boxed{100} = -50t$ Subtract 100 from both sides.

$\dfrac{d - \boxed{100}}{-50} = t$ Divide both sides by -50.

$\boxed{2} - \dfrac{d}{50} = t$ Simplify the left side.

B Interpret the inverse function.

The inverse function gives the $\underline{\text{time } t \text{ (in hours)}}$ that Mr. Williams has left to travel as a function of the $\underline{\text{distance } d \text{ (in miles)}}$ that he has driven.

© Houghton Mifflin Harcourt Publishing Company

Essential Question

How do you find the inverse of a function, and how is the original function related to its inverse?

To find the inverse of a function, replace $f(x)$ with y, solve for x, and then switch x and y. The output of a function is the input of the inverse function. The output of the inverse function is the input of the function. Because the coordinates of the ordered pairs are reversed, the graphs of the function and the inverse function are reflections across the line $y = x$.

Summarize

Have students write a journal entry that explains how they can draw the graph of an inverse function if they are given only the graph of the original function.

Where skills are taught	Where skills are practiced
3 EXAMPLE	EXS. 1–6
4 EXAMPLE	EXS. 7–10
5 EXAMPLE	EXS. 11, 12

Exercise 13a: Students extend their knowledge of inverse functions to find the inverse of a rational function.

Exercise 13b: Students graph a rational function and its inverse on the same coordinate plane and describe the relationship between the two graphs.

Exercise 13c: Students give the domain and range of a rational function and its inverse and describe the relationship between the domains and ranges.

Exercises 14 and 15: Students graph the inverse of a function given only the graph of the function. Have students look for points with integer coordinates.

REFLECT

5a. Use the inverse function to find the time that Mr. Williams has left to travel when he has driven 75 miles.

$t = 2 - \frac{75}{50} = 2 - 1.5 = 0.5$ hour

PRACTICE

Find the inverse function $f^{-1}(x)$ for each function $f(x)$.

1. $f(x) = x - 3$

$f^{-1}(x) = \underline{\quad x + 3 \quad}$

2. $f(x) = \frac{x}{3}$

$f^{-1}(x) = \underline{\quad 3x \quad}$

3. $f(x) = \frac{x+1}{6}$

$f^{-1}(x) = \underline{\quad 6x - 1 \quad}$

4. $f(x) = -0.25x$

$f^{-1}(x) = \underline{\quad -4x \quad}$

5. $f(x) = \frac{1}{2}x + 3$

$f^{-1}(x) = \underline{\quad 2(x - 3) \quad}$

6. $f(x) = 9 - 3x$

$f^{-1}(x) = \underline{\quad -\frac{1}{3}x + 3 \quad}$

Graph each function and its inverse.

7. $f(x) = x + 2$

$f^{-1}(x) = \underline{\quad x - 2 \quad}$

8. $f(x) = \frac{1}{4}x + \frac{1}{4}$

$f^{-1}(x) = \underline{\quad 4x - 1 \quad}$

9. $f(x) = -\frac{1}{3}x - \frac{2}{3}$

$f^{-1}(x) = \underline{\quad -3x - 2 \quad}$

10. $f(x) = -5x$

$f^{-1}(x) = \underline{\quad -\frac{1}{5}x \quad}$

11. The function $A(h) = \frac{1}{2}(20)h$ gives the area A (in square inches) of a triangle with a base of 20 inches and height h (in inches). Write and interpret the inverse of this function.

$h(A) = \frac{A}{10}$; the inverse function gives the height h (in inches) of a triangle having a

base of 20 inches and area A (in square inches).

12. The function $a(t) = 8t + 10$ gives the amount a (in dollars) that you pay when you rent a kayak for \$10 and use it for time t (in hours). Write and interpret the inverse of this function.

$t(a) = \frac{a - 10}{8}$; the inverse function gives the time t (in hours) that

you can rent a kayak for an amount a (in dollars).

13. Consider the rational function $f(x) = \frac{6}{x+2}$.

a. What is the inverse of the function? $f^{-1}(x) = \frac{6}{x} - 2$

b. Graph the function and its inverse on the same coordinate plane. Then graph the line $y = x$. Describe the relationship between the graphs of $f(x)$ and $f^{-1}(x)$.

The graphs are reflections of each other

across the line $y = x$.

c. Give the domain and range of $f(x)$ and the domain and range of $f^{-1}(x)$. What is the relationship between the domains and ranges?

$f(x)$: domain: $\{x \mid x \neq -2\}$, range: $\{y \mid y \neq 0\}$;

$f^{-1}(x)$: domain: $\{x \mid x \neq 0\}$, range: $\{y \mid y \neq -2\}$;

the domain of one function is the range of the other, and vice versa.

Graph the inverse of each function $f(x)$ whose graph is shown. Then write the rules for both $f(x)$ and $f^{-1}(x)$.

14.

$f(x) = 2x + 2$

$f^{-1}(x) = \frac{1}{2}x - 1$

15.

$f(x) = -\frac{1}{4}x - 3$

$f^{-1}(x) = -4x - 12$

© Houghton Mifflin Harcourt Publishing Company

Assign these pages to help your students practice and apply important lesson concepts. For additional exercises, see the Student Edition.

Answers

Additional Practice

1. $f^{-1}(x) = \dfrac{x + 10}{15}$

2. $f^{-1}(x) = -\dfrac{x - 10}{4}$

3. $f^{-1}(x) = -\dfrac{x - 12}{9}$

4. $f^{-1}(x) = \dfrac{x - 2}{5}$

5. $f^{-1}(x) = x - 6$

6. $f^{-1}(x) = x - \dfrac{1}{2}$

7. $f^{-1}(x) = -12x$

8. $f^{-1}(x) = 4x + 12$

9. $f^{-1}(x) = \dfrac{6x - 1}{3}$, or $f^{-1}(x) = 2x - \dfrac{1}{3}$

10. $f^{-1}(x) = \dfrac{1}{2}x + 2$

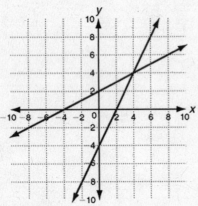

11. $f^{-1}(x) = \dfrac{2}{5}(x + 2)$

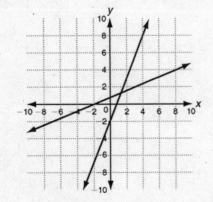

12. **a.** $c = \dfrac{d + 1.5}{0.15}$

   b. $c = 130$

   c. $112

Problem Solving

1. **a.** $p = 1.09(3n + 5)$

   b. $\dfrac{p - 5.45}{3.27} = n$

   c. $n = \dfrac{42.51}{3.27} = 13$

   d. The price has increased by $1.

2. **a.** $76.30

   b. $2.00

3. C   **4.** B

Additional Practice

Use inverse operations to write the inverse of each function.

1. $f(x) = 15x - 10$

2. $f(x) = 10 - 4x$

3. $f(x) = 12 - 9x$

_____

_____

_____

4. $f(x) = 5x + 2$

5. $f(x) = x + 6$

6. $f(x) = x + \dfrac{1}{2}$

_____

_____

_____

7. $f(x) = -\dfrac{x}{12}$

8. $f(x) = \dfrac{x - 12}{4}$

9. $f(x) = \dfrac{3x + 1}{6}$

_____

_____

_____

Graph each function. Then write and graph its inverse.

10. $f(x) = 2x - 4$

11. $f(x) = \dfrac{5}{2}x - 2$

_____

_____

Solve.

12. Dan works at a hardware store. The employee discount is determined by the formula $d = 0.15 (c - 10)$. Use the inverse of this function to find the cost of the item for which Dan received an $18.00 discount.

a. Find the inverse function that models cost as a function of the discount.   _____

b. Evaluate the inverse function for $d = 18$.   _____

c. What was Dan's final cost for this item?   _____

© Houghton Mifflin Harcourt Publishing Company

Problem Solving

Sally and Janelle pay a total of $47.96 to camp for three nights at a state park. This includes a one-time park entrance fee of $5 and 9% sales tax. They paid $12 per night to stay for three nights last year, and the one-time park entrance fee was $5.

1. By how much per night has the price changed since last year?

a. Write an equation for the total price, p, as a function of the price per night, n.   _____

b. Find the inverse function that models the price per night as a function of the total price.   _____

c. Evaluate the inverse function to find n, the price per night.   _____

d. By how much has the price per night changed since last year?   _____

2. Sally is thinking about whether they want to stay at the park next year. Assume that the entrance fee and the sales tax rate will not change.

a. If the price per night does not increase from this year's price, how much will it cost to stay for five nights next year?

_____

b. If the park management quotes them a price of $87.20 for five nights next year, what is the increase in the price per night?

_____

Choose the letter for the best answer.

3. If Sally and Janelle decide that they want to spend five nights at this same park in the future and spend no more than $100, what is the maximum price per night that they can pay?

A $16.00

B $16.50

C $17.00

D $17.50

4. If the price of a camping vacation can be expressed as a function of the number of nights, what does the inverse function represent?

F Number of nights as a function of the price per night

G Number of nights as a function of the price of the vacation

H Price of the vacation as a function of the price per night

J Price of the vacation as a function of the number of nights

© Houghton Mifflin Harcourt Publishing Company

Logarithmic Functions
Going Deeper

Essential question: *What are the characteristics of logarithmic functions?*

COMMON CORE **Standards for Mathematical Content**

CC.9-12.F.IF.2 Use function notation, evaluate functions for inputs in their domains, and interpret statements that use function notation in terms of a context.

CC.9-12.F.IF.7 Graph functions expressed symbolically and show key features of the graph ...*

CC.9-12.F.IF.7e Graph ... logarithmic functions, showing intercepts and end behavior, ...*

CC.9-12.F.BF.5(+) Understand the inverse relationship between exponents and logarithms and use this relationship to solve problems involving logarithms and exponents.

Vocabulary

logarithm

logarithmic function

Prerequisites

Basic exponential functions

Inverses of functions

Math Background

The inverse of an exponential function is a logarithmic function. In the exponential function $f(x) = 5^x$, you input 2 and get 25 as the output. In the corresponding logarithmic function, written $f(x) = \log_5 x$, you input 25 and get 2 as the output because $5^2 = 25$. That is, the logarithm is the exponent that the base must be raised to in order to obtain a given number.

The base of a logarithm can be any positive number other than 1, but two bases are used so frequently that they have special names. The common logarithm has a base of 10, and the natural logarithm has a base of e. The number e is defined as the limit of $\left(1 + \frac{1}{x}\right)^x$ as x approaches infinity. Students will investigate this limit in a later lesson.

INTRODUCE

Write these equations with empty boxes on the board. Have students determine the missing values.

$2^{\square} = 16$ **4** $7^{\square} = 49$ **2** $10^{\square} = 100{,}000$ **5**

$10^{\square} = 0.001$ **−3** $2^{\square} = \frac{1}{2}$ **−1** $e^{\square} = 1$ **0**

TEACH

1 EXPLORE

Questioning Strategies

- How do you know that $f(x) = 2^x$ is a one-to-one function? **Each y-value has only one x-value and the function's graph passes the horizontal line test.**

- How do you determine the ordered pairs for the graph of the inverse function? **Exchange the x- and y-coordinates.**

- How do you know that the graph of the inverse function has no horizontal asymptotes? **The graph of the exponential function has no vertical asymptotes.**

Differentiated Instruction

Have kinesthetic learners fold their paper over the line $y = x$ to check their graph of $f^{-1}(x)$.

2 ENGAGE

Questioning Strategies

- In the expression $\log_b y = x$, what does b represent? **b is the base in a power.**

- In the expression $\log_b y = x$, what does x represent? **x is the exponent in the power.**

- In the expression $\log_b y = x$, what does y represent? **y is the value of b^x.**

Teaching Strategy

When discussing Reflect Question 2c, input each x-coordinate from the table for $f^{-1}(x)$ in **1 EXPLORE** into $f^{-1}(x) = \log_2 x$. Show that if each input is written as a power ($2^{-2}, 2^{-1}, 2^0, 2^1,$ and 2^2), then the outputs are the exponents in those powers.

Name _____ Class _____ Date _____

Logarithmic Functions
Going Deeper

Essential question: *What are the characteristics of logarithmic functions?*

Recall that if $f(x)$ is a one-to-one function, then the graphs of $f(x)$ and its inverse, $f^{-1}(x)$, are reflections of each other about the line $y = x$. The domain of $f(x)$ is the range of $f^{-1}(x)$, and the range of $f(x)$ is the domain of $f^{-1}(x)$.

PREP FOR CC.9-12.F.IF.7e

1 EXPLORE   Graphing the Inverse of an Exponential Function

The graph of $f(x) = 2^x$ is shown. Graph $f^{-1}(x)$ by following these steps.

A Complete the table by writing the image of each point on the graph of $f(x)$ after a reflection across the line $y = x$.

Point on the graph of $f(x)$	Point on the graph's image
$(-2, 0.25)$ →	$(0.25, -2)$
$(-1, 0.5)$ →	$(0.5, -1)$
$(0, 1)$ →	$(1, 0)$
$(1, 2)$ →	$(2, 1)$
$(2, 4)$ →	$(4, 2)$

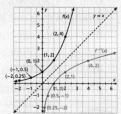

B Plot and label the image of each point on the coordinate plane.

C Use the images of the points to sketch the graph of $f^{-1}(x)$.

REFLECT

1a. What are the domain and range of $f^{-1}(x)$?

Domain: all real numbers greater than 0; Range: all real numbers

1b. Does the graph of $f^{-1}(x)$ have any asymptotes? Explain how you know.

The y-axis is a vertical asymptote; this is because the x-axis is a horizontal

asymptote for the graph of $f(x)$.

1c. How do the values of $f^{-1}(x)$ change as x increases without bound?

As x increases without bound, $f^{-1}(x)$ increases without bound.

CC.9-12.F.BF.5(+)

2 ENGAGE   Defining Logarithmic Functions

A *logarithm* is the exponent to which a base must be raised in order to obtain a given value. For example, $2^3 = 8$, so the logarithm base 2 of 8 is 3, and you write $\log_2 8 = 3$.

> **Definition of Logarithm**
>
> For positive numbers y and b ($b \neq 1$), the **logarithm** of y with base b is written $\log_b y$ and is defined as follows:
>
> $$\log_b y = x \text{ if and only if } b^x = y.$$

This definition means that every statement about exponents can be converted into an equivalent statement about logarithms, and vice versa. Note that you read $\log_b x$ as "the logarithm base b of x" or "log base b of x."

A **logarithmic function** with base b is the inverse of the exponential function with base b. For instance, the inverse of $f(x) = 2^x$ is $f^{-1}(x) = \log_2 x$, the graph of which you sketched in the Explore.

The table describes two special logarithms.

Special Logarithms		
Name	**Base**	**Notation**
Common logarithm	10	Write log x instead of $\log_{10} x$.
Natural logarithm	e	Write ln x instead of $\log_e x$.

> The number e is the value that the expression $\left(1 + \frac{1}{x}\right)^x$ approaches as x increases without bound. e is an irrational number, approximately 2.72.

REFLECT

2a. Explain, in terms of a logarithmic function, how to write $7^2 = 49$ as an equivalent statement involving a logarithm.

The base of the logarithmic function is 7; it accepts 49 as input and gives 2

as output, so $\log_7 49 = 2$.

2b. Explain, in terms of an exponential function, how to write log $1000 = 3$ as an equivalent statement involving an exponent.

The base of the exponential function is 10; it accepts 3 as input and gives

1000 as output, so $10^3 = 1000$.

2c. The input of $f(x) = 2^x$ is an exponent and the output is a power of 2. Describe the input and output of $f^{-1}(x) = \log_2 x$. Give a specific example.

The input is a power of 2 and the output is the corresponding exponent.

For example, when the input value is 32 (which is 2^5), the output value is 5.

2d. Find $\ln \frac{1}{e}$ by letting $\ln \frac{1}{e} = x$ and writing this statement in an equivalent form that involves an exponent. Explain your reasoning from that point on.

If $\ln \frac{1}{e} = x$, then $e^x = \frac{1}{e}$; since $\frac{1}{e} = e^{-1}$, $x = -1$.

Questioning Strategies

- Can you input a negative number for x in $f(x) = \log_2 x$? **No, there is no power of 2 that will result in a negative number.**

- What is the base in Reflect Question 3c? How do you know? **The base is 10. When the base is not shown, it is understood to be 10.**

EXTRA EXAMPLE

Find each value of $f(x) = \log_3 x$.

A. $f(9)$ **2**   **B.** $f\left(\frac{1}{81}\right)$ **−4**

C. $f(3)$ **1**   **D.** $f(27)$ **3**

E. $f\left(\frac{1}{243}\right)$ **−5**

MATHEMATICAL PRACTICE — **Highlighting the Standards**

The Reflect questions for **3** **EXAMPLE** address Mathematical Practice Standard 2 (Reason abstractly and quantitatively). Having students answer more questions like 3b and 3c will help them better understand logarithms.

For example, have students find the two integers that $f(40)$ lies between for $f(x) = \log_4 x$ and then explain why it lies between them. ($f(40)$ lies between 2 and 3 because $4^2 = 16$ and $4^3 = 64$.)

Also, have students estimate more outputs that are not whole numbers. For example, have them estimate $f(8,000)$ for $f(x) = \log x$ and explain their reasoning. ($f(8,000)$ is about 3.9 because 8,000 is between 1,000, or 10^3, and 10,000, or 10^4, but closer to 10^4.)

Teaching Strategies

Point out that the *base* is written as a subscript, so it is the lowest number in the equation, or the number closest to the *bottom*.

Until students get comfortable with the notation for common logarithms, they can write in the base of 10 to remind themselves that 10 is the base.

Differentiated Instruction

Oral learners will benefit from reading each function rule out loud. For example, in part B, they should say they are looking for *the logarithm, base 2, of x when x is 64*. Remind them that the logarithm is the exponent, so they are looking for the exponent when the base is 2 and the value is 64.

4 **EXAMPLE**

Questioning Strategies

- What are the intercepts? **The x-intercept is 1. There is no y-intercept.**

- Why is $(b, 1)$ on the graph of every function in the form $f(x) = \log_b x$? **Any number to the first power is equal to itself. Also, $(1, b)$ is on the graph of the inverse function $f(x) = b^x$.**

Teaching Strategy

Discuss how all the numbers in the x-column are powers of $\frac{1}{2}$. The domain is all real numbers, but these are the easiest to evaluate.

EXTRA EXAMPLE

Graph $f(x) = \log_5 x$. **The graph is a smooth curve that passes through (0.2, −1), (1, 0), (5, 1), and (25, 2).**

3 EXAMPLE   CC.9-12.F.BF.5(+)   Evaluating Logarithmic Functions

Find each value of $f(x) = \log_2 x$.

A $f(16)$

Write the function's input as a power of 2. The function's output is the exponent.

$16 = 2^{\underline{4}}$, so $f(16) = \underline{4}$

B $f(64)$

$64 = 2^{\underline{6}}$, so $f(64) = \underline{6}$

C $f\left(\frac{1}{32}\right)$

$\frac{1}{32} = 2^{\underline{-5}}$, so $f\left(\frac{1}{32}\right) = \underline{-5}$

D $f\left(\frac{1}{8}\right)$

$\frac{1}{8} = 2^{\underline{-3}}$, so $f\left(\frac{1}{8}\right) = \underline{-3}$

E $f(1)$

$1 = 2^{\underline{0}}$, so $f(1) = \underline{0}$

REFLECT

3a. Is it possible to evaluate $f(0)$? Why or why not?

No; it is not possible to write 0 as a power of 2.

3b. For $f(x) = \log_2 x$, between which two integers does $f(40)$ lie? Explain.

$f(40)$ must be between 5 and 6, since 40 is between 32 and 64;

that is, 40 is between 2^5 and 2^6, so $\log_2 40$ is between 5 and 6.

3c. Estimate $g(95)$ for $g(x) = \log x$, without using a calculator. Explain.

$g(95)$ is very close to 2, because 95 is between 10^1 and 10^2, but

much closer to 10^2.

3d. Without using a calculator, explain how you know that $\ln 20 > \log 20$.

$\ln 20$ has a base of e and $\log 20$ has a base of 10. Because $e < 10$, the power

of e that equals 20 must be greater than the power of 10 that equals 20.

4 EXAMPLE   CC.9-12.F.IF.7e   Graphing a Logarithmic Function

Graph $f(x) = \log_{\frac{1}{2}} x$.

A What is the range of $f(x)$? (Think: what powers can you raise $\frac{1}{2}$ to?) all real numbers
What is the domain of $f(x)$? (Think: what values can be obtained
by raising $\frac{1}{2}$ to a power?) $x > 0$

B Complete the table of values.

x	$f(x)$
$\frac{1}{4}$	2
$\frac{1}{2}$	1
1	0
2	−1
4	−2
8	−3

C Plot the points. Connect them with a smooth curve.

REFLECT

4a. How is the graph of $f(x) = \log_{\frac{1}{2}} x$ related to the graph of $f(x) = \log_2 x$ from the Explore?
Why does this make sense?

The graph of $f(x) = \log_{\frac{1}{2}} x$ is a reflection in the x-axis of the graph

of $f(x) = \log_2 x$. Because $\frac{1}{2} = 2^{-1}$, $\left(\frac{1}{2}\right)^m = 2^{-m}$ for any value of m; if

you let $x = \left(\frac{1}{2}\right)^m = 2^{-m}$, then $\log_{\frac{1}{2}} x = m$ and $\log_2 x = -m$, so the two

logarithmic functions have opposite values for any given value of x.

4b. What point do the graphs of $f(x) = \log_{\frac{1}{2}} x$ and $f(x) = \log_2 x$ have in common? Why?

$(1, 0)$ appears on both graphs because $\left(\frac{1}{2}\right)^0 = 1$ and $2^0 = 1$.

4c. Describe the end behavior of $f(x) = \log_{\frac{1}{2}} x$.

As x approaches 0, $f(x)$ increases without bound. As x increases

without bound, $f(x)$ decreases without bound.

4d. How is the graph of $f(x) = \log_{\frac{1}{2}} x$ related to the graph of $f(x) = \left(\frac{1}{2}\right)^x$?

The graph of $f(x) = \log_{\frac{1}{2}} x$ is a reflection of the graph of $f(x) = \left(\frac{1}{2}\right)^x$ in the

line $y = x$.

Essential Question

What are the characteristics of logarithmic functions?

A logarithmic function is an inverse of an exponential function, so the output is the exponent needed to raise the base to obtain a specific value. The graph is a reflection of its corresponding exponential function across the line $y = x$.

Summarize

Have students make a graphic organizer to compare and contrast exponential and logarithmic functions. One possibility is shown below.

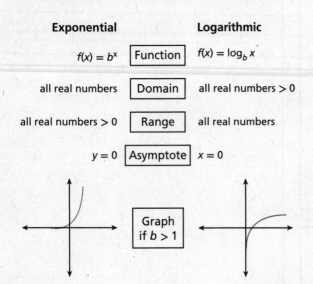

Exponential		Logarithmic
$f(x) = b^x$	Function	$f(x) = \log_b x$
all real numbers	Domain	all real numbers > 0
all real numbers > 0	Range	all real numbers
$y = 0$	Asymptote	$x = 0$
	Graph if $b > 1$	

Where skills are taught	Where skills are practiced
1 EXPLORE	EX. 1
3 EXAMPLE	EXS. 2–13
4 EXAMPLE	EXS. 17, 18, 20

Exercises 14 and 15: Students estimate the value of a common logarithm and a natural logarithm by determining the powers of 10 or e that are just below and just above the given input value.

Exercise 16: Students use the definition of a logarithm to determine that the log, base b, of b, must be 1.

Exercise 19: Given a graph of a logarithmic function, students determine its function rule.

Exercise 21: Given two points on the graph of $f(x) = \log_b x$, students determine the value of b.

Exercise 22: Given a real-world scenario for the exponential function $f(x) = 2^x$, students describe the input and output of the inverse logarithmic function in terms of the scenario, evaluate the function for a given input, and then determine an area function and its inverse for a section of paper folded x times.

PRACTICE

1. The graph of $f(x) = 3^x$ is shown.

    a. Use the labeled points to help you draw the graph of $f^{-1}(x)$. Label the corresponding points on $f^{-1}(x)$.

    b. Write the inverse function, $f^{-1}(x)$, using logarithmic notation.

      $f^{-1}(x) = \log_3 x$

    c. State the domain and range of $f^{-1}(x)$.

      D: positive real numbers; R: all real numbers

Find each value of $f(x) = \log_4 x$.

2. $f(16)$
   2

3. $f\left(\frac{1}{64}\right)$
   −3

4. $f(4)$
   1

Find each value of $f(x) = \log x$.

5. $f(10{,}000)$
   4

6. $f(0.1)$
   −1

7. $f\left(\frac{1}{100}\right)$
   −2

Find each value of $f(x) = \log_{\frac{1}{4}} x$.

8. $f(16)$
   −2

9. $f(1)$
   0

10. $f\left(\frac{1}{64}\right)$
   3

Evaluate each expression.

11. $\log_8 64$
   2

12. $\log_2 1024$
   10

13. $\log 1{,}000{,}000$
   6

14. For $f(x) = \log x$, between what two integers does $f(6)$ lie? Explain.

$f(6)$ must be between 0 and 1, since 6 is between 1 and 10; that is, 6 is between 10^0 and 10^1, so log 6 is between 0 and 1.

15. Explain how you can estimate the value of ln 10 without using a calculator.

e is a bit less than 3, so 10 is between e^2 and e^3. This means that ln 10 is between 2 and 3. It is closer to 2 because 10 is closer to e^2.

16. What is the value of $\log_b b$ for $b > 0$ and $b \neq 1$? Explain.

$\log_b b = 1$ because $b^1 = b$.

Graph each logarithmic function.

17. $f(x) = \log_4 x$

18. $f(x) = \log_{\frac{1}{3}} x$

19. The graph of what logarithmic function is shown? Explain your reasoning.

$f(x) = \log_{\frac{1}{10}} x$; the graph passes through $(10, -1)$, so $\log_b 10 = -1$ and $b = 10^{-1} = \frac{1}{10}$.

20. Name some values you would choose for x if you were plotting points to sketch the graph of $f(x) = \log x$ without using a calculator. Explain.

Sample answer: $\frac{1}{10}$, 1, and 10; these are powers of 10 with integer exponents $(10^{-1}, 10^0,$ and $10^1)$ giving the points $\left(\frac{1}{10}, -1\right)$, $(1, 0)$, and $(10, 1)$.

21. The graph of $f(x) = \log_b x$ passes through the points $(1, 0)$ and $(36, 2)$. What is the value of b? Explain.

6; $\log_b 36 = 2$, so $b^2 = 36$ and $b = 6$.

22. When you fold a sheet of paper in half x times, the function $f(x) = 2^x$ gives the number of sections that are created by the folds.

    a. Describe the input and output of the function $f^{-1}(x) = \log_2 x$ in the problem context.

      The input is the number of sections and the output is the number of folds needed to make that many sections.

    b. Use $f^{-1}(x)$ to find the number of folds needed to create 64 sections.

      $f^{-1}(64) = \log_2 64 = 6$, so 6 folds are needed.

    c. Assume that a sheet of paper has an area of 1. Write an exponential function $g(x)$ that gives the area of a section of the paper after being folded in half x times.

      $g(x) = \left(\frac{1}{2}\right)^x$

    d. Write the rule for $g^{-1}(x)$ and describe the function's input and output.

      $g^{-1}(x) = \log_{\frac{1}{2}} x$; the input is the area of a section and the output is the number of folds needed to make a section having that area.

Assign these pages to help your students practice and apply important lesson concepts. For additional exercises, see the Student Edition.

Answers

Additional Practice

1. $\log_3 2187 = 7$ **2.** $\log_{12} 144 = 2$

3. $\log_5 125 = 3$ **4.** $10^5 = 100,000$

5. $4^5 = 1024$ **6.** $9^3 = 729$

7. 6   **8.** 1

9. 0   **10.** 2

11. 0   **12.** 4

13. Domain: $\{x \mid x > 0\}$; range: all real numbers

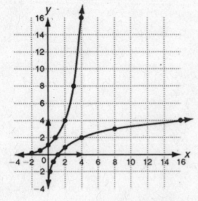

14. Domain: $\{x \mid x > 0\}$; range: all real numbers

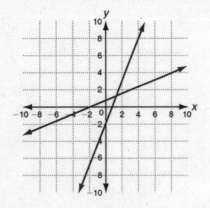

15. a. $\text{pH} = -\log(0.000316)$

b. 3.5

Problem Solving

1. a. $\text{pH} = -\log(0.0000629)$

b. $\text{pH} = 4.2$

2. a. $\text{pH} = -\log(0.0000032)$

b. $\text{pH} = 5.5$

c. Rainwater in eastern Ohio has a lower pH than that in central California by 1.3 units.

3. D   **4.** J

5. A   **6.** H

Additional Practice

Write each exponential equation in logarithmic form.

1. $3^7 = 2187$

2. $12^2 = 144$

3. $5^3 = 125$

_____   _____   _____

Write each logarithmic equation in exponential form.

4. $\log_{10} 100{,}000 = 5$

5. $\log_4 1024 = 5$

6. $\log_9 729 = 3$

_____   _____   _____

Evaluate by using mental math.

7. $\log 1{,}000{,}000$

8. $\log 10$

9. $\log 1$

_____   _____   _____

10. $\log_4 16$

11. $\log_8 1$

12. $\log_5 625$

_____   _____   _____

Use the given x-values to graph each function. Then graph its inverse. Describe the domain and range of the inverse function.

13. $f(x) = 2^x$; $x = -2, -1, 0, 1, 2, 3, 4$

14. $f(x) = \left(\dfrac{1}{2}\right)^x$; $x = -3, -2, -1, 0, 1, 2, 3$

Solve.

15. The hydrogen ion concentration in moles per liter for a certain brand of tomato-vegetable juice is 0.000316.

   a. Write a logarithmic equation for the pH of the juice. _____

   b. What is the pH of the juice? _____

Problem Solving

The acidity of rainwater varies from location to location. Acidity is measured in pH and is given by the function $pH = -\log[H^+]$, where $[H^+]$ represents the hydrogen ion concentration in moles per liter. The table gives the $[H^+]$ of rainwater in different locations.

1. Find the acidity of rainwater in eastern Ohio.

   a. Substitute the hydrogen ion concentration for rainwater in eastern Ohio in the function for pH.

   b. Evaluate the function. What is the acidity of rainwater in eastern Ohio to the nearest tenth of a unit?

Hydrogen Ion Concentration of Rainwater	
Location	$[H^+]$ (moles per liter)
Central California	0.0000032
Eastern Texas	0.0000192
Eastern Ohio	0.0000629

2. Find how the acidity of rainwater in central California compares to the acidity of rainwater in eastern Ohio.

   a. Write a function for the acidity of rainwater in central California. _____

   b. Evaluate the function. What is the acidity of rainwater in central California to the nearest tenth of a unit? _____

   c. Compare the pH of rainwater in the two locations. Is the pH of rainwater in eastern Ohio greater than or less than that in central California? By how much? _____

Choose the letter for the best answer.

3. What is the pH of rainwater in eastern Texas?

   A $pH = 3.7$ C $pH = 4.4$
   B $pH = 4.0$ D $pH = 4.7$

4. Nick makes his own vegetable juice. It has a hydrogen ion concentration of 5.9×10^{-6} moles per liter. What is the pH of his vegetable juice?

   F $pH = 4.9$ H $pH = 5.1$
   G $pH = 5.0$ J $pH = 5.2$

5. What is the pH of a sample of irrigation water with a hydrogen ion concentration of 8.3×10^{-7} moles per liter?

   A $pH = 6.1$ C $pH = 6.3$
   B $pH = 6.2$ D $pH = 6.4$

6. What is the pH of a shampoo sample with a hydrogen ion concentration of 1.7×10^{-8} moles per liter?

   F $pH = 7.4$ H $pH = 7.8$
   G $pH = 7.6$ J $pH = 8.0$

Properties of Logarithms
Going Deeper

Essential question: *How do you prove properties of logarithms?*

CC.9-12.F.IF.2 ... evaluate functions for inputs in their domains ...

CC.9-12.F.BF.5(+) Understand the inverse relationship between exponents and logarithms and use this relationship to solve problems involving logarithms and exponents.

Prerequisites

Properties of exponents

Logarithmic functions as inverses of exponential functions

Math Background

Because of the inverse relationship between logarithms and exponents, the properties of logarithms are similar to the properties of exponents. For example, to find a product of powers, such as $x^5(x^2)$, keep the base and add the exponents: x^{5+2}. To find the log of a product, such as $\log_b 5(2)$, add the log of each factor: $\log_b 5 + \log_b 2$.

INTRODUCE

Have students simplify these expressions to review properties of exponents. Students should state the names of the properties used. Then ask students to propose a similar property for logarithms.

$x^4 x^3$ x^7; **Product of Powers Property**

$\dfrac{x^6}{x^2}$ x^4; **Quotient of Powers Property**

$(x^5)^3$ x^{15}; **Power of a Power Property**

TEACH

1 EXPLORE

Materials
graphing calculator

Questioning Strategies
- What is the base for logarithms written log *x*? for logarithms written ln *x*? **The base for log *x* is 10. The base for ln *x* is e.**

- How do you enter *e* on a graphing calculator?

  Press [2nd] [÷]. (with *e* above the ÷ key)

2 ENGAGE

Questioning Strategies
- Which property of exponents is similar to the Product Property of Logarithms? Why? **Product of Powers Property; both use addition to rewrite an expression involving multiplication.**

- Which property of exponents is similar to the Quotient Property of Logarithms? Why? **Quotient of Powers Property; both use subtraction to rewrite an expression involving division.**

- How is the Power Property of Logarithms similar to the Power of a Power Property? In $(x^m)^n$, there are *n* factors of x^m. Because $n \log_b m$ represents multiplication, you can think of it as *n* factors of $\log_b m$.

Teaching Strategy
Give students examples of each property of logarithms using integers. Have students append these examples to the table given in ② ENGAGE. Examples could include the following:

$$\log_3 9(27) = \log_3 9 + \log_3 27 = 2 + 3 = 5$$

$$\log_3 \frac{27}{9} = \log_3 27 - \log_3 9 = 3 - 2 = 1$$

$$\log_3 27^4 = 4(\log_3 27) = 4(3) = 12$$

Avoid Common Errors
Students sometimes employ the Product Property of Logarithms when there is no product. Show them that a logarithm is not distributive.

$$\log_2 (8 + 32) \neq \log_2 8 + \log_2 32$$

Students also may be tempted to write a difference of logarithms as a quotient, an improper use of the Quotient Property of Logarithms. Demonstrate the following:

$$\log_2 32 - \log_2 8 \neq \frac{\log_2 32}{\log_2 8}.$$

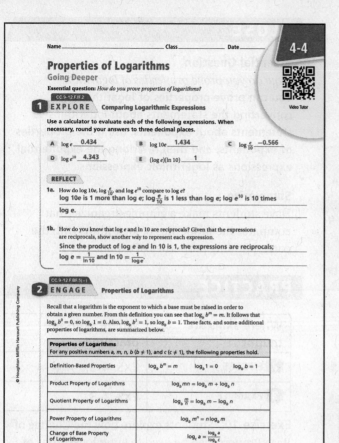

Name_____ Class_____ Date_____

4-4

Properties of Logarithms
Going Deeper

Essential question: *How do you prove properties of logarithms?*

CC.9-12.F.IF.2

1 EXPLORE Comparing Logarithmic Expressions

Use a calculator to evaluate each of the following expressions. When necessary, round your answers to three decimal places.

A $\log e$ __0.434__

B $\log 10e$ __1.434__

C $\log \frac{e}{10}$ __−0.566__

D $\log e^{10}$ __4.343__

E $(\log e)(\ln 10)$ __1__

REFLECT

1a. How do $\log 10e$, $\log \frac{e}{10}$, and $\log e^{10}$ compare to $\log e$?

__log 10e is 1 more than log e; log $\frac{e}{10}$ is 1 less than log e; log e^{10} is 10 times__

__log e.__

1b. How do you know that $\log e$ and $\ln 10$ are reciprocals? Given that the expressions are reciprocals, show another way to represent each expression.

__Since the product of log e and ln 10 is 1, the expressions are reciprocals;__

__log e = $\frac{1}{\ln 10}$ and ln 10 = $\frac{1}{\log e}$.__

CC.9-12.F.BF.5(+)

2 ENGAGE Properties of Logarithms

Recall that a logarithm is the exponent to which a base must be raised in order to obtain a given number. From this definition you can see that $\log_b b^m = m$. It follows that $\log_b b^0 = 0$, so $\log_b 1 = 0$. Also, $\log_b b^1 = 1$, so $\log_b b = 1$. These facts, and some additional properties of logarithms, are summarized below.

Properties of Logarithms	
For any positive numbers a, m, n, b ($b \neq 1$), and c ($c \neq 1$), the following properties hold.	
Definition-Based Properties	$\log_b b^m = m$ $\log_b 1 = 0$ $\log_b b = 1$
Product Property of Logarithms	$\log_b mn = \log_b m + \log_b n$
Quotient Property of Logarithms	$\log_b \frac{m}{n} = \log_b m - \log_b n$
Power Property of Logarithms	$\log_b m^n = n\log_b m$
Change of Base Property of Logarithms	$\log_c a = \frac{\log_b a}{\log_b c}$

© Houghton Mifflin Harcourt Publishing Company

REFLECT

2a. Use the definition of a logarithm to explain why $\log 10 = 1$ and $\ln e = 1$.

__By the definition of a logarithm, log 10 = $\log_{10} 10^1$ = 1 and ln e = $\log_e e^1$ = 1.__

2b. Use the Product Property of Logarithms to explain why $\log 10e$ is 1 more than $\log e$.

__By the Product Property of Logarithms, log 10e = log 10 + log e = 1 + log e.__

2c. Use the Quotient Property of Logarithms to explain why $\log \frac{e}{10}$ is 1 less than $\log e$.

__By the Quotient Property of Logarithms, log $\frac{e}{10}$ = log e − log 10 = log e − 1.__

2d. Use the Power Property of Logarithms to explain why $\log e^{10}$ is 10 times $\log e$.

__By the Power Property of Logarithms, log e^{10} = 10 log e.__

2e. Use the Change of Base Property to change the base of $\ln 10$ from e to 10. What does the result tell you about $\ln 10$?

__ln 10 = $\frac{\log 10}{\log e}$ = $\frac{1}{\log e}$; ln 10 is the reciprocal of log e.__

2f. What is the relationship between $\log e$ and $\log \frac{1}{e}$? Explain your reasoning.

__They are opposites; by the Quotient Property of Logarithms, log $\frac{1}{e}$ =__

__log 1 − log e = 0 − log e = −log e.__

CC.9-12.F.BF.5(+)

3 EXAMPLE Proving the Product Property of Logarithms

Prove the Product Property of Logarithms.

A Given positive numbers m, n, and b ($b \neq 1$), show that $\log_b mn = \log_b m + \log_b n$.

To prove this property, convert statements about logarithms to statements about exponents. Then use properties of exponents.

Let $\log_b m = p$ and let $\log_b n = q$.

By the definition of a logarithm, $m = b^p$ and __$n = b^q$__.

B $\log_b mn = \log_b \left(\boxed{b^p b^q} \right)$ Substitution

$= \log_b b^{\boxed{p+q}}$ Product of Powers Property of Exponents

$= \boxed{p+q}$ Definition of a logarithm

$= \log_b m + \log_b n$ Substitution

So, $\log_b mn = \log_b m + \log_b n$.

© Houghton Mifflin Harcourt Publishing Company

Questioning Strategies

Can you extend the Product Property of Logarithms to three factors? If so, give an example. Yes; *Sample answer:* $\log_2 64 = \log_2 (2)(4)(8) = \log_2 2 + \log_2 4 + \log_2 8 = 1 + 2 + 3 = 6$ and $2^6 = 64$.

EXTRA EXAMPLE

Prove that you can extend the Product Property of Logarithms to three factors, or that $\log_b kmn = \log_b k + \log_b m + \log_b n$. Let $\log_b k = p$, $\log_b m = q$, and $\log_b n = r$. By the definition of a logarithm, $k = b^p$, $m = b^q$, and $n = b^r$. By substitution, $\log_b kmn = \log_b (b^p b^q b^r)$. By the Product of Powers Property of Exponents, $\log_b (b^p b^q b^r) = \log_b b^{p+q+r}$, By the definition of a logarithm, $\log_b b^{p+q+r} = p + q + r$, which equals $\log_b k + \log_b m + \log_b n$ by substitution.

| MATHEMATICAL PRACTICE | Highlighting the Standards |

3 EXAMPLE and many of the practice exercises address Mathematical Practice Standard 3 (Construct viable arguments and critique the reasoning of others). Students write formal proofs for the properties, verify the properties by showing they work in certain cases, and confirm properties by graphing equivalent equations on a graphing calculator.

CLOSE

Essential Question

How do you prove properties of logarithms?
You can prove properties of logarithms by converting the statements about logarithms to statements about exponents, using the properties of exponents, and then rewriting the exponential expressions as logarithmic expressions.

Summarize

Have students make a graphic organizer that compares the properties of logarithms with the corresponding properties of exponents.

PRACTICE

Where skills are taught	Where skills are practiced
2 ENGAGE	EXS. 4–9
3 EXAMPLE	EXS. 1–3

Exercise 10: Students explore how the Change of Base Property can be used to enter logarithms of any base on a graphing calculator. Then, they use their results to evaluate $\log_2 5$.

Exercises 11 and 12: Students use their graphing calculators to confirm the Quotient and Power Properties of Logarithms. They graph functions with equivalent function rules and see that the graphs coincide.

Exercise 13: Students identify, explain, and correct an error commonly made when using the Power Property of Logarithms.

Exercise 14: Students use properties of logarithms to rewrite a formula involving the intensity of sound. Then, they use the rewritten formula to answer a question about the intensity of a sound with a given sound level.

REFLECT

3a. Suppose $m = n$ in $\log_b mn$. What result do you get when you apply the Product Property of Logarithms? This result is a particular case of what other property of logarithms? Explain.

When $m = n$, $\log_b mn = \log_b (m \cdot m) = \log_b m + \log_b m = 2\log_b m$; this result is a

particular case of the Power Property of Logarithms when $n = 2$: $\log_b m^2 = 2\log_b m$

PRACTICE

1. Prove the Quotient Property of Logarithms. Justify each step of your proof.

Let $\log_b m = p$ and $\log_b n = q$. Then $m = b^p$ and $n = b^q$. (Def. of a logarithm)

$\log_b \frac{m}{n} = \log_b \frac{b^p}{b^q}$	(Substitution)
$= \log_b b^{p-q}$	(Quotient of Powers Property of Exponents)
$= p - q$	(Definition of a logarithm)
$= \log_b m - \log_b n$	(Substitution)

2. Prove the Power Property of Logarithms. Justify each step of your proof.

Let $\log_b m = p$. Then $m = b^p$. (Definition of a logarithm)

$\log_b m^n = \log_b (b^p)^n$	(Substitution)
$= \log_b b^{pn}$	(Power of a Power Property of Exponents)
$= pn$	(Definition of a logarithm)
$= (\log_b m)(n)$	(Substitution)
$= n\log_b m$	(Commutative Property)

3. When n is a positive integer, show how you can prove the Power Property of Logarithms using the Product Property of Logarithms. (*Hint:* When n is a positive integer, $m^n = m \cdot m \cdot m \cdot \cdots \cdot m$ where m appears as a factor n times.)

When n is a positive integer, $\log_b m^n = \log_b (m \cdot m \cdot m \cdot \cdots \cdot m) = \log_b m + $

$\log_b m + \log_b m + \cdots + \log_b m = n \log_b m$.

Simplify each expression.

4. $\log_3 3^4$
_____4_____

5. $\log_7 7^5$
_____5_____

6. $\log_6 36^9$
_____18_____

7. $\log_{\frac{1}{10}} 10^3$
_____−3_____

8. $\log_2 14 - \log_2 7$
_____1_____

9. $\log 25 + \log 4$
_____2_____

© Houghton Mifflin Harcourt Publishing Company

---

10. Your calculator has keys for evaluating only common logarithms and natural logarithms. Explain why you don't need a generic logarithm key where you must specify the base. Then describe how you can evaluate $\log_2 5$ using either one of your calculator's logarithm keys. Finally, find the value of $\log_2 5$ to 3 decimal places using each key to demonstrate that you get the same result.

You can use the Change of Base Property to convert any base to base 10 or

base e; enter log 5 divided by log 2 or ln 5 divided by ln 2; the result is 2.322

in both cases.

11. On a graphing calculator, graph $y = \log \frac{10}{x}$ and $y = 1 - \log x$ in the same viewing window. What do you notice? Which property of logarithms explains what you see? Why?

The graphs coincide. The Quotient Property of Logarithms explains this because

$\log \frac{10}{x} = \log 10 - \log x = 1 - \log x$.

12. On a graphing calculator, graph $y = \log 10^x$ and $y = x \log 10$ in the same viewing window.

a. What do you notice? Which property of logarithms explains what you see? Why?

The graphs coincide. The Power Property of Logarithms explains this because

$\log 10^x = x \log 10$.

b. What linear function are both functions equivalent to? Explain.

$y = x$; $y = \log 10^x = x$ by definition of a logarithm, and $y = x \log 10 = x \cdot 1 = x$

by a definition-based property of logarithms ($\log_b b = 1$).

13. Error Analysis A student simplified $(\log_3 81)^2$ as shown at right. Explain and correct the student's error.

The property applies to expressions of the form

$\log_b m^n$, not to expressions of the form $(\log_b m)^n$.

The correct answer is $(\log_3 81)^2 = (4)^2 = 16$.

$(\log_3 81)^2$	
$= 2\log_3 81$	Power Property of Logs
$= 2\log_3 3^4$	Write 81 as a power of 3.
$= 2 \cdot 4$	Definition of logarithm
$= 8$	Multiply.

14. The formula $L = 10\log \frac{I}{I_0}$ gives the sound level L (in decibels) for a sound with intensity I (in watts per square meter). I_0 is the threshold of human hearing, 10^{-12} watts/m².

a. Rewrite the formula by using the Quotient Property of Logarithms, substituting 10^{-12} for I_0 and simplifying.

$L = 10(\log I - \log I_0) = 10(\log I - \log 10^{-12}) = 10(\log I + 12)$

b. Show how to use the formula from part (a) to find the intensity of a sound if its sound level L is 120 decibels.

Solve $120 = 10(\log I + 12)$. Dividing both sides by 10 gives $12 = \log I + 12$,

so $0 = \log I$ and $I = 1$. The intensity is 1 watt/m².

© Houghton Mifflin Harcourt Publishing Company

Assign these pages to help your students practice and apply important lesson concepts. For additional exercises, see the Student Edition.

Answers

Additional Practice

1. $\log_3 243 = 5$ **2.** $\log_2 128 = 7$

3. $\log_{10} 10,000 = 4$ **4.** $\log_6 216 = 3$

5. $\log_3 81 = 4$ **6.** $\log_4 4096 = 6$

7. $\log_2 8 = 3$ **8.** $\log_{10} 100 = 2$

9. $\log_4 64 = 3$ **10.** $\log_2 64 = 6$

11. $\log_3 243 = 5$ **12.** $\log_6 36 = 2$

13. 6   **14.** $x - 5$

15. 30   **16.** 1

17. 5   **18.** 8

19. 0   **20.** 3.10

21. 1.43

22. $1.26 \times 10^{18.1}$ ergs

Problem Solving

1. a. $7.8 = \frac{2}{3} \log \left(\frac{E}{10^{11.8}} \right)$

   b. $23.5 = \log E$

   c. Yes; by the definition of logarithm;
     $E = 10^{23.5}$

   d. They are both correct; $10^{23.5} = 3.16 \times 10^{23}$

2. A   **3.** G

4. C   **5.** F

Additional Practice

Express as a single logarithm. Simplify, if possible.

1. $\log_3 9 + \log_3 27$

2. $\log_2 8 + \log_2 16$

3. $\log_{10} 80 + \log_{10} 125$

4. $\log_6 8 + \log_6 27$

5. $\log_3 6 + \log_3 13.5$

6. $\log_4 32 + \log_4 128$

Express as a single logarithm. Simplify, if possible.

7. $\log_2 80 - \log_2 10$

8. $\log_{10} 4000 - \log_{10} 40$

9. $\log_4 384 - \log_4 6$

10. $\log_2 1920 - \log_2 30$

11. $\log_3 486 - \log_3 2$

12. $\log_6 180 - \log_6 5$

Simplify, if possible.

13. $\log_4 4^6$

14. $\log_5 5^{x-5}$

15. $7^{\log_7 30}$

16. $12^{\log_{12} 1}$

17. $\log_8 8^5$

18. $\log_3 9^4$

Evaluate. Round to the nearest hundredth.

19. $\log_{12} 1$

20. $\log_3 30$

21. $\log_5 10$

Solve.

22. The Richter magnitude of an earthquake, M, is related to the energy released in ergs, E, by the formula $M = \frac{2}{3}\log\left(\frac{E}{10^{11.8}}\right)$. Find the energy released by an earthquake of magnitude 4.2. _____

Problem Solving

Trina and Willow are researching information on earthquakes. One of the largest earthquakes in the United States, centered at San Francisco, occurred in 1906 and registered 7.8 on the Richter scale. The Richter magnitude of an earthquake, M, is related to the energy released in ergs, E, by the formula $M = \frac{2}{3}\log\left(\frac{E}{10^{11.8}}\right)$.

1. Find the amount of energy released by the earthquake in 1906.

   a. Substitute 7.8 for magnitude, M, in the equation. _____

   b. Solve for the value of $\log E$.

   c. Willow says that E is equal to 10 to the power of the value of $\log E$. Is she correct? What property or definition can be used to find the value of E? Explain.

   d. Trina says the energy of the 1906 earthquake was 3.16×10^{23} ergs. Willow says the energy was $10^{23.5}$ ergs. Who is correct? How do you know?

Choose the letter for the best answer.

2. An earthquake in 1811 in Missouri measured 8.1 on the Richter scale. About how many times as much energy was released by this earthquake as by the California earthquake of 1906?

   A 2.8

   B 3.0

   C 3.6

   D 5.7

3. Another large earthquake in California measured 7.9 on the Richter scale. Which statement is true?

   F 0.1 times as much energy was released by the larger earthquake.

   G The difference in energy released is 1.31×10^{23} ergs.

   H The energy released by the second earthquake was 3.26×10^{23} ergs.

   J The total energy released by the two earthquakes is equal to the energy released by an 8.0 earthquake.

4. Larry wrote the following: $\log 10^{0.0038} = 3.8 \times 10^{-3}$. Which property of logarithms did he use?

   A Product Property

   B Quotient Property

   C Inverse Property

   D Power Property

5. Vijay wants to change $\log_5 7$ to base 10. Which expression should he use?

   F $\dfrac{\log_{10} 7}{\log_{10} 5}$

   G $\dfrac{\log_{10} 5}{\log_{10} 7}$

   H $\dfrac{\log_{10} 7}{\log_5 5}$

   J $\dfrac{\log_7 5}{\log_{10} 7}$

Notes

Exponential and Logarithmic Equations and Inequalities
Going Deeper

Essential question: *What is the general process for solving exponential and logarithmic equations?*

CC.9-12.A.SSE.3c Use the properties of exponents to transform expressions for exponential functions.

CC.9-12.A.CED.1 Create equations ... in one variable and use them to solve problems. Include equations arising from ... exponential functions. *

CC.9-12.A.REI.11 Explain why the *x*-coordinates of the points where the graphs of the equations $y = f(x)$ and $y = g(x)$ intersect are the solutions of the equation $f(x) = g(x)$; find the solutions approximately, e.g., using technology to graph the functions, make tables of values, ... Include ... exponential, and logarithmic functions. *

CC.9-12.F.IF.7 Graph functions expressed symbolically ... using technology for more complicated cases.*

CC.9-12.F.IF.7e Graph exponential ... functions ... *

CC.9-12.F.BF.5(+) Understand the inverse relationship between exponents and logarithms and use this relationship to solve problems involving logarithms and exponents.

CC.9-12.F.LE.4 For exponential models, express as a logarithm the solution to $ab^{ct} = d$ where *a, c,* and *d* are numbers and the base is 2, 10, or *e*; evaluate the logarithm using technology.*

Prerequisites

Exponential growth and decay functions

Properties of exponents

Interest compounded continuously

Solving exponential equations

Properties of logarithms

Math Background

In the first half of this lesson, students will learn how to solve exponential equations algebraically and with a table or graph using their graphing calculators. The equations they solve algebraically are all in a form that can be solved by first rewriting the equation so that each side is a power with the same base and then setting the exponents equal to each other. This results in an equation that is not exponential (usually linear, sometimes quadratic) and that can usually be solved quite easily.

In the second half of this lesson, students will solve exponential equations by taking the logarithm of both sides. Students should notice the similarities between the Property of Equality for Logarithmic Equations and the Property of Equality for Exponential Equations.

Students will also solve some logarithmic equations graphically. They will use the Change of Base Property from the previous lesson to graph logarithmic equations with bases other than 10 or *e*.

INTRODUCE

Write $2^{2x} = 16$ on the board and ask what the value of $2x$ is and why. **4; because $2^4 = 16$** Ask for the value of *x.* **2** Ask students which of these could be solved the same way and why: $2^{2x} = 64$ or $2^{2x} = 50$. **$2^{2x} = 64$ because 64 is a power of 2 and 50 is not**

Ask students how they can solve $2^{x+3} = 64$ algebraically. **Write 64 as 2^6 and solve $x + 3 = 6$.**

Ask why they cannot use the same method to solve $2^{x+3} = 50$. **You cannot write 50 as an integer power of 2.**

Name_____ Class_____ Date_____

Exponential and Logarithmic Equations and Inequalities
Going Deeper

Essential question: *What is the general process for solving exponential and logarithmic equations?*

An exponential equation is an equation in which the variable appears only as an exponent. The following property is useful for solving some types of exponential equations.

Property of Equality for Exponential Equations

For any positive number b other than 1, if $b^x = b^y$, then $x = y$.

CC.9-12.A.SSE.3c

1 EXAMPLE   Solving Exponential Equations Algebraically

Solve each exponential equation.

A $2^{x-1} = 32$

$2^{x-1} = 2^{\boxed{5}}$ Write 32 as a power of 2.

$x - 1 = \boxed{5}$ Because the bases are equal, the exponents are equal.

$x = \boxed{6}$ Solve for x.

B $9^{2x} = 27^{x+1}$

$(3^2)^{2x} = \left(3^{\boxed{3}} \right)^{x+1}$ Write both bases as powers with a base of 3.

$3^{2 \cdot 2x} = 3^{\boxed{3(x+1)}}$ Power of a power property

$3^{4x} = 3^{\boxed{3x+3}}$ Simplify.

$4x = \boxed{3x+3}$ Because the bases are equal, the exponents are equal.

$x = \boxed{3}$ Solve for x.

REFLECT

1a. Show how you can check that the solutions of the equations are correct.

Part A: Substitute 6 for x in the original equation: $2^{6-1} = 2^5 = 32$. Part B:

Substitute 3 for x: $9^{2x} = 9^{2(3)} = 9^6 = 531,441$ and $27^{x+1} = 27^{3+1} = 27^4 = 531,441$

1b. In the property of equality for exponential equations, explain why b cannot be equal to 1.

If $b = 1$, the exponents are not necessarily equal ($1^5 = 1^6$, but $5 \neq 6$).

Chapter 4   221   Lesson 5

1c. How would you solve the equation in part A if 32 were replaced by 0.5?

Rewrite 0.5 as 2^{-1}. Equating the exponents gives $x - 1 = -1$ and so $x = 0$.

CC.9-12.A.REI.11

2 EXAMPLE   Solving an Exponential Equation with a Table

The equation $y = 4.1(1.33)^x$ models the population of the United States, in millions, from 1790 to 1890. In this equation, x is the number of decades since 1790, and y is the population in millions. In what year did the population reach 45 million?

A Write an equation and make a table of values to solve the equation.

When the population is 45 million, $y = \underline{\quad 45 \quad}$

To find the year when the population reached 45 million, solve the equation $45 = 4.1(1.33)^x$

Enter the expression $4.1(1.33)^x$ for Y_1 in your calculator's equation editor.

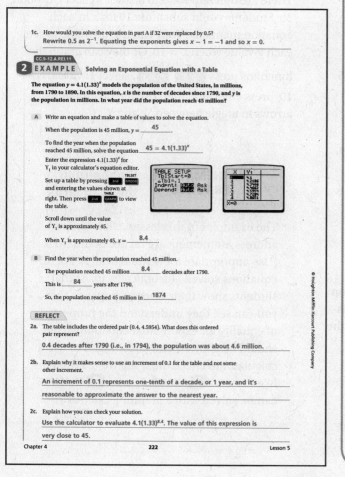

Set up a table by pressing [2nd] [WINDOW] and entering the values shown at right. Then press [2nd] [GRAPH] to view the table.

Scroll down until the value of Y_1 is approximately 45.

When Y_1 is approximately 45, $x = \underline{\quad 8.4 \quad}$

B Find the year when the population reached 45 million.

The population reached 45 million $\underline{\quad 8.4 \quad}$ decades after 1790.

This is $\underline{\quad 84 \quad}$ years after 1790.

So, the population reached 45 million in $\underline{\quad 1874 \quad}$

REFLECT

2a. The table includes the ordered pair (0.4, 4.5954). What does this ordered pair represent?

0.4 decades after 1790 (i.e., in 1794), the population was about 4.6 million.

2b. Explain why it makes sense to use an increment of 0.1 for the table and not some other increment.

An increment of 0.1 represents one-tenth of a decade, or 1 year, and it's

reasonable to approximate the answer to the nearest year.

2c. Explain how you can check your solution.

Use the calculator to evaluate $4.1(1.33)^{8.4}$. The value of this expression is

very close to 45.

Chapter 4   222   Lesson 5

TEACH

1 EXAMPLE

Questioning Strategies

- How could you state the property of equality for exponential equations simply in words? **If two powers are equal and their bases are the same, then the exponents are equal.**

- Why do you have to rewrite the base on one side in part A and rewrite the base on both sides in part B? **In part A, 32 is a power of 2. In part B, 27 is not a power of 9, but both 9 and 27 are powers of 3.**

Avoid Common Errors

In part B, stress that students should use parentheses when rewriting the right side of the equation. Otherwise, they may forget to use the distributive property and write the exponent on that side as $3x + 1$.

EXTRA EXAMPLE

Solve the exponential equation.

A. $4^{x+5} = 64$ $x = -2$ **B.** $125^{x-4} = 25^x$ $x = 12$

2 EXAMPLE

Questioning Strategies

- Why is it not possible to solve this equation as you solved the equation in Example 1? **You cannot write $(1.33)^x$ and the quotient of 45 and 4.1 as powers with a common base.**

- Why are increments of 0.1 used in setting up the table? **Each tenth represents one year, so the table displays in years, rather than decades, since 1790.**

- In the table, the y-value of 45 is between $x = 8.4$ and $x = 8.5$. Why choose 8.4? **The population reached 45 million *before* 1875 ($x = 8.5$), so it occurred *during* the year 1874 ($x = 8.4$).**

EXTRA EXAMPLE

The equation $y = 1.3(1.04)^x$ models the population of a city, in millions, from 1950 to 2010, where x is the number of years after 1950. In what year did the population reach 5 million? **1984**

Teaching Strategy

Instead of scrolling down a long list, students can first use increments of 1 for x to see that the number of decades is between 8 and 9. Then, they can go back to TBLSET and start the x-values at 8 and increase them by tenths to fine-tune the table by year.

3 EXAMPLE

Questioning Strategies

- Why is graphing and finding the point of intersection a better method than using the table as in Example 2? **It would be difficult to increment the x-values so that the two y-values would be equal. After graphing, the intersect feature will give a more accurate value for the intersection.**

- Why should you round the y-value of the point of intersection to the hundredths place? **The y-value represents dollars, with the hundredths place representing cents.**

EXTRA EXAMPLE

Sylvester invested $700 at 2.5% annual interest compounded continuously. Judy invested $650 at 3.8% annual interest compounded continuously. When will they have the same amount in their accounts? What will the amount be when this occurs? **after approximately 5.7 years; $807.22**

Teaching Strategy

There are different ways to answer Reflect Question 3b. Students could substitute 10 for x in each equation manually. They can use the table to see each y-value when $x = 10$. Or they can graph the functions press **2nd** **TRACE** (CALC), select **1: value,** type 10, press enter, and then use the up and down arrows to toggle between Y_1 and Y_2.

.·**MATHEMATICAL**   **Highlighting**
  PRACTICE   **the Standards**

The examples in this lesson allow you to address Mathematical Practice Standard 5 (Use appropriate tools strategically). For all equations solved algebraically, insist that students show their work on paper so that you can see they understand the property of equality for exponential equations. They should be allowed and encouraged to use a calculator to check those answers. Problems like those in **2 EXAMPLE** and **3 EXAMPLE** can be solved with a graphing calculator.

2d. How could you solve the equation by using your calculator to graph $y = 4.1(1.33)^x$?

Graph $y = 45$ and find the x-coordinate of the point where this line intersects

the graph of $y = 4.1(1.33)^x$.

CC.9-12.A.REI.11

3 EXAMPLE Solving an Exponential Equation by Graphing

Camilla invested $300 at 4% interest compounded continuously. Diego invested $275 at 6% interest compounded continuously. When will they have the same amount in their accounts? What will the amount be when this occurs?

A Write equations to represent the amount in each account. Use the fact that when an amount P is invested in an account that earns interest at a nominal rate r compounded n times per year, the amount in the account after t years is $A(t) = Pe^{rt}$.

Camilla: $A(t) = 300 \cdot e^{0.04 \cdot t}$ Substitute 300 for P and 0.04 for r.

Diego: $A(t) = 275 \cdot e^{0.06 \cdot t}$ Substitute 275 for P and 0.06 for r.

B Graph the equations.

Enter the equation for Camilla's account as Y_1 in your calculator's equation editor. Enter the equation for Diego's account as Y_2.

Graph both equations in the same viewing window. A good viewing in this situation is $0 \le x \le 10$ with a tick mark every 1 unit and $0 \le y \le 500$ with a tick mark every 50 units.

C Find the point of intersection of the graphs.

Press **2nd** **TRACE** and select **5:intersect** to find the point of intersection of the graphs.

The point of intersection is approximately __(4.35, 357.02)__

So, Camilla and Diego will have the same amount in their accounts after

approximately __4.35__ years.

At this time, the amount in each account will be __$357.02__

REFLECT

3a. Who has more money in his or her account after 3 years? How can you tell from the graphs?

Camilla; at $x = 3$, the curve representing her account is above the curve

representing Diego's account.

3b. Suppose Camilla and Diego leave their money in their accounts for 10 years. At that time, who will have more money in his or her account? How much more?

Diego will have $53.54 more than Camilla.

3c. How can you observe the difference in the accounts after 10 years from the graphs of the equations?

The difference is the vertical distance between the graphs at $x = 10$.

You know that you can sometimes solve an exponential equation by writing both sides as powers with the same base. When that method is not possible, you can take a logarithm of both sides of the equation. This is justified by the following property.

> **Property of Equality for Logarithmic Equations**
> For any positive numbers x, y, and b ($b \neq 1$), $\log_b x = \log_b y$ if and only if $x = y$.

CC.9-12.F.BF.5(+)

4 EXAMPLE Taking the Common Logarithm of Both Sides

Solve $2^{x-3} = 85$. Give the exact solution and an approximate solution to three decimal places.

$2^{x-3} = 85$ Original equation

$\log 2^{x-3} = \log 85$ Take the common logarithm of both sides.

$(x-3) \log 2 = \log 85$ Power Property of Logarithms

$\dfrac{(x-3) \log 2}{\log 2} = \dfrac{\log 85}{\log 2}$ Divide both sides by log 2.

$x - 3 = \dfrac{\log 85}{\log 2}$ Simplify.

$x = \dfrac{\log 85}{\log 2} + 3$ Solve for x to find the exact solution.

$x \approx 9.409$ Evaluate. Round to three decimal places.

REFLECT

4a. Why do you use the Power Property of Logarithms?

This moves the variable out of the exponent.

4b. How can you use estimation to check if your answer is reasonable?

Replace x with 9.4 in the original equation. The left side is approximately $2^{6.4}$,

which is between 2^6 and 2^7, or between 64 and 128. So it is reasonable that this

value is equal to 85.

EXAMPLE

Questioning Strategies

- What is the purpose of dividing both sides of the equation by log 2? **The purpose is to isolate the variable expression $x - 3$ on one side of the equation.**

- How do you get the value of x in the last step? **Evaluate log 85 and log 2. Divide the value of log 85 by the value of log 2. Add that quotient to 3.**

Avoid Common Errors

When finding the approximate value of x, be sure to close the parentheses for log 85 before dividing by log 2. Students should enter $\log(85) / \log(2) + 3$ into their graphing calculators.

Teaching Strategy

An alternate approach to **4 EXAMPLE** is to write the equation as a logarithmic equation, isolate the variable, and use the Change of Base Property.

$2^{x-3} = 85$ is equivalent to $\log_2 85 = x - 3$.

Then $x = \log_2 85 + 3 = \dfrac{\log 85}{\log 2} + 3$.

EXTRA EXAMPLE

Solve $3^{x+4} = 2500$. Give the exact solution and an approximate solution to three decimal places.

$x = \dfrac{\log 2500}{\log 3} - 4 \approx 3.122$

5 EXAMPLE

Questioning Strategies

- Why does $\ln e = 1$? **$\ln e = \log_e e$ and $e^1 = e$.**

- Compare solving an exponential equation using natural logarithms with solving an exponential equation using common logarithms. **The methods are identical. The only difference is the type of logarithm used.**

EXTRA EXAMPLE

Sonya has $1400 to invest for 5 years. She wants to have $2100 at the end of the 5-year period. What interest rate does she need if the interest is compounded continuously? **about 8.1%**

> ⋮ **MATHEMATICAL PRACTICE** **Highlighting the Standards**
>
> **4 EXAMPLE** and **5 EXAMPLE** offer an opportunity to address Mathematical Practice Standard 6 (Attend to precision). Discuss how much accuracy is lost or gained by rounding to fewer or greater decimal places. In Reflect Question 4b, substituting 9.4 results in about 84.449, while substituting 9.409 results in about 84.977. In this case, the difference is not very great. Both numbers are close to 85.
>
> In Reflect Question 5b, substituting 0.173 results in $998.85, while substituting 0.2 results in $1112.77. Using two more decimal places to 0.17329 results in $1000.01. Here, the differences in the results are more significant.

6 EXAMPLE

Questioning Strategies

- Why is the goal to get a single logarithmic expression on one side of the equation? **You can use the definition of a logarithm to solve the equation.**

- What is the purpose of using the definition of a logarithm? **It results in a linear equation that can be solved easily.**

continued

You can also take the natural logarithm of both sides of an equation. It makes sense to take the natural logarithm, rather than the common logarithm, when the base is e.

5 EXAMPLE   Taking the Natural Logarithm of Both Sides

Adam has $500 to invest for 4 years. He wants to double his money during this time. What interest rate does Adam need for this investment, assuming the interest is compounded continuously?

A   Write an equation.

The formula for interest compounded continuously is $A = Pe^{rt}$ where A is the amount in the account, P is the principal, r is the annual rate of interest, and t is the time in years. $P = \underline{500}$ and A is the final amount after $t = 4$ years, so $A = \underline{1000}$.

The equation is $\underline{1000 = 500e^{4r}}$.

B   Solve the equation for r.

$1000 = 500\ e^{4r}$	Write the equation.
$2 = e^{4r}$	Divide both sides by 500.
$\ln 2 = \ln e^{4r}$	Take the natural logarithm of both sides.
$\ln 2 = 4r \ln e$	Power Property of Logarithms
$\ln 2 = \boxed{4r}$	Use the fact that $\ln e = 1$.
$\dfrac{\ln 2}{4} = \dfrac{4r}{4}$	Divide both sides by 4.
$\dfrac{\ln 2}{4} = r$	Solve for r to find the exact answer.
$0.173 \approx r$	Evaluate. Round to three decimal places.

So, Adam needs an interest rate of approximately $\underline{17.3}$ %.

REFLECT

5a. What is the benefit of taking the natural logarithm of both sides of the equation, rather than the common logarithm?

This gives ln e on one side of the equation, and ln e simplifies to 1.

5b. Describe two different ways to use your calculator to check your answer.

(1) Evaluate $500e^{4 \cdot 0.173}$ to check that this value is close to 1000.

(2) Graph $y = 1000$ and $y = 500e^{4x}$ and find the point of intersection. The value of x should be about 0.173.

To solve a logarithmic equation in the form $\log_b x = a$, first rewrite the equation in exponential form ($b^a = x$) by using the definition of a logarithm. As you will see in the second part of the following example, you may first need to isolate the logarithmic expression on one side of the equation.

6 EXAMPLE   Solving a Logarithmic Equation Algebraically

Solve each logarithmic equation.

A $\log_3(x + 1) = 2$

$3^{\boxed{2}} = x + 1$	Definition of logarithm
$9 = x + 1$	Simplify.
$8 = x$	Solve for x.

B $7 + \log_3(5x - 4) = 10$

$\log_3(5x - 4) = \boxed{3}$	Subtract 7 from both sides.
$3^{\boxed{3}} = 5x - 4$	Definition of logarithm
$27 = 5x - 4$	Simplify.
$31 = 5x$	Add 4 to both sides.
$6.2 = x$	Solve for x.

REFLECT

6a. How can you check your solution to part A by substitution?

Substitute 8 for x in the original equation and check that the two sides are equal:

$\log_3(8 + 1) = \log_3 9 = 2$.

6b. Your calculator has keys for evaluating only logarithms with a base of 10 or e. Use the Change of Base Property to rewrite the equation from part A so that the base of the logarithm is 10 or e. Then explain how to use graphing to check your solution.

$\dfrac{\log(x + 1)}{\log 3} = 2$ or $\dfrac{\ln(x + 1)}{\ln 3} = 2$. To check the solution, graph $y = \dfrac{\log(x + 1)}{\log 3}$ and $y = 2$, or $y = \dfrac{\ln(x + 1)}{\ln 3}$ and $y = 2$, and find the intersection point's x-coordinate.

6c. Explain how you could use graphing to check your solution to part B.

Graph $y = 7 + \dfrac{\log(5x - 4)}{\log 3}$ and $y = 10$, or $y = 7 + \dfrac{\ln(5x - 4)}{\ln 3}$ and $y = 10$, and find the intersection point's x-coordinate.

© Houghton Mifflin Harcourt Publishing Company

6 EXAMPLE continued

EXTRA EXAMPLE

Solve each logarithmic equation.

A. $\log_4 (2x - 4) = 3$ **34**

B. $6 \log (3x + 1) = 12$ **33**

Avoid Common Errors

Students often try to use the definition of a logarithm before the logarithmic expression is isolated on one side of the equation. Remind students that the equation must be in the form "logarithm =" before they can solve it.

Teaching Strategy

Tell students that when solving logarithmic equations, it is possible to get extraneous solutions (solutions that do not make the original equation true). It is good practice to always check any answers by substituting them back into the original equation.

7 EXAMPLE

Questioning Strategies

- What quadrant or quadrants should your viewing window display? **Quadrant I**

- In Reflect Question 7c, could you subtract 2.7 as the first step? Why or why not? **Yes; it doesn't matter whether you subtract 2.7 first or 4.4 log x first as long as your second step is to subtract the other term.**

Teaching Strategy

Have students set their viewing windows so that x-values range from 0 to 2000 and y-values range from 0 to 20. Otherwise, the calculator may not detect the point of intersection.

EXTRA EXAMPLE

Two students performed an experiment involving temperature change and used regression to create equations with natural logarithms. Their equations are shown below. For both equations, x represents elapsed time in minutes and y represents the corresponding temperature in degrees Celsius.

Student A: $y = 10 + 6.9 \ln x$

Student B: $y = 10.2 + 6.7 \ln x$

After how many minutes do the two formulas give the same temperature? **about 2.7 minutes**

CLOSE

Essential Question

What is the general process for solving exponential and logarithmic equations?

To solve an exponential equation, take either the common logarithm or the natural logarithm of both sides, use the Power Property of Logarithms to remove the variable from the exponent, and then solve for the variable. To solve a logarithmic equation, write the equation in the form $\log_b x = a$ and use the definition of a logarithm to eliminate the logarithmic expression. Then solve the resulting equation for the variable.

Summarize

In their journals, have students list the various ways to solve exponential equations and the various ways to solve logarithmic equations.

7 EXAMPLE · CC.9-12.A.REI.11 · Solving a Logarithmic Equation by Graphing

A telescope's limiting magnitude m is the brightness of the faintest star that can be seen using the telescope. The limiting magnitude depends on the diameter d (in millimeters) of the telescope's objective lens. The table gives two formulas relating m to d. One is a standard formula used in astronomy. The other is a proposed new formula based on data gathered from users of telescopes of various lens diameters.

Formulas for determining limiting magnitude from lens diameter	
Standard formula	$m = 2.7 + 5 \log d$
Proposed formula	$m = 4.5 + 4.4 \log d$

For what lens diameter do the two formulas give the same limiting magnitude?

A Use a graphing calculator. Enter $2.7 + 5 \log x$ as Y_1 and enter $4.5 + 4.4 \log x$ as Y_2.

B Graph the two functions in the same viewing window. Use a window where $0 \le x \le 2000$ with a tick mark every 100 units and $0 \le y \le 20$ with a tick mark every 5 units.

C Press [2nd] [TRACE] and choose **5:intersect** to find the point of intersection of the graphs.

The coordinates of the point of intersection are ___(1000, 17.7)___

So, the two formulas give the same limiting magnitude for a lens diameter of ___1000 mm___

REFLECT

7a. What is the limiting magnitude that corresponds to this lens diameter? How do you know?

17.7; this is the y-coordinate of the point of intersection.

7b. What equation can you write in order to solve the problem algebraically?

$2.7 + 5 \log x = 4.5 + 4.4 \log x$

7c. Show how to solve the equation algebraically. Justify each step. (*Hint:* First get all logarithmic expressions on one side of the equation and all non-logarithmic expressions on the other side of the equation.)

$2.7 + 5 \log x = 4.5 + 4.4 \log x$	(Original equation)
$2.7 + 0.6 \log x = 4.5$	(Subtract $4.4 \log x$ from both sides.)
$0.6 \log x = 1.8$	(Subtract 2.7 from both sides.)
$\log x = \frac{1.8}{0.6} = 3$	(Divide both sides by 0.6.)
$x = 10^3$	(Definition of logarithm)
$x = 1000$	(Evaluate.)

PRACTICE

Solve each exponential equation algebraically.

1. $16^{3x} = 64^{x+2}$

$x = 2$

2. $\left(\frac{2}{5}\right)^{x+7} = \left(\frac{4}{25}\right)^{10}$

$x = 13$

3. $27^x = \frac{1}{9}$

$x = -\frac{2}{3}$

4. $6^{5x-1} = 36$

$x = \frac{3}{5}$

5. $0.01^{x+1} = 1000^{x-9}$

$x = 5$

6. $625 = \left(\frac{1}{25}\right)^{x+3}$

$x = -5$

7. $6^{x^2} = 36^8$

$x = \pm 4$

8. $0.75^{5x-2} = \left(\frac{27}{64}\right)^{x-6}$

$x = -8$

9. $\left(\frac{1}{3}\right)^{x+2} = 81^{x-1}$

$x = \frac{2}{5}$

10. Show that you can solve $\frac{1}{4} = 16^{x+5}$ by writing both sides of the equation with a base of 2 or with a base of 4.

$2^{-2} = (2^4)^{x+5} \rightarrow 2^{-2} = 2^{4x+20} \rightarrow -2 = 4x + 20 \rightarrow -22 = 4x \rightarrow -5.5 = x$

$4^{-1} = (4^2)^{x+5} \rightarrow 4^{-1} = 4^{2x+10} \rightarrow -1 = 2x + 10 \rightarrow -11 = 2x \rightarrow -5.5 = x$

11. The equation $y = 87.3(1.07)^x$ models the population of a city, in thousands, from 1980 to 2010. In this equation, x is the number of years since 1980, and y is the population in thousands.

a. In what year did the population reach 150,000? ___1988___

b. In what year did the population reach 250,000? ___1995___

12. In the lower stratosphere (between 36,152 feet and 82,345 feet), the equation $p = 473.1e^{1.73 - 0.000048h}$ represents the atmospheric pressure p in pounds per square foot at altitude h feet.

a. At what altitude does the pressure equal 150 lb/ft²? ___59,972 ft___

b. At what altitude does the pressure equal 300 lb/ft²? ___45,532 ft___

13. Rima and Trevor both bought a car in 2010. Rima's car cost $17,832 and Trevor's car cost $22,575. Rima's car is depreciating at a rate of 11% per year and Trevor's car is depreciating at a rate of 13.5% per year.

a. Write each car's value as a function of time t (in years since 2010).

Rima: $V(t) = 17,832(0.89)^t$; Trevor: $V(t) = 22,575(0.865)^t$

b. During what year will the cars have an equal value? At that time, what will the value of the cars be?

In 2018, both cars will be worth about $6796.

Where skills are taught	Where skills are practiced
1 EXAMPLE	EXS. 1–10
2 EXAMPLE	EX. 11
3 EXAMPLE	EXS. 12, 13
4 EXAMPLE	EXS. 14–16, 18, 20–22
5 EXAMPLE	EXS. 17, 19, 24
6 EXAMPLE	EXS. 28–33
7 EXAMPLE	EXS. 37, 38

Exercise 23: Students see that a logarithmic equation can have no solution.

Exercise 25: Given the effective rate for interest compounded continuously, students solve an exponential equation to find the annual interest rate by taking the natural logarithm of both sides. Students may need to be reminded to convert the effective rate to a decimal when writing the equation.

Exercise 26: Students solve the equation they created in the previous unit for the population of the United States from 1790 to 1890 to find the number of decades required to reach a given population.

Exercise 27: Students identify and correct an error a student made in solving an exponential equation.

Exercises 34–36: Students use properties of exponents to write sums and differences of logarithmic expressions as single logarithmic expressions so they can use the definition of a logarithm to solve logarithmic equations.

Solve. Give the exact solution and an approximate solution to three decimal places.

14. $6^x = 15$

$$x = \frac{\log 15}{\log 6}$$

$$x \approx 1.511$$

15. $4^{2x} = 200$

$$x = \frac{\log 200}{2 \log 4}$$

$$x \approx 1.911$$

16. $10^x = 35$

$$x = \log 35$$

$$x \approx 1.544$$

17. $10 + e^{\frac{x}{3}} = 4270$

$$x = 3 (\ln 4260)$$

$$x \approx 25.071$$

18. $2^{9-x} + 3 = 62$

$$x = -\frac{\log 59}{\log 2} + 9$$

$$x \approx 3.117$$

19. $e^{8x+1} = 530$

$$x = \frac{\ln 530 - 1}{6}$$

$$x \approx 0.879$$

20. $3^{2x-1} = 14$

$$x = \frac{\log 14}{2 \log 3} + \frac{1}{2}$$

$$x \approx 1.701$$

21. $210 + 4^x = 3 \cdot 4^x$

$$x = \frac{\log 105}{\log 4}$$

$$x \approx 3.357$$

22. $11^{1-x} = 8$

$$x = 1 - \frac{\log 8}{\log 11}$$

$$x \approx 0.133$$

23. What happens if you take the common logarithm of both sides of $5^x = -6$ in order to solve the equation? Why does this happen?

You get $x = \frac{\log (-6)}{\log 5}$, which cannot be evaluated because logarithms are not defined for negative numbers. This happens because the original equation has no solution.

24. Kendra wants to double her investment of $4000. How long will this take if the annual interest rate is 4% compounded continuously? How long will this take if the annual interest rate is 8% compounded continuously? What effect does doubling the interest rate have on the time it takes the investment to double?

About 17.3 years; about 8.7 years; doubling the interest rate halves the doubling time.

25. An account that earns interest at an annual rate of r earns more interest each year if the account is compounded, say n times per year (at a rate of r/n), than if it is compounded annually. The actual interest rate R earned is called the effective rate and r is called the nominal rate. For interest that is compounded continuously, R is given by $R = e^r - 1$. What is the nominal interest rate if R is 5.625%? Round to the nearest hundredth of a percent.

5.47%

26. The equation $y = 4.1(1.33)^x$ models the population of the U.S., in millions, from 1790 to 1890. In this equation, x is the number of decades since 1790, and y is the population in millions. How many decades after 1790 did the population reach 28 million? Write an expression for the exact answer and give an approximate answer to the nearest tenth.

$\frac{\log \left(\frac{28}{4.1}\right)}{\log 1.33}$ decades ≈ 6.7 decades

© Houghton Mifflin Harcourt Publishing Company

---

27. Error Analysis Identify and correct the error in the student work shown at right.

In the last line, $\frac{\ln 20}{\ln 10} \neq \ln 2$. The correct solution is $\frac{\ln 20}{\ln 10} \approx 1.301$.

$$10^x = 20$$
$$\ln 10^x = \ln 20$$
$$x \ln 10 = \ln 20$$
$$x = \frac{\ln 20}{\ln 10} = \ln 2 \approx 0.693$$

Solve each logarithmic equation. Round to three decimal places if necessary.

28. $\log_7 (x - 5) = 2$

54

29. $\log_4 (8x) = 3$

8

30. $\log (7x - 1) = -1$

0.157

31. $\ln (4x - 1) = 9$

2026.021

32. $11 + \log_4 (x + 1) = 15$

255

33. $3 = \ln (3x + 3)$

5.695

Solve by using the Product or Quotient Property of Logarithms so that one side is a single logarithm. Round to three decimal places if necessary.

34. $\log 20 + \log 10x = 5$

500

35. $\ln x - \ln 6 = 3$

120.513

36. $2.4 = \log 7 + \log 3x$

11.961

For Exercises 37 and 38, use graphing to solve.

37. Charles collected data on the atmospheric pressure (ranging from 4 to 15 pounds per square inch) and the corresponding altitude above the surface of Earth (ranging from 1 to 30,000 feet). He used regression to write two functions that give the altitude above the surface of Earth given the atmospheric pressure.

$$f(x) = 66,990 - 24,747 \ln x$$
$$g(x) = -2870x + 40,393$$

a. At what atmospheric pressure(s) do the equations give the same altitude?

approximately 5.6 psi and 12.5 psi

b. At what altitude(s) above Earth do these atmospheric pressures occur?

approximately 24,254 feet and 4415 feet

38. Elena and Paul determined slightly different equations to model the recommended height, in inches, of a tabletop for children x years old.

Elena: $y = 12.2 + 5.45 \ln x$

Paul: $y = 12.5 + 5.2 \ln x$

For what age do the models give the same tabletop height? What is that height?

about 3.3 years; 18.7 inches

© Houghton Mifflin Harcourt Publishing Company

Assign these pages to help your students practice and apply important lesson concepts. For additional exercises, see the Student Edition.

Answers

Additional Practice

1. $x \approx 0.9307$

2. $x \approx 4.5449$

3. $x = -4$

4. $x = 3$

5. $x \approx -6.67$

6. $x = 6$

7. $x = -8$

8. $x = -0.6$

9. $x = 5$

10. $x = 256$

11. $x = 9$

12. $x = 22$

13. $x = 10^{15}$

14. $x = 20$

15. $x = 16$

16. $x = 56$

17. $x = \pm 2$

18. $x = -1, -2$

19. $x < 11$

20. $x = 10,000$

21. $x = 4$

22. 2009

Problem Solving

1. a. 437 mg

   b. $C(t) = C_0(1 - 0.15)^t$

   c. 2.3 h

2. a. He can graph the equation $102 = 437(0.85)^t$ and find the value of t where $C(t)$ is 102.

b. $y = 102$ and $y = 437(0.85)^t$

c.
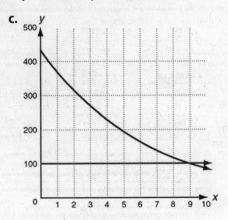

3. D

4. H

Additional Practice

Solve and check.

1. $5^{2x} = 20$

2. $12^{2x-8} = 15$

3. $2^{x+6} = 4$

_____

4. $16^{5x} = 64^{x+7}$

5. $243^{0.2x} = 81^{x+5}$

6. $25^x = 125^{x-2}$

_____

7. $\left(\frac{1}{2}\right)^x = 16^2$

8. $\left(\frac{1}{32}\right)^{2x} = 64$

9. $\left(\frac{1}{27}\right)^{x-6} = 27$

_____

Solve.

10. $\log_4 x^5 = 20$

11. $\log_3 x^6 = 12$

12. $\log_4 (x-6)^3 = 6$

_____

13. $\log x - \log 10 = 14$

14. $\log x + \log 5 = 2$

15. $\log (x+9) = \log (2x-7)$

_____

16. $\log (x+4) - \log 6 = 1$

17. $\log x^2 + \log 25 = 2$

18. $\log (x-1)^2 = \log (-5x-1)$

_____

Use a table and graph to solve.

19. $2^{x-5} < 64$

20. $\log x^3 = 12$

21. $2^x 3^x = 1296$

_____

Solve.

22. The population of a small farming community is declining at a rate of 7% per year. The decline can be expressed by the exponential equation $P = C(1 - 0.07)^t$, where P is the population after t years and C is the current population. If the population was 8,500 in 2004, when will the population be less than 6,000?

_____

_____

Problem Solving

While John and Cody play their favorite video game, John drinks 4 cups of coffee and a cola, and Cody drinks 2 cups of brewed tea and a cup of iced tea. John recalls reading that up to 300 mg of caffeine is considered a moderate level of consumption per day. The rate at which caffeine is eliminated from the bloodstream is about 15% per hour.

Caffeine Content of Some Beverages	
Beverage	Caffeine (mg per serving)
Brewed coffee	103
Brewed tea	36
Iced tea	30
Cola	25

1. John wants to know how long it will take for the caffeine in his bloodstream to drop to a moderate level.

   a. How much caffeine did John consume?

   _____

   b. Write an equation showing the amount of caffeine in the bloodstream as a function of time.

   _____

   c. How long, to the nearest tenth of an hour, will it take for the caffeine in John's system to reach a moderate level?

   _____

2. a. Cody thinks that it will take at least 8 hours for the level of caffeine in John's system to drop to the same level of caffeine that Cody consumed. Explain how he can use his graphing calculator to prove that.

   _____

   b. What equations did Cody enter into his calculator?

   _____

   c. Sketch the resulting graph.

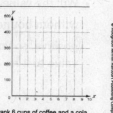

Choose the letter for the best answer.

3. About how long would it take for the level of caffeine in Cody's system to drop by a factor of 2?

   A 0.2 hour

   B 1.6 hours

   C 2.7 hours

   D 4.3 hours

4. If John drank 6 cups of coffee and a cola, about how long would it take for the level of caffeine in his system to drop to a moderate level?

   F 0.5 hour

   G 1.6 hours

   H 4.7 hours

   J 5.3 hours

Notes

The Natural Base, e
Going Deeper

Essential question: *How does the graph of* $f(x) = e^x$ *compare to graphs of exponential functions with other bases?*

COMMON CORE **Standards for Mathematical Content**

CC.9-12.A.CED.2 Create equations in two or more variables to represent relationships between quantities; graph equations on coordinate axes with labels and scales.* ,

CC.9-12.F.IF.2 Use function notation, evaluate functions for inputs in their domains, ...

CC.9-12.F.IF.7 Graph functions expressed symbolically and show key features of the graph, by hand in simple cases ...*

CC.9-12.F.IF.7e Graph exponential ... functions, showing intercepts and end behavior, ...*

CC.9-12.F.BF.3 Identify the effect on the graph of replacing $f(x)$ by $f(x) + k$, $kf(x)$, $f(kx)$, and $f(x + k)$ for specific values of k (both positive and negative) ...

CC.9-12.F.LE.2 Construct ... exponential functions, ... given ... a description of a relationship, ...*

CC.9-12.F.LE.5 Interpret the parameters in a ... exponential function in terms of a context.*

Also: CC.9-12.A.SSE.3, CC.9-12.A.SSE.3c, CC.9-12.F.IF.4*, CC.9-12.F.IF.8, CC.9-12.F.IF.8b

Vocabulary

e

Prerequisites

Graphing basic exponential functions

Transforming exponential growth functions

Math Background

Like π, e is an irrational number, so its decimal form never repeats and never terminates. Its value is approximately 2.718. The function $f(x) = e^x$ is special in mathematics because it is the only exponential function $f(x) = b^x$ whose derivative is equal to itself. For that reason, e is sometimes called the *natural base*.

INTRODUCE

Have students find the values of $\frac{1}{x}$ for $x = 1$, 10, 100, and 1000. Then, have them find the values of $1 + \frac{1}{x}$ for the same values. Ask them to describe what happens as x becomes greater.

TEACH

1 EXPLORE

Materials
graphing calculator

Questioning Strategies

- How do you enter the expression in part A into a graphing calculator? **Enter (1 + 1/X)^X.**

- Will the value of $1 + \frac{1}{x}$ ever reach 1 as x increases without bound? Why or why not? **No; $\frac{1}{x}$ is always positive, so you are always adding a positive value to 1 no matter how great x becomes.**

The Natural Base, e
Going Deeper

Essential question: *How does the graph of $f(x) = e^x$ compare to graphs of exponential functions with other bases?*

CC.9-12.F.IF.2

1 EXPLORE Investigating $\left(1 + \frac{1}{x}\right)^x$

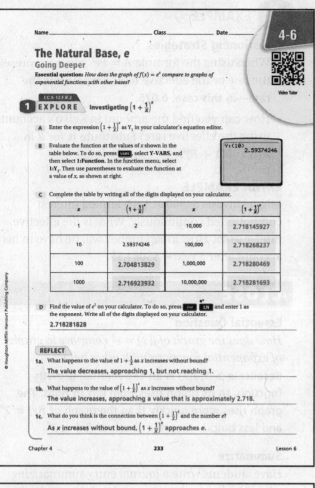

A Enter the expression $\left(1 + \frac{1}{x}\right)^x$ as Y_1 in your calculator's equation editor.

B Evaluate the function at the values of x shown in the table below. To do so, press $\boxed{\text{VARS}}$, select **Y-VARS**, and then select **1:Function**. In the function menu, select **1:Y₁**. Then use parentheses to evaluate the function at a value of x, as shown at right.

$Y_1(10)$
2.59374246

C Complete the table by writing all of the digits displayed on your calculator.

x	$\left(1+\frac{1}{x}\right)^x$	x	$\left(1+\frac{1}{x}\right)^x$
1	2	10,000	2.718145927
10	2.59374246	100,000	2.718268237
100	2.704813829	1,000,000	2.718280469
1000	2.716923932	10,000,000	2.718281693

D Find the value of e^1 on your calculator. To do so, press $\boxed{\text{2nd}}$ $\boxed{\text{LN}}$ e^x and enter 1 as the exponent. Write all of the digits displayed on your calculator.

2.718281828

REFLECT

1a. What happens to the value of $1 + \frac{1}{x}$ as x increases without bound?

The value decreases, approaching 1, but not reaching 1.

1b. What happens to the value of $\left(1 + \frac{1}{x}\right)^x$ as x increases without bound?

The value increases, approaching a value that is approximately 2.718.

1c. What do you think is the connection between $\left(1 + \frac{1}{x}\right)^x$ and the number e?

As x increases without bound, $\left(1 + \frac{1}{x}\right)^x$ approaches e.

CC.9-12.F.IF.7e

2 ENGAGE The Natural Base, e

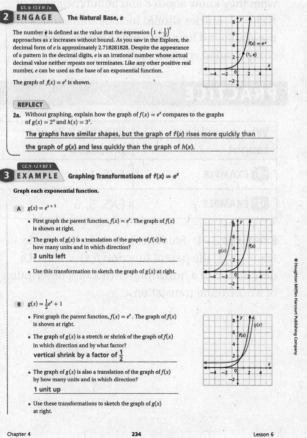

The number e is defined as the value that the expression $\left(1 + \frac{1}{x}\right)^x$ approaches as x increases without bound. As you saw in the Explore, the decimal form of e is approximately 2.718281828. Despite the appearance of a pattern in the decimal digits, e is an irrational number whose actual decimal value neither repeats nor terminates. Like any other positive real number e can be used as the base of an exponential function.

The graph of $f(x) = e^x$ is shown.

REFLECT

2a. Without graphing, explain how the graph of $f(x) = e^x$ compares to the graphs of $g(x) = 2^x$ and $h(x) = 3^x$.

The graphs have similar shapes, but the graph of $f(x)$ rises more quickly than the graph of $g(x)$ and less quickly than the graph of $h(x)$.

CC.9-12.F.BF.3

3 EXAMPLE Graphing Transformations of $f(x) = e^x$

Graph each exponential function.

A $g(x) = e^{x+3}$

• First graph the parent function, $f(x) = e^x$. The graph of $f(x)$ is shown at right.

• The graph of $g(x)$ is a translation of the graph of $f(x)$ by how many units and in which direction?

3 units left

• Use this transformation to sketch the graph of $g(x)$ at right.

B $g(x) = \frac{1}{2}e^x + 1$

• First graph the parent function, $f(x) = e^x$. The graph of $f(x)$ is shown at right.

• The graph of $g(x)$ is a stretch or shrink of the graph of $f(x)$ in which direction and by what factor?

vertical shrink by a factor of $\frac{1}{2}$

• The graph of $g(x)$ is also a translation of the graph of $f(x)$ by how many units and in which direction?

1 unit up

• Use these transformations to sketch the graph of $g(x)$ at right.

Notes

Questioning Strategies

- What is $f(0)$? What does this tell you about the graph of $f(x) = e^x$? **1; the graph passes through the point (0, 1).**

- Does the graph of $f(x) = e^x$ ever intersect the x-axis? Why or why not? **Not; there is no value of x for which $e^x = 0$. As x decreases without bound, e^x approaches but never reaches 0.**

::: MATHEMATICAL PRACTICE · Highlighting the Standards

Reflect Question 2a offers an opportunity to implement Mathematical Practice Standard 7 (Look for and make use of structure). Students must recognize that graphs of exponential growth functions rise faster as the base increases and that $2 < e < 3$.
:::

Avoid Common Errors

Students are used to letters representing variables and may get confused when working with e. Remind them that, like π, e is a constant representing an irrational number.

3 EXAMPLE

Questioning Strategies

- In part A, how do you know that the graph of $g(x)$ will be a translation of the graph of $f(x)$ to the left? **The expression $x + 3$ equals $x - (-3)$, so h is negative.**

- In part B, how do you know that the shrink is vertical and not horizontal? **$f(x)$, and not x, is being multiplied by the constant.**

EXTRA EXAMPLE
Graph the exponential function.

A. $g(x) = e^x - 4$ **It is the graph of $f(x) = e^x$ translated 4 units down.**

B. $g(x) = e^{-\frac{1}{2}x}$ **It is the graph of $f(x) = e^x$ stretched horizontally by a factor of 2 and reflected across the y-axis.**

4 EXAMPLE

Questioning Strategies

- When using the formula $A = Pe^{rt}$, does r represent the rate or the effective rate? **r represents the rate—in this case, 0.025.**

- How can you find the amount in Keiko's account using the effective rate? **Substitute it for R in $A(t) = P(1 + R)^t$.**

EXTRA EXAMPLE
Miguel invests \$4800 at 1.9% annual interest compounded continuously. What is the effective rate? **1.918%** How much money will he have in his account after 3 years? **\$5081.55**

CLOSE

Essential Question
How does the graph of $f(x) = e^x$ compare to graphs of exponential functions with other bases? **Because $e > 1$, $f(x)$ is an exponential growth function, so its graph rises from left to right. The graph rises more quickly than the graph of $f(x) = 2^x$ and less quickly than the graph of $f(x) = 3^x$.**

Summarize
Have students write a journal entry summarizing what they know about e and about the graph of $f(x) = e^x$. Entries should include translations of the graph and how e is used to find interest compounded continuously.

PRACTICE

Where skills are taught	Where skills are practiced
3 EXAMPLE	EXS. 1, 2
4 EXAMPLE	EXS. 5, 6

Exercises 3–4: Students write a function rule when given the parent function $f(x) = e^x$ and a description of a horizontal shrink or a description of a horizontal translation.

REFLECT

3a. Describe how the graph of $g(x)$ compares to the graph of $f(x) = e^x$.

The graph of $g(x)$ is a horizontal shrink by a factor of $\frac{1}{3}$.

The *effective rate of interest* on a deposit is the actual rate of interest earned, depending on the frequency of compounding. (*Nominal interest* does not take into account the frequency of compounding.) When an amount P is invested in an account earning interest at a nominal rate r compounded n times per year, the amount $A(t)$ in the account after t years is given by

$$A(t) = P\left(1 + \frac{r}{n}\right)^{nt}.$$

Consider what happens when the number n of compounding periods increases without bound; that is, when interest is compounded *continuously*.

$A(t) = P\left(1 + \frac{r}{n}\right)^{nt}$	Compound interest formula
$= P\left(1 + \frac{r}{mr}\right)^{mrt}$	Let $m = \frac{n}{r}$, so $n = mr$.
$= P\left(1 + \frac{1}{m}\right)^{mrt}$	Simplify.
$= P\left[\left(1 + \frac{1}{m}\right)^{m}\right]^{rt}$	Change the base of the exponential function.
$= Pe^{rt}$	As n increases without bound, so does m, and $\left(1 + \frac{1}{m}\right)^{m}$ approaches e.

So, when interest is compounded continuously, $A(t) = Pe^{rt}$ and the effective rate R is $e^r - 1$.

CC.9-12.F.IF.2
4 EXAMPLE Calculating Interest Compounded Continuously

Keiko invests $2700 and earns 2.5% annual interest compounded continuously. What is the effective rate? How much will be in the account after 5 years?

A Find the effective rate.

$R = e^r - 1$	Use the formula for effective rate.
$= e^{\boxed{0.025}} - 1$	Substitute 0.025 for r.
$\approx \boxed{0.02532}$	Evaluate. Round to 5 decimal places.

So, the effective rate is about 2.532%.

B Find the amount after 5 years.

$A(t) = Pe^{rt}$	Use the formula for interest compounded continuously.
$A(5) = \boxed{2700} \cdot e^{\boxed{0.025} \cdot \boxed{5}}$	Substitute 2700 for P, 0.025 for r, and 5 for t.
$\approx \boxed{3059.50}$	Evaluate. Round to the nearest hundredth.

So, the amount in Keiko's account after 5 years is $\boxed{\$3059.50}$.

© Houghton Mifflin Harcourt Publishing Company

REFLECT

4a. Why does the variable n not appear in the formula $A(t) = Pe^{rt}$?

It is incorporated in the definition of e.

PRACTICE

Graph each exponential function.

1. $f(x) = e^{3x}$

2. $f(x) = e^{-x} + 2$

The graph of $f(x) = e^x$ is shown. Write the function rules for $g(x)$ and $h(x)$ based on the descriptions given. Then sketch the graphs of $g(x)$ and $h(x)$ on the same coordinate plane.

3. The graph of $g(x)$ is a horizontal shrink of the graph of $f(x)$ by a factor of $\frac{1}{3}$.

$g(x) = e^{3x}$

4. The graph of $h(x)$ is a horizontal translation of the graph of $f(x)$ to the right 3 units.

$h(x) = e^{x-3}$

5. Carl invests $3200 in an account that earns 3.1% annual interest compounded continuously. What is the effective rate? How much money will he have in his account after 7 years?

3.149%; $3975.50

6. You plan to invest $1000 in an account for one year. How much more money will you have at the end of the year if you choose an account that earns 6% annual interest compounded continuously versus an account that earns 6% annual interest compounded quarterly? Explain.

About $0.48; with continuously compounded interest, the amount is $1000e^{0.06} \approx 1061.84$, as compared to $1000\left(1 + \frac{0.06}{4}\right)^{4} \approx 1061.36$.

© Houghton Mifflin Harcourt Publishing Company

Assign these pages to help your students practice and apply important lesson concepts. For additional exercises, see the Student Edition.

Answers

Additional Practice

1.

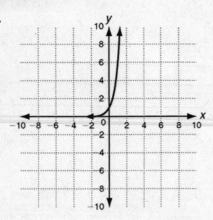

2.

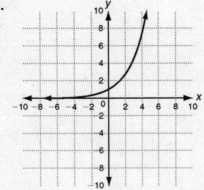

3.

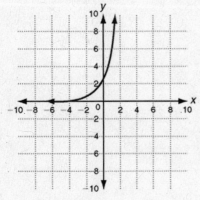

4.

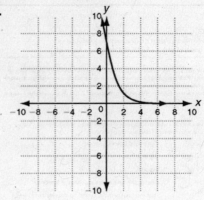

5. $x + 2$

6. $2x$

7. x^7

8. $3x + 1$

9. 1

10. $2x + y$

11. $6074.36

12. 0.000693

Problem Solving

1. 194

2. $k = 0.0934$

3.

Year	2006	2007	2008	2009	2010
t	3	4	5	6	7
Population, P_t	257	282	309	340	373

4. C

5. C

6. C

7. D

Additional Practice

Graph.

1. $f(x) = e^{2x}$

2. $f(x) = e^{0.5x}$

3. $f(x) = e^{1+x}$

4. $f(x) = e^{2-x}$

Simplify.

5. $\ln e^{x+2}$ _____

6. $e^{\ln 2x}$ _____

7. $e^{7\ln x}$ _____

8. $\ln e^{3x+1}$ _____

9. $\ln e$ _____

10. $\ln e^{2x+y}$ _____

Solve.

11. Use the formula $A = P\,e^{rt}$ to compute the total amount for an investment of $4500 at 5% interest compounded continuously for 6 years.

_____

12. Use the natural decay function, $N(t) = N_0 e^{-kt}$, to find the decay constant for a substance that has a half-life of 1000 years.

_____

Problem Solving

Irene reads that the 2004 census of whooping cranes tallied 213 birds at one wildlife refuge in Texas. This number exceeded the 2003 record by 19. If the population of whooping cranes can be modeled using the exponential growth function $P_t = P_0\,e^{kt}$, the population, P_t, at time t can be found, where P_0 is the initial population and k is the growth factor. Predict the population of whooping cranes over the next few years.

1. What was the size of the population of whooping cranes in 2003? _____

2. Use the population figures for 2003 and 2004 to find the growth factor, k.

_____

3. Complete the table to predict the population of whooping cranes through 2010.

Year	2006	2007	2008	2009	2010
t	3				
Population, P_t					

Choose the letter for the best answer.

4. Irene wants to know when the population of whooping cranes will exceed 1000. Using the 2003 population as P_0, which year is the best prediction?

   A 2017

   B 2019

   C 2021

   D 2023

5. Irene wonders how the 2010 whooping crane population would change if the growth factor doubled. Which statement is true?

   F The population would increase by a factor of e^2.

   G The population would increase by a factor of $e^{0.0934}$.

   H The population would increase by a factor of $e^{(0.0934)\,(7)}$.

   J The population would increase by a factor of $7e^2$.

6. How long will it take for an investment in an account paying 6% compounded continuously to double?

   A 10.2 years

   B 10.8 years

   C 11.6 years

   D 12.4 years

7. Darlene has a sample of a fossil that has 33% of its original carbon-14. Carbon-14 has a half-life of 5730 years. The decay constant for carbon-14 is 1.2×10^{-4}. Find the age of the fossil.

   F About 7820 years

   G About 8450 years

   H About 8980 years

   J About 9240 years

Notes

Transforming Exponential and Logarithmic Functions
Going Deeper

Essential question: *How does changing the values of a, h, and k affect the graph of* $f(x) = a \log_b (x - h) + k$*?*

COMMON CORE Standards for Mathematical Content

CC.9-12.F.IF.7 Graph functions expressed symbolically and show key features of the graph ...*

CC.9-12.F.IF.7e Graph ... logarithmic functions, showing intercepts and end behavior, ...*

CC.9-12.F.BF.3 Identify the effect on the graph of replacing $f(x)$ by $f(x) + k$, $k f(x)$, ... and $f(x + k)$ for specific values of k (both positive and negative); find the value of k given the graphs ...

Prerequisites

Transforming exponential functions

Graphing logarithmic functions

Math Background

Students will explore transformations of the graphs of logarithmic functions. As with previous types of functions, they will see how changing the values of a, h, and k in $f(x) = a \log_b (x - h) + k$ translate, shrink, or stretch the graph of the parent function $f(x) = a \log_b x$.

INTRODUCE

Review with students how changing the values of a, h, and k affected the graphs of the parent functions of quadratic, polynomial, rational, and exponential functions. Then, have students evaluate the functions below and compare their answers with what they would get if they evaluated the parent functions at the same values.

$g(8)$ for $g(x) = 3 \log_2 x$ **9**

$g(4)$ for $g(x) = \log_2 x + 4$ **6**

$g(1)$ for $g(x) = \log_2 \left(x - \dfrac{1}{2}\right)$ **−1**

TEACH

1 EXAMPLE

Questioning Strategies

• What is the difference between $\log_2 (x - 3)$ and $\log_2 x - 3$? **In the first, 3 is subtracted from x, and then the log is taken. In the second, the log of x is taken, and then 3 is subtracted.**

• What are the equations of the asymptotes for the graphs of $f(x)$, $g(x)$, and $h(x)$? **$x = 0$ for f(x) and $x = 3$ for g(x) and h(x).**

• Which parameter, h or k, changes the domain of the function? Why? **h; because it causes the graph to shift horizontally**

• If you were finding values of $g(x)$ or $h(x)$ for an x-value less than 3.5 and an x-value greater than 11, which x-values would you use and why? **Sample answer: 3.25 and 19; because after 3 is subtracted from each, the value is an integer power of 2 (2^{-2} and 2^4).**

EXTRA EXAMPLE

The graph of $f(x) = \log_{\frac{1}{2}} x$ is shown. Graph $g(x) = \log_{\frac{1}{2}}(x + 4)$ and $h(x) = \log_{\frac{1}{2}} (x + 4) - 1$.

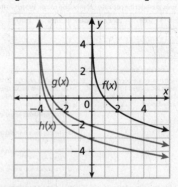

The graph of $g(x)$ is the graph of $f(x)$ shifted 4 units left, and the graph of $h(x)$ is the graph of $g(x)$ shifted 1 unit down.

Name_____ Class_____ Date_____

Transforming Exponential and Logarithmic Functions
Going Deeper

Essential question: *How does changing the values of a, h, and k affect the graph of*
$f(x) = a\log_b(x - h) + k$?

A general logarithmic function has the form $f(x) = a\log_b(x - h) + k$ where $b > 0$
($b \neq 1$) and a, h, and k are real numbers. The effect of changing the parameters a, h, and k in a logarithmic function is similar to the effect of changing these parameters in other types of functions.

Video Tutor

CC.9-12.F.BF.3
1 EXAMPLE Changing the Values of h and k

The graph of $f(x) = \log_2 x$ is shown. Graph $g(x) = \log_2(x - 3)$ and
$h(x) = \log_2(x - 3) + 2$.

A Complete the table of values.

x	g(x)	h(x)
3.5	−1	1
4	0	2
5	1	3
7	2	4
11	3	5

B Plots the points from your table.

C Use the points to help you sketch and label the graphs of g(x) and h(x).

REFLECT

1a. How does the graph of g(x) compare to the graph of f(x)?

The graph of g(x) is the graph of f(x) translated 3 units right.

1b. How does the graph of h(x) compare to the graph of f(x)?

The graph of h(x) is the graph of f(x) translated 3 units right and 2 units up.

1c. In general, how do you think the graph of $j(x) = \log_b(x - h) + k$ is related to the
graph of the parent function, $f(x) = \log_b(x)$?

The graph of j(x) is a translation of the graph of f(x) by |h| units to the right

when h > 0 or |h| units to the left when h < 0 and by |k| units up when k > 0 or

|k| units down when k < 0.

Chapter 4   239   Lesson 7

© Houghton Mifflin Harcourt Publishing Company

CC.9-12.F.BF.3
2 EXAMPLE Changing the Value of a

The graph of $f(x) = \log_{\frac{1}{3}} x$ is shown. Graph $g(x) = 2\log_{\frac{1}{3}} x$ and
$h(x) = -\frac{1}{2}\log_{\frac{1}{3}} x$.

A Complete the table of values.

x	g(x)	h(x)
1	0	0
2	−2	$\frac{1}{2}$
4	−4	1
8	−6	$\frac{3}{2}$

B Plots the points from your table.

C Use the points to help you sketch and label the graphs of g(x) and h(x).

REFLECT

2a. For $a > 0$, how do you think the value of a affects the graph of $j(x) = a\log_b x$?

The graph of j(x) is a vertical stretch of the graph of $f(x) = \log_b x$

by a factor of a when a > 1, and a vertical shrink of the graph of

$f(x) = \log_b x$ by a factor of a when 0 < a < 1.

2b. How does the value of a affect the graph of $j(x) = a\log_b x$ when $a < 0$?

In addition to the vertical stretch/shrink described above, the graph of

$f(x) = \log_b x$ is reflected across the x-axis.

2c. The graph of $j(x) = a\log_b x$ always has what point in common with the graph of
$f(x) = \log_b x$? Explain why.

(1, 0) because a vertical stretch/shrink and, possibly, a reflection in the x-axis

do not affect points on the x-axis.

2d. Without graphing, explain how the graph of $j(x) = 0.25\log_{\frac{1}{3}}(x + 6)$ would compare
to the graph of f(x). Discuss asymptotes, end behavior, and intercepts.

The graph of j(x) would be the graph of f(x) shrunk vertically by a factor of

0.25 and shifted 6 units to the left. The end behavior as x increases without

bound would not change, but the vertical asymptote would shift from x = 0 to

x = −6, and the x-intercept would change from 1 to −5.

Chapter 4   240   Lesson 7

© Houghton Mifflin Harcourt Publishing Company

Notes

Questioning Strategies

- How did the value of a affect the graphs of *exponential* functions? How does this compare with its effect on the graphs of logarithmic functions? **For exponential functions, it stretched the graph vertically by a factor of a for $a > 1$ and shrunk the graph vertically by a factor of a for $0 < a < 1$. The effect is the same for logarithmic functions.**

- Why does a negative value of a reflect the graph across the x-axis? **The y-values are opposites, so points above the x-axis are moved below the x-axis and vice versa.**

- What are the equations of the asymptotes for the graphs of $f(x)$, $g(x)$, and $h(x)$? **$x = 0$ for each.**

EXTRA EXAMPLE

The graph of $f(x) = \log_2 x$ is shown. Graph $g(x) = -3 \log_2 x$ and $h(x) = \frac{1}{4} \log_2 x$.

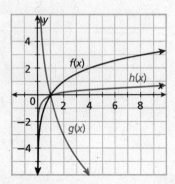

Relative to the graph of $f(x)$, the graph of $g(x)$ is vertically stretched by a factor of 3 and reflected across the x-axis, and the graph of $h(x)$ is shrunk vertically by a factor of $\frac{1}{4}$.

Teaching Strategy

Have students graph $j(x) = \frac{1}{2} \log_{\frac{1}{2}} x$ on the grid along with $g(x)$ and $h(x)$ so they can see that the graph of $j(x)$ is a reflection of the graph of $h(x)$ across the x-axis.

Questioning Strategies

- What other point could you use to find k? Explain. **(1, 0); the point moves to (−1, 0) after the translation to the left. It stays at (−1, 0) after the reflection, since it is on the x-axis. It then moves down to (−1, −1).**

- How do you know the value of a is −1? **The graph is a reflection across the x-axis, so the value of a must be negative. Since the graph is not vertically stretched or shrunk, the value of a must be −1.**

EXTRA EXAMPLE

The graph of $g(x)$ is the graph of $f(x) = \log_3 x$ after a horizontal translation and a vertical stretch. Write the equation of $g(x)$. $g(x) = 2 \log_3 (x - 3)$

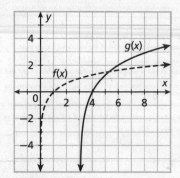

> **MATHEMATICAL PRACTICE** **Highlighting the Standards**
>
> 3 EXAMPLE addresses Mathematical Practice Standard 7 (Look for and make use of structure). Students should realize that a, h, and k affect the graph of the logarithmic function $f(x)$ in the same manner that they affect the other types of functions they studied earlier. Using this knowledge, students can write a function rule for $g(x)$.

Differentiated Instruction

Visual learners can use colored pencils to sketch each of the intermediate steps in obtaining the graph of $g(x)$ from the graph of $f(x)$: first the horizontal translation, then the reflection across the x-axis, and finally the vertical translation.

3 EXAMPLE CC.9-12.F.BF.3 Writing an Equation from a Graph

The graph of $g(x)$ is the graph of $f(x) = \log_{\frac{1}{4}} x$ after a horizontal translation, a reflection in the x-axis, and a vertical translation. Write the equation of $g(x)$.

A Let $g(x) = a \log_{\frac{1}{4}}(x - h) + k$. Find the value of h.

The vertical asymptote of $g(x)$ is the line $\underline{x = -2}$.

The vertical asymptote of the parent function $f(x)$ is $x = 0$. This means $f(x)$ is translated $\underline{\quad 2 \quad}$ units to the left and so $h = \underline{\quad -2 \quad}$.

B Find the value of a.

Since the graph of the parent function $f(x)$ is reflected across the x-axis, the sign of a is $\underline{\text{negative}}$. Since it was given that the transformation did not involve a stretch, $a = \underline{\quad -1 \quad}$.

C Find the value of k.

Consider the point $(4, -1)$ on the graph of $f(x)$ and the sequence of transformations that maps it to the corresponding point on the graph of $g(x)$.

The horizontal translation maps $(4, -1)$ to $(2, -1)$. Then the reflection across the x-axis maps $(2, -1)$ to $(2, 1)$. Finally, the vertical translation maps $(2, 1)$ to $(2, 0)$.

The final transformation is a translation of $\underline{\quad 1 \quad}$ unit(s) down, so $k = \underline{\quad -1 \quad}$.

D Write the equation.

Using the values of the parameters from above, $g(x) = \underline{-\log_{\frac{1}{4}}(x + 2) - 1}$.

REFLECT

3a. How can you use the x-intercept of the graph of $g(x)$ to check that you wrote a correct equation?

The x-intercept is 2. Check that the ordered pair $(2, 0)$ satisfies the equation.

$-\log_{\frac{1}{4}}(2 + 2) - 1 = -\log_{\frac{1}{4}} 4 - 1 = -(-1) - 1 = 1 - 1 = 0$

3b. Given the graph of a function $f(x) = ab^{x-h} + k$, which parameter $(a, h,$ or $k)$ is determined by the location of the graph's asymptote? Given the graph of a function $g(x) = a \log_b(x - h) + k$, which parameter $(a, h,$ or $k)$ is determined by the location of the graph's asymptote? Explain each of your answers.

k, because the parent function's graph has a horizontal asymptote that is affected only by a vertical translation, which k controls;

h, because the parent function's graph has a vertical asymptote that is affected only by a horizontal translation, which h controls.

PRACTICE

The graph of $f(x) = \log_3 x$ is shown. Write the function rules for $g(x)$ and $h(x)$ based on the descriptions given. Then sketch and label the graphs of $g(x)$ and $h(x)$ on the same coordinate plane.

1. The graph of $g(x)$ is the translation of the graph of $f(x)$ to the right 4 units and up 3 units.

$g(x) = \log_3(x - 4) + 3$

2. The graph of $h(x)$ is the reflection of the graph of $f(x)$ over the x-axis followed by a translation down 2 units

$h(x) = -\log_3 x - 2$

The graph of $f(x) = \log_{\frac{1}{3}} x$ is shown. Write the function rules for $g(x)$ and $h(x)$

based on the descriptions given. Then sketch and label the graphs of $g(x)$ and $h(x)$ on the same coordinate plane.

3. The graph of $g(x)$ is a vertical shrink of the graph of $f(x)$ by a factor of $\frac{1}{3}$ and a reflection across the x-axis.

$g(x) = -\frac{1}{3} \log_{\frac{1}{3}} x$

4. The graph of $h(x)$ is a vertical stretch of the graph of $f(x)$ by a factor of 2 and a translation 3 units up.

$h(x) = 2 \log_{\frac{1}{3}} x + 3$

Use the graphs of $f(x)$, $g(x)$, and $h(x)$ for Exercises 5 and 6.

5. The graph of $g(x)$ is the graph of $f(x) = \log_2 x$ after a vertical shrink and a horizontal translation. Write the equation of $g(x)$.

$g(x) = \frac{1}{2} \log_2(x + 4)$

6. The graph of $h(x)$ is the graph of $f(x) = \log_2 x$ after a horizontal translation, a reflection in the x-axis, and a vertical translation. Write the equation of $h(x)$.

$h(x) = -\log_2(x + 1) + 2$

Essential Question

How does changing the values of a, h, and k affect the graph of $f(x) = a \log_b (x - h) + k$*?*

The graph is stretched vertically for $|a| > 1$ and shrunk vertically for $0 < |a| < 1$. If a is negative, the graph is reflected across the *x*-axis as well. If h is positive, the graph is translated right, and if h is negative, it is translated left. If k is positive, the graph is translated up, and if k is negative, it is translated down.

Summarize

Have students create a table describing the effects of changing a, h, and k on the six types of functions they have studied so far. Students should list quadratic, polynomial, rational, radical, exponential, and logarithmic in that order. Students can revisit this table when they graph trigonometric functions.

Where skills are taught	Where skills are practiced
1 EXAMPLE	EX. 1
2 EXAMPLE	EXS. 2–4
3 EXAMPLE	EXS. 5, 6

Exercise 7: Students complete a table showing how changing the values of a, h, and k in $g(x) = a \log_b (x - h) + k$ affect the asymptote and the points $(1, 0)$ and $(b, 1)$ for the graph of the parent function $f(x) = \log_b x$.

Exercise 8: Students explore horizontal stretches and shrinks. They see how a horizontal stretch or shrink by a factor of $\frac{1}{c}$ has the same effect as a vertical translation by the logarithm of c.

7. The table below lists some characteristics of the graph of the function $f(x) = \log_b x$. Complete the table by listing the corresponding characteristics of the graph of $g(x) = a \log_b (x - h) + k$.

Function	Asymptote	Reference point 1	Reference point 2
$f(x) = \log_b x$	$x = 0$	$(1, 0)$	$(b, 1)$
$g(x) = a \log_b (x - h) + k$	$x = h$	$(1 + h, k)$	$(b + h, a + k)$

8. In this exercise, you will make a conjecture about horizontal stretches and shrinks of the graphs of logarithmic functions.

a. Let $f(x) = \log_2 8x$ and $g(x) = \log_2 x + 3$. Complete the table. Then graph $f(x)$ and $g(x)$ on the coordinate plane at right.

x	f(x)	g(x)
1	3	3
2	4	4
4	5	5
8	6	6

b. Describe the graphs of $f(x)$ and $g(x)$ as transformations of the parent base 2 logarithmic function.

The graph of $f(x)$ is a horizontal shrink by a factor of $\frac{1}{8}$;

The graph of $g(x)$ is a translation up 3 units.

c. Let $h(x) = \log_2 \frac{1}{2} x$ and $j(x) = \log_2 x - 1$. Complete the table. Then graph $h(x)$ and $j(x)$ on the coordinate plane at right.

x	h(x)	j(x)
1	−1	−1
2	0	0
4	1	1
8	2	2

Continued

d. Describe the graphs of $h(x)$ and $j(x)$ as transformations of the parent base 2 logarithmic function.

The graph of $h(x)$ is a horizontal stretch by a factor of 2;

The graph of $j(x)$ is a translation down 1 unit.

e. The rules for the functions $f(x)$ and $h(x)$ have the form $\log_2 cx$ while the rules for the functions $g(x)$ and $j(x)$ have the form $\log_2 x + k$. Write the values of k in $g(x)$ and $j(x)$ as logarithms with base 2.

$3 = \log_2 8$ and $-1 = \log_2 \frac{1}{2}$

f. Summarize the relationship between a horizontal stretch or horizontal shrink of the graph of a logarithmic function and a translation of the graph.

A horizontal stretch or shrink by a factor of $\frac{1}{c}$ is equivalent to a

vertical translation by k where $k = \log_b c$.

Assign these pages to help your students practice and apply important lesson concepts. For additional exercises, see the Student Edition.

Answers

Additional Practice

1.

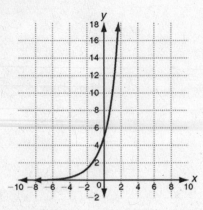

$y = 0$; it is the graph of $f(x) = 2^x$ stretched vertically by a factor of 5.

2.

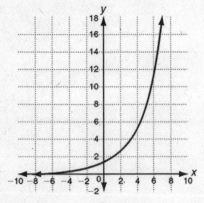

$y = 0$; it is the graph of $f(x) = 5^x$ stretched horizontally by a factor of 4.

3.

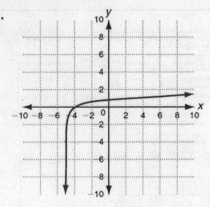

$x = -5$; it is the graph of $f(x) = \log x$ translated 5 units left.

4.

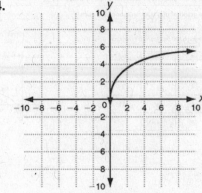

$x = 0$; it is the graph of $f(x) = \ln x$ translated 3 units up.

5. $g(x) = \log(-x + 1) - 4$

6. $g(x) = 2 \cdot 8^{5x - 3}$ 　　7. 8.7%

Problem Solving

1. **a.** About 3 ft tall

   b. About 0.45 ft; that is the initial height of the plant.

2. **a.** $g(t) = \ln t$

   b. The parent function is translated 1.25 units left and stretched vertically by a factor of 2.

   c. B

3. A 　　　　　　　4. H

Additional Practice

Graph each function. Find the asymptote. Tell how the graph is transformed from the graph of its parent function.

1. $f(x) = 5(2^x)$

2. $f(x) = 5^{\frac{x}{4}}$

_____

3. $f(x) = \log(x + 5)$

4. $f(x) = 3 + \ln x$

_____

Write each transformed function.

5. The function $f(x) = \log(x + 1)$ is reflected across the y-axis and translated down 4 units.

_____

6. The function $f(x) = -8^{x-3}$ is reflected across the x-axis, compressed horizontally by a factor of 0.2, and stretched vertically by a factor of 2.

_____

Solve.

7. The function $A(t) = Pe^{rt}$ can be used to calculate the growth of an investment in which the interest is compounded continuously at an annual rate, r, over t years. What annual rate would double an investment in 8 years?

_____

Problem Solving

Alex is studying a new species of hybrid plant. The average height of the plant can be modeled by the function $h(t) = 2 \ln(t + 1.25)$, where h is the height in feet and t is the number of weeks after planting.

1. Alex graphs the function to see the rate an average plant grows.

   a. About how tall can he expect the plant to be after 3 weeks?

   _____

   b. What is the y-intercept? What does it tell Alex about the plant?

   _____

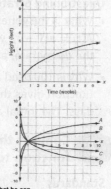

2. Alex plants seeds and finds that the height is now modeled by the parent function.

   a. Give the parent function $g(t)$. _____

   b. Describe how the function $h(t)$ is transformed from the parent function.

   _____

   c. Choose the letter of the graph that represents the parent function.

   _____

Alex experiments with different fertilizers and finds that he can change the growth curve of the hybrid plant. Choose the letter for the best answer.

3. Alex finds that the height of the plants can now be modeled by the function $f(t) = 1.5 \ln(t + 1) + 0.4$. Which statement describes the transformation from the parent function?

   A Translation 0.4 unit up and 1 unit left; vertical stretch by 1.5

   B Translation 1 unit up and 0.4 unit right; vertical stretch by 1.5

   C Translation 0.4 unit down and 1 unit left; horizontal stretch by 1.5

   D Translation 1 unit down and 0.4 unit right; horizontal stretch by 1.5

4. Alex looks at the graph of the growth of his plants after trying a different fertilizer. The graph is transformed from the parent function by a vertical compression by a factor of 0.5 and a translation 1 unit right. Which function describes this transformation?

   F $k(t) = 2 \ln(t + 1)$

   G $k(t) = 2 \ln(t - 1)$

   H $k(t) = 0.5 \ln(t - 1)$

   J $k(t) = 0.5 \ln(t + 1)$

Curve Fitting with Exponential and Logarithmic Models
Focus on Modeling

Essential question: *How can you model the time it takes a radioactive substance to decay as a function of the percent of the substance remaining?*

COMMON CORE Standards for Mathematical Content

The following standards are addressed in this lesson. (An asterisk indicates that a standard is also a Modeling standard.) For more detailed information, see each section of the lesson.

Algebra: CC.9-12.A.CED.2*, CC.9-12.A.CED.4*

Functions: CC.9-12.F.IF.2, CC.9-12.F.IF.4*, CC.9-12.F.BF.1*, CC.9-12.F.BF.1a*

Prerequisites

- Exponential decay functions
- Using the definition of a logarithm
- Using properties of logarithms

Math Background

In this lesson, students write and interpret exponential and logarithmic functions that model the half-life of a radioactive isotope. They use their knowledge from previous lessons to model the radioactive decay with an exponential decay function and then convert that function to a logarithmic function. Students then use the Change of Base Property, as well as other properties, to convert the function to one involving a common logarithm that can be analyzed using a graphing calculator.

INTRODUCE

All living things contain carbon-14. When a plant or animal dies, the carbon-14 in it begins to decay, or change to another substance. The process is very slow. It takes 5730 years for just half of it to decay, then another 5730 years for half of the remaining amount to decay, and so on. By using a method similar to the one in this lesson, scientists can determine the amount of carbon-14 in a fossil and can use that amount to determine its age.

TEACH

1 **Model radioactive decay with an exponential function.**

Standards

CC.9-12.A.CED.2 Create equations in two ... variables to represent relationships between quantities ...*

CC.9-12.F.IF.2 Use function notation, evaluate functions for inputs in their domains, and interpret statements that use function notation in terms of a context.

CC.9-12.F.IF.4 For a function that models a relationship between two quantities, interpret key features of ... tables in terms of the quantities, ...*

CC.9-12.F.BF.1 Write a function that describes a relationship between two quantities.*

CC.9-12.F.BF.1a Determine an explicit expression ... from a context.*

Questioning Strategies

- What is the general exponential decay function? $A(t) = a(1 - r)^t$ where a is the initial amount, r is the decay rate, and t is a number of time periods

- Why is 100 used as the initial amount? The function gives the percent remaining after t days. The initial amount on day 0 was 100%.

2 **Convert the exponential decay function to a logarithmic function.**

Standards

CC.9-12.A.CED.4 Rearrange formulas to highlight a quantity of interest, using the same reasoning as in solving equations.*

CC.9-12.F.IF.2 Use function notation, evaluate functions for inputs in their domains, and interpret statements that use function notation in terms of a context.

continued

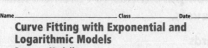

Name_____ Class_____ Date_____

Curve Fitting with Exponential and Logarithmic Models
Focus on Modeling

4-8

Video Tutor

Essential question: *How can you model the time it takes a radioactive substance to decay as a function of the percent of the substance remaining?*

Radioactive substances decay to other substances over time. The half-life of a radioactive substance is the time it takes for one-half of the substance to decay. How can you determine the length of time it takes a given radioactive substance to decay to a specified percent?

1 Model radioactive decay with an exponential function.

A   The isotope bismuth-210 has a half-life of 5 days. Complete the table showing the decay of a sample of bismuth-210.

Number of Half-Lives	Number of Days (t)	Percent of Isotope Remaining (p)
0	0	100
1	5	50
2	10	25
3	15	12.5
4	20	6.25

B   Write the decay rate r as a fraction. ____ $r = \frac{1}{2}$

C   Write an expression for the number of half-lives in t days. ____ $\frac{t}{5}$

D   Write an exponential decay function that models this situation. The function $p(t)$ should give the percent of the isotope remaining after t days.

$$p(t) = 100\left(\frac{1}{2}\right)^{\frac{t}{5}}$$

REFLECT

1a. Show how to check that your model is correct by letting $t = 10$ and comparing the resulting value of $p(t)$ to the value in the table.

When $t = 10$, $p(t) = 100\left(\frac{1}{2}\right)^{\frac{10}{5}} = 100\left(\frac{1}{2}\right)^{2} = 100\left(\frac{1}{4}\right) = 25$, which matches

the percent in the table.

Chapter 4   247   Lesson 8

© Houghton Mifflin Harcourt Publishing Company

1b. Find $p(t)$ when $t = 0$, 1, and 8. Explain what these values represent.

$p(0) = 100$; after 0 days, 100% remains. $p(1) \approx 87$; after 1 day,

about 87% remains. $p(8) \approx 33$; after 8 days, about 33% remains.

1c. Every 5 days, the amount of bismuth-210 decreases by 50%. By what percent does the amount of bismuth-210 decrease *each day*? Explain.

About 13%; $p(t) = 100\left(\frac{1}{2}\right)^{\frac{t}{5}} = 100\left(\frac{1}{2}\right)^{\frac{1}{5} \cdot t} \approx 100(0.87)^{t}$ where t is the number of

days. This shows that the decay factor is approximately 0.87, so the decay rate

is approximately 0.13 or 13% per day.

1d. Describe the end behavior of $p(t)$ as t increases without bound.

As t increases without bound, $p(t)$ approaches 0.

2 Convert the exponential decay function to a logarithmic function.

A   The function $p(t) = 100\left(\frac{1}{2}\right)^{\frac{t}{5}}$ gives the percent of bismuth-210 that remains after t days. Describe the domain and range of this function.

The domain is the number of days that have passed ($t \geq 0$). The range is the

percent of bismuth-210 ($0 < p(t) \leq 100$) remaining after t days.

B   Write the inverse of the decay function by solving for t. Use p in place of $p(t)$.

$p = 100\left(\frac{1}{2}\right)^{\frac{t}{5}}$ Given

$\frac{p}{100} = \left(\frac{1}{2}\right)^{\frac{t}{5}}$ Divide both sides by 100.

$\log_{\frac{1}{2}}\left(\frac{p}{100}\right) = \frac{t}{5}$ Definition of logarithm

$5\log_{\frac{1}{2}}\left(\frac{p}{100}\right) = t$ Multiply both sides by 5.

REFLECT

2a. Describe the domain and range of the logarithmic function.

The domain is the percent of bismuth-210 ($0 < p \leq 100$) remaining after t days.

The range is the number of days ($t(p) \geq 0$) needed to reach that percent.

2b. Verify that the logarithmic model is correct by substituting 50 for p. What is the resulting value of t? Explain why this result makes sense.

$t = 5\log_{\frac{1}{2}}\left(\frac{50}{100}\right) = 5\log_{\frac{1}{2}}\left(\frac{1}{2}\right) = 5 \cdot 1 = 5$. This result makes sense because when

$p = 50$, 50% of the bismuth-210 remains, and $t = 5$ means 5 days have passed,

which is the correct half-life.

© Houghton Mifflin Harcourt Publishing Company

Chapter 4   248   Lesson 8

Notes

Chapter 4   248   Lesson 8

2 continued

Questioning Strategies

• Can *p* equal 0? Explain. No; the remaining percent gets close to 0 but never reaches it.

• In part A, is the domain a discrete or continuous set? Explain. Continuous; you can find the percent for any number of days, including fractional parts of a day.

3 Convert to a common logarithm.

Standards
CC.9-12.A.CED.4 Rearrange formulas ...*

CC.9-12.F.IF.2 Use function notation ...

Questioning Strategies
• What is the benefit of using the common logarithm instead of the natural logarithm? In step 3B, it allows you to evaluate log 100 as 2.

• Without using a calculator, how can you tell that $t = 33.22 - 16.61 \log p$ results in 0 for $p = 100$? log 100 = 2, and 2(−16.61) is −33.22, the opposite of 33.22.

Technology
Have students graph both the exponential and the logarithmic functions from this lesson, as well as the line $y = x$, on their calculators. They should see that the graphs of the functions are reflections across the line, so the functions are inverses of one another.

4 Compare times to reach certain levels.

Standards
CC.9-12.F.IF.2 ... evaluate functions for inputs in their domains, and interpret statements ... in terms of a context.

CC.9-12.F.IF.4 For a function that models a relationship between two quantities, interpret key features of ... tables in terms of the quantities, ...*

Questioning Strategies
• Based only on the rule for the function, should the function's graph rise or fall from left to right? Why? Fall; the function has the form $g(x) = a \log x + k$ where the value of *a* is negative, so when the graph of the parent function $f(x) = \log x$, which rises, is reflected over the *x*-axis, the graph falls.

• When you move down the table, how are you moving along the graph? from right to left (toward the *y*-axis)

CLOSE

Essential Question
How can you model the time it takes a radioactive substance to decay as a function of the percent of the substance remaining?
First, write the exponential function that gives the percent of the substance remaining after *t* days. Then, find the inverse of this function and convert the inverse to a logarithmic function with base 10.

Summarize
In their journals, have students repeat parts 1–3 to write a function for carbon-14, which has a half-life of 5730 years. In this function, *t* will represent years, not days. $t = 38069 - 19035 \log p$

EXTEND

CC.9-12.A.CED.2 Create equations in two ... variables to represent relationships between quantities ...* (Ex. 1)

CC.9-12.F.BF.1 Write a function that describes a relationship between two quantities.* (Ex. 1)

CC.9-12.F.BF.1a Determine an explicit expression ... from a context.* (Ex. 1)

CC.9-12.F.IF.2 ... evaluate functions for inputs in their domains, and interpret statements ... in terms of a context. (Ex. 2)

3 Convert to a common logarithm.

A Rewrite your logarithmic function with a common logarithm. Where appropriate, round to two decimal places.

$t = 5 \log_{\frac{1}{2}}\left(\frac{p}{100}\right)$ Given

$= 5 \cdot \dfrac{\log \frac{p}{100}}{\log \frac{1}{2}}$ Change of Base Property

$= \dfrac{5}{\log \frac{1}{2}} \cdot \log \frac{p}{100}$ Write the denominator as part of the first factor.

$\doteq -16.61 \log \frac{p}{100}$ Evaluate the first factor. Round to two decimal places.

B Write the function without a fraction.

$t = -16.61 \left(\log\; p\; -\; \log\; 100\right)$ Quotient Property of Logarithms

$= -16.61 \left(\log\; p\; -\; 2\;\right)$ Evaluate log 100.

$= -16.61 \log\; p\; +\; 33.22$ Distributive Property

$= 33.22 - 16.61 \log\; p$ Commutative Property of Addition

REFLECT

3a. What is the benefit of rewriting the function so that it involves a common logarithm?

It is easier to evaluate the expression for a given value of p using a calculator

when the logarithm is a common logarithm.

3b. The final form of the logarithmic function includes rounded numbers. Check the accuracy of the function by substituting 50 for p and evaluating the expression with your calculator. Do you get the expected result? Explain.

Substituting 50 for p gives $t \approx 5.000108$, which is very close to the exact

value of 5.

3c. Explain how you can find out how long it takes until 5% of the bismuth-210 remains. Round to the nearest tenth of a day.

Substitute 5 for p in the logarithmic function. This gives $t \approx 21.6$, so it takes

about 21.6 days until 5% of the bismuth-210 remains.

3d. To emphasize that t is a function of p, write the equation of the logarithmic function using function notation.

$t(p) = 33.22 - 16.61 \log p$

4 Compare times to reach certain levels.

You can use your calculator, as follows, to compare the amounts of time it takes the percent of bismuth-210 to drop from 100% to 75%, from 75% to 50%, and from 50% to 25%.

A Enter the logarithmic function from step 3 into the equation editor of your graphing calculator.

B Press `2nd` `WINDOW`. Then set the TblStart value at 100 and the $\triangle$Tbl value to −25.

C Look at the table of values. How many days does it take for the percent to drop from 100% to 75%? from 75% to 50%? from 50% to 25%?

It takes about 2 days to drop from 100% to 75%, about 3 days to drop from

75% to 50%, and 5 days to drop from 50% to 25%.

REFLECT

4a. Why is there an ERROR message in the table in the row corresponding to the value $x = 0$?

In the model, the percent of bismuth-210 that remains never reaches 0.

4b. Make a conjecture about how the amount of time it takes for bismuth-210 to drop from 70% to 60% compares to the amount of time it takes to drop from 20% to 10%. Then check your conjecture using a graphing calculator.

Possible conjecture: The time to drop from 70% to 60% will be shorter than

the time to drop from 20% to 10%. Actual times: about 1.1 days; 5 days.

EXTEND

1. As a sample of bismuth-210 decays, the sample is transformed into a mixture of bismuth-210 and other isotopes in its decay chain. The time needed for the amount of the other isotopes to reach a certain percent of the sample can be obtained from the logarithmic model for bismuth-210 by replacing p in the function's rule. Write a function that gives the time t needed for the amount of the other isotopes to reach p percent of the sample. (*Hint:* Consider how the percent of bismuth-210 and the percent of the other isotopes are related.)

$t = 33.22 - 16.61 \log (100 - p)$

2. Use the function you wrote in Exercise 1 to determine the time needed for the other isotopes to reach 75% of the sample amount. Explain why your result makes sense.

10 days; this makes sense because it takes 10 days for bismuth-210 to decay

to the point where 25% of the isotope is remaining. At that point, the other

isotopes have reached 75% of the sample amount.

Notes

ADDITIONAL PRACTICE AND PROBLEM SOLVING

Assign these pages to help your students practice and apply important lesson concepts. For additional exercises, see the Student Edition.

Answers

Additional Practice

1. No
2. Yes; 6

3. Yes; 3
4. No

5. $f(x) = 29(0.49)^x$
6. $f(x) = 3.8(1.15)^x$

7. **a.** $f(x) = 0.97(1.16)^x$

b. 15 cm

c. $367.36

8. **a.** $f(x) = 1.14 + 8.42 \ln x$

b. 9.4 s

c. 35.6 m/s

Problem Solving

1. **a.** $W(t) = 47.34(1.13)^t$

b. 2016

2. **a.** $T(t) = 1809.17 - 510.69 \ln t$

b. 2009

3. C
4. G

5. D
6. F

Additional Practice

Determine whether f is an exponential function of x. If so, find the constant ratio.

1.

x	−1	0	1	2	3
f(x)	9	3	1	0.3	0.9

2.

x	−1	0	1	2	3
f(x)	0.01	0.03	0.15	0.87	5.19

3.

x	−1	0	1	2	3
f(x)	$\frac{5}{6}$	$\frac{5}{2}$	7.5	22.5	67.5

4.

x	−1	0	1	2	3
f(x)	1	0.5	0.33	0.25	0.2

Use exponential regression to find a function that models the data.

5.

x	1	2	3	4	5
f(x)	14	7.1	3.4	1.8	0.8

6.

x	2	12	22	32	42
f(x)	5	20	80	320	1280

Solve.

7. a. Bernice is selling seashells she has found at the beach. The price of each shell depends on its length. Find an exponential model for the data.

Length of Shell (cm)	5	8	12	20	25
Price ($)	2	3.5	5	18	40

b. What is the length of a shell selling for $9.00? _____

c. If Bernice found a 40 cm Conch shell. How much could she sell it for? _____

8. a. Use logarithmic regression to find a function that models this data.

Time (min)	1	2	3	4	5
Speed (m/s)	1.5	6.2	10.6	12.9	14.8

b. When will the speed exceed 20 m/s? _____

c. What will the speed be after 1 hour? _____

Problem Solving

1. A small group of farmers joined together to grow and sell wheat in 1985. The table shows how their production of wheat increased over 20 years.

Wheat Produced by Growers Co-op						
Years After 1985	3	6	10	13	16	20
Wheat (tons)	70	105	150	210	340	580

a. Find an exponential model for the data. _____

b. Use the model to predict when their wheat production will exceed 2000 tons. _____

2. The table shows the U.S. production of tobacco from 1997 to 2002.

Tobacco Production						
Years After 1996	1	2	3	4	5	6
Tobacco (× 100,000 pounds)	1787	1480	1293	1053	992	890

a. Find a logarithmic model for the data. _____

b. Use the model to predict when tobacco production could fall below 50,000,000 pounds. _____

Robert recently discovered a forgotten student loan bill. The amount due after 10 years is now $10,819.33. He found some old statements and determined that after 7 years the bill was $8831.80 and after 5 years he owed $7714.03. Choose the letter for the best answer.

3. Which function models the data?

A $S(x) = 5000(1.07)^x$

B $S(x) = 1.07(5000)^x$

C $S(x) = 5500(1.07)^x$

D $S(x) = 1.07(5500)^x$

4. How much did Robert borrow initially?

F $5750

G $5500

H $5250

J $5000

5. Robert is planning to pay the loan in full next year. How much will he owe then?

A $12,092.14

B $11,925.07

C $11,869.33

D $11,576.69

6. What is the interest rate on Robert's student loan?

F 7%

G 6%

H 5%

J 4%

This page provides students with the opportunity to apply concepts from the Common Core in real-world problem situations. There are three different levels of performance tasks:

⭐ **Novice:** These are short word problems that require students to apply the math they have learned in straightforward, real-world situations.

⭐⭐ **Apprentice:** These are more involved problems that guide students step-by-step through more complex tasks. These exercises include more complicated reasoning, writing, and open-ended elements.

⭐⭐⭐ **Expert:** These are open-ended, non-routine problems that, instead of stepping the students through, ask them to choose their own methods for solving and justify their answers and reasoning.

Sample answers

1. $C(t) = 15(1 + 0.02)^t$
$C(10) = 15(1 + 0.02)^{10} \approx \$18.28$

2. 253 years

3. Scoring Guide:

Task	Possible points
a	1 point for the formula $\log\left(\frac{A}{P}\right) = nt \log\left(1 + \frac{r}{n}\right)$, and 1 point for showing appropriate work
b	3 points for correctly finding the formula $n\left(10^{\frac{1}{nt}\log\left(\frac{A}{P}\right)} - 1\right) = r$ OR equivalent
c	1 point for the correct interest rate of about 0.0375 or 3.75%

Total possible points: 6

CHAPTER 4

Performance Tasks

COMMON CORE

CC-9-12.A.CED.2
CC-9-12.A.CED.4
CC-9-12.F.IF.4
CC-9-12.F.BF.5
CC-9-12.F.LE.5

⭐ **1.** Ten years ago, a printing company charged $15 to produce 100 ten-page brochures. Every year, the cost increased by 2%. Write an exponential function to model the cost increases and use the function to find the cost of 100 ten-page brochures today.

⭐ **2.** A smoke detector contains a small amount of the radioactive element americium-241. How long will it take for one-third of the americium-241 to decay if its half-life is 432.2 years? Round your answer to the nearest whole year.

⭐⭐ **3.** Aaron invested $4000 in an account that paid an interest rate r compounded quarterly. After 10 years he has $5809.81. The compound interest formula is $A = P\left(1 + \frac{r}{n}\right)^{nt}$, where P is the principal (the initial investment), A is the total amount of money (principal plus interest), r is the annual interest rate, t is the time in years, and n is the number of compounding periods per year.

   a. Divide both sides of the formula by P and then use logarithms to rewrite the formula without an exponent. Show your work.

   b. Using your answer for part **a** as a starting point, solve the compound interest formula for the interest rate, r.

   c. Use your equation from part **a** to determine the interest rate.

continued

⭐⭐⭐ **4.** The spread of a virus can be modeled by exponential growth, but its growth is limited by the number of individuals that can be infected. For such situations, the function $P(t) = \frac{Kpe^{rt}}{K + p(e^{rt} - 1)}$ can be used, where $P(t)$ is the infected population t days after the first infection, p is the initial infected population, K is the total population that can be infected, and r is the rate the virus spreads, written as a decimal.

   a. A town of 10,000 people starts with 2 infected people and a virus growth rate of 20%. When will the growth of the infected population start to level off, and how many people will be infected at that point? Explain your reasoning, and include any graphs you draw, with or without technology.

   b. When will the infected population equal the uninfected population?

---

4. Scoring Guide:

Task	Possible points
a	1 point for noting that the population growth levels off at $t \approx 60$ days, and 1 point for noting that the infected population at that point is about 9700. 2 points for an appropriate explanation with or without a graph:
b	1 point for finding that the uninfected population and the infected population will both be 5000 when the graphs of the two functions intersect at about $t = 43$, and 1 point for an explanation involving algebra or a graph.

Total possible points: 4

COMMON CORE CORRELATION

Standard	Items
CC.9-12.A.CED.1*	6, 11
CC.9-12.A.CED.2*	9
CC.9-12.A.REI.11*	5, 11, 14
CC.9-12.F.IF.2	1
CC.9-12.F.IF.4*	10
CC.9-12.F.IF.7e*	7, 15
CC.9-12.F.BF.1*	9
CC.9-12.F.BF.3	4, 13
CC.9-12.F.BF.4a	8
CC.9-12.F.BF.5(+)	3, 15
CC.9-12.F.LE.3	12
CC.9-12.F.LE.4*	2

TEST PREP DOCTOR ⊕

Multiple Choice: Item 1
- Students who chose **B** remembered that a negative exponent gives the reciprocal of the base, but thought they should also take the reciprocal of the exponent.
- Students who chose **D** may have thought that the base is $\frac{1}{3}$.

Multiple Choice: Item 2
- Students who chose **F** took the square root of 319.
- Students who chose **G** multiplied both sides of the equation by 2 after using the Power Property of Logarithms.
- Students who chose **J** wrote 2 log 10 as log 20.

Multiple Choice: Item 4
- Students who chose **G** or **J** thought that adding a positive value to x translates the graph to the right, when in fact subtracting a positive value from x does so. They may have mixed up the rules for h and k.
- Students who chose **H** or **J** thought that $|a| > 1$ represents a compression. They may have mixed up the rules for vertical and horizontal compressions.

Multiple Choice: Item 5
- Students who chose **C** chose the y-coordinate of the point of intersection.
- Students who chose **D** may have used the common logarithm instead of the natural logarithm.

Multiple Choice: Item 6
- Students who chose **F** or **J** used a logarithmic expression for calculating compound interest instead of an exponential expression.
- Students who chose **H** identified the equation that could be used if the interest was compounded annually rather than continuously.

Multiple Choice: Item 10
- Students who chose **F** may have used 4.5 or the product of 4.5 and 0.5 for the value of b.
- Students who chose **G** or **J** may have forgotten that multiplying x by a negative number reflects the graph across the y-axis, reversing its end behavior.

Constructed Response: Item 13
- Students may answer $g(x) = -\log_{\frac{1}{3}} x - 2$ by counting the number of units between $(3, -1)$ and $(3, -3)$, forgetting that the point was first reflected to $(3, 1)$.

Constructed Response: Item 14
- Students who answered 0.05 did not enclose the exponent in each function in parentheses on their graphing calculators. They ended up graphing $y = 5^x + 2$ and $y = 64x$.

Name _____ Class _____ Date _____

MULTIPLE CHOICE

1. If $f(x) = \log_5 x$, what is $f\left(\frac{1}{5}\right)$?

  A. −2   **C.** $\frac{1}{2}$

  B. $-\frac{1}{2}$ **D.** 2

2. Which is the solution of $10^{2x} = 319$?

  F. log 17.86   **H.** $\frac{\log 319}{2}$

  G. 2 log 319   **J.** $\frac{\log 319}{\log 20}$

3. Which equation has the same solution as $\log_5 (x + 7) = 5$?

  A. $4^{x+7} = 5$ **C.** $5^{x+7} = 4$

  B. $4^5 = x + 7$ **D.** $5^4 = x + 7$

4. The graph of $g(x)$ is the graph of $f(x) = \log x$ translated 6 units to the right and compressed vertically by a factor of $\frac{1}{4}$. Which is the equation of $g(x)$?

  F. $g(x) = \frac{1}{4} \log (x - 6)$

  G. $g(x) = \frac{1}{4} \log (x + 6)$

  H. $g(x) = 4 \log (x - 6)$

  J. $g(x) = 4 \log (x + 6)$

5. Miguel and Dee determined slightly different equations to model the recommended chair seat height, in inches, for children x years old.

  Miguel: $y = 4.37 \ln x + 5.52$

  Dee: $y = 4.52 \ln x + 5.35$

  For what age do the two models give the same chair seat height?

  A. about 3.1 years old

  B. about 5.0 years old

  C. about 10.5 years old

  D. about 12.6 years old

6. Latrell wants to double an investment of $3500 that earns interest at an annual rate of 6% compounded continuously. Which equation can he solve to find the doubling time t for this investment?

  F. $7000 = 3500 \ln 0.06t$

  G. $7000 = 3500 e^{0.06t}$

  H. $7000 = 3500(1.06)^t$

  J. $7000 = 3500 \log_{1.06} t$

7. Alicia graphed an exponential function that has a y-intercept of 3. Which of the following functions could she have graphed?

  A. $g(x) = 5^{x-3}$ **C.** $g(x) = 5^x + 3$

  B. $g(x) = 3(5)^x$ **D.** $g(x) = 5^{3x}$

8. What is the inverse of $f(x) = 2x + 9$?

  F. $f^{-1}(x) = \frac{x}{2} - 9$

  G. $f^{-1}(x) = \frac{1}{2x + 9}$

  H. $f^{-1}(x) = \frac{x - 9}{2}$

  J. $f^{-1}(x) = \frac{2}{x - 9}$

9. An initial population of 900 frogs decreases at a rate of 14% per year. Which function gives the population after x years?

  A. $f(x) = 900(1.14)^x$

  B. $f(x) = 900(0.86)^x$

  C. $f(x) = 900(0.14)^x$

  D. $f(x) = 900 - 0.86^x$

10. The graph of $f(x)$ decreases as x decreases and increases as x increases. Which of these could be the function described?

  F. $f(x) = 4.5(0.5)^x$ **H.** $h(x) = 4.5^{0.5x}$

  G. $g(x) = 4.5^{-2x}$ **J.** $j(x) = 4.5^{-0.5x}$

© Houghton Mifflin Harcourt Publishing Company

CONSTRUCTED RESPONSE

11. Ron invests $1200 at 4.5% compounded continuously and Dina invests $1500 at 3% compounded continuously. When will they have the same amount in their accounts?

  A. about 7 years   **C.** about 14 years

  B. about 8 years   **D.** about 15 years

12. As x increases without bound, the graph of which function rises at the fastest rate?

  F. $f(x) = 3^x$

  G. $g(x) = 3x^2$

  H. $h(x) = 5x + 30$

  J. $j(x) = x^4 + 1$

13. The graph of $g(x)$ is a reflection in the x-axis and a vertical translation of the graph of $f(x) = \log_\frac{1}{3} x$. Write the equation of $g(x)$.

$g(x) = -\log_\frac{1}{3} x - 4$

14. Explain how you can solve the exponential equation $5^{x+2} = 4^{3x}$ using your graphing calculator. Then give the approximate solution to two decimal places.

Graph $y = 5^{x+2}$ and $y = 4^{3x}$ in the

same viewing window. Use the

calculator's Intersect tool to find

the x-coordinate of the point of

intersection of the graphs.

The approximate solution is $x = 1.26$.

15. Consider the function $f(x) = \log_5 x$.

  a. Complete the table.

x	$f(x)$
$\frac{1}{5}$	−1
1	0
5	1
25	2

  b. Sketch the graph of $f(x)$.

  c. Give the equation of any asymptote for the graph of $f(x)$.

    $x = 0$

  d. The function $g(x)$ is the inverse of $f(x)$. Write the equation for $g(x)$.

    $g(x) = 5^x$

  e. Name three points on the graph of $g(x)$ and tell how you can determine them by looking at the table or graph of $f(x)$.

    $(-1, \frac{1}{5})$, (0, 1), (2, 25); $g(x)$ and $f(x)$

    are inverses, so x- and y-values are

    switched.

  f. The graph of $g(x)$ is the reflection of the graph of $f(x)$ across what line?

    $y = x$

© Houghton Mifflin Harcourt Publishing Company

CHAPTER 5

Rational and Radical Functions

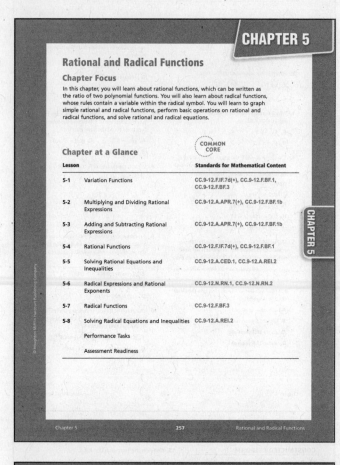

Rational and Radical Functions

CHAPTER 5

Chapter Focus

In this chapter, you will learn about rational functions, which can be written as the ratio of two polynomial functions. You will also learn about radical functions, whose rules contain a variable within the radical symbol. You will learn to graph simple rational and radical functions, perform basic operations on rational and radical functions, and solve rational and radical equations.

Chapter at a Glance

COMMON CORE

Lesson		Standards for Mathematical Content
5-1	Variation Functions	CC.9-12.F.IF.7d(+), CC.9-12.F.BF.1, CC.9-12.F.BF.3
5-2	Multiplying and Dividing Rational Expressions	CC.9-12.A.APR.7(+), CC.9-12.F.BF.1b
5-3	Adding and Subtracting Rational Expressions	CC.9-12.A.APR.7(+), CC.9-12.F.BF.1b
5-4	Rational Functions	CC.9-12.F.IF.7d(+), CC.9-12.F.BF.1
5-5	Solving Rational Equations and Inequalities	CC.9-12.A.CED.1, CC.9-12.A.REI.2
5-6	Radical Expressions and Rational Exponents	CC.9-12.N.RN.1, CC.9-12.N.RN.2
5-7	Radical Functions	CC.9-12.F.BF.3
5-8	Solving Radical Equations and Inequalities	CC.9-12.A.REI.2
	Performance Tasks	
	Assessment Readiness	

CHAPTER 5

Chapter 5   257   Rational and Radical Functions

COMMON CORE
PROFESSIONAL
DEVELOPMENT **CC.9-12.N.RN.2**

Students have extended the properties of integer exponents to define the meaning of rational exponents, leading to the notation for radicals in terms of rational exponents. They understand that $5^{\frac{1}{3}} = \sqrt[3]{5}$ because $\left[5^{\frac{1}{3}}\right]^3 = 5$. Students will take this concept further and rewrite expressions involving radicals and rational exponents.

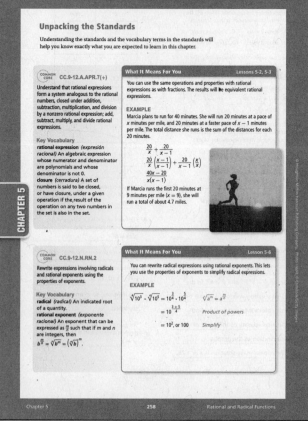

Unpacking the Standards

Understanding the standards and the vocabulary terms in the standards will help you know exactly what you are expected to learn in this chapter.

COMMON CORE **CC.9-12.A.APR.7(+)**

Understand that rational expressions form a system analogous to the rational numbers, closed under addition, subtraction, multiplication, and division by a nonzero rational expression; add, subtract, multiply, and divide rational expressions.

Key Vocabulary
rational expression *(expresión racional)* An algebraic expression whose numerator and denominator are polynomials and whose denominator is not 0.
closure *(cerradura)* A set of numbers is said to be closed, or have closure, under a given operation if the result of the operation on any two numbers in the set is also in the set.

What It Means For You   Lessons 5-2, 5-3

You can use the same operations and properties with rational expressions as with fractions. The results will be equivalent rational expressions.

EXAMPLE
Marcia plans to run for 40 minutes. She will run 20 minutes at a pace of x minutes per mile, and 20 minutes at a faster pace of $x - 1$ minutes per mile. The total distance she runs is the sum of the distances for each 20 minutes.

$$\frac{20}{x} + \frac{20}{x-1}$$
$$\frac{20}{x}\left(\frac{x-1}{x-1}\right) + \frac{20}{x-1}\left(\frac{x}{x}\right)$$
$$\frac{40x - 20}{x(x-1)}$$

If Marcia runs the first 20 minutes at 9 minutes per mile ($x = 9$), she will run a total of about 4.7 miles.

CHAPTER 5

COMMON CORE **CC.9-12.N.RN.2**

Rewrite expressions involving radicals and rational exponents using the properties of exponents.

Key Vocabulary
radical *(radical)* An indicated root of a quantity.
rational exponent *(exponente racional)* An exponent that can be expressed as $\frac{m}{n}$ such that if m and n are integers, then $b^{\frac{m}{n}} = \sqrt[n]{b^m} = \left(\sqrt[n]{b}\right)^m$.

What It Means For You   Lesson 5-6

You can rewrite radical expressions using rational exponents. This lets you use the properties of exponents to simplify radical expressions.

EXAMPLE

$$\sqrt[4]{10^3} \cdot \sqrt[4]{10^5} = 10^{\frac{3}{4}} \cdot 10^{\frac{5}{4}} \qquad \sqrt[n]{a^m} = a^{\frac{m}{n}}$$
$$= 10^{\frac{3+5}{4}} \qquad \textit{Product of powers}$$
$$= 10^2, \text{ or } 100 \qquad \textit{Simplify}$$

Chapter 5   258   Rational and Radical Functions

CC.9-12.F.IF.7*

Students have graphed linear, quadratic, and polynomial functions and identified the characteristics of the graphs such as zeros, intercepts, and end behavior. They will extend this knowledge to graphing a rational function and identifying characteristics of the graph. They will also need to use previously developed concepts of domain and range of rational functions.

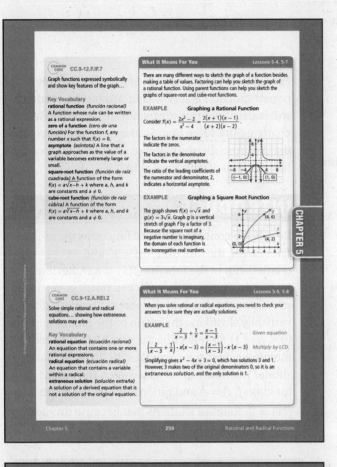

CC.9-12.F.IF.7

Graph functions expressed symbolically and show key features of the graph…

Key Vocabulary

rational function *(función racional)* A function whose rule can be written as a rational expression.

zero of a function *(cero de una función)* For the function f, any number x such that $f(x) = 0$.

asymptote *(asíntota)* A line that a graph approaches the value of a variable becomes extremely large or small.

square-root function *(función de raíz cuadrada)* A function of the form $f(x) = a\sqrt{x - h} + k$ where a, h, and k are constants and $a \neq 0$.

cube-root function *(función de raíz cúbica)* A function of the form $f(x) = a\sqrt[3]{x - h} + k$ where a, h, and k are constants and $a \neq 0$.

What It Means For You
Lessons 5-4, 5-7

There are many different ways to sketch the graph of a function besides making a table of values. Factoring can help you sketch the graph of a rational function. Using parent functions can help you sketch the graphs of square-root and cube-root functions.

EXAMPLE   **Graphing a Rational Function**

Consider $f(x) = \dfrac{2x^2 - 2}{x^2 - 4} = \dfrac{2(x+1)(x-1)}{(x+2)(x-2)}$.

The factors in the numerator indicate the zeros.

The factors in the denominator indicate the vertical asymptotes.

The ratio of the leading coefficients of the numerator and denominator, 2, indicates a horizontal asymptote.

EXAMPLE   **Graphing a Square Root Function**

The graph shows $f(x) = \sqrt{x}$ and $g(x) = 3\sqrt{x}$. Graph g is a vertical stretch of graph f by a factor of 3. Because the square root of a negative number is imaginary, the domain of each function is the nonnegative real numbers.

CC.9-12.A.REI.2

Solve simple rational and radical equations… showing how extraneous solutions may arise.

Key Vocabulary

rational equation *(ecuación racional)* An equation that contains one or more rational expressions.

radical equation *(ecuación radical)* An equation that contains a variable within a radical.

extraneous solution *(solución extraña)* A solution of a derived equation that is not a solution of the original equation.

What It Means For You
Lessons 5-5, 5-8

When you solve rational or radical equations, you need to check your answers to be sure they are actually solutions.

EXAMPLE

$$\frac{2}{x-3} + \frac{1}{x} = \frac{x-1}{x-3} \qquad \textit{Given equation}$$

$$\left(\frac{2}{x-3} + \frac{1}{x}\right) \cdot x(x-3) = \left(\frac{x-1}{x-3}\right) \cdot x(x-3) \qquad \textit{Multiply by LCD}$$

Simplifying gives $x^2 - 4x + 3 = 0$, which has solutions 3 and 1. However, 3 makes two of the original denominators 0, so it is an *extraneous solution*, and the only solution is 1.

Key Vocabulary

asymptote *(asíntota)* A line that a graph approaches as the value of a variable becomes extremely large or small.

branch of a hyperbola *(rama de una hipérbola)* One of the two symmetrical parts of the hyperbola.

closure *(cerradura)* A set of numbers is said to be closed, or have closure, under a given operation if the result of the operation on any two numbers in the set is also in the set.

cube-root function *(función de raíz cúbica)* A function of the form $f(x) = a\sqrt[3]{x - h} + k$ where a, h, and k are constants and $a \neq 0$.

end behavior *(comportamiento extremo)* The trends in the y-values of a function as the x-values approach positive and negative infinity.

excluded values *(valores excluidos)* Values of x for which a function or expression is not defined.

exponent *(exponente)* The number that indicates how many times the base in a power is used as a factor.

extraneous solution *(solución extraña)* A solution of a derived equation that is not a solution of the original equation.

inverse variation *(variación inversa)* A relationship between two variables, x and y, that can be written in the form $y = \frac{k}{x}$, where k is a nonzero constant and $x \neq 0$.

radical *(radical)* An indicated root of a quantity.

radical equation *(ecuación radical)* An equation that contains a variable within a radical.

rational equation *(ecuación racional)* An equation that contains one or more rational expressions.

rational exponent *(exponente racional)* An exponent that can be expressed as $\frac{m}{n}$ such that if m and n are integers, then $b^{\frac{m}{n}} = \sqrt[n]{b^m} = \left(\sqrt[n]{b}\right)^m$.

rational expression *(expresión racional)* An algebraic expression whose numerator and denominator are polynomials and whose denominator is not 0.

rational function *(función racional)* A function whose rule can be written as a rational expression.

square-root function *(función de raíz cuadrada)* A function of the form $f(x) = a\sqrt{x - h} + k$ where a, h, and k are constants and $a \neq 0$.

zero of a function *(cero de una función)* For the function f, any number x such that $f(x) = 0$.

CHAPTER 5

Variation Functions
Going Deeper

Essential question: *What is the effect of changing the value of a on the graph of* $f(x) = \frac{a}{x}$?

COMMON CORE **Standards for Mathematical Content**

CC.9-12.A.CED.2 Create equations in two or more variables to represent relationships between quantities; graph equations on coordinate axes with labels and scales.*

CC.9-12.F.IF.2 Use function notation, evaluate functions for inputs in their domains ...

CC.9-12.F.IF.4 For a function that models a relationship between two quantities, interpret key features of graphs and tables in terms of the quantities, and sketch graphs showing key features given a verbal description of the relationship.*

CC.9-12.F.IF.7 Graph functions expressed symbolically and show key features of the graph ...*

CC.9-12.F.IF.7d(+) Graph rational functions, identifying zeros and asymptotes when suitable factorizations are available, and showing end behavior.*

CC.9-12.F.BF.1 Write a function that describes a relationship between two quantities.*

CC.9-12.F.BF.1a Determine an explicit expression ... from a context.*

CC.9-12.F.BF.3 Identify the effect on the graph of replacing $f(x)$ by ... $k f(x)$ ... for specific values of k (both positive and negative) ...

Also: CC.9-12.F.IF.5*, CC.9-12.F.IF.6*

Prerequisites
Transformations of parent functions

Math Background
Students have previously explored the parent functions $f(x) = x^2$ and $f(x) = x^n$. Students investigated the relationship between variations of the parent functions and the corresponding transformations of their graphs.

For rational functions of the form $f(x) = \frac{a}{x}$, the parent function is $f(x) = \frac{1}{x}$. In this lesson, students will learn about transformations that are a result of changing the value of a. Students should recognize that because division by zero is undefined, x cannot have a value of zero for $f(x) = \frac{a}{x}$.

INTRODUCE

Revisit the concept of parent functions by referencing the function $f(x) = x^n$ and its relationship to the function $f(x) = ax^n$. Review how changing the value of a can result in vertically stretching the graph of the parent function ($a > 1$), vertically shrinking the graph of the parent function ($0 < a < 1$), or reflecting the graph of the parent function across the x-axis ($a < 0$). Explain that a similar relationship exists between the parent function $f(x) = \frac{1}{x}$ and rational functions of the form $f(x) = \frac{a}{x}$. Remind students that because division by zero is undefined, $x \neq 0$ for $f(x) = \frac{a}{x}$.

TEACH

1 ENGAGE

Questioning Strategies
- Is it possible to substitute zero for x in the function $f(x) = \frac{1}{x}$? Explain. **No; division by zero is undefined.**

- The domain of $f(x) = \frac{1}{x}$ is $\{x \mid x \neq 0\}$. How is this reflected in the function's graph? **The graph approaches the line $x = 0$ but never actually reaches it.**

continued

Name _____ Class _____ Date _____

5-1

Variation Functions
Going Deeper

Essential question: *What is the effect of changing the value of a on the graph of* $f(x) = \frac{a}{x}$?

Video Tutor

CC.9-12.F.IF.7d(+)

1 ENGAGE Understanding the Parent Function $f(x) = \frac{1}{x}$

The function $f(x) = \frac{1}{x}$ is the parent function of all functions of the form $g(x) = \frac{a}{x}$. The graph of $f(x) = \frac{1}{x}$ consists of two separate curves, one in Quadrant III and one in Quadrant I, called *branches*. As you can see from the tables and graph below, the ends of the branches approach the axes, which are called the graph's *asymptotes*.

$x < 0$	
x	$f(x)$
-5	$-\frac{1}{5}$
-2	$-\frac{1}{2}$
-1	-1
$-\frac{1}{2}$	-2
$-\frac{1}{5}$	-5

$x > 0$	
x	$f(x)$
$\frac{1}{5}$	5
$\frac{1}{2}$	2
1	1
2	$\frac{1}{2}$
5	$\frac{1}{5}$

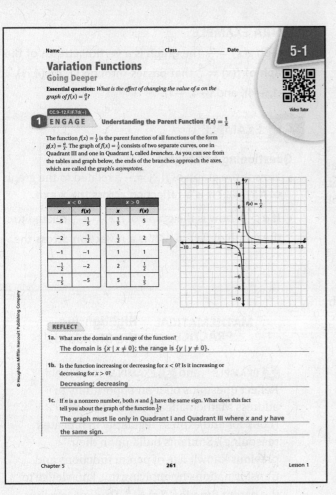

REFLECT

1a. What are the domain and range of the function?

The domain is $\{x \mid x \neq 0\}$; the range is $\{y \mid y \neq 0\}$.

1b. Is the function increasing or decreasing for $x < 0$? Is it increasing or decreasing for $x > 0$?

Decreasing; decreasing

1c. If n is a nonzero number, both n and $\frac{1}{n}$ have the same sign. What does this fact tell you about the graph of the function $\frac{1}{x}$?

The graph must lie only in Quadrant I and Quadrant III where x and y have

the same sign.

1d. If n is a nonzero number, then both $\left(n, \frac{1}{n}\right)$ and $\left(\frac{1}{n}, n\right)$ are points on the graph of the function. What does this fact tell you about the symmetry of the graph?

The graph is symmetric about the line $y = x$.

1e. The function's *end behavior* is determined by what happens to the value of $f(x)$ as the value of x increases or decreases without bound. The notation $x \to +\infty$, which is read "x approaches positive infinity," means that x is increasing without bound, while the notation $x \to -\infty$, which is read "x approaches negative infinity," means that x is decreasing without bound. Complete each table and then describe the function's end behavior.

x increases without bound.	
x	$f(x) = \frac{1}{x}$
100	0.01
1000	0.001
10,000	0.0001
100,000	0.00001

x decreases without bound.	
x	$f(x) = \frac{1}{x}$
-100	-0.01
-1000	-0.001
$-10,000$	-0.0001
$-100,000$	-0.00001

As $x \to +\infty$, $f(x) \to$ ___0___   As $x \to -\infty$, $f(x) \to$ ___0___

1f. The break in the function's graph at $x = 0$ is called an *infinite discontinuity*. To see why this is so, complete each table and then describe the function's behavior. The notation $x \to 0^+$ means that x approaches 0 from the right, while the notation $x \to 0^-$ means that x approaches 0 from the left.

x approaches 0 from the right.	
x	$f(x) = \frac{1}{x}$
0.01	100
0.001	1000
0.0001	10,000
0.00001	100,000

x approaches 0 from the left.	
x	$f(x) = \frac{1}{x}$
-0.01	-100
-0.001	-1000
-0.0001	$-10,000$
-0.00001	$-100,000$

As $x \to 0^+$, $f(x) \to$ ___$+\infty$___   As $x \to 0^-$, $f(x) \to$ ___$-\infty$___

Teaching Strategies

As students look at the table of values for $f(x) = \frac{1}{x}$, have them locate each corresponding point on the graph in the order that the points are listed in the table. Encourage students to observe how the points get closer and closer to the x- and y-axes as x decreases without bound, as x approaches 0, and as x increases without bound. Ask: Will the graph ever actually touch or cross the line $x = 0$? Will the graph ever actually touch or cross the line $y = 0$?

2 EXAMPLE

Questioning Strategies

• If the graph of a function $g(x) = \frac{a}{x}$ passes through $(1, 3)$, $(3, 1)$, $(-1, -3)$, and $(-3, -1)$, what is the value of a? **3**

• If the graph of $g(x) = \frac{a}{x}$ passes through $(0.1, 6)$, $(0.2, 3)$, $(-0.1, -6)$, and $(-0.2, -3)$, what is the value of a? **0.6**

• If $a > 1$, is the graph of $g(x) = \frac{a}{x}$ closer to or farther from the x- and y-axes than the graph of the parent function? **farther from the axes**

• If $0 < a < 1$, is the graph of $g(x) = \frac{a}{x}$ closer to or farther from the x- and y-axes than the graph of the parent function? **closer to the axes**

Differentiated Instruction

Visual learners may benefit from finding the value of $g(x) = \frac{2}{x}$ as x increases from -4 to 4:

$$-\frac{2}{4}, \, -\frac{2}{2}, \, -\frac{2}{1}, \, -\frac{2}{0.5}, \, \frac{2}{0.5}, \, \frac{2}{1}, \, \frac{2}{2}, \, \frac{2}{4}$$

As they simplify each fraction in the sequence, have them follow the path of the corresponding points on the graph of $g(x) = \frac{2}{x}$, paying close attention to what happens as x increases from -0.5 to 0.5.

Repeat the process for $g(x) = \frac{0.4}{x}$ as the values of x increase from -2 to 2:

$$-\frac{0.4}{2}, \, -\frac{0.4}{1}, \, -\frac{0.4}{0.4}, \, -\frac{0.4}{0.2}, \, -\frac{0.4}{0.1}, \, \frac{0.4}{0.1}, \, \frac{0.4}{0.2}, \, \frac{0.4}{1}, \, \frac{0.4}{2}$$

Have them pay close attention to what happens as x increases from -0.1 to 0.1.

EXTRA EXAMPLE

Graph $g(x) = \frac{4}{x}$. The graph is a vertical stretch of the graph of $f(x) = \frac{1}{x}$ that passes through $(1, 4)$, $(4, 1)$, $(-1, -4)$, and $(-4, -1)$.

3 EXAMPLE

Questioning Strategies

• How is the graph of $f(x) = -\frac{1}{x}$ related to the graph of $f(x) = \frac{1}{x}$? It is a reflection across the x-axis.

• If $a > 0$, how is the graph of $f(x) = -\frac{a}{x}$ related to the graph of $f(x) = \frac{a}{x}$? It is a reflection across the x-axis.

⋮ **MATHEMATICAL**   **Highlighting**
  PRACTICE   **the Standards**

2 EXAMPLE   and **3** EXAMPLE   and their Reflect questions offer an opportunity to address Mathematical Practice Standard 8 (Look for and express regularity in repeated reasoning). Students build upon their previous knowledge of parent functions and transformations by applying this knowledge to the parent function $f(x) = \frac{1}{x}$. Students explore how changing the value of a in the function $f(x) = \frac{a}{x}$ transforms the graph of the function by shrinking, stretching, and/or reflecting.

EXTRA EXAMPLE

Graph $g(x) = -\frac{4}{x}$. The graph is a vertical stretch and reflection over the x-axis of the graph of $f(x) = \frac{1}{x}$ that passes through $(1, -4)$, $(4, -1)$, $(-1, 4)$, and $(-4, 1)$.

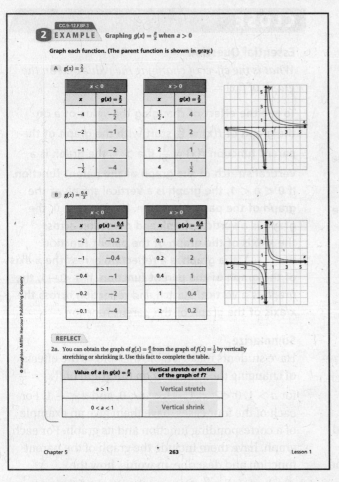

2 **E X A M P L E** CC.9-12.F.BF.3 Graphing $g(x) = \frac{a}{x}$ when $a > 0$

Graph each function. (The parent function is shown in gray.)

A $g(x) = \frac{2}{x}$

x < 0		x > 0	
x	$g(x) = \frac{2}{x}$	x	$g(x) = \frac{2}{x}$
−4	$-\frac{1}{2}$	$\frac{1}{2}$	4
−2	−1	1	2
−1	−2	2	1
$-\frac{1}{2}$	−4	4	$\frac{1}{2}$

B $g(x) = \frac{0.4}{x}$

x < 0		x > 0	
x	$g(x) = \frac{0.4}{x}$	x	$g(x) = \frac{0.4}{x}$
−2	−0.2	0.1	4
−1	−0.4	0.2	2
−0.4	−1	0.4	1
−0.2	−2	1	0.4
−0.1	−4	2	0.2

REFLECT

2a. You can obtain the graph of $g(x) = \frac{a}{x}$ from the graph of $f(x) = \frac{1}{x}$ by vertically stretching or shrinking it. Use this fact to complete the table.

Value of a in $g(x) = \frac{a}{x}$	Vertical stretch or shrink of the graph of f
a > 1	Vertical stretch
0 < a < 1	Vertical shrink

Chapter 5   263   Lesson 1

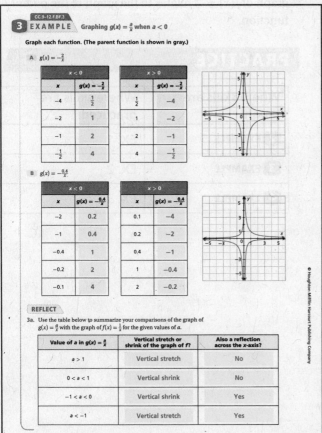

3 **E X A M P L E** CC.9-12.F.BF.3 Graphing $g(x) = \frac{a}{x}$ when $a < 0$

Graph each function. (The parent function is shown in gray.)

A $g(x) = -\frac{2}{x}$

x < 0		x > 0	
x	$g(x) = -\frac{2}{x}$	x	$g(x) = -\frac{2}{x}$
−4	$\frac{1}{2}$	$\frac{1}{2}$	−4
−2	1	1	−2
−1	2	2	−1
$-\frac{1}{2}$	4	4	$-\frac{1}{2}$

B $g(x) = -\frac{0.4}{x}$

x < 0		x > 0	
x	$g(x) = -\frac{0.4}{x}$	x	$g(x) = -\frac{0.4}{x}$
−2	0.2	0.1	−4
−1	0.4	0.2	−2
−0.4	1	0.4	−1
−0.2	2	1	−0.4
−0.1	4	2	−0.2

REFLECT

3a. Use the table below to summarize your comparisons of the graph of $g(x) = \frac{a}{x}$ with the graph of $f(x) = \frac{1}{x}$ for the given values of a.

Value of a in $g(x) = \frac{a}{x}$	Vertical stretch or shrink of the graph of f?	Also a reflection across the x-axis?
a > 1	Vertical stretch	No
0 < a < 1	Vertical shrink	No
−1 < a < 0	Vertical shrink	Yes
a < −1	Vertical stretch	Yes

Chapter 5   264   Lesson 1

Questioning Strategies

• What is the domain of the function $t(r) = \frac{30}{r}$ from a purely mathematical perspective? **The domain is $\{r \mid r \neq 0\}$.**

• Does the domain of the function accurately reflect the possible values of r in the context of this problem? Explain. **No; in addition to the rate not being equal to zero, the rate cannot have a negative value. Also, assuming Mrs. Jacobs obeys speed limits, her rate would always be the posted speed limit or less.**

Avoid Common Errors

When graphing a function that represents a real-world inverse variation situation, students may graph both branches of the function even though the context of the problem requires that only positive values be used. Ask: What if the graph also consisted of the branch in Quadrant III? Have students identify several points on that branch of the graph and analyze whether those points represent solutions that make sense in the context of the situation. Finally, encourage students to read every real-world problem carefully, identifying practical restrictions on values for any variables and solutions.

EXTRA EXAMPLE

Each day, Jim rides his bike 7 miles to work. His commuting time depends on his average speed, which varies from day to day. If r is his average speed and t is time, write and graph an equation that gives his commuting time as a function of his average speed. $t(r) = \frac{7}{r}$; **The graph is a vertical stretch of the graph of $f(x) = \frac{1}{x}$ that passes through (1, 7) and (7, 1), consisting only of the branch in Quadrant I (horizontal axis labeled r and vertical axis labeled $t(r)$).**

CLOSE

Essential Question

What is the effect of changing the value of a on the graph of $f(x) = \frac{a}{x}$?

To see the effect of changing the value of a on the graph of $f(x) = \frac{a}{x}$, start with the graph of the parent function $f(x) = \frac{1}{x}$. If $a > 1$, the graph is a vertical stretch of the graph of the parent function. If $0 < a < 1$, the graph is a vertical shrink of the graph of the parent function. If $-1 < a < 0$, the graph is a vertical shrink and reflection across the x-axis of the graph of the parent function. If $a = -1$, the graph is a reflection across the x-axis of the graph of the parent function. If $a < -1$, the graph is a vertical stretch and reflection across the x-axis of the graph of the parent function.

Summarize

Have students make a table that shows the effects of changing the value of a on the graph of $f(x) = \frac{a}{x}$ for $a > 1$, $0 < a < 1$, $-1 < a < 0$, and $a < -1$. For each of the four cases, have them give an example of a corresponding function and its graph. For each graph, have them include the graph of the parent function and describe, in words, how the graph of $f(x) = \frac{a}{x}$ relates to the graph of the parent function.

PRACTICE

Where skills are taught	Where skills are practiced
2 EXAMPLE	EX. 1
3 EXAMPLE	EX. 2
4 EXAMPLE	EX. 3

Inverse Variation When the relationship between two real-world quantities x and y has the form $y = \frac{a}{x}$ for some nonzero constant a, the relationship is called *inverse variation* and y is said to *vary inversely* as x.

4 **EXAMPLE** CC.9-12.F.BF.1 **Writing and Graphing an Equation for Inverse Variation**

Mrs. Jacobs drives 30 miles to her job in the city. Her commuting time depends on her average speed, which varies from day to day as a result of weather and traffic conditions. Write and graph an equation that gives her commuting time as a function of her average speed.

A Use the formula $d = rt$ where d is distance, r is rate (average speed), and t is time to write t as a function of r given that $d = 30$.

$rt =$ 30 The product of rate and time gives distance.

$t = \dfrac{30}{r}$ Solve for t.

B Use the table to help you graph the function $t(r)$.

r	$t(r)$
10	3
15	2
30	1
60	0.5

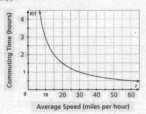

Average Speed (miles per hour)

REFLECT

4a. Why does the graph consist only of the branch in Quadrant I?

Rate and time have only positive values in this problem.

4b. Do equal changes in average speed result in equal changes in commuting time? Give an example to support your answer.

No; going from 10 mi/h to 20 mi/h decreases the commuting time by 1.5 h, but going from 20 mi/h to 30 mi/h decreases the commuting time by only 0.5 h.

PRACTICE

For each function, plot the points at which $x = \pm 1$, then draw the complete graph.

1. $f(x) = \frac{0.3}{x}$

2. $f(x) = -\frac{4}{x}$

3. Shaun is paid $20 each week to mow a lawn. The time he spends mowing varies from week to week based on factors such as how much the grass has grown and how wet the grass is. His effective hourly pay rate is therefore a function of the time he spends mowing.

a. Use the formula $p = rt$ where p is total pay, r is hourly pay rate, and t is time to write r as a function of t given that $p = 20$. Describe the relationship between r and t.

$r = \frac{20}{t}$; r varies inversely as t.

b. Use the table below to help you graph the function $r(t)$.

t	$r(t)$
0.5	40
1	20
2	10
2.5	8

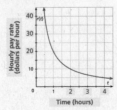

Time (hours)

Assign these pages to help your students practice and apply important lesson concepts. For additional exercises, see the Student Edition.

Answers

Additional Practice

1.

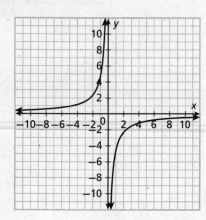

2.

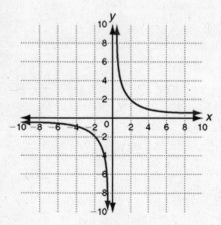

3.

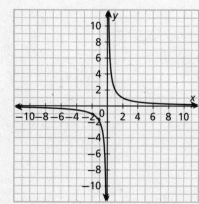

4.

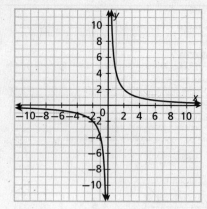

5. $y = \dfrac{4}{x}$

6. $y = \dfrac{15}{x}$

7. 13 chaperones   **8.** $10,000

Problem Solving

1. a. $t = \dfrac{k}{s}$

   b. $k = 975$

   c. It is the total number of student hours that it takes to build a 7-foot sailboat.

   d. 81.25 h

2. 13 students

3. C   **4.** B

5. a. $V = \dfrac{kT}{P}$

   b. $23\dfrac{1}{3}$ liters

5-1

Additional Practice

Graph each function.

1. $y = -\dfrac{5}{x}$

2. $y = \dfrac{15}{x}$

3. $y = \dfrac{2}{x}$

4. $y = \dfrac{4}{x}$

Determine the function of the form $y = \dfrac{a}{x}$ **represented by each data set.**

5.

x	2	3	4
y	8	12	16

6.

x	3	1	0.5
y	5	15	30

Chapter 5   267   Lesson 1

Problem Solving

Last semester five of Mr. Dewayne's students built a 7-foot sailboat in 195 working hours. The time, t, that it takes for a group of students to build a sailboat varies inversely as the number of students. Mr. Dewayne uses this data to plan activities for next semester.

1. How many working hours would it take 12 students to build the same kind of sailboat?

   a. Write an equation relating the time required to the number of students working.   _____

   b. Find the constant k.   _____

   c. Explain the meaning of k in terms of student hours.

   _____

   d. Solve the equation to answer the question.   _____

2. How many students would be needed to build a 7-foot sailboat in 75 working hours?

Choose the letter for the best answer.

3. Which equation represents the number of hours it would take 15 students to build a 7-foot sailboat?

   A $\dfrac{195}{5} = \dfrac{t}{15}$

   B $\dfrac{t}{195} = \dfrac{15}{5}$

   C $(195)(5) = 15t$

   D $195t = (5)(15)$

4. How many students must Mr. Dewayne get to participate in order to build a 7-foot sailboat in 65 hours?

   A 14 students

   B 15 students

   C 16 students

   D 17 students

5. The volume V of a gas varies inversely as the pressure P and directly as the temperature T.

   a. Write an equation representing this relationship.

   _____

   b. A certain gas has a volume of 10 liters and a pressure of 1.5 atmospheres. If the gas is held at a constant temperature, and the pressure is increased to 3.5 atmospheres, what volume will the gas take up?

   _____

Chapter 5   268   Lesson 1

Multiplying and Dividing Rational Expressions

Going Deeper

Essential question: *How do you find products and quotients of rational expressions?*

◌ COMMON **Standards for**
◌ CORE **Mathematical Content**

CC.9-12.A.SSE.1 Interpret expressions that represent a quantity in terms of its context.*

CC.9-12.A.SSE.1b Interpret complicated expressions by viewing one or more of their parts as a single entity.*

CC.9-12.A.APR.7(+) Understand that rational expressions form a system analogous to the rational numbers, closed under addition, subtraction, multiplication, and division by a nonzero rational expression; ... multiply, and divide rational expressions.

CC.9-12.F.BF.1 Write a function that describes a relationship between two quantities.*

CC.9-12.F.BF.1b Combine standard function types using arithmetic operations.*

Also: CC.9-12.N.Q.1*

Prerequisites

Multiplying polynomials

Factoring polynomials

Excluded values

Math Background

Students are familiar with factoring polynomials, as well as with multiplying polynomials. In the previous lesson, they learned to simplify rational expressions. In this lesson, they will use these skills to multiply and divide rational expressions.

INTRODUCE

Point out to students that the process of multiplying and dividing rational expressions follows the same general steps as the process of multiplying and dividing rational numbers: First, if division is involved, rewrite to multiply by the reciprocal of the divisor instead. Then, write the product of the numerators over the product of the denominators. Finally, simplify the answer, if possible. Point out that for rational expressions, unlike rational numbers, the factoring that is needed to simplify the answer should be done *before* multiplying to avoid having difficult-to-factor polynomials in the

numerator and denominator at the end. Students may find it helpful to multiply and divide a couple of rational numbers before attempting to multiply and divide rational expressions.

TEACH

1 EXAMPLE

Questioning Strategies

• Would the product be the same if you multiplied the numerators and denominators and then factored each numerator and denominator? **Yes, the expressions would be equivalent.**

• What is the purpose of factoring each numerator and denominator before multiplying the numerators and denominators? **To have the product in factored form so that common factors in the numerator and denominator can be divided out.**

EXTRA EXAMPLE

Find the product: $\dfrac{4x}{x^2 + x - 6} \cdot \dfrac{2x - 4}{x^2 + x} \cdot \dfrac{8}{(x + 1)(x + 3)}$

2 EXAMPLE

Questioning Strategies

• How is the process for dividing rational expressions related to the process for multiplying rational expressions? **Dividing by an expression is equivalent to multiplying by its reciprocal. Once division is converted to multiplication, you can carry out the steps for multiplying rational expressions.**

• Why is $x = 0$ an excluded value? **The denominator $x^2 - 4x$ equals 0 when $x = 0$.**

Avoid Common Errors

When identifying excluded values for quotients of rational expressions, students may consider values that cause the denominators to be zero, but they may not consider values that cause the divisor itself to be 0. For example, the divisor $\dfrac{x^2 - 36}{x^2 - 4x}$ will have a value of 0 when $x = 6$ or $x = -6$, so these values must also be excluded values.

continued

Name_____ Class_____ Date_____

Multiplying and Dividing Rational Expressions
Going Deeper

5-2

Essential question: *How do you find products and quotients of rational expressions?*

Video Tutor

CC.9-12.A.APR.7(+)

1 EXAMPLE Multiplying Rational Expressions

Find the product: $\dfrac{5x}{x^2 + x - 2} \cdot \dfrac{3x - 3}{x^2 + 3x}$

$$\dfrac{5x}{x^2 + x - 2} \cdot \dfrac{3x - 3}{x^2 + 3x} = \dfrac{5x}{(x+2)(x-1)} \cdot \dfrac{3(x-1)}{x(x+3)}$$

Factor each numerator and denominator, if possible.

$$= \dfrac{15x(x-1)}{x(x+2)(x-1)(x+3)}$$

Multiply the numerators, and multiply the denominators.

$$= \dfrac{15}{(x+2)(x+3)}$$

Simplify the product by dividing out any common factors in the numerator and the denominator.

REFLECT

1a. As a check on your work, show that $\dfrac{5x}{x^2 + x - 2} \cdot \dfrac{3x-3}{x^2 + 3x}$ and the simplified expression for the product have the same value when $x = 2$.

$$\dfrac{5(2)}{2^2 + 2 - 2} \cdot \dfrac{3(2) - 3}{2^2 + 3(2)} = \dfrac{10}{4} \cdot \dfrac{3}{10} = \dfrac{3}{4}, \quad \dfrac{15}{(2+2)(2+3)} = \dfrac{15}{20} = \dfrac{3}{4}$$

1b. Suppose you decide to check your work by showing that the two expressions have the same value when $x = 0$. Describe what happens, and explain why it happens.

The expression $\dfrac{3x-3}{x^2 + 3x}$ is undefined when $x = 0$ because the denominator

contains x as a factor, so you cannot find a value for $\dfrac{5x}{x^2 + x - 2} \cdot \dfrac{3x - 3}{x^2 + 3x}$;

on the other hand, the expression $\dfrac{15}{(x+2)(x+3)}$ is defined when $x = 0$.

1c. The *excluded values* for a rational expression are any values of the variable for which the expression is undefined. Also, two expressions are *equivalent expressions* provided they have the same value for every value of the variable unless they are both undefined for that value of the variable. In order for the simplified expression for the product to be equivalent to $\dfrac{5x}{x^2 + x - 2} \cdot \dfrac{3x - 3}{x^2 + 3x}$, what excluded values must it have?

$x = -3, x = -2, x = 0,$ and $x = 1$

Chapter 5   269   Lesson 2

© Houghton Mifflin Harcourt Publishing Company

CC.9-12.A.APR.7(+)

2 EXAMPLE Dividing Rational Expressions

Find the quotient: $\dfrac{x - 6}{x^2 + 2x - 24} \div \dfrac{x^2 - 36}{x^2 - 4x}$

$$\dfrac{x-6}{x^2 + 2x - 24} \div \dfrac{x^2 - 36}{x^2 - 4x} = \dfrac{x-6}{x^2 + 2x - 24} \cdot \dfrac{x^2 - 4x}{(x^2 - 36)}$$

Multiply by the reciprocal.

$$= \dfrac{x-6}{(x-4)(x+6)} \cdot \dfrac{x(x-4)}{(x+6)(x-6)}$$

Factor numerators and denominators.

$$= \dfrac{x(x-6)(x-4)}{(x-4)(x+6)(x+6)(x-6)}$$

Multiply the expressions.

$$= \dfrac{x}{(x+6)^2}$$

Simplify.

REFLECT

2a. What are the excluded values for the simplified expression for the quotient?

$x = -6, x = 0, x = 4,$ and $x = 6$

2b. As a check on your work, show that $\dfrac{x-6}{x^2 + 2x - 24} \div \dfrac{x^2 - 36}{x^2 - 4x}$ and the simplified expression for the quotient have the same value when $x = 1$.

$$\dfrac{1 - 6}{1^2 + 2(1) - 24} \div \dfrac{1^2 - 36}{1^2 - 4(1)} = \dfrac{5}{21} \div \dfrac{35}{3} = \dfrac{5}{21} \cdot \dfrac{3}{35} = \dfrac{1}{49}, \quad \dfrac{1}{(1 + 6)^2} = \dfrac{1}{49}$$

CC.9-12.F.BF.1b

3 EXAMPLE Modeling with a Quotient of Rational Expressions

The expression $\dfrac{35E - 125}{E(E - 5)}$ represents the total gas consumed (in gallons) when Mr. Garcia drives 25 miles on a highway and 10 miles in a city to get to work. In the expression, E represents the fuel efficiency (in miles per gallon) of Mr. Garcia's car at highway speeds. Use the expression to find the average rate of gas consumed on the trip.

A Find the total distance that Mr. Garcia drives.   25 + 10 = 35 miles

B Use the verbal model to write an expression involving division for the average rate of gas consumed.

Average rate of gas consumed	=	Total gas consumed	÷	Total distance traveled

Average rate of gas consumed = $\dfrac{35E - 125}{E(E - 5)} \div 35$

Chapter 5   270   Lesson 2

© Houghton Mifflin Harcourt Publishing Company

EXTRA EXAMPLE

Find the quotient: $\dfrac{x-5}{x^2+3x-10} \div \dfrac{x^2-25}{x^2-2x} \cdot \dfrac{x}{(x+5)^2}$

3 EXAMPLE

Questioning Strategies

- What are the steps to carry out the division in part C? $\dfrac{35E-125}{E(E-5)}$ is multiplied by $\dfrac{1}{35}$, the reciprocal of 35, to get $\dfrac{35E-125}{35E(E-5)}$. Then, the numerator is factored as $5(7E-25)$. Finally, the common factor of 5 is divided out, resulting in the simplified expression $\dfrac{7E-25}{7E(E-5)}$.

- Suppose the fuel efficiency of Mr. Garcia's car at highway speeds is $E = 30$ miles per gallon. Evaluate the expression $\dfrac{35E-125}{E(E-5)}$ to get the total gas consumed on his trip to work. Then divide this total by the 35 miles he drives to get the average rate of gas consumed. How does this result help you check the expression that you wrote in part C? Show that it checks. About 1.23 gallons; about 0.035 gallon per mile; evaluate the expression in part C to see if you get the same average rate of gas consumed; $\dfrac{7(30)-25}{7(30)(30-5)} \approx 0.035$

MATHEMATICAL PRACTICE   **Highlighting the Standards**

3 EXAMPLE and its Reflect questions offer an opportunity to address Mathematical Practice Standard 4 (Model with mathematics). Students use rational expressions to model the relationship between fuel economy and rate of gas consumption. Students see how operations on rational expressions can be applied to real-world situations.

EXTRA EXAMPLE

The expression $\dfrac{70E+200}{E(E+10)}$ represents the total gas consumed (in gallons) when Ann drives her truck 20 miles in a city and 50 miles on a highway to make a delivery. In the expression, E represents the fuel efficiency (in miles per gallon) of Ann's truck at city speeds. Use the expression to find the average rate of gas consumed on the trip. $\dfrac{7E+20}{7E(E+10)}$

CLOSE

Essential Question

How do you find products and quotients of rational expressions?

To find a product of rational expressions, factor each numerator and denominator, multiply the numerators and denominators, and simplify the resulting rational expression that is the product. To find a quotient of rational expressions, multiply by the reciprocal of the divisor and then follow the steps for multiplying rational expressions.

Summarize

Have students make a table that shows the steps they followed to multiply the rational expressions in 1 EXAMPLE and to divide the rational expressions in 2 EXAMPLE. Then have them identify the similarities and differences between the steps they followed.

PRACTICE

Where skills are taught	Where skills are practiced
1 EXAMPLE	EXS. 1–4
2 EXAMPLE	EXS. 4–8
3 EXAMPLE	EX. 9

c Carry out the division to get a combined expression for the average rate of gas consumed.

$$\text{Average rate of gas consumed} = \frac{35E - 125}{35E(E - 5)} = \frac{7E - 25}{7E(E - 5)}$$

REFLECT

3a. What unit of measurement applies to the expression for the average rate of gas consumed? Explain.

Gallons per mile; total gas consumed is measured in gallons, and total distance traveled is measured in miles, so the quotient of gas consumed to distance traveled is measured in gallons per mile.

3b. Mr. Garcia's car has a highway fuel efficiency of E miles per gallon and a city fuel efficiency of $(E - 5)$ miles per gallon. If the distances driven on the highway and in the city are equal, then the average rate of gas consumed is given by $\left(\frac{1}{E} + \frac{1}{E-5}\right) \div 2 = \frac{E-5}{E(E-5)} + \frac{E}{E(E-5)}$. Carry out the operations in this expression to get a combined expression for the average rate of gas consumed. (Remember that to add two fractions with a common denominator, you keep the denominator and add the numerators.)

$$\left(\frac{E-5}{E(E-5)} + \frac{E}{E(E-5)}\right) \div 2 = \frac{2E-5}{E(E-5)} \div 2 = \frac{2E-5}{2E(E-5)}$$

3c. Suppose Mr. Garcia drives 10 miles on a highway and 10 miles in a city to get to work. The combined expression for the total gas consumed is $\frac{10}{E} + \frac{10}{E-5}$, or $\frac{10(E-5)}{E(E-5)} + \frac{10E}{E(E-5)}$. Simplify the expression and then divide it by the total distance traveled to get a combined expression for the average rate of gas consumed. Compare this result with the one in the previous Reflect question.

Total gas consumed = $\frac{10(E-5)}{E(E-5)} + \frac{10E}{E(E-5)} = \frac{10(E-5) + 10E}{E(E-5)} = \frac{20E - 50}{E(E-5)}$, total distance

traveled = 20; average rate of gas used = $\frac{20E-50}{E(E-5)} \div 20 = \frac{20E-50}{20E(E-5)} = \frac{2E-5}{2E(E-5)}$,

the expressions are identical.

3d. Show that $\left(\frac{d_1(E-5)}{E(E-5)} + \frac{d_2 E}{E(E-5)}\right) \div (d_1 + d_2) = \frac{2E-5}{2E(E-5)}$ when $d_1 = d_2$ but not when $d_1 \neq d_2$.

If $d_1 = d_2$, then $\left(\frac{d_1(E-5)}{E(E-5)} + \frac{d_2 E}{E(E-5)}\right) \div (d_1 + d_2) = \left(\frac{d_1(E-5)}{E(E-5)} + \frac{d_1 E}{E(E-5)}\right) \div (d_1 + d_1) =$

$d_1\left(\frac{E-5}{E(E-5)} + \frac{E}{E(E-5)}\right) \div 2d_1 = d_1\left(\frac{2E-5}{E(E-5)}\right) \div 2d_1 = \frac{d_1(2E-5)}{2d_1 E(E-5)} = \frac{2E-5}{2E(E-5)}$, but d_1

cannot be substituted for d_2 when $d_1 \neq d_2$, so $\left(\frac{d_1(E-5)}{E(E-5)} + \frac{d_2 E}{E(E-5)}\right) \div (d_1 + d_2)$

can only be rewritten as $\frac{(d_1 + d_2)E - 5d_1}{(d_1 + d_2)E(E-5)}$.

PRACTICE

Find each product or quotient. State all excluded values.

1. $\frac{4x}{x-3} \cdot \frac{3x-9}{x^2}$

   $\frac{12}{x}$; 0, 3

2. $\frac{3x+15}{x-2} \cdot \frac{7x-14}{x^2+5x}$

   $\frac{21}{x}$; −5, 0, 2

3. $\frac{x+1}{x^2+7x-8} \cdot \frac{x-1}{5x+5}$

   $\frac{1}{5(x+8)}$; −8, ±1

4. $\frac{x^2+5x+6}{x^2-x+2} \cdot \frac{2x^2+8x+6}{x^2-3x-10}$

   $\frac{2(x+3)^2}{(x-2)(x-5)}$; −2, −1, 2, 5

5. $\frac{5}{x^2-2x} \div \frac{3x}{x-2}$

   $\frac{5}{3x^2}$; 0, 2

6. $\frac{7x-21}{x^2+7x} \div \frac{x-3}{x^2-5x}$

   $\frac{7(x-5)}{x+7}$; −7, 0, 3, 5

7. $\frac{x^2+5x-6}{4x} \div \frac{x+6}{x^2-x}$

   $\frac{(x-1)^2}{4}$; −6, 0, 1

8. $\frac{x^2+5x+4}{x^2+4x} \div \frac{x^2-2x+1}{x^2-1}$

   $\frac{(x-1)}{x}$; −4, −1, 0, 1

9. On his trip to work, Mr. Garcia drives at a speed of s miles per hour on the highway and $(s - 30)$ miles per hour in the city. Recall that the distances he drives are 25 miles on the highway and 10 miles in the city.

a. Write an expression for the time that he spends driving on the highway and the time that he spends driving in the city.

Highway time = $\frac{25}{s}$; city time = $\frac{10}{s-30}$

b. His total time can be represented by the sum $\frac{25(s-30)}{s(s-30)} + \frac{10s}{s(s-30)}$. Rewrite this sum as a combined expression.

Total time = $\frac{25}{s} + \frac{10}{s-30} = \frac{35s-750}{s(s-30)}$

c. Find his average speed on the trip by dividing the total distance that he travels by the total time. Write the average speed as a quotient and then carry out the division.

Average speed = $35 \div \frac{35s-750}{s(s-30)} = \frac{35s(s-30)}{35s-750} = \frac{7s(s-30)}{7s-150}$

Assign these pages to help your students practice and apply important lesson concepts. For additional exercises, see the Student Edition.

Answers

Additional Practice

1. $\dfrac{x+2}{x-4}; x \neq -1, x \neq 4$

2. $2x^2; x \neq 0$

3. $\dfrac{-x^2}{2x-3}; x \neq 1, x \neq \dfrac{3}{2}$

4. $\dfrac{x^2+5x}{x+4}; x \neq 4, x \neq -4$

5. $\dfrac{x-4}{2x+1}; x \neq -1, x \neq -\dfrac{1}{2}$

6. $\dfrac{3}{x+5}; x \neq 3, x \neq -5$

7. $2x - 2$

8. $\dfrac{x-1}{x+2}$

9. $\dfrac{x^2}{2}$

10. $\dfrac{x+2}{x+3}$

11. $x = 11$

12. $x = -3$

13. $1 + \dfrac{At}{2v_0}$

Problem Solving

1. a. $T_1 = 2\pi r_1$

   b. $T_2 = 2\pi (r_1 + 5)$

   c. $\dfrac{r_1 + 5}{r_1}$

2. a.
   $$\frac{(r_1 + 10)(r_1 - 5)}{(r_1^2 - 25)} = \frac{(r_1 + 10)(r_1 - 5)}{(r_1 + 5)(r_1 - 5)} = \frac{r_1 + 10}{r_1 + 5};$$

   Mari is correct.

3. a. $\dfrac{T_2}{T_1} = 1.071$

   b. $\dfrac{T_3}{T_2} = 1.067$

   c. $\dfrac{T_3}{T_1} = 1.143$

4. D

5. A

Name_____ Class_____ Date_____

Additional Practice

Simplify. Identify any x-values for which the expression is undefined.

1. $\dfrac{x^2 + 3x + 2}{x^2 - 3x - 4}$

2. $\dfrac{4x^6}{2x^4}$

3. $\dfrac{x^2 - x^3}{2x^2 - 5x + 3}$

4. $\dfrac{x^3 + x^2 - 20x}{x^2 - 16}$

5. $\dfrac{3x^2 - 9x - 12}{6x^2 + 9x + 3}$

6. $\dfrac{9 - 3x}{15 - 2x - x^2}$

Multiply. Assume all expressions are defined.

7. $\dfrac{4x + 16}{2x + 6} \cdot \dfrac{x^2 + 2x - 3}{x + 4}$

8. $\dfrac{x + 3}{x - 1} \cdot \dfrac{x^2 - 2x + 1}{x^2 + 5x + 6}$

Divide. Assume all expressions are defined.

9. $\dfrac{5x^6}{x^2 y} \div \dfrac{10x^2}{y}$

10. $\dfrac{x^2 - 2x - 8}{x^2 - 2x - 15} \div \dfrac{2x^2 - 8x}{2x^2 - 10x}$

Solve. Check your solution.

11. $\dfrac{x^2 + x - 12}{x - 3} = 15$

12. $\dfrac{2x^2 + 8x - 10}{2x^2 + 14x + 20} = 4$

Solve.

13. The distance, d, traveled by a car undergoing constant acceleration, a, for a time, t, is given by $d = v_0 t + \dfrac{1}{2}at^2$, where v_0 is the initial velocity of the car.

Two cars are side by side with the same initial velocity. One car accelerates, $a = A$, and the other car does not accelerate, $a = 0$. Write an expression for the ratio of the distance traveled by the accelerating car to the distance traveled by the nonaccelerating car as a function of time.

Problem Solving

Anders designs a running field that consists of three concentric tracks as shown in the diagram.

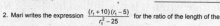

1. How do the lengths of each track compare?

   a. Write an equation for the length of the inner track, T_1, in terms of radius, r_1.

   b. Write an equation for the length of the middle track, T_2, in terms of radius r_1.

   c. Then write a rational expression for the ratio of the length of track T_2 to the length of track T_1 in terms of radius r_1.

2. Mari writes the expression $\dfrac{(r_1 + 10)(r_1 - 5)}{r_1^2 - 25}$ for the ratio of the length of the outer track, T_3, to that of the middle track, T_2. Anders thinks that is the wrong expression. Simplify Mari's expression to determine if she is correct. Explain.

3. Anders sets the radius of the inner track, T_1, at 70 meters.

   a. How many times as long is the middle track, T_2, than the inner track, T_1?

   b. How many times longer is the outer track, T_3, than the middle track, T_2?

   c. How many times longer is the outer track, T_3, than the inner track, T_1?

Choose the letter for the best answer.

4. How many times as large is the area enclosed by the outer track, T_3, than the area enclosed by the inner track, T_1?

   A $\left(\dfrac{10}{r_1}\right)$ B $\left(\dfrac{10}{r_1}\right)^2$

   C $\left(\dfrac{r_1 + 10}{r_1}\right)$ D $\left(\dfrac{r_1 + 10}{r_1}\right)^2$

5. What is the ratio of the area between the inner track and the outer track to the area enclosed by the inner track?

   A $20\left(\dfrac{r_1 + 5}{r_1^2}\right)$ B $\dfrac{(r_1 + 10)^2 - 1}{r_1^2}$

   C $\pi\left(\dfrac{r_1 + 10}{r_1}\right)^2$ D $\pi\left(\dfrac{10}{r_1}\right)^2$

Notes

Adding and Subtracting Rational Expressions
Going Deeper

Essential question: How do you find sums and differences of rational expressions?

CC.9-12.A.SSE.1 Interpret expressions that represent a quantity in terms of its context.*

CC.9-12.A.SSE.1b Interpret complicated expressions by viewing one or more of their parts as a single entity.*

CC.9-12.A.APR.7(+) ... add, subtract ... rational expressions.

CC.9-12.F.BF.1 Write a function that describes a relationship between two quantities.*

CC.9-12.F.BF.1b Combine standard function types using arithmetic operations.*

Also: CC.9-12.N.Q.1*

Prerequisites
Multiplying polynomials
Factoring polynomials

Math Background
Students are familiar with the process of multiplying polynomials as well as the reverse process of factoring polynomials. In this lesson, they will use these skills to add and subtract rational expressions.

INTRODUCE

Point out to students that the process of adding and subtracting rational expressions follows the same general steps as the process of adding and subtracting rational numbers: First, write the fractions with a common denominator, if necessary. Then, add or subtract the numerators and write the result over the common denominator. Finally, simplify the answer, if possible. Students may find it helpful to add and subtract a couple of rational numbers before attempting to add and subtract rational expressions.

TEACH

1 EXAMPLE

Questioning Strategies
- When working with equivalent expressions, how can you determine excluded values of the simplified form of the expression? **Look at the denominator after the expression in the denominator has been factored, but before any common factors have been divided out. For each factor, any value that makes the factor equal to zero is an excluded value.**

Avoid Common Errors
Encourage students to always use the factored but unsimplified form of a rational expression to identify any excluded values.

EXTRA EXAMPLE
Simplify: $\dfrac{3x-6}{x^2-5x+6}$. Identify any excluded values. $\dfrac{3}{x-3}; x \neq 3; x \neq 2$

2 EXAMPLE

Questioning Strategies
- Does the value of the second expression of the sum change when it is multiplied by $\dfrac{x-1}{x-1}$? **No, $\dfrac{x-1}{x-1} = 1$ and multiplying by 1 changes only the form of the expression, not its value.**

- Why is $x = 0$ used to check the work instead of $x = 1$ or some other value of x? **When $x = 0$, the x^2- and x-terms evaluate to 0, which simplifies the calculations.**

EXTRA EXAMPLE
Find the sum: $\dfrac{x+3}{x^2-2x-8} + \dfrac{3}{x+2} \cdot \dfrac{4x-9}{(x+2)(x-4)}$

Video Tutor

Adding and Subtracting Rational Expressions
Going Deeper

Name_____ Class_____ Date_____

5-3

Essential question: How do you find sums and differences of rational expressions?

PREP FOR CC.9–12.A.APR.7(+)

1 **EXAMPLE** Simplifying a Rational Expression

Simplify: $\dfrac{2x-8}{x^2-6x+8}$

Factor the numerator and the denominator. If there are any common factors, divide them out.

$$\dfrac{2x-8}{x^2-6x+8}=\dfrac{2\left(\boxed{x-4}\right)}{\left(\boxed{x-2}\right)(x-4)}$$
Factor the numerator and the denominator.

$$=\dfrac{2}{\left(\boxed{x-2}\right)}$$
There is a common factor, so divide it out.

REFLECT

1a. The *excluded values* for a rational expression are any values of the variable for which the expression is undefined. What are the excluded values for $\dfrac{2x-8}{x^2-6x+8}$? What are the excluded values of the simplified form of this expression?

$x=2$ and $x=4$; $x=2$ only

1b. The expression $\dfrac{2x-8}{x^2-6x+8}$ and its simplified form are called *equivalent expressions*. Equivalent expressions must have the same value for every value of the variable unless they are both undefined for that value of the variable. Is this true for $\dfrac{2x-8}{x^2-6x+8}$ and its simplified form when $x=4$? If not, what can you do to make it true?

No; consider $x=4$ to be an excluded value for the simplified form.

1c. Show that the expression $\dfrac{2x-8}{x^2-6x+8}$ and its simplified form have the same value when $x=0$. How is this helpful? (Think about what you would know if the two expressions did *not* have the same value.)

$\dfrac{2(0)-8}{0^2-6(0)+8}=-1$; $\dfrac{2}{0-2}=-1$; it suggests that the expressions are equivalent.

1d. **Error Analysis** A student says that you can divide out 8 and x to simplify the expression $\dfrac{2x-8}{x^2-6x+8}$ as $\dfrac{2}{x-6}$. Find the error in this reasoning.

Sample answer: 8 and x are not factors of the numerator and denominator, so you can't divide them out. Also, when $x=0$, the expressions aren't equal: $-1\neq-\dfrac{1}{3}$.

© Houghton Mifflin Harcourt Publishing Company

CC.9–12.A.APR.7(+)

2 **EXAMPLE** Adding Rational Expressions

Find the sum: $\dfrac{x+2}{x^2+5x-6}+\dfrac{3}{x+6}$

$$\dfrac{x+2}{x^2+5x-6}+\dfrac{3}{x+6}=\dfrac{x+2}{(x+6)(x-1)}+\dfrac{3}{x+6}$$
Factor the first expression's denominator.

$$=\dfrac{x+2}{(x+6)(x-1)}+\dfrac{3}{x+6}\cdot\dfrac{x-1}{x-1}$$
Multiply the second expression by a form of 1 so that both expressions will have the same denominator.

$$=\dfrac{x+2}{(x+6)(x-1)}+\dfrac{3\left(\boxed{x-1}\right)}{(x+6)\left(\boxed{x-1}\right)}$$
Carry out the multiplication.

$$=\dfrac{x+2+3\left(\boxed{x-1}\right)}{(x+6)(x-1)}$$
Now that both expressions have the same denominator, you can add the numerators.

$$=\dfrac{4x-1}{(x+6)(x-1)}$$
Simplify the numerator.

REFLECT

2a. As a check on your work, show that $\dfrac{x+2}{x^2+5x-6}+\dfrac{3}{x+6}$ and the expression for the sum have the same value when $x=0$.

$\dfrac{0+2}{0^2+5(0)-6}+\dfrac{3}{0+6}=-\dfrac{1}{3}+\dfrac{1}{2}=\dfrac{1}{6}$; $\dfrac{4(0)-1}{(0+6)(0-1)}=\dfrac{1}{6}$

CC.9–12.A.APR.7(+)

3 **EXAMPLE** Subtracting Rational Expressions

Find the difference: $\dfrac{x-5}{x+2}-\dfrac{x+2}{x-5}$

$$\dfrac{x-5}{x+2}-\dfrac{x+2}{x-5}=\dfrac{x-5}{x+2}\cdot\dfrac{x-5}{x-5}-\dfrac{x+2}{x-5}\cdot\dfrac{x+2}{x+2}$$
Multiply each expression by a form of 1 so that both expressions will have the same denominator.

$$=\dfrac{\left(x-5\right)^2}{(x+2)(x-5)}-\dfrac{\left(x+2\right)^2}{(x+2)(x-5)}$$
Carry out the multiplications.

$$=\dfrac{\left(x-5\right)^2-\left(x+2\right)^2}{(x+2)(x-5)}$$
Now that both expressions have the same denominator, you can subtract the numerators.

$$=\dfrac{\left(x^2-10x+25\right)-\left(x^2+4x+4\right)}{(x+2)(x-5)}$$
Square the binomials in the numerator.

$$=\dfrac{-14x+21}{(x+2)(x-5)}$$
Simplify the numerator.

© Houghton Mifflin Harcourt Publishing Company

3 EXAMPLE

Questioning Strategies

- After rational expressions have been subtracted, why is it important to check whether the numerator of the expression for the difference is factorable? **If the numerator is factorable, it may be possible that the expression for the difference can be simplified further.**

Avoid Common Errors

When students subtract a numerator that has more than one term, they may subtract only the first term and then add the remaining terms. Remind students that each term in the numerator must be subtracted. Some students may benefit from adding the opposite rather than subtracting.

MATHEMATICAL PRACTICE	Highlighting the Standards

2 EXAMPLE and **3 EXAMPLE** and their Reflect questions offer an opportunity to address Mathematical Practice Standard 8 (Look for and express regularity in repeated reasoning). Students observe that rational expressions can be both added and subtracted by multiplying one or both expressions by a form of 1 so that the denominators are the same.

EXTRA EXAMPLE

Find the difference: $\dfrac{x-4}{x+3} - \dfrac{x+3}{x-4}$. $\dfrac{-14x+7}{(x+3)(x-4)}$

4 EXAMPLE

Questioning Strategies

- What form of 1 is $\dfrac{25}{E}$ multiplied by so that both expressions have the same denominator? $\dfrac{E-5}{E-5}$
- What form of 1 is $\dfrac{10}{E-5}$ multiplied by so that both expressions have the same denominator? $\dfrac{E}{E}$

EXTRA EXAMPLE

The fuel efficiency of Ann's truck when driven at a typical city speed is E miles per hour. Highway driving increases the fuel efficiency by 10 miles per gallon. Ann drives 20 miles in a city and 50 miles on a highway to make a delivery. Write a rational expression that gives the total amount of gas consumed on Ann's delivery trip. $\dfrac{70E+200}{E(E+10)}$

CLOSE

Essential Question

How do you find sums and differences of rational expressions?

If the expressions have the same denominator, add or subtract the numerators by combining like terms. If the expressions have different denominators, multiply one or both expressions by a form of 1 so that the denominators are the same and then add or subtract the numerators by combining like terms.

Summarize

Have students make a table that shows the steps they followed to add the rational expressions in **2 EXAMPLE** and to subtract the rational expressions in **3 EXAMPLE**. Then have them identify the similarities and differences between the steps they followed.

PRACTICE

Where skills are taught	Where skills are practiced
1 EXAMPLE	EXS. 1–3
2 EXAMPLE	EXS. 4–6
3 EXAMPLE	EXS. 7–9
4 EXAMPLE	EX. 10

Exercise 11: Students investigate the property of closure for the set of all rational expressions, and come to the understanding that rational expressions form a system analogous to the set of rational numbers.

REFLECT

3a. As a check on your work, show that $\frac{x-5}{x+2} - \frac{x+2}{x-5}$ and the expression for the difference have the same value when $x = 0$.

$$\frac{0-5}{0+2} - \frac{0+2}{0-5} = -\frac{5}{2} - \left(-\frac{2}{5}\right) = -\frac{25}{10} + \frac{4}{10} = -\frac{21}{10}, \quad \frac{-14(0) + 21}{(0+2)(0-5)} = -\frac{21}{10}$$

3b. In the expression for the difference, is the numerator factorable? If so, can the expression be simplified? Explain.

The numerator can be factored as $-7(2x - 3)$; the expression cannot be simplified because there are no common factors in the numerator and denominator.

CC.9-12.F.BF.1b

4 EXAMPLE Modeling with a Sum of Rational Expressions

The fuel efficiency of Mr. Garcia's car when driven at a typical highway speed is E miles per gallon. City driving reduces the fuel efficiency by 5 miles per gallon. Mr. Garcia drives 25 miles on a highway and 10 miles in a city to get to work. Write a rational expression that gives the total amount of gas consumed on Mr. Garcia's trip to work.

A Divide the distance traveled by the fuel efficiency to find an expression for the amount of gas consumed on each portion of the trip.

$$\text{Gas consumed on highway} = \frac{25}{E} \qquad \text{Gas consumed in city} = \frac{10}{E - 5}$$

B Use the verbal model to write an expression involving addition for the total gas consumed.

Total gas consumed	=	Gas consumed on highway	+	Gas consumed in city

$$\text{Total gas consumed} = \frac{25}{E} + \frac{10}{E - 5}$$

C Carry out the addition to get a combined expression for the total gas consumed.

$$\text{Total gas consumed} = \frac{25(E - 5) + 10E}{E(E - 5)} = \frac{35E - 125}{E(E - 5)}$$

REFLECT

4a. Use unit analysis to show why dividing distance traveled by fuel efficiency gives the amount of gas consumed.

$$\text{miles} \div \frac{\text{miles}}{\text{gallons}} = \text{miles} \cdot \frac{\text{gallons}}{\text{miles}} = \text{gallons}$$

© Houghton Mifflin Harcourt Publishing Company

PRACTICE

Simplify each expression.

1. $\frac{2x - 4}{3x - 6}$

$\frac{2}{3}$

2. $\frac{4x + 8}{8x + 4}$

$\frac{x + 2}{2x + 1}$

3. $\frac{2x - 10}{x^2 - 3x - 10} \cdot$

$\frac{2}{x + 2}$

Find each sum or difference.

4. $\frac{x-5}{x+3} + \frac{x+4}{x-2}$

$\frac{2x^2 + 22}{(x + 3)(x - 2)}$

5. $\frac{3x}{2x+6} + \frac{x}{x^2 + 7x + 12}$

$\frac{3x^2 + 14x}{2(x + 4)(x + 3)}$

6. $\frac{1}{x^2 + 2x + 1} + \frac{1}{x^2 - 1}$

$\frac{2x}{(x + 1)^2(x - 1)}$

7. $\frac{7}{x^2 - 4x + 4} - \frac{3x}{x - 2}$

$\frac{-3x^2 + 6x + 7}{(x - 2)^2}$

8. $\frac{x+2}{x-1} - \frac{x+8}{3x^2 + 3x - 6}$

$\frac{3x^2 + 11x + 4}{3(x + 2)(x - 1)}$

9. $\frac{x}{x^2 - 2x + 1} - \frac{x}{x^2 - 1}$

$\frac{2x}{(x - 1)^2(x + 1)}$

10. Anita exercises by running and walking. When she runs, she burns c Calories per minute for a total of 500 Calories. When she walks, she burns $(c - 8)$ Calories per minute for a total of 100 Calories.

  a. Write an expression for the time that she spends running and another expression for the time that she spends walking.

  Running time $= \frac{500}{c}$; walking time $= \frac{100}{c - 8}$

  b. Write two equivalent expressions for her total time.

  Total time $= \frac{500}{c} + \frac{100}{c - 8} = \frac{600c - 4000}{c(c - 8)}$

11. a. In the second row of the table, write the result after performing the operation given in the first row of the table.

$\frac{x}{x+2} + \frac{1}{x^2-4}$	$\frac{x}{x+2} - \frac{1}{x^2-4}$	$\frac{x}{x+2} \cdot \frac{1}{x^2-4}$	$\frac{x}{x+2} \div \frac{1}{x^2-4}$
$\frac{(x-1)^2}{(x+2)(x-2)}$	$\frac{x^2 - 2x - 1}{(x+2)(x-2)}$	$\frac{x}{(x+2)^2(x-2)}$	$x(x - 2)$

  b. Do the results support or refute the claim that the set of all rational expressions is closed under all four basic operations? Explain.

  Support; all results are rational expressions including the last, which can be written as $\frac{x^2 - 2x}{1}$.

  c. Based on closure, what subset of real numbers is the set of rational expressions most like?

  The set of rational numbers

© Houghton Mifflin Harcourt Publishing Company

Assign these pages to help your students practice
and apply important lesson concepts. For
additional exercises, see the Student Edition.

Answers

Additional Practice

1. $15x^3y^6$

2. $(x-1)(x+2)(x-3)$

3. $\dfrac{6x-8}{x+4}; x \neq -4$ **4.** $\dfrac{-2x+14}{2x-5}; x \neq \dfrac{5}{2}$

5. $\dfrac{2x^2+7x+4}{x^2-x-12}; x \neq 4, x \neq -3$

6. $\dfrac{2x^2-5x-7}{x^2-3x-18}; x \neq 6, x \neq -3$

7. $\dfrac{x^2-4x+2}{x^2-2x-15}; x \neq -3, x \neq 5$

8. $\dfrac{-2x^2-3x+6}{x^2-7x-18}; x \neq -2, x \neq 9$

9. $\dfrac{x^2-4x+3}{x^2+11x+30}$ **10.** $\dfrac{12x-24}{x^3+3x^2+x+3}$

11. $2.6\overline{6}$ packages per hour

Problem Solving

1. **a.** $\dfrac{d}{6} + \dfrac{d}{3}$

     b. $2d$

     c. $\dfrac{2d}{\frac{d}{6}+\frac{d}{3}}$

     d. Vicki is correct. Possible answer: Lorena
calculated the average speed as if it took
the same amount of time for each leg of the
trip. Vicki took into consideration the time
for each leg.

2. 4.8 knots   **3.** D

4. C   **5.** B

6. D

Notes

Additional Practice

Find the least common multiple for each pair.

1. $3x^2y^8$ and $5x^3y^2$

2. $x^2 + x - 2$ and $x^2 - x - 6$

Add or subtract. Identify any x-values for which the expression is undefined.

3. $\dfrac{2x-3}{x+4} + \dfrac{4x-5}{x+4}$

4. $\dfrac{x+12}{2x-5} - \dfrac{3x-2}{2x-5}$

5. $\dfrac{x+4}{x^2-x-12} + \dfrac{2x}{x-4}$

6. $\dfrac{3x^2-1}{x^2-3x-18} - \dfrac{x+2}{x-6}$

7. $\dfrac{x+2}{x^2-2x-15} + \dfrac{x}{x+3}$

8. $\dfrac{x+6}{x^2-7x-18} - \dfrac{2x}{x-9}$

Simplify. Assume all expressions are defined.

9. $\dfrac{\dfrac{x-1}{x+5}}{\dfrac{x+6}{x-3}}$

10. $\dfrac{\dfrac{12}{x+3}}{\dfrac{x^2+1}{x-2}}$

Solve.

11. A messenger is required to deliver 10 packages per day. Each day, the messenger works only for as long as it takes to deliver the daily quota of 10 packages. On average, the messenger is able to deliver 2 packages per hour on Saturday and 4 packages per hour on Sunday. What is the messenger's average delivery rate on the weekend?

Problem Solving

Vicki and Lorena motor downstream at about 6 knots (nautical miles per hour) in their boat. The return trip is against the current, and they can motor at only about 3 knots.

1. Vicki wants to find the average speed for the entire trip.

   a. Write an expression for the time it takes to travel downstream plus the time it takes for the return trip if the distance in each direction is d.

   b. What is the total distance they travel downstream and upstream in terms of d?

   c. Write an expression for their average speed using the expressions for the total time and the total distance.

   d. Vicki says that the average speed is 4 knots. Lorena says that the average speed is 4.5 knots. Explain who is correct and why.

2. If they delay the return trip until the current changes direction, they can motor back at 4 knots. What is the average speed for the entire trip under these conditions?

Zak runs at an average speed of 7.0 miles per hour during the first half of a race and an average speed of 5.5 miles per hour during the second half of a race. Choose the letter for the best answer.

3. Which expression gives Zak's average speed for the entire race?

   A $\dfrac{(7+5.5)}{2}$

   B $\dfrac{12.5(7+5.5)d}{2}$

   C $\dfrac{(38.5)d}{(7+5.5)}$

   D $\dfrac{2(38.5)d}{(7+5.5)d}$

4. If Zak runs the race in 1.25 hours, what is the length of the race in miles?

   A 3.85

   B 6.25

   C 7.7

   D 12.5

5. In a later race, Zak increased his average speed during the second half of the race to 6.0 miles per hour. What is his average speed for this race in miles per hour?

   A 6.42

   B 6.46

   C 6.52

   D 6.56

6. It took Zak 1.6 hours to run this later race. What is the length of this race in miles?

   A 5.17

   B 7.28

   C 9.55

   D 10.34

Rational Functions
Extension: Translating the Graph of $g(x) = \frac{a}{x}$

Essential question: *How does changing the values of the parameters affect the graph of more complicated rational functions?*

CC.9-12.A.APR.6 Rewrite simple rational expressions in different forms; write $a(x)/b(x)$ in the form $q(x) + r(x)/b(x)$, where $a(x)$, $b(x)$, $q(x)$, and $r(x)$ are polynomials with the degree of $r(x)$ less than the degree of $b(x)$, using inspection, long division, ...

CC.9-12.A.CED.2 Create equations in two or more variables to represent relationships between quantities; graph equations on coordinate axes with labels and scales.*

CC.9-12.F.IF.2 Use function notation, evaluate functions for inputs in their domains, and interpret statements that use function notation in terms of a context.

CC.9-12.F.IF.4 For a function that models a relationship between two quantities, interpret key features of graphs and tables in terms of the quantities, and sketch graphs showing key features given a verbal description of the relationship.*

CC.9-12.F.IF.7 Graph functions expressed symbolically and show key features of the graph, by hand in simple cases and using technology for more complicated cases.*

CC.9-12.F.IF.7d(+) Graph rational functions, identifying zeros and asymptotes when suitable factorizations are available, and showing end behavior.*

CC.9-12.F.BF.1 Write a function that describes a relationship between two quantities.*

CC.9-12.F.BF.1a Determine an explicit expression ... from a context.*

CC.9-12.F.BF.3 Identify the effect on the graph of replacing $f(x)$ by ... $f(x) + k$ ... and $f(x + k)$ for specific values of k (both positive and negative) ...

Also: CC.9-12.F.IF.5*, CC.9-12.F.IF.9*

Vocabulary

rational function

Prerequisites

Graphing and translating $f(x) = \frac{a}{x}$

Polynomial long division

Math Background

Previously, students graphed rational functions of the form $f(x) = \frac{a}{x}$ by transforming the graph of the parent function $f(x) = \frac{1}{x}$. Students will now extend that knowledge by investigating how the values of h and k are related to the graph of $f(x) = \frac{a}{x - h} + k$. Students should recall that the graph of the polynomial function $f(x) = (x - h)^n + k$ is translated h units horizontally and k units vertically from the graph of the parent function $f(x) = x^n$. In this lesson, they will see that changing the values of h and k affect the graph of $f(x) = \frac{a}{x - h} + k$ in the same way. Also, students will graph rational functions in the general form $f(x) = \frac{p(x)}{q(x)}$, where $p(x)$ and $q(x)$ are polynomial functions and $q(x) \neq 0$. Finally, students will graph rational functions of the form $f(x) = \frac{bx + c}{dx + e}$, where $bx + c$ and $dx + e$ are both linear functions. Although such functions can be graphed by rewriting in the graphing form, students will also learn how to graph these functions without rewriting them first.

INTRODUCE

Ask students to recall what they know about the graph of the polynomial function $f(x) = (x - h)^n + k$ and the effects of changing the values of h and k. Ask them to predict the effects of changing the values of h and k on the graph of the rational function $f(x) = \frac{a}{x - h} + k$. Students will begin graphing functions of the form $f(x) = \frac{bx + c}{dx + e}$ by first rewriting them in the graphing form $f(x) = \frac{a}{x - h} + k$.

Review the process for using the graphing form to determine the horizontal asymptote $y = k$, the vertical asymptote $x = h$, and reference points $(1 + h, a + k)$ and $(-1 + h, -a + k)$. Also review the process of polynomial long division, which students will use to rewrite functions in graphing form.

Name_____ Class_____ Date_____

5-4

Rational Functions

Extension: Translating the Graph of $g(x) = \frac{a}{x}$

Essential question: *How does changing the values of the parameters affect the graph of more complicated rational functions?*

You have seen that the graphs of functions of the form $g(x) = \frac{a}{x}$ are vertical stretches or shrinks, coupled with a reflection in the x-axis when $a < 0$, of the graph of the parent function $f(x) = \frac{1}{x}$. In this lesson, you will learn how the graphs of more complicated rational functions are related to the graph of the parent function.

CC.9-12.F.IF.7d(+)

1 EXAMPLE Graphing $s(x) = \frac{a}{x-h} + k$ when $a = 1$

Graph the function $s(x) = \frac{1}{x-3} + 2$.

A Determine the graph's horizontal asymptote. You know from examining the end behavior of the parent function that its graph has the x-axis as a horizontal asymptote. Now consider the end behavior of the given function.

x increases without bound.			x decreases without bound.	
x	$s(x) = \frac{1}{x-3} + 2$		**x**	$s(x) = \frac{1}{x-3} + 2$
103	2.01		−97	1.99
1003	2.001		−997	1.999
10,003	2.0001		−9997	1.9999
100,003	2.00001		−99,997	1.99999

As $x \to +\infty$, $s(x) \to$ ___2___   As $x \to -\infty$, $s(x) \to$ ___2___

So, the graph's horizontal asymptote is the line ___$y = 2$___

B Determine the graph's vertical asymptote. You know that the parent function is undefined when $x = 0$. You also know from examining the behavior of the parent function near $x = 0$ that the graph has the y-axis as a vertical asymptote.

For what value of x is the given function undefined? ___$x = 3$___

Complete the tables below to show that the graph's vertical asymptote is the line $x = 3$.

x approaches 3 from the right.			x approaches 3 from the left.	
x	$s(x) = \frac{1}{x-3} + 2$		**x**	$s(x) = \frac{1}{x-3} + 2$
3.01	102		2.99	−98
3.001	1002		2.999	−998
3.0001	10,002		2.9999	−9998
3.00001	100,002		2.99999	−99,998

As $x \to 3^+$, $s(x) \to$ ___$+\infty$___   As $x \to 3^-$, $s(x) \to$ ___$-\infty$___

C Identify the coordinates of two reference points. You know that one branch of the graph of the parent function $f(x) = \frac{1}{x}$ includes the point $(1, 1)$ while the other branch includes the point $(-1, -1)$. These points are 1 unit to the right and 1 unit to the left of the vertical asymptote. What are the corresponding points on the graph of $s(x) = \frac{1}{x-3} + 2$?

(4, 3) and (2, 1)

D Draw the graph by first drawing the horizontal and vertical asymptotes as dashed lines and then plotting the reference points. Each branch of the graph should pass through one of the reference points and approach the asymptotes. (The graph of the parent function is shown in gray.)

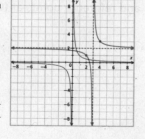

REFLECT

1a. Describe how to graph $s(x) = \frac{1}{x-3} + 2$ as a transformation of the graph of $f(x) = \frac{1}{x}$.

Translate the graph of f right 3 units and up 2 units.

1b. What are the domain and range of the function $s(x) = \frac{1}{x-3} + 2$?

$D = \{x \mid x \neq 3\}$; $R = \{y \mid y \neq 2\}$

Questioning Strategies

- How is the process of graphing a rational function of the form $f(x) = \frac{1}{x-h} + k$ related to the process of graphing a polynomial function of the form $f(x) = (x-h)^n + k$? **In both cases, you start with the graph of the parent function and translate the graph h units horizontally and k units vertically.**

- Why is the function $s(x) = \frac{1}{x-3} + 2$ undefined for the value $x = 3$? **because $x - 3$ equals 0, and division by zero is undefined**

Teaching Strategies

Encourage students to use mental math when completing the tables in parts A and B. For instance, when determining the value of $s(x)$ for $x = 103$, students should follow the order of operations and perform these calculations mentally: The difference of 103 and 3 is 100. The reciprocal of 100 is 0.01. The sum of 0.01 and 2 is 2.01, which is the value of $s(x)$.

When graphing the function in part D, students may need to plot other points besides the reference points. For instance, they can plot $(-1, 1.75)$, $(2.5, 0)$, $(3.5, 4)$, and $(5, 2.5)$. But they should recognize that each branch of the graph will follow the asymptotes as you move away from the reference points.

EXTRA EXAMPLE

Graph the function $s(x) = \frac{1}{x-4} + 1$. The graph is a translation of the graph of $f(x) = \frac{1}{x}$ with horizontal asymptote at $y = 1$, vertical asymptote at $x = 4$, and reference points at $(3, 0)$ and $(5, 2)$.

Questioning Strategies

- What horizontal and vertical translations are performed on the graph of $g(x) = \frac{3}{x}$ to obtain the graph of $s(x) = \frac{3}{x+2} + 1$? Given that the asymptotes of the graph of $g(x)$ are $x = 0$ and $y = 0$, what asymptotes do you get for the graph of $h(x)$ when you perform the translations on the asymptotes for the graph of $g(x)$? **Translate 2 units left and 1 unit up; $x = -2$ and $y = 1$**

- After graphing $s(x) = \frac{3}{x+2} + 1$ by plotting horizontal and vertical asymptotes of $y = 1$ and $x = -2$ and reference points $(-1, 4)$ and $(-3, -2)$, how could you check that you have graphed the function correctly? **Since the graph also appears to include the points $(-5, 0)$ and $(1, 2)$, substitute these values into the function.**

Differentiated Instruction

After the horizontal and vertical asymptotes of the graph have been identified, visual learners may benefit from drawing horizontal and vertical arrows to find the reference points.

They already know that the graph of $g(x) = \frac{3}{x}$ includes the reference points $(1, 3)$ and $(-1, -3)$, and that the horizontal and vertical asymptotes of the graph of $s(x) = \frac{3}{x+2} + 1$ intersect at $(-2, 1)$. By starting at the intersection and drawing a pair of arrows 1 unit right and 3 units up to get to the translation of $(1, 3)$, and a second pair 1 unit left and 3 units down to get to the translation of $(-1, -3)$, they will identify the reference points of $(-1, 4)$ and $(-3, -2)$.

EXTRA EXAMPLE

Graph the function $s(x) = \frac{2}{x+1} + 3$. The graph is a translation of the graph of $f(x) = \frac{2}{x}$ with horizontal asymptote at $y = 3$, vertical asymptote at $x = -1$, and reference points at $(0, 5)$ and $(-2, 1)$.

You have seen how to graph $s(x) = \frac{a}{x-h} + k$ when $a = 1$. The method is the same when $a \neq 1$, except that you translate the graph of $g(x) = \frac{a}{x}$ rather than the graph of $f(x) = \frac{1}{x}$.

CC.9-12.F.IF.7d(+)

2 EXAMPLE Graphing $s(x) = \frac{a}{x-h} + k$ when $a \neq 1$

Graph the function $s(x) = \frac{3}{x+2} + 1$.

A Identify the graph's horizontal asymptote. _____ $y = 1$

B Identify the graph's vertical asymptote. _____ $x = -2$

C Identify the coordinates of two reference points. You know that one branch of the graph of $g(x) = \frac{3}{x}$ includes the point $(1, 3)$ while the other branch includes the point $(-1, -3)$. These points are 1 unit to the right and 1 unit to the left of the vertical asymptote. What are the coordinates of the corresponding points on the graph of $s(x) = \frac{3}{x+2} + 1$?

_____ $(-1, 4)$ and $(-3, -2)$

D Draw the graph by first drawing the horizontal and vertical asymptotes as dashed lines and then plotting the reference points. Each branch of the graph should pass through one of the reference points and approach the asymptotes. (The graph of $g(x) = \frac{3}{x}$ is shown in gray.)

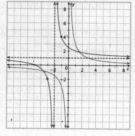

REFLECT

2a. Describe how to graph $s(x) = \frac{3}{x+2} + 1$ as a transformation of the graph of $f(x) = \frac{1}{x}$.

Vertically stretch the graph of f by a factor of 3, then translate the stretched graph 2 units left and 1 unit up.

2b. Complete the table to summarize the characteristics of the graphs of the functions listed there.

	$f(x) = \frac{1}{x}$	$g(x) = \frac{a}{x}$	$s(x) = \frac{a}{x-h} + k$
Horizontal Asymptote	$y = 0$	$y = 0$	$y = k$
Vertical Asymptote	$x = 0$	$x = 0$	$x = h$
Reference Points	$(1, 1), (-1, -1)$	$(1, a), (-1, -a)$	$(1 + h, a + k),$ $(-1 + h, -a + k)$

A **rational function** has the form $f(x) = \frac{p(x)}{q(x)}$ where $p(x)$ and $q(x)$ are polynomial functions and $q(x) \neq 0$. The functions that you have learned to graph are rational functions because they can be written as the ratio of two polynomials. For instance, you can write $f(x) = \frac{2}{x+1} + 3$ as $f(x) = \frac{2}{x+1} + 3 = \frac{2}{x+1} + \frac{3(x+1)}{x+1} = \frac{3x+5}{x+1}$. Notice that the numerator and denominator of this function are both linear. Because the process of writing $f(x) = \frac{a}{x-h} + k$ as $f(x) = \frac{bx+c}{dx+e}$ is reversible, you have a means of graphing rational functions with linear numerators and denominators by putting them in the *graphing form* $f(x) = \frac{a}{x-h} + k$.

CC.9-12.F.IF.7d(+)

3 EXAMPLE Graphing $f(x) = \frac{bx+c}{dx+e}$ when $d = 1$

Graph the function $f(x) = \frac{3x+2}{x-1}$.

A Use long division to write the function in graphing form.

$$x - 1 \overline{)3x + 2} \quad \text{with quotient } 3$$

Divide $3x$ by x and write down the quotient, 3.

$$\begin{array}{r} 3 \\ x-1{\overline{\smash{\big)}\,3x+2}} \\ \underline{3x - 3} \\ 5 \end{array}$$

Multiply the divisor, $x - 1$, by the quotient and subtract the result from the dividend, $3x + 2$, to get the remainder, 5.

So, the division of $3x + 2$ by $x - 1$ results in a quotient of 3 with a remainder of 5. Use the relationship below to rewrite the function's rule.

$$\frac{\text{dividend}}{\text{divisor}} = \text{quotient} + \frac{\text{remainder}}{\text{divisor}}$$

$$\frac{3x+2}{x-1} = 3 + \frac{5}{x-1}$$

Write the function in graphing form: _____ $f(x) = \frac{5}{x-1} + 3$

Questioning Strategies

- How can you use what you know about translating the graph of $f(x) = \frac{a}{x}$ to graph $f(x) = \frac{3x + 2}{x - 1}$? Rewrite the function in graphing form as $f(x) = \frac{5}{x - 1} + 3$; translate the graph of $f(x) = \frac{5}{x}$ right 1 unit and up 3 units.

- When $f(x) = \frac{3x + 2}{x - 1}$ is written in graphing form, what are the values of a, h, and k? 5, 1, 3

Differentiated Instruction

Interpersonal learners may benefit from working in pairs, with one student graphing $f(x) = \frac{3x + 2}{x - 1}$ by rewriting the function in graphing form and the other graphing the function by making a table of values and plotting points. Students should compare the strategies by identifying at least one advantage and one disadvantage for each method. Then have them swap methods to complete the Extra Example.

EXTRA EXAMPLE

Graph the function $f(x) = \frac{2x - 5}{x - 4}$. The horizontal asymptote is $y = 2$. The vertical asymptote is $x = 4$. The reference points are $(5, 5)$ and $(3, -1)$.

Questioning Strategies

- How are the domain and the range of $f(x) = \frac{3x + 4}{4x - 5}$ related to the graph of the function? The domain is $\{x \mid x \neq 1.25\}$ and the vertical asymptote is $x = 1.25$, so the value excluded from the domain is where the vertical asymptote occurs. The range is $\{y \mid y \neq 0.75\}$, and the horizontal asymptote is $y = 0.75$, so the value excluded from the range is also where the horizontal asymptote occurs.

- How can you use the graphing form of $f(x) = \frac{3x + 4}{4x - 5}$ to determine reference points on each side of the vertical asymptote? The graphing form $f(x) = \frac{1.9375}{x - 1.25} + 0.75$ represents a translation of the graph of $f(x) = \frac{1.9375}{x}$, which includes reference points $(1, 1.9375)$ and $(-1, -1.9375)$. The graphing form tells you that the graph is translated 1.25 units to the right and 0.75 units up, so the translated reference points are $(2.25, 2.6875)$ and $(0.25, -1.1875)$.

EXTRA EXAMPLE

Graph the function $f(x) = \frac{2x + 4}{5x - 3}$. The horizontal asymptote is $y = 0.4$, the vertical asymptote is $x = 0.6$, and the reference points are $\left(0, -\frac{4}{3}\right)$ and $(1, 3)$.

B Use the graphing form to complete the information below about the graph. Then graph the function.

- Horizontal asymptote: $y = 3$
- Vertical asymptote: $x = 1$
- Reference point that is 1 unit to the right of the vertical asymptote: $(2, 8)$
- Reference point that is 1 unit to the left of the vertical asymptote: $(0, -2)$

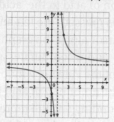

REFLECT

3a. Describe how you can find the vertical asymptote of the graph of $f(x) = \frac{3x + 2}{x - 1}$ without writing the function in graphing form first.

The vertical asymptote occurs at the value of x for which the function is undefined, which is when the denominator equals 0.

3b. If you divide the numerator and denominator of $f(x) = \frac{3x + 2}{x - 1}$ by x, you get $f(x) = \frac{3 + \frac{2}{x}}{1 - \frac{1}{x}}$. Use this form of the function to complete the table.

	The numerator approaches this value.	The denominator approaches this value.	The function approaches this value.
As x increases without bound	3	1	$\frac{3}{1} = 3$
As x decreases without bound	3	1	$\frac{3}{1} = 3$

3c. What does the table above tell you about the graph of the function?
The line $y = 3$ is a horizontal asymptote for the graph.

The Reflect questions on the previous page suggest another way to find the asymptotes of the graph of $f(x) = \frac{bx + c}{dx + e}$.

- To find the vertical asymptote, set the denominator equal to 0 and solve for x. (You are finding the value of x for which the function is undefined. This value is sometimes called an *excluded value* because it cannot be included in the function's domain.)
- To find the horizontal asymptote, divide the numerator and the denominator of the function's rule by x, and then determine what value the function approaches as x increases or decreases without bound.

CC.9-12.F.IF.7d(+)

4 EXAMPLE Graphing $f(x) = \frac{bx + c}{dx + e}$ when $d \neq 1$

Graph the function $f(x) = \frac{3x + 4}{4x - 5}$.

A Find the vertical asymptote. Set $4x - 5$ equal to 0 and solve for x to get
$x = \underline{1.25}$

B Find the horizontal asymptote. Rewrite the function rule as $f(x) = \frac{3 + \frac{4}{x}}{4 - \frac{5}{x}}$.
As x increases or decreases without bound, the y-value that the value of $f(x)$ approaches is $y = \underline{0.75}$

C Draw the graph after determining a reference point on each side of the vertical asymptote.

- A reference point to the right of the vertical asymptote: *Sample answer: About (2, 3.3)*
- A reference point to the left of the vertical asymptote: *Sample answer: (0, −0.8)*

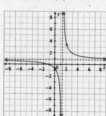

5 **EXAMPLE**

Questioning Strategies

- What would be the rule for $C(a)$ if the initial amount of acid were 3 mL instead of 5 mL? Explain.

$C(a) = \dfrac{a + 3}{a + 18}$; the concentration of acid in the acid-and-water mix would be $\dfrac{3}{3 + 15} = \dfrac{3}{18} \approx$ 16.7%, and when the additional amount a of acid is added, $C(a) = \dfrac{3 + a}{(3 + a) + 15} = \dfrac{a + 3}{a + 18}$.

- How could you graph $C(a) = \dfrac{a + 5}{a + 20}$ without using a graphing calculator? **You know that the graph begins at (0, 0.25). You can also determine that the graph has $C(a) = 1$ as its horizontal asymptote (which is the function's end behavior as a increases without bound). Make a table of values for several positive values of a, such as $a = 10, 20,$ and 30. Plot the points and draw a smooth curve that approaches the line $C(a) = 1$ for greater values of a.**

Technology

After students have graphed $C(a) = \dfrac{a + 5}{a + 20}$ using a graphing calculator, they can use the ⬚TRACE⬚ function to explore the relationship between the additional amount a of acid added and the concentration of acid in the acid-and-water mix. After ⬚TRACE⬚ is pressed, the left and right arrow keys move the cursor along the graph. As the cursor moves, its x- and y-coordinates are updated at the bottom of the viewing window. The x-value represents the amount a of acid added to the mix. The corresponding y-value represents, as a decimal, the percent of acid in the acid-and-water mix.

EXTRA EXAMPLE

An artist mixes 2 mL of red paint with 18 mL of white paint. The concentration of red in the red-and-white mix is $\dfrac{2}{2 + 18} = \dfrac{2}{20} = 10\%$.

If the painter adds more red to the mix, then the concentration of red C becomes a function of the additional amount r of red added to the mix. Write a rule for the function $C(r)$ and then graph the function using a graphing calculator. $C(r) = \dfrac{r + 2}{r + 20}$; graph the function on a graphing calculator with viewing window set to $x \geq 0$ and $0 \leq y \leq 1$.

<table>
<tr><td>⋰
MATHEMATICAL
PRACTICE
⋱</td><td>**Highlighting the Standards**</td></tr>
</table>

5 **EXAMPLE** and its Reflect questions offer an opportunity to address Mathematical Practice Standard 5 (Use appropriate tools strategically). Students write a rational function to model a real-world situation and then use a graphing calculator to graph the function. Although the vertical asymptote of the graph intersects the x-axis at a negative value of x, the reasonable domain for the function consists of only nonnegative values. Students manipulate the model by setting the viewing window of the graphing calculator to show only the portion of the graph that is relevant to the real-world situation.

REFLECT

4a. State the domain and range of the function.

$D = \{x \mid x \neq 1.25\}; R = \{y \mid y \neq 0.75\}$

4b. Follow the steps below to write $f(x) = \frac{3x+4}{4x-5}$ in graphing form.

Step 1: Divide the numerator and denominator by the coefficient of x in the denominator.

$f(x) = \dfrac{x + 1 \quad \boxed{0.75}}{x - \quad \boxed{1.25}}$

Step 2: Divide the numerator in Step 1 by the denominator in Step 1 using long division.

$x - \boxed{1.25} \enclose{longdiv}{\boxed{0.75}\,x + 1}$
$\dfrac{0.75 \quad \boxed{0.9375}}{x -}$
1.9375

Step 3: Write the function in graphing form.

$f(x) = \dfrac{\boxed{1.9375}}{x - \quad \boxed{1.25}} + \boxed{0.75}$

How does the graphing form help you check the graph that you drew?

It confirms that the vertical asymptote is $x = 1.25$ and the horizontal asymptote

is $y = 0.75$.

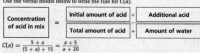 CC.9-12.F.BF.1

5 EXAMPLE Modeling with Rational Functions

A chemist mixes 5 mL of an acid with 15 mL of water. The concentration of acid in the acid-and-water mix is $\frac{5}{5+15} = \frac{5}{20} = 25\%$. If the chemist adds more acid to the mix, then the concentration C becomes a function of the additional amount a of acid added to the mix. Write a rule for the function $C(a)$ and then graph the function using a graphing calculator.

A Use the verbal model below to write the rule for $C(a)$.

| Concentration of acid in mix | = | Initial amount of acid + Additional acid |
| | | Total amount of acid + Amount of water |

$C(a) = \dfrac{5 + a}{(5 + a) + 15} = \dfrac{a + 5}{a + 20}$

B Determine a good viewing window by answering the following questions.

- What is a reasonable domain for the function? That is, what values can the variable a have in this situation?
  The amount of acid added must be nonnegative, so $a \geq 0$.

- What concentration of acid does pure water have? What concentration of acid does pure acid have? So, what are the possible values of $C(a)$?
  Pure water is 0% acid; pure acid is 100% acid; $0\% \leq C(a) \leq 100\%$ or $0 \leq C(a) \leq 1$

- On a graphing calculator, you will let x represent a and y represent $C(a)$. Specify a viewing window by stating the least and greatest x-values and the least and greatest y-values that you will use.
  Answers for the greatest x-value will vary. *Sample answer:* $0 \leq x \leq 20$; $0 \leq y \leq 1$

C Press ⬚ and set the viewing window. (Choose appropriate scales for the two axes.) Then press ⬚ and enter the rule for the function. Finally, press ⬚ to see the graph. It should look like the one shown.

REFLECT

5a. Analyze the function's rule to determine the vertical asymptote of the function's graph. Why is the asymptote irrelevant in this situation?
Vertical asymptote: $x = -20$; only nonnegative values of x are being considered.

5b. Analyze the function's rule to determine the horizontal asymptote of the function's graph. What is the relevance of the asymptote in this situation?
Horizontal asymptote: $y = 1$; when the chemist adds lots of acid to the mix, the
concentration of acid in the mix approaches that of pure acid (concentration = 1).

PRACTICE

Identify the asymptotes of the graph of each function.

1. $f(x) = \frac{5}{x-4}$
$x = 4, y = 0$

2. $f(x) = \frac{0.2}{x} - 1$
$x = 0, y = -1$

3. $f(x) = \frac{-4}{x+1} + 3$
$x = -1, y = 3$

4. $f(x) = \frac{11}{x-9} + 9$
$x = 9, y = 9$

Essential Question

How does changing the values of the parameters affect the graph of more complicated rational functions?

Changing the values of h and k will result in a translation of the graph of $f(x) = \dfrac{a}{x-h} + k$. The graph of $f(x) = \dfrac{a}{x-h} + k$ is the graph of $f(x) = \dfrac{a}{x}$ translated h units horizontally and k units vertically. The horizontal asymptote will be $y = k$, the vertical asymptote will be $x = h$, and the reference points will be $(1 + h, a + k)$ and $(-1 + h, -a + k)$.

When a rational function is given in the form $f(x) = \dfrac{bx + c}{dx + e}$, rewrite the function in graphing form $h(x) = \dfrac{a}{x-h} + k$ in order to determine how the graph of the function is related to the graph of its parent function.

Summarize

Have students make a table that shows the effects of changing the values of h and k on the graph of $f(x) = \dfrac{a}{x-h} + k$ for $a = 1$ and $a \neq 1$. For each of the two cases, have them give an example of a corresponding function and its graph. For each graph, have them include the graph of the parent function and describe, in words, how the graph of $f(x) = \dfrac{a}{x-h} + k$ relates to the graph of the parent function.

Also have them make a table showing the steps for graphing a function of the form $f(x) = \dfrac{bx + c}{dx + e}$ by two methods: (1) writing the function in graphing form before graphing and (2) graphing the function without writing the function in graphing form first.

PRACTICE

Where skills are taught	Where skills are practiced
1 EXAMPLE	EX. 5
2 EXAMPLE	EXS. 1–4, 6–8
3 EXAMPLE	EXS. 9, 10
4 EXAMPLE	EX. 11
5 EXAMPLE	EX. 12

Graph each function.

5. $f(x) = \frac{1}{x-2} + 4$

6. $f(x) = -\frac{1}{x+1} - 2$

7. $f(x) = \frac{0.5}{x-1} - 3$

8. $f(x) = -\frac{2}{x+3} + 1$

Write each function in graphing form and then graph the function.

9. $f(x) = \frac{3x-14}{x-5}$ $f(x) = \frac{1}{x-5} + 3$

10. $f(x) = -\frac{4x+5}{x+2}$ $f(x) = \frac{3}{x+2} - 4$

---

11. Graph $f(x) = \frac{2x+1}{5x-2}$ after finding the asymptotes and plotting a reference point on each side of the vertical asymptote.

- Vertical asymptote: $x = 0.4$
- Horizontal asymptote: $y = 0.4$
- A reference point to the right of the vertical asymptote: Sample answer: (1, 1)
- A reference point to the left of the vertical asymptote: Sample answer: (0, −0.5)

12. A baseball team has won 18 games and lost 12. Its current percent of wins is $\frac{18}{18+12} = \frac{18}{30} = 0.6$, or 60%. Suppose the team experiences a winning streak where every game played is a win. Then its percent P of wins becomes a function of the number w of wins in the streak.

a. Use the verbal model below to write a rule for $P(w)$.

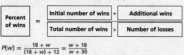

Percent of wins	=	Initial number of wins + Additional wins
		Total number of wins + Number of losses

$P(w) = \frac{18 + w}{(18 + w) + 12} = \frac{w + 18}{w + 30}$

b. Before graphing the function on a graphing calculator, decide what a good viewing window would be. Explain your reasoning.

Answers will vary, but students should recognize that x (representing w) should be nonnegative and that y (representing P(w)) should be between 0 and 1.

c. Again, before graphing the function on a graphing calculator, state what the graph's y-intercept is and whether the graph is increasing or decreasing. Explain your reasoning.

The y-intercept is 0.6 because that is the initial percent of wins; the graph is increasing because winning more games increases the percent of wins.

d. Graph the function on a graphing calculator. Describe the end behavior in terms of the context of the problem.

The graph approaches the horizontal asymptote y = 1, which represents a perfect winning percentage.

ADDITIONAL PRACTICE AND PROBLEM SOLVING

Assign these pages to help your students practice and apply important lesson concepts. For additional exercises, see the Student Edition.

Answers

Additional Practice

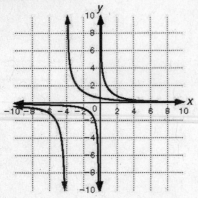

1. Translate 4 units left and vertically stretched by a factor of 2

2. Vertical asymptote: $x = 3$; horizontal asymptote: $y = 5$; domain: $\{x \mid x \neq 3\}$; range: $\{y \mid y \neq 5\}$

3. Vertical asymptote: $x = -8$; horizontal asymptote: $y = -1$; domain: $\{x \mid x \neq -8\}$; range: $\{y \mid y \neq -1\}$

4. a. Zeros: -5 and 1

   b. Vertical asymptote: $x = -1$

   c. Horizontal asymptote: none

   d.

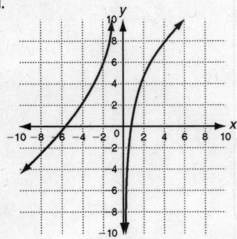

5. a. The asymptote is 250; it is the average number of people who will visit the store each day, long after the store opens.

   b. 283

Problem Solving

1. a. $f(x) = \left(\frac{420}{x}\right) + 70$

   b.

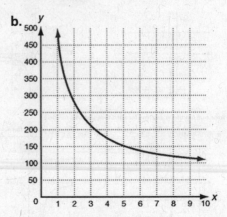

   c. $154; $130; $112

   d. $y = 70$; possible answer: no matter how many people go on the trip, the cost per person cannot be less than $70.

2. a. $f(x) = \left(\frac{1000}{x}\right) + 145$

   b. $345.00; $287.90; $245.00

   c. $133.00

3. A   4. C

Name_____ Class_____ Date_____

Additional Practice

Using the graph of $f(x) = \frac{1}{x}$ as a guide, describe the transformation and graph the function.

1. $g(x) = \frac{2}{x+4}$

_____

Identify the asymptotes, domain, and range of each function.

2. $g(x) = \frac{1}{x-3} + 5$ _____
_____

3. $g(x) = \frac{1}{x+8} - 1$ _____
_____

Identify the zeros and asymptotes of the function. Then graph.

4. $f(x) = \frac{x^2 + 4x - 5}{x+1}$

   a. Zeros:
   _____

   b. Vertical asymptote:
   _____

   c. Horizontal asymptote:
   _____

   d. Graph.

Solve.

5. The number, n, of daily visitors to a new store can be modeled by the function $n = \frac{250x + 1000}{x}$, where x is the number of days the store has been open.

   a. What is the asymptote of this function and what does it represent? _____

   b. To the nearest integer, how many visitors can be expected on day 30? _____

Problem Solving

Members of a high school cheerleading squad plan a trip to support their robotics team at a regional competition. The trip will cost $70 per person plus a $420 deposit for the bus.

1. Find the total cost of the trip per cheerleader.

   a. Write a function that represents the total cost of the trip per cheerleader.

   _____

   b. Graph the function on your graphing calculator. Sketch a graph to represent the function.

   c. Use your graph to determine the cost per person if
   5 cheerleaders go on the trip. _____
   7 cheerleaders go on the trip. _____
   10 cheerleaders go on the trip. _____

   d. What is the horizontal asymptote of the function? What does it mean in terms of the cost per person of the trip?

   _____

2. Stanton invites the cheerleaders to support the school's dive team at their next competition. The trip will cost $145 per person plus a $1000 deposit.

   a. Write a function to represent the cost of the trip per person. _____

   b. What is the cost per person if
   5 cheerleaders go on the trip? _____
   7 cheerleaders go on the trip? _____
   10 cheerleaders go on the trip? _____

   c. What is the increased cost for each of 10 cheerleaders to go with the dive team rather than to go with the robotics team? _____

Choose the letter for the best answer.

3. The deposit for the bus on the robotics trip increases to $550. By how much does the cost per person increase if 10 cheerleaders go on the trip?

   A $13
   B $37
   C $83
   D $112

4. There are 15 cheerleaders signed up to go to the competition with the dive team. What is the cost per person to the nearest dollar?

   A $76
   B $103
   C $212
   D $304

Solving Rational Equations and Inequalities
Going Deeper

Essential question: *What methods are there for solving rational equations?*

COMMON CORE **Standards for Mathematical Content**

CC.9-12.A.CED.1 Create equations ... in one variable and use them to solve problems.*

CC.9-12.A.REI.2 Solve simple rational ... equations in one variable, and give examples showing how extraneous solutions may arise.

CC.9-12.A.REI.11 Explain why the x-coordinates of the points where the graphs of the equations $y = f(x)$ and $y = g(x)$ intersect are the solutions of the equation $f(x) = g(x)$; find the solutions approximately, e.g., using technology to graph the functions ... Include cases where $f(x)$ and/or $g(x)$ are linear, ... rational ... functions.*

Also: CC.9-12.A.SSE.1*, CC.9-12.A.SSE.1b*

Vocabulary
Extraneous solutions

Prerequisites
Multiplying rational expressions
Finding zeros of polynomial functions

Math Background
Students are familiar with methods for multiplying rational expressions and solving polynomial equations. In this lesson, students will combine these skills to solve rational equations.

INTRODUCE

Review techniques for factoring polynomials. Also, review the process for identifying excluded values in rational expressions.

TEACH

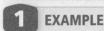

Questioning Strategies
• If the two sides of the equation are graphed as $y = \dfrac{2}{x-1}$ and $y = \dfrac{6}{x^2 - x}$, will the two graphs intersect, and if so, where? **Yes, the graphs will intersect at (3, 1), or when $x = 3$.**

• How does finding the LCM of the denominators of the rational expressions and multiplying each side of the equation by the LCM turn the rational equation into a polynomial equation? **After the multiplication of both sides by the LCM has been carried out, common factors in the numerators and denominators can be divided out. The resulting denominators on each side are 1, and since the numerators are both polynomials, the equation becomes a polynomial equation.**

Differentiated Instruction
After seeing the relationship between solving rational equations and solving polynomial equations, analytical learners may recall that when solving polynomial equations, the first step is often to rewrite the equation so that one side of the equation is set equal to 0. Analytical learners may benefit from rewriting this rational equation as $\dfrac{2}{x-1} - \dfrac{6}{x^2-1} = 0$. They can then use what they know about subtracting rational expressions to solve the equation, and draw additional conclusions about the parallels between solving rational and polynomial equations.

EXTRA EXAMPLE
Solve $\dfrac{4}{x-3} = \dfrac{8}{x^2-3x}$. $x = 2$

2 EXAMPLE

Questioning Strategies
• Why is the first step of the solution to factor the denominator of the rational expression on the right side of the equation? **Factoring the denominator makes it easier to determine the LCM.**

continued

Chapter 5   293   Lesson 5

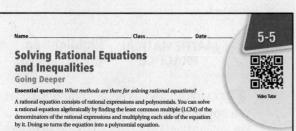

Name_____ Class_____ Date_____

5-5

Video Tutor

Solving Rational Equations and Inequalities
Going Deeper

Essential question: *What methods are there for solving rational equations?*

A rational equation consists of rational expressions and polynomials. You can solve a rational equation algebraically by finding the least common multiple (LCM) of the denominators of the rational expressions and multiplying each side of the equation by it. Doing so turns the equation into a polynomial equation.

CC.9-12.A.REI.2

1 EXAMPLE   Solving a Rational Equation Algebraically

Solve $\frac{2}{x-1} = \frac{6}{x^2-x}$.

$\frac{2}{x-1} = \frac{6}{x^2-x}$	Write the equation.
$\frac{2}{x-1} = \frac{6}{x(x-1)}$	Factor each denominator.
$\frac{2}{x-1} \cdot x(x-1) = \frac{6}{x(x-1)} \cdot x(x-1)$	Multiply each side by the LCM.
$\frac{2x(x-1)}{x-1} = \frac{6x(x-1)}{x(x-1)}$	Carry out the multiplication.
$2x = 6$	Simplify each side.
$x = 3$	Solve for x.

REFLECT

1a. Evaluate each side of the equation when $x = 3$. What conclusion can you draw?

$\frac{2}{3-1} = 1$; $\frac{6}{3^2-3} = \frac{6}{6} = 1$; both sides have the same value, so 3 is a solution.

1b. What are the excluded values for each rational expression in the equation? Is the solution of the equation among the excluded values? Why is it important to know whether a solution is among the excluded values?

1 is an excluded value for $\frac{2}{x-1}$; 0 and 1 are excluded values for $\frac{6}{x^2-x}$; 3 is not among the excluded values; if 3 were an excluded value, it wouldn't be a solution because at least one of the rational expressions would be undefined.

Chapter 5   293   Lesson 5

© Houghton Mifflin Harcourt Publishing Company

When solving rational equations algebraically, you must always check any apparent solutions to see if they are excluded values. If they are, then they are called **extraneous solutions** and must be rejected.

CC.9-12.A.REI.2

2 EXAMPLE   Solving Rational Equations Having Extraneous Solutions

Solve $\frac{x}{x-2} + \frac{1}{x-4} = \frac{2}{x^2-6x+8}$.

A Find the LCM of the denominators and multiply each side by it. Be sure to distribute the LCM to both rational expressions on the left side.

$\frac{x}{x-2} + \frac{1}{x-4} = \frac{2}{x^2-6x+8}$

$\frac{x}{x-2} + \frac{1}{x-4} = \frac{2}{(x-2)(x-4)}$

$\left[\frac{x}{x-2} + \frac{1}{x-4}\right](x-2)(x-4) = \frac{2}{(x-2)(x-4)} \cdot (x-2)(x-4)$

$\frac{x(x-2)(x-4)}{x-2} + \frac{(x-2)(x-4)}{x-4} = \frac{2(x-2)(x-4)}{(x-2)(x-4)}$

$x(x-4) + (x-2) = 2$

$x^2 - 3x - 2 = 2$

$x^2 - 3x - 4 = 0$

B Solve the resulting quadratic equation by factoring.

$(x+1)(x-4) = 0$

$x + 1 = 0$ or $x - 4 = 0$

$x = -1$ or $x = 4$

C Classify each apparent solution as either an actual solution or an extraneous solution.

* -1 is an ____actual____ solution.
* 4 is an ____extraneous____ solution.

REFLECT

2a. Evaluate the left and right sides of the equation when $x = -1$.

$\frac{-1}{-1-2} + \frac{1}{-1-4} = \frac{1}{3} + \left(-\frac{1}{5}\right) = \frac{5}{15} - \frac{3}{15} = \frac{2}{15}$; $\frac{2}{(-1)^2-6(-1)+8} = \frac{2}{15}$

Chapter 5   294   Lesson 5

© Houghton Mifflin Harcourt Publishing Company

- After multiplying both sides of the equation by the LCM, why is the equation rewritten as $x^2 - 3x - 4 = 0$ before being solved by factoring? **Simplifying the left side reveals that it is a quadratic expression. In order to solve the resulting quadratic equation by factoring and applying the Zero Product Property, one side of the equation must be 0.**

Avoid Common Errors

To make sure that students reject all extraneous solutions, have them evaluate the equation for each actual solution to double check that there are no excluded values that they may have overlooked.

EXTRA EXAMPLE

Solve $\dfrac{x}{x-3} + \dfrac{1}{x-5} = \dfrac{2}{x^2 - 8x + 15}$. $x = -1$

($x = 5$ is an extraneous solution.)

3 EXAMPLE

Questioning Strategies

- What steps would you follow to algebraically solve the equation that models the canoe trip? **Multiply each side of $\dfrac{6}{4+s} + \dfrac{6}{4-s} = 4$ by the LCM $(4 + s)(4 - s)$ and simplify to get $4s^2 - 16 = 0$. The solutions of the equation are $x = 2$ and $x = -2$, but only the positive value is reasonable in the context of the problem.**

- How would the equation that models the canoe trip change if the total trip time were 5 hours instead of 4 hours? **The right side of the equation would change from 4 to 5: $\dfrac{6}{4+s} + \dfrac{6}{4-s} = 5$.**

EXTRA EXAMPLE

Suppose you paddle a kayak at a steady speed of 5 miles per hour. You go 8 miles downstream and then 8 miles upstream to get back to where you started. The trip takes 5 hours. What is the speed of the current? **3 miles per hour**

```
MATHEMATICAL    Highlighting
   PRACTICE      the Standards
```

3 EXAMPLE and its Reflect questions offer an opportunity to address Mathematical Practice Standard 5 (Use appropriate tools strategically). When modeling a real-life situation by writing and solving a rational equation, students use a graphing calculator to find the solution quickly, allowing them to focus on interpreting the solution's meaning.

CLOSE

Essential Question

What methods are there for solving rational equations?

Rational equations can be solved algebraically by finding the LCM of the denominators of the rational expressions and multiplying each side of the equation by that LCM. When the equation is simplified, the result is a polynomial equation that can be solved by factoring, graphing, and other methods. Rational equations also can be solved by graphing. For example, each side of a rational equation may be entered as a function. The solution is the x-coordinate(s) of the point(s) at which the graphs intersect.

Summarize

Have students make a table that shows different methods that can be used to solve rational equations. For each method, have them list the steps they would follow to solve a rational equation using that method. Also, have them describe how they would classify each apparent solution as an actual or extraneous solution when solving a rational equation using that method.

PRACTICE

Where skills are taught	Where skills are practiced
1 EXAMPLE	EXS. 1–4
2 EXAMPLE	EXS. 5–7
3 EXAMPLE	EX. 8

3 EXAMPLE Modeling with Rational Equations

CC.9-12.A.CED.1

If you're in a canoe on a river and not paddling, you will travel in the same direction and at the same speed as the river's current. When you paddle *with* the current (downstream), the canoe's speed is the *sum* of your paddling speed and the current's speed. When you paddle *against* the current (upstream), the canoe's speed is the *difference* of your paddling speed and the current's speed.

Suppose you paddle a canoe at a steady speed of 4 miles per hour. You go 6 miles downstream and then 6 miles upstream to get back to where you started. The trip takes 4 hours. What is the speed of the current?

A Write expressions for the canoe's downstream and upstream speeds. Let s be the speed of the current.

Downstream speed = $4 + s$ Upstream speed = $4 - s$

B Divide the distance traveled in each direction by the canoe's speed in that direction to find the time for that part of the trip.

Downstream time = $\dfrac{6}{4+s}$ Upstream time = $\dfrac{6}{4-s}$

C Use the verbal model to write an equation that models the canoe trip.

| Downstream time | + | Upstream time | = | Total trip time |

$$\frac{6}{4+s} + \frac{6}{4-s} = 4$$

D Solve the equation. Although can you solve the equation using algebra, you can also solve it using a graphing calculator. Treat the left side of the equation as a rational function $f(x)$. (You will need to substitute x for s when you enter the function on the graphing calculator.) Treat the right side of the equation as the constant function $g(x) = 4$.

• What viewing window should you use for graphing? Why?

  Answers will vary. *Sample answer*: $0 \le x \le 4$ and $0 \le y \le 5$ because both the current's speed x and the trip time y are nonnegative, the current's speed will not exceed your paddling speed, and the trip time is 4 hours.

• Enter the functions and graph them. At what point do the graphs intersect? Interpret the coordinates of this point in the context of the problem.

  (2, 4); the current's speed is 2 miles per hour, which results in a trip time of 4 hours.

© Houghton Mifflin Harcourt Publishing Company

REFLECT

3a. The graph of $f(x)$ has a vertical asymptote at $x = 4$. Based on the context of the problem, why *should* there be a vertical asymptote at $x = 4$?

As the current's speed approaches 4 miles per hour (which is your paddling speed), the canoe's speed will approach 0, which means that your upstream time will grow without bound.

3b. Solve the equation in part C algebraically. How many solutions does the equation have? Do all the solutions make sense in the context of the problem? Why or why not?

$s = \pm 2$; there are two solutions, but the negative one doesn't make sense because the current's speed must be positive.

PRACTICE

Solve each equation.

1. $\dfrac{3}{x+1} = \dfrac{1}{x^2-1}$

$\dfrac{4}{3}$

2. $\dfrac{2}{x} = x - 1$

$-1, 2$

3. $\dfrac{3}{2x} - \dfrac{5}{3x} = 2$

$-\dfrac{1}{12}$

4. $\dfrac{x}{4} + 3 = \dfrac{x+4}{x-2}$

$-10, 4$

5. $\dfrac{x}{x-1} - \dfrac{3}{x} = \dfrac{1}{x^2-x}$

2

6. $\dfrac{4}{x^2-4} - \dfrac{1}{x+2} = \dfrac{x-1}{x-2}$

-4

7. Explain why the equation $\dfrac{x+1}{x-3} = \dfrac{4}{x-3}$ has no solution.

The only apparent solution, $x = 3$, is extraneous.

8. You paddle a canoe at a steady speed on a river where the current's speed is 1 kilometer per hour. You go 7.7 kilometers downstream and then 7.7 kilometers upstream to get back to where you started. The trip takes 3.6 hours.

a. Write a rational equation that models the problem. State what the variable in your equation represents.

$\dfrac{7.7}{s+1} + \dfrac{7.7}{s-1} = 3.6$ where s is your paddling speed

b. Solve the equation and state the solution in terms of the context of the problem.

$s = 4.5$; your paddling speed is 4.5 kilometers per hour

© Houghton Mifflin Harcourt Publishing Company

Assign these pages to help your students practice and apply important lesson concepts. For additional exercises, see the Student Edition.

Answers

Additional Practice

1. $x = -1$ or $x = 6$

2. $x = 8$

3. $x = 3$ or $x = -1$

4. no solution.

5. $-3 < x < -1$　　**6.** $x \leq 0$ or $x > 2$

7. $-5 < x \leq 0$　　　**8.** $0 \leq x < 3$

9. $x < -4$ or $x \geq -1$

10. $-\frac{22}{5} < x < -3$

11. $2 < x < \frac{9}{4}$　　**12.** $5 < x \leq 15$

13. About 45.5 miles per hour

Problem Solving

1. **a.** $\frac{1}{j}$

　　b. $\left[\frac{1}{4} (2.5) \right] + \left[\frac{1}{j} (2.5) \right] = 1$

　　c. $6\frac{2}{3}$ h

2. **a.** $\frac{1}{n}$

　　b. $\left[\frac{1}{n} \left(\frac{1}{3} \right) \right] + \left[\frac{1}{\frac{1}{2}} \left(\frac{1}{3} \right) \right] = 1$

　　c. 1h

3. C　　　　　　**4.** A

Additional Practice

Solve each equation.

1. $x - \dfrac{6}{x} = 5$

2. $\dfrac{15}{4} = \dfrac{6}{x} + 3$

_____

3. $x = \dfrac{3}{x} + 2$

4. $\dfrac{4}{x^2 - 4} = \dfrac{1}{x - 2}$

_____

Solve each inequality by using a graphing calculator and a table.

5. $\dfrac{6}{x + 1} < -3$

6. $\dfrac{x}{x - 2} \geq 0$

_____

7. $\dfrac{2x}{x + 5} \leq 0$

8. $\dfrac{-x}{x - 3} \geq 0$

_____

Solve each inequality algebraically.

9. $\dfrac{12}{x + 4} \leq 4$

10. $\dfrac{7}{x + 3} < -5$

_____

11. $\dfrac{x}{x - 2} > 9$

12. $\dfrac{2x}{x - 5} \geq 3$

_____

Solve.

13. The time required to deliver and install a computer at a customer's location
is $t = 4 + \dfrac{d}{r}$, where t is time in hours, d is the distance, in miles, from the
warehouse to the customer's location, and r is the average speed of the
delivery truck. If it takes 6.2 hours for the employee to deliver and install a
computer for a customer located 100 miles from the warehouse, what is
the average speed of the delivery truck?

_____

Problem Solving

Norton and Jessie have a lawn service business. Sometimes they
work by themselves, and sometimes they work together. They want to
know if it is worthwhile to work together on some jobs.

1. Norton can mow a large lawn in about 4.0 hours. When Norton and Jesse work
together, they can mow the same lawn in about 2.5 hours. Jesse wants to
know how long it would take her to mow the lawn if she worked by herself.

   a. Write an expression for Jessie's rate, using j
   for the number of hours she would take to
   mow the lawn by herself.   _____

   b. Write an equation to show the amount of work
   completed when they work together.   _____

   c. How long would it take Jessie to mow the lawn
   by herself?   _____

2. Jessie can weed a garden in about 30 minutes. When Norton helps her,
they can weed the same garden in about 20 minutes. Norton wants to
know how long it would take him to weed the garden if he worked by himself.

   a. Write an expression for Norton's rate, using n for
   the number of hours he would take to weed the
   garden by himself.   _____

   b. Write an equation to show the amount of work
   completed when they work together.   _____

   c. How long would it take Norton to weed the
   garden by himself?   _____

Choose the letter for the best answer.

3. Norton can edge a large lawn in about
3.0 hours. Jessie can edge a similar lawn
in about 2.5 hours. Which equation could
be used to find the time it would take
them to edge that lawn if they worked
together?

   A $\dfrac{1}{3} - \dfrac{1}{2.5} = \dfrac{1}{t}$

   B $\dfrac{1}{3} - \dfrac{1}{2.5} = t$

   C $\dfrac{1}{3} + \dfrac{1}{2.5} = \dfrac{1}{t}$

   D $\dfrac{1}{3} + \dfrac{1}{2.5} = t$

4. When Jessie helps Norton trim trees,
they cut Norton's time to trim trees in half.
What can be said about the time it would
take Jessie to do the job alone?

   A Jessie would take the same amount
   of time as Norton.

   B Jessie would take half the time that
   Norton takes.

   C Jessie would take twice the time that
   Norton takes.

   D There is not enough information.

Radical Expressions and Rational Exponents
Going Deeper

Essential question: *How are radicals and rational exponents related?*

COMMON **Standards for**
CORE **Mathematical Content**

CC.9-12.N.RN.1 Explain how the definition of the meaning of rational exponents follows from extending the properties of integer exponents to those values, allowing for a notation for radicals in terms of rational exponents.

CC.9-12.N.RN.2 Rewrite expressions involving radicals and rational exponents using the properties of exponents.

Vocabulary
radical expression

Prerequisites
Square roots and cube roots
Properties of integer exponents

Math Background
In Grade 8, students learned that the properties of exponents apply to real numbers with integer exponents. In this lesson, students will apply the properties of exponents to real numbers with rational exponents and then use them to simplify expressions that contain radicals or rational exponents.

INTRODUCE

Review the properties of integer exponents with students. Make sure students understand that x is the same as x^1, $x^2 \cdot x^3 = x^5$, and $\dfrac{x^2}{x^3} = x^{-1}$. Students should also understand that $x^2 + x^2 = 2x^2$ (by the distributive property, not by a property of exponents) and that $x^2 + x^3$ cannot be simplified.

TEACH

1 ENGAGE

Questioning Strategies
- When you convert between radical form and rational exponent form, what are the restrictions on the radicand and index? **Conversions are done for all real numbers for which the radical is defined. The index must be a positive integer and the power of the radicand must be an integer.**

- After converting a radical expression to rational exponent form, what is another way to describe the rational exponent? **The rational exponent is the ratio of integers such that the numerator is the power of the radicand and the denominator is the index of the radical.**

Differentiated Instruction
To help students learn the properties of rational exponents, you may want to have students add a column to the table that includes examples of each property.

2 EXAMPLE

Questioning Strategies
- When you simplify the rational exponent, what does it mean if the simplified form is an integer? if it is a fraction? **If the exponent is an integer, the final form will not contain a radical sign. If the exponent is a fraction, the final form will contain a radical sign.**

EXTRA EXAMPLE
Simplify each expression. Assume all variables are positive.

A. $\sqrt[4]{(xy)^{12}}$ $x^3 y^3$

B. $\dfrac{\sqrt[3]{a}}{\sqrt[6]{a}}$ $\sqrt[6]{a}$

continued

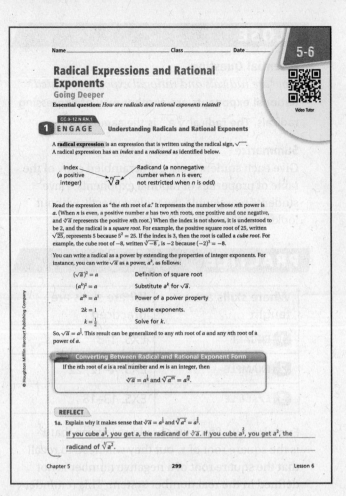

Radical Expressions and Rational Exponents
Going Deeper

Essential question: How are radicals and rational exponents related?

CC.9-12.N.RN.1

1 ENGAGE   Understanding Radicals and Rational Exponents

A **radical expression** is an expression that is written using the radical sign, $\sqrt{\ }$. A radical expression has an *index* and a *radicand* as identified below.

Index (a positive integer) → $\sqrt[n]{a}$ ← Radicand (a nonnegative number when *n* is even; not restricted when *n* is odd)

Read the expression as "the *n*th root of *a*." It represents the number whose *n*th power is *a*. (When *n* is even, a positive number *a* has two *n*th roots, one positive and one negative, and $\sqrt[n]{a}$ represents the positive *n*th root.) When the index is not shown, it is understood to be 2, and the radical is a *square root*. For example, the positive square root of 25, written $\sqrt{25}$, represents 5 because $5^2 = 25$. If the index is 3, then the root is called a *cube root*. For example, the cube root of −8, written $\sqrt[3]{-8}$, is −2 because $(-2)^3 = -8$.

You can write a radical as a power by extending the properties of integer exponents. For instance, you can write $\sqrt{a}$ as a power, a^k, as follows:

$(\sqrt{a})^2 = a$	Definition of square root
$(a^k)^2 = a$	Substitute a^k for $\sqrt{a}$.
$a^{2k} = a^1$	Power of a power property
$2k = 1$	Equate exponents.
$k = \frac{1}{2}$	Solve for *k*.

So, $\sqrt{a} = a^{\frac{1}{2}}$. This result can be generalized to any *n*th root of *a* and any *n*th root of a power of *a*.

> **Converting Between Radical and Rational Exponent Form**
>
> If the *n*th root of *a* is a real number and *m* is an integer, then
>
> $$\sqrt[n]{a} = a^{\frac{1}{n}} \text{ and } \sqrt[n]{a^m} = a^{\frac{m}{n}}.$$

REFLECT

1a. Explain why it makes sense that $\sqrt[3]{a} = a^{\frac{1}{3}}$ and $\sqrt[3]{a^2} = a^{\frac{2}{3}}$.

If you cube $a^{\frac{1}{3}}$, you get *a*, the radicand of $\sqrt[3]{a}$. If you cube $a^{\frac{2}{3}}$, you get a^2, the radicand of $\sqrt[3]{a^2}$.

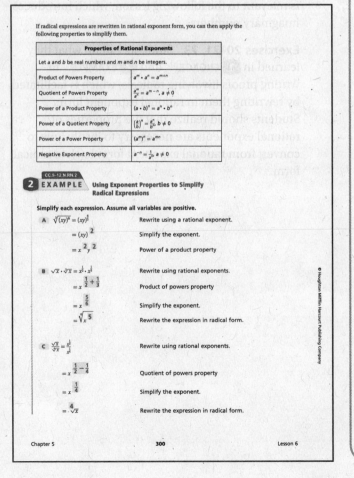

If radical expressions are rewritten in rational exponent form, you can then apply the following properties to simplify them.

Properties of Rational Exponents	
Let *a* and *b* be real numbers and *m* and *n* be integers.	
Product of Powers Property	$a^m \cdot a^n = a^{m+n}$
Quotient of Powers Property	$\frac{a^m}{a^n} = a^{m-n}, a \neq 0$
Power of a Product Property	$(a \cdot b)^n = a^n \cdot b^n$
Power of a Quotient Property	$\left(\frac{a}{b}\right)^n = \frac{a^n}{b^n}, b \neq 0$
Power of a Power Property	$(a^m)^n = a^{mn}$
Negative Exponent Property	$a^{-n} = \frac{1}{a^n}, a \neq 0$

CC.9-12.N.RN.2

2 EXAMPLE   Using Exponent Properties to Simplify Radical Expressions

Simplify each expression. Assume all variables are positive.

A $\sqrt[3]{(xy)^6} = (xy)^{\frac{6}{3}}$ Rewrite using a rational exponent.

$= (xy)^2$ Simplify the exponent.

$= x^2 y^2$ Power of a product property

B $\sqrt{x} \cdot \sqrt[3]{x} = x^{\frac{1}{2}} \cdot x^{\frac{1}{3}}$ Rewrite using rational exponents.

$= x^{\frac{1}{2} + \frac{1}{3}}$ Product of powers property

$= x^{\frac{5}{6}}$ Simplify the exponent.

$= \sqrt[6]{x^5}$ Rewrite the expression in radical form.

C $\frac{\sqrt{x}}{\sqrt[4]{x}} = \frac{x^{\frac{1}{2}}}{x^{\frac{1}{4}}}$ Rewrite using rational exponents.

$= x^{\frac{1}{2} - \frac{1}{4}}$ Quotient of powers property

$= x^{\frac{1}{4}}$ Simplify the exponent.

$= \sqrt[4]{x}$ Rewrite the expression in radical form.

MATHEMATICAL PRACTICE **Highlighting the Standards**

2 EXAMPLE provides an opportunity to address Mathematical Practice Standard 7 (Look for and make use of structure). Students should review the properties of rational exponents to find structure in the samples and then apply the structure in each step of the simplifying process. Make sure students can justify the appropriate steps using the properties.

3 **EXAMPLE**

Questioning Strategies

• How would the example be different if the expression were $27(x^9)^{\frac{2}{3}}$? What would the answer be in this case? **The rational exponent would apply only to the variable part, x^9. The final answer would be $27x^6$.**

EXTRA EXAMPLE
Simplify $(81x^8)^{\frac{3}{4}}$. **$27x^6$**

Technology
Encourage the use of graphing calculators to check the results of simplifying numerical radical expressions and numerical expressions with rational exponents. Ask students to use the following sample problems to practice entering expressions correctly into their calculators:

Enter $\sqrt[3]{6^2}$ as 6 ^ (2/3); enter $32^{\frac{3}{2}}$ as 32 ^ (3/2); enter $25^{-\frac{1}{2}}$ as 25 ^ (−1/2). Make sure students understand the importance of including parentheses.

CLOSE

Essential Question
How are radicals and rational exponents related?
· Rational exponents are another way of expressing radicals. The radical $\sqrt[n]{a^m}$ is the same as $a^{\frac{m}{n}}$.

Summarize
Give each student a cut up, scrambled copy of the table of properties of rational exponents. Have students reassemble the table correctly without looking at the table in this lesson.

PRACTICE

Where skills are taught	Where skills are practiced
1 ENGAGE	EXS. 1–3
2 EXAMPLE	EXS. 4–12, 22
3 EXAMPLE	EXS. 13–18

Exercise 19: Students should recognize that $x^{\frac{1}{2}}$ is the square root of x, but they will need to recall that the square root of a negative number is not defined in the real number system. This reminder is relevant to the following lesson, which introduces imaginary numbers.

Exercises 20–21, 23: Students extend what they learned in **1** ENGAGE and **2** EXAMPLE to writing proofs involving radicals, which is facilitated by rewriting them in rational exponent form. Students should realize that the properties of rational exponents are necessary to justify how to convert from rational exponent form back to radical form.

REFLECT

2a. In parts B and C, you started with an expression in radical form, converted to rational exponent form, and then converted back to radical form to record the answer. Explain the purpose of each conversion.

The first conversion made it possible to apply the properties of rational exponents to simplify the expression. The second conversion let you write the simplified expression is in its original radical form.

2b. Can $\sqrt{a} \cdot \sqrt{b}$ be simplified? Refer to the properties of exponents to support your answer.

No, it cannot. In rational exponent form, the expression is $a^{\frac{1}{2}} \cdot b^{\frac{1}{3}}$. Because the bases are different, the product of powers property does not apply, and the expression cannot be simplified.

2c. Use the properties of exponents to prove that $\sqrt[3]{a} \cdot \sqrt[3]{b} = \sqrt[3]{ab}$.

$\sqrt[3]{a} \cdot \sqrt[3]{b}$ in rational exponent form is $a^{\frac{1}{3}} \cdot b^{\frac{1}{3}}$. Use the power of a product property to write this as $(ab)^{\frac{1}{3}}$. Convert back to radical form to get $\sqrt[3]{ab}$.

CC.9-12.N.RN.2

3 EXAMPLE Simplifying Expressions Involving Rational Exponents

$(27x^9)^{\frac{2}{3}} = (3^3)^{\frac{2}{3}}(x^9)^{\frac{2}{3}}$ Power of a product property

$= 3^{3 \cdot \frac{2}{3}} x^{9 \cdot \frac{2}{3}}$ Power of a power property

$= 3^2 x^6$ Simplify exponents.

$= 9x^6$ Evaluate the numerical power.

REFLECT

3a. Show that you get the same simplified form of $(27x^9)^{\frac{2}{3}}$ if you simplify $[(27x^9)^2]^{\frac{1}{3}}$. That is, square $27x^9$ and then raise to the $\frac{1}{3}$ power.

$[(27x^9)^2]^{\frac{1}{3}} = [(3^3)^2(x^9)^2]^{\frac{1}{3}} = [3^6 x^{18}]^{\frac{1}{3}} = (3^6)^{\frac{1}{3}}(x^{18})^{\frac{1}{3}} = 3^{6 \cdot \frac{1}{3}} x^{18 \cdot \frac{1}{3}} = 3^2 x^6 = 9x^6$

3b. What is the simplified form of $(27x^9)^{-\frac{2}{3}}$? How is it related to the simplified form of $(27x^9)^{\frac{2}{3}}$?

$\frac{1}{9x^6}$; they are reciprocals.

Chapter 5   301   Lesson 6

© Houghton Mifflin Harcourt Publishing Company

PRACTICE

Write each radical expression in rational exponent form. Assume all variables are positive.

1. $\sqrt[5]{d}$ $d^{\frac{1}{5}}$

2. $\sqrt[3]{b^2}$ $b^{\frac{2}{3}}$

3. $\sqrt[4]{m^3}$ $m^{\frac{3}{4}}$

Simplify each expression. Assume all variables are positive.

4. $\sqrt[4]{y^2 z}$ $y^{\frac{1}{2}}\sqrt[4]{z}$

5. $\sqrt{x^4 y}$ $x^2\sqrt{y}$

6. $\sqrt{49x^2 y^4}$ $7xy^2$

7. $\sqrt[3]{x} \cdot \sqrt[4]{x}$ $\sqrt[12]{x^7}$

8. $\sqrt{(3x)(12x^3)}$ $6x^2$

9. $\sqrt{xy} \cdot \sqrt{x^3 y^5}$ $x^2 y^3$

10. $\frac{\sqrt[3]{x}}{\sqrt[5]{x}}$ $\sqrt[15]{x}$

11. $\sqrt{\frac{8x^4}{y^5}}$ $\frac{2x^2}{y^3}$

12. $\sqrt{\frac{x}{y^4}}$ $\frac{\sqrt{x}}{y^2}$

13. $(8x^3)^{\frac{2}{3}}$ $4x^2$

14. $\left(\frac{x^{\frac{1}{4}}}{y^{-1}}\right)^{12}$ $x^3 y^{12}$

15. $\left(\frac{4x^2}{y^6}\right)^{\frac{1}{2}}$ $\frac{2x}{y^3}$

16. $(216a^9)^{\frac{1}{3}}$ $6a^3$

17. $(a^4 b^{-6})^{-\frac{3}{2}}$ $\frac{b^9}{a^6}$

18. $(16b^{-2})^{-\frac{1}{2}}$ $\frac{b}{4}$

19. Explain why the expression $x^{\frac{1}{2}}$ is undefined when $x < 0$.

In radical form, $x^{\frac{1}{2}} = \sqrt{x}$ and the square root of a negative number is undefined in the real number system.

20. Use the properties of exponents to show that $\sqrt[5]{\frac{a}{b}} = \frac{\sqrt[5]{a}}{\sqrt[5]{b}}$.

In rational exponent form, $\sqrt[5]{\frac{a}{b}} = \left(\frac{a}{b}\right)^{\frac{1}{5}}$. Use the power of a quotient property to write $\left(\frac{a}{b}\right)^{\frac{1}{5}}$ as $\frac{a^{\frac{1}{5}}}{b^{\frac{1}{5}}}$. Convert back to radical form to get $\frac{\sqrt[5]{a}}{\sqrt[5]{b}}$.

21. Show that $\sqrt[n]{a^m} = (\sqrt[n]{a})^m$.

$\sqrt[n]{a^m} = a^{\frac{m}{n}} = a^{\frac{1}{n} \cdot m} = \left(a^{\frac{1}{n}}\right)^m = (\sqrt[n]{a})^m$

22. Error Analysis A student simplified the expression $\sqrt[3]{x^2} \cdot \sqrt{x}$ by writing $\sqrt[3]{x^2} \cdot \sqrt{x} = x^{\frac{2}{3}} \cdot x^{\frac{1}{2}} = x^{\frac{2}{3} + \frac{1}{2}} = x^{\frac{7}{6}} = x^2$. Describe and correct the student's error.

$\sqrt[3]{x^2} = x^{\frac{2}{3}}$, not $x^{\frac{2}{3}}$; $\sqrt[3]{x^2} \cdot \sqrt{x} = x^{\frac{2}{3}} \cdot x^{\frac{1}{2}} = x^{\frac{2}{3} + \frac{1}{2}} = x^{\frac{7}{6}} = x^{1 + \frac{1}{6}} = x^1 \cdot x^{\frac{1}{6}} = x\sqrt[6]{x}$

23. In the expression $\sqrt[n]{a^m}$, suppose m is a multiple of n. That is, $m = kn$ where k is an integer. Show how to obtain the simplified form of $\sqrt[n]{a^m}$. If a is a nonzero rational number, is $\sqrt[n]{a^m}$ rational or irrational? Explain.

$\sqrt[n]{a^m} = \sqrt[n]{a^{kn}} = a^{\frac{kn}{n}} = a^k$; rational because raising a nonzero rational number a to the kth power is equivalent to the product consisting of k factors of a (if $k > 0$) or k factors of $\frac{1}{a}$ (if $k < 0$), and the set of rational numbers is closed under multiplication.

Chapter 5   302   Lesson 6

© Houghton Mifflin Harcourt Publishing Company

Assign these pages to help your students practice and apply important lesson concepts. For additional exercises, see the Student Edition.

Answers

Additional Practice

1. $5x^3$ 2. $\dfrac{x^2}{3}$

3. $2x$ 4. 32

5. 9   6. 16

7. $51^{\frac{4}{5}}$ 8. $169^{\frac{3}{2}}$

9. 36^2 10. 256

11. 9   12. 5

13. 144   14. $\dfrac{1}{3}$

15. $\dfrac{1}{4}$ 16. $-3x^2$

17. $25x$ 18. $\dfrac{3}{2}$

19. About $0.15c$

Problem Solving

1. a. $d(12) = 50\left(2^{-\frac{12}{12}}\right)$

   b. 25 cm

   c. $\dfrac{1}{2}$

2.

Notes Higher than the Root Note	2	4	6	8	10	12
Distance of Fret from Bridge (cm)	44.5	39.7	35.4	31.5	28.1	25

3. A   4. D

5. C   6. C

Name_____ Class_____ Date_____

Additional Practice

Simplify each expression. Assume all variables are positive.

1. $\sqrt[3]{125x^9}$

2. $\sqrt[4]{\dfrac{x^8}{81}}$

3. $\sqrt[3]{\dfrac{64x^3}{8}}$

_____   _____   _____

Write each expression in radical form, and simplify.

4. $64^{\frac{5}{6}}$

5. $27^{\frac{2}{3}}$

6. $(-8)^{\frac{4}{3}}$

_____   _____   _____

Write each expression using rational exponents.

7. $\sqrt[5]{51^4}$

8. $(\sqrt{169})^3$

9. $\sqrt[7]{36^{14}}$

_____   _____   _____

Simplify each expression.

10. $4^{\frac{3}{2}} \cdot 4^{\frac{5}{2}}$

11. $\dfrac{27^{\frac{4}{3}}}{27^{\frac{2}{3}}}$

12. $\left(125^{\frac{2}{3}}\right)^{\frac{1}{2}}$

13. $(27 \cdot 64)^{\frac{2}{3}}$

14. $\left(\dfrac{1}{243}\right)^{\frac{3}{5}}$

15. $64^{-\frac{1}{3}}$

16. $(-27x^6)^{\frac{1}{3}}$

17. $\dfrac{(25x)^{\frac{3}{2}}}{5 \cdot x^{\frac{1}{2}}}$

18. $(4x)^{-\frac{1}{2}} \cdot (9x)^{\frac{1}{2}}$

Solve.

19. In every atom, electrons orbit the nucleus with a certain characteristic velocity known as the Fermi–Thomas velocity, equal to $\dfrac{Z^{\frac{2}{3}}}{137}$ c, where Z is the number of protons in the nucleus and c is the speed of light. In terms of c, what is the characteristic Fermi-Thomas velocity of the electrons in Uranium, for which Z = 92?

_____

Problem Solving

Louise is building a guitar-like instrument. It has small metal bars, called frets, positioned across its neck so that it can produce notes of a specific scale on each string. The distance a fret should be placed from the bridge is related to a string's root note length by the function

$d(n) = r\left(2^{-\frac{n}{12}}\right)$, where r is the length of the root note string and n is

the number of notes higher than that string's root note. Louise wants to know where to place frets to produce different notes on a 50-cm string.

1. Find the distance from the bridge for a fret that produces a note exactly one octave (12 notes) higher than the root note.

   a. Substitute values for r and n in the given function. _____

   b. How far from the bridge should the fret be placed? _____

   c. What fraction of the string length is the distance of this fret from the bridge? _____

2. Complete the table to find the distance from the bridge, for frets that produce every other note of an entire scale on this string.

Notes Higher than the Root Note	2	4	6	8	10	12
Distance of Fret from Bridge (cm)						

Choose the letter for the best answer.

3. Rafael made a ceramic cube in art class. The cube has a volume of 336 cm³. What is the side length of the cube to the nearest centimeter?

   A 7
   B 12
   C 18
   D 56

4. Yolanda has an exercise ball with a volume of 7234 in.³. Find the radius of the exercise ball to the nearest inch.

   A 24
   B 21
   C 19
   D 12

5. Which formula could you use to find the area of one side of a cube if the volume were given?

   A $A = V^{\frac{3}{2}}$ C $A = V^{\frac{2}{3}}$

   B $A = V^{-\frac{3}{2}}$ D $A = V^{-\frac{2}{3}}$

6. A party tent in the shape of a hemisphere has a volume of 14,130 m³. What is the area of the ground that the tent covers in square meters?

   A 653.1   C 1121.5
   B 706.5   D 1256.0

5-7 Radical Functions
Going Deeper

Essential question: *How can you graph transformations of the parent square root and cube root functions?*

COMMON CORE Standards for Mathematical Content

CC.9-12.F.IF.7 Graph functions expressed symbolically and show key features of the graph ...*

CC.9-12.F.IF.7b Graph square root, cube root ... functions ...*

CC.9-12.F.BF.3 Identify the effect on the graph of replacing $f(x)$ by $f(x) + k$, $kf(x)$, ... and $f(x + k)$ for specific values of k (both positive and negative); find the value of k given the graphs. ...

Also: CC.9–12.F.IF.9

Prerequisites

Inverses of quadratic functions

Inverses of cubic functions

Math Background

Students will explore how changing the values of a, h, and k in a square root or cube root function affect its graph. They will find that changing a parameter affects the graph in the same way it did for other functions they have encountered. Students will also write an equation given the graph of one of these transformed radical functions.

INTRODUCE

Remind students that the parent quadratic function is $f(x) = x^2$ and that the vertex form of a quadratic function is $f(x) = a(x - h)^2 + k$. Next, write the equation of the parent square root function, $f(x) = \sqrt{x}$. Ask students how to write $af(x)$, $f(x) + k$ and $f(x - h)$. $f(x) = a\sqrt{x}$, $f(x) = \sqrt{x} + k$, $f(x) = \sqrt{x - h}$

Show students that the general form for a square root function is $f(x) = a\sqrt{x - h} + k$, and in the parent function, $a = 1$, $h = 0$, and $k = 0$. Finally, ask the students how to write the general form for a cube root function. $f(x) = a\sqrt[3]{x - h} + k$

TEACH

1 EXAMPLE

Questioning Strategies

- For the x-values shown in the table in part A, what are the output values of the parent function? From the top down, they are 0, 1, 2, 3, and 4.

- In part A, how do the output values for the transformed function $g(x)$ compare with the corresponding output values for the parent function? The $g(x)$-values are 3 times the parent function values.

- For the x-values shown in the table in part B, what are the output values of the parent function? From the top down, they are −2, −1, 0, 1, and 2.

- In part B, how do the output values for the transformed function $g(x)$ compare with the corresponding output values for the parent function? The $g(x)$-values are 0.5 times the parent function values.

EXTRA EXAMPLES

Graph each radical function. Then describe the graph as a transformation of the graph of the parent function.

A. $g(x) = 0.25\sqrt{x}$ The graph of $g(x)$ passes through (0, 0), (1, 0.25), (4, 0.5), (9, 0.75), and (16, 1). It is a vertical shrink of the graph of the parent function by a factor of 0.25.

B. $g(x) = 2.5\sqrt[3]{x}$ The graph of $g(x)$ passes through (−8, −5), (−1, −2.5), (0, 0), (1, 2.5), and (8, 5). It is a vertical stretch of the graph of the parent function by a factor of 2.5.

Differentiated Instruction

Visual learners may benefit from plotting the points (4, 2), (4, 6), (16, 4), and (16, 12) on the grid in part A. Have them count the units between the x-axis and (4, 2) and between the x-axis and (4, 6) to "see" the stretch by a factor of 3. Repeat for (16, 4) and (16, 12).

Name _____ Class _____ Date _____

5-7

Radical Functions
Going Deeper

Essential question: *How can you graph transformations of the parent square root and cube root functions?*

You can transform the parent square root and parent cube root functions by changing the values of *a*, *h*, and *k* in the general forms of the equations shown below.

$$f(x) = a\sqrt{x - h} + k \qquad f(x) = a\sqrt[3]{x - h} + k$$

Video Tutor

CC.9-12.F.BF.3

1 EXAMPLE Changing the Value of *a*

Graph each radical function. Then describe the graph as a transformation of the graph of the parent function. (The graph of the parent function is shown.)

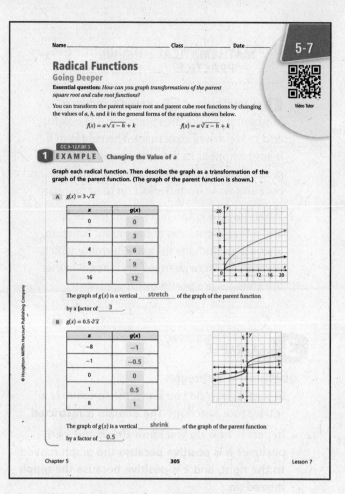

A $g(x) = 3\sqrt{x}$

x	g(x)
0	0
1	3
4	6
9	9
16	12

The graph of $g(x)$ is a vertical ___stretch___ of the graph of the parent function

by a factor of ___3___.

B $g(x) = 0.5\sqrt[3]{x}$

x	g(x)
−8	−1
−1	−0.5
0	0
1	0.5
8	1

The graph of $g(x)$ is a vertical ___shrink___ of the graph of the parent function

by a factor of ___0.5___.

© Houghton Mifflin Harcourt Publishing Company

REFLECT

1a. In part A, why does it make sense to use *x*-values of 0, 1, 4, 9, and 16 when finding points on the graph of $g(x)$?

The rule for $g(x)$ involves finding the square root of x, so using x-values that are

perfect squares will make the calculations easier.

1b. Explain how you know in part B that the graph of $g(x)$ is a vertical shrink of the graph of the parent function.

For a given x-value, the value of $g(x)$ is half the value of the parent function.

1c. Generalize from your observations to complete the sentences below.

For $g(x) = a\sqrt{x}$ or $g(x) = a\sqrt[3]{x}$:

• when $|a| > 1$, the graph of $g(x)$ is a vertical ___stretch___ of the graph of the parent function.

• when $0 < |a| < 1$, the graph of $g(x)$ is a vertical ___shrink___ of the graph of the parent function.

CC.9-12.F.BF.3

2 EXAMPLE Changing the Values of *h* and *k*

Graph each radical function. Then describe the graph as a transformation of the graph of the parent function, and give its domain and range. (The graph of the parent function is shown.)

A $g(x) = \sqrt{x + 4} - 3$

x	g(x)
−4	−3
−3	−2
0	−1
5	0
12	1

The graph of $g(x)$ is a translation of the graph of the parent function 4 units

___left___ and ___3___ units down.

Domain: $\{x \mid x \geq$ ___−4___ $\}$　Range: $\{y \mid y \geq$ ___−3___ $\}$

© Houghton Mifflin Harcourt Publishing Company

---

2 EXAMPLE

Questioning Strategies

- In part A, how can you determine the x-intercept just by analyzing the function rule? **The x-intercept is the value of x when $g(x) = 0$. If $g(x) = 0$, then $\sqrt{x+4}$ equals 3. This means the radicand must equal 9, so x must be 5.**

- Does the graph of the square root function have a vertical or horizontal asymptote? Explain. **No; the graph does not *approach* a value, but it does have a *starting point*.**

- In the function $g(x) = 5 + \sqrt{x+1}$, is 5 the value of a or of k? Explain. **It is the value of k. It is being added to the radical. The function can be rewritten as $g(x) = \sqrt{x+1} + 5$.**

EXTRA EXAMPLE

Graph each radical function. Then describe the graph as a transformation of the graph of the parent function and give its domain and range.

A. $g(x) = \sqrt{x-3} - 5$ **The graph of $g(x)$ starts at $(3, -5)$ and passes through $(4, -4)$, $(7, -3)$, $(12, -2)$, and $(19, -1)$. It is a translation 3 units right and 5 units down; domain: $\{x \mid x \geq 3\}$; range: $\{y \mid y \geq -5\}$**

B. $g(x) = \sqrt[3]{x+6} + 2$ **The graph of $g(x)$ passes through $(-14, 0)$, $(-7, 1)$, $(-6, 2)$, $(-5, 3)$, and $(2, 4)$. It is a translation 6 units left and 2 units up; domain: all real numbers; range: all real numbers**

Teaching Strategy

In part A, have students add a column for $\sqrt{x+4}$ between x and $g(x)$. Have them plot the ordered pairs that result from this intermediate step to see that the graph is first shifted 4 units left. Similarly, they can add a middle column for the results of $\sqrt[3]{x-2}$ in part B to see that the graph is first shifted 2 units right.

MATHEMATICAL PRACTICE — Highlighting the Standards

1 EXAMPLE and **2 EXAMPLE** address Mathematical Practice Standard 7 (Look for and make use of structure). The values of a, h, and k appear in the same positions in the general square root and cube root functions and have the same overall effect on their graphs.

When given a graph of a parent function and a transformation of the parent function, encourage students to first determine which parameters were changed and then whether the changes are positive or negative.

3 EXAMPLE

Questioning Strategies

- In part A, how do you know the function is a square root function? **The domain is restricted.**

- In part B, how do you know that h and k are positive? **h is positive because the graph moved to the right, and k is positive because the graph moved up.**

EXTRA EXAMPLE

Write the equation of the square root or cube root function whose graph is shown.

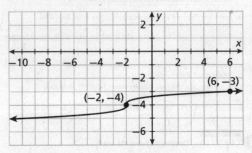

$g(x) = 0.5 \sqrt[3]{x+2} - 4$

B $g(x) = \sqrt[3]{x-2} + 4$

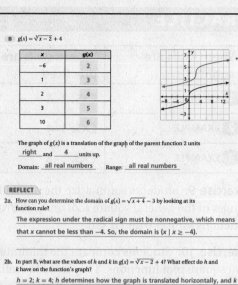

x	g(x)
−6	2
1	3
2	4
3	5
10	6

The graph of $g(x)$ is a translation of the graph of the parent function 2 units

__right__ and __4__ units up.

Domain: __all real numbers__   Range: __all real numbers__

REFLECT

2a. How can you determine the domain of $g(x) = \sqrt{x+4} - 3$ by looking at its function rule?

The expression under the radical sign must be nonnegative, which means

that x cannot be less than −4. So, the domain is $\{x \mid x \geq -4\}$.

2b. In part B, what are the values of h and k in $g(x) = \sqrt[3]{x-2} + 4$? What effect do h and k have on the function's graph?

$h = 2; k = 4;$ h determines how the graph is translated horizontally, and k

determines how the graph is translated vertically.

2c. Generalize from your observations to complete the sentences below.

For $g(x) = \sqrt{x-h} + k$ and $g(x) = \sqrt[3]{x-h} + k$:

- the graph of $g(x)$ is a translation of the parent function $|h|$ units
  __left__ if $h < 0$ and h units __right__ if $h > 0$.

- the graph of $g(x)$ is a translation of the parent function $|k|$ units
  __down__ if $k < 0$ and k units __up__ if $k > 0$.

CC.9-12.F.BF.3

3 EXAMPLE Writing the Equation of a Radical Function

Write the equation of the square root or cube root function whose graph is shown.

A Identify the function type. The shape of the graph indicates a __square root__ function.

B Identify the values of h and k.

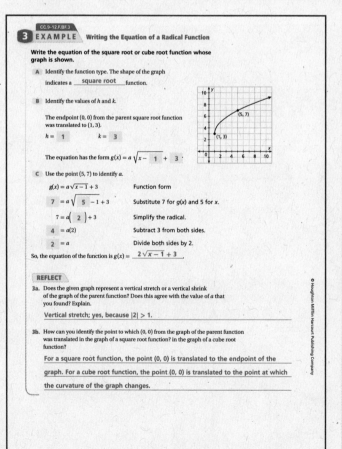

The endpoint (0, 0) from the parent square root function was translated to (1, 3).

$h =$ __1__ $k =$ __3__

The equation has the form $g(x) = a\sqrt{x - \boxed{1}} + \boxed{3}$

C Use the point (5, 7) to identify a.

$g(x) = a\sqrt{x-1} + 3$	Function form
$7 = a\sqrt{\boxed{5} - 1} + 3$	Substitute 7 for $g(x)$ and 5 for x.
$7 = a\left(\boxed{2}\right) + 3$	Simplify the radical.
$\boxed{4} = a(2)$	Subtract 3 from both sides.
$\boxed{2} = a$	Divide both sides by 2.

So, the equation of the function is $g(x) = $ __$2\sqrt{x-1} + 3$__.

REFLECT

3a. Does the given graph represent a vertical stretch or a vertical shrink of the graph of the parent function? Does this agree with the value of a that you found? Explain.

Vertical stretch; yes, because $|2| > 1$.

3b. How can you identify the point to which (0, 0) from the graph of the parent function was translated in the graph of a square root function? in the graph of a cube root function?

For a square root function, the point (0, 0) is translated to the endpoint of the

graph. For a cube root function, the point (0, 0) is translated to the point at which

the curvature of the graph changes.

Essential Question

How can you graph transformations of the parent square root and cube root functions?

The general form a square root function is $f(x) = a\sqrt{x - h} + k$. The general form of a cube root function is $f(x) = a\sqrt[3]{x - h} + k$.

For both functions, use a to stretch the graph vertically if $|a|$ is greater than 1 and to shrink the graph vertically if $|a|$ is between 0 and 1. If a is negative, the graph is also reflected across the x-axis.

Use h to translate the graph to the right if h is positive and to the left if h is negative.

Use k to translate the graph up if k is positive and down if k is negative.

Summarize

Have students write a journal entry explaining how to find the equation of a transformed square root function given the starting point and another point on the graph.

Where skills are taught	Where skills are practiced
1 EXAMPLE	EXS. 1–4
2 EXAMPLE	EXS. 1–4
3 EXAMPLE	EXS. 5–8

Exercise 9: Students summarize the domains and ranges of the general square root and cube root functions for $a > 0$ and $a < 0$.

Exercise 10: Students compare the minimums of two square root functions. They need to realize that in square root functions with $a > 0$, the minimum occurs at the graph's starting point.

PRACTICE

Graph each radical function. Then describe the graph as a transformation of the graph of the parent function, and give its domain and range. (The graph of the parent function is shown.)

1. $f(x) = 0.5\sqrt{x+2}$

vertical shrink by a factor of $\frac{1}{2}$;

translation 2 units left

Domain: $\{x \mid x \geq -2\}$

Range: $\{y \mid y \geq 0\}$

2. $f(x) = 2\sqrt[3]{x} - 4$

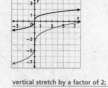

vertical stretch by a factor of 2;

translation 4 units down

Domain: all real numbers

Range: all real numbers

3. $f(x) = -\sqrt{x} + 5$

reflection across the x-axis;

translation 5 units up

Domain: $\{x \mid x \geq 0\}$

Range: $\{y \mid y \leq 5\}$

4. $f(x) = -\sqrt[3]{x-1}$

reflection across the x-axis;

translation 1 unit right

Domain: all real numbers

Range: all real numbers

Write the equation of the square root or cube root function whose graph is shown.

5. $f(x) = $ _____ $3\sqrt{x} + 2$

6. $f(x) = $ _____ $\sqrt[3]{x} + 1$

7. $f(x) = $ _____ $\sqrt{x-3} - 1$

8. $f(x) = $ _____ $2\sqrt[3]{x} - 2$

9. Complete the chart by writing the domains and ranges of each function type in terms of h and k.

Function Type	When $a > 0$		When $a < 0$	
Square Root Functions $f(x) = a\sqrt{x-h} + k$	Domain: $x \geq h$		Domain: $x \geq h$	
	Range: $y \geq k$		Range: $y \leq k$	
Cube Root Functions $f(x) = a\sqrt[3]{x-h} + k$	Domain: all real numbers		Domain: all real numbers	
	Range: all real numbers		Range: all real numbers	

10. Which function has a greater minimum value, $f(x) = \sqrt{x-4} - 1$ or the function whose graph is shown?

the graphed function

ADDITIONAL PRACTICE AND PROBLEM SOLVING

Assign these pages to help your students practice and apply important lesson concepts. For additional exercises, see the Student Edition.

Answers

Additional Practice

1. $\{x \mid x \geq -4\}; \{y \mid y \geq 0\}$

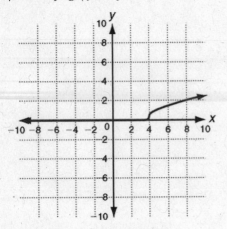

2. all real numbers; all real numbers

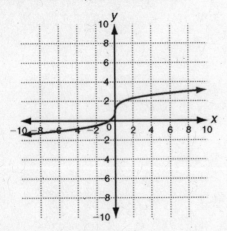

3. Vertical stretch by a factor of 4 and translate 8 units left

4. Reflection across the x-axis, horizontal compression by a factor of $\frac{1}{3}$, and translate 2 units up

5. $g(x) = 7\sqrt{-x} - 3$

6. $g(x) = -\sqrt{2(x - 2)}$

7. 0.29 cm

Problem Solving

1. **a.** $d(a) = 3.56\sqrt{\frac{5}{9}}\, a$

b.

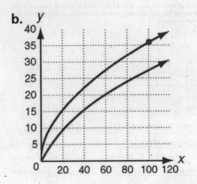

c. 36 km; 27 km

2. B   3. C

4. D   5. A

6. D

Additional Practice

Graph each function, and identify its domain and range.

1. $f(x) = \sqrt{x-4}$

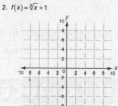

2. $f(x) = \sqrt[3]{x} + 1$

Domain: _____
Range: _____

Domain: _____
Range: _____

Using the graph of $f(x) = \sqrt{x}$ as a guide, describe the transformation.

3. $g(x) = 4\sqrt{x+8}$ _____

4. $g(x) = -\sqrt{3x} + 2$ _____

Use the description to write the square root function g.

5. The parent function $f(x) = \sqrt{x}$ is reflected across
the y-axis, vertically stretched by a factor of 7, and
translated 3 units down. _____

6. The parent function $f(x) = \sqrt{x}$ is translated 2 units right,

compressed horizontally by a factor of $\frac{1}{2}$, and reflected

across the x-axis. _____

Solve.

7. For a gas with density, n, measured in atoms per cubic centimeter, the

average distance, d, between atoms is given by $d = \left(\dfrac{3}{4\pi n}\right)^{\frac{1}{3}}$. The gas in a

certain region of space has a density of just 10 atoms per cubic centimeter.
Find the average distance between the atoms in that region of space.

_____

Problem Solving

On Earth the distance, d, in kilometers, that one can see to the
horizon is a function of altitude, a, in meters, and can be found using
the function $d(a) = 3.56\sqrt{a}$. To find the corresponding distance to the
horizon on Mars, the function must be stretched horizontally by a

factor of about $\dfrac{9}{5}$.

1. a. Write the function that corresponds to the
given transformation.

_____

b. Use a graphing calculator to graph the
function and the parent function. Sketch
both curves on the coordinate plane.

c. Use your graph to determine the
approximate distance to the horizon from
an altitude of 100 meters:

on Earth _____
on Mars _____

Choose the letter for the best answer.

2. Which equation represents the radius of
a sphere as a function of the volume of
the sphere?

A $r = \sqrt[3]{\dfrac{3\pi}{4V}}$ C $r = \sqrt[3]{\dfrac{4V}{3\pi}}$

B $r = \sqrt[3]{\dfrac{3V}{4\pi}}$ D $r = \sqrt[3]{\dfrac{4\pi}{3V}}$

4. Harry made a symmetrical design by
graphing four functions, one in each
quadrant. The graph of which function is
in the third quadrant?

A $f(x) = 4\sqrt{x}$ C $f(x) = -4\sqrt{x}$

B $f(x) = 4\sqrt{-x}$ D $f(x) = -4\sqrt{-x}$

6. The hypotenuse of a right isosceles
triangle can be written $H = \sqrt{2x^2}$,
where x is the length of one of the legs.
Which function models the hypotenuse
when the legs are lengthened by a factor
of 2?

A $H = \sqrt{2x^2} + 2$ C $H = \sqrt{4x^2}$

B $H = \sqrt{2x^2} + 4$ D $H = \sqrt{8x^2}$

3. Alice graphed a function that is found
only in the first quadrant. Which function
could she have used?

A $f(x) = \sqrt{x} + 2$ C $f(x) = \sqrt{x} + 2$

B $f(x) = -\sqrt{x}$ D $f(x) = \sqrt{x-2}$

5. The side length of a cube can be

represented by $s = \sqrt{\dfrac{T}{6}}$, where T

is the surface area of the cube. What

transformation is shown by $s = \sqrt{\dfrac{T}{3}}$?

A Horizontal compression by a factor of
0.5

B Horizontal stretch by a factor of 2

C Vertical compression by a factor of
0.5

D Vertical stretch by a factor of 2

Solving Radical Equations and Inequalities
Going Deeper

Essential question: *How can you solve equations involving square roots and cube roots?*

CC.9-12.A.REI.2 Solve simple ... radical equations in one variable, and give examples showing how extraneous solutions may arise.

CC.9-12.A.REI.11 Explain why the x-coordinates of the points where the graphs of the equations $y = f(x)$ and $y = g(x)$ intersect are the solutions of the equation $f(x) = g(x)$; find the solutions approximately, e.g. using technology to graph the functions, make tables of values, or find successive approximations.*

Also: CC.9-12.A.CED.1*

Vocabulary
extraneous solution

Prerequisites
Graphing square root and cube root functions

Math Background
Students will use inverse operations to solve radical equations, which are equations in which the variable is in the radicand. The inverse of taking a root is raising to a power. For example, the cube root of 27 is 3, and 3 cubed is 27.

Squaring both sides of an equation may produce a solution that the original equation does not have. For example, the solution of $x = 4$ is 4. If both sides of $x = 4$ are squared, the result is $x^2 = 16$. This equation has two solutions: 4 and -4. Because of this, students must check that any solutions that result from squaring both sides of an equation are not extraneous (not a solution to the original equation).

While students solve only square and cube root equations in this lesson, extraneous solutions could appear when solving radical equations with nth roots when n is even.

INTRODUCE

Ask students the following chain of questions. What is 5 cubed? **125** What is the cube root of 125? **5** What is 10 cubed? **1000** What is the cube root of 1000? **10** What is 6 squared? **36** What are the square roots of 36? **6 and −6** What is −5 squared? **25** What are the square roots of 25? **5 and −5**

How is cubing and finding cube roots different from squaring and finding square roots?

If you cube a number and then find the cube root of that number, you get the original number, and only the original number, back. However, if you square a number and then find the square roots of that number, you get both the original number and its opposite back.

TEACH

1 EXAMPLE

Questioning Strategies
- In part A, why do you square both sides of the equation? to eliminate the square root
- In part B, why do you cube both sides of the equation? to eliminate the cube root
- What would be the first step in solving $\sqrt{x - 2} + 7 = 12$? Why? Subtract 7 from both sides to isolate the radical.

EXTRA EXAMPLE
Solve each equation.
A. $\sqrt{x - 5} = 4$ $x = 21$
B. $\sqrt[3]{\dfrac{x}{5}} = 2$ $x = 40$

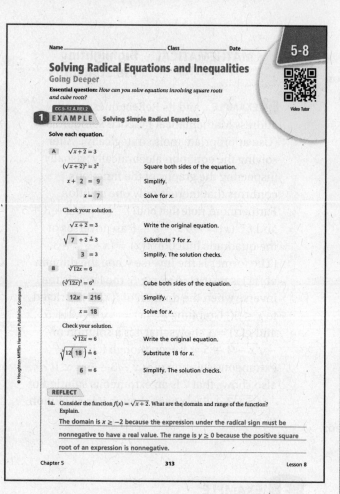

Name_____ Class_____ Date_____

5-8

Video Tutor

Solving Radical Equations and Inequalities
Going Deeper

Essential question: *How can you solve equations involving square roots and cube roots?*

CC.9-12.A.REI.2

1 EXAMPLE Solving Simple Radical Equations

Solve each equation.

A $\sqrt{x+2} = 3$

$(\sqrt{x+2})^2 = 3^2$ Square both sides of the equation.

$x + 2 = 9$ Simplify.

$x = 7$ Solve for x.

Check your solution.

$\sqrt{x+2} = 3$ Write the original equation.

$\sqrt{7+2} \stackrel{?}{=} 3$ Substitute 7 for x.

$3 = 3$ Simplify. The solution checks.

B $\sqrt[3]{12x} = 6$

$(\sqrt[3]{12x})^3 = 6^3$ Cube both sides of the equation.

$12x = 216$ Simplify.

$x = 18$ Solve for x.

Check your solution.

$\sqrt[3]{12x} = 6$ Write the original equation.

$\sqrt[3]{12(18)} \stackrel{?}{=} 6$ Substitute 18 for x.

$6 = 6$ Simplify. The solution checks.

REFLECT

1a. Consider the function $f(x) = \sqrt{x+2}$. What are the domain and range of the function? Explain.

The domain is $x \geq -2$ because the expression under the radical sign must be

nonnegative to have a real value. The range is $y \geq 0$ because the positive square

root of an expression is nonnegative.

© Houghton Mifflin Harcourt Publishing Company

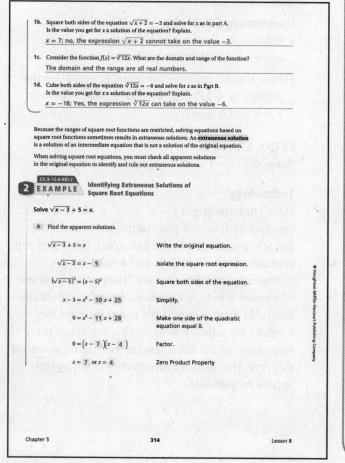

1b. Square both sides of the equation $\sqrt{x+2} = -3$ and solve for x as in Part A. Is the value you get for x a solution of the equation? Explain.

$x = 7$; no, the expression $\sqrt{x+2}$ cannot take on the value -3.

1c. Consider the function $f(x) = \sqrt[3]{12x}$. What are the domain and range of the function?

The domain and the range are all real numbers.

1d. Cube both sides of the equation $\sqrt[3]{12x} = -6$ and solve for x as in Part B. Is the value you get for x a solution of the equation? Explain.

$x = -18$; Yes, the expression $\sqrt[3]{12x}$ can take on the value -6.

Because the ranges of square root functions are restricted, solving equations based on square root functions sometimes results in *extraneous solutions*. An **extraneous solution** is a solution of an intermediate equation that is not a solution of the original equation.

When solving square root equations, you must check all apparent solutions in the original equation to identify and rule out extraneous solutions.

CC.9-12.A.REI.2

2 EXAMPLE Identifying Extraneous Solutions of Square Root Equations

Solve $\sqrt{x-3} + 5 = x$.

A Find the apparent solutions.

$\sqrt{x-3} + 5 = x$ Write the original equation.

$\sqrt{x-3} = x - 5$ Isolate the square root expression.

$(\sqrt{x-3})^2 = (x-5)^2$ Square both sides of the equation.

$x - 3 = x^2 - 10x + 25$ Simplify.

$0 = x^2 - 11x + 28$ Make one side of the quadratic equation equal 0.

$0 = (x-7)(x-4)$ Factor.

$x = 7$ or $x = 4$ Zero Product Property

© Houghton Mifflin Harcourt Publishing Company

Questioning Strategies

- Why do you not square both sides of the equation as the first step? **Squaring both sides as the first step does not eliminate the radical from the equation.**

- After squaring and obtaining a quadratic equation, how would you solve the equation if you could not factor it? **Use the quadratic formula.**

EXTRA EXAMPLE

Solve $x - 5 = \sqrt{3x - 5}$. The solution is $x = 10$. ($x = 3$ is an extraneous solution.)

Teaching Strategy

After students find that 7 is a solution and 4 is an extraneous solution, have them substitute 4 for x in each equation in the solution while working backward to see in which step the 4 quit being a solution.

$x = 7$ or $x = 4$
True: 4 = 4 (Only one part of an *or* statement needs to be satisfied.)
$0 = (x - 7)(x - 4)$
True: $x = 4$ makes the right side equal to $-3(0)$, or 0.
$0 = x^2 - 11x + 28$
True: $4^2 - 11(4) + 28 = 0$
$x - 3 = x^2 - 10x + 25$
True: $4 - 3 = 1$ and $4^2 - 10(4) + 25 = 1$.
$(\sqrt{x - 3})^2 = (x - 5)^2$
True: $(\sqrt{4 - 3})^2 = 1$ and $(4 - 5)^2 = 1$.
$\sqrt{x - 3} = x - 5$
False: $\sqrt{4 - 3} = 1$, but $4 - 5 = -1$.

Students should discover that the extraneous solution was introduced when both sides were squared.

2 EXAMPLE and its Reflect questions address Mathematical Practice Standard 5 (Use appropriate tools strategically). After solving the equation algebraically, visually inspecting the graphs of the functions confirms that there is only one solution. Furthermore, note that both $f^{-1}(x) = \sqrt{x - 3} + 5$ and $f^{-1}(x) = -\sqrt{x - 3} + 5$ are inverses of the quadratic function $f(x) = (x - 5)^2 + 3$. (The former is the inverse when the domain of $f(x)$ is restricted to $x \geq 5$; the latter is the inverse when the domain of $f(x)$ is restricted to $x \leq 5$.) Graphing $f^{-1}(x) = -\sqrt{x - 3} + 5$ and $g(x) = x$ shows that 4 is a solution of $-\sqrt{x - 3} + 5 = x$ even though it is an extraneous solution of $\sqrt{x - 3} + 5 = x$. It also shows that 7 is an extraneous solution of $-\sqrt{x - 3} + 5 = x$ even though it is a solution of $\sqrt{x - 3} + 5 = x$.

3 EXAMPLE

Questioning Strategies

- What is the first step in isolating the radical expression? **subtracting 3 from both sides**

- How do you cube the binomial $(x - 2)$? **Use the pattern $(a + b)^3 = a^3 + 3a^2b + 3ab^2 + b^3$ with $a = x$ and $b = -2$.**

EXTRA EXAMPLE

Solve $\sqrt[3]{13x - 1} - 4 = x - 5$. **$x = -2$, 0, and 5**

Technology

Have students graph $y = x^3 - 7x^2 + 12x$ (the cubic expression obtained after setting one side of the equation equal to 0 in the Example). Have students find the x-intercepts. **0, 3, and 4** Ask why the x-intercepts are the solutions. **They are the values of x when $y = 0$.** Ask students how they could use the Table feature to find the solutions. **Find the x-values for which $y = 0$.** Finally, ask about the limitations of the Table feature for finding solutions this way. **The x-values for which $y = 0$ may not appear in the table.**

B Check each apparent solution in the original equation to identify extraneous solutions.

Check $x = 7$.

$\sqrt{x-3} + 5 = x$	Write the original equation.
$\sqrt{7-3} + 5 \doteq 7$	Substitute 7 for x.
$2 + 5 = 7$	Simplify. $x = 7$ is a solution.

Check $x = 4$.

$\sqrt{x-3} + 5 = x$	Write the original equation.
$\sqrt{4-3} + 5 \doteq 4$	Substitute 4 for x.
$1 + 5 \neq 4$	Simplify. $x = 4$ is not a solution.

Because $x = 4$ is extraneous, the only solution is $x = 7$.

REFLECT

2a. Use a graphing calculator to graph the functions $f(x) = \sqrt{x-3} + 5$ and $g(x) = x$ on the same screen. How could you use the graph to solve the equation $\sqrt{x-3} + 5 = x$?

Find the x-coordinate of the point where the graphs of $f(x)$ and $g(x)$ intersect.

This x-coordinate, 7, is the solution of the equation.

2b. What types of functions are $f(x)$ and $g(x)$?

$f(x)$ is a square root function, and $g(x)$ is a linear function.

2c. Does the graph show the extraneous solution of $\sqrt{x-3} + 5 = x$? Explain.

No; the graph shows that $f(x)$ and $g(x)$ have different values when $x = 4$,

so the graph does not show the extraneous solution.

2d. Use a graphing calculator to graph the functions $h(x) = -\sqrt{x-3} + 5$ and $g(x) = x$ on the same screen. What do you notice about the point of intersection?

The x-coordinate of the point where the graphs of $h(x)$ and $g(x)$ intersect,

4, is the extraneous solution of $\sqrt{x-3} + 5 = x$.

CC.9-12.A.REI.2

3 EXAMPLE   **Solving Cube Root Equations**

Solve $2\sqrt[3]{x^2 - 8} + 3 = 2x - 1$.

$2\sqrt[3]{x^2 - 8} + 3 = 2x - 1$	Write the equation.
$2\sqrt[3]{x^2 - 8} = 2x - 4$	Isolate the cube root expression.
$\sqrt[3]{x^2 - 8} = x - 2$	Divide both sides by 2.
$\left(\sqrt[3]{x^2 - 8}\right)^3 = (x - 2)^3$	Cube both sides of the equation.
$x^2 - 8 = x^3 - 6x^2 + 12x - 8$	Expand $(x - 2)^3$.
$0 = x^3 - 7x^2 + 12x$	Make one side of the equation equal 0.
$0 = x(x - 4)(x - 3)$	Factor.
$x = 0, x = 4, \text{ or } x = 3$	Zero Product Property

Check your solutions.

$2\sqrt[3]{x^2 - 8} + 3 = 2x - 1$	$2\sqrt[3]{x^2 - 8} + 3 = 2x - 1$	$2\sqrt[3]{x^2 - 8} + 3 = 2x - 1$
$2\sqrt[3]{0^2 - 8} + 3 \doteq 2(0) - 1$	$2\sqrt[3]{4^2 - 8} + 3 \doteq 2(4) - 1$	$2\sqrt[3]{3^2 - 8} + 3 \doteq 2(3) - 1$
$2(-2) + 3 \doteq -1$	$2(2) + 3 \doteq 7$	$2(1) + 3 \doteq 5$
$-1 = -1$	$7 = 7$	$5 = 5$

REFLECT

3a. Explain how you could use a graph to check your solutions.

Graph $f(x) = 2\sqrt[3]{x^2 - 8} + 3$ and $g(x) = 2x - 1$ on the same coordinate

plane. Find the x-coordinates of the points where the graph of $f(x)$

intersects the graph of $g(x)$. These x-coordinates are the solutions of

$2\sqrt[3]{x^2 - 8} + 3 = 2x - 1$.

3b. Cube root equations that have no restrictions on the variable do not yield extraneous solutions when solved. Why is it still important to check your solutions?

Checking solutions is still important, because it may identify an

algebraic or arithmetic error in the solving process.

Essential Question

How can you solve equations involving square roots and cube roots? Isolate the radical expression. If it is a square root, square both sides of the equation. If it is a cube root, cube both sides of the equation. Continue to solve by isolating the variable.

For square root equations, check for extraneous solutions by substituting the solution(s) back into the original equation.

Summarize

Have students write an entry in their journals that compares and contrasts solving square root equations and cube root equations, using examples as appropriate. The entry should include a discussion of extraneous solutions in the case of square root equations.

Where skills are taught	Where skills are practiced
1 EXAMPLE	EXS. 1–6
2 EXAMPLE	EXS. 7–11
3 EXAMPLE	EXS. 12–14

Exercises 15 and 16: Students solve a square root equation and a cube root equation by graphing. Students can use their graphing calculators and then draw a sketch of the solution on the coordinate grid.

Exercises 17–19: Students solve real-world problems that can be modeled by either a square root function or a cube root function.

PRACTICE

Solve each equation.

1. $\sqrt{x+5} = 5$

$x = 20$

2. $\sqrt[3]{4x} = -2$

$x = -2$

3. $\sqrt[3]{3x} = 9$

$x = 27$

4. $\sqrt[3]{x+1} = 6$

$x = 215$

5. $\sqrt{4x-7} = 5$

$x = 8$

6. $\sqrt[3]{x-4} + 3 = -1$

$x = -60$

7. $\sqrt{-3x-5} = x + 3$

$x = -2$

8. $\sqrt{12+2x} = x + 2$

$x = 2$

9. $\sqrt{-6x-14} = x + 1$

no real solutions

10. $\sqrt{2x-7} = x - 5$

$x = 8$

11. $\sqrt{9x+90} = x + 6$

$x = 6$

12. $\sqrt[3]{1-x^2} = x + 1$

$x = 0, x = -1, x = -3$

13. $\sqrt[3]{9x^2+22x+8} = x + 2$

$x = 0, x = -2, x = 5$

14. $\sqrt[3]{x^2-x-1} = x - 1$

$x = 0, x = 2$

Solve each equation by graphing.

15. $2\sqrt{x+1} = 3x + 2$

$x = 0$

16. $2\sqrt[3]{x+1} + 3 = -2x + 1$

$x = -1$

© Houghton Mifflin Harcourt Publishing Company

---

17. The function $s(l) = 1.34\sqrt{l}$ models the maximum speed s in knots for a sailboat with length l in feet at the waterline.

a. Use the model to find the length of a sailboat with a maximum speed of 12 knots. Round to the nearest foot.

80 feet

b. Explain how you can check your solution using a graphing calculator. Then use the method you described to check your result.

Graph the functions $f(x) = 12$ and $g(x) = 1.34\sqrt{x}$. Find the x-coordinate of the

point where the graphs intersect.

18. The function $a(h) = 20\sqrt[3]{h-8.3} + 40$ models the age a in years of a sassafras tree that is h meters high.

a. Use the model to find the height of the sassafras tree when it was 50 years old. Round to the nearest tenth of a meter.

8.4 meters

b. Explain how you can check your solution using a graphing calculator. Then use the method you described to check your result.

Graph the functions $f(x) = 50$ and $g(x) = 20\sqrt[3]{x-8.3} + 40$. Find the

x-coordinate at the point of intersection of the two graphs.

19. When a car skids to a stop on a dry asphalt road, the equation $s = \sqrt{21d}$ models the relationship between the car's speed s in miles per hour at the beginning of the skid and the distance d in feet that the car skids.

a. Use the model to find the distance that a car will skid to a stop if it is traveling at 40 miles per hour at the beginning of the skid. Round to the nearest foot.

76 feet

b. Use the model to find the distance that a car will skid to a stop if it is traveling at 20 miles per hour at the beginning of the skid. Round to the nearest foot. Compare this result with the result from part (a), where the speed was twice as great.

19 feet; a speed that is twice as great results in a skid that is 4 times as long.

c. A car skids to a stop and leaves skid marks that are 65 feet long. The speed limit on the road is 35 miles per hour. Was the car speeding when it went into the skid? Explain.

Yes; possible explanation: If the car were traveling at 35 mi/h, its skid marks

would have been about 58 ft long. Since the skid marks were longer than this,

the car must have been speeding.

© Houghton Mifflin Harcourt Publishing Company

Assign these pages to help your students practice and apply important lesson concepts. For additional exercises, see the Student Edition.

Answers

Additional Practice

1. $x = 43$ 2. $x = 20$

3. $x = 6$ 4. $x = \frac{1}{2}$

5. $x = -15$ 6. $x = \frac{1}{4}$

7. No solutions, since both -1 and -7 are extraneous

8. $x = 32$ 9. $x = 7$

10. $x = -52$ 11. $-2 \le x \le 1$

12. $x > 40$ 13. $\frac{1}{2} \le x \le 8$

14. $x > 44$ 15. 25 years

Problem Solving

1. Directly

2. a. $d = \frac{s^2}{30f}$

    b. About 58 ft

    c. No; possible answer: his skid marks were only 52 ft, not 58 ft.

    d. About 33 mi/h

3. a. About 9 ft

    b. By at least 15 ft

4. B   5. A

Name_____ Class_____ Date_____ **5-8**

Additional Practice

Solve each equation.

1. $\sqrt{x+6}=7$

_____

2. $\sqrt{5x}=10$

_____

3. $\sqrt{2x+5}=\sqrt{3x-1}$

_____

4. $\sqrt{x+4}=3\sqrt{x}$

_____

5. $\sqrt[3]{x-6}=\sqrt[3]{3x+24}$

_____

6. $3\sqrt[3]{x}=\sqrt[3]{7x+5}$

_____

7. $\sqrt{-14x+2}=x-3$

_____

8. $(x+4)^{\frac{1}{2}}=6$

_____

9. $4(x-3)^{\frac{1}{2}}=8$

_____

10. $4(x-12)^{\frac{1}{3}}=-16$

_____

Solve each inequality.

11. $\sqrt{3x+6}\le 3$

_____

12. $\sqrt{x-4}+3>9$

_____

13. $\sqrt{x+7}\ge\sqrt{2x-1}$

_____

14. $\sqrt{2x-7}>9$

_____

Solve.

15. A biologist is studying two species of animals in a habitat. The population, p_1, of one of the species is growing according to $p_1=500t^{\frac{3}{2}}$ and the population, p_2, of the other species is growing according to $p_2=100t^2$ where time, t, is measured in years. After how many years will the populations of the two species be equal?

_____

Problem Solving

The formula $s=\sqrt{30fd}$ can be used to estimate the speed, s, in miles per hour that a car is traveling when it goes into a skid, where f is the coefficient of friction and d is the length of the skid marks in feet.

1. How does the speed vary as the length of the skid marks?

2. Kody skids to a stop on a street with a speed limit of 35 mi/h. His skid marks measure 52 ft, and the coefficient of friction is 0.7. Kody says that he was driving only about 30 mi/h. Kody wants to prove that he was not speeding.

   a. Solve the equation for d in terms of s.   _____

   b. How long would the skid marks be if he had been driving at a speed of 35 mi/h?   _____

   c. Was Kody speeding or not? Explain how you know.

   _____

   d. Find his actual speed.   _____

3. Ashley skids to a stop on a street with a speed limit of 15 mi/h to avoid a dog who runs into the street about 20 ft ahead of her. Ashley claims to have been going less than 15 mi/h. The coefficient of friction is 0.7.

   a. If Ashley were driving the speed limit, by what distance would she have missed the dog?

   _____

   b. If Ashley were driving less than 10 mi/h, by what distance would she have missed the dog?

   _____

Choose the letter for the best answer.

4. Barney was driving at 25 mi/h. A car pulls out 30 ft ahead of him. Which statement is true?

   A Barney hits the car.

   B Barney stops less than a foot from the car.

   C Barney misses the car by 3 ft.

   D Barney's skid marks measure 23 ft.

5. On a busy highway with a speed limit of 70 mi/h, a truck ahead of Verna jack-knifes across the road. Verna skids to a stop 10 ft short of the truck. Her skid marks measure 260 ft. Was Verna speeding?

   A Yes; her speed was 73.9 mi/h.

   B Yes; her speed was 75.3 mi/h.

   C No; her speed was 70 mi/h.

   D No; her speed was only 63 mi/h.

This page provides students with the opportunity to apply concepts from the Common Core in real-world problem situations. There are three different levels of performance tasks:

⭐ **Novice:** These are short word problems that require students to apply the math they have learned in straightforward, real-world situations.

⭐⭐ **Apprentice:** These are more involved problems that guide students step-by-step through more complex tasks. These exercises include more complicated reasoning, writing, and open-ended elements.

⭐⭐⭐ **Expert:** These are open-ended, non-routine problems that, instead of stepping the students through, ask them to choose their own methods for solving and justify their answers and reasoning.

Sample answers

1. No; the graph of $E(x)$ has a horizontal asymptote at $y = 0$, so the amount per employee can never be $0.

2. Randall ate $1 - \frac{1}{p} = \frac{p-1}{p}$ of the pepperoni pizza and $1 - \frac{1}{p+4} = \frac{p+3}{p+4}$ of the cheese pizza.

3. Scoring Guide:

Task	Possible points
a	1 point for writing the largest allowable volume as $\frac{4}{3}\pi r^3$ and 1 point for writing the smallest allowable volume as $\frac{4}{3}\pi(r - 0.04)^3$.
b	2 points for correctly writing the equation $\dfrac{\frac{4}{3}\pi(r-0.04)^3}{\frac{4}{3}\pi r^3} = 0.9206$ OR equivalent
c	1 point for correctly solving the equation for r, the largest allowable radius of 1.47 inches, and 1 point for correctly determining that the smallest allowable radius of a baseball is $1.47 - 0.04 = 1.43$ inches

Total possible points: 6

CHAPTER 5

Performance Tasks

COMMON CORE
CC.9-12.A.CED.1
CC.9-12.A.CED.3
CC.9-12.A.APR.1
CC.9-12.A.APR.7
CC.9-12.F.IF.7d

★ **1.** A small company has a budget of $1500 to spend on office supplies for its workers. The function $E(x) = \frac{1500}{x}$ gives the amount that the company can spend on each employee. Is it possible for the amount of money per employee to be $0? Explain what feature of the graph of $E(x)$ tells you this.

★ **2.** Randall and Tiana ordered a pepperoni pizza and a cheese pizza of the same size. All the pieces of the pepperoni pizza were the same size, as were all the pieces of the cheese pizza, but the cheese pizza was cut into 4 more pieces than the pepperoni pizza. Tiana ate one piece of each pizza. Randall ate the rest of both pizzas. If the pepperoni pizza was cut into p pieces, what fraction of each pizza did Randall eat?

★ **3.** In Major League baseball, the smallest allowable volume of a baseball is 92.06% of the largest allowable volume, and the range of allowable radii is 0.04 inches.
  a. Suppose r is the largest allowable radius of a baseball in inches. Write expressions for the largest allowable volume of the baseball and the smallest allowable volume of the baseball, both in terms of r.
  b. Write an equation that shows that the ratio of the smallest allowable volume to the largest allowable volume is 0.9206.

continued

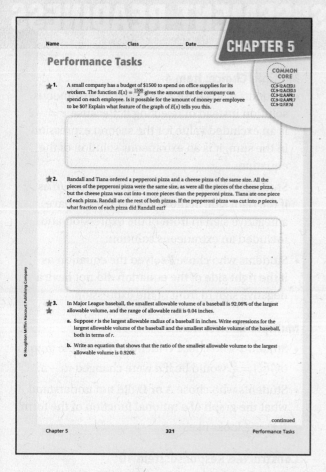

  c. Solve the equation in part **a** for r, and round r to the nearest hundredth of an inch. What are the smallest allowable radius and the largest allowable radius of a baseball?

★★★ **4.** Eva and Ty started jogging at the same time from opposite ends of a straight trail. Both jogged at a constant, but different, speed. When each of them reached the opposite end, he or she turned around and went back to where they started. The first time they met along the trail, they were 3 miles from Ty's end of the trail, and the second time they met, they had each turned around and were 2 miles from Eva's end of the trail.
  a. Let the length of the trail be m miles. What was the total distance run by Ty and the total distance run by Eva the first time they met?
  b. What was the total distance run by Ty and the total distance run by Eva the second time they met?
  c. Set up an equation and solve for m to find the length of the trail. Why must the ratio of the total distances run the first time they met be equal to the ratio of the total distances run the second time they met?

---

4. Scoring Guide:

Task	Possible points
a	1 point for correctly determining the total distance run by Ty the first time they met: 3 miles 1 point for correctly determining the total distance run by Eva the first time they met: $m - 3$ miles
b	1 point for correctly determining the total distance run by Ty the second time they met: $m + 2$ miles 1 point for correctly determining the total distance run by Eva the second time they met: $2m - 2$ miles
c	1 point for correctly setting the ratio of the total distances run the first time they met equal to the ratio of the total distances run the second time they met and solving for m, and then calculating how far both Eva and Ty ran in total once they were finished : $$\frac{3}{m-3} = \frac{m+2}{2m-2}$$ $$3(2m - 2) = (m + 2)(m - 3)$$ $$6m - 6 = m^2 - 3m + 2m - 6$$ $$6m - 6 = m^2 - m - 6$$ $$0 = m^2 - 7m$$ $$0 = m(m - 7)$$ $$m = 0 \text{ or } m = 7$$ The length of the trail is 7 miles in total. 1 point for correctly explaining that the ratio of the total distances run the first time they met must be equal to the ratio of the total distances run the second time they met because both are jogging at constant speeds and both had been jogging the same amount of time when they met. Therefore, since rate · time = distance, their distances must always be in proportion to each other.

Total possible points: 6

COMMON CORE CORRELATION

Standard	Items
CC.9-12.N.RN.2	8, 9
CC.9-12.A.APR.6	5
CC.9-12.A.APR.7(+)	12, 13
CC.9-12.A.CED.1*	13
CC.9-12.A.CED.2*	3, 11
CC.9-12.A.REI.2	1, 4
CC.9-12.A.REI.11*	13
CC.9-12.F.IF.4*	11
CC.9-12.F.IF.7b*	10
CC.9-12.F.IF.7d(+)*	6, 7, 13
CC.9-12.F.BF.1*	3, 11, 13
CC.9-12.F.BF.3	2, 10, 13

TEST PREP DOCTOR ⊕

Multiple Choice: Item 1
- Students who chose **A** or **C** may have incorrectly factored $x^2 - 7x - 18$, the polynomial that arises after squaring both sides of the equation and getting one side equal to 0.
- Students who chose **B** chose the extraneous solution.

Multiple Choice: Item 3
- Students who chose **A** placed the variable x in the numerator rather than in the denominator.
- Students who chose **B** both incorrectly placed x in the numerator and mixed up the cost that was shared (the dinner) and the cost that was not shared (the dessert).
- Students who chose **D** mixed up the shared cost and the cost that was not shared.

Multiple Choice: Item 4
- Students who chose **F** included an extraneous solution instead of rejecting it. Because $x = -2$ is an excluded value for the second expression in the sum, it is an extraneous solution of the equation.
- Students who chose **G** solved the equation as if the right side of the equation did not have a negative sign in front of the expression and included an extraneous solution.
- Students who chose **J** solved the equation as if the right side of the equation did not have a negative sign in front of the expression.

Multiple Choice: Item 7
- Students who chose **C** identified what the graph of $f(x) = \frac{a}{x}$ would be if a were changed to $-a$.
- Students who chose **A** or **D** did not understand what the graph of a rational function of the form $f(x) = \frac{a}{x}$ looks like.

Constructed Response: Item 10
- Students whose graphs start at $(-1, 2)$ used -1 for h and translated the parent graph left.

Constructed Response: Item 12
- Students who found an incorrect product may have factored or simplified incorrectly or did not simplify at all.
- Students who found an incorrect quotient may not have multiplied by the reciprocal of the divisor.
- Students who found an incorrect sum may have incorrectly factored the denominator of the second expression, incorrectly determined the LCM for the denominators, or multiplied the first expression incorrectly when multiplying by a form of 1 so that both expressions would have the same denominator.
- Students who found an incorrect difference may have added instead of subtracted, or made any of the errors listed above.

CHAPTER 5 — COMMON CORE — ASSESSMENT READINESS

Name _____ Class _____ Date _____

MULTIPLE CHOICE

1. What is the solution of the equation $\sqrt{x+27} = x - 3$?

A. $x = -9$ C. $x = 2$

B. $x = -2$ (D.) $x = 9$

2. Which best describes the graph of $g(x) = 4\sqrt[3]{x}$ as a transformation of the graph of $f(x) = \sqrt[3]{x}$?

(F.) vertical stretch by a factor of 4

G. vertical compression by a factor of $\frac{1}{4}$

H. translation 4 units up

J. translation 4 units to the right

3. A group of x friends splits the cost of a family-style dinner for $50. In addition to the cost of the dinner, each person orders a $5 dessert. Which function gives the amount $A(x)$ that each person pays?

A. $A(x) = \frac{x}{50} + 5$ (C.) $A(x) = \frac{50}{x} + 5$

B. $A(x) = \frac{x}{5} + 50$ D. $A(x) = \frac{5}{x} + 50$

4. What are the solutions of the equation $\frac{x}{x-1} + \frac{1}{x+2} = -\frac{3}{x^2+x-2}$?

F. $-1, -2$ (H.) -1

G. $-4, 1$ J. -4

5. Which function is the graphing form of $f(x) = \frac{4x+3}{x-1}$?

A. $f(x) = \frac{4}{x-1} + 7$

B. $f(x) = \frac{4}{x-1} - 1$

C. $f(x) = \frac{-1}{x-1} + 4$

(D.) $f(x) = \frac{7}{x-1} + 4$

6. The graph of which function is shown?

F. $f(x) = \frac{1}{x+1} + 1$

(G.) $f(x) = \frac{1}{x+1} - 1$

H. $f(x) = \frac{1}{x-1} + 1$

J. $f(x) = \frac{1}{x-1} - 1$

7. In which quadrants does the graph of $f(x) = \frac{3}{x}$ lie?

A. I and II   C. II and IV

(B.) I and III   D. III and IV

8. What is $\sqrt[5]{n^3}$ in rational exponent form?

F. $n^{\frac{5}{3}}$ H. n^{15}

(G.) $n^{\frac{3}{5}}$ J. n^8

9. Ron began simplifying the expression $\sqrt{a} \cdot \sqrt[3]{a}$ by writing $a^{\frac{1}{2}} \cdot a^{\frac{1}{3}}$. What is the next step that he should take?

A. Write $a^{\frac{1}{2}} \cdot a^{\frac{1}{3}}$ as $a^{\frac{1}{2} \cdot \frac{1}{3}}$.

B. Write $a^{\frac{1}{2}} \cdot a^{\frac{1}{3}}$ as $\frac{1}{a^{\frac{1}{2} \cdot \frac{1}{3}}}$.

(C.) Write $a^{\frac{1}{2}} \cdot a^{\frac{1}{3}}$ as $a^{\frac{1}{2} + \frac{1}{3}}$.

D. Write $a^{\frac{1}{2}} \cdot a^{\frac{1}{3}}$ as $\frac{1}{a^{\frac{1}{2} + \frac{1}{3}}}$.

CONSTRUCTED RESPONSE

10. Graph $g(x) = \sqrt{x-1} + 2$ on the coordinate plane below. Then describe the graph of $g(x)$ as a transformation of the graph of the parent function $f(x) = \sqrt{x}$.

The graph of $g(x)$ is a translation of

the graph of $f(x)$ right 1 unit and up

2 units.

11. Kelsey is making bracelets to sell at a craft fair. She spends $50 on a jewelry-making kit and $.50 on beads for each bracelet. She plans to sell the bracelets for $3 each.

a. Write and simplify a rule for the profit-per-bracelet function $P(b)$ if she sells b bracelets.

$P(b) = \frac{3b - (50 + 0.5b)}{b} = -\frac{50}{b} + 2.5$

b. As the number of bracelets sold increases, what happens to the profit per bracelet?

The profit per bracelet

approaches $2.50.

12. Use the expressions $\frac{x}{x+1}$ and $\frac{1}{x^2+x}$ to complete the following.

a. Find the product of the expressions.

$\frac{x}{x+1} \cdot \frac{1}{x(x+1)} = \frac{1}{(x+1)^2}$

b. Find the quotient of the expressions (first expression divided by second expression).

$\frac{x}{x+1} \div \frac{1}{x(x+1)} =$

$\frac{x}{x+1} \cdot \frac{x(x+1)}{1} = x^2$

c. Find the sum of the expressions.

$\frac{x}{x+1} + \frac{1}{x(x+1)} = \frac{x^2+1}{x(x+1)}$

d. Find the difference of the expressions (first expression minus second expression).

$\frac{x}{x+1} - \frac{1}{x(x+1)} = \frac{x^2-1}{x(x+1)} = \frac{x-1}{x}$

13. While canoeing on a river, your paddling speed is twice the river's current. You travel 3 miles downstream and then 3 miles upstream to get back to where you started.

a. Write a rule for $T(s)$, the function that gives your total trip time (in hours) as a function of the current's speed s (in miles per hour). The rule should involve a sum of two rational expressions. Carry out the addition to simplify the rule as much as possible.

$T(s) = \frac{3}{2s+s} + \frac{3}{2s-s} = \frac{1}{s} + \frac{3}{s} = \frac{4}{s}$

b. Use the coordinate plane below to graph $T(s)$. Include axis labels and scales.

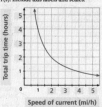

c. How is the graph of $T(s)$ related to the graph of the parent function $f(s) = \frac{1}{s}$?

Vertical stretch by a factor of 4

d. Use the graph to estimate the current's speed when the total trip time is 2.5 hours.

About 1.6 miles per hour

e. Write and solve an equation to find the current's speed exactly when the total trip time is 2.5 hours.

$\frac{4}{s} = 2.5$; $s = 1.6$ miles per hour

© Houghton Mifflin Harcourt Publishing Company

CHAPTER 6

Properties and Attributes of Functions

Properties and Attributes of Functions

Chapter Focus

In this chapter, you will learn about the properties and attributes of functions. You will learn how to compare, transform, perform arithmetic operations on, and invert functions. You will also investigate piecewise functions and model real-world situations with square root functions.

Chapter at a Glance

Lesson		COMMON CORE Standards for Mathematical Content
6-1	Multiple Representations of Functions	CC.9-12.A.SSE.3c, CC.9-12.F.IF.8b, CC.9-12.F.BF.1, CC.9-12.F.LE.3, CC.9-12.S.ID.6a, CC.9-12.S.ID.6b
6-2	Comparing Functions	CC.9-12.F.IF.9
6-3	Piecewise Functions	CC.9-12.F.IF.2, CC.9-12.F.IF.5, CC.9-12.F.IF.7b, CC.9-12.F.BF.1
6-4	Transforming Functions	CC.9-12.F.BF.3
6-5	Operations with Functions	CC.9-12.F.BF.1b
6-6	Functions and Their Inverses	CC.9-12.A.CED.2, CC.9-12.F.BF.4, CC.9-12.F.BF.4a, CC.9-12.F.BF.4d(+)
6-7	Modeling Real-World Data	CC.9-12.A.CED.2, CC.9-12.F.IF.4, CC.9-12.F.IF.7b, CC.9-12.F.BF.1, CC.9-12.F.BF.4d(+), CC.9-12.S.ID.6a
	Performance Tasks	
	Assessment Readiness	

COMMON CORE PROFESSIONAL DEVELOPMENT

CC.9-12.F.IF.7b*

Building on their knowledge of linear, quadratic, and exponential functions, students will graph piecewise-defined functions such as step functions and absolute value functions. Instruction should include highlighting domain and range and the usefulness of domain and range when examining piecewise-defined functions.

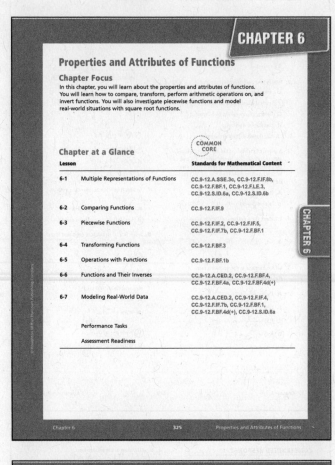

Unpacking the Standards

Understanding the standards and the vocabulary terms in the standards will help you know exactly what you are expected to learn in this chapter.

COMMON CORE CC.9-12.F.IF.7b
Graph … piecewise-defined functions, including step functions and absolute value functions.

Key Vocabulary
piecewise function *(función a trozos)* A function that is a combination of one or more functions.
step function *(función escalón)* A piecewise function that is constant over each interval in its domain.
absolute-value function *(función de valor absoluto)* A function whose rule contains absolute-value expressions.

What It Means For You   Lesson 6-3

You can use piecewise-defined functions to model applications that are described by different functions over different parts of their domain.

EXAMPLE
The function for topsoil prices is a step function consisting of three constant functions:

$y = 10$, for $0 \leq x < 5$,
$y = 7$, for $5 \leq x < 25$
$y = 5$, for $x \geq 25$

Topsoil Prices

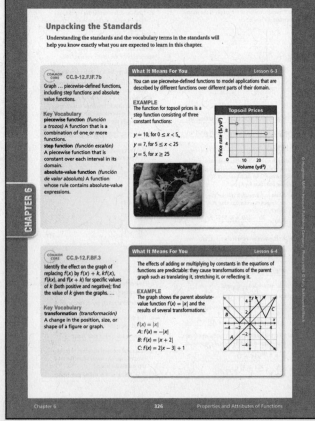

COMMON CORE CC.9-12.F.BF.3
Identify the effect on the graph of replacing $f(x)$ by $f(x) + k$, $kf(x)$, $f(kx)$, and $f(x + k)$ for specific values of k (both positive and negative); find the value of k given the graphs. …

Key Vocabulary
transformation *(transformación)* A change in the position, size, or shape of a figure or graph.

What It Means For You   Lesson 6-4

The effects of adding or multiplying by constants in the equations of functions are predictable: they cause transformations of the parent graph such as translating it, stretching it, or reflecting it.

EXAMPLE
The graph shows the parent absolute-value function $f(x) = |x|$ and the results of several transformations.

$f(x) = |x|$
$A: f(x) = -|x|$
$B: f(x) = |x + 2|$
$C: f(x) = 2|x - 3| + 1$

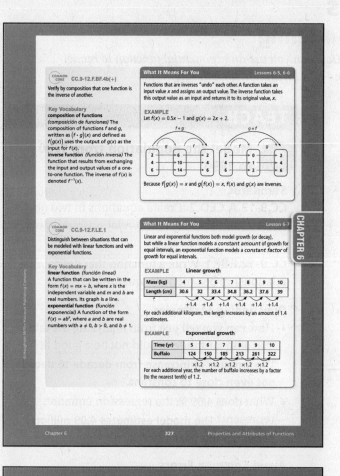

COMMON CORE CC.9-12.F.BF.4b(+)

Verify by composition that one function is the inverse of another.

Key Vocabulary

composition of functions
(composición de funciones) The composition of functions f and g, written as $(f \circ g)(x)$ and defined as $f(g(x))$ uses the output of $g(x)$ as the input for $f(x)$.

inverse function *(función inversa)* The function that results from exchanging the input and output values of a one-to-one function. The inverse of $f(x)$ is denoted $f^{-1}(x)$.

What It Means For You — Lessons 6-5, 6-6

Functions that are inverses "undo" each other. A function takes an input value x and assigns an output value. The inverse function takes this output value as an input and returns it to its original value, x.

EXAMPLE

Let $f(x) = 0.5x - 1$ and $g(x) = 2x + 2$.

Because $f(g(x)) = x$ and $g(f(x)) = x$, $f(x)$ and $g(x)$ are inverses.

COMMON CORE CC.9-12.F.LE.1

Distinguish between situations that can be modeled with linear functions and with exponential functions.

Key Vocabulary

linear function *(función lineal)*
A function that can be written in the form $f(x) = mx + b$, where x is the independent variable and m and b are real numbers. Its graph is a line.

exponential function *(función exponencial)* A function of the form $f(x) = ab^x$, where a and b are real numbers with $a \neq 0$, $b > 0$, and $b \neq 1$.

What It Means For You — Lesson 6-7

Linear and exponential functions both model growth (or decay), but while a linear function models a *constant amount* of growth for equal intervals, an exponential function models a *constant factor* of growth for equal intervals.

EXAMPLE — Linear growth

Mass (kg)	4	5	6	7	8	9	10
Length (cm)	30.6	32	33.4	34.8	36.2	37.6	39

+1.4 +1.4 +1.4 +1.4 +1.4 +1.4

For each additional kilogram, the length increases by an amount of 1.4 centimeters.

EXAMPLE — Exponential growth

Time (yr)	5	6	7	8	9	10
Buffalo	124	150	185	213	261	322

×1.2 ×1.2 ×1.2 ×1.2 ×1.2

For each additional year, the number of buffalo increases by a factor (to the nearest tenth) of 1.2.

Chapter 6 — 327 — Properties and Attributes of Functions

CHAPTER 6

In previous courses, students have worked with the line of best fit to describe a situation that can be modeled with a linear function. Students saw that linear functions have a constant rate of change. Using their knowledge of linear and exponential functions and rates of change, students will formalize the difference between situations that can be modeled by linear functions and exponential functions based on rate of change.

CHAPTER 6

Key Vocabulary

absolute-value function *(función de valor absoluto)* A function whose rule contains absolute-value expressions.

composition of functions *(composición de funciones)* The composition of functions f and g, written as $(f \circ g)(x)$ and defined as $f(g(x))$, uses the output of $g(x)$ as the input for $f(x)$.

cube-root function *(función de raíz cúbica)* A function of the form $f(x) = a\sqrt[3]{x-h} + k$ where a, h, and k are constants and $a \neq 0$.

end behavior *(comportamiento extremo)* The trends in the y-values of a function as the x-values approach positive and negative infinity.

exponential function *(función exponencial)* A function of the form $f(x) = ab^x$, where a and b are real numbers with $a \neq 0$, $b > 0$, and $b \neq 1$.

greatest integer function *(función de entero mayor)* A function denoted by $f(x) = [x]$ or $f(x) = \lfloor x \rfloor$ in which the number x is rounded down to the greatest integer that is less than or equal to x.

inverse function *(función inversa)* The function that results from exchanging the input and output values of a one-to-one function. The inverse of $f(x)$ is denoted $f^{-1}(x)$.

linear function *(función lineal)* A function that can be written in the form $f(x) = mx + b$, where x is the independent variable and m and b are real numbers. Its graph is a line.

one-to-one function *(función uno a uno)* A function in which each y-value corresponds to only one x-value. The inverse of a one-to-one function is also a function.

parabola *(parábola)* The shape of the graph of a quadratic function. Also, the set of points equidistant from a point F, called the focus, and a line d, called the *directrix*.

piecewise function *(función a trozos)* A function that is a combination of one or more functions.

quadratic function *(función cuadrática)* A function that can be written in the form $f(x) = ax^2 + bx + c$, where a, b, and c are real numbers and $a \neq 0$, or in the form $f(x) = a(x - h)^2 + k$, where a, h, and k are real numbers and $a \neq 0$.

residual *(residuo)* The signed vertical distance between a data point and a line of fit.

square root function *(función de raíz cuadrada)* A function of the form $f(x) = a\sqrt{x-h} + k$ where a, h, and k are constants and $a \neq 0$.

step function *(función escalón)* A piecewise function that is constant over each interval in its domain.

transformation *(transformación)* A change in the position, size, or shape of a figure or graph.

vertex form of a quadratic function *(forma en vértice de una función cuadrática)* A quadratic equation written in the form $f(x) = a(x - h)^2 + k$, where a, h, and k are constants and (h, k) is the vertex.

CHAPTER 6

Chapter 6 — 328 — Properties and Attributes of Functions

6-1 Multiple Representations of Functions
Focus on Modeling

Essential question: *How can you use an exponential function to model population growth and find an annual growth rate?*

COMMON Standards for
CORE Mathematical Content

The following standards are addressed in this lesson. (An asterisk indicates that a standard is also a Modeling standard.) For more detailed information, see each section of the lesson.

Algebra: CC.9-12.A.SSE.3, CC.9-12.A.SSE.3c, CC.9-12.A.CED.2*

Functions: CC.9-12.F.IF.4*, CC.9-12.F.IF.7*, CC.9-12.F.IF.7e*, CC.9-12.F.IF.8, CC.9-12.F.IF.8b, CC.9-12.F.BF.1*, CC.9-12.F.BF.1a*, CC.9-12.F.LE.3*

Statistics and Probability: CC.9-12.S.ID.6*, CC.9-12.S.ID.6a*, CC.9-12.S.ID.6b*

Prerequisites
- Graphing an exponential function
- Interpreting an exponential growth function
- Finding a regression equation
- Finding and interpreting residuals

Math Background
In this lesson, students enter population data into their graphing calculators to determine an exponential regression equation. They use the graph of the exponential equation and residuals to determine whether the model is a good fit for the data and use properties of exponents to write an equivalent equation to gain new information about the situation. They see that while the model is a good fit for the given time period, it is a poor fit for times beyond it. In the extension, they compare the exponential model to a quadratic model.

INTRODUCE
Population can grow very quickly. As an example, have students use the census table and find the differences from one decade to the next. Students should see that each difference increases over the difference before it.

TEACH

1 Model the population from 1790 to 1890.

Standards
CC.9-12.A.CED.2 Create equations in two or more variables to represent relationships between quantities...*

CC.9-12.F.BF.1 Write a function that describes a relationship between two quantities.*

Questioning Strategies
- How can you tell just from analyzing the table that a linear model would not be a good fit?
  The amount of increase from decade to decade is not even close to constant.
- What does 4.09 in the regression equation represent? The model estimates 4.09 million people in the year 1790.

Avoid Common Errors
In answering Reflect Question 1a, students might say that the growth rate is 33% per year. Remind them that the *x*-values represent decades, not years.

2 Determine how well the model fits the data.

Standards
CC.9-12. A.CED.2 ... graph equations on coordinate axes with labels and scales.*

CC.9-12.F.IF.4 For a function that models a relationship between two quantities, interpret key features of graphs in terms of the quantities, ...*

CC.9-12.F.IF.7e Graph exponential...functions, showing intercepts and end behavior ...*

CC.9-12.S.ID.6 Represent data on two quantitative variables on a scatter plot, and describe how the variables are related.*

CC.9-12.S.ID.6b Informally assess the fit of a function by plotting and analyzing residuals.*

continued

Name _____ Class _____ Date _____

6-1

Multiple Representations of Functions
Focus on Modeling

Essential question: *How can you use an exponential function to model population growth and find an annual growth rate?*

COMMON CORE
CC-9-12.A.SSE.3c
CC-9-12.F.IF.8b
CC-9-12.F.BF.1*
CC-9-12.F.LE.3*,
CC-9-12.S.ID.6a*,
CC-9-12.S.ID.6b*

The United States government performs a census every 10 years. The census data from 1790 to 1890 are given in the table below. How can you use the data to predict the population in 1845 and 1990?

1 Model the population from 1790 to 1890.

A   Complete the table. Round the population (in millions) to the nearest tenth.

Census Year	Decades Since First Census	Population	Population (in millions)
1790	0	3,929,214	3.9
1800	1	5,308,483	5.3
1810	2	7,239,881	7.2
1820	3	9,638,453	9.6
1830	4	12,866,020	12.9
1840	5	17,069,453	17.1
1850	6	23,191,876	23.2
1860	7	31,443,321	31.4
1870	8	39,818,449	39.8
1880	9	50,189,209	50.2
1890	10	62,979,766	63.0

B   Use your graphing calculator to determine the exponential regression equation for the data as follows.
   • Let the x-values be the number of decades since 1790. Enter these values in list L_1.
   • Let the y-values be the population in millions. Enter these values in list L_2.
   • Find the exponential regression equation by pressing [STAT], selecting the CALC menu, and then selecting 0:ExpReg.

Write the exponential regression equation below, rounding the values of a and b to two decimal places.

$y = 4.09(1.33)^x$

REFLECT

1a. Write the regression equation in the form of an exponential growth function, $y = a(1 + r)^t$. What does r represent?

$y = 4.09(1 + 0.33)^t$; r represents the population's growth rate of 33% per decade.

2 Determine how well the model fits the data.

A   Plot the 11 data points (*decades since first census, population in millions*) on the coordinate plane below.

B   Graph the exponential regression equation on the same coordinate plane.

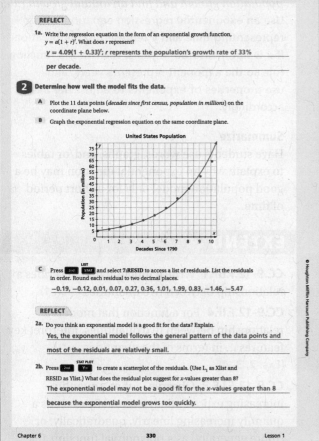

United States Population

C   Press [2nd] [STAT] and select 7:RESID to access a list of residuals. List the residuals in order. Round each residual to two decimal places.

−0.19, −0.12, 0.01, 0.07, 0.27, 0.36, 1.01, 1.99, 0.83, −1.46, −5.47

REFLECT

2a. Do you think an exponential model is a good fit for the data? Explain.

Yes, the exponential model follows the general pattern of the data points and most of the residuals are relatively small.

2b. Press [2nd] [Y=] to create a scatterplot of the residuals. (Use L_1 as Xlist and RESID as Ylist.) What does the residual plot suggest for x-values greater than 8?

The exponential model may not be a good fit for the x-values greater than 8 because the exponential model grows too quickly.

Questioning Strategies

- What does the absolute value of a residual reveal? **the distance between a data value and the corresponding output value from the model**

- What does the sign of a residual reveal? **whether the data value is greater or less than the corresponding output value from the model**

- For which decade (0–10) is the residual positive and its absolute value the greatest? For which decade is the residual negative and its absolute value the greatest? **7; 10**

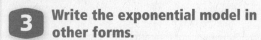
Write the exponential model in other forms.

Standards

CC.9-12.A.SSE.3 … produce an equivalent form of an expression to reveal and explain properties of the quantity represented by the expression.

CC.9-12.A.SSE.3c Use the properties of exponents to transform expressions for exponential functions.

CC.9-12.F.IF.8 Write a function defined by an expression in different but equivalent forms to reveal and explain different properties of the function.

CC.9-12.F.IF.8b Use properties of exponents to interpret expressions for exponential functions.

Questioning Strategies

- Why does raising 1.33 to the one-tenth power give the growth factor per year? **When rewriting the function with an exponent of 10x representing years, you have to rewrite the base as 1.33 to the one-tenth power to produce an equivalent expression, and this base represents the annual growth factor. (In general, if the growth factor for n years is g, then the annual growth factor is the nth root of g.)**

- Will using the equation in Reflect Question 3b for $x = 5$ give the same result as using the original equation for $x = 5$? **Not exactly; 1.03 was rounded in part B.**

4 **Use the model to make predictions.**

Standards

CC.9-12.S.ID.6a … use functions fitted to data to solve problems in the context of the data.*

Questioning Strategies

- How can you check the reasonableness of the prediction for 1845? **See whether it is between the populations given for 1840 and 1850 in the table.**

- How do you find the value of x when the year is 1990? **Find 1990 − 1790 and divide by 10.**

⋮ MATHEMATICAL PRACTICE   **Highlighting the Standards**

Answering the questions about the predictions addresses Mathematical Practice Standard 3 (Construct viable arguments and critique the reasoning of others). Let students discuss among themselves why the model was good for 1845 but very poor for 1990. Encourage students to look for a pattern in the residuals and think about the form of an exponential growth function.

CLOSE

Essential Question

How can you use an exponential function to model population growth and find an annual growth rate?
Use an exponential regression equation with x representing time and y representing population. If x is not measured in years, rewrite the function rule so the exponent represents years, and use properties of exponents to adjust the base accordingly.

Summarize

Have students use words, graphs, and/or tables to explain why an exponential function may be a good population model only for a short period of time.

EXTEND

CC.9-12.F.BF.1 Write a function that describes a relationship between two quantities.* (Ex. 1)

CC.9-12.F.IF.4 For a function that models a relationship between two quantities, interpret key features … in terms of the quantities, …*
(Exs. 2, 3, 4)

CC.9-12.F.LE.3 Observe … that a quantity increasing exponentially eventually exceeds a quantity increasing linearly, quadratically, or (more generally) as a polynomial function. (Ex. 5)

3 Write the exponential model in other forms.

A What property of exponents tells you that $y = 4.09\left(1.33^{\frac{1}{10}}\right)^{10x}$ is an equivalent form of the exponential model?

Power of a power property

B Rewrite $y = 4.09\left(1.33^{\frac{1}{10}}\right)^{10x}$ by evaluating the base. Round the base to two decimal places.

$y = 4.09(1.03)^{10x}$

C Based on the rewritten model, what was the annual growth rate of the U.S. population for the period 1790–1890?

about 3%

REFLECT

3a. What does x represent in the rewritten model?

x still represents the number of decades since 1790.

3b. Suppose a student used the equation $y = 4.09(1.03)^x$ as an exponential model for the population. What would these x-values represent?

x would represent the number of years since 1790.

4 Use the model to make predictions.

A Use the exponential model you wrote in step 1B to predict the population in 1845. State what value you used for x.

about 19.6 million; $x = 5.5$

B Use the exponential model you wrote in step 1B to predict the population in 1990. State what value you used for x.

about 1.23 billion; $x = 20$

REFLECT

4a. How confident are you of the predicted population for 1845? Explain.

Very confident because the model fits the data well for x-values from 0 to 8, and the prediction used an x-value of 5.5.

4b. Knowing that a residual is the difference between an actual value and a predicted value, would you say that your prediction of the population in 1845 might be a little too high or a little too low? Explain.

A little too low because the residuals for 1840 and 1850 were both positive, so the model underestimates those population values and probably does the same for 1845.

© Houghton Mifflin Harcourt Publishing Company

4c. The census for 1990 showed that the U.S. population was 248,718,302. Compare this to your prediction. What does this tell you about the growth rate of the population for the period 1890–1990 relative to the growth rate for the period 1790–1890?

The actual population in 1990 was about one-fifth of the population that the model predicted. For the period 1890–1990, the population must have grown at a rate less than 33% per decade (or 3% per year).

4d. Explain the difference between the predicted population and the actual population for 1990.

The prediction is based on an exponential model that grows very quickly. The residuals indicate that the actual population would not keep up with the model, and $x = 20$ is far beyond the data used to develop the model.

EXTEND

1. Use the data in the population table (still stored in your calculator as L_1 and L_2) to determine the quadratic regression equation. Round the values of a, b, and c to three decimal places.

$y = 0.638x^2 - 0.684x + 5.046$

2. List the residuals for the quadratic regression in order. Round each residual to the nearest hundredth.

$-1.15, 0.30, 0.97, 0.86, 0.38, -0.48, -0.72, -0.13, -0.62, -0.39, 0.97$

3. Is the quadratic regression equation a better fit for the data than the exponential model? Explain.

Yes, the quadratic model has fewer large residuals than the exponential model.

4. Use the quadratic model to predict the population in 1990. Compare this prediction to the one you obtained from the exponential model.

246.57 million; this is much closer to the actual population than the prediction that was obtained from the exponential model.

5. On your calculator, graph the data and both regression equations in the same window. Discuss how the graphs compare. (*Hint:* To make the graphs, perform the regressions again with the arguments shown at right. This stores the regression equations as Y_1 and Y_2.)

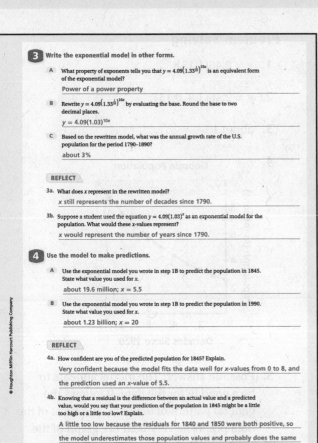

ExpReg L₁,L₂,Y₁

QuadReg L₁,L₂,Y₂

Both graphs start out about the same and model the data well, but then the graph of the exponential model rises more steeply than the graph of the quadratic model.

© Houghton Mifflin Harcourt Publishing Company

Assign these pages to help your students practice and apply important lesson concepts. For additional exercises, see the Student Edition.

Answers

Additional Practice

1. $y = 4.37(1.05)^x$

2. $y = 7.80(0.95)^x$

3. $y = 1.2(1 - 0.15)^t$

4. $y = 3.85(1 + 0.07)^t$

5. $y = 3.35(1.02)^{10x}$

6. The growth rate per decade, 18%, is about 9 times the growth rate per year, 2%.

7. Possible answer: The model appears to be a good fit for the data. It follows the general pattern of the data, and most of the data points lie very near the graph of the exponential equation.

8. Possible answer: No. The fit of the model becomes more questionable for values of x greater than 6. It isn't reasonable to assume that the model would produce a reasonable estimate for $x = 15$.

Problem Solving

1. $y = 2.46(1.15)^x$

2. $y = 2.46(1 + 0.15)^x$

3. about 1%

4.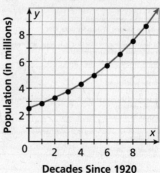
Georgia Population

5. Possible answer: The model appears to be a good fit for the data. It follows the general pattern of the data, and most of the data points lie very near the graph of the exponential equation.

6. A

7. J

Name_____ Class_____ Date_____   **6-1**

Additional Practice

Use a graphing calculator to determine the exponential regression equation for the data. Round the values of *a* and *b* to two decimal places.

1.

x	0	5	10	15	20
f(x)	4.2	5.7	7.3	9	11

2.

x	−1	0	1	2	3
f(x)	8.2	7.8	7.4	7.1	6.8

_____   _____

Write the equation in the form of an exponential growth function, $y = a(1 + r)^t$, or an exponential decay function, $y = a(1 - r)^t$.

3. $y = 1.2(0.85)^t$ _____   4. $y = 3.85(1.07)^t$ _____

The population of the city of Lincoln over the period from 1970 to 2010 can be modeled by the equation $y = 3.35(1.18)^x$ where *x* is the number of decades since 1970.

5. Write an equivalent model that represents the *annual* change in population (to two decimal places) over that same period. _____

6. Compare the growth rate per decade with the growth rate per year.

A scatterplot of a data set and the graph of an exponential model for the data are shown.

7. Tell whether the model does or does not appear to be a good fit for the data. Explain your reasoning.

_____

8. Can you use your model to predict the value of *y* for *x* = 15? Explain why you would or would not want to do so.

_____

_____

Chapter 6   333   Lesson 1

Problem Solving

The table shows the population (in millions) of the state of Georgia according to census results for 1920–2010.

Decades since 1920	Population (in millions)	Decades since 1920	Population (in millions)
0	2.90	5	4.59
1	2.91	6	5.46
2	3.12	7	6.48
3	3.44	8	8.19
4	3.94	9	9.69

1. Use a graphing calculator to find the exponential regression equation for the data. Round the values of *a* and *b* to two decimal places. _____

2. Rewrite your equation from Exercise 1 so that it demonstrates the growth rate per decade. _____

3. What is the growth rate per *year* (to two decimal places)? _____

The coordinate grid shows a scatterplot of the data.

4. Use the grid to graph your equation from Exercise 1.

5. Explain why the model is or is not a good fit for the data.

_____

_____

_____

Use the table above and your answers to Exercises 1–5. Choose the letter for the best answer.

6. Use your graph to predict the population of Georgia in 1995.

   A 7 million

   B 9 million

   C 70 million

   D 90 million

7. Use the table and your equation to approximate the residual for 1960.

   F 0.36

   G 0.23

   H −0.23

   J −0.36

Chapter 6   334   Lesson 1

Chapter 6   **334**   Lesson 1

Comparing Functions
Going Deeper

Essential question: How can you compare two different functions each presented in a different way?

COMMON CORE **Standards for Mathematical Content**

CC.9-12.F.IF.9 Compare properties of two functions each represented in a different way (algebraically, graphically, numerically in tables, or by verbal descriptions).

CC.9-12.F.LE.3 Observe using graphs and tables that a quantity increasing exponentially eventually exceeds a quantity increasing linearly, quadratically, or (more generally) as a polynomial function.

Prerequisites
Multiple representations of functions

Math Background
Students have learned characteristics of linear, quadratic, exponential, logarithmic, polynomial, radical, and rational functions in previous lessons. In this lesson, students will use what they have learned about these functions, their equations, and their graphs to compare different types of functions represented in different ways.

INTRODUCE

As a review, ask students (or groups of students) to look through their textbooks to find examples of different types of functions represented in different ways. Pair the functions and discuss how the functions in each pair might be compared.

TEACH

1 EXAMPLE

Questioning Strategies
- How can you identify a function given in a table? Graph the function and use the graph. Or, if the changes in the independent variable are constant, consider the first or second differences or ratios of consecutive function values.

- How do you find any minima and maxima of a function? Look at the graph of the function. Maxima (or minima) are y-coordinates of points that are higher (or lower) than all nearby points.

EXTRA EXAMPLE
The function f has equation $f(x) = (x - 1)^2(x - 3)^2$. The function g is shown in the table.

x	−2	−1	0	1	2
$g(x)$	3	0	−1	0	3

Classify the functions. Compare any maxima and minima and where the graphs are increasing or decreasing.

f is a fourth-degree polynomial function and g is a quadratic function. f has local minima at (1, 0) and (3, 0) and a local maximum at (2, 1). g has a minimum at (0, −1) and no maxima. f decreases for x-values from −∞ to 1 and from 2 to 3, and increases for x-values from 1 to 2 and from 3 to ∞. g decreases for x-values from −∞ to 0 and increases for x-values from 0 to ∞.

2 EXPLORE

Questioning Strategies
- Suppose that the equation of g doesn't change, but the growth factor of f decreases to 1.5. Will $f(x)$ always be less than $g(x)$? No; eventually $f(x)$ will be greater than $g(x)$. For example, when $x = 13$, $f(x) \approx 194.6$ and $g(x) = 171$.

CLOSE

Essential Question
How can you compare two different functions each presented in a different way?
Determine key characteristics of the functions such as minima, maxima, and end behavior. Then compare these characteristics.

PRACTICE

Where skills are taught	Where skills are practiced
1 EXAMPLE	EX. 1
2 EXPLORE	EX. 1

Name _____ Class _____ Date _____

6-2

Comparing Functions
Going Deeper

Essential question: *How can you compare two different functions each presented in a different way?*

Video Tutor

CC.9-12.F.IF.9

1 EXAMPLE Identifying and Comparing Functions

Classify each of the functions *f* and *h* shown below. Then compare any maxima and minima, and the intervals where the graphs are increasing or decreasing.

x	h(x)
−5	4
−2	2
1	0
4	−2

A Graph *h* on the same set of axes as *f*. Connect the points with a smooth line or curve.

The graph shows that *f* is a ___nonlinear___ ___polynomial___ function and that *h* is a

___linear___ function.

B *f* has a local maximum at ___(−1, 5)___ and a local minimum at

___(1, −5)___. The function increases for *x*-values from negative infinity to ___−1___,

___decreases___ for *x*-values from −1 to ___1___, then ___increases___ for *x*-values

from ___1___ to ___positive infinity___.

h has ___no___ minima or maxima. The function ___decreases___ for *x*-values

from ___negative infinity___ to ___positive infinity___.

REFLECT

1a. Could you have used tables to compare *f* and *h*? Is there an advantage to using graphs instead?

Yes; Sample answer: Using graphs makes it easier to compare end behavior.

1b. What type of function is $g(x) = (x − 1)^2$? Compare any maxima and minima of *g* to those for the function *f* in Explore 1.

Quadratic; *g* has a minimum of 0, which is greater than the local minimum of −5

for *f*. *g* doesn't have a maximum value, local or otherwise, unlike *f*.

© Houghton Mifflin Harcourt Publishing Company

Chapter 6   335   Lesson 2

CC.9-12.F.LE.3

2 EXPLORE Identifying Functions and Comparing End Behavior

A Classify functions *f* and *g*.

x	−1	0	1	2	3	4
f(x)	0.5	1	2	4	8	16

$g(x) = x^2 + 2$

The table for *f* shows that changes in *x* are constant, and the ratios of the values of *f*(*x*)
are constant, so *f* is ___exponential___.

g is ___quadratic___ because the function rule is written in the form

$g(x) = ax^2 + c$

B Graph both functions and investigate their end behavior.

End behavior of *f*:

As *x* approaches positive infinity $(x \to +\infty)$, *f*(*x*) approaches ___+∞___

As *x* approaches negative infinity $(x \to -\infty)$, *f*(*x*) approaches ___0___

End behavior of *g*:

As *x* approaches positive infinity $(x \to +\infty)$, *g*(*x*) approaches ___+∞___

As *x* approaches negative infinity $(x \to -\infty)$, *g*(*x*) approaches ___+∞___

REFLECT

2a. In Explore 2, is *f*(*x*) always less than *g*(*x*)? Explain.

No; Sample answer: Making extended tables for *f* and *g* shows that $f(x) \geq$

g(*x*) for *x* ≥ 5. Because the values of *f*(*x*) continue to double while the values

of *g*(*x*) increase more slowly, *f*(*x*) will be greater than *g*(*x*) from that point on.

PRACTICE

1. Classify each of the functions shown below. Then compare the end behavior of the functions.

$j(x) = \frac{1}{x} + 3$ The function *k* has constant first differences of
                               −2 and a *y*-intercept at (0, 3).

j is rational and *k* is linear; For *j*, as *x* approaches positive infinity, *j*(*x*) approaches

3, and as *x* approaches negative infinity, *j*(*x*) approaches 3. For *k*, as *x* approaches

positive infinity, *k*(*x*) approaches negative infinity, and as *x* approaches negative

infinity, *k*(*x*) approaches positive infinity.

© Houghton Mifflin Harcourt Publishing Company

Chapter 6   336   Lesson 2

Assign these pages to help your students practice
and apply important lesson concepts. For
additional exercises, see the Student Edition.

Answers

Additional Practice

1. As $x \rightarrow -\infty$, $f(x) \rightarrow \infty$ and $g(x) \rightarrow \infty$
   and as $x \rightarrow \infty$, $f(x) \rightarrow \infty$ and $g(x) \rightarrow -\infty$

2. As $x \rightarrow -\infty$, $f(x) \rightarrow -\infty$ and $g(x) \rightarrow -\infty$
   and as $x \rightarrow \infty$, $f(x) \rightarrow \infty$ and $g(x) \rightarrow -\infty$

3. As $x \rightarrow -\infty$, $f(x) \rightarrow -\infty$ and $g(x) \rightarrow 0$
   and as $x \rightarrow \infty$, $f(x) \rightarrow -\infty$ and $g(x) \rightarrow \infty$

4. As $x \rightarrow -\infty$, $f(x) \rightarrow 0$ and $g(x) \rightarrow -\infty$
   and as $x \rightarrow \infty$, $f(x) \rightarrow 0$ and $g(x) \rightarrow \infty$

5. $f(x) = -2x^2 + 3$

6. $f(x) = x^3 - 1$ 7. 2.25

Problem Solving

1. D

2. H

3. 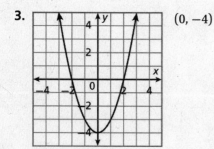   (0, −4)

4. 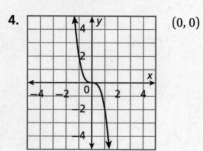   (0, 0)

Additional Practice

Compare the end behavior for each pair of functions.

1. $f(x) = x^4 - x^2 + 4x$ and $g(x) = -5x + 2$

_____

_____

2. $f(x) = x^3$ and $g(x) = -x^2$

_____

_____

3. $f(x) = -x^4 - 3x^3$ and $g(x) = \sqrt{x}$

_____

_____

4. $f(x) = \frac{1}{x}$ and $g(x) = x \ln 2$

_____

_____

Determine which function matches the graphical representation shown.

5.

_____

6.

_____

7. Find the average rate of change for the data in the following chart, over the given range.

x	2	4	6	8	10	12	14
y	1.5	6	10.5	15	19.5	24	28.5

_____

© Houghton Mifflin Harcourt Publishing Company

Problem Solving

Sketch the graph of the function.

1. The quadratic function passes through points (–2, 0) and (2, 0). Find the point that represents the vertex.

Solution:
Step 1: Plot the zeros.
Step 2: Find the vertex.
$(x + 2)(x - 2) = x^2 - 4$
vertex: (0, -4)
Step 3: Sketch the graph.

2. The cubic function passes through points (–2, 16), (–1, 2), (1, –2), and (2, –16). Find the point that represents the zero.

Determine which function matches the graph shown.

3.

A $y = \ln x$

B $y = \log x$

C $y = \dfrac{1}{x+2}$

4.

F $y = x^2 + 1$

G $y = x^2 - 2x + 1$

H $y = x^4 - 2x^2 + 1$

© Houghton Mifflin Harcourt Publishing Company

Piecewise Functions
Going Deeper

Essential question: *How are piecewise functions and step functions different from other functions?*

COMMON Standards for
CORE   Mathematical Content

CC.9-12.A.CED.2 Create equations in two ... variables to represent relationships between quantities; graph equations on coordinate axes with labels and scales.*

CC.9-12.F.IF.2 Use function notation, evaluate functions for inputs in their domains, and interpret statements that use function notation in terms of a context.

CC.9-12.F.IF.4 For a function that models a relationship between two quantities, interpret key features of graphs and tables in terms of the quantities, and sketch graphs showing key features given a verbal description of the relationship.*

CC.9-12.F.IF.5 Relate the domain of a function to its graph and, where applicable, to the quantitative relationship it describes.*

CC.9-12.F.IF.7 Graph functions expressed symbolically and show key features of the graph ...*

CC.9-12.F.IF.7b Graph ... piecewise-defined functions, including step functions ...*

CC.9-12.F.BF.1 Write a function that describes a relationship between two quantities.*

CC.9-12.F.BF.1a Determine an explicit expression ... from a context.*

Also: CC.9-12.N.Q.1*

Vocabulary
greatest integer function

piecewise function

step function

Prerequisites
Functions

Linear functions

Math Background

A piecewise function is defined by at least two different rules that apply to different parts of the domain. To evaluate a piecewise function, substitute the value of x into the rule for the part of the domain that includes that value of x. If the graph of a piecewise function resembles a set of stairs, the function is defined by a constant value over each part of its domain. This type of piecewise function is referred to as a "step" function. An example of this is the greatest integer function, $f(x) = [\![x]\!]$. The greatest integer function can also be written as shown below.

$$f(x) = \begin{cases} \vdots & \\ -2 & \text{if } -2 \le x < -1 \\ -1 & \text{if } -1 \le x < 0 \\ 0 & \text{if } 0 \le x < 1 \\ 1 & \text{if } 1 \le x < 2 \\ 2 & \text{if } 2 \le x < 3 \\ \vdots & \end{cases}$$

INTRODUCE

The table below shows U.S. postal rates in 2011 for first class letters. Ask students the following questions: What is the cost of mailing a letter that weighs 0.8 ounce? 1.5 ounces? 2 ounces? 2.9 ounces? $0.44; $0.61; $0.61; $0.78

Weight Not Over	Postage
1 oz	$0.44
2 oz	$0.61
3 oz	$0.78

Piecewise Functions
Going Deeper

6-3

Video Tutor

Essential question: *How are piecewise functions and step functions different from other functions?*

A **piecewise function** is a function whose definition changes over different parts of its domain. The **greatest integer function** is a piecewise function whose rule is denoted by [x], which represents the greatest integer less than or equal to x. To evaluate a piecewise function for a given value of x, substitute the value of x into the rule for the part of the domain that includes x.

CC.9-12.F.IF.2

1 EXAMPLE Evaluating Piecewise Functions

A Find $f(-3)$, $f(-0.2)$, $f(0)$, and $f(2)$ for $f(x) = \begin{cases} -x & \text{if } x < 0 \\ x+1 & \text{if } x \geq 0 \end{cases}$

$-3 < 0$, so use the rule $f(x) = -x$: $f(-3) = -(-3) = \underline{3}$

$-0.2 < 0$, so use the rule $f(x) = -x$: $f(-0.2) = -(-0.2) = \underline{0.2}$

$0 \geq 0$, so use the rule $f(x) = x + 1$: $f(0) = 0 + 1 = \underline{1}$

$2 \geq 0$, so use the rule $f(x) = x + 1$: $f(2) = \underline{2} + 1 = \underline{3}$

B Find $f(-3)$, $f(-2.9)$, $f(0.7)$, and $f(1.06)$ for $f(x) = [x]$.

The greatest integer function $f(x) = [x]$ can also be written as shown below. Complete the rules for the function before evaluating it.

$$f(x) = \begin{cases} \vdots \\ -3 & \text{if } -3 \leq x < -2 \\ -2 & \text{if } -2 \leq x < -1 \\ -1 & \text{if } -1 \leq x < 0 \\ 0 & \text{if } 0 \leq x < 1 \\ 1 & \text{if } 1 \leq x < 2 \\ 2 & \text{if } 2 \leq x < 3 \\ \vdots \end{cases}$$

For any number x that is less than −2 and greater than or equal to −3, the greatest of the integers less than or equal to x is −3.

-3 is in the interval $-3 \leq x < -2$, so $f(-3) = -3$.

-2.9 is in the interval $-3 \leq x < -2$, so $f(-2.9) = \underline{-3}$.

0.7 is in the interval $\underline{0 \leq x < 1}$, so $f(0.7) = \underline{0}$.

1.06 is in the interval $\underline{1 \leq x < 2}$, so $f(1.06) = \underline{1}$.

© Houghton Mifflin Harcourt Publishing Company

REFLECT

1a. Why should the parts of the domain of a piecewise function $f(x)$ have no common x-values?

You want only one rule to apply to a given x-value so that you get only one

f(x)-value, since a function must give a unique output for each input.

1b. For positive numbers, how is applying the greatest integer function different from the method of rounding to the nearest whole number?

When you round a positive number to the nearest whole number, you round down

if the tenths digit is 4 or less and you round up if the tenths digit is 5 or greater. For

the greatest integer function, you always round down.

CC.9-12.F.IF.7b

2 EXAMPLE Graphing Piecewise Functions

Graph each function.

A $f(x) = \begin{cases} -x & \text{if } x < 0 \\ x+1 & \text{if } x \geq 0 \end{cases}$

Complete the table. Use the values to help you complete the graph. Extend the pattern to cover the entire domain on the grid.

x	−3	−2	−1	−0.9	−0.1
f(x)	3	2	1	0.9	0.1

x	0	0.1	0.9	1	2
f(x)	1	1.1	1.9	2	3

The transition from one rule, −x, to the other, x + 1, occurs at x = 0. Show an open dot at (0, 0) because the point is not part of the graph. Show a closed dot at (0, 1) because the point is part of the graph.

B $f(x) = [x]$

Complete the table. Use the values to help you complete the graph. Extend the pattern to cover the entire domain on the grid.

x	−4	−3.9	−3.1	−3	−2.9
f(x)	−4	−4	−4	−3	−3

x	−2.1	−2	−1.5	−1	0
f(x)	−3	−2	−2	−1	0

x	1	1.5	2	3	4
f(x)	1	1	2	3	4

© Houghton Mifflin Harcourt Publishing Company

Notes

1 EXAMPLE

Questioning Strategies

- What are the domain and range of the function in part A? **domain: all real numbers; range: all real numbers**

- What are the domain and range of the function in part B? **domain: all real numbers; range: all integers**

Teaching Strategy

Help students remember that you always round down for the greatest integer function by telling them that the function is sometimes called the "floor" function.

EXTRA EXAMPLE

A. Find $f(-3), f(-0.1), f(0),$ and $f(1)$

for the following: $f(x) = \begin{cases} x & \text{if } x < 0 \\ -x - 1 & \text{if } x \ge 0 \end{cases}$.

$-3, -0.1, -1, -2$

B. Find $f(-2), f(-1.3), f(0.9),$ and $f(2.12)$
for $f(x) = [\![x]\!]$. **$-2, -2, 0, 2$**

2 EXAMPLE

Questioning Strategies

- How is the graph of $g(x) = -x$ with domain negative real numbers related to the graph of $f(x)$ in part A? **The graph of $g(x)$ is the left side of the graph of $f(x)$.**

- Why are the "steps" in the graph of $f(x)$ in part B closed on the left and open on the right? **$f(x) = x$ when x is an integer.**

Avoid Common Errors

Students make errors when they use the normal rules of rounding to find values for $f(x) = [\![x]\!]$. Caution them to always round down.

EXTRA EXAMPLE

Graph each function.

A. $f(x) = \begin{cases} x & \text{if } x < 0 \\ -x - 1 & \text{if } x \ge 0 \end{cases}$

The graph consists of two rays; one ray has an open circle at (0, 0) continuing downward and left, passing through the points (−1, −1) and (−3, −3); the other ray has a closed circle at (0, −1) and continues downward and right, passing through (1, −2), and (3, −4).

B. $f(x) = [\![x]\!] - 1$

The graph has solid circles at ..., (−2, −3), (−1, −2), (0, −1), (1, 0), (2, 1), ... each of which is connected by a solid line to an open circle one unit to the right.

3 EXAMPLE

Questioning Strategies

- Why is the graph in part C continuous? **A gap in either time or distance traveled would not make sense in the context of the problem.**

- Why does the graph in part C include a section that is horizontal? **The student stopped traveling for one minute, so the distance traveled during that time period did not change.**

⋰ **MATHEMATICAL   Highlighting**
PRACTICE   the Standards
⋱

Example 3 addresses Mathematical Practice Standard 4 (Model with mathematics). Draw students' attention to the use of multiple representations for the piecewise function. Specifically, ask students why using a table or graph may be helpful in visualizing the different rules for a specific piecewise function representing a real-world situation.

Teaching Strategy

In the table for part B, stress the importance of recognizing the t-values that correspond to the endpoints of each part of the domain.

continued

2a. Why does the first graph use rays and not lines?

Each rule has a separate domain. If the graph contained lines, the domains would

overlap. Since each rule is an inequality with one endpoint, the graph contains rays.

2b. The greatest integer function is an example of a **step function**, a piecewise function that is constant for each rule. Use the graph of the greatest integer function to explain why such a function is called a step function.

The sections of the graph are horizontal segments and look like a set of stairs.

2c. Does the greatest integer function have a maximum or minimum value? Explain.

No; there is no point on the graph that is higher or lower than all other points.

CC.9–12.F.BF.1

3 EXAMPLE Writing and Graphing a Piecewise Function

On his way to class from his dorm room, a college student walks at a speed of 0.05 mile per minute for 3 minutes, stops to talk to a friend for 1 minute, and then to avoid being late for class, runs at a speed of 0.10 mile per minute for 2 minutes. Write a piecewise function for the student's distance from his dorm room during this time. Then graph the function.

A Express the student's distance traveled d (in miles) as a function of time t (in minutes). Write an equation for the function $d(t)$.

$$d(t) = \begin{cases} 0.05\ t & \text{if } 0 \le t \le 3 \\ 0.15 & \text{if } 3 < t \le 4 \\ 0.15 + 0.10\,(t-4) & \text{if } 4 < t \le 6 \end{cases}$$

← He travels at 0.05 mile per minute for 3 minutes.
← Distance traveled is constant for 1 minute.
← Add the distance traveled at 0.10 mile per minute to the distance already traveled.

B Complete the table.

t	0	1	2	3
d(t)	0	0.05	0.10	0.15

t	4	5	6
d(t)	0.15	0.25	0.35

C Complete the graph.

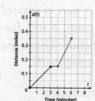

3a. Why is the second rule for the function $d(t) = 0.15$ instead of $d(t) = 0$?

$d(t)$ represents distance traveled, and the student has traveled 0.15 mile when $t = 3$.

3b. Why is the third rule for the function $d(t) = 0.15 + 0.10(t-4)$?

The distance already traveled during the first 4 minutes is 0.15 mile. During the next

2 minutes, he is traveling at 0.10 mile per minute for only the time beyond 4 minutes.

CC.9–12.F.IF.5

4 EXAMPLE Writing a Function When Given a Graph

Write the equation for each function whose graph is shown.

A

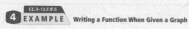

B

Find the equation for each ray:

* Find the slope m of the line that contains the ray on the left. Use $(-4, -2)$ and $(-1, 1)$.

$$m = \frac{1 - (-2)}{-1 - (-4)} = \frac{3}{3} = 1$$

Substitute this value of m along with the coordinates of $(-1, 1)$ into $y = mx + b$ and solve for b.

$$y = mx + b$$
$$1 = 1(-1) + b$$
$$2 = b$$

So, $y = 1x + 2$.

* The equation of the line that contains the horizontal ray is $y = 3$.

The equation for the function is:

$$f(x) = \begin{cases} x + 2 & \text{if } x \le -1 \\ 3 & \text{if } x > -1 \end{cases}$$

Write a rule for each horizontal line segment.

$$f(x) = \begin{cases} -4 & \text{if } -2 \le x < -1 \\ -2 & \text{if } -1 \le x < 0 \\ 0 & \text{if } 0 \le x < 1 \\ 2 & \text{if } 1 \le x < 2 \\ 4 & \text{if } 2 \le x < 3 \end{cases}$$

Although the graph shows the function's domain to be $-2 \le x < 3$, assume that the domain consists of all real numbers and that the graph continues its stair-step pattern for $x < -2$ and $x \ge 3$.

Notice that each function value is ___2___ times the corresponding value of the greatest integer function.

The equation for the function is:

$$f(x) = 2\ [x]$$

EXTRA EXAMPLE

A parent drives from home to the grocery store at 0.9 mile per minute for 4 minutes, stops to buy snacks for the team for 2 minutes, and then drives to the soccer field at a speed of 0.7 mile per minute for 3 minutes. Write a piecewise function for the parent's distance from home to the soccer field during this time. Then graph the function.

$$d(t) = \begin{cases} 0.9t & \text{if } 0 \leq t \leq 4 \\ 3.6 & \text{if } 4 < t \leq 6 \\ 3.6 + 0.7(t-6) & \text{if } 6 < t \leq 9 \end{cases}$$

The graph is a line segment from (0, 0) to (4, 3.6), a line segment from (4, 3.6) to (6, 3.6) and a line segment from (6, 3.6) to (9, 5.7).

4 EXAMPLE

Questioning Strategies

- How is the graph in part A related to the graph of $g(x) = 3$? The graph of $g(x) = 3$ restricted to the domain values $x > -1$ is the upper part of the graph of $f(x)$.

- In part B, how are $f(x)$ and the greatest integer function related? The range values of $f(x)$ are twice those of the corresponding range values of the greatest integer function.

EXTRA EXAMPLE

Write the equation for each function whose graph is shown.

A.

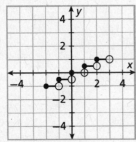

$f(x) = \frac{1}{2} [\![x]\!]$ for $-2 \leq x < 3$

B.

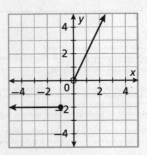

$$f(x) = \begin{cases} -2 & \text{if } x \leq -1 \\ 2x & \text{if } x > 0 \end{cases}$$

CLOSE

Essential Question

How are piecewise functions and step functions different from other functions?
A piecewise function's rule has two or more parts; each part is applied to a different subset of the domain. A step function is a special piecewise function whose graph consists of horizontal line segments.

Summarize

Have students write a journal entry in which they describe how to graph a step function and explain why the function is called a step function.

PRACTICE

Where skills are taught	Where skills are practiced
2 EXAMPLE	EXS. 1–3
3 EXAMPLE	EXS. 7–8
4 EXAMPLE	EXS. 4–6

REFLECT

4a. When writing a piecewise function from a graph, how do you determine the domain of each rule?

For each piece of the function, determine the interval on the x-axis that corresponds to that piece. An open circle on the graph indicates the x-value is not in the domain for that piece.

4b. How can you use y-intercepts to check that your answer in part A is reasonable?

Extend the first ray to see that it passes through (0, 2), which agrees with the equation $y = x + 2$. The second ray passes through (0, 3), which agrees with the equation $y = 0x + 3$.

PRACTICE

Graph each function.

1. $f(x) = \begin{cases} -x + 1 & \text{if } x < 0 \\ x & \text{if } x \geq 0 \end{cases}$

2. $f(x) = \begin{cases} -1 & \text{if } x < 1 \\ 2x - 2 & \text{if } x \geq 1 \end{cases}$

3. $f(x) = [\![x]\!] + 1$

Write the equation for each function whose graph is shown.

4.

5.

6.

$f(x) = \begin{cases} x + 1 & \text{if } x < 0 \\ 2 & \text{if } x \geq 0 \end{cases}$

$f(x) = \begin{cases} -x - 1 & \text{if } x < 0 \\ 1 & \text{if } 0 \leq x < 2 \\ \frac{1}{2}x + 1 & \text{if } x \geq 2 \end{cases}$

$f(x) = [\![x]\!] - 2$

---

7. A garage charges the following rates for parking (with an 8 hour limit):

    $4 per hour for the first 2 hours

    $2 per hour for the next 4 hours

    No additional charge for the next 2 hours

a. Write a piecewise function that gives the parking cost C (in dollars) in terms of the time t (in hours) that a car is parked in the garage.

$C(t) = \begin{cases} 4t & \text{if } 0 \leq t \leq 2 \\ 8 + 2(t - 2) & \text{if } 2 < t \leq 6 \\ 16 & \text{if } 6 < t \leq 8 \end{cases}$

b. Graph the function. Include labels to show what the axes represent and to show the scales on the axes.

8. The cost to send a package between two cities is $8.00 for any weight less than 1 pound. The cost increases by $4.00 when the weight reaches 1 pound and again each time the weight reaches a whole number of pounds after that.

a. For a package having weight w (in pounds), write a function in terms of $[\![w]\!]$ to represent the shipping cost C (in dollars).

$C(w) = 8 + 4 [\![w]\!]$

b. Complete the table.

Weight (pounds) w	Cost (dollars) C(w)
0.5	8
1	12
1.5	12
2	16
2.5	16

c. Graph the function. Show the costs for all weights less than 5 pounds.

Assign these pages to help your students practice and apply important lesson concepts. For additional exercises, see the Student Edition.

Answers

Additional Practice

1. $-16, 0$ 2. $10, -3$

3. $-12, 25$ 4. $15, 4\frac{1}{2}$

5.

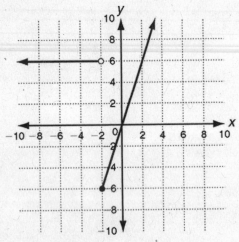

6.

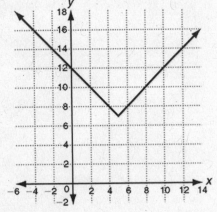

7. a. $f(x) = \begin{cases} 20x & \text{if } x \le 7 \\ 17x + 21 & \text{if } x > 7 \end{cases}$

   b. $191   c. $57

Problem Solving

1.

Hours per Week (t)	Roscoe's Earnings, $E(t)$				
	Hours $\le$ 40($9.50 per h)		Hours > 40($13.00 per h)		Total Earnings
30	30	$285	0	$0	$285
40	40	$380	0	$0	$380
50	40	$380	10	$130	$510
60	40	$380	20	$260	$640

2. No

3. Possible answer: The graph shows two straight-line segments that intersect where $t = 40$. The slope of a segment is the rate of pay for that interval: 9.5 or 13.

4. $E(t) = \begin{cases} 9.5t & \text{if } 0 \le t \le 40 \\ 13(t - 40) + 380 & \text{if } 40 < t \le 60 \end{cases}$

5. A   6. G

Additional Practice

Evaluate each piecewise function for $x = -8$ and $x = 5$.

1. $f(x) = \begin{cases} 2x & \text{if } x < 0 \\ 0 & \text{if } x \geq 0 \end{cases}$

2. $g(x) = \begin{cases} 2-x & \text{if } x \leq 5 \\ -x^2 & \text{if } 5 < x < 8 \\ 6 & \text{if } 8 \leq x \end{cases}$

_____

_____

3. $h(x) = \begin{cases} 2x+4 & \text{if } x \leq -8 \\ -1 & \text{if } -8 < x < 5 \\ x^2 & \text{if } 5 \leq x \end{cases}$

4. $k(x) = \begin{cases} 15 & \text{if } x \leq -5 \\ x & \text{if } -5 < x < 1 \\ 7 - \dfrac{x}{2} & \text{if } 1 < x \end{cases}$

_____

_____

Graph each function.

5. $f(x) = \begin{cases} 6 & \text{if } x < -2 \\ 3x & \text{if } -2 \leq x \end{cases}$

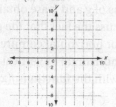

6. $g(x) = \begin{cases} 12 - x & \text{if } x \leq 5 \\ x + 2 & \text{if } 5 < x \end{cases}$

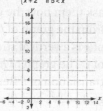

Solve.

7. An airport parking garage costs $20 per day for the first week. After that, the cost decreases to $17 per day.

   a. Write a piecewise function for the cost of parking a car for x days.

   _____

   b. What is the cost to park for 10 days?

   _____

   c. Ms. Anderson went on two trips. On the first, she parked at the garage for 5 days; on the second, she parked at the garage for 8 days. What was the difference in the cost of parking between the two trips?

   _____

Problem Solving

Roscoe earns $9.50 per hour at the woodcrafts store for up to 40 hours per week. For each hour over 40 hours he earns $13.00 per hour. Company policy limits his hours to no more than 60 per week. Roscoe wants to know how much he can earn in a week.

1. Complete the table to show his earnings for 30, 40, 50, and 60 hours per week.

Hours per Week (t)	Roscoe's Earnings, E(t)			
	Hours ≤ 40 ($9.50 per h)		Hours > 40 ($13.00 per h)	Total Earnings
30	30	$285	0	$0	$285
40					
50					
60					

2. Graph earnings as a function of hours worked, using the data from the table. Roscoe thinks the points lie in a straight line. Is he correct?

   _____

3. Draw line segments to join the points, including the point that represents earnings for 0 hours worked. Describe the graph in terms of line segments and the slope of each segment. Explain the meaning of the slope in terms of rate of pay.

   _____
   _____

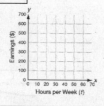

4. Use the slope and a point on each line segment to write a piecewise function for earnings E(t) as a function of hours worked (t).

   _____

Choose the letter for the best answer.

5. How much will Roscoe earn if he works 56.5 hours in one week?

   A $594.50
   B $610.00
   C $625.50
   D $734.50

6. Roscoe earned $471 last week. How many hours did he work?

   F 45
   G 47
   H 49
   J 51

Notes

Transforming Functions
Extension: Transformations of Exponential Functions

Essential question: *How do transformations of exponential functions compare with transformations of other function types?*

COMMON **Standards for**
CORE **Mathematical Content**

CC.9-12.F.BF.3 Identify the effect on the graph of replacing $f(x)$ by $f(x) + k$, $k f(x)$, $f(kx)$, and $f(x + k)$ for specific values of k (both positive and negative); find the value of k given the graphs....

Prerequisites

Transforming linear functions

Transforming quadratic functions

Transforming polynomial functions

Math Background

Students have seen transformations of linear, quadratic, and polynomial functions. Each of these families has a unique parent function. However, in the family of exponential functions, each of the functions $y = 2^x$, $y = 3^x$, $y = 4^x$, and so on, is itself the parent function of a family of exponential functions.

In Examples 1 and 2, students may wonder why they can ignore the value of h in finding equations of exponential growth or decay functions. The general equation $g(x) = ab^{x-h} + k$ (for either an exponential growth or decay function) has been simplified algebraically by multiplying a and b^{-h}.

INTRODUCE

Ask students to identify the parent function of the functions $f(x) = x$, $g(x) = 2x$, and $h(x) = x + 2$. Then ask them how the graphs of g and h are obtained from the graph of f. Discuss the fact that the graph of g is a vertical stretch or horizontal compression of f. The graph of h is a horizontal or vertical translation of f. Repeat with the functions $f(x) = x^2$, $g(x) = 2x^2$, and $h(x) = x^2 + 2$.

TEACH

1 EXAMPLE

Questioning Strategies

• How is the graph of $g(x) = ab^x + k$ affected by changes in k? **Changes in k will translate the graph up or down.**

• How does finding k help you to determine a? **Finding k tells you how to translate the graph before comparing the y-intercept to that of the parent function in order to find a.**

EXTRA EXAMPLE

Write an equation of the exponential growth function $g(x)$ whose graph is shown.

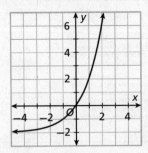

$g(x) = 2(2)^x - 2$

6-4

Transforming Functions
Extension: Transformations of Exponential Functions

Essential question: *How do transformations of exponential functions compare with transformations of other function types?*

Video Tutor

The following table summarizes how the values of the parameters a, h, and k affect the graph of an exponential growth function $f(x) = ab^{x-h} + k$.

Parameter	Effect
h	If $h > 0$, the graph of the parent function is translated $|h|$ units to the right. If $h < 0$, the graph of the parent function is translated $|h|$ units to the left.
k	If $k > 0$, the graph of the parent function is translated $|k|$ units up. If $k < 0$, the graph of the parent function is translated $|k|$ units down.
a	If $a > 1$, the graph of the parent function is stretched vertically by a factor of a. If $0 < a < 1$, the graph of the parent function is shrunk vertically by a factor of a.

Using the properties of exponents, you can rewrite the expression $ab^{x-h} + k$ as follows:

$$ab^{x-h} + k = ab^x \cdot b^{-h} + k = (ab^{-h})b^x + k$$

where ab^{-h} is a constant because a, b, and h are constants. This means that the parameter h in the function $f(x) = ab^{x-h} + k$ can be eliminated by combining it with the parameter a. Therefore, when you are asked to find the equation of an exponential growth function, you can assume that it has the form $f(x) = ab^x + k$.

CC.9-12.F.BF.3

1 EXAMPLE Writing an Exponential Growth Equation from a Graph

A Find the value of k. $y = 1$ is a horizontal asymptote of the graph of g, so the parent function is transformed vertically. $k = \underline{\ 1\ }$.

B If g is transformed so the x-axis is the asymptote of the graph, the y-intercept of the graph is 2. The y-intercept of the parent exponential growth function $f(x) = b^x$ is 1, so f is stretched vertically by a factor of 2, and $a = \underline{\ 2\ }$.

$g(x) = ab^x + k$

C The graph of g passes through $(1, 7)$. If g is transformed as in part B, then the graph passes through $(1, 6)$. A shrink produces the graph of the parent function passing through $(1, \underline{\ 3\ })$. The graph of the parent function passes through $(1, b)$, so $b = \underline{\ 3\ }$.

D The equation of g is $g(x) = \underline{\ 2(3^x) + 1\ }$.

Questioning Strategies

- How do you know immediately that k will be negative? **Because the asymptote is below the x-axis ($y = 0$).**

- Describe another way to find the value of b using the point $(-1, 5)$. **When you reverse the vertical translation, you get $(-1, 6)$. When you reverse the stretch by 2, you get $(-1, 3)$. The graph of every function in the form $y = b^x$ ($0 < b < 1$) includes the point $\left(-1, \frac{1}{b}\right)$, so $b = \frac{1}{3}$.**

EXTRA EXAMPLE

Write an equation of the exponential decay function $g(x)$ whose graph is shown.

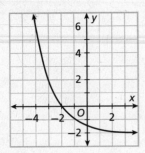

$g(x) = \frac{1}{2}\left(\frac{1}{2}\right)^x - 2$

Essential Question

How do transformations of exponential functions compare with transformations of other function types? **Like other families of functions, exponential functions can be transformed. The graph of $g(x) = ab^x + k$ is a vertical stretch and translation of the graph of $f(x) = b^x$.**

Summarize

Have students draw coordinate axes and a rough sketch of $y = 2^x$. Ask them to sketch $y = 0.5(2^x)$, $y = 2^x + 2$, and $y = 0.5(2^x) + 2$ on the same axes. Ask them to describe how they altered the sketch of $y = 2^x$ to produce the others. Then have them draw new coordinate axes and repeat the exercise, starting with $y = \left(\frac{1}{2}\right)^x$ instead of $y = 2^x$.

MATHEMATICAL PRACTICE	Highlighting the Standards

This lesson provides opportunities to address Mathematical Practices Standard 7 (Look for and make use of structure). Students should see that vertical stretches and vertical translations of graphs of exponential functions correspond to predictable changes in the equations of the functions.

Where skills are taught	Where skills are practiced
1 EXAMPLE	EXS. 1–4
2 EXAMPLE	EXS. 5–7

REFLECT

2a. What is the parent function of g?

The parent function is $f(x) = \left(\frac{1}{3}\right)^x$.

2b. How is the graph of g related to the graph of its parent function?

The graph of f is stretched vertically by a factor of 2 and translated down

1 unit to give the graph of g.

Consider two linear functions $f(x) = x$ and $g(x) = 3x$. By simply multiplying by 3, you can transform f into g. Can an exponential function be transformed into another through a combination of a vertical translation and stretching or shrinking?

3 CC.9-12.F.BF.3
EXAMPLE **The Uniqueness of Parent Functions**

A Let $f(x) = 3^x$ and $g(x) = ab^x + k$. Transform f by stretching/shrinking it vertically by a factor of a and translating vertically by k units. What is the equation of transformed f?

$f(x) = a(3)^x + k$

B Compare the equations of transformed f and g. If f and g are equal, what must be true about b?

$b = 3$

REFLECT

3a. What conclusion can you draw concerning the possibility of transforming $f(x) = 3^x$ into a different exponential function $g(x) = ab^x + k$, with $b \neq 3$? Explain.

It can't be done. In any proposed transformation, b must equal 3.

3b. Through translation and stretching or shrinking, can you transform $f(x) = 3^x$ into $g(x) = 6^x$? Explain.

No. Transforming f(x) through translation and stretching/shrinking will produce

$f(x) = p \cdot 3^x + q$ for some constants p and q. But they cannot change the base

$b = 3$.

3c. Do you agree or disagree with the following statement? "The functions $y = 2^x$, $y = 3^x$, $y = 4^x$, and so on, are each parent functions of an exponential family and not simply transformations of one another." Explain your reasoning.

Agree. Transformations cannot change the base of an exponential function.

PRACTICE

1. **Error Analysis** A student is told that the graph shown at right is a vertical translation of $f(x) = 1.5^x$ and determines that the equation of the function must be $f(x) = 1.5^x - 3$ because the y-intercept is -3. Explain and correct the error in the student's reasoning.

The y-intercept of the parent function is (0, 1), not

(0, 0), so the graph was translated 4 units down.

The equation is $f(x) = 1.5^x - 4$.

Write an equation of the exponential function g(x) whose graph is shown.

2.

$g(x) = 2^x + 2$

3.

$g(x) = 2(2)^x$

4.

$g(x) = 3^x - 4$

5.
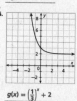

$g(x) = \left(\frac{1}{3}\right)^x + 2$

6.
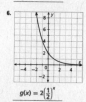

$g(x) = 2\left(\frac{1}{2}\right)^x$

7.
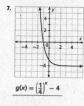

$g(x) = \left(\frac{1}{4}\right)^x - 4$

Consider the functions $f(x) = 2(5^x)$ and $g(x) = 2\left(\frac{1}{5}\right)^x$.

8. Can you describe a vertical translation, vertical shrink, vertical compression, or some combination of those transformations of f that will produce g? Explain.

No; f and g are both exponential parent functions. None of those, alone or in

combination, will produce another exponential function with a different base.

9. Can you describe a different type of transformation of f that will produce g? Explain.

Yes; a reflection of f across the y-axis. The equation of the transformed function is

$y = 2(5^{-x})$, which is equivalent to $y = 2\left(\frac{1}{5}\right)^x$.

Assign these pages to help your students practice and apply important lesson concepts. For additional exercises, see the Student Edition.

Answers

Additional Practice

1. $h(x) = 3^x + 3$

2. $h(x) = 3^{x+3}$

3. $h(x) = -2\left(\frac{1}{2}\right)^x$

4. $h(x) = \left(\frac{1}{3}\right)^x - 1$

5. $h(x) = 2^{2-x} + 1$

6. $h(x) = 4^{-x} + 1$

Problem Solving

1. vertical compression by a factor of $\frac{1}{2}$

2. shift of the graph by 10 units to the right

3. horizontal stretch by a factor of 2

4. C

5. J

6. B

Additional Practice

Write an equation of the exponential function $h(x)$ whose graph is shown.

1. _____

2. _____

3. _____

4. _____

5. _____

6. _____

Problem Solving

A dose of a synthetic compound breaks down in the bloodstream over time. The amount of the compound in the blood with an initial dose of A_0 mg, under some conditions, is given by $A = A_0 (0.97^t)$, where t is the time in minutes. The standard dose is 20 mg. Describe how each of the following changes would be reflected in the model.

1. The initial dose is changed from 20 mg to 10 mg.

_____

2. The breakdown of the compound does not begin for 10 minutes.

_____

3. The breakdown time period is decreased from one-minute intervals to 30-second intervals.

_____

The half-life of a radioactive material is the time it takes for half of the amount of material to decay. The function $N(t) = N_0 \left(\frac{1}{2} \right)^{t/t_{1/2}}$ can be used to calculate the remaining undecayed amount of material, where N_0 is the initial amount of material, $t_{1/2}$ is the half-life of the substance, and t is time.

4. Suppose sample A contains 10 lb of material and sample B contains 20 lb of the same material. Which sample will have half of its mass decay first?

   A sample A

   B sample B

   C They will both reach half of their respective initial mass simultaneously.

   D not enough information

5. Suppose the half-life of a substance were twice as long. What kind of transformation would the graph of the function undergo?

   F vertical stretch by 2

   G vertical shift by 2

   H horizontal compression by $\frac{1}{2}$

   J none of the above

6. Which of the following changes is a reflection of the graph of
$$N(t) = N_0 \left(\frac{1}{2} \right)^{t/t_{1/2}} ?$$

   A choosing a substance with a different half-life

   B graphing the amount of decayed material in the sample

   C starting with more of the substance

   D graphing the "third-life" of the substance

6-5 Operations with Functions
Going Deeper

Essential question: When you perform operations with functions, how does the graph of the resulting function compare with the original graphs?

COMMON CORE Standards for Mathematical Content

CC.9-12.F.BF.1b Combine standard function types using arithmetic operations.

Prerequisites

Polynomials

Multiplying polynomials

Dividing polynomials

Comparing functions

Math Background

Students know how to graph linear, quadratic, polynomial, exponential, logarithmic, rational, and radical functions. They know how to add, subtract, multiply, and divide functions algebraically. In this lesson, they will combine all of those skills to deepen their understanding of operations with functions by exploring graphic representations of the sum, difference, product, and quotient of two functions.

INTRODUCE

Review the linear function $f(x) = x$ and its graph. Ask students what will happen to the graph of f if a number, such as 3, is added to the function. Investigate adding and subtracting a few more numbers. Then discuss how adding or subtracting a constant to f affects the graph of the function.

TEACH

1 EXAMPLE

Questioning Strategies

• For part A, what will the graph of $f + g$ look like if $f(x) = 2$? **The graph of $f + g$ will be the graph of g translated 2 units up.**

• Suppose f and g are both constant functions. What will the graph of $f + g$ look like? **a horizontal line**

EXTRA EXAMPLE

Given $f(x) = x^2 - 8x + 15$ and $g(x) = -2$, what do the graphs of f and $f + g$ look like? Find $(f + g)(x)$ algebraically. **The graph of f is a parabola with vertex $(4, -1)$ and x-intercepts 3 and 5. The graph of $f + g$ is the graph of f translated 2 units up; $(f + g)(x) = x^2 - 8x + 13$.**

2 EXAMPLE

Questioning Strategies

• In part A, is the graph of $f - g$ a translation of the graph of f? Explain. **No; the graph of $f - g$ is narrower than the graph of f, so it cannot be a translation of the graph.**

• Suppose h is a constant function. What type of function would $f - h$ be? **a quadratic function**

Avoid Common Errors

When subtracting functions algebraically, it is important to distribute the negative sign to all of the terms of the second function. Remind students to draw parentheses around the second function when subtracting it from the first function. Otherwise, students may mistakenly subtract only the first term of the second function.

EXTRA EXAMPLE

Given $f(x) = x^2 + 3$ and $g(x) = x + 5$, what do the graphs of f, g, and $f - g$ look like? Find $(f - g)(x)$ algebraically. **The graph of f is a parabola with vertex $(0, 3)$ passing through $(-1, 4)$ and $(1, 4)$. The graph of g is a line with a slope of 1 and a y-intercept of 5. The graph of $f - g$ is a parabola with vertex $\left(\frac{1}{2}, -\frac{9}{4}\right)$ and x-intercepts -1 and 2; $(f - g)(x) = x^2 - x - 2$.**

6-5

Operations with Functions
Going Deeper

Essential question: *When you perform operations with functions, how does the graph of the resulting function compare with the original graphs?*

Video Tutor

The sum of two functions, $f + g$, can be found graphically using the graphs of f and g.

1 CC.9-12.F.BF.1b
EXAMPLE   Adding Functions Graphically and Algebraically

Given $f(x) = 4$ and $g(x) = \frac{2}{5}x - 2$, sketch the graph of $f + g$ using the graphs of f and g. Then find $f + g$ algebraically and use your answer to check your graph.

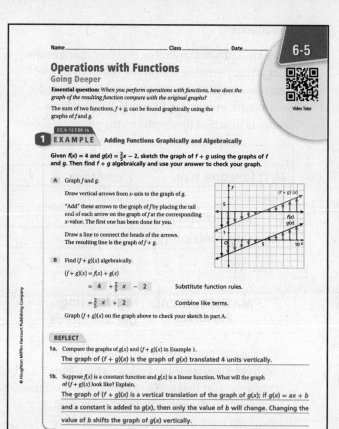

A   Graph f and g.

Draw vertical arrows from x-axis to the graph of g.

"Add" these arrows to the graph of f by placing the tail end of each arrow on the graph of f at the corresponding x-value. The first one has been done for you.

Draw a line to connect the heads of the arrows. The resulting line is the graph of $f + g$.

B   Find $(f + g)(x)$ algebraically.

$(f + g)(x) = f(x) + g(x)$

$\qquad = \;4\; + \frac{2}{5}x - 2$ Substitute function rules.

$\qquad = \frac{2}{5}x + 2$ Combine like terms.

Graph $(f + g)(x)$ on the graph above to check your sketch in part A.

REFLECT

1a.   Compare the graphs of $g(x)$ and $(f + g)(x)$ in Example 1.

The graph of $(f + g)(x)$ is the graph of $g(x)$ translated 4 units vertically.

1b.   Suppose $f(x)$ is a constant function and $g(x)$ is a linear function. What will the graph of $(f + g)(x)$ look like? Explain.

The graph of $(f + g)(x)$ is a vertical translation of the graph of $g(x)$; if $g(x) = ax + b$

and a constant is added to $g(x)$, then only the value of b will change. Changing the

value of b shifts the graph of $g(x)$ vertically.

© Houghton Mifflin Harcourt Publishing Company

The difference of two functions, $f - g$, can be found graphically using the graphs of f and g. When the graph of f lies above the graph of g, the difference $f - g$ is positive. When the graph of f lies below the graph of g, the difference $f - g$ is negative.

2 CC.9-12.F.BF.1b
EXAMPLE   Subtracting Functions Graphically and Algebraically

Given $f(x) = \frac{1}{2}x^2 - 4x + 11$ and $g(x) = -\frac{1}{4}x^2 + 2x + 2$, sketch the graph of $f - g$ using the graphs of f and g. Then find $f - g$ algebraically and use your answer to check your graph.

A   Graph f and g.

Draw vertical arrows from the graph of g to the graph of f. Two have been done for you.

Redraw the arrows with the tail end of each arrow on the x-axis at corresponding x-values.

Make a smooth curve to connect the arrowheads. The resulting curve is the graph of $f - g$.

B   Find $f - g$ algebraically.

$(f - g)(x) = f(x) - g(x)$

$\qquad = \frac{1}{2}x^2 - 4x + 11 - \left(-\frac{1}{4}x^2 + 2x + 2\right)$ Substitute function rules.

$\qquad = \frac{1}{2}x^2 - 4x + 11 + \frac{1}{4}x^2 - 2x - 2$ Distributive Property

$\qquad = \frac{3}{4}x^2 - 6x + 9$ Combine like terms.

Graph $f - g$ on the graph above to check your sketch in part A.

REFLECT

2a.   Compare the graphs of f and $f - g$ in Example 2.

Both graphs open up and have the same axis of symmetry. However, the graph of

$f - g$ is steeper and its vertex is 6 units lower.

2b.   Suppose f and g are quadratic functions, and the coefficients of the x^2-terms are not equal. What will the graph of $f - g$ look like? Explain.

The function $f - g$ will be a quadratic function, so the graph of $f - g$ will be a

parabola. If the coefficient of x^2 in $f - g$ is positive, then the parabola opens up. If

the coefficient of x^2 is negative, then the parabola opens down.

© Houghton Mifflin Harcourt Publishing Company

Notes

Questioning Strategies

- Suppose f and g are both linear functions. What type of function will fg be? **quadratic**

- In part B, why is 1 an excluded value of $\frac{f}{g}$? When $x = 1$, $g(x) = 0$, so $\frac{f}{g}$ is undefined.

EXTRA EXAMPLE

Given $f(x) = 2x^2 - 18$ and $g(x) = x + 3$, find the given function. Then compare the graph of the resulting function to the graphs of the original function.

A fg $(fg)(x) = 2x^3 + 6x^2 - 18x - 54$; The graph of $(fg)(x)$ shows a cubic function with a local maximum of $(-3, 0)$ and a local minimum of $(1, -64)$. The graph of $f(x)$ is a parabola with vertex $(0, -18)$ and x-intercepts -3 and 3. The graph of $g(x)$ is a line with a slope of 1 and a y-intercept of 3.

B $\frac{f}{g}$ $\left(\frac{f}{g}\right)(x) = 2x - 6$, where $x \neq -3$; The graph of $\frac{f}{g}$ shows a line with a slope of 2 and a y-intercept of -6 with an open circle at $(-3, -12)$. The graph of f is a parabola with vertex $(0, -18)$ and x-intercepts -3 and 3. The graph of g is a line with a slope of 1 and a y-intercept of 3.

Differentiated Instruction

To help students who may be overwhelmed by having to graph all of the functions in Example 3, divide students into groups to complete Example 3. Groups of three students will work well because each student can graph one function. Then all group members can compare the graphs of the functions.

CLOSE

Essential Question

When you perform operations with functions, how does the graph of the resulting function compare with the original graphs?

The graph of the resulting function depends on the graphs of the original functions and the operation being performed. When comparing graphs, consider the general shape and characteristics of each graph.

Summarize

Have students make a table that summarizes the operations performed with the different types of functions in this lesson. Such a table is started below, with entries for Example 1. Then have students describe any patterns they see.

	Example 1
First function type	constant
Operation	addition
Second function type	linear
Resulting function type	linear

MATHEMATICAL PRACTICE — Highlighting the Standards

Exercises 5 and 6 provide opportunities to address Mathematical Practices Standard 7 (Look for and make use of structure). Students can see how the structure of the function resulting from operations on functions is related to the structure of the original functions. For example, students can see that multiplying a linear function by a constant function will result in a linear function. Students can use this observation to help them determine the type of function that will result when a quadratic function is multiplied by a constant function.

PRACTICE

Where skills are taught	Where skills are practiced
1 EXAMPLE	EXS. 1–2
2 EXAMPLE	EXS. 3–4
3 EXAMPLE	EXS. 5–6

Exercise 7: Students make conjectures about the result of operations performed with two functions, in which one function is a constant function.

3 EXAMPLE Multiplying and Dividing Functions
CC.9-12.F.BF.1b

Given $f(x) = x^2 - 6x + 5$ and $g(x) = x - 1$, find the given function. Then compare the graph of the resulting function to the graphs of the original functions.

A fg

$(fg)(x) = f(x) \cdot g(x)$

$= (x^2 - 6x + 5) \cdot (x - 1)$

$= x^3 - 6x^2 + 5x - x^2 + 6x - 5$

$= x^3 - 7x^2 + 11x - 5$

Graph f, g, and fg on the same set of axes.

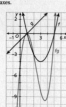

The graph of fg shows a cubic function.

The graph of f is a parabola, and the graph of g is a line.

B $\dfrac{f}{g}$

$\left(\dfrac{f}{g}\right)(x) = \dfrac{f(x)}{g(x)}$

$= \dfrac{x^2 - 6x + 5}{x - 1}$

$= \dfrac{(x - 1)(x - 5)}{x - 1}$

$= x - 5$, where $x \neq 1$

Graph f, g, and $\dfrac{f}{g}$ on the same set of axes.

The graph of $\dfrac{f}{g}$ is the graph of g translated down 4 units, where $x \neq 1$.

REFLECT

3a. Explain why the graph of the product of the quadratic function and the linear function shows a cubic function in part A of Example 3.

A quadratic function is a polynomial function of degree 2, and a linear function is a polynomial function of degree 1. The degree of the product of the functions is the sum of the degrees of the functions. So the product is a polynomial function of degree 3, which is a cubic function.

3b. Is the graph of the quotient of a quadratic function and a linear function always a line? Explain.

No; if the linear function is a factor of the quadratic function, then the graph of the quotient will be a line. However, if the linear function is not a factor of the quadratic function, then the graph of the quotient will not be a line.

PRACTICE

Sketch the graph of the sum or difference of the functions using the graphs of $f(x)$ and $g(x)$. Then find the sum or difference of the functions algebraically and use your answer to check your sketch.

1. $f(x) = \frac{1}{4}x + 3$, $g(x) = -\frac{1}{4}x + 2$
$(f + g)(x) = \underline{\qquad 5 \qquad}$

2. $f(x) = 2^x$, $g(x) = 3$
$(f + g)(x) = \underline{\qquad 2^x + 3 \qquad}$

3. $f(x) = \log_3 x + 5$, $g(x) = 6$
$(f - g)(x) = \underline{\qquad \log_3 x - 1 \qquad}$

4. $f(x) = x + 4$, $g(x) = x^2 - 2x + 4$
$(f - g)(x) = \underline{\qquad -x^2 + 3x \qquad}$

Find each function using $f(x)$ and $g(x)$. Then compare the graph of the resulting function to the graphs of the original functions.

5. Find $(fg)(x)$ when $f(x) = \frac{1}{3}x + 2$ and $g(x) = 3$.

$x + 6$; the graph of fg is a line like the graphs of f and g. However, the graph of fg has the steepest slope and the greatest y-intercept.

6. Find $\left(\dfrac{f}{g}\right)(x)$ when $f(x) = x^3 - 4x^2 + x + 6$ and $g(x) = x - 2$.

$x^2 - 2x - 3$, where $x \neq 2$; the graph of $\dfrac{f}{g}$ is a parabola with an excluded value, while the graph of f shows a cubic function and the graph of g is a line.

7. In Exercises 2, 3, and 5, one of the given functions is a constant function. How does adding or subtracting a constant to a function appear to affect the graph of the function? How does multiplying a function by a constant appear to affect the graph of a function?

Adding or subtracting a constant appears to translate the graph; multiplying a function by a constant appears to stretch or shrink the graph.

Assign these pages to help your students practice and apply important lesson concepts. For additional exercises, see the Student Edition.

Answers

Additional Practice

1. $x^2\sqrt{x}$ 2. $x^2 + x - 8$

3. $x^2 - x + 8$ 4. $\dfrac{x}{2}$

5. $x^3 - 8x^2$ 6. $\dfrac{1}{2x^3}$

7. $x\sqrt{x}$ 8. $\sqrt{\dfrac{x}{2x}}$

9. $-x^2 + x - 8$ 10. 243

11. $-\dfrac{4}{10}$ 12. -192

13. 1

14. 54

15. 68

16. The function $\left(\dfrac{f}{g}\right)(x)$ is not defined at $x = 2$.

Problem Solving

1. $3x^2 - 7x + 1$ 2. $-0.5x^2 + x - 3$

3. Answers will vary.

4. $I(t) = -t + 3750$

Additional Practice

Use the following functions for Exercises 1–16.

$$f(x) = \frac{1}{2x} \qquad g(x) = x^2 \qquad h(x) = x - 8 \qquad k(x) = \sqrt{x}$$

Find each function.

1. $(gk)(x)$

2. $(g + h)(x)$

3. $(g - h)(x)$

4. $(fg)(x)$

5. $(gh)(x)$

6. $\left(\frac{f}{g}\right)(x)$

7. $\left(\frac{g}{k}\right)(x)$

8. $(fk)(x)$

9. $(h - g)(x)$

Find each value.

10. $(gk)(9)$

11. $\left(\frac{g}{h}\right)(-2)$

12. $(gh)(-4)$

13. $\left(\frac{f}{f}\right)(732)$

14. $\left(\frac{g}{f}\right)(3)$

15. $(fg)(136)$

16. Find $\left(\frac{f}{g}\right)(2)$ when $f(x) = x^3 - 5x^2 + 7x - 2$ and $g(x) = x - 2$.

Problem Solving

In an airport, Roberta is walking on a moving walkway, in the direction the walkway is moving. Her speed relative to the walkway is given by the function $G(x) = 2x^2 - 4x + 2$. The walkway's speed relative to the ground is given by the function $H(x) = 1.5x^2 - 3x - 1$.

1. Write an expression showing Roberta's total speed, relative to the ground.

_____

2. Shortly after stepping on the walkway, Roberta realizes she forgot to buy a postcard in the gift shop behind her. She turns around and walks backwards, against the flow of the walkway. Write an expression showing Roberta's total speed, relative to the ground, after she has turned around.

_____

3. Write a pair of functions (of x) j and k such that the following equation is true:

$$\left(\frac{j}{k}\right)(2) = 5$$

$j(x) = $ _____ $k(x) = $ _____

4. An industrial engineer models a company's sales, in units sold, with the function $S(t) = 18t - 1950$ and the company's factory's output, in units produced, by $P(t) = 17t + 1800$. Write a function representing the inventory of the company's warehouse, which holds the units the company produces but has not yet sold.

$I(t) = $ _____

Notes

Functions and Their Inverses
Going Deeper

Essential question: *What are the inverses of quadratic and cubic functions and how do you find them?*

COMMON CORE **Standards for Mathematical Content**

CC.9-12.A.CED.2 Create equations in two … variables to represent relationships between quantities; graph equations on coordinate axes with labels and scales.*

CC.9-12.F.IF.2 Use function notation, evaluate functions for inputs in their domains, and interpret statements that use function notation in terms of a context.

CC.9-12.F.IF.7 Graph functions expressed symbolically and show key features of the graph …*

CC.9-12.F.IF.7a Graph … quadratic functions …*

CC.9-12.F.IF.7b Graph square root, cube root, … functions …*

CC.9-12.F.IF.7c Graph polynomial functions …*

CC.9-12.F.BF.4 Find inverse functions.

CC.9-12.F.BF.4a Solve an equation of the form $f(x) = c$ for a simple function f that has an inverse and write an expression for the inverse.

CC.9-12.F.BF.4d(+) Produce an invertible function from a non-invertible function by restricting the domain.

Also: CC.9-12.A.CED.4*, CC.9-12.F.BF.3

Vocabulary

one-to-one function

square root function

cube root function

Prerequisites

Quadratic functions

Finding cube roots

Graphing polynomial functions

Inverses of functions

Inverses of quadratic functions

Math Background

The domain of a quadratic function needs to be restricted in order for the inverse of the function to also be a function. If the domain of a quadratic function is not restricted, then reflecting its graph across the line $y = x$ yields a graph that fails the vertical line test.

If $a^3 = b$, then a is the cube root of b. Every real number has a single cube root. This is in contrast to square roots, where positive real numbers have two square roots, 0 has one square root (itself), and negative real numbers have no (real) square roots.

INTRODUCE

Have students evaluate the function $f(x) = x^2$ for $x = -2, -1, 0, 1,$ and 2 and write the resulting ordered pairs. (−2, 4), (−1, 1), (0, 0), (1, 1), (2, 4) Have students switch the coordinates and explain whether the inverse is also a function. (4, −2), (1, −1), (0, 0), (1, 1), (4, 2); no; 4 is paired with both −2 and 2, and 1 is paired with both −1 and 1.

6-6

Functions and Their Inverses
Going Deeper

Essential question: *What are the inverses of quadratic and cubic functions and how do you find them?*

Video Tutor

PREP FOR CC.9-12.F.BF.4d(+)

1 ENGAGE   Understanding One-to-One Functions

A function is **one-to-one** if each output of the function is paired with exactly one input. Only one-to-one functions have inverses that are also functions.

Recall that the graph of $f^{-1}(x)$ is the reflection of the graph of $f(x)$ across the line $y = x$.

Linear functions with nonzero slopes are always one-to-one, so their inverses are always functions.

Quadratic functions with unrestricted domains are not one-to-one. The reflection of the parabola labeled $g(x)$ across the line $y = x$ is not a function.

REFLECT

1a. Why is a linear function with a nonzero slope a one-to-one function? Why is a linear function not one-to-one if the slope is 0?

If the slope of a linear function is nonzero, then every y-value is paired with exactly one x-value. If the slope is 0, then there is only one y-value, which is paired with every x-value.

1b. Why is the quadratic function $g(x)$ not one-to-one?

Because the parabola is symmetric with respect to the y-axis, there are two x-values that correspond to each y-value greater than 0.

1c. Explain why the reflection of the graph of $g(x)$ across the line $y = x$ is not a function.

Each x-value in the domain (except 0) is paired with more than one y-value.

1d. Consider the quadratic function $g(x) = x^2$. How could you restrict its domain so that the resulting function is one-to-one? Explain. Graph the function for the restricted domain.

Sample answer: Restrict the domain to $x \geq 0$. For this domain, every y-value will correspond to exactly one x-value.

CC.9-12.F.BF.4d(+)

2 EXAMPLE   Graphing the Inverse of $f(x) = ax^2$ with $x \geq 0$

Graph the function $f(x) = 0.5x^2$ for the domain $x \geq 0$. Then graph its inverse, $f^{-1}(x)$, and write a rule for the inverse function.

A Complete a table of values to graph $f(x)$ for nonnegative values of x.

x	f(x)
0	0
1	0.5
2	2
3	4.5
4	8

B Complete the table below by finding the image of each point on the graph of $f(x)$ after a reflection across the line $y = x$. To reflect a point across $y = x$, switch the x- and y-coordinates of the point.

Points on the graph of f(x)	0, 0	1, 0.5	2, 2	3, 4.5	4, 8
Points on the graph of $f^{-1}(x)$	0, 0	0.5, 1	2, 2	4.5, 3	8, 4

C Use the table from part B to graph $f^{-1}(x)$.

D Write a rule for $f^{-1}(x)$.

$y = 0.5x^2$ Replace $f(x)$ with y.

$2y = x^2$ Multiply both sides by 2.

$\sqrt{2y} = x$ Use the definition of positive square root.

$\sqrt{2x} = y$ Switch x and y to write the inverse.

$\sqrt{2x} = f^{-1}(x)$ Replace y with $f^{-1}(x)$.

1 ENGAGE

Questioning Strategies

- Give an example of a linear function that is not one-to-one. **Sample answer: $f(x) = 2$**

- In Reflect Question 1d, what is another way to restrict the domain of $g(x)$ to obtain a one-to-one function? What does the graph of $g(x)$ with this restricted domain look like? **Restrict the domain to $x \leq 0$. The graph is the part of the parabola in Quadrant II along with the vertex (0, 0).**

Differentiated Instruction

Explain the *horizontal line test*: Given the graph of a function, if every possible horizontal line that passes through the graph intersects it in only one point, then the function is a one-to-one function. So, the vertical line test determines whether a relation is a function, and the horizontal line test determines whether it is also one-to-one.

> **MATHEMATICAL PRACTICE**   **Highlighting the Standards**
>
> **1 ENGAGE** includes opportunities to address Mathematical Practice Standard 2 (Reason abstractly and quantitatively). Have students use mapping diagrams and the given graphs to compare and contrast linear functions with nonzero slopes, linear functions with zero slope, and quadratic functions, and discuss why they are or are not one-to-one functions.

2 EXAMPLE

Questioning Strategies

- Why is the domain restricted to nonnegative numbers? **so that the inverse is a function**

- In part C, how can you visually check whether the graph of $f^{-1}(x)$ is correct? **The graph should be a reflection of the graph of $f(x)$ across the line $y = x$.**

- In part D, why multiply both sides by 2 to isolate x^2? **The multiplicative inverse of 0.5 is 2.**

EXTRA EXAMPLE

Graph the function $f(x) = 3x^2$ for the domain $x \geq 0$. Then graph its inverse, $f^{-1}(x)$, and write a rule for the inverse function. **The graph of $f(x)$ is a curve in the first quadrant passing through (0, 0), (1, 3), and (2, 12). The graph of $f^{-1}(x)$ is a curve in the first quadrant passing through (0, 0), (3, 1), and (12, 2).** $f^{-1}(x) = \sqrt{\frac{x}{3}}$

Teaching Strategy

Have students state the sequence of operations performed on x in both the function and its inverse. For $f(x)$, square x and take half of the result. For $f^{-1}(x)$, multiply x by 2 and take the positive square root of the result.

Avoid Common Errors

Students sometimes fail to draw the radical sign far enough to the right to cover the expression they wish to cover. For example, they may write $f(x) = \sqrt{3}x$ instead of $f(x) = \sqrt{3x}$.

3 ENGAGE

Questioning Strategies

- What points do the graphs of $f(x)$ and $g(x)$ have in common? **(0, 0) and (1, 1)**

- Do you think the graphs of the functions have other points in common? Explain. **No; when $x > 1$, $f(x) > x$ and $g(x) < x$, and when $0 < x < 1$, $f(x) < x$ and $g(x) > x$ so $f(x)$ never equals $g(x)$ for any other points on the graphs.**

Differentiated Instruction

When answering Reflect Question 3a, visual learners may benefit from sketching the graphs of $f(x)$ and $g(x)$ in different colors when $a = 2$ and then when $a = 0.5$ as examples of the effect of $|a|$ on the graphs.

REFLECT

2a. When solving the equation $2y = x^2$ for x in part D, you use the definition of a positive square root. Why can you ignore negative square roots?

Because the domain of $f(x)$ is restricted to $x \geq 0$, x cannot be negative.

2b. How else could you restrict the domain of $f(x)$ in order to get an inverse that is a function? What is the inverse function given that restriction?

The domain could be restricted to any interval where the function is one-to-one; for example, $x \leq 0$, where the inverse would be $f^{-1}(x) = -\sqrt{2x}$.

3 ENGAGE CC.9-12.F.BF.4

Understanding Square Root Functions

A quadratic function of the form $f(x) = ax^2$ for $x \geq 0$ is a one-to-one function, so its inverse is also a function. In general, the inverse of $f(x) = ax^2$ for $x \geq 0$ is the *square root function* $g(x) = \sqrt{\frac{x}{a}}$.

A **square root function** is a function whose rule involves $\sqrt{x}$. The parent square root function is $g(x) = \sqrt{x}$. The graph shows that $g(x) = \sqrt{x}$ is the inverse of $f(x) = x^2$ for $x \geq 0$.

A square root function is defined only for values of x that make the expression under the radical sign nonnegative.

REFLECT

3a. What are the domain and range of the parent square root function $g(x) = \sqrt{x}$? Explain.

The expression under the radical sign must be nonnegative, so the domain of the function is $x \geq 0$. The square root of a real number is never negative, so the range of the function is $y \geq 0$.

3b. When $a > 1$, the graph of $f(x) = ax^2$ for $x \geq 0$ is a vertical stretch by a factor of a of the graph of the parent quadratic function for $x \geq 0$. When $a > 1$, is the graph of $g(x) = \sqrt{\frac{x}{a}}$ a horizontal stretch or a horizontal shrink by a factor of a of the graph of the parent square root function? Explain.

When reflected across the line $y = x$, a vertical stretch of the graph of the parent quadratic function for $x \geq 0$ results in a graph that is a horizontal stretch of the parent square root function. So, the graph of $g(x)$ is a horizontal stretch by a factor of a of the parent square root function.

---

4 EXAMPLE CC.9-12.A.CED.2

Modeling the Inverse of a Quadratic Function

The function $d(t) = 16t^2$ gives the distance d in feet that a dropped object falls in t seconds. Write and graph the inverse function $t(d)$ to find the time t in seconds it takes for an object to fall a distance of d feet. Then estimate how long it will take a penny dropped into a well to fall 48 feet.

A Write the inverse function.

The original function is a ___quadratic___ function with a domain restricted to $t \geq$ ___0___

The function fits the pattern $f(x) = ax^2$ for $x \geq 0$, so its inverse will have the form $g(x) = \sqrt{\frac{x}{a}}$.

Original Function	Inverse Function
$d(t) = 16t^2$ for $t \geq 0$	$t(d) = \sqrt{\dfrac{d}{16}}$ for $d \geq 0$

B Complete the table of values and use it to graph the function $t(d)$.

d	0	4	16	36	64	100
t	0	0.5	1	1.5	2	2.5

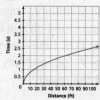

C Use the function $t(d)$ to estimate how long it will take a penny to fall 48 feet.

$t(d) = \sqrt{\dfrac{d}{16}}$ Write the function.

$t(48) = \sqrt{\dfrac{48}{16}}$ Substitute 48 for d.

$t(48) = \sqrt{3}$ Simplify.

$t(48) \approx 1.7$ Use a calculator to estimate.

So, it will take about ___1.7___ seconds for a penny to fall 48 feet.

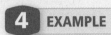

4 EXAMPLE

Questioning Strategies

- Is the graph of $d(t)$ a vertical stretch or a vertical shrink of the graph of the parent quadratic function? **a vertical stretch**

- Is the graph of $t(d)$ a horizontal stretch or shrink of the graph of the parent square root function? **a horizontal stretch**

- If you did not know the pattern to find the inverse of a function in the form $f(x) = ax^2$, how could you find the inverse of $d(t)$? **Perform inverse operations on t in the reverse order they were applied: divide by 16 and then take the positive square root of the result.**

- In part C, how does the graph confirm your estimate? **For $d = 48$, the point on the graph for t is between 1.5 and 2.**

EXTRA EXAMPLE
The function $A(s) = 6s^2$ gives the surface area A of a cube with side length s. Write and graph the inverse function $s(A)$ to find the side length of a cube with surface area A. Then, estimate the side length of a cube whose surface area is 500 square centimeters. **$s(A) = \sqrt{\frac{A}{6}}$; the graph is a curve in the first quadrant that passes through (0, 0), (6, 1), (24, 2), (54, 3), and (96, 4); about 9.1 centimeters**

5 ENGAGE

Questioning Strategies

- How do the domain and range of a cube root function compare with the domain and range of a square root function? Why? **Both the domain and range of a cube root function are all real numbers. The domain and range of a square root function are all nonnegative real numbers. This is because you cannot take the square root of a negative number, but you can take the cube root of a negative number.**

- How do you know that $f(x) = x^3$ is a one-to-one function? **Each output is paired with exactly one input, which means that the graph of the function passes the horizontal line test.**

- Why is there no need to restrict the domain of a cubic function before finding its inverse? **Because it is a one-to-one function, its inverse is also a function.**

- Look at the table of values for $g(x)$. What is the next greatest value of x for which $g(x)$ is an integer? How did you determine that? **For $x = 27$, $g(x) = 3$. One way to determine this is to extend the table for $f(x)$ and find $f(x)$ when $x = 3$.**

Differentiated Instruction
Visual learners may benefit from graphing $f(x)$ and $g(x)$ on the same coordinate plane, each in a different color, and then drawing the line $y = x$.

6 EXAMPLE

Questioning Strategies

- When finding the inverse of $f(x) = x^2$ for $x \geq 0$, you use the definition of a positive square root. In part D, why don't you use the definition of a positive cube root? **Positive real numbers have two square roots (one positive and one negative), but you want only the positive square root due to the restriction $x \geq 0$. Real numbers have a single cube root, so you're simply finding *the* cube root.**

- In part D, how can you write the radicand $2x$ in the form $\frac{x}{a}$? What is a? **Multiplying x by 2 is the same as dividing x by $\frac{1}{2}$, so $g(x) = \sqrt[3]{2x} = \sqrt[3]{\frac{x}{0.5}}$; $a = 0.5$**

EXTRA EXAMPLE
Graph the function $f(x) = -\frac{1}{2}x^3$. Then graph its inverse, $f^{-1}(x)$, and write a rule for the inverse function. **The graph of $f(x)$ is a curve passing through $(-2, 4)$, $(-1, 0.5)$, $(0, 0)$, $(1, -0.5)$, and $(2, -4)$. The graph of $f^{-1}(x)$ is a curve passing through $(4, -2)$, $(0.5, -1)$, $(0, 0)$, $(-0.5, 1)$, and $(-4, 2)$. $f^{-1}(x) = \sqrt[3]{-2x}$**

Teaching Strategy
Have students state the sequence of operations performed on x in both the function and its inverse. **For $f(x)$, cube x and take half of the result. For $f^{-1}(x)$, multiply x by 2 and take the cube root of the result.**

Technology
To cube a number on a graphing calculator, enter the base followed by the caret key ⌃ and the exponent, 3. To take a cube root, enter the base followed by ⌃ (1/3), making sure to enclose the fractional exponent in parentheses.

continued

REFLECT

4a. Explain why the domain is restricted to $t \geq 0$ for the original function $d(t) = 16t^2$.

The domain is restricted because t represents time in seconds, which can only be nonnegative.

4b. Describe another way that you could estimate the time it would take a penny to fall 48 feet.

Sample answer: Set $d(t)$ equal to 48 in the original function $d(t) = 16t^2$. Then solve for t.

---

5 ENGAGE   CC 9-12.F.BF.4a   **Understanding the Cube Root Function**

A table of values for the parent cubic function, $f(x) = x^3$, is shown below, along with its graph.

x	f(x)
−2	−8
−1	−1
0	0
1	1
2	8

Because $f(x) = x^3$ is a one-to-one function, its inverse is also a function. The inverse of $f(x) = x^3$ is the *cube root function* $g(x) = \sqrt[3]{x}$.

A **cube root function** is a function whose rule involves $\sqrt[3]{x}$. The parent cube root function is $g(x) = \sqrt[3]{x}$.

A table of values for $g(x) = \sqrt[3]{x}$ is shown below, along with its graph.

x	g(x)
−8	−2
−1	−1
0	0
1	1
8	2

REFLECT

5a. Explain how the values in the tables for $f(x) = x^3$ and $g(x) = \sqrt[3]{x}$ show that the graphs of these functions are reflections of each other across the line $y = x$.

The x- and y-coordinates in the table for $f(x)$ are switched in the table for $g(x)$.

5b. Is $g(x) = \sqrt[3]{x}$ also a one-to-one function? Explain.

Yes; each y-value is paired with exactly one x-value.

5c. What are the domain and range of $f(x) = x^3$?

Both the domain and range of $f(x)$ are all real numbers.

5d. What are the domain and range of $g(x) = \sqrt[3]{x}$?

Both the domain and range of $g(x)$ are also all real numbers.

---

6 EXAMPLE   CC 9-12.F.BF.4   **Graphing the Inverse of $f(x) = ax^3$**

Graph the function $f(x) = 0.5x^3$. Then graph its inverse, $f^{-1}(x)$, and write a rule for the inverse function.

A Complete the table of values to graph the function $f(x) = 0.5x^3$.

x	f(x)
−2	−4
−1	−0.5
0	0
1	0.5
2	4

B Complete the table below by finding the image of each point on the graph of $f(x)$ after a reflection across the line $y = x$.

Points on the graph of f(x)	(−2, −4)	(−1, −0.5)	(0, 0)	(1, 0.5)	(2, 4)
Points on the graph of f⁻¹(x)	(−4, −2)	(−0.5, −1)	(0, 0)	(0.5, 1)	(4, 2)

△ **MATHEMATICAL PRACTICE** **Highlighting the Standards**

6 EXAMPLE includes opportunities to address Mathematical Practice Standard 8 (Look for and express regularity in repeated reasoning). In Reflect Question 6a, students find that the inverse of the general cubic function $f(x) = ax^3$ is $f^{-1}(x) = \sqrt[3]{\frac{x}{a}}$. Have students compare these two general functions to the general quadratic and square root functions they found previously: $f(x) = ax^2$ for $x \geq 0$ and $f^{-1}(x) = \sqrt{\frac{x}{a}}$. Ask students what they think the inverses of $f(x) = ax^4$ and $f(x) = ax^5$ would be.

Essential Question

What are the inverses of quadratic and cubic functions and how do you find them?

A square root function is the inverse of a quadratic function whose domain is restricted. The inverse of $f(x) = ax^2$ for $x \geq 0$ is $f^{-1}(x) = \sqrt{\frac{x}{a}}$.

The inverse of $f(x) = ax^3$ is the function $f^{-1}(x) = \sqrt[3]{\frac{x}{a}}$. Algebraically, substitute y for $f(x)$, solve for x, and then switch x and y. Graphically, graph the function and reflect the graph across the line $y = x$, which switches the coordinates in each ordered pair for $f(x)$ and thereby results in ordered pairs for $f^{-1}(x)$.

Summarize

Create a graphic organizer that compares and contrasts inverse linear, quadratic, and cubic functions. One possibility is shown below.

	Linear	Quadratic	Cubic
Equations	$f(x) = ax$ $f^{-1}(x) = \frac{x}{a}$	$f(x) = ax^2$ $f^{-1}(x) = \sqrt{\frac{x}{a}}$	$f(x) = ax^3$ $f^{-1}(x) = \sqrt[3]{\frac{x}{a}}$
Graphs	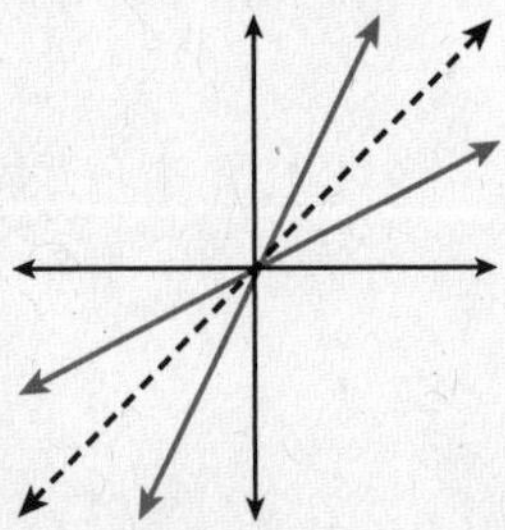	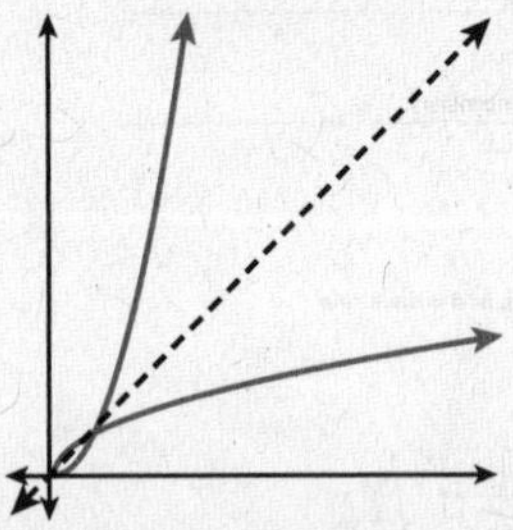	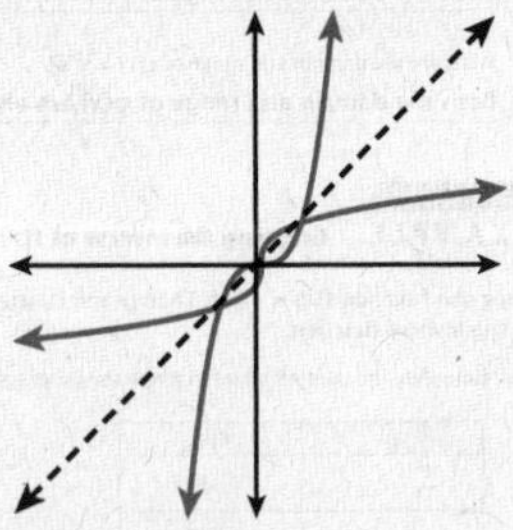
Restrictions	$f(x)$ must have nonzero slope.	Domain of $f(x)$ restricted to nonnegative values	No restrictions

C Use the table from part B to graph $f^{-1}(x)$.

D Write a rule for $f^{-1}(x)$.

$y = 0.5x^3$	Replace $f(x)$ with y.
$2\ \ y = x^3$	Solve for x. Multiply both sides by 2.
$\sqrt[3]{2y} = x$	Use the definition of cube root.
$\sqrt[3]{2}\ \ x = y$	Switch x and y to write the inverse.
$\sqrt[3]{2x} = f^{-1}(x)$	Replace y with $f^{-1}(x)$.

REFLECT

6a. What is the inverse of the function $f(x) = ax^3$?

$f^{-1}(x) = \sqrt[3]{\dfrac{x}{a}}$

6b. When $0 < a < 1$, the graph of $f(x) = ax^3$ is a vertical shrink by a factor of a of the graph of the parent cubic function. When $0 < a < 1$, is the graph of $f^{-1}(x) = \sqrt[3]{\dfrac{x}{a}}$ a horizontal stretch or a horizontal shrink by a factor of a of the graph of the parent cube root function? Explain.

When reflected across the line $y = x$, a vertical shrink of the

graph of the parent cubic function results in a graph that is a

horizontal shrink of the graph of the parent cube root function.

So, the graph of $f^{-1}(x)$ is a horizontal shrink by a factor of a of

the graph of the parent cube root function.

6c. Complete the chart below by describing the graph of each function as a transformation of the graph of its parent function.

Value of a	$f(x) = ax^3$	$g(x) = \sqrt[3]{\dfrac{x}{a}}$
$a > 1$	vertical stretch by a factor of a	horizontal stretch by a factor of a
$0 < a < 1$	vertical shrink by a factor of a	horizontal shrink by a factor of a

---

PRACTICE

Graph the function $f(x)$ for the domain $x \geq 0$. Then graph its inverse, $f^{-1}(x)$, and write a rule for the inverse function.

1. $f(x) = 2x^2$

$f^{-1}(x) =$ $\sqrt{\dfrac{x}{2}}$

2. $f(x) = -x^2$

$f^{-1}(x) =$ $\sqrt{-x}$

3. $f(x) = \frac{1}{3}x^2$

$f^{-1}(x) =$ $\sqrt{3x}$

4. $f(x) = -\frac{1}{2}x^2$

$f^{-1}(x) =$ $\sqrt{-2x}$

5. A company manufactures square tabletops that are covered by 16 square tiles. If s is the side length of each tile in inches, then the area A of a tabletop in square feet is given by $A(s) = \frac{1}{9}s^2$.

a. Write and graph the inverse function $s(A)$ to find the side length of the tiles in inches for a tabletop with an area of A square feet.

$s(A) = \sqrt{9A}$

b. What is the side length of the tiles that make up a tabletop with an area of 4 square feet?

6 inches

Where skills are taught	Where skills are practiced
2 EXAMPLE	EXS. 1–4
3 EXAMPLE	EXS. 5, 6, 13
6 EXAMPLE	EXS. 9–12

Exercises 7 and 8: These exercises are extensions of Reflect Question 3b, which showed that the graph of $g(x) = \sqrt{\frac{x}{a}}$ is a horizontal stretch of the parent square root function by a factor of a when $a > 1$ (and, through similar reasoning, a horizontal shrink by a factor of a when $0 < a < 1$). When completing Exercises 7 and 8, some students may compare the graph of $g(x)$ with the given graph of the parent square root function and see vertical stretches and shrinks instead of horizontal stretches and shrinks. If so, this would be an opportunity to show students that the constant a can be pulled out of the radicand. For instance, in Exercise 7, you can rewrite $g(x)$ as $g(x) = \sqrt{\frac{x}{3}} = \sqrt{\frac{1}{3}} \cdot \sqrt{x} \approx 0.58\sqrt{x}$. This shows that the graph of $g(x)$ can be characterized as either a horizontal stretch by a factor of 3 or a vertical shrink by a factor of 0.58. In Exercise 8, you

can write $g(x)$ as either $g(x) = \sqrt{\frac{x}{0.25}}$ or $g(x) = 2\sqrt{x}$. The former tells you that the graph of $g(x)$ is a horizontal shrink of the parent square root function by a factor of 0.25, while the latter tells you that the graph of $g(x)$ is a vertical stretch by a factor of 2.

Exercise 14: Students analyze a cubic function that is not a one-to-one function. Point out how this function is not in the form $f(x) = ax^3$, as are those studied in the lesson.

Exercises 15 and 16: Students describe the graphs of cube root functions that involve multiplying the function by a or multiplying x by a as horizontal or vertical stretches or shrinks of the graph of the parent cube root function. While students should be familiar with the transformation in Exercise 15, they may have trouble with the transformation in Exercise 16. This exercise is an extension of Reflect Questions 6a–6c. Students will need to rewrite $g(x)$ as $g(x) = \sqrt[3]{8x} = \sqrt[3]{\frac{x}{0.125}}$ in order to see that its graph is a horizontal stretch by a fator of 0.125 of the graph of the parent cube root function. Alternatively, students can rewrite $g(x)$ as $g(x) = \sqrt[3]{8x} = \sqrt[3]{8} \cdot \sqrt[3]{x} = 2\sqrt[3]{x}$ and characterize the graph of $g(x)$ as a vertical stretch by a factor of 2 of the graph of the parent cube root function.

6. The function $A(r) = \pi r^2$ gives the area A in square meters of a circle with a radius of r meters.

a. Write and graph the inverse function $r(A)$ to find the radius in meters of a circle with an area of A square meters.

$$r(A) = \sqrt{\dfrac{A}{\pi}}$$

b. Estimate the radius of a circular swimming pool that has a surface area of 120 square meters.

6.2 meters

Graph each square root function $g(x)$. (The graph of the parent function is shown.) Then describe $g(x)$ as a transformation of the parent square root function.

7. $g(x) = \sqrt{\dfrac{x}{3}}$

Horizontal stretch by a factor of 3

8. $g(x) = \sqrt{4x}$

Horizontal shrink by a factor of $\dfrac{1}{4}$

Graph the function $f(x)$. Then graph its inverse, $f^{-1}(x)$, and write a rule for the inverse function.

9. $f(x) = 2x^3$

$f^{-1}(x) = \quad \sqrt[3]{\dfrac{x}{2}}$

10. $f(x) = -x^3$

$f^{-1}(x) = \quad \sqrt[3]{-x}$

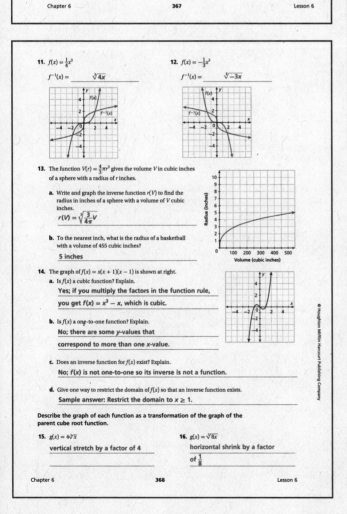

---

11. $f(x) = \dfrac{1}{4}x^3$

$f^{-1}(x) = \quad \sqrt[3]{4x}$

12. $f(x) = -\dfrac{1}{3}x^3$

$f^{-1}(x) = \quad \sqrt[3]{-3x}$

13. The function $V(r) = \dfrac{4}{3}\pi r^3$ gives the volume V in cubic inches of a sphere with a radius of r inches.

a. Write and graph the inverse function $r(V)$ to find the radius in inches of a sphere with a volume of V cubic inches.

$$r(V) = \sqrt[3]{\dfrac{3}{4\pi}V}$$

b. To the nearest inch, what is the radius of a basketball with a volume of 455 cubic inches?

5 inches

14. The graph of $f(x) = x(x+1)(x-1)$ is shown at right.

a. Is $f(x)$ a cubic function? Explain.

Yes; if you multiply the factors in the function rule, you get $f(x) = x^3 - x$, which is cubic.

b. Is $f(x)$ a one-to-one function? Explain.

No; there are some y-values that correspond to more than one x-value.

c. Does an inverse function for $f(x)$ exist? Explain.

No; $f(x)$ is not one-to-one so its inverse is not a function.

d. Give one way to restrict the domain of $f(x)$ so that an inverse function exists.

Sample answer: Restrict the domain to $x \geq 1$.

Describe the graph of each function as a transformation of the graph of the parent cube root function.

15. $g(x) = 4\sqrt[3]{x}$

vertical stretch by a factor of 4

16. $g(x) = \sqrt[3]{8x}$

horizontal shrink by a factor of $\dfrac{1}{8}$

Notes

Assign these pages to help your students practice and apply important lesson concepts. For additional exercises, see the Student Edition.

Answers

Additional Practice

1. $k^{-1}(x) = \dfrac{x-5}{10}$; function;
   domain: $(-\infty, +\infty)$ range: $(-\infty, +\infty)$

2. $d^{-1}(x) = -\dfrac{x}{2} + 3$; function;
   domain: $(-\infty, +\infty)$ range: $(-\infty, +\infty)$

3. $y = 5 \pm \sqrt{x}$; not a function;
   domain: $(-\infty, +\infty)$ range: $[0, +\infty)$

4. $g^{-1}(x) = -2x + 4$; function;
   domain: $(-\infty, +\infty)$ range: $(-\infty, +\infty)$

5. $h^{-1}(x) = \pm\sqrt{x^2 + 9}$; not a function;
   domain: $[0, +\infty)$ range: $(-\infty, -3]$ and
   $[3, +\infty)$

6. $b^{-1}(x) = \log^{-1} \dfrac{x}{2}$ or $b^{-1}(x) = 10^{\frac{x}{2}}$;
   function; domain:$(-\infty, +\infty)$ range: $(0, +\infty)$

7. $m^{-1}(x) = 5 + \ln x$; function; domain: $(0, +\infty)$
   range: $(0, +\infty)$

8. $w^{-1}(x) = 3 \pm 2\sqrt[6]{x}$; not a function;
   domain: $(0, +\infty)$ range: $(-\infty, +\infty)$

9a. $f^{-1}(x) = \dfrac{1}{30}x - 100$

9b. Number of months she has saved

9c. 33 months   9d. 5 years

Problem Solving

1. a. $L(h) = 2.5\pi h$; $h(L) = \dfrac{L}{2.5\pi}$

   b. $h(L)$ gives the height of a can for a given lateral surface area.

   c. 4.5 in.

2. C   3. F

4. B   5. J

Additional Practice

Find the inverse of each function. Determine whether the inverse is a function and state its domain and range.

1. $k(x) = 10x + 5$

2. $d(x) = 6 - 2x$

3. $f(x) = (x - 5)^2$

4. $g(x) = \dfrac{4 - x}{2}$

5. $h(x) = \sqrt{x^2 - 9}$

6. $b(x) = 2\log x$

7. $m(x) = e^{x - 5}$

8. $w(x) = \left(\dfrac{x - 3}{2}\right)^6$

Solve.

9. So far, Rhonda has saved $3000 for her college expenses. She plans to save $30 each month. Her college fund can be represented by the function $f(x) = 30x + 3000$.

   a. Find the inverse of $f(x)$.

   b. What does the inverse represent?

   c. When will the fund reach $3990?

   d. How long will it take her to reach her goal of $4800?

Problem Solving

A juice drink manufacturer is designing an advertisement for a national sports event on its cans. The lateral surface area of the cans is given by the function $L(h) = 2.5\pi h$, where h is the height of the can. The total surface area of the can is given by the function $T(h) = 2.5\pi(h + 1.25)$.

1. The graphic designer needs to know how the height of the can varies as a function of the lateral surface area.

   a. Find the inverse, $h(L)$, of the function $L(h)$.

   b. Explain the meaning of the inverse function.

   c. If the lateral surface area of one can is 35.34 in^2, what is the height of this can?

Choose the letter for the best answer.

2. The manufacturer produces cans in different sizes. The height of one can is 5.5 in. The designer is planning to use only half the lateral surface area of this can. What is this area?

   A 8.8 in^2

   B 11.0 in^2

   C 21.6 in^2

   D 43.2 in^2

3. The designer is studying the possibility of using the total surface area of each can. Which function gives height, $h(T)$, as a function of total surface area, T?

   F $h(T) = \dfrac{T}{2.5\pi} - 1.25$

   G $h(T) = \dfrac{T}{2.5\pi} + 1.25$

   H $h(T) = (2.5\pi)(T - 1.25)$

   J $h(T) = (2.5\pi)(T + 1.25)$

4. The total surface area of one size of can is 45.16 in^2. What is the height of this can?

   A 3.5 in.

   B 4.5 in.

   C 5.5 in.

   D 6.5 in.

5. The designer updates an old advertisement that covers the lateral surface area, L, of a can to create a new advertisement that covers the total surface area, T, of the can. Which function gives this area?

   F $T = (2.5\pi)(L + 1.25)$

   G $T = (2.5\pi)(L - 1.25)$

   H $T = L - 2.5\pi(1.25)$

   J $T = L + 2.5\pi(1.25)$

Notes

Modeling Real-World Data
Focus on Modeling

Essential question: *How can you model age as a function of body mass index given a data set?*

COMMON
CORE
Standards for
Mathematical Content

The following standards are addressed in this lesson. (An asterisk indicates that a standard is also a Modeling standard.) For more detailed information, see each section of the lesson.

Algebra: CC.9-12.A.CED.2*, CC.9-12.A.SSE.3, CC.9-12.A.SSE.3b

Functions: CC.9-12.F.IF.2, CC.9-12.F.IF.4*, CC.9-12.F.IF.7*, CC.9-12.F.IF.7b*, CC.9-12.F.IF.8, CC.9-12.F.IF.8a, CC.9-12.F.BF.1*, CC.9-12.F.BF.1a*, CC.9-12.F.BF.4, CC.9-12.F.BF.4d(+)

Statistics and Probability: CC.9-12.S.ID.6*, CC.9-12.S.ID.6a*

Prerequisites

- Writing a quadratic function in vertex form
- Finding a regression equation
- Inverses of quadratic functions
- Writing a rule for a square root function given a graph

Math Background

In this lesson, students obtain a quadratic function by using their calculators to perform quadratic regression on a set of data. The calculator gives the equation in standard form. Students use previously learned skills to rewrite the equation in vertex form. They then find the inverse of the quadratic model.

INTRODUCE

Children's physical characteristics, such as size and weight, tend to follow predictable trends as children grow. Given a child's age, you can predict his or her height within a few inches, although there are always exceptions. Another fairly predictable characteristic is a child's body mass index, or BMI, which is a measure used to determine healthy body mass based on height.

TEACH

1 **Write a model of boys' median BMI as a function of age.**

Standards

CC.9-12.A.CED.2 Create equations in two ... variables to represent relationships between quantities ...*

CC.9-12.F.IF.2 Use function notation ...

CC.9-12.F.BF.1 Write a function that describes a relationship between two quantities.*

CC.9-12.F.BF.1a Determine an explicit expression ... from a context.*

CC.9-12.S.ID.6 Represent data on two quantitative variables on a scatter plot, and describe how the variables are related.*

CC.9-12.S.ID.6a Fit a function to the data ...*

Questioning Strategies

- How do you know, before performing the regression, that the value of a in the equation will be positive? **The graph opens upward.**
- In finding significant digits, which numbers are always significant? **1, 2, 3, 4, 5, 6, 7, 8, and 9**
- When are zeros significant? **when they appear between nonzero digits or after a nonzero digit following a decimal point**

2 **Write the quadratic model in vertex form.**

Standards

CC.9-12.A.CED.2 Create equations in two ... variables to represent relationships between quantities ...*

CC.9-12.A.SSE.3 Choose and produce an equivalent form of an expression to reveal and explain properties of the quantity represented by the expression.

CC.9-12.A.SSE.3b Complete the square in a quadratic expression to reveal the maximum or minimum value of the function it defines.

CC.9-12.F.IF.2 Use function notation ... and interpret statements that use function notation in terms of a context.

continued

Name_____ Class_____ Date_____ 6-7

Modeling Real-World Data
Focus on Modeling

Essential question: *How can you model age as a function of body mass index given a data set?*

COMMON CORE
CC.9-12.A.CED.2*,
CC.9-12.F.IF.4*,
CC.9-12.F.IF.7b*,
CC.9-12.F.BF.1*,
CC.9-12.F.BF.4d(+),
CC.9-12.S.ID.6a*

Body mass index (BMI) is a measure used to determine healthy body mass based on a person's height. BMI is calculated by dividing a person's mass in kilograms by the square of his or her height in meters. The median BMI measures for a group of boys ages 2 to 10 years are given in the chart below.

Age of Boys	2	3	4	5	6	7	8	9	10
Median BMI	16.6	16.0	15.6	15.4	15.4	15.5	15.8	16.2	16.6

How can you use the data to develop a model for predicting the age of a boy with a given BMI?

1 Write a model of boys' median BMI as a function of age.

A Create a scatter plot for the data in the table, treating age as the independent variable x and median BMI as the dependent variable y.

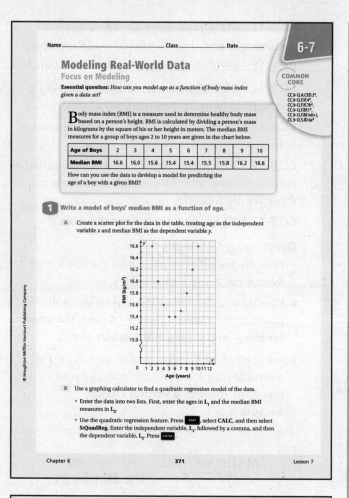

B Use a graphing calculator to find a quadratic regression model of the data.

- Enter the data into two lists. First, enter the ages in L_1 and the median BMI measures in L_2.

- Use the quadratic regression feature. Press [STAT], select **CALC**, and then select **5:QuadReg**. Enter the independent variable, L_1, followed by a comma, and then the dependent variable, L_2. Press [ENTER].

© Houghton Mifflin Harcourt Publishing Company

- The values for a, b, and c correspond to the values in the standard form of a quadratic function, $f(x) = ax^2 + bx + c$. Record each value to three significant digits to complete the quadratic model below.

$$f(x) = \boxed{0.0763} x^2 - \boxed{0.897} x + \boxed{18.0}$$

REFLECT

1a. Explain why it is appropriate to use a quadratic model for this data set, rather than another type of model, such as linear or cubic.

The data points appear to lie on a curve that approximates a parabola.

1b. Use a calculator to make a scatter plot of the data and then graph $f(x)$ on the same screen. Is the model a good fit for the data? Explain.

Yes; the curve appears to pass through or near almost all of the

data points.

2 Write the quadratic model in vertex form.

Complete the square to write the function in vertex form, $f(x) = a(x - h)^2 + k$.

$f(x) = 0.0763x^2 - 0.897x + 18.0$ Write the equation in standard form.

$f(x) = 0.0763\left(x^2 - 11.76x\right) + 18.0$ Factor the variable terms so that the coefficient of x^2 is 1.

$f(x) = 0.0763\left(x^2 - 11.76x + \boxed{}\right) + 18.0 - \boxed{}$ Set up for completing the square.

$f(x) = 0.0763\left(x^2 - 11.76x + \boxed{34.5744}\right) + 18.0 - 0.0763 \cdot \boxed{34.5744}$ Complete the square: $\left(\frac{11.76}{2}\right)^2 = \boxed{34.5744}$

$f(x) = 0.0763\left(x - \boxed{5.88}\right)^2 + \boxed{15.4}$ Write the expression in parentheses as a binomial squared. Simplify the product being subtracted, rounding to 3 significant digits.

REFLECT

2a. Based on the vertex form of the equation, what is the approximate vertex of the graph of $f(x)$? Explain how you determined your answer.

(5.88, 15.4); for an equation in vertex form, the coordinates of the vertex

are (h, k). For $f(x)$, $h = 5.88$ and $k = 15.4$.

© Houghton Mifflin Harcourt Publishing Company

2 continued

CC.9-12.F.IF.8 Write a function defined by an expression in different but equivalent forms to reveal and explain different properties of the function.

CC.9-12.F.IF.8a Use the process of ... completing the square in a quadratic function to show ... extreme values ...

CC.9-12.F.BF.1 Write a function that describes a relationship between two quantities.*

CC.9-12.F.BF.1a Determine an explicit expression ... from a context.*

CC.9-12.F.BF.4 Find inverse functions.

CC.9-12.F.BF.4d(+) Produce an invertible function from a non-invertible function by restricting the domain.

Questioning Strategies

- How do you determine the constant term in the trinomial when completing the square? **Divide the coefficient of the x-term by 2 and square the result.**

- Why is the product of 0.0763 and 34.5744, instead of 34.5744, subtracted from the equation? **Because the trinomial is multiplied by 0.0763, the amount added to the trinomial to complete the square, 34.5744, is multiplied by 0.0763, so the product of 0.0763 and 34.5744 must be subtracted to maintain balance.**

- How do you factor the perfect square trinomial into a squared binomial? **The square root of 34.5744 is 5.88 (to three significant digits), and the x-term is negative, so the trinomial factors as $(x - 5.88)^2$.**

3 **Graph and write the inverse of the quadratic model.**

Standards

CC.9-12.A.CED.2 Create equations in two ... variables to represent relationships between quantities; graph equations on coordinate axes with labels and scales.*

CC.9-12.F.IF.2 Use function notation, evaluate functions for inputs in their domains, and interpret statements that use function notation in terms of a context.

CC.9-12.F.IF.4 For a function that models a relationship between two quantities, interpret key features of graphs and tables in terms of the quantities, and sketch graphs showing key features ...*

CC.9-12.F.IF.7 Graph functions expressed symbolically and show key features of the graph ...*

CC.9-12.F.IF.7b Graph square root ... functions.*

CC.9-12.F.BF.1 Write a function that describes a relationship between two quantities.*

CC.9-12.F.BF.1a Determine an explicit expression ... from a context.*

CC.9-12.S.ID.6 Represent data on two quantitative variables on a scatter plot, and describe how the variables are related.*

CC.9-12.S.ID.6a Fit a function to the data ...*

Questioning Strategies

- How do you reflect a point over the line $y = x$? **Switch the x and y coordinates.**

- How do you determine the axis labels in the graph of the inverse function? **Switch the labels for the x- and y-axes in the graph of $f(x)$.**

- Is the graph of $f^{-1}(x)$ a vertical stretch or a vertical shrink of the parent square root function? Explain. **a vertical stretch; because $a > 1$**

MATHEMATICAL PRACTICE | **Highlighting the Standards**

The steps in this lesson address Mathematical Practice Standard 6 (Attend to precision). All of the steps require students to round to 3 significant digits. You may need to review how to determine significant digits. In decimal numbers, zeros to the right of the decimal point, but to the left of the first nonzero digit, are not significant, because they are placeholders. For example, in 0.005060, the two zeros between the decimal point and the 5 are not significant. The other two zeros are significant.

Discuss the balance between using enough digits to give a certain degree of accuracy and using few enough digits to keep the handling of the equations manageable.

In step 3, students round coordinates to the nearest tenth. This rounding should occur only in the final step. Rounding in intermediate steps compromises accuracy by compounding round-off errors.

2b. Do the coordinates you found for the vertex agree with the information in the scatter plot? Explain.

Yes, the data in the scatter plot can be modeled by a parabola with a vertex close to (5.88, 15.4).

2c. Interpret the meaning of the vertex in the context of the problem.

The vertex gives the age (about 5.88 years) at which boys' median BMI is least (about 15.4).

2d. Give the domain of $f(x)$ based on the data set.

$\{x \mid 2 \le x \le 10\}$

3 Graph and write the inverse of the quadratic model.

A Because $f(x)$ is quadratic, it is not one-to-one and its inverse is not a function. Restrict the domain of $f(x)$ to values of x for which $f(x)$ is increasing so that its inverse will be a function. What is the restricted domain of $f(x)$?

$\{x \mid 5.88 \le x \le 10\}$

B Enter the coordinates of the vertex in the first row of the table below. Complete the table of values and use it to graph $f(x)$ with the restricted domain. Round the values of $f(x)$ to the nearest tenth.

x	f(x)
5.88	15.4
7	15.5
8	15.7
9	16.1
10	16.7

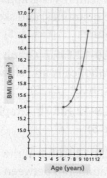

C Find the images of each of the points in the table in part B after reflection over the line $y = x$. Record the coordinates of the points below.

(15.4, 5.88), (15.5, 7), (15.7, 8), (16.1, 9), (16.7, 10)

D Plot the points from part C and draw a smooth curve through them to graph the inverse function, $f^{-1}(x)$.

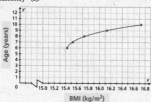

E Write a rule for $f^{-1}(x)$.

$$f(x) = 0.0763\left(x - 5.88\right)^2 + 15.4 \qquad \text{Write equation of } f(x).$$

$$y = 0.0763\left(x - 5.88\right)^2 + 15.4 \qquad \text{Replace } f(x) \text{ with } y.$$

$$y - 15.4 = 0.0763\left(x - 5.88\right)^2 \qquad \text{Subtract 15.4 from both sides.}$$

$$\tfrac{1}{0.0763}\left(y - 15.4\right) = \left(x - 5.88\right)^2 \qquad \text{Divide both sides by 0.0763.}$$

$$\sqrt{\tfrac{1}{0.0763}}\sqrt{y - 15.4} = x - 5.88 \qquad \text{Use the definition of positive square root.}$$

$$\sqrt{\tfrac{1}{0.0763}}\sqrt{y - 15.4} + 5.88 = x \qquad \text{Add 5.88 to both sides.}$$

$$\sqrt{\tfrac{1}{0.0763}}\sqrt{x - 15.4} + 5.88 = y \qquad \text{Switch } x \text{ and } y \text{ to write inverse.}$$

$$3.62\sqrt{x - 15.4} + 5.88 \approx f^{-1}(x) \qquad \text{Simplify and replace } y \text{ with } f^{-1}(x).$$

So, the inverse function is $f^{-1}(x) \approx 3.62\sqrt{x - 15.4} + 5.88$.

REFLECT

3a. The quadratic function $f(x)$ models boys' median BMI as a function of age. What does $f^{-1}(x)$ model?

boy's age as a function of median BMI

Notes

Essential Question

How can you model age as a function of body mass index given a data set?

The graph of BMI as a function of age appears to be parabolic, so use a quadratic regression equation with *x* representing age and *y* representing BMIs. Restrict the domain so that the function is a one-to-one function and then find its inverse, which is a square root function that accepts BMIs as inputs and gives ages as outputs.

Summarize

In their journals, have students explain why they must be able to identify the vertex of the graph of a quadratic function to determine the inverse function.

Standards

CC.9-12.A.CED.2 Create equations in two variables ... to represent relationships between quantities ...* (Ex. 5)

CC.9-12.F.IF.2 Use function notation, evaluate functions for inputs in their domains ... (Exs. 1, 2, 3, 5)

CC.9-12.F.IF.4 For a function that models a relationship between two quantities, interpret key features of graphs and tables in terms of the quantities, and sketch graphs showing key features ...* (Exs. 4, 5)

CC.9-12.F.IF.7 Graph functions expressed symbolically and show key features of the graph ...* (Ex. 5)

CC.9-12.F.IF.7b Graph square root ... functions.* (Ex. 5)

CC.9-12.F.BF.1 Write a function that describes a relationship between two quantities.* (Ex. 5)

CC.9-12.F.BF.1a Determine an explicit expression ... from a context.* (Ex. 5)

CC.9-12.F.BF.4 Find inverse functions. (Ex. 5)

CC.9-12.F.BF.4d(+) Produce an invertible function from a non-invertible function by restricting the domain. (Ex. 5)

3b. Why does it make sense to make the least x-value in the domain of $f(x)$ be 5.88 when finding the inverse function?

5.88 is the x-coordinate of the vertex of the graph of the quadratic model.

The function is one-to-one to the left or right of the vertex.

3c. What are the domain and range of $f(x)$? of $f^{-1}(x)$?

Domain of $f(x)$: $\{x \mid 5.88 \le x \le 10\}$; range of $f(x)$: $\{y \mid 15.4 \le y \le 16.7\}$;

domain of $f^{-1}(x)$: $\{x \mid 15.4 \le x \le 16.7\}$; range of $f^{-1}(x)$: $\{y \mid 5.88 \le y \le 10\}$

3d. Use a graphing calculator to graph $f(x)$, $f^{-1}(x)$, and the line $y = x$ in the same window. How can you use these graphs to check that you found the inverse function correctly?

If the inverse was found correctly, then the two graphs should appear

to be reflections across the line $y = x$.

EXTEND

Use the inverse function $f^{-1}(x)$ to make predictions for Exercises 1 and 2.
(In Exercise 2, allow the domain to include x-values greater than 10.)

1. A boy over the age of 6 has a BMI of 15.9. How old do you expect him to be, to the nearest tenth of a year?

8.4 years old

2. A boy over the age of 6 has a BMI of 20.4. How old do you expect him to be, to the nearest tenth of a year?

14.0 years old

3. Which of your predictions, the one in Exercise 1 or the one in Exercise 2, do you think is more reliable? Explain your reasoning.

The prediction in Exercise 1 is more reliable. The original data set had a maximum

age of 10 years. Because the age in Exercise 2 is outside the age range of the

original data set, it is less likely to be reliable.

4. Over what interval, if any, does the inverse function $f^{-1}(x)$ increase? Over what interval, if any, does it decrease? Does this make sense given what you know about $f(x)$?

The function increases throughout its domain. There is no interval for which it

decreases. Because $f(x)$ increases throughout its restricted domain, it makes sense

that its inverse will also increase throughout its domain.

---

5. The model you found for $f^{-1}(x)$ applies to boys aged 5.88 years or older. Consider how you could change your model so that it applies to boys aged 5.88 years or younger.

a. How else could you restrict the domain of $f(x) = 0.0763(x - 5.88)^2 + 15.4$ to find an inverse that is a function?

Restrict the domain to $2 \le x \le 5.88$.

b. Complete the table of values and use it to graph $f(x)$ with the restricted domain. Round the values of $f(x)$ to the nearest hundredth.

x	$f(x)$
2	16.55
3	16.03
4	15.67
5.88	15.4

BMI (kg/m²) vs Age (years)

c. What is the range of $f(x)$ with the restricted domain?

$15.4 \le y \le 16.55$

d. Graph the inverse of $f(x)$ with the restricted domain. Give the domain and range of the inverse.

Domain:

$15.4 \le x \le 16.55$

Range:

$2 \le y \le 5.88$

Age (years) vs BMI (kg/m²)

e. The equation of $f^{-1}(x)$ when the domain of $f(x)$ is restricted to $\{x \mid 5.88 \le x \le 10\}$ is $f^{-1}(x) = 3.62\sqrt{x - 15.4} + 5.88$. What is the equation of $f^{-1}(x)$ when the domain of $f(x)$ is restricted to $\{x \mid 2 \le x \le 5.88\}$? Explain.

$f^{-1}(x) = -3.62\sqrt{x - 15.4} + 5.88$; writing the rule proceeds exactly as in part

E of step 3, except that you use a negative square root instead of a positive

square root.

Notes

Assign these pages to help your students practice and apply important lesson concepts. For additional exercises, see the Student Edition.

Answers

Additional Practice

1. Exponential

2. Linear

3. Quadratic

4. Square root

5. $f(x) = 2x^2 - 9$

6. $f(x) = -0.4x + 6$

7. $f(x) = 2.18(1.577)^x$

8. $f(x) = 0.816\sqrt{x}$

9. $f(x) = 0.44x^2 + 0.2x + 0.36$

10. $f(x) = 1.318x^{0.378}$

11. **a.** $f(x) = 657.3(1.02)^x$

   b. 1634 people

Problem Solving

1. The independent variable (x) is the year. The dependent variable (y) is the population.

2. Possible answer: The first few points appear to be linear, but the later points start a curve upward. For the data to be linear, the first differences must be constant.

3. **a.** 88, 92, 97, 108, 108, 120

   b. 4, 5, 11, 0, 12

   c. 1, 6, −11, 12

   d. All ratios round to 1.08.

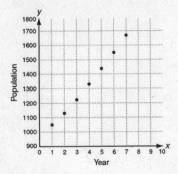

4. Exponential function, because the ratios between y-values are almost constant

5. D   **6.** H

Additional Practice

Use constant differences or ratios to determine which parent function would best model the given data set.

1.

x	12	16	20	24	28
y	0.8	3.6	16.2	72.9	328.05

_____

2.

x	13	19	25	31	37	43
y	−1	17	35	53	71	89

_____

3.

x	2	7	12	17	22
y	−100	−55	40	185	380

_____

4.

x	0.10	0.37	0.82	1.45	2.26
y	0.3	0.6	0.9	1.2	1.5

_____

Write a function that models the data set.

5.

x	2.2	2.6	3.0	3.4	3.8
y	0.68	4.52	9.0	14.12	19.88

_____

6.

x	−5	0	5	10	15	20
y	8	6	4	2	0	−2

_____

7.

x	0.3	0.7	1.1	1.5	1.9
y	2.5	3	3.6	4.32	5.184

_____

8.

x	0.06	0.375	0.96	1.815	2.94
y	0.2	0.5	0.8	1.1	1.4

_____

9.

x	−6	1	8	15	22
y	15	1	30.12	102.36	217.72

_____

10.

x	0.32	2.07	4.8	8.51	13.2
y	0.9	1.6	2.3	3.0	3.7

_____

Solve.

11. The table shows the population growth of a small town.

Years after 1974	1	6	11	16	21	26	31
Population	662	740	825	908	1003	1095	1200

a. Write a function that models the data.

b. Use your model to predict the population in 2020. _____

Problem Solving

The table shows the population of Lincoln Valley over the last 7 years. The town council is developing long-range plans and is considering how the population might grow in the future if the current trend continues.

Lincoln Valley Population 2000–2006						
Year	1	2	3	4	5	6	7
Population	1049	1137	1229	1326	1434	1542	1662

1. What is the independent variable? What is the dependent variable? Assign x or y to each variable.

_____

2. Make a scatter plot of the data. Do the data form a linear pattern? For this to be true, explain what must be true about finite differences.

_____

3. Use the table of data.
   a. Find the first differences.

   b. Find the second differences.

   c. Find the third differences.

   d. Find the ratios between y-values.

4. What kind of function will best describe the data? Justify your conclusion.

_____

Choose the letter for the best answer.

5. Which function best models the given data?

   A $y = 101.9x + 932.1$

   B $y = 3.1x^2 + 77.0x + 969.6$

   C $y = 996.6x^{0.233}$

   D $y = 974.9(1.08)^x$

6. Predict the population of Lincoln Valley in 2012.

   F 2270

   G 2450

   H 2650

   J 2860

Notes

This page provides students with the opportunity to apply concepts from the Common Core in real-world problem situations. There are three different levels of performance tasks:

⭐ **Novice:** These are short word problems that require students to apply the math they have learned in straightforward, real-world situations.

⭐⭐ **Apprentice:** These are more involved problems that guide students step-by-step through more complex tasks. These exercises include more complicated reasoning, writing, and open-ended elements.

⭐⭐⭐ **Expert:** These are open-ended, non-routine problems that, instead of stepping the students through, ask them to choose their own methods for solving and justify their answers and reasoning.

Sample answers

1. For insurance policy A, let the function $f(x) = x - d$ represent your monthly income after the income loss, and let the function $g(x) = x + d$ represent your monthly income after receiving the payment from policy A. Your monthly income would be $g(f(x)) = (x - d) + d = x$. For insurance policy B, let the function $f(x) = (1 - p)(x)$ represent your monthly income after the income loss, and let the function $g(x) = (1 + p)(x)$ represent your monthly income after receiving the payment from policy B. Your monthly income would be $g(f(x)) = (1 + p)((1 - p)(x)) = (1 - p^2)(x)$. Since $1 - p^2$ is less than 1, your monthly income under insurance policy B would be less than that under insurance policy A, so insurance policy A pays out more.

2. The transformations that must be applied to the function $f(t) = e^t$ to produce the function $a(t) = 325e^{-0.2166t}$ are a vertical stretch, a horizontal stretch, and a reflection across the y-axis.

3. Scoring Guide:

Task	Possible points
a	1 point total for correctly writing the three points (0, 0), (1, 15), (2, 24), and 1 point for correctly finding the quadratic function $y = -3x^2 + 18x$
b	1 point for correctly writing the two points (3, 28) and (4, 32), and 1 point for correctly finding the function $y = 4x + 16$
c	1 point for correctly writing the piecewise function: $$y = \begin{cases} -3x^2 + 18x & \text{if } 0 \le x \le 2 \\ 4x + 16 & \text{if } x > 2 \end{cases}$$ 1 point for correctly noting that both parts of the piecewise function give a result of (2, 24)

Total possible points: 6

Name_____ Class_____ Date_____

Performance Tasks

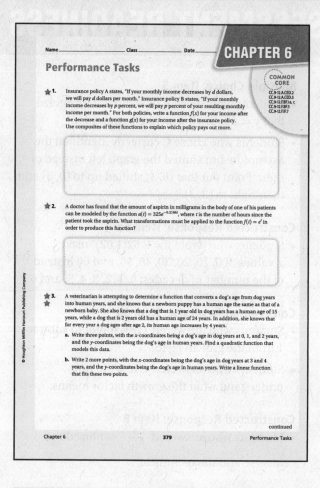

★ 1. Insurance policy A states, "If your monthly income decreases by d dollars, we will pay d dollars per month." Insurance policy B states, "If your monthly income decreases by p percent, we will pay p percent of your resulting monthly income per month." For both policies, write a function $f(x)$ for your income after the decrease and a function $g(x)$ for your income after the insurance policy. Use composites of these functions to explain which policy pays out more.

CC.9-12.A.CED.2
CC.9-12.A.CED.3
CC.9-12.F.BF.1a, c
CC.9-12.F.BF.3
CC.9-12.F.IF.7

★ 2. A doctor has found that the amount of aspirin in milligrams in the body of one of his patients can be modeled by the function $a(t) = 325e^{-0.2166t}$, where t is the number of hours since the patient took the aspirin. What transformations must be applied to the function $f(t) = e^t$ in order to produce this function?

★ 3. A veterinarian is attempting to determine a function that converts a dog's age from dog years into human years, and she knows that a newborn puppy has a human age the same as that of a newborn baby. She also knows that a dog that is 1 year old in dog years has a human age of 15 years, while a dog that is 2 years old has a human age of 24 years. In addition, she knows that for every year a dog ages after age 2, its human age increases by 4 years.

a. Write three points, with the x-coordinates being a dog's age in dog years at 0, 1, and 2 years, and the y-coordinates being the dog's age in human years. Find a quadratic function that models this data.

b. Write 2 more points, with the x-coordinates being the dog's age in dog years at 3 and 4 years, and the y-coordinates being the dog's age in human years. Write a linear function that fits these two points.

continued

© Houghton Mifflin Harcourt Publishing Company

---

c. Write a piecewise function that converts a dog's age in dog years into human years. Does it matter which part of the function you use to convert 2 dog years into human years? Why or why not?

★ 4. A single person's federal income tax bracket is determined by his or her taxable income as shown in the table.

2011 Federal Income Tax Brackets	
Tax Rate	Taxable Income
10%	$0 to $8,500
15%	$8,500 to $34,500
25%	$34,500 to $83,600
28%	$83,600 to $174,400
33%	$174,400 to $379,150
35%	$379,150 and above

a. A person with $50,000 in taxable income pays 10% on the income up to $8,500, 15% on the income between $8,500 and $34,500, and 25% on the income between $34,500 and $50,000. How much would the person pay in income tax?

b. Write a piecewise function $T(n)$ that can be used to calculate the amount of federal income tax owed based on taxable income. Then use the function to verify the amount of income tax you calculated in part **a**, showing your work.

c. What percentage of their entire income would a person with $50,000 in taxable income actually pay in income tax?

© Houghton Mifflin Harcourt Publishing Company

---

4. Scoring Guide:

Task	Possible points
a	1 point for correctly calculating and adding the amount of income tax paid at the 10% rate, the 15% rate, and the 25% rate to determine the amount paid in income tax: $850 + $3,900 + $3,875 = $8,625
b	3 points for correctly writing the piecewise function: $T(n) =$ $\begin{cases} 0.1n & \text{if } n \leq 8,500 \\ 0.15(n - 8,500) + 850 & \text{if } 8,500 < n \leq 34,500 \\ 0.25(n - 34,500) + 4,750 & \text{if } 34,500 < n \leq 83,600 \\ 0.28(n - 83,600) + 17,025 & \text{if } 83,600 < n \leq 174,400 \\ 0.33(n - 174,400) + 42,449 & \text{if } 174,400 < n \leq 379,150 \\ 0.35(n - 379,150) + 110,016.5 & \text{if } n > 379,150 \end{cases}$ 1 point for correctly verifying the amount of income tax calculated in part **a**: $T(50,000) = 0.25(50,000 - 34,500) + 4,750$ $= 0.25(15,500) + 4,750$ $= 3,875 + 4,750$ $= \$8,625$
c	1 point for correctly calculating the percentage a person with $50,000 in taxable income would actually pay in income tax: $\dfrac{8,625}{50,000} = 0.1725 = 17.25\%$

Total possible points: 6

COMMON CORE CORRELATION

Standard	Items
CC.9-12.A.SSE.3c	6
CC.9-12.A.CED.2*	6, 7
CC.9-12.F.IF.2	7
CC.9-12.F.IF.7b*	4, 7
CC.9-12.F.IF.8b	6
CC.9-12.F.IF.9	2
CC.9-12.F.BF.1*	3, 7
CC.9-12.F.BF.1b	1
CC.9-12.F.BF.3	5
CC.9-12.F.BF.4d(+)	3, 8
CC.9-12.S.ID.6a*	6
CC.9-12.S.ID.6b*	6

TEST PREP DOCTOR ⊕

Multiple Choice: Item 3

- Students who chose **A** found a by dividing 1 by 4.9, but they forgot to take the square root of the result.
- Students who chose **C** found a by taking the square root of 4.9.
- Students who chose **D** used the value of a from the original function.

Multiple Choice: Item 4

- Students who chose **F** confused the general shapes of the graphs of a square root function and cube root function.
- Students who chose **H** read the coordinates in (8, 2) in the reverse order.
- Students who chose **J** took the reciprocal instead of the inverse of the parent cubic function.

Multiple Choice: Item 5

- Students who chose **A** or **D** did not recognize that $y = 2$ is the horizontal asymptote.
- Students who chose **C** correctly identified the asymptote but shifted the graph left instead of right. Point out that (0, 1) shifted up to (0, 3) and then right to (3, 3).

Constructed Response: Item 6a

- Students who wrote $y = 2.62(1.02)^x$ used x-values of 0, 10, 20, 30, 40, 50, and 60 instead of the number of decades: 0, 1, 2, 3, 4, 5, and 6.

Constructed Response: Item 6b

- Students who answered 118% forgot to subtract 1 from the growth factor.
- Students who answered 1.18% did not understand what the growth factor means.

Constructed Response: Item 8

- Students who answered $\frac{1}{x^2 + 3}$ confused the inverse and the reciprocal.

Name _____ Class _____ Date _____

MULTIPLE CHOICE

1. Given $f(x) = -5x - 2$ and $g(x) = 2x - 7$, find $h(x) = f(x) - g(x)$.

   A. $h(x) = -3x - 9$

   B. $h(x) = -7x - 9$

   C. $h(x) = -7x + 5$

   D. $h(x) = -7x - 5$

2. You graph the function $f(x) = 300(1.015)^x$, which gives the total amount in your account after x years of interest that is compounded annually. The function $g(x)$ gives the amount in your account if you make the same initial investment, but at a rate of interest of 2.3% compounded annually. How would the graph of $g(x)$ compare to the graph of $f(x)$?

   F. It would have the same y-intercept, but rise more quickly over time.

   G. It would have the same y-intercept, but rise less quickly over time.

   H. It would have a greater y-intercept and rise more quickly over time.

   J. It would have a greater y-intercept and rise less quickly over time.

3. The function $d(t) = 4.9t^2$ models the distance in meters an object falls after t seconds where $t \geq 0$. Which function $t(d)$ best models the time in seconds that it will take an object to fall d meters?

   A. $t(d) = 0.20\sqrt{d}$

   B. $t(d) = 0.45\sqrt{d}$

   C. $t(d) = 2.2\sqrt{d}$

   D. $t(d) = 4.9\sqrt{d}$

4. Which function is graphed below?

   F. $f(x) = \sqrt{x}$ H. $f(x) = x^3$

   G. $f(x) = \sqrt[3]{x}$ J. $f(x) = \dfrac{1}{x^3}$

5. The graph below is a horizontal and vertical translation of the graph of $f(x) = \left(\frac{3}{4}\right)^x$.

   What is the equation of the graph?

   A. $y = \left(\frac{3}{4}\right)^{x-2} + 3$ C. $y = \left(\frac{3}{4}\right)^{x+3} + 2$

   B. $y = \left(\frac{3}{4}\right)^{x-3} + 2$ D. $y = \left(\frac{3}{4}\right)^{x+2} + 3$

CONSTRUCTED RESPONSE

6. The table shows the total world population from 1950 to 2010 according to data from the U.S. Census Bureau.

Year	Population (in billions)
1950	2.6
1960	3.0
1970	3.7
1980	4.5
1990	5.3
2000	6.1
2010	6.9

   a. Find the exponential regression equation, using the number of decades since 1950 as x-values. Round the values of a and b to two decimal places.

   $y = 2.62(1.18)^x$

   b. What is the population's growth rate? Tell how you know.

   18% per decade because 1.18 is the growth factor $1 + r$, so $r = 0.18$.

   c. Show how to transform the equation to find the annual growth rate.

   $y = 2.62\left(1.18^{\frac{1}{10}}\right)^{10x} \rightarrow$

   $y = 2.62(1.017)^{10x}$; the annual growth rate is about 1.7%.

   d. Do you think the exponential model is a good fit for the data? Use residuals to explain.

   Yes; the residuals are all relatively close to 0. (They are approximately:

   $-0.02, -0.10, 0.03, 0.16, 0.17, 0.03,$

   -0.29.)

   e. Would you use the model to predict the world population in the year 3000? Explain.

   No; exponential functions grow very quickly and a prediction that far beyond the given data would likely be much too high.

7. A taxicab driver charges $6.00 for any distance less than 1 mile. For distances of 1 mile or more, he charges $6.00 plus $3.00 for each complete mile.

   a. Write the equation for the function $C(d)$, which gives the cost C (in dollars) of riding in the taxicab for a distance d (in miles).

   $C(d) = 6 + 3[\![d]\!]$

   b. Graph the function to show the costs for all distances less than 5 miles. Include labels and scales on your graph.

8. Find the inverse function of $f(x) = x^2 + 3$ by using algebra. Include any necessary restrictions on the domain of $f(x)$.

   Restrict the domain of $f(x)$ to $x \geq 0$.

   $f(x) = x^2 + 3 \rightarrow y = x^2 + 3$

   $y - 3 = x^2$

   $\sqrt{y - 3} = x$

   Switch x and y to write the inverse:

   $\sqrt{x - 3} = y$. So, $f^{-1}(x) = \sqrt{x - 3}$.

© Houghton Mifflin Harcourt Publishing Company

CHAPTER 7

Probability

CHAPTER 7

Probability

Chapter Focus
Probability theory is the branch of mathematics concerned with situations involving chance. You will learn how to use set theory to help you calculate basic probabilities and will investigate the role of permutations and combinations in probability. You will also learn how to determine the probability of mutually exclusive events, overlapping events, independent events, and dependent events. Along the way, you will perform simulations.

Chapter at a Glance

COMMON CORE

Lesson		Standards for Mathematical Content
7-1	Permutations and Combinations	CC.9-12.S.CP.9(+)
7-2	Theoretical and Experimental Probability	CC.9-12.S.MD.6(+)
7-3	Independent and Dependent Events	CC.9-12.S.CP.2, CC.9-12.S.CP.3, CC.9-12.S.CP.4, CC.9-12.S.CP.8(+)
7-4	Two-Way Tables	CC.9-12.S.CP.3, CC.9-12.S.CP.6
7-5	Compound Events	CC.9-12.S.CP.7
	Performance Tasks	
	Assessment Readiness	

CHAPTER 7

Chapter 7   383   Probability

COMMON CORE PROFESSIONAL DEVELOPMENT **CC.9-12.S.CP.9(+)***

In previous courses, students listed the elements of a sample space using tables, organized lists, and diagrams, and found probability using the ratio of the number of favorable outcomes to total number of possible outcomes. In this chapter, students take a more sophisticated approach to probability by identifying patterns used to develop formulas. These include permutations and combinations formulas, as well as formulas for conditional probability, probability of mutually exclusive and overlapping events, and the Addition Rule.

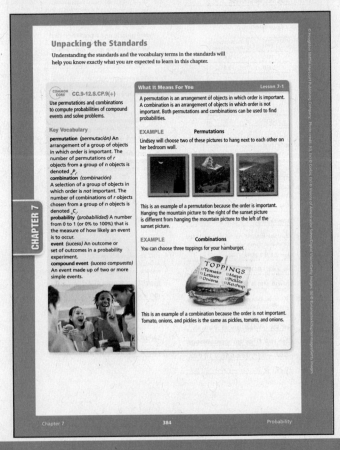

Unpacking the Standards
Understanding the standards and the vocabulary terms in the standards will help you know exactly what you are expected to learn in this chapter.

COMMON CORE **CC.9-12.S.CP.9(+)**
Use permutations and combinations to compute probabilities of compound events and solve problems.

Key Vocabulary
permutation *(permutación)* An arrangement of a group of objects in which order is important. The number of permutations of r objects from a group of n objects is denoted $_nP_r$.
combination *(combinación)* A selection of a group of objects in which order is *not* important. The number of combinations of r objects chosen from a group of n objects is denoted $_nC_r$.
probability *(probabilidad)* A number from 0 to 1 (or 0% to 100%) that is the measure of how likely an event is to occur.
event *(suceso)* An outcome or set of outcomes in a probability experiment.
compound event *(suceso compuesto)* An event made up of two or more simple events.

What It Means For You   Lesson 7-1
A permutation is an arrangement of objects in which order is important. A combination is an arrangement of objects in which order is not important. Both permutations and combinations can be used to find probabilities.

EXAMPLE   **Permutations**
Lindsey will choose two of these pictures to hang next to each other on her bedroom wall.

This is an example of a permutation because the order is important. Hanging the mountain picture to the right of the sunset picture is different from hanging the mountain picture to the left of the sunset picture.

EXAMPLE   **Combinations**
You can choose three toppings for your hamburger.

TOPPINGS
Tomato   Mayo
Lettuce Pickles
Onions   Ketchup

This is an example of a combination because the order is not important. Tomato, onions, and pickles is the same as pickles, tomato, and onions.

CHAPTER 7

Chapter 7   384   Probability

CC.9-12.S.CP.4*

Students have studied relationships in bivariate data by plotting ordered pairs in a coordinate plane to create a scatter plot. In a two-way table, the variables are categorical and quantities are frequencies. In this chapter, students will use two-way tables to organize data categorized by two variables. Students can use two-way tables to calculate or to approximate conditional probability, and to develop a formula for conditional probability.

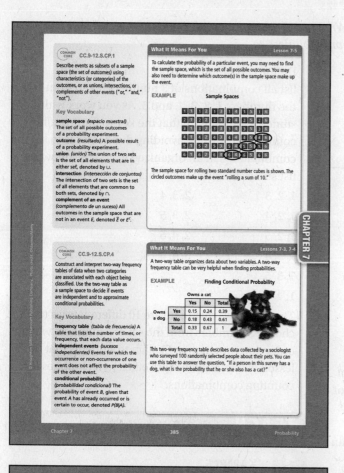

CC.9-12.S.CP.1

Describe events as subsets of a sample space (the set of outcomes) using characteristics (or categories) of the outcomes, or as unions, intersections, or complements of other events ("or," "and," "not").

Key Vocabulary

sample space *(espacio muestral)* The set of all possible outcomes of a probability experiment.
outcome *(resultado)* A possible result of a probability experiment.
union *(unión)* The union of two sets is the set of all elements that are in either set, denoted by ∪.
intersection *(intersección de conjuntos)* The intersection of two sets is the set of all elements that are in common to both sets, denoted by ∩.
complement of an event *(complemento de un suceso)* All outcomes in the sample space that are not in an event *E*, denoted $\bar{E}$ or E^c.

What It Means For You Lesson 7-5

To calculate the probability of a particular event, you may need to find the sample space, which is the set of all possible outcomes. You may also need to determine which outcome(s) in the sample space make up the event.

EXAMPLE **Sample Spaces**

The sample space for rolling two standard number cubes is shown. The circled outcomes make up the event "rolling a sum of 10."

CC.9-12.S.CP.4

Construct and interpret two-way frequency tables of data when two categories are associated with each object being classified. Use the two-way table as a sample space to decide if events are independent and to approximate conditional probabilities.

Key Vocabulary

frequency table *(tabla de frecuencia)* A table that lists the number of times, or frequency, that each data value occurs.
independent events *(sucesos independientes)* Events for which the occurrence or non-occurrence of one event does not affect the probability of the other event.
conditional probability *(probabilidad condicional)* The probability of event *B*, given that event *A* has already occurred or is certain to occur, denoted *P*(*B*|*A*).

What It Means For You Lessons 7-3, 7-4

A two-way table organizes data about two variables. A two-way frequency table can be very helpful when finding probabilities.

EXAMPLE **Finding Conditional Probability**

	Owns a cat		
	Yes	No	Total
Owns a dog Yes	0.15	0.24	0.39
No	0.18	0.43	0.61
Total	0.33	0.67	1

This two-way frequency table describes data collected by a sociologist who surveyed 100 randomly selected people about their pets. You can use this table to answer the question, "If a person in this survey has a dog, what is the probability that he or she also has a cat?"

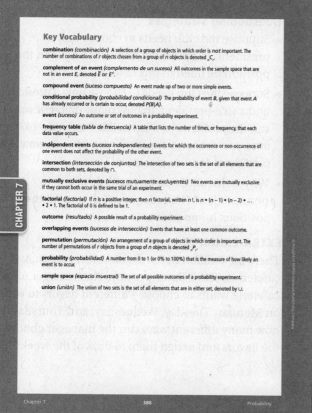

Key Vocabulary

combination *(combinación)* A selection of a group of objects in which order is *not* important. The number of combinations of *r* objects chosen from a group of *n* objects is denoted $_nC_r$.

complement of an event *(complemento de un suceso)* All outcomes in the sample space that are not in an event *E*, denoted $\bar{E}$ or E^c.

compound event *(suceso compuesto)* An event made up of two or more simple events.

conditional probability *(probabilidad condicional)* The probability of event *B*, given that event *A* has already occurred or is certain to occur, denoted *P*(*B*|*A*).

event *(suceso)* An outcome or set of outcomes in a probability experiment.

frequency table *(tabla de frecuencia)* A table that lists the number of times, or frequency, that each data value occurs.

independent events *(sucesos independientes)* Events for which the occurrence or non-occurrence of one event does not affect the probability of the other event.

intersection *(intersección de conjuntos)* The intersection of two sets is the set of all elements that are common to both sets, denoted by ∩.

mutually exclusive events *(sucesos mutuamente excluyentes)* Two events are mutually exclusive if they cannot both occur in the same trial of an experiment.

factorial *(factorial)* If *n* is a positive integer, then *n* factorial, written *n* !, is $n \cdot (n-1) \cdot (n-2) \cdot \ldots \cdot 2 \cdot 1$. The factorial of 0 is defined to be 1.

outcome *(resultado)* A possible result of a probability experiment.

overlapping events *(sucesos de intersección)* Events that have at least one common outcome.

permutation *(permutación)* An arrangement of a group of objects in which order is important. The number of permutations of *r* objects from a group of *n* objects is denoted $_nP_r$.

probability *(probabilidad)* A number from 0 to 1 (or 0% to 100%) that is the measure of how likely an event is to occur.

sample space *(espacio muestral)* The set of all possible outcomes of a probability experiment.

union *(unión)* The union of two sets is the set of all elements that are in either set, denoted by ∪.

Permutations and Combinations
Going Deeper

Essential question: *What are permutations and combinations and how can you use them to calculate probabilities?*

:::: COMMON **Standards for**
: CORE : **Mathematical Content**
::::

CC.9-12.S.CP.9(+) Use permutations and combinations to compute probabilities of compound events and solve problems.*

Vocabulary
permutation

factorial

combination

Prerequisites
Probability and set theory

Permutations and probability

Math Background
A compound event is an event that consists of more than one outcome. To find the probability of a compound event, find the ratio of the number of outcomes in the event to the number of outcomes in the sample space. Counting the number of outcomes in the event and in the sample space can often be the most challenging part of calculating a probability. Permutations and combinations are two tools for counting outcomes.

INTRODUCE

Define *permutation*. Work with students to list all permutations of the numbers 1, 2, and 3. You may want to construct a tree diagram as shown below. The diagram shows that there are 6 different permutations of the numbers.

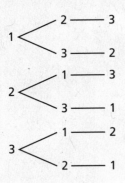

Define *combination*. Work with students to list all combinations of 3 numbers taken from the numbers 1, 2, 3, 4, and 5. As you work with students, emphasize that the key to finding all combinations while avoiding duplicates is to list the combinations in an organized way. The following list shows one way to do this:

1, 2, 3	2, 3, 4
1, 2, 4	2, 3, 5
1, 2, 5	2, 4, 5
1, 3, 4	3, 4, 5
1, 3, 5	
1, 4, 5	

The list shows that there are 10 different ways to choose 3 numbers from the set of 5 numbers when order does not matter. Explain to students that this lesson will introduce more efficient techniques for counting combinations.

TEACH

1 EXAMPLE

Questioning Strategies
- Suppose the club needs to choose only a president. In how many different ways can the position be filled in this case? **7**
- Suppose the club needs to choose only a president and a vice-president. In how many different ways can the positions be filled in this case? Why? **42; once you choose a president, you have 6 remaining candidates for vice-president.**
- Why is this situation an example of a permutation? **The order in which you fill the positions is important.**

EXTRA EXAMPLE
There are 6 different flavors of frozen yogurt. A cafeteria offers 1 flavor per day. The manager of the cafeteria wants to choose 4 different flavors to serve on Monday, Tuesday, Wednesday, and Thursday. In how many different ways can the manager choose the flavors and assign them to days of the week? **360**

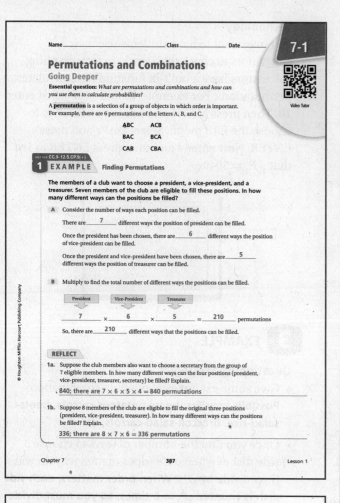

Name_____ Class_____ Date_____

7-1

Video Tutor

Permutations and Combinations
Going Deeper

Essential question: *What are permutations and combinations and how can you use them to calculate probabilities?*

A **permutation** is a selection of a group of objects in which order is important. For example, there are 6 permutations of the letters A, B, and C.

ABC	ACB
BAC	BCA
CAB	CBA

PREP FOR CC.9-12.S.CP.9(+)

1 EXAMPLE Finding Permutations

The members of a club want to choose a president, a vice-president, and a treasurer. Seven members of the club are eligible to fill these positions. In how many different ways can the positions be filled?

A Consider the number of ways each position can be filled.

There are ___7___ different ways the position of president can be filled.

Once the president has been chosen, there are ___6___ different ways the position of vice-president can be filled.

Once the president and vice-president have been chosen, there are ___5___ different ways the position of treasurer can be filled.

B Multiply to find the total number of different ways the positions can be filled.

President	Vice-President	Treasurer

___7___ × ___6___ × ___5___ = ___210___ permutations

So, there are ___210___ different ways that the positions can be filled.

REFLECT

1a. Suppose the club members also want to choose a secretary from the group of 7 eligible members. In how many different ways can the four positions (president, vice-president, treasurer, secretary) be filled? Explain.

840; there are 7 × 6 × 5 × 4 = 840 permutations

1b. Suppose 8 members of the club are eligible to fill the original three positions (president, vice-president, treasurer). In how many different ways can the positions be filled? Explain.

336; there are 8 × 7 × 6 = 336 permutations

© Houghton Mifflin Harcourt Publishing Company

The process you used in the example can be generalized to give a formula for permutations. To do so, it is helpful to use factorials. For a positive integer n, n **factorial**, written $n!$, is defined as follows.

$$n! = n \cdot (n-1) \cdot (n-2) \cdot \ldots \cdot 3 \cdot 2 \cdot 1$$

That is, $n!$ is the product of n and all the positive integers less than n. Note that $0!$ is defined to be 1.

In the example, the number of permutations of 7 objects taken 3 at a time is

$$7 \cdot 6 \cdot 5 = \frac{7 \cdot 6 \cdot 5 \cdot 4 \cdot 3 \cdot 2 \cdot 1}{4 \cdot 3 \cdot 2 \cdot 1} = \frac{7!}{4!} = \frac{7!}{(7-3)!}.$$

This can be generalized as follows.

Permutations

The number of permutations of n objects taken r at a time is given by

$$_nP_r = \frac{n!}{(n-r)!}.$$

Recall that the probability of an event is equal to the number of outcomes that result in the event, divided by the number of all possible outcomes.

CC.9-12.S.CP.9(+)

2 EXAMPLE Using Permutations to Calculate a Probability

Every student at your school is assigned a four-digit code, such as 6953, to access the computer system. In each code, no digit is repeated. What is the probability that you are assigned a code with the digits 1, 2, 3, and 4 in any order?

A Let S be the sample space. Find $n(S)$.

The sample space consists of all permutations of 4 digits taken from the 10 digits 0 through 9.

$$n(S) = {}_{10}P_4 = \frac{10!}{(10-4)!} = \frac{10!}{6!} = \frac{10 \cdot 9 \cdot 8 \cdot 7 \cdot 6 \cdot 5 \cdot 4 \cdot 3 \cdot 2 \cdot 1}{6 \cdot 5 \cdot 4 \cdot 3 \cdot 2 \cdot 1} = \underline{5040}$$

B Let A be the event that your code has the digits 1, 2, 3, and 4. Find $n(A)$.

The event consists of all permutations of 4 digits chosen from the 4 digits 1 through 4.

$$n(A) = {}_4P_4 = \frac{4!}{(4-4)!} = \frac{4!}{0!} = \frac{4 \cdot 3 \cdot 2 \cdot 1}{1} = \underline{24}$$

C Find $P(A)$.

$$P(A) = \frac{n(A)}{n(S)} = \frac{24}{5040} = \frac{1}{210}$$

So, the probability that your code has the digits 1, 2, 3, and 4 is ___$\frac{1}{210}$___.

© Houghton Mifflin Harcourt Publishing Company

You may want to have students use their calculators to check their work. In fact, graphing calculators have a built-in function that calculates permutations. For example, to find $_{10}P_4$, first enter 10. Then press MATH and use the arrow keys to choose the PRB menu. Select **2:nPr** and press ENTER. Now enter 4 and then press ENTER to see that $_{10}P_4 = 5040$.

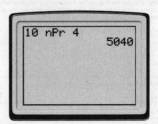

MATHEMATICAL PRACTICE — Highlighting the Standards

The process of developing a formula for permutations is a good opportunity to address Standard 8 (Look for and express regularity in repeated reasoning). Have students calculate the number of permutations in various situations "by hand"; that is, by reasoning about the situation and using multiplication, as in the first example. Then ask students what patterns they notice. A common element of every solution should be the product of a string of descending, consecutive integers. Once students have been introduced to factorial notation, the formula for the number of permutations of n objects taken r at a time should seem natural.

3 EXAMPLE

Questioning Strategies

• Give some examples of possible combinations. **Possible answers: beets-potatoes-carrots, beets-salad-rice, broccoli-salad-carrots, etc.**

• Once you find the number of ways to choose 3 side dishes when order does matter, why do you then divide by $_3P_3$? **When order matters, each side dish is counted $_3P_3 = 6$ times, so you must divide by 6 to count each combination just once.**

EXTRA EXAMPLE

A winner on a game show gets to choose 4 prize boxes from a set of 10 prize boxes. In how many different ways can the contestant choose 4 prize boxes? **210**

Teaching Strategies

You may wish to show students a different way of solving the problem in the first example. There are 8 choices for the first side dish, 7 choices for the second side dish, and 6 choices for the third side dish. This is $8 \times 7 \times 6 = 336$ possibilities. However, each combination is counted $3! = 6$ times, so the number of combinations is $336 \div 6 = 56$.

2 EXAMPLE

Questioning Strategies

• What are some examples of four-digit codes in the sample space? **Possible answers: 7421, 9605, 7534**

• Is the code 4878 in the sample space? Why or why not? **No; no digit may be repeated in a code.**

• What are some examples of four-digit codes in event A? **Possible answers: 1234, 2314, 4231**

• Is the code 4215 in event A? Why or why not? **No; codes in event A consist of the digits 1, 2, 3, and 4 in any order.**

EXTRA EXAMPLE

To buy concert tickets at a Web site, you must first type a random code consisting of 5 letters, such as JQBKN. (This prevents computer programs from purchasing the tickets.) In each code, no letter is repeated. When you buy concert tickets at the Web site, what is the probability that your code will consist of the letters A, E, I, O, and U in any order? $\frac{1}{65,780}$

REFLECT

2a. What is the probability that you are assigned the code 1234? Explain.

$\frac{1}{5040}$; in this case $n(A) = 1$, so $P(A) = \frac{n(A)}{n(S)} = \frac{1}{5040}$.

A **combination** is a grouping of objects in which order does not matter. For example, when you choose 3 letters from the letters A, B, C, and D, there are 4 different combinations.

ABC   ABD   ACD   BCD

PREP FOR CC.9-12.S.CP.9(+)

3 EXAMPLE   Finding Combinations

A restaurant offers 8 side dishes. When you order an entree, you can choose 3 of the side dishes. In how many ways can you choose 3 side dishes?

Side Dishes	
Beets	Rice
Potatoes	Broccoli
Carrots	Cole slaw
Salad	Apple sauce

A   First find the number of ways to choose 3 sides dishes when order does matter. This is the number of permutations of 8 objects taken 3 at a time.

$_8P_3 = \frac{8!}{(8-3)!} = \frac{8!}{5!} = \frac{8 \cdot 7 \cdot 6 \cdot \cancel{5} \cdot \cancel{4} \cdot \cancel{3} \cdot \cancel{2} \cdot \cancel{1}}{\cancel{5} \cdot \cancel{4} \cdot \cancel{3} \cdot \cancel{2} \cdot \cancel{1}} = \underline{336}$

B   In this problem, order does not matter, since choosing beets, carrots, and rice is the same as choosing rice, beets, and carrots.

Divide the result from Step A by $_3P_3$, which is the number of ways the 3 side dishes can be ordered.

$_3P_3 = \frac{3!}{(3-3)!} = \frac{3!}{0!} = \underline{6}$

So, the number of ways you can choose 3 side dishes is $\frac{336}{6} = \underline{56}$.

REFLECT

3a.   Suppose the restaurant offers a special on Mondays that allows you to choose 4 side dishes. In how many ways can you choose the side dishes?

_____ 70 _____

3b.   In general, are there more ways or fewer ways to select objects when order does not matter? Why?

Fewer; when order does not matter, multiple selections are counted as the same

combination.

The process you used in the example can be generalized to give a formula for combinations. In order to find $_8C_3$, the number of combinations of 8 objects taken 3 at a time, you first found the number of permutations of 8 objects taken 3 at a time, then you divided by 3! That is,

$$_8C_3 = \frac{8!}{(8-3)!} \div 3! \text{ or } \frac{8!}{3!(8-3)!}.$$

This can be generalized as follows.

Combinations

The number of combinations of n objects taken r at a time is given by

$_nC_r = \frac{n!}{r!(n-r)!}$.

CC.9-12.S.CP.9(+)

4 EXAMPLE   Using Combinations to Calculate a Probability

There are 5 boys and 6 girls in a school play. The director randomly chooses 3 of the students to meet with a costume designer. What is the probability that the director chooses all boys?

A   Let S be the sample space. Find $n(S)$.

The sample space consists of all combinations of 3 students taken from the group of 11 students.

$n(S) = {}_{11}C_3 = \frac{11!}{3!(11-3)!} = \frac{11!}{3! \cdot 8!} = \frac{11 \cdot 10 \cdot 9 \cdot \cancel{8} \cdot \cancel{7} \cdot \cancel{6} \cdot \cancel{5} \cdot \cancel{4} \cdot \cancel{3} \cdot \cancel{2} \cdot \cancel{1}}{3 \cdot 2 \cdot 1 \cdot \cancel{8} \cdot \cancel{7} \cdot \cancel{6} \cdot \cancel{5} \cdot \cancel{4} \cdot \cancel{3} \cdot \cancel{2} \cdot \cancel{1}} = \underline{165}$

B   Let A be the event that the director chooses all boys. Find $n(A)$.

Suppose the 11 students are $B_1, B_2, B_3, B_4, B_5, G_1, G_2, G_3, G_4, G_5, G_6$, where the Bs represent boys and the Gs represent girls.

The combinations in event A are combinations like $B_2B_4B_5$ and $B_1B_3B_4$. That is, event A consists of all combinations of 3 boys taken from the set of 5 boys.

So, $n(A) = {}_5C_3 = \frac{5!}{3!(5-3)!} = \frac{5!}{3! \cdot 2!} = \frac{5 \cdot 4 \cdot \cancel{3} \cdot \cancel{2} \cdot \cancel{1}}{\cancel{3} \cdot \cancel{2} \cdot \cancel{1} \cdot 2 \cdot 1} = \underline{10}$

C   Find $P(A)$.

$P(A) = \frac{n(A)}{n(S)} = \frac{10}{165} = \underline{\frac{2}{33}}$

So, the probability that the director chooses all boys is $\underline{\frac{2}{33}}$.

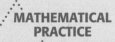

MATHEMATICAL PRACTICE

Highlighting the Standards

To address Standard 7 (Look for and make use of structure) ask students to explain how the formula for the number of combinations of n objects taken r at a time is related to the formula for the number of permutations of n objects taken r at a time. Students should see that the number of permutations divided by $r!$ is equal to the number of combinations.

4 EXAMPLE

Questioning Strategies

• Does this problem involve permutations or combinations? Why? Combinations; the order in which the students are chosen does not matter.

• Based on your answer, is the director likely to choose all boys? Explain. No; this is not likely, since the probability is only $\frac{2}{33}$.

EXTRA EXAMPLE

A box contains 4 bottles of orange juice and 5 bottles of grapefruit juice. You randomly choose 3 of the bottles to serve at a school breakfast. What is the probability that you choose 3 bottles of grapefruit juice? $\frac{5}{42}$

Teaching Strategies

You might want to revisit the example once students have learned about the probability of dependent events. At that point, students will have another way to solve the problem. Specifically, the probability of choosing 3 boys is the probability that the first student is a boy times the probability that the second student is a boy given that the first student was a boy times the probability that the third student is a boy given that the first two students were boys. This probability is $\frac{5}{11} \cdot \frac{4}{10} \cdot \frac{3}{9} = \frac{2}{33}$.

CLOSE

Essential Question

What are permutations and combinations and how can you use them to calculate probabilities?
A permutation is a selection of a group of objects in which order is important. You can use permutations to find the number of outcomes in a sample space and/or the number of outcomes in an event.

A combination is a grouping of objects in which order does not matter. You can use combinations to find the number of outcomes in a sample space and/or the number of outcomes in an event.

Summarize

Have students make graphic organizers to summarize what they know about permutations and what they know about combinations. Samples are shown.

Definition	Example
A permutation is a selection of a group of objects in which order is important.	Permutations of A, B, and C: ABC ACB BAC BCA CAB CBA

Permutations

Formula	Factorials
$_nP_r = \dfrac{n!}{(n-r)!}$	n factorial ($n!$) is the product of n and all the positive integers less than n. 0! is 1.

Definition	Example
A combination is a grouping of objects in which order does not matter.	Combinations of 2 letters from A, B, C, and D: AB AC AD BC BD CD

Combinations

Formula	Factorials
$_nC_r = \dfrac{n!}{r!(n-r)!}$	n factorial ($n!$) is the product of n and all the positive integers less than n. 0! is 1.

PRACTICE

Where skills are taught	Where skills are practiced
1 EXAMPLE	EXS. 1–4
2 EXAMPLE	EXS. 5–6
3 EXAMPLE	EXS. 8–9
4 EXAMPLE	EXS. 10–13

Exercise 7: Students apply what they learned to critique another student's work.

Exercises 14–15: Students use reasoning to state a generalization about combinations.

REFLECT

4a. Is the director more likely to choose all boys or all girls? Why?

All girls; $_6C_3 = 20$, so $P(\text{all girls}) = \frac{20}{165} = \frac{4}{33}$, which is greater than the

probability of choosing all boys, $\frac{2}{33}$

PRACTICE

1. An MP3 player has a playlist with 12 songs. You select the shuffle option for the playlist. In how many different orders can the songs be played?

479,001,600

2. There are 10 runners in a race. Medals are awarded for 1st, 2nd, and 3rd place. In how many different ways can the medals be awarded?

720

3. There are 9 players on a baseball team. In how many different ways can the coach choose players for first base, second base, third base, and shortstop?

3024

4. You have 15 photographs of your school. In how many different ways can you arrange 6 of them in a line for the cover of the school yearbook?

3,603,600

5. A bag contains 9 tiles, each with a different number from 1 to 9. You choose a tile, put it aside, choose a second tile, put it aside, and then choose a third tile. What is the probability that you choose tiles with the numbers 1, 2, and 3 in that order?

$\frac{1}{362,880}$

6. There are 11 students on a committee. To decide which 3 of these students will attend a conference, 3 names are chosen at random by pulling names one at a time from a hat. What is the probability that Sarah, Jamal, and Mai are chosen in any order?

$\frac{1}{165}$

7. **Error Analysis** A student solved the problem at right. The student's work is shown. Did the student make an error? If so, explain the error and provide the correct answer.

The student made an error; $n(A)$

should be 1 since the tiles must

appear in the order B-E-A-D. The

correct probability is $\frac{1}{360}$.

A bag contains 6 tiles with the letters A, B, C, D, E, and F. You choose 4 tiles one at a time without looking and line up the tiles as you choose them. What is the probability that your tiles spell BEAD?

Let S be the sample space and let A be the event that the tiles spell BEAD.

$n(S) = {}_6P_4 = \frac{6!}{(6-4)!} = \frac{6!}{2!} = 360$

$n(A) = {}_4P_4 = \frac{4!}{(4-4)!} = \frac{4!}{0!} = 4! = 24$

So, $P(A) = \frac{n(A)}{n(S)} = \frac{24}{360} = \frac{1}{15}$

8. A cat has a litter of 6 kittens. You plan to adopt 2 of the kittens. In how many ways can you choose 2 of the kittens from the litter?

15

9. An amusement park has 11 roller coasters. In how many ways can you choose 4 of the roller coasters to ride during your visit to the park?

330

10. A school has 5 Spanish teachers and 4 French teachers. The school's principal randomly chooses 2 of the teachers to attend a conference. What is the probability that the principal chooses 2 Spanish teachers?

$\frac{5}{18}$

11. There are 6 fiction books and 8 nonfiction books on a reading list. Your teacher randomly assigns you 4 books to read over the summer. What is the probability that you are assigned all nonfiction books?

$\frac{10}{143}$

12. A bag contains 26 tiles, each with a different letter of the alphabet written on it. You choose 3 tiles from the bag without looking. What is the probability that you choose the tiles containing the letters A, B, and C?

$\frac{1}{2600}$

13. You are randomly assigned a password consisting of 6 different characters chosen from the digits 0 to 9 and the letters A to Z. As a percent, what is the probability that you are assigned a password consisting of only letters?

$\approx 11.8\%$

14. Calculate $_{10}C_6$ and $_{10}C_4$.

a. What do you notice about these values? Explain why this makes sense.

$_{10}C_6 = {}_{10}C_4 = 210$; it makes sense that these values are equal because every

combination of 6 objects that are selected has a corresponding combination

of 4 objects that are not selected.

b. Use your observations to help you state a generalization about combinations.

In general, $_nC_r = {}_nC_{n-r}$.

15. Use the formula for combinations to make a generalization about $_nC_n$. Explain why this makes sense.

Using the formula for combinations and the fact that $0! = 1$, $_nC_n = \frac{n!}{n!(n-n)!} =$

$\frac{n!}{n!(0!)} = \frac{n!}{n!} = 1$; this makes sense because there is only 1 combination of n objects

taken n at a time.

© Houghton Mifflin Harcourt Publishing Company

Assign these pages to help your students practice and apply important lesson concepts. For additional exercises, see the Student Edition.

Answers

Additional Practice

1. 8 T-shirts   **2.** 24 packages

3. 720   **4.** 720

5. 60,360   **6.** 90 ways

7. 2184 ways   **8.** 120

9. 3   **10.** 336

11. a. 91 ways

   b. 462 ways

   c. 2300 ways

Problem Solving

1. a. $12 \times 11 \times 10 = 1320$

   b. Permutation; possible answer: the order of the 3 numbers matters.

2. a. 720 codes

   b. 5040 codes

   c. 151,200 codes

3. a. 78 ways

   b. Combination; possible answer: the order in which she chooses the locks does not matter.

4. Because order matters, *combination locks* represent permutations.

5. C   **6.** J

Additional Practice

Use the Fundamental Counting Principle.

1. The soccer team is silk-screening T-shirts. They have 4 different colors of T-shirts and 2 different colors of ink. How many different T-shirts can be made using one ink color on a T-shirt? _____

2. A travel agent is offering a vacation package. Participants choose the type of tour, a meal plan, and a hotel class from the table below.

Tour	Meal	Hotel
Walking	Restaurant	4-Star
Boat	Picnic	3-Star
Bicycle		2-Star
		1-Star

How many different vacation packages are offered? _____

Evaluate.

3. $\dfrac{3!6!}{3!}$

4. $\dfrac{10!}{7!}$

5. $\dfrac{9!-6!}{(9-6)!}$

Solve.

6. In how many ways can the debate team choose a president and a secretary if there are 10 people on the team? _____

7. A teacher is passing out first-, second-, and third-place prizes for the best student actor in a production of *Hamlet*. If there are 14 students in the class, in how many different ways can the awards be presented? _____

Evaluate.

8. $_5P_4$

9. $_3C_2$

10. $_8P_3$

Solve.

11. Mrs. Marshall has 11 boys and 14 girls in her kindergarten class this year.

a. In how many ways can she select 2 girls to pass out a snack? _____

b. In how many ways can she select 5 boys to pass out new books? _____

c. In how many ways can she select 3 students to carry papers to the office? _____

Problem Solving

Rosalie is looking at locks. The label *combination lock* confuses her. She wonders about the number of possible permutations or combinations a lock can have.

1. She looks at one circular lock with 12 positions. To open it she turns the dial clockwise to a first position, then counterclockwise to a second position, then clockwise to a third position

a. Write an expression for the number of 3-position codes that are possible, if no position is repeated.

_____

b. Explain how this represents a combination or a permutation.

_____

2. Rosalie looks at cable locks. Each position can be set from 0 to 9. How many different codes are possible for each lock if no digits are repeated in each code?

a. a 3-digit cable lock

_____

b. a 4-digit cable lock

_____

c. a 6-digit cable lock

_____

3. Rosalie needs 2 cable locks, but there are 13 types of locks to choose from.

a. In how many ways can she choose 2 different locks? _____

b. Explain how this represents a permutation or a combination.

_____

4. Explain why you think Rosalie might be confused by the label *combination lock*.

_____

Rosalie wants to lock her bicycle near the library. There are 7 slots still open in the bike rack. Choose the letter for the best answer.

5. Rosalie arrives at the same time as 2 other cyclists. In how many ways can they arrange their bikes in the open slots?

A 7   C 210
B 35   D 343

6. Suppose Rosalie arrived just ahead of the 2 other cyclists and selected a slot. In how many ways can the others arrange their bikes in the open slots?

F 2   H 24
G 15   J 30

Theoretical and Experimental Probability
Connection: Making Fair Decisions

Essential question: *How can you use probability to help you make fair decisions?*

Standards for Mathematical Content

CC.9-12.S.MD.6(+) Use probabilities to make fair decisions (e.g., drawing by lots, using a random number generator).*

Prerequisites
Probability and Set Theory

Math Background
Students have already considered the connection between probability and fair decision-making. In this lesson, they investigate the connection between these ideas from a somewhat different perspective. The scenario presented in this lesson is based on the famous "Problem of Points," which was originally investigated by the French mathematicians Blaise Pascal and Pierre de Fermat in 1654.

INTRODUCE

Remind students that they have already seen an example of the role probability can play in making fair decisions. Previously, students used probability to help them simulate choosing a random sample and a convenience sample. Explain that in this lesson, students will use probability to determine how a game prize should be divided between two competitors.

TEACH

1 ENGAGE

Questioning Strategies
- At the start, does one student have a greater chance of winning than the other? Explain. No; both students have an equal chance of winning since the game depends solely upon chance and since each student has an equal chance of winning each coin toss.
- What is the greatest number of coin tosses that might be needed to play the game from start to finish? 39

2 EXPLORE

Questioning Strategies
- How can you make an organized list of all possible results of 4 coin tosses? First, assume there are no tails among the 4 tosses; then, assume there is 1 tail among the 4 tosses and put it in each of the possible positions; then, assume there are 2 tails; and so on.
- How many different outcomes of 4 coin tosses are there? 16

MATHEMATICAL PRACTICE **Highlighting the Standards**

To address Standard 5 (Use appropriate tools strategically) you might have students think about how they can use their calculators to simulate the remainder of the game between Lee and Rory. Students can use the calculator's random-number generator to simulate flipping a coin (1 = heads, 2 = tails), keep track of their results, and pool their findings with those of other students. Over the course of many trials, students should find that their simulations lead to a win for Lee about $\frac{11}{16}$ of the time and a win for Rory about $\frac{5}{16}$ of the time.

CLOSE

Essential Question
How can you use probability to help you make fair decisions? You can use probability to help determine how a game prize should be divided between two equally-skilled players when the game is interrupted before someone has won.

Summarize
Have students write a journal entry in which they summarize the Problem of Points and explain how probability is used to solve the problem.

Name_____ Class_____ Date_____

7-2

Theoretical and Experimental Probability
Connection: Making Fair Decisions

Essential question: *How can you use probability to help you make fair decisions?*

Probability theory arose from a need to make decisions fairly. In fact, the decision-making situation that you will investigate in this lesson is based on a famous problem that was studied by the French mathematicians Blaise Pascal and Pierre de Fermat in the 17th century. Their work on the problem launched the branch of mathematics now known as probability.

Video Tutor

PREP FOR CC.9-12.S.MD.6(+)

1 ENGAGE   Introducing the Problem of Points

Two students, Lee and Rory, find a box containing 100 baseball cards. To determine who should get the cards, they decide to play a game with the rules shown at right.

As Lee and Rory are playing the game they get interrupted and are unable to continue. When they are interrupted, Lee has 18 points and Rory has 17 points.

How should the 100 baseball cards be divided between the students given that the game was interrupted at this moment? This is known as the "Problem of Points."

> **Game Rules**
> - One of the students repeatedly tosses a coin.
> - When the coin lands heads up, Lee gets a point.
> - When the coin lands tails up, Rory gets a point.
> - The first student to reach 20 points wins the game and gets the baseball cards.

REFLECT

1a. Which student has a greater probability of winning the game if it were to continue until someone reaches 20 points? Why?

Lee has a greater probability of winning since Lee needs only 2 more points, while Rory still needs 3.

1b. If the students divide the baseball cards between themselves, which student do you think should get a greater number of cards? Why?

Lee should get a greater number of cards, because Lee had a greater number of points when the game was interrupted.

1c. Describe one way you might divide the baseball cards between Lee and Rory.

Possible answer: Since a total of 35 points were scored, Lee should get $\frac{18}{35}$ of the cards (i.e., 51 cards) and Rory should get $\frac{17}{35}$ of the cards (i.e., 49 cards).

© Houghton Mifflin Harcourt Publishing Company

Chapter 7   395   Lesson 2

You may have decided that it would be fair to divide the baseball cards in proportion to the number of points each student scored, as summarized at right.

However, this solution doesn't work well if the game is interrupted very early. If Rory won the first point and ended the game, it would not be fair to give Rory all the cards just because Rory had 1 point and Lee had 0 points.

The following solution is the one proposed by Blaise Pascal and Pierre de Fermat.

> **One Method of Dividing the Cards**
> - A total of $17 + 18 = 35$ points were scored.
> - Lee scored 18 points, so Lee gets $\frac{18}{35}$ of the cards.
> - Rory scored 17 points, so Rory gets $\frac{17}{35}$ of the cards.

CC.9-12.S.MD.6(+)

2 EXPLORE   Solving the Problem of Points

Consider the different ways the game might have continued if it had not been interrupted.

A What is the maximum number of coin tosses that would have been needed for someone to win the game?   **4**

B Make an organized list to show all possible results of these coin tosses. The list has been started below. Look for patterns to help you complete the list.
(H = heads; T = Tails)

0T, 4H	1T, 3H	2T, 2H	3T, 1H	4T, 0H
HHHH	THHH	TTHH	TTTH	TTTT
	HTHH	THTH	TTHT	
	HHTH	THHT	THTT	
	HHHT	HTTH	HTTT	
		HTHT		
		HHTT		

C Circle the above outcomes in which Lee wins the game.

In how many outcomes would Lee win?   **11**

In how many outcomes would Rory win?   **5**

D What is the probability that Lee would have won had the game continued? $\frac{11}{16}$

What is the probability that Rory would have won had the game continued? $\frac{5}{16}$

REFLECT

2a. Based on your work in the Explore, what do you think is a fair way to divide the baseball cards?

Lee should get $\frac{11}{16}$ of the cards (i.e., 69 cards) and Rory should get $\frac{5}{16}$ of the cards (i.e., 31 cards).

© Houghton Mifflin Harcourt Publishing Company

Chapter 7   396   Lesson 2

Assign these pages to help your students practice and apply important lesson concepts. For additional exercises, see the Student Edition.

Answers

Additional Practice

1. five tosses

2. $2^5 = 32$

3.

0P, 5B	1P, 4B	2P, 3B	3P, 2B	4P, 1B	5P, 0B
BBBBB	PBBBB	PPBBB	PPPBB	PPPPB	PPPPP
	BPBBB	PBPBB	PPBPB	PPPBP	
	BBPBB	PBBPB	PBPPB	PPBPP	
	BBBPB	PBBBP	BPPPB	PBPPP	
	BBBBP	BPPBB	PPBBP	BPPPP	
		BPBPB	PBPBP		
		BPBBP	BPPBP		
		BBPPB	PBBPP		
		BBPBP	BPBPP		
		BBBPP	BBPPP		

4. Yes, because each is a sequence of equally-likely coin flips.

5. Pierre $\dfrac{6}{32} = \dfrac{3}{16}$, Blaise $\dfrac{26}{32} = \dfrac{13}{16}$

6. $\dfrac{{}_5C_5 + {}_5C_4 + {}_5C_3 + {}_5C_2}{(\text{\# of possible outcomes})} = \dfrac{1 + 5 + 10 + 10}{32} = \dfrac{13}{16}$

Problem Solving

1. $\dfrac{2}{3}$

2. $\dfrac{2}{3}$

3. Pierre must win four consecutive rolls, before Blaise wins one roll.

4. *PPPP, PPPB, PPB, PB, B*

5. Because the probabilities of each are not equal

6.
$$PPPP = \left(\dfrac{1}{3}\right)^4 = \dfrac{1}{81}$$
$$PPPB = \left(\dfrac{1}{3}\right)^3 \cdot \dfrac{2}{3} = \dfrac{2}{81}$$
$$PPB = \left(\dfrac{1}{3}\right)^2 \cdot \dfrac{2}{3} = \dfrac{2}{27}$$
$$PB = \dfrac{1}{3} \cdot \dfrac{2}{3} = \dfrac{2}{9}$$
$$B = \dfrac{2}{3}$$

7. $\dfrac{1}{81}$

Additional Practice

Solve.

1. A fruit bowl contains 4 green apples and 7 red apples. What is the probability that a randomly selected apple will be green? _____

2. When two number cubes labeled 1–6 are rolled, what is the probability that the result will be two 4's? _____

3. Joanne is guessing which day in November is Bess's birthday. Joanne knows that Bess's birthday does not fall on an odd-numbered day. What is the probability that Joanne will guess the correct day on her first try? _____

4. Tom has a dollar's worth of dimes and a dollar's worth of nickels in his pocket.

    a. What is the probability he will randomly select a nickel from his pocket? _____

    b. What is the probability he will randomly select a dime from his pocket? _____

5. Clarice has 7 new CDs; 3 are classical music and the rest are pop music. If she randomly grabs 3 CDs to listen to in the car on her way to school, what is the probability that she will select only classical music? _____

6. Find the probability that a point chosen at random inside the larger circle shown here will also fall inside the smaller circle.

_____

Frank is playing darts. The results of his throws are shown in the table below. Assume that his results continue to follow this trend.

Color Hit	Number of Throws
Blue	12
Red	5
White	2

Find the experimental probability of each event.

7. Frank's next throw will hit white. _____

8. Frank's next throw will hit blue. _____

9. Frank's next throw will hit either red or white. _____

10. Frank's next throw will NOT hit red. _____

Problem Solving

As part of a grant to improve bus routes to and from school, Hogan and Jane gather traffic flow statistics for one intersection. They make a table to show their findings for between 7:45 A.M. and 8:00 A.M. on a Monday morning.

1. Analyze the statistics.

    a. Write and evaluate an expression for $P(N)$, the probability that a vehicle will turn north.

    _____

    b. Write and evaluate an expression for the probability that a vehicle will turn north or go straight through the intersection.

    _____

    c. Write and evaluate an expression for the probability that a vehicle will not turn north.

    _____

Traffic Direction	Number of Vehicles
Straight through	282
Turn north	94
Turn south	188

2. The police department gathers statistics on Tuesday. Officers count a total of 608 vehicles, of which 380 go straight through the intersection, 76 turn north, and the rest turn south.

    a. What is the probability that a vehicle will turn north? _____

    b. What is the probability that a vehicle will turn north or go straight through the intersection? _____

    c. What is the probability that a vehicle will not turn north? _____

3. Does this represent theoretical or experimental probability? Explain.

Math Assessment Survey

Activity	Group Projects	Keep a Journal	Multiple Choice	Word Problems
Student Response	57	18	35	10

A teacher surveys students on how they would prefer to have work assessed in math class. Choose the letter for the best answer.

4. What is the probability that a randomly chosen student prefers assessment through a group project?

    A $\frac{1}{12}$ C $\frac{19}{40}$

    B $\frac{53}{120}$ D $\frac{21}{40}$

5. Which expression gives the probability that a randomly chosen student will not want multiple-choice questions?

    F $\frac{7}{24}$ H $1 - \frac{7}{24}$

    G $1 + \frac{7}{24}$ J $35 - \frac{7}{24}$

Notes

Independent and Dependent Events
Going Deeper

Essential question: *How do you find the probability of independent and dependent events?*

⋯⋯⋯
COMMON Standards for
CORE Mathematical Content
⋯⋯⋯

CC.9-12.S.CP.2 Understand that two events *A* and *B* are independent if the probability of *A* and *B* occurring together is the product of their probabilities, and use this characterization to determine if they are independent.*

CC.9-12.S.CP.3 … interpret independence of *A* and *B* as saying that the conditional probability of *A* given *B* is the same as the probability of *A*, and the conditional probability of *B* given *A* is the same as the probability of *B*.*

CC.9-12.S.CP.4 Construct and interpret two-way frequency tables of data when two categories are associated with each object being classified. Use the two-way table as a sample space to decide if events are independent ….*

CC.9-12.S.CP.5 Recognize and explain the concept of … independence in everyday language and everyday situations.*

CC.9-12.S.CP.8(+) Apply the general Multiplication Rule in a uniform probability model, $P(A \text{ and } B) = P(A)\,P(B\,|\,A) = P(B)\,P(A\,|\,B)$, and interpret the answer in terms of the model.*

Vocabulary
independent events

dependent events

Prerequisites
Probability and Set Theory

Conditional Probability

Independent Events

Math Background
In this lesson, students learn two different ways to identify independent events. For two events *A* and *B*, if $P(A) = P(A\,|\,B)$, then the events are independent. Also, if $P(A \text{ and } B) = P(A) \cdot P(B)$, then the events are independent.

Then students use what they have learned about conditional probability to develop the Multiplication Rule. This rule can be used to find the probability of dependent events.

INTRODUCE

Define *independent events*. Ask students to suggest examples of independent events. Be sure to discuss examples from everyday life, such as the event that it is cloudy tomorrow and the event that there is a math test tomorrow. The events are independent since the occurrence of one event does not affect the occurrence of the other.

Define *dependent events*. To illustrate the difference between independent events and dependent events, discuss two different ways of choosing two colored marbles from a bag: 1) with replacement and 2) without replacement.

When you choose with replacement, you select the first marble, note its color, and put the marble back in the bag before choosing the second marble. In this case, the two selections are independent events. The sample space for the two events is the same.

When you choose without replacement, you select the first marble, put it aside, and then choose the second marble. In this case, the two selections are dependent events because the marble you choose first changes the sample space for your second selection.

TEACH

 EXAMPLE

Questioning Strategies
• What percent of all flights are late? Where do you find this information? **10%; look at the bottom row of the table.**

• What percent of all domestic flights are late? Where do you find this information? **10%; look at the "Domestic Flight" row of the table.**

• What percent of all international flights are late? Where do you find this information? **10%; Look at the "International Flight" row of the table.**

continued

Name_____ Class_____ Date_____

7-3

Independent and Dependent Events
Going Deeper

Essential question: *How do you find the probability of independent and dependent events?*

Two events are **independent events** if the occurrence of one event does not affect the occurrence of the other event. For example, rolling a 1 on a number cube and choosing an ace at random from a deck of cards are independent events.

If two events *A* and *B* are independent events, then the fact that event *B* has occurred does not affect the probability of event *A*. In other words, for independent events *A* and *B*, $P(A) = P(A \mid B)$. You can use this as a criterion to determine whether two events are independent.

CC.9-12.S.CP.4

1 EXAMPLE Determining If Events are Independent

An airport employee collects data on 180 random flights that arrive at the airport. The data is shown in the two-way table. Is a late arrival independent of the flight being an international flight? Why or why not?

	Late Arrival	On Time	TOTAL
Domestic Flight	12	108	120
International Flight	6	54	60
TOTAL	18	162	180

A Let event *A* be the event that a flight arrives late. Let event *B* be the event that a flight is an international flight.

To find $P(A)$, first note that there is a total of ___180___ flights.

Of these flights, there is a total of ___18___ late flights.

So, $P(A) = \dfrac{18}{180} = $ ___10%___

To find $P(A \mid B)$, first note that there is a total of ___60___ international flights.

Of these flights, there is a total of ___6___ late flights.

So, $P(A \mid B) = \dfrac{6}{60} = $ ___10%___

B Compare $P(A)$ and $P(A \mid B)$.

So, a late arrival is independent of the flight being an international flight because

___$P(A) = P(A \mid B)$, which means that events A and B are independent events.___

REFLECT

1a. In the example, you compared $P(A)$ and $P(A \mid B)$. Suppose you compare $P(B)$ and $P(B \mid A)$. What do you find? What does this tell you?

___$P(B) = P(B \mid A) = 33.3\%$; this also shows A and B are independent events.___

Chapter 7   399   Lesson 3

© Houghton Mifflin Harcourt Publishing Company

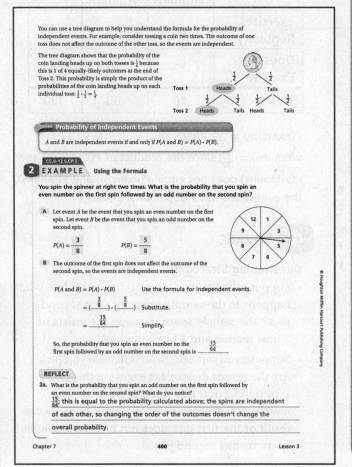

You can use a tree diagram to help you understand the formula for the probability of independent events. For example, consider tossing a coin two times. The outcome of one toss does not affect the outcome of the other toss, so the events are independent.

The tree diagram shows that the probability of the coin landing heads up on both tosses is $\frac{1}{4}$ because this is 1 of 4 equally-likely outcomes at the end of Toss 2. This probability is simply the product of the probabilities of the coin landing heads up on each individual toss: $\frac{1}{2} \cdot \frac{1}{2} = \frac{1}{4}$.

Probability of Independent Events

A and *B* are independent events if and only if $P(A \text{ and } B) = P(A) \cdot P(B)$.

CC.9-12.S.CP.3

2 EXAMPLE Using the Formula

You spin the spinner at right two times. What is the probability that you spin an even number on the first spin followed by an odd number on the second spin?

A Let event *A* be the event that you spin an even number on the first spin. Let event *B* be the event that you spin an odd number on the second spin.

$$P(A) = \frac{3}{8} \qquad P(B) = \frac{5}{8}$$

B The outcome of the first spin does not affect the outcome of the second spin, so the events are independent events.

$P(A \text{ and } B) = P(A) \cdot P(B)$ Use the formula for independent events.

$= \left(\dfrac{3}{8}\right) \cdot \left(\dfrac{5}{8}\right)$ Substitute.

$= \dfrac{15}{64}$ Simplify.

So, the probability that you spin an even number on the first spin followed by an odd number on the second spin is $\dfrac{15}{64}$.

REFLECT

2a. What is the probability that you spin an odd number on the first spin followed by an even number on the second spin? What do you notice?

___$\frac{15}{64}$; this is equal to the probability calculated above; the spins are independent___

___of each other, so changing the order of the outcomes doesn't change the___

___overall probability.___

Chapter 7   400   Lesson 3

© Houghton Mifflin Harcourt Publishing Company

EXTRA EXAMPLE

A doctor collects data on 120 randomly-chosen patients. The data are shown in the two-way table. Is taking vitamins independent of exercising regularly? Why or why not?

	Takes Vitamins	No Vitamins	TOTAL
Exercises Regularly	28	48	76
Does Not Exercise	12	32	44
TOTAL	40	80	120

No; the events are not independent because P(exercise) does not equal P(exercise|vitamins).

MATHEMATICAL PRACTICE   **Highlighting the Standards**

Standard 6 (Attend to precision) states that mathematically proficient students "try to use clear definitions in discussion with others." Have students communicate their results from this lesson orally and in writing. Ask them to check that they are using terms correctly. In particular, be sure students understand that the word *independent* has a specific meaning in probability theory that may be different from its meaning in everyday conversation.

---

2   EXAMPLE

Questioning Strategies

• What is the sample space for each spin? {1, 3, 5, 6, 7, 8, 9, 12}

• On any given spin, are you more likely to spin an even number or an odd number? Why? Odd; 5 of the 8 numbers on the spinner are odd.

• Why are the events in this problem independent events? The outcome of the first spin does not affect the outcome of the second spin.

EXTRA EXAMPLE

A number cube has the numbers 3, 5, 6, 8, 10, and 12 on its faces. You roll the number cube twice. What is the probability that you roll an odd number on both rolls? $\frac{1}{9}$

Avoid Common Errors

Students sometimes confuse independent events and mutually exclusive events. This may lead students to add the probabilities of event A and event B in the second example. If students do add the probabilities, they will find that $P(A) + P(B) = 1$, which would mean that $A \cap B$ is a certainty. This result, which does not make sense in the context of the problem, should alert students that they may have made an error.

3   EXAMPLE

Questioning Strategies

• Which column or row of the table do you look at to calculate $P(A)$? the bottom row of the table

• Which column or row of the table do you look at to calculate $P(B)$? the right-most column of the table

EXTRA EXAMPLE

The two-way table shows the data from the first extra example. Show that a patient taking vitamins and a patient exercising regularly are not independent events.

	Takes Vitamins	No Vitamins	TOTAL
Exercises Regularly	28	48	76
Does Not Exercise	12	32	44
TOTAL	40	80	120

P(exercise) $= \frac{19}{30}$; P(vitamins) $= \frac{1}{3}$; P(exercise and vitamins) $= \frac{7}{30}$; since the product of P(exercise) and P(vitamins) does not equal P(exercise and vitamins), the events are not independent events.

4   ENGAGE

Questioning Strategies

• Suppose the first marble you choose is blue. What happens to the sample space for your second pick? The sample space changes; it consists of 1 blue marble and 2 black marbles.

• Suppose you replace the first marble you pick. Are the events dependent events in this case? Why or why not? No; if you replace the first marble, the events are independent because the result of the first pick does not affect the sample space for the second pick.

The formula for the probability of independent events gives you another way to determine whether two events are independent. That is, two events A and B are independent events if $P(A \text{ and } B) = P(A) \cdot P(B)$.

3 EXAMPLE Showing that Events are Independent

The two-way table shows the data from the first example. Show that a flight arriving on time and a flight being a domestic flight are independent events.

	Late Arrival	On Time	TOTAL
Domestic Flight	12	108	120
International Flight	6	54	60
TOTAL	18	162	180

A Let event A be the event that a flight arrives on time. Let event B be the event that a flight is a domestic flight.

To find $P(A)$, $P(B)$, and $P(A \text{ and } B)$ note that there is a total of __180__ flights.

There is a total of __162__ on-time flights.

So, $P(A) = \dfrac{162}{180} = \dfrac{9}{10}$.

There is a total of __120__ domestic flights.

So, $P(B) = \dfrac{120}{180} = \dfrac{2}{3}$.

There is a total of __108__ on-time domestic flights.

So, $P(A \text{ and } B) = \dfrac{108}{180} = \dfrac{3}{5}$.

B Compare $P(A \text{ and } B)$ and $P(A) \cdot P(B)$.

$P(A) \cdot P(B) = (\dfrac{9}{10}) \cdot (\dfrac{2}{3}) = \dfrac{3}{5}$

So, the events are independent events because

$P(A \text{ and } B) = P(A) \cdot P(B)$.

REFLECT

3a. Describe a different way you can show that a flight arriving on time and a flight being a domestic flight are independent events.

Let events A and B be as in the example and show that $P(A) = P(A \mid B)$.

---

4 ENGAGE Introducing Dependent Events

Two events are **dependent events** if the occurrence of one event affects the occurrence of the other event.

Suppose you have a bag containing 2 blue marbles and 2 black marbles. You choose a marble without looking, put it aside, and then choose a second marble. Consider the following events.

Event A: The first marble you choose is blue.

Event B: The second marble you choose is black.

Events A and B are dependent events, because the marble you choose for your first pick changes the sample space for your second pick. That is, the occurrence of event A affects the probability of event B.

Recall that you developed the following formula for conditional probability.

$$P(B \mid A) = \dfrac{P(A \text{ and } B)}{P(A)}$$

Multiplying both sides by $P(A)$ results in $P(A) \cdot P(B \mid A) = P(A \text{ and } B)$. This is known as the Multiplication Rule.

Multiplication Rule

$P(A \text{ and } B) = P(A) \cdot P(B \mid A)$, where $P(B \mid A)$ is the conditional probability of event B, given that event A has occurred.

You can use the Multiplication Rule to find the probability of dependent or independent events. Note that when A and B are independent events, $P(B \mid A) = P(B)$ and the rule may be rewritten as $P(A \text{ and } B) = P(A) \cdot P(B)$, which is the rule for independent events.

REFLECT

4a. How can you write the Multiplication Rule in a different way by starting with the formula for the conditional probability $P(A \mid B)$ and multiplying both sides of that equation by $P(B)$?

$P(A \mid B) = \dfrac{P(A \text{ and } B)}{P(B)}$; multiplying both sides by $P(B)$ results in

$P(A \text{ and } B) = P(B) \cdot P(A \mid B)$.

5 EXAMPLE Finding the Probability of Dependent Events

There are 5 tiles with the letters A, B, C, D, and E in a bag. You choose a tile without looking, put it aside, and then choose another tile. Find the probability that you choose a consonant followed by a vowel.

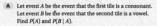

A Let event A be the event that the first tile is a consonant.
Let event B be the event that the second tile is a vowel.
Find $P(A)$ and $P(B \mid A)$.

$P(A) = \dfrac{3}{5}$ Of the 5 tiles, 3 are consonants.

© Houghton Mifflin Harcourt Publishing Company

Notes

Questioning Strategies

• Why are these events dependent events? **The tile you choose first changes the sample space for your second pick. That is, the occurrence of event A affects the probability of event B.**

• How many consonants and vowels are in the bag? **3 consonants, 2 vowels**

EXTRA EXAMPLE
You choose a marble at random from the bag shown here. You put the marble aside and then choose another marble. Find the probability that you choose a gray marble followed by a blue marble. $\frac{4}{15}$

Teaching Strategies
The student page shows two different ways to determine the probability: 1) by using the formula for the Multiplication Rule and 2) by making a tree diagram. Students can also determine the probability by thinking about permutations. The number of outcomes in the sample space is $_5P_2 = 20$. The number of favorable outcomes (that is, outcomes consisting of a consonant followed by a vowel) is $3 \cdot 2 = 6$, since there are 3 consonants and 2 vowels in the bag. Thus, the required probability is $\frac{6}{20}$, or $\frac{3}{10}$.

MATHEMATICAL PRACTICE **Highlighting the Standards**

Standard 1 (Make sense of problems and persevere in solving them) discusses the need for students to plan a "solution pathway" when they are confronted with a new problem. The example in this lesson can serve as an illustration to students that a single problem may have many correct solution pathways. If possible, take some time to discuss the pros and cons of the various methods so that students will feel more confident in choosing a solution pathway the next time they see a similar problem.

CLOSE

Essential Question
How do you find the probability of independent and dependent events? Use the Multiplication Rule: $P(A \text{ and } B) = P(A) \cdot P(B \mid A)$, where $P(B \mid A)$ is the conditional probability of event B, given that event A has occurred.
For independent events, $P(B \mid A) = P(B)$

Summarize
Have students make a graphic organizer or chart in which they summarize the probability formulas that apply to independent events and dependent events. A sample is shown below.

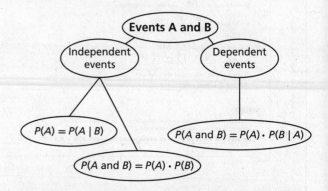

PRACTICE

Where skills are taught	Where skills are practiced
1 EXAMPLE	EX. 1
3 EXAMPLE	EX. 2
5 EXAMPLE	EX. 3–6

$P(B \mid A) = \dfrac{2}{4} = \dfrac{1}{2}$ Of the 4 remaining tiles, 2 are vowels.

B Use the Multiplication Rule.

$P(A \text{ and } B) = P(A) \cdot P(B \mid A)$ Use the Multiplication Rule.

$= \left(\dfrac{3}{5} \right) \cdot \left(\dfrac{1}{2} \right)$ Substitute.

$= \dfrac{3}{10}$ Multiply.

So, the probability that you choose a consonant followed by a vowel is $\dfrac{3}{10}$.

REFLECT

5a. Complete the tree diagram below. Then explain how you can use it to check your answer.

1st tile

2nd tile B C   D E A C   D E A B   D E A B   C E A B   C D

The tree diagram has 20 "branches" and 6 of these (circled) correspond to a

consonant followed by a vowel; so, the probability of a consonant followed

by a vowel is $\dfrac{6}{20} = \dfrac{3}{10}$.

5b. What does your answer tell you about the likelihood of choosing a consonant followed by a vowel?

The outcome is unlikely (it will theoretically occur 30% of the time).

PRACTICE

1. A farmer wants to know if an insecticide is effective in preventing small insects called aphids from living on tomato plants. The farmer checks 80 plants. The data is shown in the two-way table. Is having aphids independent of being sprayed with the insecticide? Why or why not?

	Has Aphids	No Aphids	TOTAL
Was sprayed with insecticide	12	40	52
Was not sprayed with insecticide	14	14	28
TOTAL	26	54	80

No; $P(\text{aphids}) = \dfrac{26}{80} = 32.5\%$ and $P(\text{aphids} \mid \text{insecticide}) = \dfrac{12}{52} \approx 23\%$; since these

probabilities are not equal, the events are not independent.

2. A student wants to know if right-handed people are more or less likely to play a musical instrument than left-handed people. The student collects data from 250 people, as shown in the two-way table. Show that being right handed and playing a musical instrument are independent events.

	Right Handed	Left Handed	TOTAL
Plays a musical instrument	44	6	50
Does not play a musical instrument	176	24	200
TOTAL	220	30	250

$P(\text{right}) = \dfrac{220}{250} = \dfrac{22}{25}$; $P(\text{plays}) = \dfrac{50}{250} = \dfrac{1}{5}$; $P(\text{right and plays}) = \dfrac{44}{250} = \dfrac{22}{125}$;

since $P(\text{right}) \cdot P(\text{plays}) = P(\text{right and plays})$, the events are independent.

3. A basket contains 6 bottles of apple juice and 8 bottles of grape juice. You choose a bottle without looking, put it aside, and then choose another bottle. What is the probability that you choose a bottle of apple juice followed by a bottle of grape juice?

$\dfrac{6}{14} \cdot \dfrac{8}{13} = \dfrac{24}{91}$

4. You have a set of ten cards that are numbered 1 through 10. You shuffle the cards and choose a card at random. You put the card aside and choose another card. What is the probability that you choose an even number followed by an odd number?

$\dfrac{5}{10} \cdot \dfrac{5}{9} = \dfrac{5}{18}$

5. There are 12 boys and 14 girls in Ms. Garcia's class. She chooses a student at random to solve a geometry problem at the board. Then she chooses another student at random to check the first student's work. Is she more likely to choose a boy followed by a girl, a girl followed by a boy, or are these both equally likely? Explain.

Equally likely; the probability of a boy followed by a girl is $\dfrac{12}{26} \cdot \dfrac{14}{25} = \dfrac{84}{325}$;

the probability of a girl followed by a boy is $\dfrac{14}{26} \cdot \dfrac{12}{25} = \dfrac{84}{325}$.

6. A bag contains 4 blue marbles and 4 red marbles. You choose a marble without looking, put it aside, and then choose another marble. Is there a greater than or less than 50% chance that you choose two marbles with different colors? Explain.

Greater than 50%; the probability of choosing blue then red is $\dfrac{4}{8} \cdot \dfrac{4}{7}$; the

probability of choosing red then blue is $\dfrac{4}{8} \cdot \dfrac{4}{7}$; the sum of these probabilities

is $\dfrac{4}{7}$, which is greater than 50%.

© Houghton Mifflin Harcourt Publishing Company

Assign these pages to help your students practice and apply important lesson concepts. For additional exercises, see the Student Edition.

Answers

Additional Practice

1. $\frac{3}{50}$ **2.** $\frac{1}{9}$

3. a. The events are dependent because $P(\text{sum} \geq 6)$ is different when it is known that a black 3 occurred.

 b. $\frac{1}{9}$

4. a. The events are dependent because $P(\text{sum} = 8)$ is different when it is known that the white cube shows an even number.

 b. $\frac{1}{12}$

5. 0.52   **6.** 0.09

7. 0.12

8. Independent; $\frac{15}{121}$

9. Dependent; $\frac{3}{43}$

Problem Solving

1. a. $P(10) = \frac{135}{440}$

 b. $P(Tr \mid 10) = \frac{6}{135}$

 c. $P(10 \text{ and } Tr) = \frac{6}{440} \approx 0.014$

2. a. $P(12) = \frac{85}{440}$

 b. $P(Tr \text{ or } Te \mid 12) = \frac{7 + 12}{85} = \frac{19}{85}$

 c. $P(12 \text{ and } (Tr \text{ or } Te)) = \frac{19}{85} \cdot \frac{85}{440} \approx 0.043$

3. a. $\frac{19}{440}$

 b. $\frac{6}{439}$

 c. $\frac{19}{440} \cdot \frac{6}{439} \approx 0.0006$

 d. Dependent; possible answer: the second student is one of the remaining 439 students.

4. D   **5.** F

Additional Practice

Find each probability.

1. A bag contains 5 red, 3 green, 4 blue, and 8 yellow marbles. Find the probability of randomly selecting a green marble, and then a yellow marble if the first marble is replaced. _____

2. A sock drawer contains 5 rolled-up pairs of each color of socks, white, green, and blue. What is the probability of randomly selecting a pair of blue socks, replacing it, and then randomly selecting a pair of white socks? _____

Two 1–6 number cubes are rolled—one is black and one is white.

3. The sum of the rolls is greater than or equal to 6 and the black cube shows a 3.

   a. Explain why the events are dependent.

   _____

   b. Find the probability. _____

4. The white cube shows an even number, and the sum is 8.

   a. Explain why the events are dependent.

   _____

   b. Find the probability. _____

The table below shows numbers of registered voters by age in the United States in 2004 based on the census. Find each probability in decimal form.

Age	Registered Voters (in thousands)	Not Registered to Vote (in thousands)
18–24	14,334	13,474
25–44	49,371	32,763
45–64	51,659	19,355
65 and over	26,706	8,033

5. A randomly selected person is registered to vote, given that the person is between the ages of 18 and 24. _____

6. A randomly selected person is between the ages of 45 and 64 and is not registered to vote. _____

7. A randomly selected person is registered to vote and is at least 65 years old. _____

A bag contains 12 blue cubes, 12 red cubes, and 20 green cubes. Determine whether the events are independent or dependent, and find each probability.

8. A green cube and then a blue cube are chosen at random with replacement. _____

9. Two blue cubes are chosen at random without replacement. _____

Problem Solving

The table shows student participation in different sports at a high school. Suppose a student is selected at random.

Sports Participation by Grade

	Track	Volleyball	Basketball	Tennis	No Sport
Grade 9	12	18	15	9	66
Grade 10	6	20	12	2	95
Grade 11	15	11	8	5	61
Grade 12	7	6	10	12	50

1. What is the probability that a student is in grade 10 and runs track?

   a. Find the probability that a student is in grade 10, $P(10)$. _____

   b. Find the probability that a student runs track, given that the student is in grade 10, $P(Tr \mid 10)$. _____

   c. Find $P(10 \text{ and } Tr) = P(10) \cdot P(Tr \mid 10)$. _____

2. What is the probability that a student is in grade 12 and runs track or plays tennis?

   a. Find the probability that a student is in grade 12, $P(12)$. _____

   b. Find the probability that a student runs track or plays tennis, given that the student is in grade 12, $P(Tr \text{ or } Te \mid 12)$. _____

   c. Find $P(12 \text{ or } (Tr \text{ or } Te))$. _____

3. During a fire drill, the students are waiting in the parking lot. What is the probability that one student is in grade 12 and runs track or plays tennis, and the student standing next to her is in grade 10 and runs track?

   a. Find the probability for the first student. _____

   b. Find the probability for the second student. _____

   c. Find the probability for the event occurring. _____

   d. Are these events independent or dependent? Explain.

Samantha is 1 of 17 students in a class of 85 who have decided to pursue a business degree. Each week, a student in the class is randomly selected to tutor younger students. Choose the letter for the best answer.

4. What is the probability of drawing a business student one week, replacing the name, and drawing the same name the next week?

   A 3.4   C 0.04

   B 0.2   D 0.002

5. What is the probability of drawing Samantha's name one week, not replacing her name, and drawing the name of another business student the next week?

   F $\dfrac{1}{85} \cdot \dfrac{16}{84}$ H $\dfrac{17}{85} \cdot \dfrac{16}{84}$

   G $\dfrac{1}{85} \cdot \dfrac{17}{84}$ J $\dfrac{17}{85} \cdot \dfrac{17}{84}$

Two-Way Tables
Going Deeper

Essential question: *How do you calculate a conditional probability?*

COMMON CORE Standards for Mathematical Content

CC.9-12.S.CP.3 Understand the conditional probability of *A* given *B* as *P(A and B)/P(B)* . . . .*

CC.9-12.S.CP.4 Construct and interpret two-way frequency tables of data when two categories are associated with each object being classified. Use the two-way table . . . to approximate conditional probabilities.*

CC.9-12.S.CP.5 Recognize and explain the concept of conditional probability . . . in everyday language and everyday situations.*

CC.9-12.S.CP.6 Find the conditional probability of *A* given *B* as the fraction of *B*'s outcomes that also belong to *A*, and interpret the answer in terms of the model.*

Vocabulary

conditional probability

Prerequisites

Probability and Set Theory

Math Background

In this lesson students will be given opportunities to work with two-way tables, which can be used to make sense of a wide range of probability and statistics problems. These tables are used to develop a formula for calculating conditional probability. This formula is given by

$$P(B \mid A) = \frac{P(A \cap B)}{P(A)}.$$

INTRODUCE

Define *conditional probability*. Give students a simple example. For instance, when you roll a number cube, the probability that you roll a 6 is $\frac{1}{6}$. The conditional probability that you roll a 6 given that you roll a number greater than 4 is $\frac{1}{2}$ since this condition effectively restricts the sample space to {5, 6}.

TEACH

1 EXAMPLE

Questioning Strategies

- What percent of the participants in the study were given the medicine? **60%**

- How many participants in the study did not get a headache? **73**

- Was a participant who got a headache more likely to have taken the medicine or not? **The participant was more likely to have not taken the medicine.**

EXTRA EXAMPLE

The manager of a produce stand wants to find out whether there is a connection between people who buy fresh vegetables and people who buy eggs. The manager collects data on 200 randomly chosen shoppers, as shown in the two-way table.

	Bought Vegetables	No Vegetables	TOTAL
Eggs	56	20	76
No Eggs	49	75	124
TOTAL	105	95	200

A. To the nearest percent, what is the probability that a shopper who bought eggs also bought vegetables? **74%**

B. To the nearest percent, what is the probability that a shopper who bought vegetables also bought eggs? **53%**

7-4

Video Tutor

Two-Way Tables
Going Deeper

Essential question: *How do you calculate a conditional probability?*

The probability that event *B* occurs given that event *A* has already occurred is called the **conditional probability** of *B* given *A* and is written $P(B \mid A)$.

CC.9-12.S.CP.6

1 EXAMPLE Finding Conditional Probabilities

One hundred people who frequently get migraine headaches were chosen to participate in a study of a new anti-headache medicine. Some of the participants were given the medicine; others were not. After one week, the participants were asked if they got a headache during the week. The two-way table summarizes the results.

	Took Medicine	No Medicine	TOTAL
Headache	12	15	27
No Headache	48	25	73
TOTAL	60	40	100

A To the nearest percent, what is the probability that a participant who took the medicine did not get a headache?

Let event *A* be the event that a participant took the medicine. Let event *B* be the event that a participant did not get a headache.

To find the probability that a participant who took the medicine did not get a headache, you must find $P(B \mid A)$. You are only concerned with participants who took the medicine, so look at the data in the "Took Medicine" column.

There were ___60___ participants who took the medicine.

Of these participants, ___48___ participants did not get a headache.

So, $P(B \mid A) = \dfrac{48}{60} = $ ___80%___

B To the nearest percent, what is the probability that a participant who did not get a headache took the medicine?

To find the probability that a participant who did not get a headache took the medicine, you must find $P(A \mid B)$. You are only concerned with participants who did not get a headache, so look at the data in the "No headache" row.

There were ___73___ participants who did not get a headache.

Of these participants, ___48___ participants took the medicine.

So, $P(A \mid B) = \dfrac{48}{73} \approx $ ___66%___

© Houghton Mifflin Harcourt Publishing Company

REFLECT

1a. In general, do you think $P(B \mid A) = P(A \mid B)$? Why or why not?

No; these conditional probabilities are not equal in the example.

1b. How can you use set notation to represent the event that a participant took the medicine and did not get a headache? Is the probability that a participant took the medicine and did not get a headache equal to either of the conditional probabilities you calculated in the example?

This is represented by $A \cap B$; $P(A \cap B) = \dfrac{48}{100} = 48\%$; this probability is not

equal to $P(B \mid A)$ or $P(A \mid B)$.

CC.9-12.S.CP.3

2 EXPLORE Developing a Formula for Conditional Probability

You can generalize your work from the previous example to develop a formula for finding conditional probabilities.

A Recall how you calculated $P(B \mid A)$, the probability that a participant who took the medicine did not get a headache.

You found that $P(B \mid A) = \dfrac{48}{60}$.

Use the table shown here to help you write this quotient in terms of events *A* and *B*.

		Event A		
		Took Medicine	No Medicine	TOTAL
	Headache	12	15	27
Event B	No Headache	$48 = n(A \cap B)$	25	$73 = n(B)$
	TOTAL	$60 = n(A)$	40	100

$P(B \mid A) = \dfrac{n(A \cap B)}{n(A)}$

B Now divide the numerator and denominator of the quotient by $n(S)$, the number of outcomes in the sample space. This converts the counts to probabilities.

$P(B \mid A) = \dfrac{n(A \cap B)\big/ n(S)}{n(A)\big/ n(S)} = \dfrac{P(A \cap B)}{P(A)}$

REFLECT

2a. Write a formula for $P(A \mid B)$ in terms of $n(A \cap B)$ and $n(B)$.
$P(A \mid B) = \dfrac{n(A \cap B)}{n(B)}$

2b. Write a formula for $P(A \mid B)$ in terms of $P(A \cap B)$ and $P(B)$.
$P(A \mid B) = \dfrac{P(A \cap B)}{P(B)}$

© Houghton Mifflin Harcourt Publishing Company

Notes

MATHEMATICAL PRACTICE

Highlighting the Standards

Standard 4 (Model with mathematics) includes the statement that mathematically proficient students are able to map relationships among important quantities using tools like two-way tables. Furthermore, "they can analyze those relationships mathematically to draw conclusions." This lesson offers many opportunities for such analyses. After the first example, ask students what conclusions they can draw about the effectiveness of the headache medicine. The data in the two-way table and the conditional probabilities indicate that the medicine is at least somewhat effective in preventing headaches.

2 EXPLORE

- What does $A \cap B$ represent? **participants who took the medicine and did not get a headache**

- How many participants are in $A \cap B$? How do you know? **48; this is the number in the cell corresponding to "Took Medicine" and "No Headache."**

- What is $n(S)$? Why? **100;100 people participated in the study.**

Teaching Strategies

English language learners may have difficulty with conditional probability because so much depends upon understanding that "What is the probability that a participant who took the medicine did not get a headache?" and "What is the probability that a participant who did not get a headache took the medicine?" are different questions. When working with such statements, you may want to prompt students to underline the words that correspond to the event that is assumed to have already occurred.

3 EXAMPLE

Questioning Strategies

- In this situation, which event can be considered to have already occurred? **the event that the card is red**

- What are the red cards in a deck of cards? **The red cards are the 13 hearts and the 13 diamonds.**

EXTRA EXAMPLE

In a standard deck of playing cards, find the probability that a face card is a king. $\frac{1}{3}$

CLOSE

Essential Question

How do you calculate a conditional probability?
You can calculate a conditional probability from a two-way table. You can also use the formula $P(B \mid A) = \frac{P(A \cap B)}{P(A)}$.

Summarize

Have students write a journal entry in which they explain conditional probability in their own words. Also, ask students to give an example of how to use the formula for conditional probability.

PRACTICE

Where skills are taught	Where skills are practiced
1 EXAMPLE	EXS. 1–2
3 EXAMPLE	EXS. 3–9

You may have discovered the following formula for conditional probability.

Conditional Probability

The conditional probability of B given A (the probability that event B occurs given that event A occurs) is given by the following formula:

$$P(B \mid A) = \frac{P(A \cap B)}{P(A)}$$

CC.9-12.S.CP.3

3 EXAMPLE Using the Conditional Probability Formula

In a standard deck of playing cards, find the probability that a red card is a queen.

A Let event Q be the event that a card is a queen. Let event R be the event that a card is red. You are asked to find $P(Q \mid R)$. First find $P(R \cap Q)$ and $P(R)$.

$R \cap Q$ represents cards that are both red and a queen; that is, red queens.

There are ___2___ red queens in the deck of 52 cards, so $P(R \cap Q) = \frac{2}{52}$

There are ___26___ red cards in the deck, so $P(R) = \frac{26}{52}$

B Use the formula for conditional probability.

$P(Q \mid R) = \frac{P(Q \cap R)}{P(R)} = \dfrac{\frac{2}{52}}{\frac{26}{52}}$ Substitute probabilities from above.

$= \dfrac{2}{26}$ Multiply numerator and denominator by 52.

$= \dfrac{1}{13}$ Simplify.

So, the probability that a red card is a queen is ___$\frac{1}{13}$___.

REFLECT

3a. How can you interpret the probability you calculated above?

If you choose a red card at random, it is very unlikely that it will be a queen
(it will be a queen about 8% of the time).

3b. Is the probability that a red card is a queen equal to the probability that a queen is red? Explain.

No; $P(R \mid Q) = \frac{1}{2}$, whereas $P(Q \mid R) = \frac{1}{13}$.

© Houghton Mifflin Harcourt Publishing Company

PRACTICE

1. In order to study the connection between the amount of sleep a student gets and his or her school performance, data was collected about 120 students. The two-way table shows the number of students who passed and failed an exam and the number of students who got more or less than 6 hours of sleep the night before.

	Passed Exam	Failed Exam	TOTAL
Less than 6 hours of sleep	12	10	22
More than 6 hours of sleep	90	8	98
TOTAL	102	18	120

   a. To the nearest percent, what is the probability that a student who failed the exam got less than 6 hours of sleep? ___56%___

   b. To the nearest percent, what is the probability that a student who got less than 6 hours of sleep failed the exam? ___45%___

   c. To the nearest percent, what is the probability that a student got less than 6 hours of sleep and failed the exam? ___8%___

2. A botanist studied the effect of a new fertilizer by choosing 100 orchids and giving 70% of these plants the fertilizer. Of the plants that got the fertilizer, 40% produced flowers within a month. Of the plants that did not get the fertilizer, 10% produced flowers within a month. Find each probability to the nearest percent. (*Hint:* Construct a two-way table.)

   a. Find the probability that a plant that produced flowers got the fertilizer. ___90%___

   b. Find the probability that a plant that got the fertilizer produced flowers. ___40%___

3. At a school fair, a box contains 24 yellow balls and 76 red balls. One-fourth of the balls of each color are labeled "Win a prize." Find each probability as a percent.

   a. Find the probability that a ball labeled "Win a prize" is yellow. ___24%___

   b. Find the probability that a ball labeled "Win a prize" is red. ___76%___

   c. Find the probability that a ball is labeled "Win a prize" and is red. ___19%___

   d. Find the probability that a yellow ball is labeled "Win a prize." ___25%___

In Exercises 4–9, consider a standard deck of playing cards and the following events: A: the card is an ace; B: the card is black; C: the card is a club. Find each probability as a fraction.

4. $P(A \mid B)$ 5. $P(B \mid A)$ 6. $P(A \mid C)$
   $\frac{1}{13}$ $\frac{1}{2}$ $\frac{1}{13}$

7. $P(C \mid A)$ 8. $P(B \mid C)$ 9. $P(C \mid B)$
   $\frac{1}{4}$ 1 $\frac{1}{2}$

© Houghton Mifflin Harcourt Publishing Company

Notes

ADDITIONAL PRACTICE AND PROBLEM SOLVING

Assign these pages to help your students practice and apply important lesson concepts. For additional exercises, see the Student Edition.

Answers

Additional Practice

1.

	Ages 10–20	Ages 21–45	Ages 46–65	65 and Older	Total
Yes	0.13	0.02	0.08	0.24	0.47
No	0.25	0.10	0.15	0.03	0.53
Total	0.38	0.12	0.23	0.27	1

2. a.

Owns an MP3 player

		Yes	No	Total
Owns a Smart Phone	Yes	0.28	0.12	0.40
	No	0.34	0.26	0.60
	Total	0.62	0.38	1

b. 0.45   c. 0.70

Problem Solving

1.

	Lowerclassmates	Upperclassmates	Total
Always	0.080	0.305	0.385
Sometimes	0.145	0.110	0.255
Never	0.060	0.300	0.360
Total	0.285	0.715	1

2. a. 0.81   b. 0.27

3. D   4. J

7-4

Notes

Additional Practice

1. The table shows the results of a customer satisfaction survey of 100 randomly selected shoppers at the mall who were asked if they would shop at an earlier time if the mall opened earlier. Make a table of joint and marginal relative frequencies.

	Ages 10–20	Ages 21–45	Ages 46–65	65 and Older
Yes	13	2	8	24
No	25	10	15	3

	Ages 10–20	Ages 21–45	Ages 46–65	65 and Older	Total
Yes					
No					
Total					

2. Jerrod collected data on 100 randomly selected students, and summarized the results in a table.

		Owns an MP3 Player	
		Yes	No
Owns a Smart phone	Yes	28	12
	No	34	26

a. Make a table of the joint relative frequencies and marginal relative frequencies. Round to the nearest hundredth where appropriate.

		Owns an MP3 player		
		Yes	No	Total
Owns a Smart Phone	Yes			
	No			
	Total			

b. If you are given that a student owns an MP3 player, what is the probability that the student also owns a smart phone? Round your answer to the nearest hundredth.

_____

c. If you are given that a student owns a smart phone, what is the probability that the student also owns an MP3 player? Round your answer to the nearest hundredth.

_____

Problem Solving

1. The table shows the number of students who would drive to school if the school provided parking spaces. Make a table of joint relative frequencies and marginal relative frequencies.

	Lowerclassmates	Upperclassmates
Always	32	122
Sometimes	58	44
Never	24	120

	Lowerclassmates	Upperclassmates	Total
Always			
Sometimes			
Never			
Total			

2. Gerry collected data and made a table of marginal relative frequencies on the number of students who participate in chorus and the number who participate in band.

		Chorus		
		Yes	No	Total
Band	Yes	0.38	0.29	0.67
	No	0.09	0.24	0.33
	Total	0.47	0.53	1.0

a. If you are given that a student is in chorus, what is the probability that the student also is in band? Round your answer to the nearest hundredth.

_____

b. If you are given that a student is not in band, what is the probability that the student is in chorus? Round your answer to the nearest hundredth.

_____

Select the best answer.

3. What is the probability if a student is not in chorus, then that student is in band?

A 0.29   B 0.38

C 0.43   D 0.55

4. What is the probability that if a student is not in band, then that student is not in chorus?

F 0.09   G 0.33

H 0.44   J 0.73

7-5 Compound Events
Going Deeper

Essential question: *How do you find the probability of mutually exclusive events and overlapping events?*

COMMON CORE Standards for Mathematical Content

CC.9-12.S.CP.7 Apply the Addition Rule, $P(A \text{ or } B) = P(A) + P(B) - P(A \text{ and } B)$, and interpret the answer in terms of the model.*

Vocabulary
mutually exclusive events
overlapping events

Prerequisites
Probability and Set Theory

Math Background
Mutually exclusive events have no outcomes in common. Thus, mutually exclusive events cannot both occur on the same trial of an experiment. Overlapping or inclusive events have one or more outcomes in common. For overlapping events A and B, $P(A \text{ or } B) = P(A) + P(B) - P(A \text{ and } B)$. In the case that A and B are mutually exclusive events, $P(A \text{ and } B) = 0$, so the rule takes on the simpler form $P(A \text{ or } B) = P(A) + P(B)$.

INTRODUCE

Define *mutually exclusive events*. Give students an example of mutually exclusive events. For example, when you roll a standard number cube, rolling a number less than 3 and rolling a 6 are mutually exclusive events because the events have no outcomes in common. Ask students to give additional examples of mutually exclusive events based on rolling a number cube.

TEACH

1 EXAMPLE

Questioning Strategies
- Why are events A and B mutually exclusive events? They have no outcomes in common.
- How is this reflected in the Venn diagram? The ovals representing the events do not intersect.

EXTRA EXAMPLE
You choose a card at random from a standard deck of playing cards. What is the probability that you choose a queen or the 7 of diamonds? $\frac{5}{52}$

2 EXAMPLE

Questioning Strategies
- Why are events A and B overlapping? They have some outcomes in common.
- How is this reflected in the Venn diagram? The ovals representing the events intersect.
- If A and B are overlapping events, what can you say about $A \cap B$? $A \cap B$ is not the empty set.

EXTRA EXAMPLE
You have a set of 20 cards that are numbered 1–20. You shuffle the cards and choose one at random. What is the probability that you choose an even number or a number greater than 15? $\frac{3}{5}$

MATHEMATICAL PRACTICE **Highlighting the Standards**

According to Standard 1 (Make sense of problems and persevere in solving them), mathematically proficient students continually ask themselves, "Does this make sense?" This lesson provides an especially good opportunity for this type of reflective thinking. Whenever students calculate a probability they should ask themselves whether the probability seems reasonable. For instance, in the second example, students find that the probability, of rolling an even number or a number greater than 7 on a dodecahedral number cube is $\frac{2}{3}$. This seems reasonable since more than half of the outcomes in the sample space are in at least one of these events.

7-5

Compound Events
Going Deeper

Essential question: *How do you find the probability of mutually exclusive events and overlapping events?*

Two events are **mutually exclusive events** if the events cannot both occur in the same trial of an experiment. For example, when you toss a coin, the coin landing heads up and the coin landing tails up are mutually exclusive events.

Video Tutor

1 EXAMPLE Finding the Probability of Mutually Exclusive Events

CC.9-12.S.CP.7

A dodecahedral number cube has 12 sides numbered 1 through 12. What is the probability that you roll the cube and the result is an even number or a 7?

A Let event A be the event that you roll an even number. Let event B be the event that you roll a 7. Let S be the sample space.

Complete the Venn diagram by writing all outcomes in the sample space in the appropriate region.

B You must find the probability of A or B.

$n(S) = \underline{\quad 12 \quad}$

$n(A \text{ or } B) = n(A) + n(B)$ A and B are mutually exclusive events.

$= \underline{\quad 6 \quad} + \underline{\quad 1 \quad}$ Use the Venn diagram to find $n(A)$ and $n(B)$.

$= \underline{\quad 7 \quad}$ Add.

So, $P(A \text{ or } B) = \dfrac{n(A \text{ or } B)}{n(S)} = \dfrac{\boxed{7}}{\boxed{12}}$.

REFLECT

1a. Does the probability you calculated seem reasonable? Why?

Yes; the probability of rolling an even number is $\frac{1}{2}$, so the probability of rolling

an even number or a 7 should be a bit greater than that.

1b. Is it always true that $n(A \text{ or } B) = n(A) + n(B)$? Explain.

This is always true when events A and B are mutually exclusive events.

1c. How is $P(A \text{ or } B)$ related to $P(A)$ and $P(B)$? Do you think this is always true?

$P(A \text{ or } B) = P(A) + P(B)$. This is always true when events A and B are mutually

exclusive events.

© Houghton Mifflin Harcourt Publishing Company

Chapter 7   413   Lesson 5

The process you used in the example can be generalized to give a formula for the probability of mutually exclusive events.

> **Mutually Exclusive Events**
>
> If A and B are mutually exclusive events, then $P(A \text{ or } B) = P(A) + P(B)$.

Two events are **overlapping events** (or *inclusive events*) if they have one or more outcomes in common.

2 EXAMPLE Finding the Probability of Overlapping Events

CC.9-12.S.CP.7

What is the probability that you roll a dodecahedral number cube and the result is an even number or a number greater than 7?

A Let event A be the event that you roll an even number. Let event B be the event that you roll a number greater than 7. Let S be the sample space.

Complete the Venn diagram by writing all outcomes in the sample space in the appropriate region.

B You must find the probability of A or B.

$n(S) = \underline{\quad 12 \quad}$

$n(A \text{ or } B) = n(A) + n(B) - n(A \text{ and } B)$ A and B are overlapping events.

$= \underline{\quad 6 \quad} + \underline{\quad 5 \quad} - \underline{\quad 3 \quad}$ Use the Venn diagram.

$= \underline{\quad 8 \quad}$ Simplify.

So, $P(A \text{ or } B) = \dfrac{n(A \text{ or } B)}{n(S)} = \dfrac{\boxed{8}}{\boxed{12}} = \dfrac{\boxed{2}}{\boxed{3}}$.

REFLECT

2a. Why is $n(A \text{ or } B)$ equal to $n(A) + n(B) - n(A \text{ and } B)$?

The number of outcomes in A or B is equal to the number of outcomes in

A plus the number of outcomes in B, except for the fact that the outcomes

in both A and B have been counted twice, so $n(A \text{ and } B)$ must be subtracted

from the total.

2b. Is $P(A \text{ or } B)$ equal to $P(A) + P(B)$ in this case? Explain.

No; $P(A \text{ or } B) = \frac{2}{3}$, but $P(A) + P(B) = \frac{1}{2} + \frac{5}{12} = \frac{11}{12}$.

© Houghton Mifflin Harcourt Publishing Company

Chapter 7   414   Lesson 5

Notes

Questioning Strategies

- How are the cards in a standard deck organized? There are 13 cards (ace, 2, 3, 4, 5, 6, 7, 8, 9, 10, jack, queen, king), each in 4 suits (hearts, clubs, diamonds, spades), for a total of 52 cards.

- What card or cards does $A \cap B$ represent? Why? $A \cap B$ is the king of hearts since the card must be both a king and a heart.

EXTRA EXAMPLE

You have a set of 26 cards with the letters A through Z. You shuffle the cards and choose one at random. What is the probability that you choose a card with a consonant or a letter in the word PROBABILITY? $\frac{12}{13}$

Differentiated Instruction

Some students may find it easier to solve the problem in the third example by making a chart that shows all of the cards in a deck of cards and then highlighting the cards in events A and B.

A ♥	A ♣	A ♦	A ♠
2 ♥	2 ♣	2 ♦	2 ♠
3 ♥	3 ♣	3 ♦	3 ♠
4 ♥	4 ♣	4 ♦	4 ♠
5 ♥	5 ♣	5 ♦	5 ♠
6 ♥	6 ♣	6 ♦	6 ♠
7 ♥	7 ♣	7 ♦	7 ♠
8 ♥	8 ♣	8 ♦	8 ♠
9 ♥	9 ♣	9 ♦	9 ♠
10 ♥	10 ♣	10 ♦	10 ♠
J ♥	J ♣	J ♦	J ♠
Q ♥	Q ♣	Q ♦	Q ♠
K ♥	K ♣	K ♦	K ♠

Teaching Strategies

Tell students that when they calculate the probabilities $P(A)$, $P(B)$, and $P(A \text{ and } B)$ for use in the Addition Rule, it is often easiest to leave the fractions in unsimplified form. For instance, in the third example, these probabilities are all expressed with a denominator of 52. This makes it easy to add and subtract the probabilities in the Addition Rule.

CLOSE

Essential Question

How do you find the probability of mutually exclusive events and overlapping events?
For mutually exclusive events A and B, $P(A \text{ or } B) = P(A) + P(B)$. For overlapping events A and B, $P(A \text{ or } B) = P(A) + P(B) - P(A \text{ and } B)$.

Summarize

Have students write a journal entry in which they write their own probability problems that involve mutually exclusive events and overlapping events. For each problem, students should identify the type of events involved, state the probability rule that applies, and show a complete solution.

PRACTICE

Where skills are taught	Where skills are practiced
1 EXAMPLE	EXS. 1–2
2 EXAMPLE	EXS. 3–4
3 EXAMPLE	EXS. 5–6

Exercise 7: Students use a two-way table to calculate probabilities.

Exercise 8: Students use a Venn diagram to calculate probabilities.

Exercise 9: Students use reasoning to write a probability rule.

In the previous example you saw that for overlapping events A and B, $n(A \cup B) = n(A) + n(B) - n(A \cap B)$. You can convert these counts to probabilities by dividing each term by $n(S)$ as shown below.

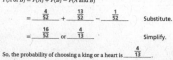

$$\frac{n(A \cup B)}{n(S)} = \frac{n(A)}{n(S)} + \frac{n(B)}{n(S)} - \frac{n(A \cap B)}{n(S)}$$

Rewriting each term as a probability results in the following rule.

Addition Rule

$$P(A \text{ or } B) = P(A) + P(B) - P(A \text{ and } B)$$

Notice that when A and B are mutually exclusive events, $P(A \text{ and } B) = 0$, and the rule becomes the simpler rule for mutually exclusive events on the previous page.

CC.9-12.S.CP.7

3 EXAMPLE Using the Addition Rule

You shuffle a standard deck of playing cards and choose a card at random. What is the probability that you choose a king or a heart?

A Let event A be the event that you choose a king. Let event B be the event that you choose a heart. Let S be the sample space.

There are 52 cards in the deck, so $n(S) = \underline{52}$.

There are 4 kings in the deck, so $n(A) = \underline{4}$ and $P(A) = \underline{\frac{4}{52}}$.

There are 13 hearts in the deck, so $n(B) = \underline{13}$ and $P(B) = \underline{\frac{13}{52}}$.

There is one king of hearts in the deck, so $P(A \text{ and } B) = \underline{\frac{1}{52}}$.

B Use the Addition Rule.

$P(A \text{ or } B) = P(A) + P(B) - P(A \text{ and } B)$

$= \underline{\frac{4}{52}} + \underline{\frac{13}{52}} - \underline{\frac{1}{52}}$ Substitute.

$= \underline{\frac{16}{52}}$ or $\underline{\frac{4}{13}}$ Simplify.

So, the probability of choosing a king or a heart is $\underline{\frac{4}{13}}$.

REFLECT

3a. What does the answer tell you about the likelihood of choosing a king or a heart from the deck?

The probability is about 31%, so the outcome is not very likely (it will occur about 31% of the time).

PRACTICE

1. A bag contains 3 blue marbles, 5 red marbles, and 4 green marbles. You choose a marble without looking. What is the probability that you choose a red marble or a green marble?
$\frac{3}{4}$

2. An icosahedral number cube has 20 sides numbered 1 through 20. What is the probability that you roll the cube and the result is a number that is less than 4 or greater than 11?
$\frac{3}{5}$

3. A bag contains 26 tiles, each with a different letter of the alphabet written on it. You choose a tile without looking. What is the probability that you choose a vowel or a letter in the word GEOMETRY?
$\frac{5}{13}$

4. You roll two number cubes at the same time. Each cube has sides numbered 1 through 6. What is the probability that the sum of the numbers rolled is even or greater than 9?
$\frac{5}{9}$

5. You shuffle a standard deck of playing cards and choose a card at random. What is the probability that you choose a face card (jack, queen, or king) or a club?
$\frac{11}{26}$

6. You have a set of 25 cards numbered 1 through 25. You shuffle the cards and choose a card at random. What is the probability that you choose a multiple of 3 or a multiple of 4?
$\frac{12}{25}$

7. The two-way table provides data on the students at a high school. You randomly choose a student at the school. Find each probability.

	Freshman	Sophomore	Junior	Senior	TOTAL
Boy	98	104	100	94	396
Girl	102	106	96	108	412
TOTAL	200	210	196	202	808

a. The student is a senior. $\frac{1}{4}$

b. The student is a girl. $\frac{103}{202}$

c. The student is a senior and a girl. $\frac{27}{202}$

d. The student is a senior or a girl. $\frac{253}{404}$

8. A survey of the 1108 employees at a software company finds that 621 employees take a bus to work and 445 employees take a train to work. Some employees take both a bus and a train, and 312 employees take only a train. To the nearest percent, what is the probability that a randomly-chosen employee takes a bus or a train to work? (*Hint:* Make a Venn diagram.)
84%

9. Suppose A and B are complementary events. Explain how you can rewrite the Addition Rule in a simpler form for this case.
Because $P(A \text{ and } B) = 0$ for complementary events, $P(A \text{ or } B) = P(A) + P(B) = 1$.

Assign these pages to help your students practice and apply important lesson concepts. For additional exercises, see the Student Edition.

Answers

Additional Practice

1. These events are mutually exclusive because each can contains only one type of vegetable.

2. $\frac{13}{40}$ 3. $\frac{1}{3}$

4. $\frac{5}{6}$ 5. $\frac{2}{3}$

6. $\frac{7}{8}$ 7. $\frac{29}{40}$

8. $\frac{4}{5}$ 9. $\frac{67}{110}$ or 0.61

10. 0.81

Problem Solving

1. a. The total number of male students; 44

   b. The total number of students in favor of the change; 54

   c. $54 - 20 = 34$

   e. $\frac{44}{100} + \frac{54}{100} - \frac{34}{100} = \frac{64}{100} = 0.64$

2. a. $100 - 44 = 56$ b. $100 - 54 = 46$

   c. The number of females who are opposed to the change; 36

   d. $\frac{56}{100} + \frac{46}{100} - \frac{36}{100} - \frac{66}{100} = 0.66$

3. $\frac{27}{100} + \frac{54}{100} - \frac{18}{100} = \frac{63}{100} = 0.63$

4. C   5. J

7-5

Additional Practice

A can of vegetables with no label has a $\frac{1}{8}$ chance of being green beans and a $\frac{1}{5}$ chance of being corn.

1. Explain why the events "green beans" or "corn" are mutually exclusive.

   _____

2. What is the probability that an unlabeled can of vegetables is either green beans or corn? _____

Ben rolls a 1–6 number cube. Find each probability.

3. Ben rolls a 3 or a 4. _____

4. Ben rolls a number greater than 2 or an even number. _____

5. Ben rolls a prime number or an odd number. _____

Of the 400 doctors who attended a conference, 240 practiced family medicine and 130 were from countries outside the United States. One-third of the family medicine practitioners were not from the United States.

6. What is the probability that a doctor practices family medicine or is from the United States? _____

7. What is the probability that a doctor practices family medicine or is not from the United States? _____

8. What is the probability that a doctor does not practice family medicine or is from the United States? _____

Use the data to fill in the Venn diagram. Then solve.

9. Of the 220 people who came into the Italian deli on Friday, 104 bought pizza and 82 used a credit card. Half of the people who bought pizza used a credit card. What is the probability that a customer bought pizza or used a credit card?

   Bought Pizza   Used credit card   _____

Solve.

10. There are 6 people in a gardening club. Each gardener orders seeds from a list of 11 different types of seeds available. What is the probability that 2 gardeners will order the same type of seeds? _____

Problem Solving

Of 100 students surveyed, 44 are male and 54 are in favor of a change to a 9-period, 4-day school week. Of those in favor, 20 are female. One student is picked at random from those surveyed.

1. What is the probability that the student is male or favors the change? Use the Venn diagram.

   School Week Survey
   A   B   C
   Male Students   In Favor of the Change

   a. What is represented by the total of $A + B$?

      _____

   b. What is represented by the total of $B + C$?

      _____

   c. How many of those in favor of the change are male? _____

   d. Find the values for A, B, and C and label the diagram.

   e. Write and evaluate an expression for the probability that the student is male or favors the change. _____

2. What is the probability that the student is female or opposes the change?

   a. How many students are female? _____

   b. How many students oppose the change? _____

   c. If you draw a Venn diagram to show females and those opposed to the change, what is the meaning and value of the overlapping area?

      _____

   d. Write and evaluate an expression for the probability that the student is female or opposes the change. _____

3. Of the students surveyed, 27 plan to start their own businesses. Of those, 18 are in favor of the change to the school week. Write and evaluate an expression for the probability that a student selected at random plans to start his or her own business or favors the change.

   _____

Sean asks each student to cast a vote for the type of class he or she would prefer. Of the students, 55% voted for online classes, 30% voted for projects, and 15% voted for following the textbook. Choose the letter for the best answer.

4. Which description best describes Sean's experiment?

   A Simple events

   B Compound events

   C Mutually exclusive events

   D Inclusive events

5. What is the probability that a randomly selected student voted for online classes or projects?

   F $\frac{33}{200}$ H $\frac{1}{4}$

   G $\frac{7}{10}$ J $\frac{17}{20}$

© Houghton Mifflin Harcourt Publishing Company

This page provides students with the opportunity to apply concepts from the Common Core in real-world problem situations. There are three different levels of performance tasks:

⭐ **Novice:** These are short word problems that require students to apply the math they have learned in straightforward, real-world situations.

⭐⭐ **Apprentice:** These are more involved problems that guide students step-by-step through more complex tasks. These exercises include more complicated reasoning, writing, and open-ended elements.

⭐⭐⭐ **Expert:** These are open-ended, non-routine problems that, instead of stepping the students through, ask them to choose their own methods for solving and justify their answers and reasoning.

Sample answers

1. $\frac{1}{6}$; no, P(Sam moves back to the beginning) $=$ $\frac{1}{3}$, and $\frac{1}{6} + \frac{1}{3} \neq 1$.

2. 40% or 0.4

3. Scoring Guide:

Task	Possible points
a	1 point for the correct answer (no), and 1 point for a correct explanation, for example: Since Mel must choose a different tea than Alice, the events are not independent.
b	2 points for a correct Venn diagram:
c	2 points for the correct answer: $\frac{8}{14} \approx 0.571$

Total possible points: 6

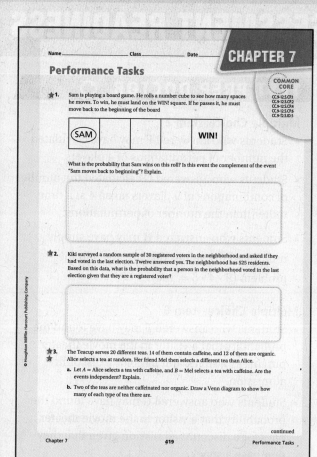

Name_____ Class_____ Date_____

Performance Tasks

COMMON CORE

CC-9-12.S.CP.1
CC-9-12.S.CP.2
CC-9-12.S.CP.4
CC-9-12.S.CP.6
CC-9-12.S.ID.5

★ **1.** Sam is playing a board game. He rolls a number cube to see how many spaces he moves. To win, he must land on the WIN! square. If he passes it, he must move back to the beginning of the board

SAM				WIN!

What is the probability that Sam wins on this roll? Is this event the complement of the event "Sam moves back to beginning"? Explain.

★ **2.** Kiki surveyed a random sample of 30 registered voters in the neighborhood and asked if they had voted in the last election. Twelve answered yes. The neighborhood has 525 residents. Based on this data, what is the probability that a person in the neighborhood voted in the last election given that they are a registered voter?

★ **3.** The Teacup serves 20 different teas. 14 of them contain caffeine, and 12 of them are organic. Alice selects a tea at random. Her friend Mel then selects a different tea than Alice.

a. Let A = Alice selects a tea with caffeine, and B = Mel selects a tea with caffeine. Are the events independent? Explain.

b. Two of the teas are neither caffeinated nor organic. Draw a Venn diagram to show how many of each type of tea there are.

continued

© Houghton Mifflin Harcourt Publishing Company

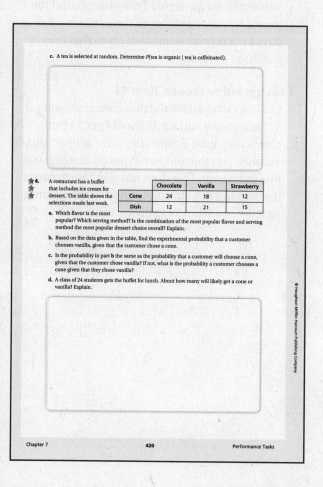

c. A tea is selected at random. Determine P(tea is organic | tea is caffeinated).

★ **4.** A restaurant has a buffet that includes ice cream for dessert. The table shows the selections made last week.

	Chocolate	Vanilla	Strawberry
Cone	24	18	12
Dish	12	21	15

a. Which flavor is the most popular? Which serving method? Is the combination of the most popular flavor and serving method the most popular dessert choice overall? Explain.

b. Based on the data given in the table, find the experimental probability that a customer chooses vanilla, given that the customer chose a cone.

c. Is the probability in part **b** the same as the probability that a customer will choose a cone, given that the customer chose vanilla? If not, what is the probability a customer chooses a cone given that they chose vanilla?

d. A class of 24 students gets the buffet for lunch. About how many will likely get a cone or vanilla? Explain.

© Houghton Mifflin Harcourt Publishing Company

4. Scoring Guide:

Task	Possible points
a	1 point total for the correct answers *vanilla* and *cone*, and 1 point for correctly noting that the most popular dessert choice is a chocolate cone, not a vanilla cone
b	1 point for the correct answer $\left(\frac{1}{3}\right)$
c	1 point total for the correct answer (no) and the correct probability $\left(\frac{6}{13}\right)$
d	1 point for the correct answer of about 18 students, and 1 point for correctly explaining that 75 of 102 or about 73.5% of customers chose either a cone or vanilla, so 73.5% of 24 students, which is $17.64 \approx 18$ students, will get a cone or vanilla.

Total possible points: 6

Standard	Items
CC.9-12.S.CP.1*	1
CC.9-12.S.CP.2*	8
CC.9-12.S.CP.3*	9
CC.9-12.S.CP.4*	5
CC.9-12.S.CP.5*	5
CC.9-12.S.CP.6*	6
CC.9-12.S.CP.7*	4
CC.9-12.S.CP.8(+)*	7
CC.9-12.S.CP.9(+)*	2, 3
CC.9-12.S.MD.6(+)*	11
CC.9-12.S.MD.7(+)*	10

TEST PREP DOCTOR ⊕

Multiple Choice: Item 2
- Students who answered **F** may have calculated the number of permutations of 4 players.
- Students who answered **G** calculated the number of combinations of 9 players taken 4 at a time, rather than the number of permutations.
- Students who answered **H** may have simply multiplied the values that are given in the problem ($9 \cdot 4 \cdot 5 = 180$).

Multiple Choice: Item 6
- Students who answered **F** may have found the probability that a visitor to the movie theater purchases a snack and pays for a discount admission.
- Students who answered **G** may have found the probability that a visitor to the movie theater pays for a discount admission given that they purchase a snack.
- Students who answered **J** may have found the probability that a visitor to the movie theater pays for a regular admission given that they purchase a snack.

Constructed Response: Item 11
- Students who answered that Naomi should get 47 fruit chews and Kayla should get 33 fruit chews may have divided the prize proportionally according to the number of points already won by each player. This does not take into account the number of points needed to win the game, so it is not a fair way to divide the prize.

Name _____ Class _____ Date _____

MULTIPLE CHOICE

1. You spin a spinner with 10 equal sections that are numbered 1 through 10. Event A is rolling an odd number. Event B is rolling a number greater than 5. What is $P(A \cap B)$?

A. $\frac{1}{8}$ C. $\frac{1}{2}$

B. $\frac{1}{5}$ D. $\frac{4}{5}$

2. There are 9 players on a basketball team. For a team photo, 4 of the players are seated on a row of chairs and 5 players stand behind them. In how many different ways can 4 players be arranged on the row of chairs?

F. 24   H. 180

G. 126   J. 3024

3. There are 5 peaches and 4 nectarines in a bowl. You randomly choose 2 pieces of fruit to pack in your lunch. What is the probability that you choose 2 peaches?

A. $\frac{5}{36}$ C. $\frac{2}{3}$

B. $\frac{5}{18}$ D. $\frac{5}{9}$

4. You shuffle the cards shown below and choose one at random. What is the probability that you choose a gray card or an even number?

1	2	4	5	7	9
10	11	13	16	18	19

F. $\frac{1}{10}$ H. $\frac{5}{6}$

G. $\frac{35}{144}$ J. 1

The two-way table provides data about 240 randomly chosen people who visit a movie theater. Use the table for Items 5 and 6.

	Discount Admission	Regular Admission	TOTAL
Purchases a snack	24	72	96
Purchases no snack	36	108	144
TOTAL	60	180	240

5. Consider the following events.

Event A: Pays for a regular admission.
Event B: Purchases a snack.

Which is the best description of the two events?

A. complementary events

B. dependent events

C. independent events

D. mutually exclusive events

6. What is the probability that a visitor to the movie theater purchases a snack given that the visitor pays for a discount admission?

F. 0.1   H. 0.4

G. 0.25   J. 0.75

7. A bag contains 8 yellow marbles and 4 blue marbles. You choose a marble, put it aside, and then choose another marble. What is the probability that you choose two yellow marbles?

A. $\frac{7}{18}$ C. $\frac{4}{9}$

B. $\frac{14}{33}$ D. $\frac{2}{3}$

© Houghton Mifflin Harcourt Publishing Company

---

8. Events A and B are independent events. Which of the following must be true?

F. $P(A \text{ and } B) = P(A) \cdot P(B)$

G. $P(A \text{ and } B) = P(A) + P(B)$

H. $P(A) = P(B)$

J. $P(B|A) = P(A|B)$

9. Which expression can you use to calculate the conditional probability of event A given that event B has occurred?

A. $P(A) + P(B) - P(A \text{ and } B)$

B. $P(B) \cdot P(A|B)$

C. $\dfrac{P(A \text{ and } B)}{P(B)}$

D. $\dfrac{P(A)}{P(B)}$

CONSTRUCTED RESPONSE

10. It is known that 1% of all mice in a laboratory have a genetic mutation. A test for the mutation correctly identifies mice that have the mutation 98% of the time. The test correctly identifies mice that do not have the mutation 96% of the time. A lab assistant tests a mouse and finds that the mouse tests positive for the mutation. The lab assistant decides that the mouse must have the mutation. Is this a good decision? Explain.

No; there is only a 19.8% probability that a mouse that tests positive for the mutation actually has the mutation.

11. Two students, Naomi and Kayla, play a game using the rules shown below. The winner of the game gets a box of 80 fruit chews.

Game Rules

- One student repeatedly tosses a coin.
- When the coin lands heads up, Naomi gets a point.
- When the coin lands tails up, Kayla gets a point.
- The first student to reach 8 points wins the game and gets the fruit chews.

The game gets interrupted when Naomi has 7 points and Kayla has 5 points. How should the 80 fruit chews be divided between the students given that the game was interrupted at this moment? Explain why your answer provides a fair way to divide the fruit chews.

Naomi should get $\frac{7}{8}$ of the fruit chews (i.e., 70 fruit chews) and Kayla should get $\frac{1}{8}$ of the fruit chews (i.e., 10 fruit chews). The game would end in at most three additional coin tosses. There are 8 possible outcomes of these tosses: 7 result in a win for Naomi, while 1 results in a win for Kayla.

© Houghton Mifflin Harcourt Publishing Company

CHAPTER 8

Data Analysis and Statistics

Data Analysis and Statistics

Chapter Focus

Statistics are used to summarize and compare sets of data as well as to generalize from a sample taken from a population to the population as a whole. You will learn how to gather data, how to calculate statistics, how to make claims based on statistics, how to describe your degree of certainty about those claims, and how to make decisions based on statistics. A knowledge of statistics is especially useful when evaluating reports in the media about surveys, studies, and experiments, and when making and analyzing decisions.

Chapter at a Glance

COMMON CORE

Lesson		Standards for Mathematical Content
8-1	Measures of Central Tendency and Variation	CC.9-12.S.ID.1, CC.9-12.S.ID.3
8-2	Data Gathering	CC.9-12.S.IC.1
8-3	Surveys, Experiments, and Observational Studies	CC.9-12.S.IC.3, CC.9-12.S.IC.6
8-4	Significance of Experimental Results	CC.9-12.S.IC.5
8-5	Sampling Distributions	CC.9-12.S.IC.4
8-6	Binomial Distributions	CC.9-12.S.IC.2, CC.9-12.S.MD.3(+), CC.9-12.S.MD.5(+)
8-7	Fitting to a Normal Distribution	CC.9-12.S.ID.4
8-8	Analyzing Decisions	CC.9-12.S.MD.7(+)
	Performance Tasks	
	Assessment Readiness	

COMMON CORE PROFESSIONAL DEVELOPMENT

CC.9-12S.IC.3*

In earlier grades, students were introduced to different ways of collecting data and making comparisons using graphical displays and summary statistics. In Advanced Algebra, students focus on how the method of data collection determines the scope and nature of conclusions that can be drawn from the collected data.

Unpacking the Standards

Understanding the standards and the vocabulary terms in the standards will help you know exactly what you are expected to learn in this chapter.

COMMON CORE CC.9-12.S.ID.2

Use statistics appropriate to the shape of the data distribution to compare center (median, ...) and spread (interquartile range, ...) of two or more different data sets.

Key Vocabulary

statistic *(estadística)* A number that describes a sample. **median of a data set** *(mediana de un conjunto de datos)* For an ordered data set with an odd number of values, the median is the middle value. For an ordered data set with an even number of values, the median is the average of the two middle values. **interquartile range (IQR)** *(rango entre cuartiles)* The difference of the third (upper) and first (lower) quartiles in a data set, representing the middle half of the data.

What It Means For You — Lesson 8-1

You can compare two data sets by comparing their medians and comparing how the data are spread around the medians.

EXAMPLE

Box-and-whisker plots help you compare the center and spread of two data sets.

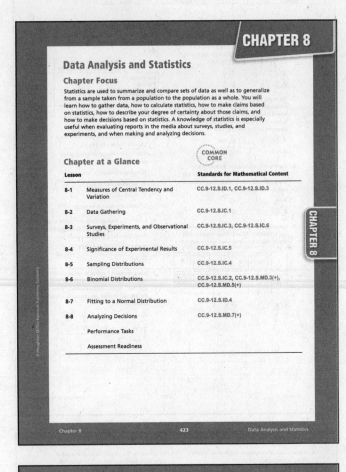

Home Runs by Season

COMMON CORE CC.9-12.S.IC.3

Recognize the purposes of and differences among sample surveys, experiments, and observational studies; explain how randomization relates to each.

Key Vocabulary

observational study *(estudio de observación)* A study that observes individuals and measures variables without controlling the individuals or their environment in any way.

What It Means For You — Lessons 8-2, 8-3

A survey allows you to measure a population variable. An observational study helps you look for associations between variables. An experiment may allow you to establish a cause-and-effect relationship between variables.

EXAMPLE

Survey: You choose 20 students at random from those taking a particular math course at your school, and you ask whether they take notes during class.

Observational Study: You observe whether 20 students taking a particular math course take notes during class, and you compare the test scores of those who take notes with those who don't.

Experiment: You randomly divide 20 students taking a particular math course into two groups of 10. One group is asked to take notes, and the other group is asked not to take notes. You then compare the test scores of the two groups to see if taking notes had an effect on the scores.

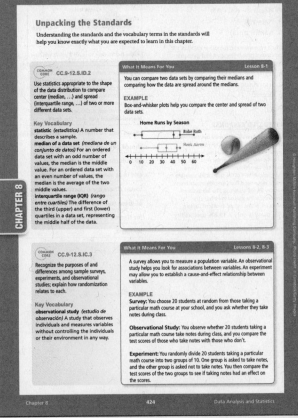

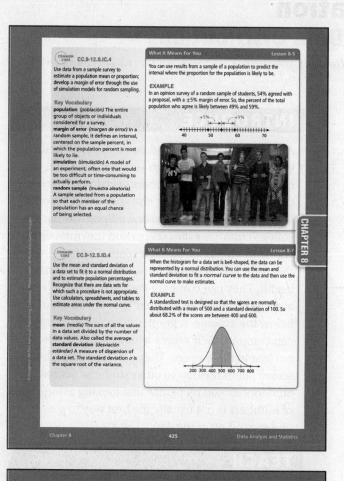

COMMON CORE PROFESSIONAL DEVELOPMENT

CC.9-12.S.ID.4*

Prior to this course, students have studied data distributions by working with line plots, histograms, and box-and-whisker plots. Students may have heard of normal distributions, but it is not likely that they have experience in using them to make specific estimates. During instruction, build on their understanding of data distributions to help them see how areas are used in normal distributions to make estimates. Students should learn that not all data are well described by a normal distribution.

Measures of Central Tendency and Variation
Extension: Data Distributions

Essential question: *How can you use shape, center, and spread to characterize a data distribution?*

COMMON CORE **Standards for Mathematical Content**

CC.9-12.S.ID.1 Represent data with plots on the real number line (dot plots, histograms, and box plots).*

CC.9-12.S.ID.3 Interpret differences in shape, center, and spread in the context of the data sets, accounting for possible effects of extreme data points (outliers).*

Vocabulary

data distribution, uniform distribution, normal distribution, skewed distribution, skewed left, skewed right, mean, median, standard deviation, interquartile range

Prerequisites

Creating line plots, histograms, and box plots

Math Background

The normal distribution, also called a Gaussian distribution or a bell-shaped curve, is likely the most well-known distribution in statistics. Normal distributions can be completely described by their mean and standard deviation. In normal distributions, 68% of all values fall within one standard deviation of the mean. Similarly, 95% of values fall within two standard deviations, and 99.7% of the values fall within three standard deviations of the mean. Normal distributions will be covered in more detail later.

The normal distribution can even be used in situations in which the data are not distributed normally. The central limit theorem states that the distribution of the means of random samples have a normal distribution for large sample sizes. So, normal distributions can be used to describe the averages of data that do not necessarily have a normal distribution themselves.

INTRODUCE

Ask students which would be most useful to them when researching colleges—a list of all of the college entrance exam scores of last year's freshman class, the average college entrance exam score of last year's freshman class, or a graph showing the college entrance exam scores and the number of students who received each score. Guide them to the understanding that the average score can be useful. They can compare their scores with the average score to see whether they are above or below the average. A graph is also useful. Students can compare their scores with all other scores, not just to the average. They can see where their scores fall in relation to other students' scores. Students should recognize that looking at long lists of numbers is not usually the best way to get an understanding of the data.

TEACH

1 EXPLORE

Questioning Strategies

- What values are on the number lines for line plots, histograms, and box plots? **the data values**

- Interpret the values on the number line for each of the three line plots. **The values on the number line in part A are birth months, with 1 representing January, 2 representing February, and so on. In part B, the values are the birth weights of the babies in kilograms from 3.0 kg to 4.0 kg, with each tick mark representing 0.1 kg. In part C, the values are mothers' ages in years.**

- What does the "height" of each vertical stack of X's in the line plots represent? **the number of times each value occurs**

- How many X's are on each line plot? Why? **There are 20 X's on each line plot because the data came from 20 babies.**

Name_____ Class_____ Date_____

8-1

Video Tutor

Measures of Central Tendency and Variation

Extension: Data Distributions

Essential question: *How can you use shape, center, and spread to characterize a data distribution?*

A **data distribution** is a set of numerical data that you can graph using a data display that involves a number line, such as a line plot, histogram, or box plot. The graph will reveal the shape of the distribution.

CC.9-12.S.ID.1

1 EXPLORE   Seeing the Shape of a Data Distribution

The table gives data about a random sample of 20 babies born at a hospital.

A Make a line plot for the distribution of birth months.

Birth month

B Make a line plot for the distribution of birth weights.

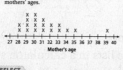
Birth weight (kg)

C Make a line plot for the distribution of mothers' ages.

Mother's age

Baby	Birth month	Birth weight (kg)	Mother's age
1	5	3.3	28
2	7	3.6	31
3	11	3.5	33
4	2	3.4	35
5	10	3.7	39
6	3	3.4	30
7	1	3.5	29
8	4	3.2	30
9	7	3.6	31
10	6	3.4	32
11	9	3.6	33
12	10	3.5	29
13	11	3.4	31
14	1	3.7	29
15	6	3.5	34
16	5	3.8	30
17	8	3.5	32
18	9	3.6	30
19	12	3.3	29
20	2	3.5	28

REFLECT

1a. Describe the shape of the distribution of birth months.

The distribution is fairly level; that is, the data are more or less evenly distributed.

© Houghton Mifflin Harcourt Publishing Company

1b. Describe the shape of the distribution of birth weights.

The distribution is mounded and symmetric.

1c. Describe the shape of the distribution of mothers' ages.

The distribution is mounded and asymmetric; that is, it trails off more to the right than to the left.

PREP FOR CC.9-12.S.ID.3

2 ENGAGE   Understanding Shape, Center, and Spread

As you saw in the Explore, data distributions can have various shapes. Some of these shapes are given names in statistics.

• A distribution whose shape is basically level (that is, it looks like a rectangle) is called a **uniform distribution**.

• A distribution that is mounded in the middle with symmetric "tails" at each end (that is, it looks bell-shaped) is called a **normal distribution**. To be a normal distribution, a data distribution has to have some additional properties besides a bell shape. You will learn more about this in later lessons.

• A distribution that is mounded but not symmetric because one "tail" is much longer than the other is called a **skewed distribution**. When the longer "tail" is on the left, the distribution is called **skewed left**. When the longer "tail" is on the right, the distribution is called **skewed right**.

The figures below show the general shape of normal and skewed distributions.

Skewed left   Symmetric   Skewed right

Shape is one way of characterizing a data distribution. Another way is by identifying the distribution's center and spread.

• The **mean** of n data values is the sum of the data values divided by n. If $x_1, x_2, \ldots, x_n$ are data values from a sample, then the mean $\bar{x}$ is given by:

$$\bar{x} = \frac{x_1 + x_2 + \cdots + x_n}{n}$$

• The **median** of n data values written in ascending order is the middle value if n is odd and is the mean of the two middle values if n is even.

• The **standard deviation** of n data values is the square root of the mean of the squared deviations from the distribution's mean. If $x_1, x_2, \ldots, x_n$ are data values from a sample, then the standard deviation s is given by:

$$s = \sqrt{\frac{(x_1 - \bar{x})^2 + (x_2 - \bar{x})^2 + \cdots + (x_n - \bar{x})^2}{n}}$$

• The **interquartile range**, or IQR, of data values written in ascending order is the difference between the median of the upper half of the data, called the *third quartile* or Q_3, and the median of the lower half of the data, called the *first quartile* or Q_1. So, IQR $= Q_3 - Q_1$.

The first quartile, the median, and the third quartile divide a set of data into four groups that each contain about 25% of the data, so the IQR tells you how spread out the middle 50% (or so) of the data are.

© Houghton Mifflin Harcourt Publishing Company

Questioning Strategies

- What information does a data display give you? the shape of the data distribution

- What information do the mean and median give you? the center of the distribution

- What information do the standard deviation and interquartile range give you? the spread of the distribution

Teaching Strategy

Students should add the vocabulary of this lesson to their vocabulary flash cards from the first lesson. Once the flash cards are complete, put students in pairs. Each student shuffles his or her flash cards. One student from each pair lays the cards down with the words up; the other student lays the cards down with the definition up. Students take turns placing a card with a definition on top of a card with the matching word. Students get a point for each correct match. Each turn begins with the student who is about to match cards either accepting or challenging the previous match. If the student correctly challenges a match, that student earns a point and the opponent loses a point. If the challenging student is incorrect, he or she loses both a point and a turn.

Emphasize to students that in this lesson, they'll be using a very rough definition of normal distribution. A symmetric graph with a peak in the middle is not necessarily a normal distribution. They will learn more about what constitutes a normal distribution in later lessons.

3 EXPLORE

Questioning Strategies

- If the baby weights were more spread out, how would you expect the standard deviation to be different? The standard deviation would be greater.

- Would your answers to the Reflect questions be different if the birth weights were given in pounds instead of kilograms? Why or why not? No; although the numbers representing the mean, median, standard deviation, and IQR would be different (representing pounds), the overall results would not change. The shape of the birth weight distribution would be the same, the mean would still equal the median, and the standard deviation and the IQR would still be significantly less than for the skewed distribution.

Avoid Common Errors

When using multiple lists in a calculator, students can confuse them. Students should write down what set of data is in each list to help them avoid any confusion while using the lists.

To distinguish a population mean from a sample mean, statisticians use the Greek letter mu, written μ, instead of $\bar{x}$. Similarly, they use the Greek letter sigma, written σ, instead of s to distinguish a population standard deviation from a sample standard deviation. Also, for a reason best left to a statistics course, the formula for the sample standard deviation sometimes has $n-1$ rather than n in the denominator of the radicand. (In this book, n will always be used.)

REFLECT

2a. Describe the shape of each distribution in the Explore using the vocabulary defined on the previous page.

Distribution of birth months is uniform; distribution of baby weights is

normal; distribution of mothers' ages is skewed right.

2b. When the center and spread of a distribution are reported, they are generally given either as the mean and standard deviation or as the median and IQR. Why do these pairings make sense?

Standard deviation depends on the mean; IQR depends on the median.

CC.9-12.S.ID.3

3 EXPLORE Relating Center and Spread to Shape

Use a graphing calculator to compute the measures of center and the measures of spread for the distribution of baby weights and the distribution of mothers' ages.

A Enter the two sets of data into two lists on a graphing calculator as shown.

B Calculate the "1-Variable Statistics" for the distribution of baby weights. Record the statistics listed below. (Note: Your calculator may report the standard deviation with a denominator of $n-1$ as "s_x" and the standard deviation with a denominator of n as "σ_x." Use the latter.)

$\bar{x} = $ ___3.5___ Median = ___3.5___

$s \approx $ ___0.14___ IQR $= Q_3 - Q_1 = $ ___0.2___

C Calculate the "1-Variable Statistics" for the distribution of mothers' ages. Record the statistics listed below.

$\bar{x} = $ ___31.15___ Median = ___30.5___

$s \approx $ ___2.6___ IQR $= Q_3 - Q_1 = $ ___3.5___

REFLECT

3a. What do you notice about the mean and median for the symmetric distribution (baby weights) as compared with the mean and median for the skewed distribution (mothers' ages)? Explain why this happens.

Mean and median for a symmetric distribution are equal, but mean and median

for a skewed distribution are not. This happens because the mean is pulled toward

the data values in the longer tail, but the median is not.

3b. One way to compare the spread of two distributions is to find the ratio (expressed as a percent) of the standard deviation to the mean for each distribution. Another way is to find the ratio (expressed as a percent) of the IQR to the median. Calculate these ratios, rounding each to the nearest percent if necessary, for the symmetric distribution (baby weights) and the skewed distribution (mothers' ages). What do you observe when you compare the corresponding ratios? Why does this make sense?

The ratio of the standard deviation to the mean is $\frac{0.14}{3.5} = 4\%$ for the symmetric

distribution and $\frac{2.6}{31.15} = 8\%$ for the skewed distribution, which indicates that the

skewed distribution has a greater spread. The ratio of the IQR to the median is $\frac{0.2}{3.5}$

$= 6\%$ for the symmetric distribution and $\frac{3.5}{30.5} = 11\%$ for the skewed distribution,

which again indicates that the skewed distribution has a greater spread. This

makes sense because the longer tail on a skewed distribution increases the spread.

3c. Which measures of center and spread would you report for the symmetric distribution? For the skewed distribution? Explain your reasoning.

Report either mean and standard deviation or median and IQR for symmetric, but

use only median and IQR for skewed because mean and standard deviation are too

sensitive to the data values in the long tail.

CC.9-12.S.ID.1

4 EXPLORE Making and Analyzing a Histogram

A Use a graphing calculator to make a histogram for the distribution of baby weights. Begin by turning on a statistics plot, selecting the histogram option, and entering the list where the data are stored.

EXPLORE

Questioning Strategies

- Why were you instructed to set Xmin to 3.15 and Xscl to 0.1? This sets the intervals so that each recorded weight shows as a different bar. By setting the minimum to 3.15 and the increment to 0.1, all weights from 3.15 kilograms to 3.25 kilograms are included in the first bar. Thus, the first bar represents 3.2 kilograms, the second bar represents 3.3 kilograms, and so on.

- How are the shapes of the line plot and the histogram for birth weight related? The shapes are the same.

- How would a histogram for the mothers' ages be different from the one for birth weights? Its shape would resemble the shape of the line plot for mothers' ages. Its right tail would be longer than its left tail, meaning that it would be skewed right.

5 EXPLORE

Questioning Strategies

- How do you find the interquartile range (IQR)? Calculate $Q_3 - Q_1$, which is the median of the upper half of the data minus the median of the lower half of the data.

- On the box plot, describe what the IQR corresponds to. the width of the box

- How would a box plot for the birth weights be different from the one for mothers' ages? It would be more symmetric. The vertical line that marks the median would be more centered within the box, and the whiskers would be about the same length.

CLOSE

Essential Question

How can you use shape, center, and spread to characterize a data distribution?
The shape of the distribution of a data set can be shown by displaying the data as a line plot, as a histogram, or as a box plot. The measures of center and spread can be used to summarize the distribution.

Summarize

Have students write a journal entry in which they draw a normal distribution and a skewed distribution. Next to the drawings, they should list the measures of center and spread that are used for each type of distribution and explain why.

B Set the viewing window. To obtain a histogram that looks very much like the line plot that you drew for this data set, use the values shown at the right. Xscl determines the width of each bar, so when Xscl = 0.1 and Xmin = 3.15, the first bar covers the interval $3.15 \leq x < 3.25$, which captures the weight of 3.2 kg.

C Draw the histogram by pressing [GRAPH]. You can obtain the heights of the bars by pressing [TRACE] and using the arrow keys.

REFLECT

4a. By examining the histogram, determine the percent of the data that fall within 1 standard deviation ($s = 0.14$) of the mean ($\bar{x} = 3.5$). That is, determine the percent of the data in the interval $3.5 - 0.14 < x < 3.5 + 0.14$, or $3.36 < x < 3.64$. Explain your reasoning.

The bars that are within 1 standard deviation of the mean have heights of 4, 6, and 4, so 14 out of 20, or 70% of the data are in the interval.

4b. Suppose one of the baby weights is chosen at random. By examining the histogram, determine the probability that the weight is more than 1 standard deviation ($s = 0.14$) above the mean ($\bar{x} = 3.5$). That is, determine the probability that the weight is in the interval $x > 3.5 + 0.14$, or 3.64. Explain your reasoning.

The bars that are more than 1 standard deviation above the mean have heights of 2 and 1, so the probability that the weight is in the interval is $\frac{3}{20} = 0.15$.

4c. Change Xscl from 0.1 to 0.2 and redraw the histogram. Notice that the histogram loses some of its symmetry. Explain why this happens.

The bars are now twice as wide, so weights of 3.2 and 3.3 are combined, weights of 3.4 and 3.5 are combined, and so on. Corresponding bars on each side of the tallest bar no longer have the same height.

4d. To create a histogram for the distribution of mothers' ages, what values of Xscl and Xmin would you use so that the histogram matches the line plot that you drew?

Xscl = 1; Xmin = 27.5

EC 9-12.S.ID.1
5 EXPLORE   Making and Analyzing a Box Plot

A Use a graphing calculator to make a box plot for the distribution of mothers' ages. Begin by turning on a statistics plot, selecting the box plot option, and entering the list where the data are stored. (There are two box plot options: one that shows outliers and one that does not. Choose the second of these.)

B Set the viewing window. Use the values shown at the right.

C Draw the box plot by pressing [GRAPH]. The box plot is based on five key values: the minimum data value, the first quartile, the median, the third quartile, and the maximum data value. You can obtain these values by pressing [TRACE] and using the arrow keys.

REFLECT

5a. How does the box plot show that the distribution is skewed right?

The part of the box to the right of the median is wider than the part to the left, and the "whisker" on the right is longer than the one on the left.

5b. Suppose one of the mothers' ages is chosen at random. Based on the box plot and not the original set of data, what can you say is the approximate probability that the age falls between the median, 30.5, and the third quartile, 32.5? Explain your reasoning.

25% or 0.25 because Q_1, the median, and Q_3 divide the data into four almost-equal parts.

5c. A data value x is considered to be an *outlier* if $x < Q_1 - 1.5(IQR)$ or $x > Q_3 + 1.5(IQR)$. Explain why a mother's age of 39 is an outlier for this data set. Redraw the box plot using the option for showing outliers. How does the box plot change?

$Q_3 + 1.5(IQR) = 32.5 + 1.5(3.5) = 37.75$, and $39 > 37.75$, so 39 is an outlier; the right "whisker" now ends at 35 and there is an isolated dot at 39.

Assign these pages to help your students practice and apply important lesson concepts. For additional exercises, see the Student Edition.

Answers

Additional Practice

1. **a.** 10.5
   b. 11.5
   c. None

2. **a.** 8.6
   b. 9
   c. 9

3. Interquartile range is 4.

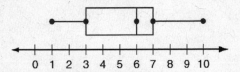

4. Interquartile range is 3.

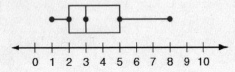

5. 6.8; 2.6   6. 278; 16.7

7. 9.3; 3.0   8. 8.4; 2.9

9. 7.01

10. **a.** 45.1
    b. 13.1
    c. 88
    d. The mean increases from ≈ 41.2 to ≈ 45.1, and the standard deviation increases from ≈ 2.1 to ≈ 13.1.

Problem Solving

1. **a.** 17, 18, 18, 18, 19, 19, 25, 26, 29, 30
   b. Minimum = 17; maximum = 30; median = 19; first quartile = 18; third quartile = 26
   c.

   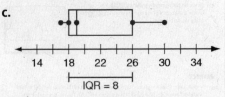

   d. Possible answer: Damien's car gets between 18 to 26 miles per gallon 50% of the time.

2. **a.** $(18 + 17 + 19 + 18 + 18 + 25 + 29 + 30 + 26 + 19)/10 = 21.9$
   b. -3.9; -4.9; -2.9; -3.9; -3.9; 3.1; 7.1; 8.1; 4.1; -2.9; 15.21; 24.01; 8.41; 15.21; 15.21; 9.61; 50.41; 65.61; 16.81; 8.41
   c. Find the square root of the mean of the $(x - \bar{x})^2$ terms.
   d. 4.78
   e. Possible answer: All but 3 data points are clustered within 1 standard deviation of the mean.

3. He is correct; possible answer: the standard deviation depends on the entire set of data values; whereas the interquartile range depends on only 2 values, the first and third quartiles.

8-1

Additional Practice

Find the mean, median, and mode of each data set.

1. { 12, 11, 17, 3, 9, 14, 16, 2 }

   a. Mean _____

   b. Median _____

   c. Mode _____

2. { 6, 9, 9, 20, 4, 5, 9, 13, 10, 1 }

   a. Mean _____

   b. Median _____

   c. Mode _____

Make a box-and-whisker plot of the data. Find the interquartile range.

3. { 3, 7, 7, 3, 10, 1, 6, 6 }

```
+--+--+--+--+--+--+--+--+--+--+
0  1  2  3  4  5  6  7  8  9 10
```

4. { 1, 2, 3, 5, 3, 5, 8, 2 }

```
+--+--+--+--+--+--+--+--+--+--+
0  1  2  3  4  5  6  7  8  9 10
```

Find the variance and standard deviation.

5. { 7, 4, 3, 9, 2 }

6. { 35, 67, 21, 16, 24, 51, 18, 32 }

7. { 19, 23, 17, 20, 25, 19, 15, 22 }

8. { 5, 12, 10, 13, 8, 11, 15, 12 }

Solve.

9. The probability distribution for the amount of rain that falls on Boston in May each year is given below. Find the expected amount of rain for Boston in May.

Inches of Rain, n	5	6	7	8
Probability	0.05	0.10	0.64	0.21

10. A biologist is growing bacteria in the lab. For a certain species of bacteria, she records these doubling times: 41 min, 45 min, 39 min, 42 min, 38 min, 88 min, 43 min, 40 min, 44 min, 39 min, 42 min, and 40 min.

   a. Find the mean of the data. _____

   b. Find the standard deviation. _____

   c. Identify any outliers. _____

   d. Describe how any outlier affects the mean and the standard deviation.

Problem Solving

Each week, Damien records the miles per gallon for his car, to the nearest whole number. Over a period of 10 weeks, the data are 18, 17, 19, 18, 18, 25, 29, 30, 26, 19. He wants to arrange and summarize his data so that he can analyze it.

1. Make a box-and-whisker plot of his data.

   a. Order the data from least to greatest. _____

   b. Identify the minimum, maximum, median, first quartile, and third quartile.

   c. Use the number line to make a box-and-whisker plot of the data. Find and label the interquartile range.

```
+----+----+----+----+----+----+
14   18   22   26   30   34
```

   d. Explain what the interquartile range represents in terms of the car's miles per gallon.

2. Find the standard deviation for the data.

   a. Write an equation and solve to find the mean.

   b. Complete the table to show the difference between the mean and each data value, and the square of that difference.

Data Value, x	18	17	19	18	18	25	29	30	26	19
$x - \bar{x}$										
$(x - \bar{x})^2$										

   c. Explain how to use the data from the table to find the standard deviation.

   d. What is the standard deviation for the data? _____

   e. Explain what the standard deviation represents in terms of the car's miles per gallon.

3. Damien thinks that the standard deviation is a more reliable measure of dispersion than the interquartile range. Is he correct? Explain.

Data Gathering
Going Deeper

Essential question: What are the different methods for gathering data about a population?

COMMON CORE **Standards for Mathematical Content**

CC.9-12.S.IC.1 Understand statistics as a process for making inferences about population parameters based on a random sample from that population.*

Vocabulary

numerical data, categorical data, population, individuals, census, parameter, sampling, statistic, representative sample, proportion

Prerequisites

Calculating the mean of a data set

Math Background

Sampling is an important aspect of statistics. It involves making observations of or gathering data from a population, either the entire population (a census) or a part of a population (a sample). Typically, the goal of sampling is to gain knowledge about a population, often to make predictions. Statistics are also used to persuade.

The predictions based on statistics have a certain amount of error associated with them. Error can come about from the sampling method used, whether intentional (sometimes done when using statistics to persuade) or unintentional. *How to Lie with Statistics*, written by Darrell Huff in 1954, outlines how errors can lead to inaccurate conclusions, such as the rather famous but inaccurate prediction of who would win the presidential election in 1948. A frequent source of errors in statistical predictions is bias, which makes it more likely that certain subsets of the population are over-represented in the sample. Sampling methods can affect the statistics gathered, and, therefore, the predictions that are based on them.

INTRODUCE

Ask students to give examples of using statistical surveys. **Answers will vary: Students may mention "4 out of 5 dentists surveyed" or political polls.** Ask students how this information might have been gathered. Prompt them if necessary: Were the data gathered from an online survey? from people on the street? from a poll conducted by telephone? Use this to introduce the idea of a sample.

TEACH

1 ENGAGE

Questioning Strategies

- What is the difference between a parameter and a statistic? **A parameter is based on a census; it represents an entire population. A statistic is based on a sample.**

- Describe how a statistic might not be representative of an entire population. **Statistics can result in accurate estimates of parameters. This will happen if the sample is representative of the population.**

- A reporter for a high school paper asked all members of the track team how many miles they run each week. What type of data is the reporter gathering? **numerical** Is this a census or a sample? Why? **It's a census of the track team—unless your intended population is the entire student body, in which case it's a sample.** Will the data be representative of the entire student body? Why or why not? **No; members of the track team most likely run more than members of the entire student body.**

Teaching Strategy

This unit contains a great deal of new vocabulary. Making flash cards will help students learn the language of statistics. They can add to their cards as the unit progresses. In addition to using the cards to study, students can play games with the flash cards, such as one student giving clues to a second who must guess what is on the card.

Name _____ Class _____ Date _____

8-2

Video Tutor

Data Gathering
Going Deeper

Essential question: *What are the different methods for gathering data about a population?*

CC.9-12.S.IC.1

1 ENGAGE — Understanding Data-Gathering Techniques

In the branch of mathematics known as statistics, you work with data. Data can be **numerical**, such as heights or salaries, or **categorical**, such as eye color or political affiliation. You collect data about a **population** by surveying or studying some or all of the **individuals** in the population.

When *all* the individuals in a population are surveyed or studied, the data-gathering technique is called a **census**. A **parameter** is a number that summarizes a characteristic of the population.

When only some of the individuals in a population are surveyed or studied, the data-gathering technique is called **sampling**. A **statistic** is a number that summarizes a characteristic of a sample. Statistics can be used to estimate parameters. Samples that result in accurate estimates are said to be **representative** of the population.

There are a variety of sampling methods, characterized by how the individuals in the sample are chosen. The table below lists a few.

Sampling Method	Description
Random	Each individual in the population has an equal chance of being selected.
Self-selected	Individuals volunteer to be part of the sample.
Convenience	Individuals are selected based on how accessible they are.
Systematic	Members of the sample are chosen according to a rule, such as every *n*th individual in the population.
Stratified	The individuals are organized into groups, and individuals from each group are selected (typically through a random sample within each group).
Cluster	The individuals are organized into groups, and all of the individuals in just some of the groups are selected (typically through a random sample of the groups).

REFLECT

1a. Give an example of numerical data and an example of categorical data other than the examples listed in the first paragraph.

Answers will vary. Sample answer: An example of numerical data is age. An example of categorical data is gender.

1b. Asking your friends is an example of what type of sampling method? Explain.

Convenience sampling, because friends are easily accessible.

© Houghton Mifflin Harcourt Publishing Company

1c. Which sampling method do you think is most likely to result in a representative sample? Why?

A random sample is most likely to be representative because the method is unbiased and gives each individual the same chance of being selected.

1d. Which sampling method do you think would be least likely to result in a representative sample? Why?

A self-selected sample is least likely to be representative because the method is biased toward individuals who have a strong interest in the results.

1e. Explain why a researcher might use a sampling method rather than a census to gather information about a population.

A census of all individuals may be too expensive, impractical, or even impossible to obtain.

CC.9-12.S.IC.1

2 EXPLORE — Finding Statistics Using Various Sampling Methods

The salaries (in thousands of dollars) of all 30 employees at a small company are listed in the table.

Salaries at a Small Company									
21	24	26	28	30	32	33	35	37	41
44	46	47	49	50	51	52	54	55	57
58	62	62	64	64	65	70	71	73	80

Use the table to generate a sample of 6 individuals using each sampling method, and then use the sample to predict the mean of the population.

A Suppose individuals whose salaries are 51, 57, 58, 65, 70, and 73 volunteer to be in the sample. Compute the self-selected sample's mean, rounding to the nearest whole number.

Mean ≈ 62

B Take a convenience sample by choosing the 6 numbers in the first two columns of the table. Record the salaries, and then compute the sample's mean, rounding to the nearest whole number.

21, 24, 44, 46, 58, 62; mean ≈ 43

C Take a systematic sample by choosing every fifth number in the list, reading from left to right in each row. Record the salaries, and then compute the sample's mean, rounding to the nearest whole number.

30, 41, 50, 57, 64, 80; mean ≈ 54

© Houghton Mifflin Harcourt Publishing Company

Questioning Strategies

- How are the salaries organized in the table? **They are in ascending order, from left to right and top to bottom.**

- Explain how taking a convenience sample different from the one described in part B could select all low salaries. **Take all of the salaries from the top row.** Explain how the convenience sample in part B avoids this issue. **It takes salaries from all three rows.** Explain why it doesn't avoid the issue completely. **It takes salaries from the left side of the table, which are lower than those on the right side.**

- With the way the table is organized, the systematic sample is almost as close to the actual mean as the random sample. Why? **The data are organized in ascending order. So taking every 5th number gets some low, some medium, and some high salaries.**

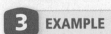

3 EXAMPLE

Questioning Strategies

- How do you know that the proportion of runners is 50%? **There are 5 entries in the table for running out of 10 total entries; $5 \div 10 = 0.5 = 50\%$**

- What proportion of the adults who get cardio exercise walk? **20%** What proportion swim? **10%** What proportion do some other form of cardio exercise? **20%** What is the total of all of the proportions, including runners? **100%** Is this 100% of all of the people surveyed? Explain. **No; it's all of the people who said they get cardio exercise, which is only 40% of the people surveyed.**

EXTRA EXAMPLE

A ski area uses the information gained from scanning season ski passes in lift lines to determine how many days out of each season the pass holders ski and how many lift rides they take each day. The table lists the data for a random sample of 15 skiers. Calculate statistics from the sample and use the statistics to make predictions about the ski habits of the approximately 10,000 season pass holders.

Number of Days	Number of Lift Rides
10	12
5	15
2	6
14	18
27	10
3	6
18	15
5	9
4	11
16	13
7	14
12	10
19	8
14	6
25	15

A. What proportion of the skiers ski 10 or more days? Of those, what proportion take 12 or more lift rides in a day? **60%; about 55.5%**

B. Use the proportions from part A to predict the total number of skiers who ski 10 or more days in a season and take 12 or more lift rides each time they ski. **about 3330**

C. Calculate the following two means from the sample data: 1) mean number of days skied and 2) mean number of lift rides taken per day. **about 12.1; 11.2**

D. Use the means from part C to predict the number of lift rides taken per season by a skier. **about 136**

D Take a random sample. Begin by labeling the data in the table with the identifiers 1–10 for the first row, 11–20 for the second row, and 21–30 for the third row. Then use a graphing calculator's random integer generator to generate 6 identifiers between 1 and 30, as shown. (If any identifiers are repeated, simply generate replacements for them until you have 6 unique identifiers.) Record the corresponding salaries, and then compute the sample's mean, rounding to the nearest whole number.

Answers will vary. Sample answer for the

identifiers shown on the calculator screen:

65, 44, 26, 54, 58, 30; mean ≈ 46

REFLECT

2a. Compute the mean of the population. Then list the four samples from best to worst in terms of how well each sample mean estimates the population mean.

Population mean ≈ 49; random, systematic, convenience, self-selected

2b. How do the best and worst sampling methods from your list compare with your answers to Reflect Questions 1c and 1d?

Answers will vary, but students should generally find that random samples

are best and self-selected samples are worst.

Some statistics, such as the mean, apply only to numerical data. For categorical data, an appropriate statistic is a **proportion**, which is the relative frequency of a category.

CC.9-12.S.IC.1

3 EXAMPLE Making Predictions from a Sample

A community health center surveyed a small random sample of adults in the community about their exercise habits. The survey asked whether the person engages in regular cardio exercise (running, walking, swimming, or other) and, if so, what the duration and frequency of exercise are.

Of the 25 people surveyed, 10 said that they do engage in regular cardio exercise. The table lists the data for those 10 people.

Calculate statistics from the sample, and use the statistics to make predictions about the exercise habits of the approximately 5000 adults living in the community.

Type of exercise	Duration (minutes spent exercising)	Frequency (times per week)
Running	30	4
Walking	20	5
Running	40	3
Running	60	6
Swimming	40	4
Other	90	2
Running	30	3
Walking	20	5
Running	30	4
Other	120	1

A Calculate the following two proportions from the sample data.

Proportion of adults who get regular cardio exercise $= \dfrac{10}{25} =$ 40 %

Proportion of runners among those who get regular cardio exercise $= \dfrac{5}{10} =$ 50 %

B Use the proportions from part A and the verbal model below to predict the number of runners among all adults living in the community.

Number of runners in the community	=	Number of adults in the community	×	Proportion of adults who get cardio exercise	×	Proportion of runners among those who get regular cardio exercise

Number of runners in the community = 5000 · 0.4 · 0.5 = 1000

C Calculate the following two means from the sample data.

Mean duration of exercise for those who get regular cardio exercise = 48 min

Mean frequency of exercise for those who get regular cardio exercise = 3.7 times per week

D Use the means from part C to predict, for those who get regular cardio exercise, the number of *hours* spent exercising each week. Show your calculations and include units.

Time spent exercising each week $\approx \dfrac{48 \text{ min} \cdot 3.7}{60 \text{ min/h}} \approx$ 3 hours

REFLECT

3a. One of the *categorical variables* in the survey was regular cardio exercise. That variable had only two possible values: yes or no. What was the other categorical variable, and what were its possible values?

Type of exercise; running, walking, swimming, other

3b. What were the two *numerical variables* in the survey, and what were their possible values?

Duration of exercise, which could be any positive number (though generally a

multiple of 10 less than, say, 240); weekly frequency of exercise, which could be

any counting number from 1 to 7

3c. How much confidence do you have in the predictions made from the results of the survey? Explain your reasoning.

Answers will vary. Students should note that the sample was random, which

makes the results representative of the population, but the sample size was small,

which may not make the results accurate.

© Houghton Mifflin Harcourt Publishing Company

MATHEMATICAL PRACTICE · Highlighting the Standards

1 ENGAGE and 3 EXAMPLE provide opportunities to address Mathematical Practice Standard 6 (Attend to precision). Students will need to be precise in their communication and their choice of vocabulary. In 3 EXAMPLE, they will need to be clear and concise about whether they are discussing the population (5000 people), the sample (25 people), those from the sample who are runners (10 people), or their projection of those of the population who are runners (1000 people). This example also provides an opportunity to practice newly learned vocabulary and to clearly state which group of people or proportion they are discussing.

CLOSE

Essential Question

What are the different methods for gathering data about a population?

A census in which information is gathered from every individual in the population can be used. If a census is impractical, a sampling method can be used. Sampling techniques include random, self-selected, convenience, systematic, stratified, and cluster.

Summarize

Have students write a journal entry discussing the different types of sampling—random, self-selected, convenience, systematic, stratified, and cluster. The entry should include a description and an example of each type, a reason why you might use each type, and a statement about how representative of the entire population each type would be.

PRACTICE

Where skills are taught	Where skills are practiced
1 ENGAGE	EXS. 1–10
3 EXAMPLE	EXS. 11–14

PRACTICE

A student council wants to know whether students would like the council to sponsor a mid-winter dance or a mid-winter carnival this year. Classify each sampling method.

1. Survey every tenth student on the school's roster. <u>systematic</u>

2. Survey all freshmen and all juniors. <u>cluster</u>

3. Survey 20 freshmen, 20 sophomores, 20 juniors, and 20 seniors. <u>stratified</u>

4. Survey those who ask the council president for a questionnaire. <u>self-selected</u>

5. Survey those who happen to be in the cafeteria at noon. <u>convenience</u>

Use the following information for Exercises 6–9.

The officers of a neighborhood association want to know whether residents are interested in beautifying the neighborhood and, if so, how much money they are willing to contribute toward the costs involved. The officers are considering the three sampling methods below.

A. Call and survey every tenth resident on the association's roster.

B. Randomly select and survey 10 residents from among those who come to the neighborhood block party.

C. Mail a survey to every resident with instructions to complete and mail the survey back.

6. Identify the population.

<u>all residents of the neighborhood</u>

7. Which sampling method is most likely to result in a representative sample of the population? Explain.

<u>Method A; if method B is used, those who do not attend the block party have</u>

<u>no chance of being represented and if method C is used, only people who feel</u>

<u>strongly are likely to mail their surveys back.</u>

8. Describe another sampling method that is likely to result in a representative sample of the population.

<u>Randomly select names from the association's roster.</u>

9. Describe the categorical and numerical data that the officers of the neighborhood association want to gather through a survey.

<u>Categorical: interest in beautifying neighborhood; numerical: amount willing to</u>

<u>contribute</u>

Use the following information for Exercises 10–14.

A community theater association plans to produce three plays for the upcoming season. The association surveys a random sample of the approximately 7000 households in the community to see if an adult member of the household is interested in attending plays and, if so, what type of plays the person prefers (comedy, drama, or musical), how many members of the household (including the person surveyed) might attend plays, and how many of the three plays those household members might attend.

Of the 50 adults surveyed, 12 indicated an interest in attending plays. The table lists the data for those 12 people.

Preferred type of play	Number of people attending	Number of plays attending
Comedy	2	1
Musical	3	2
Musical	1	2
Drama	2	3
Comedy	3	2
Comedy	2	3
Musical	4	1
Drama	2	3
Comedy	2	2
Musical	2	3
Comedy	5	1
Drama	1	2

10. Describe the categorical and numerical data gathered in the survey.

<u>Categorical: interest in attending plays, preferred type of play;</u>

<u>numerical: number of household members who might attend plays,</u>

<u>how many plays they might attend</u>

11. Calculate the proportion of adults who indicated an interest in attending plays. Then calculate the proportion of those interested in attending plays who prefer dramas.

<u>$\frac{12}{50} = 24\%$; $\frac{3}{12} = 25\%$</u>

12. Approximately 15,000 adults live in the community. Predict the number of adults who prefer plays that are dramas. Show your calculations.

<u>$15{,}000 \cdot 0.24 \cdot 0.25 = 900$</u>

13. For an adult with an interest in attending plays, calculate the mean number of household members who might attend plays. Then calculate the mean number of plays that those household members might attend. Round each mean to the nearest tenth.

<u>mean number attending $\approx$ 2.4; mean number of plays $\approx$ 2.1</u>

14. The theater association plans to sells tickets to the plays for $40 each. Predict the amount of revenue from ticket sales. Show your calculations and include units.

<u>Predicted number of households with an adult having an interest in attending</u>

<u>plays = 7000 $\cdot$ 0.24 = 1680; predicted number of tickets sold =</u>

<u>1680 households $\cdot \frac{2.4 \text{ people}}{\text{household}} \cdot \frac{2.1 \text{ tickets}}{\text{person}} = 8476.2$ tickets;</u>

<u>predicted revenue from ticket sales = 8467.2 tickets $\cdot \frac{\$40}{\text{ticket}} = \$338{,}688$</u>

ADDITIONAL PRACTICE AND PROBLEM SOLVING

Assign these pages to help your students practice and apply important lesson concepts. For additional exercises, see the Student Edition.

Answers

Additional Practice

1. B

2. A

3. B

4. A

5. 500 students

6. 100 students

Problem Solving

1. 902 students

2. 132 students

3. 1034 students

4. 352 students

5. Yes; the sample is a convenience sample so it is likely to be biased.

6. No; the population may be underrepresented because the sample only includes mall shoppers.

7. A

8. G

8-2

Name_____ Class_____ Date_____

Additional Practice

Decide which sampling method, A or B, is less likely to result in a biased sample.

1. A representative of a mall wants to know whether the mall's customers would shop at a new audio equipment store in the mall.

   A. He asks every 5th person walking into an electronics store if they would shop at a new audio equipment store in the mall.

   B. He asks every 5th person walking into the main mall entrance if they would shop at a new audio equipment store in the mall.

   _____

2. A researcher wants to know the average amount of debt college students expect to have.

   A. She surveys 50 randomly-selected students on several college campuses with different tuitions and with different kinds of programs.

   B. She surveys 100 randomly-selected students at an expensive medical school.

   _____

Decide which survey is more likely to result in a sample that is representative of the population.

3. The manager of a movie theater wants to know what type of movies his customers prefer.

   A. He asks every 3rd customer coming out of a comedy movie.

   B. He asks every 10th customer who enters the theater during a day when the theater is showing an assortment of movie types.

   _____

4. The chef at a restaurant wants to get feedback on the quality of his food.

   A. He has each server at the restaurant survey 5 customers during each shift for a week.

   B. He has the servers at the restaurant survey every customer on a night when family members of employees get a discount.

   _____

100 students out of 1000 at a school were surveyed. The results are recorded in each problem below. Predict the number of students in the entire population that would answer similarly.

5. 50 ride the bus to school.   _____

6. 10 transferred from another school.   _____

Problem Solving

100 students out of 1100 at a school were surveyed. The results are recorded in each problem below. For Exercises 1–4, predict the number of students in the population that would answer similarly.

1. 82 students said they would take a study hall or resource period if it were offered. **Solution: 82 x 11 = 902**   __902 students__

2. 12 students said they were members of the after-school music program. ____ x ____ = 132   _____

3. 94 students said they used the Internet for their homework.   _____

4. 32 students said they drove to school.   _____

5. The principal wanted to know if he should allow cell phones in the classroom. He surveyed the students in Algebra 2 class. Decide whether the sampling method could result in a biased sample. Explain your reasoning.

   _____

6. A discount store chain wants to know how often families in a certain area would shop regularly at a discount store. Their representative surveys 100 people at a mall in the same area. Are his results likely to be representative of the population? Explain.

   _____

Select the best answer.

7. The director of the Glee Club would like to know if her Booster Club parents would do a fundraiser. Which sampling method is most likely to yield an accurate prediction of the population?

   A Survey every 3rd Booster Club parent who comes to a fundraiser meeting.

   B Survey every 10th Booster Club parent who comes to a fundraiser meeting.

   C Survey only the parents who respond to a letter from the director.

8. The principal of the school would like to determine if the cafeteria should sell snacks during non-lunch hour periods. Which sampling method is most likely to yield an accurate prediction of the population?

   F Survey every 20th student who enters the cafeteria during lunch hour.

   G Survey 50 random students each from the 9th, 10th, 11th, and 12th grades.

   H Survey the first 25 students that walk into the school.

Surveys, Experiments, and Observational Studies
Going Deeper

Essential question: *What kinds of statistical research are there, and which ones can establish cause-and-effect relationships between variables?*

Standards for Mathematical Content

CC.9-12.S.IC.3 Recognize the purposes of and differences among sample surveys, experiments, and observational studies; explain how randomization relates to each.*

CC.9-12.S.IC.6 Evaluate reports based on data.*

Vocabulary
survey, observational study, factor, experiment, treatment, randomized comparative experiment, treatment group, control group

Prerequisites
Data-gathering techniques

Math Background
Students are familiar with various data-gathering techniques and understand the advantages of using random samples. Students have analyzed examples of surveys and evaluated how well the results represent the population based on the sampling technique used. Students understand that accurate predictions can be made based on data obtained from a sample only if that sample accurately represents the population. However, even if the sample is representative of the population, there are other factors that can prevent a survey or another kind of study from yielding accurate results.

INTRODUCE

Review the various data-gathering techniques students have learned. Also, have students look back at some of the surveys in the examples and exercises in that lesson. Ask students to identify possible ways that the results of the surveys could have been influenced by how the survey questions were worded. Guide students to discover other factors that could also affect the accuracy of the data gathered, such as who asks the questions in an interview and whether a survey can be completed anonymously.

TEACH

1 EXAMPLE

Questioning Strategies

- Are biased questions in a survey always intentional on the part of the person designing the survey? **No, the bias could be completely unintentional, which is why it is a good idea to have someone uninvolved with the survey look at the questions before the survey is administered.**

- Many surveys are conducted over the telephone. How could using only landline phones to conduct a survey affect the outcome? **People with only cell phones will not be included. Those people may be younger or more urban than people with landline phones and therefore be underrepresented in the survey.**

Teaching Strategy

Students may benefit from acting out interview and telephone surveys. Have students design survey questions, including questions that may be biased. Challenge the class to identify potential sources of error for each survey and suggest ways that the accuracy of the survey can be improved.

EXTRA EXAMPLE

Ken, an artist, conducts one-on-one interviews with a random sample of people at the opening night of his latest exhibit to have them rate the quality of his artwork. Explain why the results of this survey are likely to be inaccurate and then suggest a way to improve the accuracy of the survey. **Because the person conducting the survey is the artist, people who do not like the artwork may not give their true opinion out of concern for Ken's feelings. A better survey would involve a neutral interviewer or allow people to respond anonymously.**

8-3

Surveys, Experiments, and Observational Studies
Going Deeper

Essential question: What kinds of statistical research are there, and which ones can establish cause-and-effect relationships between variables?

A **survey** measures characteristics of interest about a population using a sample selected from the population. A sample needs to be representative of the population in order for the measurements obtained from the sample to be accurate. Random sampling is generally the best way to ensure representation.

Even when random sampling is used for a survey, the survey's results can have errors. Some of the sources of errors are:

- *Biased questions:* The wording of questions in a survey can influence the way people respond to the questions. Survey questions need to be worded in a neutral, unbiased way.

- *Interviewer effect:* If the questions in a survey are being asked by an interviewer, the person being interviewed may give inaccurate responses to avoid being embarrassed. For instance, if the questions involve sensitive issues, the person may not tell the truth, or if the questions involve complex or unfamiliar issues, the person may resort to guessing.

- *Nonresponse:* Some people may be difficult or impossible to contact, or they may simply refuse to participate once contacted. If nonresponse rates are higher for certain subgroups of a population, such as the elderly, then those subgroups will be underrepresented in the survey results.

CC.9-12.S.IC.3

1 EXAMPLE Detecting Errors in Surveys

Explain why the results of each survey are likely to be inaccurate and then suggest a way to improve the accuracy of the survey.

A Mrs. Ruben, the owner of a business, conducts one-on-one interviews with a random sample of employees to have them rate how satisfied they are with different aspects of their jobs.

Because the person conducting the survey is the owner of the business, the employees may not be completely open about any job dissatisfaction they may have, since they may feel that their job security is at stake. A better survey would involve a neutral interviewer or allow the employees to respond anonymously.

B In a random sample of town residents, a survey asks, "Are you in favor of a special tax levy to renovate the dilapidated town hall?"

The question is biased because the word "dilapidated" suggests that the town hall is in a complete state of disrepair, which makes it seem that a renovation is urgently needed. The question could begin with a factual list of repairs that need to be made, followed by "Are you in favor of a special tax levy to make these repairs?"

REFLECT

1a. Even if the survey question in part B is revised to give a factual list of repairs that need to be made to the town hall, do the people surveyed have enough information to give an informed and accurate response? Explain.

No, because most people responding to the survey will want to know the amount of the tax levy; without that knowledge, they may be likely to respond negatively out of fear that their taxes will increase too much.

An **observational study** can be used to determine whether an existing condition, called a **factor**, in a population is related to a characteristic of interest. For instance, an observational study might be used to find the incidence of heart disease among those who smoke. In the study, being a smoker is the factor, and having heart disease is the characteristic of interest.

In an observational study, the condition already exists in the population. In an **experiment**, the condition is created by imposing a **treatment** on the sample. For instance, an experiment might be conducted by having a group of people with eczema take a vitamin E pill daily, and then observing whether their symptoms improve. In the experiment, taking the vitamin E pill is the treatment, and improvement of symptoms is the characteristic of interest.

CC.9-12.S.IC.3

2 EXAMPLE Identifying Observational Studies and Experiments

Determine whether each research study is an observational study or an experiment. Identify the factor if it is an observational study or the treatment if it is an experiment. Also identify the characteristic of interest.

A Researchers measure the cholesterol of 50 subjects who report that they eat fish regularly and 50 subjects who report that they do not eat fish regularly.

Observational study; factor: eating fish regularly; characteristic of interest: cholesterol level

B Researchers have 100 subjects with high cholesterol take fish oil pills daily for two months. They monitor the cholesterol of the subjects during that time.

Experiment; treatment: taking fish oil tablets daily; characteristic of interest: cholesterol level

REFLECT

2a. Suppose the researchers in part A find that considerably more people who eat fish regularly have normal cholesterol levels than those who do not eat fish regularly. Is it reasonable to conclude that eating fish regularly has an effect on cholesterol? Explain.

No; there may be other factors that the people who eat fish regularly have in common, such as regular exercise, and it may be those factors that have an effect on cholesterol.

© Houghton Mifflin Harcourt Publishing Company

Notes

EXAMPLE

Identifying Strategies

Suppose the researcher had picked a trial that could differ from subjects who took the fish pill and lower cholesterol that could ...

EXTRA EXAMPLE

2 EXAMPLE

Questioning Strategies

- Suppose the researchers in part B find that considerably more subjects who took the fish oil pills had lower cholesterol after two months. Is it reasonable to conclude that taking fish oil pills has an effect of lowering cholesterol? Explain. **Yes; if taking the fish oil pills was the only difference between the two groups of subjects, the treatment of taking a fish oil pill could be determined to have an effect of lowering cholesterol.**

- What is an example of a situation for which an observational study would be better than an experiment? **If the treatment being imposed in an experiment could be harmful, then an observational study would be better. For example, if researchers want to study whether eating fried food every day increases cholesterol, it would be better to conduct an observational study of people who already report that they eat fried food every day rather than ask people to engage in the potentially harmful behavior as a treatment in an experiment.**

Avoid Common Errors

Results of observational studies are often incorrectly interpreted as establishing a cause-and-effect relationship. Remind students that observational studies can establish only an association between a factor and a characteristic of interest.

EXTRA EXAMPLE

Researchers measure the bone density of 50 subjects who report that they take a daily multivitamin and 50 subjects who report that they do not take a daily multivitamin. Determine whether the research study is an observational study or an experiment. Identify the factor if it is an observational study or the treatment if it is an experiment. Also, identify the characteristic of interest. **observational study; factor: taking a daily multivitamin; characteristic of interest: bone density**

3 EXAMPLE

Questioning Strategies

- In the research study in part A, how would the experiment be affected if subjects in the control group simply did not take any tablet at all? **If subjects in the control group did not take a tablet, then the placebo effect could make it difficult to interpret the results of the experiment. If the treatment group had different outcomes from the control group, researchers could not tell whether the result was actually due to the zinc in the tablet or merely the effect of taking a pill.**

- In the research study in part B, could the control group be subjects who did not study for the test? Explain. **The focus of the research is the effect of having a classmate involved in the studying process, not the effect of studying itself. If the control group were subjects who did not study for the test, then the focus of the research would be more on the effect of studying versus not studying.**

Differentiated Instruction

Visual learners may benefit by thinking of ways to present the results of a randomized comparative experiment. For instance, for the experiment in part A, the results might be presented in a bar graph, with a bar for the treatment group and a bar for the control group. The height of a bar would indicate the mean duration of the colds for the group.

EXTRA EXAMPLE

To see whether honey has an effect on the duration of a sore throat, half the subjects took lozenges containing honey at the onset of a sore throat, and half took lozenges without any honey. The durations of the sore throats were then recorded. Identify the control group and the treatment group in the experiment. Assume all subjects were selected randomly. **control group: subjects who took lozenges without honey; treatment group: subjects who took lozenges with honey**

2b. In medical research, subjects sometimes respond to a treatment even if the treatment, called a *placebo*, is designed not to have an effect. (For instance, a placebo may be a pill with no active ingredients.) If the researchers in part B find that taking fish oil pills lowers cholesterol, what should they do to rule out the possibility of a placebo effect?

Give a placebo pill to a second group of subjects to see what happens to

their cholesterol.

Whether a study is observational or experimental, it should be *comparative* in order to establish a connection between the factor or treatment and the characteristic of interest. For instance, determining the rate of car accidents among people who talk on cell phones while driving is pointless unless you compare it with the rate of car accidents among people who don't talk on cell phones while driving and find that it is significantly different.

While a comparative observational study can suggest a relationship between two variables, such as cell phone use while driving and car accidents, it cannot establish a cause-and-effect relationship because there can be *confounding variables* (also called *lurking variables*) that influence the results. For instance, perhaps people who talk on cell phones while driving are more likely to drive aggressively, so it is the aggressive driving (not the cell phone use) that leads to a higher rate of car accidents.

In an experiment, randomization can remove the problem of a confounding variable by distributing the variable among the groups being compared so that its influence on the groups is more or less equal. Therefore, the best way to establish a cause-and-effect relationship between two variables is through a **randomized comparative experiment** where subjects are randomly divided into two groups: the **treatment group**, which is given the treatment, and the **control group**, which is not.

3 EXAMPLE CC.9-12.S.IC.3 **Identifying Control Groups and Treatment Groups**

Identify the control group and treatment group in each experiment. Assume all subjects of the research are selected randomly.

A To see whether zinc has an effect on the duration of a cold, half the subjects took tablets containing zinc at the onset of cold symptoms, and half took tablets without any zinc. The durations of the colds were then recorded.

Control group: _Subjects who took tablets without zinc_

Treatment group: _Subjects who took tablets with zinc_

B To see whether reviewing for a test with a classmate improves test scores, half the subjects studied with a classmate prior to taking a test, and half studied for the test alone. The test scores were then recorded.

Control group: _Subjects who studied for the test alone_

Treatment group: _Subjects who studied for the test with a classmate_

© Houghton Mifflin Harcourt Publishing Company

REFLECT

3a. How does using a control group help a researcher interpret the results of an experiment? How does using randomization help?

A control group provides a basis for comparison, so the researcher can observe

the magnitude of the effect that the manipulated variable has on the treatment

group. Randomization assures the researcher that any observed difference in effect

between the treatment and control groups is due to the manipulated variable and

not some other variable.

When you encounter media reports of statistical research in your daily life, you should judge any reported conclusions on the basis of how the research was conducted. Among the questions you should consider are:

• Is the research a survey, an observational study, or an experiment? In broad terms, a survey simply measures variables, an observational study attempts to find a relationship between variables, and an experiment attempts to establish a cause-and-effect relationship between variables.

• Was randomization used in conducting the research? As you know, random sampling is considered the best way to obtain a representative sample from a population and therefore get accurate results. Randomization also helps to dilute the effect of confounding variables.

• Does the report include the details of the research, such as sample size, statistics, and margins of error?

4 EXAMPLE CC.9-12.S.IC.6 **Evaluating a Media Report**

Evaluate the article about the effect of doctor empathy on the duration and severity of a cold.

A Is this a survey, an observational study, or an experiment? How do you know?

Experiment, because a treatment (standard

or enhanced interaction with a doctor) was

imposed

B Was randomization used in the research? If so, how?

Yes; subjects were randomly assigned to

a control group or one of two treatment

groups.

C Does the report include the details of the research? If not, what information is missing?

The report includes the number of subjects

but no statistics (measures of cold duration/

severity).

Caring Doctors Shorten and Ease the Common Cold

Researchers have found that among patients with colds, those who gave their doctors perfect scores on a questionnaire measuring empathy had colds that did not last as long and were less severe. Empathy on the part of doctors included making patients feel at ease, listening to their concerns, and showing compassion.

A total of 350 subjects who were experiencing the onset of a cold were randomly assigned to one of three groups: no doctor-patient interaction, standard interaction, and enhanced interaction. Only subjects in the third group saw doctors who had been coached on being empathetic.

© Houghton Mifflin Harcourt Publishing Company

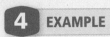

Questioning Strategies

- How could you rewrite the second paragraph of the article if the research involved a survey instead of an experiment? **A total of 350 subjects completed a survey that asked them to rate their doctors on level of empathy when subjects interacted with the doctors at the onset of a cold. Subjects also answered questions on how they thought the level of empathy affected the duration of the cold.**

- How could you rewrite the second paragraph of the article if the research involved an observational study instead of an experiment? **A total of 350 subjects reported the duration of a cold. Subjects also reported whether they had no interaction with a doctor, standard interaction with a doctor, or interaction with a doctor who seemed especially empathetic.**

MATHEMATICAL PRACTICE — Highlighting the Standards

4 EXAMPLE and its Reflect questions offer an opportunity to address Mathematical Practice Standard 3 (Construct viable arguments and critique the reasoning of others). By looking at media reports about research studies and identifying the type of statistical research based on given information, students can determine whether or not the conclusions in the media report are valid. For example, if the research is an observational study rather than an experiment, students will be able to critique any conclusions that try to establish a cause-and-effect relationship between variables.

Avoid Common Errors

Remind students that the placebo effect can occur even in research where medicine and pills are not involved. When designing experiments, researchers must be aware that a treatment can have an effect simply because the subjects in the treatment group are receiving it.

EXTRA EXAMPLE

A news article says that students who study with classical music playing in the background score higher on math tests than students who study with no music playing. The article reports that 200 students were randomly assigned to one of two groups: 1) studying with classical music playing and 2) studying with no music playing. Subjects in the group with classical music playing had higher scores on the math test. Is this a survey, an observational study, or an experiment? How do you know? **Experiment, because a treatment (classical music playing while studying) was imposed**

CLOSE

Essential Question

What kinds of statistical research are there, and which ones can establish cause-and-effect relationships between variables?
Statistical research can include surveys, observational studies, and experiments. While surveys measure variables and observational studies may show associations between variables, only experiments can establish cause-and-effect relationships between variables.

Summarize

Have students make a table comparing surveys, observational studies, and experiments. For each type of research, describe how data are gathered and what conclusions can be determined from the results.

PRACTICE

Where skills are taught	Where skills are practiced
1 EXAMPLE	EXS. 1, 2
2 EXAMPLE	EXS. 3, 4
3 EXAMPLE	EX. 5
4 EXAMPLE	EXS. 6, 7

REFLECT

4a. What information would you want to see before deciding on the validity of the study?

Possible answers: how the length and severity of each cold was measured; the mean length of cold for each group; how empathy was measured on the questionnaires.

4b. Describe a confounding variable that might have affected the results of the research. How did the researchers deal with such confounding variables?

Answers will vary. Sample answer: Overall health could have been a confounding variable if healthier subjects happened to see the empathetic doctors and then had shorter/milder colds; researchers randomly assigned subjects to control and treatment groups so each group would have subjects in various states of overall health.

PRACTICE

Explain why the results of each survey are likely to be inaccurate and then suggest a way to improve the accuracy of the survey.

1. A store offers its customers a chance to win a cash prize if they call a toll-free number and participate in a survey of customer satisfaction.

Survey respondents are self-selected and may be inclined to rate their satisfaction high in the belief that doing so will increase their chance of winning the cash prize; randomly ask customers to complete a quick survey as they are leaving the store (regardless of whether they made a purchase).

2. In a random sample of parents in a school district, a survey asks, "Are you willing to pay a small fee for each school sport that your child participates in?"

The question is biased because of the word "small," which suggests that parents should be willing to pay the fee; the question should give the amount of the fee so that parents can decide if it's acceptable.

For Exercises 3 and 4, determine whether each research study is an observational study or an experiment. Identify the factor if it is an observational study or the treatment if it is an experiment. Also identify the characteristic of interest.

3. Researchers found that patients who had been taking a bone-loss drug for more than five years, a high percent also had an uncommon type of fracture in the thigh bone.

Observational study; factor: taking a bone-loss drug for more than five years; characteristic of interest: uncommon type of fracture in the thigh bone

4. Researchers found that when patients with chronic illnesses were randomly divided into two groups, the group that got regular coaching by phone from health professionals to help them manage their illnesses had lower monthly medical costs than the group that did not get the coaching.

Experiment; treatment: regular coaching by phone from health professionals; characteristic of interest: monthly medical costs

5. Is the research study in Exercise 4 a comparative randomized experiment? If so, identify the treatment group and the control group.

Yes; treatment group: patients who got regular coaching by phone from health professionals; control group: patients who did not get coaching

6. Evaluate the article about doctors working when sick.

a. Is this a survey, an observational study, or an experiment? How do you know?

Survey; the only variable is doctors who work while sick

b. Was randomization used in the research? If so, how?

The article does not say whether random sampling was used.

c. Does the report include the details of the research? If not, what information is missing?

Yes; the sample size is given, and sample proportions are reported.

d. What is your overall evaluation of the report? Why?

Anonymity allowed honest responses, but the results may not apply to all doctors since only doctors-in-training were surveyed.

> **Doctors Work When Sick**
>
> Doctors know that they can get sick from their patients, but when they are sick themselves, do they stay away from their patients? Researchers asked 537 doctors-in-training to anonymously report whether they had worked while sick during the past year. The researchers found that 58% said they had worked once while sick and 31% said they had worked more than once while sick.

7. Evaluate the article about antibiotic use in infants.

a. Is this a survey, an observational study, or an experiment? How do you know?

Observational study; compared two variables (antibiotic use and occurrence of asthma/allergies), but no treatment imposed

b. Was randomization used in the research? If so, how?

The article does not say whether subjects were chosen at random.

c. Does the report include the details of the research? If not, what information is missing?

Yes; the sample size is given, and the increased risks of developing asthma/allergies are given.

d. What is your overall evaluation of the report? Why?

While the study provides reason for caution when doctors give infants antibiotics, it does not establish a cause-and-effect relationship.

> **Antibiotic Use Tied to Asthma and Allergies**
>
> Antibiotic use in infants is linked to asthma and allergies, says a study involving 1401 children. Researchers asked mothers how many doses of antibiotics their children received before 6 months of age as well as whether their children had developed asthma or allergies by age 6. Children who received just one dose of antibiotics were 40% more likely to develop asthma or allergies. The risk jumped to 70% for children who received two doses.

Notes

Assign these pages to help your students practice and apply important lesson concepts. For additional exercises, see the Student Edition.

Answers

Additional Practice

1. Given on worksheet.

2. Experiment; the park ranger applies a treatment (planting near the lake) to some of the individuals (all 20 trees the ranger planted).

3. Observational study; the caretaker gathers data without controlling the individuals or applying a treatment.

4. Given on worksheet.

5. The treatment is *taking the class online*. The treatment group is the online class. The control group is the in-person class.

6. It would not be ethical to impose the treatment (being a smoker) to a group of people, so the study is best addressed through an observational study. I would set up the study by randomly selecting a group of 20 people who already smoke and 20 people who do not. Then, I would track the individuals in the study for a year and have them report the number of minor sicknesses they get.

Problem Solving

1. The teacher applies a treatment (playing music during tests) to some of the individuals (the class). This situation is an example of an experiment.

2. No; observational study

3. Treatment: applying heat to flower seeds. Treatment group: 50 randomly chosen seeds that were heated. Control group: another 50 randomly chosen seeds left at room temperature.

4. Treatment: using a fuel additive. Treatment group: volunteers that use fuel with the additive. Control group: volunteers that use plain fuel.

5. A

6. G

Name_____ Class_____ Date_____

Additional Practice

Explain whether each situation is an experiment or an observational study. The first problem has been completed for you.

1. A park ranger measures the change in height of all trees of a similar species and age over a month. Half the trees are within a quarter of a mile from a large lake and half are further away.

   Observational study; the park ranger gathers data without controlling the individuals or applying a treatment.

2. A park ranger plants 10 trees within a quarter of a mile from a large lake and 10 trees of a similar species and age further than half of a mile from the lake. He then measures the growth of all trees over a month.

   _____

3. A caretaker at a zoo records the sleeping habits of the wildcats at the zoo for a month.

   _____

The study described below is a randomized comparative experiment. Describe the treatment, the treatment group, and the control group. The first problem has been completed for you.

4. A researcher feeds one group of rats high-fat and high-calorie foods like cheesecake, bacon, and pastries. She feeds a second group of rats a normal, nutritious diet. For two weeks, the researcher records how many calories each rat eats daily, as well as how often it goes to its feeding bowl. She compares the data from the one group to the data from the other and finds that the rats that eat the nutritious food get hungry less often and eat a smaller number of calories overall.

   The treatment is feeding high-fat and high-calorie foods. The treatment group is the rats that were fed the diet that was not nutritious. The control group is the rats that were fed the nutritious diet.

5. A college professor wants to know if students learn as well in an online class as in person. He decides to offer the same course both online and in a classroom. Students who sign up for the course are told they will be assigned to either class randomly. The professor then gives the same test to both classes and compares the scores.

   _____

Explain whether the research topic is best addressed through an experiment or an observational study. Then explain how you would set up the experiment or observational study.

6. Does being a smoker cause people to get minor sicknesses more often?

   _____

   _____

Chapter 8   449   Lesson 3

Problem Solving

Explain whether each situation is an experiment or an observational study.

1. A teacher plays music during all tests given in a one-month period and compares the class grades with a similar class that does not have music played during tests.

   Solution: The teacher applies a treatment (playing music during tests) to some of the individuals (the class). This situation is an example of an experiment.

2. A real estate developer records the listing and selling prices of all homes in one area to determine the difference in the listing price and the selling price.

   Does the real estate developer control the individuals or apply a treatment? _____

   Is the situation an experiment or an observational study? _____

The study described below is a randomized controlled experiment. Describe the treatment, the treatment group, and the control group.

3. At a seed farm, 50 randomly chosen seeds were treated to temperatures above 100°F, and 50 other randomly chosen seeds were left at normal temperatures. At the end of the growing season, the heated group sprouted 20% faster than the non-heated group.

   _____

   _____

4. An engineer recruits 40 volunteers, and randomly assigns them to two groups. One group fills their cars with gasoline with an additive. The other group fills their cars with plain gasoline. The group that uses the additive sees a 5% decrease in fuel efficiency.

   _____

   _____

Choose the method that would be least biased.

5. An ice cream company wants to test whether the quality of ingredients it uses affects the taste of the product.

   A randomized comparative experiment

   B observational study

   C survey

6. An auto manufacturer wants to measure the fuel efficiency of a new hybrid car.

   F randomized comparative experiment

   G observational study

   H survey

Chapter 8   450   Lesson 3

8-4

Significance of Experimental Results

Going Deeper

Essential question: *In an experiment, when is the difference between the control group and treatment group likely to be caused by the treatment?*

COMMON CORE Standards for Mathematical Content

CC.9-12.S.IC.5 Use data from a randomized experiment to compare two treatments; use simulations to decide if differences between parameters are significant.*

Vocabulary

null hypothesis, significant result, resampling, permutation test

Prerequisites

Randomized comparative experiments

Math Background

In this lesson, students use reasoning to either accept or reject a null hypothesis for a randomized comparative experiment, which says that any result obtained from the experiment is due to chance. Working under the assumption that the null hypothesis is true, students use the data from an experiment to generate a resampling distribution, which is approximately normal. If the experimental result falls somewhere in the middle 90% (or 95% or even 99%) of the resampling distribution, there is no reason to reject the null hypothesis, so the result is not significant. But if the result falls outside the middle (making the result very unusual), the null hypothesis is rejected and the result is called significant. (The level of significance is determined by the probability of getting the result or one that is even more extreme.)

INTRODUCE

Revisit some of the randomized comparative experiments described in previous lessons. Ask students to think about how they could determine whether differences between the control and treatment groups in these experiments were significant (that is, likely to be caused by the treatment and not simply due to chance).

TEACH

1 EXAMPLE

Questioning Strategies

- The word *null* is defined in the dictionary as meaning "without consequence." How does this relate to the meaning of *null hypothesis*? **The null hypothesis states that there is no significant difference between the control and treatment groups. This is another way of saying that the treatment had no consequence.**

- Why does a result have to be rare (that is, have a very low probability of occurrence) for the null hypothesis to be rejected? Why couldn't any result that shows a difference between the treatment and control groups be evidence that the treatment has an effect? **There is always going to be some variation within a group and therefore some difference between two groups regardless of whether a treatment has an effect. This is why the null hypothesis says that any difference between the groups is simply due to chance. Only when a difference between the treatment and control groups is rare should the null hypothesis be called into question and the treatment deemed to have an effect.**

continued

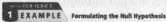

Name_____ Class_____ Date_____

8-4

Video Tutor

Significance of Experimental Results
Going Deeper

Essential question: In an experiment, when is a difference between the control group and treatment group likely to be caused by the treatment?

You can think of every randomized comparative experiment as a test of a *null hypothesis*. The **null hypothesis** states that any difference between the control group and the treatment group is due to chance. In other words, the null hypothesis is the assumption that the treatment has no effect.

In statistics, an experimental result is called **significant** if the likelihood that it occurred by chance alone is very low. A low probability of getting the result by chance is evidence in favor of rejecting the null hypothesis. A significant result, however, does not *prove* that the treatment has an effect; the null hypothesis may still be true, and a rare event may simply have occurred. Nevertheless, standard practice in statistics is to reject the null hypothesis in favor of the *alternative* hypothesis that the result is due to the treatment.

CC.9-12.S.IC.5

1 EXAMPLE Formulating the Null Hypothesis

For each experiment, state the null hypothesis.

A A potential growth agent is sprayed on the leaves of 12 emerging ferns twice a week for a month. Another 12 emerging ferns are not sprayed with the growth agent. The mean stalk lengths of the two groups of ferns are compared after a month.

The null hypothesis is that the mean stalk lengths of the two groups of ferns will

be about the same.

B Ten people with colds are treated with a new formula from an existing brand of cold medicine. Ten other people with colds are treated with the original formula. The mean recovery times for the two groups are compared.

The null hypothesis is that the mean recovery times for the two groups will be

about the same.

REFLECT

1a. Suppose in part A that the treated ferns had a mean stalk length that is twice the mean stalk length of the untreated ferns. Should the researcher reject the null hypothesis? Does the experimental result prove that the growth agent works? Explain.

Yes, the researcher should reject the null hypothesis because the difference

between the control group and the treatment group is so dramatic. No, the result

does not prove that the growth agent works; it only provides evidence that

rejecting the assumption that the growth agent has no effect is reasonable.

1b. Suppose in part B that the mean recovery time for both groups is 5 days. Should the researcher reject the null hypothesis? Does the experimental result prove that the new formula is no more effective than the original formula? Explain.

No, the researcher should not reject the null hypothesis because there is no

difference between the control group and the treatment group. No, the result does

not prove that the new formula is no more effective than the old; it only supports

the reasonableness of the assumption that the new formula is no more effective.

1c. In the U.S. legal system, a defendant is assumed innocent until guilt is proved beyond a reasonable doubt. How is this situation like rejecting a null hypothesis?

A null hypothesis (like innocence) is assumed to be true unless the experimental

evidence (like evidence of guilt) allows you to reject the null hypothesis

(innocence).

Suppose a company that offers an SAT prep course wants to demonstrate that its course raises test scores. The company recruits 20 students and randomly assigns half of them to a treatment group, where subjects take the course before taking the SAT, and half to a control group, where subjects do not take the course before taking the SAT. The table below shows the SAT scores of the 10 students in each group. How can you tell whether the course actually improved the scores of the students in the treatment group?

	SAT Scores				
Treatment Group	1440	1610	1430	1700	1690
	1570	1480	1620	1780	2010
Control Group	1150	1500	1050	1600	1460
	1860	1350	1750	1680	1330

One thing you could do is compute the mean SAT score for each group to see if the means are different. Obviously, the company expects the treatment group's mean to be greater than the control group's mean. But even if that is the case, how do you know that the difference in the means can be attributed to the treatment and not to chance? In other words, how do you know if the difference is *significant*?

The null hypothesis for this experiment is that the SAT prep course has no effect on a student's score. Under this assumption, it doesn't matter whether a student is in the treatment group or the control group. Since each group is a sample of the students, the means of the two samples should be about equal. In fact, any random division of the 20 students into two groups of 10 should result in two means whose difference is relatively small and a matter of chance. This technique, called **resampling**, allows you to create a distribution of the differences of means for every possible pairing of groups with 10 students in each. You can *test* the null hypothesis by using this distribution to find the likelihood, given that the null hypothesis is true, of getting a difference of means at least as great as the actual experimental difference. The test is called a **permutation test**.

Notes

Teaching Strategy

Although stating a null hypothesis will probably not be intuitive for students, most students will be very comfortable stating a hypothesis in a more "positive" way. For example, a student will probably have no problem understanding a hypothesis like "Students who stay up late at night have trouble getting up early in the morning." Point out that in an experimental situation, this could be stated as the null hypothesis by saying that "there will be no difference in the number of times students who stay up late and students who do not stay up late have trouble getting up early in the morning." Have students take turns stating hypotheses about their everyday lives; then, have the entire class restate the hypotheses as null hypotheses.

EXTRA EXAMPLE

At a car dealership, 20 identical new cars were given a rust-proofing treatment. Another 20 identical new cars were not given the rust proofing treatment. After three years, the two groups of cars are compared for mean area of rust spots. State the null hypothesis for this experiment. **The null hypothesis is that the mean area of rust spots for the two groups of cars will be about the same.**

2 EXAMPLE

Questioning Strategies

- In part C, would it be possible to have a simulation in which the mean score difference between Group A and Group B is greater than the mean score difference between the control and treatment groups? Explain. **Yes; if the calculator's random integer generator happens to assign the ten highest SAT scores to Group A and the ten lowest SAT scores to Group B, then the difference between the mean scores for Group A and Group B will be greater than the difference between the mean scores for the control and treatment groups.**

- Do the results of the three simulations in part C tell you anything about the significance of the difference in mean scores between the control group and the treatment group? **Answers will vary depending on the outcomes of the simulations. Students will generally find that the absolute value of the difference between the mean score for Group A and the mean score for Group B is much less than the difference between the control and the treatment groups. However, three simulations are not enough to get an accurate sense of the resampling distribution.**

- If 90 simulations were used for the permutation test in parts B through E, how could you use the information given in part F to determine the least difference in mean scores for the control and the treatment groups that would be significant? Explain your reasoning. **According to the information given in part F, if $P > 0.10$, then the results are not significant. This means that the difference for which the P-value is equal to 0.10 will be the least difference in mean scores for the control and the treatment groups that is significant. If 90 simulations were used for the permutation test, then to get a P-value of 0.10, you would need $0.10(90) = 9$ results at least as great as the least significant difference. By examining an ordered list of the differences from the 90 simulations, you could count down from the greatest difference to the ninth-greatest difference, which is the least of the significant differences.**

- Why would this method be impractical without using a computer? **For all but the smallest data sets, resampling, calculating the means of the resampled groups, and plotting them is a lot of work.**

continued

2 EXAMPLE CC.9-12.S.IC.5 Using a Permutation Test

Use the table of SAT scores on the previous page to construct a resampling distribution for the difference of means, assuming that the null hypothesis is true. Then determine the significance of the actual experimental result.

A State the null hypothesis in terms of the difference of the two group means.

The difference of the two group means is about 0.

B Calculate the mean score for the treatment group, $\bar{x}_T$, and the mean score for the control group, $\bar{x}_C$. Then find the difference of the means.

$\bar{x}_T = \underline{1633}$ $\bar{x}_C = \underline{1473}$ $\bar{x}_T - \bar{x}_C = \underline{160}$

C Label the data in the table on the previous page with the identifiers 1 through 20. Then follow these steps to complete each table below:

* Use a calculator's random integer generator to generate a list of 10 identifiers between 1 and 20 with no identifiers repeated.
* Record the scores that correspond to those identifiers as the scores for Group A. Record the remaining 10 scores as the scores for Group B.
* Find $\bar{x}_A$, $\bar{x}_B$, and $\bar{x}_A - \bar{x}_B$, and record them in the table.

Sample answers appear in each table.

Simulation 1					Means	Difference of means
Group A	1750	1460	1330	1480	1570	$\bar{x}_A = 1536$	
	1610	1700	1350	1430	1680		$\bar{x}_A - \bar{x}_B = -34$
Group B	1440	1690	1620	1780	2010	$\bar{x}_B = 1570$	
	1150	1500	1050	1600	1860		

Simulation 2					Means	Difference of means
Group A	1570	1680	1150	1350	1610	$\bar{x}_A = 1559$	
	1750	1440	2010	1330	1700		$\bar{x}_A - \bar{x}_B = 12$
Group B	1430	1690	1480	1620	1780	$\bar{x}_B = 1547$	
	1500	1050	1600	1460	1860		

Simulation 3					Means	Difference of means
Group A	1600	1860	1460	1330	1350	$\bar{x}_A = 1551$	
	1610	1780	1750	1150	1620		$\bar{x}_A - \bar{x}_B = -4$
Group B	1440	1430	1700	1690	1570	$\bar{x}_B = 1555$	
	1480	2010	1500	1050	1680		

D Report the differences of means that you found for simulations 1–3 to your teacher so that he or she can create a frequency table and histogram of the class results. You should make your own copy of the frequency table and histogram using the table and the grid below.

Interval	Frequency
$-320 \le x < -240$	1
$-240 \le x < -160$	7
$-160 \le x < -80$	19
$-80 \le x < 0$	26
$0 \le x < 80$	23
$80 \le x < 160$	11
$160 \le x < 240$	2
$240 \le x < 320$	1

Sample results for 90 simulations are shown.

E Explain how you can use the frequency table or the histogram to find the probability that a difference of means is *at least as great* as the difference that you recorded in part B. Then find that probability.

Divide the sum of the frequencies for the intervals $160 \le x < 240$ and

$240 \le x < 320$ by the sum of all frequencies (total number of simulations); sample

answer using the sample frequencies from part D: $(2 + 1)/90 \approx 0.03$.

F The probability that you found in part E is called a *P-value*. The *P-value* determines the significance of the experimental result. Statisticians commonly use the following levels of significance:

* When $P > 0.10$, the result is *not significant*.
* When $0.05 < P \le 0.10$, the result is *marginally significant*.
* When $0.01 < P \le 0.05$, the result is *significant*.
* When $P \le 0.01$, the result is *highly significant*.

Using the *P-value* that you obtained in part E, characterize the significance of the experimental result for the SAT scores.

Answers depend on the class data. For the sample data above, the result is significant.

G State the conclusion that you can draw from the permutation test.

Reject the null hypothesis that the SAT prep course has no effect in favor of the

alternative hypothesis that the course has a positive effect.

- A critic of the experiment pointed out that students taking the SAT prep course spent more time studying for the test, and that the extra time spent studying, not the course itself, was the reason for the observed difference in the mean scores of the treatment and control groups. Do you agree or disagree? Explain. **Disagree: The amount of time that a student is willing or able to study for the test is a factor that was randomly distributed between the two groups, so its influence on the results is inconsequential. What distinguished the treatment group from the control group was the course itself. The students taking the course might actually have spent less time, on average, studying for the test than the students not taking the course.**

MATHEMATICAL PRACTICE **Highlighting the Standards**

2 EXAMPLE and its Reflect questions offer an opportunity to address Mathematical Practice Standard 5 (Use appropriate tools strategically). Students use their graphing calculators to generate random numbers that they then use to assign the SAT scores to Group A or Group B in the simulations they run for the permutation test. They can also use their calculators to calculate $\bar{x}_A$, $\bar{x}_B$, and $\bar{x}_A - \bar{x}_B$ for each simulation.

Avoid Common Errors

In part E, when students use the frequency table or histogram in the permutation test to find the probability that a difference of means is at least as great as the difference they recorded for the control and treatment groups in the experiment, they may include only the frequencies for the interval in which the difference occurs. Remind students that they must find the sum of frequencies for all the intervals including and above the difference.

EXTRA EXAMPLE

In another experiment for the same company that offers the SAT prep course, $\bar{x}_T = 1652$ and $\bar{x}_C = 1370$. Based on the result in **2 EXAMPLE**, predict whether or not the null hypothesis can be rejected for this experiment. Explain your reasoning. **The null hypothesis is quite likely to be rejected. In 2 EXAMPLE, $\bar{x}_T - \bar{x}_C = 160$. In this experiment, $\bar{x}_T - \bar{x}_C = 282$. Since the difference is much greater in this experiment, the difference will probably be significant.**

CLOSE

Essential Question

In an experiment, when is the difference between the control group and treatment group likely to be caused by the treatment?
In an experiment, the null hypothesis states that any difference between the control group and the treatment group is due to chance. If the difference between the control group and the treatment group has a very low probability of occurring by chance alone, then the null hypothesis is rejected, and the standard practice in statistics is to attribute the cause of the difference to the treatment. You can use a permutation test to determine whether a difference between means in the control group and treatment group is significant.

Summarize

Have students make a graphic organizer outlining the steps for formulating a null hypothesis and using a permutation test to determine whether experimental results are significant.

PRACTICE

Where skills are taught	Where skills are practiced
1 EXAMPLE	EXS. 1, 2
2 EXAMPLE	EXS. 3, 4

REFLECT

2a. The reason that the test is called a *permutation* test is that the process of resampling assigns different permutations of the labels "treatment" and "control" to the 20 SAT scores. Although the number of permutations of n distinct objects is $n!$, the objects in this case are 10 "treatment" labels and 10 "control" labels, so the 20 labels are not distinct. When a set of n objects contains n_1 copies of the first object, n_2 copies of the second object, . . ., and n_t copies of the last object, then the formula for the number of permutations of the n objects becomes $\dfrac{n!}{n_1! \cdot n_2! \cdot \cdots \cdot n_t!}$.

Use this formula to find the number of permutations of the labels for the SAT scores. Did your class generate all possible resamples?

$\dfrac{20!}{10! \cdot 10!} = 184{,}756;$ no

2b. Suppose your class had generated all possible resamples. Explain why the distribution would be perfectly symmetric and centered on 0.

For every treatment group and control group for which a difference of means

equals x, you can switch the labels on the two groups and obtain a difference

of means that equals $-x$. The sum of all possible differences of means is 0, so

the mean of the differences is 0.

2c. Explain why it makes sense to call the test of significance in part F a *one-tailed* test?

The P-value is calculated using only one tail of the resampling distribution.

PRACTICE

1. King County, Washington, recently required all restaurant chains to post Calorie counts for menu items. Researchers gathered data on the average Calorie per transaction at a Mexican restaurant chain both before and after the regulation went into effect.

a. State the null hypothesis in terms of the difference in the average Calorie per transaction before and after Calorie counts were posted.

The difference in the average Calorie per transaction before and after

Calorie counts were posted is about 0.

b. The researchers found a slight increase in the average Calorie per transaction once the regulation went into effect, but the result was not statistically different from 0. What does this result mean in terms of accepting or rejecting the null hypothesis?

The null hypothesis should not be rejected, because the result shows no

evidence that posting Calorie counts affects people's menu choices.

For Exercises 2–4, use the following information.

A textbook company has created an electronic version of one of its books and wants to know what effect, if any, using the e-book has on student learning. With the permission of the school district, a teacher who has two classes that already use the textbook agrees to participate in a research study. One of the classes uses the e-book for the next unit of instruction while the other class continues to use the print version of the book. After teaching the unit, the teacher gives the same test to both classes. The mean score for the class using the e-book is 82.3, while the mean score for the class using the print book is 78.2.

2. State the null hypothesis in terms of the difference of the mean test scores.

The difference of the mean test scores using the e-book and the print

book is about 0.

3. Identify the treatment group and its mean test score, $\bar{x}_T$, as well as the control group and its mean test score, $\bar{x}_C$. Then find $\bar{x}_T - \bar{x}_C$.

Treatment group: class using e-book; $\bar{x}_T = 82.3$; control group: class using

print book; $\bar{x}_C = 78.2$; $\bar{x}_T - \bar{x}_C = 4.1$

4. The resampling distribution for the difference of mean test scores, given that the null hypothesis is true, is normal with a mean of 0 and a standard error of 2. The distribution is shown at the right.

a. Describe how the resampling distribution is obtained from the students' test scores.

Determine all possible permutations of the labels

"e-book" and "print" for the individual test scores from both classes. For each

permutation, calculate the mean test score for each group and find the difference

of the means. The resampling distribution consists of all differences of means.

b. Write an interval that captures the middle 95% of the differences of means in the resampling distribution. If the experimental result falls within this interval, the result is not significant; if it falls outside the interval, the result is significant. Which is the case?

$-4 \le x \le 4$; the experimental result is significant.

c. Explain why the test of significance in part b is called a *two-tailed* test.

A result that falls in either tail (outside the middle 95%) is significant.

d. Should the null hypothesis be accepted or rejected? What does acceptance or rejection mean in this situation?

Reject the null hypothesis, which means that there is enough evidence to reject

the assumption that the e-book had no effect on student learning in favor of

the assumption that it had an effect.

ADDITIONAL PRACTICE AND PROBLEM SOLVING

Assign these pages to help your students practice and apply important lesson concepts. For additional exercises, see the Student Edition.

Answers

Additional Practice

1. Given in worksheet.

2. **a.** It will take the same amount of time for the water to boil whether salt is added or not.

   b. There is a very slight difference between the two groups that is likely to be caused by chance, so the null hypothesis cannot be rejected based on this experiment.

3. **a.** If it takes Carly more or less than 15 minutes to get to school, the difference is caused by chance.

   b. 3

   C. It is not likely that Carly's claim is true because |3| > 1.96 and so the null hypothesis was rejected with 95% certainty.

Problem Solving

1. ice: 25 lb, newspaper: 35 lb

2. ice: 21 lb, newspaper: 30 lb

3. ice: 27 lb, newspaper: 40 lb

4. Yes, the minimum, median, and maximum weights for the newspaper are higher than for the ice. Therefore, Martin and Leandra should reject the null hypothesis, which means that frozen newspaper is stronger than ice.

5. B

6. H

7. A

8. G

Additional Practice

1. The makers of a light bulb claim that their light bulbs last longer than the leading brand. A researcher tests this claim by finding the mean length of time that 25 bulbs of each brand last. State the null hypothesis for the experiment.

_____

2. A pharmaceutical company is testing a new drug to see whether it lowers cholesterol in women. They randomly divide 150 volunteers into two groups. The volunteers in each group have their cholesterol monitored for one month to establish a baseline. Then one group is given the drug for a one month period, and the other group is given a placebo for a one month period. The mean change in cholesterol before and after treatment is found for each group. State the null hypothesis for the experiment.

_____

3. A study investigates how many numbers in a list a person can memorize in order in 30 seconds. Volunteers are randomly assigned either to a group simply shown the list or to a group taught a memorization strategy before being shown the list. A report on the study's results includes the statement, "After comparing the means of the groups, the null hypothesis is rejected with a P-value of 0.01." What does this statement say about the results of the study?

_____

_____

_____

For Exercises 4 and 5, use the following information.

The results of an experiment are resampled 80 times by randomly assigning them to a "control" or a "treatment" group, and the differences in the means are found for each resampling. The table gives the results of the differences x.

4. In the original experiment, the difference of the means was 8. What is the P-value for this result?

_____

5. Using a one-tailed test, what is the significance of the experimental result?

_____

Interval	Frequency
$-16 \leq x < -12$	1
$-12 \leq x < -8$	6
$-8 \leq x < -4$	10
$-4 \leq x < 0$	18
$0 \leq x < 4$	23
$4 \leq x < 8$	13
$8 \leq x < 12$	7
$12 \leq x < 16$	2

Problem Solving

For Exercises 1–3, use the following information.

In a lab comparing handle strengths of two kinds of paper bags, students add weight to each bag and record the weight at which its handles fail. The results are shown below.

	Trial 1	Trial 2	Trial 3	Trial 4	Trial 5
Bag A	25 lb	22 lb	27 lb	26 lb	21 lb
Bag B	35 lb	37 lb	30 lb	31 lb	40 lb

1. What is the difference of the means for the two groups? _____

2. State the null hypothesis of the experiment.

3. Dee uses a graphing calculator to randomly resample the data 100 times. The distribution of the resampling difference of means $\bar{x}_B - \bar{x}_A$ has a mean of -0.2 and a standard error of 3.8. Is the difference of means from Exercise 1 significant? Explain.

_____

_____

For Exercises 4 and 5, use the following information.

Students record how long it takes a given amount of water to boil using identical burners. Half of the students do not add salt to the water (control) and half add a teaspoon of salt (treatment). The boiling times in seconds are shown in the chart below.

Control	65	78	64	71	75
Treatment	61	70	73	69	64

4. The resampling distribution for the difference of mean boiling times is normal with a mean of 0 and a standard error of about 3.3. Are the experimental results significant? Explain.

_____

_____

5. Adding salt to water raises the boiling point a very small amount. Explain how this can be consistent with the information in Exercise 4.

_____

_____

Sampling Distributions
Extension: Confidence Intervals and Margins of Error

Essential question: *How do you calculate a confidence interval and a margin of error for a population proportion or mean?*

⌐COMMON⌐ **Standards for**
⌐ CORE ⌐ **Mathematical Content**

CC.9-12.S.IC.4 Use data from a sample survey to estimate a population mean or proportion; develop a margin of error through the use of simulation models for random sampling.*

Vocabulary

sampling distribution, standard error of the mean, standard error of the proportion, confidence interval, margin of error

Prerequisites

Data distributions,
Data-gathering techniques

Math Background

In this lesson, students will construct data distributions obtained from different samples of the same population. Students should understand that the mean and standard deviation obtained for a certain characteristic of a sample usually will not match the mean and standard deviation for the entire population, nor will it necessarily match the statistics obtained for a different sample of the same population.

Students will learn in this lesson how to characterize the data obtained from different samples. They will build on this knowledge when they use sample statistics to make predictions about population parameters.

This lesson includes the study of sampling distributions for populations whose mean or proportion is not known. Students will learn how to determine, with a certain degree of confidence, that the population mean or proportion is within a particular range of values.

INTRODUCE

To introduce students to the idea of a sampling distribution, have students work in groups of equal size to conduct a quick survey. The survey should consist of a single question calling for a numerical response, such as: How long (in minutes) did it take you to get to school today? Each group of students should calculate the sum of the responses within the group as well as the mean of the responses, reporting these results to you. After pointing out that each group represents a sample of the entire class, you can use the reported means to generate a line plot, which represents a sampling distribution. Have students examine the sampling distribution and make a conjecture about what the class mean is. (You may want to have students write down their conjectures so that the most accurate ones can be determined later.) You can then calculate the class mean by adding together the sums that the groups reported to you and dividing by the number of students in the class.

8-5

Sampling Distributions
Extension: Confidence Intervals and Margins of Error

Essential question: *How do you calculate a confidence interval and a margin of error for a population proportion or mean?*

CC.9-12.S.IC.4

1 EXPLORE   Developing a Sampling Distribution

Video Tutor

The table provides data about the first 50 people to join a new gym. For each person, the table lists his or her member ID number, age, and sex.

ID	Age	Sex	ID	Age	Sex	ID	Age	Sex	ID	Age	Sex	ID	Age	Sex
1	30	M	11	38	F	21	74	F	31	32	M	41	46	M
2	48	M	12	24	M	22	21	M	32	28	F	42	34	F
3	52	M	13	48	F	23	29	F	33	35	M	43	44	F
4	25	F	14	45	M	24	48	M	34	49	M	44	68	M
5	63	F	15	28	F	25	37	M	35	18	M	45	24	F
6	50	F	16	39	M	26	52	F	36	56	F	46	34	F
7	18	F	17	37	F	27	25	F	37	48	F	47	55	F
8	28	F	18	63	M	28	44	M	38	38	M	48	39	M
9	72	M	19	20	M	29	29	F	39	52	F	49	40	F
10	25	F	20	81	F	30	66	M	40	33	F	50	30	F

A   Use your calculator to find the mean age μ and standard deviation σ for the population of the gym's first 50 members. Round to the nearest tenth.

$\mu =$ __41.2__ ; $\sigma =$ __15.3__

B   Use your calculator's random number generator to choose a sample of 5 gym members. Find the mean age $\bar{x}$ for your sample. Round to the nearest tenth.

$\bar{x} =$ __Answers will vary.__

C   Report your sample mean to your teacher. As other students report their sample means, create a class histogram below. To do so, shade a square above the appropriate interval as each sample mean is reported. For sample means that lie on an interval boundary (such as 39.5), shade a square on the interval to the right (39.5 to 40.5).

A sample histogram is shown.

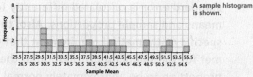

Sample Mean

D   Calculate the mean of the sample means $\mu_{\bar{x}}$ and the standard deviation of the sample means $\sigma_{\bar{x}}$. **Sample answers are shown.**

$\mu_{\bar{x}} =$ __39.8__ ; $\sigma_{\bar{x}} =$ __7.9__

© Houghton Mifflin Harcourt Publishing Company

E   Now use your calculator's random number generator to choose a sample of 15 gym members. Find the mean $\bar{x}$ for your sample. Round to the nearest tenth.

$\bar{x} =$ __Answers will vary.__

F   Report your sample mean to your teacher and make a class histogram below.
A sample histogram is shown.

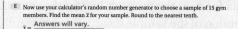

Sample Mean

G   Calculate the mean of the sample means $\mu_{\bar{x}}$ and the standard deviation of the sample means $\sigma_{\bar{x}}$. **Sample answers are shown.**

$\mu_{\bar{x}} =$ __40.8__ ; $\sigma_{\bar{x}} =$ __3.4__

REFLECT

1a. In the class histograms, how does the mean of the sample means compare with the population mean?

The mean of the sample means is close to the population mean.

1b. What happens to the standard deviation of the sample means as the sample size increases?

The standard deviation of the sample means decreases.

1c. What happens to the shape of the histogram as the sample size increases?

The histogram gets closer to the shape of a normal distribution.

The histograms that you made are *sampling distributions*. A **sampling distribution** shows how a particular statistic varies across all samples of *n* individuals from the same population. You have worked with the sampling distribution of the sample mean, $\bar{x}$.

The mean of the sampling distribution of the sample mean is denoted $\mu_{\bar{x}}$. The standard deviation of the sampling distribution of the sample mean is denoted $\sigma_{\bar{x}}$ and is also called the **standard error of the mean.**

You may have discovered that $\mu_{\bar{x}}$ is close to $\bar{x}$ regardless of the sample size and that $\sigma_{\bar{x}}$ decreases as the sample size *n* increases. These observations were based on simulations. When you consider *all* possible samples of *n* individuals, you arrive at one of the major theorems of statistics.

© Houghton Mifflin Harcourt Publishing Company

Notes

Questioning Strategies

- Describe the population parameters in words. The average age of the first 50 people who joined the gym is just over 41. There is a large spread in the data; the standard deviation is 15.3.

- Why isn't the answer in part B the same as in part A? Because the mean of the sample is based on only 5 data values from the population.

- How can you change the way a sample is selected to make the sample mean better match the population mean? Increase the sample size. As the sample size increases, the sample mean approaches the population mean.

Teaching Strategy

In parts C and F of the Explore, you may want to create a class histogram on the board and have students come up and add their sample means one at a time. You may also want to draw a vertical line on the histogram at the population mean to drive home the point that the sample means are clustering around the population mean.

2 EXAMPLE

Questioning Strategies

- What allows you to assume that the sampling distribution is approximately normal? the Central Limit Theorem

- What interval captures 68% of the means for random samples of 36 boxes? 68% of the means fall between $323 - 3.3 = 319.7$ g and $323 + 3.3 = 326.3$ g.

EXTRA EXAMPLE

The safety placard on an elevator states that up to 8 people (660 kilograms) can ride the elevator at one time. Suppose the mean mass of a group of 8 people is 600 kilograms with a standard deviation of 76 kilograms. You choose a random sample of 16 groups of 8 people.

A. What is the probability that your sample has a mean mass of at most 660 kilograms (the maximum mass the elevator can safely carry)? 99.93%

B. What interval captures 95% of the means for random samples of 16 groups? Describe what this interval means in words. 562 to 638; 95%

of the groups of 8 will have a mass between 562 kilograms and 638 kilograms, well within the maximum mass the elevator can safely carry.

3 EXPLORE

Questioning Strategies

- What is the difference between this sampling distribution and the one in the first Explore? The one in the first Explore was a distribution of sample means, while this is a distribution of sample proportions.

- Compare the "Properties of the Sampling Distribution of the Sample Proportion" box with the "Properties of the Sampling Distribution of the Sample Mean" box in the first Explore. In both cases, the mean of the sampling distribution equals the population parameter, but the standard error is calculated differently for sample means and sample proportions. Also, there is a specific mathematical requirement that must be met for the sampling distribution of the sample proportion to be approximately normal.

Teaching Strategy

To help students see the parallel between the formula for $\sigma_{\hat{p}}$ in the property box for the sampling distribution of the sample proportion and the formula for $\sigma_{\bar{x}}$ in the property box for the sampling distribution of the sample mean, you may want to derive a formula for the standard deviation of a population consisting of categorical data that either do or do not meet a criterion: Let each data value that meets the criterion be 1, and let each data value that doesn't meet the criterion be 0. This effectively converts the categorical data into numerical data. If you find the sum of the 1s and 0s and divide by the number N of data values, you get the population proportion p for the criterion. So, the number of 1s is Np, and the number of 0s is $N(1 - p)$. The deviation of each 1 from the population proportion is $1 - p$, while the deviation of each 0 from the population proportion is $0 - p$, or $-p$. Therefore, the standard deviation is given by $\sigma = \sqrt{\dfrac{Np(1 - p)^2 + N(1 - p)(-p)^2}{N}}$, which can be simplified through algebraic manipulation to $\sigma = \sqrt{p(1 - p)}$. This means that the standard deviation of the sampling distribution of the sample proportion is

$\sigma_{\hat{p}} = \sqrt{\dfrac{p(1 - p)}{n}} = \dfrac{\sqrt{p(1 - p)}}{\sqrt{n}} = \dfrac{\sigma}{\sqrt{n}}$, which exactly matches the formula for $\sigma_{\bar{x}}$.

Properties of the Sampling Distribution of the Sample Mean

If a random sample of size n is selected from a population with mean μ and standard deviation σ, then

(1) $\mu_{\bar{x}} = \mu$,

(2) $\sigma_{\bar{x}} = \dfrac{\sigma}{\sqrt{n}}$, and

(3) the sampling distribution of the sample mean is normal if the population is normal; for all other populations, the sampling distribution of the mean approaches a normal distribution as n increases.

The third property stated above is known as the Central Limit Theorem.

All normal distributions have the following properties, sometimes collectively called the 68-95-99.7 rule:

- 68% of the data fall within 1 standard deviation of the mean.
- 95% of the data fall within 2 standard deviation of the mean.
- 99.7% of the data fall within 3 standard deviation of the mean.

You will learn more about the specific properties of normal distributions later in this chapter.

CC.9-12.S.IC.4

2 EXAMPLE   Using the Sampling Distribution of the Sample Mean

Boxes of Cruncho cereal have a mean mass of 323 g with a standard deviation of 20 g. You choose a random sample of 36 boxes of the cereal. What interval captures 95% of the means for random samples of 36 boxes?

- Write the given information about the population and the sample.

  $\mu = \underline{\ 323\ }$ $\sigma = \underline{\ 20\ }$ $n = \underline{\ 36\ }$

- Find the mean of the sampling distribution of the sample mean and the standard error of the mean.

  $\mu_{\bar{x}} = \mu = \underline{\ 323\ }$ $\sigma_{\bar{x}} = \dfrac{\sigma}{\sqrt{n}} = \dfrac{20}{6} \approx \underline{\ 3.3\ }$

The sampling distribution of the sample mean is approximately normal. In a normal distribution, 95% of the data fall within 2 standard deviations of the mean.

$\mu_{\bar{x}} - 2\sigma_{\bar{x}} = \underline{\ 323\ } - 2\left(\underline{\ 3.3\ }\right) = \underline{\ 316.4\ }$

$\mu_{\bar{x}} + 2\sigma_{\bar{x}} = \underline{\ 323\ } + 2\left(\underline{\ 3.3\ }\right) = \underline{\ 329.6\ }$

So, 95% of the sample means fall between $\underline{\ 316.4\ }$ g and $\underline{\ 329.6\ }$ g.

REFLECT

2a. When you choose a sample of 36 boxes, is it possible for the sample to have a mean mass of 315 g? Is it likely? Explain.

It is possible, but unlikely since a mean of 315 g lies more than 2 standard

deviations from $\mu_{\bar{x}}$.

CC.9-12.S.IC.4

3 EXPLORE   Developing Another Sampling Distribution

Use the table of data from the first Explore. This time you will develop a sampling distribution based on a sample proportion rather than a sample mean.

A Find the proportion p of gym members in the population who are female.

$p = \underline{\ 0.6\ }$

B Use your calculator's random number generator to choose a sample of 5 gym members. Find the proportion of female members $\hat{p}$ for your sample.

$\hat{p} = \underline{\text{Answers will vary.}}$

C Report your sample proportion to your teacher. As other students report their sample proportions, create a class histogram at right.
A sample histogram is shown.

D Calculate the mean of the sample proportions $\mu_{\hat{p}}$ and the standard deviation of the sample proportions $\sigma_{\hat{p}}$. Round to the nearest hundredth.
Sample answers are shown.

$\mu_{\hat{p}} = \underline{\ 0.68\ }$; $\sigma_{\hat{p}} = \underline{\ 0.21\ }$

E Now use your calculator's random number generator to choose a sample of 10 gym members. Find the proportion of female members $\hat{p}$ for your sample.

$\hat{p} = \underline{\text{Answers will vary.}}$

F Report your sample proportion to your teacher. As other students report their sample proportions, create a class histogram at right. A sample histogram is shown.

G Calculate the mean of the sample proportions $\mu_{\hat{p}}$ and the standard deviation of the sample proportions $\sigma_{\hat{p}}$. Round to the nearest hundredth.
Sample answers are shown.

$\mu_{\hat{p}} = \underline{\ 0.55\ }$; $\sigma_{\hat{p}} = \underline{\ 0.16\ }$

Notes

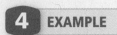

EXAMPLE

Questioning Strategies

- How is this example different from **2** EXAMPLE ? This example involves a proportion rather than a mean

- How is the solving technique similar to the previous example? In both cases, you (1) write down facts about the population and the sample, (2) find the mean of the sampling distribution and the standard error, and (3) determine an interval that captures 95% of the means or porportions in the sampling distribution based on the fact that it is approximately normal

- What is different in this solution from the solution in **2** EXAMPLE ? part C—checking that the sampling distribution is approximately normal

EXTRA EXAMPLE

About 28% of students at a large school play varsity sports. You choose a random sample of 60 students. What interval captures 68% of the proportions for random samples of 60 students? 68% of the sample proportions lie between 22.2% and 33.8%.

MATHEMATICAL PRACTICE — Highlighting the Standards

This lesson includes many opportunities to address Mathematical Practice Standard 6 (Attend to precision). Students should know the vocabulary for the unit coming into this lesson. For instance, students will need to distinguish between the population mean and the sampling mean, between the standard deviation and the standard error of the mean, and between sampling distributions of sample means and sampling distributions of sample proportions. Students will need to use precision in their communication and interpret statistical symbols correctly.

EXPLORE

Questioning Strategies

- Suppose that all numbers in the given situation stay the same. However, you surveyed a random sample of 25 students, not 50 students. What are the reasonably likely values of the sample proportion $\hat{p}$? Explain.

  If $p = 0.3$ and $n = 25$, then $\mu_{\hat{p}} = p = 0.3$ and $\sigma_{\hat{p}} = \sqrt{\dfrac{0.3(1 - 0.3)}{25}} \approx 0.092$. Because reasonably likely values of $\hat{p}$ lie within two standard deviations of $\mu_{\hat{p}}$, you have $\mu_{\hat{p}} - 2\sigma_{\hat{p}} = 0.3 - 2(0.092) \approx 0.12$ and $\mu_{\hat{p}} + 2\sigma_{\hat{p}} = 0.3 + 2(0.092) \approx 0.48$. So, for a random sample of 25 students, the reasonably likely values of the sample proportion $\hat{p}$ lie between 0.12 and 0.48.

- Suppose that all numbers in the given situation stay the same. However, you surveyed a random sample of 100 students, not 50 students. What are the reasonably likely values of the sample proportion $\hat{p}$? Explain.

  If $p = 0.3$ and $n = 100$, then $\mu_{\hat{p}} = p = 0.3$ and $\sigma_{\hat{p}} = \sqrt{\dfrac{0.3(1 - 0.3)}{100}} \approx 0.046$. Because reasonably likely values of $\hat{p}$ lie within two standard deviations of $\mu_{\hat{p}}$, you have $\mu_{\hat{p}} - 2\sigma_{\hat{p}} = 0.3 - 2(0.046) \approx 0.21$ and $\mu_{\hat{p}} + 2\sigma_{\hat{p}} = 0.3 + 2(0.046) \approx 0.39$. So, for a random sample of 100 students, the reasonably likely values of the sample proportion $\hat{p}$ lie between 0.21 and 0.39.

continued

REFLECT

3a. In the class histograms, how does the mean of the sample proportions compare with the population proportion?

The mean of the sample proportions is close to the population proportion.

3b. What happens to the standard deviation of the sample proportions as the sample size increases?

The standard deviation of the sample proportions decreases.

When you work with the sampling distribution of a sample proportion, p represents the proportion of individuals in the population that have a particular characteristic (that is, the proportion of "successes") and $\hat{p}$ is the proportion of successes in a sample. The mean of the sampling distribution of the sample proportion is denoted $\mu_{\hat{p}}$. The standard deviation of the sampling distribution of the sample proportion is denoted $\sigma_{\hat{p}}$ and is also called the **standard error of the proportion**.

Properties of the Sampling Distribution of the Sample Proportion

If a random sample of size n is selected from a population with proportion of successes p, then

(1) $\mu_{\hat{p}} = p$,

(2) $\sigma_{\hat{p}} = \sqrt{\dfrac{p(1-p)}{n}}$, and

(3) if both np and $n(1-p)$ are at least 10, then the sampling distribution of the sample proportion is approximately normal.

CC.9-12.S.IC.4
4 EXAMPLE Using the Sampling Distribution of the Sample Proportion

About 40% of the students at a university live off campus. You choose a random sample of 50 students. What interval captures 95% of the proportions for random samples of 50 students?

A Write the given information about the population and the sample, where a success is a student who lives off campus.

$p = $ ___0.4___ $n = $ ___50___

B Find the mean of the sampling distribution of the sample proportion and the standard error of the proportion.

$\mu_{\hat{p}} = p = $ ___0.4___ $\sigma_{\hat{p}} = \sqrt{\dfrac{p(1-p)}{n}} = \sqrt{\dfrac{0.4\,(1 - 0.4)}{50}} \approx$ ___0.069___

C Check that np and $n(1-p)$ are both at least 10.

$np = $ ___50___ $\cdot$ ___0.4___ $= $ ___20___ $n(1-p) = $ ___50___ $\cdot$ ___0.6___ $= $ ___30___

Since np and $n(1-p)$ are both greater than 10, the sampling distribution is approximately normal.

D In a normal distribution, 95% of the data fall within 2 standard deviations of the mean.

$\mu_{\hat{p}} - 2\sigma_{\hat{p}} = $ ___0.4___ $- 2\big($ ___0.069___ $\big) = $ ___0.262___

$\mu_{\hat{p}} + 2\sigma_{\hat{p}} = $ ___0.4___ $+ 2\big($ ___0.069___ $\big) = $ ___0.538___

So, 95% of the sample proportions fall between ___26.2%___ and ___53.8%___.

REFLECT

4a. How likely is it that a random sample of 50 students includes 31 students who live off campus? Explain.

This is very unlikely since $\frac{31}{50}$ = 62% and this proportion is more than 3 standard deviations from the mean of the sampling distribution.

Previously, you investigated sampling from a population whose parameter of interest (mean or proportion) is known. In many real-world situations, you collect sample data from a population whose parameter of interest is not known. Now you will learn how to use sample statistics to make inferences about population parameters.

CC.9-12.S.IC.4
5 EXPLORE Analyzing Likely Population Proportions

You survey a random sample of 50 students at a large high school and find that 30% of the students have attended a school football game. You cannot survey the entire population of students, but you would like to know what population proportions are reasonably likely in this situation.

A Suppose the proportion p of the population that has attended a school football game is 30%. Find the reasonably likely values of the sample proportion $\hat{p}$.

In this case, $p = $ ___0.3___ and $n = $ ___50___.

$\mu_{\hat{p}} = p = $ ___0.3___ and $\sigma_{\hat{p}} = \sqrt{\dfrac{p(1-p)}{n}} = \sqrt{\dfrac{0.3\,(1 - 0.3)}{50}} \approx$ ___0.065___

The reasonably likely values of $\hat{p}$ fall within 2 standard deviations of $\mu_{\hat{p}}$.

$\mu_{\hat{p}} - 2\sigma_{\hat{p}} = $ ___0.3___ $- 2\big($ ___0.065___ $\big) = $ ___0.17___

$\mu_{\hat{p}} + 2\sigma_{\hat{p}} = $ ___0.3___ $+ 2\big($ ___0.065___ $\big) = $ ___0.43___

© Houghton Mifflin Harcourt Publishing Company

- How does the sample size affect the reasonably likely values of the sample proportion $\hat{p}$? Explain. **As the sample size increases, the range of the reasonably likely values of the sample proportion $\hat{p}$ decreases.**

- In Reflect Question 5c, you drew the conclusion that a population proportion between 30% and 50% would be reasonably likely for the sample size of 50 students. Could you draw this same conclusion if all numbers in the given situation stayed the same except that the sample size was 100 instead of 50? Explain your reasoning. **No; a population proportion between 30% and 50% would no longer be reasonably likely. If you drew the graph for a sample size of 100 students, the horizontal line segment at the level of 0.3 would extend from 0.21 to 0.39. A vertical line at $\hat{p} = 0.4$ would not intersect this line segment, which means that with a sample size of 100 students, a population proportion of 30% is not reasonably likely for a sample proportion of 0.4.**

Avoid Common Errors

In part A of the Explore, students may want to use 0.4 instead of 0.3 for the value of $\mu_{\hat{p}}$. Remind students that 40% is a *sample* proportion. The value of $\mu_{\hat{p}}$, however, is equal to the *population* proportion, which is unknown. In part A, you *assume* that the population proportion is 30%, and that is the value that you use for $\mu_{\hat{p}}$.

6 EXAMPLE

Questioning Strategies

- Based on the given random sample, one researcher states that between 68% and 84% of four-year-olds in the United States can write their names. Based on the same random sample, another researcher states that between 65% and 87% of four-year-olds in the United States can write their names. If both researchers have made a reasonable statement, what could be the reason for the discrepancy? **The first researcher is making the statement with 95% confidence, while the second researcher is making the statement with 99% confidence.**

- If you make a statement "with confidence," this implies that you have a degree of certainty about the statement. If this is the case, then why does the range of values for the percent of four-year-olds who can write their name increase rather than decrease as the confidence level increases? **If the range of possible values is greater, then you can be more confident that the actual value is going to fall within that range than within a smaller range of values.**

Teaching Strategy

Students may benefit from seeing some real-world situations in which statistics are reported with a specified level of confidence. Academic journals in fields ranging from science and medicine to psychology and business often display detailed information resulting from surveys in a table format, often with a confidence level indicated at the bottom. Although the statistics used may go beyond what is covered in this lesson, students can see that level of confidence is a component of many statistical analyses.

EXTRA EXAMPLE

Based on the given information, what is the 90% confidence interval for the proportion p of four-year-olds in the United States who can write their names? **between 0.69 and 0.83**

B On the graph, draw a horizontal line segment at the level of 0.3 on the vertical axis to represent the interval of likely values of $\hat{p}$ that you found above.

C Now repeat the process for $p = 0.35$, 0.4, 0.45, and so on to complete the graph. You may wish to divide up the work with other students and pool your findings.

D Draw a vertical line at 0.4 on the horizontal axis. This represents $\hat{p} = 0.4$. The line segments that this vertical line intersects are the population proportions for which a sample proportion of 0.4 is reasonably likely.

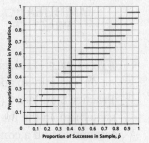

REFLECT

5a. Is it possible that 30% of all students at the school have attended a football game? Is it likely? Explain.

It is both possible and likely; in part A of the Explore, you found that for $p = 0.3$, the interval of likely sample proportions (for a sample of 50 students) is 0.17 to 0.43, which includes $\hat{p} = 0.4$.

5b. Is it possible that 60% of all students at the school have attended a football game? Is it likely? Explain.

It is possible, but not likely; for $p = 0.6$, the interval of likely sample proportions (for a sample of 50 students) is 0.46 to 0.74, which does not include $\hat{p} = 0.4$.

5c. Based on your graph, which population proportions do you think are reasonably likely? Why?

30% to 50%; for these population proportions, the intervals of likely sample proportions include $\hat{p} = 0.4$.

A **confidence interval** is an approximate range of values that is likely to include an unknown population parameter. The *level* or *degree* of a confidence interval, such as 95%, gives the probability that the interval includes the true value of the parameter.

Recall that when data are normally distributed, 95% of the values fall within 2 standard deviations of the mean. Using this idea in the Explore, you found a 95% confidence interval for the proportion of all students who have attended a school football game.

To develop a formula for a confidence interval, notice that the vertical bold line segment in the figure, which represents the 95% confidence interval you found in the Explore, is about the same length as the horizontal bold line segment. The horizontal bold line segment has endpoints $\mu_{\hat{p}} - 2\sigma_{\hat{p}}$ and $\mu_{\hat{p}} + 2\sigma_{\hat{p}}$ where $\hat{p} = 0.4$. Since the bold line segments intersect at (0.4, 0.4), the vertical bold line segment has these same endpoints.

The above argument shows that you can find the endpoints of the confidence interval by finding the endpoints of the horizontal segment centered at $\hat{p}$. You know how to do this using the formula for the standard error of the sampling distribution of the sample proportion from earlier in this lesson. Putting these ideas together gives the following result.

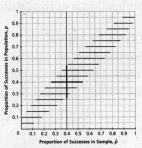

A Confidence Interval for a Population Proportion

A $c\%$ confidence interval for the proportion p of successes in a population is given by

$$\hat{p} - z_c\sqrt{\frac{\hat{p}(1 - \hat{p})}{n}} \le p \le \hat{p} + z_c\sqrt{\frac{\hat{p}(1 - \hat{p})}{n}}$$

where $\hat{p}$ is the sample proportion, n is the sample size, and z_c depends upon the desired degree of confidence.

In order for this interval to describe the value of p reasonably accurately, three conditions must be met.

1. There are only two possible outcomes associated with the parameter of interest. The population proportion for one outcome is p, and the proportion for the other outcome is $1 - p$.

2. $n\hat{p}$ and $n(1 - \hat{p})$ must both be at least 10.

3. The size of the population must be at least 10 times the size of the sample, and the sample must be random.

Use the values in the table below for z_c. (Note that for greater accuracy you should use 1.96 rather than 2 for $z_{95\%}$.)

Desired degree of confidence	90%	95%	99%
Value of z_c	1.645	1.96	2.576

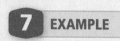
Questioning Strategies

- Suppose the confidence level in the situation is reduced to 95%. Would the confidence interval for the mean test score among all students be wider or narrower than the confidence interval for the mean test score among all students when the confidence level is 99%? Explain your reasoning. **The confidence interval for a 95% confidence level will be narrower than the confidence interval for a 99% confidence level. As the confidence interval becomes wider, it is more likely that the mean test score among all students will fall within that confidence interval; therefore, the confidence level increases.**

- You determined in Reflect Question 7b that the formula for a confidence interval given in the example should be used only when the scores are normally distributed. Give an example of a way that scores could be distributed so that the given formula for a confidence interval should *not* be used and explain why. **The distribution of the scores could be uniform, skewed left, or skewed right. For example, two populations could have the same mean and standard deviation, but one could be skewed right with a few very high scores and many relatively low scores, while the other population could be skewed left with a few very low scores and many relatively high scores. When a distribution is skewed, conclusions based on the use of the given formula for a confidence interval are invalid.**

MATHEMATICAL PRACTICE

Highlighting the Standards

7 EXAMPLE and its Reflect questions offer an opportunity to address Mathematical Practice Standard 7 (Look for and make use of structure). In the previous example, students learned to find a confidence interval for a proportion. In this example, students learn to find a confidence interval for a mean. In the previous example, students not only learned the formula for the confidence interval of a proportion, but also came to understand the underlying concepts of how the formula was derived. When students now use the formula for the confidence interval of a mean, they are already familiar with the basic structure of the formula. For example, in both formulas, an amount based on the standard error and the confidence level is both subtracted from and added to either the sample proportion or the sample mean to find the confidence interval.

Avoid Common Errors

Remind students that the formula used in this example will produce valid results only when the population is normally distributed.

EXTRA EXAMPLE

For the given situation, what is the 90% confidence interval for the mean score among all students at the school? **between 566 and 654**

6 EXAMPLE Finding a Confidence Interval for a Proportion

In a random sample of 100 four-year-old children in the United States, 76 were able to write their name. Find a 95% confidence interval for the proportion p of four-year-olds in the United States who can write their name.

A Determine the sample size n, the proportion $\hat{p}$ of four-year-olds in the sample who can write their name, and the value of z_c for a 95% confidence interval.

$$n = \underline{100} \qquad \hat{p} = \underline{0.76} \qquad z_c = \underline{1.96}$$

B Substitute the values of n, $\hat{p}$, and z_c into the formulas for the endpoints of the confidence interval. Then simplify and round to two decimal places.

$$\hat{p} - z_c\sqrt{\frac{\hat{p}(1-\hat{p})}{n}} = \underline{0.76} - \underline{1.96}\sqrt{\frac{\underline{0.76}\left(1 - \underline{0.76}\right)}{\underline{100}}} \approx \underline{0.68}$$

$$\hat{p} + z_c\sqrt{\frac{\hat{p}(1-\hat{p})}{n}} = \underline{0.76} + \underline{1.96}\sqrt{\frac{\underline{0.76}\left(1 - \underline{0.76}\right)}{\underline{100}}} \approx \underline{0.84}$$

So, you can state with 95% confidence that the proportion of all four-year-olds in the United States who can write their name lies between __0.68__ and __0.84__.

REFLECT

6a. Find the 99% confidence interval for p and describe how increasing the degree of confidence affects the range of values. Why does this make sense?

$0.65 \le p \le 0.87$; as the degree of confidence increases, the range of values gets

broader; this makes sense because in order to have a greater degree of confidence

in whether the population proportion has been "captured," you have to cast a

wider net.

You can use reasoning similar to the argument in the Explore to develop a formula for a confidence interval for a population mean.

A Confidence Interval for a Population Mean

A $c\%$ confidence interval for the mean μ in a normally distributed population is given by

$$\bar{x} - z_c\frac{\sigma}{\sqrt{n}} \le \mu \le \bar{x} + z_c\frac{\sigma}{\sqrt{n}}$$

where $\bar{x}$ is the sample mean, n is the sample size, σ is the population standard deviation, and z_c depends upon the desired degree of confidence.

Note that it is assumed that the population is normally distributed and that you know the population standard deviation σ. In a more advanced statistics course, you can develop a confidence interval formula that does not depend upon a normally distributed population or knowing the population standard deviation.

© Houghton Mifflin Harcourt Publishing Company

---

7 EXAMPLE Finding a Confidence Interval for a Mean

In a random sample of 20 students at a large high school, the mean score on a standardized test is 610. Given that the standard deviation of all scores at the school is 120, find a 99% confidence interval for the mean score among all students at the school.

A Determine the sample size n, the sample mean $\bar{x}$, the population standard deviation σ, and the value of z_c for a 99% confidence interval.

$$n = \underline{20} \qquad \bar{x} = \underline{610}$$

$$\sigma = \underline{120} \qquad z_c = \underline{2.576}$$

B Substitute the values of n, $\bar{x}$, σ, and z_c into the formulas for the endpoints of the confidence interval. Then simplify and round to the nearest whole number.

$$\bar{x} - z_c\frac{\sigma}{\sqrt{n}} = \underline{610} - \underline{2.576}\frac{\underline{120}}{\sqrt{\underline{20}}} \approx \underline{541}$$

$$\bar{x} + z_c\frac{\sigma}{\sqrt{n}} = \underline{610} + \underline{2.576}\frac{\underline{120}}{\sqrt{\underline{20}}} \approx \underline{679}$$

So, you can state with 99% confidence that the mean score among all students at the school lies between __541__ and __679__.

REFLECT

7a. What is the 99% confidence interval when the sample size increases to 50? Describe how increasing the sample size affects the confidence interval.

$566 \le \mu \le 654$; as the sample size increases, the confidence

interval gets narrower.

7b. What do you assume about the test scores of all students at the school in order to use the formula for the confidence interval?

You assume the scores are normally distributed.

In the previous example, you found the 99% confidence interval $541 \le \mu \le 679$, which is a range of values centered at $\mu = 610$. You can write the confidence interval as 610 ± 69, where 69 is the *margin of error*. The **margin of error** is half the length of a confidence interval.

© Houghton Mifflin Harcourt Publishing Company

Essential Question

How do you calculate a confidence interval and a margin of error for a population proportion or mean?

The mean of the sampling distribution of the sample mean is equal to the population mean. Similarly, the mean of the sampling distribution of the sample proportion is equal to the population proportion.

To calculate a confidence interval for a population proportion, use the formula

$$\hat{p} - z_c \sqrt{\frac{\hat{p}(1 - \hat{p})}{n}} \le p \le \hat{p} + z_c \sqrt{\frac{\hat{p}(1 - \hat{p})}{n}},$$ where

p is the proportion of successes in a population, $\hat{p}$ is the sample proportion, n is the sample size, and z_c is the confidence level. To calculate a confidence interval for a population mean, use the formula

$$\bar{x} - z_c \frac{\sigma}{\sqrt{n}} \le \mu \le \bar{x} + z_c \frac{\sigma}{\sqrt{n}},$$ where μ is the mean

in a normally distributed population, $\bar{x}$ is the sample mean, n is the sample size, σ is the population standard deviation, and z_c depends on the desired degree of confidence. For both the population proportion and the population mean, the margin of error is half the length of the confidence interval.

Summarize

Each student should create a flow chart to summarize the steps in the lesson's first two examples.

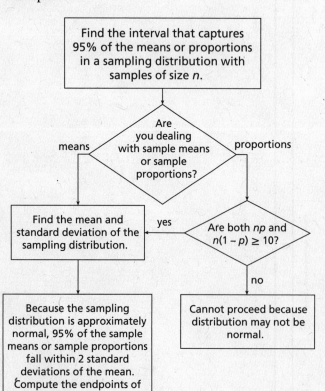

Have students make a graphic organizer outlining the processes for calculating a confidence interval for a population proportion and a population mean. Include information about calculating the margin of error, as well as steps for choosing a sample size.

Where skills are taught	Where skills are practiced
2 EXAMPLE	EXS. 1–4
6 EXAMPLE	EXS. 5, 6
7 EXAMPLE	EXS. 7–8

Exercise 9: Students derive a formula for estimating the margin of error E for the proportion of successes in a population.

Margin of Error for a Population Proportion

The margin of error E for the proportion of successes in a population with sample proportion $\hat{p}$ and sample size n is given by

$$E = z_c \sqrt{\frac{\hat{p}(1 - \hat{p})}{n}}$$

where z_c depends on the degree of the confidence interval.

Margin of Error for a Population Mean

The margin of error E for the mean in a normally distributed population with standard deviation σ, sample mean $\bar{x}$, and sample size n is given by

$$E = z_c \frac{\sigma}{\sqrt{n}}$$

where z_c depends on the degree of the confidence interval.

From the above formulas, it is clear that the margin of error decreases as the sample size n increases. This suggests using a sample that is as large as possible; however, it is often more practical to determine a margin of error that is acceptable and then calculate the required sample size.

PRACTICE

Bags of SnackTime Popcorn have a mean mass of 15 ounces with a standard deviation of 1.5 ounces. A quality control inspector selects a random sample of 40 bags of popcorn at the factory. Find each of the following.

1. What is the population mean? _15 oz_

2. What is the sample mean? _15 oz_

3. What is the sample standard deviation? _0.24 oz_

4. The interval that captures 95% of the proportions for random samples of 40 bags of popcorn

   Between 14.76 oz and 15.24 oz

5. In a random sample of 100 U.S. households, 37 had a pet dog.

   a. Do the data satisfy the three conditions for the confidence interval formula for a population proportion? Why or why not?

   Yes; (1) there are only two outcomes associated with the parameter: either having a dog or not having a dog; (2) $n\hat{p} = 100(0.37) = 37$ and $n(1 - \hat{p}) = 100(0.63) = 63$, so both are greater than 10; (3) the population of households in the United States is far greater than $10n = 10(100) = 1000$.

   b. Find a 90% confidence interval for the proportion p of U.S. households that have a pet dog.

   $0.29 \leq p \leq 0.45$

---

   c. Find a 95% confidence interval for the proportion p of U.S. households that have a pet dog.

   $0.275 \leq p \leq 0.465$

6. In a quality control study, 200 cars made by a particular company were randomly selected and 13 were found to have defects in the electrical system.

   a. Give a range for the percent p of all cars made by the company that have defective electrical systems, assuming you want to have a 90% degree of confidence.

   $3.6\% \leq p \leq 9.4\%$

   b. What is the margin or error?

   0.029 or 2.9%

   c. How does the margin of error change if you want to report the range of percents p with a 95% degree of confidence?

   The margin or error increases to 0.034 or 3.4%.

7. The mean annual salary for a random sample of 300 kindergarten through 12th grade teachers in a particular state is $50,500. The standard deviation among the state's entire population of teachers is $3,700. Find a 95% confidence interval for the mean annual salary μ for all kindergarten through 12th grade teachers in the state.

   $\$50{,}081 \leq \mu \leq \$50{,}919$

8. You survey a random sample of 90 students at a university whose students' grade-point averages (GPAs) have a standard deviation of 0.4. The surveyed students have a mean GPA of 3.1.

   a. How likely is it that the mean GPA among all students at the university is 3.25? Explain.

   This is very unlikely. The 99% confidence interval for μ is $2.99 \leq \mu \leq 3.21$ and 3.25 lies outside this range.

   b. What are you assuming about the GPAs of all students at the university? Why?

   The GPAs are normally distributed; this assumption is necessary in order to use the formula for the confidence interval for a population mean.

9. The margin of error E for the proportion of successes in a population may be estimated by $\frac{1}{\sqrt{n}}$ where n is the sample size. Explain where this estimate comes from. (Hint: Assume a 95% confidence interval.)

   $z_c = 1.96 \approx 2$ and $\hat{p}$ is assumed to be 0.5, so $E = z_c \sqrt{\frac{\hat{p}(1 - \hat{p})}{n}} = 2\sqrt{\frac{0.5(0.5)}{n}}$, which simplifies to $\frac{1}{\sqrt{n}}$.

Assign these pages to help your students practice and apply important lesson concepts. For additional exercises, see the Student Edition.

Answers

Additional Practice

1. systematic sample

2. cluster sample

3. simple random sample

4. convenience sample

5. Method c is likely to be the most accurate method because every junior has an equal chance of being selected.

6. Given on worksheet.

7. No; 47% ± 4% = 43% to 51% and 53% ± 4% = 49% to 57%. The intervals overlap, so the survey does not indicate the majority's preference.

Problem Solving

1. No; 56% ± 7% = 49% to 63%. 44% ± 7% = 37% to 51%. The intervals overlap, so the poll does not clearly indicate the outcome of the voting.

2. Yes; 52% ± 1% = 51% to 53%. 48% ± 1% = 47% to 49%. The intervals do not overlap, so the poll clearly indicates the majority's preference.

3. No; 53% ± 3% = 50% to 56%. 47% ± 3% = 44% to 50%. The intervals overlap, so the poll does not clearly indicate the majority's preference.

4. Yes; 58% ± 5% = 53% to 63%. 42% ± 5% = 37% to 47%. The intervals do not overlap, so the poll clearly indicates the majority's preference.

5. B

6. H

7. C

8. F

8-5

Additional Practice

For Exercises 1–3, use the following information: The mean height of the population of male high school students in a school district is 67.2 inches with a standard deviation of 2.8 inches.

1. Random samples are drawn from the population. What is the mean of the sampling distribution of the sample mean?

   _____

2. What is the standard error of the mean for a random sample of 25 students? for a random sample of 64 students?

   _____

3. What interval captures 95% of the sample means for a sample size of 64 students?

   _____

For Exercises 4 and 5, use the following information: From a random sample of 30 customers who bought a soft-serve frozen yogurt cone, 26% chose chocolate-vanilla swirl.

4. Find $n\hat{p}$ and $n(1 - \hat{p})$ where n is the sample size and $\hat{p}$ is the sample proportion.

   _____

5. Is it reasonable to use this sample to construct a confidence interval for the population proportion of customers who would choose chocolate-vanilla swirl? Explain.

   _____

6. In a random sample of 44 students from a school of 1290 students, 60% chose red and blue for the new school colors over red and white. Find a 90% confidence interval for the proportion p of students at the school who prefer red and blue. Can you conclude with 90% confidence that the majority of students prefer red and blue?

   _____

7. In a random sample of 550 students in a state, the mean math score on a standardized test was 22.6. Find a 95% confidence interval for the population mean score μ for the state given that the standard deviation is 4.8.

   _____

Find the margin of error E for the statistic at the given confidence level.

8. population proportion, if sample proportion $\hat{p} = 0.11$ and sample size $n = 124$; 99% _____

9. population mean, if standard deviation $\sigma = 6.8$ and sample size $n = 1000$; 95% _____

Problem Solving

Out of a random sample of $n = 40$ students from a high school with more than 2000 students, $\hat{p} = 58\%$ say that their morning travel time to school is less than 30 minutes.

1. Can you use the data to construct a reasonably accurate confidence interval for the proportion of students with a morning travel time of less than 30 minutes? Explain.

   _____

2. Can you conclude that the morning travel time for the majority of the students is less than 30 minutes at the 90%, 95%, or 99% confidence level? Explain.

   _____
   _____

3. If you increase the sample size to $n = 125$ students and obtain the same sample proportion of $\hat{p} = 0.58$, does this change your answer to Exercise 2? Explain.

   _____
   _____

For Exercises 4 and 5, a random sample is drawn from a population with a normally distributed statistic with mean μ and standard deviation $\sigma = 20$.

4. What is the margin of error E for estimating μ from the sample mean at the 95% confidence level for a sample size of $n = 100$? _____

5. How can you use the margin of error formula to find the minimum sample size so that $E \leq 2.0$ at the 95% confidence level? What is this sample size?

   _____

6. What is the relationship between the margin of error E for a population proportion when the sample proportion is $\hat{p} = 0.2$ and when the sample proportion is $\hat{p} = 0.5$ for a given confidence level and sample size?

   _____

Notes

Binomial Distributions
Extension: Probability Distributions

Essential question: What is a probability distribution and how is it displayed?

COMMON CORE Standards for Mathematical Content

CC.9-12.S.ID.1 Represent data with plots on the real number line (… histograms …).*

CC.9-12.S.IC.2 Decide if a specified model is consistent with results from a given data-generating process, e.g., using simulation.*

CC.9-12.S.MD.3(+) Develop a probability distribution for a random variable...

CC.9-12.S.MD.5(+) Weigh the possible outcomes of a decision by assigning probabilities to payoff values...

Vocabulary
random variable, probability distribution, cumulative probability

Prerequisites
Data gathering techniques

Probability

Math Background
Theoretical probability describes how frequently an event is expected to occur based on analysis of possible outcomes. Experimental probability describes how frequently an event has occurred based on historical data. Both types of probabilities involve forming ratios of "successful" occurrences (the event occurred) to all occurrences (the event did or did not occur). Probabilities, therefore, are numbers (expressed as decimals, fractions, or percents) between and including 0 and 1.

In this lesson, students will graph probability distributions. While the two distributions are similar, there is one very important difference. For probability distributions, the sum of the areas of the rectangles in the histogram (or the area under the probability curve) is equal to 1 because the events in a probability distribution are mutually exclusive and represent all possibilities.

INTRODUCE

Review with students what probability is and what the characteristics of probabilities are, such as $0 \leq P(A) \leq 1$ and $P(A) + P(\text{not } A) = 1$ for any event A. Ask students to calculate the following: A spinner is divided into four equal quadrants that are orange, yellow, green, and purple. What is the probability the spinner will land on purple? $\frac{1}{4}$

TEACH

1 ENGAGE

Questioning Strategies

• In the last lesson, you saw histograms for data distributions. In this lesson, you are seeing histograms for probability distributions. Compare the values on the *x*-axis of a histogram for a data distribution and for a probability distribution. **For a data distribution, the *x*-axis shows data values (or groups of data values). For a probability distribution, the *x*-axis shows possible outcomes (that is, the values of the random variable).**

• Compare the values on the *y*-axis of a histogram for a data distribution and for a probability distribution. **For a data distribution, the *y*-axis shows the frequency of each data value (or group of data values). For a probability distribution, the *y*-axis shows the probability of each outcome.**

• If one bar is taller than another in a histogram for a data distribution, what does that tell you? What about a histogram for a probability distribution? **For a data distribution, a taller bar tells you that a data value (or group of data values) has a greater frequency. For a probability distribution, a taller bar tells you that an outcome has a greater probability.**

Name_____ Class_____ Date_____

8-6

Binomial Distributions
Extension: Probability Distributions

Essential question: *What is a probability distribution and how is it displayed?*

Video Tutor

© Houghton Mifflin Harcourt Publishing Company

CC.9-12.S.MD.5(+)
1 ENGAGE   Introducing Probability Distributions

A **random variable** is a variable whose value is determined by the outcome of a probability experiment. For example, when you roll a number cube, you can use a random variable X to represent the number you roll. The possible values of X are 1, 2, 3, 4, 5, and 6.

A **probability distribution** is a data distribution that gives the probabilities of the values of a random variable. A probability distribution can be represented by a histogram in which the values of the random variable—that is, the possible outcomes—are on the horizontal axis, and probabilities are on the vertical axis. The figure shows the probability distribution for rolling a number cube.

When the values of a random variable are consecutive whole numbers, as is the case for rolling a number cube, the probability distribution typically shows bars that each have a width of 1 and is centered on a value of the variable. The area of each bar therefore equals the probability of the corresponding outcome, and the combined areas of the bars is the sum of the probabilities, which is 1.

A **cumulative probability** is the probability that a random variable is less than or equal to a given value. You can find cumulative probabilities from a histogram by adding the areas of the bars for all outcomes less than or equal to the given value.

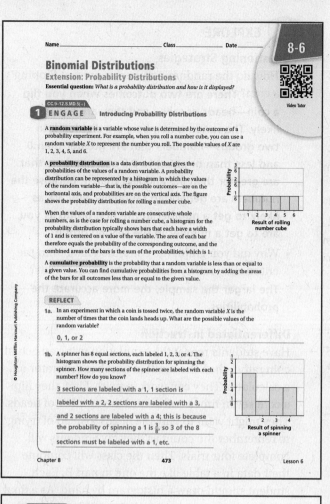

Result of rolling number cube

REFLECT

1a. In an experiment in which a coin is tossed twice, the random variable X is the number of times that the coin lands heads up. What are the possible values of the random variable?

0, 1, or 2

1b. A spinner has 8 equal sections, each labeled 1, 2, 3, or 4. The histogram shows the probability distribution for spinning the spinner. How many sections of the spinner are labeled with each number? How do you know?

3 sections are labeled with a 1, 1 section is

labeled with a 2, 2 sections are labeled with a 3,

and 2 sections are labeled with a 4; this is because

the probability of spinning a 1 is $\frac{3}{8}$, so 3 of the 8

sections must be labeled with a 1, etc.

Result of spinning a spinner

CC.9-12.S.MD.5(+)
2 EXAMPLE   Displaying a Probability Distribution

You roll two number cubes at the same time. Let X be a random variable that represents the sum of the numbers rolled. Make a histogram to show the probability distribution for X.

A Complete the frequency table to show the number of ways that you can get each sum in one roll of the number cubes.

Sum	2	3	4	5	6	7	8	9	10	11	12
Frequency	1	2	3	4	5	6	5	4	3	2	1

B Add the frequencies you found in part A to find the total number of possible outcomes.

The total number of possible outcomes is ___36___.

C Divide each frequency by the total number of outcomes to find the probability of each sum. Complete the table.

Sum	2	3	4	5	6	7	8	9	10	11	12
Probability	$\frac{1}{36}$	$\frac{2}{36}$	$\frac{3}{36}$	$\frac{4}{36}$	$\frac{5}{36}$	$\frac{6}{36}$	$\frac{5}{36}$	$\frac{4}{36}$	$\frac{3}{36}$	$\frac{2}{36}$	$\frac{1}{36}$

D Create a histogram with the sums on the horizontal axis and the probabilities on the vertical axis. Complete the histogram below by labeling the axes and drawing a bar to represent the probability of each sum.

Sum

© Houghton Mifflin Harcourt Publishing Company

REFLECT

2a. The probability that you roll a sum less than or equal to 5 is written $P(X \leq 5)$. What is this probability? How is it represented in the histogram?

The probability is $\frac{10}{36}$. This is the sum of the areas of the bars for the

outcomes 2, 3, 4, and 5.

Questioning Strategies

- How many ways can you roll a 2? Describe them.
  Both cubes must land showing a 1, so there is one way.

- One number cube is red and the other is blue. Describe how many ways you can roll a sum of 3.
  The red cube can show a 1, and the blue cube can show a 2, or vice versa, so there are two ways.

- One number cube is red and the other is blue. Describe how many ways you can roll a sum of 4.
  The red cube can show a 1, and the blue cube can show a 3, or vice versa. The red cube can show a 2, and the blue cube can show a 2. So, there is a total of three ways.

- One number cube is red, and the other is blue. Describe how many ways you can roll a sum of 5.
  The red cube can show a 1, and the blue cube can show a 4, or vice versa. The red cube can show a 2, and the blue cube can show a 3, or vice versa. So, there is a total of four ways.

- What is the sum of the probabilities in the table in part C? Will that always be the case? Explain.
  1; Yes, if all possibilities are accounted for and they are mutually exclusive, the sum must be 1.

EXTRA EXAMPLE

A spinner has four equal sections that are labeled 1, 2, 3, and 4. You spin the spinner twice and find the sum of the two numbers it lands on. Let X be a random variable that represents the sum of the two numbers.

A. Complete the table.

Sum	2	3	4	5	6	7	8
Frequency	1	2	3	4	3	2	1
Probability	$\frac{1}{16}$	$\frac{2}{16}$	$\frac{3}{16}$	$\frac{4}{16}$	$\frac{3}{16}$	$\frac{2}{16}$	$\frac{1}{16}$

B. Make a histogram of the probability distribution.

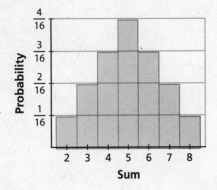

Questioning Strategies

- How do the random numbers represent flipping a coin? There are two outcomes when you flip a coin—heads or tails—and they are equally likely. The random numbers are divided into two groups—numbers that are greater than 0 and less than or equal to 0.5 and numbers that are greater than 0.5 and less than 1. Because the numbers are generated randomly, you are as likely to get a number in the first group as you are to get a number in the second group.

- Why did you graph the combined data from the entire class rather than just your own results? The larger the sample, the more accurate the probabilities.

Differentiated Instruction

Have students repeat the simulation using an actual coin rather than the random number generator on a calculator. They can work in pairs. First, they flip a coin seven times and record the number of heads. They might want to tally the heads instead of trying to remember the count as they go. Students will complete four trials. Then the class will combine their data in a table like the one in part B. Each student should draw a histogram by hand. As a final activity, they can compare their actual results with their randomly generated results.

In the example, you used theoretical probabilities to define a probability distribution. You can also use experimental probabilities to define a probability distribution.

EXPLORE Using a Simulation

CC.9-12.S.IC.2

You flip a coin 7 times in a row. Use a simulation to determine the probability distribution for the number of times the coin lands heads up.

A When you flip a coin, the possible outcomes are heads and tails. You will use your calculator to generate random numbers between 0 and 1, assigning heads to numbers less than or equal to 0.5 and tails to numbers greater than 0.5.

To do the simulation, press MATH and then select **PRB**. Choose **1:rand** and press ENTER.

Now press ENTER 7 times to generate 7 random numbers. This simulates one trial (that is, one set of 7 coin flips). Record the number of heads in the table. For example, on the calculator screen shown here, there are 3 numbers less than or equal to 0.5, so there are 3 heads.

Carry out three more trials and record your results in the table.

Trial	1	2	3	4
Number of Heads				

Answers will vary.

B Report your results to your teacher in order to combine everyone's results. Use the combined class data to complete the table below. To find the relative frequency for an outcome, divide the frequency of the outcome by the total number of trials in the class.

Number of Heads	0	1	2	3	4	5	6	7
Frequency								
Relative Frequency								

Answers will vary.

C Enter the outcomes (0 through 7) into your calculator as list L_1. Enter the relative frequencies as list L_2.

D Make a histogram by turning on a statistics plot, selecting the histogram option, and using L_1 for Xlist and L_2 for Freq. Set the viewing window as shown. Then press GRAPH. A sample histogram is shown below.

Chapter 8 475 Lesson 6

REFLECT

3a. Describe the shape of the probability distribution.

The distribution is mounded and roughly symmetric.

3b. Based on the histogram, what is $P(X \leq 3)$? That is, what is the probability of getting 3 or fewer heads when you flip a coin 7 times? Explain.

Answers will vary; the probability should be close to 0.5; this probability is the sum of the areas of the bars for the outcomes 0, 1, 2, and 3.

3c. If you flipped a coin 7 times and got 7 heads, would this cause you to question whether the coin is fair? Why or why not?

Sample answer: Perhaps; the probability of getting 7 heads with a fair coin is about 1%, which is very unlikely.

4 EXAMPLE Analyzing a Probability Distribution

CC.9-12.S.MD.3(+)

The histogram shows the theoretical probability distribution for the situation in the Explore. Use the distribution to answer each question.

A What is the probability of getting 4 or more heads?

$P(X \geq 4) = P(X = 4) + P(X = 5) + P(X = 6) + P(X = 7)$

So, the probability of getting 4 or more heads is

_0.273_ + _0.164_ + _0.055_ + _0.008_ = _0.5_ .

B What is the probability of getting at least 1 head?

An easy way to calculate this probability is to use the complement of the event. The complement of getting at least 1 head is getting 0 heads. Use the histogram to find $P(X = 0)$ and subtract it from 1.

$P(X = 0) =$ _0.008_

So, the probability of getting at least 1 head is

$1 -$ _0.008_ = _0.992_ .

REFLECT

4a. Why are the probabilities in the histogram you made in the Explore different from the probabilities given in the histogram above?

The histogram in the Explore was based on experimental probabilities, so there is randomness in the results.

Chapter 8 476 Lesson 6

Notes

Chapter 8 476 Lesson 6

4 EXAMPLE

Questioning Strategies

- Describe what information the histogram conveys about the outcome of three heads compared with the outcome of four heads. **The probability of getting three heads is the same as getting four heads—0.273. The probability of either of these events is greater than the probability of getting fewer than three heads or more than four heads.**

- Describe in words what the shape of the histogram shows. **The shape is symmetric with high probabilities in the middle tapering to low probabilities at the ends. So, you are least likely to get no heads or seven heads when flipping a coin seven times. You are slightly more likely to get one head or six heads, and even more likely to get two heads or five heads. You are most likely to get three heads or four heads.**

EXTRA EXAMPLE

You flip a coin 4 times in a row. The histogram shows the theoretical probability distribution for this situation.

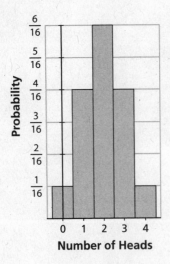

A. What is the probability of getting 3 or more heads? $\frac{5}{16}$

B. What is the probability of getting at most 2 heads? $\frac{11}{16}$

2 EXAMPLE, **3 EXPLORE**, and **4 EXAMPLE** include opportunities to address Mathematical Practice Standard 7 (Look for and make use of structure). Students will use histograms to display probability distributions. They will recognize the difference between a theoretically generated probability distribution and an experimentally generated probability distribution. They will be able to explain why theoretical and experimental probability distributions are not necessarily the same and when they should expect them to be more alike (which happens as you increase the number of trials in a probability experiment).

CLOSE

Essential Question

What is a probability distribution and how is it displayed?

A probability distribution is a distribution that shows the likelihood of each outcome of a probability experiment. It can be displayed as a histogram with possible outcomes on the *x*-axis and probabilities on the *y*-axis.

Summarize

Have students write a journal entry. They should choose between the probability distribution in **2 EXAMPLE** and the one in **4 EXAMPLE** and summarize it in their entry. Students should include a description of the scenario, a histogram of the probability distribution, and examples of probabilities that can be determined from the histogram.

PRACTICE

Where skills are taught	Where skills are practiced
2 EXAMPLE	EXS. 1, 2
4 EXAMPLE	EXS. 3–6

4b. What do you think would happen to the histogram you made in the Explore if you included data from 1000 additional trials?

The histogram would approach the shape of the histogram that shows the

theoretical probabilities.

4c. Why does it make sense that the histogram that shows the theoretical probabilities is symmetric?

Getting 0 heads means getting 7 tails, but getting 7 tails is just as likely as getting

7 heads, so $P(X = 0) = P(X = 7)$. By similar reasoning, $P(X = 1) = P(X = 6)$,

$P(X = 2) = P(X = 5)$, and $P(X = 3) = P(X = 4)$.

PRACTICE

1. The spinner at right has three equal sections. You spin the spinner twice and find the sum of the two numbers the spinner lands on.

a. Let X be a random variable that represents the sum of the two numbers. What are the possible values of X?

2, 3, 4, 5, and 6

b. Complete the table.

Sum	2	3	4	5	6
Probability	$\frac{1}{9}$	$\frac{2}{9}$	$\frac{1}{3}$	$\frac{2}{9}$	$\frac{1}{9}$

c. Make a histogram of the probability distribution.

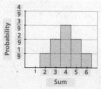

d. What is the probability that the sum is not 2? How is this probability represented in the histogram?

The probability is $\frac{8}{9}$. This is the sum of the areas of the bars for the

outcomes 3, 4, 5, and 6.

© Houghton Mifflin Harcourt Publishing Company

2. You roll two number cubes at the same time. Let X be a random variable that represents the absolute value of the difference of the numbers rolled.

a. What are the possible values of X?

0, 1, 2, 3, 4, and 5

b. Complete the table.

Difference	0	1	2	3	4	5
Probability	$\frac{6}{36}$	$\frac{10}{36}$	$\frac{8}{36}$	$\frac{6}{36}$	$\frac{4}{36}$	$\frac{2}{36}$

c. Is this probability distribution symmetric? Why or why not?

No; the probability distribution is skewed right because the histogram

would have its greatest probability for the outcome 1 and would trail

off toward the right.

A trick coin is designed to land heads up with a probability of 80%. You flip the coin 7 times. The histogram shows the probability distribution for the number of times the coin lands heads up. ("0+" means slightly greater than 0.) Use the histogram for Exercises 3–6.

3. What is the probability of getting 6 or 7 heads?

0.577

4. What is the probability of getting 4 or more heads? Explain.

0.967; this is the sum of the areas of the bars corresponding to 4, 5, 6,

and 7 heads

5. Is the probability of getting an even number of heads the same as the probability of getting an odd number of heads? Explain.

No; the probability of getting an even number of heads is about

$0 + 0.004 + 0.115 + 0.367 = 0.486$, while the probability of getting

an odd number of heads is about $0 + 0.029 + 0.275 + 0.210 = 0.514$.

6. Suppose you flip a coin 7 times and get 7 heads. Based on what you know now, would you question whether the coin is fair? Why or why not?

Sample answer: Yes; although it is possible to get 7 heads with a fair coin

(the probability is about 1%), it is much more likely to happen with a trick

coin (the probability of getting 7 heads with the trick coin is 21%).

© Houghton Mifflin Harcourt Publishing Company

Assign these pages to help your students practice and apply important lesson concepts. For additional exercises, see the Student Edition.

Answers

Additional Practice

1. a. 1, 2, 3, 4, 6, 8, 9, 12, 16

b.

Product	1	2	3	4	6	8	9	12	16
Probability	$\frac{1}{16}$	$\frac{1}{8}$	$\frac{1}{8}$	$\frac{3}{16}$	$\frac{1}{8}$	$\frac{1}{8}$	$\frac{1}{16}$	$\frac{1}{8}$	$\frac{1}{6}$

c.

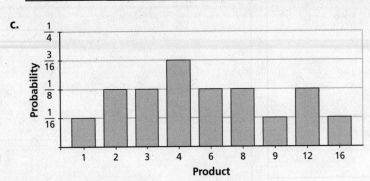

2. A fair coin will have a symmetric probability distribution, centered on "an equal number of heads and tails." This is true for any number of flips.

Problem Solving

1. a. $\frac{1}{6}$

b. $n = 5; r = 3; p = \frac{1}{6}; q = \frac{5}{6}$

c. $P(3) = {}_5C_3 \left(\frac{1}{6}\right)^3 \left(\frac{5}{6}\right)^2$

d. 0.032

2.

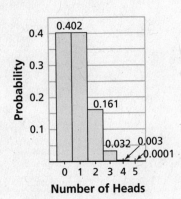

3. a. Find the sum of the probabilities of 1, 2, 3, 4, and 5 students buying a bag of trail mix, $P(1) + P(2) + P(3) + P(4) + P(5)$.

b. Find the probability that no student will buy a bag of trail mix and subtract that probability from 1.

c. 0.6

Additional Practice

1. You roll two four-sided number cubes at the same time. Let X be a random variable that represents the product of the numbers rolled.

   a. What are the possible values of X?

   _____

   b. Complete the table.

Control									
Probability									

   c. Draw a histogram of the probability distribution.

2. Describe the probability distribution for flipping a fair coin. Does this depend on the number of flips?

   _____

   _____

© Houghton Mifflin Harcourt Publishing Company

Problem Solving

Sales records for the snack machines show that 1 of every 6 students buys a bag of trail mix. There are 5 students waiting to use the machines. Melanie uses the formula for binomial probability, $P(r) = {}_nC_r p^r q^{n-r}$, to determine the number of students expected to buy trail mix. (The expression ${}_nC_r$ means $\dfrac{n!}{(r!)(n-r!)}$).

1. What is the probability of exactly 3 students buying a bag of trail mix?

   a. What is the probability of each student buying a bag of trail mix?   _____

   b. Define each variable used in the formula and give its value.
   _____

   c. Write the binomial formula, substituting these values.   _____

   d. Solve the equation to give the probability of exactly 3 students buying a bag of trail mix.   _____

2. Repeat the process to find the probability of exactly 0, 1, 2, 4, and 5 students buying a bag of trail mix. Use these results to graph a probability distribution.

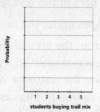

3. What is the probability of at least 1 student buying a bag of trail mix?

   a. Describe a method to solve involving the sum of probabilities.
   _____

   b. Describe a method to solve that uses the formula $P(E) + P(\text{not } E) = 1$.
   _____

   c. Use either method to determine the probability of at least 1 student buying a bag of trail mix.   _____

© Houghton Mifflin Harcourt Publishing Company

Notes

Fitting to a Normal Distribution
Going Deeper

Essential question: *How do you find percents of data and probabilities of events associated with normal distributions?*

COMMON CORE Standards for Mathematical Content

CC.9-12.S.ID.4 Use the mean and standard deviation of a data set to fit it to a normal distribution and to estimate population percentages. Recognize that there are data sets for which such a procedure is not appropriate. Use calculators, ... and tables to estimate areas under the normal curve.*

Vocabulary

standard normal distribution, *z*-score

Prerequisites

Probability distributions

Math Background

The general shape of a normal probability distribution is that of a bell. The exact shape of the bell is determined by the distribution's mean and standard deviation. The graph of a normal probability distribution is called a *normal curve* and is given by the equation

$$y = \frac{1}{\sqrt{2\pi\sigma^2}} e^{-(x-\mu)^2/2\sigma^2}$$

where μ is the mean and σ is the standard deviation. The mean and standard deviation can be found from the data and the equation for the normal curve can then be written, although students are not asked to do that in this lesson. Students should, however, be able to draw a histogram from data and sketch a smooth, "best-fit" normal curve by hand.

INTRODUCE

Ask students to recall how to find the mean and standard deviation of a set of data. Have them state in words what those statistics describe. Then have them sketch curves representing three normal distributions on the same coordinate plane—each distribution with the same mean, but one with a small standard deviation, the second with a larger standard deviation, and the third with the largest standard deviation.

Students' curves should all be centered at the same location (the mean). One will be narrow and tall (small σ), one will be medium height and broader (medium σ), and the last will be short and wide (large σ). Students are likely to draw the curves all the same height, but with varying widths. This is a good opportunity to discuss the fact that for a normal *probability* distribution, the area under the curve must equal 1, so a normal curve where the standard deviation is greater will not rise as high as a normal curve where the standard deviation is less.

TEACH

1 EXPLORE

Questioning Strategies

- Look at the first table—weight and frequency. How do you know the histogram is symmetric by looking at the table? **The frequencies of the highest and lowest weights are the same, the frequencies of the second-highest and second lowest weights are the same, and so on.**

- Look at the table in step A. Describe what the relative frequency means with respect to baby weight. **It is the percent (in decimal form) of babies with that weight.**

- Why is the sum of the relative frequencies 1? **because the sum represents the whole sample, or in terms of percent, 100% of the sample**

- Why were the adjustments to the heights of the bars made in step B? **to make the sum of all the areas of the bars in the histogram 1**

- What is the area under the normal curve? **1**

- What value does the area under the normal curve between two specific *x*-values represent? **the probability the outcome will be between those two *x*-values, in this case the probability a baby's birth weight will be between those two weights**

- Why does the normal curve in step E lie directly on top of the histogram? **because you used the mean and standard deviation of the baby weights to define the normal curve**

Fitting to a Normal Distribution
Going Deeper

Essential question: *How do you find percents of data and probabilities of events associated with normal distributions?*

CC.9-12.S.ID.4

1 EXPLORE Substituting a Normal Curve for a Symmetric Histogram

Previously, you used a graphing calculator to create a histogram for a set of 20 baby weights. The baby weights had a mean of 3.5 kg and a standard deviation of 0.14 kg. Because the histogram was perfectly symmetric, you learned that it represents a *normal distribution*. The table below gives the frequency of each weight from the data set.

Weight (kg)	3.2	3.3	3.4	3.5	3.6	3.7	3.8
Frequency	1	2	4	6	4	2	1

You can use a graphing calculator to draw a smooth bell-shaped curve, called a *normal curve*, that captures the shape of the histogram. A normal curve has the property that the area under the curve (and above the *x*-axis) is 1. This means that you must adjust the heights of the bars in the histogram so that the sum of the areas of the bars is 1.

A Convert the frequency table above to a relative frequency table by using the fact that there are 20 data values.

Weight (kg)	3.2	3.3	3.4	3.5	3.6	3.7	3.8
Relative frequency	$\frac{1}{20}$ = 0.05	0.1	0.2	0.3	0.2	0.1	0.05

What is the sum of the relative frequencies? ___1___

B For a given baby weight, the relative frequency is the area that you want the bar to have. Since you used a bar width of 0.1 when you created the histogram, the area of the bar is $0.1h$ where h is the height of the bar. You want $0.1h$ to equal the relative frequency f, so solve $0.1h = f$ for h to find the adjusted bar height.

Weight (kg)	3.2	3.3	3.4	3.5	3.6	3.7	3.8
Adjusted bar height	$\frac{0.05}{0.1}$ = 0.5	1	2	3	2	1	0.5

C Enter each weight from the table in part B into L_1 on your graphing calculator. Then enter each adjusted bar height into L_2.

D Turn on a statistics plot and select the histogram option. For Xlist, enter L_1. For Freq, enter L_2. Set the graphing window as shown. Then press GRAPH.

E Your calculator has a built-in function called a *normal probability density function*, which you can access by pressing 2nd VARS and selecting the first choice from the DISTR (distribution) menu. When entering this function to be graphed, you must include the mean and standard deviation of the distribution as shown below. When you press GRAPH, the calculator will draw a normal curve that fits the histogram.

REFLECT

1a. Describe the end behavior of the normal probability density function.

$f(x)$ approaches 0 as x increases or decreases without bound.

1b. If the area under the normal curve is 1, then what is the area under the curve to the left of the mean, 3.5? Describe how to obtain this area using the bars in the histogram. Show that your method gives the correct result.

0.5; add the areas of the first three bars plus the half the area of the fourth

bar: $0.05 + 0.1 + 0.2 + \frac{1}{2}(0.3) = 0.5$ (since bar area = relative frequency)

1c. Explain how you can use the bars in the histogram to estimate the area under the curve within 1 standard deviation of the mean, which is the interval from $3.5 - 0.14 = 3.36$ to $3.5 + 0.14 = 3.64$ on the *x*-axis. Then find the estimate.

The interval "captures" the middle three bars, so the sum of the areas of those

bars should give an estimate of the area under the curve: $0.2 + 0.3 + 0.2 = 0.7$

1d. Explain how you can use the bars in the histogram to estimate the area under the curve within 2 standard deviations of the mean, which is the interval from $3.5 - 2(0.14) = 3.22$ to $3.5 + 2(0.14) = 3.78$ on the *x*-axis. Then find the estimate.

The interval "captures" the middle five bars, so the sum of the areas of those

bars gives an estimate of the area under the curve: $0.1 + 0.2 + 0.3 + 0.2 + 0.1 = 0.9$

Notes

Questioning Strategies

- State your answer to the last question in part A in terms of the context of the problem. **95% of the pennies produced have masses between 2.46 grams and 2.54 grams.**

- State your answer to the last question in part B in terms of the context of the problem. What does this mean for the other pennies? **16% of the pennies produced have a mass greater than 2.52 grams. This means that 84% of the pennies produced have a mass less than 2.52 grams.**

EXTRA EXAMPLE

Suppose the masses of boxes of Mega Munch cereal coming off an assembly line are normally distributed with a mean of 454.0 grams and a standard deviation of 3.9 grams. Find each of the following.

A. the percent of cereal boxes that have a mass between 446.2 grams and 461.8 grams **95%**

B. the probability that a randomly chosen box has a mass greater than 457.9 grams **16%**

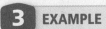 **EXAMPLE**

Questioning Strategies

- Describe in words how the number 0.4 is determined in part A and what that number means. **You find 0.4 by subtracting the mean from the given value of 65 and then dividing that result by the standard deviation. The number 0.4 means that the given value of 65 is 0.4 standard deviation away from the mean.**

- How do you find the decimal in the table for the second statement of part A? **Read across the "0" row until you intersect the ".4" column.**

- What is the meaning of the number read from the standard normal table for a given z-score? **The number is the probability that a data value has a z-score less than or equal to the given z-score.**

- How do you find the probability that a data value exceeds a given z-score? **Subtract the probability obtained from the standard normal table for the given z-score from 1.**

Teaching Strategy

To help students understand the z-score formula, have them consider a normal distribution with mean μ and standard deviation σ. Let x be a data value from this distribution. Ask: If $x = \mu$, what is the corresponding z-score? $z = \dfrac{\mu - \mu}{\sigma} = \dfrac{0}{\sigma} = 0$ If $x = \mu + \sigma$, what is the corresponding z-score? $z = \dfrac{(\mu + \sigma) - \mu}{\sigma} = \dfrac{\sigma}{\sigma} = 1$ These questions should help students see that the z-score formula associates the mean of a normal distribution with 0, the mean of the standard normal distribution. Likewise, the formula associates one standard deviation more than the mean of a normal distribution with 1, the standard deviation of the standard normal distribution. At this point, students should be able to predict that when $x = \mu - \sigma$, $z = -1$.

EXTRA EXAMPLE

Suppose a compact fluorescent light bulb produced by a certain manufacturer lasts, on average, 10,000 hours. The standard deviation is 720 hours. Find each of the following.

A. the percent of light bulbs that burn out within 11,000 hours **about 92%**

B. the probability that a randomly chosen light bulb burns out between 9200 hours and 10,800 hours **about 0.73**

Normal Curves All normal curves have the following properties, sometimes collectively called the *68-95-99.7 rule*:

* 68% of the data fall within 1 standard deviation of the mean.
* 95% of the data fall within 2 standard deviations of the mean.
* 99.7% of the data fall within 3 standard deviations of the mean.

The figure at the left below illustrates the 68-95-99.7 rule.

A normal curve's symmetry allows you to separate the area under the curve into eight parts and know the percent of the data in each part, as shown at the right below.

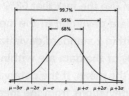
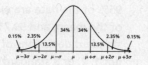

$\mu-3\sigma$ $\mu-2\sigma$ $\mu-\sigma$ μ $\mu+\sigma$ $\mu+2\sigma$ $\mu+3\sigma$

0.15% 2.35% 13.5% 34% 34% 13.5% 2.35% 0.15%

$\mu-3\sigma$ $\mu-2\sigma$ $\mu-\sigma$ μ $\mu+\sigma$ $\mu+2\sigma$ $\mu+3\sigma$

CC.9-12.S.ID.4

2 EXAMPLE Finding Areas Under a Normal Curve

Suppose the masses (in grams) of pennies minted in the United States after 1982 are normally distributed with a mean of 2.50 g and a standard deviation of 0.02 g. Find each of the following.

A The percent of pennies that have a mass between 2.46 g and 2.54 g

* How far below the mean is 2.46 g?
  How many standard deviations is this? — **0.04 g; 2 standard deviations**

* How far above the mean is 2.54 g?
  How many standard deviations is this? — **0.04 g; 2 standard deviations**

* What percent of the data in a normal distribution fall within *n* standard deviations of the mean where *n* is the number of standard deviations you found in the preceding questions? — **95%**

B The probability that a randomly chosen penny has a mass greater than 2.52 g

* How far above the mean is 2.52 g?
  How many standard deviations is this? — **0.02 g; 1 standard deviation**

* When the area under a normal curve is separated into eight parts as shown above, which of those parts satisfy the condition that the penny's mass be greater than 2.52 g? (Give the percent of data that fall within each part.) — **13.5%, 2.35%, 0.15%**

* Find the sum of the percents. Express this probability as a decimal as well. — **16%; 0.16**

© Houghton Mifflin Harcourt Publishing Company

REFLECT

2a. In the second normal curve shown on the previous page, explain how you know that the area under the curve between $\mu + \sigma$ and $\mu + 2\sigma$ represents 13.5% of the data if you know that the percent of the data within 1 standard deviation of the mean is 68% and the percent of the data within 2 standard deviations of the mean is 95%.

The difference between 95% and 68% is 27%; the symmetry of the curve tells you

that this difference is split evenly between the interval from $\mu - 2\sigma$ to $\mu - \sigma$ and

the interval from $\mu + \sigma$ to $\mu + 2\sigma$, so each interval represents 13.5% of the data.

2b. Another way to approach part B of the Example is to recognize that since the mound in the middle of the distribution (between $\mu - \sigma$ and $\mu + \sigma$) represents 68% of the data, the remainder of the data, 100% − 68% = 32%, must be in the two tails. Complete the reasoning to obtain the desired probability.

The desired probability is the percent of data in just one tail, which is half

of 32%, or 16%.

The Standard Normal Curve The **standard normal distribution** has a mean of 0 and a standard deviation of 1. A data value *x* from a normal distribution with mean μ and standard deviation σ can be standardized by finding its **z-score** using the formula $z = \frac{x - \mu}{\sigma}$.

Areas under the *standard normal curve* to the left of a given z-score have been computed and appear in the *standard normal table* below. This table allows you to find a greater range of percents and probabilities than you can using μ and multiples of σ as on the previous page. For instance, the intersection of the shaded row and column of the table tells you that the value of $P(z \leq 1.3)$ is 0.9032. (In the table, ".0000+" means slightly more than 0, and "1.0000−" means slightly less than 1.)

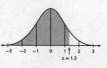

-3 -2 -1 0 1 2 3
z = 1.3

© Houghton Mifflin Harcourt Publishing Company

Standard Normal Table									
z	.0	.1	.2	.3	.4	.5	.6	.7	.8	.9
−3	.0013	.0010	.0007	.0005	.0003	.0002	.0002	.0001	.0001	.0000+
−2	.0228	.0179	.0139	.0107	.0082	.0062	.0047	.0035	.0026	.0019
−1	.1587	.1357	.1151	.0968	.0808	.0668	.0548	.0446	.0359	.0287
−0	.5000	.4602	.4207	.3821	.3446	.3085	.2743	.2420	.2119	.1841
0	.5000	.5398	.5793	.6179	.6554	.6915	.7257	.7580	.7881	.8159
1	.8413	.8643	.8849	.9032	.9192	.9332	.9452	.9554	.9641	.9713
2	.9772	.9821	.9861	.9893	.9918	.9938	.9953	.9965	.9974	.9981
3	.9987	.9990	.9993	.9995	.9997	.9998	.9998	.9999	.9999	1.000−

MATHEMATICAL PRACTICE   Highlighting the Standards

2 EXAMPLE and **3** EXAMPLE include opportunities to address Mathematical Practice Standard 1 (Make sense of problems and persevere in solving them). Students will need to look for entry points into normal distribution problems. First, they will need to confirm the distribution is, indeed, normal. Then they will plan a solution pathway by determining whether the questions are based on integer multiples of the standard deviation, a special case that can be solved quickly, or not. If not, students will need to convert data values to z-scores and use the standard normal table. They will need to determine how to approach the problem—if the answer comes directly from one probability, or if they need to calculate several probabilities and add or subtract them. Finally, students will need to use their knowledge of normal distributions to gain insight into the solution. If they determine their answers don't make sense, they may need to change course and approach the problem differently.

Essential Question

How do you find percents of data and probabilities of events associated with normal distributions?
If a given data value is 1, 2, or 3 standard deviations from the mean, you can use the fact that 68% of the data are within 1 standard deviation of the mean, 95% of the data are within 2 standard deviations of the mean, and 99.7% of the data are within 3 standard deviations of the mean. If the data value is not 1, 2, or 3 standard deviations from the mean, you can calculate z-scores and use the standard normal table.

Summarize

Have students write a journal entry explaining how to use the standard normal table to find the probability of an event, given the mean and standard deviation of a normal distribution.

PRACTICE

Where skills are taught	Where skills are practiced
2 EXAMPLE	EXS. 1–6
4 EXAMPLE	EXS. 7–12

Exercise 13: Students extend what they learned in **1** EXPLORE to explain when normal distributions can be applied to data.

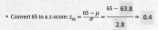

3 EXAMPLE Using the Standard Normal Table

CC.9-12.S.ID.4

Suppose the heights (in inches) of adult females in the United States are normally distributed with a mean of 63.8 inches and a standard deviation of 2.8 inches. Find each of the following.

A The percent of women who are no more than 65 inches tall

- Convert 65 to a z-score: $z_{65} = \dfrac{65 - \mu}{\sigma} = \dfrac{65 - 63.8}{2.8} \approx 0.4$

- Recognize that the phrase "no more than 65 inches" means that $z \le z_{65}$. Read the decimal from the appropriate row and column of the standard normal table: 0.6554

- Write the decimal as a percent, rounding to the nearest whole percent: about 66%

B The probability that a randomly chosen woman is between 60 inches and 63 inches tall

- Convert 60 to a z-score: $z_{60} = \dfrac{60 - \mu}{\sigma} = \dfrac{60 - 63.8}{2.8} \approx -1.4$

- Convert 63 to a z-score: $z_{63} = \dfrac{63 - \mu}{\sigma} = \dfrac{63 - 63.8}{2.8} \approx -0.3$

- Because the standard normal table gives areas under the standard normal curve to the left of a given z-score, you find $P(z_{60} \le z \le z_{63})$ by subtracting $P(z \le z_{60})$ from $P(z \le z_{63})$. Complete the following calculation using the appropriate values from the table:

$P(z_{60} \le z \le z_{63}) = P(z \le z_{63}) - P(z \le z_{60}) = 0.3821 - 0.0808 = 0.3013$

- Round the decimal to the nearest hundredth: about 0.30

REFLECT

3a. Using the result of part A, you can find the percent of females who are at least 65 inches tall without needing the table. Find the percent and explain your reasoning.

about 34%; the percent of females who are at least 65 inches tall is what's left

of the area under the curve (which is 1 or 100%) after you remove the percent of

females who are no more than 65 inches tall.

3b. How does the probability that a randomly chosen female has a height between 64.6 inches and 67.6 inches compare with your answer in part B? Why?

The probability is the same because of the symmetry of the curve.

© Houghton Mifflin Harcourt Publishing Company

PRACTICE

Suppose the scores on a test given to all juniors in a school district are normally distributed with a mean of 74 and a standard deviation of 8. Find each of the following.

1. The percent of juniors whose score is no more than 90 ___97.5%___

2. The percent of juniors whose score is between 58 and 74 ___47.5%___

3. The percent of juniors whose score is at least 74 ___50%___

4. The probability that a randomly chosen junior has a score above 82 ___0.16___

5. The probability that a randomly chosen junior has a score between 66 and 90 ___0.815___

6. The probability that a randomly chosen junior has a score below 74 ___0.5___

Suppose the heights (in inches) of adult males in the United States are normally distributed with a mean of 69.4 inches and a standard deviation of 3.2 inches. Find each of the following.

7. The percent of men who are no more than 68 inches tall ___about 34%___

8. The percent of men who are between 70 and 72 inches tall ___about 21%___

9. The percent of men who are at least 66 inches tall ___about 86%___

10. The probability that a randomly chosen man is greater than 71 inches tall ___about 0.31___

11. The probability that a randomly chosen man is between 63 and 73 inches tall ___about 0.84___

12. The probability that a randomly chosen man is less than 76 inches tall ___about 0.98___

13. The calculator screen on the left shows the probability distribution when six coins are flipped and the number of heads is counted. The screen on the right shows the probability distribution when six dice are rolled and the number of 1s is counted. For which distribution is it reasonable to use a normal curve as an approximation? Why?

0 1 2 3 4 5 6
Probability of getting a given number of heads when 6 coins are flipped

0 1 2 3 4 5 6
Probability of getting a given number of 1s when 6 dice are rolled

Use a normal curve for the distribution of heads when 6 coins are

flipped because the distribution is symmetric.

© Houghton Mifflin Harcourt Publishing Company

ADDITIONAL PRACTICE AND PROBLEM SOLVING

Assign these pages to help your students practice and apply important lesson concepts. For additional exercises, see the Student Edition.

Answers

Additional Practice

1. 0.84

2. Given on worksheet.

3. 0.02

4. 0.16

5. 0.68

6. 7; No, more than half of the wait times are below the mean.

Problem Solving

1. a. 0.84

   b. 0.93

   c. 0.02

   d. 0.99

   e. 0.68

   f. 0.62

2. B

3. H

8-7

Additional Practice

1. In a plant shop, the heights of young plants are normally distributed with a mean of 50 mm and a standard deviation of 4 mm. Count grid squares in the graph to estimate the probability that a plant chosen at random by a customer will be less than 54 mm tall.

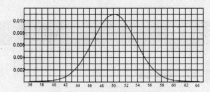

_____

Scores on a test are normally distributed with a mean of 80 and a standard deviation of 5. Use the table below to find each probability. The first probability has been found for you.

$z = \dfrac{x - \mu}{\sigma}$	−2	−1	0	1	2
Area Under Standard Normal Curve	0.02	0.16	0.5	0.84	0.98

2. A randomly selected student scored below 80. $z = \dfrac{80 - 80}{5} = 0$, so P(below 80) = 0.5

3. A randomly selected student scored above 90. _____

4. A randomly selected student scored below 75. _____

5. A randomly selected student scored between 75 and 85. _____

6. The wait times, in minutes, of 10 customers in line at a grocery store are given below. The mean wait time is 7 minutes. How many data points fall below the mean? Use your answer to explain whether the data appear to be normally distributed.

16	15	10	7	5
5	4	3	3	2

Problem Solving

The scores on a test are normally distributed with a mean of 70 and a standard deviation of 6. Use the table below to answer the questions.

z	−2.5	−2	−1.5	−1	−0.5	0	0.5	1	1.5	2	2.5
Area	0.01	0.02	0.07	0.16	0.31	0.5	0.69	0.84	0.93	0.98	0.99

1. a. Estimate the probability that a randomly selected student scored less than 76.

   Solution: $z = \dfrac{76 - 70}{6} = \dfrac{6}{6} = 1$ 0.84

   b. Estimate the probability that a randomly selected student scored less than 79.

   $z = \dfrac{-70}{6} = \dfrac{}{6} =$ _____

   c. Estimate the probability that a randomly selected student scored greater than 82. _____

   d. Estimate the probability that a randomly selected student scored greater than 55. _____

   e. Estimate the probability that a randomly selected student scored between 64 and 76. _____

   f. Estimate the probability that a randomly selected student scored between 67 and 79. _____

A student is analyzing a set of normally distributed data, but the data provided is incomplete. The student knows that the mean of the data is 120. The student also knows that 84% of the data are less than 130.

2. What is the standard deviation for this data?

   A −10

   B 10

   C 120

3. Use the table of z-scores above to determine which statement about this data is true.

   F About 90% of the values are greater than 140.

   G About 50% of the values are greater than 130.

   H About 68% of the values are between 110 and 130.

8-8 Analyzing Decisions
Going Deeper

Essential question: *How can you use probability to help you analyze decisions?*

CC.9-12.S.CP.4 Construct and interpret two-way frequency tables of data when two categories are associated with each object being classified .... *

CC.9-12.S.MD.7(+) Analyze decisions and strategies using probability concepts (e.g., product testing, medical testing ...).*

Prerequisites

Probability and set theory

Mutually exclusive and overlapping events

Conditional probability

Independent events

Dependent events

Math Background

At the heart of this lesson is Bayes's Theorem, a probability formula named after the English mathematician Thomas Bayes (1702–1761). The theorem is useful when you want to "reverse" a conditional probability. For example, you might know the probability that someone who has tuberculosis tests positive for the disease, but you may want to know the probability that someone who tests positive actually has tuberculosis. Bayes's Theorem is generally the appropriate tool for calculating this probability. Note that the theorem can appear daunting when presented as a formula. However, any problem that can be solved by the formula can also be solved by constructing a two-way table. Because this latter method may seem more intuitive, it is the method used in the first example of the lesson.

INTRODUCE

Explain to students that they will learn how to use probability to analyze a decision. Point out that many ideas from this unit will come together in this lesson, including two-way tables, conditional probability, and complementary events.

TEACH

 EXAMPLE

Questioning Strategies

- You start by assuming a population of 1,000,000. Does this choice affect the solution of the problem? Why or why not? **No; you can use any population because this does not affect the relevant percents and probabilities.**

- How can you check that you have filled in the two-way table correctly? **The sum of the values in the "Total" column should be 1,000,000; the sum of the values in the "Total" row should be 1,000,000.**

EXTRA EXAMPLE

You want to hand out coupons for a local restaurant to students who live off campus at a rural college. You know that 1% of the students live off campus and that 98% of the students who live off campus ride a bike. Also, 92% of the students who live on campus do not have a bike. You decide to give a coupon to any student you see who is riding a bike. Is this a good decision? Why or why not? **No; the probability that a student who is riding a bike lives off campus is only 11%.**

Teaching Strategies

The results of the first example are likely to seem unintuitive and surprising to students. To help them understand why there is only a 33.2% probability that someone who tests positive for the virus actually has the virus, point out that the vast majority of the population (99.5%) does not have the virus. Even though false positives only occur 1% of the time for this group of people, these positive results greatly outweigh the relatively smaller number of true positives for people who actually have the virus.

Name_____ Class_____ Date_____

8-8

Analyzing Decisions
Going Deeper

Essential question: *How can you use probability to help you analyze decisions?*

You can use a two-way table and what you know about probability to help you evaluate decisions.

Video Tutor

CC.9–12.S.MD.7(+)

1 EXAMPLE   Analyzing a Decision

A test for a virus correctly identifies someone who has the virus (by returning a positive result) 99% of the time. The test correctly identifies someone who does not have the virus (by returning a negative result) 99% of the time. It is known that 0.5% of the population has the virus. A doctor decides to treat anyone who tests positive for the virus. Is this a good decision?

A In order to analyze the decision, you need to know the probability that someone who tests positive actually has the virus.

Make a two-way table. Begin by assuming a large overall population of 1,000,000. This value appears in the cell at the lower right, as shown.

- Use the fact that 0.5% of the population has the virus to complete the rightmost column.
- Use the fact that the test correctly identifies someone who has the virus 99% of the time to complete the "Has the virus" row.
- Use the fact that the test correctly identifies someone who does not have the virus 99% of the time to complete the "Does not have the virus" row.
- Finally, complete the bottom row of the table by finding totals.
- Check your work by verifying that the numbers in the bottom row have a sum of 1,000,000.

	Tests Positive	Tests Negative	TOTAL
Has the virus	4,950	50	5,000
Does not have the virus	9,950	985,050	995,000
TOTAL	14,900	985,100	1,000,000

B Use the table to find the the probability that someone who tests positive actually has the virus.

There is a total of ___14,900___ people who test positive.

Of these people, ___4,950___ people actually have the virus.

So, the probability that some who tests positive has the virus is ___33.2%___.

REFLECT

1a. Do you think the doctor made a good decision in treating everyone who tests positive for the virus? Why or why not?

Possible answer: No; there is only a 33.2% probability that someone who tests positive actually has the virus.

The method that you used in the example can be generalized. The generalization is known as Bayes's Theorem.

Bayes's Theorem

Given two events A and B with $P(B) \neq 0$, $P(A \mid B) = \dfrac{P(B \mid A) \cdot P(A)}{P(B)}$.

The following example shows how you can use Bayes's Theorem to help you analyze a decision.

CC.9–12.S.MD.7(+)

2 EXAMPLE   Using Bayes's Theorem

The principal of a school plans a school picnic for June 2. A few days before the event, the weather forecast predicts rain for June 2, so the principal decides to cancel the picnic. Consider the following information.

- In the school's town, the probability that it rains on any day in June is 3%.
- When it rains, the forecast correctly predicts rain 90% of the time.
- When it does not rain, the forecast incorrectly predicts rain 5% of the time.

Do you think the principal made a good decision? Why or why not?

A Let event A be the event that it rains on a day in June. Let event B be the event that the forecast predicts rain. To evaluate the decision to cancel the picnic, you want to know $P(A \mid B)$, the probability that it rains given that the forecast predicts rain.

In order use Bayes's Theorem to calculate $P(A \mid B)$, you must find $P(B \mid A)$, $P(A)$, and $P(B)$. For convenience, find these probabilities as decimals.

$P(B \mid A)$ is the probability of a prediction of rain given that it actually rains. This value is provided in the given information.

$P(B \mid A) = $ ___0.9___

$P(A)$ is the probability of rain on any day in June. This value is also provided in the given information.

$P(A) = $ ___0.03___

$P(B)$ is the probability of a prediction of rain. This value is not provided in the given information. In order to calculate $P(B)$, make a tree diagram, as shown on the following page.

Questioning Strategies

- What conditional probability do you need to know to evaluate the principal's decision? You need to know the probability that it rains given a forecast of rain.

- How can you find the missing probabilities on the right side of the tree diagram? Use the fact that the sum of the probabilities of complementary events is 1, as well as the given information that the forecast predicts rain 5% of the time when it does not rain.

EXTRA EXAMPLE

A veterinarian knows that 1.5% of all dogs have a particular condition. According to a recent study, 91% of dogs that have the condition also have patches of missing fur. Also, 3% of dogs that do not have the condition have patches of missing fur. The veterinarian sees a dog which has patches of missing fur and decides to treat the dog for the condition. Is this a good decision? Why or why not? No; the probability that a dog which has patches of missing fur has the condition is only 31.6%.

MATHEMATICAL PRACTICE **Highlighting the Standards**

Standard 4 (Model with mathematics) discusses the need for students to interpret mathematical results in the context of the situation. This lesson offers many opportunities for students to practice this skill. When students use Bayes's Theorem to find a conditional probability, the specific value they find for the probability is less important than understanding what this value means. In the problems presented in this lesson, interpreting the mathematical result is the essential step in determining whether a good decision was made.

CLOSE

Essential Question

How can you use probability to help you analyze decisions? You can use a two-way table and/or Bayes's Theorem to use given information to calculate a conditional probability. Then, you can use the conditional probability to evaluate a decision that may have been made based on the given information.

Summarize

Have students write a journal entry in which they compare two methods of analyzing a decision: 1) making a two-way table and 2) using Bayes's Theorem. Prompt students to describe the pros and cons of each method.

PRACTICE

Where skills are taught	Where skills are practiced
1 EXAMPLE	EXS. 1, 3
2 EXAMPLE	EX. 2

Exercise 4: Students use reasoning and algebra to justify the formula in Bayes's Theorem.

B Make a tree diagram to find $P(B)$. The values on the "branches" show the probability of the associated event. Complete the right side of the tree diagram by writing the correct probabilities. Remember that the probabilities of events that are complements must add up to 1.

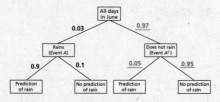

```
                        All days
                        in June
              0.03                    0.97
          Rains                           Does not rain
         (Event A)                          (Event A^C)
      0.9      0.1                     0.05        0.95
  Prediction   No prediction      Prediction      No prediction
  of rain      of rain            of rain         of rain
```

$P(B)$ is the probability that there is a prediction of rain when it actually rains plus the probability that there is a prediction of rain when it does not rain.

$$P(B) = P(A) \cdot P(B|A) + P(A^C) \cdot P(B|A^C)$$

$= 0.03 \cdot 0.9 + \underline{\ 0.97\ } \cdot \underline{\ 0.05\ }$ Substitute values from the tree diagram.

$= \underline{\ 0.0755\ }$ Simplify.

C Use Bayes's Theorem to find $P(A|B)$.

$$P(A|B) = \frac{P(B|A) \cdot P(A)}{P(B)}$$ Use Bayes's Theorem.

$= \dfrac{\underline{\ 0.9\ } \cdot \underline{\ 0.03\ }}{\underline{\ 0.0755\ }}$ Substitute.

$\approx \underline{\ 0.358\ }$ Simplify. Round to the nearest thousandth.

So, as a percent, the probability that it rains given that the forecast predicts rain is approximately __35.8%__.

REFLECT

2a. Do you think the principal made a good decision when canceling the picnic? Why or why not?

No; the probability that it actually rains on June 2 given a forecast of rain

is only 35.8%.

2b. What would $P(A)$, the probability that it rains on any day in June, have to be for the value of $P(A|B)$ to be greater than 50%? Explain.

$P(A)$ would have to be greater than about 5.26% for $P(A|B)$ to exceed 50%;

let $P(A) = x$ and $P(B) = 0.5$, then solve $0.5 = \dfrac{0.9 \cdot x}{x \cdot 0.9 + (1 - x) \cdot 0.05}$.

PRACTICE

1. It is known that 2% of the population has a certain allergy. A test correctly identifies people who have the allergy 98% of the time. The test correctly identifies people who do not have the allergy 94% of the time. A doctor decides that anyone who tests positive for the allergy should begin taking anti-allergy medication. Do you think this a good decision? Why or why not?

No; there is only a 25% probability that someone who tests positive actually

has the allergy.

2. Company X supplies 20% of the MP3 players to an electronics store and Company Y supplies the remainder. The manager of the store knows that 80% of the MP3 players in the last shipment from Company X were defective, while only 5% of the MP3 players from Company Y were defective. The manager chooses an MP3 player at random and finds that it is defective. The manager decides that the MP3 player must have come from Company X. Do you think this is a good decision? Why or why not?

Yes; there is an 80% probability that the defective MP3 player came from

Company X.

3. You can solve Example 2 using a two-way table. Consider a population of 10,000 randomly chosen June days. Complete the table. Then explain how to find the probability that it rains given that the forecast predicts rain.

	Rains	Does not rain	TOTAL
Prediction of rain	270	485	755
No prediction of rain	30	9215	9245
TOTAL	300	9700	10,000

Using the "Prediction of rain" row, the probability that it rains given that the

forecast predicts rain is $\frac{270}{755} \approx 35.8\%$.

4. Explain how to derive Bayes's Theorem using the Multiplication Rule. (*Hint:* The Multiplication Rule can be written as $P(A \text{ and } B) = P(B) \cdot P(A|B)$ or as $P(A \text{ and } B) = P(A) \cdot P(B|A)$.)

Setting the right sides of the two versions of the Multiplication Rule equal to

each other yields $P(B) \cdot P(A|B) = P(A) \cdot P(B|A)$. Dividing both sides by $P(B)$ gives

Bayes's Theorem.

ADDITIONAL PRACTICE AND PROBLEM SOLVING

Assign these pages to help your students practice and apply important lesson concepts. For additional exercises, see the Student Edition.

Answers

Additional Practice

1. $P(spam \mid phrase) = \dfrac{P(phrase \mid spam)\,P(spam)}{P(Phrase)}$

2. $0.5 = \dfrac{0.99(N)}{0.99(N) + 0.01(1-N)}$ at least 0.01 or 1% of the population

3.

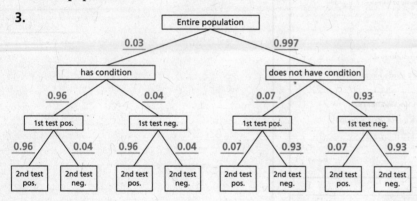

Problem Solving

1.

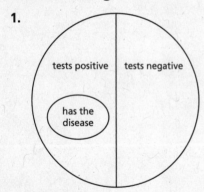

2. **a.** the probability that a subject tests positive for the disease

   b. the probability that a subject has the disease

   c. the probability that a subject who has the disease tests positive for the disease

   d. the probability that a subject who tests positive for the disease has the disease

   e. $P(B) = 0.02$, $P(A|B) = 1$

8-8

Name _____ Class _____ Date _____

Additional Practice

1. Bayes' Theorem can be applied to filter for spam e-mail messages. These filters often look for the presence of specific phrases. Write an equation showing how to calculate the probability that a given message is spam, given that it contains a certain phrase.

_____

2. Suppose a test for a drug returns true positive results for 99% of users and 99% true negative results for non-users. What percentage of the population would have to be users of the drug in order to say that a positive test result was more likely than not to indicate use of the drug? Set up an equation and solve it.

_____

_____ % of the population

3. A certain test for a genetic condition correctly identifies a person with the condition 96% of the time and correctly identifies a person without the condition 93% of the time. It is known that 0.3% of the population has the condition. In order to improve accuracy, a researcher runs the test twice on each subject. Fill out the tree diagram.

_____

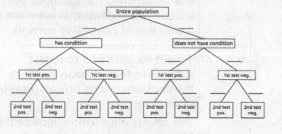

Problem Solving

1. Suppose a medical screening test for a disease always returns a positive result if the subject has the disease, but also returns false positives in 55% of subjects without the disease. Draw a Venn diagram to illustrate this situation.

2. Let A be the event "tests positive for the disease" and let B be the event "has the disease". The disease occurs naturally in 2% of the population.

a. What is the meaning of P(A)?

_____

b. What is the meaning of P(B)?

_____

c. What is the meaning of P(A|B)?

_____

d. What is the meaning of P(B|A)?

_____

e. Which of these four values are given by the problem, and what is their value?

_____

3. a. Choose one of the four values mentioned in exercise 2 to complete the equation. _____ = P(has disease and tests positive) + P(doesn't have disease and tests positive)

b. What is the value of your answer for part a?

_____

4. What is the probability that a subject who tests positive for the disease has the disease?

_____

© Houghton Mifflin Harcourt Publishing Company

This page provides students with the opportunity to apply concepts from the Common Core in real-world problem situations. There are three different levels of performance tasks:

⭐ **Novice:** These are short word problems that require students to apply the math they have learned in straightforward, real-world situations.

⭐⭐ **Apprentice:** These are more involved problems that guide students step-by-step through more complex tasks. These exercises include more complicated reasoning, writing, and open-ended elements.

⭐⭐⭐ **Expert:** These are open-ended, non-routine problems that, instead of stepping the students through, ask them to choose their own methods for solving and justify their answers and reasoning.

Sample answers

1a. Power-Pump Gym: mean 32, standard deviation 10; Smithville Racket Club: mean 39, standard deviation 20

b. Possible answer: the ages at the racket club are more spread out; the gym has younger members on average.

2a. Observational study; possible explanation: it would be easiest to observe customers and record results. Customers would be unlikely to answer a survey, and an experiment could give biased results if the customers are aware of the experiment.

b. Possible answer: the number of sandwiches ordered

3. Scoring Guide:

Task	Possible points
a	3 points total, 1 for each aspect of the survey with possible answers including: the number of people surveyed, whether the survey was random, and how the survey was conducted such as exactly what group was surveyed (a particular region for example), or how the 12% was determined (for example, does it include respondents that were not sure if they would cancel DVR service)
b	1 point for each of 3 complete statements that correctly relate to the decision-making process. Possible statements: This affects the decision because the 29% of customers that buy DVR service may still decrease by about 12%. Also, customers interested in buying the DVR service may not, if they know that they cannot fast-forward through ads. Lastly, customers in general may be dissatisfied with a negative change in the service and look for alternative services.

Total possible points: 6

CHAPTER 8

Performance Tasks

COMMON
CORE
CC.9-12.S.ID.2
CC.9-12.S.ID.4
CC.9-12.S.IC.3
CC.9-12.S.IC.6

⭐ **1.** Samples of the ages of members of two different athletic clubs in Smithville are shown.

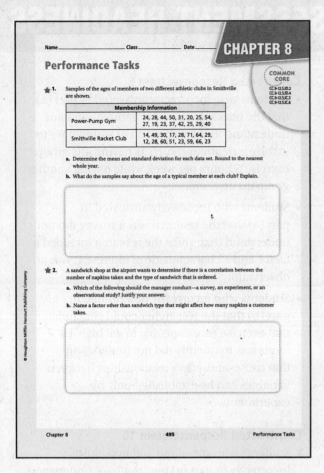

Membership Information	
Power-Pump Gym	24, 28, 44, 50, 31, 20, 25, 54, 27, 19, 23, 37, 42, 25, 29, 40
Smithville Racket Club	14, 49, 30, 17, 28, 71, 64, 29, 12, 28, 60, 51, 23, 59, 66, 23

  a. Determine the mean and standard deviation for each data set. Round to the nearest whole year.

  b. What do the samples say about the age of a typical member at each club? Explain.

⭐ **2.** A sandwich shop at the airport wants to determine if there is a correlation between the number of napkins taken and the type of sandwich that is ordered.

  a. Which of the following should the manager conduct—a survey, an experiment, or an observational study? Justify your answer.

  b. Name a factor other than sandwich type that might affect how many napkins a customer takes.

⭐⭐ **3.** A cable company wants to know if customers that pay for DVR service (to record shows) would cancel it if the ads in the shows could not be skipped during playback. A report from a survey shows that only 12% of customers that pay for DVR would cancel it.

  a. Name at least three aspects of the survey that you would want to know more about to help determine if the report is valid.

  b. The cable company ultimately wants more of its customers to pay for DVR service, since only 29% of customers currently subscribe to this service. How might this information affect the company's decision to disable fast-forwarding of ads? Write 3 statements about your reasoning.

⭐⭐⭐ **4.** The United States Association of Table Tennis (USATT) uses a rating system for members. The ratings are normally distributed with a mean of 1400 and a standard deviation of 490.

  a. Ernesto says that about a third of all members have ratings between 900 and 1400. Is this correct? Explain.

  b. An "expert" player is considered to have a rating of at least 1900. About what percent of members are *not* "experts"? Show your work.

  c. Ernesto is a member of the New York chapter of the USATT. He surveys the members in his chapter. Why might Ernesto's results not match the distribution of the national ratings?

---

4. Scoring Guide:

Task	Possible points
a	1 point for the correct answer (yes) and 1 point for correctly explaining that about 34.1% of members have a rating between the mean and one standard deviation below the mean—because $1400 - 490 = 910$ is a little more than 900, and 34.1% is a little more than one third.
b	2 points for a correct answer of about 84%
c	2 points for correctly explaining that the members of a particular club do not constitute a random sample of the entire USATT. A random sample would mean that each member of the USATT had an equal chance of being selected for the sample.

Total possible points: 6

COMMON CORE CORRELATION

Standard	Items
CC.9-12.S.ID.1*	6
CC.9-12.S.ID.3*	2
CC.9-12.S.ID.4*	5, 8, 10, 11
CC.9-12.S.IC.1*	3, 8
CC.9-12.S.IC.2*	4
CC.9-12.S.IC.3*	1, 9
CC.9-12.S.IC.4*	7, 8
CC.9-12.S.IC.5*	6, 10
CC.9-12.S.IC.6*	7

TEST PREP DOCTOR ✚

Multiple Choice: Item 1

- Students who chose **A** may have thought that because 50 people were involved in the research and something was measured, the research was an experiment.

- Students who chose **C** may have overlooked the fact that only people with colds were recruited for the research.

- Students who chose **D** may not have understood the concept of statistical research.

Multiple Choice: Item 2

- Students who chose **F** did not recognize that a normal distribution would be symmetric.

- Students who chose **G** probably confused the concepts of a distribution's being skewed left and skewed right.

- Students who chose **J** may not have known what a uniform distribution is.

Constructed Response: Item 9

- Students who incorrectly answered in part (a) that the research was an experiment did not understand that an experiment would have to involve a treatment, such as having one group exercise 5 hours per week while having another group do no exercise.

- Students who incorrectly answered in part (a) that the research was a survey did not understand that, since the research included a factor and a characteristic of interest, it was an observational study.

- Students who incorrectly determined in part (b) that the researcher could conclude that exercise causes people to eat high-fat foods less frequently did not understand that cause-and-effect relationships between variables can be established only by experiments.

Constructed Response: Item 10

- Students who stated the null hypothesis incorrectly in part (a) may not have understood that the form of a null hypothesis is that the treatment will have no effect and that any difference between the control group and the treatment group is due to chance.

- Students who stated the interval as $-0.14 \leq x \leq 0.14$ found the interval for the middle 68%, not the middle 95%. Students who stated the interval as $-0.42 \leq x \leq 0.42$ found the interval for the middle 99.7%, not the middle 95%. These students did not understand that the interval that captures the middle 95% of the differences of the means is the mean plus or minus two standard deviations, not one or three standard deviations.

- Students who said that the null hypothesis should not be rejected may not have understood that the mean difference in hair growth between the control and treatment groups was 0.3 inches, which falls outside of the range of $-0.28 \leq x \leq 0.28$. These students may not have understood that because the mean difference falls outside this range, the null hypothesis that any difference was due to chance was very unlikely to be true.

Name _____ Class _____ Date _____

MULTIPLE CHOICE

1. What type of research, described below, is being conducted?

A researcher recruits 50 people with colds and measures the level of stress they were under during the week prior to the start of the cold.

A. Experiment

(B.) Observational study

C. Survey

D. None of these

2. Identify the word or phrase that completes this statement: The mean of the data in the distribution shown is greater than the median because the distribution is __?__.

F. normal   (H.) skewed right

G. skewed left   J. uniform

3. You want to estimate a population mean by taking a sample from the population and finding the sample's mean. Which sampling technique gives the best estimate?

A. Convenience sampling

(B.) Random sampling

C. Self-selected sampling

D. Systematic sampling

4. Suppose you roll a die repeatedly and make a histogram of the results (number of 1s, number of 2s, and so on). If the die is fair, which shape will the histogram have?

F. Normal   H. Skewed right

G. Skewed left   (J.) Uniform

5. A normal distribution has a mean of 10 and a standard deviation of 1.5. In which interval does the middle 95% of the data fall?

A. $-3 \leq x \leq 3$ (C.) $7 \leq x \leq 13$

B. $8.5 \leq x \leq 11.5$ D. $5.5 \leq x \leq 14.5$

6. A researcher recorded the heights of 5 plants grown in soil treated with a fertilizer and 5 plants grown in soil not treated with the fertilizer. The mean height of the treatment group was 24 cm, while the mean height of the control group was 22 cm. A histogram of the differences of means for 50 resamples of the data under the assumption that the fertilizer had no effect on the plants' growth is shown.

Based on the histogram, what is the probability that a difference of means is *at least as great* as the experimental result?

F. 0.01   H. 0.1

(G.) 0.02   J. 0.2

7. A newspaper reports on a survey of likely voters in an upcoming local election. The survey showed that 57% support candidate Robertson with a margin of error of 4%. Which statement about all voters in the election is most likely to be accurate?

A. Between 55% and 59% favor Robertson.

(B.) Between 53% and 61% favor Robertson.

C. Between 53% and 57% favor Robertson.

D. Between 57% and 61% favor Robertson.

CONSTRUCTED RESPONSE

8. Researchers plan to use a survey to find the percent of workers who are employed full-time in a state. The researchers are aiming for a 3% margin of error at a 95% confidence level. Can they attain this result by polling 1000 randomly selected workers? Justify your answer.

No; to find the minimum sample size, you must solve the margin-of-error formula $E = z_c \cdot \sqrt{\frac{\hat{p}(1 - \hat{p})}{n}}$ for n and then substitute 0.03 for E, 1.96 for z_c, and 0.5 as an estimate for $\hat{p}$. Doing so gives $n \approx 1067.1$, so to get a 3% margin of error at a 95% confidence level, the researchers would have to poll at least 1068 people.

9. A researcher finds that people who exercise for at least 5 hours per week eat high-fat foods less often than people who exercise less than 5 hours per week.

a. What type of research is this? Explain how you know.

Observational study; the researcher starts with an existing condition (amount of exercise) and checks for a characteristic of interest (consumption of high-fat foods).

b. Can the researcher conclude that exercise causes people to eat high-fat foods less frequently? Explain.

No; although the study may show an association between exercise and consumption of high-fat foods, it cannot establish a cause-and-effect relationship. There are likely other factors at work, such as overall health-consciousness.

10. In a randomized comparative experiment, 100 people used a hair growth agent for two months and 100 people did not. The mean hair growth among people who used the agent was 1.3 inches, and the mean hair growth among people who did not use it was 1.0 inch.

a. State the null hypothesis for this experiment in terms of the effect of the treatment and in terms of the difference of the means.

The treatment has no effect on hair growth; the difference of the means is about 0.

b. Given that the null hypothesis is true, the resampling distribution for the difference of means is normal with a mean of 0 inches and a standard deviation of 0.14 inch. State the interval that captures the middle 95% of the differences of the means.

$2(-0.14) \leq x \leq 2(0.14)$, or $-0.28 \leq x \leq 0.28$

c. Should the null hypothesis be rejected? Explain why or why not.

Yes; because the observed result falls outside the middle 95% of the differences of means, it is a very unlikely result.

11. Suppose the upper arm length (in centimeters) of adult males in the United States is normally distributed with a mean of 39.4 cm and a standard deviation of 2.3 cm.

a. What percent of adult males have an upper arm length no greater than 41.7 cm? Explain how you know.

84%; 41.7 cm is 1 standard deviation above the mean; in a normal distribution, the percent of data less than the mean is 50%, and the percent of data between the mean and 1 standard deviation above the mean is 34%.

b. What is the probability that a randomly chosen adult male has an upper arm length greater than 44 cm? Explain how you know.

0.025; 44 cm is 2 standard deviations above the mean; in a normal distribution, the percent of data between 2 and 3 standard deviations above the mean is 2.35%, and the percent of data greater than 3 standard deviations above the mean is 0.15%.

CHAPTER 9

Sequences and Series

COMMON CORE
PROFESSIONAL
DEVELOPMENT **CC.9-12.F.IF.3**

Sequences can be confusing to students, but you can help students understand them by making clear connections to students' prior knowledge of functions. Make sure students understand the idea of recursion. Defining a function recursively means that you apply an operation (or series of operations) to a term to generate the next term. You can provide simple examples of this, such as "Start with 5 and add 4 to get the next term." Repeating the process illustrates recursion: $5 + 4 = 9$, $9 + 4 = 13$, $13 + 4 = 17$, and so on. In this case, you are recursively adding 4 to each term to get the next term. This sequence can be recursively defined as $a_n = a_{(n-1)} + 4$. In order to use this formula to find the value of a specific term, you need to know the value of the previous term. This idea is central to recursion. An explicit rule for a sequence defines the sequence as a general rule by the number of the term rather than the value of the terms. The sequence above can be defined explicitly as $a_n = 4(n-1) + 5$. To find the value of a specific term with this formula, you need only know the number of the term. You don't need to know the values of any other terms.

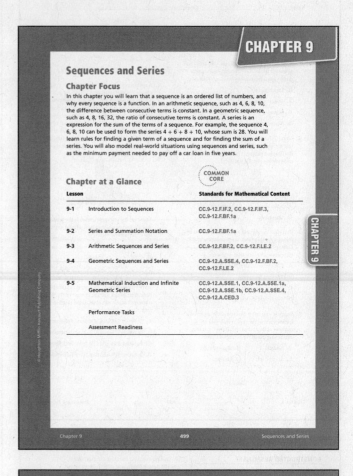

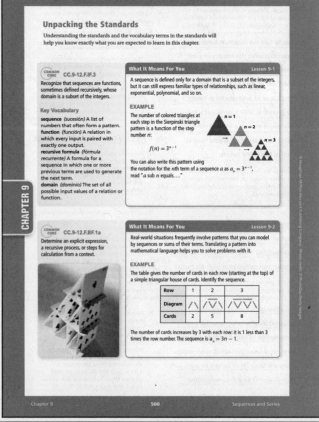

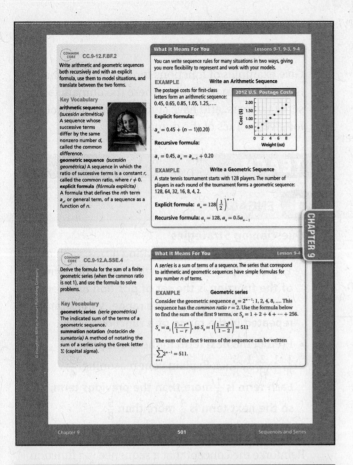

CC.9-12.F.BF.2

Write arithmetic and geometric sequences both recursively and with an explicit formula, use them to model situations, and translate between the two forms.

Key Vocabulary

arithmetic sequence *(sucesión aritmética)* A sequence whose successive terms differ by the same nonzero number d, called the *common difference*.

geometric sequence *(sucesión geométrica)* A sequence in which the ratio of successive terms is a constant r, called the *common ratio*, where $r \neq 0$.

explicit formula *(fórmula explícita)* A formula that defines the nth term a_n, or general term, of a sequence as a function of n.

What It Means For You   Lessons 9-1, 9-3, 9-4

You can write sequence rules for many situations in two ways, giving you more flexibility to represent and work with your models.

EXAMPLE   **Write an Arithmetic Sequence**

The postage costs for first-class letters form an arithmetic sequence: 0.45, 0.65, 0.85, 1.05, 1.25,....

Explicit formula:

$a_n = 0.45 + (n - 1)(0.20)$

Recursive formula:

$a_1 = 0.45,\ a_n = a_{n-1} + 0.20$

2012 U.S. Postage Costs

EXAMPLE   **Write a Geometric Sequence**

A state tennis tournament starts with 128 players. The number of players in each round of the tournament forms a geometric sequence: 128, 64, 32, 16, 8, 4, 2.

Explicit formula: $a_n = 128\left(\dfrac{1}{2}\right)^{n-1}$

Recursive formula: $a_1 = 128,\ a_n = 0.5a_{n-1}$

CC.9-12.A.SSE.4

Derive the formula for the sum of a finite geometric series (when the common ratio is not 1), and use the formula to solve problems.

Key Vocabulary

geometric series *(serie geométrica)* The indicated sum of the terms of a geometric sequence.

summation notation *(notación de sumatoria)* A method of notating the sum of a series using the Greek letter Σ (capital *sigma*).

What It Means For You   Lesson 9-4

A *series* is a sum of terms of a sequence. The series that correspond to arithmetic and geometric sequences have simple formulas for any number n of terms.

EXAMPLE   **Geometric series**

Consider the geometric sequence $a_n = 2^{n-1}$: 1, 2, 4, 8, ... This sequence has the *common ratio* $r = 2$. Use the formula below to find the sum of the first 9 terms, or $S_9 = 1 + 2 + 4 + \cdots + 256$.

$S_n = a_1\left(\dfrac{1 - r^n}{1 - r}\right)$, so $S_9 = 1\left(\dfrac{1 - 2^9}{1 - 2}\right) = 511$

The sum of the first 9 terms of the sequence can be written

$\displaystyle\sum_{n=1}^{9} 2^{n-1} = 511$.

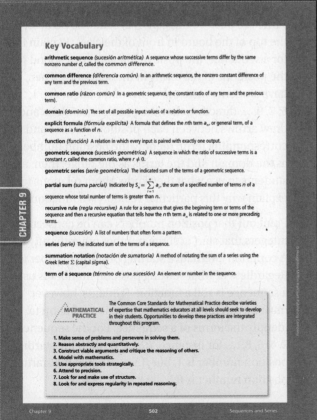

Key Vocabulary

arithmetic sequence *(sucesión aritmética)* A sequence whose successive terms differ by the same nonzero number d, called the *common difference*.

common difference *(diferencia común)* In an arithmetic sequence, the nonzero constant difference of any term and the previous term.

common ratio *(razón común)* In a geometric sequence, the constant ratio of any term and the previous term).

domain *(dominio)* The set of all possible input values of a relation or function.

explicit formula *(fórmula explícita)* A formula that defines the nth term a_n, or general term, of a sequence as a function of n.

function *(función)* A relation in which every input is paired with exactly one output.

geometric sequence *(sucesión geométrica)* A sequence in which the ratio of successive terms is a constant r, called the *common ratio*, where $r \neq 0$.

geometric series *(serie geométrica)* The indicated sum of the terms of a geometric sequence.

partial sum *(suma parcial)* Indicated by $S_n = \displaystyle\sum_{i=1}^{n} a_i$, the sum of a specified number of terms n of a sequence whose total number of terms is greater than n.

recursive rule *(regla recursiva)* A rule for a sequence that gives the beginning term or terms of the sequence and then a recursive equation that tells how the nth term a_n is related to one or more preceding terms.

sequence *(sucesión)* A list of numbers that often form a pattern.

series *(serie)* The indicated sum of the terms of a sequence.

summation notation *(notación de sumatoria)* A method of notating the sum of a series using the Greek letter Σ (capital *sigma*).

term of a sequence *(término de una sucesión)* An element or number in the sequence.

MATHEMATICAL PRACTICE

The Common Core Standards for Mathematical Practice describe varieties of expertise that mathematics educators at all levels should seek to develop in their students. Opportunities to develop these practices are integrated throughout this program.

1. Make sense of problems and persevere in solving them.
2. Reason abstractly and quantitatively.
3. Construct viable arguments and critique the reasoning of others.
4. Model with mathematics.
5. Use appropriate tools strategically.
6. Attend to precision.
7. Look for and make use of structure.
8. Look for and express regularity in repeated reasoning.

The study of arithmetic and geometric sequences can be made clearer to students by connecting them thoughtfully to students' prior knowledge of linear and exponential functions. Sequences are functional relationships whose domain is restricted to natural numbers, so everything students have learned about functions still applies. Like linear functions, the distinct points that make up the graph of an arithmetic sequence lie along a straight line. They also have constant first differences between successive output values. The points that make up the graphs of geometric sequences lie along exponential curves. Like exponential functions, successive outputs of geometric sequences have constant ratios.

Introduction to Sequences
Going Deeper

Essential question: Why is a sequence a function?

COMMON **Standards for**
CORE **Mathematical Content**

CC.9-12.F.IF.2 Use function notation, evaluate functions for inputs in their domains, and interpret statements that use function notation in terms of a context.

CC.9-12.F.IF.3 Recognize that sequences are functions, sometimes defined recursively, whose domain is a subset of the integers.

CC.9-12.F.BF.1 Write a function that describes a relationship between two quantities.*

CC.9-12.F.BF.1a Determine an explicit expression, a recursive process ... from a context.*

Vocabulary

sequence

term

explicit rule

recursive rule

Prerequisites

Discrete linear functions

Discrete exponential functions

Math Background

Students are familiar with the concept of functions and know that a function assigns exactly one output to each input. Students understand that a function has a domain and a range, and they have previously evaluated functions for inputs in their domains. Students have also written functions for real-world situations, and understand the use of function notation to both interpret and express statements in terms of a context.

INTRODUCE

Review the basics of functions by using function notation in all explanations. Make sure that students understand that each input of a function is associated with exactly one output. Review the concepts of domain and range by again focusing on the relationship between input and output values.

Give examples of functions for which the domain is restricted, in particular where the domain is the set of integers, and have students evaluate functions for given values of the domain.

TEACH

1 ENGAGE

Questioning Strategies

- Can a sequence with repeating terms, such as 1, 1, 2, 2, 3, 3, ..., be a function? **Yes, the domain of the function is the set of position numbers, and the set of terms is the range. Values can be repeated in the range of a function.**

- Predict the next term in the sequence $\frac{1}{8}, \frac{1}{4}, \frac{3}{8}, \frac{1}{2}, \frac{5}{8}$, ... Explain your reasoning. $\frac{3}{4}$; **Each term is $\frac{1}{8}$ more than the previous term, so the next term is $\frac{1}{8}$ more than $\frac{5}{8}$.**

Teaching Strategy

Reinforce the concept that a sequence is a function by emphasizing the domain and range of a sequence. Write the positive integers 1, 2, 3, and so on across the top of the board in front of the class. Explain that, for a sequence, the positive integers correspond to the positions of the terms in the sequence. Then, have students write the terms of the sequence 1, 3, 5, 7, 9, ... directly below the position numbers and draw arrows between each position number and its corresponding term. Identify the position numbers as the domain and the terms as the range; then, ask students to use what they know about relations to explain why this particular relation is a function.

Point out that position numbers can be consecutive integers that start at some number other than 1. A common alternative starting position number is 0. Regardless of what starting position number is used, a sequence is still a function. Students, however, must be careful when using function notation to identify the terms of a sequence. For the sequence 2, 4, 6, 8, ..., for instance, $f(3) = 6$ when the starting position number is 1, but $f(3) = 8$ when the starting position number is 0.

Name_____ Class_____ Date_____

9-1

Video Tutor

Introduction to Sequences
Going Deeper

Essential question: *Why is a sequence a function?*

CC.9-12.F.IF.3

1 ENGAGE **Understanding Sequences**

A **sequence** is an ordered list of numbers or other items. Each element in a sequence is called a **term**. For instance, in the sequence 1, 3, 5, 7, 9, ..., the second term is 3.

Each term in a sequence can be paired with a position number, and these pairings establish a function whose domain is the set of position numbers and whose range is the set of terms, as illustrated below. The position numbers are consecutive integers that typically start at either 1 or 0.

Position number	n	1	2	3	4	5	Domain
Term of sequence	$f(n)$	1	3	5	7	9	Range

For the sequence shown in the table, you can write $f(4) = 7$, which can be interpreted as "the fourth term of the sequence is 7."

REFLECT

1a. The domain of the function f defining the sequence 2, 5, 8, 11, 14, ... is the set of consecutive integers starting with 0. What is $f(4)$? Explain how you determined your answer.

14; because the domain starts with 0, $f(4)$ is the fifth term of the sequence, which is 14.

1b. How does your answer to Question 1a change if the domain of the function is the set of consecutive integers starting with 1?

Now $f(4)$ represents the fourth term of the sequence, which is 11.

1c. Predict the next term in the sequence 48, 42, 36, 30, 24, ... Explain your reasoning.

Sample answer: 18; each term is 6 less than the previous term, so the next term will be 6 less than 24.

1d. Why is the relationship between the position numbers and the terms of a sequence a function?

Each position number corresponds to exactly one term.

1e. Give an example of a sequence from your everyday life. Explain why your example represents a sequence.

Sample answer: The numbers of my combination lock (24, 8, 44) form a sequence. The numbers are a sequence because their order matters.

© Houghton Mifflin Harcourt Publishing Company

Chapter 9   503   Lesson 1

Some numerical sequences can be described by using algebraic rules. An **explicit rule** for a sequence defines the nth term as a function of n.

CC.9-12.F.IF.2

2 EXAMPLE **Using an Explicit Rule to Generate a Sequence**

Write the first 4 terms of the sequence $f(n) = n^2 + 1$. Assume that the domain of the function is the set of consecutive integers starting with 1.

n	$n^2 + 1$	$f(n)$
1	$1^2 + 1 = 1 + 1$	2
2	$2^2 + 1 = 4 + 1$	5
3	$3^2 + 1 = 9 + 1$	10
4	$4^2 + 1 = 16 + 1$	17

The first 4 terms are ___2, 5, 10, and 17___.

REFLECT

2a. How could you use a graphing calculator to check your answer?

Sample answer: Enter the equation $y = x^2 + 1$ and make a table.

2b. Explain how to find the 20th term of the sequence.

Evaluate $n^2 + 1$ for $n = 20$; $f(20) = 401$.

A **recursive rule** for a sequence defines the nth term by relating it to one or more previous terms.

CC.9-12.F.IF.2

3 EXAMPLE **Using a Recursive Rule to Generate a Sequence**

Write the first 4 terms of the sequence with $f(1) = 3$ and $f(n) = f(n - 1) + 2$ for $n \geq 2$. Assume that the domain of the function is the set of consecutive integers starting with 1.

The first term is given: $f(1) = 3$. Use $f(1)$ to find $f(2)$, $f(2)$ to find $f(3)$, and so on. In general, $f(n - 1)$ refers to the term that precedes $f(n)$.

n	$f(n - 1) + 2$	$f(n)$
2	$f(2 - 1) + 2 = f(1) + 2 = 3 + 2$	5
3	$f(3 - 1) + 2 = f(2) + 2 = 5 + 2$	7
4	$f(4 - 1) + 2 = f(3) + 2 = 7 + 2$	9

The first 4 terms are ___3, 5, 7, and 9___.

© Houghton Mifflin Harcourt Publishing Company

Chapter 9   504   Lesson 1

Questioning Strategies

- What is the fifth term of $f(n) = n^2 + 1$? **26**

- What sequence is generated by the rule $f(n) = 3n$ when the domain is the set of consecutive integers starting with 1? Explain your reasoning. **The sequence generated is 3, 6, 9, 12, …; each term is three times the corresponding position number.**

- What is the tenth term of the sequence $f(n) = 3n$ when the domain is the set of consecutive integers starting with 1? Explain how to find it. **30; evaluate $3n$ for $n = 10$.**

Avoid Common Errors

Be sure students pay attention to the domain of the function that defines a sequence. While 1 is typically used as the first number in the domain, some other number (typically 0) can be used instead. A change in the function's inputs will result in a change in the function's outputs, thereby creating a different sequence. For instance, if the domain of $f(n) = n^2 + 1$ is {0, 1, 2, 3, …} rather than {1, 2, 3, 4, …}, then the function generates the sequence 1, 2, 5, 10, … rather than the sequence 2, 5, 10, 17, … .

EXTRA EXAMPLE

Write the first four terms of the sequence $f(n) = n^3 + 1$. Assume that the domain of the function is the set of consecutive integers starting with 1. **The first four terms are 2, 9, 28, and 65.**

3 **EXAMPLE**

Questioning Strategies

- Is it possible to generate the second term of the sequence $f(n) = f(n - 1) + 2$ without knowing that $f(1) = 3$? Explain. **No; since the second term is calculated by using the term before it, it is necessary to know the first term.**

- How is the sequence $f(n) = 3n$ related to the sequence $f(1) = 3$ and $f(n) = f(n - 1) + 3$ for $n \geq 2$? **Both rules generate the same sequence: 3, 6, 9, 12, … .**

- If you know only that the rule for the sequence is $f(n) = f(n - 1) + 2$ and that $f(4) = 9$, is it possible to determine that $f(1) = 3$? **Yes, if you know that $f(4) = 9$, the recursive rule tells you that adding 2 to $f(3)$ gives $f(4)$, so $f(3)$ is 7. Again, the recursive rule tells you that adding 2 to $f(2)$ gives $f(3)$, so $f(2)$ is 5. Finally, the recursive rule tells you that adding 2 to $f(1)$ gives $f(2)$, so $f(1) = 3$.**

Differentiated Instruction

Visual learners may benefit by drawing diagrams that illustrate how the nth term of a sequence with a recursive rule is generated by the terms that come before it. Students can use arrows to show how previous terms become the inputs to generate the terms that follow.

MATHEMATICAL PRACTICE | **Highlighting the Standards**

3 **EXAMPLE** and its Reflect questions offer an opportunity to address Mathematical Practice Standard 7 (Look for and make use of structure). Students explore the concept of a recursive rule as they generate each term of a sequence by referencing a term or terms that came before it. Students must interpret sequence rules expressed using function notation in the context of recursion. As they use a recursive rule to generate a sequence and find a specific term in the sequence, students must understand the structure of a function that is defined in terms of itself.

EXTRA EXAMPLE

Write the first four terms of the sequence with $f(1) = 2$ and $f(n) = f(n - 1) + 3$ for $n \geq 2$. Assume that the domain of the function is the set of consecutive integers starting with 1. **The first four terms are 2, 5, 8, and 11.**

REFLECT

3a. Describe how to find the 12th term of the sequence.

Add 2 to the 11th term of the sequence.

3b. Suppose you want to find the 50th term of a sequence. Would you rather use a recursive rule or an explicit rule? Explain your reasoning.

Sample answer: explicit; with an explicit rule, you can calculate the 50th term

directly; with a recursive rule, you have to find the first 49 terms before you

can find the 50th term.

4 **E X A M P L E**   Modeling a Sequence

A male honeybee has one female parent, and a female honeybee has one male and one female parent. In the diagram below, a male honeybee is represented by M in row 1. His parent is represented by F in row 2. Her parents are represented by M and F in row 3, and so on. Write a recursive rule for a sequence that describes the number of bees in each row.

A Extend the diagram to show rows 5, 6, and 7.

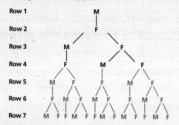

Row 1   M
Row 2   F
Row 3   M   F
Row 4   F   M   F
Row 5   M   F   F   M   F
Row 6   F M   F M   F   F M   F
Row 7   M F F M   F F M   F M   F F M   F

B Complete the table to show the number of bees in each row.

Row (position number)	1	2	3	4	5	6	7
Number of bees (term of sequence)	1	1	2	3	5	8	13

C Write a recursive rule for the sequence in the table. Assume that the domain of the function is the set of consecutive integers starting with 1.

- First, write the rule in words.

  The first two terms are both ___1___. Every other term is the __sum__ of the previous two terms.

- Then, write the rule algebraically.

  $f(1) = f(2) = $ __1__ and   The first and second terms are both 1.

  $f(n) = f\left(n - \boxed{1}\right) + f(n-2)$ for $n \geq \boxed{3}$ Each successive term is the sum of the preceding two terms.

REFLECT

4a. If you continued the pattern in the diagram, how many bees would be in the 8th row? Explain how you determined your answer.

21; add the numbers of bees in the 7th and 6th rows: 13 + 8 = 21.

4b. The sequence given in the table, 1, 1, 2, 3, 5, 8, 13, …, is called the Fibonacci sequence. An explicit rule for the Fibonacci sequence is $f(n) = \frac{1}{\sqrt{5}}\left(\frac{1+\sqrt{5}}{2}\right)^n - \frac{1}{\sqrt{5}}\left(\frac{1-\sqrt{5}}{2}\right)^n$ where the values of n are consecutive integers starting with 1. Use the explicit rule to show that $f(1) = 1$. Then use a calculator and the explicit rule to find the 9th term of the Fibonacci sequence.

$\frac{1}{\sqrt{5}}\left(\frac{1+\sqrt{5}}{2}\right) - \frac{1}{\sqrt{5}}\left(\frac{1-\sqrt{5}}{2}\right) = \frac{1+\sqrt{5} - (1-\sqrt{5})}{2\sqrt{5}} = \frac{2\sqrt{5}}{2\sqrt{5}} = 1$; 34

4c. Now use the recursive rule to find the 9th term of the Fibonacci sequence. Does your result agree with the result from the explicit rule?

$f(9) = f(8) + f(7) = 21 + 13 = 34$; yes

4d. Which rule for the Fibonacci sequence would be easier to use if you did not have a calculator? Explain.

Sample answer: recursive; to find terms using the recursive rule, you only need to

add whole numbers, but to find terms using the explicit rule, you have to perform

operations with radical expressions.

4e. The number of petals on many flowers is equal to a *Fibonacci number*, that is, one of the terms in the Fibonacci sequence. Based on this fact, is a flower more likely to have 20 petals or 21 petals? Explain.

21; 21 is a Fibonacci number, but 20 is not.

Questioning Strategies

- Why is the condition $n \geq 3$ imposed on $f(n) = f(n-1) + f(n-2)$ in the rule for generating the Fibonacci sequence? Since the first two terms are given, this part of the rule for generating the Fibonacci sequence is used only to generate the terms for $n \geq 3$, which is the third term and beyond.

- When writing the explicit rule $f(n) = \frac{1}{\sqrt{5}}\left(\frac{1+\sqrt{5}}{2}\right)^{n} - \frac{1}{\sqrt{5}}\left(\frac{1-\sqrt{5}}{2}\right)^{n}$ to generate the Fibonacci sequence, is it necessary to also include $f(1) = 1$ and $f(2) = 1$ as part of the rule? No, when an explicit rule is used to generate a sequence, each term is a function of the position number, not the term before it. So, when using the explicit rule to generate the Fibonacci sequence, $f(1)$ and $f(2)$ are generated by the explicit rule.

Teaching Strategy

Students may be interested to learn more about the Fibonacci sequence. Encourage them to research the origins of Fibonacci numbers and the many ways in which the sequence appears in nature. In addition to bee reproduction and patterns of flower petals, the Fibonacci sequence has also been seen in other natural patterns, such as the branchings of trees, the arrangement of petals, leaves, and seed heads on plants, and the spirals of seashells. Students may be interested to learn that there is an academic journal devoted solely to the study of the Fibonacci sequence.

EXTRA EXAMPLE

The first two terms of a sequence are both 2. Every other term is the sum of the previous two terms. Write a recursive rule for the sequence.
$f(1) = f(2) = 2$ and $f(n) = f(n-1) + f(n-2)$ for $n \geq 3$

CLOSE

Essential Question

Why is a sequence a function?
Each term in a sequence is associated with a position number, usually the set of consecutive integers starting with 1 or 0. Since each position number is associated with exactly one term, a numerical sequence is a function in which the domain is the set of position numbers and the range is the set of terms.

Summarize

Have students make a table comparing explicit and recursive rules for sequences. For each type of rule, give an example of a function that uses that type of rule to define a numerical sequence, describe how to use that rule to generate a sequence, and explain how to use the rule to find the nth term of a sequence.

PRACTICE

Where skills are taught	Where skills are practiced
2 EXAMPLE	EXS. 1–4, 10, 11
3 EXAMPLE	EXS. 5–8
4 EXAMPLE	EXS. 9, 12

Exercises 13–15: Given a table that represents a function, students write an explicit rule for the sequence defined by the function.

Exercises 16–18: Given a table that represents a function, students write a recursive rule for the sequence defined by the function.

PRACTICE

Write the first four terms of each sequence. Assume that the domain of the function is the set of consecutive integers starting with 1.

1. $f(n) = (n-1)^2$

0, 1, 4, 9

2. $f(n) = \frac{n+1}{n+3}$

$\frac{1}{2}, \frac{3}{5}, \frac{2}{3}, \frac{5}{7}$

3. $f(n) = 4(0.5)^n$

2, 1, 0.5, 0.25

4. $f(n) = \sqrt{n-1}$

0, 1, $\sqrt{2}$, $\sqrt{3}$

5. $f(1) = 2$ and $f(n) = f(n-1) + 10$ for $n \geq 2$ ___2, 12, 22, 32___

6. $f(1) = 16$ and $f(n) = \frac{1}{2}f(n-1)$ for $n \geq 2$ ___16, 8, 4, 2___

7. $f(1) = 1$ and $f(n) = 2f(n-1) + 1$ for $n \geq 2$ ___1, 3, 7, 15___

8. $f(1) = f(2) = 1$ and $f(n) = f(n-2) - f(n-1)$ for $n \geq 3$ ___1, 1, 0, −1___

9. Each year for the past 4 years, Donna has gotten a raise equal to 5% of the previous year's salary. Her starting salary was $40,000.

   a. Complete the table to show Donna's salary over time.

   b. Write a recursive rule for the sequence in the table. Assume that the domain of the function is the set of consecutive integers starting with 0, so the first term of the sequence is $f(0)$.

   $f(0) = 40,000$ and $f(n) = 1.05f(n-1)$ for

   $n \geq 1$

   c. What is $f(7)$, rounded to the nearest whole number? What does $f(7)$ represent in this situation?

   56,284; Donna's salary 7 years after she began working if she keeps getting the

   same raise each year

Year (position number)	Salary ($) (term of sequence)
0	40,000
1	42,000
2	44,100
3	46,305
4	48,620.25

Write the 12th term of each sequence. Assume that the domain of the function is the set of consecutive integers starting with 1.

10. $f(n) = 3n - 2$ ___34___

11. $f(n) = 2n(n+1)$ ___312___

---

12. The diagram shows the first four figures in a pattern of dots.

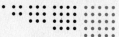

   a. Draw the next figure in the pattern.

   b. Use the pattern to complete the table.

   c. Write an explicit rule for the sequence in the table. Assume that the domain of the function is the set of consecutive integers starting with 1.

   $f(n) = n^2$

   d. How many dots will be in the 10th figure of the pattern?

   100

Figure (position number)	Number of dots (term of sequence)
1	1
2	4
3	9
4	16
5	25

Write an explicit rule for each sequence. Assume that the domain of the function is the set of consecutive integers starting with 1.

13.

n	f(n)
1	6
2	7
3	8
4	9
5	10

$f(n) = n + 5$

14.

n	f(n)
1	3
2	6
3	9
4	12
5	15

$f(n) = 3n$

15.

n	f(n)
1	1
2	$\frac{1}{2}$
3	$\frac{1}{3}$
4	$\frac{1}{4}$
5	$\frac{1}{5}$

$f(n) = \frac{1}{n}$

Write a recursive rule for each sequence. Assume that the domain of the function is the set of consecutive integers starting with 1.

16.

n	f(n)
1	8
2	9
3	10
4	11
5	12

$f(1) = 8$ and $f(n) =$ $f(n-1) + 1$ for $n \geq 2$

17.

n	f(n)
1	2
2	4
3	8
4	16
5	32

$f(1) = 2$ and $f(n) =$ $2f(n-1)$ for $n \geq 2$

18.

n	f(n)
1	27
2	24
3	21
4	18
5	15

$f(1) = 27$ and $f(n) =$ $f(n-1) - 3$ for $n \geq 2$

Assign these pages to help your students practice and apply important lesson concepts. For additional exercises, see the Student Edition.

Answers

Additional Practice

1. 1, 3, 9, 27, 81

2. 2, 1, −1, −5, −13

3. −2, 3, 8, 63, 3968

4. 1, 4, −2, 10, −14

5. −1, 1, −3, 13, 141

6. −2, 0, 1, $\frac{1}{2}$, $\frac{3}{4}$

7. −2, 0, 4, 10, 18

8. 1, 6, 15, 28, 45

9. 0, 4, 18, 48, 100

10. 4, 2, 1, $\frac{1}{2}$, $\frac{1}{4}$

11. 1, −2, 4, −8, 16

12. −1, 0, 3, 8, 15

13. $a_n = 8n$

14. $a_n = 0.1n^2$

15. $a_n = n^2 + 2$

16. $a_n = 3\left(\frac{1}{2}\right)^n$

17. $a_n = 3n - 5$

18. $a_n = 5(0.2)^{n-1}$

19. 31, 63

20. a.

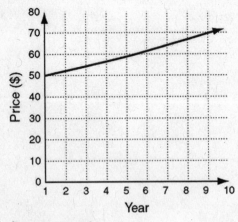

b. Exponential

c. $61 per week

Problem Solving

1. a. $\frac{2}{3}$; $\frac{2}{3}$; −3; −2; 1.5; 1

b. The ratios are constant; so the sequence is exponential.

c. $a_n = 13.5\left(\frac{2}{3}\right)^{n-1}$

d. 1.2 mm

2. a. 10 min, 8 min, 6 min, 4 min

b. 6.6 min

3. B

4. F

Additional Practice

Find the first 5 terms of each sequence.

1. $a_1 = 1, a_n = 3(a_{n-1})$

2. $a_1 = 2, a_n = 2(a_{n-1} + 1) - 5$

3. $a_1 = -2, a_n = (a_{n-1})^2 - 1$

_____

_____

_____

4. $a_1 = 1, a_n = 6 - 2(a_{n-1})$

5. $a_1 = -1, a_n = (a_{n-1} - 1)^2 - 3$

6. $a_1 = -2, a_n = \dfrac{2 - a_{n-1}}{2}$

_____

_____

_____

7. $a_n = (n-2)(n+1)$

8. $a_n = n(2n - 1)$

9. $a_n = n^3 - n^2$

_____

_____

_____

10. $a_n = \left(\dfrac{1}{2}\right)^{n-3}$

11. $a_n = (-2)^{n-1}$

12. $a_n = n^2 - 2n$

_____

_____

_____

Write a possible explicit rule for the *n*th term of each sequence.

13. 8, 16, 24, 32, 40, ...

14. 0.1, 0.4, 0.9, 1.6, 2.5, ...

15. 3, 6, 11, 18, 27, ...

_____

_____

_____

16. $\dfrac{3}{2}, \dfrac{3}{4}, \dfrac{3}{8}, \dfrac{3}{16}, \dfrac{3}{32}, ...$

17. −2, 1, 4, 7, 10, ...

18. 5, 1, 0.2, 0.04, 0.008, ...

_____

_____

_____

Solve.

19. Find the number of line segments in the next two iterations.

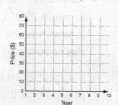

_____

20. Jim charges $50 per week for lawn mowing and weeding services. He plans to increase his prices by 4% each year.

a. Graph the sequence.

b. Describe the pattern.

_____

_____

c. To the nearest dollar, how much will he charge per week in 5 years?

_____

(Graph with y-axis "Price ($)" marked 0–80 and x-axis "Year" marked 1–10)

© Houghton Mifflin Harcourt Publishing Company

Problem Solving

Tina is working on some home improvement projects involving repeated tasks. She wants to analyze her work patterns.

1. Tina is hammering nails into wallboard. With the first hit, a nail goes in 13.5 millimeters; with the second, it goes in an additional 9 mm; with the third, it goes in an additional 6 mm; and with the fourth it goes in 4 mm further. Suppose this pattern continues. Predict how far the nail would go in with the seventh hit.

a. Complete the table to find first differences, second differences, and ratios.

Distance	13.5mm	9mm	6mm	4mm
Ratios	$\dfrac{2}{3}$			
First Differences	−4.5			
Second Differences				

b. How do you know whether the rule for the sequence of distances that the nail goes in is linear, quadratic, or exponential?

_____

c. Write a possible rule for a_n, the *n*th term in the sequence.

_____

d. If this pattern continues, how far would the nail go in with the seventh hit?

_____

2. Tina builds a fence for her neighbor. It takes her 10 minutes to pound the first fence post into the ground. The neighbor predicts that Tina should improve her time on each successive fence post according to the rule $a_n = F - 2(n - 1)$, where F is the time for the first fence post, and a_n is the time it takes to pound in the *n*th post.

a. Use the rule to find the time it should take Tina to pound each of the first 4 fence posts into the ground.

_____

b. If the rule that describes Tina's time on each successive post is $a_n = F - 1.5^{n-1}$, how long will it take her to pound the fourth fence post into the ground?

_____

The label on Pete's blue jeans states that, when washed, the jeans will lose 5% of their color. Choose the letter for the best answer.

3. Which rule describes the percent of color left in the blue jeans after *n* washings?

A $a_n = 100(0.05)^n$

B $a_n = 100(0.95)^n$

C $a_n = 100(0.95)^n$

D $a_n = 100(0.05)^n$

4. How much of the original color will be left after 8 washings?

F 66%

G 60%

H 40%

J 34%

© Houghton Mifflin Harcourt Publishing Company

Notes

Series and Summation Notation
Going Deeper

Essential question: *How can you derive and apply formulas for the sum of a linear or quadratic series?*

COMMON CORE **Standards for Mathematical Content**

CC.9-12.F.BF.1a Determine an explicit expression, a recursive process, or steps for calculation from a context.*

Vocabulary

series

partial sum

summation notation

Prerequisites

Introduction to sequences

Math Background

When students are introduced to the summation notation $\sum_{k=1}^{n} k$, they will see 1 referred to as the first value of k, and n referred to as the last value of k. In more formal language, k is called the *index of summation*, 1 is called the *lower limit of summation*, and n is called the *upper limit of summation*. If students visualize a horizontal row of the terms of a series, they will see why the terms *lower* and *upper* are used to describe limits of the terms.

INTRODUCE

Give students the following sequence: 2, 4, 6, 8, 10, ... Have them organize the sequence in a table where the first row gives the term number, n, and the second row lists the term value, a_n. Tell students to use the table to write an explicit rule for the nth term of the sequence. Then start investigating sums of consecutive terms in the sequence, such as the sum of the first 3 and the sum of the first 4 terms. Point out that writing out sums can become tedious, especially if there are many terms. Have students use the explicit rule to write a verbal description of the sum of the first 12 terms of the sequence, such as "The sum of the first 12 terms of the sequence 2n." Tell students that they will learn a way to express this statement symbolically.

TEACH

1 ENGAGE

Questioning Strategies

- How many partial sums can be found for the sequence in **1 ENGAGE**? Explain. **Infinitely many; the sequence is an infinite sequence, so there are infinitely many partial sums that can be found.**

- What does the coefficient of k in the explicit formula $2k - 1$ represent? **The coefficient of k is 2, which is the common difference of the terms in the sequence.**

- For a series written in summation notation, is it possible for the first value of k or the last value of k to be numbers other than positive integers? Explain. **No; these numbers represent the relative positions of terms in a sequence, so both must be positive integers.**

Teaching Strategy

Explain to students that a series may not always start with the first value of the corresponding sequence. To emphasize this point, have students expand and simplify each of the following series:

$$\sum_{k=1}^{5}(2k-1), \sum_{k=2}^{5}(2k-1), \sum_{k=3}^{5}(2k-1), \sum_{k=4}^{5}(2k-1)$$

Remind students to pay close attention to the starting value of k when working with summation notation.

Differentiated Instruction

Some students may have difficulty understanding the symbolic nature of summation notation. For these students, write a verbal description of the summation notation in **1 ENGAGE**, such as "the sum of $2k - 1$ for values of k from 1 to 5." Encourage students to write this verbal description next to the summation notation so they can make reference to it, if needed. Students can continue to use these verbal descriptions until they feel comfortable with the symbolic notation.

Name_____ Class_____ Date_____

9-2

Series and Summation Notation

Extension: Summation of Linear and Quadratic Series

Essential question: *How can you derive and apply formulas for the sum of a linear or quadratic series?*

CC.9-12.F.BF.1a

1 ENGAGE   Investigating Series and Summation Notation

Video Tutor

The sum of the terms of a sequence is called a **series**. Many sequences are infinite and therefore do not have defined sums. For these sequences, *partial sums* can be found. A **partial sum**, represented by S_n, is the sum of a specified number, *n*, of terms of a sequence. Examples of partial sums of a sequence of odd integers are shown below.

Sequence: 1, 3, 5, 7, 9, ...

$S_1 = 1$ Sum of first term

$S_2 = 1 + 3 = 4$ Sum of first 2 terms

$S_3 = 1 + 3 + 5 = 9$ Sum of first 3 terms

$S_4 = 1 + 3 + 5 + 7 = 16$ Sum of first 4 terms

A series can be represented using **summation notation**, in which the Greek letter $\sum$ (capital *sigma*) is used to represent the sum of a sequence defined by a rule. The series $1 + 3 + 5 + 7 + 9$ is written in summation notation below.

$$\sum_{k=1}^{5} (2k - 1)$$

     ← Last value of *k*
     ← Explicit formula for sequence
     ← First value of *k*

In summation notation, an explicit formula for the sequence is needed as shown above. When writing a formula for a sequence, it is helpful to examine the first and second differences of the terms and the ratios of the terms.

REFLECT

1a. Explain the difference between a sequence and a series.

A sequence is an ordered set of numbers called terms. A series is the sum of the terms of a sequence.

1b. Without making any calculations, determine whether the two series below have the same sum. Explain your reasoning.

$$\sum_{k=1}^{7} 4(k + 12) \qquad \sum_{k=3}^{9} 4(k + 12)$$

No; both series are the sum of 7 terms from the same sequence. However, the first series is the sum of the first 7 terms and the second series is the sum of the third through ninth terms. These terms are different, so the sums are different.

CC.9-12.F.BF.1a

2 EXAMPLE   Using Summation Notation and Evaluating Series

A Write the series $\frac{3}{5} + \frac{3}{10} + \frac{3}{15} + \frac{3}{20} + \frac{3}{25}$ in summation notation.

Find a rule for the *k*th term of the series. Notice that the denominators of the terms are multiples of 5. The numerator of each term is 3. So the terms of the series can be written as follows:

$$a_k = \frac{3}{5k} \text{ where } k = 1, 2, 3, 4, 5$$

Notice that the first value of *k* is 1 and the last value of *k* is 5.

The summation notation for the series is $\sum_{k=1}^{6} \frac{3}{5k}$.

B Expand the series $\sum_{k=3}^{6} (-1)^k (k + 4)$ and evaluate.

$$\sum_{k=3}^{6} (-1)^k (k + 4) = (-1)^3(3 + 4) + (-1)^4(4 + 4) + (-1)^5(5 + 4) + (-1)^6(6 + 4)$$

$$= (-1)(7) + (1)(8) + (-1)(9) + (1)(10)$$

$$= 2$$

REFLECT

2a. In part B of Example 2, suppose the rule for the *k*th term of the series is $(-1)^{k+1}(k + 4)$. How will this affect the answer? Explain.

The terms of the new sequence will have opposite signs, so the sum will have an opposite sign. The terms will be 7, −8, 9, −10 instead of −7, 8, −9, 10, and the new sum will be −2 instead of 2.

2b. The first term of the series $\sum_{k=a}^{b} k$ is *a* and the last term of the series is *b*. Given that the series has *c* terms, write a rule for finding the value of *b* in terms of *a* and *c*.

$b = a + c - 1$

Formulas can be used to find sums of some common series. In a *constant series*, such as $2 + 2 + 2 + 2$, each term has the same value.

$$\sum_{k=1}^{n} c = \underbrace{c + c + c + \ldots + c}_{n \text{ terms}} = nc$$

You can see that the sum of a constant series with *n* terms of value *c* can be expressed as *nc*. How can you find formulas for the sums of non-constant series?

Questioning Strategies

- In part A, suppose the series changes to $-\frac{3}{5} + \frac{3}{10} + \left(-\frac{3}{15}\right) + \frac{3}{20} + \left(-\frac{3}{25}\right)$. How does this change the explicit rule used in the summation notation? In general, how do you write a rule for a series in which every other term has a negative sign?

  The explicit rule becomes $(-1)^k\left(\frac{3}{5k}\right)$; If the odd-numbered terms of the series are negative, then $(-1)^k$ should be included in the explicit rule. If the even-numbered terms of the series are negative, then include $(-1)^{k+1}$ in the explicit rule.

- In part B, how many terms are in the series? What values of k are used to generate the terms?

  4; $k = 3, 4, 5, 6$

EXTRA EXAMPLE

A Write the series $-3 + (-7) + (-11) + (-15) + (-19) + (-23)$ in summation notation.

$$\sum_{k=1}^{6}(-4k + 1)$$

B Expand the series $\sum_{k=2}^{7}(8k + 10)$ and evaluate.

$26 + 34 + 42 + 50 + 58 + 66 = 276$

Teaching Strategy

When students write a series in summation notation, suggest they start by numbering each term in the series. It may seem obvious, but tell students to use 1 for the first term, 2 for the second term, and so on. In doing so, students see how the term number relates to the term, which will help them write an explicit rule for the series.

Technology

Students can use their graphing calculators to evaluate a series by using the *summation* feature. Tell them to follow the prompts for the explicit rule, the variable used in the explicit rule, the lower limit, and the upper limit.

Questioning Strategies

- What does the variable n represent? What is the value of n in the series in part A? **The last value of k; 6**

- What is the sum of the integers from 1 to 52? **1378**

- What is an advantage of using a formula to find the sum of a series? **Finding the sum of a series using a formula is usually faster than expanding the series and calculating the sum.**

Teaching Strategy

To help students understand the derivation of the formula for the sum of the first n positive integers, relate the story of how Carl Friedrich Gauss added the numbers from 1 to 100 in his head when he was in elementary school. Tell students that he began by visualizing the series:

$$1 + 2 + 3 + 4 + \ldots + 97 + 98 + 99 + 100.$$

Then he found the sum of the first and last terms $(1 + 100)$, the sum of the second and second-to-last terms $(2 + 99)$, the sum of the third and third-to-last terms $(3 + 98)$, and so on. All of these sums equal 101, and he realized that there are 50 sums of 101 in the series. So the sum is $50(101) = 5{,}050$. As you tell this story, write the series on the board and draw lines to connect the paired terms. Tell students that there are 50 sums because 100 terms are divided into pairs. Then relate Gauss's reasoning to the formula derived in **3 EXPLORE**.

Questioning Strategies

- In Part B, what other formulas are used to derive the formula? **The formula for the sum of a constant series and the formula for the sum of the first n positive integers**

- Given the formula for the sum of the squares of the first n positive integers, does it make sense that the formula was derived from series involving cubed terms? Explain. **Yes; the formula is a cubic expression.**

3 EXPLORE Deriving a Formula for the Sum of Positive Integers

CC.9-12.F.BF.1a

Derive a formula for the sum of the first n positive integers.

A Consider the partial sum $\sum_{k=1}^{6} k$, which can be called S_6.

Write S_6 twice, the second time with the order reversed. Then add the two equations term by term.

$$S_6 = 1 + 2 + 3 + 4 + 5 + 6$$
$$S_6 = 6 + 5 + 4 + 3 + 2 + 1$$

Solve for S_6. Notice that the sum is the product of the number of terms, 6, and the sum of the first and last terms, 7, divided by 2.

$$2S_6 = 7 + 7 + 7 + 7 + 7 + 7$$
$$S_6 = \frac{6(7)}{2} = 21$$

B Now consider the general sum $\sum_{k=1}^{n} k$, which can be called S_n.

Write the series twice, as in part A, and then add the two equations.

$$S_n = 1 \quad + \quad 2 \quad + \quad 3 \quad + \dots + (n-2) + (n-1) + n$$
$$S_n = n \quad + (n-1) + (n-2) + \dots + \quad 3 \quad + \quad 2 \quad + 1$$

$$2S_n = (n+1) + (n+1) + (n+1) + \dots + (n+1) + (n+1) + (n+1)$$

n terms

$$2S_n = n(n+1)$$
$$S_n = \frac{n(n+1)}{2}$$

REFLECT

3a. Expand and evaluate to find the sum of the series $\sum_{k=1}^{9} k$. Show that you get the same sum by using the formula in part B of Explore 3.

$1+2+3+4+5+6+7+8+9 = 45$; $\frac{9(10)}{2} = 45$. The sums are the same.

3b. The terms of the series at the right are rearranged to form 4 terms of 9. Explain how this suggests the formula for the sum of the first n integers in part B of Explore 3.

In the product 4(9), 4 is half the number of terms and 9 is the sum of the first and last terms. For n terms, this product can be written as $\frac{n}{2}(1+n)$, which is $\frac{n(n+1)}{2}$.

$$\sum_{k=1}^{8} k = 1+2+3+4+5+6+7+8$$
$$= (1+8) + (2+7) + (3+6) + (4+5)$$
$$= 9+9+9+9$$
$$= 4(9)$$
$$= 36$$

4 EXPLORE Deriving a Formula for the Sum of Squares of Integers

CC.9-12.F.BF.1a

Derive a formula for the sum of the squares of the first n positive integers.

A To derive the formula for $\sum_{k=1}^{n} k^2$, use the series $\sum_{k=1}^{n} k^3$ and $\sum_{k=1}^{n} (k-1)^3$.

Notice the result when you find the difference of these series.

$$\sum_{k=1}^{n} k^3 = 1^3 + 2^3 + 3^3 + \dots + (n-2)^3 + (n-1)^3 + n^3$$
$$\sum_{k=1}^{n} (k-1)^3 = 0^3 + 1^3 + 2^3 + 3^3 + \dots + (n-2)^3 + (n-1)^3$$

$$\sum_{k=1}^{n} [k^3 - (k-1)^3] = 0 + 0 + 0 + 0 + \dots + 0 + 0 + n^3$$

B Use the result from part A to find a formula for the sum of $= \sum_{k=1}^{n} k^2$.

$n^3 = \sum_{k=1}^{n} [k^3 - (k-1)^3]$	Write result from part A.
$n^3 = \sum_{k=1}^{n} (3k^2 - 3k + 1)$	Simplify the explicit rule.
$n^3 = \sum_{k=1}^{n} 3k^2 - \sum_{k=1}^{n} 3k + \sum_{k=1}^{n} 1$	Separate into three sums.
$n^3 = 3\sum_{k=1}^{n} k^2 - 3\sum_{k=1}^{n} k + \sum_{k=1}^{n} 1$	Move constant factors outside of sigma.
$n^3 = 3\sum_{k=1}^{n} k^2 - 3\left(\frac{n(n+1)}{2}\right) + n$	Substitute formulas for $\sum_{k=1}^{n} k$ and $\sum_{k=1}^{n} 1$.
$\sum_{k=1}^{n} k^2 = \frac{n^3}{3} + \frac{n(n+1)}{2} - \frac{n}{3}$	Rewrite equation to isolate $\sum_{k=1}^{n} k^2$.
$\sum_{k=1}^{n} k^2 = \frac{2n^3 + 3n^2 + n}{6}$	Write expression with a common denominator.
$\sum_{k=1}^{n} k^2 = \frac{n(n+1)(2n+1)}{6}$	Factor numerator.

MATHEMATICAL PRACTICE — Highlighting the Standards

3 EXPLORE and 4 EXPLORE provide opportunities to address Mathematical Practices Standard 7 (Look for and make use of structure). In 3 EXPLORE, students derive the formula for the sum of the first n positive integers. In doing so, students must understand the structure of the series to rearrange the terms to find the common sums used in the formula. In 4 EXPLORE, students derive the formula for the sum of the squares for integers from 1 to n. Students begin by expanding and rearranging the terms of two series given in summation notation. Their knowledge of the structure of these series allows them to simplify the difference of the series. This difference is essential in the derivation of the formula.

5 EXAMPLE

Questioning Strategies

- What is a verbal description of the series given in Part A? **The sum of the integers from 1 to 44**

- What is a verbal description of the series given in Part B? **The sum of the squares of the integers from 1 to 17**

EXTRA EXAMPLE

Evaluate each series.

A $\displaystyle\sum_{k=1}^{33} k$ 561

B $\displaystyle\sum_{k=1}^{21} k^2$ 3311

Differentiated Instruction

Give advanced students the properties below for the sequences a_k and b_k.

$$\sum_{k=1}^{n} ca_k = c\sum_{k=1}^{n} a_k; \quad \sum_{k=1}^{n}(a_k + b_k) = \sum_{k=1}^{n} a_k + \sum_{k=1}^{n} b_k$$

Then challenge them to use the properties in conjunction with the formulas fo r sums to evaluate series like the ones below.

$$\sum_{k=1}^{31} 4k^2 \qquad \sum_{k=1}^{56}(k+9) \qquad \sum_{k=1}^{22}(7k^2 + 15)$$

Essential Question

How can you derive and apply formulas for the sum of a linear or quadratic series? To derive the formula for the sum of a linear series, begin by expanding the series $\displaystyle\sum_{k=1}^{n} k$ twice and adding the two series together. Pair the terms to form sums of $n + 1$. Then multiply $n + 1$ by the number of these sums in one of the series (n) to find the sum of the two series, and then divide that sum by 2. To derive the formula for the sum of a quadratic series, use the fact that $n^3 = \displaystyle\sum_{k=1}^{n}[k^3 - (k-1)^3]$. Then use various properties and the formulas for a constant series and a linear series to transform the equation into $\displaystyle\sum_{k=1}^{n} k^2 = \frac{n(n+1)(2n+1)}{6}$.

Summarize

Have students make a table that summarizes the formulas for the sum of a constant series, a linear series, and a quadratic series. Each entry in the table should include the following:

- the series written in summation notation for values of k from 1 to n

- an abbreviated form of the expanded series for values of k from 1 to n

- the formula for the sum of the series

- an example of such a series, with its sum

PRACTICE

Where skills are taught	Where skills are practiced
2 EXAMPLE	EXS. 1–10
5 EXAMPLE	EXS. 11–13

Exercises 14: Students investigate a method for finding the sum of consecutive integers not starting at 1.

Exercises 15: Students examine whether two seemingly different series written in summation notation can have the same sum.

REFLECT

4a. Use the formula in part B to find the sum of the series $\sum_{k=1}^{5} k^2$. Show that you get the same sum by expanding and evaluating the series.

$\frac{5(6)(11)}{6} = 55;\ 1^2 + 2^2 + 3^2 + 4^2 + 5^2 = 55$. The sums are the same.

4b. One of the steps in part B uses the fact that $\sum_{k=1}^{n} ck = c\sum_{k=1}^{n} k$ for any constant c. Prove this fact by using the Distributive Property on the expanded series.

$\sum_{k=1}^{n} ck = c(1) + c(2) + c(2) + \ldots + c(n) = c(1 + 2 + 3 + \ldots + n) = c\sum_{k=1}^{n} k$

5 EXAMPLE Using Summation Formulas

CC.9-12.F.BF.1a

Evaluate each series.

A $\sum_{k=1}^{44} k$

$\sum_{k=1}^{44} k = \frac{n(n+1)}{2}$ Use the formula derived in Explore 3.

$= \frac{44(44+1)}{2}$ Substitute 44 for n.

$= 990$ Simplify.

B $\sum_{k=1}^{17} k^2$

$\sum_{k=1}^{17} k^2 = \frac{n(n+1)(2n+1)}{6}$ Use the formula derived in Explore 4.

$= \frac{17(17+1)[2(17)+1]}{6}$ Substitute 17 for n.

$= 1,785$ Simplify.

REFLECT

5a. Suppose the series in part A started with $k = 8$. Would you be able to use the formula derived in Explore 3 to find the sum of the series? Explain.

No; the formula is for the first n integers. If $k = 8$, then the sum of the first seven integers is excluded from the sum.

5b. Let n be any integer. Is the sum of the series $\sum_{k=1}^{n} k^2$ an integer? Explain.

Yes; all of the terms of the series are integers, and the sum of integers is an integer.

© Houghton Mifflin Harcourt Publishing Company

PRACTICE

Write each series in summation notation.

1. $8 + 9 + 10 + 11 + 12 + 13 + 14 + 15$

$\sum_{k=1}^{8} (k + 7)$

2. $-3 + (-6) + (-9) + (-12) + (-15)$

$\sum_{k=1}^{5} (-3k)$

3. $1 + \frac{1}{4} + \frac{1}{9} + \frac{1}{16}$

$\sum_{k=1}^{4} \frac{1}{k^2}$

4. $\frac{1}{2} + \frac{2}{3} + \frac{3}{4} + \frac{4}{5} + \frac{5}{6} + \frac{6}{7}$

$\sum_{k=1}^{6} \frac{k}{k+1}$

5. $11 + 101 + 1,001 + 10,001 + 100,001$

$\sum_{k=1}^{5} (10^k + 1)$

6. $-2 + 4 + (-6) + 8 + (-10) + 12$

$\sum_{k=1}^{6} (-1)^k (2k)$

Expand each series and evaluate.

7. $\sum_{k=1}^{5} (3k - 2)$

$1 + 4 + 7 + 10 + 13 = 35$

8. $\sum_{k=3}^{9} 4k$

$12 + 16 + 20 + 24 + 28 +$

$32 + 36 = 168$

9. $\sum_{k=1}^{7} (-1)^k (11k)$

$-11 + 22 + (-33) + 44 +$

$(-55) + 66 + (-77) = -44$

10. $\sum_{k=5}^{11} (k-1)(k+4)$

$36 + 50 + 66 + 84 +$

$104 + 126 + 150 = 616$

Evaluate each series using a summation formula.

11. $\sum_{k=1}^{14} 6.2$ **62**

12. $\sum_{k=1}^{77} k$ **3,003**

13. $\sum_{k=1}^{20} k^2$ **2,870**

14. Follow the steps below to find the sum of the series $\sum_{k=16}^{31} k$.

a. Solve the equation $\sum_{k=1}^{31} k = \sum_{k=1}^{15} k + \sum_{k=16}^{31} k$ for $\sum_{k=16}^{31} k$. $\sum_{k=16}^{31} k = \sum_{k=1}^{31} k - \sum_{k=1}^{15} k$

b. Use your rewritten equation to find the sum of the series $\sum_{k=16}^{31} k$.   **376**

15. Do the series $\sum_{k=1}^{n} (k+2)(k+7)$ and $\sum_{k=1}^{n-1} (k+3)(k+8)$ have the same sum? Explain.

Yes; $\sum_{k=1}^{n} (k+2)(k+7) = (3)(8) + (4)(9) + \ldots + (n+1)(n+6) + (n+2)(n+7)$ and

$\sum_{k=1}^{n-1} (k+3)(k+8) = (3)(8) + (4)(9) + \ldots + (n+1)(n+6) + (n+2)(n+7)$.

The expanded series are the same, so the series have the same sum.

© Houghton Mifflin Harcourt Publishing Company

Assign these pages to help your students practice and apply important lesson concepts. For additional exercises, see the Student Edition.

Answers

Additional Practice

1. $\displaystyle\sum_{k=1}^{5}(-2)^k$ **2.** $\displaystyle\sum_{k=1}^{4}\left(\frac{1}{10}\right)^k$

3. $\displaystyle\sum_{k=1}^{6}(5k-11)$ **4.** $\displaystyle\sum_{k=1}^{6}\frac{1}{3k}$

5. $\displaystyle\sum_{k=1}^{5}(6k+1)$ **6.** $\displaystyle\sum_{k=1}^{7}(-1)^k$

7. **a.** $1+\dfrac{5}{4}+\dfrac{6}{4}+\dfrac{7}{4}+2$

    b. $7\dfrac{1}{2}$

8. **a.** $\dfrac{1}{5}+1+5+25$

    b. $31\dfrac{1}{5}$

9. **a.** $4-8+16-32+64$

    b. 44

10. **a.** $10+8+6+4+2+0-2-4-6-8$

    b. 10

11. 27   **12.** 820

13. 385

14. **a.** $\displaystyle\sum_{k=1}^{n}3^k$

    b. $\displaystyle\sum_{k=1}^{7}3^k$

    c. 3279

Problem Solving

1. **a.** $a_k = 4(0.9)^{k-1}$

    b. $\displaystyle\sum_{k=1}^{8}4(0.9)^{k-1}$

    c. 22.8 mm

2. $a_k = 4(0.9)^{k-1} + \dfrac{1}{2}$

    b. $\displaystyle\sum_{k=1}^{8}0.5 + 4(0.9)^{k-1}$

    c. 26.8 mm

    d. 7 weeks

3. C   **4.** G

Additional Practice

Write each series in summation notation.

1. $-2 + 4 - 8 + 16 - 32$

_____

2. $\dfrac{1}{10} + \dfrac{1}{100} + \dfrac{1}{1,000} + \dfrac{1}{10,000}$

3. $-6 - 1 + 4 + 9 + 14 + 19$

_____

4. $\dfrac{1}{3} + \dfrac{1}{6} + \dfrac{1}{9} + \dfrac{1}{12} + \dfrac{1}{15} + \dfrac{1}{18}$

5. $7 + 13 + 19 + 25 + 31$

_____

6. $-1 + 1 - 1 + 1 - 1 + 1 - 1$

Expand each series and evaluate.

7. $\displaystyle\sum_{k=4}^{8} \dfrac{k}{4}$

   a. Expand. _____

   b. Simplify. _____

8. $\displaystyle\sum_{k=1}^{4} 5^{k-2}$

   a. Expand. _____

   b. Simplify. _____

9. $\displaystyle\sum_{k=2}^{6} (-2^{k})$

   a. Expand. _____

   b. Simplify. _____

10. $\displaystyle\sum_{k=30}^{39} (70 - 2k)$

   a. Expand. _____

   b. Simplify. _____

Evaluate each series.

11. $\displaystyle\sum_{k=12}^{20} 3$

12. $\displaystyle\sum_{k=1}^{40} k$

13. $\displaystyle\sum_{k=1}^{10} k^{2}$

Solve.

14. One day, Hannah starts a new online Internet club by convincing two of her friends to join. The next day, each member convinces two more people to join. The third day of the club, each member convinces two more people to join, and so on for a full week.

   a. Write a series that represents the number of club members at the end of n days.

   b. Write a series that represents the number of club members at the end of one week.

   c. How many members will the club have at the end of a week?

Problem Solving

Todd joins a fitness club. During the first week of training, his biceps increase by 4 millimeters. The trainer says Todd can expect his biceps to continue to increase each week, but only by about 90% of the increase of the week before.

1. Todd wants to know how much his biceps will increase in 8 weeks.

   a. Write a rule for the kth term in the sequence that represents the amount of muscle increase each week.

   b. Write the summation notation using $\sum$ for the first 8 terms.

   c. Expand the series and evaluate to find the amount by which Todd's biceps will increase in 8 weeks.

2. Todd thinks that, if he works out extra hard each week, his biceps should increase by at least an additional half-millimeter each week. If this is true, how much will his biceps increase after 8 weeks?

   a. Write a rule for the kth term in the sequence that represents the minimum amount of muscle increase each week.

   b. Use summation notation to represent the minimum total amount of muscle increase after 8 weeks.

   c. What is the minimum increase in size in Todd's biceps after 8 weeks?

   d. At this rate, how many weeks would it take to reach or exceed the total muscle increase predicted by the trainer?

Rodrigo puts his change into a bowl each evening. On Monday he puts 2 quarters in the bowl and decides to try and increase the amount each evening by at least 10 cents over the evening before. Choose the letter for the best answer.

3. Which series represents the minimum amount in the bowl Saturday morning?

   A $\displaystyle\sum_{k=1}^{5} 0.1(0.5)^{k-1}$

   B $\displaystyle\sum_{k=1}^{5} 0.5(0.1)^{k-1}$

   C $\displaystyle\sum_{k=1}^{5} 0.5 + 0.1(k-1)$

   D $\displaystyle\sum_{k=1}^{5} 0.1 + 0.5(k-1)$

4. What is the minimum amount in the bowl the following Monday morning?

   F $3.50

   G $5.60

   H $6.80

   J $7.60

Notes

Arithmetic Sequences and Series
Going Deeper

Essential question: *How can you write a rule for an arithmetic sequence?*

COMMON **Standards for**
CORE **Mathematical Content**

CC.9-12.F.BF.1 Write a function that describes a relationship between two quantities.*

CC.9-12.F.BF.1a Determine an explicit expression, a recursive process ... from a context.*

CC.9-12.F.BF.2 Write arithmetic ... sequences both recursively and with an explicit formula, use them to model situations, and translate between the two forms.*

CC.9-12.F.LE.2 Construct linear ... functions, including arithmetic ... sequences, given a graph, a description of a relationship, or two input-output pairs (include reading these from a table).*

Vocabulary
arithmetic sequence
common difference

Prerequisites
Sequences

Math Background
Previously, students became familiar with sequences and learned to use functions to define sequences. Many of the sequences students have explored were arithmetic sequences, although the sequences were not defined as such.

INTRODUCE

Review the basic concepts about sequences that students have learned. Remind students that sequences are defined by functions, emphasizing how the domain and range of a function are related to the position numbers and terms of a sequence. Review the distinction between recursive and explicit rules.

TEACH

1 EXAMPLE

Questioning Strategies

- What would be the meaning in the context of the situation if $f(1)$ was equal to 20 instead of 60 in the recursive rule? It would mean that the starting balance was $20.

- In part C, why does the explicit rule for the sequence involve multiplying the common difference by $n - 1$ and not n? Month 1 ($n = 1$) represents the initial account balance, $60. A monthly deposit of $20 (the common difference) is made starting with month 2 ($n = 2$). So, the explicit rule must generate the sequence $f(1) = 60 + 0 \cdot 20$, $f(2) = 60 + 1 \cdot 20$, $f(3) = 60 + 2 \cdot 20$, ... The number of 20s added to 60 is always 1 less than the month number.

- Which rule, the recursive rule or the explicit rule, would be more useful in determining the balance at the end of the 45th month? Explain your reasoning. The explicit rule is more useful because you can easily evaluate $f(45) = 940$ to find the balance at the end of the 45th month. To use the recursive rule, you would have to start with $f(1)$ and calculate the balance for each successive month up to month 45.

Differentiated Instruction
Kinesthetic learners may benefit by acting out the situation using counters to represent the money in the account.

EXTRA EXAMPLE
The table shows end-of-month balances in a bank account that does not earn interest. Write a recursive rule and an explicit rule for the arithmetic sequence described by the table.

Month	n	1	2	3	4	5
Account Balance ($)	$f(n)$	50	80	110	140	170

$f(1) = 50$ and $f(n) = f(n - 1) + 30$ for $n \geq 2$;
$f(n) = 50 + 30(n - 1)$

Name_____ Class_____ Date_____

9-3

Arithmetic Sequences and Series
Going Deeper

Essential question: *How can you write a rule for an arithmetic sequence?*

In an **arithmetic sequence**, the difference between consecutive terms is constant. The constant difference is called the **common difference**, often written as d.

Video Tutor

CC.9-12.F.BF.2

1 EXAMPLE   Writing Rules for an Arithmetic Sequence

The table shows end-of-month balances in a bank account that does not earn interest. Write a recursive and an explicit rule for the arithmetic sequence described by the table.

Month	n	1	2	3	4	5
Account Balance ($)	$f(n)$	60	80	100	120	140

A Find the common difference by calculating the differences between consecutive terms.

$80 - 60 = $ **20**

$100 - 80 = $ **20**

$120 - 100 = $ **20**

$140 - 120 = $ **20**

The common difference, d, is __**20**__.

B Write a recursive rule for the sequence.

$f(1) = $ **60**   and   The first term is __**60**__.

$f(n) = f(n - 1) + 20$ for $n \geq 2$ Every other term is the __**sum**__ of the previous term and the common difference.

C Write an explicit rule for the sequence by writing each term as the sum of the first term and a multiple of the common difference.

n	$f(n)$
1	$60 + 20(0) = 60$
2	$60 + 20(1) = 80$
3	$60 + 20(\boxed{2}) = 100$
4	$60 + 20(\boxed{3}) = 120$
5	$60 + 20(\boxed{4}) = 140$

Generalize the results from the table: $f(n) = $ **60** $ + 20(n -$ **1** $)$

REFLECT

1a. Explain how you know that the sequence 1, 2, 4, 8, 16, … is not an arithmetic sequence.

The differences between consecutive terms are not constant.

1b. An arithmetic sequence has a common difference of 3. If you know that the third term of the sequence is 15, how can you find the fourth term?

Add the common difference to the third term to get 18 as the fourth term.

CC.9-12.F.BF.2

2 EXPLORE   Writing General Rules for Arithmetic Sequences

Use the arithmetic sequence 6, 9, 12, 15, 18, … to help you write a recursive rule and an explicit rule for any arithmetic sequence. For the general rules, the values of n are consecutive integers starting with 1.

A Find the common difference.

Numbers

6, 9, 12, 15, 18, …

Common difference = **3**

Algebra

$f(1), f(2), f(3), f(4), f(5), …$

Common difference = d

B Write a recursive rule.

Numbers

$f(1) = $ **6**   and

$f(n) = f(n - 1) + $ **3**   for $n \geq 2$

Algebra

Given $f(1)$,

$f(n) = f(n - 1) + $ d for $n \geq 2$

C Write an explicit rule.

Numbers

$f(n) = $ **6** $ + $ **3** $(n - 1)$

Algebra

$f(n) = $ $f(1)$ $ + $ d $(n - 1)$

REFLECT

2a. The first term of an arithmetic sequence is 4 and the common difference is 10. Explain how you can find the 6th term of the sequence.

Evaluate the explicit rule for an arithmetic sequence when $n = 6$:

$f(6) = 4 + 10(6 - 1) = 54.$

2b. What information do you need to know in order to find the 8th term of an arithmetic sequence by using its recursive rule?

The 7th term and the common difference

2c. What is the recursive rule for the sequence $f(n) = 2 + (-3)(n - 1)$?

$f(1) = 2$ and $f(n) = f(n - 1) - 3$ for $n \geq 2$

© Houghton Mifflin Harcourt Publishing Company

Questioning Strategies

- What is a recursive rule for an arithmetic sequence with a first term of 10 and a common difference of -4?
$f(1) = 10$ and $f(n) = f(n - 1) - 4$ for $n \geq 2$

- What is an explicit rule for an arithmetic sequence with a first term of $\frac{1}{2}$ and a common difference of $\frac{3}{4}$? $f(n) = \frac{1}{2} + \frac{3}{4}(n - 1)$

- If you know the second term and the common difference of an arithmetic sequence, can you write an explicit rule for the sequence? If so, explain how. **Yes; you can subtract the common difference from the second term to get the first term. Then, you can substitute the first term and the common difference into the general explicit rule to get the explicit rule for the sequence.**

Teaching Strategy

After students have written the general algebraic formulas for recursive and explicit rules for arithmetic sequences, review the process for substituting values for variables in a formula. In both the general recursive and explicit rules, values must be inserted for $f(1)$, the first term in the sequence, and d, the common difference. Remind students that the qualification $n \geq 2$ must be included in the recursive rule and guide students to understand why this is the case. Also, point out that the common difference d is added to $f(n - 1)$ in the recursive rule, while d is multiplied by $n - 1$ in the explicit rule.

/ MATHEMATICAL
/ PRACTICE

Highlighting the Standards

2 EXPLORE and its Reflect questions address Mathematical Practice Standard 2 (Reason abstractly and quantitatively). Students use a specific arithmetic sequence to help them obtain general rules, both recursive and explicit, for arithmetic sequences. They can then use the general rules to obtain rules for other specific arithmetic sequences and to transform a rule given in one form into the other form (recursive to explicit or explicit to recursive).

Questioning Strategies

- How is the domain of a linear function restricted if the function defines an arithmetic sequence? **The domain is restricted to a subset of the set of integers.**

- Why is the slope of a linear function that defines an arithmetic sequence equal to the common difference of the arithmetic sequence? **The slope of a linear function describes the vertical change for 1 unit of horizontal change in the graph of the function. If 1 unit of horizontal change corresponds to a change of 1 in the position number for the sequence, then the vertical change corresponds to the common difference between two terms.**

Differentiated Instruction

Visual learners may benefit by enhancing the graph in **3** EXAMPLE . For instance, by drawing arrows to identify rise and run, students may be able to more clearly see the relationship between the slope of the linear function and the common difference of the arithmetic sequence.

EXTRA EXAMPLE

If the points plotted on the graph in **3** EXAMPLE were changed to $(1, 25)$, $(2, 75)$, $(3, 125)$, and $(4, 175)$, what explicit rule would you write for the sequence shown in the graph?
$f(n) = 25 + 50(n - 1)$

---

3 EXAMPLE CC.9-12.F.LE.2 **Relating Arithmetic Sequences and Linear Functions**

The graph shows how the cost of a rafting trip depends on the number of passengers. Write an explicit rule for the sequence of costs.

Whitewater Rafting

A Represent the sequence in a table.

n	1	2	3	4
$f(n)$	75	100	125	150

B Examine the sequence.

Is the sequence arithmetic? Explain how you know.

Yes; the difference between consecutive terms is constant.

What is the common difference? ___25___

C Write an explicit rule for the sequence.

$f(n) = f(1) + d(n-1)$ Write the general rule.

$f(n) = $ _75_ $+$ _25_ $(n-1)$ Substitute _75_ for $f(1)$ and _25_ for d.

So, the sequence has the rule $f(n) = 75 + 25(n-1)$, where n is the number of passengers and $f(n)$ is the cost of the trip in dollars.

REFLECT

3a. An arithmetic sequence is equivalent to a linear function with a restricted domain. On the graph above, draw the line that passes through the given points. Then write a linear function of the form $f(n) = mn + b$ for the line that you drew and give the function's domain.

$f(n) = 25n + 50; \{1, 2, 3, 4\}$

3b. Show that the explicit rule for the sequence is equivalent to the linear function. Justify the steps you take.

$f(n) = 75 + 25(n-1)$	Explicit rule
$f(n) = 75 + 25n - 25$	Distributive property
$f(n) = 25n + 50$	Commutative and associative properties

3c. What is the relationship between the slope of the line that you drew and the common difference of the arithmetic sequence?

The slope is equal to the common difference.

Subscript Notation You have used function notation to describe sequences. You can also describe sequences by using subscript notation. In subscript notation, a_n represents the nth term of the sequence. For example, $a_5 = 8$ means that the 5th term of a sequence is 8.

The explicit rule for an arithmetic sequence using subscript notation is
$a_n = a_1 + d(n-1)$.

4 EXAMPLE CC.9-12.F.LE.2 **Writing an Arithmetic Sequence Given Two Terms**

Each day Xavier waters his plants using water from a rain barrel. On May 6, the barrel held 45 gallons of water, and on May 11, the barrel held 30 gallons of water.

The amount of water in the barrel over time is an arithmetic sequence where a_n is the number of gallons on the nth day in May. Write an explicit rule for the sequence using subscript notation.

A Identify the given terms in the sequence.

$a_6 = 45$ There were 45 gallons in May 6, so the 6th term of the sequence is 45.

$a_{11} = 30$ There were 30 gallons in May 11, so the __11th__ term of the sequence is __30__.

B Find the common difference.

The common difference is equal to the slope of the related linear function.

$m = \dfrac{y_2 - y_1}{x_2 - x_1}$ Slope formula

$m = \dfrac{30 - 45}{11 - 6}$ Use (6, 45) for (x_1, y_1) and (11, 30) for (x_2, y_2).

$m = -3$ Simplify.

The common difference is __−3__.

C Find the first term of the sequence.

$a_n = a_1 + d(n-1)$ Write the explicit rule.

$45 = a_1 + -3\left(6 - 1\right)$ Substitute 45 for a_n, 6 for n, and __−3__ for d.

$45 = a_1 + -15$ Simplify.

$60 = a_1$ Solve for a_1.

D Write the explicit rule.

$a_n = a_1 + d(n-1)$ Write the general rule.

$a_n = 60 + -3(n-1)$ Substitute __60__ for a_1 and __−3__ for d.

Questioning Strategies

- How is an explicit rule for an arithmetic sequence written using function notation related to an explicit rule for an arithmetic sequence written using subscript notation? **When position numbers start with 1, the variable n is used in both notations to represent the nth term of the sequence, which in both cases is found by adding the first term to the product of $(n - 1)$ and the common difference.**

- How can you determine by what number of gallons the amount of water in the rain barrel increases or decreases each day? **Since the common difference is -3, this tells you that the amount of water in the rain barrel decreases by 3 gallons each day.**

- How can you find how much water is in the rain barrel on May 13? **Evaluate the explicit rule for $n = 13$: $a_{13} = 60 + (-3)(13 - 1) = 24$. There are 24 gallons of water in the rain barrel on May 13.**

- What is the recursive rule for the arithmetic sequence that describes the amount of water in the rain barrel over time? **$a_1 = 60$ and $a_n = a_{n-1} - 3$ for $n \geq 2$**

Avoid Common Errors

Students may use the wrong sign in rules for arithmetic sequences when the common difference is a negative number. Remind students that the common difference is the difference between a term and the one *before* it, and this difference will be negative if a term is less than the one before it.

EXTRA EXAMPLE

What would be the explicit rule for the sequence in **4 EXAMPLE** if on May 5 the barrel held 50 gallons of water and on May 15 the barrel held 30 gallons of water? $a_n = 58 + (-2)(n - 1)$

CLOSE

Essential Question

How can you write a rule for an arithmetic sequence?

To write a recursive rule, assume $f(1)$ is given and use the general formula $f(n) = f(n - 1) + d$ for $n \geq 2$, where d is the common difference. To write an explicit rule, use the general formula $f(n) = f(1) + d(n - 1)$, where $f(1)$ is the first term in the sequence and d is the common difference.

Summarize

Have students make a graphic organizer outlining the process for writing explicit and recursive rules for sequences. Include details about how the first term of the sequence and the common difference are incorporated into each rule.

PRACTICE

Where skills are taught	Where skills are practiced
1 EXAMPLE	EXS. 1–4
3 EXAMPLE	EX. 5
4 EXAMPLE	EXS. 6–8

Exercises 9–12: Given a rule for an arithmetic sequence, students write a recursive rule as an explicit rule, or an explicit rule as a recursive rule.

Exercise 13: Students write an explicit rule for an arithmetic sequence to solve a problem that involves finding the nth term of the sequence.

REFLECT

4a. Why does it make sense that the common difference is negative in this situation?

The amount of water decreased from May 6 to May 11. A decrease

indicates that an amount is being subtracted, so the common difference

will be negative.

4b. Explain how you could determine when the rain barrel will be empty (assuming no more water is added to the barrel).

Find n when $f(n) = 0$. Solve the equation $0 = 60 + (-3)(n - 1)$ to get $n = 21$.

The barrel will be empty on May 21.

PRACTICE

Write a recursive rule and an explicit rule for each arithmetic sequence.

1. $3, 7, 11, 15, \ldots$

$f(1) = 3$ and $f(n) = f(n - 1) + 4$ for $n \geq 2$; $f(n) = 3 + 4(n - 1)$

2. $19, 9, -1, -11, \ldots$

$f(1) = 19$ and $f(n) = f(n - 1) - 10$ for $n \geq 2$; $f(n) = 19 + (-10)(n - 1)$

3. $1, \frac{5}{2}, 4, \frac{11}{2}, \ldots$

$f(1) = 1$ and $f(n) = f(n - 1) + \frac{3}{2}$ for $n \geq 2$; $f(n) = 1 + \frac{3}{2}(n - 1)$

4. Carrie borrowed money interest-free to pay for a car repair. She is repaying the loan in equal monthly payments.

Monthly Payment Number	n	1	2	3	4	5
Loan Balance ($)	$f(n)$	840	720	600	480	360

a. Explain how you know that the sequence of loan balances is arithmetic.

The difference between consecutive loan balances is a constant, −120.

b. Write recursive and explicit rules for the sequence of loan balances.

$f(1) = 840$ and $f(n) = f(n - 1) - 120$ for $n \geq 2$; $f(n) = 840 + (-120)(n - 1)$

c. How many months will it take Carrie to pay off the loan? Explain.

8 months; $f(8) = 0$, so the 8th payment brings the loan balance to 0.

d. How much did Carrie borrow? Explain.

$960; the initial balance is $f(0) = 960$.

---

5. The graph shows the lengths of the rows formed by various numbers of grocery carts when they are nested together.

Nested Grocery Carts

a. Write an explicit rule for the sequence of row lengths.

$f(n) = 38 + 12(n - 1)$

b. What is the length of a row of 25 nested carts?

326 inches, or 27 feet 2 inches

6. Jen is planting beans on a triangular plot of ground. The numbers of beans in each row form an arithmetic sequence where a_n is the number of beans in row n.

a. She plants 7 beans in the second row and 22 beans in the seventh row. Write an explicit rule for the sequence using subscript notation.

$a_n = 4 + 3(n - 1)$

b. How many beans does she plant in the fifth row? ___16___

Write an explicit rule for each arithmetic sequence based on the given terms from the sequence.

7. $a_3 = 30$ and $a_5 = 78$

$a_n = 14 + 8(n - 1)$

8. $a_5 = 8.8$ and $a_7 = 8.4$

$a_n = 9.6 + (-0.2)(n - 1)$

Each given rule represents an arithmetic sequence. If the given rule is recursive, write it as an explicit rule. If the given rule is explicit, write it as a recursive rule. Assume that $f(1)$ is the first term of the sequence.

9. $f(n) = 6 + 5(n - 1)$

$f(1) = 6$; $f(n) = f(n - 1) + 5$ for $n \geq 2$

10. $a_n = 2.5 + (-4)(n - 1)$

$a_1 = 2.5$; $a_n = a_{n-1} - 4$ for $n \geq 2$

11. $f(1) = 8$; $f(n) = f(n - 1) - 2$ for $n \geq 2$

$f(n) = 8 + (-2)(n - 1)$

12. $a_1 = -5$; $a_n = a_{n-1} + 7$ for $n \geq 2$

$a_n = -5 + 7(n - 1)$

13. Each stair on a staircase has a height of 7.5 inches.

a. Write an explicit rule for an arithmetic sequence that gives the height (in inches) of the nth stair above the base of the staircase.

$f(n) = 7.5 + 7.5(n - 1)$

b. What is the fourth term of the sequence, and what does it represent in this situation?

30; the fourth stair is 30 inches above the base of the staircase.

Assign these pages to help your students practice
and apply important lesson concepts. For
additional exercises, see the Student Edition.

Answers

Additional Practice

1. $-17; -44$

2. Not arithmetic

3. $\frac{1}{2}; \frac{33}{10}$

4. Not arithmetic

5. 142

6. -0.7

7. -30.1

8. 49.75

9. 17, 31, 45

10. 5, 14

11. 18, 29, 40, 51

12. 29, 23, 17, 11, 5, -1

13. 28.8

14. 12.5

15. 22.6

16. -23.25

17. 19 tables

Problem Solving

1. a. $a_n = a_1 + (n-1)d$

b. Let $a_n = a_{20}$ and $a_1 = a_{12}$; replace 1 in
$(n-1)$ with 12; replace n in $(n-1)$ with 20;
substitute 385 and 665 for a_{12} and a_{20}; and
calculate d.

c. 35; possible answer: the number of pages
Violet must read each day

d. 0 pages; $385 = a_1 + (35)(12-1)$; so $a_1 = 0$;
and a_1 represents the number of pages for
day 1.

e. $a_5 = 0 + (35)(5-1)$; 140 pages

2. a. $a_n = a_1 + (n-1)(2)$; 20 pages

b. $S_n = 6\left(\frac{10+20}{2}\right)$; 90 pages

3. D

4. G

9-3

Additional Practice

Determine whether each sequence could be arithmetic. If so, find the common difference and the next term.

1. 41, 24, 7, –10, –27, ...

2. 6, –6, 6, –6, 6, –6, 6, –6, ...

3. $\dfrac{4}{5}, \dfrac{13}{10}, \dfrac{9}{5}, \dfrac{23}{10}, \dfrac{14}{5}, ...$

4. 2, 4, 8, 16, 32, 64, ...

Find the 12th term of each arithmetic sequence.

5. 21, 32, 43, 54, 65, ...

6. 3.7, 3.3, 2.9, 2.5, 2.1, ...

7. 1.8, –1.1, –4, –6.9, –9.8, ...

8. –8, –2.75, 2.5, 7.75, 13, ...

Find the missing terms in each arithmetic sequence.

9. 3, __, __, __, 59, ...

10. –4, __, __, 23, ...

11. 7, __, __, __, __, 62, ...

12. 35, __, __, __, __, __, __, –7, ...

Find the 10th term of each arithmetic sequence.

13. $a_4 = 12$ and $a_7 = 20.4$

14. $a_3 = 37$ and $a_{17} = -12$

15. $a_{13} = -5$ and $a_{18} = -51$

16. $a_{25} = 18$ and $a_{41} = 62$

Solve.

17. A banquet hall uses tables that seat 4, one person on each side. For a large party, the tables are positioned end to end in a long row. Two tables will seat 6, three tables will seat 8, and four tables will seat 10. How many tables should be set end to end to seat 40?

_____

Problem Solving

Violet has the book and the assignment for her literature class. Counting today, Monday, as day 1, she sees that she must read through page 385 by day 12, and through page 665 by day 20.

1. If Violet reads an equal number of pages each day, how many pages will she have read by this Friday?

   a. First write a rule for the *n*th term of an arithmetic sequence that represents the number of pages, a_n, that she will have read after *n* days.   _____

   b. Explain how to find the common difference by using the rule with the given data.

   _____

   c. What is the common difference, and what does it mean in terms of Violet's assignment?

   _____

   d. How many pages must Violet read today, Monday? Explain how you know this.

   _____

   e. Use the rule to find the number of pages Violet will have read by Friday.   _____

2. Violet looks at the table of contents in her book. She sees that each of the first 6 chapters is 2 pages longer than the preceding chapter, with the first chapter having 10 pages.

   a. How many pages are in the sixth chapter? Write a rule for the number of pages, a_n, in chapter *n*. Then solve for $n = 6$.   _____

   b. How pages are in the first 6 chapters? Use the formula for the sum of the first *n* terms of an arithmetic sequence.   _____

Choose the letter for the best answer.

3. Violet reads the first 385 pages by day 6. Which expression gives the minimum pages she must read each day to finish 665 pages by day 20?

   A $6\left(\dfrac{665 + 385}{2}\right)$

   B $\dfrac{665 - 385}{6}$

   C $14\left(\dfrac{665 + 385}{2}\right)$

   D $\dfrac{665 - 385}{14}$

4. Page 385 of Violet's book is 15 pages before the end of a 40-page chapter. If chapter 1 contains 10 pages, which chapter contains page 385?

   F Chapter 15

   G Chapter 16

   H Chapter 19

   J Chapter 25

Geometric Sequences and Series
Going Deeper

Essential question: *How can you write a rule for a geometric sequence and find the sum of a finite geometric series?*

COMMON
CORE
Standards for Mathematical Content

CC.9-12.A.SSE.1 Interpret expressions that represent a quantity in terms of its context.*

CC.9-12.A.SSE.1a Interpret parts of an expression, such as terms, factors, and coefficients.*

CC.9-12.A.SSE.1b Interpret complicated expressions by viewing one or more of their parts as a single entity.*

CC.9-12.A.SSE.4 Derive the formula for the sum of a finite geometric series (when the common ratio is not 1), and use the formula to solve problems.*

CC.9-12.F.BF.1 Write a function that describes a relationship between two quantities.*

CC.9-12.F.BF.1a Determine an explicit expression, a recursive process ... from a context.*

CC.9-12.F.BF.2 Write ... geometric sequences both recursively and with an explicit formula, use them to model situations, and translate between the two forms.*

CC.9-12.F.LE.2 Construct ... exponential functions, including ... geometric sequences, given a graph, a description of a relationship, or two input-output pairs (include reading these from a table).*

Vocabulary
geometric sequence

common ratio

series

geometric series

Prerequisites
Arithmetic sequences

Math Background

Previously, students studied arithmetic sequences and wrote general recursive and explicit rules for them. Students used these rules to solve real-world problems involving arithmetic sequences. In this lesson, they will study the same aspects of geometric sequences as they learn to recognize a geometric sequence by seeing that each term is related to the previous term by a common ratio. Students will use the general rules for geometric sequences to write both recursive and explicit rules for specific sequences. Students will also learn about geometric series, which are formed by adding the terms of a geometric sequence.

INTRODUCE

Review what students have previously learned about arithmetic sequences. Make sure that students understand how to use the general recursive and explicit rules for arithmetic sequences to write specific rules, including how recursive rules can be rewritten as explicit rules and vice versa.

Name_____ Class_____ Date_____

Geometric Sequences and Series
Going Deeper

Essential question: *How can you write a rule for a geometric sequence and find the sum of a finite geometric series?*

In a **geometric sequence**, the ratio of consecutive terms is constant. The constant ratio is called the **common ratio**, often written as *r*.

Video Tutor

CC.9-12.F.BF.2

1 EXAMPLE Writing Rules for a Geometric Sequence

Makers of Japanese swords in the 1400s repeatedly folded and hammered the metal to form layers. The folding process increased the strength of the sword.

The table shows how the number of layers depends on the number of folds. Write a recursive rule and an explicit rule for the geometric sequence described by the table.

Number of Folds	n	1	2	3	4	5
Number of Layers	$f(n)$	2	4	8	16	32

A Find the common ratio by calculating the ratios of consecutive terms.

$\frac{4}{2} = $ 2 $\frac{8}{4} = $ 2 $\frac{16}{8} = $ 2 $\frac{32}{16} = $ 2

The common ratio, r, is ___2___

B Write a recursive rule for the sequence.

$f(1) = $ 2 and   The first term is ___2___

$f(n) = f(n-1) \cdot $ 2 for $n \geq 2$ Every other term is the ___product___ of the previous term and the common ratio.

C Write an explicit rule for the sequence by writing each term as the product of the first term and a power of the common ratio.

n	$f(n)$
1	$2(2)^0 = 2$
2	$2(2)^1 = 4$
3	$2(2)^2 = 8$
4	$2(2)^3 = 16$
5	$2(2)^4 = 32$

Generalize the results from the table: $f(n) = $ 2 $\cdot 2^{n-1}$

© Houghton Mifflin Harcourt Publishing Company

REFLECT

1a. Explain how you know that the sequence 4, 12, 36, 108, 324, … is a geometric sequence.

The ratios of consecutive terms are constant; the common ratio is 3.

1b. A geometric sequence has a common ratio of 5. If you know that the 6th term of the sequence is 30, how could you find the 7th term?

Multiply the 6th term by the common ratio to get 150 as the 7th term.

CC.9-12.F.BF.2

2 EXPLORE Writing General Rules for Geometric Sequences

Use the geometric sequence 6, 24, 96, 384, 1536, … to help you write a recursive rule and an explicit rule for any geometric sequence. For the general rules, the values of n are consecutive integers starting with 1.

A Find the common ratio.

Numbers	**Algebra**
6, 24, 96, 384, 1536, …	$f(1), f(2), f(3), f(4), f(5), …$
Common ratio = 4	Common ratio = r

B Write a recursive rule.

Numbers	**Algebra**
$f(1) = $ 6 and	Given $f(1)$,
$f(n) = f(n-1) \cdot $ 4 for $n \geq 2$	$f(n) = f(n-1) \cdot$ r for $n \geq 2$

C Write an explicit rule.

Numbers	**Algebra**
$f(n) = $ 6 $\cdot$ 4^{n-1}	$f(n) = f(1) \cdot$ r^{n-1}

REFLECT

2a. The first term of a geometric sequence is 81 and the common ratio is $\frac{1}{3}$. Explain how you could find the 4th term of the sequence.

Evaluate the explicit rule for a geometric sequence for $n = 4$: $f(4) = 81\left(\frac{1}{3}\right)^{4-1} = 3$.

2b. What information do you need to know in order to find the 5th term of a geometric sequence by using its explicit rule?

The first term and the common ratio

2c. What is the recursive rule for the sequence $f(n) = 5(4)^{n-1}$?

$f(1) = 5$ and $f(n) = f(n-1) \cdot 4$ for $n \geq 2$

© Houghton Mifflin Harcourt Publishing Company

1 EXAMPLE

Questioning Strategies

- In part C, why does the explicit rule for the sequence involve raising the common ratio to the power $n - 1$ and not n? **Fold 1 ($n = 1$) results in 2 layers. The number of layers doubles with fold 2 ($n = 2$) and each subsequent fold. So, the explicit rule must generate the sequence $f(1) = 2 \cdot 2^0$, $f(2) = 2 \cdot 2^1$, $f(3) = 2 \cdot 2^2$, ... The power of 2 that the initial 2 layers is multiplied by is always 1 less than the fold number.**

- Which rule, the recursive rule or the explicit rule, would be more useful in determining the number of layers in the sword metal after the 12th fold? Explain your reasoning. **The explicit rule is more useful because you can easily evaluate $f(12) = 4{,}096$ to find the number of layers after the 12th fold. To use the recursive rule, you would have to start with $f(1)$ and calculate the number of layers for each successive fold.**

- How would the recursive rule and explicit rule change if the table included a starting value of 1 layer with 0 folds? **Recursive rule: $f(0) = 1$ and $f(n) = f(n - 1) \cdot 2$ for $n \geq 1$; explicit rule: $f(n) = 2^n$**

Differentiated Instruction

Kinesthetic learners may benefit by acting out the situation by folding sheets of paper to represent the sheets of metal folded by the sword smiths.

EXTRA EXAMPLE

n	1	2	3	4	5
$f(n)$	5	10	20	40	80

Write a recursive rule and an explicit rule for the geometric sequence described by the table.

$f(1) = 5$ and $f(n) = f(n - 1) \cdot 2$ for $n \geq 2$;
$f(n) = 5 \cdot 2^{n - 1}$

Questioning Strategies

- What is a recursive rule for a geometric sequence with a first term of 3 and a common ratio of -2? $f(1) = 3$ and $f(n) = f(n - 1) \cdot (-2)$ for $n \geq 2$

- What is an explicit rule for a geometric sequence with a first term of $\frac{5}{6}$ and a common ratio of $\frac{1}{3}$? $f(n) = \frac{5}{6} \cdot \left(\frac{1}{3}\right)^{n - 1}$

- If you know the second term and the common ratio of a geometric sequence, can you write an explicit rule for the sequence? If so, explain how. **Yes; you can divide the second term by the common ratio to get the first term. Then, you can substitute the first term and the common ratio into the general explicit rule to get the explicit rule for the sequence.**

Teaching Strategy

After students have written the general algebraic formulas for recursive and explicit rules for geometric sequences, compare the process for substituting values for the variables in the formulas for geometric sequences with the process for arithmetic sequences. Point out the similarities such as the use of a common difference in arithmetic sequences and the use of a common ratio in geometric sequences. Also, point out the differences such as how the common difference is added in a recursive rule for an arithmetic sequence, while the common ratio is multiplied in a recursive rule for a geometric sequence.

MATHEMATICAL PRACTICE   **Highlighting the Standards**

2 EXPLORE and its Reflect questions address Mathematical Practice Standard 2 (Reason abstractly and quantitatively). Students use a specific geometric sequence to help them obtain general rules, both recursive and explicit, for geometric sequences. They can then use the general rules to obtain rules for other specific geometric sequences and to transform a rule given in one form into the other form (recursive to explicit or explicit to recursive).

---

3 EXAMPLE — Relating Geometric Sequences and Exponential Functions

CC.9-12.F.LE.2

The graph shows the heights to which a ball bounces after it is dropped.
Write an explicit rule for the sequence of bounce heights.

A Represent the sequence in a table.

n	1	2	3	4
$f(n)$	100	80	64	51.2

Ball Bounces

B Examine the sequence.

Is the sequence geometric? Explain.

Yes; the ratio of consecutive terms is constant.

What is the common ratio? __0.8__

C Write an explicit rule for the sequence.

$f(n) = f(1) \cdot r^{n-1}$ Write the general rule.

$f(n) = $ __100__ $\cdot$ __0.8__$^{n-1}$ Substitute __100__ for $f(1)$ and __0.8__ for r.

So, the sequence has the rule $f(n) = 100(0.8)^{n-1}$ where n is the bounce

number and $f(n)$ is the __height of the bounce in centimeters__.

REFLECT

3a. A geometric sequence is equivalent to an exponential function with a restricted domain. On the graph above, draw an exponential curve that passes through the given points. Then write an exponential function of the form $f(n) = ab^n$ for the curve that you drew and give the function's domain.

$f(n) = 125(0.8)^n$; {1, 2, 3, 4}

3b. Show that the explicit rule for the sequence is equivalent to the exponential function. Justify the steps you take.

$f(n) = 100 \cdot 0.8^{n-1}$	Explicit rule
$f(n) = 100 \cdot 0.8^n \cdot 0.8^{-1}$	Product of powers rule
$f(n) = 125(0.8)^n$	Commutative and associative properties

The explicit and recursive rules for a geometric sequence can also be written in subscript notation.

Explicit: $a_n = a_1 \cdot r^{n-1}$

Recursive: a_1 is given and $a_n = a_{n-1} \cdot r$ for $n \geq 2$

4 EXAMPLE — Writing a Geometric Sequence Given Two Terms

CC.9-12.F.LE.2

The shutter speed settings on a camera form a geometric sequence where a_n is the shutter speed in seconds and n is the setting number. The fifth setting on the camera is $\frac{1}{60}$ second, and the seventh setting on the camera is $\frac{1}{15}$ second. Write an explicit rule for the sequence using subscript notation.

A Identify the given terms in the sequence.

$a_5 = \frac{1}{60}$ The fifth setting is $\frac{1}{60}$ second, so the 5th term of the sequence is $\frac{1}{60}$.

$a_7 = \frac{1}{15}$ The seventh setting is $\frac{1}{15}$ second, so the __7th__ term of the sequence is __$\frac{1}{15}$__.

B Find the common ratio.

$a_7 = a_6 \cdot r$ Write the recursive rule for a_7.

$a_6 = $ __a_5__ $\cdot r$ Write the recursive rule for a_6.

$a_7 = $ __a_5__ $\cdot$ __r__ $\cdot r$ Substitute the expression for a_6 into the rule for a_7.

$\frac{1}{15} = $ __$\frac{1}{60}$__ $\cdot r^2$ Substitute $\frac{1}{15}$ for a_7 and __$\frac{1}{60}$__ for a_5.

$4 = r^2$ Multiply both sides by 60.

$2 = r$ Definition of positive square root

C Find the first term of the sequence.

$a_n = a_1 \cdot r^{n-1}$ Write the explicit rule.

$\frac{1}{60} = a_1 \cdot$ __2__$^{5-1}$ Substitute $\frac{1}{60}$ for a_n, __2__ for r, and 5 for n.

$\frac{1}{60} = a_1 \cdot$ __16__   Simplify.

$\frac{1}{960} = a_1$ Divide both sides by 16.

D Write the explicit rule.

$a_n = a_1 \cdot r^{n-1}$ Write the general rule.

$a_n = $ __$\frac{1}{960}$__ $\cdot$ __2__$^{n-1}$ Substitute __$\frac{1}{960}$__ for a_1 and __2__ for r.

Questioning Strategies

- How is the domain of an exponential function restricted if the function defines a geometric sequence? **The domain is restricted to a subset of the set of integers.**

- Compare the graph of a geometric sequence for which the common ratio r is greater than 1 with the graph of a geometric sequence for which $0 < r < 1$. **The graph for the geometric sequence with $r > 1$ rises from left to right as x increases, at first slowly and then at an increasingly fast rate. The graph for $0 < r < 1$ falls from left to right as x increases, at first quickly and then at an increasingly slower rate. The graph for $r > 1$ is similar to the graph of an exponential growth function, while the graph for $0 < r < 1$ is similar to the graph of an exponential decay function.**

Avoid Common Errors

When looking at the graph with points plotted for only four values of n, students may incorrectly determine that a geometric sequence is equivalent to a linear function rather than an exponential function. To avoid this misunderstanding, have students extend the table and graph.

EXTRA EXAMPLE

If the points plotted on the graph in **3** EXAMPLE were changed to (1, 800), (2, 400), (3, 200), and (4, 100), what explicit rule would you write for the sequence shown in the graph? $f(n) = 800 \cdot 0.5^{n-1}$

Questioning Strategies

- How is an explicit rule for a geometric sequence written using function notation related to an explicit rule for a geometric sequence written using subscript notation? **When the position numbers start with 1, the variable n is used in both notations to represent the nth term of the sequence, which in both cases is found by multiplying the first term by the common ratio raised to the power of $(n - 1)$.**

- What is the relationship between the common ratio 2 and the shutter speed of the camera? **The time that the shutter takes to open and close is increased by a factor of 2 each time the setting number is increased by 1.**

- At what setting is the shutter speed of this camera about 1 second? Explain. **setting 11;**
  $$a_{11} = \frac{1}{960} \cdot 2^{11-1} = \frac{1}{960} \cdot 1024 \approx 1.07$$

- What is the recursive rule for the geometric sequence that describes the shutter speed on the camera in relation to the setting number n?
  $$a_1 = \frac{1}{960} \text{ and } a_n = a_{n-1} \cdot 2 \text{ for } n \geq 2$$

Teaching Strategy

Students may be interested in learning more about geometric sequences and photography. Encourage them to explore the relationship between shutter speed and exposure time. Point out that f-stop settings on a camera can also be described by a geometric sequence, with each increasing f-stop corresponding to an aperture, or lens opening, with half the light-gathering area as the previous f-stop.

EXTRA EXAMPLE

What would be the explicit rule for the geometric sequence in **4** EXAMPLE if the second shutter speed setting was $\frac{1}{500}$ and the fourth shutter speed setting was $\frac{1}{125}$? $a_n = \frac{1}{1000} \cdot 2^{n-1}$

REFLECT

4a. When finding the common ratio, why can you ignore the negative square root of 4 when solving the equation $4 = r^2$?

If r were negative, some of the terms of the sequence would be negative.

Negative terms do not make sense in this situation because the terms

represent shutter speeds.

4b. If you graphed the explicit rule for the sequence, what would the graph look like?

The graph would be a set of discrete points showing exponential growth.

CC.9-12.A.SSE.4
5 EXPLORE Investigating a Geometric Series

A Start with a rectangular sheet of paper and assume the sheet has an area of 1 square unit. Cut the sheet in half and lay down one of the half-pieces. Then cut the remaining piece in half, and lay down one of the quarter-pieces. Continue the process: At each stage, cut the remaining piece in half, and lay down one of the halves. As you lay pieces down, arrange them to rebuild the original sheet of paper.

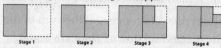

Stage 1   Stage 2   Stage 3   Stage 4

B Complete the table below by expressing the total area of the paper that has been laid down in two ways:

* as the sum of the areas of the pieces that have been laid down, and
* as the difference of 1 and the area of the remaining piece.

Stage	Sum of the areas of the pieces that have been laid down	Difference of 1 and the area of the remaining piece
1	$\frac{1}{2}$	$1 - \frac{1}{2} = \frac{1}{2}$
2	$\frac{1}{2} + \frac{1}{4} = \frac{3}{4}$	$1 - \frac{1}{4} = \frac{3}{4}$
3	$\frac{1}{2} + \frac{1}{4} + \frac{1}{8} = \frac{7}{8}$	$1 - \frac{1}{8} = \frac{7}{8}$
4	$\frac{1}{2} + \frac{1}{4} + \frac{1}{8} + \frac{1}{16} = \frac{15}{16}$	$1 - \frac{1}{16} = \frac{15}{16}$

REFLECT

5a. Describe the sequence formed by the areas of the pieces that have been laid down.

It is a geometric sequence with common ratio $\frac{1}{2}$.

5b. Make a generalization: What is the total area of the paper that has been laid down at the nth stage? Write the area as a sum and as a difference.

$\frac{1}{2} + \frac{1}{4} + \cdots + \left(\frac{1}{2}\right)^n$ or $1 - \left(\frac{1}{2}\right)^n$

A **series** is the expression formed by adding the terms of a sequence. A **geometric series** is the expression formed by adding the terms of a geometric sequence. In the Explore, the areas $\frac{1}{2}, \frac{1}{4}, \frac{1}{8}$, and $\frac{1}{16}$ form a geometric sequence. The expression $\frac{1}{2} + \frac{1}{4} + \frac{1}{8} + \frac{1}{16}$ is a geometric series. You can derive a formula for the sum of a geometric series.

CC.9-12.A.SSE.4
6 EXPLORE Deriving a Formula for the Sum of a Geometric Series

Consider the geometric series $a_1 + a_1r + a_1r^2 + a_1r^3 + \cdots + a_1r^{n-1}$. The series has n terms. Let S_n be the sum of the geometric series.

A Find a simplified expression for $S_n - rS_n$.

$S_n = a_1 + a_1r + a_1r^2 + a_1r^3 + \cdots + a_1r^{n-1}$ Write S_n.

$rS_n = a_1r + a_1r^2 + a_1r^3 + a_1r^4 + \cdots + a_1r^n$ Multiply each term of S_n by r.

Align like terms and subtract.

$S_n = a_1 + a_1r + a_1r^2 + a_1r^3 + \cdots + a_1r^{n-1}$

$rS_n = \qquad a_1r + a_1r^2 + a_1r^3 + \cdots + a_1r^{n-1} + a_1r^n$

$S_n - rS_n = a_1 + 0 + 0 + 0 + \cdots + 0 - a_1r^n$

So, $S_n - rS_n = \underline{a_1 - a_1r^n}$.

B Factor and divide by $1 - r$.

$S_n - rS_n = a_1 - a_1r^n$ Write the result from part A.

$S_n(1 - r) = a_1\left(1 - r^n\right)$ Factor both sides.

$S_n = a_1\left(\dfrac{1 - r^n}{1 - r}\right)$ Divide both sides by $1 - r$.

© Houghton Mifflin Harcourt Publishing Company

Questioning Strategies

- What happens to the total area of the pieces laid down as the number n of stages increases? **As n increases, the total area of the pieces laid down gets closer to 1, the area of the paper.**

- Suppose you take a sheet of paper with an area of 1 square unit and cut it into two pieces with one piece having twice the area of the other. This means that one piece has an area of $\frac{2}{3}$ square unit while the other has an area of $\frac{1}{3}$ square unit. You lay down the larger piece. You cut the remaining piece into two pieces with one piece having twice the area of the other, and you lay down the larger piece. You continue this process of cutting the remaining piece into two pieces having a 2 : 1 ratio of areas and laying down the larger piece. Complete the table.

Stage	Sum of the areas of the pieces that have been laid down	Difference of 1 and the area of the remaining piece
1	$\frac{2}{3}$	$1 - \frac{1}{3} = \frac{2}{3}$
2	$\frac{2}{3} + \frac{2}{3}\left(\frac{1}{3}\right) = \frac{8}{9}$	$1 - \frac{1}{9} = \frac{8}{9}$
3	$\frac{2}{3} + \frac{2}{3}\left(\frac{1}{3}\right) + \frac{2}{3}\left(\frac{1}{9}\right) = \frac{26}{27}$	$1 - \frac{1}{27} = \frac{26}{27}$

- Generalize the second column of the table above: What is the sum of the areas of the pieces that have been laid down at the nth stage?
$\frac{2}{3} + \frac{2}{3}\left(\frac{1}{3}\right) + \frac{2}{3}\left(\frac{1}{9}\right) + \cdots + \frac{2}{3}\left(\frac{1}{3}\right)^{n-1}$

- Generalize the third column of the table above: What is the difference of 1 and the area of the remaining piece at the nth stage? $1 - \left(\frac{1}{3}\right)^{n}$

Differentiated Instruction

Learners who have trouble visualizing area may benefit from using a strip of paper instead of a sheet of paper. By starting with a strip of paper whose length is taken to be 1 unit, they can fold it in half, cut at the crease, and lay down one of the halves. By repeating the process and laying down the successive halves end to end, students will still be able to complete the table in part B of the Explore, but they will be focused on length rather than area.

6 EXPLORE

Questioning Strategies

- When cutting paper into pieces having a 2 : 1 ratio of areas, you found the sum of the areas of the pieces that have been laid down to be $\frac{2}{3} + \frac{2}{3}\left(\frac{1}{3}\right) + \frac{2}{3}\left(\frac{1}{9}\right) + \cdots + \frac{2}{3}\left(\frac{1}{3}\right)^{n-1}$. Explain why this is a finite geometric series. **The terms form a geometric sequence with $a_1 = \frac{2}{3}$ and $r = \frac{1}{3}$.**

- When cutting paper into pieces having a 2 : 1 ratio of areas, you found difference of 1 and the area of the remaining piece to be $1 - \left(\frac{1}{3}\right)^{n}$. What is true about this difference and the sum of the areas of the pieces laid down? **They are equal.**

- Show that $\frac{2}{3} + \frac{2}{3}\left(\frac{1}{3}\right) + \frac{2}{3}\left(\frac{1}{9}\right) + \cdots + \frac{2}{3}\left(\frac{1}{3}\right)^{n-1} = 1 - \left(\frac{1}{3}\right)^{n}$ using the formula for the sum of a finite geometric series.
$\frac{2}{3} + \frac{2}{3}\left(\frac{1}{3}\right) + \frac{2}{3}\left(\frac{1}{9}\right) + \cdots$
$+ \frac{2}{3}\left(\frac{1}{3}\right)^{n-1} = \frac{2}{3}\left(\dfrac{1 - \left(\frac{1}{3}\right)^{n}}{1 - \frac{1}{3}}\right) = \frac{2}{3}\left(\dfrac{1 - \left(\frac{1}{3}\right)^{n}}{\frac{2}{3}}\right) =$
$1 - \left(\frac{1}{3}\right)^{n}$

Avoid Common Errors

Students may come away from Reflect Questions 6a and 6b with the mistaken idea that the formula for the sum of a finite geometric series with n terms is 1 minus the common ratio raised to the nth power. Point out that this formula is the result of a specific situation where the first term and the common ratio are both $\frac{1}{2}$. Emphasize to students that they should use the general formula $S_n = a_1\left(\dfrac{1 - r^n}{1 - r}\right)$ to find the sum of a finite geometric series.

REFLECT

6a. In the first Explore, you found that $\frac{1}{2} + \left(\frac{1}{2}\right)^2 + \left(\frac{1}{2}\right)^3 + \cdots + \left(\frac{1}{2}\right)^n = 1 - \left(\frac{1}{2}\right)^n$.

Show that you get the same sum for the geometric series by using the formula you derived above.

$a_1 = \frac{1}{2}$ and $r = \frac{1}{2}$, so $S_n = a_1\left(\frac{1-r^n}{1-r}\right) = \frac{1}{2}\left(\frac{1-\left(\frac{1}{2}\right)^n}{1-\frac{1}{2}}\right) = \frac{1}{2}\left(\frac{1-\left(\frac{1}{2}\right)^n}{\frac{1}{2}}\right) = 1 - \left(\frac{1}{2}\right)^n$

6b. What restrictions are there on the values of r that can be used in the formula for the sum of a geometric series?

The value of r cannot be 1, because $1 - r$ is in a denominator in the

formula for the sum, and division by zero is undefined.

Sum of a Finite Geometric Series

The sum S_n of the geometric series $a_1 + a_1 r + a_1 r^2 + a_1 r^3 + \cdots + a_1 r^{n-1}$ is

$$S_n = a_1\left(\frac{1-r^n}{1-r}\right)$$

where r is the common ratio, $r \neq 1$, and n is the number of terms.

CC.9-12.A.SSE.4

7 EXAMPLE Finding the Distance Traveled by a Bouncing Ball

The following geometric sequence models n bounce heights of a ball, where the heights are measured in inches. (The initial height from which the ball is dropped before the first bounce is not part of this sequence.)

$$80, 80(0.8), 80(0.8)^2, \ldots, 80(0.8)^{n-1}$$

Based on the model, what is the total vertical distance that the ball travels in 10 bounces?

A Write a geometric series for the total vertical distance the ball travels.

On the first bounce, the ball travels 80 inches up and 80 inches down. On the second bounce, it travels 64 inches up and 64 inches down. On every bounce, the ball travels twice the bounce height. So, the following geometric sequence models the 10 distances traveled.

160, 160 (0.8), 160 (0.8)^2, ..., 160 (0.8)^9

The following geometric series models the total distance traveled.

$S_n = 160 + $ 160 $(0.8) + $ 160 $(0.8)^2 + \cdots + $ 160 $(0.8)^9$

B Use the formula for the sum of a finite geometric series.

In this case, $n = $ 10 , $a_1 = $ 160 , and $r = $ 0.8 .

$S_n = a_1\left(\frac{1-r^n}{1-r}\right)$ Write the sum formula.

$= 160 \left(\dfrac{1-0.8^{10}}{1-0.8}\right)$ Substitute the values of n, a_1, and r.

$\approx$ 714   Round to the nearest inch.

So, the ball travels approximately ___714___ inches in 10 bounces.

REFLECT

7a. Write and simplify an expression for the total distance the ball travels in n bounces. Check that your expression gives the correct result when $n = 10$.

$S_n = 800(1 - (0.8)^n)$; when $n = 10$, $S_{10} = 800(1 - (0.8)^{10}) \approx 714$.

An *annuity* is an account that is increased (or decreased) by equal deposits (or payments) that are made at regular intervals. The *future value* of an annuity is the total amount in the account at some time in the future.

CC.9-12.A.SSE.4

8 EXAMPLE Determining the Future Value of an Annuity

You deposit $1000 into a savings account at the end of each year for 10 years. The account earns 3% interest that is compounded annually. What is the future value of the annuity in 10 years?

A Develop a general formula for the future value of an annuity.

Suppose you deposit P dollars into the account at the end of each year for n years, and the account earns interest compounded annually at a rate i.

At the end of the first year, the total value of the annuity is P. At the end of the second year, interest is applied to the first deposit and there is a new deposit of P dollars, for a total value of $P(1 + i) + P$. Complete the table.

Year	Total Value of Annuity at End of Year
1	P
2	$P(1 + i) + P$
3	$P(1 + i)^2 + P(1 + i) + P$
⋮	⋮
n	$P(1 + i)^{n-1} + P(1 + i)^{n-2} + \cdots + P(1 + i)^2 + P(1 + i) + P$

© Houghton Mifflin Harcourt Publishing Company

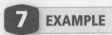

7 EXAMPLE

Questioning Strategies

- Although the initial height from which the ball was dropped is not part of the given sequence, you can still determine that height. State what it is and explain your reasoning. **100 inches; the ball rebounds to 80% of its previous height on each bounce, so 80% of the drop height h must equal the first bounce height, 80, and solving $0.8h = 80$ for h gives $h = 100$.**

- To find the total vertical distance that the ball travels in 10 bounces, you doubled all the bounce heights before finding their sum. What is another method for solving the problem? Show that your method gives the same answer. **First find the sum of the bounce heights and then double the result:**

$$80 + 80(0.8) + \cdots + 80(0.8)^9 = 80\left(\frac{1 - 0.8^{10}}{1 - 0.8}\right) \approx$$

357 and 2(357) = 714 inches.

EXTRA EXAMPLE
For the model given in **7 EXAMPLE**, what is the total distance the ball travels in 12 bounces? **about 745 in.**

8 EXAMPLE

Questioning Strategies

- How is the given formula for the future value of an annuity related to the formula for the sum of a finite geometric series? **The variable A, which represents the future value of the annuity (the sum of all of the previous deposits and the interest earned on those deposits), corresponds to the variable S_n. Both formulas contain the variable n to represent the number of terms, which is the number of years for the annuity. The expression $i + 1$, which represents the interest rate, corresponds to the common ratio r.**

- What will be the future value of an annuity in 20 years if the annual deposits are $6000 and the interest rate is 4%? Explain how you found the answer. **about $178,668.47; use the formula to find**

$$A = 6000\left(\frac{1.04^{20} - 1}{0.04}\right).$$

EXTRA EXAMPLE
What will be the future value of the annuity in **8 EXAMPLE** in 20 years? **about $26,870.37**

CLOSE

Essential Question
How can you write a rule for a geometric sequence and find the sum of a finite geometric series?
To write a recursive rule, assume $f(1)$ is given and use the general rule $f(n) = f(n - 1) \cdot r$ for $n \geq 2$, where r is the common ratio. To write an explicit rule, use the general rule $f(n) = f(1) \cdot r^{n - 1}$, where $f(1)$ is the first term in the sequence and r is the common ratio.

To find the sum of a finite geometric series, first find a simplified expression for $S_n - rS_n$ where $S_n = a_1 + a_1r + a_1r^2 + \ldots + a_1r^{n - 2} + a_1r^{n - 1}$; then, factor $S_n - rS_n$ and divide by $1 - r$. The result is $S_n = a_1\left(\frac{1 - r^n}{1 - r}\right)$, which is the formula for the sum of a finite geometric series.

Complete the equation for the total value A after n years.

$$A = P + P(1 + i) + P(1 + i)^2 + \cdots + P(1 + i)^{n-2} + P(1 + i)^{n-1}$$

This is a geometric series with $a_1 = \underline{P}$ and $r = \underline{1 + i}$, so its sum is

$$A = a_1\left(\frac{1 - r^n}{1 - r}\right) = P\left(\frac{1 - (1 + i)^n}{1 - (1 + i)}\right) = P\left(\frac{(1 + i)^n - 1}{(1 + i) - 1}\right) = P\left(\frac{(1 + i)^n - 1}{i}\right).$$

B Use the formula to find the future value of the annuity.

$$A = P\left(\frac{(1 + i)^n - 1}{i}\right) \qquad \text{Write the formula.}$$

$$= 1000\left(\frac{1.03^{10} - 1}{0.03}\right) \qquad \text{Substitute 1000 for } P, 0.03 \text{ for } i, \text{ and 10 for } n.$$

$$\approx \underline{11,463.88} \qquad \text{Round to 2 decimal places.}$$

So, the value of the annuity in 10 years is $\underline{\$11,463.88}$

REFLECT

8a. Does your answer seem reasonable? How do you know?

Yes; the sum of the deposits is $10,000, so it makes sense that the total value of

the annuity is more than $10,000 when the interest is taken into account.

8b. The total interest earned on an annuity is the future value minus the sum of the deposits. Write a formula for the total interest I of an annuity after n years with annual deposits of P dollars and interest compounded annually at rate i.

$$I = P\left(\frac{(1 + i)^n - 1}{i}\right) - nP$$

PRACTICE

Write a recursive rule and an explicit rule for each geometric sequence.

1. $9, 27, 81, 243, \ldots$

$f(1) = 9$ and $f(n) = f(n - 1) \cdot 3$, for $n \geq 2$; $f(n) = 9(3)^{n-1}$

2. $5, -5, 5, -5, \ldots$

$f(1) = 5$ and $f(n) = f(n - 1) \cdot (-1)$, for $n \geq 2$; $f(n) = 5(-1)^{n-1}$

3. $12, 3, \frac{3}{4}, \frac{3}{16}, \ldots$

$f(1) = 12$ and $f(n) = f(n - 1) \cdot \frac{1}{4}$, for $n \geq 2$; $f(n) = 12 \cdot \left(\frac{1}{4}\right)^{n-1}$

---

4. The table shows the beginning-of-month balances, rounded to the nearest cent, in Marla's savings account for the first few months after she made an initial deposit in the account.

Month	n	1	2	3	4
Account Balance ($)	$f(n)$	2010.00	2020.05	2030.15	2040.30

a. Explain how you know that the sequence of account balances is geometric.

The ratio of consecutive account balances is approximately constant (1.005)

b. Write recursive and explicit rules for the sequence of account balances.

$f(1) = 2010$ and $f(n) = f(n - 1) \cdot 1.005$, for $n \geq 2$; $f(n) = 2010 (1.005)^{n-1}$

c. What amount did Marla deposit initially? Explain.

$2000; the initial amount is $f(0) = 2000$.

5. The graph shows the number of players in the first four rounds of the U.S. Open women's singles tennis tournament.

a. Write an explicit rule for the sequence of players in each round.

$f(n) = 128\left(\frac{1}{2}\right)^{n-1}$

b. How many rounds are there in the tournament? (*Hint:* In the last round, only 2 players are left.)

7 rounds

U.S. Open
Women's Singles

6. The numbers of points that a player must accumulate to reach the next level of a video game form a geometric sequence, where a_n is the number of points needed to complete level n.

a. A player needs 1000 points to complete level 2 and 8,000,000 points to complete level 5. Write an explicit rule for the sequence using subscript notation.

$a_n = 50(20)^{n-1}$

b. How many points are needed for level 7? $\underline{3,200,000,000}$

Write an explicit rule for each geometric sequence based on the given terms from the sequence. Assume that the common ratio r is positive.

7. $a_2 = 12$ and $a_4 = 192$

$a_n = 3 \cdot 4^{n-1}$

8. $a_5 = 0.32$ and $a_7 = 0.0128$

$a_n = 200(0.2)^{n-1}$

Notes

Summarize

Have students make a graphic organizer outlining the process for writing explicit and recursive rules for geometric sequences. Include details about how the first term of the sequence and the common ratio are incorporated into each rule. Also, have students make a graphic organizer outlining the process for finding the sum of a geometric series. Include details about how the first term of the series, the number of terms, and the common ratio are incorporated into the formula.

PRACTICE

Where skills are taught	Where skills are practiced
1 EXAMPLE	EXS. 1–4
3 EXAMPLE	EX. 5
4 EXAMPLE	EXS. 6–8
7 EXAMPLE	EXS. 14, 18-20
8 EXAMPLE	EXS. 15, 16

Exercises 9 and 10: Given a rule for a geometric sequence, students write a recursive rule as an explicit rule, or an explicit rule as a recursive rule.

Exercise 11: Students write an explicit rule for a geometric sequence to solve a problem that involves finding the nth term of the sequence.

Exercises 12 and 13: Students rewrite a finite geometric series in terms of the first term and the common ratio, and then they find the sum of the series.

Exercise 17: Students use the formula for the future value of an annuity to find the yearly deposit required to reach a certain value after a given number of years.

Each rule represents a geometric sequence. If the given rule is recursive, write it as an explicit rule. If the given rule is explicit, write it as a recursive rule. Assume that $f(1)$ is the first term of the sequence.

9. $f(n) = 6(3)^{n-1}$

$f(1) = 6; f(n) = f(n-1) \cdot 3$ for $n \geq 2$

10. $f(1) = 10; f(n) = f(n-1) \cdot 8$ for $n \geq 2$

$f(n) = 10(8)^{n-1}$

11. An economist predicts that the cost of food will increase by 4% per year for the next several years.

a. Use the economist's prediction to write an explicit rule for a geometric sequence that gives the cost in dollars of a box of cereal in year n given that it costs $3.20 in year 1.

$f(n) = 3.20(1.04)^{n-1}$

b. What is the fourth term of the sequence, and what does it represent in this situation?

about 3.60; the cost of the box of cereal is predicted to be about $3.60 in year 4.

For each finite geometric series, n indicates the number of terms. Rewrite each series in the form $a_1 + a_1r + a_1r^2 + \cdots + a_1r^{n-1}$. Then find the sum.

12. $4 + 12 + 36 + \cdots + 8748$; $n = 8$

$4 + 4(3) + 4(3)^2 + \cdots + 4(3)^7$;

13,120

13. $10 + 5 + 2.5 + \cdots + 0.000003125$; $n = 6$

$10 + 10(0.5) + 10(0.5)^2 + \cdots + 10(0.5)^5$;

19.6875

14. A ball is dropped from a height of 16 feet and allowed to bounce repeatedly. On the first bounce it rises to a height of 12 feet and then on each subsequent bounce it rises to 75% of its previous height.

a. Write a geometric sequence that models the first n bounce heights, in feet.

$12, 12(0.75), 12(0.75)^2, 12(0.75)^3, \ldots, 12(0.75)^{n-1}$

b. Write a geometric series to model the total vertical distance the ball travels as a result of n bounces. (Exclude the distance traveled before the first bounce.)

$24 + 24(0.75) + 24(0.75)^2 + 24(0.75)^3 + \cdots + 24(0.75)^{n-1}$

c. How far does the ball travel vertically as a result of the first 3 bounces? Show two ways to find the answer—by adding the first three terms of the series and by using a formula.

$24 + 24(0.75) + 24(0.75)^2 = 24 + 18 + 13.5 = 55.5$ feet;

$S_3 = a_1\left(\dfrac{1-r^n}{1-r}\right) = 24\left(\dfrac{1-(0.75)^3}{1-0.75}\right) = 55.5$ feet

d. How far does the ball travel vertically as a result of the first 9 bounces?

about 88.8 feet

15. Ali deposits $2000 into an account at the end of each year for 4 years. The account earns 5% interest compounded annually.

a. Complete the table to show the value of each deposit as well as the total value of the account at the end of the fourth year. For example, the value of the first deposit is $2000(1.05)^3 = 2315.25.

Value of first deposit	$2315.25
Value of second deposit	$2205.00
Value of third deposit	$2100.00
Value of fourth deposit	$2000.00
Total value of account	$8620.25

b. Use the formula for the sum of a finite geometric series to find the total value of the account at the end of the fourth year.

about $24,724.52; $A = P\left(\dfrac{(1+r)^n - 1}{r}\right) = 800\left(\dfrac{(1.06)^{18} - 1}{0.06}\right) \approx 24{,}724.52$

16. Mr. Ortiz wants to save money for his grandson's future college costs. He plans to deposit $800 into an account at the end of each year. The account earns 6% interest compounded annually. What will be the value of the account in 18 years? Justify your answer.

$8620.25; $A = P\left(\dfrac{(1+i)^n - 1}{i}\right) = 2000\left(\dfrac{(1.05)^4 - 1}{0.05}\right) = 8620.25$

17. Ms. Turner wants to accumulate $50,000 for her daughter's future college costs in 12 years. How much does she need to deposit into an account at the end of each year if the account earns 4% interest compounded annually? Explain.

about $3327.61; solve $50{,}000 = P\left(\dfrac{(1.04)^{12} - 1}{0.04}\right)$ for P.

18. In a single-elimination tournament, a competitor is eliminated after one loss. Suppose a single-elimination tennis tournament has 64 players. In the first round, 32 matches are played. In each subsequent round, the number of matches decreases by one half. How many matches are played in the tournament? Show how to find the answer two ways—by direct calculation and by a formula.

63; $32 + 16 + 8 + 4 + 2 + 1 = 63$; $S_6 = 32\left(\dfrac{1 - (0.5)^6}{0.5}\right) = 63$

19. Nick works for a cleaning company. It takes him 2 hours 30 minutes to clean an office the first time. If he decreases his time by 5% on each subsequent visit, how much time will he spend cleaning the office during 10 visits? Justify your answer.

about 20.063 hours or 20 hours 4 minutes; $S_{10} = 2.5\left(\dfrac{1 - (0.95)^{10}}{1 - 0.95}\right) \approx 20.063$

20. Midori earns $850 in her first month at a part time job. If she gets a 1% raise in each subsequent month, how much will she earn in a year? Justify your answer.

about $10,780.13; $S_{12} = 850\left(\dfrac{1 - (1.01)^{12}}{1 - 1.01}\right) = -85{,}000(1 - (1.01)^{12}) \approx 10{,}780.13$

Assign these pages to help your students practice and apply important lesson concepts. For additional exercises, see the Student Edition.

Answers

Additional Practice

1. Geometric; $r = -3$

2. Arithmetic; $d = 11$ 3. Neither

4. Geometric; $r = 0.8$ 5. 3.125

6. 100,000,000,000

7. 2460.375   8. $-39,366$

9. 384   10. $\pm 12,800$

11. $\pm \dfrac{4}{27}$ 12. ± 972

13. ± 4 14. ± 10

15. $\pm \sqrt{6}$ 16. 15,302

17. $-13,107$ 18. 111,111,111

Problem Solving

1. **a.** $a_n = a_1 (r^{n-1})$

   b. $a_1 = 100$; because all the sunlight reaches layer 1

   c. $r = 0.9$; r represents the fraction of sunlight that passes through a layer.

   d. $a_7 = 100(0.9)^{(7-1)}$; 53%

   e. 15 layers

2. **a.** 18%

   b. 7 layers

3. D   4. H

Name_____ Class_____ Date_____

Additional Practice

Determine whether each sequence could be geometric or arithmetic. If possible, find the common ratio or difference.

1. 1.1, –3.3, 9.9, –29.7, 89.1, …

2. –18, –7, 4, 15, 26, …

3. 1, 2, 6, 24, 120, 720, …

4. 3125, 2500, 2000, 1600, 1280, …

Find the 10th term of each geometric sequence.

5. 1600, 800, 400, 200, …

6. 0.0000001, 0.00001, 0.001, 0.1, …

7. –64, 96, –144, 216, …

8. 2, –6, 18, –54, …

Find the 8th term of each geometric sequence with the given terms.

9. $a_3 = 12$ and $a_6 = 96$

10. $a_{15} = 100$ and $a_{17} = 25$

11. $a_{11} = -4$ and $a_{13} = -36$

12. $a_3 = -4$ and $a_5 = -36$

Find the geometric mean of each pair of numbers.

13. 2 and 8

14. 4 and 25

15. 2 and 3

Find the indicated sum for each geometric series.

16. S_7 for 14, 42, 126, 378, …

17. $\sum_{k=1}^{8} (-4)^{k-1}$

Solve.

18. Deanna received an e-mail asking her to forward it to 10 other people. Assume that no one breaks the chain and that there are no duplicate recipients. How many e-mails will have been sent after 8 generations, including Deanna's?

Problem Solving

Crystal works at a tree nursery during the summer. She wonders why the lower branches of one particular type of tree drop off. The nurseryman explains that each layer of branches absorbs about 10% of the sunlight and lets the rest through to the next layer. If a layer receives less than 25% of the sunlight, those branches will drop off.

1. Crystal counts 7 distinct healthy layers on one tree. She wants to know how many more layers the tree will grow before starting to lose layers of branches.

   a. Write the rule for the nth term, a_n, of a geometric sequence.

   b. If a_n represents the percent of sunlight reaching layer n, what is the value of a_1? How do you know?

   c. What is the value of r? What does it represent?

   d. Write the rule to find the percent of sunlight reaching layer 7. Solve for a_7.

   e. About how many layers of branches will this tree have before a bottom layer drops off?

2. The nurseryman points to a denser type of tree and states that only about 75% of sunlight gets through to each lower layer, but that a layer of this type of tree needs only about 15% of the original sunlight to survive.

   a. What percent of sunlight gets through to layer 7 of this tree?

   b. How many layers of branches could this type of tree support?

Jackson usually runs 8 laps around the football field and consistently completes the first lap in 3 minutes. During one practice session, his coach notes that it takes him 15% longer to complete each lap than the previous lap. Choose the letter for the best answer.

3. How long does it take Jackson to complete the eighth lap?

   A 5.25 min

   B 6.03 min

   C 6.93 min

   D 7.98 min

4. How long does it take Jackson to complete all 8 laps?

   F 9.18 min

   G 20.39 min

   H 41.18 min

   J 61.18 min

Mathematical Induction and Infinite Geometric Series
Connection: Modeling with Finite Geometric Series

Essential question: *How can you analyze the balance due on a loan?*

Standards for Mathematical Content

The following standards are addressed in this lesson. (An asterisk indicates that a standard is also a Modeling standard.) For more detailed information, see each section of the lesson.

Algebra: CC.9-12.A.SSE.1*, CC.9-12.A.SSE.1a*, CC.9-12.A.SSE.1b*, CC.9-12.A.SSE.4, CC.9-12.A.CED.3*

Prerequisites
- Interest compounded monthly
- Geometric sequences
- Finite geometric series

Math Background
Students use what they know about arithmetic and geometric sequences to create a spreadsheet that models monthly payments and balance due on a car loan. Students then extend the model by deriving a formula from the sum of a finite geometric series to calculate the minimum monthly payment required to pay off a car loan for a given principal, interest rate, and number of payments.

INTRODUCE

Begin by asking how many students are interested in learning more about buying a car. Encourage students to discuss cars they would like to buy and have them research how much those cars cost. Explain that in this lesson students will explore getting a car loan and making monthly payments.

TEACH

1 **Use a spreadsheet to determine if a given payment will pay off a loan.**

Standards
CC.9-12.A.SSE.1 Interpret expressions that represent a quantity in terms of its context.*
CC.9-12.A.SSE.1a Interpret parts of an expression, such as terms, factors, and coefficients.*

CC.9-12.A.SSE.1b Interpret complicated expressions by viewing one or more of their parts as a single entity.*

Questioning Strategies
- How does using the Fill command in step F calculate the balance at the end of each period? **When the Fill command is used for a cell that contains a formula, any cell references in that formula are updated relative to the new location. So, for payment period 3, which is located in row 9, the formula in cell B9 becomes =D8*(1+$B$2/12) and now calculates the new balance at the end of period 3 based on the balance after the payment in period 2. The formula in cell D9 is also updated to =B9−C9 to calculate the balance after payment has been made in period 3. This updating process continues through payment period 60.**

- What would happen if you omitted the dollar signs in the cell reference $B$2 when you entered the formula =D7*(1+$B$2/12) in cell B8? **If a cell reference has dollar signs in a formula, it means that the associated row and/or column will not be updated relative to the new location when the Fill command is used. If $B$2 did not have the dollar signs, the formula in cell B9 would be updated to =D8*(1+B3/12), and the new balance would be calculated using the monthly payment of $350 instead of the annual interest rate of 0.06.**

- When you set up cells in step A for values you will change by hand, why do you *not* set up a cell for the number of payment periods? **The number of payment periods is not treated as a variable in any calculation in the spreadsheet. The number of payment periods is represented by the number of rows in the table.**

Mathematical Induction and Infinite Geometric Series

Connection: Modeling with Finite Geometric Series

Essential question: *How can you analyze the balance due on a loan?*

Video Tutor

Suppose that you want to borrow $19,000 to buy a car. You can get a 5-year loan with an annual interest rate of 6%. Payments are to be made at the end of each month. You want to know if monthly payments of $350 will pay off the loan in 5 years. If not, you'd like to know the minimum monthly payment that will work.

1 Use a spreadsheet to determine if a given payment will pay off a loan.

A Enter the items at the top of your spreadsheet, as shown, for the principal, the annual interest rate, and the monthly payment. As you experiment with the spreadsheet later, these will be the only values you will change by hand; all other values will be calculated by the spreadsheet, using formulas you enter.

	A	B	C	D	E
1	Principal	19000			
2	Annual rate	0.06			
3	Monthly payment	350			
4					
5					

B In row 6, enter the column headings Payment Period, Balance at End of Period (this is the balance due before the payment is made), Payment Applied, and Balance After Payment.

C In cell A7, enter 1 for the first payment period. The balance at the end of this period is the principal ($19,000) plus the interest for one month ($\frac{1}{12}$ of 6% of $19,000). Enter the formula = B1*(1 + $B$2/12) in cell B7 to calculate this. In cell C7, enter the formula = $B$3. This tells the spreadsheet to use the monthly payment you entered above as the amount in the Payment Applied column. In cell D7, enter the formula = B7 − C7 to subtract the payment and find the balance after payment. Once you hit Enter, your spreadsheet should look like the one below. (*Hint:* Cells that show dollar amounts should be formatted as "currency.")

	A	B	C	D	E
1	Principal	19000			
2	Annual rate	0.06			
3	Monthly payment	350			
4					
5					
6	Payment Period	Balance at End of Period	Payment Applied	Balance After Payment	
7	1	$19,095.00	$350.00	$18,745.00	

© Houghton Mifflin Harcourt Publishing Company

D There are 12 payments per year for 5 years, so there will be 60 payments. Use the Fill command and choose "Series" to enter payment periods 2 through 60 in the Payment Period column.

E In cell B8, enter the formula = D7*(1 + $B$2/12). This calculates the balance at the end of the second month by adding the monthly interest to the balance after payment from the previous period. In cell C8, enter the formula = $B$3. In cell D8, enter the formula = B8 − C8.

F Select cells B8 through D8. Use the Fill command to fill columns B, C, and D for payment periods 3 through 60.

	A	B	C	D	E
1	Principal	19000			
2	Annual rate	0.06			
3	Monthly payment	350			
4					
5					
6	Payment Period	Balance at End of Period	Payment Applied	Balance After Payment	
7	1	$19,095.00	$350.00	$18,745.00	
8	2	$18,838.73	$350.00	$18,488.73	
9	3	$18,581.17	$350.00	$18,231.17	
10	4	$18,322.32	$350.00	$17,972.32	
11	5	$18,062.19	$350.00	$17,712.19	

G According to your spreadsheet, can you pay off the loan in 5 years with monthly payments of $350? How do you know?

No; the balance due after the 60th payment is $1208.64.

REFLECT

1a. Describe what the formula = B1*(1 + $B$2/12) in cell B7 calculates based on what B1 and 1 + $B$2/12 represent in the context of the problem. Include a description of what $B$2/12 represents and how it is obtained.

The formula calculates the principal plus interest at the end of month 1

because B1 represents the principal and 1 + $B$2/12 represents the growth

factor due to the interest. In the growth factor, $B$2/12 represents the

monthly interest rate, which is obtained by dividing the annual rate by 12.

1b. You could have entered the formula = B1 + B1*$B$2/12 in cell B7 instead of = B1*(1 + $B$2/12). What do the terms of this alternate formula represent?

B1 represents the principal; B1*$B$2/12 represents the interest for month 1.

1c. Using monthly payments of $350, how long will it take to pay off the loan? Explain how you can use the spreadsheet to answer this question.

5 years 4 months; Use the Fill command to fill columns B, C, and D

until the amount in column D is zero or less. After payment 64, the

balance due is −$177.54.

© Houghton Mifflin Harcourt Publishing Company

Notes

2 Use a spreadsheet to calculate the payment needed to pay off a loan.

Standards
CC.9-12.A.CED.3 ... interpret solutions as viable or non-viable in a modeling context.*

Questioning Strategies
- How could you analyze the effect of getting a loan with a different interest rate? **You can enter the new interest rate in cell B2. The spreadsheet will automatically use the new interest rate to recalculate all the amounts for each payment period.**

- Will it be possible to pay off the $19,000 loan in 5 years with a monthly payment of $350 if you have a loan with an interest rate of 5%? Explain your reasoning. **No; with an interest rate of 5% on the loan there is still a balance due of $581.69 after the 60th payment.**

- With what interest rate would it be possible to pay off the $19,000 loan in 5 years with a monthly payment of $350? Explain. **You could pay off the $19,000 loan in 5 years with a monthly payment of $350 if you had an interest rate of 4%. If you enter 0.04 into cell B2 and press Enter, the balance due after the 60th payment is −$5.71, meaning the loan has been paid off.**

- What if the best interest rate you could get was 5%? Explain how it would be possible to pay off the $19,000 loan in 5 years. **If you increase your monthly payment by $9 each month to $359, the balance due after the 60th payment is −$30.37, meaning the loan has been paid off.**

- How could you modify your spreadsheet to analyze loan payments for a 3-year or a 4-year loan? **Since there are 12 periods per year, a 3-year loan would have 36 payments and a 4-year loan would have 48 payments. You can look at the first 36 or 48 rows of the 5-year spreadsheet you currently have set up to see what has been paid at the end of a 3-year or 4-year period.**

- Describe how you could create a separate area on the spreadsheet to analyze loan payments for a 3-year loan. **You could enter information for a 3-year loan in columns F, G, and H. In cell F7, enter =B1*(1+$B$2/12); in cell G7, enter =$B$3; and in cell H7, enter =F7−G7. After pressing Enter, the cells should contain the same amounts as cells B7 through D7. Then, in cell F8, enter =H7*(1+$B$2/12); in cell G8, enter =$B$3; and in cell H8, enter =F8−G8. Use the Fill command to fill columns F, G, and H for payment periods 3 through 36.**

3 Use a geometric series to calculate the payment needed to pay off a loan.

Standards
CC.9-12.A.SSE.4 Derive the formula for the sum of a finite geometric series (when the common ratio is not 1), and use the formula to solve problems.*

Questioning Strategies
- Using the formula derived from the sum of a finite geometric series, what would be the value of r for an annual interest rate of 5%? Explain. **The value of r for a 5% annual interest rate would be approximately 0.004. The monthly interest rate is $\frac{1}{12}$ the annual interest rate, so divide 0.05 by 12.**

Continued

2 Use a spreadsheet to calculate the payment needed to pay off a loan.

A Experiment with different monthly payment amounts. To do so, change the value in cell B3. Be sure to keep track of the final balance after payment at the end of the 60th payment period. What is the minimum monthly payment that pays off the loan in 5 years?

$367.33

B What happens when you enter a monthly payment of $95? Explain why this happens.

The balance after payment is $19,000 every month. The interest for the first month is $95, so a $95 monthly payment pays only the interest and none of the principal.

C Is it possible to pay off the loan (in any amount of time) with a monthly payment that is less than $95? How do you know?

No; any monthly payment less than $95 will result in a balance due after the first payment of more than $19,000 and then increasing subsequent balances due.

REFLECT

2a. Assume you make the monthly payment from part A above. At the end of 5 years, what is the balance due after the last payment? Explain what it means.

−$0.47; You have paid $0.47 too much.

2b. Assume you make the monthly payment from part A above for 59 payments and then $0.47 less than that amount for the 60th payment. At the end of 5 years, what is the total amount of interest you have paid? Explain.

$3039.33; 59 × $367.33 + $366.86 = $22,039.33; $22,039.33 − $19,000 = $3039.33

2c. Explain why the total amount of interest paid at the end of 5 years is not simply 6% of $19,000 multiplied by 5.

6% of $19,000 multiplied by 5 is $1140 · 5 = $5700; this is the simple interest you would owe if you waited 5 years before repaying the loan all at once, but you are making monthly payments and interest is compounding monthly.

2d. Suppose you want to make monthly payments of $350 and plan to take a 5-year loan with an annual interest rate of 6%. What is the most expensive loan you can afford? Explain how you found your answer.

$18,103.94; Experiment by changing the principal until the balance due after the 60th payment is zero or less. In this case, the balance due after the 60th payment is −$0.01.

© Houghton Mifflin Harcourt Publishing Company

---

3 Use a geometric series to calculate the payment needed to pay off a loan.

A You can use what you know about the sum of a finite geometric series to derive a formula that can be used to calculate a monthly loan payment. To begin, set up variables as follows.

P = principal

R = annual interest rate expressed as a decimal

r = monthly interest rate expressed as a decimal

m = monthly payment

Explain how r is related to R.

$r = \dfrac{R}{12}$ because the monthly interest rate is $\frac{1}{12}$ of the annual interest rate.

B You can use P, r, and m to write an expression for the loan balance B after you make a payment at the end of each month.

At the end of the first month, before the monthly payment is applied, the loan balance is the principal P plus the interest for the month rP, for a total of $P + rP$, or $P(1 + r)$.

At the end of the first month, after the monthly payment is applied, what is the loan balance?

$P(1 + r) - m$

At the end of the second month, before the monthly payment is applied, you owe the balance after payment from the first month plus interest, which is $[P(1 + r) - m](1 + r)$, or $P(1 + r)^2 - m(1 + r)$.

At the end of the second month, after the monthly payment is applied, what is the loan balance?

$P(1 + r)^2 - m(1 + r) - m$

Complete the table.

Period	Balance at End of Period	Balance After Payment (B)
1	$P(1 + r)$	$P(1 + r) - m$
2	$P(1 + r)^2 - m(1 + r)$	$P(1 + r)^2 - m(1 + r) - m$
3	$P(1 + r)^3 - m(1 + r)^2 - m(1 + r)$	$P(1 + r)^3 - m(1 + r)^2 - m(1 + r) - m$
4	$P(1 + r)^4 - m(1 + r)^3 - m(1 + r)^2 - m(1 + r)$	$P(1 + r)^4 - m(1 + r)^3 - m(1 + r)^2 - m(1 + r) - m$

© Houghton Mifflin Harcourt Publishing Company

- How can you use the formula you wrote to calculate the monthly payment to pay off a loan with principal P, monthly interest rate r, and n monthly payments to determine the monthly payment required to pay off the $19,000 loan in 5 years with an annual interest rate of 5%? Substitute 0.004 instead of 0.005 for r in the formula $m = \dfrac{rP(1 + r)^n}{(1 + r)^2 - 1}$:

  $m = \dfrac{0.004(19{,}000)(1.004)^{60}}{(1.004)^{60} - 1} \approx 356.82$. So, the required monthly payment would be $356.82.

- How does the minimum monthly payment you found for a 5% annual interest rate using the formula compare with the minimum monthly payment you found for a 5% annual interest rate using the spreadsheet? Explain. **Using the spreadsheet, the minimum monthly payment for a 5% annual interest rate was about $359, while using the formula the monthly payment was about $357. The difference is due to a rounding error in the formula when the interest rate 0.05 is divided by 12 to get r. If 0.00417 is substituted for r instead of 0.004, the monthly payment is $358.59, which is just about the same as the spreadsheet result.**

- How can you rewrite the formula you wrote in part E to calculate the principal P that you can pay off if you take out a loan with monthly interest rate r, n monthly payments, and a monthly payment of m dollars?

  $P = \dfrac{m(1 - (1 + r)^{-n})}{r}$

- How can you use the formula in the previous question to determine the amount of money you could spend on a car if you can get a loan at a 5.4% annual interest rate for 5 years and you can afford a monthly payment of only $250?

  $P = \dfrac{250(1 - (1 + 0.0045)^{-60})}{0.0045} \approx 13{,}119.89$; you could spend about $13,000 on a car.

MATHEMATICAL PRACTICE **Highlighting the Standards**

This lesson addresses Mathematical Practice Standard 2 (Reason abstractly and quantitatively). In the first part of the lesson, students experiment with monthly payments to determine what monthly payment results in an ending balance closest to 0. Here, the spreadsheet removes the burden of performing tedious calculations so that students can focus on quantitative reasoning. In the second part of the lesson, students generalize the situation in order to derive a formula that replaces the need for a spreadsheet. Here, students engage in abstract reasoning, and they check the correctness of the formula by comparing what the formula gives as a monthly payment against what they found by trial and error using the spreadsheet.

CLOSE

Essential Question

How can you analyze the balance due on a loan?
Use a spreadsheet or derive a formula to calculate a monthly payment. By starting with the formula for the sum of a finite geometric series, you can write a formula to calculate the monthly payment required to pay off any loan with principal P, monthly interest rate r, and n monthly payments.

Summarize

Have students write a one-page summary of how to use a finite geometric series model to write a formula to analyze the balance due on a loan.

EXTEND

Standards
CC.9-12.A.SSE.4 Derive the formula for the sum of a finite geometric series (when the common ratio is not 1), and use the formula to solve problems.* (Exs. 1–6)

C Extend the pattern in the Balance After Payment column. Complete the formula for B, the balance after payment at the end of the nth period.

$$B = P(1+r)^n - m(1+r)^{n-1} - m(1+r)^{n-2} - \cdots - m(1+r) - m$$

Simplify the formula by factoring.

$$B = P(1+r)^n - m\left[(1+r)^{n-1} + (1+r)^{n-2} + \cdots + (1+r) + 1\right]$$

The expression $(1+r)^{n-1} + (1+r)^{n-2} + \cdots + (1+r) + 1$ is a finite geometric series.

How many terms are in the series? $\underline{\quad n \quad}$

What is the common ratio? $\underline{\quad 1+r \quad}$

D The sum S_n of the finite geometric series $a_1 r^{n-1} + a_1 r^{n-2} + \cdots + a_1 r + a_1$ is
$S_n = \dfrac{a_1(1-r^n)}{1-r}$ where r is the common ratio and n is the number of terms.
Replace the finite geometric series $(1+r)^{n-1} + (1+r)^{n-2} + \cdots + (1+r) + 1$ with the expression for its sum, and simplify.

$$B = P(1+r)^n - m \cdot \dfrac{1[1-(1+r)^n]}{1-(1+r)} = P(1+r)^n - m \cdot \dfrac{(1+r)^n - 1}{r}$$

E You are interested in knowing what monthly payment will result in a balance B that is equal to 0 after n payments. Set $B = 0$ in the above equation and then solve for m and simplify. This will give you a formula you can use to calculate the monthly payment needed to pay off a loan with principal P, monthly interest rate r, and n monthly payment periods.

$$m = \dfrac{rP(1+r)^n}{(1+r)^n - 1}$$

F Show how to use the formula to find the minimum monthly payment needed to pay off a 5-year \$19,000 loan with an annual interest rate of 6%.

$$m = \dfrac{rP(1+r)^n}{(1+r)^n - 1} = \dfrac{0.005(19,000)(1.005)^{60}}{(1.005)^{60} - 1} \approx 367.32$$

REFLECT

3a. How does the minimum monthly payment that you found using the formula compare to the minimum monthly payment that you found using the spreadsheet?

They are about the same.

3b. If you could increase the number of monthly payments (say, from 60 to 72), what do you expect would happen to the amount of the monthly payment?

The monthly payment would decrease.

© Houghton Mifflin Harcourt Publishing Company

Chapter 9   545   Lesson 5

EXTEND

1. Suppose you want to borrow \$19,000 and you find a 5-year loan with an annual interest rate of 5%. By how much do you lower your monthly payments by taking this loan instead of the 6% loan? How much do you save over the life of the loan?

\$8.78; 60 · \$8.78 = \$526.80

2. You would like your monthly payments to be no more than \$300. Suppose you get a \$19,000 loan with an annual interest rate of 6%, but you are able to choose the term (length) of the loan. Enter the formula for the monthly payment m into your calculator as a function of the number of payments, n. Then use the calculator's table feature to find the shortest term for the loan that results in monthly payments of no more than \$300.

77 months

3. A friend claims that if you borrow half the amount (\$9,500 instead of \$19,000), you will cut your monthly payments in half. Is your friend correct? Explain.

Yes; $m = \dfrac{0.005(9500)(1.005)^{60}}{(1.005)^{60} - 1} \approx 183.66$

4. In general, how is the monthly payment affected when the amount borrowed is multiplied by some factor, and the interest rate and number of periods are kept the same? Explain.

The monthly payment is multiplied by the same factor because m is directly proportional to P. m is directly proportional to P because

$m = \dfrac{rP(1+r)^n}{(1+r)^n - 1} = \dfrac{r(1+r)^n}{(1+r)^n - 1} \cdot P$, and $\dfrac{r(1+r)^n}{(1+r)^n - 1}$ is constant.

5. Use the formula $m = \dfrac{rP(1+r)^n}{(1+r)^n - 1}$ to explain why the monthly payment m decreases when the number n of monthly payments increases. Assume that the principal P and interest rate r are constant. (*Hint:* Let $x = (1+r)^n$. Determine what happens to x as n increases. Then determine what happens to $m = rP \cdot \dfrac{x}{x-1}$.)

As n increases, $x = (1+r)^n$ increases because the base $1+r$ is greater than 1.

As x increases, the fraction $\dfrac{x}{x-1}$ decreases (toward 1), so $m = rP \cdot \dfrac{x}{x-1}$ decreases.

6. What alternate form of the formula $m = \dfrac{rP(1+r)^n}{(1+r)^n - 1}$ do you get if you multiply the numerator and denominator by $(1+r)^{-n}$? What is the advantage of using this alternate form when calculating m?

$m = \dfrac{rP}{1 - (1+r)^{-n}}$; there are fewer steps in the calculation process.

© Houghton Mifflin Harcourt Publishing Company

Chapter 9   546   Lesson 5

Notes

Assign these pages to help your students practice
and apply important lesson concepts. For
additional exercises, see the Student Edition.

Answers

Additional Practice

1. 109 months, or 9 years 1 month

2. $1590

3. $467

4. 62 months, or 5 years 2 months

5. Find the cell just before the balance goes
   negative. The sum of those complete
   payments, plus the remaining balance, is the
   total amount paid.

6. $91,944

7. $16,131

Problem Solving

1. $21,738

2. $18,839

3. 25 months sooner

4. B

5. G

6. A

Name_____ Class_____ Date_____

Additional Practice

Suppose that you want to borrow $80,000 to start a business. You can get a loan with an annual interest rate of 7%. Payments are made at the end of each month.

Use a spreadsheet to help you answer the following questions.

1. To the nearest month, how long will it take to pay off the loan if you make monthly payments of $1000?

   _____

2. To the nearest ten dollars, how high does the monthly payment have to be in order to pay off the loan in 5 years?

   _____

3. To the nearest dollar, what is the minimum monthly payment to *ever* pay off the loan?

   _____

Suppose that you find a competing bank that offers an $80,000 loan at 5.5% annual interest, but with a minimum monthly payment of $1500.

4. To the nearest month, how long will it take to pay off the loan, using the minimum payment?

   _____

5. Using your spreadsheet, how can you calculate the total amount paid over the lifetime of a loan?

   _____
   _____

6. To the nearest dollar, what is the total cost of the 5.5% loan (at $1500 per month)?

   _____

7. To the nearest dollar, how much does the 5.5% loan (at $1500 per month) save you versus the 7% loan (at $1000 per month), over the life of the loan?

   _____

Problem Solving

A *balloon payment* is a type of loan that is not fully repaid over the time interval, leaving a balance due at the end as a final payment. The final payment is called a *balloon payment* because its size includes the remaining balance on the loan.

Suppose you take out a loan for $19,000, with an annual interest rate of 6%. Because this is a balloon loan, the monthly payment is only $100, and whatever balance remains at the end of 2.5 years (30 months) will need to be paid as a lump sum.

1. What is the total cost of the loan?

   _____

2. To the nearest dollar, how much is the final payment of the loan?

   _____

3. Compared to a non-balloon loan of the same principal and interest rate, but with a monthly payment of $400, how much sooner will the balloon loan come due?

   _____

Kristi finds that she can afford a $320 monthly car payment.

4. If Kristi qualifies for an annual interest rate of 4.7% for a 5-year loan, what is the most expensive car she can afford?

   A $16,000
   B $17,000
   C $18,000
   D $19,000

5. Kristi is offered an adjustable-rate loan, where the interest rate is 0% for the first year and rises to 9% for the remaining four years of the loan. If she buys the car she calculated she could afford in question 4 and does not change her monthly payment, will she have paid the loan off at the end of 5 years?

   F Yes
   G No
   H Not enough information

6. What is the highest rate to which her interest rate could rise for Kristi to be able to pay off an adjustable-rate loan on the car you answered for question 4 by the end of five years?

   A 7.7%   C 8.1%
   B 7.8%   D 8.4%

This page provides students with the opportunity to apply concepts from the Common Core in real-world problem situations. There are three different levels of performance tasks:

⭐ **Novice:** These are short word problems that require students to apply the math they have learned in straightforward, real-world situations.

⭐⭐ **Apprentice:** These are more involved problems that guide students step-by-step through more complex tasks. These exercises include more complicated reasoning, writing, and open-ended elements.

⭐⭐⭐ **Expert:** These are open-ended, non-routine problems that, instead of stepping the students through, ask them to choose their own methods for solving and justify their answers and reasoning.

Sample answers

1. base level: $6 \cdot 6 = 36$ glasses; second level: $5 \cdot 5 = 25$ glasses; third level: $4 \cdot 4 = 16$ glasses; fourth level: $3 \cdot 3 = 9$ glasses; fifth level: $2 \cdot 2 = 4$ glasses; sixth level: 1 glass; $36 + 25 + 16 + 9 + 4 + 1 = 91$ glasses

2. $\sum_{k=1}^{n} 3k$; No. Each level has $3k$ blocks, where k is the level number. Since 32 is not divisible by 3, no level could have 32 blocks.

3. Scoring Guide:

Task	Possible points
a	1 point for identifying the sequence as geometric, and 1 point for writing the rule as either $a_n = 1000(3)^n$ or $a_n = 3000(3)^{n-1}$
b	1 point for correct answer of $n = 9$, and 1 point for the explanation that there are $18 \div 2 = 9$ triplings in 18 hours, so $n = 9$.
c	2 points for correct number of bacteria: 19,683,000

Total possible points: 6

Name_____ Class_____ Date_____

Performance Tasks

★ 1. A contestant on a game show needs to make a pyramid of stacked wineglasses. Each wineglass not on the base level is supported by the four glasses below it, as shown. The base of the pyramid is 6 glasses by 6 glasses. If the contestant successfully builds the entire pyramid, how many glasses does she use? Show your work.

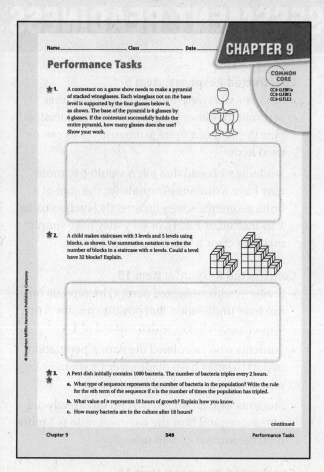

★ 2. A child makes staircases with 3 levels and 5 levels using blocks, as shown. Use summation notation to write the number of blocks in a staircase with n levels. Could a level have 32 blocks? Explain.

★ 3. A Petri dish initially contains 1000 bacteria. The number of bacteria triples every 2 hours.

a. What type of sequence represents the number of bacteria in the population? Write the rule for the nth term of the sequence if n is the number of times the population has tripled.

b. What value of n represents 18 hours of growth? Explain how you know.

c. How many bacteria are in the culture after 18 hours?

continued

★★★ 4. Prove $1 + 3 + 5 + \ldots + (2n - 1) = n^2$ for all natural numbers n using induction.

4. Scoring Guide:

Task	Possible points
	6 points for a complete, correct proof. Students' proofs should show that the formula is true for $n = 1$, and a proof that if the statement is true for k, it is true for $k + 1$, as shown below, or equivalent: $1 + 3 + 5 + \ldots + (2k - 1) = k^2$ $1 + 3 + 5 + \ldots + (2k - 1) + [2(k + 1) - 1]$ $= k^2 + [2(k + 1) - 1]$ Add the next term, $2(k + 1) - 1$, to both sides. $1 + 3 + 5 + \ldots + (2k - 1) + [2(k + 1) - 1]$ $= k^2 + 2k + 2 - 1$ Expand the right side. $[1 + 3 + 5 + \ldots + (2k - 1)] + [2(k + 1) - 1]$ $= k^2 + 2k + 1$ Collect like terms on the right side. $[1 + 3 + 5 + \ldots + (2k - 1)] + [2(k + 1) - 1]$ $= (k + 1)^2$ Factor the perfect square trinomial on the right side. Because the statement is true for 1 and for $k + 1$, it is true for all natural numbers.

Total possible points: 6

Standard	Items
CC.9-12.A.SSE.1*	3, 6, 10
CC.9-12.A.SSE.4*	5, 6, 9, 11
CC.9-12.F.IF.2	4, 8, 11
CC.9-12.F.IF.3	1
CC.9-12.F.BF.2*	4, 7, 8, 11
CC.9-12.F.LE.2*	2, 8, 11

TEST PREP DOCTOR ⊕

Multiple Choice: Item 1
- Students who chose **A** did not understand the difference between a recursive and an explicit rule.
- Students who chose **B** did not understand the difference between a recursive and an explicit rule, and they did not understand that the domain of a sequence is a subset of the set of integers.
- Students who chose **D** did not understand that the domain of a sequence is a subset of the set of integers.

Multiple Choice: Item 2
- Students who chose **F** or **G** did not recognize that the pattern in the graph is exponential and used an arithmetic sequence to model the situation rather than a geometric sequence.
- Students who chose **H** used 0.10 for the common ratio r instead of 1.10, not understanding that if $0 < r < 1$, the graph would be falling from left to right instead of rising.

Multiple Choice: Item 4
- Students who chose **F** used n instead of $n - 1$ in the explicit rule $f(n) = 450 - 25(n - 1)$.
- Students who chose **H** or **J** mixed up the first term and the common difference when writing the explicit rule.

Constructed Response: Item 9
- Students who were unable to calculate total earnings for either job may not have understood how the sum of a finite geometric series can be used here.
- Students who said that job A would pay more may have written the formula for the sum of a finite geometric series incorrectly (such as using 1.05 instead of 1.005), or they may have simply made an error when evaluating the sum.

Constructed Response: Item 10
- Students who answered part (a) incorrectly may not have understood that position numbers in a sequence can begin with 0 instead of 1.
- Students who calculated the wrong population in part (b) may have made an error when evaluating the rule for the sequence.
- Students who answered part (c) incorrectly did not understand how the common ratio is 1 more than the annual growth rate.

Constructed Response: Item 11
- Students who wrote a rule for an arithmetic sequence instead of a geometric sequence in part (a) may not have recognized that the terms have a common ratio, not a common difference.
- Students who wrote the rule $f(1) = 100,000$ and $f(n) = f(n - 1) \cdot 0.95$ for $n \geq 2$ in part (a) did not understand the difference between a recursive rule and an explicit rule.
- Students who used a different value for 0.95 in the formula in part (a) did not correctly calculate the common ratio between consecutive terms in the sequence.
- Students who were not able to write a formula in part (b) may not have understood how the sum of a finite geometric series can be used to solve the problem.
- Students who calculated the wrong total in part (b) may have written the formula for the sum of a finite geometric series incorrectly, or they may have simply made an error when evaluating the formula.

Name _____ Class _____ Date _____

MULTIPLE CHOICE

1. Which rule defines a sequence recursively?

  A. $f(n) = 4n + 2$
    domain: $\{0, 1, 2, 3, 4\}$

  B. $f(n) = 4n + 2$
    domain: {all real numbers}

  (C) $f(0) = 2, f(n) = f(n-1) + 4$ if $n \geq 1$
    domain: $\{0, 1, 2, 3, 4\}$

  D. $f(0) = 2, f(n) = f(n-1) + 4$ if $n \geq 1$
    domain: {all real numbers}

2. A college currently has 4990 students. A faculty committee made the following graph to show their plan for recommended enrollments for the next four years.

Which sequence is the best model for the committee's recommendations?

  F. $f(n) = 4990 + 500n$

  G. $f(n) = 4990 + 1.10n$

  H. $f(n) = 4990(0.10)^n$

  (J.) $f(n) = 4990(1.10)^n$

3. The sequence $a_n = a_0(1 + r)^n$ can be used to find the value of a car n years after 2005. Which expression represents the value of the car in 2005?

  (A.) a_0 **C.** $a_0(1 + r)$

  B. $1 + r$ **D.** $(1 + r)^n$

4. The following rule represents the sequence of balances Hector owes on a loan, where $f(n)$ is the balance he owes in dollars after making n equal payments.

$$f(1) = 450, f(n) = f(n-1) - 25 \text{ if } n \geq 2$$

Which is an explicit rule for the sequence?

  F. $f(n) = 450 - 25n$

  (G.) $f(n) = 475 - 25n$

  H. $f(n) = 450n - 25$

  J. $f(n) = 475n - 25$

5. Deon is deriving a formula for S_n, the sum of the finite geometric series $a_1 + a_1 r + a_1 r^2 + a_1 r^3 + \cdots + a_1 r^{n-1}$. What is $S_n - rS_n$?

  A. $a_1 + a_1 r^n$

  (B.) $a_1 - a_1 r^n$

  C. $a_1 + a_1 + a_1 r + a_1 r^2 + \cdots + a_1 r^{n-2}$

  D. $a_1 - a_1 - a_1 r - a_1 r^2 - \cdots - a_1 r^{n-2}$

6. Which expression is equal to $(1 + r)^{n-1} + (1 + r)^{n-2} + \cdots + (1 + r)^2 + (1 + r) + 1$?

  F. $\dfrac{1 - r^n}{1 - r}$ **H.** $\dfrac{1 - (1 + r)^n}{r}$

  G. $\dfrac{1 + r^n}{1 + r}$ **(J.)** $\dfrac{(1 + r)^n - 1}{r}$

7. A sheet of paper is 0.1 mm thick. The paper is folded in half repeatedly, and the sequence of thicknesses (in millimeters) is 0.1, 0.2, 0.4, 0.8, ... What is a rule for this sequence if 0.1 is term 0?

  A. $f(n) = 0.1(0.5)^n$

  B. $f(n) = 0.5(0.1)^n$

  C. $f(n) = 2(0.1)^n$

  (D.) $f(n) = 0.1(2)^n$

CONSTRUCTED RESPONSE

8. The table shows the weight of Tom's truck as he loads it with bags of cement.

Bags of Cement n	Truck Weight (lb) $f(n)$
0	2988
1	3068
2	3148
3	3228
4	3308

a. Write a recursive rule for the sequence of truck weights.

  $f(0) = 2988, f(n) = f(n-1) + 80$

  if $n \geq 1$

b. Write an explicit rule for the sequence of truck weights.

  $f(n) = 2988 + 80n$

c. Is the sequence arithmetic, geometric, or neither? Explain.

  Arithmetic; differences are constant.

9. Morgan is considering two job offers. If she takes job A, she will earn $3600 in her first month and then will get a 0.5% raise every month for 2 years. If she takes job B, she will earn $3800 per month to start and will get a 1% raise at the end of every 3-month interval for 2 years. Which job will pay more during the first 2 years? Justify your answer.

  Job B will pay more.

  Job A: Use $S_n = a_1\left(\dfrac{1 - r^n}{1 - r}\right)$ with

  $a_1 = 3600, r = 0.005,$ and $n = 24$:

  $S_{24} = 3600\left(\dfrac{1 - (1.005)^{24}}{1 - 1.005}\right) \approx 91,555$

  Job B: Use $S_n = a_1\left(\dfrac{1 - r^n}{1 - r}\right)$ with

  $a_1 = 3800, r = 0.01,$ and $n = 8$,

  but note that the total pay is 3 times S_8:

  $3 \cdot S_8 = 3 \cdot 3800\left(\dfrac{1 - (1.01)^8}{1 - 1.01}\right) \approx 94,457$

10. The sequence $a_n = 14,000(1.03)^n$ is a model for the population of a town, where n is the number of years after 2010.

a. What is a_0? What does it represent?

  14,000; the population in 2010,

  based on the model

b. What is a_4? What does it represent?

  15,757; the population in 2014,

  based on the model

c. What is the common ratio for the sequence? How can you use the common ratio to find the town's annual growth rate?

  1.03; subtract 1 and express

  the result as a percent to find

  the annual growth rate, 3%.

11. Ms. Hudson donated $100,000 in the year 2000 to establish a scholarship account for her former college. The table shows end-of-year balances in the account over the next several years as scholarships were awarded.

Year	Year-End Balance (Dollars)
2000	100,000.00
2001	95,000.00
2002	90,250.00
2003	85,737.50
2004	81,450.63

a. Write an explicit formula for the sequence of year-end balances. Let $n = 0$ represent the year 2000.

  $f(n) = 100,000(0.95)^n$

b. Suppose the balance changed only as a result of awarding scholarships in the years 2001 through 2010 according to the pattern indicated in the table. How much scholarship money was awarded in total during those 10 years? Justify your answer.

  $40,126.31; $S_{10} = \dfrac{5000\left(1 - (0.95)^{10}\right)}{1 - 0.95}$

  $\approx 40,126.31$

CHAPTER 10

Trigonometric Functions

Trigonometric Functions

Chapter Focus

In this chapter, you will learn about the three basic trigonometric functions. These functions are related to the trigonometric ratios of angles in right triangles that you learned about in Geometry. Trigonometric functions are defined on a circle centered at the origin with radius 1 unit. You will also learn how to use the Laws of Sine and Cosine to evaluate parts of a triangle.

Chapter at a Glance

Lesson		Standards for Mathematical Content
10-1	Right-Angle Trigonometry	CC.9-12.N.Q.1, CC.9-12.A.CED.4, CC.9-12.G.C.5
10-2	Angles of Rotation	CC.9-12.F.TF.1
10-3	The Unit Circle	CC.9-12.F.TF.2, CC.9-12.F.TF.3(+)
10-4	Inverses of Trigonometric Functions	CC.9-12.F.TF.6(+), CC.9-12.F.TF.7(+)
10-5	The Law of Sines	CC.9-12.G.SRT.10(+), CC.9-12.G.SRT.11(+)
10-6	The Law of Cosines	CC.9-12.G.SRT.10(+), CC.9-12.G.SRT.11(+)
	Performance Tasks	
	Assessment Readiness	

COMMON CORE PROFESSIONAL DEVELOPMENT

CC.9-12.F.TF.3(+)

Students will combine their prior knowledge of special triangles and trigonometric ratios to determine the values of sine, cosine, and tangent for $\frac{\pi}{3}$, $\frac{\pi}{4}$, and $\frac{\pi}{6}$ geometrically. Students will connect coordinates of a point on the unit circle to side lengths of a right triangle to be able to determine trigonometric ratios based on the unit circle. Instruction should emphasize the connection between trigonometric functions on the unit circle and graphing of trigonometric functions in the coordinate plane to model periodic situations.

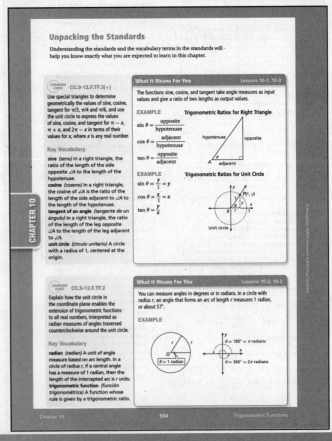

Unpacking the Standards

Understanding the standards and the vocabulary terms in the standards will help you know exactly what you are expected to learn in this chapter.

CC.9-12.F.TF.3(+)

Use special triangles to determine geometrically the values of sine, cosine, tangent for π/3, π/4, and π/6, and use the unit circle to express the values of sine, cosine, and tangent for π − x, π + x, and 2π − x in terms of their values for x, where x is any real number.

Key Vocabulary

sine *(seno)* In a right triangle, the ratio of the length of the side opposite ∠A to the length of the hypotenuse.
cosine *(coseno)* In a right triangle, the cosine of ∠A is the ratio of the length of the side adjacent to ∠A to the length of the hypotenuse.
tangent of an angle *(tangente de un ángulo)* In a right triangle, the ratio of the length of the leg opposite ∠A to the length of the leg adjacent to ∠A.
unit circle *(círculo unitario)* A circle with a radius of 1, centered at the origin.

What It Means For You   Lessons 10-1, 10-3

The functions sine, cosine, and tangent take angle measures as input values and give a ratio of two lengths as output values.

EXAMPLE   Trigonometric Ratios for Right Triangle

$$\sin \theta = \frac{\text{opposite}}{\text{hypotenuse}}$$
$$\cos \theta = \frac{\text{adjacent}}{\text{hypotenuse}}$$
$$\tan \theta = \frac{\text{opposite}}{\text{adjacent}}$$

EXAMPLE   Trigonometric Ratios for Unit Circle

$$\sin \theta = \frac{y}{1} = y$$
$$\cos \theta = \frac{x}{1} = x$$
$$\tan \theta = \frac{y}{x}$$

Unit circle

CC.9-12.F.TF.2

Explain how the unit circle in the coordinate plane enables the extension of trigonometric functions to all real numbers, interpreted as radian measures of angles traversed counterclockwise around the unit circle.

Key Vocabulary

radian *(radian)* A unit of angle measure based on arc length. In a circle of radius r, if a central angle has a measure of 1 radian, then the length of the intercepted arc is r units.
trigonometric function *(función trigonométrica)* A function whose rule is given by a trigonometric ratio.

What It Means For You   Lessons 10-2, 10-3

You can measure angles in degrees or in radians. In a circle with radius r, an angle that forms an arc of length r measures 1 radian, or about 57°.

EXAMPLE

$\theta = 180° = \pi$ radians
$\theta = 360° = 2\pi$ radians
$\theta = 1$ radian

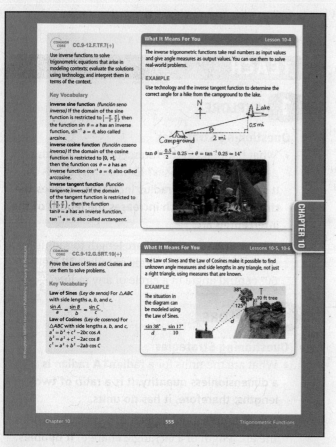

CC.9-12.F.TF.7(+)

Use inverse functions to solve trigonometric equations that arise in modeling contexts; evaluate the solutions using technology, and interpret them in terms of the context.

Key Vocabulary

inverse sine function *(función seno inverso)* If the domain of the sine function is restricted to $\left[-\frac{\pi}{2}, \frac{\pi}{2}\right]$, then the function $\sin \theta = a$ has an inverse function, $\sin^{-1} a = \theta$, also called *arcsine*.

inverse cosine function *(función coseno inverso)* If the domain of the cosine function is restricted to $[0, \pi]$, then the function $\cos \theta = a$ has an inverse function $\cos^{-1} a = \theta$, also called *arccosine*.

inverse tangent function *(función tangente inversa)* If the domain of the tangent function is restricted to $\left(-\frac{\pi}{2}, \frac{\pi}{2}\right)$, then the function $\tan \theta = a$ has an inverse function, $\tan^{-1} a = \theta$, also called *arctangent*.

What It Means For You — Lesson 10-4

The inverse trigonometric functions take real numbers as input values and give angle measures as output values. You can use them to solve real-world problems.

EXAMPLE

Use technology and the inverse tangent function to determine the correct angle for a hike from the campground to the lake.

$$\tan \theta = \frac{0.5}{2} = 0.25 \rightarrow \theta = \tan^{-1} 0.25 \approx 14°$$

CC.9-12.G.SRT.10(+)

Prove the Laws of Sines and Cosines and use them to solve problems.

Key Vocabulary

Law of Sines *(Ley de senos)* For $\triangle ABC$ with side lengths a, b, and c, $\frac{\sin A}{a} = \frac{\sin B}{b} = \frac{\sin C}{c}$.

Law of Cosines *(Ley de cosenos)* For $\triangle ABC$ with side lengths a, b, and c,
$a^2 = b^2 + c^2 - 2bc \cos A$
$b^2 = a^2 + c^2 - 2ac \cos B$
$c^2 = a^2 + b^2 - 2ab \cos C$

What It Means For You — Lessons 10-5, 10-6

The Law of Sines and the Law of Cosines make it possible to find unknown angle measures and side lengths in any triangle, not just a right triangle, using measures that are known.

EXAMPLE

The situation in the diagram can be modeled using the Law of Sines.

$$\frac{\sin 38°}{d} = \frac{\sin 17°}{10}$$

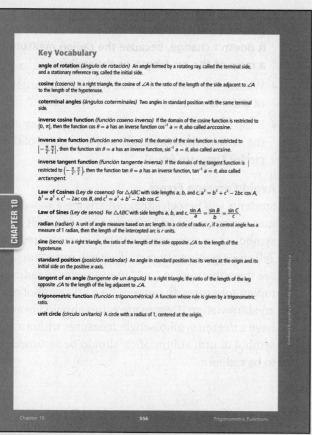

Key Vocabulary

angle of rotation *(ángulo de rotación)* An angle formed by a rotating ray, called the terminal side, and a stationary reference ray, called the initial side.

cosine *(coseno)* In a right triangle, the cosine of $\angle A$ is the ratio of the length of the side adjacent to $\angle A$ to the length of the hypotenuse.

coterminal angles *(ángulos coterminales)* Two angles in standard position with the same terminal side.

inverse cosine function *(función coseno inverso)* If the domain of the cosine function is restricted to $[0, \pi)$, then the function $\cos \theta = a$ has an inverse function $\cos^{-1} a = \theta$, also called *arccosine*.

inverse sine function *(función seno inverso)* If the domain of the sine function is restricted to $\left[-\frac{\pi}{2}, \frac{\pi}{2}\right]$, then the function $\sin \theta = a$ has an inverse function, $\sin^{-1} a = \theta$, also called *arcsine*.

inverse tangent function *(función tangente inversa)* If the domain of the tangent function is restricted to $\left(-\frac{\pi}{2}, \frac{\pi}{2}\right)$, then the function $\tan \theta = a$ has an inverse function, $\tan^{-1} a = \theta$, also called *arctangent*.

Law of Cosines *(Ley de cosenos)* For $\triangle ABC$ with side lengths a, b, and c, $a^2 = b^2 + c^2 - 2bc \cos A$, $b^2 = a^2 + c^2 - 2ac \cos B$, and $c^2 = a^2 + b^2 - 2ab \cos C$.

Law of Sines *(Ley de senos)* For $\triangle ABC$ with side lengths a, b, and c, $\frac{\sin A}{a} = \frac{\sin B}{b} = \frac{\sin C}{c}$.

radian *(radián)* A unit of angle measure based on arc length. In a circle of radius r, if a central angle has a measure of 1 radian, then the length of the intercepted arc is r units.

sine *(seno)* In a right triangle, the ratio of the length of the side opposite $\angle A$ to the length of the hypotenuse.

standard position *(posición estándar)* An angle in standard position has its vertex at the origin and its initial side on the positive x-axis.

tangent of an angle *(tangente de un ángulo)* In a right triangle, the ratio of the length of the leg opposite $\angle A$ to the length of the leg adjacent to $\angle A$.

trigonometric function *(función trigonométrica)* A function whose rule is given by a trigonometric ratio.

unit circle *(círculo unitario)* A circle with a radius of 1, centered at the origin.

COMMON CORE PROFESSIONAL DEVELOPMENT

CC.9-12.F.TF.7(+)*

Students have used inverse operations to solve linear, quadratic, polynomial, and exponential equations. This concept will now be extended to solving trigonometric equations. When trigonometric equations are used to model a real-world situation, instruction should stress the importance of interpreting the meaning and reasonableness of solutions in the context.

Right-Angle Trigonometry
Connection: Radian Measure

Essential question: *What is radian measure, and how are radians related to degrees?*

COMMON CORE **Standards for Mathematical Content**

CC.9-12.N.Q.1 Use units as a way to understand problems ...; choose and interpret units consistently in formulas ....*

CC.9-12.A.CED.4 Rearrange formulas to highlight a quantity of interest, using the same reasoning as in solving equations.*

CC.9-12.G.C.5 Derive using similarity the fact that the length of the arc intercepted by an angle is proportional to the radius, and define the radian measure of the angle as the constant of proportionality ....

Vocabulary

intercepted arcs

radian measure

Prerequisites

Circles, arcs, and angles

Math Background

Radians are a unit of angle measure. Radians are different from degrees, but it is possible to convert between degrees and radians. A radian can be defined as the measure of an angle in standard position on a circle of radius r centered at the origin whose terminal side intercepts an arc of length r. This means radians are dimensionless (radians are defined as the ratio of two lengths).

INTRODUCE

Review basic facts about circles. Students should understand the difference between the radius, the diameter, and the circumference of a circle. Remind students that π is the ratio of the circumference to the diameter of any circle. Since the radius is half the diameter, the circumference C is equal to $2\pi r$. Students should also recall that a circle measures 360°.

TEACH

1 EXPLORE

Questioning Strategies

• What happens to the intercepted arc length s as the radius increases? Explain why this is so. **It increases. As the radius increases, so does the circumference, which increases the length of the intercepted arc.**

• What will be the ratio of arc length to radius for a 60° central angle in a circle of radius 10 feet? for a 60° central angle in a circle of any radius? $\frac{\pi}{3}$; $\frac{\pi}{3}$

2 EXPLORE

Questioning Strategies

• What are the units for a radian? **A radian is a dimensionless quantity. It is a ratio of two lengths; therefore, it has no units.**

• If you double the diameter of a circle, how does the arc length of a 60° angle change? **It doubles.**

• If you double the diameter of a circle, how does the radian measure of a 60° angle change? **It doesn't change, because the radian measure is a ratio of the arc length to the radius.**

• What is the radian measure for a central angle of 180°? π

• If the radian measure is 1, what can you say about the arc length of the angle and the radius of the circle? **They are equal.**

Avoid Common Errors

Students will perceive that radians are a way of measuring angles and may seek to add a unit symbol or an abbreviation to radian measures. Tell students that although they will sometimes see the abbreviation "rad" used to refer to radians, radian measures do not require a unit symbol or an abbreviation. Degree measures should always have a degree symbol; angle measures without a symbol or unit abbreviation should be assumed to be radians.

continued

Name_____ Class_____ Date_____

10-1

Video Tutor

Right-Angle Trigonometry
Connection: Radian Measure

Essential question: *What is radian measure, and how are radians related to degrees?*

CC.9-12.G.C.5

1 EXPLORE   Finding the Ratio of Arc Length to Radius

The diagram shows three circles centered at point O. The arcs between the sides of the 60° central angle are called **intercepted arcs**.

$\overset{\frown}{AB}$ is on the circle with radius 1 unit,

$\overset{\frown}{CD}$ is on the circle with radius 2 units, and

$\overset{\frown}{EF}$ is on the circle with radius 3 units.

Each intercepted arc has a different length, but because the arcs are intercepted by the same central angle, each length is the *same fraction* of the circumference of the circle containing the arc.

A Determine the fraction of each circle's circumference that the length of each arc represents.

- How many degrees are in a circle? ___360°___
- What fraction of the total number of degrees in a circle is 60°? ___$\frac{1}{6}$___
- So, what fraction of the circumference of each circle is the length of each intercepted arc? ___$\frac{1}{6}$___

B Complete the table below. To find the length of the intercepted arc, use the fraction that you found in part A. Give all answers in terms of π.

Radius, r	Circumference, C $(C = 2\pi r)$	Length of Intercepted Arc, s	Ratio of Arc Length to Radius, $\frac{s}{r}$
1	$2\pi(1) = 2\pi$	$\frac{1}{6} \cdot 2\pi = \frac{\pi}{3}$	$\frac{\pi}{3} \div 1 = \frac{\pi}{3}$
2	$2\pi(2) = 4\pi$	$\frac{1}{6} \cdot 4\pi = \frac{2\pi}{3}$	$\frac{2\pi}{3} \div 2 = \frac{\pi}{3}$
3	$2\pi(3) = 6\pi$	$\frac{1}{6} \cdot 6\pi = \pi$	$\pi \div 3 = \frac{\pi}{3}$

REFLECT

1a. What do you notice about the ratios in the fourth column of the table?

They are all equal.

© Houghton Mifflin Harcourt Publishing Company

1b. When the ratio of the values of one variable y to the corresponding values of another variable x is a constant k, y is said to be *proportional* to x, and the constant k is called the *constant of proportionality*. Because $\frac{y}{x} = k$, you can solve for y to get $y = kx$. In the case of arcs intercepted by a 60° central angle, is arc length s proportional to radius r? If so, what is the constant of proportionality, and what equation gives s in terms of r?

Yes; $\frac{\pi}{3}$; $s = \frac{\pi}{3} \cdot r$

1c. Suppose the central angle is 90° instead of 60°. Would arc length s still be proportional to radius r? If so, would the constant of proportionality still be the same? Explain.

Although s is still proportional to r, the constant of proportionality would

become $\frac{\pi}{2}$ because a 90° angle represents $\frac{1}{4}$ of a circle, so (for instance) on

a circle of radius 2, $s = \frac{1}{4} \cdot 4\pi = \pi$, $r = 2$, and $\frac{s}{r} = \frac{\pi}{2}$.

Radian Measure In the Explore and its Reflect questions, you should have reached the following conclusions:

1. When a central angle intercepts arcs on circles that have a common center, the ratio of each arc length s to radius r is constant.

2. When the degree measure of the central angle changes, the constant also changes.

These facts allow you to create an alternative way of measuring angles. Instead of degree measure, you can use *radian measure*, defined as follows: If a central angle in a circle of radius r intercepts an arc of length s, then the angle's **radian measure** is $\theta = \frac{s}{r}$.

CC.9-12.A.CED.4

2 EXPLORE   Relating Radians to Degrees

Let the degree measure of a central angle in a circle with radius r be $d°$, as shown. You can derive formulas that relate the *angle's* degree measure and its radian measure.

A Find the length s of the intercepted arc $\overset{\frown}{XY}$ using the verbal model below. Give the length in terms of π, and simplify.

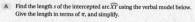

$$\text{Length of arc} = \frac{\text{Degrees in arc}}{\text{Degrees in circle}} \cdot \text{Circumference of circle}$$

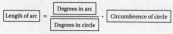

$$s = \frac{d°}{360°} \cdot 2\pi r = \frac{\pi r \cdot d°}{180°}$$

© Houghton Mifflin Harcourt Publishing Company

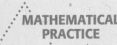

MATHEMATICAL PRACTICE   Highlighting the Standards

1 EXPLORE and **2** EXPLORE include opportunities to address Mathematical Practice Standard 2 (Reason abstractly and quantitatively). Students will explore the relationship between arc length and radius for various intercepted arcs. They will derive the conversion factor between radians and degrees and understand that radians are dimensionless quantities. Students will practice converting between degrees and radians.

3 EXAMPLE

Questioning Strategies

- How can you check that you are using your conversion factor between degrees and radians correctly? When you convert an angle measure from degrees to radians, the ratio of the degree measure to the radian measure should be about 57.3°.

- As a quick check of your conversion, you can look at values. If $0° < d° < 180°$, between what values will the corresponding radians be? $0 < \theta < \pi$. If $180° < d° < 360°$, between what values will the corresponding radians be? $\pi < \theta < 2\pi$

EXTRA EXAMPLES

A. Use the formula $\theta = \dfrac{\pi}{180°} \cdot d°$ to convert each degree measure to radian measure. Simplify the result: 10°, 20°, 30°. $\dfrac{\pi}{18}, \dfrac{\pi}{9}, \dfrac{\pi}{6}$

B. Use the formula $d° = \dfrac{180°}{\pi} \cdot \theta$ to convert each radian measure to degree measure. Simplify the result: $\dfrac{7\pi}{6}, \dfrac{4\pi}{3}, \dfrac{3\pi}{2}$. 210°, 240°, 270°

CLOSE

Essential Question

What is radian measure, and how are radians related to degrees?

A radian is a unit of angle measure. The radian measure of a central angle of a circle is equal to the ratio of the intercepted arc length to the radius of the circle. It is related to degrees by the formula $\theta = \dfrac{\pi}{180°} \cdot d°$, where θ represents radian measure and $d°$ represents degree measure.

Summarize

Have students write a journal entry describing what radian measure is and showing how to convert between radians and degrees. Students should explain the conversion formulas in words.

PRACTICE

Where skills are taught	Where skills are practiced
3 EXAMPLE	EXS. 1, 2

Exercise 3: Students extend what they learned in **1** EXPLORE and **2** EXPLORE to find the radian measure of a central angle whose intercepted arc is equal in length to the radius of the circle.

Exercise 4: Students extend what they learned in **1** EXPLORE and **2** EXPLORE to the unit circle.

Exercise 5: Students extend what they learned in **1** EXPLORE and **2** EXPLORE to find the radian measure of a pizza slice and the diameter of the pizza, given an arc length.

B Use the result from part A to write the angle's radian measure θ in terms of d to find a formula for converting degrees to radians.

$$\theta = \frac{s}{r} = \frac{\frac{\pi r \cdot d^\circ}{180^\circ}}{r} = \frac{\pi}{180^\circ} \cdot d^\circ$$

C Solve the equation from part B for d° to find a formula for converting radians to degrees.

$$d^\circ = \frac{180^\circ}{\pi} \cdot \theta$$

REFLECT

2a. What radian measure is equivalent to 360°? Why does this make sense?

2π; 360° is a complete circle, so the arc length is the circumference of the circle, $2\pi r$. The ratio of the arc length to the radius is 2π.

Radian measures are usually written in terms of π, using fractions, such as $\frac{2\pi}{3}$, rather than mixed numbers.

3 EXAMPLE CC.9-12.N.Q.1 **Converting Between Radians and Degrees**

A Use the formula $\theta = \frac{\pi}{180^\circ} \cdot d^\circ$ to convert each degree measure to radian measure. Simplify the result.

Degree measure	Radian measure
15°	$\frac{\pi}{180^\circ} \cdot 15^\circ = \frac{\pi}{12}$
45°	$\frac{\pi}{180^\circ} \cdot 45^\circ = \frac{\pi}{4}$
90°	$\frac{\pi}{180^\circ} \cdot 90^\circ = \frac{\pi}{2}$
120°	$\frac{\pi}{180^\circ} \cdot 120^\circ = \frac{2\pi}{3}$
135°	$\frac{\pi}{180^\circ} \cdot 135^\circ = \frac{3\pi}{4}$
165°	$\frac{\pi}{180^\circ} \cdot 165^\circ = \frac{11\pi}{12}$

B Use the formula $d^\circ = \frac{180^\circ}{\pi} \cdot \theta$ to convert each radian measure to degree measure. Simplify the result.

Radian measure	Degree measure
$\frac{\pi}{6}$	$\frac{180^\circ}{\pi} \cdot \frac{\pi}{6} = 30^\circ$
$\frac{\pi}{3}$	$\frac{180^\circ}{\pi} \cdot \frac{\pi}{3} = 60^\circ$
$\frac{5\pi}{12}$	$\frac{180^\circ}{\pi} \cdot \frac{5\pi}{12} = 75^\circ$
$\frac{7\pi}{12}$	$\frac{180^\circ}{\pi} \cdot \frac{7\pi}{12} = 105^\circ$
$\frac{5\pi}{6}$	$\frac{180^\circ}{\pi} \cdot \frac{5\pi}{6} = 150^\circ$
π	$\frac{180^\circ}{\pi} \cdot \pi = 180^\circ$

REFLECT

3a. Which is greater, 1° or 1 radian? Explain.

1 radian; it is equivalent to $\frac{180^\circ}{\pi} \approx 57^\circ$.

3b. A radian is sometimes called a "dimensionless" quantity. Use unit analysis and the definition of radian to explain why this description makes sense.

A radian is a ratio of two lengths. The units in the numerator and denominator are the same, so they divide out, leaving no units.

PRACTICE

1. Convert each degree measure to radian measure. Simplify the result.

Degree measure	18°	24°	72°	84°	108°	126°	132°
Radian measure	$\frac{\pi}{10}$	$\frac{2\pi}{15}$	$\frac{2\pi}{5}$	$\frac{7\pi}{15}$	$\frac{3\pi}{5}$	$\frac{7\pi}{10}$	$\frac{11\pi}{15}$

2. Convert each radian measure to degree measure. Simplify the result.

Radian measure	$\frac{\pi}{15}$	$\frac{\pi}{5}$	$\frac{4\pi}{15}$	$\frac{3\pi}{10}$	$\frac{8\pi}{15}$	$\frac{13\pi}{15}$	$\frac{9\pi}{10}$
Degree measure	12°	36°	48°	54°	96°	156°	162°

3. When a central angle of a circle intercepts an arc whose length equals the radius of the circle, what is the angle's radian measure? Explain.

1; in the formula $\theta = \frac{s}{r}$, $s = r$, so $\theta = 1$.

4. A *unit circle* has a radius of 1. What is the relationship between the radian measure of a central angle in a unit circle and the length of the arc that it intercepts? Explain.

They are equal; in the formula $\theta = \frac{s}{r}$, $r = 1$, so $\theta = s$.

5. A pizza is cut into 8 equal slices.

a. What is the radian measure of the angle in each slice? $\frac{\pi}{4}$

b. If the length along the outer edge of the crust of one slice is about 7 inches, what is the *diameter* of the pizza to the nearest inch?
(Use the formula $\theta = \frac{s}{r}$, but note that it gives you the radius of the pizza.) 18 inches

Assign these pages to help your students practice
and apply important lesson concepts. For
additional exercises, see the Student Edition.

Answers

Additional Practice

1. $75°$

2. $\dfrac{43\pi}{36}$ radians

3. $-290°$

4. $-\pi$ radians

5. $300°$

6. $210°$

7. $\dfrac{20\pi}{9}$ radians

8. $54°$

9. $\dfrac{7\pi}{36}$ radians

10. $-\dfrac{1}{2}$

11. 1

12. $-\dfrac{\sqrt{3}}{3}$

13. $-\dfrac{\sqrt{2}}{2}$

14. $-\dfrac{\sqrt{2}}{2}$

15. $\sqrt{3}$

16. $\dfrac{1}{2}; -\dfrac{\sqrt{3}}{2}; -\dfrac{\sqrt{3}}{3}$

17. $\dfrac{\sqrt{2}}{2}; -\dfrac{\sqrt{2}}{2}; -1$

18. $\dfrac{\sqrt{3}}{2}; \dfrac{1}{2}; \sqrt{3}$

19. $-\dfrac{1}{2}; \dfrac{\sqrt{3}}{2}; -\dfrac{\sqrt{3}}{3}$

20. $-\dfrac{\sqrt{3}}{2}; -\dfrac{1}{2}; \sqrt{3}$

21. $-\dfrac{\sqrt{2}}{2}; -\dfrac{\sqrt{2}}{2}; 1$

22. 2073 mi

Problem Solving

1. a. $r = \dfrac{\pi}{2}$

   b. $\theta = \dfrac{2\pi}{6}$ or $\dfrac{\pi}{3}$

   c. $S = r\theta = \dfrac{\pi}{2} \cdot \dfrac{\pi}{3} = \dfrac{\pi^2}{6}$

   d. 1.64 in.

   e. Yes; possible answer: because the arc length
of the fragment is very close to the arc
length that would be expected for a plate of
diameter π

2. $\dfrac{1}{4}$

3. C

4. H

5. B

6. F

Additional Practice

Name_____ Class_____ Date_____

Convert each measure from degrees to radians or from radians to degrees.

1. $\dfrac{5\pi}{12}$

_____

2. 215°

_____

3. $-\dfrac{29\pi}{18}$

_____

4. −180°

_____

5. $\dfrac{5\pi}{3}$

_____

6. $\dfrac{7\pi}{6}$

_____

7. 400°

_____

8. $\dfrac{3\pi}{10}$

_____

9. 35°

_____

Use the unit circle to find the exact value of each trigonometric function.

10. $\cos\dfrac{2\pi}{3}$

_____

11. $\tan\dfrac{5\pi}{4}$

_____

12. $\tan\dfrac{5\pi}{6}$

_____

13. sin 315°

_____

14. cos 225°

_____

15. tan 60°

_____

Use a reference angle to find the exact value of the sine, cosine, and tangent of each angle.

16. 150°

_____

17. −225°

_____

18. −300°

_____

19. $\dfrac{11\pi}{6}$

_____

20. $-\dfrac{2\pi}{3}$

_____

21. $\dfrac{5\pi}{4}$

_____

Solve.

22. San Antonio, Texas, is located about 30° north of the equator. If Earth's radius is about 3959 miles, approximately how many miles is San Antonio from the equator?

_____

Chapter 10   561   Lesson 1

Problem Solving

Gabe is spending two weeks on an archaeological dig. He finds a fragment of a circular plate that his leader thinks may be valuable. The arc length of the fragment is about $\dfrac{1}{6}$ the circumference of the original complete plate and measures 1.65 inches.

1. A similar plate found earlier has a diameter of 3.14 inches. Could Gabe's fragment match this plate?

   a. Write an expression for the radius, r, of the earlier plate. _____

   b. What is the measure, in radians, of a central angle, θ, that intercepts an arc that is $\dfrac{1}{6}$ the length of the circumference of a circle? _____

   c. Write an expression for the arc length, S, intercepted by this central angle. _____

   d. How long would the arc length of a fragment be if it were $\dfrac{1}{6}$ the circumference of the plate? _____

   e. Could Gabe's plate be a matching plate? Explain.

   _____

2. Toby finds another fragment of arc length 2.48 inches. What fraction of the outer edge of Gabe's plate would it be if this fragment were part of Gabe's plate? _____

The diameter of a merry-go-round at the playground is 12 feet. Elijah stands on the edge and his sister pushes him around. Choose the letter for the best answer.

3. How far does Elijah travel if he moves through an angle of $\dfrac{5\pi}{4}$ radians?

   A 12.0 ft   C 23.6 ft

   B 15.1 ft   D 47.1 ft

4. Through what angle does Elijah move if he travels a distance of 80 feet around the circumference?

   F $\dfrac{40}{3}\pi$ radians   H $\dfrac{40}{3}$ radians

   G $\dfrac{80}{3}$ radians   J $\dfrac{20}{3}$ radians

Virgil sets his boat on a 1000-yard course keeping a constant distance from a rocky outcrop. Choose the letter for the best answer.

5. If Virgil keeps a distance of 200 yards, through what angle does he travel?

   A 5π radians   C 10 radians

   B 5 radians   D 10π radians

6. If Virgil keeps a distance of 500 yards, what fraction of the circumference of a circle does he cover?

   F $\dfrac{1}{\pi}$ H $\dfrac{3}{4\pi}$

   G $\dfrac{\pi}{3}$ J $\dfrac{3\pi}{4}$

Chapter 10   562   Lesson 1

Angles of Rotation
Extension: The Unit Circle

Essential question: *What is an angle of rotation, and how is it measured?*

COMMON Standards for
CORE Mathematical Content

CC.9-12.F.TF.1 Understand radian measure of an angle as the length of the arc on the unit circle subtended by the angle.

Vocabulary

angle of rotation

standard position

initial side

terminal side

unit circle

coterminal

Prerequisites

Circles, arcs, and angles

Radian measure

Math Background

Students are familiar with angles from their study of geometry. However, those angles all measured 180° or less. Students will now be exposed to angles with measures of more than 180°, including angles with measures more than 360°, and to negative angle measures.

The unit circle is a circle with a radius of one unit, centered at the origin. Any point on the circle (x, y) will satisfy the equation $x^2 + y^2 = 1$. This results from the Pythagorean theorem by using the radius of 1 as the hypotenuse. Students will use this Pythagorean relationship to derive the trigonometric identity $\sin^2 \theta + \cos^2 \theta = 1$ later in this unit.

INTRODUCE

In this lesson, students will investigate angles of rotation. These angles are not confined to angles with measures less than 180°, as angles often are in geometry courses. Angles of rotation may measure more than 180° or have negative measures. Remind students that there are 360° in one revolution. Ask them how many degrees there are in two revolutions, in three revolutions, or in one and a half revolutions.

TEACH

1 ENGAGE

Questioning Strategies

- What is the difference between a 180° angle of rotation and a −180° angle of rotation? They have the same terminal side, but the positive angle has a counterclockwise rotation while the negative angle has a clockwise rotation.

- What is the difference between a 90° angle of rotation and a −90° angle of rotation? The positive angle has its terminal side along the positive *y*-axis. The negative angle has its terminal side along the negative *y*-axis.

Teaching Strategy

Introducing students to the unit circle provides an opportunity to further develop students' understanding of units of measure. Point out to students that although the measure of a central angle in a unit circle and the length of its intercepted arc are *numerically* equal, they don't have the same units. Arcs are measured in units of length. Angles are measured in radians, which are unitless.

2 EXAMPLE

Questioning Strategies

- How would the drawing of a 90° angle differ from the drawing in part A? The arrow for a 90° angle would start at the positive *x*-axis and end at the positive *y*-axis. It would not go around in a complete circle.

- In part B, why does the arrow go clockwise to the terminal side? to indicate that the angle measure is negative

continued

Name_____ Class_____ Date_____

10-2

Angles of Rotation
Extension: The Unit Circle

Essential question: *What is an angle of rotation, and how is it measured?*

Video Tutor

© Houghton Mifflin Harcourt Publishing Company

CC.9-12.F.TF.1

1 ENGAGE   **Understanding Angles of Rotation**

In trigonometry, an **angle of rotation** is an angle formed by the starting and ending positions of a ray that rotates about its endpoint. The angle is in **standard position** in a coordinate plane when the starting position of the ray, or **initial side** of the angle, is on the positive x-axis and has its endpoint at the origin. To show the amount and direction of rotation, a curved arrow is drawn to the ending position of the ray, or **terminal side** of the angle.

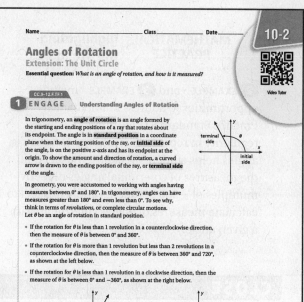

In geometry, you were accustomed to working with angles having measures between 0° and 180°. In trigonometry, angles can have measures greater than 180° and even less than 0°. To see why, think in terms of *revolutions*, or complete circular motions. Let θ be an angle of rotation in standard position.

- If the rotation for θ is less than 1 revolution in a counterclockwise direction, then the measure of θ is between 0° and 360°.

- If the rotation for θ is more than 1 revolution but less than 2 revolutions in a counterclockwise direction, then the measure of θ is between 360° and 720°, as shown at the left below.

- If the rotation for θ is less than 1 revolution in a clockwise direction, then the measure of θ is between 0° and −360°, as shown at the right below.

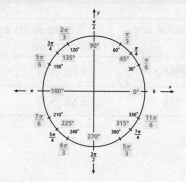

In general, when a rotation is counterclockwise, the measure of θ is positive, and when a rotation is clockwise, the measure of θ is negative.

In the illustrations above, the measures of angles of rotation are given in degrees, but if a circle is introduced into the coordinate plane, you can think in terms of arc lengths and use radian measure instead.

The **unit circle** is a circle that has a radius of 1 unit and is centered at the origin. Think of θ, an angle of rotation in standard position, as traversing an arc on the unit circle. Recall that radian measure was defined in Lesson 8-1 as $\theta = \frac{s}{r}$ where s is the arc length and r is the radius of the circle. Since r = 1 in this case, the radian measure of θ is simply the arc length: θ = s. (Note: Throughout this unit, the symbol θ will be used to represent both an angle of rotation and its measure. For instance, "angle θ" refers to an angle, while "θ = π" refers to an angle's measure.)

REFLECT

1a. The unit circle below shows the measures of angles of rotation that are commonly used in trigonometry. Radian measures appear outside the circle, and equivalent degree measures appear inside the circle. Provide the missing measures.

$$\frac{\pi}{2} \quad 90°$$
$$\frac{2\pi}{3} \quad 120° \qquad 60° \quad \frac{\pi}{3}$$
$$\frac{3\pi}{4} \quad 135° \qquad 45° \quad \frac{\pi}{4}$$
$$\frac{5\pi}{6} \quad 150° \qquad 30° \quad \frac{\pi}{6}$$
$$\pi \quad 180° \qquad\qquad 0° \quad 0$$
$$\frac{7\pi}{6} \quad 210° \qquad 330° \quad \frac{11\pi}{6}$$
$$225° \qquad 315° \quad \frac{7\pi}{4}$$
$$\frac{5\pi}{4} \quad 240° \qquad 300° \quad \frac{5\pi}{3}$$
$$\frac{4\pi}{3} \quad 270° \quad \frac{5\pi}{3}$$
$$\frac{3\pi}{2}$$

1b. Explain how you can use the diagram above to draw an angle of rotation with a measure of 570°.

Subtract 360° from 570° to get 210°; the angle represents 1 counterclockwise

revolution plus 210° more.

© Houghton Mifflin Harcourt Publishing Company

EXTRA EXAMPLE
Draw each angle of rotation with the given measure.

A. 720°

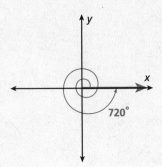

B. $-\dfrac{11\pi}{4}$

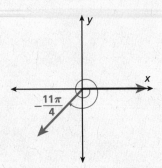

3 EXAMPLE

Questioning Strategies
- How else could you find coterminal angles in parts A and B? **In part A, you could add or subtract any multiple of 360° to or from −30°. In part B, you could add or subtract any multiple of 2π to or from $\dfrac{4\pi}{3}$.**

EXTRA EXAMPLE
Find the measure of a positive angle and a negative angle that are coterminal with each given angle.

A. −45°   315°, −405°

B. $\dfrac{\pi}{3}$ $\dfrac{7\pi}{3}$, $-\dfrac{5\pi}{3}$

CLOSE

Essential Question
What is an angle of rotation, and how is it measured?
An angle of rotation is an angle formed by the starting and ending positions of a ray that rotates about its endpoint. If the initial side is the positive x-axis and the endpoint is the origin, the angle is in standard position. You can measure an angle of rotation in degrees or radians, with the measure of an angle formed by a clockwise rotation being negative and the measure of an angle formed by a counterclockwise rotation being positive.

Summarize
Have students write a journal entry describing angles of rotation and coterminal angles. They should mention positive and negative angles, as well as radians and degrees.

PRACTICE

Where skills are taught	Where skills are practiced
2 EXAMPLE	EXS. 1–4
3 EXAMPLE	EXS. 5–8

---

2 EXAMPLE Drawing Angles of Rotation

Draw each angle of rotation with the given measure.

A 450°

Recognize that 450° represents 1 revolution counterclockwise (360°) plus 90° more. Draw the angle's initial side on the positive x-axis. Then draw a spiraling arrow from the initial side in a counterclockwise direction. The spiral should complete a full circle and then go a quarter of a circle farther. Draw the angle's terminal side where the arrow ends.

B $-\frac{5\pi}{4}$

Recognize that $-\frac{5\pi}{4}$ represents $\frac{1}{2}$ revolution clockwise $(-\pi)$ plus $-\frac{\pi}{4}$ more. Draw the angle's initial side on the positive x-axis. Then draw a spiraling arrow from the initial side in a clockwise direction. The spiral should complete a half circle and then go an eighth of a circle farther. Draw the angle's terminal side where the arrow ends.

REFLECT

2a. Is the measure of an angle of rotation in standard position completely determined by the position of its terminal side? Explain.

No; there are infinitely many angles of rotation that could be drawn in standard position with a given terminal side.

Angles of rotation in standard position that have the same terminal side are called **coterminal**.

3 EXAMPLE Finding Coterminal Angles

Find the measure of a positive angle and a negative angle that are coterminal with each given angle.

A −30°

For a positive coterminal angle, add 360°: −30° + 360° = ___330°___

For a negative coterminal angle, subtract 360°: −30° − 360° = ___−390°___

B $\frac{4\pi}{3}$

For a positive coterminal angle, add 2π: $\frac{4\pi}{3} + 2\pi =$ ___$\frac{10\pi}{3}$___

For a negative coterminal angle, subtract 2π: $\frac{4\pi}{3} - 2\pi =$ ___$-\frac{2\pi}{3}$___

© Houghton Mifflin Harcourt Publishing Company

REFLECT

3a. Describe a general method for finding the measure of *any* angle that is coterminal with a given angle.

Add or subtract a multiple of 360° or 2π from the given angle's measure.

3b. Find the measure between 720° and 1080° of an angle that is coterminal with an angle that has a measure of −30°. Explain your method.

1050°; 720 and 1080 are consecutive multiples of 360, and −30 + 1080 = 1050

PRACTICE

Draw the angle of rotation with each given measure.

1. −180°

2. 405°

3. $-\frac{2\pi}{3}$

4. $\frac{15\pi}{4}$

Find the measure of a positive angle and a negative angle that are coterminal with each given angle.   Answers may vary. Sample answers are given.

5. −10° ___350°; −370°___

6. 500° ___140°; −220°___

7. $-\frac{7\pi}{6}$ ___$\frac{5\pi}{6}$; $\frac{19\pi}{6}$___

8. $\frac{11\pi}{4}$ ___$\frac{3\pi}{4}$; $-\frac{5\pi}{4}$___

© Houghton Mifflin Harcourt Publishing Company

Assign these pages to help your students practice and apply important lesson concepts. For additional exercises, see the Student Edition.

Answers

Additional Practice

1.

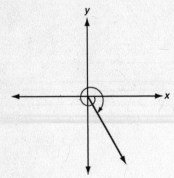

2.

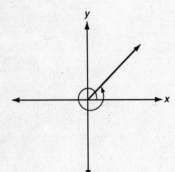

3.

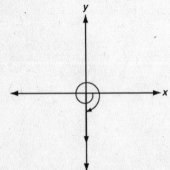

4. 65°, −295°   **5.** 44°, −676°

6. 280°, −80°   **7.** 641°, −79°

8. 356°, −364°   **9.** 23°, −337°

10. 31°   **11.** 35°

12. 15°   **13.** 61°

14. 20°   **15.** 55°

16. $\sin \theta = \dfrac{\sqrt{2}}{2}$; $\cos \theta = -\dfrac{\sqrt{2}}{2}$;

$\tan \theta = -1$; $\cot \theta = -1$;

$\csc \theta = \sqrt{2}$; $\sec \theta = -\sqrt{2}$

17. $\sin \theta = \dfrac{9\sqrt{85}}{85}$; $\cos \theta = \dfrac{2\sqrt{85}}{85}$;

$\tan \theta = \dfrac{9}{2}$; $\cot \theta = \dfrac{2}{9}$;

$\csc \theta = \dfrac{\sqrt{85}}{9}$; $\sec \theta = \dfrac{\sqrt{85}}{2}$

18. $\sin \theta = -\dfrac{5\sqrt{74}}{74}$; $\cos \theta = -\dfrac{7\sqrt{74}}{74}$;

$\tan \theta = \dfrac{5}{7}$; $\cot \theta = \dfrac{7}{5}$;

$\csc \theta = -\dfrac{\sqrt{74}}{5}$; $\sec \theta = \dfrac{\sqrt{74}}{7}$

19. 8100°

Problem Solving

1. 180°   **2.** 60°

3. a. $\dfrac{330}{360} \times 60$ min

b. 55 min

c. 25 min

d. 150°

4. a. 2 h 20 min

b. $2\dfrac{1}{3}$

c. 60°

5. a. $\tan \theta = \dfrac{3}{2}$

b. 2.2 km

6. A   **7.** J

Additional Practice

Name_____ Class_____ Date_____ **10-2**

Draw an angle with the given measure in standard position.

1. −420°

2. 405°

3. −450°

Find the measures of a positive angle and a negative angle that are coterminal with each given angle.

4. $\theta = 425°$

5. $\theta = -316°$

6. $\theta = -800°$

7. $\theta = 281°$

8. $\theta = -4°$

9. $\theta = 743°$

Find the measure of the reference angle for each given angle.

10. $\theta = 211°$

11. $\theta = -755°$

12. $\theta = -555°$

13. $\theta = 119°$

14. $\theta = -160°$

15. $\theta = 235°$

P is a point on the terminal side of θ in standard position. Find the exact value of the six trigonometric functions for θ.

16. $P(-5, 5)$

17. $P(2, 9)$

18. $P(-7, -5)$

Solve.

19. A circus performer trots her pony into the ring. The pony circles the ring 22 times as the performer flips and turns on the pony's back. At the end of the act, the pony exits on the side of the ring opposite its point of entry. Through how many degrees does the pony trot during the entire act?

Chapter 10   567   Lesson 2

Problem Solving

Isabelle and Karl agreed to meet at the rotating restaurant at the top of a tower in the town center. The restaurant makes one full rotation each hour.

1. Isabelle waits for Karl, who arrives 30 minutes later. Through how many degrees does the restaurant rotate between the time that Isabelle arrives and the time that Karl arrives? _____

2. Since the restaurant is busy, they don't get menus for another ten minutes. How much farther has the restaurant rotated? _____

3. By the time they are served dinner, the restaurant has rotated to an angle 30° short of its orientation when Isabelle arrived.

   a. Write an expression for the length of time that Isabelle has been there. _____

   b. How long has she been there? _____

   c. How long has Karl been there? _____

   d. How far has the restaurant rotated since Karl arrived? _____

4. When their bill comes, it includes a note that the restaurant has rotated 840° since Isabelle arrived.

   a. How long has it been since they were served dinner? _____

   b. How many rotations has the restaurant made since Isabelle arrived? _____

   c. How far is the restaurant from its orientation when Karl arrived? _____

5. On their way out, they stop and look at a map. A museum is located at a point northeast of the tower with coordinates (3, 2).

   a. Write the trigonometric function for the angle that the line from the tower to the museum makes with a line due north from the tower. _____

   b. Isabelle says that the museum is exactly 4 kilometers from the tower. How much farther north is the museum than the tower? _____

An advertisement on a kiosk near the bus stop rotates through 765° while Aaron waits for his bus. Choose the letter for the best answer.

6. What is the difference in the orientation of the advertisement between when Aaron arrived at the bus stop and when the bus came?

   A 45°

   B 90°

   C 315°

   D 405°

7. If the advertisement rotates at a rate of one rotation every 10 minutes, how long does Aaron wait for his bus?

   F Less than 2 min

   G Between 2 min and 10 min

   H Between 10 min and 20 min

   J More than 20 min

Chapter 10   568   Lesson 2

10-3

The Unit Circle
Connection: The Sine, Cosine, and Tangent Functions

Essential question: *How can the sine, cosine, and tangent functions be defined using the unit circle?*

COMMON CORE Standards for Mathematical Content

CC.9-12.F.IF.1 Understand that a function from one set (called the domain) to another set (called the range) assigns to each element of the domain exactly one element of the range. If f is a function and x is an element of its domain, then $f(x)$ denotes the output of f corresponding to the input x. The graph of f is the graph of the equation $y = f(x)$.

CC.9-12.F.TF.2 Explain how the unit circle in the coordinate plane enables the extension of trigonometric functions to all real numbers, interpreted as radian measures of angles traversed counterclockwise around the unit circle.

CC.9-12.F.TF.3(+) Use special triangles to determine geometrically the values of sine, cosine, tangent for $\frac{\pi}{3}$, $\frac{\pi}{4}$, and $\frac{\pi}{6}$, and use the unit circle to express the values of sine, cosine, and tangent for x, $\pi + x$, and $2\pi - x$ in terms of their values for x, where x is any real number.

Vocabulary
reference angle

Prerequisites
Sine, cosine, and tangent
Special right triangles

Math Background
The sine, cosine, and tangent functions—sometimes called circular functions—are used when modeling periodic motion. Periodic motion is a motion that has a pattern that is repeated at regular intervals. Examples include the swinging of a pendulum and the progress of a wave (light, sound, or ocean waves).

This lesson connects students' past experience with triangle trigonometry to the study of circular trigonometry. Later in the unit, students will investigate real-world applications of trigonometry involving periodic motion.

There are many real-world applications of trigonometric functions. Early trigonometric relationships were used around 200 BCE in describing astronomical observations.

Today these functions are also used in the following fields: acoustics, music, optics, electronics, probability, medical imaging, surveying, architecture, electrical engineering, civil engineering, cartography, and computer game development, to name a few.

INTRODUCE

Ask students to recall the sine, cosine, and tangent ratios from geometry. Then ask them what mnemonics they use to remember these ratios. One popular method is using the alphabet for sine and cosine (cosine goes with adjacent and sine goes with opposite—the earlier letters in the alphabet belong together). Another method is the mnemonic SOHCAHTOA.

Next, have students review the values of the sine, cosine, and tangent for the special angles. Also, have them find the corresponding radian measure for those angles. Gather the information in a table on the board, such as the one below.

Angle	Radians	Sine	Cosine	Tangent
30°	$\frac{\pi}{6}$	$\frac{1}{2}$	$\frac{\sqrt{3}}{2}$	$\frac{\sqrt{3}}{3}$
45°	$\frac{\pi}{4}$	$\frac{\sqrt{2}}{2}$	$\frac{\sqrt{2}}{2}$	1
60°	$\frac{\pi}{3}$	$\frac{\sqrt{3}}{2}$	$\frac{1}{2}$	$\sqrt{3}$

TEACH

 EXPLORE

Questioning Strategies
• The sine, cosine, and tangent are ratios of the lengths of sides for what type of triangle?
  right triangle

continued

10-3

The Unit Circle
Connection: The Sine, Cosine, and Tangent Functions

Essential question: *How can the sine, cosine, and tangent functions be defined using the unit circle?*

Video Tutor

CC.9–12.F.TF.2

1 EXPLORE   Extending the Definitions of Sine, Cosine, and Tangent

In geometry, you learned that sine, cosine, and tangent are ratios of the lengths of the sides of a right triangle. In particular, if θ is an acute angle in a right triangle, then:

$\sin\theta = \dfrac{\text{opposite}}{\text{hypotenuse}}$

$\cos\theta = \dfrac{\text{adjacent}}{\text{hypotenuse}}$

$\tan\theta = \dfrac{\text{opposite}}{\text{adjacent}}$

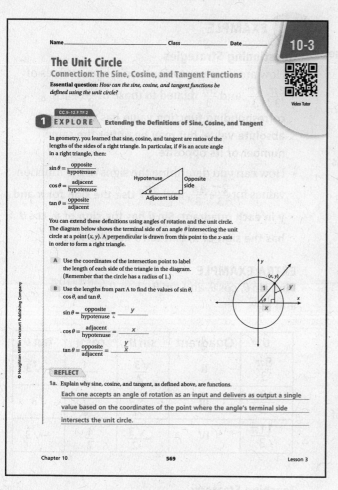

Hypotenuse / Opposite side / Adjacent side / θ

You can extend these definitions using angles of rotation and the unit circle. The diagram below shows the terminal side of an angle θ intersecting the unit circle at a point (x, y). A perpendicular is drawn from this point to the x-axis in order to form a right triangle.

A Use the coordinates of the intersection point to label the length of each side of the triangle in the diagram. (Remember that the circle has a radius of 1.)

B Use the lengths from part A to find the values of $\sin\theta$, $\cos\theta$, and $\tan\theta$.

$\sin\theta = \dfrac{\text{opposite}}{\text{hypotenuse}} = \dfrac{y}{}$

$\cos\theta = \dfrac{\text{adjacent}}{\text{hypotenuse}} = \dfrac{x}{}$

$\tan\theta = \dfrac{\text{opposite}}{\text{adjacent}} = \dfrac{y}{x}$

REFLECT

1a. Explain why sine, cosine, and tangent, as defined above, are functions.

Each one accepts an angle of rotation as an input and delivers as output a single

value based on the coordinates of the point where the angle's terminal side

intersects the unit circle.

© Houghton Mifflin Harcourt Publishing Company

1b. Although you can think of x and y as lengths when the terminal side of θ lies in Quadrant I, you know that the values of x and/or y are negative in other quadrants. Dropping the idea of lengths and simply accepting that $\sin\theta = y$, $\cos\theta = x$, and $\tan\theta = \dfrac{y}{x}$ no matter where the terminal side of θ lies, complete the table by stating the sign of each function's values in each quadrant.

Trigonometric function	Sign of Function's Values in Quadrant			
	I	II	III	IV
$\sin\theta$	positive	positive	negative	negative
$\cos\theta$	positive	negative	negative	positive
$\tan\theta$	positive	negative	positive	negative

1c. Are the sine, cosine, and tangent functions defined at all points on the unit circle? If not, identify the points where each function is not defined, and state any restrictions on the value of θ.

Sine and cosine are always defined, so there are no restrictions on θ;

tangent is undefined at $(0, 1)$ and $(0, -1)$, so θ cannot equal odd multiples

of 90°.

1d. What are the maximum and minimum x- and y-coordinates of points on the unit circle? What does this mean for the range of the sine and cosine functions?

The maximum x-coordinate and the maximum y-coordinate are 1, and the

minimum x-coordinate and the minimum y-coordinate are -1; the range of sine is

$\{\sin\theta \mid -1 \le \sin\theta \le 1\}$, and the range of cosine is $\{\cos\theta \mid -1 \le \cos\theta \le 1\}$.

1e. Each table lists several points on the unit circle near $(0, 1)$. If each point is on the terminal side of an angle θ, find the value of $\tan\theta$. Then describe what happens to $\tan\theta$ the closer θ gets to 90°.

The values of $\tan\theta$ appear to increase

and decrease without bound.

Point on terminal side of θ	Value of $\tan\theta$
$\left(\frac{3}{5}, \frac{4}{5}\right)$	$\frac{4}{3}$
$\left(\frac{5}{13}, \frac{12}{13}\right)$	$\frac{12}{5}$
$\left(\frac{7}{25}, \frac{24}{25}\right)$	$\frac{24}{7}$

Point on terminal side of θ	Value of $\tan\theta$
$\left(-\frac{3}{5}, \frac{4}{5}\right)$	$-\frac{4}{3}$
$\left(-\frac{5}{13}, \frac{12}{13}\right)$	$-\frac{12}{5}$
$\left(-\frac{7}{25}, \frac{24}{25}\right)$	$-\frac{24}{7}$

© Houghton Mifflin Harcourt Publishing Company

- Why does sin $\theta = y$ and cos $\theta = x$? **The hypotenuse is 1, so sin $\theta = \frac{y}{1} = y$ and cos $\theta = \frac{x}{1} = x$.**

- In the table giving the domain and range of the trigonometric functions, why is the range for sine and cosine between -1 and 1 inclusive? **The sine and cosine are defined using the unit circle. The greatest value either x or y can have is 1 and the least value is -1. Therefore, the range of both functions is between -1 and 1 inclusive.**

Avoid Common Errors

Students are likely to look at the range of the sine function and the range of the cosine function and come to the conclusion that the tangent also has a range of -1 to 1 inclusive. To help them see that this is not the case, have them use string to make right triangles in the first quadrant on the unit circle. As θ increases, they should see that x decreases and y increases. In fact, they should see that x approaches 0 as y approaches 1. Because of this, the ratio of y to x increases rapidly toward infinity. Thus, as θ gets close to 90° or $\frac{\pi}{2}$, the ratio of y to x becomes very large, much greater than 1.

2 EXPLORE

Questioning Strategies

- If you reflect a point (x, y) over the y-axis, what happens to the values of x and y? **The value of x becomes the opposite of the original value; the value of y remains the same.**

- If you reflect a point (x, y) over the x-axis, what happens to the values of x and y? **The value of x remains the same; the value of y becomes the opposite of the original value.**

- A ray in the first quadrant that makes an angle θ with the positive x-axis is reflected across the y-axis. What angle does the reflected ray make with the negative x-axis? **θ**

3 EXAMPLE

Questioning Strategies

- How are the sine, cosine, and tangent values of $\frac{2\pi}{3}$, $\frac{4\pi}{3}$, and $\frac{5\pi}{3}$ related to those of $\frac{\pi}{3}$? **Each corresponding function value has the same absolute value, but may be either the same number or its opposite.**

- How can you determine the signs of the function values for $\frac{2\pi}{3}$, $\frac{4\pi}{3}$, and $\frac{5\pi}{3}$? **Use the sign for x and y in each quadrant. Sin θ has the sign of y, cos θ has the sign of x, and tan θ has the sign of $\frac{y}{x}$.**

EXTRA EXAMPLE

Find sin θ, cos θ, and tan θ when $\theta = \frac{8\pi}{3}$, $\frac{10\pi}{3}$, and $\frac{11\pi}{3}$.

θ	Quadrant	sin θ	cos θ	tan θ
$\frac{8\pi}{3}$	II	$\frac{\sqrt{3}}{2}$	$-\frac{1}{2}$	$-\sqrt{3}$
$\frac{10\pi}{3}$	III	$-\frac{\sqrt{3}}{2}$	$-\frac{1}{2}$	$\sqrt{3}$
$\frac{11\pi}{3}$	IV	$-\frac{\sqrt{3}}{2}$	$\frac{1}{2}$	$-\sqrt{3}$

Teaching Strategy

After students write the coordinates of point P in step A, ask them to apply the Pythagorean theorem to the triangle shown on the unit circle in step A. Since the hypotenuse of the triangle for trigonometric functions will always be 1, students can check their values for special angles by confirming that the sum of the squares of the leg lengths is equal to the length of the hypotenuse squared, or 1.

Avoid Common Errors

Later in the unit students will use calculators to evaluate trigonometric functions. Calculators can be set to interpret angles in either degrees or radians. If students assume their calculators are set to degrees when they are actually set to radians, their answers will be wrong. Students should check which mode their calculators are in prior to using them for trigonometry problems. A simple way to check is to type in one of the well-known values, such as sin 30°. If the value given is not 0.5, the calculator is probably in radian mode.

continued

Domain and Range The table below describes the domain and range of each trigonometric function.

Function	Domain	Range
Sine ($\sin \theta = y$)	θ can be any angle of rotation.	$-1 \le \sin \theta \le 1$
Cosine ($\cos \theta = x$)	θ can be any angle of rotation.	$-1 \le \cos \theta \le 1$
Tangent $\left(\tan \theta = \frac{y}{x}\right)$	θ cannot be an odd multiple of 90° or $\frac{\pi}{2}$.	All real numbers

CC.9–12.F.TF.3(+)

2 EXPLORE Identifying Reference Angles

Let θ' be an angle with a measure between 0 and $\frac{\pi}{2}$, and let (x, y) be the coordinates of the point of intersection of the terminal side of θ' and the unit circle. You can find three other angles related to θ' through reflections in the axes.

A Draw the reflection of the terminal side of θ' in the y-axis. Consider this to be the terminal side of an angle θ with a measure between 0 and 2π. Label the coordinates of the point of intersection of the terminal side of θ and the unit circle.

- In what quadrant is the terminal side of θ? Q. II

- Due to the reflection, the positive angle that the terminal side of θ makes with the *negative x*-axis is θ'. What is the sum of the measures of θ and θ'? π

- Write θ' in terms of θ. $\theta' = \pi - \theta$

B Draw the reflection of the terminal side of θ' in the x-axis. Consider this to be the terminal side of an angle θ with a measure between 0 and 2π. Label the coordinates of the point of intersection of the terminal side of θ and the unit circle.

- In what quadrant is the terminal side of θ? Q. IV

- Due to the reflection, the positive angle that the terminal side of θ makes with the *positive x*-axis is θ'. What is the sum of the measures of θ and θ'? 2π

- Write θ' in terms of θ. $\theta' = 2\pi - \theta$

C Draw the reflection of the terminal side of θ' in *both* axes. (First reflect in one axis, then reflect the image in the other axis.) Consider this to be the terminal side of an angle θ with a measure between 0 and 2π. Label the coordinates of the point of intersection of the terminal side of θ and the unit circle.

- In what quadrant is the terminal side of θ? Q. III

- Due to the reflection, the positive angle that the terminal side of θ makes with the *negative x*-axis is θ'. By how much do the measures of θ and θ' differ? π

- Write θ' in terms of θ. $\theta' = \theta - \pi$

REFLECT

2a. The **reference angle** θ' for an angle θ with a measure between 0 and 2π is the acute angle formed by the terminal side of θ and the x-axis.

For θ in Quadrant I, $\theta' = \theta$.

For θ in Quadrant II, $\theta' = \pi - \theta$.

For θ in Quadrant III, $\theta' = \theta - \pi$.

For θ in Quadrant IV, $\theta' = 2\pi - \theta$.

You can use reference angles to find the values of sine, cosine, and tangent of θ if the values are known for θ'. Suppose that $\sin \theta' = y$ and $\cos \theta' = x$ as in the Explore. Complete the table using the coordinates of the intersection points from the Explore.

	Quadrant I $0 < \theta < \frac{\pi}{2}$	Quadrant II $\frac{\pi}{2} < \theta < \pi$	Quadrant III $\pi < \theta < \frac{3\pi}{2}$	Quadrant IV $\frac{3\pi}{2} < \theta < 2\pi$
$\sin \theta$	y	y	$-y$	$-y$
$\cos \theta$	x	$-x$	$-x$	x
$\tan \theta$	$\frac{y}{x}$	$\frac{y}{-x}$	$\frac{-y}{-x}$	$\frac{-y}{x}$

2b. Explain how to use the diagram at right to determine the values of $\sin \theta$ and $\cos \theta$ when the values are known for the reference angle θ'.

The absolute value of each function is the same for θ and θ'. The sign of each function depends on the quadrant that contains the terminal side of θ. The sign of the x-coordinate gives the sign of $\cos \theta$, and the sign of the y-coordinate gives the sign of $\sin \theta$.

$(-, +)$ $(+, +)$

$(-, -)$ $(+, -)$

MATHEMATICAL PRACTICE **Highlighting the Standards**

This lesson, particularly the use of reference angles in **3 EXAMPLE**, includes opportunities to address Mathematical Practice Standard 8 (Look for and express regularity in repeated reasoning). Students apply the patterns they discovered in **1 EXPLORE** and **2 EXPLORE** about signs of trigonometric functions and reference angles to reason through the values of the trigonometric functions for special angles $\frac{\pi}{3}$, $\frac{2\pi}{3}$, $\frac{4\pi}{3}$, and $\frac{5\pi}{3}$.

CLOSE

Essential Question

How can the sine, cosine, and tangent functions be defined using the unit circle?

The functions can be defined using the unit circle so that the y-value of the point where the terminal side of an angle of rotation intersects the unit circle is its sine, the x-value is its cosine, and the ratio of y to x is its tangent.

Summarize

After finishing the Practice exercises students should create a single table in their journals showing the sine, cosine, and tangent values for all the special angles. The angles should be entered in numerical order from 0 radians to $\frac{11\pi}{6}$ radians.

PRACTICE

Where skills are taught	Where skills are practiced
3 EXAMPLE	EX. 1

Exercise 2: Students extend what they learned in **3 EXAMPLE** to finding the sine, cosine, and tangent of the quadrantal angles.

Special Angles In geometry, you studied two special right triangles: 30°-60°-90° and 45°-45°-90° triangles. You can use these triangles to find exact values for the trigonometric functions of angles with measure 30°, 45°, and 60° $\left(\text{or, in radians, } \frac{\pi}{6}, \frac{\pi}{4}, \text{ and } \frac{\pi}{3}\right)$ or of any angle having one of these angles as a reference angle.

CC.9-12.F.TF.3(+)

3 EXAMPLE Finding Sine, Cosine, and Tangent of Special Angles

Find $\sin\theta$, $\cos\theta$, and $\tan\theta$ when $\theta = \frac{\pi}{3}, \frac{2\pi}{3}, \frac{4\pi}{3},$ and $\frac{5\pi}{3}$.

A The diagram shows an angle of $\frac{\pi}{3}$ and the unit circle. Use the side-length relationships in a 30°-60°-90° triangle to label the side lengths of the triangle formed by dropping a perpendicular from the point P where the angle's terminal side intersects the unit circle.

What are the coordinates of P? $\underline{\left(\frac{1}{2}, \frac{\sqrt{3}}{2}\right)}$

B Find each function value.

$\sin\frac{\pi}{3} = \dfrac{\sqrt{3}}{2}$

$\cos\frac{\pi}{3} = \dfrac{1}{2}$

$\tan\frac{\pi}{3} = \sqrt{3}$

C Recognize that $\frac{\pi}{3}$ is the reference angle for $\frac{2\pi}{3}, \frac{4\pi}{3},$ and $\frac{5\pi}{3}$.
Complete the table, remembering that the quadrant in which the terminal side of an angle lies determines the signs of the trigonometric functions of the angle.

θ	Quadrant	$\sin\theta$	$\cos\theta$	$\tan\theta$
$\frac{2\pi}{3}$	II	$\frac{\sqrt{3}}{2}$	$-\frac{1}{2}$	$-\sqrt{3}$
$\frac{4\pi}{3}$	III	$-\frac{\sqrt{3}}{2}$	$-\frac{1}{2}$	$\sqrt{3}$
$\frac{5\pi}{3}$	IV	$-\frac{\sqrt{3}}{2}$	$\frac{1}{2}$	$-\sqrt{3}$

REFLECT

3a. Explain why $\frac{\pi}{3}$ is the reference angle for $\frac{2\pi}{3}, \frac{4\pi}{3},$ and $\frac{5\pi}{3}$.
$\frac{2\pi}{3}$ is in Q. II, so subtract $\frac{2\pi}{3}$ from π to get the reference angle: $\pi - \frac{2\pi}{3} = \frac{\pi}{3}$.
$\frac{4\pi}{3}$ is in Q. III, so subtract π from $\frac{4\pi}{3}$ to get the reference angle: $\frac{4\pi}{3} - \pi = \frac{\pi}{3}$;
$\frac{5\pi}{3}$ is in Q. IV, so subtract $\frac{5\pi}{3}$ from 2π to get the reference angle: $2\pi - \frac{5\pi}{3} = \frac{\pi}{3}$.

3b. Explain how to find $\sin\theta$, $\cos\theta$, and $\tan\theta$ when $\theta = \frac{16\pi}{3}$.
Subtract 2 revolutions (4π) from θ to get $\frac{4\pi}{3}$, which is in Q. III; so, $\sin\theta = -\frac{\sqrt{3}}{2}$,
$\cos\theta = -\frac{1}{2}$, and $\tan\theta = \sqrt{3}$.

PRACTICE

1. Each table lists four angles that have the same reference angle. Find the sine, cosine, and tangent of each angle.

θ	$\sin\theta$	$\cos\theta$	$\tan\theta$
$\frac{\pi}{6}$	$\frac{1}{2}$	$\frac{\sqrt{3}}{2}$	$\frac{\sqrt{3}}{3}$
$\frac{5\pi}{6}$	$\frac{1}{2}$	$-\frac{\sqrt{3}}{2}$	$-\frac{\sqrt{3}}{3}$
$\frac{7\pi}{6}$	$-\frac{1}{2}$	$-\frac{\sqrt{3}}{2}$	$\frac{\sqrt{3}}{3}$
$\frac{11\pi}{6}$	$-\frac{1}{2}$	$\frac{\sqrt{3}}{2}$	$-\frac{\sqrt{3}}{3}$

θ	$\sin\theta$	$\cos\theta$	$\tan\theta$
$\frac{\pi}{4}$	$\frac{\sqrt{2}}{2}$	$\frac{\sqrt{2}}{2}$	1
$\frac{3\pi}{4}$	$\frac{\sqrt{2}}{2}$	$-\frac{\sqrt{2}}{2}$	-1
$\frac{5\pi}{4}$	$-\frac{\sqrt{2}}{2}$	$-\frac{\sqrt{2}}{2}$	1
$\frac{7\pi}{4}$	$-\frac{\sqrt{2}}{2}$	$\frac{\sqrt{2}}{2}$	-1

2. If the terminal side of an angle falls on one of the axes, the angle is called a *quadrantal angle*. The table below lists the four quadrantal angles from 0 to 2π (not including 2π). Complete the table by giving the coordinates of the point where each angle's terminal side intersects the unit circle, and then find the values of sine, cosine, and tangent.

θ	Intersection point	$\sin\theta$	$\cos\theta$	$\tan\theta$
0	$(1, 0)$	0	1	0
$\frac{\pi}{2}$	$(0, 1)$	1	0	Undefined
π	$(-1, 0)$	0	-1	0
$\frac{3\pi}{2}$	$(0, -1)$	-1	0	Undefined

Notes

ADDITIONAL PRACTICE AND PROBLEM SOLVING

Assign these pages to help your students practice and apply important lesson concepts. For additional exercises, see the Student Edition.

Answers

Additional Practice

1. $\frac{4}{5}; \frac{3}{5}; \frac{4}{3}$ **2.** $\frac{9}{41}; \frac{40}{41}; \frac{9}{40}$

3. $\frac{12}{13}; \frac{5}{13}; \frac{12}{5}$ **4.** $6\sqrt{3}$

5. $\frac{44\sqrt{3}}{3}$ **6.** 7

7. $\sin \theta = \frac{12}{13}; \cos \theta = \frac{5}{13}; \tan \theta = \frac{12}{5}$

$\csc \theta = \frac{13}{12}; \sec \theta = \frac{13}{5}; \cot \theta = \frac{5}{12}$

8. $\sin \theta = \frac{3}{5}; \cos \theta = \frac{4}{5}; \tan \theta = \frac{3}{4}$

$\csc \theta = \frac{5}{3}; \sec \theta = \frac{5}{4}; \cot \theta = \frac{4}{3}$

9. $\sin \theta = \frac{9}{41}; \cos \theta = \frac{40}{41}; \tan \theta = \frac{9}{40}$

$\csc \theta = \frac{41}{9}; \sec \theta = \frac{41}{40}; \cot \theta = \frac{40}{9}$

10. 47 ft   **11.** 162 ft

12. 4817 m

Problem Solving

1. a. a

   b. $\tan 75° = \frac{a}{180}$

   c. 672 yd

2. a. 380 yd

   b. $\cos 60° = \frac{380}{c}$

   c. 760 yd

3. B   **4.** H

5. D   **6.** J

Name_____ Class_____ Date_____

Additional Practice

Find the value of the sine, cosine, and tangent functions for θ.

1.

60, 36, 48, θ

2.

27, 123, 120, θ

3.

36, 39, 15, θ

_____

Use a trigonometric function to find the value of x.

4.

60°, 6, x

5.

22, 30°, x

6.

7√2, 45°, x

_____

Find the values of the six trigonometric functions for θ.

7.

θ, 26, 24

8.

21, 28, θ

9.

40, 41, θ

_____

_____

Solve.

10. A water slide is 26 feet high. The angle between the slide and the water is 33.5°. What is the length of the slide?

11. A surveyor stands 150 feet from the base of a viaduct and measures the angle of elevation to be 46.2°. His eye level is 6 feet above the ground. What is the height of the viaduct to the nearest foot?

12. The pilot of a helicopter measures the angle of depression to a landing spot to be 18.8°. If the pilot's altitude is 1640 meters, what is the horizontal distance to the landing spot to the nearest meter?

Problem Solving

Kayla is fishing near the ferry landing near her home. She wonders how far the ferries actually travel when they cross the river. To find out, she puts a fishing pole upright on the riverbank directly across from the ferry landing. Then she walks down the bank 180 yards and measures an angle of 75° between the lines to her fishing pole and the ferry landing on the opposite bank.

Ferry landing, a, b, 75°, Fishing pole marker, 180 yards

1. Find the distance directly across the river.

   a. On the diagram, name the side of the triangle that represents the distance Kayla wants to determine.

   b. Write a trigonometric function that relates the known distance and angle to the required distance.

   c. Find the distance to the nearest yard directly across the river.

2. Kayla walks another 200 yards down the riverbank. At this point the ferries seem to come straight at her at an angle of 60° to the line to her fishing pole. If the boats travel along this line to compensate for the current, how far do they travel?

   a. How far is she from her fishing pole now?

   b. Write the trigonometric function that relates this distance and angle to the required distance, c.

   c. What is the distance that the ferries travel if they travel along this line?

At a hot-air balloon festival, Luis watches a hot-air balloon rise from a distance of 200 yards. Choose the letter for the best answer.

3. From Luis's position, the balloon seems to hover at an angle of elevation of 50°. Which trigonometric function gives the height of the balloon, h?

   A 200 sin 50°   C $\dfrac{200}{\cos 50°}$

   B 200 tan 50°   D $\dfrac{200}{\cot 50°}$

4. After a short while, the balloon seems to hover at an angle of 75°. How high is it off the ground now?

   F 193 yd
   G 207 yd
   H 746 yd
   J 773 yd

Olivia has a pool slide that makes an angle of 25° with the water. The top of the slide stands 4.5 feet above the surface of the water. Choose the letter for the best answer.

5. How far out into the pool will the slide reach?

   A 2.1 ft
   B 5.0 ft
   C 7.6 ft
   D 9.7 ft

6. The slide makes a straight line into the water. How long is the slide?

   F 5.0 ft
   G 7.6 ft
   H 9.7 ft
   J 10.6 ft

Inverses of Trigonometric Functions

Essential question: *How can you construct the inverse of a trigonometric function?*

COMMON CORE **Standards for Mathematical Content**

CC.9-12.A.CED.1 Create equations ... in one variable and use them to solve problems.

CC.9-12.F.TF.6(+) Understand that restricting a trigonometric function to a domain on which it is always increasing or always decreasing allows its inverse to be constructed.

CC.9-12.F.TF.7(+) Use inverse functions to solve trigonometric equations that arise in modeling contexts; evaluate the solutions using technology, and interpret them in terms of the context.

Vocabulary

arcsine

arccosine

arctangent

Prerequisites

Right-angle trigonometry

The unit circle

Math Background

Inverse trigonometric functions are used in a wide variety of applications. They can be used to find an angle of elevation or angle of depression, the angle made by two vectors in a physics application, or the angle formed by two sides of a triangle in plane geometry.

INTRODUCE

Start by discussing one-to-one functions and what it means for a function to be one-to-one. Ask students why one-to-one functions are important, leading into a discussion of inverses and inverse functions. Show students the graphs of sine, cosine, and tangent. Lead them to the conclusion that the domains of these functions must be restricted in order to obtain the inverse trigonometric functions.

TEACH

1 EXPLORE

Questioning Strategies

- How can you use a 30°-60°-90° triangle to calculate the sine and cosine of a 60° angle? Draw a 30°-60°-90° triangle with the 60° angle at the center of the unit circle and its shorter leg along the positive *x*-axis. The hypotenuse of the triangle measures 1, the side opposite the 60° angle is its sine, which measures $\frac{\sqrt{3}}{2}$, and the side adjacent to the 60° angle is its cosine, which measures $\frac{1}{2}$.

- Is there more than one angle with the same sine? Yes. There are infinitely many angles with the same sine.

2 ENGAGE

Questioning Strategies

- On which interval is the function $y = \sin x$ strictly increasing? On the interval $-\frac{\pi}{2} \leq x \leq \frac{\pi}{2}$

- On which interval is the function $y = \cos x$ strictly decreasing? On the interval $0 \leq x \leq \pi$

- On which interval is the function $y = \tan x$ strictly increasing? On the interval $-\frac{\pi}{2} < x < \frac{\pi}{2}$

Avoid Common Errors

Students may use the same domain for sine, cosine, and tangent when finding their inverses. Stress the importance of having a one-to-one function before taking the inverse. This will help students avoid this mistake.

Name_____ Class_____ Date_____

10-4

Video Tutor

Inverses of Trigonometric Functions
Going Deeper

Essential Question: *How can you construct the inverse of a trigonometric function?*

CC.9-12.F.TF.6(+)
CC.9-12.F.TF.7(+)

1 EXPLORE Exploring the Inverse of a Trigonometric Function

A Complete the following table:

$\sin 60° = \dfrac{\sqrt{3}}{2}$	$\cos 60° = \dfrac{1}{2}$	$\tan 60° = \sqrt{3}$
$\sin 120° = \dfrac{\sqrt{3}}{2}$	$\cos 300° = \dfrac{1}{2}$	$\tan 240° = \sqrt{3}$
$\sin 420° = \dfrac{\sqrt{3}}{2}$	$\cos 420° = \dfrac{1}{2}$	$\tan 420° = \sqrt{3}$

B Based on the table, what is the angle whose sine is equal to $\dfrac{\sqrt{3}}{2}$?

Impossible to say; based on the table, the answer could be 60°, 120° or 420°.

What is the angle whose cosine is equal to $\dfrac{1}{2}$?

Impossible to say; based on the table, the answer could be 60°, 300° or 420°.

What is the angle whose tangent is equal to $\sqrt{3}$?

Impossible to say; based on the table, the answer could be 60°, 240° or 420°.

REFLECT

1a. What problem did you have when trying to find the answers to part B?

There is more than one possible angle that satisfies the requirements.

1b. What must be true of any relation in order for it to be considered a function?

Each input must correspond to only one output.

1c. What would you need to change in order to create inverse trigonometric functions based on the data in the table above?

Restrict the domain before finding the inverse so that there is only one output for a given input.

The inverse sine function, denoted Sin⁻¹(x), is also called the arcsine function. Likewise, inverse cosine is known as arccosine and inverse tangent is known as arctangent.

CC.9-12.F.TF.6(+)

2 ENGAGE Identifying the Domain of Inverse Trigonometric Functions

Complete the table:

Words	Symbol	Domain	Range
The inverse sine function, $\sin^{-1}a = \theta$, where $\sin \theta = a$	$\sin^{-1}a$	$\{a: -1 \le a \le 1\}$	$\left\{\theta: -\dfrac{\pi}{2} \le \theta \le \dfrac{\pi}{2}\right\}$ or $\{\theta: -90° \le \theta \le 90°\}$
The inverse cosine function, $\cos^{-1}a = \theta$, where $\cos \theta = a$	$\cos^{-1}a$	$\{a: -1 \le a \le 1\}$	$\{\theta: 0 \le \theta \le \pi\}$ or $\{\theta: 0° \le \theta \le 180°\}$
The inverse tangent function, $\tan^{-1}a = \theta$, where $\tan \theta = a$	$\tan^{-1}a$	$\{a: -\infty < a < \infty\}$	$\left\{\theta: -\dfrac{\pi}{2} < \theta < \dfrac{\pi}{2}\right\}$ or $\{\theta: -90° < \theta < 90°\}$

REFLECT

2a. In which two quadrants is the range of $\sin^{-1}x$?

Quadrants I and IV

2b. Why is the range of $\sin^{-1}x$ restricted to those two quadrants?

$\sin x$ is strictly increasing on the interval $\left[-\dfrac{\pi}{2}, \dfrac{\pi}{2}\right]$. This ensures that the inverse function exists.

2c. Why is the range of $\cos^{-1}x$ different from the range of $\sin^{-1}x$ even though the two functions have the same domain?

$\sin x$ is strictly increasing on the interval $\left[-\dfrac{\pi}{2}, \dfrac{\pi}{2}\right]$. $\cos x$ is strictly decreasing on the interval $[0, \pi]$. The functions must be either strictly increasing or strictly decreasing in order for the inverse to exist; $\cos x$ is not strictly increasing or decreasing on the interval $\left[-\dfrac{\pi}{2}, \dfrac{\pi}{2}\right]$.

CC.9-12.F.TF.6(+)

3 EXAMPLE Evaluating Inverse Trigonometric Functions

Evaluate the inverse trigonometric function. Give your answer in both radians and degrees.

$\text{Tan}^{-1}1$

$1 = $ __Tan θ__ . Find the value of θ on the interval $-\dfrac{\pi}{2} \le \theta \le \dfrac{\pi}{2}$ whose __Tangent__ is __1__

© Houghton Mifflin Harcourt Publishing Company

3 EXAMPLE

Questioning Strategies

- On what interval must the tangent function be restricted before you can take its inverse? $-\frac{\pi}{2} < x < \frac{\pi}{2}$

- How do you know that an angle drawn in the unit circle has a tangent equal to 1? **The x- and y-coordinates of the point on the circle are equal.**

EXTRA EXAMPLE

What is the value of $\text{Cos}^{-1}\left(\frac{1}{2}\right)$? $\frac{\pi}{3}$

4 EXAMPLE

Questioning Strategies

- In which quadrants is sine positive? In which quadrants is it negative?
  Sine is positive in quadrants I and II.
  Sine is negative in quadrants III and IV.

- When you use a calculator to find the inverse sine of a number, why won't the calculator return an angle between 90° and 180°? **The calculator returns the principal value of inverse sine, which is a value between $-\frac{\pi}{2}$ and $\frac{\pi}{2}$ radians.**

- How can you use a reference angle to find angles with the same sine in different quadrants?
  If the reference angle is in Quadrant I, subtract from 180° to find the Quadrant II angle with the same sine. If the reference angle is negative, add its absolute value to 180° to find the Quadrant III angle with the same sine.

EXTRA EXAMPLE

Solve $\cos x = -0.2$ for $180° \leq x \leq 270°$. $258.5°$

CLOSE

Essential Question

How can you construct the inverse of a trigonometric function?

First restrict the domain of the trigonometric function because only one-to-one functions have inverses. After an appropriate domain is found, switch the values of x and y to find values of the inverse function.

Summarize

Have students write a journal entry in which they describe how to construct the inverses of trigonometric functions. They should write about how the domains of each trigonometric function must be restricted in order for it to be one-to-one. Tell students to include graphs of the trigonometric functions, highlighting how the domains must be restricted in order for the functions to have an inverse. Have the students write about why the calculator may not give the desired answer to a problem involving an inverse trigonometric function.

> **MATHEMATICAL PRACTICE** — **Highlighting the Standards**
>
> Exercises 1–12 provide opportunities to address Mathematical Practices Standard 2 (Reason abstractly and quantitatively). As students calculate the inverse trigonometric functions, they use abstract, quantitative reasoning. Exercises 13–14 address Mathematical Practices Standard 1 (Make sense of problems and persevere in solving them).

PRACTICE

Where skills are taught	Where skills are practiced
3 EXAMPLE	EXS. 1–6
4 EXAMPLE	EXS. 7–12

Exercises 13–14: These exercises are real-world examples of the uses of inverse trigonometric functions.

Sketch the angle in the unit circle shown.

Label the *x*- and *y*- coordinates of the point at which the terminal side of the angle intersects the unit circle.

Use the unit circle to find the measure of the angle.

$$\text{Tan}^{-1}1 = \underline{\frac{\pi}{4}}\ \text{radians, or}\ \underline{45}\ °.$$

REFLECT

3a. How does the unit circle help you find the values of the inverse trigonometric functions?

By seeing the angle graphed on the unit circle with the values of *x* and *y*, it is

easier to identify the angle with the desired sine, cosine, or tangent.

CC.9–12.F.TF.7(+)

4 EXAMPLE   Solving Trigonometric Equations

Solve each equation to the nearest tenth. Use the given restrictions.

A $\sin\theta = 0.2$ for $0° \le \theta \le 90°$

The given restriction is the same as that of the ___inverse sine___ function.

$\theta = \sin^{-1}(0.2) \approx \underline{11.5°}$ (from the calculator)

B $\sin\theta = 0.2$ for $90° \le \theta \le 180°$

The given restriction is not the same as that of the ___inverse sine___ function.

Find the angle in Quadrant ___II___ that has the same sine value as the given angle.

To use the reference angle in Quadrant II, subtract from ___180°___.

$\theta = \underline{180° - 11.5°} \approx \underline{168.5°}$

REFLECT

4a. Why does the calculator return only one value when you use the $\sin^{-1}x$ key, even though there are multiple correct answers?

The calculator computes $\text{Sin}^{-1}x$, which is an invertible function.

4b. How can you use your calculator to find the inverse sine of an angle in a domain that is different from the domain of $\sin^{-1}x$?

Use the calculator to find $\text{Sin}^{-1}x$. Use this as a reference angle to find the measure

of the angle in the other quadrants.

PRACTICE

Evaluate each inverse trigonometric function. Give your answer in degrees and radians.

1. $\text{Sin}^{-1}\left(-\frac{\sqrt{2}}{2}\right)$

$-45°, -\frac{\pi}{4}$

2. $\text{Tan}^{-1}\sqrt{3}$.

$60°, \frac{\pi}{3}$

3. $\text{Cos}^{-1}(-1)$

$180°, \pi$

4. $\text{Cos}^{-1}\left(-\frac{\sqrt{2}}{2}\right)$

$135°, \frac{3\pi}{4}$

5. $\text{Sin}^{-1}1$

$90°, \frac{\pi}{2}$

6. $\text{Tan}^{-1}\left(-\frac{\sqrt{3}}{3}\right)$

$-30°, -\frac{\pi}{6}$

Solve each equation to the nearest tenth of a degree. Use the given restrictions.

7. $\sin x = 0.1, 0° \le x \le 90°$

$5.7°$

8. $\cos x = -0.6, 180° \le x \le 270°$.

$233.1°$

9. $\cos x = 0.5, 270° \le x \le 360°$

$300°$

10. $\tan x = 1.6, 180° \le x \le 270°$

$238°$

11. $\tan x = -6.2, 90° \le x \le 180°$

$99.2°$

12. $\sin x = 0.9, 0° \le x \le 90°$

$64.2°$

13. A 6-foot-tall man is standing 20 feet away from a tree. He notices a cat in the tree, 56 feet above the ground. What is the angle between the man's line of sight to the cat and a horizontal line at the man's eye level? Round to the nearest tenth of a degree.

68.2

14. A helicopter is flying 1,200 feet in the air. The pilot spots a fire on the ground. The distance on the ground between the fire and the spot directly below the plane is 4,890 feet.

a. Draw a diagram for the situation in the space provided. Clearly label the altitude of the helicopter, the pilot's line of sight, the fire, and the ground distance between the fire and the spot directly below the plane.

b. What is the angle of depression of the pilot's line of sight to the fire? Round to the nearest tenth of a degree.

$13.8°$

ADDITIONAL PRACTICE AND PROBLEM SOLVING

Assign these pages to help your students practice and apply important lesson concepts. For additional exercises, see the Student Edition.

Answers

Additional Practice

1. $\dfrac{4\pi}{3} + 2\pi n;\ \dfrac{5\pi}{3} + 2\pi n$

2. $\dfrac{2\pi}{3} + 2\pi n;\ \dfrac{4\pi}{3} + 2\pi n$

3. $0 + 2\pi n;\ \pi + 2\pi n$

4. $\dfrac{5\pi}{4} + 2\pi n;\ \dfrac{7\pi}{4} + 2\pi n$

5. $\dfrac{3\pi}{4} + 2\pi n;\ \dfrac{5\pi}{4} + 2\pi n$

6. $\dfrac{\pi}{6} + 2\pi n;\ \dfrac{7\pi}{6} + 2\pi n$ 7. $\dfrac{3\pi}{2};\ 270°$

8. $\dfrac{5\pi}{3};\ 300°$ 9. $0;\ 0°$

10. $\dfrac{\pi}{3};\ 60°$ 11. $\dfrac{11\pi}{6};\ 330°$

12. $\dfrac{\pi}{4};\ 45°$ 13. $26.7°$

14. $233.2°$ 15. $247.5°$

16. $109.5°$ 17. $259.6°$

18. $95.7°$ 19. $71°$

Problem Solving

1. Possible answer: Subtract his height from any height measurements.

2. a.

b. $\theta = \tan^{-1}\left(\dfrac{27.25}{100}\right)$

c. $15.2°$

d. Yes; since the actual angle of elevation is less than the assumed angle of elevation, the building is less than 33 ft tall.

---

3. a. $18.4°$

b. $18.9°$

c. The inn is more than 40 ft tall. Since the angle of elevation is greater than 18.9°, the building is taller than 40 ft.

4. a. $20 \tan 55.9° + 5.5 = 35.0$ ft

b. $\tan^{-1}\left(\dfrac{35 - 5.75}{50}\right) = 30.3°$

10-4

Additional Practice

Find all possible values of each expression.

1. $\sin^{-1}\left(-\dfrac{\sqrt{3}}{2}\right)$

2. $\cos^{-1}\left(-\dfrac{1}{2}\right)$

3. $\tan^{-1}0$

_____

_____

_____

4. $\sin^{-1}\left(-\dfrac{\sqrt{2}}{2}\right)$

5. $\cos^{-1}\left(-\dfrac{\sqrt{2}}{2}\right)$

6. $\tan^{-1}\left(\dfrac{\sqrt{3}}{3}\right)$

_____

_____

_____

Evaluate each inverse trigonometric function. Give your answer in both radians and degrees.

7. $\text{Sin}^{-1}(-1)$

8. $\text{Tan}^{-1}\left(-\sqrt{3}\right)$

9. $\text{Cos}^{-1}1$

_____

_____

_____

10. $\text{Sin}^{-1}\left(\dfrac{\sqrt{3}}{2}\right)$

11. $\text{Tan}^{-1}\left(-\dfrac{\sqrt{3}}{3}\right)$

12. $\text{Cos}^{-1}\left(\dfrac{\sqrt{2}}{2}\right)$

_____

_____

_____

Solve each equation to the nearest tenth. Use the given restrictions.

13. $\sin\theta = 0.45$, for $0° < \theta < 90°$

14. $\sin\theta = 0.801$, for $90° < \theta < 270°$

_____

_____

15. $\tan\theta = 2.42$, for $180° < \theta < 360°$

16. $\cos\theta = -0.334$, for $0° < \theta < 180°$

_____

_____

17. $\cos\theta = -0.181$, for $180° < \theta < 360°$

18. $\tan\theta = -10$, for $90° < \theta < 270°$

_____

_____

Solve.

19. A 21-foot ladder is leaning against a building. The base of the ladder is 7 feet from the base of the building. To the nearest degree, what is the measure of the angle that the ladder makes with the ground?

_____

Problem Solving

Rafe is concerned that some recently constructed buildings in his town do not comply with code restrictions. New buildings are limited to a maximum of 40 feet in height.

1. When working with angles of elevation from his eye level, Rafe realizes that he must allow for his own height, 5 feet 9 inches, in his calculations. Explain how he can do this.

_____

2. On the building plans, the height of the new bank is 33 feet. Rafe calculates what the angle of elevation should be from 100 feet away if the bank is 33 feet tall.

   a. Label the diagram to show the height of the bank that Rafe will use in his calculations. Mark the angle of elevation.

   b. Write a trigonometric function for the assumed angle of elevation, θ.

Bank

Rafe: 5 ft 9 in.

100 ft

   c. To the nearest tenth of a degree, what is the assumed angle of elevation?

   _____

   d. Using a clinometer, Rafe measures the angle of elevation to be 14.2°. Does the bank comply with the building code? Explain.

   _____

3. On the plans, the height of the new inn is 39 feet. Rafe finds the angle of elevation and compares it to what he measures.

   a. Predict the angle of elevation of the highest point on this building from a distance of 100 feet and allowing for Rafe's height. _____

   b. Predict the angle of elevation of the highest point on a building that is 40 feet tall, allowing for Rafe's height. _____

   c. If Rafe measures an angle of elevation of 19.0°, how does the height of the inn compare to its declared height of 39 feet? Explain.

   _____

   _____

4. Carrie says the angle of elevation of the top of the flagpole at school is 55.9° from a distance of 20 feet away and allowing for her height of 5 feet 6 inches.

   a. Write and evaluate an expression for the height of the flagpole to the nearest tenth of a foot. _____

   b. What should be the angle of elevation if Rafe measures it from a distance of 50 feet away? Write and evaluate an expression.

   _____

Notes

The Law of Sines
Going Deeper

Essential question: *How can you prove the Law of Sines and use it to find side lengths and angle measures in a triangle?*

COMMON CORE **Standards for Mathematical Content**

CC.9-12.G.SRT.10(+) Prove the Laws of Sines and Cosines and use them to solve problems.

CC.9-12.G.SRT.11(+) Understand and apply the Law of Sines and the Law of Cosines to find unknown measurements in right and non-right triangles (e.g., surveying problems, resultant forces).

Vocabulary
Law of Sines

Prerequisites
Right-angle trigonometry

Angles of rotation

The unit circle

Math Background
The Law of Sines is used extensively in ship navigation. To describe the locations of objects relative to a vessel, the sea captain uses bearings. A bearing is the measure of the angle between a ray pointing north, south, east, or west that passes through an object and a ray drawn from that object to another object. The Law of Sines can be used with bearings to find the distance between objects in the ocean.

INTRODUCE

Start the lesson by reminding students of the formula for area of a triangle, $A = \frac{1}{2}bh$. Draw an acute triangle on the board and ask students to describe how to find the area of the triangle. They should realize that any side of the triangle may be considered to be the base. Remind students how the sine function is defined within a right triangle, and ask them to consider the right triangles created when an altitude is draw in the acute triangle.

TEACH

1 EXPLORE

Questioning Strategies
- In the diagram on the left, what is the length of the side opposite angle A? **a**
- In the diagram on the left, what is the length of the base if h is the height? **b**

Differentiated Instruction
Some students may have trouble working with the three different expressions for the area of a triangle. It may be helpful to provide a numerical example to show students that the area of the triangle is the same, regardless of which base and altitude are used to calculate it.

2 EXAMPLE

Questioning Strategies
- What do the three expressions represent? **area of a triangle**
- Why does multiplying by 2 get rid of the $\frac{1}{2}$ in each of the expressions? **The product of $\frac{1}{2}$ and 2 is 1.**

Name _____ Class _____ Date _____

The Law of Sines
Going Deeper

Essential question: *How can you prove the Law of Sines and use it to find side lengths and angle measures in a triangle?*

CC.9-12.G.SRT.10(+)

1 EXPLORE   The Area of a Triangle

One formula for area of a triangle is Area $= \frac{1}{2} bh$. This formula can be written in different ways using sines.

A In the triangle on the left, $\sin A = \frac{\text{opposite}}{\text{hypotenuse}} = \frac{h}{c}$.

Multiply both sides by c to obtain an expression for h: $h = \underline{\ c \sin A \ }$

Rewrite the formula for area using this expression: Area $= \underline{\ \frac{1}{2} bc \sin A \ }$

B In the triangle on the left, $\sin C = \frac{\text{opposite}}{\text{hypotenuse}} = \frac{h}{a}$.

Multiply both sides by a to obtain an expression for h: $h = \underline{\ a \sin C \ }$

Rewrite the formula for area using this expression: Area $= \underline{\ \frac{1}{2} ab \sin C \ }$

C The triangle on the right is the same as the one on the left but choosing a different height. Relative to this height h, the base of $\triangle ABC$ is now c.

In the triangle on the right, $\sin B = \frac{\text{opposite}}{\text{hypotenuse}} = \frac{h}{a}$.

Multiply both sides by a to obtain an expression for h: $h = \underline{\ a \sin B \ }$

Rewrite the formula for area using this expression: Area $= \underline{\ \frac{1}{2} ac \sin B \ }$

REFLECT

1a. Why are the formulas in parts A, B and C all equal?

All of the formulas represent the area of the same triangle.

1b. Can you express the height of the triangle using the cosine of one angle? Explain why or why not.

No. The cosine ratio includes the adjacent side and the hypotenuse. The height is the side opposite the angle, so you must use sine.

The formulas for the area of a triangle are summarized below.

For $\triangle ABC$,

Area $= \frac{1}{2} bc \sin A$

Area $= \frac{1}{2} ac \sin B$

Area $= \frac{1}{2} ab \sin C$

CC.9-12.G.SRT.10(+)

2 EXPLORE   Deriving the Law of Sines

From the results above, set the three expressions for area equal to each other. This yields:

$\frac{1}{2} bc \sin A = \frac{\frac{1}{2} ac \sin B}{} = \frac{\frac{1}{2} ab \sin C}{}$

Multiply by 2: $bc \sin A = \frac{ac \sin B}{} = \frac{ab \sin C}{}$

Divide by abc: $\frac{\sin A}{a} = \frac{\sin B}{b} = \frac{\sin C}{c}$

The Law of Sines:

For $\triangle ABC$, the Law of Sines states that

$\frac{\sin A}{a} = \frac{\sin B}{b} = \frac{\sin C}{c}$.

The Law of Sines can be used to solve triangles. If you know two sides and a non-included angle of the triangle (SSA case), there may be zero, one, or two possible triangles. Because of this, SSA is called the *ambiguous case*.

CC.9-12.G.SRT.11(+)

3 EXPLORE   The Ambiguous Case

Solve the triangle: $\angle C = 48°$, $c = 4.4$ and $a = 5.6$.

A Use the Law of Sines to find the measure of angle A:

$\frac{\sin A}{a} = \frac{\sin C}{c}$, or $\frac{\sin A}{5.6} = \frac{\sin 48°}{4.4}$

Cross-multiply: $4.4 \sin A = 5.6 \sin 48°$

Use the inverse sine function of your calculator to find the measure of $\angle A$: $\angle A \approx \underline{\ 71° \ }$

Calculate the measure of $\angle B$: $\angle B = 180° - \underline{\ 71° \ } - \underline{\ 48° \ } = \underline{\ 61° \ }$

Use the Law of Sines again to find b: $\frac{\sin C}{c} = \frac{\sin B}{b}$, or $\frac{\sin 48°}{4.4} = \frac{\sin 61°}{b}$

$b = \underline{\ 5.2 \ }$

Questioning Strategies

- How do you find the measure of angle A given $\sin A$? **Use the inverse sine function on the calculator.**

- Why do you need to calculate the supplement of angle A in part C? **You need to check if another triangle is possible from the given information.**

- How do you know that two triangles can be solved using the given information? **The sum of the supplement of angle A and angle C is less than 180°.**

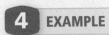

4 EXAMPLE

Questioning Strategies

- Which angle is opposite the southern boundary?
  Angle B

- Which angle is opposite the western boundary?
  Angle C

- Which ratio will you set equal to the ratio $\dfrac{\sin B}{\text{southern boundary}}$ to find the length of the western boundary? $\dfrac{\sin C}{\text{western boundary}}$

EXTRA EXAMPLE
Connie built a triangular fence between posts A, B, and C. The distance from post A to post B is 100 m. The angle between side AC and side BC is 120°. The angle between side AB and side BC is 15°. What is the distance between posts A and C? **29.9 m**

Avoid Common Errors
Students commonly forget to check for other possible triangles. Remind them that there is a Quadrant I angle and a Quadrant II angle that have a given positive sine, and that two different triangles may be possible when using the Law of Sines.

CLOSE

Essential Question
How can you prove the Law of Sines and use it to find side lengths and angle measures in a triangle?
The Law of Sines can be derived by finding the area of the same triangle in three different ways. The Law of Sines is found by equating the three expressions for area and simplifying the resulting equations. The Law of Sines is used to solve a triangle when two angles and a side or two sides and a non-included angle are known.

Summarize
Encourage students to write the formula for the Law of Sines in their notebooks. Students should reflect on solving triangles using the Law of Sines, noting specifically that some triangles cannot be solved with this formula, and some solutions may result in the ambiguous case.

MATHEMATICAL PRACTICE	Highlighting the Standards

Exercises 1–9 provide opportunities to address Mathematical Practices Standard 2 (Reason abstractly and quantitatively). As students solve triangles, they use abstract, quantitative reasoning. Exercise 11, addresses Mathematical Practices Standard 1 (Make sense of problems and persevere in solving them).

PRACTICE

Where skills are taught	Where skills are practiced
3 EXPLORE	EX. 10
4 EXAMPLE	EXS. 1–9, 11

B   Sketch the triangle from part A.

C   Find the supplement of ∠A from part A to see if there is a second possible triangle. 109°

Why can this angle also be used to solve the triangle?

The sine of 109° is equal to the sine of 71°.

Calculate the measure of ∠B using this value of A: ∠B = 180° − 109° − 48° = 23°

Use the Law of Sines again to find b: $\frac{\sin C}{c} = \frac{\sin B}{b}$, or $\frac{\sin 48°}{4.4} = \frac{\sin 23°}{b}$

b = 2.3

D   Sketch the triangle from part C.

CC.9-12.G.SRT.11(+)

4   **E X A M P L E**   Solving a Triangle Application

In a triangular park, the southern boundary measures 410 feet. The eastern boundary forms a 100° angle with the southern boundary. The western boundary forms a 60° angle with the southern boundary. What is the length of the western boundary?

A   Subtract the two given angles from 180° to find the measure of ∠B the angle opposite the southern boundary:

180° − 100° − 60° = 20°

B   Use the Law of Sines to find the length of the western boundary:

$\frac{\sin B}{410} = \frac{\sin C}{c}$, or $\frac{\sin 20°}{410} = \frac{\sin 100°}{c}$

Cross-multiply: c sin 20° = 410 sin 100°

The length of the western boundary is _____ 1,180.5 ft

REFLECT

4a.   In which situation(s) would you be unable to use the Law of Sines to solve a triangle?

If you are given three sides (SSS) or two sides and an included angle (SAS)

PRACTICE

Solve for the indicated quantity.

1. BC 18.4

2. DF 22.9

3. XZ 21.0

4. ST 4.8

5. MO 27.9

6. GH 8.8

7. PR 82.0

8. XY 27.0

9. UW 55.7

10. A triangle has side lengths 12 and 18 and a non-included angle that measures 65°. How many triangles are possible with these measurements? Explain how you know.

One. The given angle cannot be opposite the side that measures 12.

Only one triangle is possible with the given angle opposite the side

that measures 18.

11. A farmer is fencing in a triangular plot that has angles 50°, 100° and 30°. The longest side of the plot is 1,200 feet. How many feet of fencing does the farmer need to fence the entire plot?

about 2,743 feet of fencing

Assign these pages to help your students practice and apply important lesson concepts. For additional exercises, see the Student Edition.

Answers

Additional Practice

1. 41.9 m^2 2. 84 ft^2

3. 114.2 cm^2

4. $m\angle N = 61°$; $n \approx 25.6$; $m \approx 17.2$

5. $m\angle P = 27°$; $r \approx 12.9$; $p \approx 6.6$

6. $m\angle D = 33°$; $e \approx 36.6$; $c \approx 40.0$

7. $m\angle Y = 64°$; $x \approx 10.4$; $y \approx 12.6$

8. $m\angle C = 44°$; $a \approx 48.9$; $b \approx 58.1$

9. $m\angle F = 73°$; $h \approx 7.7$; $f \approx 8.5$

10. 0 triangles

11. 1 triangle; $c \approx 11.3 \text{ cm}$; $m\angle B = 56°$; $m\angle C = 39°$

12. 1 triangle; $c \approx 10.3 \text{ cm}$; $m\angle B = 36°$; $m\angle C = 24°$

13. 38.0 cm; 40.3 cm

Problem Solving

1. **a.** $A = \frac{1}{2}(100)(53.2)\sin(40)°$

   b. 1709.8 yd^2

2. **a.** $221.6 - (100 + 53.2) = 68.4 \text{ yd}$

   b. $\dfrac{\sin S}{53.2} = \dfrac{\sin 40°}{68.4}$; so $\angle S = 30°$

   c. Possible answer: $180° - (30° + 40°) = 110°$. Or, if student uses the Law of Sines, check the work.

3. **a.** $45°$

   b. $\dfrac{40 \sin 80°}{\sin 45°} = 55.7 \text{ yd}$

4. B   5. F

Additional Practice

Find the area of each triangle. Round to the nearest tenth.

1. (triangle: 39°, 12.8 m, 54°, 8.1 m)

2. (triangle: 16 ft, 30°, 21 ft)

3. (triangle: 8 cm, 100°, 29 cm)

Solve each triangle. Round to the nearest tenth.

4. (triangle LMN: L, 83°, n, m, M 36°, N, 29)

5. (triangle with 118°, 8.4, P, 38°, Q)

6. (triangle D E G: D, c, 66° E, 22, 62°, G)

7. (triangle XYZ: Y, 13, x, 68° Z, 48° X, y)

8. (triangle ABC: B, 80°, 41°, a, A 56°, b, C)

9. (triangle FGH: G, 47°, h, 60° H, F, 6.5)

An artist is designing triangular mosaic tiles. Determine the number of triangles he can form from the given side and angle measures. Then solve the triangles. Round to the nearest tenth.

10. $a = 8$ cm, $b = 10$ cm, $A = 60°$

11. $a = 18$ cm, $b = 15$ cm, $A = 85°$

12. $a = 22$ cm, $b = 15$ cm, $A = 120°$

Solve.

13. Ann is creating a triangular frame. Two angles and the included side of the frame measure 64°, 58°, and 38 centimeters, respectively. What are the lengths of the other two sides of the frame to the nearest tenth of a centimeter?

_____

Problem Solving

In the middle of town, State and Elm streets meet at an angle of 40°. A triangular pocket park between the streets stretches 100 yards along State Street and 53.2 yards along Elm Street. Hoa and Cat walk around the pocket park every day at lunchtime.

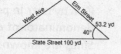

1. Hoa would like to know the area of the pocket park.

   a. Write a formula for the area of the pocket park using the given dimensions.

   _____

   b. What is the area of the pocket park to the nearest tenth of a square yard?

   _____

2. Cat determines that the total distance around the pocket park is 221.6 yards.

   a. Write and evaluate an expression for the length of the park along West Avenue.

   _____

   b. Use the Law of Sines to find ∠S to the nearest degree, the angle that West Avenue makes with State Street.

   _____

   c. Write an expression for the angle that West Avenue makes with Elm Street.

   _____

3. West Avenue makes angles of 55° with Main Street and 80° with Third Street. The distance from Main to Third along West Avenue is 40 yards. Hoa contracts to design a pocket park for the acute-angled triangular area enclosed by these streets.

   a. What is the measure of the third angle of the triangular area? _____

   b. Write and evaluate an expression for the distance from West Avenue to Third Street along Main Street. _____

Choose the letter for the best answer.

4. Hoa wants to plant palm trees 8 feet apart along the side of the park on Third Street. Which expression gives the number of trees she will need?

   A $\dfrac{40 \sin 55°}{\sin 45°}$

   B $\dfrac{5 \sin 55°}{\sin 45°}$

   C $\dfrac{5 \sin 45°}{\sin 55°}$

   D $\dfrac{40 \sin 45°}{\sin 55°}$

5. What is the area of the new pocket park that Hoa is designing?

   F 913 yd^2

   G 1004 yd^2

   H 1207 yd^2

   J 1398 yd^2

10-6

The Law of Cosines
Going Deeper

Essential question: *How can you prove and use the Law of Cosines to find side lengths and angle measures in a triangle?*

COMMON CORE **Standards for Mathematical Content**

CC.9-12.G.SRT.10(+) Prove the Laws of Sines and Cosines and use them to solve problems.

CC.9-12.G.SRT.11(+) Understand and apply the Law of Sines and the Law of Cosines to find unknown measurements in right and non-right triangles (e.g., surveying problems, resultant forces).

Prerequisites
The Law of Sines

Math Background
To solve a triangle means to find all of its side lengths and angle measures. Students have done some of this work before by using the Triangle Sum Theorem and the Pythagorean Theorem. They have also learned the Law of Sines, which can be applied when the given information about the triangle fits the pattern of AAS, ASA, or SSA. None of these methods allows for solving all types of triangles. The Law of Cosines can be used to solve any triangle about which sufficient information is known.

INTRODUCE

Tell students that there are six measures in any triangle: three side lengths, and three angle measures. To solve a triangle means to find all six measures. Ask them whether they could use the Law of Sines to solve a triangle when only the three side lengths are known. Students should realize that they must know at least one angle measure in order to set up the ratios used in the Law of Sines. In this lesson, they will learn another method for solving triangles. Tell students that any triangle can be solved if you know at least three of those measures (with the exception of knowing only the three angle measures). Show students the Law of Sines.

TEACH

1 EXPLORE

Questioning Strategies

- The Law of Sines can be used to solve the triangle in part A, but not those in parts B and C. Why not? **In part A, both the numerator and denominator of one of the ratios in the Law of Sines are known. In parts B and C, there is no ratio in which you know both the numerator and denominator.**

- Could you solve the triangle in part B if you didn't know c but you knew that $a = 5.1$? Explain. **Yes. Then you would know both the numerator and denominator of one of the ratios in the Law of Sines.**

Name_____ Class_____ Date_____

10-6

Video Tutor

The Law of Cosines
Going Deeper

Essential question: *How can you prove and use the Law of Cosines to find side lengths and angle measures in a triangle?*

CC.9-12.G.SRT.10 (+)
CC.9-12.G.SRT.11 (+)

1 EXPLORE Understanding Limitations on the Law of Sines

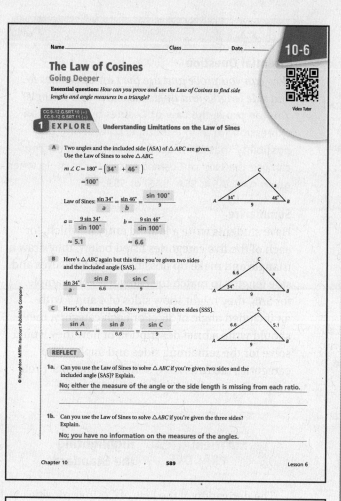

A Two angles and the included side (ASA) of △ ABC are given. Use the Law of Sines to solve △ABC.

$$m \angle C = 180^\circ - \left(34^\circ + 46^\circ \right)$$

$$= 100^\circ$$

Law of Sines: $\dfrac{\sin 34^\circ}{a} = \dfrac{\sin 46^\circ}{b} = \dfrac{\sin 100^\circ}{9}$

$a = \dfrac{9 \sin 34^\circ}{\sin 100^\circ}$ $b = \dfrac{9 \sin 46^\circ}{\sin 100^\circ}$

≈ 5.1 ≈ 6.6

B Here's △ ABC again but this time you're given two sides and the included angle (SAS).

$$\dfrac{\sin 34^\circ}{a} = \dfrac{\sin B}{6.6} = \dfrac{\sin C}{9}$$

C Here's the same triangle. Now you are given three sides (SSS).

$$\dfrac{\sin A}{5.1} = \dfrac{\sin B}{6.6} = \dfrac{\sin C}{9}$$

REFLECT

1a. Can you use the Law of Sines to solve △ ABC if you're given two sides and the included angle (SAS)? Explain.

No; either the measure of the angle or the side length is missing from each ratio.

1b. Can you use the Law of Sines to solve △ABC if you're given the three sides? Explain.

No; you have no information on the measures of the angles.

© Houghton Mifflin Harcourt Publishing Company

The Law of Sines can be used to solve triangles when you are given AAS, ASA, or SSA. When given other information, you can use the Law of Cosines. The Law of Cosines is similar to the Pythagorean Theorem in that it uses relationships between the squares of the side lengths.

CC.9-12.G.SRT.10 (+)

2 EXPLORE Deriving the Law of Cosines

For △ABC, find an expression for a^2. Consider the cases that ∠A is acute or obtuse.

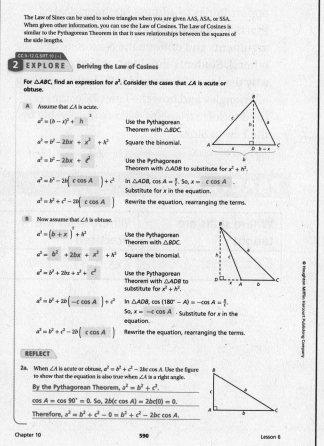

A Assume that ∠A is acute.

$a^2 = (b - x)^2 + h^2$ Use the Pythagorean Theorem with △BDC.

$a^2 = b^2 - 2bx + x^2 + h^2$ Square the binomial.

$a^2 = b^2 - 2bx + c^2$ Use the Pythagorean Theorem with △ADB to substitute for $x^2 + h^2$.

$a^2 = b^2 - 2b(\ c \cos A \ ) + c^2$ In △ADB, $\cos A = \dfrac{x}{c}$. So, $x = \ c \cos A$. Substitute for x in the equation.

$a^2 = b^2 + c^2 - 2b(\ c \cos A \ )$ Rewrite the equation, rearranging the terms.

B Now assume that ∠A is obtuse.

$a^2 = \left(b + x \right)^2 + h^2$ Use the Pythagorean Theorem with △BDC.

$a^2 = \ b^2 + 2bx + x^2 + h^2$ Square the binomial.

$a^2 = b^2 + 2bx + x^2 + c^2$ Use the Pythagorean Theorem with △ADB to substitute for $x^2 + h^2$.

$a^2 = b^2 + 2b(\ -c \cos A \ ) + c^2$ In △ADB, $\cos (180^\circ - A) = -\cos A = \dfrac{x}{c}$. So, $x = \ -c \cos A$. Substitute for x in the equation.

$a^2 = b^2 + c^2 - 2b(\ c \cos A \ )$ Rewrite the equation, rearranging the terms.

REFLECT

2a. When ∠A is acute or obtuse, $a^2 = b^2 + c^2 - 2bc \cos A$. Use the figure to show that the equation is also true when ∠A is a right angle.

By the Pythagorean Theorem, $a^2 = b^2 + c^2$.

$\cos A = \cos 90^\circ = 0$. So, $2b(c \cos A) = 2bc(0) = 0$.

Therefore, $a^2 = b^2 + c^2 - 0 = b^2 + c^2 - 2bc \cos A$.

© Houghton Mifflin Harcourt Publishing Company

Questioning Strategies

- Why do you need to consider the case that $\angle A$ may be acute, obtuse, or right? **The relationship between the side lengths and *x* changes depending on the measure of $\angle A$. So, the expression for *x* changes. You need to check each of the three cases.**

3 EXAMPLE

Questioning Strategies

- In part A, how could you find m$\angle B$ and m$\angle C$? **Use the Law of Sines, since you now know the numerator and denominator of one of the ratios.**

- Why is the quadratic formula used to solve part B but not part A? **After substitution in part A, the only variable term in the quadratic equation is a^2. That equation can be solved by taking the square root of both sides. After substitution in part B, the quadratic equation that remains includes both c^2 and *c*. The quadratic formula can be used to solve that equation.**

EXTRA EXAMPLE
In $\triangle ABC$, $\angle A = 44°$, $b = 6$, and $c = 7$. Find a. Round your answer to the nearest tenth.
$a \approx 5.0$

A ship's navigator picks up signals from two radio transmitters on shore. One transmitter is 70 miles from the ship, and the other is 130 miles from the ship. The angle between the two incoming signals is 130°. To the nearest mile, how far apart are the transmitters?
183 miles

CLOSE

Essential Question
How can you prove and use the Law of Cosines to find side lengths and angle measures in a triangle?
You can prove the Law of Cosines by deriving an expression for a^2 in a triangle, considering the possibility that $\angle A$ is acute, obtuse, or right. You can use the Law of Cosines to solve a triangle when given AAS, ASA, SSA, SAS, or SSS.

Summarize
Have students write a journal entry in which, for each of the five categories listed below, they draw a triangle and make up possible angle measures and side lengths to match the category. For example, for SAS, they might show sides of 4 and 7 with an included angle of 36°. For each category, they should write a brief description of how they would solve for the remaining sides and angles. The categories are AAS, ASA, SSA, SAS, and SSS. (You may wish to include HL as well.)

MATHEMATICAL PRACTICE	**Highlighting the Standards**

The derivation of the Law of Cosines provides opportunities to address Mathematical Practices Standard 3 (Construct viable arguments and critique the reasoning of others). Students should be able to explain why the Law of Sines is insufficient for solving all triangles and how the Law of Cosines is used to solve triangles that are unsolvable by the Law of Sines.

PRACTICE

Where skills are taught	Where skills are practiced
3 EXAMPLE	EXS. 1–13

For $\triangle ABC$, the Law of Cosines states that:

$$a^2 = b^2 + c^2 - 2bc \cos A$$
$$b^2 = a^2 + c^2 - 2ac \cos B$$
$$c^2 = a^2 + b^2 - 2ab \cos C$$

CC.9-12.G.SRT.10 (+)
CC.9-12.G.SRT.11 (+)

3 EXAMPLE Using the Law of Cosines

Find the length of the unknown side of the triangle.

A $a^2 = b^2 + c^2 - 2bc \cos A$ Law of Cosines

$a^2 = 40^2 + 45^2 - 2(40)(45)\cos 51°$ Substitute for the variables.

$= 1359.45$ Simplify.

$a = \sqrt{1359.45} \approx 36.9$ Take the square root.

B   A pilot is flying 50 miles from Benton (B) to Colfax (C) but heavy winds have thrown the plane off course at a 27° angle. When the wind stops, the plane is 40 miles from Colfax. How far did it fly at an angle to the true course?

$b^2 = a^2 + c^2 - 2ac \cos B$ Law of Cosines

$40^2 = 50^2 + c^2 - 2(50)(c)\cos 27°$ Substitute for the variables.

$0 = c^2 - 89.1 c + 900$ Simplify and rearrange terms.

$c = \dfrac{-(-89.1) \pm \sqrt{(-89.1^2) - 4(1)(900)}}{2(1)}$ Use the quadratic formula to solve.

$c = 77.5$ miles or 11.6 miles   Simplify.

REFLECT

3a. In Part B, you need to find c. Why was the b^2 form of the Law of Cosines used?

You are given $\angle B$, so you needed the form of the Law with cos B in it.

3b. You can use the Law of Cosines alone to solve any triangle, whereas the Law of Sines works only in certain triangles. Why might you ever choose to use the Law of Sines?

The Law of Sines is less complicated than the Law of Cosines and leads to

easier calculations.

© Houghton Mifflin Harcourt Publishing Company

PRACTICE

Solve each triangle. Round answers to the nearest tenth.

1. $a = 38, b = 31, c = 35$ $m\angle A = 70.0°, m\angle B = 50.1°, m\angle C = 59.9°$

2. $a = 20, c = 24, m\angle B = 47°$ $b = 17.9, m\angle A = 54.7°, m\angle C = 78.3°$

3. $m\angle A = 78.3°, b = 7, c = 11$ $a = 11.8, m\angle B = 35.6°, m\angle C = 66.1°$

4. $a = 4, b = 6, c = 3$ $m\angle A = 36.3°, m\angle B = 117.3°, m\angle C = 26.4°$

5. $a = 17, b = 20, m\angle C = 48°$ $m\angle A = 55.7°, m\angle B = 76.3°, c = 15.3$

6. $a = 13.7, m\angle A = 25.4°, m\angle B = 78°$ $b = 31.2, c = 31.1, m\angle C = 76.6°$

7. $m\angle A = 114°, b = 23, c = 26$ $a = 41.1, m\angle B = 30.7°, m\angle C = 35.3°$

8. $a = 8, b = 24, c = 18$ $m\angle A = 14.6°, m\angle B = 130.8°, m\angle C = 34.6°$

9. $m\angle C = 35°, b = 24, a = 18$ $c = 13.9, m\angle B = 96.9°, m\angle A = 48.1°$

10. $b = 2, c = 5, m\angle A = 60°$ $a = 4.4, m\angle B = 23.4°, m\angle C = 96.6°$

11. Given $\triangle DEF$, $d = 9.2$, $e = 5$, and $f = 10.1$. Find $m\angle E$. Round your answer to the nearest tenth of a degree.

$m\angle E \approx 29.6°$

12. When measured from the level of the river, the angles of elevation to the top and the bottom of a bridge are 56° and 42° respectively. The height of the bridge is 40 feet. How far above the river is the bottom of the bridge? Round your answer to the nearest tenth of a foot.

61.9 ft

13. Two sides of a parallelogram measure 10 cm and 15 cm. The angle formed by the two sides measures 35°. Find the lengths of the diagonals of the parallelogram. Round your answer to the nearest tenth of a centimeter.

8.9 cm and 23.9 cm

© Houghton Mifflin Harcourt Publishing Company

Notes

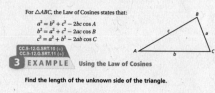

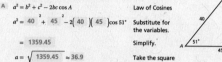

Assign these pages to help your students practice and apply important lesson concepts. For additional exercises, see the Student Edition.

Answers

Additional Practice

1. $m \approx 16.6$; $m\angle L \approx 28.7°$; $m\angle N \approx 57.3°$

2. $n \approx 10.7$; $m\angle L \approx 134.5°$; $m\angle M \approx 9.5°$

3. $m \approx 28.7$; $m\angle L \approx 65.9°$; $m\angle N \approx 49.1°$

4. $m\angle L \approx 84.8°$; $m\angle M \approx 55.1°$; $m\angle N \approx 40.1°$

5. $l \approx 43.5$; $m\angle M \approx 25.4°$; $m\angle N \approx 117.6°$

6. $m\angle L \approx 25.5°$; $m\angle M \approx 26.9°$; $m\angle N \approx 127.6°$

7. $m\angle L \approx 27.2°$; $m\angle M \approx 101°$; $m\angle N \approx 51.8°$

8. $m \approx 10.1$; $m\angle L \approx 44.7°$; $m\angle N \approx 117.3°$

9. $m\angle L \approx 68°$; $m\angle M \approx 59.4°$; $m\angle N \approx 52.6°$

10. 30 min   11. 94.1 ft^2

Problem Solving

1. **a.** $c^2 = 72^2 + 60^2 - 2(72)(60)\cos 105°$

   b. 105 m

2. **a.** $\angle F = \cos^{-1}\left(\dfrac{(50^2 + 20^2 - 49^2)}{2(50)(20)}\right)$

   b. 75.6°

3. **a.** $A = \sqrt{59.5(9.5)(39.5)(10.5)}$

   b. 484.2 m^2

4. A   5. F

Additional Practice

Use the given measurements to solve each triangle. Round to the nearest tenth.

1.

2.

3.

4.

5.

6.

7.

8.

9.

Solve.

10. A postal airplane leaves Island A and flies 91 miles to Island B. It drops off and picks up mail and flies 63 miles to Island C. After unloading and loading mail, the plane returns to Island A at an average rate of 300 miles per hour. How long does it take the pilot to travel from Island C to Island A?

_____

11. A statue is erected on a triangular marble base. The lengths of the sides of the triangle are 12 feet, 16 feet, and 18 feet. What is the area of the region at the base of the statue?

_____

Problem Solving

Standing on a small bluff overlooking a local pond, Clay wants to calculate the width of the pond.

1. From point C, Clay walks the distances $\overline{CA}$ and $\overline{CB}$. Then he measures the angle between these line segments.

   a. Use the Law of Cosines to write an equation for the distance $\overline{AB}$.

   _____

   b. What is the distance to the nearest meter from A to B?

   _____

2. From another point F, Clay measures 20 meters to D and 50 meters to E. Reece says that last summer this area dried out so much that he could walk the 49 meters from D to E.

   a. Use the Law of Cosines to write an equation for the measure of the angle between $\overline{DF}$ and $\overline{EF}$.

   _____

   b. What is the measure of this angle?

   _____

3. Reece tells Clay that when the area defined by Δ DEF dries out, it becomes covered with a grass native to this area of the country. Clay wants to know the area of this section.

   a. Use Heron's Formula to write an expression for the area.

   _____

   b. Find the area to the nearest tenth of a square meter.

   _____

A local naturalist says that a triangular area on the north sides of the pond is a turtle habitat. The lengths of the sides of this area are 15 meters, 25 meters, and 36 meters. Choose the letter for the best answer.

4. What is the area of this triangular turtle habitat?

   A 150.7 m²

   B 213.2 m²

   C 1012.9 m²

   D 3075 m²

5. Which expression gives the measure of the angle between the sides of the habitat that measure 15 meters and 25 meters?

   F $\cos^{-1}(-0.595)$

   G $\cos(-0.595)$

   H $\cos(0.595)$

   J $\cos^{-1}(0.595)$

Notes

This page provides students with the opportunity to apply concepts from the Common Core in real-world problem situations. There are three different levels of performance tasks:

⭐ Novice: These are short word problems that require students to apply the math they have learned in straightforward, real-world situations.

⭐⭐ Apprentice: These are more involved problems that guide students step-by-step through more complex tasks. These exercises include more complicated reasoning, writing, and open-ended elements.

⭐⭐⭐ Expert: These are open-ended, non-routine problems that, instead of stepping the students through, ask them to choose their own methods for solving and justify their answers and reasoning.

Sample answers

1. 17.5°

2. 64.9 inches

3. Scoring Guide:

Task	Possible points
a	1 point for finding 210π, and 1 point for appropriate work
b	1 point for the linear distance 3958 cm, and 1 point for appropriate work
c	1 point for the linear distance 4006 cm, and 1 point for appropriate work

Total possible points: 6

Performance Tasks

CHAPTER 10

COMMON CORE
CC.9-12.F.TF.1
CC.9-12.F.TF.7
CC.9-12.G.SRT.8

★ **1.** When a road has a 6% grade, it rises a vertical distance of 6 ft over a horizontal distance of 100 ft. One of the steepest roads in the U.S. is in San Francisco. Filbert Street between Hyde and Leavenworth has a grade of 31.5%. What is the angle that corresponds to this grade? Round to the nearest tenth of a degree.

★ **2.** Marija wants to stitch around the outside edge of a triangular banner. The banner is an isosceles triangle, with a vertex angle of 35° and a base of 15 inches. To the nearest tenth of an inch, how many inches will Marija stitch?

★★ **3.** A DVD's rotational speed varies from 1530 revolutions per minute (rpm) when the inner edge is being read to 630 rpm when the outer edge is being read.

   a. What is the total rotation of the DVD in radians after 10 seconds if the computer is reading data on the outer edge? Write your answer in terms of π and show your work.

   b. In 10 seconds, what linear distance is covered by the part of the DVD that passes under the reader head from part a, which is about 6 cm from the center of the DVD? Round to the nearest centimeter and show your work.

   c. If the computer is reading data on the inner edge (about 2.5 cm from the center of the DVD), what linear distance is covered by the part of the DVD that passes under the reader head in 10 seconds? Round to the nearest centimeter and show your work.

continued

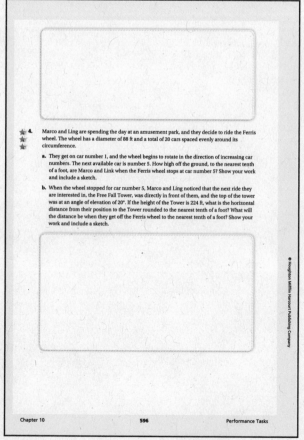

★★★ **4.** Marco and Ling are spending the day at an amusement park, and they decide to ride the Ferris wheel. The wheel has a diameter of 88 ft and a total of 20 cars spaced evenly around its circumference.

   a. They get on car number 1, and the wheel begins to rotate in the direction of increasing car numbers. The next available car is number 5. How high off the ground, to the nearest tenth of a foot, are Marco and Link when the Ferris wheel stops at car number 5? Show your work and include a sketch.

   b. When the wheel stopped for car number 5, Marco and Ling noticed that the next ride they are interested in, the Free Fall Tower, was directly in front of them, and the top of the tower was at an angle of elevation of 20°. If the height of the Tower is 224 ft, what is the horizontal distance from their position to the Tower rounded to the nearest tenth of a foot? What will the distance be when they get off the Ferris wheel to the nearest tenth of a foot? Show your work and include a sketch.

4. Scoring Guide:

Task	Possible points
a	1 point for 30.4 ft, and 2 points for work and a sketch like the one shown: 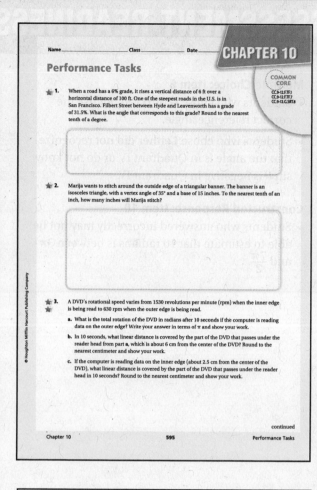
b	2 points for values of 531.9 ft and 573.7 ft, and 1 point for appropriate work and a sketch like the one shown: From the sketch, $\tan 20° = \dfrac{193.6}{d} \rightarrow d = 531.9$ ft From the bottom of the Ferris wheel to the base of the Tower, add $44 \sin 72° \approx 41.8$ ft: $531.9 + 41.8 = 573.7$ ft

Total possible points: 6

Standard	Items
CC.9-12.F.IF.2	6
CC.9-12.F.TF.1	1
CC.9-12.F.TF.2	10
CC.9-12.F.TF.3(+)	2, 4, 6
CC.9-12.F.TF.7(+)*	5
CC.9-12.G.SRT.9(+)	9
CC.9-12.G.SRT.10(+)	7, 11
CC.9-12.G.SRT.11(+)	7, 8, 11
CC.9-12.G.C.5	3

TEST PREP DOCTOR ✚

Multiple Choice: Item 1

- Students who chose **A** used the given ratio of arc length to circumference without multiplying by 2π, the number of radians in a full circle.

- Students who chose **B** multiplied the given ratio of arc length to circumference by π instead of 2π.

- Students who chose **D** did not stay within the constraints stated for θ.

Multiple Choice: Item 3

- Students who chose **A** determined that the arc is $\frac{3}{4}$ of the full circumference, but did not multiply by 2π to obtain the radian measure of the angle.

- Students who chose **B** divided the radius by the arc length instead of dividing the arc length by the radius.

- Students who chose **D** did not stay within the constraints stated for θ.

Multiple Choice: Item 6

- Students who chose **G** or **H** did not use the correct reference angle.

- Students who chose **J** either did not recognize that the angle is in Quadrant IV or do not know $\sin \theta$ is negative in Quadrant IV.

Constructed Response: Item 10

- Students who answered incorrectly may not be able to estimate that 10 radians is between 3π and $\frac{7\pi}{2}$.

Name _____ Class _____ Date _____

MULTIPLE CHOICE

1. An angle θ whose vertex is at the center of a unit circle intercepts an arc whose length is $\frac{2}{3}$ of the circle's circumference. What is the radian measure of θ if $0 < \theta < 2\pi$?

A. $\frac{2}{3}$

B. $\frac{2\pi}{3}$

C. $\frac{4\pi}{3}$

D. $-\frac{4\pi}{3}$

2. For which value of θ does $\tan \theta = 1$?

F. $\frac{\pi}{6}$

G. $\frac{\pi}{4}$

H. $\frac{\pi}{3}$

J. $\frac{\pi}{2}$

3. An angle θ whose vertex is at the center of a circle of radius 4 units intercepts an arc whose length is 6π units. What is the radian measure of θ if $0 < \theta < 2\pi$?

A. $\frac{3}{4}$

B. $\frac{2}{3\pi}$

C. $\frac{3\pi}{2}$

D. $-\frac{\pi}{2}$

4. If $0 < \theta < \frac{\pi}{2}$, which of the following is equal to $\sin \theta$?

F. $\sin\left(\frac{\pi}{2} + \theta\right)$

G. $\sin(\pi - \theta)$

H. $\sin(\pi + \theta)$

J. $\sin(2\pi - \theta)$

5. Solve the equation $\sin \theta = 0.4$ to the nearest tenth. Use the restrictions $90° < \theta < 180°$.

A. $\theta = 23.6°$

B. $\theta = 113.6°$

C. $\theta = 156.4°$

D. $\theta = 203.6°$

6. If $f(\theta) = \sin \theta$, what is $f\left(\frac{5\pi}{3}\right)$?

F. $\frac{\sqrt{3}}{2}$

G. $-\frac{1}{2}$

H. $\frac{1}{2}$

J. $\frac{\sqrt{3}}{2}$

7. Solve the triangle. $m\angle N = 120°$, $m\angle P = 28°$, and $m = 10$ cm. Round to the nearest tenth.

A. $m\angle M = 32°$, $n \approx 6.1$ cm, $p \approx 8.9$ cm

B. $m\angle M = 32°$, $n \approx 16.3$ cm, $p \approx 8.9$ cm

C. $m\angle M = 32°$, $n \approx 6.1$ cm, $p \approx 11.3$ cm

D. $m\angle M = 32°$, $n \approx 16.3$ cm, $p \approx 11.3$ cm

8. Use the given measurements to solve $\triangle ABC$. Round to the nearest tenth.

F. $b = 10.1$ in.; $m\angle A = 100.9°$; $m\angle C = 25.8°$

G. $b = 8.8$ in.; $m\angle A = 115.5°$; $m\angle C = 11.2°$

H. $b = 10.9$ in.; $m\angle A = 93.2°$; $m\angle C = 33.5°$

J. $b = 10.5$ in.; $m\angle A = 96.9°$ $m\angle C = 29.8°$

CONSTRUCTED RESPONSE

9. You are using the figure below to derive a formula for the area of a triangle that involves the sine ratio.

First you note that $\sin C = \frac{h}{b}$ and, therefore, $h = b \sin C$. How do you complete the derivation of the formula?

The area of the triangle is Area $= \frac{1}{2}ah$.

So, by substitution, Area $= \frac{1}{2}ab \sin C$.

10. If $\theta = 10$ radians, explain how you know that $\cos \theta < 0$ without using a calculator to find $\cos \theta$.

$3\pi \approx 9.42$ and $\frac{7\pi}{2} \approx 10.99$, so

$3\pi < \theta < \frac{7\pi}{2}$, or $2\pi + \pi < \theta < 2\pi + \frac{3\pi}{2}$.

This means that the terminal side of

θ rotates counterclockwise one full

revolution plus enough to put it in

Quadrant III, where cosine is negative.

11. Two airplanes leave an airport at the same time. One airplane flies due east at a speed of 300 miles per hour. The other airplane flies north-northeast at a speed of 350 miles per hour. The angle between the two directions is 67.5°.

a. Where is the plane that flies due east relative to the airport after 2.5 hours? Explain your reasoning.

750 miles due east of the airport;

$2.5 \text{ h} \times 300 \frac{\text{mi}}{\text{h}} = 750 \text{ mi}$

b. Where is the plane that flies north-northeast relative to the airport after 2.5 hours? Explain your reasoning.

875 miles north-northeast of the

airport; $2.5 \text{ h} \times 350 \frac{\text{mi}}{\text{h}} = 875 \text{ mi}$

c. If the planes are at the same altitude, how far apart are they after 2.5 hours? Round your answer to the nearest mile. Explain your reasoning.

909 miles; Let P_1 and P_2 be the

distances traveled by the two

planes. Use the law of cosines to

find the distance between the

planes, d. Then you get the result

$d^2 = (P_1)^2 + (P_2)^2 - 2(P_1)(P_2) \cos 67.5°$

$d^2 = 750^2 + 875^2 - 2(750)(875) \cos 67.5°$

$d^2 \approx 825,853$

$d \approx 909$ miles

Trigonometric Graphs and Identities

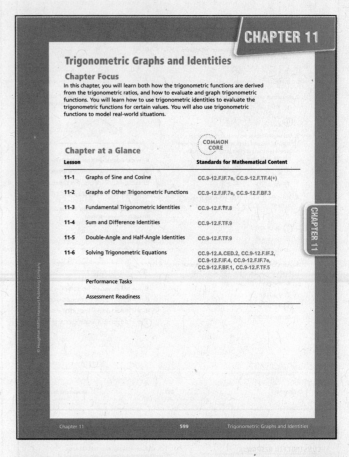

Trigonometric Graphs and Identities

Chapter Focus

In this chapter, you will learn both how the trigonometric functions are derived from the trigonometric ratios, and how to evaluate and graph trigonometric functions. You will learn how to use trigonometric identities to evaluate the trigonometric functions for certain values. You will also use trigonometric functions to model real-world situations.

Chapter at a Glance

COMMON CORE

Lesson		Standards for Mathematical Content
11-1	Graphs of Sine and Cosine	CC.9-12.F.IF.7e, CC.9-12.F.TF.4(+)
11-2	Graphs of Other Trigonometric Functions	CC.9-12.F.IF.7e, CC.9-12.F.BF.3
11-3	Fundamental Trigonometric Identities	CC.9-12.F.TF.8
11-4	Sum and Difference Identities	CC.9-12.F.TF.9
11-5	Double-Angle and Half-Angle Identities	CC.9-12.F.TF.9
11-6	Solving Trigonometric Equations	CC.9-12.A.CED.2, CC.9-12.F.IF.2, CC.9-12.F.IF.4, CC.9-12.F.IF.7e, CC.9-12.F.BF.1, CC.9-12.F.TF.5
	Performance Tasks	
	Assessment Readiness	

COMMON CORE PROFESSIONAL DEVELOPMENT   **CC.9-12.F.IF.7e***

In this chapter, students are introduced to periodic functions. Periodic functions repeat over a given period. In the case of some trigonometric functions, this creates a continuous wave-looking graph. It's important that students recognize that the wave consists of repeating parts. Thus, understanding one period of the graph allows one to understand any part of the graph. Make sure that students understand this concept, and help them to learn the periods and common values for common periodic functions like sine and cosine. Once the idea of periodicity is clear, students can apply their previous knowledge of transformations to identify key attributes of trigonometric functions and their graphs, including the midline and amplitude.

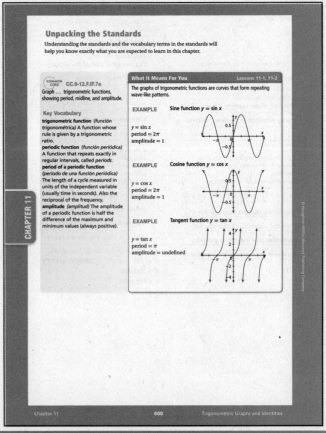

Unpacking the Standards

Understanding the standards and the vocabulary terms in the standards will help you know exactly what you are expected to learn in this chapter.

COMMON CORE **CC.9-12.F.IF.7e**

Graph … trigonometric functions, showing period, midline, and amplitude.

Key Vocabulary

trigonometric function *(función trigonométrica)* A function whose rule is given by a trigonometric ratio.

periodic function *(función periódica)* A function that repeats exactly in regular intervals, called *periods*.

period of a periodic function *(periodo de una función periódica)* The length of a cycle measured in units of the independent variable (usually time in seconds). Also the reciprocal of the frequency.

amplitude *(amplitud)* The amplitude of a periodic function is half the difference of the maximum and minimum values (always positive).

What It Means For You   Lessons 11-1, 11-2

The graphs of trigonometric functions are curves that form repeating wave-like patterns.

EXAMPLE   Sine function $y = \sin x$

$y = \sin x$
period $= 2\pi$
amplitude $= 1$

EXAMPLE   Cosine function $y = \cos x$

$y = \cos x$
period $= 2\pi$
amplitude $= 1$

EXAMPLE   Tangent function $y = \tan x$

$y = \tan x$
period $= \pi$
amplitude $=$ undefined

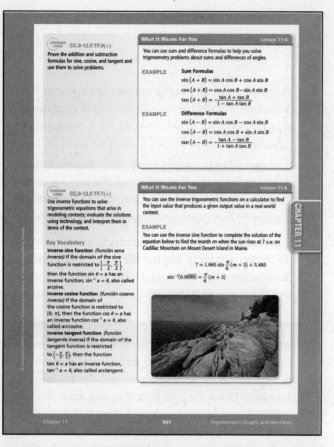

COMMON CORE
PROFESSIONAL
DEVELOPMENT

CC.9-12.F.TF.9(+)

Trigonometric identities allow students to manipulate trigonometric expressions to simplify them and solve problems. Encourage students to understand key identities and the rationale behind them. Students need not memorize every identity they see. If students understand a few key identities, they can use reasoning to derive other identities that are useful in a given problem situation.

COMMON CORE CC.9-12.F.TF.9(+)

Prove the addition and subtraction formulas for sine, cosine, and tangent and use them to solve problems.

What It Means For You — Lesson 11-4

You can use sum and difference formulas to help you solve trigonometry problems about sums and differences of angles.

EXAMPLE **Sum Formulas**

$\sin(A + B) = \sin A \cos B + \cos A \sin B$

$\cos(A + B) = \cos A \cos B - \sin A \sin B$

$\tan(A + B) = \dfrac{\tan A + \tan B}{1 - \tan A \tan B}$

EXAMPLE **Difference Formulas**

$\sin(A - B) = \sin A \cos B - \cos A \sin B$

$\cos(A - B) = \cos A \cos B + \sin A \sin B$

$\tan(A - B) = \dfrac{\tan A - \tan B}{1 + \tan A \tan B}$

COMMON CORE CC.9-12.F.TF.7(+)

Use inverse functions to solve trigonometric equations that arise in modeling contexts; evaluate the solutions using technology, and interpret them in terms of the context.

What It Means For You — Lesson 11-6

You can use the inverse trigonometric functions on a calculator to find the input value that produces a given output value in a real-world context.

EXAMPLE

You can use the inverse sine function to complete the solution of the equation below to find the month m when the sun rises at 7 A.M. on Cadillac Mountain on Mount Desert Island in Maine.

$$7 = 1.665 \sin \frac{\pi}{6}(m + 3) + 5.485$$

$$\sin^{-1}(0.9099) = \frac{\pi}{6}(m + 3)$$

Key Vocabulary

inverse sine function *(función seno inverso)* If the domain of the sine function is restricted to $\left[-\frac{\pi}{2}, \frac{\pi}{2}\right]$, then the sin $\theta = a$ has an inverse function, $\sin^{-1} a = \theta$, also called *arcsine*.

inverse cosine function *(función coseno inverso)* If the domain of the cosine function is restricted to $[0, \pi]$, then the function cos $\theta = a$ has an inverse function cos$^{-1} a = \theta$, also called *arccosine*.

inverse tangent function *(función tangente inversa)* If the domain of the tangent function is restricted to $\left(-\frac{\pi}{2}, \frac{\pi}{2}\right)$, then the function tan $\theta = a$ has an inverse function, tan$^{-1} a = \theta$, also called *arctangent*.

Chapter 11   601   Trigonometric Graphs and Identities

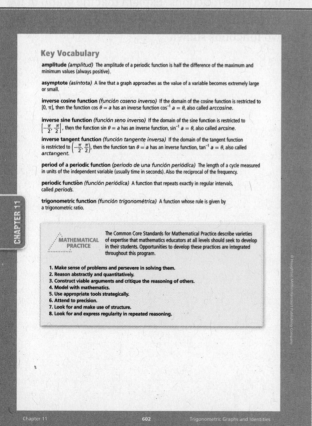

Key Vocabulary

amplitude *(amplitud)* The amplitude of a periodic function is half the difference of the maximum and minimum values (always positive).

asymptote *(asíntota)* A line that a graph approaches as the value of a variable becomes extremely large or small.

inverse cosine function *(función coseno inverso)* If the domain of the cosine function is restricted to $[0, \pi]$, then the function cos $\theta = a$ has an inverse function cos$^{-1} a = \theta$, also called *arccosine*.

inverse sine function *(función seno inverso)* If the domain of the sine function is restricted to $\left[-\frac{\pi}{2}, \frac{\pi}{2}\right]$, then the function sin $\theta = a$ has an inverse function, sin$^{-1} a = \theta$, also called *arcsine*.

inverse tangent function *(función tangente inversa)* If the domain of the tangent function is restricted to $\left(-\frac{\pi}{2}, \frac{\pi}{2}\right)$, then the function tan $\theta = a$ has an inverse function, tan$^{-1} a = \theta$, also called *arctangent*.

period of a periodic function *(periodo de una función periódica)* The length of a cycle measured in units of the independent variable (usually time in seconds). Also the reciprocal of the frequency.

periodic function *(función periódica)* A function that repeats exactly in regular intervals, called *periods*.

trigonometric function *(función trigonométrica)* A function whose rule is given by a trigonometric ratio.

MATHEMATICAL PRACTICE

The Common Core Standards for Mathematical Practice describe varieties of expertise that mathematics educators at all levels should seek to develop in their students. Opportunities to develop these practices are integrated throughout this program.

1. Make sense of problems and persevere in solving them.
2. Reason abstractly and quantitatively.
3. Construct viable arguments and critique the reasoning of others.
4. Model with mathematics.
5. Use appropriate tools strategically.
6. Attend to precision.
7. Look for and make use of structure.
8. Look for and express regularity in repeated reasoning.

Chapter 11   602   Trigonometric Graphs and Identities

11-1 Graphs of Sine and Cosine
Going Deeper

Essential question: *What are the key features of the graphs of the sine, cosine, and tangent functions?*

COMMON CORE Standards for Mathematical Content

CC.9-12.F.IF.7 Graph functions expressed symbolically and show key features of the graph … *

CC.9-12.F.IF.7e Graph … trigonometric functions, showing period, midline, and amplitude.*

CC.9-12.F.TF.4(+) Use the unit circle to explain … periodicity of trigonometric functions.

Vocabulary

periodic

period

midline

amplitude

Prerequisites

The sine, cosine, and tangent functions

Graphing the sine and cosine functions

Math Background

Students will first use function values for special angles to graph the sine and cosine functions over one revolution around the unit circle. Students should notice that the values of the functions are never less than −1 or greater than 1. They will then move on to graph the functions over several revolutions around the unit circle, and will learn about the periodicity of the functions. Students might observe that the graphs of the sine and cosine functions have the same shape, with one being a horizontal translation of the other. This transformation involves a trigonometric identity that is beyond the scope of this lesson. However, students will explore other transformations of trigonometric functions later in this unit.

The tangent function is discontinuous. In simple terms, that means that you cannot draw the graph of the function without lifting your pencil point off the paper. A slightly more complex definition for continuous functions is that small changes in the input of a function (in this case, θ) yield small changes in the output. Clearly, as θ passes through $\frac{\pi}{2}$, small changes in the input

yield huge changes in the output (from $+\infty$ to $-\infty$). A mathematically rigorous definition of continuous is $\lim_{x \to a} f(x) = f(a)$. In other words, for a continuous function, as θ approaches $\frac{\pi}{2}$ from either side, the function gives the same value. The tangent function does not meet this definition; as θ increases toward $\frac{\pi}{2}$, $f(\theta)$ approaches positive infinity. As θ decreases toward $\frac{\pi}{2}$, $f(\theta)$ approaches negative infinity. Continuity is something students in calculus will be concerned with. But the idea of a discontinuous function can be introduced here, using the simple pencil-on-paper definition.

INTRODUCE

Ask students to explain the difference between the graphs of the sine function and the cosine function. Draw the sine function and draw the cosine function immediately below it. Ask students to define the tangent function in terms of the sine and cosine functions. Explain that the graph of the tangent function will represent the quotient of the two functions shown.

Name _____ Class _____ Date _____

11-1

Graphs of Sine and Cosine
Going Deeper

Essential question: What are the key features of the graphs of the sine, cosine, and tangent functions?

Video Tutor

CC.9–12.F.IF.7e

1 EXPLORE Graphing $f(\theta) = \sin \theta$

Graph $f(\theta) = \sin \theta$ for $0 \leq \theta \leq 2\pi$.

A Complete the axis labels on the coordinate plane below. The θ-axis shows angle measures in radians. The $f(\theta)$-axis shows the function values.

B Complete the table of values.

θ	0	$\frac{\pi}{6}$	$\frac{\pi}{2}$	$\frac{5\pi}{6}$	π	$\frac{7\pi}{6}$	$\frac{3\pi}{2}$	$\frac{11\pi}{6}$	2π
$f(\theta) = \sin \theta$	0	0.5	1	0.5	0	−0.5	−1	−0.5	0

C Plot the points from the table and draw a smooth curve through them.

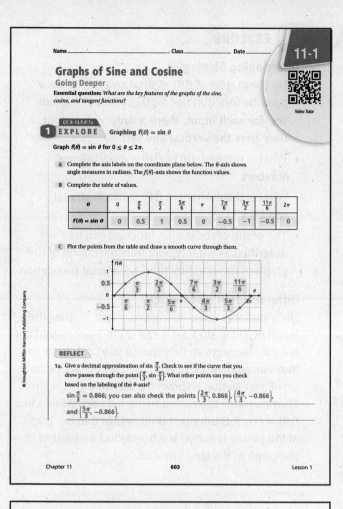

REFLECT

1a. Give a decimal approximation of $\sin \frac{\pi}{3}$. Check to see if the curve that you drew passes through the point $\left(\frac{\pi}{3}, \sin \frac{\pi}{3}\right)$. What other points can you check based on the labeling of the θ-axis?

$\sin \frac{\pi}{3} \approx 0.866$; you can also check the points $\left(\frac{2\pi}{3}, 0.866\right)$, $\left(\frac{4\pi}{3}, -0.866\right)$, and $\left(\frac{5\pi}{3}, -0.866\right)$.

© Houghton Mifflin Harcourt Publishing Company

1b. On the interval $0 \leq \theta \leq 2\pi$, where does the sine function have positive values? Where does it have negative values?

$0 < \theta < \pi$; $\pi < \theta < 2\pi$

1c. List the θ-intercepts of the graph of $f(\theta) = \sin \theta$ on the interval $0 \leq \theta \leq 2\pi$. What do you think the next positive θ-intercept will be? Explain.

0, π, 2π; 3π because it is terminal with π just as 2π is coterminal with 0

1d. What are the minimum and maximum values of $f(\theta) = \sin \theta$ on the interval $0 \leq \theta \leq 2\pi$? Where do the extreme values occur in relation to the θ-intercepts?

The minimum is −1, and the maximum is 1; the extreme values occur exactly halfway between the θ-intercepts.

1e. Describe a rotation that will map the curve onto itself over the interval $0 \leq \theta \leq 2\pi$.

A rotation of 180° clockwise or counterclockwise about the point $(\pi, 0)$ will map the curve onto itself.

CC.9–12.F.IF.7e

2 EXPLORE Graphing $f(\theta) = \cos \theta$

Graph $f(\theta) = \cos \theta$ for $0 \leq \theta \leq 2\pi$.

A Complete the axis labels on the coordinate plane below. The θ-axis shows angle measures in radians. The $f(\theta)$-axis shows the function values.

B Complete the table of values.

θ	0	$\frac{\pi}{3}$	$\frac{\pi}{2}$	$\frac{2\pi}{3}$	π	$\frac{4\pi}{3}$	$\frac{3\pi}{2}$	$\frac{5\pi}{3}$	2π
$f(\theta) = \cos \theta$	1	0.5	0	−0.5	−1	−0.5	0	0.5	1

C Plot the points from the table and draw a smooth curve through them.

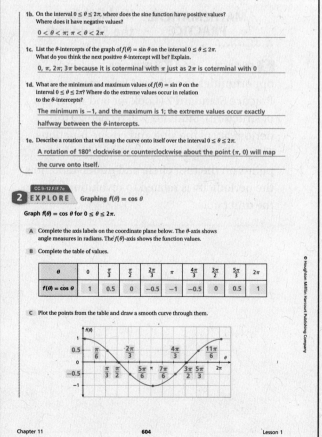

© Houghton Mifflin Harcourt Publishing Company

1 EXPLORE

Questioning Strategies

- Is this graph a function? Explain. Yes; each input corresponds to only one output.

- Is the inverse of $f(\theta) = \sin \theta$ a function? Explain. No; the function is not one-to-one. For example, $\sin 0 = 0$, $\sin \pi = 0$ and $\sin 2\pi = 0$.

- What do you think the graph of $f(\theta) = \sin \theta$ would look like if you extended the graph from 2π to 4π? Why? The graph from 2π to 4π would look exactly like the graph from 0 to π because the angles from 2π to 4π have the same sine values as their reference angles from 0 to 2π.

2 EXPLORE

Questioning Strategies

- Compare the ranges for the graphs of $f(\theta) = \sin \theta$ and $f(\theta) = \cos \theta$. The ranges are the same (–1 to 1 for both functions).

- Compare the zeros for the graphs of $f(\theta) = \sin \theta$ and $f(\theta) = \cos \theta$. The zeros for $\sin \theta$ are 0 and π. For $\cos \theta$ they are $\frac{\pi}{2}$ and $\frac{3\pi}{2}$. The zeros differ by $\frac{\pi}{2}$.

3 ENGAGE

Questioning Strategies

- What does one period of the sine graph or the cosine graph correspond to on the unit circle? one complete revolution of the terminal side around the unit circle

- For $0 \le \theta \le 2\pi$, at what value(s) of θ does a crest occur for $\sin \theta$? for $\cos \theta$? $\frac{\pi}{2}$; 0 and 2π

- For $0 \le \theta \le 2\pi$, at what value(s) of θ does a trough occur for $\sin \theta$? for $\cos \theta$? $\frac{3\pi}{2}$; π

Questioning Strategies

- Do the graphs of $f(\theta) = \sin \theta$ and $f(\theta) = \cos \theta$ pass the function test for $0 \le \theta \le 4\pi$? Explain. Yes; for each input, there is only one output. They pass the vertical line test.

- What is the domain of $f(\theta) = \sin \theta$? all real numbers

- What is the domain of $f(\theta) = \cos \theta$? all real numbers

- The graph of the cosine function can be described as what type of transformation of the graph of the sine function? horizontal translation

Differentiated Instruction

Have students use construction paper to draw the graph of $f(\theta) = \sin \theta$ for $0 \le \theta \le 2\pi$. They should cut out the sine wave so they have a physical shape to move around. Students can then set the shape on a set of axes so that it shows the function $f(\theta) = \sin \theta$. They can slide the cutout to the left until it looks like $f(\theta) = \cos \theta$. Students should realize that the graph of the cosine function is a horizontal translation of the graph of the sine function.

┈┈┈┈┈┈
MATHEMATICAL
PRACTICE

Highlighting the Standards

3 ENGAGE and **4** EXPLORE include opportunities to address Mathematical Practice Standard 7 (Look for and make use of structure). Students will recognize the periodicity of the sine and cosine functions. They will compare points on the graphs to points on the unit circle and understand how the periodicity is related to revolutions about the unit circle.

REFLECT

2a. On the interval $0 \le \theta \le 2\pi$, where does the cosine function have positive values? Where does it have negative values?

$0 < \theta < \dfrac{\pi}{2}$ and $\dfrac{3\pi}{2} < \theta < 2\pi$; $\dfrac{\pi}{2} < \theta < \dfrac{3\pi}{2}$

2b. List the θ-intercepts of the graph of $f(\theta) = \cos \theta$ on the interval $0 \le \theta \le 2\pi$. What do you think the next positive θ-intercept will be? Explain.

$\dfrac{\pi}{2}, \dfrac{3\pi}{2}; \dfrac{5\pi}{2}$ because $\dfrac{5\pi}{2}$ is terminal with $\dfrac{\pi}{2}$

2c. What are the minimum and maximum values of $f(\theta) = \cos \theta$ on the interval $0 \le \theta \le 2\pi$? Where do the extreme values occur in relation to the θ-intercepts?

The minimum is −1, and the maximum is 1; the extreme values occur exactly

halfway between the θ-intercepts.

3 **ENGAGE**   Understanding the Properties of the Graphs

In the preceding Explores, you graphed the sine and cosine functions over the interval $0 \le \theta \le 2\pi$, which represents all angles of rotation within the first counterclockwise revolution that starts at 0. What you drew are not the complete graphs, however. They are simply one *cycle* of the graphs.

As you will see in the next Explore, the graphs of sine and cosine consist of repeated cycles that form a wave-like shape. When a function repeats its values over regular intervals on the horizontal axis as the sine and cosine functions do, the function is called **periodic**, and the length of the interval is called the function's **period**.

The wave-like shape of the sine and cosine functions has a "crest" (where the function's maximum value occurs) and a "trough" (where the function's minimum value occurs). Halfway between the "crest" and the "trough" is the graph's **midline**. The distance that the "crest" rises above the midline or the distance that the "trough" falls below the midline is called the graph's **amplitude**.

REFLECT

3a. Complete the table.

Function	Properties of Function's Graph		
	Period	Midline	Amplitude
$f(\theta) = \sin \theta$	2π	The θ-axis	1
$f(\theta) = \cos \theta$	2π	The θ-axis	1

4 **EXPLORE**   Extending the Graphs of Sine and Cosine

Use the cycle shown for the first counterclockwise revolution (starting at 0 and ending at 2π) to extend the graphs of the sine and cosine functions to the right (second counterclockwise revolution) and to the left (first clockwise revolution).

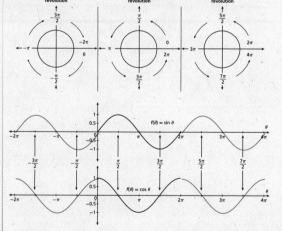

REFLECT

4a. The graphs show that sine and cosine are periodic functions. Explain why this is so by referring to angles of rotation and the unit circle.

One revolution gives all values of the functions. Subsequent revolutions repeat

those values.

4b. The graphs show that $\sin(-\theta) = -\sin \theta$ and $\cos(-\theta) = \cos \theta$. Explain why this is so by referring to angles of rotation and the unit circle.

The angles θ and $-\theta$ intersect the unit circle at points that have the same

x-coordinate (cosine value) but opposite y-coordinates (sine value).

Questioning Strategies

- Look at the graph of $f(\theta) = \tan \theta$. Does it meet the requirements to be a function? Explain. **Yes; each input maps to only one output.**

- What is the domain of $f(\theta) = \tan \theta$? **all real numbers except odd multiples of $\frac{\pi}{2}$** How does this compare with the domains of the sine function and the cosine function? **The domains for the sine and cosine functions are all real numbers.**

- What is the range of $f(\theta) = \tan \theta$? **all real numbers** How does this compare to the ranges of the sine function and the cosine function? **The sine function and the cosine function both have a range from −1 to 1, as opposed to the range of the tangent function, which is all real numbers.**

Teaching Strategy

Students might be uncomfortable with the graph of the tangent function due to the multiple vertical asymptotes. However, they are familiar with other functions that have asymptotes. Ask students to make a table for and then a graph of $f(x) = \frac{1}{x}$. Recommend that they create a table showing $x = \pm0.001, \pm0.01, \pm0.1, \pm1, \pm2, \pm3, \pm4, \pm5,$ and ±10. Ask students to describe what happens to $f(x)$ as x gets closer and closer to 0 from the positive side and then from the negative side. Students should realize that the y-axis is an asymptote for this function and that what the function approached from the positive side $(+\infty)$ is different from what it approaches from the negative side $(-\infty)$. Use this as a springboard into the tangent function and its asymptotes.

Questioning Strategies

- What interval between 0 and 2π shows one complete cycle of the tangent function? $\frac{\pi}{2} \leq \theta \leq \frac{3\pi}{2}$

- How does the graph of the tangent function behave as θ increases from $\frac{\pi}{4}$ to $\frac{\pi}{2}$? **The graph of the tangent function climbs more steeply as θ increases.**

- How can you use the graph of the tangent function from $\frac{\pi}{2}$ to $\frac{3\pi}{2}$ to draw more of the graph of $f(\theta) = \tan \theta$? **The graph of each period of $f(\theta) = \tan \theta$ is a horizontal translation of the graph from $\frac{\pi}{2}$ to $\frac{3\pi}{2}$ by a multiple of π. You can keep shifting the original graph left or right by π to get more of the graph**

MATHEMATICAL PRACTICE | Highlighting the Standards

6 **EXPLORE** includes opportunities to address Mathematical Practice Standard 7 (Look for and make use of structure). Students will recognize the periodicity of the tangent function. They will compare points on the graph with points on the unit circle and understand how the periodicity is related to revolutions about the unit circle.

5 EXPLORE Graphing $f(\theta) = \tan \theta$

Graph $f(\theta) = \tan \theta$ for $0 \le \theta \le 2\pi$.

A Complete the axis labels on the coordinate plane in part D. The θ-axis shows angle measures in radians. The $f(\theta)$-axis shows the function values.

B Complete the table of values. The dashes that appear as function values for $\theta = \frac{\pi}{2}$ and $\theta = \frac{3\pi}{2}$ indicate that $f(\theta)$ is undefined.

θ	0	$\frac{\pi}{4}$	$\frac{\pi}{2}$	$\frac{3\pi}{4}$	π	$\frac{5\pi}{4}$	$\frac{3\pi}{2}$	$\frac{7\pi}{4}$	2π
$f(\theta) = \tan \theta$	0	1	—	-1	0	1	—	-1	0

C Examine the behavior of the function near $\theta = \frac{\pi}{2}$ and $\theta = \frac{3\pi}{2}$. For each table below, use a calculator set in radian mode to find the approximate values of $\sin \theta$ and $\cos \theta$, then use the fact that $\tan \theta = \frac{\sin \theta}{\cos \theta}$ to find the value of $\tan \theta$. Note that $\frac{\pi}{2} \approx 1.5708$ and $\frac{3\pi}{2} \approx 4.7124$. After examining the values of $\tan \theta$, complete the summary statement below the table.

θ	$\sin \theta$	$\cos \theta$	$\tan \theta$
1.50	0.997	0.071	14.0
1.55	0.9998	0.0208	48.07
1.57	0.9999997	0.0007963	1255.808

θ	$\sin \theta$	$\cos \theta$	$\tan \theta$
1.65	0.997	-0.079	-12.6
1.60	0.9996	-0.0292	-34.23
1.58	0.999958	-0.009204	-108.644

As $\theta \to \frac{\pi}{2}^{-}$, $\tan \theta \to$ ___ $+\infty$ ___ .

As $\theta \to \frac{\pi}{2}^{+}$, $\tan \theta \to$ ___ $-\infty$ ___ .

θ	$\sin \theta$	$\cos \theta$	$\tan \theta$
4.50	-0.9775	-0.2108	4.637
4.70	-0.99992	-0.01239	80.704
4.71	-0.999997	-0.002389	418.584

θ	$\sin \theta$	$\cos \theta$	$\tan \theta$
5.00	-0.959	0.284	-3.38
4.75	-0.9993	0.0376	-26.58
4.72	-0.99997	0.00761	-131.40

As $\theta \to \frac{3\pi}{2}^{-}$, $\tan \theta \to$ ___ $+\infty$ ___ .

As $\theta \to \frac{3\pi}{2}^{+}$, $\tan \theta \to$ ___ $-\infty$ ___ .

© Houghton Mifflin Harcourt Publishing Company

D Draw the vertical asymptotes found in part C as dashed lines. Then plot the points from part B and draw smooth curves that pass through the plotted points and approach the asymptotes.

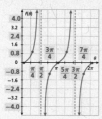

REFLECT

5a. What is the relationship between $\frac{\pi}{4}$ and 0.8? Why is 0.8 a good interval to use for the vertical axis?

Sample answer: As a decimal, $\frac{\pi}{4} \approx 0.8$; intervals of 0.8 along the vertical axis produce

a graph of the tangent function that is not distorted horizontally or vertically.

5b. On the interval $0 \le \theta \le 2\pi$, where does the tangent function have positive values? Where does it have negative values?

$0 < \theta < \frac{\pi}{2}$ and $\pi < \theta < \frac{3\pi}{2}$; $\frac{\pi}{2} < \theta < \pi$ and $\frac{3\pi}{2} < \theta < 2\pi$

5c. List the θ-intercepts of the graph of $f(\theta) = \tan \theta$ on the interval $0 \le \theta \le 2\pi$. What do you think the next positive θ-intercept will be? Explain.

$0, \pi, 2\pi$; 3π because it is coterminal with π just as 2π is coterminal with 0

5d. How many times does the tangent function run through all of its values on the interval $0 \le \theta \le 2\pi$? What, then, is the function's period?

Twice; π

5e. Does the tangent function have minimum or maximum values? Explain.

No; the value of the tangent function can be any real number, so there is no

maximum value or minimum value.

5f. The points where $\tan \theta = \pm 1$ serve as handy reference points when graphing the tangent function. What line lies halfway between them? (Note that this line is called the graph's *midline* even though the tangent function does not have minimum or maximum values.)

The θ-axis

© Houghton Mifflin Harcourt Publishing Company

Essential Question

What are the key features of the graphs of the sine, cosine, and tangent functions?

The graph of the sine function has an amplitude of 1, a period of 2π, θ-intercepts at $n\pi$, maximums at $\theta = \frac{\pi}{2} + 2n\pi$, and minimums at $\theta = \frac{3\pi}{2} + 2n\pi$, where n is an integer.

The graph of the cosine function has an amplitude of 1, a period of 2π, θ-intercepts at $\frac{\pi}{2} + n\pi$, maximums at $\theta = 2n\pi$, and minimums at $\theta = \pi + 2n\pi$, where n is an integer.

The graph of the tangent function has a period of π, vertical asymptotes at $\theta = \frac{\pi}{2} + n\pi$, and θ-intercepts at $n\pi$, where n is an integer.

Summarize

Have students draw a sine graph and a cosine graph in their journals, one below the other and to the same scale. They should clearly label which is which. They should include labels on the axes, clearly marking the θ-values corresponding to the intercepts and to the maximum and minimum values.

Immediately below these, students should draw a tangent function to the same scale. They should include labels on the axes, clearly mark the value of θ for the intercepts, and label the asymptotes. As a final step, students should include the summary table from Reflect question 6g under the graphs.

6 EXPLORE CC.9-12.F.TF.4(+) Extending the Graph of Tangent

Use the cycle shown for the first counterclockwise revolution (starting at 0 and ending at 2π) to extend the graph of the tangent function to the right (second counterclockwise revolution) and to the left (first clockwise revolution).

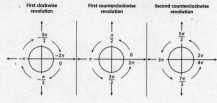

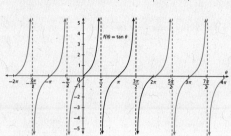

REFLECT

6a. The graph shows that tangent is a periodic function. Explain why this is so by referring to angles of rotation and the unit circle.

One revolution gives all values of the function twice. Subsequent revolutions repeat those values.

6b. Error Analysis A student says that there are 8 cycles of the tangent function on the interval $-8\pi \leq \theta \leq 8\pi$, because $\frac{16\pi}{2\pi} = 8$. Explain the error in the student's reasoning.

The period of the tangent function is π, not 2π, so there are $\frac{16\pi}{\pi} = 16$ cycles of the tangent function on the interval $-8\pi \leq \theta \leq 8\pi$.

6c. The graph shows that $\tan(-\theta) = -\tan\theta$. Explain why this is so by referring to angles of rotation and the unit circle.

The angles θ and $-\theta$ intersect the unit circle at points that have the same x-coordinate (cosine value) but opposite y-coordinates (sine value), so the ratio of y to x for $-\theta$ is the opposite of the ratio of y to x for θ.

6d. Show that $\tan(-\theta) = -\tan\theta$ using these facts: $\tan\theta = \frac{\sin\theta}{\cos\theta}$, $\sin(-\theta) = -\sin\theta$, and $\cos(-\theta) = \cos\theta$.

$\tan(-\theta) = \frac{\sin(-\theta)}{\cos(-\theta)} = \frac{-\sin\theta}{\cos\theta} = -\frac{\sin\theta}{\cos\theta} = -\tan\theta$

6e. A function is called *even* if $f(-x) = x$ for all x, and it is called *odd* if $f(-x) = -f(x)$ for all x. Which of the trigonometric functions (sine, cosine, and tangent) are even? Which are odd?

cosine; sine and tangent

6f. The graph of $f(\theta) = \tan\theta$ has θ-intercepts at multiples of π and has vertical asymptotes at odd multiples of $\frac{\pi}{2}$. Use the fact that $\tan\theta = \frac{\sin\theta}{\cos\theta}$ to explain how the θ-intercepts and vertical asymptotes of the tangent function are related to the θ-intercepts of the sine and cosine functions.

Tangent's θ-intercepts occur when $\tan\theta = 0$, which is when $\sin\theta = 0$, so tangent has the same θ-intercepts as sine. Tangent's vertical asymptotes occur when $\tan\theta$ is undefined, which is when $\cos\theta = 0$, so tangent has vertical asymptotes where cosine has θ-intercepts.

6g. Complete the table to summarize the properties of the graphs of the sine, cosine, and tangent functions. If a function does not have a property, say so.

Function	Properties of Function's Graph				
	θ-intercepts	Vertical asymptotes	Period	Midline	Amplitude
$f(\theta) = \sin\theta$	Multiples of π	None	2π	The θ-axis	1
$f(\theta) = \cos\theta$	Odd multiples of $\frac{\pi}{2}$	None	2π	The θ-axis	1
$f(\theta) = \tan\theta$	Multiples of π	Odd multiples of $\frac{\pi}{2}$	π	The θ-axis	None

ADDITIONAL PRACTICE AND PROBLEM SOLVING

Assign these pages to help your students practice and apply important lesson concepts. For additional exercises, see the Student Edition.

Answers

Additional Practice

1. not periodic

2. not periodic

3. not periodic

4. periodic; period is π

5. periodic; period is 2

Problem Solving

1. $x = \dfrac{\pi}{4} + 2\pi n$ for $n \in \mathbb{Z}$

2. $\cot(x)$ is not defined at values of x where $\sin(x)$ is equal to 0, that is, $x = \pi n$ for $n \in \mathbb{Z}$.

3.

θ	0	$\dfrac{\pi}{6}$	$\dfrac{\pi}{2}$	$\dfrac{5\pi}{6}$	π	$\dfrac{7\pi}{6}$	$\dfrac{3\pi}{2}$	$\dfrac{11\pi}{6}$	2π
2θ	0	$\dfrac{\pi}{3}$	π	$\dfrac{5\pi}{3}$	2π	$\dfrac{7\pi}{3}$	3π	$\dfrac{11\pi}{3}$	4π
$f(\theta) = \sin 2\theta$	0	$\dfrac{\sqrt{3}}{2}$	0	$-\dfrac{\sqrt{3}}{2}$	0	$\dfrac{\sqrt{3}}{2}$	0	$-\dfrac{\sqrt{3}}{2}$	0

4.

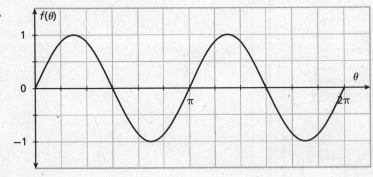

5. 1 and -1

6. π

Additional Practice

Identify whether each function is periodic. If the function is periodic, give the period.

1.

2.

_____ _____

3.

4.

_____ _____

5.

_____

Problem Solving

1. Use the periodicity of the sine and cosine graphs to write an expression showing the general form of the values for which $\cos(x) = \sin(x)$.

_____

2. The *cotangent* function, abbreviated cot(x), is the multiplicative inverse of the tangent function. On the interval $0 \le x \le 2\pi$, where is cot(x) not defined?

_____

Consider the function $f(\theta) = \sin(2\theta)$.

3. Complete the table of values.

θ	0	$\dfrac{\pi}{6}$	$\dfrac{\pi}{2}$	$\dfrac{5\pi}{6}$	π	$\dfrac{7\pi}{6}$	$\dfrac{3\pi}{2}$	$\dfrac{11\pi}{6}$	2π
2θ									
$f(\theta) = \sin 2\theta$									

4. Plot the points from the table and draw a smooth sinusoidal curve through them.

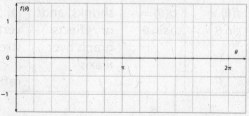

5. What do the maximum and minimum values of $f(\theta) = \sin(2\theta)$ on the interval $0 \le \theta \le 2\pi$ appear to be?

_____

6. What is the period of $f(\theta) = \sin(2\theta)$? _____

Notes

Graphs of Other Trigonometric Functions

Extension: Transformations of Trigonometric Graphs

Essential question: *How do the constants a, b, h, and k in the functions* $g(\theta) = a \sin b(\theta - h) + k$, $g(\theta) = a \cos b(\theta - h) + k$, *and* $g(\theta) = a \tan b(\theta - h) + k$ *affect their graphs?*

COMMON CORE Standards for Mathematical Content

CC.9-12.F.IF.7 Graph functions expressed symbolically and show key features of the graph ... *

CC.9-12.F.IF.7e Graph ... trigonometric functions, showing period, midline, and amplitude.*

CC.9-12.F.BF.3 Identify the effect on the graph of replacing $f(x)$ by $f(x) + k$, $kf(x)$, $f(kx)$, and $f(x + k)$ for specific values of k (both positive and negative); find the value of k given the graphs. ...

Also: CC.9-12.F.IF.4*

Prerequisites

Graphing the sine and cosine functions,
Graphing the tangent function
Stretching, shrinking, and reflecting trigonometric graphs

Math Background

Periodic motion is often modeled using sine and cosine functions. The general form of the sine function is $y = a \sin b(x - h) + k$. (The other trig functions can be written similarly.) The initial conditions describing the real-world situation are incorporated in the constants a, b, h, and k. In the first part of this lesson, students will study the effect of different values of a and b. In the second part of this lesson, they will study the effect of different values of h and k and begin to apply trigonometric functions to real-world situations.

In the first part of this lesson, students learn the effects of the values of a and b on the sine, cosine, and tangent functions of the form $g(\theta) = a \sin b(\theta)$, etc. Students see that changing the values of these constants has the same effect on these trigonometric functions as on other types of functions. The graphs of the trigonometric functions are shrunk, stretched, and reflected depending on the values of a and b.

In the second part of this lesson, students will study the effects of h and k on trigonometric functions

of the form $g(\theta) = a \sin b(\theta - h) + k$, etc., and they will discover that changing these values translates the graphs of the parent functions horizontally or vertically in much the same manner as with previously studied functions. The value of h for trigonometric functions has a special meaning. It indicates the horizontal translation and is called the *phase shift* of the function.

INTRODUCE

Ask students to recall the parent quadratic function $f(x) = x^2$. Ask them to recall what effects the coefficient of the x^2-term has on the function. Have students summarize the results in the first row of the table. Have them make predictions for the second row.

Parent Function	Function	Effects of Coefficient	Specific Effects
$f(x) = x^2$	$g(x) = ax^2$	vertically stretches, shrinks, and/ or reflects graph over x-axis.	$\|a\| < 1$ vertically shrinks $\|a\| > 1$ vertically stretches $a < 0$ reflects
$f(\theta) = \sin \theta$	$g(\theta) = a \sin \theta$	vertically stretches, shrinks, and/ or reflects graph over θ-axis	$\|a\| < 1$ vertically shrinks $\|a\| > 1$ vertically stretches $a < 0$ reflects

Name _____ Class _____ Date _____

11-2

Graphs of Other Trigonometric Functions
Extension: Transformations of Trigonometric Graphs

Essential question: *How do the constants a, b, h, and k in the functions*
$g(\theta) = a \sin b(\theta - h) + k$, $g(\theta) = a \cos b(\theta - h) + k$, *and* $g(\theta) = a \tan b(\theta - h) + k$
affect their graphs?

Video Tutor

CC.9-12.F.IF.7e

1 ENGAGE   Recognizing Key Points and Asymptotes on Parent Graphs

In this lesson you will graph functions of the form $g(\theta) = a \sin b\theta$, $g(\theta) = a \cos b\theta$, and $g(\theta) = a \tan b\theta$. You have already seen the graphs of the *parent* functions (when $a = 1$ and $b = 1$). One cycle of the graph of each parent function is shown below along with five key points or asymptotes from that cycle.

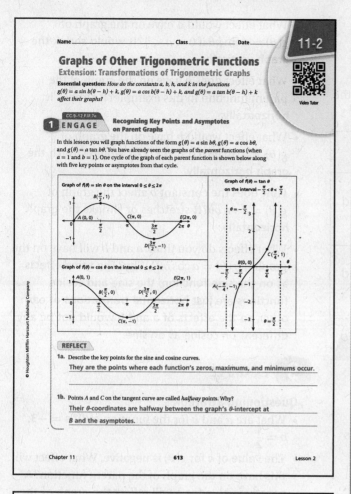

Graph of $f(\theta) = \sin \theta$ on the interval $0 \le \theta \le 2\pi$

Graph of $f(\theta) = \cos \theta$ on the interval $0 \le \theta \le 2\pi$

Graph of $f(\theta) = \tan \theta$ on the interval $-\frac{\pi}{2} < \theta < \frac{\pi}{2}$

REFLECT

1a. Describe the key points for the sine and cosine curves.

They are the points where each function's zeros, maximums, and minimums occur.

1b. Points A and C on the tangent curve are called *halfway* points. Why?

Their θ-coordinates are halfway between the graph's θ-intercept at

B and the asymptotes.

CC.9-12.F.BF.3

2 ENGAGE   Understanding Transformations of Trigonometric Graphs

If $f(\theta)$ is one of the three parent trigonometric functions, then the constants a and b in $g(\theta) = af(b\theta)$ alter the graph of $f(\theta)$ in particular ways. Notice that the constant a appears *outside* the function and therefore acts on f's output values, while the constant b appears *inside* the function and therefore acts on f's input values. For instance, consider the function $g(\theta) = 3 \sin 2\theta$ whose parent function is $f(\theta) = \sin \theta$. The mapping diagram below shows what happens when $0, \frac{\pi}{4}, \frac{\pi}{2}, \frac{3\pi}{4}$, and π are used as inputs for g.

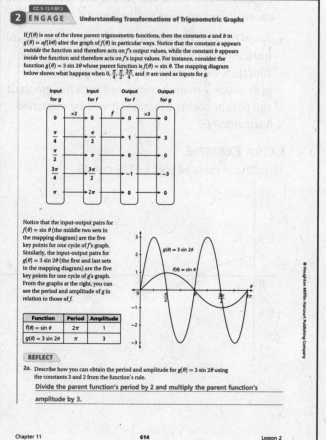

Notice that the input-output pairs for $f(\theta) = \sin \theta$ (the middle two sets in the mapping diagram) are the five key points for one cycle of f's graph. Similarly, the input-output pairs for $g(\theta) = 3 \sin 2\theta$ (the first and last sets in the mapping diagram) are the five key points for one cycle of g's graph. From the graphs at the right, you can see the period and amplitude of g in relation to those of f.

Function	Period	Amplitude
$f(\theta) = \sin \theta$	2π	1
$g(\theta) = 3 \sin 2\theta$	π	3

REFLECT

2a. Describe how you can obtain the period and amplitude for $g(\theta) = 3 \sin 2\theta$ using the constants 3 and 2 from the function's rule.

Divide the parent function's period by 2 and multiply the parent function's

amplitude by 3.

© Houghton Mifflin Harcourt Publishing Company

Again recalling the parent quadratic function $f(x) = x^2$, ask students what effects the h and k values had on the graph of $g(x) = (x - h)^2 + k$. Have students summarize the results in the first row of the table below and make predictions for the second row.

Parent Function	Function	Specific Effects
$f(x) = x^2$	$g(x) = (x - h)^2 + k$	h translates horizontally, and k translates vertically.
$f(\theta) = \sin\theta$	$g(\theta) = \sin(\theta - h) + k$	h translates horizontally, and k translates vertically.

TEACH

1 ENGAGE

Questioning Strategies

• Why are the five points indicated on the graphs of the sine and cosine functions key points for these graphs? **These points correspond to the minimum, maximum, and zeros for one period of the functions. These are the points that will be transformed to create the graph of the transformed functions.**

• Why are the three points and the asymptotes shown key features of the graph of the tangent function? **Point A is where the value of the tangent is −1, the θ-coordinate of point B is the zero of the function, and point C is where the value of the tangent is 1. These are the points, along with the vertical asymptotes, that will be transformed to create the graph of the transformed tangent function.**

2 ENGAGE

Questioning Strategies

• What are the values of a and b for $g(\theta)$? **a = 3; b = 2**

• What effect does a have on the graph of the parent function in this example? **It stretches it vertically.**

• What effect would a have on the graph of $g(\theta) = a\sin b\theta$ if $0 < a < 1$? **It would shrink the graph vertically.**

• What effect does b have on the graph of the parent function in this example? **It shrinks it horizontally.**

• What effect would b have on the graph of $g(\theta) = a\sin b\theta$ if $0 < b < 1$? **It would stretch the graph horizontally.**

• How does the constant b affect the graph of $g(\theta) = a\sin b\theta$? **It stretches or shrinks the graph horizontally.**

• What effects do you think a and b will have on the graph of $g(\theta) = a\cos b\theta$? Why? **The same effects as on the sine function; the sine and cosine functions are just horizontal translations of each other, so the effects of a and b would not be any different on cosine as on sine.**

3 EXAMPLE

Questioning Strategies

• What are a and b for the function $g(\theta)$? **a = −3; b = $\frac{1}{2}$**

• The value of a for $g(\theta)$ is negative. What effect will this have on the graph of the parent function? **A negative value for a will reflect the graph of the parent function over the horizontal axis.**

• Knowing that the graph of $f(\theta) = \sin 2\theta$ is shrunk horizontally from the graph of the parent sine function, how do you expect the graph of $g(\theta) = \cos\frac{\theta}{2}$ to look compared with the graph of the parent cosine function? **It will be stretched horizontally**

EXTRA EXAMPLE
Graph one cycle of $g(\theta) = 0.25\cos 2\theta$

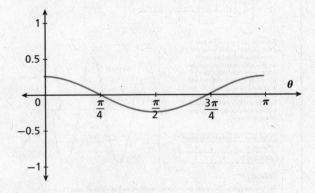

2b. In terms of transformations, the change in the period is the result of horizontally shrinking the graph of f by a factor of $\frac{1}{2}$ (since $\pi = \frac{1}{2}(2\pi)$). How would you characterize the change in the amplitude in terms of transformations?

The result of vertically stretching the graph of f by a factor of 3

CC.9-12.F.IF.7e

3 EXAMPLE Graphing $g(\theta) = a \cos b\theta$

Graph one cycle of $g(\theta) = -3 \cos \frac{\theta}{2}$.

A Determine the function's period. One cycle of the graph of the parent function, $f(\theta) = \cos \theta$, begins at 0 and ends at 2π. One cycle of the graph of g also begins at 0 but ends when $\frac{\theta}{2} = 2\pi$, or $\theta = 4\pi$.

So, the function's period is $\underline{4\pi}$.

B Use the period to determine the five key input values for g. Those five values divide the interval $0 \le \theta \le 4\pi$ into four equal parts. So, the first input value is 0, and the second is $\frac{4\pi}{4} = \pi$. These values are entered in the first column of the table at the right. Complete the rest of the first column.

C Determine the output values for the key input values. Remember that g multiplies each output value from the parent function by -3. For instance, when $\theta = 0$, the parent function's output value is 1, but the output value for g is $-3 \cdot 1 = -3$. Complete the second column of the table.

Key input-output pairs	
θ	$g(\theta)$
0	-3
π	0
2π	3
3π	0
4π	-3

D Plot the key points on the coordinate plane shown. Then use them to draw one cycle of the graph of $g(\theta) = -3 \cos \frac{\theta}{2}$. One cycle of the graph of the parent function is shown in gray for comparison.

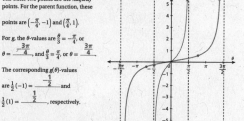

REFLECT

3a. Describe how the graph of f is transformed to obtain the graph of g.

Horizontal stretch by a factor of 2; vertical stretch by a factor of 3; reflection in the θ-axis

3b. Error Analysis A student said that the amplitude of the graph of g is -3. Describe and correct the student's error.

Amplitude is defined as the maximum *distance* that a wave-like curve rises above or falls below its midline, so the amplitude is 3, not -3.

CC.9-12.F.IF.7e

4 EXAMPLE Graphing $g(\theta) = a \tan b\theta$

Graph one cycle of $g(\theta) = \frac{1}{2} \tan \frac{\theta}{3}$.

A Determine the graph's asymptotes. The graph of the parent function, $f(\theta) = \tan \theta$, has asymptotes at $\theta = -\frac{\pi}{2}$ and $\theta = \frac{\pi}{2}$. The graph of g has asymptotes at $\frac{\theta}{3} = -\frac{\pi}{2}$, or $\theta = \underline{-\frac{3\pi}{2}}$, and $\frac{\theta}{3} = \frac{\pi}{2}$, or $\theta = \underline{\frac{3\pi}{2}}$.

B Determine the graph's three key points.

* One point is where the graph crosses its midline (the θ-axis). For the parent function, this occurs when $\theta = 0$. For g, this occurs when $\frac{\theta}{3} = 0$, or $\theta = \underline{0}$. So, the graph of g crosses its midline at the point $\underline{(0, 0)}$.

* The other two points are the *halfway* points. For the parent function, these points are $\left(-\frac{\pi}{4}, -1\right)$ and $\left(\frac{\pi}{4}, 1\right)$.

For g, the θ-values are $\frac{\theta}{3} = -\frac{\pi}{4}$, or $\theta = \underline{-\frac{3\pi}{4}}$, and $\frac{\theta}{3} = \frac{\pi}{4}$, or $\theta = \underline{\frac{3\pi}{4}}$.

The corresponding $g(\theta)$-values are $\frac{1}{2}(-1) = \underline{-\frac{1}{2}}$ and $\frac{1}{2}(1) = \underline{\frac{1}{2}}$, respectively.

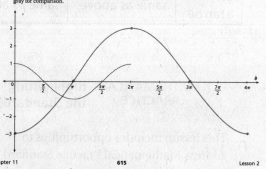

C Use the asymptotes and key points to draw one cycle of the graph of g. One cycle of the parent function's graph is shown in gray.

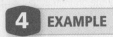 **EXAMPLE**

Questioning Strategies

- What effect do you think *a* would have on the graph of the parent tangent function if $a < 0$? **The graph would be reflected in the horizontal axis.**

- What effect do you think *b* would have on the graph of the parent tangent function if *b* were 3 instead of $\frac{1}{3}$? **The function would be shrunk horizontally by a factor of $\frac{1}{3}$.**

EXTRA EXAMPLE

Graph one cycle of $g(\theta) = -0.5 \tan 3\theta$.

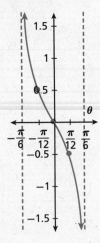

Technology

Students can use their graphing calculators to explore the effects of various values of *a* and *b* on the parent trigonometric functions. Students can graph a parent function and then graph a transformed function to see what effects *a* and *b* have on the parent function.

Teaching Strategy

Summarize the effects of *a* and *b* on the trigonometric functions using the table below. You can put a partially blank table on the board and have students work in pairs to complete it. Then reassemble as a class and ask the pairs to contribute their answers. Discuss the answers and correct any misconceptions. Be sure all students know the correct answers for their charts.

Function	Effects of Coefficient(s)	Specific Effects
$g(\theta) = a \sin b\theta$	*a*: vertically stretch, shrink, or reflect graph *b*: stretch or shrink horizontally	$\|a\| < 1$ vertical shrink $\|a\| > 1$ vertical stretch $a < 0$ reflection over θ-axis $b > 1$ horizontal shrink $0 < b < 1$ horizontal stretch
$g(\theta) = a \cos b\theta$	same as above	same as above
$g(\theta) = a \tan b\theta$	same as above	same as above

MATHEMATICAL PRACTICE   **Highlighting the Standards**

This lesson includes opportunities to address Mathematical Practice Standard 5 (Use appropriate tools strategically). Students should be able to quickly sketch the graphs of the parent functions for sine, cosine, and tangent by hand. They should understand the effects of *a* and *b* so they can predict how the graphs of specific equations will look prior to graphing them. If there are discrepancies between their predictions and their graphs, students should be able to resolve the discrepancies and locate any errors. One way to resolve discrepancies is to use a graphing calculator or another graphing technology to graph the transformed function and compare it with what the student has graphed.

REFLECT

4a. Describe how the graph of f is transformed to obtain the graph of g.
Horizontal stretch by a factor of 3; vertical shrink by a factor of $\frac{1}{2}$

---

5 ENGAGE   CC.9-12.F.BF.3   **Understanding Transformations of Trigonometric Graphs**

You have learned how the constants a and b in the functions $f(\theta) = a \sin b\theta$, $f(\theta) = a \cos b\theta$, and $f(\theta) = a \tan b\theta$ affect the period and amplitude of their graphs. Now you will examine how the constants h and k in $g(\theta) = f(\theta - h) + k$ alter the graph of $f(\theta)$.

Notice that the constant h appears *inside* the function and therefore acts on f's input values, while the constant k appears *outside* the function and therefore acts on f's output values. For instance, consider the function $g(\theta) = 3 \sin 2\left(\theta - \frac{\pi}{2}\right) + 1$, the result of introducing the constants $h = \frac{\pi}{2}$ and $k = 1$ in the function $f(\theta) = 3 \sin 2\theta$. The mapping diagram below shows what happens when $\frac{\pi}{2}, \frac{3\pi}{4}, \pi, \frac{5\pi}{4},$ and $\frac{3\pi}{2}$ are used as inputs for g.

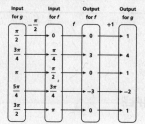

Notice that the input-output pairs for $f(\theta) = 3 \sin 2\theta$ (the middle two sets in the mapping diagram) are the five key points for one cycle of f's graph. Similarly, the input-output pairs for $g(\theta) = 3 \sin 2\left(\theta - \frac{\pi}{2}\right) + 1$ (the first and last sets in the mapping diagram) are the five key points for one cycle of g's graph. From the graphs at the right, you can see that g's graph is a translation of f's graph.

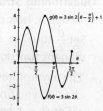

Chapter 11   617   Lesson 2

REFLECT

5a. In terms of the constants $h = \frac{\pi}{2}$ and $k = 1$, describe how the graph of f is translated to obtain the graph of g.
The graph of f is translated $\frac{\pi}{2}$ units to the right and 1 unit up.

5b. The constants h and k in $g(\theta) = f(\theta - h) + k$ change where a cycle begins and ends as well as what the maximum and minimum values are, but do the constants change the period and amplitude? Explain.
No; the length of the cycle (which is the period) and half the difference between the maximum and minimum values (which is the amplitude) do not change.

---

6 EXAMPLE   CC.9-12.F.IF.7e   Graphing $g(\theta) = a \cos b(\theta - h) + k$

Graph one cycle of $g(\theta) = 0.5 \cos 3\left(\theta - \frac{\pi}{3}\right) - 1.5$.

A Think about the related function $f(\theta) = 0.5 \cos 3\theta$.

* What is the period of f? $\frac{2\pi}{3}$

* Use the period to determine the five key input-output pairs for f. Complete the table.

Key input-output pairs for f	θ	0	$\frac{\pi}{6}$	$\frac{\pi}{3}$	$\frac{\pi}{2}$	$\frac{2\pi}{3}$
	$f(\theta)$	0.5	0	−0.5	0	0.5

B Think about the graph of $g(\theta) = 0.5 \cos 3\left(\theta - \frac{\pi}{3}\right) - 1.5$ in relation to the graph of f.

* How must the graph of f be translated horizontally and vertically to obtain the graph of g? (Note that $k < 0$ in this case.)
Translate $\frac{\pi}{3}$ units to the right and 1.5 units down.

* Complete the table to show the effect of the horizontal and vertical translations on the key input-output pairs for f. Remember that a horizontal translation affects only the input values and a vertical translation affects only the output values.

Key input-output pairs for g	θ	$\frac{\pi}{3}$	$\frac{\pi}{2}$	$\frac{2\pi}{3}$	$\frac{5\pi}{6}$	π
	$g(\theta)$	−1	−1.5	−2	−1.5	−1

Chapter 11   618   Lesson 2

Questioning Strategies

- What is the value of a in $g(\theta)$ and how does it affect the graph of the parent function? **3; vertical stretch**

- What is the value of b in $g(\theta)$ and how does it affect the graph of the parent function? **2; horizontal shrink**

- What is the value of h in $g(\theta)$ and how does it affect the graph of the parent function? **$\frac{\pi}{2}$; horizontal translation to the right**

- Look at the input column for g (the first column). How were these points chosen? **The period of f is π. So for g, $\theta - \frac{\pi}{2}$ must go from 0 to π to complete a full cycle. To make the initial input for f be 0, the initial input for g must be $\frac{\pi}{2}$ since this makes $\theta - \frac{\pi}{2}$ equal to 0.**

- What happens to the mid-line of this function? Why? **It moves up 1; because $k = 1$**

- What values of k would cause this function to have no real zeros? Why? **$k > 3$; $k < -3$; both values translate the function so that it does not cross the horizontal axis.**

Teaching Strategy

Students may wonder how to determine the key points when graphing a function of the form $g(\theta) = a\sin(\theta - h) + k$. Remind them that for sine (and cosine) the key points are the turning points and the zeros, as they were in the previous lesson. To show students a complete use of key points, you may wish to have students start with the key points for $f(\theta) = \sin\theta$ and use them to generate the key points for $f(\theta) = 3\sin2\theta$. These key points can then be used to generate the key points for $g(\theta) = 3\sin2(\theta - \frac{\pi}{2}) + 1$. You may wish to have students perform a similar process for the tangent function that involves key points and asymptotes.

6 **EXAMPLE**

Questioning Strategies

- In step A, how do you find the period of f? **Set 3θ equal to 2π. Then, solve for θ.**

- How do you find the key input values of θ for g? **You set $\theta - \frac{\pi}{3}$ equal to each of the key inputs for f and solve each equation for θ.**

EXTRA EXAMPLE

Graph one cycle of $g(\theta) = \frac{1}{4}\cos[2(\theta - \pi)] + 2$.

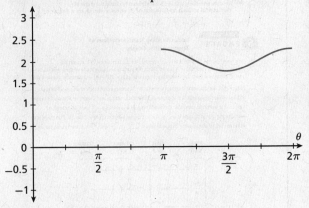

7 **EXAMPLE**

Questioning Strategies

- In step A, how do you find the period of f? **Set $\frac{\theta}{2}$ equal to π, which is the period for the tangent function. Then, solve for θ.**

- The asymptotes of the graph of f are at $-\pi$ and π. How do you find the asymptotes for the graph of g? **Set $\theta + \pi$ equal to each of these values and solve the equation for θ.**

EXTRA EXAMPLE

Graph one cycle of $g(\theta) = -2\tan\left[\frac{1}{2}(\theta - \frac{\pi}{2})\right] + 1$.

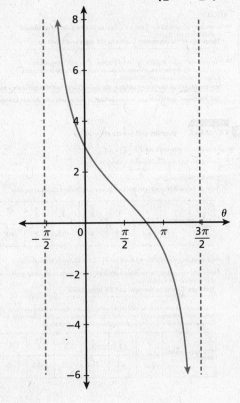

continued

C Plot the key points for the graph of *g* and use them to draw one cycle of the graph. One cycle of the graph of *f* is shown in gray for comparison.

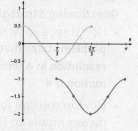

REFLECT

6a. If $g(\theta) = 0.5 \cos 3\left(\theta + \frac{\pi}{3}\right) - 1.5$ instead of $g(\theta) = 0.5 \cos 3\left(\theta - \frac{\pi}{3}\right) - 1.5$, what changes about how the graph of *f* is translated to obtain the graph of *g*?

The graph of *f* is translated to the left $\frac{\pi}{3}$ units rather than to the right $\frac{\pi}{3}$ units.

CC.9-12.F.IF.7e
7 EXAMPLE Graphing $g(\theta) = a \tan b(\theta - h) + k$

Graph one cycle of $g(\theta) = 2 \tan \frac{1}{2}(\theta + \pi) + 3$.

A Think about the related function $f(\theta) = 2 \tan \frac{\theta}{2}$.

- What is the period of *f*? ___2π___
- Use the period to determine the key features of the graph of *f*. Complete the table.

Key features of the graph of *f*	Equations of asymptotes	Coordinates of midline crossing	Coordinates of halfway points
	$\theta = -\pi, \theta = \pi$	(0,0)	$\left(-\frac{\pi}{2}, -2\right), \left(\frac{\pi}{2}, 2\right)$

B Think about the graph of $g(\theta) = 2 \tan \frac{1}{2}(\theta + \pi) + 3$ in relation to the graph of *f*.

- How must the graph of *f* be translated horizontally and vertically to obtain the graph of *g*? (Note that $h < 0$ in this case.)

Translate π units to the left and 3 units up.

- Complete the table to show the effect of the horizontal and vertical translations on the key features of the graph of *f*.

Key features of the graph of *f*	Equations of asymptotes	Coordinates of midline crossing	Coordinates of halfway points
	$\theta = -2\pi, \theta = 0$	$(-\pi, 3)$	$\left(-\frac{3\pi}{2}, 1\right), \left(-\frac{\pi}{2}, 5\right)$

© Houghton Mifflin Harcourt Publishing Company

C Use the key features for the graph of *g* to draw one cycle of the graph. One cycle of the graph of *f* is shown in gray for comparison.

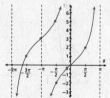

REFLECT

7a. Only one of the constants *h* and *k* affects the asymptotes for the graph of a tangent function. Which constant is it, and why?

h; because the asymptotes are vertical, they are affected by shifts left or right, but not shifts up or down.

7b. Only one of the constants *h* and *k* affects the midline for the graph of a trigonometric function. Which constant is it, and why?

k; because the midline is horizontal, it is affected by shifts up or down, but not shifts left or right.

CC.9-12.F.IF.7e
8 EXAMPLE Modeling the Motion of a Paddle Wheel

A side view of a riverboat's paddle wheel is shown. The paddle wheel has a diameter of 16 feet and rotates at a rate of 1 revolution every 4 seconds. Its lowest point is 2 feet below the water line.

The function $h(t) = 8 \sin \frac{\pi}{2}(t - 1) + 6$ models the motion of the paddle labeled *P*. The function gives the "height" (which is negative when the paddle is below the water line) at time *t* (in seconds). Graph the function on the interval $0 \le t \le 6$.

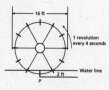

16 ft

1 revolution every 4 seconds

Water line

2 ft

P

A Complete the table for the related function $f(t) = 8 \sin \frac{\pi}{2}t$.

Key input-output pairs for *f*	*t*	0	1	2	3	4
	f(t)	0	8	0	−8	0

© Houghton Mifflin Harcourt Publishing Company

Questioning Strategies

- How do you know that t goes from 0 to 4? **The problem states that the wheel completes a revolution in 4 seconds. So the period of the motion is 4.**

- How do you find the key input values for h, given the key inputs for f? **Set $t - 1$ equal to each of the key inputs of f and solve for t.**

Extra Example

A different paddle wheel has a diameter of 20 feet, and 3 feet of it dips under the water. It rotates once every 8 seconds. The function that models the motion of the wheel is $h(t) = 10 \sin \frac{\pi}{4}(t - 1) + 7$. Graph the function on the interval $0 \le t \le 16$.

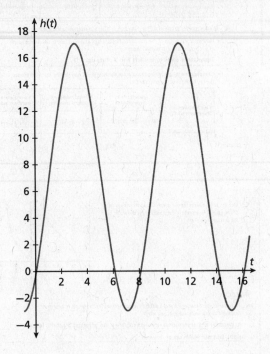

:::: MATHEMATICAL PRACTICE | **Highlighting the Standards**

This lesson, particularly **6** EXAMPLE , includes opportunities to address Mathematical Practice Standard 6 (Attend to precision). Students will need to be very precise about which function (f or g) they are describing. The inputs for f and g are likely to be different, so students will need to clearly state which function they are working with and how the two functions relate. (See the mapping diagram in **5** ENGAGE .) Insist on clear, concise communication when students are describing the key points and the period of the functions.

Differentiated Instruction

A suggested activity in the previous lesson was to create cutouts of the sine function. Students can use those cutouts to model horizontal and vertical translations. Have students carefully draw axes and label $\frac{\pi}{6}, \frac{\pi}{4}, \frac{\pi}{3}, \frac{\pi}{2}, \frac{2\pi}{3}, \frac{3\pi}{4}, \frac{5\pi}{6}$, and π to match their cutouts. They should label similar intervals from -2π to 2π on the x-axis and label from -5 to 5 on the y-axis. Give students equations with different values of h and k ($a = b = 1$) and have them move their cutouts to show the graph of the equation.

Suggested equations include $f(\theta) = \sin(\theta - \frac{\pi}{2})$, $f(\theta) = \sin(\theta - \pi)$, $f(\theta) = \sin(\theta - 2\pi)$, $f(\theta) = \sin(\theta + \frac{\pi}{2})$, and similar variations of the cosine function.

B Identify the translations to obtain the graph of *h* from the graph of *f*, then complete the table for *h*.

Amount and direction of horizontal translation: _1 unit to the right_

Amount and direction of vertical translation: _6 units up_

Key input-output pairs for h	*t*	1	2	3	4	5
	h(t)	6	14	6	−2	6

C Plot the key points for the graph of *h* and use them to draw one cycle of the graph. One cycle of the graph of *f* is shown in gray for comparison.

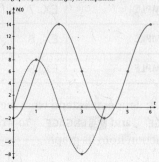

D Extend the graph one quarter of a cycle to the left and to the right in order to show the graph over the interval $0 \le t \le 6$.

REFLECT

8a. What is the significance of the graph's *t*-intercepts in the context of the situation?

They represent each time paddle *P* breaks the surface of the water.

8b. What is the significance of the maximum and minimum values of *h* in the context of the situation?

The maximum represents the height of paddle *P* when it reaches the top of the wheel, and the minimum represents the "height" of the paddle when it reaches the bottom of the wheel.

PRACTICE

For Exercises 1–3, complete each table with the key points or asymptotes for one cycle of the graph of each function, then graph the cycle. (One cycle of the graph of the parent function is shown in gray.)

1. $g(\theta) = -2 \sin 4\theta$

Key input-output pairs	
θ	$g(\theta)$
0	0
$\frac{\pi}{8}$	−2
$\frac{\pi}{4}$	0
$\frac{3\pi}{8}$	2
$\frac{\pi}{2}$	0

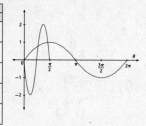

2. $g(\theta) = 0.75 \cos \frac{2\theta}{3}$

Key input-output pairs	
θ	$g(\theta)$
0	0.75
$\frac{3\pi}{4}$	0
$\frac{3\pi}{2}$	−0.75
$\frac{9\pi}{4}$	0
3π	0.75

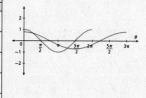

Essential Question

How do the constants a, b, h, and k in the functions $g(\theta) = a \sin b(\theta - h) + k$, $g(\theta) = a \cos b(\theta - h) + k$, *and* $g(\theta) = a \tan b(\theta - h) + k$ *affect their graphs?*
For sine and cosine, changing *a* changes the amplitude. For tangent, changing *a* stretches or shrinks the graph vertically.

For all three functions, changing *b* changes the period of the function.

For the graphs of $y = a \sin b(x - h) + k$, $y = a \cos b(x - h) + k$, and $y = a \tan b(x - h) + k$, changing the value of *h* translates the graph horizontally, and changing the value of *k* translates the graph vertically.

Summarize

Students should graph the parent functions of the three trigonometric functions. On the same axes, they should graph equations of the form $g(\theta) = a \sin b\theta$, $g(\theta) = a \cos b\theta$, or $g(\theta) = a \tan b\theta$ for each function. Students should ensure they use values for *a* and *b* to illustrate all the different effects on the graphs.

Students should then add to their summary. They should graph equations of the form $g(\theta) = a \sin b(\theta - h) + k$, $g(\theta) = a \cos b(\theta - h) + k$, and $g(\theta) = a \tan b(\theta - h) + k$, choosing values for *h* and *k* to show different vertical and horizontal translations. (*a* and *b* can be 1 since students have already shown the effects of these coefficients in their summaries.) The goal is to have the graphs of the parent function, a stretched, shrunk, and/or reflected function, and a translated function next to one another so the effects of the values *a, b, h,* and *k* are readily apparent.

Where skills are taught	Where skills are practiced
3 EXAMPLE	EXS. 1, 2
4 EXAMPLE	EX. 3
6 EXAMPLE	EX. 7
7 EXAMPLE	EX. 8
8 EXAMPLE	EX. 9

Exercise 4: Students extend what they learned in **1** ENGAGE and **2** ENGAGE to write the rule for a sine function from its graph.

Exercise 5: Students extend what they learned in **2** ENGAGE to express the period and amplitude of the graph of $g(\theta) = a \sin b\theta$ in terms of *a* and *b*.

Exercise 6: Students extend what they learned in **4** EXAMPLE to express the period of the graph of $g(\theta) = a \tan b\theta$ and to express the halfway points for one cycle of the graph in terms of *a* and *b*.

3. $g(\theta) = -\tan 2\theta$

Key features of graph	
Equation of left asymptote	$\theta = -\frac{\pi}{4}$
Equation of right asymptote	$\theta = \frac{\pi}{4}$
Coordinates of midline crossing	$(0, 0)$
Coordinates of left halfway point	$\left(-\frac{\pi}{8}, 1\right)$
Coordinates of right halfway point	$\left(\frac{\pi}{8}, -1\right)$

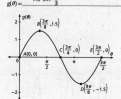

4. One cycle of the graph of a sine function is shown along with the five key points for the cycle. Use the points to determine a rule for the function.

$g(\theta) = \underline{\quad 1.5 \sin \frac{4\theta}{3} \quad}$

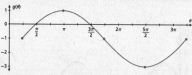

5. What are the period and amplitude of the graph of $g(\theta) = a \sin b\theta$ where $a \neq 0$ and $b > 0$? (Give your answers in terms of a and b.)

Period $= \frac{2\pi}{b}$; amplitude $= |a|$

6. What is the period of the graph of $g(\theta) = a \tan b\theta$ where $a \neq 0$ and $b > 0$? What are the coordinates of the halfway points on one cycle of the graph? (Give your answers in terms of a and b.)

Period $= \frac{\pi}{b}$; halfway points at $\left(-\frac{\pi}{4b}, -a\right)$ and $\left(\frac{\pi}{4b}, a\right)$

---

7. Graph one cycle of $g(\theta) = 2 \sin \frac{2}{3}\left(\theta - \frac{\pi}{4}\right) - 1$ by first completing the table of key input-output pairs for the related function $f(\theta) = 2 \sin \frac{2}{3}\theta$, then completing the table for g, and finally using the table for g to graph the cycle.

θ	0	$\frac{3\pi}{4}$	$\frac{3\pi}{2}$	$\frac{9\pi}{4}$	3π
$f(\theta)$	0	2	0	-2	0

θ	$\frac{\pi}{4}$	π	$\frac{7\pi}{4}$	$\frac{5\pi}{2}$	$\frac{13\pi}{4}$
$g(\theta)$	-1	1	-1	-3	-1

8. Graph one cycle of $g(\theta) = \frac{1}{2} \tan 2\left(\theta + \frac{\pi}{2}\right) + \frac{1}{2}$ by first completing the table of key features for the graph of the related function $f(\theta) = \frac{1}{2} \tan 2\theta$, then completing the table for g, and finally using the table for g to graph the cycle.

	Graph of f	Graph of g
Asymptotes	$\theta = -\frac{\pi}{4}$, $\theta = \frac{\pi}{4}$	$\theta = -\frac{3\pi}{4}$, $\theta = -\frac{\pi}{4}$
Midline crossing	$(0, 0)$	$\left(-\frac{\pi}{2}, \frac{1}{2}\right)$
Halfway points	$\left(-\frac{\pi}{8}, -\frac{1}{2}\right)$, $\left(\frac{\pi}{8}, \frac{1}{2}\right)$	$\left(-\frac{5\pi}{8}, 0\right)$, $\left(-\frac{3\pi}{8}, 1\right)$

9. Suppose a working scale model of a riverboat has a paddle wheel that is 8 inches in diameter, rotates at a rate of 1 revolution every 2 seconds, and dips 0.5 inch below the water line. The function $h(t) = 4 \sin \pi(t - 0.5) + 3.5$ gives the "height" (in inches) of one paddle at time t (in seconds). Graph the function on the interval $0 \leq t \leq 4$.

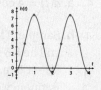

Assign these pages to help your students practice and apply important lesson concepts. For additional exercises, see the Student Edition.

Answers

Additional Practice

1. Amplitude: 5; period: 2

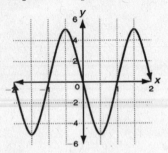

2. Amplitude: 3; period: 1

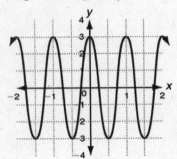

3. x-intercepts: $\frac{3\pi}{4}$, $\frac{7\pi}{4}$; phase shift: $\frac{\pi}{4}$ radians to the left

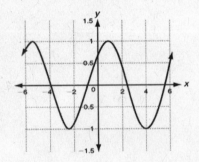

4. x-intercepts: $\frac{3\pi}{4}$, $\frac{7\pi}{4}$; phase shift: $\frac{\pi}{4}$ radians to the right

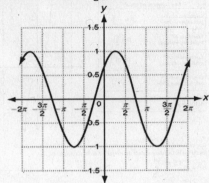

5. **a.**

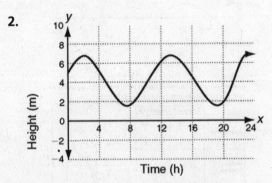

b. 500 Hz

Problem Solving

1. **a.** 2.5   **b.** 12   **c.** 2 units right

d. 4 units up   **e.** 6.5 m at 2:00 A.M.

f. 1.5 m at 8:00 A.M.

2.

3. 2

4. **a.** $d(t) = 4 \cos\left(\frac{\pi}{6}\right)(t - 2) + 2.5$

b. Sample: The max depth of the water would still be 6.5 m, but the min depth would be −1.5 m. The bay would dry out. The frequency of high tide and low tide would not change.

5. 2 h and 14 h   **6.** A   **7.** H

Additional Practice

Using $f(x) = \sin x$ or $g(x) = \cos x$ as a guide, graph each function. Identify the amplitude and period.

1. $b(x) = -5\sin \pi x$

2. $k(x) = 3\cos 2\pi x$

_____

_____

Using $f(x) = \sin x$ or $g(x) = \cos x$ as a guide, graph each function. Identify the x-intercepts and phase shift.

3. $h(x) = \sin\left(x + \dfrac{\pi}{4}\right)$

4. $h(x) = \cos\left(x - \dfrac{\pi}{4}\right)$

_____

_____

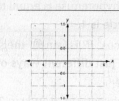
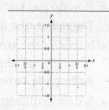

Solve.

5. a. Use a sine function to graph a sound wave with a period of 0.002 second and an amplitude of 2 centimeters.

   b. Find the frequency in hertz for this sound wave.

_____ s

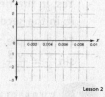

Problem Solving

As a result of the tide, the depth of the water in the bay varies with time. According to the harbormaster, the depth can be modeled by the function $d(t) = 2.5\cos\left(\dfrac{\pi}{6}\right)(t - 2) + 4$, where t is the number of hours since midnight, and d is the depth in meters.

1. Identify the following features of the graph of the function.
   a. Amplitude _____
   b. Period _____
   c. Phase shift _____
   d. Vertical shift _____
   e. What is the maximum depth and when does that occur?

   _____
   f. What is the minimum depth and when does that occur?

   _____

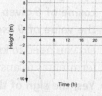

2. Graph the function for 24 hours.
3. How many high tides occur in 24 hours?
4. Jim thinks that the amplitude and the vertical shift should be reversed.
   a. Write the equation for this new function. _____
   b. Explain how water depth and frequency of tides would change using Jim's function.

_____

_____

5. Petra thinks that the original function is correct, except for the period, which should be 24. If so, how many hours after midnight would the first high and low tides occur?

_____

Jim looks at equations for the depth of water in different locations. Choose the letter for the best answer.

6. Which function represents a location that will dry out?

   A $d(t) = 5\cos\dfrac{\pi}{12}(t - 1) + 4$

   B $d(t) = 4\cos\dfrac{\pi}{8}(t - 2) + 4.5$

   C $d(t) = 3\cos\dfrac{\pi}{6}(t - 3) + 5$

   D $d(t) = 2\cos\dfrac{\pi}{4}(t - 4) + 5.5$

7. How deep is the water at 1:00 A.M. in a location where the water depth t hours after midnight is modeled by

   $d(t) = 1.25\cos\dfrac{\pi}{12}(t - 1) + 6$?

   F 4.75 m
   G 5.75 m
   H 7.25 m
   J 8.25 m

Notes

Fundamental Trigonometric Identities
Going Deeper

Essential question: *How can you use a given value of one of the trigonometric functions to calculate the values of the other functions?*

COMMON CORE Standards for Mathematical Content

CC.9-12.F.TF.8 Prove the Pythagorean Identity $\sin^2 \theta + \cos^2 \theta = 1$ and use it to calculate trigonometric ratios.

Also: CC.9-12.A.REI.4, CC.9-12.A.REI.4b

Prerequisites

Pythagorean Theorem

The sine, cosine, and tangent functions

Math Background

Students should be familiar with the Pythagorean Theorem from their work in Geometry. Since the sine and cosine functions are defined by using a right triangle with its hypotenuse connecting the origin to the unit circle, the Pythagorean Theorem can be used to generate an identity involving these functions. This identity, $\sin^2 \theta + \cos^2 \theta = 1$, is one of the Pythagorean identities, and it, along with other trigonometric identities, can be used to find the value of one trigonometric function given the value of another.

INTRODUCE

Students are familiar with laws and identities involving exponents and logarithms. Let students know that trigonometric functions have their own set of identities. The first they will study is based on the Pythagorean Theorem. An important fact to remember about identities is that they are relationships that are true for all values of x (or θ).

TEACH

1 EXPLORE

Questioning Strategies

- How do you know the hypotenuse is equal to 1? **The radius of a unit circle is 1.**
- Is $(\cos \theta)^2$ the same as $\cos^2 \theta$? Is $(\sin \theta)^2$ the same as $\sin^2 \theta$? **Yes, they are just different ways of writing the same thing.**
- Is there a difference between $\sin^2 \theta$ and $\sin 2\theta$? **Yes, in the first you take the sine of θ and square it; in the second you are taking the sine of 2θ. For example, $\sin^2 \frac{\pi}{6} = \left(\frac{1}{2}\right)^2 = \frac{1}{4}$ but $\sin 2\left(\frac{\pi}{6}\right) = \sin \frac{\pi}{3} = \frac{\sqrt{3}}{2}$.**

2 EXAMPLE

Questioning Strategies

- Is $1 - \sin^2 \theta$ ever negative? Why or why not? **No; $-1 \le \sin \theta \le 1$, so $0 \le \sin^2 \theta \le 1$ and $1 - \sin^2 \theta$ can never be less than 0.**
- Do you need to know the precise value of θ to answer part A? Why or why not? **No; the Pythagorean identity allows you to find the cosine of θ given the sine of θ without knowing the value of θ itself.**
- Do you need to know the quadrant where θ terminates to answer part B? Why or why not? **Yes; the sign of the answer varies depending on the quadrant where θ terminates.**

EXTRA EXAMPLE

Find the approximate value of each trigonometric function.

A. Given $\sin \theta = -0.544$, where $\frac{3\pi}{2} < \theta < 2\pi$, find $\cos \theta$. **0.839**

B. Given $\cos \theta = -0.123$, where $\frac{\pi}{2} < \theta < \pi$, find $\sin \theta$. **0.992**

continued

Name_____ Class_____ Date_____

Fundamental Trigonometric Identities
Going Deeper

Essential question: *How can you use a given value of one of the trigonometric functions to calculate the values of the other functions?*

You may have noticed that because $\sin \theta = y$, $\cos \theta = x$, and $\tan \theta = \frac{y}{x}$ you can write the identity $\tan \theta = \frac{\sin \theta}{\cos \theta}$. In the following Explore, you will derive another identity based on the Pythagorean Theorem, which is why the identity is known as a *Pythagorean* identity.

Video Tutor

1 EXPLORE   CC.9-12.F.TF.8   Deriving a Pythagorean Identity

The terminal side of an angle θ intersects the unit circle at the point (a, b), as shown.

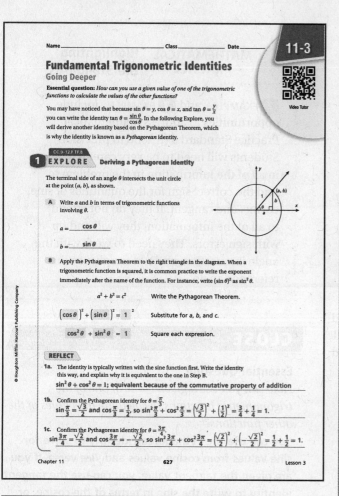

A Write a and b in terms of trigonometric functions involving θ.

$a = \underline{\quad \cos \theta \quad}$

$b = \underline{\quad \sin \theta \quad}$

B Apply the Pythagorean Theorem to the right triangle in the diagram. When a trigonometric function is squared, it is common practice to write the exponent immediately after the name of the function. For instance, write $(\sin \theta)^2$ as $\sin^2 \theta$.

$a^2 + b^2 = c^2$ Write the Pythagorean Theorem.

$\left(\cos \theta \right)^2 + \left(\sin \theta \right)^2 = 1^2$ Substitute for a, b, and c.

$\cos^2 \theta + \sin^2 \theta = 1$ Square each expression.

REFLECT

1a. The identity is typically written with the sine function first. Write the identity this way, and explain why it is equivalent to the one in Step B.

$\sin^2 \theta + \cos^2 \theta = 1$; equivalent because of the commutative property of addition

1b. Confirm the Pythagorean identity for $\theta = \frac{\pi}{3}$.

$\sin \frac{\pi}{3} = \frac{\sqrt{3}}{2}$ and $\cos \frac{\pi}{3} = \frac{1}{2}$, so $\sin^2 \frac{\pi}{3} + \cos^2 \frac{\pi}{3} = \left(\frac{\sqrt{3}}{2} \right)^2 + \left(\frac{1}{2} \right)^2 = \frac{3}{4} + \frac{1}{4} = 1$.

1c. Confirm the Pythagorean identity for $\theta = \frac{3\pi}{4}$.

$\sin \frac{3\pi}{4} = \frac{\sqrt{2}}{2}$ and $\cos \frac{3\pi}{4} = -\frac{\sqrt{2}}{2}$, so $\sin^2 \frac{3\pi}{4} + \cos^2 \frac{3\pi}{4} = \left(\frac{\sqrt{2}}{2} \right)^2 + \left(-\frac{\sqrt{2}}{2} \right)^2 = \frac{1}{2} + \frac{1}{2} = 1$.

Rewriting the Identity You can rewrite the identity $\sin^2 \theta + \cos^2 \theta = 1$ to express one trigonometric function in terms of the other. As shown below, each alternate version of the identity involves positive and negative square roots. You determine which sign to use based on knowing the quadrant in which the terminal side of θ lies.

Solve for $\sin \theta$:

$\sin^2 \theta + \cos^2 \theta = 1$

$\sin^2 \theta = 1 - \cos^2 \theta$

$\sin \theta = \pm \sqrt{1 - \cos^2 \theta}$

Solve for $\cos \theta$:

$\sin^2 \theta + \cos^2 \theta = 1$

$\cos^2 \theta = 1 - \sin^2 \theta$

$\cos \theta = \pm \sqrt{1 - \sin^2 \theta}$

2 EXAMPLE   CC.9-12.F.TF.8   Using the Pythagorean Identity

Find the approximate value of each trigonometric function.

A Given that $\sin \theta = 0.766$ where $0 < \theta < \frac{\pi}{2}$, find $\cos \theta$.

$\cos \theta = \pm \sqrt{1 - \sin^2 \theta}$ Use the identity solved for $\cos \theta$.

$= \pm \sqrt{1 - \left(0.766 \right)^2}$ Substitute for $\sin \theta$.

$\approx \pm 0.643$ Evaluate using a calculator. Round to the nearest thousandth.

The terminal side of θ lies in Quadrant $\underline{\quad I \quad}$, where $\cos \theta \underline{\; > \;} 0$.

So, $\cos \theta \approx \underline{\quad 0.643 \quad}$.

B Given that $\cos \theta = -0.906$ where $\pi < \theta < \frac{3\pi}{2}$, find $\sin \theta$.

$\sin \theta = \pm \sqrt{1 - \cos^2 \theta}$ Use the identity solved for $\sin \theta$.

$= \pm \sqrt{1 - \left(-0.906 \right)^2}$ Substitute for $\cos \theta$.

$\approx \pm 0.423$ Evaluate using a calculator. Round to the nearest thousandth.

The terminal side of θ lies in Quadrant $\underline{\quad III \quad}$, where $\sin \theta \underline{\; < \;} 0$.

So, $\sin \theta \approx \underline{\quad -0.423 \quad}$.

REFLECT

2a. In part A, suppose $\frac{\pi}{2} < \theta < \pi$ instead of $0 < \theta < \frac{\pi}{2}$. How does this affect the value of $\cos \theta$?

If $\frac{\pi}{2} < \theta < \pi$, then the terminal side of θ lies in Quadrant II. Cosine is negative in Quadrant II, so the value of $\cos \theta$ would be negative.

© Houghton Mifflin Harcourt Publishing Company

Teaching Strategy

Encourage students to make a sketch prior to attempting to solve the problems in 2 EXAMPLE . The given information should make it clear which quadrant the terminal side of the angle lies in. If students know the values of sine and cosine for $0, \frac{\pi}{2}, \pi$, and $\frac{3\pi}{2}$, they can estimate where the terminal side should be. For example, in part B, the angle is in the third quadrant. Since the cosine is very close to -1, the terminal side makes a very small angle with the negative x-axis. In part A, the sine is 0.766, so students will know only that the terminal side is in Quadrant I, but not necessarily its position relative to the other axes. Even if students can only surmise the correct quadrant, a diagram will still be helpful. Once they've sketched the angle, students can write down the signs for all three trigonometric functions in that quadrant and refer to their sketches throughout the problem.

3 EXAMPLE

Questioning Strategies

- Is there another way to begin this problem besides writing $\sin\theta$ in terms of $\cos\theta$? Yes, you can write $\cos\theta$ in terms of $\sin\theta$.

- Write the Pythagorean identity with $\cos\theta$ written in terms of $\sin\theta$. $\sin^2\theta + \left(\dfrac{\sin\theta}{\tan\theta}\right)^2 = 1$

- If you do not remember the two identities from this lesson, how can you derive them?
  Recall that a point in Quadrant I on the unit circle has coordinates $P(\cos\theta, \sin\theta)$. Draw a right triangle with hypotenuse $\overline{OP}$, where O is the origin. The side lengths of this triangle are $\cos\theta$, $\sin\theta$, and 1. Use the Pythagorean Theorem to arrive at the identity $\sin^2\theta + \cos^2\theta = 1$. Use the definition of the tangent ratio to arrive at the identity $\tan\theta = \dfrac{\sin\theta}{\cos\theta}$.

EXTRA EXAMPLE

Given that $\tan\theta = 1.648$ where $0 < \theta < \dfrac{\pi}{2}$, find the approximate values of $\sin\theta$ and $\cos\theta$.
$\sin\theta = 0.855$; $\cos\theta = 0.519$

---

2 EXAMPLE and 3 EXAMPLE include opportunities to address Mathematical Practice Standard 6 (Attend to precision). Students will need to be very careful to take in all of the information in the problem to find the correct sign for the quantities of sine, cosine, and tangent. If they do not attend to all of the information, they will end up with sign errors. They need to work with the angle in question, and not simply use the reference angle.

CLOSE

Essential Question

How can you use a given value of one of the trigonometric functions to calculate the values of the other functions?

You can use the Pythagorean identity to solve for sine values from cosine values and vice versa. If you are given the tangent value, you can use the tangent identity to write the sine in terms of the cosine, or vice versa, and then substitute into the Pythagorean identity to find the cosine and sine.

Summarize

Have students write a journal entry summarizing the two trigonometric identities presented in this lesson. They should make a heading for each of the identities $\left(\sin^2\theta + \cos^2\theta = 1 \text{ and } \tan\theta = \dfrac{\sin\theta}{\cos\theta}\right)$; then, list any rewritten forms below the primary identities.

PRACTICE

Where skills are taught	Where skills are practiced
2 EXAMPLE	EXS. 1–8
3 EXAMPLE	EXS. 9–12

2b. In part B, suppose $\frac{3\pi}{2} < \theta < 2\pi$ rather than $\pi < \theta < \frac{3\pi}{2}$. How does this affect the value of $\sin\theta$?

If $\frac{3\pi}{2} < \theta < 2\pi$, then the terminal side of θ lies in Quadrant IV. Sine is negative in Quadrant IV, so the value of $\sin\theta$ would not change.

2c. In part A, explain how to find the approximate value of $\tan\theta$. Then find it.

Use the identity $\tan\theta = \frac{\sin\theta}{\cos\theta}$, $\tan\theta = \frac{0.766}{0.643} \approx 1.191$

Other Identities If you multiply both sides of the identity $\tan\theta = \frac{\sin\theta}{\cos\theta}$ by $\cos\theta$, you get the identity $\sin\theta = \tan\theta\cos\theta$. And if you divide both sides of $\sin\theta = \tan\theta\cos\theta$ by $\tan\theta$, you get the identity $\cos\theta = \frac{\sin\theta}{\tan\theta}$.

3 EXAMPLE Using an Identity That Involves Tangent

Given that $\tan\theta \approx -2.327$ where $\frac{\pi}{2} < \theta < \pi$, find the approximate values of $\sin\theta$ and $\cos\theta$.

A Write $\sin\theta$ in terms of $\cos\theta$.

$\sin\theta = \tan\theta\cos\theta$ Use the identity $\sin\theta = \tan\theta\cos\theta$.

$\approx\ -2.327\ \cos\theta$ Substitute the value of $\tan\theta$.

B Use the Pythagorean identity to find $\cos\theta$. Then find $\sin\theta$.

$\sin^2\theta + \cos^2\theta = 1$ Use the Pythagorean identity.

$\left(-2.327\ \cos\theta\right)^2 + \cos^2\theta \approx 1$ Substitute for $\sin\theta$.

$5.415\ \cos^2\theta + \cos^2\theta \approx 1$ Square.

$6.415\ \cos^2\theta \approx 1$ Combine like terms.

$\cos^2\theta \approx\ 0.156$ Solve for $\cos^2\theta$.

$\cos\theta \approx \pm\ 0.395$ Solve for $\cos\theta$.

The terminal side of θ lies in Quadrant ___II___, where $\cos\theta\ \underline{<}\ 0$.

So, $\cos\theta \approx\ \underline{-0.395}$, and $\sin\theta \approx -2.327\cos\theta \approx\ \underline{0.919}$.

© Houghton Mifflin Harcourt Publishing Company

REFLECT

3a. When you multiplied the given value of $\tan\theta$ with the calculated value of $\cos\theta$ in order to find the value of $\sin\theta$, was the product positive or negative? Explain why this is the result you'd expect.

Positive; $\sin\theta$ should be positive in Quadrant II.

3b. If $\tan\theta = 1$ where $0 < \theta < \frac{\pi}{2}$, show that you can solve for $\sin\theta$ and $\cos\theta$ exactly using the Pythagorean identity. Why is this so?

If $\tan\theta = 1$, then $\sin\theta = \cos\theta$, so $\sin^2\theta + \cos^2\theta = 1$ becomes $2\sin^2\theta = 1$, which gives $\sin\theta = \cos\theta = \frac{\sqrt{2}}{2}$; in this case, θ is a special angle: $\frac{\pi}{4}$.

PRACTICE

Find $\sin\theta$ and $\tan\theta$ for each given value of $\cos\theta$.

1. $\cos\theta = 0.596, 0 < \theta < \frac{\pi}{2}$

$\sin\theta \approx\ \underline{0.803}$, $\tan\theta \approx\ \underline{1.347}$

2. $\cos\theta = 0.985, \frac{3\pi}{2} < \theta < 2\pi$

$\sin\theta \approx\ \underline{-0.173}$, $\tan\theta \approx\ \underline{-0.176}$

3. $\cos\theta = -0.342, \frac{\pi}{2} < \theta < \pi$

$\sin\theta \approx\ \underline{0.940}$, $\tan\theta \approx\ \underline{-2.749}$

4. $\cos\theta = -0.819, \pi < \theta < \frac{3\pi}{2}$

$\sin\theta \approx\ \underline{-0.574}$, $\tan\theta \approx\ \underline{0.701}$

Find $\cos\theta$ and $\tan\theta$ for each given value of $\sin\theta$.

5. $\sin\theta = 0.186, 0 < \theta < \frac{\pi}{2}$

$\cos\theta \approx\ \underline{0.983}$, $\tan\theta \approx\ \underline{0.189}$

6. $\sin\theta = 0.756, \frac{\pi}{2} < \theta < \pi$

$\cos\theta \approx\ \underline{-0.655}$, $\tan\theta \approx\ \underline{-1.154}$

7. $\sin\theta = -0.644, \frac{3\pi}{2} < \theta < 2\pi$

$\cos\theta \approx\ \underline{0.765}$, $\tan\theta \approx\ \underline{-0.842}$

8. $\sin\theta = -0.328, \pi < \theta < \frac{3\pi}{2}$

$\cos\theta \approx\ \underline{-0.945}$, $\tan\theta \approx\ \underline{0.347}$

Find $\sin\theta$ and $\cos\theta$ for each given value of $\tan\theta$.

9. $\tan\theta = 0.301, 0 < \theta < \frac{\pi}{2}$

$\sin\theta \approx\ \underline{0.288}$, $\cos\theta \approx\ \underline{0.958}$

10. $\tan\theta = 2.416, \pi < \theta < \frac{3\pi}{2}$

$\sin\theta \approx\ \underline{-0.923}$, $\cos\theta \approx\ \underline{-0.382}$

11. $\tan\theta = -0.739, \frac{\pi}{2} < \theta < \pi$

$\sin\theta \approx\ \underline{0.594}$, $\cos\theta \approx\ \underline{-0.804}$

12. $\tan\theta = -3.305, \frac{3\pi}{2} < \theta < 2\pi$

$\sin\theta \approx\ \underline{-0.958}$, $\cos\theta \approx\ \underline{0.290}$

© Houghton Mifflin Harcourt Publishing Company

Assign these pages to help your students practice and apply important lesson concepts. For additional exercises, see the Student Edition.

Answers

Additional Practice

1. $\cos^4\theta - \sin^4\theta + \sin^2\theta = (\cos^2\theta + \sin^2\theta)$
$(\cos^2\theta - \sin^2\theta) + \sin^2\theta$ $(1)(\cos^2\theta - \sin^2\theta)$
$+ \sin^2\theta = \cos^2\theta$

2. $\dfrac{\cos^2\theta}{\sin^2\theta} - \cos^2\theta = \dfrac{\cos^2\theta}{\sin^2\theta} - \dfrac{\sin^2\theta\cos^2\theta}{\sin^2\theta} =$

$\dfrac{\cos^2\theta - \sin^2\theta\cos^2\theta}{\sin^2\theta} = \dfrac{\cos^2\theta(1 - \sin^2\theta)}{\sin^2\theta} =$

$\left(\dfrac{\cos^2\theta}{\sin^2\theta}\right)(1 - \sin^2\theta) = \left(\dfrac{\cos^2\theta}{\sin^2\theta}\right)(\cos^2\theta)$

3. $\tan^2\theta - \tan^2\theta\sin^2\theta = \sin^2\theta$

$\tan^2\theta(1 - \sin^2\theta) = \sin^2\theta$

$\tan^2\theta(\cos^2\theta) = \sin^2\theta$

$\dfrac{\sin^2\theta}{\cos^2\theta}(\cos^2\theta) = \sin^2\theta$

$\sin^2\theta = \sin^2\theta$

4. $\dfrac{1 + \dfrac{\cos\theta}{\sin\theta}}{\dfrac{\cos\theta}{\sin\theta}(\sin\theta + \cos\theta)} =$

$\dfrac{\dfrac{\sin\theta + \cos\theta}{\sin\theta}}{\dfrac{\cos\theta(\sin\theta + \cos\theta)}{\sin\theta}} =$

$\dfrac{\sin\theta + \cos\theta}{\cos\theta(\sin\theta + \cos\theta)} = \dfrac{1}{\cos\theta}$

5. $\cos\theta \approx 0.416$
$\sin\theta \approx -0.909$

6. $\cos\theta \approx -0.989$
$\sin\theta \approx 0.142$

7. $9.6°$

Problem Solving

1. a. $mg\sin\theta = \mu mg\cos\theta$

b. $\dfrac{\sin\theta}{\cos\theta} = 1.5$

c. $\tan\theta = 1.5$

d. $56.3°$

2. a. $mg\sin\theta = (1.3)mg\cos\theta$

b. $52.4°$

c. Possible answer: With the new shoes he should be able to push off at a greater angle (by about 4°) to the vertical.

3. D   4. G

Additional Practice

Prove each trigonometric identity.

1. $\cos^4\theta - \sin^4\theta + \sin^2\theta = \cos^2\theta$

2. $\left(\dfrac{\cos^2\theta}{\sin^2\theta}\right)\cos^2\theta = \left(\dfrac{\cos^2\theta}{\sin^2\theta}\right) - \cos^2\theta$

_____   _____

3. $\tan^2\theta - \tan^2\theta\sin^2\theta = \sin^2\theta$

4. $\dfrac{1+\dfrac{\cos\theta}{\sin\theta}}{\dfrac{\cos\theta}{\sin\theta}(\sin\theta+\cos\theta)} = \dfrac{1}{\cos\theta}$

_____   _____

Find $\sin\theta$ and $\cos\theta$ for each given value of $\tan\theta$.

5. $\tan\theta \approx -2.185,\ \dfrac{3\pi}{4} < \theta < 2\pi$

6. $\tan\theta \approx -0.143,\ \dfrac{\pi}{2} < \theta < \pi$

_____   _____

Solve.

7. Use the equation $mg\sin\theta = \mu mg\cos\theta$ to determine the angle at which a waxed wood block on an inclined plane of wet snow begins to slide. Assume $\mu = 0.17$.

_____

Problem Solving

The advertisement for a new shoe promises runners less slip. The coefficient of friction (μ) between concrete and a new material used in the sole of this shoe is 1.5. The force of friction that causes slip is equal to $mg\sin\theta$, where m is a runner's mass and g is the acceleration due to gravity. The force that prevents slip is $\mu mg\cos\theta$.

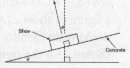

Shoe

Concrete

1. Mukisa wants to know what this new shoe will do for his performance.

   a. At the instant of slip, the force that causes slip is equal to the force that prevents it. Write an equation to show this relationship.   _____

   b. Rewrite the equation with trigonometric expressions on one side of the equation, and substitute the coefficient of friction for the new material.   _____

   c. Use a trigonometric identity to rewrite the equation using only the tangent function.   _____

   d. Solve for θ, the angle at which the new shoe will start to slip.   _____

2. Mukisa wonders how his old shoes compare to these new shoes. The label on the box of his old shoes states that the coefficient of friction is 1.3.

   a. Write an equation to find the angle at which a shoe with a coefficient of friction of 1.3 will slip.   _____

   b. At what angle will this shoe start to slip?   _____

   c. Suggest how the new shoes might improve Mukisa's performance.
   _____

An advertisement states, "Use this wax and your skis will slide better than silk on silk!" The coefficient of friction for silk on silk is 0.25. The coefficient of friction for waxed wood on wet snow is 0.14. The equation $mg\sin\theta = \mu mg\cos\theta$ can be used to find the angle at which a material begins to slide. Choose the letter for the best answer.

3. Which expression gives the angle at which silk begins to slide on silk?

   A $\cos^{-1}(0.25)$

   B $\sin\left(\dfrac{1}{0.25}\right)$

   C $\tan\left(\dfrac{1}{0.25}\right)$

   D $\tan^{-1}(0.25)$

4. At what angle would a waxed wooden ski begin to slide on wet snow?

   F 2°

   G 8°

   H 12°

   J 14°

Sum and Difference Identities
Going Deeper

Essential question: *How can you prove addition and subtraction identities for trigonometric functions?*

COMMON CORE Standards for Mathematical Content

CC.9-12.F.TF.9(+) Prove the addition and subtraction formulas for sine, cosine, and tangent and use them to solve problems.*

Prerequisites

Fundamental Trigonometric Identities

Math Background

A trigonometric identity is an equation, such as $\cos^2\theta + \sin^2\theta = 1$, that is true for all values of the variable. The simplest identities arise from analyses of the relationship among the side lengths in a right triangle and involve only one angle per identity. This lesson introduces the first of the multiple-angle identities, the sum and difference identities. Because the number of identities that can be derived is limitless (the great majority of the equations in this lesson can be regarded as identities), the aim is to develop those that are simple and useful. Explore 3 furnishes a good example of this, the derivation of an identity for $\tan(A + B)$. All of the equations in the derivation are identities, and the last one, achieved through a shrewd division of numerator and denominator by $\cos A \cos B$, yields an identity that is simple and useful.

INTRODUCE

Ask students to provide some real-world examples of situations in which a scientist or engineer might draw a 30° angle. For example, a geographical surveyor might take a sighting on a mountainside at a 30° angle of elevation. Review how to find sin 30°, cos 30°, and tan 30°. Then return to the real-world example and suggest that the surveyor increases the angle of elevation of the sighting by 45°. Review how to find sin 45°, cos 45°, and tan 45°. In this lesson, students will learn how to extend their knowledge of familiar angles (such as 30° and 45° angles) to less familiar angles (such as 75° angles).

TEACH

1 EXPLORE

Questioning Strategies

- The figure depicts $\angle(A - B)$ in a unit circle for the purpose of deriving an identity for $\cos(A - B)$. Describe how you would draw a figure to show $\angle(A + B)$ for the purpose of deriving an identity for $\cos(A + B)$. **Draw $\angle A$ as shown. Use the terminal side of $\angle A$ as the initial side of $\angle B$. Then $\angle(A + B)$ has initial side on the x-axis and terminal side joining the origin with the point $(\cos(A + B), \sin(A + B))$ on the unit circle.**

- In part E, $\angle(A - B)$ is rotated clockwise to align its initial side with the x-axis. Explain why the distance d in part E is equal to the distance d in part B. **Rotation preserves angle measures. Because the measure of $\angle(A - B)$ does not change, the distance between the endpoints of the angle on the unit circle does not change.**

11-4

Video Tutor

Sum and Difference Identities
Going Deeper

Essential question: *How can you prove addition and subtraction identities for trigonometric functions?*

The trigonometric identities you've worked with such as $\tan\theta = \frac{\sin\theta}{\cos\theta}$ and $\cos^2\theta + \sin^2\theta = 1$ have all involved a single angle. However, many science, engineering, and navigation problems involve two or more angles. Start by deriving an identity for $\cos(A - B)$, the cosine of the difference of two angles.

1 EXPLORE   Deriving Sum and Difference Identities for Cosine

CC 9 12.1 TF.9

A The figure depicts the difference of two angles A and B. Explain why the point of intersection of the terminal side of $\angle B$ and the unit circle has coordinates $(\cos B, \sin B)$. You may refer to the detail of the reference triangle shown below the graph.

In the reference triangle, $\cos B = \frac{x}{1}$, so x,

the x-coordinate of the point, is $\cos B$.

Similarly, $\sin B = \frac{y}{1}$, so y, the y-coordinate

of the point, is $\sin B$.

Note that similar reasoning explains the coordinates of the other point, $(\cos A, \sin A)$.

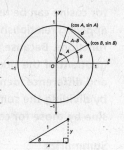

B Now look at the line segment joining the two points $(\cos A, \sin A)$ and $(\cos B, \sin B)$. The key to deriving the identity is to find two ways to express d, the distance between the points on the two sides of $\angle(A - B)$. Start by using the distance formula.

$$d = \sqrt{\left(\cos A - \cos B\right)^2 + \left(\sin A - \sin B\right)^2}$$

C To find an expression for d^2, square both sides and expand the resulting expression.

$$d^2 = \left(\cos A - \cos B\right)^2 + \left(\sin A - \sin B\right)^2$$

$$d^2 = \cos^2 A - 2\left(\cos A\right)\left(\cos B\right) + \cos^2 B + \sin^2 A - 2\left(\sin A\right)\left(\sin B\right) + \left(\sin^2 B\right)$$

D Recall the identity $\sin^2\theta + \cos^2\theta = 1$. Use this identity to substitute for $\cos^2 A + \sin^2 A$ and $\cos^2 B + \sin^2 B$.

$$d^2 = \boxed{2} - 2\cos A \cos B - 2\sin A \sin B$$

© Houghton Mifflin Harcourt Publishing Company

E Find a second expression for d^2. The figure shows $\angle(A - B)$ rotated clockwise to align one side with the x-axis. Once again, use the distance formula to find d, which is now the distance between the points $(\cos(A - B), \sin(A - B))$ and $(1, 0)$.

$$d = \sqrt{\left(\cos(A - B) - 1\right)^2 + \left(\sin(A - B) - 0\right)^2}$$

F Again, find an expression for d^2 by squaring both sides and expanding the resulting expression.

$$d^2 = \left(\cos(A - B) - 1\right)^2 + \left(\sin(A - B) - 0\right)^2$$

$$d^2 = \cos^2(A - B) - 2\cos(A - B) + 1 + \sin^2(A - B)$$

G As before, use the identity $\sin^2\theta + \cos^2\theta = 1$ to simplify the expression.

$$d^2 = \boxed{2} - 2\cos(A - B)$$

H To find an identity for $\cos(A - B)$, equate the two expressions for d^2 from part D and part G and simplify.

$$2 - 2\cos(A - B) = 2 - 2\cos A \cos B - 2\sin A \sin B \qquad \text{Equate the expressions.}$$

$$-1 + \cos(A - B) = -1 + \cos A \cos B + \sin A \sin B \qquad \text{Divide both sides by } -2.$$

$$\cos(A - B) = \cos A \cos B + \sin A \sin B \qquad \text{Add 1 to both sides.}$$

REFLECT

1a. Use $\cos(-B) = \cos B$ and $\sin(-B) = -\sin B$ and the identity for $\cos(A - B)$ to find an identity for $\cos(A + B)$.

$$\cos(A + B) = \cos[A - (-B)]$$

$$= \cos A \cos(-B) + \sin A \sin(-B)$$

$$= \cos A \cos B + \sin A (-\sin B)$$

$$= \cos A \cos B - \sin A \sin B$$

The sum and difference identities for cosine are:

$$\cos(A + B) = \cos A \cos B - \sin A \sin B$$
$$\cos(A - B) = \cos A \cos B + \sin A \sin B$$

You can use these results to find the sum and difference identities for the sine and tangent functions.

© Houghton Mifflin Harcourt Publishing Company

Questioning Strategies

- In part A, you show that $\cos(90° - \theta) = \sin\theta$. Use what you know about right triangles to explain these identities. **In a right triangle, if one acute angle measures θ, then the other acute angle measures $(90° - \theta)$. The side opposite the angle that measures θ is the side adjacent to the angle that measures $(90° - \theta)$, so the ratios for $\sin\theta$ and $\cos(90° - \theta)$ are equal.**

- In part C, how is the identity for $\cos(A + B)$ used to find an identity for $\sin(A - B)$? **You must recognize $\cos([90° - A] + B)$ as the cosine of the sum of two angles.**

Technology

Have students choose complementary angle pairs such as 16° and 74° and use their calculators to check that the cosine of one angle equals the sine of the other, and vice-versa.

3 EXPLORE

Questioning Strategies

- How are the identities for $\cos(A + B)$ and $\sin(A + B)$ used to derive an identity for $\tan(A + B)$? **$\tan(A + B)$ is the quotient of $\sin(A + B)$ divided by $\cos(A + B)$.**

- Why might you want to use the identities from part B rather than the identities you found in part A? **After simplifying, there are fewer trigonometric functions to evaluate.**

CLOSE

Essential Question

How can you prove addition and subtraction identities for trigonometric functions?
The difference identity for cosine can be developed by reasoning about $\angle(A - B)$ drawn in a unit circle. The addition identity for cosine follows from this directly. The sum and difference identities for cosine can be used to prove those for sine by applying relationships between the sine and cosine functions. Because the tangent function is the quotient of the sine and cosine functions, the sum and difference identities for tangent can be found by dividing the sum and difference identities for sine by those for cosine.

Summarize

Have students write journal entries in which they describe similarities and differences between the sum and difference identities for the cosine and sine functions. Have students describe methods they can use to memorize the identities. For example, in the sum and difference identities for cosine, the product pairs include the same trigonometric function while in the sum and difference identities for sine, the product pairs include different functions. These visual cues may help students commit the identities to memory.

> **MATHEMATICAL PRACTICE** **Highlighting the Standards**
>
> The derivation of the sum and difference identities provides opportunities to address Mathematical Practices Standard 3 (Construct viable arguments and critique the reasoning of others). The derivation of the difference identity for cosine in particular is quite challenging and requires careful thinking and precise reasoning to understand the nuances of the proof.

2 EXPLORE   Deriving Sum and Difference Identities for Sine

CC.9–12.F.TF.9

A Before you can derive the sum and difference identities for sine, you need to develop two intermediate identities. The first will give an expression for $\cos(90° - \theta)$.

$\cos(90° - \theta) = \cos 90° \cos \theta + \sin 90° \sin \theta$ Use the difference identity for cosine.

$= \boxed{0} \cos \theta + \boxed{1} \sin \theta$ Simplify.

$= \sin \theta$

B For the second intermediate identity, use the one you just derived to find an expression for $\sin(90° - \theta)$.

$\sin(90° - \theta) = \cos\left(90° - \boxed{90° - \theta}\right)$ Substitute $(90° - \theta)$ for θ in the identity from part A.

$= \cos\left(90° - \boxed{90°} + \boxed{\theta}\right)$ Simplify.

$= \cos \theta$

C Now use the two intermediate identities and the difference identity for cosine to find the difference identity for sine.

$\sin(A - B) = \cos\left(90° - \boxed{A - B}\right)$ Substitute $(A - B)$ for θ in the identity from part A.

$= \cos\left([90° - A] + \boxed{B}\right)$ Distributive and Associative properties

$= \cos(90° - A)\cos B - \sin\left(90° - A\right)\sin B$ Sum identity for cosine

$= \sin A \cos B - \cos A \sin B$ Identity from part A

D To find the sum identity for sine, use the difference identity for sine, and write $(A + B)$ as $[A - (-B)]$.

$\sin(A + B) = \sin[A - (-B)].$

$\sin[A - (-B)] = \sin A \cos(-B) + \cos A \sin(-B)$ Difference identity for sine

$= \sin A \boxed{\cos B} + \cos A \boxed{\sin B}$

The sum and difference identities for sine are:

$\sin(A + B) = \sin A \cos B + \cos A \sin B$
$\sin(A - B) = \sin A \cos B - \cos A \sin B$

REFLECT

2a. Show how you can use the values of cos 30°, cos 45°, sin 30°, and sin 45° to find:

cos 15°

$\cos 15° = \cos(45° - 30°) = \cos 45° \cos 30° + \sin 45° \sin 30°$

sin 75°

$\sin 75° = \sin(30° + 45°) = \sin 45° \cos 30° + \cos 45° \sin 30°$

3 EXPLORE   Deriving Sum and Difference Identities for Tangent

CC.9–12.F.TF.9

A Since $\tan \theta = \dfrac{\sin \theta}{\cos \theta}$ and since you know identities for $\cos(A \pm B)$ and $\sin(A \pm B)$, you can write identities for $\tan(A + B)$ and $\tan(A - B)$.

$$\tan(A + B) = \frac{\sin(A + B)}{\cos(A + B)} = \frac{\sin A \cos B + \cos A \sin B}{\cos A \cos B - \sin A \sin B}$$

$$\tan(A - B) = \frac{\sin(A - B)}{\cos(A - B)} = \frac{\sin A \cos B - \cos A \sin B}{\cos A \cos B + \sin A \sin B}$$

B Those will work, but there's a step you can take to make the tangent identities simpler. Divide the numerator and denominator of each term by cos A cos B.

$$\tan(A + B) = \frac{\sin A \cos B + \cos A \sin B}{\cos A \cos B - \sin A \sin B}$$

$$= \frac{\dfrac{\sin A \cos B}{\cos A \cos B} + \dfrac{\cos A \sin B}{\cos A \cos B}}{\dfrac{\cos A \cos B}{\cos A \cos B} - \left(\dfrac{\sin A}{\cos A}\right)\left(\dfrac{\sin B}{\cos B}\right)}$$

$$= \frac{\tan A + \tan B}{1 - \tan A \tan B}$$

You can use the same approach to write an identity for $\tan(A - B)$.

The sum and difference identities for tangent are:

$\tan(A + B) = \dfrac{\tan A + \tan B}{1 - \tan A \tan B}$
$\tan(A - B) = \dfrac{\tan A - \tan B}{1 + \tan A \tan B}$

REFLECT

3a. Explain how you could find sum and difference identities for the secant, cosecant, and cotangent functions.

Use the reciprocals of the sum and difference identities for the cosine, the sine,

and the tangent functions, respectively.

Assign these pages to help your students practice and apply important lesson concepts. For additional exercises, see the Student Edition.

Answers

Additional Practice

1. $-\dfrac{1}{2}$

2. $-\dfrac{\sqrt{2}}{2}$

3. $2 + \sqrt{3}$

4. $\dfrac{\sqrt{3}}{3}$

5. $\dfrac{\sqrt{6} - \sqrt{2}}{4}$

6. $-\dfrac{\sqrt{2}}{2}$

7. $\sin\left(x - \dfrac{3\pi}{2}\right) = \cos x;$

$\sin x \cos\left(\dfrac{3\pi}{2}\right) - \sin\left(\dfrac{3\pi}{2}\right)\cos x = \cos x$

$\sin x \cdot 0 - (-1)\cos x = \cos x$

$\cos x = \cos x$

8. $\cos\left(x - \dfrac{\pi}{2}\right) = \sin x$

$\cos x \cos \dfrac{\pi}{2} + \sin x \sin \dfrac{\pi}{2} = \sin x$

$\cos x \cdot 0 + \sin x \cdot 1 = \sin x$

$\sin x = \sin x$

9. $\dfrac{21}{221}$

10. $-\dfrac{220}{221}$

11. $-\dfrac{21}{220}$

12. $-\dfrac{171}{221}$

13. $-\dfrac{140}{220}$

14. $\dfrac{171}{140}$

15. a. $\begin{bmatrix} \cos 60° & -\sin 60° \\ \sin 60° & \cos 60° \end{bmatrix}\begin{bmatrix} 1 & 10 & 2 \\ 0 & 0 & 6 \end{bmatrix}$

b. $\begin{bmatrix} 0.50 & 5.00 & -4.20 \\ 0.87 & 8.66 & 4.73 \end{bmatrix}$

c. $A'(0.50, 0.87)$, $B'(5, 8.66)$, $C'(-4.2, 4.73)$

16. 207 m

Problem Solving

1. a. $\begin{bmatrix} \cos 60° & -\sin 60° \\ \sin 60° & \cos 60° \end{bmatrix}$

$\begin{bmatrix} 1 & 2 & 4 & 2 \\ 1 & 0 & -3 & -2 \end{bmatrix}$

b. $\begin{bmatrix} -0.37 & 1 & 4.60 & 2.73 \\ 1.37 & 1.73 & 1.96 & 0.73 \end{bmatrix}$

c. $P'(-0.37, 1.37)$, $Q'(1, 1.73)$, $R'(4.60, 1.96)$, and $S'(2.73, 0.73)$

2. $\begin{bmatrix} -1.37 & -1.73 & -1.96 & -0.73 \\ 0.37 & 1 & 4.60 & 2.73 \end{bmatrix}$

$P''(-1.37, -0.37)$, $Q''(-1.73, 1)$, $R''(-1.96, 4.60)$, and $S''(-0.73, 2.73)$

3.

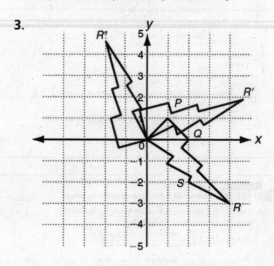

4. A

5. H

11-4

Notes

Additional Practice

Find the exact value of each expression.

1. cos120°

2. sin315°

3. tan255°

4. $\tan\dfrac{7\pi}{6}$

5. $\sin\dfrac{\pi}{12}$

6. $\cos\dfrac{3\pi}{4}$

Prove each identity.

7. $\sin\left(x - \dfrac{3\pi}{2}\right) = \cos x$

8. $\cos\left(x - \dfrac{\pi}{2}\right) = \sin x$

Find each value if $\cos A = \dfrac{12}{13}$ with $0° \le A \le 90°$ and if $\sin B = \dfrac{8}{17}$ with $90° \le B \le 180°$.

9. $\sin(A + B)$

10. $\cos(A + B)$

11. $\tan(A + B)$

12. $\sin(A - B)$

13. $\cos(A - B)$

14. $\tan(A - B)$

Solve.

15. Find the coordinates, to the nearest hundredth, of the vertices of triangle ABC with $A(1, 0)$, $B(10, 0)$, and $C(2, 6)$ after a 60° rotation about the origin.

a. Write the matrices for the rotation and for the points. _____

b. Find the matrix product. _____

c. Write the coordinates. _____

16. A hill rises from the horizontal at a 15° angle. The road leading straight up the hill is 800 meters long. How much higher is the top of the hill than the base of the hill? _____

Problem Solving

Caitlin is designing a rotating graphic for her website. She explores what it will look like if it flashes in different positions.

1. Use rotation matrices to find the coordinates of the figure $PQRS$ after a 60° rotation about the origin.

a. Write matrices for a 60° rotation and for the points P, Q, R, and S in the figure.

$R_{60°} = \left[\right]$

$PQRS = \left[\right]$

b. Find the matrix product. $R_{60°} \times PQRS = \left[\right]$

c. Name the coordinates of P', Q', R', S' to the nearest hundredth after a 60° rotation.

_____

2. a. Write the matrix product that gives the coordinates of the figure after a rotation of 150°.

$R_{150°} \times PQRS = \left[\right]$

b. Name the coordinates of $P''Q''R''S''$ to the nearest hundredth.

_____

3. Graph the two rotations on the plane above to see where Caitlin's rotating graphic will flash. Label R' and R''.

Choose the letter for the best answer.

4. Which expression gives the exact value of sin150°?

A sin90°cos60° + cos90°sin60°

B sin90°cos60° − cos90°sin60°

C cos180°cos30° + sin180°sin30°

D cos180°cos30° − sin180°sin30°

5. What is the exact value of cos75°?

F $\dfrac{\sqrt{2} - \sqrt{6}}{2}$

G $\dfrac{\sqrt{6} + \sqrt{2}}{4}$

H $\dfrac{\sqrt{6} - \sqrt{2}}{4}$

J $\dfrac{\sqrt{6} + \sqrt{2}}{2}$

Double-Angle and Half-Angle Identities
Going Deeper

Essential question: *How can you prove trigonometric identities involving double-angles and half-angles?*

CC.9-12.F.TF.9 Prove the addition and subtraction formulas for sine, cosine, and tangent and use them to solve problems.

Prerequisites
Right-Angle Trigonometry
The Unit Circle

Math Background
The father of modern trigonometry is a Greek mathematician named Hipparchus of Nicea (190 B.C.–120 B.C.). He was the first mathematician to keep a table of calculated values of various trigonometric functions.

INTRODUCE

Start the lesson by reminding students that they should be able to find the exact values of sine, cosine, and tangent for certain angles (0°, 30°, 45°, 60°, 90°, etc.) without a calculator. Motivate the lesson by telling students that in this lesson, they will learn identities that will allow them to find exact values of sine, cosine, and tangent of other angles. Before deriving any of the identities in this lesson, remind students of the Pythagorean identity: $\sin^2 \theta + \cos^2 \theta = 1$.

TEACH

1 EXPLORE

Questioning Strategies
- What is the angle sum identity for sine?
  $\sin (A + B) = \sin A \cos B + \cos A \sin B$
- What is the angle sum identity for cosine?
  $\cos (A + B) = \cos A \cos B - \sin A \sin B$.
- How can you use the identity $\sin^2 \theta + \cos^2 \theta = 1$ to obtain an expression that is equivalent to $\sin^2 \theta$? **Subtract $\cos^2 \theta$ from both sides to obtain $\sin^2 \theta = 1 - \cos^2 \theta$.**

2 EXPLORE

Questioning Strategies
- How do you know which version of the double-angle identity for cosine to use in part A? **Use the version that includes the sine function. To derive $\sin \frac{\theta}{2}$, use $\cos 2\theta = 1 - 2\sin^2 \theta$**
- How do you know which version of the double-angle identity for cosine to use in part B? **Use the version that includes only the cosine function. To derive $\cos \frac{\theta}{2}$, use $\cos 2\theta = 2\cos^2 \theta - 1$.**
- How can you use the angle sum identity for cosine to show that $\cos (90° - \theta) = \sin \theta$?
  $\cos (90° - \theta) = \cos 90° \cos \theta + \sin 90°$
  $\sin \theta = 0 + 1 \cdot \sin \theta = \sin\theta$

CLOSE

Essential Question
How can you prove trigonometric identities involving double-angles and half-angles?
To prove the double-angle identities, write the double angle as a sum of two angles and use the angle sum identities. To prove the half-angle identities, consider the double-angle identities, rearrange to solve for the term of interest, and then halve the angle.

Summarize
Have students write a journal entry in which they describe how to derive the double-angle and half-angle identities for sine, cosine and tangent. The derivation of the double-angle identities should come from the identities for addition of two angles. The derivation of the half-angle identities should come from the double-angle identities.

Name _____ Class _____ Date _____

11-5

Double-Angle and Half-Angle Identities
Going Deeper

Essential question: *How can you prove trigonometric identities involving double-angles and half-angles?*

Video Tutor

CC.9-12.F.TF.9

1 EXPLORE Deriving the Double-Angle Identities

A You can think of $\sin 2\theta$ as $\sin(\theta + \theta)$.

Using the angle sum identity for sine, this is equivalent to $\underline{\sin\theta\cos\theta + \cos\theta\sin\theta}$

Simplify to obtain the identity $\sin 2\theta = 2\sin\theta\cos\theta$.

B The derivation of $\cos 2\theta$ is similar. Rewrite 2θ as the sum of two angles.

$\cos 2\theta = \underline{\cos(\theta + \theta)}$

Using the angle sum identity for cosine, this is equivalent to $\underline{\cos\theta\cos\theta - \sin\theta\sin\theta}$

This identity can be rewritten as $\cos 2\theta = \cos^2\theta - \sin^2\theta$.

This identity can be written in two other ways:

Using the identity $\sin^2\theta + \cos^2\theta = 1$, you know that $\sin^2\theta = \underline{1 - \cos^2\theta}$

Substitute for $\sin^2\theta$ in $\cos^2\theta - \sin^2\theta$ to obtain $\underline{2\cos^2\theta - 1}$

Likewise you can use the identity $\sin^2\theta + \cos^2\theta = 1$ to find that $\cos^2\theta = \underline{1 - \sin^2\theta}$

Substitute for $\cos^2\theta$ in $\cos^2\theta - \sin^2\theta$ to obtain $\underline{1 - 2\sin^2\theta}$

C Since $\tan\theta = \dfrac{\sin\theta}{\cos\theta}$ it follows that $\tan 2\theta = \dfrac{\sin 2\theta}{\cos 2\theta}$.

Use the identities you derived in parts A and B to simplify the double angle identity for tangent:

$$\frac{\sin 2\theta}{\cos 2\theta} = \frac{2\sin\theta\cos\theta}{\cos^2\theta - \sin^2\theta}$$

Divide the numerator and the denominator by $\cos^2\theta$ to obtain

$$\frac{2\sin\theta\cos\theta \cdot \dfrac{1}{\cos^2\theta}}{(\cos^2\theta - \sin^2\theta)\dfrac{1}{\cos^2\theta}} = \frac{\dfrac{2\sin\theta\cos\theta}{\cos^2\theta}}{\dfrac{\cos^2\theta}{\cos^2\theta} - \dfrac{\sin^2\theta}{\cos^2\theta}} = \frac{2\tan\theta}{1-\tan^2\theta}$$

The double-angle formulas are summarized in the table below.

Double-Angle Identities		
$\sin 2\theta = 2\sin\theta\cos\theta$	$\cos 2\theta = \cos^2\theta - \sin^2\theta$ $\cos 2\theta = 2\cos^2\theta - 1$ $\cos 2\theta = 1 - 2\sin^2\theta$	$\tan 2\theta = \dfrac{2\tan\theta}{1-\tan^2\theta}$

REFLECT

1a. Use the fact that $\sin 45° = \cos 45° = \dfrac{\sqrt{2}}{2}$ and the double-angle identity for sine to show that $\sin 90° = 1$.

$\sin 90° = 2\sin 45°\cos 45° = 2 \cdot \dfrac{\sqrt{2}}{2} \cdot \dfrac{\sqrt{2}}{2} = 2 \cdot \dfrac{2}{4} = \dfrac{4}{4} = 1.$

CC.9-12.F.TF.9

2 EXPLORE Deriving the Half-Angle Identities

A To derive an identity for $\sin\dfrac{\theta}{2}$, solve $\cos 2\theta = 1 - 2\sin^2\theta$ for $\sin\theta$.

Since $\cos 2\theta = 1 - 2\sin^2\theta$, $-2\sin^2\theta$ is equal to $\underline{\cos 2\theta - 1}$

Thus $\sin^2\theta = \dfrac{1-\cos 2\theta}{2}$ and $\sin\theta = \pm\sqrt{\dfrac{1-\cos 2\theta}{2}}$.

Replace θ with $\dfrac{\theta}{2}$ to obtain the half-angle formula for sine:

$\sin\dfrac{\theta}{2} = \pm\sqrt{\dfrac{1-\cos\theta}{2}}$

B The derivation of $\cos\dfrac{\theta}{2}$ is similar. Solve $\cos 2\theta = 2\cos^2\theta - 1$ for $\cos\theta$.

Since $\cos 2\theta = 2\cos^2\theta - 1$, $2\cos^2\theta$ is equal to $\underline{\cos 2\theta + 1}$

Thus $\cos^2\theta = \dfrac{1+\cos 2\theta}{2}$ and $\cos\theta = \pm\sqrt{\dfrac{1+\cos 2\theta}{2}}$.

Replace θ with $\dfrac{\theta}{2}$ to obtain the half-angle formula for cosine:

$\cos\dfrac{\theta}{2} = \pm\sqrt{\dfrac{1+\cos\theta}{2}}$

C To derive an identity for $\tan\dfrac{\theta}{2}$, use the fact that $\tan\theta = \dfrac{\sin\theta}{\cos\theta}$ for any angle.

$$\tan\frac{\theta}{2} = \frac{\sin\dfrac{\theta}{2}}{\cos\dfrac{\theta}{2}} = \pm\frac{\sqrt{\dfrac{1-\cos\theta}{2}}}{\sqrt{\dfrac{1+\cos\theta}{2}}} = \pm\sqrt{\frac{1-\cos\theta}{2} \cdot \frac{2}{1+\cos\theta}} = \pm\sqrt{\frac{1-\cos\theta}{1+\cos\theta}}$$

REFLECT

2a. Why is there $\pm$ outside the square root symbol for the half-angle identities? How can you determine if the value is positive or negative?

A positive number has two square roots, the positive square root and the negative square root. The sign will depend on the quadrant in which the angle terminates.

2b. Use the half-angle identity and the fact that $\cos(90° - \theta) = \sin\theta$ to explain why

$\sin\left(45° - \dfrac{\theta}{2}\right) = \pm\sqrt{\dfrac{1-\sin\theta}{2}}$.

$45° - \dfrac{\theta}{2}$ is half of $90° - \theta$, so $\sin\left(45° - \dfrac{\theta}{2}\right) = \pm\sqrt{\dfrac{1-\cos(90°-\theta)}{2}}$ according to the half-angle identity. Then substitute $\sin\theta$ for $\cos(90° - \theta)$ under the radical.

© Houghton Mifflin Harcourt Publishing Company

Assign these pages to help your students practice and apply important lesson concepts. For additional exercises, see the Student Edition.

Answers

Additional Practice

1. $\dfrac{120}{169}; \dfrac{119}{169}; \dfrac{120}{119}$ **2.** $\dfrac{\sqrt{141}}{25}; \dfrac{22}{25}; \dfrac{\sqrt{141}}{22}$

3. $-\dfrac{4\sqrt{5}}{9}; \dfrac{1}{9}; -4\sqrt{5}$ **4.** $-\dfrac{60}{61}; \dfrac{11}{61}; -\dfrac{60}{11}$

5. $2\cos^2\theta = \cos 2\theta + 1$

$2\cos^2\theta = \cos^2\theta - \sin^2\theta + 1$

$2\cos^2\theta = \cos^2\theta - (1 - \cos^2\theta) + 1$

$2\cos^2\theta = \cos^2\theta - 1 + \cos^2\theta + 1$

$2\cos^2\theta = 2\cos^2\theta$

6. $\tan\theta = \dfrac{1 - \cos 2\theta}{\sin 2\theta}$

$\tan\theta = \dfrac{1 - (1 - 2\sin^2\theta)}{2\sin\theta\cos\theta}$

$\tan\theta = \dfrac{1 - 1 + 2\sin^2\theta}{2\sin\theta\cos\theta}$

$\tan\theta = \dfrac{\sin\theta}{\cos\theta}; \tan\theta = \tan\theta$

7. $\sqrt{\dfrac{2 - \sqrt{2}}{2 + \sqrt{2}}}$ **8.** $-\dfrac{\sqrt{2 - \sqrt{3}}}{2}$

9. $\sqrt{\dfrac{2 - \sqrt{3}}{2}}$ **10.** $\dfrac{\sqrt{5}}{5}; -\dfrac{2\sqrt{5}}{5}; -\dfrac{1}{2}$

11. $\dfrac{\sqrt{30}}{6}; -\dfrac{\sqrt{6}}{6}; -\sqrt{5}$

12. a. $\tan\theta = \dfrac{9}{25}$

b. $\dfrac{100 \cdot 2\left(\dfrac{9}{25}\right)}{1 - \left(\dfrac{9}{25}\right)^2}$ **c.** 83ft

Problem Solving

1. a. $\sin 2\theta = 2\sin\theta\cos\theta$

b. $d(\theta) = \dfrac{3v_0^2 \sin 2\theta}{32}$

c. $35 = \dfrac{3(20)^2 \sin 2\theta}{32}$

d. $\sin 2\theta = 0.933$

e. $34.5°$

2. a.

Angle of Elevation (°)	Horizontal Distance (yd)
15	18.75
25	28.73
35	35.24
45	37.50
55	35.24

b. $45°$

3. $26.5°$

4. Possible answer: For this initial velocity and target distance, $\sin 2\theta \approx 1.32$, which is outside the possible range of values for the sine of an angle; so he is incorrect.

5. C   **6.** G

Additional Practice

Find sin 2θ, cos 2θ, and tan 2θ for each.

1. $\cos\theta = -\dfrac{12}{13}$ for $\pi < \theta < \dfrac{3\pi}{2}$

2. $\sin\theta = \dfrac{\sqrt{6}}{10}$ for $0 < \theta < \dfrac{\pi}{2}$

_____

3. $\sin\theta = -\dfrac{2}{3}$ for $\dfrac{3\pi}{2} < \theta < 2\pi$

4. $\tan\theta = -\dfrac{5}{6}$ for $\dfrac{\pi}{2} < \theta < \pi$

_____   _____

Prove each identity.

5. $2\cos^2\theta = \cos 2\theta + 1$

6. $\tan\theta = \dfrac{1 - \cos 2\theta}{\sin 2\theta}$

_____

Use half-angle identities to find the exact value of each trigonometric expression.

7. $\tan 22.5°$

8. $\cos\dfrac{7\pi}{12}$

9. $\sin\dfrac{11\pi}{12}$

_____   _____   _____

Find $\sin\dfrac{\theta}{2}$, $\cos\dfrac{\theta}{2}$, and $\tan\dfrac{\theta}{2}$ for each.

10. $\cos\theta = \dfrac{3}{5}$ and $270° < \theta < 360°$

11. $\sin\theta = -\dfrac{\sqrt{5}}{3}$ and $180° < \theta < 270°$

_____

Solve.

12. A water-park slide covers 100 feet of horizontal space and is 36 feet high.

a. Write a trigonometric relation in terms of θ, the angle that the slide makes with the water surface. _____

b. A new replacement slide will create an angle with the water surface that measures twice that of the original slide. The new slide will use the same horizontal space as the old slide. Write an expression that can be evaluated to find the height of the new slide. _____

c. What is the height of the new slide to the nearest foot? _____

Problem Solving

Chris set a new personal best in football with a 35-yard kick. He wants to improve his distance. His coach suggests using the formula $d(\theta) = \dfrac{3v_0^2\,\sin\theta\,\cos\theta}{16}$, which gives the horizontal distance, d, in yards, as a function of the angle of elevation, θ, at which the ball is kicked with an initial velocity of v_0 yards per second.

1. What is the angle of elevation of the ball when Chris kicks it with an initial velocity of 20 yards per second and the ball covers 35 yards.

a. What double-angle identity can you use to rewrite the function in terms of $\sin 2\theta$? _____

b. Rewrite the function in terms of $\sin 2\theta$. _____

c. Substitute the known values in the equation. _____

d. Solve for $\sin 2\theta$. _____

e. What is the angle at which he kicked the ball? _____

2. Chris wonders how the horizontal distance would change if he kicked the ball with the same velocity but at a different angle.

a. Complete the table to show the horizontal distance, to the nearest hundredth yard, for the given angles.

b. At what angle must Chris kick the ball to cover the greatest horizontal distance?

Angle of Elevation (°)	Horizontal Distance (yd)
15	
25	
35	
45	
55	

3. What is the least angle at which Chris must kick the ball if he wants to cover at least 30 yards horizontally?

_____

4. Chris thinks he can kick the ball with an initial velocity of 18 yards per second and make a horizontal distance of 40 yards. Is he correct? Explain.

_____

Choose the letter for the best answer.

5. If Chris kicks the ball with an initial velocity of only 15 yards per second and an angle of elevation of 45°, what is the maximum horizontal distance the ball will cover?

  A 12.06 yd   C 21.09 yd
  B 14.92 yd   D 29.83 yd

6. At what angle can Chris kick the ball to cover a horizontal distance of 36 yards, if he kicks the ball with an initial velocity of 20 yards per second?

  F 18.5°   H 44.1°
  G 36.9°   J 73.7°

Solving Trigonometric Equations
Focus on Modeling

Essential question: *How can you model the height of a gondola on a rotating Ferris wheel?*

Standards for Mathematical Content

The following standards are addressed in this lesson. (An asterisk indicates that a standard is also a Modeling standard.) For more detailed information, see each section of the lesson.

Number and Quantity: CC.9-12.N.Q.1*

Algebra: CC.9-12.A.CED.2*

Functions: CC.9-12.F.IF.2, CC.9-12.F.IF.4*, CC.9-12.F.IF.7*, CC.9-12.F.IF.7e*, CC.9-12.F.BF.1*, CC.9-12.F.BF.1a*, CC.9-12.F.BF.3, CC.9-12.F.TF.5*
Geometry: CC.9-12.G.SRT.5

Prerequisites

- Angles of rotation and radian measure
- Graphing the sine and cosine functions
- Stretching, shrinking, and reflecting trigonometric graphs
- Translating trigonometric graphs

Math Background

In this lesson, students analyze the motion of a Ferris wheel. Students model the motion using a sine function. They find the values for *a, b, h,* and *k* in $h(t) = a \sin b(t - h) + k$ that describe this particular motion; then, they graph the function.

INTRODUCE

Even though the Ferris wheel is not particularly exciting compared with more modern rides, it is a staple of amusement parks and traveling carnivals. Large wheels with enclosed gondolas, such as the almost-450-foot-tall London Eye, are being erected in tourist areas to give a bird's eye view of the area. It took hundreds of people and seven years to build the London Eye. In this lesson, students will model the height of a gondola on a Ferris wheel as a function of time using a trigonometric function.

TEACH

1 **Choose a coordinate system and a trigonometric function.**

Standards

CC.9-12.G.SRT.5 Use ... similarity criteria to solve problems and to prove relationships in geometric figures.

CC.9-12.F.TF.5 Choose trigonometric functions to model periodic phenomena with specified amplitude, frequency, and midline.*

Questioning Strategies

- What is the radius of the wheel? **6 ft**
- How high off the ground is the bottom of the wheel? **1 ft**
- What is the height above the *x*-axis of point *G*? **0 ft**
- What is the height above the *x*-axis of point *G´*? **6 ft**
- Which function (sine, cosine, or tangent) will give a value of 0 when the terminal side of θ is the positive *x*-axis and a maximum when the terminal side of θ is the positive *y*-axis? **sine**

2 **Write and revise a model for height as a function of angle.**

Standards

CC.9-12. A.CED.2 Create equations in two ... variables to represent relationships between quantities; ... *

CC.9-12.F.IF.2 Use function notation, evaluate functions for inputs in their domains, and interpret statements that use function notation in terms of a context.

CC.9-12.F.BF.1 Write a function that describes a relationship between two quantities.*

CC.9-12.F.BF.1a Determine an explicit expression ... from a context.*

CC.9-12.F.TF.5 Choose trigonometric functions to model periodic phenomena with specified amplitude, frequency, and midline.*

continued

Name_____ Class_____ Date_____

11-6

COMMON CORE

Solving Trigonometric Equations
Focus on Modeling

Essential question: *How can you model the height of a gondola on a rotating Ferris wheel?*

CC-9-12.A.CED.2*,
CC-9-12.F.IF.2,
CC-9-12.F.IF.4*,
CC-9-12.F.IF.7e*,
CC-9-12.F.BF.1*,
CC-9-12.F.TF.5*

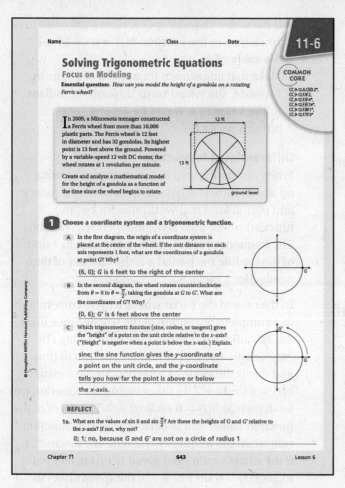

In 2009, a Minnesota teenager constructed a Ferris wheel from more than 10,000 plastic parts. The Ferris wheel is 12 feet in diameter and has 32 gondolas. Its highest point is 13 feet above the ground. Powered by a variable-speed 12 volt DC motor, the wheel rotates at 1 revolution per minute.

Create and analyze a mathematical model for the height of a gondola as a function of the time since the wheel begins to rotate.

1 Choose a coordinate system and a trigonometric function.

A In the first diagram, the origin of a coordinate system is placed at the center of the wheel. If the unit distance on each axis represents 1 foot, what are the coordinates of a gondola at point *G*? Why?

(6, 0); *G* is 6 feet to the right of the center

B In the second diagram, the wheel rotates counterclockwise from $\theta = 0$ to $\theta = \frac{\pi}{2}$, taking the gondola at *G* to *G'*. What are the coordinates of *G'*? Why?

(0, 6); *G'* is 6 feet above the center

C Which trigonometric function (sine, cosine, or tangent) gives the "height" of a point on the unit circle relative to the *x*-axis? ("Height" is negative when a point is below the *x*-axis.) Explain.

sine; the sine function gives the *y*-coordinate of a point on the unit circle, and the *y*-coordinate tells you how far the point is above or below the *x*-axis.

REFLECT

1a. What are the values of $\sin 0$ and $\sin \frac{\pi}{2}$? Are these the heights of *G* and *G'* relative to the *x*-axis? If not, why not?

0; 1; no, because *G* and *G'* are not on a circle of radius 1

Chapter 11   643   Lesson 6

1b. The diagram shows the terminal side of an angle θ intersecting a circle of radius 1 at point *P* and a circle of radius *r* at point *P'*. A perpendicular is drawn from each point to the *x*-axis, forming two right triangles. You know that the *y*-coordinate of *P* is $\sin \theta$. Explain why you can write the proportion $\frac{y}{\sin \theta} = \frac{r}{1}$ to find the *y*-coordinate of *P'*. Then solve the proportion for *y*.

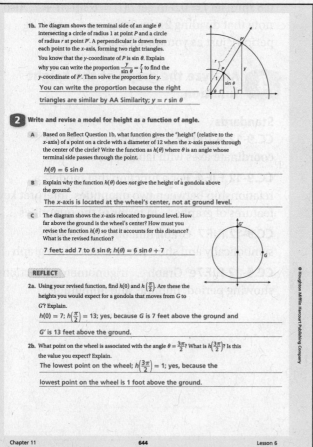

You can write the proportion because the right triangles are similar by AA Similarity; $y = r \sin \theta$

2 Write and revise a model for height as a function of angle.

A Based on Reflect Question 1b, what function gives the "height" (relative to the *x*-axis) of a point on a circle with a diameter of 12 when the *x*-axis passes through the center of the circle? Write the function as $h(\theta)$ where θ is an angle whose terminal side passes through the point.

$h(\theta) = 6 \sin \theta$

B Explain why the function $h(\theta)$ does *not* give the height of a gondola above the ground.

The *x*-axis is located at the wheel's center, not at ground level.

C The diagram shows the *x*-axis relocated to ground level. How far above the ground is the wheel's center? How must you revise the function $h(\theta)$ so that it accounts for this distance? What is the revised function?

7 feet; add 7 to 6 sin θ; $h(\theta) = 6 \sin \theta + 7$

REFLECT

2a. Using your revised function, find $h(0)$ and $h\left(\frac{\pi}{2}\right)$. Are these the heights you would expect for a gondola that moves from *G* to *G'*? Explain.

$h(0) = 7$; $h\left(\frac{\pi}{2}\right) = 13$; yes, because *G* is 7 feet above the ground and *G'* is 13 feet above the ground.

2b. What point on the wheel is associated with the angle $\theta = \frac{3\pi}{2}$? What is $h\left(\frac{3\pi}{2}\right)$? Is this the value you expect? Explain.

The lowest point on the wheel; $h\left(\frac{3\pi}{2}\right) = 1$; yes, because the lowest point on the wheel is 1 foot above the ground.

Chapter 11   644   Lesson 6

Questioning Strategies

• What physical characteristic of the Ferris wheel does the value of a in $h(\theta) = a \sin \theta + k$ represent? the radius of the wheel

• What physical characteristic of the Ferris wheel does the value of k in $h(\theta) = a \sin \theta + k$ represent? the height of the center of the wheel above the ground

Teaching Strategy

Another way for students to determine the values for the function $h(\theta) = 6 \sin \theta$ is to ask them to recall the general function $h(\theta) = a \sin b\theta$. Ask them what effect a and b have on the graph. Students should remember that a changes the amplitude and b changes the period. They should recognize the wheel has a maximum "height" of 6 feet and a minimum of −6 feet, so the amplitude of the function's graph must be 6. Hence, the function is $h(\theta) = 6 \sin \theta$.

 Revise the model to make height a function of time.

Standards

CC.9-12.N.Q.1 Use units as a way to understand problems and guide the solution of multi-step problems; ...*

CC.9-12.A.CED.2 Create equations in two ... variables to represent relationships between quantities; ... *

CC.9-12.F.IF.2 Use function notation, evaluate functions for inputs in their domains, ...

CC.9-12.F.BF.1 Write a function that describes a relationship between two quantities.*

CC.9-12.F.BF.1a Determine an explicit expression ... from a context.*

Questioning Strategies

• Have students re-read the initial problem description on the first page of the lesson. What is the rotational speed of the wheel? 1 revolution per minute

• In part C, show the dimensional analysis used to convert from radians per minute to radians. $\frac{2\pi}{\text{min}} \cdot t \text{ min} = 2\pi t$

• To check your answer above, find the angle through which the wheel has turned when $t = 1$ min. 2π

• If the wheel changes speed, what parameter must you adjust in the function $h(t) = a \sin bt + k$? the value of b
Make that adjustment for a speed of 2 rpm. In 1 minute, the wheel turns through 4π radians, so the value of b would be 4π and $h(t) = 6 \sin 4\pi t + 7$.

Differentiated Instruction

When discussing step 3, you may want to bring up the reciprocal relationship between *frequency* and *period* for a real-world sine (or cosine) function where time is the independent variable. The frequency f is the number of cycles in 1 unit of time, while the period p is the amount of time needed for 1 cycle. So, $f = \frac{1}{p}$ and $p = \frac{1}{f}$.

In the case of the Ferris wheel, a cycle corresponds to a complete revolution of the wheel. Since there are 2π radians in 1 revolution, multiplying f by 2π gives the number of radians per unit of time, and this is the value of b needed for the function $h(t) = 6 \sin bt + 7$. In other words, the function can be written as $h(t) = 6 \sin 2\pi f t + 7$. This form of the function allows you to easily change the function rule when the frequency changes. For instance, if the wheel's rotational speed is 1 rpm, let $f = 1$ to get $h(t) = 6 \sin 2\pi t + 7$; if the speed slows to 0.5 rpm, let $f = 0.5$ to get $h(t) = 6 \sin \pi t + 7$. Also, note that dividing 2π by $2\pi f$ gives $\frac{1}{f}$, or p (the period), just as you would expect.

 Analyze the graph of the height function.

Standards

CC.9-12.A.CED.2 ...; graph equations on coordinate axes with labels and scales.*

CC.9-12.F.IF.4 For a function that models a relationship between two quantities, interpret key features of graphs ... in terms of the quantities ... .*

CC.9-12.F.IF.7 Graph functions expressed symbolically and show key features of the graph ... *

CC.9-12.F.IF.7e Graph ... trigonometric functions, showing period, midline, and amplitude.*

continued

3 Revise the model to make height a function of time.

A The wheel's rotational speed is given in revolutions per minute. The unit analysis below shows that you can convert this rate into another form. Complete the unit analysis.

$$\frac{\text{revolutions}}{\text{minute}} \times \frac{\text{radians}}{\text{revolution}} = \frac{\text{radians}}{\text{minute}}$$

B How many radians are in 1 revolution? What, then, is the wheel's rotational speed in radians per minute?

   2π; 2π radians per minute

C You can use the rotational speed in radians per minute to write angle θ (measured in radians) in terms of time t (measured in minutes). Explain how, and give the result.

   Multiply 2π radians per minute by minutes to get the angle measure; $\theta = 2\pi t$

D Returning to the revised function $h(\theta)$ that you wrote in part C of step 2, you can now replace θ with an expression involving t so that $h(\theta)$ becomes $h(t)$. Write the rule for $h(t)$.

   $h(t) = 6 \sin 2\pi t + 7$

REFLECT

3a. When the wheel begins to turn, a gondola at point G moves to points G', G'', G''', and returns to G. Determine the time t (in minutes) that it takes the gondola to reach each point. Then evaluate $h(t)$ to confirm that the model gives the correct heights above the ground.

t	0	$\frac{1}{4}$	$\frac{1}{2}$	$\frac{3}{4}$	1
$h(t)$	7	13	7	1	7

3b. Suppose the speed of the motor that powers the wheel is reduced so that the wheel rotates at a speed of 1 revolution every 2 minutes (or 0.5 revolution per minute). How does the height function change?

   The height function becomes $h(t) = 6 \sin \pi t + 7$.

3c. What is the period of the height function in part D? What is the amplitude? Explain your reasoning.

   1 minute; 6 feet; *Sample answer:* the wheel makes one complete revolution, or

   1 complete cycle, in 1 minute. The minimum height is 1 foot and the maximum

   height is 13 feet, so the amplitude is $0.5(13 - 1) = 6$ feet.

4 Analyze the graph of the height function.

A The table in Reflect Question 3a gives the five key points for one cycle of the height function. Use the table to graph the cycle, then repeat the cycle as needed to show the graph over the interval $0 \le t < 5$. Complete the labels and scales on the axes below before graphing.

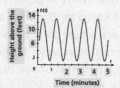

B During any cycle, when is the height function increasing and when is it decreasing? Give your answers in terms of quarters of a cycle, and then explain why your answers make sense in terms of a gondola on a rotating Ferris wheel. (Remember that the gondola starts at the point $(6, 7)$ in the coordinate system from part C of step 2 and that the wheel rotates counterclockwise.)

   The function increases during the first and fourth quarters of a cycle; it

   decreases during the second and third quarters; this makes sense because a

   gondola at $(6, 7)$ rises to $(0, 13)$, then drops to $(-6, 7)$ and continues to drop

   to $(0, 1)$, and finally rises to $(6, 7)$ to complete the cycle.

C During the interval $0 \le t < 5$, how many times is a gondola at a given height between 1 foot and 13 feet above the ground? Explain how you know from the graph and from the context of a gondola on a rotating Ferris wheel.

   10 times; a horizontal line drawn between 1 and 13 on the vertical axis

   intersects the graph 10 times; on each of the 5 rotations, the gondola is at

   the same height once on the way up and once on the way down.

REFLECT

4a. What is the equation of the midline of the height function? Explain your reasoning.

   $h(t) = 7$; the halfway point between the maximum and minimum values is 7 feet.

4b. At which times during the interval $0 \le t < 5$ is the height of the gondola on the midline?

   0 min, 0.5 min, 1 min, 1.5 min, 2 min, 2.5 min, 3 min, 3.5 min, 4 min, and

   4.5 min

© Houghton Mifflin Harcourt Publishing Company

continued

Questioning Strategies

- How many revolutions does the wheel complete in 5 minutes? **5** How many cycles should appear in the graph of the sine function? **5**

- At what times during the interval $0 \le t < 5$ is the gondola at its highest point? **0.25 min, 1.25 min, 2.25 min, 3.25 min, and 4.25 min**

- At what times during the interval $0 \le t < 5$ is the gondola at its lowest point? **0.75 min, 1.75 min, 2.75 min, 3.75 min, and 4.75 min**

5 Generalize the height function to any gondola.

Standards

CC.9-12.A.CED.2 Create equations in two ... variables to represent relationships between quantities; ... *

CC.9-12.F.IF.2 Use function notation, evaluate functions for inputs in their domains, and interpret function notation in terms of a context.

CC.9-12.F.IF.7 Graph functions expressed symbolically and show key features of the graph ...*

CC.9-12.F.IF.7e Graph ... trigonometric functions, showing period, midline, and amplitude.*

CC.9-12.F.BF.1 Write a function that describes a relationship between two quantities.*

CC.9-12.F.BF.1a Determine an explicit expression ... or steps for calculations from a context.*

CC.9-12.F.BF.3 Identify the effect on the graph of replacing $f(x)$ by ... $f(x + k)$ for specific values of k (both positive and negative; ...

Questioning Strategies

- Describe the height function in words. **For the gondola that starts at (6, 7), the function gives the gondola's height above the ground at any time t measured in minutes.**

- Where on the wheel is the gondola at (0, 1) located? **It is at the bottom of the wheel.**

- Given the graph of the height function for the gondola that starts at (6, 7), how can the graph of the height function for any other gondola be obtained through a transformation? Explain your reasoning. **All gondolas follow the same path around the wheel and therefore run through the same cycle of heights above the ground, but they do so at different times. So, given the graph of the height function for one gondola, you can simply translate the graph horizontally to obtain the graph for any other gondola. The**

magnitude of the horizontal shift depends on the gondola's position on the wheel relative to the gondola that starts at (6, 7).

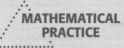 **Highlighting the Standards**

Modeling circular motion using a trigonometric function supports Mathematical Practice Standard 4 (Model with mathematics). Draw students' attention to how they used the information given in the problem to "customize" the sine function. Each constant in the model can be related to some physical characteristic in the problem situation.

CLOSE

Essential Question

How can you model the height of a gondola on a rotating Ferris wheel?

Use the function $h(t) = a \sin bt + k$ where a is the radius of the wheel, b is 2π times the speed (in revolutions per minute) of the wheel, and k is the height of the center of the wheel above the ground. This function gives the height h at time t of the gondola that starts at (a, k) when the center of the wheel is located at $(0, k)$. For any other gondola, introduce a time shift t' that depends on that gondola's position relative to the gondola at (a, k). Then the height function becomes $h(t) = a \sin b(t + t') + k$.

Summarize

Have students write a one-page summary of how to model circular motion using a trigonometric function.

EXTEND

Standards

CC.9-12.A.CED.2 Create equations in two ... variables to represent relationships between quantities; ... *(Ex. 1)

CC.9-12.F.BF.1 Write a function that describes a relationship between two quantities.* (Ex. 1)

CC.9-12.F.BF.1a Determine an explicit expression ... from a context.* (Ex. 1)

4c. Suppose someone who doesn't know the rotational speed of the wheel is given only the rule for the height function or only the function's graph. Explain how the rotational speed can be determined from each.

The function has the form $h(t) = a \sin bt + k$, and the period of such functions

is $\frac{2\pi}{b}$; since $b = 2\pi$ for $h(t)$, the period is $\frac{2\pi}{2\pi} = 1$, which means that the wheel

completes a revolution in 1 minute; the graph shows that the cycle that starts at

$t = 0$ ends at $t = 1$, so again the wheel completes a revolution in 1 minute.

4d. Suppose the speed of the motor that powers the wheel is reduced so that the wheel rotates at a speed of 1 revolution every 2 minutes (or 0.5 revolution per minute). How does the graph of the height function change? Explain why.

The graph becomes stretched horizontally because each cycle takes twice as long.

5 Generalize the height function to any gondola.

A The height function is based on the gondola at $(6, 7)$ because that point is on the terminal side of angle θ when $\theta = 0$. You can think of the gondolas at other points as either being ahead of the gondola at $(6, 7)$ or being behind it. For instance, consider a gondola at $(0, 1)$. Give an angle θ_1 between 0 and 2π that shows how far ahead the gondola at $(0, 1)$ is relative to the one at $(6, 7)$. Alternatively, give an angle θ_2 between -2π and 0 that shows how far behind it is. How are θ_1 and θ_2 related?

$\theta_1 = \frac{3\pi}{2}$; $\theta_2 = -\frac{\pi}{2}$; they are coterminal angles that differ by 2π.

B The independent variable for the height function is time rather than angle. Convert θ_1 to time t_1 and θ_2 to time t_2 (both times in minutes). By how much do t_1 and t_2 differ? Why does this make sense?

$t_1 = \frac{3}{4}$; $t_2 = -\frac{1}{4}$; they differ by 1 because a cycle lasts 1 minute.

C The height function $h(t)$ based on the gondola at $(6, 7)$ performs several actions to produce an output of height for an input of time. The table lists those actions as well as the results of the actions when $t = 0$ is used as input. Complete the table by providing the missing numerical results. (The unit of measurement for each result is given in parentheses.)

Actions	Results for $h(t)$
Accept a time as input.	0 (minutes)
Convert time to an angle.	0 (radians)
Find "height" relative to wheel's center.	0 (feet)
Output height above ground.	7 (feet)

D A height function based on the gondola at $(0, 1)$ has to perform one more action than $h(t)$ does. This action is a "time shift" that changes the input time $t = 0$ to the time that represents how far ahead or behind the gondola at $(0, 1)$ is relative to the gondola at $(6, 7)$. In the table, the column for $h_1(t)$ uses time t_1 and angle θ_1 from parts A and B of step 5. Complete the column for $h_2(t)$ using time t_2 and angle θ_2.

Actions	Results for $h_1(t)$	Results for $h_2(t)$
Accept a time as input.	0 (minutes)	0 (minutes)
Convert to time ahead or time behind.	$\frac{3}{4}$ (minutes)	$-\frac{1}{4}$ (minutes)
Convert time to an angle.	$\frac{3\pi}{2}$ (radians)	$-\frac{\pi}{2}$ (radians)
Find "height" relative to wheel's center.	-6 (feet)	-6 (feet)
Output height above ground.	1 (feet)	1 (feet)

E Based on the table above, one height function for the gondola at $(0, 1)$ is

$h_1(t) = 6 \sin 2\pi \left(t + \frac{3}{4} \right) + 7$. Write a rule for the other height function $h_2(t)$.

$h_2(t) = 6 \sin 2\pi \left(t - \frac{1}{4} \right) + 7$

REFLECT

5a. The graph of $h_1(t)$ on the interval $0 \le t < 1$ is shown. Using the same coordinate plane, graph $h_2(t)$ on the interval $0 \le t < 1$. What do you notice?

The graphs are identical.

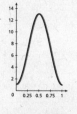

5b. Describe the impact that a "time shift" in the rule for the height function has on the graph of the function. For instance, how is the graph of $h_1(t)$ related to graph of $h(t)$ if both functions have unrestricted domains?

The "time shift" produces a horizontal shift in the graph.

EXTEND

1. Suppose a Ferris wheel has a radius of r feet, rotates counterclockwise at a speed of s revolutions per minute, and has a center whose distance above the ground is c feet (where $c > r$). Relative to the gondola at the rightmost point on the wheel, suppose a gondola has a "time shift" of t_1 minutes. Write a rule for the height h (in feet) of that gondola as a function of the time t (in minutes) since the wheel begins to rotate.

$h(t) = r \sin 2\pi s(t + t_1) + c$

Assign these pages to help your students practice and apply important lesson concepts. For additional exercises, see the Student Edition.

Answers

Additional Practice

1. $H(t) = 7 \sin\left(\frac{2\pi x}{12} + \frac{\pi}{2}\right) + 94 = 7 \sin\left(\frac{\pi x}{6} + \frac{\pi}{2}\right) + 94$

or $H(t) = 7 \cos\left(\frac{2\pi x}{12}\right) + 94 = 7 \cos\left(\frac{\pi x}{6}\right) + 94$

2. $V(t) = -0.3 \sin\left(\frac{\pi}{2}x + \frac{\pi}{2}\right) + 2.7$ or

$V(t) = -0.3 \cos\left(\frac{\pi}{2}x\right) + 2.7$

3.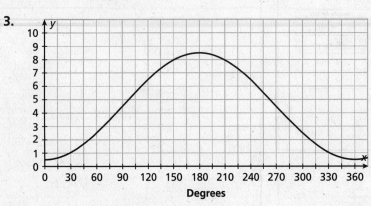

4. 2.5 feet above the ground

5. $\theta = 180°$

Problem Solving

1. 85 degrees

2. 45 degrees

3. up by 65

4. d

5. 20

6. a

7. 52 weeks (1 year)

8. b; $b = \dfrac{2\pi}{\text{period}}$

9. horizontal shift

10. 0

11. $y = 20 \sin\left(\frac{2\pi}{52}x\right) + 65$ or $y = 20 \sin\left(\frac{\pi}{26}x\right) + 65$

Name_____ Class_____ Date_____

Additional Practice

1. The hour hand on a grandfather clock is 7 inches long. The pin that the hand rotates about sits 7 feet (94 inches) off the floor. Write an equation that models the height H of the tip of the hour hand in inches as a function of time t in hours after midnight.

_____

2. During normal breathing, the lung volume of a typical adult human male fluctuates in a periodic way between 2.4 and 3 liters, with a breath occurring every 4 seconds. Write a function to model lung volume V as a function of time t during normal breathing. Assume that at $t = 0$ seconds the lungs have just finished exhaling.

_____

The height H in feet above the ground of a seat on a carousel can be modeled by $H(\theta) = -4\cos\theta + 4.5$.

3. Graph the height of the seat for $0° \le \theta \le 360°$.

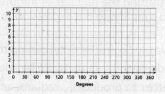

4. How high is the seat when $\theta = 60°$?

_____

5. When is the seat at its lowest?

_____

Solve.

6. The height of the water at a pier on a certain day can be modeled by $h(t) = 4.8\sin\frac{\pi}{6}(t + 3.5) + 9$, where h is the height in feet and t is the time in hours after midnight. When is the height of the water 6 feet?

_____

Problem Solving

Martha has been collecting data on the average daily temperature in her city for the past year. After plotting the data, she suspects the temperature follows a periodic pattern, so she wants to use a trigonometric model to make future temperature predictions. Help Martha build her model.

She chooses to begin with the general formula $y = a\sin(bx + c) + d$.

1. What is the upper range of the data? _____

2. What is the lower range of the data? _____

3. What is the vertical shift of the data, compared to the parent sine function? _____

4. To which parameter in the formula does the vertical translation correspond? _____

5. What is the amplitude? _____

6. To which parameter in the formula does the amplitude correspond? _____

7. What is the period? _____

8. To which parameter in the formula does the period relate, and what is the relationship? _____

9. What does the last parameter represent? _____

10. What is the value of the final parameter, in this model? _____

11. What is the equation of Martha's model? _____

This page provides students with the opportunity to apply concepts from the Common Core in real-world problem situations. There are three different levels of performance tasks:

⭐ **Novice:** These are short word problems that require students to apply the math they have learned in straightforward, real-world situations.

⭐⭐ **Apprentice:** These are more involved problems that guide students step-by-step through more complex tasks. These exercises include more complicated reasoning, writing, and open-ended elements.

⭐⭐⭐ **Expert:** These are open-ended, non-routine problems that, instead of stepping the students through, ask them to choose their own methods for solving and justify their answers and reasoning.

Sample answers

1. The domain of the model function is 0 cm to however far the car can travel before it is no longer viewed, and the range of the function is 0 cm to $2 \cdot 36 = 72$ cm, which is the diameter of the car tire. Since the height of the tape mark goes through a full cycle during one revolution of the car tire, the period of the function is the circumference of the car tire, or $2 \cdot \pi \cdot 36 = 72\pi$ cm. Finally, the amplitude of the function is the radius of the car tire, or 36 cm.

2. $D(t) = 6\cos\left(\frac{\pi}{30}t\right) + 96$

3. Scoring Guide:

Task	Possible points
a	1 point for correctly determining that the close is $6.5 \cdot 60 = 390$ minutes after the open, and 1 point for correctly substituting the number of minutes for t and simplifying the expression to $\frac{5\pi}{12}$.
b	1 point for correctly determining that $\frac{\pi}{6}$ radians and $\frac{\pi}{4}$ radians can be added together to produce $\frac{5\pi}{12}$ radians, and 1 point for correctly identifying the angle sum identity that can help you find the closing price of the stock as $\sin\left(\frac{\pi}{6} + \frac{\pi}{4}\right) = \sin\frac{\pi}{6}\cos\frac{\pi}{4} + \cos\frac{\pi}{6}\sin\frac{\pi}{4}$
c	1 point for correctly calculating the closing price of the stock, and 1 point for doing so using the angle sum formula and the results of part **b**: $$P(t) = -0.72\sin\left(\frac{5\pi}{12}\right) + 24$$ $$= -0.72\sin\left(\frac{\pi}{6} + \frac{\pi}{4}\right) + 24$$ $$= -0.72\left(\sin\frac{\pi}{6}\cos\frac{\pi}{4} + \cos\frac{\pi}{6}\sin\frac{\pi}{4}\right) + 24$$ $$= -0.72\left(\frac{1}{2} \cdot \frac{\sqrt{2}}{2} + \frac{\sqrt{3}}{2} \cdot \frac{\sqrt{2}}{2}\right) + 24$$ $$= -0.72\left(\frac{\sqrt{2}}{4} + \frac{\sqrt{6}}{4}\right) + 24$$ $$= -0.72\left(\frac{\sqrt{2} + \sqrt{6}}{4}\right) + 24$$ $$\approx \$23.30$$

Total possible points: 6

Performance Tasks

★ **1.** Janis placed a tape mark on the top outer edge of a car tire with a 36-cm radius and took a video of the tire's motion. Janis then created a trigonometric function to model the height of the tape mark above the ground as a function of the total distance traveled by the car in centimeters. What are the domain, range, period, and amplitude of the model function? Explain your answers.

★ **2.** The center of a circular wall clock is 8 feet, or 96 inches, from a classroom floor, and the minute hand is 6 inches long. Ross wants to model the distance of the tip of the minute hand from the floor as a function of the number of minutes past 12:00 PM by using the cosine function. Write the model function, where $D(t)$ is the distance from the floor in inches and t is the number of minutes past 12:00 PM.

★ **3.** The New York Stock Exchange is usually open on business days from 9:30 AM to 4:00 PM Eastern Time. On a particular trading day, the price in dollars of a stock traded on the exchange could be modeled by the function $P(t) = -0.72 \sin\left(\frac{\pi}{192}(t - 310)\right) + 24$, where $P(t)$ was the price and t was the number of minutes since the open. Use this information to find the closing price of the stock that day.

a. How many minutes is the close after the open? Substitute the number of minutes for t and simplify the expression $\frac{\pi}{192}(t - 310)$, leaving π in the expression.

continued

---

b. The expression in part **a** can be rewritten as the sum of $\frac{\pi}{4}$ and what other angle measurement? What is the angle sum identity that can help you find the closing price of the stock?

c. Use the angle sum identity from part **b** to help find the closing price of the stock.

★★★ **4.** Belinda recorded the dew point in her hometown in degrees Fahrenheit each day for a year (not a leap year) and entered the data into her graphing calculator, with x representing the number of days since January 1 and $x = 0$ as January 1. She then performed a sinusoidal regression as shown.

```
SinReg
y=a*sin(bx+c)+d
a=25.00036565
b=.0172134442
c=-1.583657028
d=39.99903543
```

a. What is the model function? What is the function's period and amplitude? (Answers can be rounded to two decimal places, but don't round when calculating.)

b. Use the model function to find the approximate dew point on February 20. Also, determine on what day(s) the model says the dew point was 55°F by using your graphing calculator.

c. What is the phase shift of the model function?

---

4. Scoring Guide:

Task	Possible points
a	1 point for determining the model function is $y \approx 25.00 \sin(0.02x - 1.58) + 40.00$, 1 point for finding the function's period to be $\frac{2\pi}{0.0172134442} \approx 365.02$, and 1 point for finding the function's amplitude to be 25.00.
b	1 point for correctly substituting 50 into the function for February 20 and calculating the approximate dew point to be 23.46°F, and 1 point for determining that the dew point was 55°F at $x = 129$ and $x = 237$, or May 10 and August 26.
c	1 point for correctly calculating the phase shift of the model function to be $\frac{-1.583657028}{0.0172134442} = -92.00$, or 92 units to the right.

Total possible points: 6

COMMON CORE CORRELATION

Standard	Items
CC.9-12.A.CED.2*	9
CC.9-12.F.IF.4*	3, 4, 5, 6, 9
CC.9-12.F.IF.7e*	6, 9
CC.9-12.F.BF.1*	9
CC.9-12.F.BF.3	7
CC.9-12.F.TF.4(+)	8
CC.9-12.F.TF.5*	9
CC.9-12.F.TF.8	1
CC.9-12.F.TF.9(+)	2

TEST PREP DOCTOR ⊕

Multiple Choice: Item 1
- Students who chose **A** or **B** did not recognize that $\sin \theta$ is negative in the fourth quadrant.
- Students who chose **C** did not take the square root when using Pythagorean identity.

Constructed Response: Item 6
- Students who incorrectly identified the amplitude may have used the greatest y-value (7) as the amplitude, or they may have used the vertical distance between the highest and lowest points on the graph (6).

Constructed Response: Item 9
- Students may have difficulty determining the argument of the sine function. Since the wheel rotates twice each second, that is 4π radians per second.

- Students may have difficulty finding that the amplitude is 9 (half the diameter of the circle made by the movement of the reflector).

- Students may not be able to determine that the center of the circle is 13 inches above the ground, which puts the midline of the function's graph at $h(t) = 13$.

Name _____ Class _____ Date _____

MULTIPLE CHOICE

1. If $\cos \theta = 0.342$ where $\frac{3\pi}{2} < \theta < 2\pi$, what is the approximate value of $\sin \theta$?

   A. 0.940

   B. 0.883

   C. −0.883

   D. −0.940 ✓

2. Which of the following uses the difference identity for the sine function to correctly prove the identity $\sin(\pi - \theta) = \sin \theta$?

   F. $\sin(\pi - \theta)$
   $= (\sin \pi) - (\sin \theta)$
   $= 0 - (\sin \theta)$
   $= \sin \theta$

   G. $\sin(\pi - \theta)$
   $= (\sin \pi)(\cos \theta) - (\cos \pi)(\sin \theta)$
   $= (0)(\cos \theta) - (1)(\sin \theta)$
   $= \sin \theta$

   H. $\sin(\pi - \theta)$ ✓
   $= (\sin \pi)(\cos \theta) - (\cos \pi)(\sin \theta)$
   $= (0)(\cos \theta) - (-1)(\sin \theta)$
   $= \sin \theta$

   J. $\sin(\pi - \theta)$
   $= (\sin \pi)(\sin \theta) - (\cos \pi)(\cos \theta)$
   $= (1)(\sin \theta) - (0)(\cos \theta)$
   $= \sin \theta$

Use the following information for Items 3–6.

In the window of a jewelry store, rings are displayed on a rotating turntable. The function

$$d(t) = 3 \sin \pi t + 4$$

models a particular ring's distance (in inches) from the window at time t (in minutes).

3. How fast (in revolutions per minute, or rpm) is the turntable rotating?

   A. 1 rpm   C. 3 rpm

   B. 2 rpm ✓   D. 4 rpm

4. What is the ring's maximum distance from the window?

   F. 1 inch   H. 5 inches

   G. 3 inches   J. 7 inches ✓

5. An employee at the jewelry store made a change to the display so that the distance function is now $d(t) = 3 \sin \pi t + 3.5$. Which of the following describes the change?

   A. The employee moved the ring closer to the center of the turntable.

   B. The employee moved the ring farther from the center of the turntable.

   C. The employee moved the turntable closer to the window. ✓

   D. The employee moved the turntable farther from the window.

© Houghton Mifflin Harcourt Publishing Company

CONSTRUCTED RESPONSE

6. a. Using the original distance function $d(t) = 3 \sin \pi t + 4$ as described on the preceding page, graph the function on the interval $0 \le t \le 6$. Include labels and scales for the axes.

   b. Identify the graph's period, amplitude, and midline.

   Period = 2; amplitude = 3; midline:

   $d(t) = 4$

7. Graph one cycle of the function $g(\theta) = 1.5 \cos 2\theta$. (One cycle of the graph of the parent function is shown in gray.)

   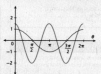

8. Use angles of rotation and the unit circle to explain why $\cos(-\theta) = \cos \theta$.

   The terminal sides of angles θ and $-\theta$

   intersect the unit circle at points that

   are reflections across the x-axis. These

   points have the same x-coordinate

   and opposite y-coordinates. Since

   cosine outputs the x-coordinate, $\cos \theta$

   and $\cos(-\theta)$ are equal.

9. A reflector is attached to a spoke on a bicycle wheel. When the wheel rotates, the reflector is 4 inches above the ground at its lowest point and 22 inches above the ground at its highest point.

   a. Write a rule for the function $h(t)$ that gives the height h (in inches) of the reflector at time t (in seconds) when the wheel rotates at a rate of 2 revolutions per second. Assume the following:

   • The x-axis is at ground level.

   • The y-axis passes through the center of the wheel.

   • The reflector starts at the point $(9, 13)$.

   Note that the wheel rotates *clockwise*, so angles of rotation must be negative.

   $h(t) = 9 \sin(-4\pi t) + 13$

   b. Graph $h(t)$ on the interval $0 \le t \le 2$. Include labels and scales for the axes.

   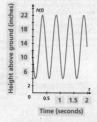

   c. Suppose the wheel's rotational speed is increased to 3 revolutions per second. How must you alter the height function's rule? What effect does this change have on the function's graph?

   $\sin(-4\pi t)$ becomes $\sin(-6\pi t)$

   in the function's rule; the period

   decreases from $\frac{1}{2}$ to $\frac{1}{3}$ second.

© Houghton Mifflin Harcourt Publishing Company

Conic Sections

Conic Sections

Chapter Focus

In this chapter you will study the conic sections. You will learn that conic sections are formed by the intersection of a double right cone and a plane. You will learn how the equation of a conic section contains and reveals information key to graphing it. You will learn to identify a conic section from its equation. Lastly, you will see how to incorporate your knowledge of conic section equations in solving nonlinear systems.

Chapter at a Glance

COMMON CORE

Lesson		Standards for Mathematical Content
12-1	Introduction to Conic Sections	CC.9-12.G.GPE.4
12-2	Circles	CC.9-12.G.GPE.1
12-3	Ellipses	CC.9-12.G.GPE.3(+)
12-4	Hyperbolas	CC.9-12.G.GPE.3(+)
12-5	Parabolas	CC.9-12.G.GPE.2
12-6	Identifying Conic Sections	CC.9-12.A.SSE.1a, CC.9-12.A.SSE.1b, CC.9-12.A.SSE.2
12-7	Solving Nonlinear Systems	CC.9-12.A.REI.7
	Performance Tasks	
	Assessment Readiness	

CHAPTER 12

COMMON CORE
PROFESSIONAL
DEVELOPMENT

CC.9-12.G.GPE.1
CC.9-12.G.GPE.2
CC.9-12.G.GPE.3(+)

In this chapter, students study equations and graphs of conics. They expand on their study of circles and parabolas from previous courses. For example, they learn the more general definition of a parabola involving its focus and directrix. Students learn to recognize circles, parabolas, ellipses, and hyperbolas based on the structures of their equations, and rewrite equations in different forms in order to identify the conic represented.

Unpacking the Standards

Understanding the standards and the vocabulary terms in the standards will help you know exactly what you are expected to learn in this chapter.

COMMON CORE **CC.9-12.G.GPE.1**
Derive the equation of a circle of given center and radius using the Pythagorean Theorem; ...

Key Vocabulary

circle *(círculo)* The set of points in a plane that are a fixed distance from a given point called the *center of the circle*.
radius of a circle *(radio de un círculo)* A segment whose endpoints are the center of a circle and a point on the circle; the distance from the center of a circle to any point on the circle.
Pythagorean Theorem *(Teorema de Pitágoras)* If a right triangle has legs of lengths a and b and a hypotenuse of length c, then $a^2 + b^2 = c^2$.

What It Means For You   Lesson 12-2

You can use the Pythagorean Theorem to derive the Distance Formula. In turn, you can use the Distance Formula to derive the equation of a circle.

EXAMPLE

For the circle shown, the distance from the center (h, k) to any point (x, y) on the circle is the radius. The center is at $(-1, 2)$ and the radius is 3. Using the Distance Formula:

$$\sqrt{(x - h)^2 + (y - k)^2} = r$$

$$\sqrt{(x - (-1))^2 + (y - 2)^2} = 3$$

$$\sqrt{(x + 1)^2 + (y - 2)^2} = 3$$

Squaring both sides of the equation gives the equation of the circle, $(x + 1)^2 + (y - 2)^2 = 9$.

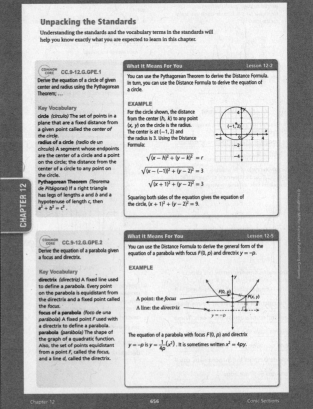

CHAPTER 12

COMMON CORE **CC.9-12.G.GPE.2**
Derive the equation of a parabola given a focus and directrix.

Key Vocabulary

directrix *(directriz)* A fixed line used to define a *parabola*. Every point on the parabola is equidistant from the directrix and a fixed point called the *focus*.
focus of a parabola *(foco de una parábola)* A fixed point F used with a directrix to define a parabola.
parabola *(parábola)* The shape of the graph of a quadratic function. Also, the set of points equidistant from a point F, called the *focus*, and a line d, called the *directrix*.

What It Means For You   Lesson 12-5

You can use the Distance Formula to derive the general form of the equation of a parabola with focus $F(0, p)$ and directrix $y = -p$.

EXAMPLE

A point: the *focus*
A line: the *directrix*

The equation of a parabola with focus $F(0, p)$ and directrix $y = -p$ is $y = \frac{1}{4p}(x^2)$. It is sometimes written $x^2 = 4py$.

COMMON CORE CC.9-12.G.GPE.3(+)

Derive the equations of ellipses and hyperbolas given the foci, using the fact that the sum or difference of distances from the foci is constant.

Key Vocabulary

conjugate axis of a hyperbola *(eje conjugado de una hipérbola)* The axis of symmetry of a hyperbola that separates the two branches of the hyperbola.

co-vertices of a hyperbola *(co-vértices de una hipérbola)* The endpoints of the conjugate axis.

co-vertices of an ellipse *(co-vértices de una elipse)* The endpoints of the minor axis.

ellipse *(elipse)* The set of all points P in a plane such that the sum of the distances from P to two fixed points F_1 and F_2, called the foci, is constant.

focus (pl. foci) of an ellipse *(foco de una elipse)* One of two fixed points F_1 and F_2 that are used to define an ellipse. For every point P on the ellipse, $PF_1 + PF_2$ is constant.

focus (pl. foci) of a hyperbola *(foco de una hipérbola)* One of two fixed points F_1 and F_2 that are used to define a hyperbola. For every point P on the hyperbola, $PF_1 - PF_2$ is constant.

hyperbola *(hipérbola)* The set of all points P in a plane such that the difference of the distances from P to two fixed points F_1 and F_2, called the foci, is a constant.

major axis of an ellipse *(eje mayor de una elipse)* The longer axis of an ellipse. The foci of the ellipse are located on the major axis, and its endpoints are the vertices of the ellipse.

minor axis of an ellipse *(eje menor de una elipse)* The shorter axis of an ellipse. Its endpoints are the co-vertices of the ellipse.

transverse axis of a hyperbola *(eje transversal de una hipérbola)* The axis of symmetry of a hyperbola that contains the vertices and foci.

What It Means For You Lessons 12-3, 12-4

You can use the Distance Formula to derive the general form of the equations of ellipses and hyperbolas given the foci.

EXAMPLE **Ellipse with Center at the Origin**

The general equation of an ellipse with center at the origin depends on whether the major axis of the ellipse is horizontal or vertical.

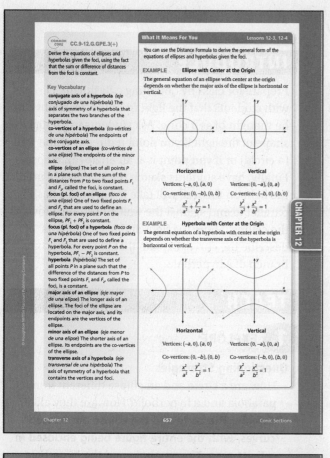

Horizontal

Vertices: $(-a, 0), (a, 0)$

Co-vertices: $(0, -b), (0, b)$

$$\frac{x^2}{a^2} + \frac{y^2}{b^2} = 1$$

Vertical

Vertices: $(0, -a), (0, a)$

Co-vertices: $(-b, 0), (b, 0)$

$$\frac{y^2}{a^2} + \frac{x^2}{b^2} = 1$$

EXAMPLE **Hyperbola with Center at the Origin**

The general equation of a hyperbola with center at the origin depends on whether the transverse axis of the hyperbola is horizontal or vertical.

Horizontal

Vertices: $(-a, 0), (a, 0)$

Co-vertices: $(0, -b), (0, b)$

$$\frac{x^2}{a^2} - \frac{y^2}{b^2} = 1$$

Vertical

Vertices: $(0, -a), (0, a)$

Co-vertices: $(-b, 0), (b, 0)$

$$\frac{y^2}{a^2} - \frac{x^2}{b^2} = 1$$

© Houghton Mifflin Harcourt Publishing Company

Key Vocabulary

axis of symmetry *(eje de simetria)* A line that divides a plane figure or a graph into two congruent reflected halves.

circle *(círculo)* The set of points in a plane that are a fixed distance from a given point called the center of the circle.

conjugate axis of a hyperbola *(eje conjugado de una hipérbola)* The axis of symmetry of a hyperbola that separates the two branches of the hyperbola.

co-vertices of a hyperbola *(co-vértices de una hipérbola)* The endpoints of the conjugate axis.

co-vertices of an ellipse *(co-vértices de una elipse)* The endpoints of the minor axis.

directrix *(directriz)* A fixed line used to define a *parabola*. Every point on the parabola is equidistant from the directrix and a fixed point called the *focus*.

ellipse *(elipse)* The set of all points P in a plane such that the sum of the distances from P to two fixed points F_1 and F_2, called the foci, is constant.

focus (pl. foci) of an ellipse *(foco de una elipse)* One of two fixed points F_1 and F_2 that are used to define an ellipse. For every point P on the ellipse, $PF_1 + PF_2$ is constant.

focus (pl. foci) of a hyperbola *(foco de una hipérbola)* One of two fixed points F_1 and F_2 that are used to define a hyperbola. For every point P on the hyperbola, $PF_1 - PF_2$ is constant.

focus of a parabola *(foco de una parábola)* A fixed point F used with a directrix to define a parabola.

hyperbola *(hipérbola)* The set of all points P in a plane such that the difference of the distances from P to two fixed points F_1 and F_2, called the foci, is a constant.

major axis of an ellipse *(eje mayor de una elipse)* The longer axis of an ellipse. The foci of the ellipse are located on the major axis, and its endpoints are the vertices of the ellipse.

minor axis of an ellipse *(eje menor de una elipse)* The shorter axis of an ellipse. Its endpoints are the co-vertices of the ellipse.

parabola *(parábola)* The shape of the graph of a quadratic function. Also, the set of points equidistant from a point F, called the *focus*, and a line d, called the directrix.

radius of a circle *(radio de un círculo)* A segment whose endpoints are the center of a circle and a point on the circle; the distance from the center of a circle to any point on the circle.

transverse axis of a hyperbola *(eje transversal de una hipérbola)* The axis of symmetry of a hyperbola that contains the vertices and foci.

vertices of an ellipse *(vértices de una elipse)* The endpoints of the major axis of the ellipse.

vertices of a hyperbola (vertices) *(vértices de una hipérbola)* The endpoints of the transverse axis of the hyperbola.

vertex of a parabola *(vértice de una parábola)* The point on the parabola that lies on the axis of symmetry.

© Houghton Mifflin Harcourt Publishing Company

Introduction to Conic Sections
Going Deeper

Essential question: *What are conic sections, and how can they be graphed?*

COMMON CORE **Standards for Mathematical Content**

CC.9-12.G.GPE.4 Use coordinates to prove simple geometric theorems algebraically. *

Prerequisites

Solving quadratic equations by graphing and factoring

Vocabulary

double right cone

conic sections

ellipse

hyperbola

parabola

Math Background

Students will be familiar with the four geometrical curves discussed in this lesson: the circle, the parabola, the ellipse, and the hyperbola. What may be new to them is the fact that each of these curves can be generated by intersecting a plane and a double right cone, thus inspiring the name *conic sections* for the group as a whole. (The circle is generally classified as a special type of ellipse rather than as a separate conic section. Three types of "degenerate" conics, the point, the line, and intersecting lines, are created when a plane passes through the apex of a double right cone at varying angles.) The conic sections have wide applications in many fields, their properties having been studied by historical figures that include Leonardo da Vinci (who studied parabolic mirrors) and Johannes Kepler (who proved that the planets move in elliptical orbits).

INTRODUCE

Prepare for class by obtaining a flashlight. Discuss with students that the light from the flashlight can be thought of as a cone. Ask students to predict the shape of the light if you point it directly at the wall (a circle) or if you point it at an angle (an ellipse). Finally, have students sketch the shape they predict the light on the wall will take if you hold a flashlight parallel to and against the wall and shine it toward the ceiling. Shine the light and have students describe the curve. Explain that the curve is one branch of a hyperbola.

TEACH

1 EXPLORE

Questioning Strategies

- How are a circle and an ellipse different from a parabola and a hyperbola? How are they alike? **Sample: The circle and the ellipse are "closed" curves, with the entire figure being enclosed in a finite area. The parabola and the hyperbola are "open," with the open ends of one U-shaped curve (the parabola) or two U-shaped curves (the hyperbola) extending to infinity. The four figures are alike in that they all can be produced by intersecting a plane and a double right cone.**

- The letter "O" can accurately be described as a circle or an ellipse, in that it can be produced by intersecting a plane and a double right cone. Can the letter "U" be accurately described a parabola? Explain? **No; to be a parabola, the open ends of a "U" would have to extend to infinity. Instead, they are finite in length. Also, the arms of a parabola are never parallel as the arms of a "U" are.**

Introduction to Conic Sections
Going Deeper

Essential question: *What are conic sections, and how can they be graphed?*

12-1

Video Tutor

CC.9-12.G.GPE.4

1 EXPLORE Sketching the Conic Sections

Find geometric shapes in a double right cone.

Each of the four figures below is a portion of a **double right cone**. (A complete double right cone extends infinitely upwards and downwards.) The first figure shows how a plane can be drawn so that the intersection of the plane and the cone is a circle. Sketch a plane intersecting each of the remaining three figures to produce the shape listed beneath the figure.

Circle   Ellipse   Parabola   Hyperbola

REFLECT

1a. The first figure above shows that the intersection of a horizontal plane and a double right cone is a circle. Explain how the shape of the intersection changes as the angle or "tilt" of the plane changes from horizontal to vertical.

When the plane is tilted at an angle less than the slant of the cone, the shape of

the intersection is an ellipse. When the plane is tilted so that it is parallel to the

side of the cone, the shape of the intersection is a U-shape (parabola). When

the plane is tilted at an angle greater than a side of the cone (including vertical),

the shape of the intersection is a double U-shape.

1b. Identify the intersection of a double right cone and a plane passing through the vertex of the cone if (a) the plane is slanted at the same angle as the cone; (b) the plane is horizontal.

(a) a line; (b) a point

1c. Can the intersection of a plane and a cone produce shapes other than the six listed in your solutions to Reflect 1a and 1b? Explain your reasoning.

No. Every possible position of the plane relative to the double right cone is accounted

for, so every possible intersection is a circle, ellipse, parabola, hyperbola, line, or point.

The shapes formed by the intersection of a plane and a double right cone are called conic sections. Along with the circle, the **conic sections** include the flattened circle, technically known as an **ellipse**; the U-shape or **parabola**; and the double-U shape or **hyperbola**.

Circle   Ellipse

Every conic section can be represented by an equation. Quadratic functions are parabolas, but most conic sections are not functions. So you will often need to use two functions to graph a conic section on a calculator.

Parabola   Hyperbola

CC.9-12.G.GPE.4

2 EXAMPLE Graphing Conic Sections

Use a graphing calculator to graph the equations $9x^2 + 25y^2 = 225$ and $9y^2 - 16x^2 = 144$.

A To draw the graph of $9x^2 + 25y^2 = 225$ using a graphing calculator, solve the equation for y.

$$9x^2 + 25y^2 = 225$$

$$25y^2 = 225 - 9x^2 \qquad \text{Subtract } 9x^2 \text{ from both sides.}$$

$$y^2 = \frac{225 - 9x^2}{25} \qquad \text{Divide both sides by 25.}$$

$$y = \pm\sqrt{\frac{225 - 9x^2}{25}} \qquad \text{Take the square root of both sides.}$$

B Write the equations you'll use to graph $9x^2 + 25y^2 = 225$ on a graphing calculator.

$$y_1 = \sqrt{\frac{225 - 9x^2}{25}} \qquad y_2 = -\sqrt{\frac{225 - 9x^2}{25}}$$

C Graph both equations using a square window on your graphing calculator. The conic section whose graph you drew is a(n) **ellipse**. The center is **(0, 0)**. The intercepts are **(5, 0)**, **(−5, 0)**, **(0, 3)**, and **(0, −3)**.

D Write the two equations you'll use to graph $9y^2 - 16x^2 = 144$.

$$y_1 = \sqrt{\frac{16x^2 + 144}{9}} \qquad y_2 = -\sqrt{\frac{16x^2 + 144}{9}}$$

E Graph both equations. The conic section whose graph you drew is a(n) **hyperbola**. The center is **(0, 0)**. The intercepts are **(0, 4)** and **(0, −4)**.

REFLECT

2. Describe similarities and differences between the graphs of the two conic sections.

Possible answer: Similarities: Both were symmetric about both axes. Both were

centered at (0, 0). Differences: The ellipse was a single closed figure while the

hyperbola was in two parts and open at both ends. The ellipse had four intercepts,

two on each axis, while the hyperbola had only two intercepts, on the y-axis.

2 EXAMPLE

Questioning Strategies

- Explain why the equation of a conic section is usually not a function. Sample: To be a function, there must be only one and only one value of y for each given value of x. Inspection of the graphs of a circle, an ellipse, and a hyperbola shows that this is not true for these curves. A vertical line that intersects any of the curves at one point will (except for the extreme right and left points of a circle and an ellipse) intersect the curve at a second point.

- Given the equation of a circle, an ellipse, or a hyperbola centered at the origin, how can you find the equations you need to graph the curve on a graphing calculator? Solve the equation for y. When y equals a positive and negative square root, graph two separate equations. Set y equal to the positive square root as one equation and y equal to the negative square root as the other.

EXTRA EXAMPLE

Identify the type of conic section, the center, and the x- and y-intercepts of the conic with the equation $9x^2 + 49y^2 = 441$. ellipse; center (0, 0); intercepts (7, 0), (−7, 0), (0, 3), (0, −3)

3 EXAMPLE

Questioning Strategies

- Why is it necessary to find the slopes of the line segments forming the angle inscribed in the semicircle? Once the slopes are known, you can check to see whether the product of the slopes is −1. If it is, the lines are perpendicular.

- How would the proof change if you were trying to prove that an angle inscribed in a semiellipse is a right angle? The proof would be identical, except that you would start with the equation of an ellipse, not the equation of a circle. Also, the result would show that the angle is not right.

EXTRA EXAMPLE

An ellipse has the equation $Ax^2 + By^2 = C$. Give the y-coordinate of any point on the ellipse (in terms of x). $\pm\sqrt{\frac{C - Ax^2}{B}}$

CLOSE

Essential Question

What are conic sections, and how can they be graphed? The conic sections are the possible shapes formed by the intersection of a plane and a double right cone. To graph a conic section, solve its equation for y. Then plot points (x, y) or, if a positive and a negative square root appear in the solution, graph two equations on a graphing calculator, one using the positive square root, the other using the negative square root.

Summarize

Have students write journal entries summarizing the main points of the lesson. They should include (1) a general description and sketch of each conic section; and (2) a sketch or description of how the section can be created by intersecting a plane and a double right cone.

MATHEMATICAL PRACTICE · · · · · · **Highlighting the Standards**

Example 2 provides opportunities for students to address Mathematical Practices Standard 5 (Use appropriate tools strategically). If students graph $y = \sqrt{\frac{225 - 9x^2}{25}}$ using graphing calculators, then they'll see only half of the ellipse with the equation $9x^2 + 25y^2 = 225$. This result suggests that the equation is not a function. Students can confirm this by graphing the other "half" of the ellipse, 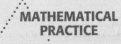 $y = -\sqrt{\frac{225 - 9x^2}{25}}$.

PRACTICE

Where skills are taught	Where skills are practiced
2 EXAMPLE	EXS. 1–12
3 EXAMPLE	EX. 13

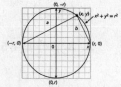

3 EXAMPLE CC.9-12.G.GPE.4 — Proving a Relationship for a Conic

From your study of geometry, recall that an angle inscribed in a semicircle is a right angle. One way to use coordinate geometry to show that this is true is to show that the slopes of the sides of the angle have a product of -1. That's because two lines whose slopes are negative reciprocals of one another (that is, the product of the slopes is -1) must be perpendicular.

A The equation of the circle is $x^2 + y^2 = r^2$. The circle has its center at the origin and a radius of r. Line segments are drawn to (x, y), a point on the circle, from $(-r, 0)$ and $(r, 0)$, the endpoints of a diameter. Use the equation of the circle to write y in terms of x.

$$x^2 + y^2 = r^2 \qquad \text{Write the equation of the circle.}$$

$$y^2 = r^2 - x^2 \qquad \text{Subtract } x^2 \text{ from both sides.}$$

$$y = \pm\sqrt{r^2 - x^2} \qquad \text{Solve for } y.$$

B So, the coordinates of any point on the circle can be expressed as $\left(x, \pm\sqrt{r^2 - x^2}\right)$.

C Now find the slopes of the sides of the angle. The endpoints of a are $(-r, 0)$ and $\left(x, \sqrt{r^2 - x^2}\right)$. The endpoints of b are $(r, 0)$ and $\left(x, \sqrt{r^2 - x^2}\right)$.

$$\text{slope } a = \frac{\sqrt{r^2 - x^2} - 0}{x - -r} = \frac{\sqrt{r^2 - x^2}}{x + r} \qquad \text{slope } b = \frac{\sqrt{r^2 - x^2} - 0}{x - r} = \frac{\sqrt{r^2 - x^2}}{x - r}$$

D Now find the product of the slopes. If the product of the slopes of two lines is -1, then their slopes are negative reciprocals of each other, and the lines are perpendicular.

$$\frac{\sqrt{r^2 - x^2}}{x + r} \cdot \frac{\sqrt{r^2 - x^2}}{x - r} = \frac{r^2 - x^2}{x^2 - r^2} \qquad [\text{slope } a] \times [\text{slope } b]$$

$$= \frac{-\left(x^2 - r^2\right)}{x^2 - r^2} \qquad \text{Factor } -1 \text{ from the numerator.}$$

$$= -1 \qquad \text{Simplify.}$$

REFLECT

3. A circle has a diameter with endpoints (x_1, y_1) and (x_2, y_2). Describe a method for finding the center of the circle and the radius.

Possible method: Find the midpoint of the line segment joining (x_1, y_1) and (x_2, y_2). This gives the coordinates of the center of the circle. Then find the distance between the center and (x_1, y_1) or (x_2, y_2). This gives the radius.

© Houghton Mifflin Harcourt Publishing Company

PRACTICE

Graph each equation on a graphing calculator. Then identify the conic section and give its intercepts, if they exist.

	Conic	x-intercepts	y-intercepts
1. $x^2 + 4y^2 = 36$	ellipse	$(6, 0), (-6, 0)$	$(0, 3), (0, -3)$
2. $y = x^2 - 4$	parabola	$(2, 0), (-2, 0)$	$(0, -4)$
3. $x^2 + y^2 = 256$	circle	$(16, 0), (-16, 0)$	$(0, 16), (0, -16)$
4. $y = \frac{1}{2}x^2$	parabola	$(0, 0)$	$(0, 0)$
5. $4x^2 - 9y^2 = 36$	hyperbola	$(3, 0), (-3, 0)$	none
6. $16x^2 + 25y^2 = 400$	ellipse	$(5, 0), (-5, 0)$	$(0, 4), (0, -4)$
7. $25x^2 - 36y^2 = 900$	hyperbola	$(6, 0), (-6, 0)$	none
8. $x = y^2 - 9$	parabola	$(-9, 0)$	$(0, 3), (0, -3)$
9. $16x^2 + 49y^2 = 784$	ellipse	$(7, 0), (-7, 0)$	$(0, 4), (0, -4)$
10. $x^2 + y^2 = 98$	circle	$(7\sqrt{2}, 0), (-7\sqrt{2}, 0)$	$(0, 7\sqrt{2}), (0, -7\sqrt{2})$
11. $4y^2 - x^2 = 100$	hyperbola	none	$(0, 5), (0, -5)$
12. $x^2 + y^2 = 81$	circle	$(9, 0), (-9, 0)$	$(0, 9), (0, -9)$

13. Compare the equations that graphed as circles with those that graphed as ellipses. What evidence can you find for the argument that a circle is a special type of ellipse?

Possible answer: All of the equations have the form $ax^2 + by^2 = c^2$ for constants a, b, and c. Circles provide a special case where $a = b$.

© Houghton Mifflin Harcourt Publishing Company

Assign these pages to help your students practice and apply important lesson concepts. For additional exercises, see the Student Edition.

Answers

Additional Practice

1. Circle; center: $(0, 0)$; intercepts: $(0, 3)$, $(0, -3)$, $(3, 0)$, $(-3, 0)$

2. Ellipse; center $(0, 0)$; intercepts: $(0, 1)$, $(0, -1)$, $(5, 0)$, $(-5, 0)$

3. Circle; center $(0, 0)$; intercepts: $(0, 4)$, $(0, -4)$, $(4, 0)$, $(-4, 0)$

4. Ellipse; center $(0, 0)$; intercepts: $(0, 7)$, $(0, -7)$, $(2, 0)$, $(-2, 0)$

5. Parabola; $(0, -3)$; opens upward

6. Hyperbola; $(0, 2)$, $(0, -2)$; vertically

7. Hyperbola; $(1, 0)$, $(-1, 0)$; horizontally

8. Parabola; $(-4, 0)$; opens right

9. Parabola; $(0, -2)$; opens upward

10. Parabola; $(3, 0)$; opens right

11. Hyperbola; $(-2, 0)$, $(2, 0)$; horizontally

12. Parabola; $(1, 0)$; opens left

13. **a.** Ellipse

    b. $(0, 2)$, $(0, -2)$, $(4, 0)$, $(-4, 0)$

    c. 320 million miles

Problem Solving

1. $\left(\frac{3}{2}, -1\right)$

2. **a.** Either $(4, 5)$ and $\left(\frac{3}{2}, -1\right)$, or $(-1, -7)$ and $\left(\frac{3}{2}, -1\right)$

   b. $6\frac{1}{2}$ units

   c. 13π units

3. **a.** Possible answer: Find the distance between point C and the center of the circle; compare this distance to the radius.

   b. Hunter is correct. Possible answer: The radius of the circle (6.5 units) is greater than the distance between point C and the center (about 5.4 units.)

4. A   5. J

6. C   7. J

Additional Practice

Graph each equation on a graphing calculator. Identify each conic section. Then describe the center and intercepts.

1. $5x^2 + 5y^2 = 45$ 2. $x^2 + 25y^2 = 25$

_____   _____

3. $4x^2 + 4y^2 = 64$ 4. $49x^2 + 4y^2 = 196$

_____   _____

Graph each equation on a graphing calculator. Identify each conic section. Then describe the vertices and the direction that the graph opens.

5. $y = x^2 - 3$ 6. $y^2 = x^2 + 4$

_____   _____

7. $x^2 - y^2 = 1$ 8. $y^2 = x + 4$

_____   _____

9. $x^2 = y + 2$ 10. $x = y^2 + 3$

_____   _____

11. $4x^2 - 5y^2 = 16$ 12. $3x + y^2 = 3$

_____   _____

Solve.

13. The orbit of an asteroid is modeled by the equation $9x^2 + 36y^2 = 144$.

    a. Identify the conic section.   _____

    b. Identify the x- and y-intercepts of the orbit.

    _____

    c. Suppose each unit of the coordinate plane represents 40 million miles.
       What is the maximum width of the asteroid's orbit?

    _____

Problem Solving

Hunter and Max draw a grid over a map of their town so that they can determine precisely where to set up a broadcast station. Hunter decides that locations A and B should be the endpoints of the diameter of a circle around the broadcast station.

1. Locate the center of the circle using the Midpoint Formula and points A and B.

   _____

2. Find the radius and the circumference of the circle.

   a. Name the coordinates of two points you can use
      with the Distance Formula to find the radius.

   _____

   b. Use the Distance Formula to find the radius.   _____

   c. What is the circumference of the circle?   _____

3. Hunter says that point C is within the circle. Max says that point C is on the circumference of the circle.

   a. Explain how they can use the Distance Formula to determine the answer.

   _____

   b. Who is correct? Why?

   _____

A broadcast station is set up at the location with coordinates (0, 2). The transmissions just reach a location with coordinates (8, 8). Choose the letter for the best answer.

4. Which point is farthest from the point
   (8, 8) and still within range of the
   broadcast station?

   A (−8, −4)   C (0, 10)

   B (−8, −8)   D (10, 2)

5. What is the maximum distance the
   broadcast transmissions will reach?

   F 6 units

   G 8 units

   H 9 units

   J 10 units

6. What is the area the broadcast
   transmissions will cover?

   A 20π   C 100π

   B 64π   D 196π

7. The broadcast transmissions just reach
   the point (x, 0). What is the value of x?

   F 8.4   H 9.2

   G 8.8   J 9.8

Notes

Circles
Going Deeper

Essential question: *How can you understand circles in terms of distances?*

CC.9-12.G.GPE.1 Derive the equation of a circle of given center and radius using the Pythagorean Theorem; complete the square to find the center and radius of a circle given by an equation. *

Prerequisites
Introduction to conic sections

Math Background
The circle is a special case of the ellipse, one whose major and minor axes are equal lengths and whose foci are concurrent at the center. Students have seen the circle as the intersection of a double right cone and a plane perpendicular to the axis of the cone. In this lesson, they turn to the definition of a circle as the set of points equidistant from a point, the center, to develop the general equation of a circle.

INTRODUCE

Prepare a length of string with a marker attached at one end. Display a coordinate plane. With a tack, tape, or some other means, attach the non-marker end of the string to an arbitrary point on the plane and draw a circle. Ask students to explain how they could use a point on the circle and the center to find the length of the string.

TEACH

 EXAMPLE

Questioning Strategies
• Why does point P have coordinates (x, k)? It is below (x, y), which has x-coordinate x, and to the left of (h, k), which has y-coordinate k.

• In Part B, you find the equation of a circle with center at $(-3, 8)$. Yet instead of -3 and 8, the equation of the circle shows $+3$ and -8 in parentheses. Why? The opposites of h and k appear in the general equation of a circle with center (h, k).

EXTRA EXAMPLE
Write the equation of a circle with center at $(4, -7)$ and radius 9. $(x - 4)^2 + (y + 7)^2 = 81$

---

2 EXAMPLE

Questioning Strategies
• Why do you add 9 to the left side of the equation in Part A? Your goal is to convert the equation to the standard form of the equation of a circle, which contains the term $(x - h)^2$. By adding 9 to $x^2 + 6x$ you partially achieve your goal by completing the square to make the term $(x + 3)^2$.

EXTRA EXAMPLE
Find the center and radius of the circle $x^2 - 10x + y^2 + 18y = -70$ center: $(5, -9)$, radius 6

CLOSE

Essential Question
How can you understand circles in terms of distances?
A circle is the set of points equidistant from a point called the *center*.

Summarize
Have students write a journal entry in which, for $(x - h)^2 + (y - k)^2 = r^2$, they explain the meaning of the equation and of each variable and constant.

MATHEMATICAL PRACTICE | Highlighting the Standards

The derivation of the equation of a circle provides opportunities to address Mathematical Practices Standard 2 (Reason abstractly and quantitatively). To complete the derivation, students must generalize a geometric relationship described in terms of distance on the coordinate place.

PRACTICE

Where skills are taught	Where skills are practiced
1 EXAMPLE	EXS. 1–2
2 EXAMPLE	EXS. 3–6

Name_____ Class_____ Date_____

Circles
Going Deeper

Essential question: *How can you understand circles in terms of distances?*

The standard form of a linear equation for a line graphed on a coordinate grid is $Ax + By = C$. Like lines, conic sections have equations that can be analyzed and used to graph them. This lesson will develop the standard form of the equation of a circle.

Video Tutor

CC.9-12.G.GPE.1

1 EXAMPLE Deriving the Equation of a Circle

Use distances on the coordinate plane to find the equation of a circle.

A   A circle is a set of points equidistant from a point called the center. The distance of each point from the center is called the radius. The figure shows a circle with its center at (h, k) and radius r. Line segments drawn from (x, y) and (h, k) intersect at point P to form a right triangle with the radius as its hypotenuse.

Use points (x, y) and (h, k) to write the coordinates of P: (x, k)

The length of the horizontal leg of the triangle is $x - h$.

The length of the vertical leg of the triangle is $y - k$.

By the Pythagorean Theorem, $\left(x - h\right)^2 + \left(y - k\right)^2 = r^2$

B   The equation you have just written is the standard form of the equation of a circle with center at (h, k) and radius r.

The standard form of the equation of a circle with its center at $(0, 0)$ and radius r is $x^2 + y^2 = r^2$.

The standard form of the equation of a circle with center at $(-3, 8)$ and radius 5 is $(x + 3)^2 + (y - 8)^2 = 25$.

REFLECT

1a. How could you find the equation of a circle if you knew only the center and a point on the circle?

You know the center (h, k). To find the radius r, use the Distance Formula to find

the distance between the center and the given point on the circle. Now that you

have h, k, and r, substitute them in the standard form of the equation of a circle.

1b. If you knew two points on a circle, could you find the equation of the circle? Explain. You can use a diagram to support your answer.

No. Two points determine a line but not a circle. Given two points,

there are an infinite number of circles that contain them. The figure

shows three different circles that all contain the same two points.

Chapter 12   665   Lesson 2

The standard form of the equation of a circle with center at (h, k) and radius r is $(x - h)^2 + (y - k)^2 = r^2$. The standard form of the equation of a circle with its center at $(0, 0)$ and radius r is $x^2 + y^2 = r^2$.

CC.9-12.G.GPE.1

2 EXAMPLE Finding the Center and Radius of a Circle

Find the center and radius of the circle $x^2 + 6x + y^2 - 2y = 15$.

A   If the equation of a circle is not written in standard form, you can convert it to standard form by completing the square.

$x^2 + 6x + y^2 - 2y = 15$

$\left(x^2 + 6x + \boxed{9}\right) + \left(y^2 - 2y + \boxed{1}\right) = 15 + \boxed{9} + \boxed{1}$

Complete the square in each trinomial by halving, then squaring, the coefficient of the middle term. Add the same numbers to both sides of the equation.

$\left(x + 3\right)^2 + \left(y - 1\right)^2 = \boxed{5}^2$

Factor the trinomials and simplify.

B   The center of the circle is $(-3, 1)$. The radius is 5 .

REFLECT

2a. What is the radius of the circle $\frac{(x - h)^2}{M} + \frac{(y - k)^2}{M} = 1$? Explain.

$\sqrt{M}$. Write the equation in standard form by multiplying both sides by M. This

gives $(x - h)^2 + (y - k)^2 = M$, meaning $r^2 = M$, or $r = \sqrt{M}$.

2b. Complete the square to find the radius and center of the circle $x^2 + ax + y^2 + by = c$.

radius: $\frac{\sqrt{a^2 + b^2 + 4c}}{2}$; center: $\left(-\frac{a}{2}, -\frac{b}{2}\right)$

PRACTICE

Find the equation of the circle with the given center and radius.

1. center $(7, -8)$, radius 12
$(x - 7)^2 + (y + 8)^2 = 144$

2. center $(-0.6, -4.7)$, radius $\sqrt{11}$
$(x + 0.6)^2 + (y + 4.7)^2 = 11$

Find the center and radius of the circle.

3. $x^2 + 14x + y^2 + 6y = 23$
center: $(-7, -3)$ radius: 9

4. $x^2 + 8x + y^2 - 6y = 0$
center: $(-4, 3)$ radius: 5

5. $x^2 + y^2 = 4x + 9$
center: $(2, 0)$ radius: $\sqrt{13}$

6. $x^2 + y^2 + 2x + 4y - 9 = 0$
center: $(-1, -2)$ radius: $\sqrt{14}$

Chapter 12   666   Lesson 2

Assign these pages to help your students practice and apply important lesson concepts. For additional exercises, see the Student Edition.

Answers

Additional Practice

1. $(x - 8)^2 + (y - 9)^2 = 100$

2. $(x + 1)^2 + (y - 5)^2 = 625$

3. $(x - 2)^2 + (y - 2)^2 = 25$

4. $(x - 3)^2 + (y + 5)^2 = 356$

5. $(x + 3)^2 + y^2 = 36$

6. $(x - 6)^2 + (y + 1)^2 = 64$

7. $(x + 3)^2 + (y + 4)^2 = 100$

8. $(x - 5)^2 + (y + 5)^2 = 25$

9. $y = -\dfrac{12}{5}x + \dfrac{169}{5}$ **10.** $y = \dfrac{4}{3}x - 10$

11. $y = \dfrac{-7}{18}x - 21$ **12.** $y = 6$

13. D, E, F

Problem Solving

1. a. $(x - 5)^2 + (y - 1)^2 = 100$

b. P, S, W

c. Q, R, T, U, V

2. a. $(x - 5)^2 + (y - 1)^2 = 225$

b. P, Q, S, T, V, W

c. 14.9 units

3. C   **4.** G

Name_____ Class_____ Date_____

Additional Practice

Write the equation of each circle.

1. Center (8, 9) and radius $r = 10$

2. Center (−1, 5) and containing the point (23, −2)

3. Center (2, 2) and containing the point (−1, 6)

4. Center (3, −5) and containing the point (−7, 11)

5. Center (−3, 0) and radius $r = 6$

6. Center (6, −1) and radius $r = 8$

7. Center (−3, −4) and containing the point (3, 4)

8. Center (5, −5) and containing the point (1, −2)

Write the equation of the line that is tangent to each circle at the given point.

9. $x^2 + y^2 = 169$; (12, 5)

10. $(x − 2)^2 + (y − 1)^2 = 25$; (6, −2)

11. $(x − 7)^2 + (y + 3)^2 = 625$; (0, −21)

12. $(x + 3)^2 + (y + 6)^2 = 144$; (−3, 6)

Solve.

13. A rock concert is located at the point (−1, 1). The music can be heard up to 4 miles away. Use the equation of a circle to find the locations that are affected. Assume each unit of the coordinate plane represents 1 mile.

© Houghton Mifflin Harcourt Publishing Company

Problem Solving

When Claire started her consulting business, she decided not to accept any clients located more than 10 miles from her home. On the graph below, her home is located at (5, 1), and her prospective clients are represented by the letters P through W.

1. Claire needs to know which prospective clients are located within a 10-mile radius of her home.

   a. Write the equation of a circle with center (5, 1) and radius 10.
   _____

   b. Which prospective clients are located within 10 miles of Claire's home?
   _____

   c. Which prospective clients are located more than 10 miles from Claire's home?
   _____

2. Claire finds that she isn't earning enough to pay the expenses from her consulting business and she needs to find some additional clients. She decides that she will drive up to 15 miles from her home to visit a client. Which prospective clients are within a 15-mile radius of her home?

   a. Write the equation of a circle with center (5, 1) and radius 15.
   _____

   b. Which prospective clients are located within 15 miles of Claire's home?
   _____

   c. How far away is a prospective client located at (10, 15)?
   _____

Claire rents an office at location (−2, −3). Choose the letter for the best answer.

3. Which of the prospective clients P through W are located more than 15 miles from Claire's office?

   A R, V

   B R, S, V

   C Q, R, V

   D Q, R, S, V

4. Which location is within 5 miles of Claire's office?

   F Post office at (2, 3)

   G Library at (2, −3)

   H Marina at (−3, 2)

   J Swimming pool at (−2, 3)

© Houghton Mifflin Harcourt Publishing Company

Ellipses
Going Deeper

Essential question: *How can you model an ellipse?*

COMMON CORE Standards for Mathematical Content

CC.9-12.G.GPE.3 Derive the equations of ellipses and hyperbolas given the foci and directrices.

Vocabulary
major axis

minor axis

Prerequisites
Radical functions

Solving radical equations and inequalities

Introduction to conic sections

Math Background
The orbits of planets and other celestial bodies are modeled using ellipses. In the 17th century, Johannes Kepler developed the first law of planetary motion, based on the observations of Tycho Brahe. Kepler discovered that the orbits of planets are elliptical, with one focus of the ellipse being the sun. This discovery was radical at the time, since many people believed the orbits of the planets to be circular. In the late 18th century, Sir Isaac Newton developed his law of universal gravity based on Kepler's findings. These two laws are important discoveries upon which discoveries in modern physics and astronomy are based.

INTRODUCE

Begin the lesson by reminding students that a circle is the set of all points that are a fixed distance from a point, the center of the circle. After going through the first Explore, ask the students how they think an ellipse should be defined, based on the definition of the circle. Explain to the students that the ellipse is the set of all points the sum of whose distances to two points (the foci) is constant.

TEACH

1 EXPLORE

Materials

pushpins

string

Questioning Strategies

- Which parts of an ellipse do the two push pins represent? the foci

- How does using string to draw the ellipse ensure that the sum of the distances from each point drawn to the foci is constant? The same amount of string is stretched out to draw each point.

2 EXPLORE

Questioning Strategies

- What is the sum of distances PF_1 and PF_2 equal to? a constant d

Teaching Strategy

Students may have trouble seeing that the sum of the distances is always a constant. Draw an ellipse and show the students that the sum of the distances from any point on the ellipse to the foci is always constant by measuring some of the distances and recording them.

Name_____ Class_____ Date_____

Ellipses
Going Deeper

Essential question: *How can you model an ellipse?*

CC.9-12.G.GPE.3

1 EXPLORE   Draw an Ellipse

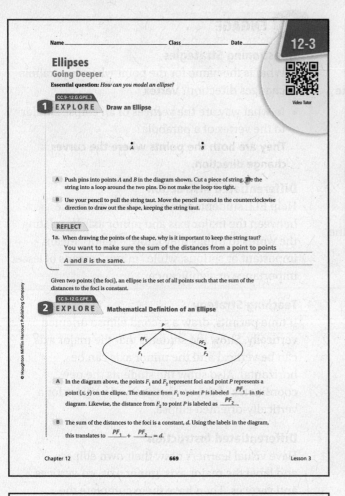

A   Push pins into points *A* and *B* in the diagram shown. Cut a piece of string. Tie the string into a loop around the two pins. Do not make the loop too tight.

B   Use your pencil to pull the string taut. Move the pencil around in the counterclockwise direction to draw out the shape, keeping the string taut.

REFLECT

1a. When drawing the points of the shape, why is it important to keep the string taut?

You want to make sure the sum of the distances from a point to points

A and B is the same.

Given two points (the foci), an ellipse is the set of all points such that the sum of the distances to the foci is constant.

CC.9-12.G.GPE.3

2 EXPLORE   Mathematical Definition of an Ellipse

A   In the diagram above, the points F_1 and F_2 represent foci and point *P* represents a point (x, y) on the ellipse. The distance from F_1 to point *P* is labeled ___PF_1___ in the diagram. Likewise, the distance from F_2 to point *P* is labeled as ___PF_2___.

B   The sum of the distances to the foci is a constant, *d*. Using the labels in the diagram, this translates to ___PF_1___ + ___PF_2___ $= d$.

Chapter 12   669   Lesson 3

REFLECT

2. How does the equation you wrote in part B reflect the definition of an ellipse?

The equation is $PF_1 + PF_2 = d$. The definition of an ellipse is the set of all points

such that the sum of the distance to two points is constant. In the equation, PF_1

and PF_2 represent distances from a point P to two other points F_1 and F_2, the foci.

This sum equals the constant d.

The standard form for the equation of a horizontal ellipse centered at the origin is $\frac{x^2}{a^2} + \frac{y^2}{b^2} = 1$, where *a* and *b* are constants and $a^2 - b^2 = c^2$, where *c* equals the distance from each focus to the center of the ellipse.

CC.9-12.G.GPE.3

3 EXAMPLE   Equations of an Ellipse

A   Find the equation of the ellipse with foci F_1 $(-3, 0)$ and F_2 $(3, 0)$ whose constant distance (sum of the distances to the foci) is 8.

Use the Distance Formula to write the distance from each focus to a point (x, y) on the ellipse.

$PF_1 = \sqrt{(x - (-3))^2 + (y - 0)^2} = \sqrt{(x+3)^2 + y^2}$

$PF_2 = \dfrac{\sqrt{(x-3)^2 + (y-0)^2}}{} = \dfrac{\sqrt{(x-3)^2 + y^2}}{}$

Write an equation of the ellipse.

$PF_1 + PF_2 = d$	Write formula.
$\sqrt{(x+3)^2 + y^2} + \sqrt{(x-3)^2 + y^2} = 8$	Substitute known values.
$\sqrt{(x+3)^2 + y^2} = 8 - \dfrac{\sqrt{(x-3)^2 + y^2}}{}$	Isolate one radical.
$(x+3)^2 + y^2 = 64 - \dfrac{16\sqrt{(x-3)^2 + y^2}}{} + (x-3)^2 + y^2$	Square each side.
$x^2 + 6x + 9 + y^2 = 64 - 16\sqrt{(x-3)^2 + y^2} + x^2 - 6x + 9 + y^2$	Simplify.
$\dfrac{12x}{} = 64 - 16\sqrt{(x-3)^2 + y^2}$	Combine like terms.
$\dfrac{12x - 64}{-16} = \sqrt{(x-3)^2 + y^2}$	Isolate the remaining radical.
$4 - \dfrac{\frac{3}{4}x}{} = \sqrt{(x-3)^2 + y^2}$	Simplify.
$\left(4 - \frac{3}{4}x\right)\left(\dfrac{4 - \frac{3}{4}x}{}\right) = (x-3)^2 + y^2$	Square each side.
$16 - 6x + \frac{9}{16}x^2 = x^2 - 6x + 9 + y^2$	Simplify.
$7 = \frac{7}{16}x^2 + y^2$	Combine like terms.
$1 = \frac{x^2}{16} + \dfrac{y^2}{7}$	Divide each side by 7 to write in standard form.

Chapter 12   670   Lesson 3

Questioning Strategies

- Which formula can you use to find the distance between two points on the coordinate plane? **the Distance Formula**

- Which expression can you use to find the distance from point $P(0, 6)$ to point $F_2(8, 0)$? $\sqrt{(0 - (8)^2 + (6 - 0)^2} = \sqrt{64 + 36} = 10$

EXTRA EXAMPLES

A What is the equation of the ellipse centered at the origin with foci $(-2, 0)$ and $(2, 0)$ and sum of the distances to the foci equal to 10? $\frac{x^2}{25} - \frac{y^2}{21} = 1$.

B What is the equation of the ellipse centered at the origin with foci $(-4, 0)$ and $(4, 0)$ that passes through the point $(0, -3)$? $\frac{x^2}{25} - \frac{y^2}{9} = 1$.

Avoid Common Errors

Remind students that to solve equations with radicals, they must first isolate the radical before squaring both sides of the equation.

Technology

Ellipses can be graphed on the TI-84 calculator by hitting the APPS key and selecting 8: Conics followed by 2: Ellipse. The calculator will display the standard form of an ellipse and prompt the user to enter values for a, b, h and k. If students want to graph ellipses to find intersection points and use the features under the CALC menu, they can solve the equation of the ellipse in terms of y and graph the two equations in the Y = menu.

Questioning Strategies

- What is the name for the point where a parabola changes direction? **Vertex**

- In what way are the vertices of an ellipse similar to the vertex of a parabola? **They are both the points where the curves change direction.**

Differentiated Instruction

Help ELL students remember the difference between the major axis and minor axis by relating the words to things they know. "Major" means important or serious, while "minor" means of lesser importance or significance.

Teaching Strategy

If time permits, draw a second ellipse oriented vertically. Show the students that the major axis can be vertical and the minor axis can be horizontal. Also show the students the new coordinates of the co-vertices and vertices for a vertically-oriented ellipse.

Differentiated Instruction

Have visual learners draw their own ellipses and label the major axis, minor axis, co-vertices and vertices. Then have them complete the following chart.

Axis	Name
longer	major
shorter	minor

Endpoints	Name
on major	vertices
on minor	co-vertices

B Find the equation of the ellipse with foci $F_1(-8, 0)$ and $F_2(8, 0)$ that passes through the point $P(0, 6)$.

Use the Distance Formula to find the sum of the distances to point P.

$PF_1 = \sqrt{(0 - (-8))^2 + (6 - 0)^2} = \sqrt{8^2 + 6^2} = \sqrt{100} = 10$

$PF_2 = \underline{\sqrt{(0 - 8)^2 + (6 - 0)^2}} = \underline{\sqrt{(-8)^2 + 6^2}} = \underline{10}$

The sum of the distances is $10 + \underline{10} = \underline{20}$

Use the Distance Formula to write the distance from each focus to a point (x, y) on the ellipse.

$PF_1 = \sqrt{(x - (-8))^2 + (y - 0)^2} = \sqrt{(x + 8)^2 + y^2}$

$PF_2 = \underline{\sqrt{(x - 8)^2 + (y - 0)^2}} = \underline{\sqrt{(x - 8)^2 + y^2}}$

Write an equation of the ellipse.

$PF_1 + PF_2 = d$	Write formula.
$\sqrt{(x + 8)^2 + y^2} + \sqrt{(x - 8)^2 + y^2} = 20$	Substitute known values.
$\sqrt{(x + 8)^2 + y^2} = 20 - \sqrt{(x - 8)^2 + y^2}$	Isolate one radical.
$(x + 8)^2 + y^2 = 400 - 40\sqrt{(x - 8)^2 + y^2} + (x - 8)^2 + y^2$	Square each side.
$x^2 + 16x + 64 + y^2 = 400 - 40\sqrt{(x - 8)^2 + y^2} + x^2 - 16x + 64 + y^2$	Simplify.
$32x = 400 - 40\sqrt{(x - 8)^2 + y^2}$	Combine like terms.
$\frac{32x - 400}{-40} = \sqrt{(x - 8)^2 + y^2}$	Isolate the remaining radical.
$10 - \frac{4}{5}x = \sqrt{(x - 8)^2 + y^2}$	Simplify.
$\left(10 - \frac{4}{5}x\right)\left(10 - \frac{4}{5}x\right) = (x - 8)^2 + y^2$	Square each side.
$100 - \frac{16x}{} + \frac{16}{25}x^2 = x^2 - 16x + 64 + y^2$	Simplify.
$\frac{36}{} = \frac{9}{25}x^2 + y^2$	Combine like terms.
$1 = \frac{x^2}{100} + \frac{y^2}{36}$	Divide each side by 7 to write in standard form.

REFLECT

3. Notice that when the sum of the distances to the foci equals 20, as in part A, the value of a^2, the denominator of the x^2 term is 100. If the sum of the distances is 8, as in part B, the value of a^2 is 16. What is the relationship between the sum of the distances and the value of a in the equation for an ellipse?

   The sum of the distances is equal to $2a$.

CC.9-12.G.GPE.3
4 ENGAGE   Parts of an Ellipse

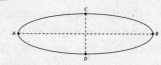

A A circle has a single radius but an ellipse has two axes. The longer of the two axes is called the **major axis**. The major axis is segment $\overline{AB}$ in the diagram above. The shorter of the two axes is called the **minor axis**. The minor axis is segment $\overline{CD}$ in the diagram above.

B The endpoints of the major axis are called vertices. The vertices in the ellipse shown are $\underline{A}$ and $\underline{B}$. The endpoints of the minor axis are called co-vertices. The co-vertices in the ellipse shown above are $\underline{C}$ and $\underline{D}$.

REFLECT

4. Consider an ellipse where the major axis and the minor axis are the same length. What happens to the values of a, b, and c? What shape is the ellipse?

   If $AB = CD$, then $a = b$, which means that both foci are the same distance from every point on the ellipse. If $a = b$, then $a^2 - b^2 = c^2$ gives $c^2 = 0$, which means the distance from the center of the ellipse to the foci is 0. So the foci coincide with the center, and the resulting shape is a circle.

CC.9-12.G.GPE.3
5 EXPLORE   The Standard Form of an Ellipse

Derive the standard form of a horizontal ellipse centered at the origin with vertices $(-a, 0)$ and $(a, 0)$, co-vertices $(0, -b)$ and $(0, b)$ and foci $F_1(-c, 0)$ and $F_2(c, 0)$.

Let $P(x, y)$ be a point on the ellipse. The distance from P to the foci are:

$PF_1 = \sqrt{(x - (-c))^2 + (y - 0)^2} = \sqrt{(x + c)^2 + y^2}$ and

$PF_2 = \sqrt{(x - c)^2 + (y - 0)^2} = \sqrt{(x - c)^2 + y^2}$

The sum of the distances to the foci is constant and is equal to the length of the major axis of the ellipse, which is $\underline{2a}$.

$\sqrt{(x + c)^2 + y^2} + \sqrt{(x - c)^2 + y^2} = \underline{2a}$

To solve the equation, you need to eliminate the radicals. Start by isolating one of the radicals. Then square both sides and simplify.

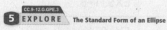

$\sqrt{(x + c)^2 + y^2} = 2a - \sqrt{(x - c)^2 + y^2}$

$(x + c)^2 + y^2 = \left(2a - \sqrt{(x - c)^2 + y^2}\right)\left(2a - \sqrt{(x - c)^2 + y^2}\right)$

© Houghton Mifflin Harcourt Publishing Company

5 EXPLORE

Questioning Strategies

- What is the length of the major axis of an ellipse in standard form? **2a**

- How can you shift a function to the left or right? **Add or subtract a positive constant to the *x*-value of the function.**

- How can you shift a function up or down? **Add or subtract a positive constant to the *y*-value of the function.**

Teaching Strategy

Lead students through the derivation of the equation for each ellipse. Instruct them to follow the procedure outlined in the student lesson.

Avoid Common Errors

Students often forget that $c^2 = a^2 - b^2$. Remind students that in an ellipse, c, the distance from the center to the focus, must be less than a, the distance from the center of the ellipse to a vertex.

Differentiated Instruction

Draw an ellipse with foci, vertices and center labeled so students can see how all the values of a, b and c are related.

CLOSE

Essential Question

How can you model an ellipse?

Horizontally-oriented ellipses can be modeled using the equation in standard form: $\frac{(x-h)^2}{a^2} + \frac{(y-k)^2}{b^2} = 1$, where the point (h, k) is the center of the ellipse, the coordinates of the foci are $(c + h, k)$ and $(-c + h, k)$ and $c^2 = a^2 - b^2$. Vertically-oriented ellipses can be modeled using the equation in standard form: $\frac{(x-h)^2}{b^2} + \frac{(y-k)^2}{a^2} = 1$, where the point (h, k) is the center of the ellipse, the coordinates of the foci are $(h, c + k)$ and $(h, -c + k)$ and $c^2 = a^2 - b^2$.

Summarize

Have students write a journal entry in which they describe how to derive the standard form for the equation of an ellipse. Tell students to include a diagram that shows the parts of an ellipse (vertices, co-vertices, major axis, minor axis, center, foci).

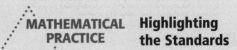
MATHEMATICAL PRACTICE — **Highlighting the Standards**

Modeling an ellipse using string and pushpins in 1 Explore provides an opportunity to address Mathematical Practices Standard 4 (Model with mathematics). Exercises 1–8 provide opportunities to address Mathematical Practices Standard 7 (Look for and make use of structure). Students match the given information with the standard form for the equation of an ellipse to find equations.

PRACTICE

Where skills are taught	Where skills are practiced
3 EXAMPLE	EXS. 1–8
4 EXAMPLE	EX. 9

$$x^2 + \frac{2cx}{} + \frac{c^2}{} + y^2 = 4a^2 - 4a\sqrt{(x-c)^2 + y^2} + \frac{(x-c)^2}{} + \frac{y^2}{}$$

$$x^2 + 2cx + c^2 + y^2 = 4a^2 - 4a\sqrt{(x-c)^2 + y^2} + x^2 - 2cx + c^2 + y^2$$

$$4cx = 4a^2 - 4a\sqrt{(x-c)^2 + y^2}$$

Now isolate the remaining radical. Again, square both sides and simplify.

$$4cx - \frac{4a^2}{} = -4a\sqrt{(x-c)^2 + y^2}$$

$$\frac{4cx - 4a^2}{-4a} = \sqrt{(x-c)^2 + y^2}$$

$$a - \frac{cx}{a} = \sqrt{(x-c)^2 + y^2}$$

$$\left(a - \frac{cx}{a}\right)\left(a - \frac{cx}{a}\right) = \frac{(x-c)^2 + y^2}{}$$

$$a^2 - 2cx + \frac{c^2 x^2}{a^2} = x^2 - 2cx + c^2 + y^2$$

$$a^2 + \frac{c^2 x^2}{a^2} = x^2 + c^2 + y^2$$

$$a^2 - c^2 = \left(\frac{a^2 - c^2}{a^2}\right)x^2 + y^2$$

Divide both sides by $a^2 - c^2$ to get 1 on the left side of the equation. Because the definition of of the standard form of an ellipse states that $c^2 = a^2 - b^2$, you know that $b^2 = a^2 - c^2$.

$$1 = \frac{x^2}{a^2} + \frac{y^2}{a^2 - c^2}$$

$$\frac{x^2}{a^2} + \frac{y^2}{b^2} = 1$$

REFLECT

5a. The standard form equation of an ellipse with center (h, k) is $\frac{(x-h)^2}{a^2} + \frac{(y-k)^2}{b^2} = 1$.

Use your knowledge of transformations of graphs to explain how to derive this equation from the equation of an ellipse centered at the origin, $\frac{x^2}{a^2} + \frac{y^2}{b^2} = 1$.

The graph of the ellipse centered at the origin is shifted horizontally h units and

vertically k units. The horizontal shift is shown in the term $x - h$. The vertical shift

is shown in the term $y - k$.

5b. The standard form of a vertical ellipse is $\frac{y^2}{a^2} + \frac{x^2}{b^2} = 1$. Write the coordinates of the

vertices, foci, and co-vertices of a vertical ellipse.

Vertices: $(0, a)$, $(0, -a)$; Foci: $(0, c)$, $(0, -c)$; Co-vertices: $(b, 0)$, $(-b, 0)$

PRACTICE

Write the equation of each ellipse described.

1. Write the equation of an ellipse with foci $(0, -\sqrt{6})$ and $(0, \sqrt{6})$ that passes through the point $(2, 0)$.

$$\frac{x^2}{4} + \frac{y^2}{10} = 1$$

2. Write the equation of an ellipse with foci $(0, -4\sqrt{5})$ and $(0, 4\sqrt{5})$ that passes through the point $(0, 10)$.

$$\frac{x^2}{20} + \frac{y^2}{100} = 1$$

3. Write the equation of an ellipse with foci $(-\sqrt{3}, 0)$ and $(\sqrt{3}, 0)$ that passes through the point $(0, -2)$.

$$\frac{x^2}{7} + \frac{y^2}{4} = 1$$

4. Write the equation of an ellipse with foci $(-3, 0)$ and $(3, 0)$ with sum of distances to the foci equal to 10.

$$\frac{x^2}{25} + \frac{y^2}{16} = 1$$

5. Write the equation of an ellipse with foci $(-6, 0)$ and $(6, 0)$ with sum of distances to the foci equal to 30.

$$\frac{x^2}{225} + \frac{y^2}{189} = 1$$

6. Write the equation of an ellipse with foci $(0, -5\sqrt{2})$ and $(0, 5\sqrt{2})$ that passes through the point $(0, 10\sqrt{3})$.

$$\frac{x^2}{250} + \frac{y^2}{300} = 1$$

7. Write the equation of an ellipse with foci $(0, 3)$ and $(0, -3)$ that passes through the point $(-7, 0)$.

$$\frac{x^2}{49} + \frac{y^2}{58} = 1$$

8. Write the equation of an ellipse with foci $(0, 10)$ and $(0, -10)$ with sum of distances to the foci equal to 44.

$$\frac{x^2}{384} + \frac{y^2}{484} = 1$$

9. Use your knowledge of x- and y- intercepts and the equation of an ellipse in standard form to explain the relationship between the intercepts of an ellipse centered at the origin and its vertices and co-vertices.

For a vertical ellipse, the y-intercepts are the vertices and the x-intercepts are the

co-vertices. For a horizontal ellipse, the y-intercepts are the co-vertices and the

x-intercepts are the vertices.

ADDITIONAL PRACTICE AND PROBLEM SOLVING

Assign these pages to help your students practice and apply important lesson concepts. For additional exercises, see the Student Edition.

Answers

Additional Practice

1. 82   **2.** 50

3. $\dfrac{x^2}{225} + \dfrac{y^2}{144} = 1$ **4.** $\dfrac{x^2}{6066} + \dfrac{y^2}{441} = 1$

5. $\dfrac{y^2}{2704} + \dfrac{x^2}{400} = 1$ **6.** $\dfrac{x^2}{3721} + \dfrac{y^2}{121} = 1$

7.

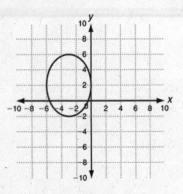

8.

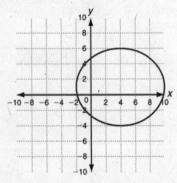

9. a. 7.5 ft tall, 5 ft wide

    b. $\dfrac{y^2}{56.25} + \dfrac{x^2}{25} = 1$

Problem Solving

1. a. $\dfrac{x^2}{182.25}$

    b. Since $182.25 > 132.25$, the major axis is horizontal.

    c. No; 13.5 ft is the distance from the center of the bridge to one side; so the width is 27 ft.

    d. $\sqrt{132.25}$; 11.5 ft

2. a. Vertices: $(17.55, 0)$, $(-17.55, 0)$; co-vertices: $(0, 23)$, $(0, -23)$

    b. $\dfrac{x^2}{308.00} + \dfrac{y^2}{529.00} = 1$

3. B   **4.** F

Additional Practice

Find the constant sum of an ellipse with the given foci and point on the ellipse.

1. $F_1(40, 0)$, $F_2(-40, 0)$, $P(0, -9)$

2. $F_1(0, -20)$, $F_2(0, 20)$, $P(15, 0)$

_____

_____

Write an equation in standard form for each ellipse with center (0, 0).

3. Vertex (15, 0), focus (9, 0)

4. Co-vertex (0, -21), focus (-75, 0)

_____

_____

5. Co-vertex (-20, 0), focus (0, 48)

6. Vertex (61, 0), focus (60, 0)

_____

_____

Graph each ellipse.

7. $\dfrac{(x+3)^2}{9} + \dfrac{(y-2)^2}{16} = 11$

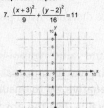

8. $\dfrac{(x-4)^2}{36} + \dfrac{(y-1)^2}{25} = 1$

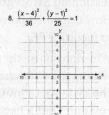

Solve.

9. Tom has a small semi-elliptical arch in his garden that he wants to enlarge. He wants to increase the height by a factor of 3 and increase the width by a factor of 2.5. The original arch can be modeled by the equation $\dfrac{y^2}{6.25} + \dfrac{x^2}{4} = 1$, measured in feet.

   a. Find the dimensions of the enlarged arch. _____

   b. Write an equation to model the enlarged arch. _____

Problem Solving

Lenore and Zane study a drawing of an ornamental bridge such as the one shown at right. It shows an elliptical arch that spans a narrow strait of water. The arch they are studying can be modeled by the following equation.

$$\dfrac{x^2}{182.25} + \dfrac{y^2}{132.25} = 1$$

1. Lenore wants to know the dimensions of the arch.

   a. Which term in the equation defines the horizontal axis?

   b. Write a comparative statement to show whether the major axis of the arch is horizontal or vertical.

   c. Lenore says that the width of the bridge is 13.5 feet. Is she correct? Explain.

   d. Write an expression for the height of the bridge. _____

2. Zane notes that this bridge is hardly high enough to pass under while standing up in a moderate-size boat. If he were to build a bridge, it would be at least 1.3 times as wide and twice as high.

   a. Find the vertices and co-vertices of Zane's bridge design.

   _____

   b. Write an equation for the design of Zane's bridge using his minimum dimensions. _____

Lenore finds architectural drawings for other bridges. Choose the letter for the best answer.

3. The equation for the arch of a bridge at the entrance to a wildlife park is $\dfrac{x^2}{225} + \dfrac{y^2}{324} = 1$. What is the width of this bridge?

   A 36 ft

   B 30 ft

   C 18 ft

   D 15 ft

4. The width and the height of one arch leading into part of an old town are both 17 feet. What is the equation for this bridge?

   F $\dfrac{x^2}{72.25} + \dfrac{y^2}{289} = 1$

   G $\dfrac{x^2}{72.25} + \dfrac{y^2}{72.25} = 1$

   H $\dfrac{x^2}{289} + \dfrac{y^2}{72.25} = 1$

   J $\dfrac{x^2}{289} + \dfrac{y^2}{289} = 1$

Hyperbolas
Going Deeper

Essential question: *Where does the standard form of the equation of a hyperbola come from?*

COMMON CORE **Standards for Mathematical Content**

CC.9-12.G.GPE.3 Derive the equations of ellipses and hyperbolas given foci and directrices.

Prerequisites

Radical functions

Solving radical equations and inequalities

Introduction to conic sections

Ellipses

Vocabulary

hyperbola

Math Background

Students have seen the graph of the function $y = \frac{1}{x}$ in their study of inverse variation. The graph of $y = \frac{1}{x}$ is a hyperbola with center $(0, 0)$ and asymptotes $x = 0$ and $y = 0$. This hyperbola is the parent function for the family of functions $y = \frac{a}{x - h} + k$, which are a special case where the equation of the hyperbola is a function. The equations seen in this lesson are not functions. The asymptotes are not horizontal and vertical lines, and the equations have two solutions for most values of x.

INTRODUCE

Start the lesson by reminding students of the equation of an ellipse from the previous lesson. Point out that another conic section can be defined given two points, the set of all points such that the difference of the distance to each of the two points is constant (rather than the sum).

TEACH

1 EXPLORE

Questioning Strategies

- How can you represent the distance from point P to focus F_1? **PF_1**

- Why do you use the absolute value symbol when writing the difference of the two distances? **The distance cannot be negative, so to ensure you don't get a negative value, use the absolute value to get the positive difference**

2 EXAMPLE

Questioning Strategies

- What formula can you use to find the distance between two points? **the Distance Formula**

EXTRA EXAMPLE

Find the constant difference of a hyperbola with foci $F_1(3, 0)$ and $F_2(-3, 0)$ that passes through the point $P(3, 8)$. **The constant difference is 2.**

Differentiated Instruction

Help visual learners by showing them a double cone and intersecting it with different planes to obtain the different conic sections. Emphasize the hyperbola. Show students that the absolute value of the difference of the distances from any point on the hyperbola to each of the foci is always constant. Measure the distance with a ruler and record the absolute value of the differences of the distances.

12-4

Video Tutor

Hyperbolas
Going Deeper

Essential question: *Where does the standard form of the equation of a hyperbola come from?*

Given two points (the foci), a **hyperbola** is defined to be the set of all points such that the absolute value of the difference of the distances to each of the two foci is constant.

CC.9-12.G.GPE.3
1 EXPLORE **Mathematical Definition of a Hyperbola**

A In the diagram above, the points F_1 and F_2 represent foci and point P represents a point (x, y) on the hyperbola. The distance from F_1 to point P is ___PF_1___. Likewise, the distance from F_2 to point P is ___PF_2___.

B The absolute value of the difference of the distances to the foci is a constant, d. In the diagram, this is $\left|\ PF_1\ -\ PF_2\ \right| = d$.

REFLECT

1. How does the equation you wrote in part B reflect the definition of a hyperbola?

   The equation is $|PF_1 - PF_2| = d$. The definition of a hyperbola is the set of all points

   such that the absolute value of the difference of the distance to two points is

   constant. In the equation, PF_1 and PF_2 represent distances from a point P to two

   other points F_1 and F_2, the foci. The absolute value of the difference of these

   quantities equals the constant d.

© Houghton Mifflin Harcourt Publishing Company

CC.9-12.G.GPE.3
2 EXAMPLE **Constant Difference of a Hyperbola**

Find the constant difference of a hyperbola with foci $F_1\,(-4, 0)$ and $F_2\,(4, 0)$ that passes through the point $P\,(5, 0)$.

Use the Distance Formula to find the difference of the distances to point P:

$PF_1 = \sqrt{(5-(-4))^2 + (0-0)^2} = \sqrt{9^2 + 0^2} = \sqrt{81} = 9$

$PF_2 = \underline{\sqrt{(5-4)^2 + (0-0)^2}} = \underline{\sqrt{1^2 + 0^2}} = \underline{1}$

The constant difference is $\left|\ \underline{9-1}\ \right| = \underline{8}$

REFLECT

2. How is finding the constant difference for a hyperbola similar to finding the constant sum for an ellipse?

   Both quantities involve the distance from foci to a point on the curve.

CC.9-12.G.GPE.3
3 ENGAGE **Parts of a Hyperbola**

A A hyperbola contains two symmetrical parts called branches. The vertices of a hyperbola are the endpoints of the transverse axis, which is contained in ___line m___ in the diagram above along with the foci. The vertices of the hyperbola above are points ___A___ and ___B___.

B The conjugate axis separates the symmetric parts of the hyperbola. The conjugate axis is the line segment ___CD___ in the diagram above. The endpoints of the conjugate axis are called co-vertices. The co-vertices in the hyperbola shown above are points ___D___ and ___C___.

© Houghton Mifflin Harcourt Publishing Company

Notes

Questioning Strategies

- What are the lines of symmetry for the hyperbola shown? segment *CD* and line *m*

- How can you remember the different formulas for vertical and horizontal formulas? Horizontal hyperbolas have x^2 first and x is the horizontal axis. Vertical hyperbolas have y^2 first and y is the vertical axis.

- If the hyperbola centered at the origin is horizontal, what is the relationship between the vertices and the x-intercepts? They are the same points.

- If the hyperbola centered at the origin is vertical, what is the relationship between the vertices and the y-intercepts? They are the same points.

Avoid Common Errors

Students often confuse the formula $c^2 = a^2 + b^2$ for a hyperbola with the relation $c^2 = a^2 - b^2$ used for an ellipse. Remind students that the foci of a hyperbola are located further from the center than the vertices. Therefore in a hyperbola, the value of c^2 (which is the square of the distance of the foci from the center) must be greater than the value of a^2 (which is the square of the distance of the vertices from the center).

Differentiated Instruction

English Language Learners may have trouble with the word *transverse*. Point out to the students that the prefix *trans-* means "across." Provide examples of other words with this prefix, such as *transportation* and *transcontinental*. The transverse axis is on a line of symmetry for a hyperbola that contains its vertices, center and foci.

Technology

Hyperbolas can be graphed on the TI-84 calculator by hitting the APPS key and selecting 8: Conics followed by 3: Hyperbola. The calculator will display the standard form of a hyperbola and prompt the user to enter values for *a*, *b*, *h* and *k*. If students want to graph hyperbolas to find intersection points and use the features under the CALC menu, they can solve the equation of the hyperbola in terms of *y* and graph the equations in the Y = menu.

Horizontal

Vertical

C There are two equations for a hyperbola centered at the origin. The formula

$\frac{x^2}{a^2} - \frac{y^2}{b^2} = 1$ is used for horizontal hyperbolas. The formula $\boxed{\frac{y^2}{a^2} - \frac{x^2}{b^2} = 1}$ is used for vertical hyperbolas.

D The asymptotes of a hyperbola are lines which the graph approaches as values of x (for horizontal) or y (for vertical) get very large. The equations of the asymptotes are $y = \pm \frac{b}{a}x$ for horizontal hyperbolas and $y = \pm \frac{a}{b}x$ for vertical hyperbolas.

E The coordinates of the vertices are $\underline{(0, -a)}$ and $\underline{(0, a)}$ for vertical hyperbolas and $\underline{(-a, 0)}$ and $\underline{(a, 0)}$ for horizontal hyperbolas.

F The coordinates of the co-vertices are $\underline{(-b, 0)}$ and $\underline{(b, 0)}$ for vertical hyperbolas and $\underline{(0, -b)}$ and $\underline{(0, b)}$ for horizontal hyperbolas.

G The distance from the center of the hyperbola to a focus is $\underline{c}$. The relation $\underline{c^2 = a^2 + b^2}$ is helpful for finding the equation of a hyperbola when you are given some of the information about it.

REFLECT

3a. Explain how you can tell if a hyperbola is vertical or horizontal based on the equation in standard form and your knowledge of x- and y-intercepts.

A vertical hyperbola centered at the origin will not have any x-intercepts.

A horizontal hyperbola centered at the origin will not have any y-intercepts. You can tell if an equation has x-intercepts by plugging in 0 for y. If the resulting equation can be solved for x, then it has x-intercepts (likewise for checking for y-intercepts).

3b. Explain how the vertices of a hyperbola centered at the origin are related to its intercepts.

The x-intercepts of a horizontal hyperbola are its vertices located at $(-a, 0)$, $(a, 0)$.

The y-intercepts of a vertical hyperbola are its vertices located at $(0, -a)$, $(0, a)$.

---

4 EXAMPLE   The Equation of a Hyperbola

A Write a standard form equation of a hyperbola centered at the origin that has foci $(-10, 0)$ and $(10, 0)$ and vertex $(\sqrt{40}, 0)$.

First write the standard form equation of a hyperbola centered at the origin. The hyperbola is $\underline{\text{horizontal}}$ because the foci are located on the $\underline{x\text{-axis}}$.

The equation is $\frac{x^2}{a^2} - \frac{y^2}{b^2} = 1$

The x-value of the vertex corresponds to the value of $\underline{a}$ in the standard form equation. Thus the equation becomes $\frac{x^2}{40} - \frac{y^2}{b^2} = 1$

The distance from the each focus to the center is the value of c. In this hyperbola c equals $\underline{10}$.

Use the relation $c^2 = a^2 + b^2$ to calculate the value of b^2.

$c^2 = a^2 + b^2 \rightarrow \underline{100} = \underline{40} + b^2$, or $b^2 = \underline{60}$

The equation of the hyperbola is $\frac{x^2}{40} - \frac{y^2}{60} = 1$

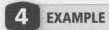

4 EXAMPLE

Questioning Strategies

- How can you tell if the hyperbola is vertical or horizontal? **Graph the vertices and foci to see which axis they are located on.**

- How are the coordinates of the vertices related to the value of a in the equation of the hyperbola in standard form? **For a horizontal hyperbola centered at the origin, the absolute value of the x-coordinate of each vertex is equal to the value of a.**

- How are the coordinates of the co-vertices related to the value of b in the equation of the hyperbola in standard form? **For a vertical hyperbola centered at the origin, the absolute value of the x-coordinate of each co-vertex is equal to the value of b.**

EXTRA EXAMPLE

A Write a standard form equation of a hyperbola centered at the origin that has foci $(-5, 0)$ and $(5, 0)$ and vertex $(-\sqrt{8}, 0)$. $\frac{x^2}{8} - \frac{y^2}{17} = 1$

B Write a standard form equation of a hyperbola centered at the origin that has vertex $(0, 6)$ and co-vertex $(-2, 0)$. $\frac{y^2}{36} - \frac{x^2}{4} = 1$

Teaching Strategy

Encourage students to write out the appropriate standard form equation of each hyperbola and fill in the values as they calculate them.

Differentiated Instruction

Some students may benefit from graphing the given information in order to determine the orientation of the hyperbola. Show students graphs of each hyperbola in the Example.

5 EXPLORE

Questioning Strategies

- How can you represent the constant difference using the Distance Formula? **Use the Distance Formula to find the distance from each focus to a point on the hyperbola.**

Teaching Strategy

Lead students through the derivation of the standard form equation of a hyperbola. Instruct them to follow the procedure outlined in the student lesson. Remind them that $c^2 = a^2 + b^2$ for a hyperbola.

6 EXAMPLE

Questioning Strategies

- What does the value of a tell you about the graph of a hyperbola? **a and $-a$ are the x-coordinates of the vertices of a horizontal hyperbola centered at the origin (and are the y-coordinates of the vertices of a vertical hyperbola).**

- What does the value of b tell you about the graph of a hyperbola? **b and $-b$ are the y-coordinates of the co-vertices of a horizontal hyperbola centered at the origin (and are the x-coordinates of the co-vertices of a vertical hyperbola).**

- What are the equations of the asymptotes of a horizontal hyperbola centered at the origin? **$y = \pm\frac{b}{a}x$**

EXTRA EXAMPLE

Describe the hyperbola $\frac{y^2}{16} - \frac{x^2}{4} = 1$. **vertical hyperbola centered at $(0, 0)$ with foci $(0, -2\sqrt{5})$ and $(0, 2\sqrt{5})$, vertices $(0, 4)$ and $(0, -4)$, co-vertices $(2, 0)$ and $(-2, 0)$, asymptotes: $y = \pm 2x$.**

B Write a standard form equation of a hyperbola centered at the origin that has vertex $(0, 5)$ and co-vertex $(2, 0)$.

First write the standard form equation of a hyperbola centered at the origin. The hyperbola is ___vertical___ because the vertex is located on the ___y-axis___.

The equation is $\dfrac{y^2}{a^2} - \dfrac{x^2}{b^2} = 1$

The y-coordinate of the vertex is the value of ___a___ in the equation.

The equation becomes: $\dfrac{y^2}{25} - \dfrac{x^2}{b^2} = 1$

The x-coordinate of the co-vertex is the value of ___b___ in the equation.

The equation for the hyperbola is $\dfrac{y^2}{25} - \dfrac{x^2}{4} = 1$

REFLECT

4a. The standard form equation of a horizontal hyperbola with center (h, k) is $\dfrac{(x-h)^2}{a^2} - \dfrac{(y-k)^2}{b^2} = 1$. Use your knowledge of transformations of graphs to explain how to get this equation from the equation of a hyperbola centered at the origin, $\dfrac{x^2}{a^2} - \dfrac{y^2}{b^2} = 1$.

The graph of the hyperbola centered at the origin is shifted horizontally h units and vertically k units. The horizontal shift is shown in the term $x - h$. The vertical shift is shown in the term $y - k$.

4b. Using the equation of the hyperbola in standard form, explain why any hyperbola centered at the origin does not contain the point $(0, 0)$.

If you plug $(0, 0)$ into the equation in standard form, you get $0 = 1$, which cannot be true. Therefore $(0, 0)$ is not on the graph of the hyperbola.

CC.9-12.G.GPE.3

5 EXPLORE   Deriving The Equation of a Hyperbola

Use the relation $c^2 = a^2 + b^2$ to derive the standard form equation for a horizontal hyperbola centered at the origin, with foci $(-c, 0)$ and $(c, 0)$ and length of the transverse axis equal to $2a$.

Use the Distance Formula to find the constant difference to a point $P(x, y)$ on the hyperbola.

$PF_1 = \sqrt{(x-(-c))^2 + (y-0)^2} = \sqrt{(x+c)^2 + y^2}$

$PF_2 = \sqrt{(x-c)^2 + (y-0)^2} = \sqrt{(x-c)^2 + y^2}$

The constant difference is $\left| \sqrt{(x+c)^2 + y^2} - \sqrt{(x-c)^2 + y^2} \right|$.

Assume that the difference is positive. Set the constant difference equal to $2a$, the length of the transverse axis.

$\sqrt{(x+c)^2 + y^2} - \sqrt{(x-c)^2 + y^2} = 2a$.

Isolate one of the radicals. Square both sides. Then simplify the result.

$\sqrt{(x+c)^2 + y^2} = 2a + \sqrt{(x-c)^2 + y^2}$

$(x+c)^2 + y^2 = \left(2a + \sqrt{(x-c)^2 + y^2}\right)\left(2a + \sqrt{(x-c)^2 + y^2}\right)$

$x^2 + 2cx + c^2 + y^2 = 4a^2 + 4a\sqrt{(x-c)^2 + y^2} + (x-c)^2 + y^2$

$x^2 + 2cx + c^2 + y^2 = 4a^2 + 4a\sqrt{(x-c)^2 + y^2} + x^2 - 2cx + c^2 + y^2$

$4cx = 4a^2 + 4a\sqrt{x^2 - 2cx + c^2 + y^2}$

Isolate the remaining radical. Square both sides. Then simplify the result.

$\dfrac{4cx - 4a^2}{4a} = \sqrt{x^2 - 2cx + c^2 + y^2}$

$\left(\dfrac{cx-a^2}{a}\right)\left(\dfrac{cx-a^2}{a}\right) = x^2 - 2cx + c^2 + y^2$

$\dfrac{c^2x^2}{a^2} - 2cx + a^2 = x^2 - 2cx + c^2 + y^2$

$\left(\dfrac{c^2-a^2}{a^2}\right)x^2 - y^2 = c^2 - a^2$

Divide by $c^2 - a^2$ to get 1 on the right side of the equation. Because $c^2 = a^2 + b^2$, you know that $b^2 = c^2 - a^2$.

$\dfrac{x^2}{a^2} - \dfrac{y^2}{c^2-a^2} = 1$

$\dfrac{x^2}{a^2} - \dfrac{y^2}{b^2} = 1$

CLOSE

Essential Question
Where does the standard form of the equation of a hyperbola come from?
The standard form of the equation of a hyperbola comes from the definition of the hyperbola itself; given two points (foci) the hyperbola is the set of all points such that the absolute value of the difference of the distances to each of the two foci is constant. The derivation of the formula arises from using the Distance Formula.

Summarize
Have students write a journal entry in which they describe how to derive the standard form for the equation of a hyperbola. Tell students to include a diagram that shows the parts of a hyperbola (vertices, co-vertices, transverse axis, conjugate axis, asymptotes). The students should include a diagram for both vertical and horizontal hyperbolas.

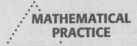

MATHEMATICAL PRACTICE   Highlighting the Standards

Exercises 1–3 provide opportunities to address Mathematical Practices Standard 7 (Look for and make use of structure). Students match the given information with the standard form for the equation of a hyperbola to find equations and graph the curves.

PRACTICE

Where skills are taught	Where skills are practiced
4 EXAMPLE	EXS. 1–3
6 EXAMPLE	EXS. 2, 3

REFLECT

5. In the equation of an ellipse, where c is the distance from a focus to the center and a is the distance from a vertex to the center, $c^2 = a^2 - b^2$. In the equation of a hyperbola, where c and a stand for the same things, $c^2 = a^2 + b^2$. Explain why this makes sense geometrically, comparing the relative distances of the foci and vertices to the center of the hyperbola and the ellipse.

In a hyperbola, the vertices are closer to the center than the foci, so it makes sense
that c^2 would be larger than a^2 in a hyperbola. In an ellipse, the foci are closer to
the center than the vertices, so it makes sense that c^2 would be smaller than a^2 for
an ellipse.

6 EXAMPLE   Graphing a Hyperbola

Graph the hyperbola $\frac{x^2}{25} - \frac{y^2}{9} = 1$.

The equation is in standard form $\frac{x^2}{a^2} - \frac{y^2}{b^2} = 1$ so the transverse axis
lies on the __x-axis__.

Since $a^2 = $ __25__, the vertices are $\left(\boxed{-5}, \boxed{0} \right)$ and $\left(\boxed{5}, \boxed{0} \right)$.

Since $b^2 = $ __9__, the co-vertices are $\left(\boxed{0}, \boxed{3} \right)$ and $\left(\boxed{0}, \boxed{-3} \right)$.

The equations for the asymptotes are $y = \boxed{\pm \frac{3}{5}x}$.

Graph the hyperbola below using the information above.

REFLECT

6. Explain how the asymptotes can help you graph the hyperbola.
The asymptotes are lines which the graph approaches but does not touch. The
asymptotes can be used as a border when sketching the curve.

PRACTICE

Write the equation of each hyperbola described.

1. Write the equation of the hyperbolas with the following characteristics:

(a) vertices $(0, -\sqrt{6})$ and $(0, \sqrt{6})$ and co-vertices $(2, 0)$ and $(-2, 0)$. $\dfrac{y^2}{6} - \dfrac{x^2}{4} = 1$

(b) vertices $(4, 0)$ and $(-4, 0)$ and co-vertices $(0, 1)$ and $(0, -1)$. $\dfrac{x^2}{16} - y^2 = 1$

(c) foci $(0, -\sqrt{5})$ and $(0, \sqrt{5})$ and vertex $(0, 1)$. $y^2 - \dfrac{x^2}{4} = 1$

(d) foci $(10, 0)$ and $(-10, 0)$ and vertex $(3, 0)$. $\dfrac{x^2}{9} - \dfrac{y^2}{91} = 1$

(e) focus $(5, 0)$ and co-vertex $(0, \sqrt{2})$ $\dfrac{x^2}{23} - \dfrac{y^2}{2} = 1$

2. For the hyperbola $\frac{x^2}{25} - \frac{y^2}{49} = 1$.

(a) Is the hyperbola vertical or horizontal? __horizontal__

(b) What are the coordinates of the vertices and co-vertices?
vertices: $(-5, 0)$ and $(5, 0)$, co-vertices $(0, 7)$ and $(0, -7)$

(c) What are the equations of the asymptotes? $y = \pm \frac{7}{5}x$

(d) Sketch the graph of the hyperbola on the axes provided.

3. For the hyperbola $\frac{y^2}{100} - \frac{x^2}{64} = 1$.

(a) Is the hyperbola vertical or horizontal?
__vertical__

(b) What are the coordinates of the vertices and co-vertices?
vertices: $(0, 10)$, $(0, -10)$, co-vertices: $(8, 0)$
and $(-8, 0)$.

(c) What are the equations of the asymptotes?
$y = \pm \frac{5}{4}x$

(d) Sketch the graph of the hyperbola on the axes provided.

Assign these pages to help your students practice and apply important lesson concepts. For additional exercises, see the Student Edition.

Answers

Additional Practice

1. 14 **2.** 16

3. $\dfrac{y^2}{144} - \dfrac{x^2}{256} = 1$ **4.** $\dfrac{x^2}{576} - \dfrac{y^2}{49} = 1$

5. $\dfrac{y^2}{289} - \dfrac{x^2}{1} = 1$ **6.** $\dfrac{x^2}{900} - \dfrac{y^2}{700} = 1$

7. Vertices: $(14, 0)$, $(-14, 0)$; co-vertices: $(0, 7)$, $(0, -7)$; asymptotes: $1, y = \dfrac{1}{2}x, y = -\dfrac{1}{2}x^2$

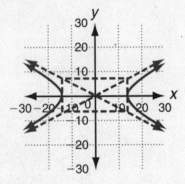

8. Vertices: $(0, 10)$, $(0, -2)$; co-vertices: $(9, 4)$, $(-9, 4)$;

asymptotes: $y = \dfrac{2}{3}x + 4, y = -\dfrac{2}{3}x + 4$

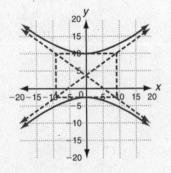

9. 167.7 million miles

Problem Solving

1. a. Since the y^2 term is negative, the transverse axis is horizontal.

b. Vertices: $(25, 0)$ and $(-25, 0)$; covertices: $(0, 45)$ and $(0, -45)$

c. The diameter of the tower is equal to the distance between the vertices.

d. 50 ft

2. a. $(0, 18)$, $(0, -18)$

b. $\dfrac{x^2}{100} - \dfrac{y^2}{324} =$

3. a. $y = \pm 1.8x; y = \pm 1.8x$

b. The asymptotes are the same.

4. C **5.** H

Additional Practice

Find the constant difference for a hyperbola with the given foci and point on the hyperbola.

1. $F_1(0, 11)$, $F_2(0, -11)$, $P(0, 7)$

2. $F_1(-9, 0)$, $F_2(9, 0)$, $P(-8, 0)$

Write an equation in standard form for each hyperbola with center (0, 0).

3. Co-vertex $(-16, 0)$, focus $(0, -20)$

4. Vertex $(24, 0)$, focus $(-25, 0)$

5. Vertex $(0, -17)$, co-vertex $(1, 0)$

6. Vertex $(30, 0)$, focus $(-40, 0)$

Find the vertices, co-vertices, and asymptotes of each hyperbola, and then graph.

7. $\dfrac{x^2}{196} - \dfrac{y^2}{49} = 1$

8. $\dfrac{(y-4)^2}{36} - \dfrac{x^2}{81} = 1$

Solve.

9. A comet's path as it approaches the sun is modeled by one branch of the hyperbola $\dfrac{y^2}{1122} - \dfrac{x^2}{39,355} = 1$, where the sun is at the corresponding focus. Each unit of the coordinate plane represents one million miles. How close does the comet come to the sun? _____

Problem Solving

A brochure for a new amusement park describes the design of the towers that characterize the park. The outline of the central and largest tower can be modeled by the hyperbola $\dfrac{x^2}{625} - \dfrac{y^2}{2025} = 1$, with dimensions in feet. The smaller towers are scaled-down versions of the central tower, and so their dimensions are in proportion to those of the central tower.

1. What is the diameter of the central tower at its narrowest part?

   a. Explain how to determine whether the transverse axis of a hyperbola is horizontal or vertical.
   _____

   b. Find the vertices and co-vertices.
   _____

   c. How can you use these data to answer the question?
   _____

   d. What is the diameter of the tower at its narrowest part? _____

2. The vertices of a smaller tower are $(10, 0)$ and $(-10, 0)$.

   a. Name the coordinates of the co-vertices. _____

   b. What is the equation for the outline of the smaller tower? _____

3. How do the asymptotes of the hyperbolas of the larger central tower and the smaller tower compare?

   a. Find the asymptotes of the two towers. _____

   b. Compare the asymptotes of the two towers. _____

Choose the letter for the best answer.

4. The hyperbola that models a third tower has vertices $(0, 9)$ and $(0, -9)$ and focus $(0, 15)$. The solution to which of the following equations gives the denominator of the y^2 term in the equation of the hyperbola?

   A $15^2 = a^2 - 9^2$

   B $15^2 = a^2 + 18^2$

   C $15^2 = b^2 + 9^2$

   D $15^2 = b^2 - 18^2$

5. The outline of a tower at the park's Welcome Center can be modeled by the equation $\dfrac{x^2}{25} - \dfrac{y^2}{81} = 1$. What are the asymptotes of the hyperbola?

   F $y = \pm 0.31x$

   G $y = \pm 0.56x$

   H $y = \pm 1.8x$

   J $y = \pm 3.24x$

Notes

Parabolas
Going Deeper

Essential question: *What are the defining features of a parabola?*

COMMON CORE Standards for Mathematical Content

CC.9-12.G.GPE.2 Derive the equation of a parabola given a focus and directrix. *

Prerequisites

Using transformations to graph quadratic equations
Properties of quadratic functions in standard form

Vocabulary

axis of symmetry

directix

focus

vertex

Math Background

Students encounter the parabola for the first time, not as a member of the family of conic sections, but as the graph of the quadratic function $y = ax^2 + bx + c$. This function and its graph model a rich variety of real-world phenomena in science, engineering, business, and a variety of other fields. Analysis of this function leads to the development of the quadratic formula for solving quadratic equations, and methods for graphing parabolas based on the locations of their vertices and axes of symmetry. A unifying characteristic of all such parabolas is that they have vertical axes of symmetries, which reveals them as special cases of the more generalized parabola introduced in this lesson, described by the general equation of conic sections $Ax^2 + Bxy + Cy^2 + Dx + Ey + F = 0$, where $B^2 - 4AC = 0$. In this lesson, students will investigate parabolas with both vertical and horizontal axes of symmetry. All conics are defined in terms of distance: the circle (the set of points equidistant from a fixed point); the ellipse (the set of points whose sum of distances from two fixed points is constant); the hyperbola (the set of points whose difference of distances from two fixed points is constant); and the parabola (the set of points equidistant from a fixed point, the focus, and a line, the directrix).

INTRODUCE

Review the use of *distance* in the definitions of the conic sections already studied: the circle, the ellipse, and the hyperbola. Ask students to propose other ways a set of points in the coordinate plane could be defined in terms of distance, and to describe and sketch the sets, if possible. (Example: The set of points equidistance from two parallel lines would be a line parallel to the given lines and equidistant between them.) If no one suggests a set of points equidistant from a point and a line, introduce the idea and ask students to sketch such a set. Close the discussion by stating that the definition describes a curve they have already encountered in their study of quadratic equations, the parabola.

TEACH

1 EXPLORE

Questioning Strategies

- In the second step of the derivation in Part A, why are $(0, p)$ and $(x, -p)$ substituted for (x_1, y_1) and (x_2, y_2)? **They are substituted to show that the distances from $(0, p)$ and $(x, -p)$ to (x, y) are equal.**

- How can you show that the standard form of the equation of a parabola $y = \frac{1}{4p} x^2$ is equivalent to  the alternate form $x^2 = 4py$? **Multiply both sides of the equation by 4p.**

2 EXAMPLE

Questioning Strategies

- Why is the equation of the first parabola given in the form "$x =$" while the equation of the second parabola is given in the form "$y =$"? **The first parabola has the x-axis as its axis of symmetry. The second parabola has the y-axis as its axis of symmetry.**

Name _____ Class _____ Date _____

12-5

Parabolas
Going Deeper

Essential question: *What are the defining features of a parabola?*

Like the circle, the ellipse, and the hyperbola, the parabola can be defined in terms of distance. A parabola is the set of all points in a plane that are the same distance from a fixed point, called the **focus**, and a fixed line, called the **directrix**. The midpoint of the shortest segment connecting the focus and the directrix is the **vertex** of the parabola. The **axis of symmetry** is a line perpendicular to the directrix and passes through the focus and the vertex.

CC.9-12.G.GPE.2

1 EXPLORE Deriving the Equation of a Parabola

Use distance on the coordinate plane to find the equation of a parabola.

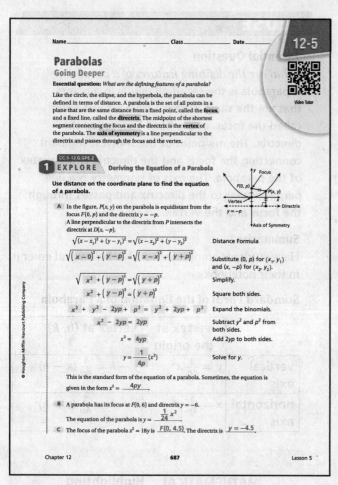

A In the figure, $P(x, y)$ on the parabola is equidistant from the focus $F(0, p)$ and the directrix $y = -p$.
A line perpendicular to the directrix from P intersects the directrix at $D(x, -p)$.

$\sqrt{(x - x_1)^2 + (y - y_1)^2} = \sqrt{(x - x_2)^2 + (y - y_2)^2}$	Distance Formula
$\sqrt{(x - 0)^2 + (y - p)^2} = \sqrt{(x - x)^2 + (y + p)^2}$	Substitute $(0, p)$ for (x_1, y_1) and $(x, -p)$ for (x_2, y_2).
$\sqrt{x^2 + (y - p)^2} = \sqrt{(y + p)^2}$	Simplify.
$x^2 + (y - p)^2 = (y + p)^2$	Square both sides.
$x^2 + y^2 - 2yp + p^2 = y^2 + 2yp + p^2$	Expand the binomials.
$x^2 - 2yp = 2yp$	Subtract y^2 and p^2 from both sides.
$x^2 = 4yp$	Add $2yp$ to both sides.
$y = \dfrac{1}{4p}(x^2)$	Solve for y.

This is the standard form of the equation of a parabola. Sometimes, the equation is given in the form $x^2 = \underline{4py}$.

B A parabola has its focus at $F(0, 6)$ and directrix $y = -6$.
The equation of the parabola is $y = \underline{\dfrac{1}{24}x^2}$.

C The focus of the parabola $x^2 = 18y$ is $\underline{F(0, 4.5)}$. The directrix is $\underline{y = -4.5}$.

REFLECT

1. In the first step of the derivation of the equation of a parabola, the points $(0, p)$ and $(x, -p)$ were substituted for (x_1, y_1) and (x_2, y_2), yielding the equation $\sqrt{(x - 0)^2 + (y - p)^2}$ $= \sqrt{(x - x)^2 + (y + p)^2}$. Compare that equation with the equation you would write if the parabola were rotated 90° so that its axis of symmetry were horizontal, as in the figure at the right. How would the remaining equations in the derivation be affected? What would the derivation yield as the standard form of the equation of a parabola with a horizontal axis of symmetry?

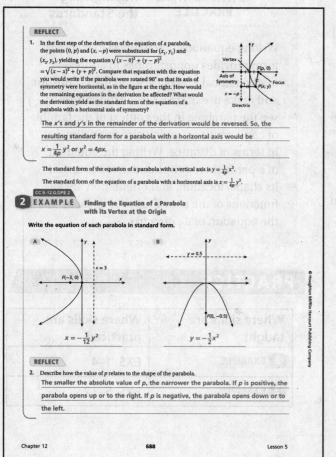

The x's and y's in the remainder of the derivation would be reversed. So, the

resulting standard form for a parabola with a horizontal axis would be

$x = \dfrac{1}{4p}y^2$ or $y^2 = 4px$.

The standard form of the equation of a parabola with a vertical axis is $y = \dfrac{1}{4p}x^2$.

The standard form of the equation of a parabola with a horizontal axis is $x = \dfrac{1}{4p}y^2$.

CC.9-12.G.GPE.2

2 EXAMPLE Finding the Equation of a Parabola with its Vertex at the Origin

Write the equation of each parabola in standard form.

A $x = -\dfrac{1}{12}y^2$

B $y = -\dfrac{1}{2}x^2$

REFLECT

2. Describe how the value of p relates to the shape of the parabola.

The smaller the absolute value of p, the narrower the parabola. If p is positive, the

parabola opens up or to the right. If p is negative, the parabola opens down or to

the left.

Questioning Strategies

- What does the sign of the fraction $\frac{1}{4p}$ in the standard form of the equation of a parabola tell you about the graph of the parabola? **If the sign is positive, the parabola opens upward or to the right. Otherwise, it opens downward or to the left.**

EXTRA EXAMPLE

A Write the equation of a parabola with focus $(0, 1)$ and directrix $y = -1$. $y = \frac{1}{4}x^2$

B Write the equation of a parabola with focus $(-2, 0)$ and directrix $x = 2$. $x = -\frac{1}{8}y^2$

3 EXAMPLE

Questioning Strategies

- In Part A, how can you find the vertex of the parabola? **The vertex is halfway between the focus (3, 8) and the point on the directrix with the same x-coordinate as the focus, that is, the point (3, 4). So the vertex is (3, 6).**

- If you know the distance from the focus of a parabola to the directrix, how can you find the value of p? **Divide the distance from the focus to the directrix by 2.**

EXTRA EXAMPLE

Write the equation of a parabola with focus $(-2, 5)$ and directrix $y = 1$. $y - 3 = \frac{1}{8}(x + 2)^2$

Technology

Parabolas with vertical axes of symmetry are functions, so students can graph them on graphing calculators simply by inputting the equations of the parabolas in the form $y = f(x)$. For parabolas with horizontal axes of symmetry, they'll need to write the equations in the form $y = f(x)$ and then input two functions: one using a positive square root and the other using a negative square root.

CLOSE

Essential Question

What are the defining features of a parabola?
A parabola is the set of all points in a plane that are the same distance from a fixed point, called the focus, and a fixed line, called the directrix. The midpoint of the shortest segment connecting the focus and the directrix is the vertex of the parabola. The axis of symmetry is a line perpendicular to the directrix and passes through the focus and the vertex.

Summarize

Have students complete the table below and enter it in their notebooks.

Standard Form of the Equation of a Parabola

	vertex at the origin	vertex at (h, k)
vertical axis	$y = \frac{1}{4p}x^2$	$y - k = \frac{1}{4p}(x - h)^2$
horizontal axis	$x = \frac{1}{4p}y^2$	$x - h = \frac{1}{4p}(y - k)^2$

MATHEMATICAL PRACTICE — Highlighting the Standards

Writing equations of parabolas in standard form provides opportunities to address Mathematical Practices Standard 7 (Look for and make use of structure). Students must see the parabola in the context of the family of conic sections, which also are defined in terms of distance. Writing the equation of a parabola requires understanding that its shape, location, and orientation are all functions of the coordinates of its focus and the equation of its directrix.

PRACTICE

Where skills are taught	Where skills are practiced
2 EXAMPLE	EXS. 1–4
3 EXAMPLE	EXS. 5–12

For the circle, the ellipse, and the hyperbola, translating the center of the conic section from $(0, 0)$ to (h, k) changed x in the standard form of the equation of the figure to $x - h$ and changed y to $y - k$. A similar transformation takes place when the vertex of a parabola is translated from $(0, 0)$ to (h, k).

Direction of Axis of Symmetry	Equation of Axis of Symmetry	Standard Form of the Equation of a Parabola with Vertex at (h, k)
Vertical	$x = h$	$y - k = \frac{1}{4p}(x - h)^2$
Horizontal	$y = k$	$x - h = \frac{1}{4p}(y - k)^2$

3 EXAMPLE Finding the Equation of a Parabola with its Vertex Not at the Origin

Use the focus and directrix to sketch the parabola. Then find the equation of the parabola.

A A parabola has focus $(3, 8)$ and directrix $y = 4$.

The vertex of the parabola is ___(3, 6)___. So $h =$ ___3___ and $k =$ ___6___.

Use the fact that p equals the distance from the focus to the vertex to find p: $p =$ ___2___.

Standard form of the equation of the parabola: ___$y - 6 = \frac{1}{8}(x - 3)^2$___

B A parabola has focus $(3, -1)$ and directrix $x = -2$.

The vertex of the parabola is ___(0.5, -1)___. So $h =$ ___0.5___ and $k =$ ___-1___.

Find p: $p =$ ___2.5___.

Standard form of the equation of the parabola: ___$x - 0.5 = \frac{1}{10}(y + 1)^2$___

REFLECT

3. During the study of quadratic functions, the standard form of a quadratic function is given as $y = ax^2 + bx + c$. Find values of a, b, and c which show that this equation is equivalent to the standard form given in this lesson $y - k = \frac{1}{4p}(x - h)^2$. Explain how you found the values.

$a = \frac{1}{4p}$, $b = \frac{-h}{2p}$, and $c = \frac{h^2 + 4pk}{4p}$. Rewrite the standard form from this lesson in the form $y = ax^2 + bx + c$. a will be the coefficient of x^2, b will be the coefficient of x, and c will be the constant.

PRACTICE

Write the equation of each parabola in standard form.

Focus	Directrix	Equation
1. $F(2, 0)$	$x = -2$	$x = \frac{1}{8}y^2$
2. $F(0, 8)$	$y = -8$	$y = \frac{1}{32}x^2$
3. $F(-20, 0)$	$x = 20$	$x = -\frac{1}{80}y^2$
4. $F\left(0, -\frac{1}{12}\right)$	$y = \frac{1}{12}$	$y = -3x^2$
5. $F(5, 5)$	$y = -3$	$y - 1 = \frac{1}{16}(x - 5)^2$
6. $F(3, 0)$	$x = -2$	$x - \frac{1}{2} = \frac{1}{10}y^2$
7. $F(4, -3)$	$y = 6$	$y - \frac{3}{2} = -\frac{1}{18}(x - 4)^2$
8. $F(8, 0)$	$y = 4$	$y - 2 = -\frac{1}{8}(x - 8)^2$
9. $F(10, -3)$	$x = 5$	$x - 7\frac{1}{2} = \frac{1}{10}(y + 3)^2$
10. $F(6, 2)$	$x = 4$	$x - 5 = \frac{1}{4}(y - 2)^2$
11. $F(7, -7)$	$x = -2$	$x - \frac{5}{2} = \frac{1}{18}(y + 7)^2$
12. $F(-1, 2)$	$y = -1$	$y - \frac{1}{2} = \frac{1}{6}(x + 1)^2$

Notes

Assign these pages to help your students practice and apply important lesson concepts. For additional exercises, see the Student Edition.

Answers

Additional Practice

1. $x = \frac{1}{18}y^2 + \frac{3}{2}$ **2.** $x = 0.1y - 1.5$

3. $y = \frac{1}{8}x^2$ **4.** $x = \frac{1}{36}y^2$

5. $x = -\frac{1}{24}y^2$ **6.** $y = -\frac{1}{12}x^2$

7. Vertex $(1, 0)$; $p = -3$; axis of symmetry $y = 0$; focus $(-2, 0)$; directrix $x = 4$

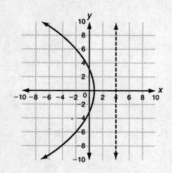

8. Vertex $(1, -2)$; $p = 1$; axis of symmetry $x = 1$; focus $(1, -1)$; directrix $y = -3$

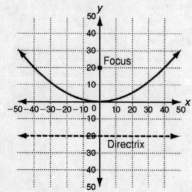

9. a. $y = \frac{1}{24}x^2$

  b. 13.5 inches

Problem Solving

1. a. $(0, 0)$

b. $4p = 80$, $p = 20$

c. $x = 0$

d. $(0, 20)$

e. $y = -20$

f.

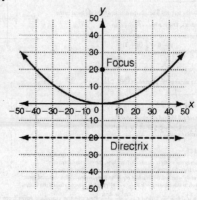

2. a. Possible answer: A parabola is the set of points in a plane that are equidistant from the focus and the directrix.

  b. $y = \frac{1}{20}x^2$

3. A   **4.** J

Additional Practice

Use the Distance Formula to find the equation of a parabola with the given focus and directrix.

1. $F(6, 0)$, $x = -3$

2. $F(1, 0)$, $x = -4$

Write the equation in standard form for each parabola.

3. Vertex $(0, 0)$, directrix $y = -2$

4. Vertex $(0, 0)$, focus $(9, 0)$

5. Focus $(-6, 0)$, directrix $x = 6$

6. Vertex $(0, 0)$, focus $(0, -3)$

Find the vertex, value of p, axis of symmetry, focus, and directrix of each parabola. Then graph.

7. $x - 1 = -\dfrac{1}{12}y^2$

8. $y + 2 = \dfrac{1}{4}(x-1)^2$

Solve.

9. A spotlight has parabolic cross sections.

   a. Write an equation for a cross section of the spotlight if the bulb is 6 inches from the vertex and the vertex is placed at the origin. _____

   b. If the spotlight has a diameter of 36 inches at its opening, find the depth of the spotlight if the bulb is 6 inches from the vertex. _____

Problem Solving

At a bungee-jumping contest, Gavin makes a jump that can be modeled by the equation $x^2 - 12x - 12y + 84 = 0$, with dimensions in feet.

1. Gavin wants to know how close he came to the ground during his jump.

   a. Classify the shape of his path. Identify the values for the coefficients of each term, and determine what conic section models his path.

   b. Write the equation of his path in standard form by completing the square.

   c. Which point on the path identifies the lowest point that Gavin reached? What are the coordinates of this point? How close to the ground was he?

2. Nicole makes a similar jump that can be modeled by the equation $x^2 - 4x - 8y + 84 = 0$. She wants to know whether she got closer to the ground than Gavin and by how much.

   a. Write the equation of Nicole's path in standard form.

   b. How close to the ground did she get?

   c. Did Nicole get closer to the ground than Gavin?

The design for a new auto racetrack can be modeled by the equation $x^2 + 4y^2 - 20x - 32y + 160 = 0$, with dimensions in kilometers. Tracey tests the track. Choose the letter for the best answer.

3. What is the standard form of the equation for the path of the racetrack?

   A $\dfrac{(x-10)^2}{1^2} + \dfrac{(y-4)^2}{2^2} = 1$

   B $\dfrac{(x-10)^2}{2^2} + \dfrac{(y-4)^2}{1^2} = 1$

   C $\dfrac{(x-4)^2}{2^2} + \dfrac{(y-10)^2}{1^2} = 1$

   D $\dfrac{(x-4)^2}{1^2} + \dfrac{(y-10)^2}{2^2} = 1$

4. While driving around the track, what is the greatest distance that Tracey will reach from the center of the track?

   F 1 km

   G 2 km

   H 10 km

   J 16 km

Identifying Conic Sections
Going Deeper

Essential question: *How can you identify a conic section by its equation?*

COMMON Standards for
CORE Mathematical Content

CC.9-12.A.SSE.1a Interpret parts of an expression, such as terms, factors, and coefficients.

CC.9-12.A.SSE.1b Interpret complicated expressions by viewing one or more of their parts as a single entity.

CC.9-12.A.SSE.2 Use the structure of an expression to identify ways to rewrite it.

Also: CC.9-12.F.BF.3

Prerequisites

Completing the square

Circles   Ellipses

Hyperbolas   Parabolas

Math Background

Students have studied circles, ellipses, hyperbolas, and parabolas. They have learned how to determine the characteristics of the graphs of these conic sections using given equations. Also, they can write equations for circles, ellipses, hyperbolas, and parabolas in standard form, either centered at the origin or at some other point.

The graph of any quadratic equation in two variables is always a conic section. Exactly what type of conic it is can be determined by putting the equation in the general quadratic form $Ax^2 + Bxy + Cy^2 + Dx + Ey + F = 0$ and then evaluating the discriminant $B^2 - 4AC$.

- If $B^2 - 4AC < 0$, the section is an ellipse.
- If $A = C$ and $B = 0$, the section is a circle.
- If $B^2 - 4AC = 0$, the section is a parabola.
- If $B^2 - 4AC > 0$, the section is a hyperbola.

INTRODUCE

Graph the parabola $y = -x^2$ on the board, label its vertex, and write its equation. Then take a flashlight and angle it on the board to fill the parabola. Move the flashlight a few units vertically and a few units horizontally, counting the units as you move the flashlight. (Try to maintain the shape of the parabola as you move the flashlight.) Trace the new location of the parabola. Ask students what the new

vertex is and how they know. Then ask students how the equation of the parabola will change.

TEACH

1 EXPLORE

Questioning Strategies

- In Part A, what is the major axis of the gray ellipse and the major axis of the black ellipse? Explain how the translation affects the location of the major axis. **Major axis of gray ellipse: $y = 0$, major axis of black ellipse: $y = -4$; the ellipse is translated down 4 units, so the major axis is also translated down 4 units.**

- In Part B, suppose the gray hyperbola is translated 6 units to the right and 1 unit down. What is an equation for the new hyperbola? $\frac{(x-6)^2}{4} - (y+1)^2 = 1$

2 ENGAGE

Questioning Strategies

- In the table for standard forms of equations of conic sections, what do the "horizontal axis" and "vertical axis" headings describe in an ellipse, a hyperbola, and a parabola? **For the equations in the horizontal axis column, the major axis of the ellipse is horizontal, the transverse axis of the hyperbola is horizontal (opens to the left and right), and the axis of symmetry of the parabola is horizontal (opens to the left or right). For the equations in the vertical axis column, the major axis of the ellipse is vertical, the transverse axis of the hyperbola is vertical (opens up and down), and the axis of symmetry of the parabola is vertical (opens up or down).**

- In the general form of an equation of a conic section, suppose $A = C$, $B = 0$ and neither A nor C are 0. What is the classification of the conic section? **circle**

continued

12-6

Identifying Conic Sections
Going Deeper

Essential question: *How can you identify a conic by its equation?*

· Video Tutor

EXT. OF CC.9-12.F.BF.3

1 EXPLORE   Translating Conic Sections

Describe the translation that maps the gray conic section onto the black conic section. Explain how translating the graph affects its equation.

A The gray ellipse maps onto the black ellipse by a translation of __2__ units to the __right__ and __4__ units __down__.

When translating the ellipse $\frac{x^2}{16} + \frac{y^2}{9} = 1$ to the ellipse $\frac{(x-2)^2}{16} + \frac{(y+4)^2}{9} = 1$, notice that __2__, the number of units to translated to the __right__, is subtracted from the *x*-values and __4__, the number of units translated __down__, is added to the *y*-values.

B The gray hyperbola maps onto the black hyperbola by a translation of __3__ units to the __left__ and __5__ units __up__.

When translating the hyperbola $\frac{x^2}{4} - y^2 = 1$ to the hyperbola $\frac{(x+3)^2}{4} - (y-5)^2 = 1$, notice that __3__, the number of units translated to the __left__, is added to the *x*-values and __5__, the number of units translated __up__, is subtracted from the *y*-values.

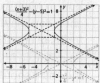

REFLECT

1a. In part A, the gray ellipse is centered at the origin. What is the center of the black ellipse? Can you determine the center of the black ellipse by looking at its equation? Explain.

(2, −4); yes; the *x*-coordinate is the number subtracted from *x*, and the *y*-coordinate is the opposite of the number added to *y*.

1b. In part B, the gray hyperbola is centered at the origin. What is the center of the black hyperbola? Can you determine the center of the black hyperbola by looking at its equation? Explain.

(−3, 5); yes; the *x*-coordinate is the opposite of the number added to *x*, and the *y*-coordinate is the number subtracted from *y*.

© Houghton Mifflin Harcourt Publishing Company

CC.9-12.A.SSE.1a
CC.9-12.A.SSE.1b

2 ENGAGE   Recognizing Equations of Conic Sections

When equations of conic sections are written in standard form, characteristics of the conic sections can be identified. In the equations below, (h, k) is the vertex of the parabola and the center of the other conic sections.

Standard Forms of Equations of Conic Sections

Circle	$(x - h)^2 + (y - k)^2 = r^2$	
	Horizontal axis	**Vertical axis**
Ellipse	$\frac{(x-h)^2}{a^2} + \frac{(y-k)^2}{b^2} = 1$	$\frac{(x-h)^2}{b^2} + \frac{(y-k)^2}{a^2} = 1$
Hyperbola	$\frac{(x-h)^2}{a^2} - \frac{(y-k)^2}{b^2} = 1$	$\frac{(y-k)^2}{a^2} - \frac{(x-h)^2}{b^2} = 1$
Parabola	$x - h = \frac{1}{4p}(y-k)^2$	$y - k = \frac{1}{4p}(x-h)^2$

Conic sections can also be written in the *general form* $Ax^2 + Bxy + Cy^2 + Dx + Ey + F = 0$. When an equation for a conic section is written in general form, you can use the expression $B^2 - 4AC$ to classify a conic section.

Classifying Conic Sections

For an equation of the form $Ax^2 + Bxy + Cy^2 + Dx + Ey + F = 0$
(A, B, and C do not all equal 0.)

Conic Section	Coefficients
Circle	$B^2 - 4AC < 0$, $B = 0$, and $A = C$
Ellipse	$B^2 - 4AC < 0$ and either $B \neq 0$ or $A \neq C$
Hyperbola	$B^2 - 4AC > 0$
Parabola	$B^2 - 4AC = 0$

REFLECT

2a. Describe how the standard forms of equations for each pair of conic sections are alike and how they are different.

Circle and ellipse: Both equations have terms that involve the expressions $(x - h)^2$ and $(y - k)^2$. In the equation for a circle, the sum of these expressions equals r^2, while in the equation for an ellipse, the expressions are divided by a^2 and b^2 and the sum equals 1. If you divided both sides of the equation of a circle by r^2, the result would look like the equation for an ellipse with $a = b$.

Ellipse and hyperbola: Both equations involve the expressions $\frac{(x-h)^2}{a^2}$ and $\frac{(y-k)^2}{b^2}$ (or $\frac{(x-h)^2}{b^2}$ and $\frac{(y-k)^2}{a^2}$). In an ellipse, the sum of the expressions is equal to 1. In a hyperbola, the difference of the expressions is equal to 1.

© Houghton Mifflin Harcourt Publishing Company

Notes

Teaching Strategy

When discussing the table of classifying conic sections, work with students to write an equation (in general form) that fits the criteria for each conic section. Tell students that the value of B in equations of conic sections with horizontal and vertical axes is 0. So, let $B = 0$ in the equations since only conic sections with horizontal and vertical axes are being covered in this unit.

3 EXAMPLE

Questioning Strategies

- Is the given equation written in general form? Explain. Yes; the equation is written in the form $Ax^2 + Bxy + Cy^2 + Dx + Ey + F = 0$, but it does not have an xy-term.

- How do you find the values of A, B, and C? A is the coefficient of the x^2-term, B is the coefficient of the xy-term, and C is the coefficient of the y^2-term.

- Is it possible to classify a conic section given its equation in general form by only rewriting the equation in standard form and not evaluating $B^2 - 4AC$? Explain. Yes; after rewriting the equation, the conic section can be classified from the standard form of the equation.

- Would you use the general form or the standard form of the equation to graph the conic section in Example 3? Explain. Standard form; characteristics of the graph are easier to see from the standard form of the equation.

EXTRA EXAMPLE

Classify the conic section $2x^2 + 32x - y + 134 = 0$. Then write an equation for the conic section in standard form. parabola; $y - 6 = 2(x + 8)^2$

Avoid Common Errors

When completing the square, remind students that the x^2-term and y^2-term must each have a coefficient of 1 to complete the square. If a constant is factored out of the binomial being used to complete the square, make sure students multiply by this constant when adding or subtracting values to balance the equation.

Differentiated Instruction

Students don't have to complete the square when rewriting equations of conic sections centered at the origin. Students will have an easier time rewriting equations like $8y^2 - x = 0$ (parabola) and $16x^2 - 25y^2 + 400 = 0$ (hyperbola) in standard form since these conic sections are centered at the origin.

CLOSE

Essential Question

How can you identify a conic section by its equation? Analyze the standard form of the equation to see if it matches one of the standard forms of equations of conic sections. If the equation is written in general form, either identify the conic section using the value of $B^2 - 4AC$, or rewrite the equation in standard form, completing the square if necessary.

Summarize

Have students make a journal entry that describes how to identify a conic section by its equation. The entry can include a table that shows the standard forms of equations for conic sections, including an example of each equation and its graph. Also, the entry should describe the two methods for identifying a conic section from the general form of its equation. Students should include a table describing the value of $B^2 - 4AC$ from the general form of the equation for each conic section.

.·°**MATHEMATICAL** **Highlighting**
.·°: **PRACTICE**   **the Standards**
:·.·...·:

Exercises 5–10 provide opportunities to address Mathematical Practices Standard 7 (Look for and make use of structure). To identify the conic sections, students analyze the structure of each equation to see whether or not it resembles one of the standard forms of equations of conic sections. If not, students need to rewrite the equation so that it is in a recognizable form.

PRACTICE

Where skills are taught	Where skills are practiced
2 ENGAGE	EXS. 1–4
3 EXAMPLE	EXS. 5–14

Exercise 15: Students investigate the values of B, D, and E in the general form of an equation for a circle, ellipse, and hyperbola centered at the origin.

2b. Use the descriptions of the coefficients of the general form of the equation for the conic section to classify the conic section.

$B = 0$ and A and C have opposite signs	hyperbola
$B = 0$ and A and C have the same sign	ellipse or circle
$B = 0$ and $A = 0$ or $C = 0$	parabola

CC.9-12.A.SSE.1b,
CC.9-12.A.SSE.2

3 EXAMPLE   Writing an Equation of a Conic Section in Standard Form

Classify the conic section $49x^2 - 25y^2 - 490x - 50y - 25 = 0$. Then write an equation for the conic section in standard form.

A Find the values of A, B, and C. Then substitute the values in the expression $B^2 - 4AC$.

$A = \underline{49}$ $B = \underline{0}$ $C = \underline{-25}$

$B^2 - 4AC = \underline{0}^2 - 4\left(\underline{49}\right)\left(\underline{-25}\right) = \underline{4,900}$

Because $B^2 - 4AC \underline{\ >\ } 0$, the conic section is $\underline{\text{a hyperbola}}$.

B To rewrite the equation in standard form, complete the square in both x and y.

$49x^2 - 25y^2 - 490x - 50y - 25 = 0$ Write equation.

$\left(49x^2 - 490x\right) - \left(25y^2 + 50y\right) = 25$ Rearrange terms.

$49\left(x^2 - 10x + ?\right) - 25\left(y^2 + 2y + ?\right) = 25 + 49(?) - 25(?)$

Begin to complete squares.

$49\left(x^2 - 10x + 25\right) - 25\left(y^2 + 2y + 1\right) = 25 + 49\left(25\right) - 25\left(1\right)$

Complete both squares.

$49\left(x - 5\right)^2 - 25\left(y + 1\right)^2 = 1,225$ Factor and simplify.

$\dfrac{(x-5)^2}{25} - \dfrac{(y+1)^2}{49} = 1$ Divide both sides by 1,225.

REFLECT

3a. Tell how to write an equation of a conic section in standard form given the general form of the equation.

Complete the square in both x and y, if needed. Then factor and simplify the resulting equation to resemble one of the standard form equations for conic sections.

3b. In Example 3, can you complete Part B without completing Part A first?

Yes; you do not need to know that the conic section is a hyperbola before writing an equation in standard form for the conic section.

PRACTICE

Find the coordinates of the center of each conic section if possible.

1. $\dfrac{(x+3)^2}{4} - \dfrac{(y-1)^2}{10} = 1$ $\underline{(-3, 1)}$

2. $x - 5 = \frac{1}{8}(y-7)^2$ $\underline{\text{no center}}$

3. $(x-4)^2 + (y+9)^2 = 36$ $\underline{(4, -9)}$

4. $\dfrac{(x+13)^2}{25} + \dfrac{y^2}{20} = 1$ $\underline{(-13, 0)}$

Identify the conic section that each equation represents.

5. $y + 2 = \frac{1}{4}(x - 7)^2$

$\underline{\text{parabola}}$

6. $(x-9)^2 + (y-3)^2 = 49$

$\underline{\text{circle}}$

7. $\dfrac{x^2}{8} + \dfrac{(y+15)^2}{9} = 1$

$\underline{\text{ellipse}}$

8. $\dfrac{(x+4)^2}{25} - \dfrac{(y-1)^2}{25} = 1$

$\underline{\text{hyperbola}}$

9. $9x^2 + 16y^2 - 36x - 32y - 92 = 0$

$\underline{\text{ellipse}}$

10. $x^2 + y^2 + 10x + 16 = 0$

$\underline{\text{circle}}$

Find the standard form of each equation by completing the square.

11. $x^2 + 10x - 12y + 73 = 0$

$y - 4 = \frac{1}{12}(x + 5)^2$

12. $-121x^2 + 81y^2 + 242x - 9922 = 0$

$\dfrac{y^2}{121} - \dfrac{(x-1)^2}{81} = 1$

13. $9x^2 + y^2 - 18x + 6y - 18 = 0$

$\dfrac{(x-1)^2}{4} + \dfrac{(y+3)^2}{36} = 1$

14. $36x^2 + 25y^2 + 144x - 150y - 531 = 0$

$\dfrac{(x+2)^2}{25} + \dfrac{(y-3)^2}{36} = 1$

15. Use the conic sections given below.

Circle: $x^2 + y^2 = 64$ Ellipse: $\dfrac{x^2}{9} + \dfrac{y^2}{36} = 1$ Hyperbola: $\dfrac{y^2}{100} - \dfrac{x^2}{81} = 1$

a. Find the center of each conic section. What do you notice?

Center of circle: (0, 0), center of ellipse: (0, 0), center of hyperbola: (0, 0); all of the conic sections are centered at the origin.

b. Write the equation for each conic section in general form.

Circle: $x^2 + y^2 - 64 = 0$, ellipse: $36x^2 + 9y^2 - 324 = 0$,

hyperbola: $-100x^2 + 81y^2 - 8100 = 0$

c. Make a conjecture about the general form of an equation of a conic section centered at the origin.

In the general form of an equation of a conic section centered at the origin,

$B = D = E = 0$.

ADDITIONAL PRACTICE AND PROBLEM SOLVING

Assign these pages to help your students practice and apply important lesson concepts. For additional exercises, see the Student Edition.

Answers

Additional Practice

1. Parabola
2. Ellipse
3. Circle
4. Parabola
5. Hyperbola
6. Ellipse
7. Parabola
8. Circle
9. Hyperbola
10. Ellipse

11. $\dfrac{(y-3)^2}{1^2} - \dfrac{(x+2)^2}{4^2} = 1$; hyperbola

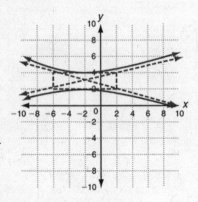

12. $\dfrac{x^2}{4^2} + \dfrac{y^2}{2^2} = 1$; ellipse

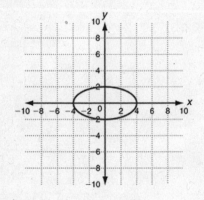

13. **a.** $y - 34 = \dfrac{1}{16}(x - 14)^2$

b. 4 miles

Problem Solving

1. **a.** $A = 1, B = 0, C = 0, B^2 - 4AC = 0$; parabola

b. $y - 4 = \left(\dfrac{1}{12}\right)(x - 6)^2$

c. Vertex; (6, 4); 4 ft off the ground

2. **a.** $y - 10 = \left(\dfrac{1}{8}\right)(x - 2)^2$

b. 10 ft

c. No; Gavin got 6 ft closer to the ground.

3. B
4. G

Additional Practice

Identify the conic section that each equation represents.

1. $x - 1 = \frac{1}{4}(y - 8)^2$

2. $\frac{(y+7)^2}{6^2} + \frac{(x-9)^2}{1^2} = 1$

3. $(x - 9)^2 + (y + 1)^2 = 3^2$

_____

4. $y + 5 = -(x - 9)^2$

5. $\frac{(y+4)^2}{4^2} - \frac{(x-4)^2}{3^2} = 1$

6. $\frac{(x-2)^2}{6^2} + \frac{(y+8)^2}{4^2} = 1$

_____

7. $y^2 + 8x + 2y + 57 = 0$

8. $x^2 + y^2 - 4x + 4y - 17 = 0$

_____

9. $x^2 - 9y^2 + 2x + 18y - 17 = 0$

10. $x^2 + 4y^2 - 2x - 16y + 1 = 0$

_____

Find the standard form of each equation by completing the square. Then identify and graph each conic.

11. $x^2 - 16y^2 + 4x + 96y - 124 = 0$

12. $x^2 + 4y^2 = 16$

_____

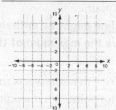
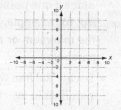

Solve.

13. A train takes a path around the town that can be modeled by the equation $x^2 + 28x + 16y = 348$. The town lies at the focus.

   a. Write the equation in standard form. _____

   b. If the measurement is in miles, how close does the train come to the town? _____

Problem Solving

At a bungee-jumping contest, Gavin makes a jump that can be modeled by the equation $x^2 - 12x - 12y + 84 = 0$, with dimensions in feet.

1. Gavin wants to know how close he came to the ground during his jump.

   a. Classify the shape of his path. Identify the values for the coefficients of each term, and determine what conic section models his path.

   b. Write the equation of his path in standard form by completing the square.

   c. Which point on the path identifies the lowest point that Gavin reached? What are the coordinates of this point? How close to the ground was he?

2. Nicole makes a similar jump that can be modeled by the equation $x^2 - 4x - 8y + 84 = 0$. She wants to know whether she got closer to the ground than Gavin and by how much.

   a. Write the equation of Nicole's path in standard form.

   b. How close to the ground did she get? _____

   c. Did Nicole get closer to the ground than Gavin?

The design for a new auto racetrack can be modeled by the equation $x^2 + 4y^2 - 20x - 32y + 160 = 0$, with dimensions in kilometers. Tracey tests the track. Choose the letter for the best answer.

3. What is the standard form of the equation for the path of the racetrack?

   A $\frac{(x-10)^2}{1^2} + \frac{(y-4)^2}{2^2} = 1$

   B $\frac{(x-10)^2}{2^2} + \frac{(y-4)^2}{1^2} = 1$

   C $\frac{(x-4)^2}{2^2} + \frac{(y-10)^2}{1^2} = 1$

   D $\frac{(x-4)^2}{1^2} + \frac{(y-10)^2}{2^2} = 1$

4. While driving around the track, what is the greatest distance that Tracey will reach from the center of the track?

   F 1 km

   G 2 km

   H 10 km

   J 16 km

Notes

Solving Nonlinear Systems
Going Deeper

Essential question: *How can you solve systems of equations involving lines and circles or parabolas?*

COMMON CORE **Standards for Mathematical Content**

CC.9-12.A.REI.7 Solve a simple system consisting of a linear equation and a quadratic equation in two variables algebraically and graphically.

Prerequisites

Solving Linear Systems

Lines, Parabola, and Circles

Math Background

In many problems, the conditions or constraints that determine a solution are found in an equation. The equation $x^2 + y^2 = 1$ has infinitely many solutions. Many times, the constraints are found in two or more equations, a system of equations.

Unlike $x^2 + y^2 = 1$, the system $\begin{cases} x^2 + y^2 = 1 \\ y = mx + b \end{cases}$,

where m and b are fixed numbers, will not have infinitely many solutions. The system can have two solutions, one solution, or even no solution at all.

INTRODUCE

Review what it means to find a solution to a system of equations. Then review the various methods for solving a pair of linear equations in two variables. In particular, review the graphical approach and the algebraic approach.

When reviewing the graphical approach, remind students using graphing calculators to experiment with different viewing windows to get a representative picture of where the graphs might intersect.

When reviewing the algebraic approach, remind students that the substitution method is often helpful. However, the elimination method may be the better option in other situations.

TEACH

1 ENGAGE

Questioning Strategies

- A parabola extends infinitely. Does this mean that a line in the plane must intersect the parabola in at least one point? Explain.

  No; for example, the line might be entirely below the minimum or above the maximum of the parabola.

- Locate the line you drew that intersects the parabola in exactly one point. What would happen if you keep the point of contact fixed but rotate the line about that point?

  The point of contact would still be a point of intersection but a second point of intersection would occur. The line and the parabola would then have two points of intersection.

2 EXAMPLE

Questioning Strategies

- In Part A, explain why writing an equation in one variable, *x*, makes sense.

  In both equations, *y* is given in terms of *x*. By equating the expressions for *y*, the result is a quadratic equation in one variable, *x*. Methods for finding solutions for *x* are factoring or the quadratic formula.

- In Part B, explain why a graphing calculator approach might be more convenient?

  If the expressions for *y* are set equal, the resulting quadratic equation would be more complicated to deal with than the quadratic equation in Part A.

EXTRA EXAMPLE

A Solve $\begin{cases} y = 2x^2 - 1 \\ y = 2x - 1 \end{cases}$.

  (0, −1) and (1, 1)

B Solve $\begin{cases} y = (x + 1)^2 - 1 \\ y = 2x - 3 \end{cases}$.

  no solution

Name_____ Class_____ Date_____

12-7

Video Tutor

Solving Nonlinear Systems
Going Deeper

Essential question: How can you solve systems of equations involving lines and circles or parabolas?

CC.9-12.A.REI.7

1 ENGAGE Investigating Different Solution Scenarios

A The coordinate grid at the left below shows a parabola. On the grid, sketch straight lines that show how many different possibilities there are for a line and the parabola to intersect. Write the number of points of intersection for each situation.

B The coordinate grid at the right below shows a circle. On the grid, sketch straight lines that show how many different possibilities there are for the graphs to intersect. Write the number of points of intersection for each situation.   Check students' work.

Samples are given.

REFLECT

1a. In how many points can two distinct lines in a plane intersect?

None if the lines are parallel and one if the lines are not parallel.

1b. On the grid below, illustrate the different ways a parabola and circle can intersect.

1c. In how many ways can a parabola and a circle intersect?

None, one, two, three, or four

Chapter 12   699   Lesson 7

© Houghton Mifflin Harcourt Publishing Company

CC.9-12.A.REI.7

2 EXAMPLE Solving a System Involving a Line and a Parabola

A Solve $\begin{cases} y = 2x^2 + 3 \\ y = 4x + 1 \end{cases}$ algebraically.

$2x^2 + 3 = 4x + 1$ Equate the expressions for y.

$2x^2 - 4x + 2 = 0$ Write in standard form.

$x^2 - 2x + 1 = 0$ Simplify.

$(x - 1)(x - 1) = 0 \rightarrow x = 1$ Solve by factoring.

$(1 , 5)$ Write the solution (x, y).

B Solve $\begin{cases} y = (x - 2)^2 + 1 \\ y = -2x + 8 \end{cases}$ using a graphing calculator.

To use a graphing calculator, enter $(x - 2)^2 + 1$ and $-2x + 8$ as the functions to graph. Choose ranges for x and for y. Check students' ranges.

Xmin = -2 Xmax = 6 Ymin = -5 Ymax = 16

The display shows there are ____two____ solutions: $(-1 , 10)$ and $(3 , 2)$. Sketch your solution display. Check students' displays.

REFLECT

2a. In Part B, how would you change the system, using a vertical translation, so that the system has exactly one solution?

Translate the line down or translate the parabola up so that the graphs touch in just one point, that is, so that the line is tangent to the parabola.

2b. How does the solution to Part A change if $y = 2x^2 + 3$ is replaced by $y = 2x^2 + 4$?

By translating the parabola vertically up one unit, the system that had one solution now has no solution. A graphing calculator can confirm a space between the graphs.

2c. How can you solve $\begin{cases} y = 0.2x^2 + 1.5x + 3 \\ y = 4.2x - 2.5 \end{cases}$ algebraically?

$0.2x^2 + 1.5x + 3 = 4.2x - 2.5$ can be rewritten as $2x^2 + 15x + 30 = 42x - 25$ to eliminate decimals. Writing in standard form gives $2x^2 - 27x + 55 = 0$. Solving by the quadratic formula results in $x = 2.5$ or $x = 11$. The solutions are $(2.5, 8)$ and $(11, 43.7)$.

Chapter 12   700   Lesson 7

© Houghton Mifflin Harcourt Publishing Company

Questioning Strategies

- In Part A, describe the graphs of the equations. The graph of $y = \frac{3}{4}x$ is a straight line through the origin. The graph of $x^2 + y^2 = 25$ is the circle with radius 5 and center at the origin.

- What conclusion can you draw about any points of intersection from your descriptions of the graphs?
  The origin is on the line and inside the circle. This suggests that the line intersects the circle in two points.

- What does the conclusion you drew about the number of points of intersection suggest with regard to solutions?
  If the line and the circle intersect in two points, then there should be two ordered pairs that satisfy the system.

- Can you easily tell whether the system in Part B has any solutions?
  No. The system consists of the circle with radius 4 and center $(-1, 1)$. The line has negative slope and y-intercept 6. This information is not enough to predict reliably.

- In Part B, explain how to solve $(x + 1)^2 + (y - 1)^2 = 16$ for y.
  First, subtract $(x + 1)^2$ from each side. Then take the square root of each side. Keep both the positive and the negative roots. Finally, add 1 to each side.

- What viewing window might be a suitable choice as a first attempt at solving the system in Part B?
  The viewing window should be big enough to show the entire circle.

EXTRA EXAMPLE

A Solve $\begin{cases} y = x + 4 \\ x^2 + y^2 = 1 \end{cases}$.

   no solution

B Solve $\begin{cases} y = -\frac{3}{4}x + \frac{33}{4} \\ x^2 + (y - 2)^2 = 25 \end{cases}$.

   $(3, 6)$

Technology

Remind students that a graphing calculator will not be useful if the viewing window is not chosen wisely. This diagram will not help solve a system consisting of a line and a circle. The circle is only partially visible and the line is not shown at all.

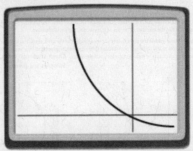

CLOSE

Essential Question
How can you solve systems of equations involving lines and circles or parabolas?
After examining the system, decide whether to use an algebraic or graphical approach. If an algebraic approach is chosen, decide what method of solution will be used.

Summarize
Have students make a flow-chart poster that illustrates the process of solving a nonlinear system of equations. Encourage students to include the determination of the number of solutions there.

MATHEMATICAL PRACTICE	Highlighting the Standards

Exercises 1–14 provide opportunities to address Mathematical Practices Standard 5 (Use appropriate tools strategically). Students learn to make choices about a solution approach depending on the circumstances of the problem.

PRACTICE

Where skills are taught	Where skills are practiced
1 ENGAGE	EXS. 1–3
2 EXAMPLE	EXS. 4–9
3 EXAMPLE	EXS. 10–14

3 EXAMPLE CC.9-12.A.REI.7 **Solving a System Involving a Line and a Circle**

A Solve $\begin{cases} y = \frac{3}{4}x \\ x^2 + y^2 = 25 \end{cases}$ algebraically.

$x^2 + \left(\frac{3}{4}x\right)^2 = 25$	Substitute.
$25x^2 - 400 = 0$	Clear fractions and simplify.
$x = -4$ or 4	Solve by factoring.
$\left(-4, -3\right)$ and $\left(4, 3\right)$	Write the solution (x, y).

B Solve $\begin{cases} y = -x + 6 \\ (x+1)^2 + (y-1)^2 = 16 \end{cases}$ using a graphing calculator.

Solve $(x + 1)^2 + (y - 1)^2 = 16$ for y.

$y = \sqrt{16 - (x+1)^2} + 1$ and $y = -\sqrt{16 - (x+1)^2} + 1$

The number of functions for the calculator function list is ___three___

The display at the left below suggests that the graphs do not intersect.

To get a closer look at the region where the graphs are close, use the Zoom feature of the calculator.

There are no points of intersection. The system has no solution.

REFLECT

3a. Explain how to change the equation of the line in the system in Part B so that the slope remains the same and the system has two solutions.

Explanations may vary. Sample explanation: Translate the line down so that it

intersects the circle in two points. Since (0, 0) is inside the circle, use a y-intercept

of 0. Replace $y = -x + 6$ with $y = -x$.

3b. Explain how you know that $\begin{cases} y = 4 \\ x^2 + y^2 = 1 \end{cases}$ has no solution without using a

graphing calculator or solving the system algebraically.

$x^2 + y^2 = 1$ is the circle with radius 1 centered at the origin. The highest point on the

circle is (0, 1). The line $y = 4$ is horizontal and above this point. The line and circle do

not intersect. Thus, there is no solution.

Chapter 12   701   Lesson 7

PRACTICE

Without solving, determine the number of solutions to each system.

1. $\begin{cases} y = -3 \\ y = x^2 \end{cases}$

___zero___

2. $\begin{cases} y = -4 \\ x^2 + y^2 = 16 \end{cases}$

___one___

3. $\begin{cases} y = 1 \\ (x-3)^2 + y^2 = 16 \end{cases}$

___two___

Solve each system of equations. If solved algebraically, give exact answers. If solved using a graphing calculator give, answers to the nearest hundredth.

4. $\begin{cases} y = 4 \\ y = x^2 + 3x \end{cases}$

___(-4, 4) and (1, 4)___

5. $\begin{cases} y = 2x - 4 \\ y = x^3 - 3 \end{cases}$

___(1, -2)___

6. $\begin{cases} y = 3x - 5 \\ y = 2x^2 - 2x + 1 \end{cases}$

___no solution___

7. $\begin{cases} y = -x + 2 \\ y = (x-2)^2 \end{cases}$

___(1, 1) and (2, 0)___

8. $\begin{cases} y = 2x - 2 \\ y = -x^2 + 2 \end{cases}$

___(-3.24, -8.47) and (1.24, 0.47)___

9. $\begin{cases} y = x - 3 \\ y = 3x^2 + 2x \end{cases}$

___no solution___

10. $\begin{cases} y = x + 4 \\ (x-3)^2 + (y-1)^2 = 9 \end{cases}$

___no solution___

11. $\begin{cases} y = -\frac{3}{4}x - \frac{25}{2} \\ x^2 + y^2 = 100 \end{cases}$

___(-6.00, -8.00)___

12. $\begin{cases} y = 2 \\ (x-2)^2 + (y-1)^2 = 1 \end{cases}$

___(2, 2)___

13. $\begin{cases} y = 2x - 5 \\ x^2 + y^2 = 4 \end{cases}$

___no solution___

14. Find b such that $\begin{cases} y = b \\ (x-5)^2 + (y+4)^2 = 25 \end{cases}$ will have no solution, one solution, and two solutions.

No solution: $b > 1$ or $b < -9$; one solution: $b = 1$ or $b = -9$;

two solutions: $-9 < b < 1$

Chapter 12   702   Lesson 7

Assign these pages to help your students practice and apply important lesson concepts. For additional exercises, see the Student Edition.

Answers

Additional Practice

1. $(9, -12), (4, 8)$ 2. $(2, 5), (-4, 8)$

3. $(3, 2), (-3, -2)$ 4. $(1, -10), (-1, 10)$

5. $(9, 12), (-9, -12)$ 6. $(-5, 0), (123, 16)$

7. $(5, 3), (-3, -5)$ 8. $(2, -1), (-2, -1)$

9. $(10, 3), (10, -3)$

10. $(5, 6), (5, -6), (-5, 6), (-5, -6)$

11. $(1, 3), (1, -3), (-1, 3), (-1, -3)$

12. $(6, 11), (6, -11), (-6, 11), (-6, -11)$

13. $(5, 3), (5, -3), (-5, 3), (-5, -3)$

14. $(9, 7), (9, -7), (-9, 7), (-9, -7)$

15. $(8, 8), (8, -8), (-8, 8), (-8, -8)$

16. $(0, 40), (40, 0)$

Problem Solving

1. a Jim's boat: ellipse; the sum of two squared terms; Janice's boat: parabola; only one squared term

   b. 4

   c. $8(x - 2)$

   d. $4x^2 + 72x - 180 = 0$

   e. $x = 2.2$ and -20.2

   f. Yes; points of possible collision are $(2.2, 1.3)$ and $(2.2, -1.3)$

2. a.

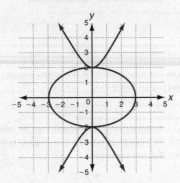

   b. Yes; point of possible collision is $(0, 2)$

3. C   4. F

Name_____ Class_____ Date_____

12-7

Additional Practice

Solve each system of equations by graphing.

1. $\begin{cases} 4x + y = 24 \\ x = \dfrac{1}{16}y^2 \end{cases}$

2. $\begin{cases} y - 4 = \dfrac{1}{4}x^2 \\ x + 2y = 12 \end{cases}$

3. $\begin{cases} 9y - 6x = 0 \\ \dfrac{x^2}{45} + \dfrac{y^2}{5} = 1 \end{cases}$

Solve each system of equations by using the substitution method.

4. $\begin{cases} x^2 + y^2 = 101 \\ 10x + y = 0 \end{cases}$

5. $\begin{cases} 3y = 4x \\ x^2 - y^2 = -63 \end{cases}$

6. $\begin{cases} 8y = x + 5 \\ x + 5 = \dfrac{1}{2}y^2 \end{cases}$

7. $\begin{cases} x^2 + y^2 = 34 \\ 3x - 3y = 6 \end{cases}$

8. $\begin{cases} x^2 + y^2 = 5 \\ y + 3 = \dfrac{1}{2}x^2 \end{cases}$

9. $\begin{cases} x^2 + y^2 = 109 \\ x - 7 = \dfrac{1}{3}y^2 \end{cases}$

Solve each system of equations by using the elimination method.

10. $\begin{cases} 2x^2 + y^2 = 86 \\ x^2 + 3y^2 = 133 \end{cases}$

11. $\begin{cases} 4x^2 + y^2 = 13 \\ 2x^2 - y^2 = -7 \end{cases}$

12. $\begin{cases} 3x^2 + 2y^2 = 350 \\ 4x^2 - 2y^2 = -98 \end{cases}$

13. $\begin{cases} 8x^2 - 3y^2 = 173 \\ 5x^2 - y^2 = 116 \end{cases}$

14. $\begin{cases} 2x^2 - 3y^2 = 15 \\ 3x^2 - 2y^2 = 341 \end{cases}$

15. $\begin{cases} 5x^2 - 3y^2 = 128 \\ 4x^2 - 2y^2 = 128 \end{cases}$

Solve.

16. The shape of a state park can be modeled by a circle with the equation $x^2 + y^2 = 1600$. A stretch of highway near the park is modeled by the equation $y = \dfrac{1}{40}(x - 40)^2$. At what points does a car on the highway enter or exit the park?

_____

Chapter 12   703   Lesson 7

Problem Solving

Jim sets a course in his fishing boat that can be modeled by the equation $4x^2 + 9y^2 = 36$. Janice has her sailboat on a path that can be modeled by the equation $x - 2 = \left(\dfrac{1}{8}\right)y^2$.

1. Janice wonders whether there is a danger of them colliding.

   a. Explain which conic section models each boat's path and why.

   _____

   b. What is the maximum number of points of intersection between two such paths? _____

   c. To solve this system of equations using the quadratic formula, what expression can be substituted for y^2 in the equation of the path of Jim's boat? _____

   d. Rewrite the equation of the path of Jim's boat in terms of x. _____

   e. Solve for x using the quadratic formula.

   _____

   f. Is there a possibility of collision? If so, name the coordinates of the point(s) of intersection.

   _____

2. Janice changes course so that her sailboat now follows a path modeled by the equation $\dfrac{y^2}{4} - x^2 = 1$ in quadrants I and II. Is there now a possibility of collision?

   a. Sketch the system of equations represented by Jim's boat's course and Janice's boat's new course.

   b. Use your graph to determine if there is now a possibility of collision. If so, give the coordinates of the point(s).

   _____

A trawler is on a course modeled by the equation $2x + y + 3 = 0$. Choose the letter for the best answer.

3. Which solution set represents possible points of collision between Jim's boat and the trawler's course?

   A $(-2.2, 1.37)$

   B $(-0.5, -2)$

   C $(-2.2, 1.37); (-0.5, -2)$

   D There is no possible collision point.

4. Janice sees the trawler. Which equation models a path that avoids a possible collision of her boat with the trawler?

   F $x - 1 = 0.5y^2$

   G $y = 0.5x + 2$

   H $y^2 - x^2 = 1$

   J $4x^2 + 3y^2 = 12$

Chapter 12   704   Lesson 7

This page provides students with the opportunity to apply concepts from the Common Core in real-world problem situations. There are three different levels of performance tasks:

⭐ **Novice:** These are short word problems that require students to apply the math they have learned in straightforward, real-world situations.

⭐⭐ **Apprentice:** These are more involved problems that guide students step-by-step through more complex tasks. These exercises include more complicated reasoning, writing, and open-ended elements.

⭐⭐⭐ **Expert:** These are open-ended, non-routine problems that, instead of stepping the students through, ask them to choose their own methods for solving and justify their answers and reasoning.

Sample answers

1a. $(x - 4)^2 + y^2 = 81$; center $(4, 0)$, radius 9

b. 4 miles; Missy's house is at $(0, 0)$ and the library is at $(4, 0)$.

2a. $x^2 + y^2 = 25$ (or $\pi x^2 + \pi y^2 = 25\pi$) and $y = x + 1$

b. $x = 3$, $y = 4$; 7π square units

3. Scoring Guide:

Task	Possible points
a	1 point for the correct expression $r = \sqrt{a^2 + b^2}$, and 1 point for a correct explanation, for example: applied the Distance Formula using points $(0, 0)$ and (a, b).
b	2 points for the correct equation $x^2 + y^2 = a^2 + b^2$.
c	1 point for the correct substitution into the equation: $(-a)^2 + (-b)^2 = a^2 + b^2$ $a^2 + b^2 = a^2 + b^2$ (true statement) 1 point for a correct justification, such as the point $(-a, -b)$ satisfies the equation of the circle, and therefore lies on the circle.

Total possible points: 6

Name_____ Class_____ Date_____

Performance Tasks

★1. Missy draws a map on the coordinate plane. She plots her house at the origin. She then draws a circle that represents all the places that are exactly 9 miles from the library.

    a. The equation $x^2 - 8x + y^2 = 65$ represents the graph of the circle that Missy drew. Complete the square to find the center and radius of the circle.

    b. How far does Missy live from the library? Explain.

★2. A company logo is created from two circles as shown. The combined area of both circles is 25π square units, and the radius of the large circle is 1 unit longer than the radius of the small circle.

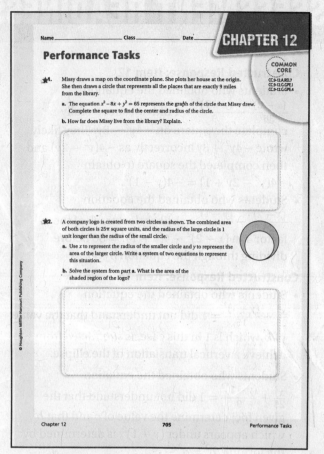

    a. Use x to represent the radius of the smaller circle and y to represent the area of the larger circle. Write a system of two equations to represent this situation.

    b. Solve the system from part **a.** What is the area of the shaded region of the logo?

★★3. Chase wants to prove the following: Given a circle with radius r and center $(0, 0)$, if (a, b) is on the circle, then the point $(-a, -b)$ is on the circle.

    a. Use the figure to write the radius r in terms of a and b. Explain what you did.

    b. Write the equation of the circle using your expression for the radius from part **a.**

    c. Use the equation to prove Chase's statement. Justify your answer.

★★4. Sherman stands on level ground and kicks a ball. If Sherman stands at the origin, the path of the ball is described by the equation $y = -0.08x^2 + x$, where x and y are both measured in feet. Six feet directly in front of Sherman, in the same direction he kicks the ball, the ground starts to slope down at a rate of -1 vertical foot for every 2 horizontal feet.

    a. Write and solve a system of equations to find where the ball lands after Sherman's kick. If the system has more than one solution, explain which solution is relevant to this situation. Write the final x and y values rounded to the nearest tenth of a foot.

    b. When the ball lands, it rolls another 5 feet down the hill. If Sherman walks from where he kicked the ball to where it stopped, how much distance does he cover? Round your answer the nearest tenth of a foot and show your work.

4. Scoring Guide:

Task	Possible points
a	1 point for writing the correct system of $y = -0.08x^2 + x$ and $y = -\frac{1}{2}x + 3$, 2 points for finding the approximate solutions (2.3, 1.9) and (16.5, –5.2), and 1 point for explaining that (16.5, –5.2) is the relevant solution because (2.3, 1.9) would be in mid-air, OR equivalent explanation.
b	2 points for correctly calculating the distance as $6 + \sqrt{(6 - 16.5)^2 + (0 - (-5.2))^2} + 5 \approx 22.7$ ft with appropriate work shown.

Total possible points: 6

COMMON CORE CORRELATION

Standard	Items
CC.9-12.A.SSE.1a*	1, 8, 10, 11, 12, 13
CC.9-12.A.SSE.1b*	1, 8, 10, 11, 12, 13
CC.9-12.A.REI.7	9
CC.9-12.G.GPE.1	2
CC.9-12.G.GPE.2	6, 7, 13, 14
CC.9-12.G.GPE.3(+)	3, 4, 5, 10, 11, 12, 15
CC.9-12.G.GPE.4	16

TEST PREP DOCTOR ⊕

Multiple Choice: Item 4

- Students who chose **F** put the center of the ellipse at $(3, -3)$ rather than $(-3, 3)$.

- Students who chose **H** mixed up the values of a and b.

- Students who chose **J** put the center of the ellipse at $(3, -3)$ rather than $(-3, 3)$ and mixed up the values of a and b.

Multiple Choice: Item 6

- Students who chose **G** or **H** did not recognize that the parabola has a vertical axis of symmetry because the directrix is a horizontal line.

- Students who chose **F** recognized that the parabola has a vertical axis of symmetry but did not recognize that the parabola opens down because the focus is below the directrix.

Constructed Response: Item 12

- Students who obtained the equation $\frac{(x-2)^2}{36} - \frac{(y-1)^2}{9} = 1$ did not successfully complete the square on $-4y^2 - 8y$. They likely wrote $-4y^2 - 8y$ incorrectly as $-4(y^2 - 2y)$ and then completed the square to obtain $-4(y^2 - 2y + 1) = -4(y - 1)^2$.

- Students who obtained the equation $\frac{(x-2)^2}{36} - \frac{(y-1)^2}{36} = 1$ likely lost track of the factor 4 in $(x - 2)^2 - 4(y + 1)^2 = 36$ before dividing through the equation by 36.

Constructed Response: Item 15

- Students who obtained the equation $\frac{x^2}{25} + \frac{(y+1)^2}{16} = 1$ did not understand that the value of k, which is 1 in this case, is *subtracted* from y to achieve a vertical translation of the ellipse.

- Students who obtained the equation $\frac{x^2}{25} + \frac{(y-1)^2}{9} = 1$ did not understand that the given foci determine the value of c and that b^2, which appears under $(y - 1)^2$, is determined by the formula $b^2 = a^2 - c^2$.

Notes

Name _____ Class _____ Date _____

MULTIPLE CHOICE

1. The equation $\frac{x^2}{33} + \frac{y^2}{49} = 1$ represents which conic section?

  A. Circle

  B. Ellipse

  C. Hyperbola

  D. Parabola

2. What is the equation of a circle with radius 7 and center $(0, 0)$?

  F. $x^2 + y^2 = 7$

  G. $x^2 + y^2 = 49$

  H. $\frac{x^2}{14} + \frac{y^2}{14} = 1$

  J. $x^2 + y^2 = 14$

3. What is the equation of an ellipse with a vertex of $(0, 3)$ and a co-vertex of $(-2, 0)$?

  A. $\frac{x^2}{4} + \frac{y^2}{9} = 1$

  B. $\frac{x^2}{3} + \frac{y^2}{2} = 1$

  C. $4x^2 + 9y^2 = 36$

  D. $-2x^2 + 3y^2 = 36$

4. A race track is modeled with the graph of an ellipse with vertices at $(2, 3)$ and $(-8, 3)$ and foci at $(1, 3)$ and $(-7, 3)$. Which is the equation of this ellipse?

  F. $\frac{(x-3)^2}{25} + \frac{(y+3)^2}{9} = 1$

  G. $\frac{(x+3)^2}{25} + \frac{(y-3)^2}{9} = 1$

  H. $\frac{(x+3)^2}{9} + \frac{(y-3)^2}{25} = 1$

  J. $\frac{(x-3)^2}{9} + \frac{(y+3)^2}{25} = 1$

5. What is the equation in standard form for the hyperbola with center $(0, 0)$, vertex $(4, 0)$, and focus $(8, 0)$?

  A. $\frac{x^2}{16} - \frac{y^2}{64} = 1$

  B. $\frac{y^2}{48} - \frac{x^2}{16} = 1$

  C. $\frac{x^2}{16} - \frac{y^2}{48} = 1$

  D. $\frac{y^2}{64} - \frac{x^2}{16} = 1$

6. What is the equation in standard form for the parabola with focus $F(0, -6)$ and directrix $y = 6$?

  F. $y = \frac{1}{24}x^2$

  G. $x = \frac{1}{24}y^2$

  H. $x = -\frac{1}{24}y^2$

  J. $y = -\frac{1}{24}x^2$

7. What is an equation in standard form for the parabola shown?

  $x = -2$ $F(2, 0)$

  A. $y = -\frac{1}{8}x^2$

  B. $y = \frac{1}{8}x^2$

  C. $x = \frac{1}{8}y^2$

  D. $x = -\frac{1}{8}y^2$

---

8. Which equation represents a hyperbola?

  F. $x^2 + 9y^2 + 6x - 90y + 225 = 0$

  G. $x^2 - 9y^2 + 6x + 90y - 225 = 0$

  H. $x^2 + y^2 + 6x - 10y + 25 = 0$

  J. $x^2 + 6x - 4y + 14 = 0$

9. Solve the system.

$$\begin{cases} y = x^2 - 1 \\ x - y = -1 \end{cases}$$

  A. $(-1, 0), (1, 0)$

  B. $(-1, 0), (2, 3)$

  C. $(-1, 0), (3, 2)$

  D. $(1, 0), (-2, 3)$

CONSTRUCTED RESPONSE

In Items 10–11, classify the conic section that each equation represents. Give the center, vertices, foci, and asymptotes if the conic section has them.

10. $\frac{x^2}{4} - \frac{y^2}{9} = 1$

hyperbola; center: $(0, 0)$; vertices:

$(\pm 2, 0)$; foci: $(\pm\sqrt{13}, 0)$; asymptotes:

$y = \pm\frac{3}{2}x$

11. $\frac{x^2}{9} + \frac{y^2}{4} = 1$

ellipse; center: $(0, 0)$; vertices: $(\pm 3, 0)$;

co-vertices: $(0, \pm 2)$; foci: $(\pm\sqrt{5}, 0)$

In Items 12–13, classify the conic section that each equation represents. Rewrite the equation in standard form.

12. $x^2 - 4y^2 - 4x - 8y = 36$

hyperbola; $\frac{(x-2)^2}{36} - \frac{(y+1)^2}{9} = 1$

13. $x^2 - 8y + 24 = 0$

parabola; $y - 3 = \frac{1}{8}x^2$

14. What is the equation of the parabola with focus $(4, -1)$ and directrix $x = 1$? Without graphing, tell the direction in which the parabola opens. How do you know?

$x - \frac{5}{2} = \frac{1}{6}(y + 1)^2$; the parabola opens

to the right. The directrix is a vertical

line and the focus is to the right of

the directrix. A parabola opens away

from its directrix toward its focus, so

the parabola opens to the right.

15. On a map of an amusement park, a ride has a track in the shape of an ellipse. The ellipse has vertices at $(5, 1)$ and $(-5, 1)$ and foci at $(3, 1)$ and $(-3, 1)$. Find the equation that can be used to describe the path of the ride.

$\frac{x^2}{25} + \frac{(y-1)^2}{16} = 1$

16. Prove that the angle inscribed in a semicircle below is a right angle.

slope of $\overline{PQ}$ is $\frac{4 - 0}{3 - (-5)} = \frac{4}{8} = \frac{1}{2}$;

slope of $\overline{QR}$ is $\frac{0 - 4}{5 - 3} = \frac{-4}{2} = -2$;

The slopes are negative reciprocals, so

the segments are perpendicular, and

the angle formed is a right angle.

Correlation of *Explorations in Core Math* to the Common Core State Standards

Standards	Algebra 1	Geometry	Algebra 2
Number and Quantity			
The Real Number System			
CC.9-12.N.RN.1 Explain how the definition of the meaning of rational exponents follows from extending the properties of integer exponents to those values, allowing for a notation for radicals in terms of rational exponents.	Lessons 6-1, 6-2		Lesson 5-6
CC.9-12.N.RN.2 Rewrite expressions involving radicals and rational exponents using the properties of exponents.	Lesson 6-2		Lesson 5-6
CC.9-12.N.RN.3 Explain why the sum or product of two rational numbers is rational; that the sum of a rational number and an irrational number is irrational; and that the product of a nonzero rational number and an irrational number is irrational.	Lesson 6-2		
Quantities			
CC.9-12.N.Q.1 Use units as a way to understand problems and to guide the solution of multi-step problems; choose and interpret units consistently in formulas; choose and interpret the scale and the origin in graphs and data displays.*	Lessons 1-8, 1-9, 3-2, 4-1, 4-9		Lessons 2-8, 10-1
CC.9-12.N.Q.2 Define appropriate quantities for the purpose of descriptive modeling.*	Lessons 4-9, 5-6		
CC.9-12.N.Q.3 Choose a level of accuracy appropriate to limitations on measurement when reporting quantities.*	Lesson 1-10		
The Complex Number System			
CC.9-12.N.CN.1 Know there is a complex number i such that $i^2 = -1$, and every complex number has the form $a + bi$ with a and b real.			Lesson 2-5
CC.9-12.N.CN.2 Use the relation $i^2 = -1$ and the commutative, associative, and distributive properties to add, subtract, and multiply complex numbers.			Lesson 2-9
CC.9-12.N.CN.3(+) Find the conjugate of a complex number; use conjugates to find moduli and quotients of complex numbers.			Lesson 2-9

(+) Advanced   * = Also a Modeling Standard

Standards	Algebra 1	Geometry	Algebra 2
CC.9-12.N.CN.7 Solve quadratic equations with real coefficients that have complex solutions.			**Lesson 2-6**
CC.9-12.N.CN.9(+) Know the Fundamental Theorem of Algebra; show that it is true for quadratic polynomials.			**Lesson 3-6**
Algebra			
Seeing Structure in Expressions			
CC.9-12.A.SSE.1 Interpret expressions that represent a quantity in terms of its context.* **a.** Interpret parts of an expression, such as terms, factors, and coefficients. **b.** Interpret complicated expressions by viewing one or more of their parts as a single entity.	Lessons 1-1, 1-8, 6-3, 7-1, 7-2, 7-6		**Lessons 2-8, 3-9, 9-5, 12-6**
CC.9-12.A.SSE.2 Use the structure of an expression to identify ways to rewrite it.	Lessons 6-5, 6-6, 7-2, 7-3, 7-4, 7-5, 7-6		**Lessons 3-6, 12-6**
CC.9-12.A.SSE.3 Choose and produce an equivalent form of an expression to reveal and explain properties of the quantity represented by the expression. **a.** Factor a quadratic expression to reveal the zeros of the function it defines. **b.** Complete the square in a quadratic expression to reveal the maximum or minimum value of the function it defines. **c.** Use the properties of exponents to transform expressions for exponential functions.	Lessons 8-3, 8-6, 8-8		**Lessons 4-5, 6-1, 6-7**
CC.9-12.A.SSE.4 Derive the formula for the sum of a finite geometric series (when the common ratio is not 1), and use the formula to solve problems.			**Lessons 9-4, 9-5**
Arithmetic with Polynomials and Rational Expressions			
CC.9-12.A.APR.1 Understand that polynomials form a system analogous to the integers, namely, they are closed under the operations of addition, subtraction, and multiplication; add, subtract, and multiply polynomials.	Lessons 6-4, 6-5		**Lessons 3-1, 3-2**
CC.9-12.A.APR.2 Know and apply the Remainder Theorem: For a polynomial $p(x)$ and a number a, the remainder on division by $x - a$ is $p(a)$, so $p(a) = 0$ if and only if $(x - a)$ is a factor of $p(x)$.			**Lessons 3-3, 3-4, 3-6**
CC.9-12.A.APR.3 Identify zeros of polynomials when suitable factorizations are available, and use the zeros to construct a rough graph of the function defined by the polynomial.			**Lesson 3-5**
CC.9-12.A.APR.4 Prove polynomial identities and use them to describe numerical relationships.			**Lesson 3-2**

(+) Advanced   * = Also a Modeling Standard

Standards	Algebra 1	Geometry	Algebra 2
CC.9-12.A.APR.5(+) Know and apply the Binomial Theorem for the expansion of $(x + y)^n$ in powers of x and y for a positive integer n, where x and y are any numbers, with coefficients determined for example by Pascal's Triangle. (The Binomial Theorem can be proved by mathematical induction or by a combinatorial argument.)			Lesson 3-2
CC.9-12.A.APR.6 Rewrite simple rational expressions in different forms; write $a(x)/b(x)$ in the form $q(x) + r(x)/b(x)$, where $a(x)$, $b(x)$, $q(x)$, and $r(x)$ are polynomials with the degree of $r(x)$ less than the degree of $b(x)$, using inspection, long division, or, for the more complicated examples, a computer algebra system.			Lesson 5-4
CC.9-12.A.APR.7(+) Understand that rational expressions form a system analogous to the rational numbers, closed under addition, subtraction, multiplication, and division by a nonzero rational expression; add, subtract, multiply, and divide rational expressions.			Lessons 5-2, 5-3
Creating Equations			
CC.9-12.A.CED.1 Create equations and inequalities in one variable and use them to solve problems.*	Lessons 1-9, 2-1, 8-6, 8-7	Lesson 1-4	Lessons 2-7, 3-9, 5-5
CC.9-12.A.CED.2 Create equations in two or more variables to represent relationships between quantities; graph equations on coordinate axes with labels and scales.*	Lessons 1-7, 3-3, 3-4, 4-5, 4-6, 4-9, 4-10, 8-1, 8-2, 8-4, 8-5, 8-10, 9-2, 9-4		Lessons 2-8, 3-9, 4-8, 6-1, 6-3, 6-6, 6-7, 11-6
CC.9-12.A.CED.3 Represent constraints by equations or inequalities, and by systems of equations and/or inequalities, and interpret solutions as viable or nonviable options in a modeling context.*	Lessons 4-9, 5-6		Lessons 2-8, 3-9, 9-5
CC.9-12.A.CED.4 Rearrange formulas to highlight a quantity of interest, using the same reasoning as in solving equations.*	Lesson 1-6	Lesson 1-5	Lessons 4-8, 10-1
Reasoning with Equations and Inequalities			
CC.9-12.A.REI.1. Explain each step in solving a simple equation as following from the equality of numbers asserted at the previous step, starting from the assumption that the original equation has a solution. Construct a viable argument to justify a solution method.	Lessons 1-2, 1-3, 1-4, 1-5, 1-7, 9-4		
CC.9-12.A.REI.2 Solve simple rational and radical equations in one variable, and give examples showing how extraneous solutions may arise.			Lessons 5-5, 5-8
CC.9-12.A.REI.3 Solve linear equations and inequalities in one variable, including equations with coefficients represented by letters.	Lessons 1-2, 1-6, 2-2, 2-3, 2-4, 2-5, 2-6, 2-7		

(+) Advanced   * = Also a Modeling Standard

Standards	Algebra 1	Geometry	Algebra 2
CC.9-12.A.REI.4 Solve quadratic equations in one variable. **a.** Use the method of completing the square to transform any quadratic equation in x into an equation of the form $(x - p)^2 = q$ that has the same solutions. Derive the quadratic formula from this form. **b.** Solve quadratic equations by inspection (e.g., for $x^2 = 49$), taking square roots, completing the square, the quadratic formula and factoring, as appropriate to the initial form of the equation. Recognize when the quadratic formula gives complex solutions and write them as $a \pm bi$ for real numbers a and b.	Lessons 8-6, 8-7, 8-8, 8-9		**Lesson 2-6**
CC.9-12.A.REI.5 Prove that, given a system of two equations in two variables, replacing one equation by the sum of that equation and a multiple of the other produces a system with the same solutions.	Lesson 5-3		
CC.9-12.A.REI.6 Solve systems of linear equations exactly and approximately (e.g., with graphs), focusing on pairs of linear equations in two variables.	Lessons 5-1, 5-2, 5-3, 5-4, 5-6		
CC.9-12.A.REI.7 Solve a simple system consisting of a linear equation and a quadratic equation in two variables algebraically and graphically.	Lesson 8-10	Lesson 12-7	**Lesson 12-7**
CC.9-12.A.REI.10 Understand that the graph of an equation in two variables is the set of all its solutions plotted in the coordinate plane, often forming a curve (which could be a line).	Lesson 4-2		
CC.9-12.A.REI.11 Explain why the x-coordinates of the points where the graphs of the equations $y = f(x)$ and $y = g(x)$ intersect are the solutions of the equation $f(x) = g(x)$; find the solutions approximately, e.g., using technology to graph the functions, make tables of values, or find successive approximations. Include cases where $f(x)$ and/or $g(x)$ are linear, polynomial, rational, absolute value, exponential, and logarithmic functions.*	Lessons 1-7, 4-6, 8-5, 9-4		**Lesson 4-5**
CC.9-12.A.REI.12 Graph the solutions to a linear inequality in two variables as a half-plane (excluding the boundary in the case of a strict inequality), and graph the solution set to a system of linear inequalities in two variables as the intersection of the corresponding half-planes.	Lesson 5-5		
Functions			
Interpreting Functions			
CC.9-12.F.IF.1 Understand that a function from one set (called the domain) to another set (called the range) assigns to each element of the domain exactly one element of the range. If f is a function and x is an element of its domain, then $f(x)$ denotes the output of f corresponding to the input x. The graph of f is the graph of the equation $y = f(x)$.	Lessons 3-2, 4-1, 9-3		**Lesson 10-3**

(+) Advanced   * = Also a Modeling Standard

Standards	Algebra 1	Geometry	Algebra 2
CC.9-12.F.IF.2 Use function notation, evaluate functions for inputs in their domains, and interpret statements that use function notation in terms of a context.	Lessons 3-2, 3-3, 3-4, 3-6, 4-1, 4-5, 4-10, 8-1, 8-2, 8-4, 9-2		Lessons 3-5, 4-4, 4-6, 4-8, 6-3, 6-6, 6-7, 9-1, 11-6
CC.9-12.F.IF.3 Recognize that sequences are functions, sometimes defined recursively, whose domain is a subset of the integers.	Lessons 3-6, 4-1		Lesson 9-1
CC.9-12.F.IF.4 For a function that models a relationship between two quantities, interpret key features of graphs and tables in terms of the quantities, and sketch graphs showing key features given a verbal description of the relationship.*	Lessons 3-1, 3-4, 4-3, 4-5, 4-6, 4-10, 8-1, 8-4		Lessons 2-8, 3-9, 4-8, 6-3, 6-7, 11-6
CC.9-12.F.IF.5 Relate the domain of a function to its graph and, where applicable, to the quantitative relationship it describes.*	Lessons 3-2, 3-4, 4-1, 8-1, 8-2, 9-3		Lessons 1-1, 6-3
CC.9-12.F.IF.6 Calculate and interpret the average rate of change of a function (presented symbolically or as a table) over a specified interval. Estimate the rate of change from a graph.*	Lessons 4-3, 4-4		Lesson 2-8
CC.9-12.F.IF.7 Graph functions expressed symbolically and show key features of the graph, by hand in simple cases and using technology for more complicated cases.* **a.** Graph linear and quadratic functions and show intercepts, maxima, and minima. **b.** Graph square root, cube root, and piecewise-defined functions, including step functions and absolute value functions. **c.** Graph polynomial functions, identifying zeros when suitable factorizations are available, and showing end behavior. **d.** (+) Graph rational functions, identifying zeros and asymptotes when suitable factorizations are available, and showing end behavior. **e.** Graph exponential and logarithmic functions, showing intercepts and end behavior, and trigonometric functions, showing period, midline, and amplitude.	Lessons 3-4, 4-1, 4-5, 4-6, 4-10, 8-1, 8-2, 8-3, 8-4, 9-2, 9-3		Lessons 2-1, 2-2, 2-8, 3-5, 3-7, 4-1, 4-2, 4-3, 4-6, 5-1, 5-4, 6-3, 6-7, 11-1, 11-2, 11-6
CC.9-12.F.IF.8 Write a function defined by an expression in different but equivalent forms to reveal and explain different properties of the function. **a.** Use the process of factoring and completing the square in a quadratic function to show zeros, extreme values, and symmetry of the graph, and interpret these in terms of a context. **b.** Use the properties of exponents to interpret expressions for exponential functions.	Lessons 4-7, 8-3, 8-6		Lessons 2-3, 2-4, 6-1, 6-7
CC.9-12.F.IF.9 Compare properties of two functions each represented in a different way (algebraically, graphically, numerically in tables, or by verbal descriptions).	Lesson 4-1		Lesson 6-2

(+) Advanced   * = Also a Modeling Standard

Standards	Algebra 1	Geometry	Algebra 2
Building Functions			
CC.9-12.F.BF.1 Write a function that describes a relationship between two quantities.* **a.** Determine an explicit expression, a recursive process, or steps for calculation from a context. **b.** Combine standard function types using arithmetic operations. **c.** (+) Compose functions.	Lessons 3-3, 3-4, 4-5, 4-10, 6-4, 8-1, 8-2, 8-4, 9-1		**Lessons 3-1, 3-9, 4-8, 5-1, 5-2, 5-3, 5-4, 6-1, 6-3, 6-5, 6-7, 9-1, 9-2, 11-6**
CC.9-12.F.BF.2 Write arithmetic and geometric sequences both recursively and with an explicit formula, use them to model situations, and translate between the two forms.*	Lesson 3-6		**Lessons 9-3, 9-4**
CC.9-12.F.BF.3 Identify the effect on the graph of replacing $f(x)$ by $f(x) + k$, $kf(x)$, $f(kx)$, and $f(x + k)$ for specific values of k (both positive and negative); find the value of k given the graphs. Experiment with cases and illustrate an explanation of the effects on the graph using technology.	Lessons 4-5, 4-10, 8-1, 8-2, 8-4, 9-2		**Lessons 1-1, 1-2, 1-3, 2-1, 3-7, 3-8, 4-6, 4-7, 5-1, 5-7, 6-4, 11-2**
CC.9-12.F.BF.4 Find inverse functions. **a.** Solve an equation of the form $f(x) = c$ for a simple function f that has an inverse and write an expression for the inverse. **b.** (+) Verify by composition that one function is the inverse of another. **c.** (+) Read values of an inverse function from a graph or a table, given that the function has an inverse. **d.** (+) Produce an invertible function from a non-invertible function by restricting the domain.	Lesson 3-3		**Lessons 4-2, 6-6, 6-7**
CC.9-12.F.BF.5(+) Understand the inverse relationship between exponents and logarithms and use this relationship to solve problems involving logarithms and exponents.			**Lessons 4-3, 4-4, 4-5**
Linear, Quadratic, and Exponential Models			
CC.9-12.F.LE.1 Distinguish between situations that can be modeled with linear functions and with exponential functions.* **a.** Prove that linear functions grow by equal differences over equal intervals, and that exponential functions grow by equal factors over equal intervals. **b.** Recognize situations in which one quantity changes at a constant rate per unit interval relative to another. **c.** Recognize situations in which a quantity grows or decays by a constant percent rate per unit interval relative to another.	Lessons 9-3, 9-5		
CC.9-12.F.LE.2 Construct linear and exponential functions, including arithmetic and geometric sequences, given a graph, a description of a relationship, or two input-output pairs (include reading these from a table).*	Lessons 3-3, 3-6, 4-6, 4-7, 9-1, 9-2, 9-3, 9-4		**Lessons 9-3, 9-4**

(+) Advanced   * = Also a Modeling Standard

Standards	Algebra 1	Geometry	Algebra 2
CC.9-12.F.LE.3 Observe using graphs and tables that a quantity increasing exponentially eventually exceeds a quantity increasing linearly, quadratically, or (more generally) as a polynomial function.*	Lesson 9-5		Lessons 4-1, 6-1
CC.9-12.F.LE.4 For exponential models, express as a logarithm the solution to $ab^{ct} = d$ where a, c, and d are numbers and the base b is 2, 10, or e; evaluate the logarithm using technology.*			Lesson 4-5
CC.9-12.F.LE.5 Interpret the parameters in a linear or exponential function in terms of a context.*	Lessons 3-3, 4-8, 4-10, 9-3, 9-4		Lesson 4-6
Trigonometric Functions			
CC.9-12.F.TF.1 Understand radian measure of an angle as the length of the arc on the unit circle subtended by the angle.			Lesson 10-2
CC.9-12.F.TF.2 Explain how the unit circle in the coordinate plane enables the extension of trigonometric functions to all real numbers, interpreted as radian measures of angles traversed counterclockwise around the unit circle.			Lesson 10-3
CC.9-12.F.TF.3(+) Use special triangles to determine geometrically the values of sine, cosine, tangent for $\pi/3$, $\pi/4$ and $\pi/6$, and use the unit circle to express the values of sine, cosines, and tangent for x, $\pi + x$, and $2\pi - x$ in terms of their values for x, where x is any real number.			Lesson 10-3
CC.9-12.F.TF.4(+) Use the unit circle to explain symmetry (odd and even) and periodicity of trigonometric functions.			Lesson 11-1
CC.9-12.F.TF.5 Choose trigonometric functions to model periodic phenomena with specified amplitude, frequency, and midline.*			Lesson 11-6
CC.9-12.F.TF.6(+) Understand that restricting a trigonometric function to a domain on which it is always increasing or always decreasing allows its inverse to be constructed.			Lesson 10-4
CC.9-12.F.TF.7(+) Use inverse functions to solve trigonometric equations that arise in modeling contexts; evaluate the solutions using technology, and interpret them in terms of the context.*			Lesson 10-4
CC.9-12.F.TF.8 Prove the Pythagorean identity $\sin^2(\theta) + \cos^2(\theta) = 1$ and use it to calculate trigonometric ratios.			Lesson 11-3
CC.9-12.F.TF.9(+) Prove the addition and subtraction formulas for sine, cosine, and tangent and use them to solve problems.			Lesson 11-4, 11-5

(+) Advanced   * = Also a Modeling Standard

Standards	Algebra 1	Geometry	Algebra 2
Geometry			
Congruence			
CC.9-12.G.CO.1 Know precise definitions of angle, circle, perpendicular line, parallel line, and line segment, based on the undefined notions of point, line, distance along a line, and distance around a circular arc.		Lessons 1-1, 1-4, 12-3	
CC.9-12.G.CO.2 Represent transformations in the plane using, e.g., transparencies and geometry software; describe transformations as functions that take points in the plane as inputs and give other points as outputs. Compare transformations that preserve distance and angle to those that do not (e.g., translation versus horizontal stretch).		Lessons 1-7, 7-2, 7-6, 9-1, 9-2, 9-3, 9-7, 10-5	
CC.9-12.G.CO.3 Given a rectangle, parallelogram, trapezoid, or regular polygon, describe the rotations and reflections that carry it onto itself.		Lesson 9-5	
CC.9-12.G.CO.4 Develop definitions of rotations, reflections, and translations in terms of angles, circles, perpendicular lines, parallel lines, and line segments.		Lessons 9-1, 9-2	
CC.9-12.G.CO.5 Given a geometric figure and a rotation, reflection, or translation, draw the transformed figure using, e.g., graph paper, tracing paper, or geometry software. Specify a sequence of transformations that will carry a given figure onto another.		Lessons 1-7, 4-1, 9-1, 9-2, 9-3, 9-4, 9-6	
CC.9-12.G.CO.6 Use geometric descriptions of rigid motions to transform figures and to predict the effect of a given rigid motion on a given figure; given two figures, use the definition of congruence in terms of rigid motions to decide if they are congruent.		Lessons 4-1, 9-1, 9-2, 9-3	
CC.9-12.G.CO.7 Use the definition of congruence in terms of rigid motions to show that two triangles are congruent if and only if corresponding pairs of sides and corresponding pairs of angles are congruent.		Lessons 4-4, 4-5	
CC.9-12.G.CO.8 Explain how the criteria for triangle congruence (ASA, SAS, and SSS) follow from the definition of congruence in terms of rigid motions.		Lessons 4-5, 4-6	
CC.9-12.G.CO.9 Prove geometric theorems about lines and angles.		Lessons 1-4, 2-6, 2-7, 3-2, 3-4, 4-5, 6-6, 12-5	
CC.9-12.G.CO.10 Prove theorems about triangles.		Lessons 4-3, 4-6, 4-9, 5-3, 5-4, 5-5, 5-6	
CC.9-12.G.CO.11 Prove theorems about parallelograms.		Lessons 6-2, 6-3, 6-4	
CC.9-12.G.CO.12 Make formal geometric constructions with a variety of tools and methods (compass and straightedge, string, reflective devices, paper folding, dynamic geometry software, etc.).		Lessons 1-2, 1-3, 3-3, 3-4	

(+) Advanced   * = Also a Modeling Standard

Standards	Algebra 1	Geometry	Algebra 2
CC.9-12.G.CO.13 Construct an equilateral triangle, a square, and a regular hexagon inscribed in a circle.		Lesson 6-1	
Similarity, Right Triangles, and Trigonometry			
CC.9-12.G.SRT.1 Verify experimentally the properties of dilations given by a center and a scale factor: **a.** A dilation takes a line not passing through the center of the dilation to a parallel line, and leaves a line passing through the center unchanged. **b.** The dilation of a line segment is longer or shorter in the ratio given by the scale factor.		Lesson 7-2	
CC.9-12.G.SRT.2 Given two figures, use the definition of similarity in terms of similarity transformations to decide if they are similar; explain using similarity transformations the meaning of similarity for triangles as the equality of all corresponding angles and the proportionality of all corresponding pairs of sides.		Lessons 7-2, 7-3	
CC.9-12.G.SRT.3 Use the properties of similarity transformations to establish the AA criterion for two triangles to be similar.		Lesson 7-3	
CC.9-12.G.SRT.4 Prove theorems about triangles.		Lessons 7-4, 8-1	
CC.9-12.G.SRT.5 Use congruence and similarity criteria for triangles to solve problems and prove relationships in geometric figures.		Lessons 4-5, 4-6, 6-2, 6-3, 6-4, 7-4, 7-5	
CC.9-12.G.SRT.6 Understand that by similarity, side ratios in right triangles are properties of the angles in the triangle, leading to definitions of trigonometric ratios for acute angles.		Lessons 5-8, 8-2	
CC.9-12.G.SRT.7 Explain and use the relationship between the sine and cosine of complementary angles.		Lesson 8-2	
CC.9-12.G.SRT.8 Use trigonometric ratios and the Pythagorean Theorem to solve right triangles in applied problems.		Lessons 5-7, 5-8, 8-2, 8-3, 8-4	
CC.9-12.G.SRT.9(+) Derive the formula $A = 1/2\ ab\ \sin(C)$ for the area of a triangle by drawing an auxiliary line from a vertex perpendicular to the opposite side.		Lesson 10-1	
CC.9-12.G.SRT.10(+) Prove the Laws of Sines and Cosines and use them to solve problems.		Lesson 8-5	**Lessons 10-5, 10-6**
CC.9-12.G.SRT.11(+) Understand and apply the Law of Sines and the Law of Cosines to find unknown measurements in right and non-right triangles (e.g., surveying problems, resultant forces).		Lessons 8-5, 8-6	**Lessons 10-5, 10-6**
Circles			
CC.9-12.G.C.1 Prove that all circles are similar.		Lesson 7-2	

(+) Advanced   * = Also a Modeling Standard

Standards	Algebra 1	Geometry	Algebra 2
CC.9-12.G.C.2 Identify and describe relationships among inscribed angles, radii, and chords.		Lessons 12-1, 12-2, 12-4, 12-6	
CC.9-12.G.C.3 Construct the inscribed and circumscribed circles of a triangle, and prove properties of angles for a quadrilateral inscribed in a circle.		Lessons 5-2, 12-4	
CC.9-12.G.C.4(+) Construct a tangent line from a point outside a given circle to the circle.		Lesson 12-5	
CC.9-12.G.C.5 Derive using similarity the fact that the length of the arc intercepted by an angle is proportional to the radius, and define the radian measure of the angle as the constant of proportionality; derive the formula for the area of a sector.		Lesson 12-3	**Lesson 10-1**
Expressing Geometric Properties with Equations			
CC.9-12.G.GPE.1 Derive the equation of a circle of given center and radius using the Pythagorean Theorem; complete the square to find the center and radius of a circle given by an equation.		Lesson 12-7	**Lesson 12-2**
CC.9-12.G.GPE.2 Derive the equation of a parabola given a focus and directrix.		Lesson 5-1	**Lesson 12-5**
CC.9-12.G.GPE.3(+) Derive the equations of ellipses and hyperbolas given the foci, using the fact that the sum or difference of distances from the foci is constant.			**Lessons 12-3, 12-4**
CC.9-12.G.GPE.4 Use coordinates to prove simple geometric theorems algebraically.		Lessons 1-6, 4-2, 4-8, 5-3, 5-4, 6-5, 12-7	**Lesson 12-1**
CC.9-12.G.GPE.5 Prove the slope criteria for parallel and perpendicular lines and use them to solve geometric problems (e.g., find the equation of line parallel or perpendicular to a given line that passes through a given point).		Lessons 3-5, 3-6, 4-7	
CC.9-12.G.GPE.6 Find the point on a directed line segment between two given points that partitions the segment in a given ratio.		Lesson 1-6	
CC.9-12.G.GPE.7 Use coordinates to compute perimeters of polygons and areas of triangles and rectangles, e.g., using the distance formula.*		Lessons 4-2, 10-4	
Geometric Measurement and Dimension			
CC.9-12.G.GMD.1 Give an informal argument for the formulas for the circumference of a circle, area of a circle, volume of a cylinder, pyramid, and cone.		Lessons 10-2, 11-2, 11-3, 12-3	
CC.9-12.G.GMD.2(+) Give an informal argument using Cavalieri's principle for the formulas for the volume of a sphere and other solid figures.		Lessons 11-2, 11-4	
CC.9-12.G.GMD.3 Use volume formulas for cylinders, pyramids, cones, and spheres to solve problems.*		Lessons 11-2, 11-3, 11-4	

(+) Advanced   * = Also a Modeling Standard

Standards	Algebra 1	Geometry	Algebra 2
CC.9-12.G.GMD.4 Identify the shapes of two-dimensional cross-sections of three-dimensional objects, and identify three-dimensional objects generated by rotations of two-dimensional objects.		Lesson 11-1	
Modeling with Geometry			
CC.9-12.G.MG.1 Use geometric shapes, their measures, and their properties to describe objects (e.g., modeling a tree trunk or a human torso as a cylinder).*		Lessons 10-2, 10-3, 12-6	
CC.9-12.G.MG.2 Apply concepts of density based on area and volume in modeling situations (e.g., persons per square mile, BTUs per cubic foot).*		Lessons 10-4, 11-2	
CC.9-12.G.MG.3 Apply geometric methods to solve design problems (e.g., designing an object or structure to satisfy physical constraints or minimize cost; working with typographic grid systems based on ratios).*		Lessons 7-5, 10-3, 11-2	
Statistics and Probability			
Interpreting Categorical and Quantitative Data			
CC.9-12.S.ID.1 Represent data with plots on the real number line (dot plots, histograms, and box plots).*	Lessons 10-2, 10-3, 10-4		Lesson 8-1
CC.9-12.S.ID.2 Use statistics appropriate to the shape of the data distribution to compare center (median, mean) and spread (interquartile range, standard deviation) of two or more different data sets.*	Lessons 10-2, 10-3, 10-4		
CC.9-12.S.ID.3 Interpret differences in shape, center, and spread in the context of the data sets, accounting for possible effects of extreme data points (outliers).*	Lesson 10-4		Lesson 8-1
CC.9-12.S.ID.4 Use the mean and standard deviation of a data set to fit it to a normal distribution and to estimate population percentages. Recognize that there are data sets for which such a procedure is not appropriate. Use calculators, spreadsheets, and tables to estimate areas under the normal curve.*			Lesson 8-8
CC.9-12.S.ID.5 Summarize categorical data for two categories in two-way frequency tables. Interpret relative frequencies in the context of the data (including joint, marginal, and conditional relative frequencies). Recognize possible associations and trends in the data.*	Lesson 10-5		

(+) Advanced   * = Also a Modeling Standard

Standards	Algebra 1	Geometry	Algebra 2
CC.9-12.S.ID.6 Represent data on two quantitative variables on a scatter plot, and describe how the variables are related.* **a.** Fit a function to the data; use functions fitted to data to solve problems in the context of the data. **b.** Informally assess the fit of a function by plotting and analyzing residuals. **c.** Fit a linear function for a scatter plot that suggests a linear association.	Lessons 3-5, 4-8, 9-4		**Lessons 1-4, 6-1, 6-7**
CC.9-12.S.ID.7 Interpret the slope (rate of change) and the intercept (constant term) of a linear model in the context of the data.*	Lessons 3-5, 4-8		
CC.9-12.S.ID.8 Compute (using technology) and interpret the correlation coefficient of a linear fit.*	Lesson 3-5		
CC.9-12.S.ID.9 Distinguish between correlation and causation.*	Lesson 3-5		
Making Inferences and Justifying Conclusions			
CC.9-12.S.IC.1 Understand statistics as a process for making inferences about population parameters based on a random sample from that population.*			**Lesson 8-2**
CC.9-12.S.IC.2 Decide if a specified model is consistent with results from a given data-generating process, e.g., using simulation.*			**Lesson 8-6**
CC.9-12.S.IC.3 Recognize the purposes of and differences among sample surveys, experiments, and observational studies; explain how randomization relates to each.*			**Lesson 8-3**
CC.9-12.S.IC.4 Use data from a sample survey to estimate a population mean or proportion; develop a margin of error through the use of simulation models for random sampling.*			**Lesson 8-5**
CC.9-12.S.IC.5 Use data from a randomized experiment to compare two treatments; use simulations to decide if differences between parameters are significant.*			**Lesson 8-4**
CC.9-12.S.IC.6 Evaluate reports based on data.*			**Lesson 8-3**
Conditional Probability and the Rules of Probability			
CC.9-12.S.CP.1 Describe events as subsets of a sample space (the set of outcomes) using characteristics (or categories) of the outcomes, or as unions, intersections, or complements of other events ("or," "and," "not").*	Lessons 10-5, 10-6	Lesson 10-6	
CC.9-12.S.CP.2 Understand that two events A and B are independent if the probability of A and B occurring together is the product of their probabilities, and use this characterization to determine if they are independent.*	Lesson 10-7	Lesson 13-3	**Lesson 7-3**

(+) Advanced   * = Also a Modeling Standard

Standards	Algebra 1	Geometry	Algebra 2
CC.9-12.S.CP.3 Understand the conditional probability of A given B as P(A and B)/P(B), and interpret independence of A and B as saying that the conditional probability of A given B is the same as the probability of A, and the conditional probability of B given A is the same as the probability of B.*	Lesson 10-7	Lessons 13-3, 13-4	**Lessons 7-3, 7-4**
CC.9-12.S.CP.4 Construct and interpret two-way frequency tables of data when two categories are associated with each object being classified. Use the two-way table as a sample space to decide if events are independent and to approximate conditional probabilities.*		Lesson 13-3	**Lesson 7-3**
CC.9-12.S.CP.5 Recognize and explain the concepts of conditional probability and independence in everyday language and everyday situations.*		Lessons 13-3, 13-4	**Lessons 7-3, 7-4**
CC.9-12.S.CP.6 Find the conditional probability of A given B as the fraction of B's outcomes that also belong to A, and interpret the answer in terms of the model.*		Lesson 13-4	**Lesson 7-4**
CC.9-12.S.CP.7 Apply the Addition Rule, P(A or B) = P(A) + P(B) − P(A and B), and interpret the answer in terms of the model.*		Lesson 13-5	**Lesson 7-5**
CC.9-12.S.CP.8(+) Apply the general Multiplication Rule in a uniform probability model, P(A and B) = P(A)P(B|A) = P(B)P(A|B), and interpret the answer in terms of the model.*	Lesson 10-7	Lesson 13-3	**Lesson 7-3**
CC.9-12.S.CP.9(+) Use permutations and combinations to compute probabilities of compound events and solve problems.*		Lesson 13-1	**Lesson 7-1**
Using Probability to Make Decisions			
CC.9-12.S.MD.3(+) Develop a probability distribution for a random variable defined for a sample space in which theoretical probabilities can be calculated; find the expected value.*			**Lesson 8-6**
CC.9-12.S.MD.5(+) Develop a probability distribution for a random variable defined for a sample space in which probabilities are assigned empirically; find the expected value.*			**Lesson 8-6**
CC.9-12.S.MD.6(+) Use probabilities to make fair decisions (e.g., drawing by lots, using a random number generator).*		Lesson 13-2	**Lesson 7-2**
CC.9-12.S.MD.7(+) Analyze decisions and strategies using probability concepts (e.g., product testing, medical testing, pulling a hockey goalie at the end of a game).*			**Lesson 8-8**

(+) Advanced   * = Also a Modeling Standard